ISBN 978-1-5282-1535-0
PIBN 10907257

Forgotten Books is a registered trademark of FB &c Ltd.
Copyright © 2018 FB &c Ltd.
FB &c Ltd, Dalton House, 60 Windsor Avenue, London, SW19 2RR.
Company number 08720141. Registered in England and Wales.

For support please visit www.forgottenbooks.com

NEW YORK CITY.

1008 PAGES
1029 PICTURES
72 COLUMNS
OF INDEX

BOSTON, MASS.

The Germania
Life Insurance Company

OF NEW YORK.

THE GERMANIA LIFE is a thoroughly representative German-American institution, with its main offices in New York, and its branches and agencies throughout the United States and Europe.

It was organized in 1860, and its career of 34 years is a continuous record of progress and prosperity. During that period it has paid to its policy-holders over Thirty Millions of Dollars, nearly $17,000,000 for losses by death, $4,000,000 for endowments and annuities, and $10,000,000 for dividends and surrendered policies.

On January 1, 1894, its status was as follows: Total Assets, $18,689,858.84; liabilities (4% standard), $17,501,930.88; surplus (4% standard), $1,187,927.86; surplus (4½% standard), $2,048,599.96; insurance in force, $69,411,918.

Its cash income in 1893 was $3,725,343.79, and the new insurance written in 1893 amounted to $13,017,757.

The Company issues all approved forms of policies, but makes a specialty of its own "Dividend Tontine Policies," which have these advantageous characteristics: They are free from restrictions, nonforfeitable, incontestable, combine insurance protection with attractive investment features, and are always payable in full, and on presentation of satisfactory proof of death; they may be made payable in one sum or in 10, 15, 20, 25, or 30 equal annual installments; thus providing for the beneficiaries a fixed annual income beyond contingency of loss.

This absolute protection against loss enjoyed by beneficiaries under the Installment Policies is secured by the payment of lower premiums than those charged for policies payable in one sum.

THE GERMANIA
LIFE INSURANCE COMPANY.

(Commenced Business in 1860.)

HOME OFFICE,   EUROPEAN BRANCH OFFICE,
No. 20 NASSAU STREET,   LEIPZIGER PLATZ 12,
NEW YORK CITY.   BERLIN, GERMANY.

Agencies in all the larger Cities of the United States of America and of the German Empire ; also in Austria, Belgium, Denmark, France, Holland, Norway and Switzerland.

ASSETS.

Bonds and Mortgages on Real Estate,		$9,996,391.55
Domestic and Foreign State, City and		
R. R. Bonds owned, Market Value,		5,059,980.58
Real Estate owned, viz :		
Office Buildings in the United States and Berlin, Germany,	$1,570,747.05	
City Property taken on Foreclosure,	478,092.72	
		2,048,839 77
Cash deposited in Banks,	155,393.26	
Cash on hand and in transit (since received),	111,057.87	
Loans on Stocks,	50,000.00	
Loans on Policies in force,	665,551.38	

Net or invested Assets, Dec.31,1893, $18,087,214.41
Interest and Rents due and accrued, . . 149,151.72
Deferred Premiums, net, ... 260,937.80
Premiums in course of transmission, net, 186,254.91

Total Assets, Dec. 31, 1893, . $18,689,858.84

LIABILITIES.

Legal Reserve on outstanding Policies (4%),	$17,281,283.00	
Reserve for extra Risks, Surrender Values, etc.,	62,594.78	
Unadjusted Claims, . .	117,470.51	
Dividends due to Policyholders,	40,582.59	
	17,501,930.88	

Surplus as regards Policy-holders, **$1,187,927.96**

If the Reserve is computed on a 4½% basis the

Surplus as regards Policy-holders is **$2,048,599.96**

In the Statement of Assets above, the securities owned by the Company are valued at the low quotations of December 31, 1893.

Every item which is not admitted by the State Insurance Department is excluded, as is usual with this Company.

Notwithstanding the great temporary depression of values, there was an increase in the Assets of nearly one million of dollars, which is equal to the average increase during the last four years. The amount of new business written in 1893 was larger than ever before, all of which goes to show that the disturbance in the money market experienced in 1893 was no impediment to the continued healthy growth of this Company.

BOARD OF DIRECTORS.

THOMAS ACHELIS,	EWALD FLEITMANN,	CARL SCHURZ,
EWALD BALTHASAR,	HERMAN MARCUSE,	CASIMIR TAG,
FRANCIS BOLTING,	EMIL OELBERMANN,	F. VON BERNUTH,
HENRY A. CAESAR,	ALBRECHT PAGENSTECHER,	HUGO WESENDONCK,
HUBERT CILLIS,	ALFRED ROELKER,	MAX A. WESENDONCK,
CORNELIUS DOREMUS,	HERMANN ROSE,	OTTO WESENDONCK.

HUGO WESENDONCK, . . . *President.*

CORNELIUS DOREMUS, . . *Vice-President.*   HUBERT CILLIS, . *Secretary and Actuary.*
MAX A. WESENDONCK, . . *Special Director.*   GUSTAV MEIDT, . *Assistant Secretary.*
CHARLES BERNACKI, M. D., *Medical Director.*

KING'S
·HANDBOOK·OF·
NEW YORK
·CITY·

·AN·OUTLINE·HISTORY·
·AND·DESCRIPTION·OF·
·THE·AMERICAN·METROPOLIS·

·WITH·OVER·ONE·THOUSAND·
·ILLUSTRATIONS·FROM·PHO-
·TOGRAPHS·MADE·EXPRESS-
·LY·FOR·THIS·WORK·

PLANNED, EDITED AND
PUBLISHED
BY MOSES KING BOSTON, MASS·

THE MATTHEWS-NORTHRUP CO., COMPLETE ART-PRINTING WORKS, BUFFALO, N. Y.

CONTENTS.

PAGES.

Index.— An extensive detailed list of pictures and complete index to subjects, names, etc., is at the close of the volume. 985–1,008

Historical.— New York of the Past, from the Earliest Times to the Present, . . . 5–46

New York of the Present.— A Comprehensive Outline Description of the Whole City — Area, Population, Wealth, Statistics. etc , ... 47–68

The Water Ways.— The Harbor and Rivers — Piers and Shipping — Fortifications and Quarantine — Exports and Imports — Oceanic and Coastwise Lines, etc., . . 69–108

Transportation and Transit.— Railroads, Steam, Elevated, Cable, Horse and Electric — Stages, etc., ... 109–140

Thoroughfares and Adornments.— Streets, Avenues, Boulevards, Alleys, Ways, Parks, Squares, Drives, Monuments, Statues, Fountains, etc., ... 141–184

Overhead and Underfoot.— Bridges, Tunnels, Sewers, Water, Aqueducts, Reservoirs, Lighting by Gas and Electricity, Telegraph, Telephone, etc., ... 185–214

Life in the Metropolis. — Hotels, Inns, Cafés, Restaurants, Apartment-Houses, Flats, Homes, Tenements, etc., ... 215–244

The Rule of the City.— The City, County, State and National Governments — Officers and Buildings, Courts, etc., ... 245–266

The General Culture.—Educational Institutions—Universities, Colleges, Academies, and Seminaries ; and Public, Private and Parochial Schools and Kindergartens, . 267–302

The Higher Culture.— Art Museums and Galleries, Scientific, Literary, Musical and Kindred Institutions, Societies and Organizations. 303–324

The Literary Culture.— Libraries, Public, Club, Society and Private, ... 325–334

Shrines of Worship.— Cathedrals, Churches, Synagogues, and other Places of Religious Worship and Work, ... 335–418

Charity and Benevolence.— Institutions and Associations for the Poor and Unfortunate — Homes and Asylums, and Temporary Relief, ... 419–456

The Sanitary Organizations.— Board of Health and Health Statistics — Hospitals, Dispensaries, Morgue, Curative Institutions, Insane and other Asylums, ... 457–492

Reformatories and Corrections.— The Police Courts, Prisons, House of Refuge, Penitentiaries, Work-House, House of Correction, etc., ... 493–504

Final Resting-Places.— Cemeteries, Burial-Places, Crematories, Church Yards and Vaults, Tombs, etc., ... 505–522

Defense and Protection.— Police Department, Military and Militia, Army and Pension Offices, Fire Department, Fire Patrol, Detectives, etc , ... 523–542

Sociability and Friendship — Clubs and Social Associations, Secret and Friendship Organizations, ... 543–574

Amusement Places.—Play-Houses, Opera-Houses, Theatres, Public Halls, Museums, Outdoor Sports, etc., ... 575–608

Journalism and Publishing.— Newspapers and Periodicals, Book, Music and other Publishing, ... 609–638

Fire and Marine Insurance.— Offices and Companies for assuming losses by fires and transit and Fire and Marine Underwriters' Associations, ... 639–662

Life-Insurance.— Companies for protection of widows, orphans and others, and for providing incomes in advanced age, etc., and Life-Insurance Associations, . . . 663–682

Miscellaneous Insurance.— Companies for providing against accidents, explosions, broken plate-glass, dishonest employees, loss of salaries, and for furnishing bonds, 683–690

Financial Institutions.— United-States Treasury and Assay Office, Clearing House, National and State Banks, Bankers, Brokers, etc., ... 691–752

Fiduciary Institutions.— Trust and Investment Companies, Savings-Banks, Safe-Deposit Companies, etc., ... 753–782

Financial and Commercial Associations.— The Custom House, Chamber of Commerce, the Stock, Produce, Cotton and other Exchanges, Board of Trade, Mercantile and other Agencies, Warehouses and Markets, ... 783–816

Architectural Features.— Development in Architecture — Notable Office-Buildings and Business Blocks. 817–842

Notable Retail Establishments.— Interesting and prominent Retail Concerns, nearly all being unquestioned leading houses in their respective lines, ... 843–870

Notable Wholesale Establishments —Some gigantic Firms and Corporations, whose yearly transactions involve millions of dollars and extend over the earth, . 871–912

Notable Manufacturers.— An outline history of some preëminent industries carried on or represented in New York, ... 913–984

PREFACE TO SECOND EDITION.

NEVER before has any one put forth an illustrated history and description of New-York City in a single volume at all comparable with "King's Handbook." This volume contains exactly 1,008 pages, more than 1,000 illustrations, thirty chapters, and an index of twenty-four pages with 72 columns, containing over 5,000 items and about 20,000 references. The text furnishes an elaborate but condensed history and description of the city itself, and also of every notable public institution and especially interesting feature. The illustrations give many reminders of the past, and furnish an extensive series of pictures of the present city, to an extent many times beyond that of any volume yet published. Every plate was made expressly for this book, and so were nearly all of the original photographs. The whole has been carefully printed on an exceptionally fine quality of paper. It is conceded to be the handsomest, the most thorough, the largest, the most costly and the most profusely illustrated book of its class ever issued for any city in the world.

The original text was prepared with the utmost care, and was the result of the painstaking work of many individuals, principally of Moses Foster Sweetser, Henri Péne du Bois, William Henry Burbank, Lyman Horace Weeks, Henry Edward Wallace, John Collins Welch, Louis Berg and Charles Putnam Tower. The manuscript underwent a thorough revision at the hands of several thousand people, each an authority on the submitted portion, and thus the book became an authentic volume. The text was amplified, rectified, and verified by Mr. Sweetser, the foremost American in this special field of literature. Valuable general assistance was also given by Mr. Tower.

Although the first edition appeared only ten months ago the present volume is not another edition in the ordinary use of the term. It is in fact a new book. Nearly every text page has been reset, and changes of every character have been made throughout the book. About 300 new engravings are inserted, some to replace former ones, but a large part appear for the first time from new originals. The book is now larger and better, with more text and more illustrations. It is indeed a picture of New York in 1893. Its success has exceeded all expectations. The first edition comprised 10,000 copies, and was exhausted in a few weeks. The present edition is 20,000 copies, more than one-half of which are needed to fill orders on hand before publication.

In the second edition the revisions and additions were made by Mr. Sweetser and the undersigned, with the coöperation of more than 3,000 people, who have kindly made revisions or substitutes for the parts in which they had direct interest. Historical works, newspapers, special reports and hundreds of other sources of information, too numerous to permit of specific acknowledgment, have been utilized.

The illustrations are almost wholly from specially-made photographs, upwards of 1,500 negatives having been made by Arthur Chiar, who has shown remarkable skill in photographing exceedingly difficult subjects. Some photographs were made by Frank E. Parshley, John S. Johnston, C. C. Langill and others. The designs for the cover linings and the series of bird's-eye views were made by the New-York Photogravure Company, the President of which is Ernest Edwards.

The entire mechanical work from cover to cover, with slight exceptions, was done by The Matthews-Northrup Company, the famous Art-Printers of Buffalo, whose establishment is one of the most complete in the world, and whose President, George E. Matthews, and Art-manager, Charles E. Sickels, are entitled to much of the credit for the artistic effect of this volume.

If it were usual to dedicate a volume of this character, this one would be dedicated to Charles F. Clark, the President of The Bradstreet Company, to whom I am indebted for substantial aid, valuable suggestions, and hearty encouragement.

And now this second edition is submitted to the public, with the hope that it will be found to be :

> "Good enough for any body,
> Cheap enough for everybody,"

and that the appreciation of the public will necessitate many editions.

MOSES KING, Editor and Publisher.

Boston, July 1, 1893.

☞ Corrections and suggestions for future editions are invited.

Historical.

New York of the Past, from the Earliest
Times to the Present.

T HE HISTORY of the city of New York, in its
Dutch, British, and American periods, abounds in
episodes of deep interest, illustrating the development
of a petty fur-trading post into the great cosmopolitan
metropolis of the Western Hemisphere. Many ponderous volumes have been devoted to this worthy theme,
with a wealth of illustration and much grace of literary style ; and yet but a part of
the wonderful story has been told. In this brief chapter an attempt is made to exhibit
a few vignettes from the nearly three centuries of annals pertaining to the Empire
City, and to give a few intimations of her lines of advance and of successful endeavor.

Manhattan was the original place-name. *Munnoh* was an Indian word for
"island"; in Abenaqui, *Menatan;* in Delaware, *Menatey*; in Chippewa, *Minis.*
Thus *Grand Menan*, in the Bay of Fundy ; and *Manati*, the ancient Indian name
of Long Island ; and *Manisees*, the old name of Block Island. *Menatan* was any
small island ; *Menates* or *Manisees, the* small island. The island on which New
York stands was sometimes spoken of as "*the* island," *Manate*, or *Manhatte ;*
sometimes as "*a* small island," *Manathan, Menatan,* or *Manhatan ;* and sometimes as "*the* small island," *Manhaates, Manattes,* and *Manados*. The same root
appears in *Manhanset, Montauk* (*Manati-auke*), and other Indian place-names.
Campanius speaks of "*Manataanung,* or *Manaates,* a place settled by the Dutch,
who built there a clever little town, which went on increasing every day."

· The first recorded visitor to this jocund region was Verrazano, a Florentine
navigator and traveller, who was serving at that time as a French corsair. He
sailed from Brittany in the *Dauphine,* in 1524, and cruised up the American coast

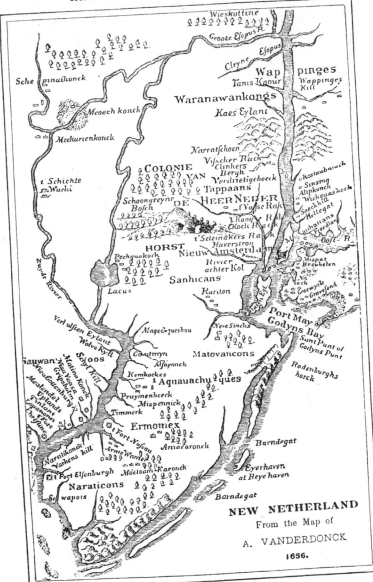

DUTCH MAP OF NEW YORK, 1656.

from Cape Fear to New-York Bay, where his ship lay at anchor for a few days, sending boats up the river and meeting a kindly reception from the natives. There is a tradition that ships of the Dutch Greenland Company entered the North River in 1598, and wintered there, the crews dwelling in a fort which they had constructed on the shore.

But the first practical and undoubted discovery of our harbor and river was due to Henry Hudson, an English mariner, at that time in the employ of a Holland trading corporation. In 1609 the Dutch East India Company sent Hudson out on a voyage of discovery; and after making landfalls at Newfoundland, Penobscot Bay, Cape Cod and Delaware Bay, he entered the harbor of New York. In his little ship, the *Halve-Maen* ("Half-Moon"), with the orange, white and blue flag of Holland floating from the mast, the bold explorer ascended the Hudson River, through the mountains, nearly to the site of Albany, trading with the native tribes

DUTCH COTTAGE AT NEW YORK, 1679.

on the way. He had hoped and fancied that the grand stream might be the long-sought northwest passage to the East Indies; and when the shoaling water above Albany indicated that it was but an ordinary river, he turned about and dropped down the stream and spread his sails for Europe. He carried back the report that the new-found country contained many fur-bearing animals; and the dwellers under the cold northern skies of Holland needed and prized furs for winter clothing. The very next year some Dutch merchants sent out a ship to trade here, and in its crew were several of the sailors of the *Half-Moon*. In 1611 Adriaen Block visited Manhattan, and carried thence to Europe two sons of an Indian chief, the first New-Yorkers to visit the Old World. The next year Block and Christiaensen were sent across in the *Tiger* and the *Fortune*, by several enterprising Amsterdam merchants, to open trade at Manhattan. Christiaensen built Fort Nassau, near the site of Albany, and started a flourishing trade with the Mohawks; and erected a group of log huts near the southern point of Manhattan (45 Broadway); and Block built here a vessel, the *Onrust* (or "Restless"), in which he explored the coast eastward

to Block Island.   This brave little vessel was the pioneer of the vast commerce of
New York, which has since that day borne its flags over all seas, and to the remotest
ports of both hemispheres.

In 1614 the States-General chartered the United New-Netherland Company, of
Amsterdam merchants, to traffic here for three years ; and under the orders of this
corporation traders penetrated far inland, and the treaty of Tawasentha was concluded with the Indians.   In 1621 the Dutch Government chartered the West India

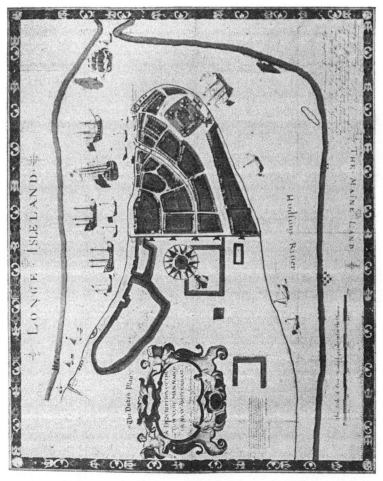

"THE DUKE'S PLAN," MADE FOR JAMES, DUKE OF YORK, ABOUT 1664.

Company, with the powers of making treaties, maintaining courts, and employing soldiers ; and three years later their ship *New Netherland* entered the North River, bearing a colony of 110 Walloons, or people of French origin from southern Holland. Some of these stayed at Manhattan, and others scattered throughout the country.

Nearly all who had come to Manhattan hitherto were transient fur-traders and servants of the company. The Walloon immigration marks the first real and permanent colonization of the new land, as a place of homes. The new-comers

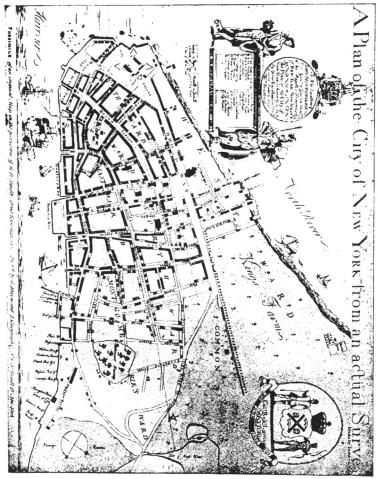

BRADFORD'S MAP OF NEW YORK, 1728.

brought their families, and also horses and cattle, sheep and swine, and farming implements and seed.

In 1625 came the first specimen of the New-York girl, now the delight of two hemispheres, in the diminutive person of Sarah Rapaelje, "the first-born Christian daughter" in the colony. The first white male child born on Manhattan Island was Jean Vigne, who appeared in 1614. His mother owned a farm at the corner of Wall and Pearl streets, and on the hill back of it stood a great windmill. Vigne was a farmer and brewer, and three times schepen of the town. He left no children.

The first director sent out by the West India Company to govern its North-River trading-post was Captain Mey; who was succeeded, in 1625, by William Verhulst. A year later four ships arrived, bringing fresh relays of colonists and 103 head of cattle.

In 1626 the *Sea-Mew* arrived in the harbor, bringing Peter Minuit, the new Director-General, and the first of the four notable rulers of the colony. His earliest official act was the purchase of Manhattan Island from the savages, the payment

being in beads, buttons and other trinkets to the value of 60 guilders (or $24). This policy of purchasing land from the Indians was followed by all the Dutch rulers and colonists.

Manhattan was then a forest-bordered island, swampy along the shores, and rising

RHINELANDER'S SUGAR-HOUSE AND RESIDENCE, BETWEEN WILLIAM AND ROSE STREETS.

inland to low hills crowned with oaks and hickories. On the line of Canal Street tidal marshes and ponds stretched from river to river, and were covered with sea-water at high tide. Wolves and panthers prowled among the rugged ledges and dense thickets beyond, whence an occasional bear sallied forth to dine at ease on the Netherland sheep; and hungry deer ran swiftly southward to trample down the settlers' crops, and enjoy the taste of their corn and wheat. Near the Battery stood a group of the mean precursors of the vast cosmopolitan civilization which was destined to rise on this site; and farther up the island, a few groups of wigwams and communal houses stood in the open valleys, near the corn and tobacco fields of the aborigines. The houses of the Dutch trading-post were of one story, including two rooms, with chimneys of wood, roofs of straw, furniture hewn out of rough planks, and wooden platters and spoons. In 1626 the village had 200 inhabitants, which were augmented to 270 by 1628. About this time it assumed the name of *Fort Amsterdam*, in memory of the metropolis of the Dutch Republic.

The United Netherlands which thus bore Manhattan as a favored child was then conspicuous in Europe in commerce and the mechanic arts. Her dauntless battalions had just shattered forever the power of Spain, and her fleets defied the mariners of England by cruising up and down the English Channel with brooms at their mast-heads. Her cultivation in literature was exemplified in Grotius and DeWitt,

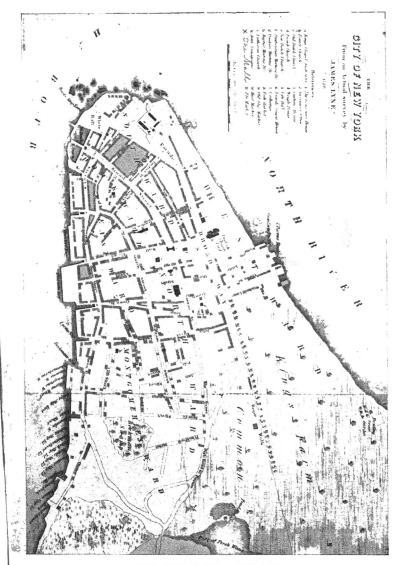

NEW YORK IN 1728, LYNE'S MAP.

THE IRREGULAR PORTION OF THE CITY, AS ORIGINALLY LAID OUT.

Barneveld and William the Silent, and by the great University of Leyden, famous throughout Christendom. In art, her Rembrandt and Rubens, Van Dyck and Teniers, were painting those pictures which are still the admiration of Europe. The most adventurous spirits of this wonderful nation sought new fields beyond the sea, and made a deep and enduring impress on the nascent city and common-wealth.

Most of Minuit's colonists were merely servants of the West India Company, without the rights of owning land, manufacturing, or trading with the Indians.

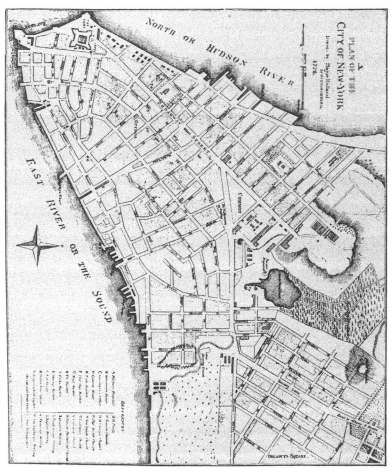

NEW YORK IN 1776.   MAJOR HOLLAND'S MAP.

They came to Manhattan only to work for the company, and of this they had enough, building cabins, stone warehouses and mills. Near the Bowling Green (on the site of No. 4 Bowling Green) they also erected Fort Amsterdam, a bastioned earth-work with three sides, and walls crested with red cedar palisades. Minuit sent his secretary, De Rasières, in the barque *Nassau* to Manomet, in Massachusetts, whence

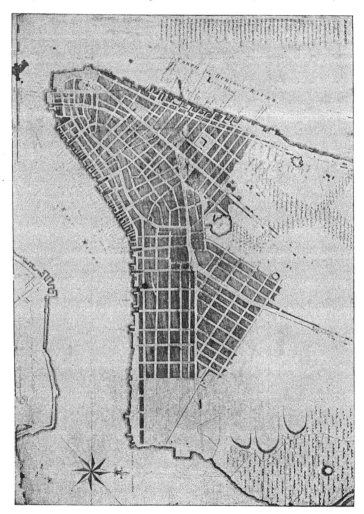

NEW YORK IN 1789. ENGRAVED BY P. R. MAVERICK.

he journeyed to Plymouth, and opened friendly communications and trade relations with the Pilgrim colony.   Boston had not yet been founded.   About the same time Huyck and Krol came hither as "consolers of the sick;" and began Christian observances in the colony by reading the Scriptures and Creeds in the upper room of the horse-mill.   Manhattan in 1629 and 1630 sent to Amsterdam 130,000 guilders' worth of goods, being a large balance in favor of the colony.   In 1631 the Manhattan ship-yard built the great ship *New Netherland*, of 800 tons and 30 guns, one of the largest vessels then afloat.

In 1633 Director-General Wouter Van Twiller reached Manhattan in the frigate *Zoutberg*, bringing in a prize Spanish caravel, and having in his company the first accredited clergyman on these shores, Dominie Everardus Bogardus, and the first professional schoolmaster, Adam Roelandsen.   While New England depended on her fisheries, and Virginia on the tobacco trade, New Netherland shipped grain to Boston and over-seas, and rich peltries to Holland.

Van Twiller brought with him 104 Dutch troops, the first soldiers to enter Manhattan; and for their proper accommodation he erected barracks, and enlarged and strengthened Fort Amsterdam. His colonists were never so happy as when draining their

"YE EXECUTION OF GOFF, YE NEGER OF MR. MOTHIUS, ON YE COMMONS."

huge pewter tankards; and to provide means for these joyous revels, he erected a profitable brewery.   The most conspicuous objects on the island were the tall windmills which he built, and whose slowly revolving arms recalled to the burghers the similar works towering over the far-away meadows of Holland.   But Van Twiller, fat and moon-faced, low of stature and dull of wit, was a shrewd trader and self-provider, and secured as his own private property Nutten (Governor's) Island and Blackwell's Island and other valuable properties. He also granted to Roelof Jans 62 acres of land along the North River, between Fulton and Christopher Streets, and reaching Broadway near Fulton Street.   In 1671 the heirs sold this domain to Governor Lovelace, and it became incorporated with the King's Farm.   This united estate was presented by Queen Anne to Trinity Church in 1703.   Van Twiller's successor, William Kieft, little, fussy, fiery and avaricious, ruled from 1638 to 1647; and built a stone tavern near Coenties Slip, the stone church of St. Nicholas, in the fort, and a distillery.   In his time hundreds of New-Englanders, flying from religious intolerance, settled in the province, and the Indian tribes of the lower Hudson swept the Dutch settlements with torch and tomahawk, and even shot guards on the walls of Fort Amsterdam.   Angered at Kieft's imposition of taxes, and at his unwise Indian policy, the burghers united against him, and inaugurated popular government here.   Scores of unarmed and friendly Indians were massacred in their camp at the foot of Grand Street by Dutch soldiers, who also slaughtered 80 more at Pavonia, without resistance, and even larger numbers at Canarsie and Greenwich. At the end of the Indian war in 1645 there were but 100 persons left at Manhattan, and 1,500 in the province. The poor little colony, the plaything of a foreign commercial corporation, drooped rapidly, especially after the West India Company began to lose money here, and so its officers planned to absorb the best lands in the new domain and to assume feudal

NEW YORK IN 1778. THOMAS KITCHIN, SENIOR'S, MAP. FROM THE LONDON MAGAZINE.

prerogatives, under the title of "Patroons." The States-General, therefore, curtailed the company's privileges greatly, and colonists began to pour in from all

NEW YORK AND EAST RIVER, FROM BROOKLYN HEIGHTS.

parts, so that in 1643 eighteen different nationalities were represented in New Amsterdam alone.

The cosmopolitan growth of the future city was prophesied early in the 17th century by the Amsterdam Chamber, which declared that when its population and navigation "should become permanently established, when the ships of New Netherland ride on every part of the ocean, then numbers, now looking to that coast with eager eyes, will be allured to embark for your island." The accuracy of this prediction has been verified to an extent quite more than desirable, especially during the last half century.

The irregular lines of the lower New-York streets are due to the fact that the colony grew for thirty years before streets were laid out, and the settlers built their cabins wherever they liked. There were but two public roads, the Boston (or Old Post) road, from the Battery along Broadway and the Bowery; and the ferry road, from the fort along the lines of Stone Street and

Hanover Square to the Brooklyn ferry at Peck Slip.   De Perel Straat (Pearl Street) was on the water side ; Water, Front and South Streets all having been reclaimed from the river.   Pearl Street is the oldest in New York, and was built upon in 1633, being followed closely by Bridge Street.   The most ancient conveyance of property now on record in New York shows that Van Steenwyck sold to Van Fees a lot of 3,300 square feet on Bridge Street for $9.60.   The first lot of land granted on Broadway (then called De Heere Straat) was in 1643, to Martin Krigier, who erected here the celebrated Krigier's Tavern, on whose site rose the King's Arms Tavern, afterwards the Atlantic Gardens (9 Broadway).

The next (and last) Director-General was Petrus Stuyvesant, a veteran of the West-Indian wars, wearing a wooden leg banded with silver.   He was an autocratic, decided and vigorous ruler ; and sturdily fought the colonists, patroons, and Home Government in the interests of the West India Company.   Lutherans, Baptists, Quakers and other dissenters from the Reformed religion were persecuted, and

NEW YORK IN 1775.   FORT GEORGE, FROM THE HARBOR.

Stuyvesant forbade the mustering of the burgher guard, and ousted the municipal council of the Nine from their honorary pew in the church.   Fearful of attack from England and New England, the gallant old soldier fortified the town in 1653 with a breastwork, ditch and sharpened palisades, running from the East River nearly to the North River, and garnished with block-houses.   This defensive wall was 2,340 feet long.   From Lombard Street it followed the crest of the bluff along the North River as far as the fort.   Fort Amsterdam, on the site of the brick block southeast of Bowling Green, was built of small Holland brick, and contained the governor's house, the church, and quarters for 300 soldiers.   It stood from 1635 until 1790–91.

The quaint little Dutch seaport was governed from its picturesque stone Stadt Huys, in front of which stood a high gallows.   Here often gathered the entire body of the people, from the black-gowned schepens and the richly-clad patroons and merchants down to the common populace, whose men were clad in jackets and wide baggy breeches, and their women in bodices and short skirts.   The site of the Stadt Huys is now occupied by No. 73 Pearl Street.   Pearl Street was then known

2

as "the Road to the Ferry" (to Brooklyn); and passed through the wall at the
Water Gate, which was strengthened by a block-house and a two-gun battery.
Before the end of the century these defenses were augmented by the Slip Battery of
ten guns, near Coenties Slip; the Stadt-Huys Battery of five guns; the Whitehall
Battery of fifteen guns; a wall with bastions and postern gates along the North
River; and stone bastions near Broadway and Nassau Street.   An arched gateway spanned Broadway where that avenue crossed the walls; and other gates
and posterns occurred at convenient points.   During the second Dutch dominion
it was the duty of the Schout (or Mayor) to walk around the city every morning
with a guard, and unlock the gates, after which he gave the keys to the commander of the fort.   At evening he locked the gates and posted sentries and
pickets at exposed points.

Outside the town wall a footpath led to the ponds near by, and because this way
had been made by the Dutch lasses going to the ponds to wash clothes, it was called
T'Maagde Paatje, or the Maidens' Path, and later Maiden Lane.   Inside the wall,
Broad Street stretched its lines of little gabled brick and stone houses, and a narrow
canal ran down its center.   Farther down came Whitehall, the fashionable quarter,

VIEW OF NEW YORK IN 1746--MIDDLE DUTCH AND FRENCH CHURCHES.

with prim, bright gardens of dahlias and tulips, and orchards surrounding its quaint
step-gabled houses of small black and yellow brick, and Stuyvesant's town house of
Whitehall.   Bowling Green was at an early day set apart for a parade-ground and
village-green, and for public festivities and solemnities, May-poles and the games of
the children; and here also great Indian councils were held.   It was for many
decades known as "The Plain"; and here, in 1658, was established the first market-
house in the city.   Every morning the village-herdsman passed through the streets,
blowing his horn, at which the settlers turned their cattle out from their yards, and
they were formed into a common herd, and driven along Pearl Street to the present
City-Hall Park, which was then known as *De Vlackte* ("The Flat").   At night
the herdsman drove back the cattle, leaving at each citizen's door his own good

milch cow. Sometimes, perchance, he lingered in the great cherry orchard, near Franklin Square, from which the modern Cherry Street derives its name ; or loitered along the edge of Beekman's Swamp, now given over to leather-dealers ; or rested under the shadow of the barn-like church, near Whitehall ; or watched the whirling arms of the windmill on State Street. Stuyvesant also founded (in 1658) the village of Niew Harlaem, on the northern part of Manhattan, and began a good highway thitherward. It was during Stuyvesant's time, in 1653, that the West India Company incorporated Niew Amsterdam as a city, with a government mod- elled on that of Amsterdam, and composed of a schout, two burgomasters and five schepens. The city thus created had 1,000 inhabitants and 120 houses. Moreover, in 1650, Dirck Van Schelluyne, the first lawyer here, had opened his practice.

Between 1656 and 1660 most of the seventeen streets were paved with cobble-stones, and provided with gutters in the middle. The first to be paved were De Hoogh Straat (Stone Street) and De Brugh Street (Bridge Street). In 1658 the

NEW YORK IN 1746--LOWER MARKET AND LANDING.

first fire-company came into existence, under the name of "The Rattle Watch." It numbered eight men, who were to stay on watch and duty from nine in the even- ing until morning drum-beat. At the same time the equipment of the fire-depart- ment was prepared, in the importation from Holland of a supply of hooks and ladders and 250 fire-buckets. The gabled ends of the houses faced the streets, and were (even in the cases of wooden edifices) decorated with a checker-work of small black and yellow bricks, all of which were imported from Holland until Stuyvesant's time. Iron figures showing the dates of their erection were fastened in the gables between their zig-zag sides. The main doors of the houses had heavy and well-polished brass knockers ; and over each cresting gable a quaint weather-cock whirled with the breeze. Sitting on the stoops or under the low eaves, or leaning over their half-doors, the burghers discussed the problems of their day amid clouds of tobacco smoke. Every house had its garden, with places for horse and cow, pigs and chickens, and a patch of cabbage and a bed of tulips. The parlor, carpeted only with fine white sand, contained the great camlet-valanced bed, with homespun linen and grotesque patch-work quilts, the iron-bound oaken chest of linen, the corner cupboard, with the small but precious store of plate and porcelain ; the tea-table, stiff Russia-leather chairs, flowered chintz curtains, quaint old pictures, and the fire-place, surrounded with storied Dutch tiles. The kitchen was the home-room, with the large square dining-table, the vrouw's spinning-wheel, the burgher's capacious chair and pipe, and the immense fire-place, with its hooks and iron pots, and chimney-corner seats sacred to children and stories. A fair city lot could still be obtained for $50, and the rent of a very good house did not exceed $20 a year. For there were many troubles still surrounding the good burghers, betwixt the aggressive Yankees on the east, the Swedes on the south, and the aboriginal citizens of the neighboring hills and valleys. As late as the year 1655 the Indians attacked the town with 1,900 warriors, in 64 canoes, and within three days killed 100 Dutch settlers and captured 150 more, mainly in the suburbs.

Under the lead of Peter Minuit, formerly Director-General of New Netherland, and with the aid of Queen Christina, Swedish colonies had been established on the Delaware River, in 1638, and subsequently enlarged and increased by many expeditions from Sweden. The Dutch West India Company claimed all this region by right of prior settlement ; and finally, in 1655, Stuyvesant assembled 600 soldiers and seven vessels in the harbor of Niew Amsterdam, and sailed around to the Scandinavian forts, which he captured in succession. Thus fell New Sweden. But the heavy cost of these hostilities and of the Indian wars drained the treasury of the West India Company, and paved the way for the approaching fall of New Netherland.

Great Britain had always claimed that the Hudson-River country belonged to her, by virtue of Cabot's discoveries in 1497, and had made several formal protests against the Dutch occupation. The claim was perhaps not well grounded ; but Britain feared the fast-increasing naval and commercial power of Holland, and determined to reduce it wherever possible. Gov. Bradford of Plymouth had asserted Great Britain's ownership of Manhattan, in a letter to Minuit ; and Captain Argal had planned to drive away the colonists, with a naval force from Virginia, as early as the year 1613. The West India Company also applied to King Charles I. for permission to trade to the ports of England and her colonies — a proceeding which did not tend to clear the Dutch title. Calvert, Lord Baltimore's secretary, informed the Dutch envoy that Maryland extended to the frontiers of New England. "And the New-Englanders claim that their domain doth reach to Maryland," answered the envoy ; "where then remains New Netherland?" To which Calvert coldly replied : "Truly, I do not know." The Connecticut Legislature in 1663 informed Stuyvesant's commissioners that it "knew of no New Netherland province." The New-England towns on Long Island, in 1663, petitioned Connecticut to annex and protect them, and after several appeals from them, and from Stuyvesant to the English and Dutch governments, the Duke of York, Lord High Admiral of Great Britain, sent out a fleet, which in 1664 appeared before the town, and seized it, subject to negotiations between the home governments. Stuyvesant cried out, that in preference to surrender, "I would much rather be carried out dead ;" but his clergy and people refused to permit a battle, and the Dutch garrison was allowed "to march out with their arms, drums beating and colors flying." Since the governments of Great Britain and Holland were in profound peace at this time, the successful naval expedition was in reality a cold-blooded and treacherous buccaneering attack ; but the Duke of York was the brother of the British King, who had granted to him all the territory between the Connecticut and Delaware Rivers. Moreover, he had more men and heavier guns at the point of dispute. Captain-General Stuyvesant retired to his Bowerie farm, where for eighteen years, until his death, he dwelt in

OLD CITY OR FEDERAL HALL, TRINITY CHURCH AND WALL STREET IN 1789.
ON THE BALCONY OF THIS FEDERAL HALL WASHINGTON WAS MADE PRESIDENT.

quiet dignity, enjoying a placid rural life.   On this lovely and tranquil estate, and on the present site of St. Mark's Church, he erected a chapel wherein he was in due time buried.

Thus closed the Dutch *régime* in New York.   Its ruling impulse, the aggrandizement of a commercial company, differed widely from the movements of religious enthusiasm or national pride which inspired the foundations of the English and French colonies in America.   From the start, it was a business community, and all its development has been near the original lines of effort.   In the present era of mercantile and industrial supremacy, when the sagacity developed by business, and the wealth created thereby, establish religious missions, equip armies, create nations and fill the homes of the people with comfort, New York, London and Paris are the three capitals of the world.   The Dutch founders, practical, sagacious and earnest,

were influenced by the refined and vivacious French Huguenots, who settled among them, and by their sturdy and enterprising fellow-colonists from New England; while the varied traits of the German Palatines, the Swedish emigrants and many other nationalities tended still further to build up here a cosmopolitan and tolerant

JUMEL MANSION, NEAR WASHINGTON HEIGHTS, ONCE WASHINGTON'S HEADQUARTERS.

community, broad in views, fearless in thought, energetic in action, and free from the limiting provincialisms of Puritan or Cavalier, or of New France or New Spain.

As soon as the town with its 1,500 inhabitants had passed under British rule, it was officially named NEW YORK, in honor of the Duke of York, its new lord.   Thus the name of the quiet old provincial town on the English River Ouse, the Eburacum of the Romans, where Constantine the Great was proclaimed emperor, became attached to the future metropolis of the Western World.   According to the monkish tradition the name was derived from that of King Ebraucus, who ruled in Yorkshire at about the same period that David reigned in Israel.   This ancient sovereign was said to have had twenty wives, twenty sons and thirty daughters ; and yet, in spite of these circumstances, he ruled over his people for three-score years.   Through the same change of name, " by a strange caprice in history, the greatest State in the Union bears the name of the last and the most tyrannical of the Stuarts."

Holland entered the following year into a two-years' war with Great Britain, whose fleets she well-nigh swept from the seas.   By the treaty of Breda, however, she yielded New York to the British, receiving in exchange Surinam and other valuable possessions, which still remain under her flag.

The first British governor was Colonel Richard Nicolls, a wise, tactful and handsome officer, who knew the Dutch and French languages as well as he did his own.

This honest gentleman ruled from 1664 until 1668, and happily conciliated the varied elements in his little principality. Colonel Francis Lovelace, the despotic governor between 1668 and 1672, ordered May races at Hempstead, bought Staten Island from the Indians, and established the first mail between New York and Boston, to be of monthly operation. He also founded the first merchants' exchange on Manhattan. It started its barterings in 1670, when the easy-going Dutch and English shopkeepers began the custom of meeting every Friday noon at the bridge over the Broad-Street canal. The hour of meeting was marked by the ringing of the Stadt-Huys bell; and the mayor was required to be at the assembly to prevent disturbance. In 1673 a Dutch fleet of twenty-three vessels and 1,600 men entered the harbor and exchanged broadsides with the fort, by which serious losses were occasioned. Then 600 stout Dutch troops were landed, at the foot of Vesey Street, and joined by 400 burghers. The army marched down Broadway to attack the fort, but this stronghold prudently surrendered, and the banner of the Dutch Republic once more floated in supremacy over the city and harbor, and up the Hudson, and over New Jersey and Long Island. The name *New York* was repudiated, and in its place the Lowland commodores ordained that *New Orange* should be the title of the city.

FRAUNCES' TAVERN, CORNER OF BROAD AND PEAPL STREETS.

The new government lasted but little more than a year, and then the province was restored by the States-General to Great Britain; and Edmund Andros, a major in Prince Rupert's cavalry, came over as governor of the territories of the Duke of York in America. In Andros's time, the canal on Broad Street was filled; the tanners were driven out of the city and reestablished their tan-pits in the remote district now between Broadway, Ann Street and Maiden Lane; the slaughter-houses were also driven into the country and settled at Smit's Vley, now the intersection of Pearl Street and Maiden Lane; all Indian slaves were set free; and the burghers secured the exclusive right of bolting and exporting flour from the province. The latter monopoly, during its sixteen years of operation, trebled the wealth of the city and ten-folded the value of its real estate, 600 houses having been built and the local fleet augmented to 60 ships.

In 1678, the aggregate value of all the estates in the province was $750,000; and a planter with $1,500, or a merchant worth $3,000, was accounted a rich man. A considerable export trade in furs and provisions, lumber and tar was carried on with European ports. The slaves on Manhattan were rated in value at about $150 each, and had been brought from Guinea and the West Indies. In 1712, when there were about 4,000 negroes in the city, a hot outbreak of race hatred occurred, and nine whites were slain by negro conspirators in Maiden Lane. The wildest excitement followed, and fears of a general insurrection; but the garrison and militia quelled the outbreak with unsparing hands. Six Africans committed suicide, and 21 were executed, most of them by hanging or by burning at the stake. One was broken on the wheel, and one hung in chains until he starved. A similar panic

FEDERAL HALL AND PART OF BROAD STREET, 1796.

broke out in 1741, when conflagrations at Fort George, on the Battery, and elsewhere, were attributed to the slaves acting in collusion with the hostile power of Spain. In this wild popular frenzy 14 negroes were burned at the stake, 18 hanged, and 71 transported.

In 1683 the governorship was devolved upon Thomas Dongan, an Irish Catholic soldier, then recently lieutenant-governor of Tangier, in Africa, and subsequently Earl of Limerick. This able and prudent statesman convened in the old fort on the Battery a council and elective assembly which enacted "The Charter of Liberties," providing for religious freedom and liberty of choice in elections, and forbidding taxation without the consent of the people. The city was now divided into six wards, although its entire assessed value of property lay under £80,000. After five years of happy rule, Governor Dongan was removed, and New York, New Jersey and the Eastern Colonies were united in the Dominion of New England, with Sir Edmund Andros as Governor-in-Chief, and Francis Nicholson in charge of New York. After the Bostonians had deposed and imprisoned Andros, Jacob Leisler, a German captain of the train-bands, seized the government of New York, and held it for over a year, during which there was one bloody fight between the local train-bands in the fort and British infantry in the town. After Governor Sloughter had arrived, Leisler was tried for treason, and convicted; and suffered the penalty of death by hanging, on the edge of Beekman's Swamp, where the *Sun* building now stands.

During the period between 1690 and 1700, New York carried on a large trade with British East-Indian pirates, sending out liquors, ammunition and other com-modities, and at the pirates' haunts exchanging these for Oriental fabrics and carpets, jewels and gold, perfumes and spices. Some of these freebooters were New-York-ers, and several successful pirate chiefs visited the city. Captain Robert Kidd, "so wickedly he did," recruited at this port most of the buccaneers who sailed with him on his last three-years' voyage to the Red Sea.

Governor Benjamin Fletcher, a luxurious soldier of fortune, and courtier, ruled New York from 1692 until 1698; and received large gifts from the pirates. His successor was the Earl of Bellomont, a pure and honorable governor, who restored the Leislerian (or people's) party to power, and hung all the pirates he could catch. Next came Lord Corn-bury, the nephew of Queen Anne, and a silly, venal and bigoted de-bauchee, who ruled here from 1702 until 1708.

BANK OF NEW YORK   MC EVER'S MANSION   CITY BANK
WALL STREET, BELOW WILLIAM, IN 1800.

The Dutch Reformed people had long been content to wor-ship in the stone church in the fort; but in 1691–93 they erected on Exchange Street (now Garden Street) the finest church in the province, a quaint and high-steepled brick structure. Next came the Church-of-England people, dissatisfied with services in the fort chapel; and to this society Gov. Fletcher in 1696 gave the reve-nue of the King's Farm for seven years, which encouraged them to build a new chapel on the site of the present Trinity. The First Presbyterian Church, now on Fifth Avenue, near 11th Street, is descended from the church of the same faith erected on Wall Street in 1719. The quaint towers of the French Huguenot and Middle Dutch Churches rose high above the gables of the houses near Broad Street.

From 1710 to 1719, the little royal court at New York was dominated by Gov. Robert Hunter, formerly a Scottish general under Marlborough, and a friend of Addison and Swift. He founded the court of chancery; fought for religious liberty; and predicted American independence. ("The colonies are infants at their mother's breast, but such as will wean themselves when they become of age.")

In 1692 the municipality cut up the Clover Pastures, and laid out Pine and Cedar Streets, and others; and further increased its dignity a year later by appointing a town-crier, dressed in proper livery, and by building a bridge across Spuyten-Duyvil Creek. Four more years passed, and then the night-watch came into existence, to patrol the streets of lonely evenings. The watchmen moved about on duty from nine o'clock until the break of day, traversing their beats every hour, with bells,

proclaiming the condition of the weather and the hour of the night.   The dark high-
ways were lighted by lanterns put out on poles from every seventh house.   In front
of the City Hall stood the cage, pillory, and whipping-post, as terrors to thieves and
slanderers, vagrants and truants; and the ducking-stool, to cool the ardor of scolds
and evil-speaking persons.   Now also began the era of street-cleaning, when each
householder was ordered to keep clean his section of street, and the street surveyor received directions to root up weeds.   In 1696 the city made its first appropriation (of £20) for cleaning the streets.   At the same time, "the street that runs
by the pie-woman's leading to the city commons" was laid out, and became Nassau
Street.

From Hunter's successor was another gentleman of Scottish origin, William Burnet,
the son of the famous Bishop of Salisbury; and after a rule of eight years, he in

NEW YORK IN 1805.

turn gave place to Col. John Montgomery, another Scot, and an old soldier and
member of Parliament.   During this period, Greenwich and Washington Streets
were made, by filling in along the North River.

With the dawn of the year 1730 a fortnightly winter stage to Philadelphia was
established.   A year thereafter the municipal authorities imported from London
two Newnham fire engines, able to throw water seventy feet high; and organized a
fire-department of twenty-four strong and discreet men.

From 1743 to 1753 the city and province were governed by Admiral George
Clinton, the son of an earl, who ruled with the rough temper of a sailor, and retired
from his administration, enriched by plunder, after many a hot contest with the
people.   During this period, in 1752, the Royal Exchange was opened, at the foot
of Broad Street, with its spacious assembly-hall for merchants, and a famous coffee-
room.   The Chamber of Commerce received its incorporation in 1770, by Royal
Charter.

In 1751 the Assembly appointed trustees to take charge of funds raised for a
college; and the next year Trinity Church offered to give the site for the proposed
institution.   In 1753 the entering class of ten members began its studies in the

vestry-room of Trinity; and in another year King's College received its charter. The building was erected in 1756–60, on the site long held by the college, between Barclay, Church and Murray Streets and College Place.

The tremendous power of New-York journalism and publishing, which is now felt all over the continent, began in the humblest way far back in 1693, when the Council invited William Bradford to settle in the city as official printer, for "£40 a year and half the benefit of his printing, besides what served the public." He issued the first bound book in New York, the *Laws of the Colony*, in 1694; and in 1725 began the publication of *The New-York Gazette*, a semi-official organ of Gov. Burnet's administration, printed weekly, on foolscap paper. Nine years later *The Weekly Journal* came into being, to resist the Government, and Zenger, its editor,

THE NEW TRINITY CHURCH AND PART OF WALL STREET.

was sent to prison, and various numbers of the paper were burned by order. The *Gazette* was the organ of the aristocracy, and the *Journal* stood as the champion of the people. After Editor Zenger had languished in prison for nine months, he was tried, and received a triumphant acquittal, to the immense delight of the people, who bitterly resented this first attempt to muzzle the press.

The Brooklyn ferry was started in the earliest days of the colony, and consisted of a flatboat worked by sweeps, the ferryman being summoned by blasts of a horn. It was not until 1755 that a packet began running semi-weekly to Staten Island; and the Paulus-Hook (Jersey-City) ferry began its trips in 1763, followed in 1774 by a ferry to Hoboken.

In the year 1765 the Stamp Act was passed, and the disruption of America and England began. The New-Yorkers forgot their old-time local controversies, and took sides in the new contest. Rivington's *Gazetteer* stigmatized the patriots as rebels, traitors, banditti, fermenters of sedition, sons of licentiousness, and the like ; and Gaine's *Mercury* and Holt's *Journal* proclaimed the Royalists to be ministerial hirelings, dependent placemen and informers.

A congress of delegates from nine colonies met at the New-York City Hall and passed a Declaration of Rights and an address to the King. When the stamped paper arrived from England, under naval escort, the Sons of Liberty refused to allow its use, and the Common Council compelled the surrender of the paper to the corporation. The city and province were then under the rule of the venerable Lieutenant-Governor Cadwallader Colden, a Scottish Jacobite and scholar, who lived in New York from 1708 until his death in 1776. He endeavored to repress the popular tumults, but prevented the fort from firing on the rioters. The military commander was Gen. Thomas Gage, who afterwards received from the New-Englanders the brevet title of "Lord Lexington, Baron of Bunker Hill." Major James of the Royal Artillery had his beautiful estate of Ranelagh near the present West Broadway ; Sir Peter Parker's estate of Vauxhall was at the foot of Warren Street ; and Murray Hill, the seat of Robert Murray, the Quaker merchant, occu_ pied the domain between Fourth and Fifth Avenues, and 36th and 40th Streets.

The Commons, now the City-Hall Park, were often crowded by assemblies of citizens, to whom the tribunes of the people, Sears and Scott, McDougall and Wil_

BROADWAY.   ALMS-HOUSE.   CITY HALL.

BUILDINGS IN CITY-HALL PARK IN 1809.

lett, Livingston and Hamilton, made fiery addresses, although strong detachments of the 16th and 24th British Regiments lay in adjacent barracks. · Thence the populace marched to the fort, at evening, bearing 500 lights, and beat against its gates, defied its grape-shot, insulted the officers, spiked the guns of the Battery, and burned Governor Colden's coach, and an effigy of the ruler. The Liberty Pole was set up on the Commons, amid hilarious festivities, attended with a barbecue, and the drink-ing of twenty-five barrels of beer and a hogshead of punch. Thrice the red-coats of the 24th Regiment cut down this emblem of popular sovereignty, but when they laid it low for the fourth time, the alarm-bells tolled, the shops were closed, and the citizens made a series of attacks on the soldiers. The hottest skirmish occurred on Golden Hill John Street), where the Sons of Liberty beleaguered and beat a large detachment of the 16th, and themselves received many bayonet-thrusts and other wounds. After this outbreak, the patriots erected on the Commons a lofty iron-bound pole, crowned by a vane bearing the word Liberty. This stood fast until the city fell into the hands of the British army. In 1770 the people erected an eques-trian statue of George III. on Bowling Green ; and also a marble statue of William

Pitt, at Wall and William Streets. When the British ships laden with taxed tea arrived at New York, the people seized the *London* and emptied all her tea-chests into the river, and compelled the *Nancy* to put about and sail back to England.

On the Sunday after the battle of Lexington, a breathless horseman galloped in over the Boston road, bearing the startling news. The citizens immediately seized the public stores and colony arms; over-rode the local authorities; formed a governing Committee of One Hundred; and enthusiastically welcomed the New-England delegates to the Continental Congress. A few weeks later, the frigate *Asia* fired a broadside through the city, injuring several people, and damaging the houses along Whitehall.

The Provincial Congress, fearing a descent on the city by royalist troops from Ireland, summoned help from New England; and Gen. Wooster marched down

OLD CUSTOM HOUSE AND VICINITY IN 1825.

with 1,800 Connecticut militia, and encamped for several weeks at Harlem, sending out detachments to cover the coast from British marauders. Under this protection the Sons of Liberty seized the Royalist supply-depots at Greenwich Village and at Turtle Bay (at the foot of East 47th Street), and removed thirty cannon from the Battery. The Tories included the landed proprietors, the recent English immigrants, and the Episcopalians; while the patriot party was made up of the Dutch and Huguenots, the New-Englanders and Scots, the Dissenters and the artisans. The influence of the principal families inclined the General Assembly and Provincial Congress strongly toward Royalism; and caused the province to move more slowly in the direction of independence than its neighbors had done. But the great mass of the people were in favor of freedom, and in time crushed out the Tory legislative influences.

During these troublous days, Isaac Sears, one of the leading New-York patriots, rode down from Connecticut, with a band of light horsemen, and destroyed the press and other apparatus of Rivington's *Royal Gazetteer*, and carried off the type to be made into bullets. Early in 1776 Gen. Charles Lee marched into New York with 1,200 Connecticut troops, and encamped on the Commons, whence his detachments disarmed the Tories, and began to fortify the city. Lee was succeeded by Lord Stirling, and he by Gen. Putnam ; and the Third New-Jersey Regiment and troops from Dutchess and Westchester Counties and from Pennsylvania entered the city.

Governor Tryon took refuge on the British fleet, and the garrison of the Royal Irish Regiment was sent away to Boston. As soon as the New-England metropolis was delivered from the enemy, Washington marched his army to New York ; and here on the 9th of July, 1776, the Continental troops were assembled by brigades to have the Declaration of Independence read to them. One brigade was drawn up on the Commons, and in the hollow square Washington sat on horseback while an aide read the historic document. The same day the citizens pulled down the gilded-lead equestrian statue of George III. on Bowling Green, and sent it off into Connecticut,

RESERVOIR OF MANHATTAN WATER WORKS ON CHAMBERS STREET, IN 1825.

where it was converted into 48,000 bullets ; and thus the Royalist troops had "melted majesty" fired at them from patriotic muskets. Three days later the British frigates *Rose* and *Phænix* sailed up the Hudson, firing on the city as they passed, and taking post above. By mid-August the hostile fleet in the Bay numbered 437 sail, bearing the armies of Howe, Clinton and Cornwallis, and the King's Guards and De Heister's Hessian division, numbering 31,000 soldiers in all. Again the *Rose* and *Phænix* sailed past the city, bound downward, and firing broad-sides through its streets and buildings.

The defences of New York (aside from the Brooklyn lines) consisted of Fort George, six guns, and the Grand Battery, 18 guns ; the Whitehall Battery ; and field-works at Coenties Slip and at Catherine, Madison, Pike, Clinton, Broome, and Pitt streets, and Grand and Mulberry streets, besides others near Trinity Church, and heavy barricades in the streets. In due time 21,000 British troops landed at Gravesend, and shattered Putnam's army of 9,000 men, holding the Brooklyn lines. Almost a fortnight later five frigates demolished the American defences at Kip's Bay (foot of East 34th Street), and scattered their garrisons in wild panic, which was communicated to the troops on Murray Hill, as the English grenadiers advanced. Putnam retreated from the city by the Bloomingdale Road. The Continentals rallied on Harlem Heights ; defeated the enemy in some hot skirmishes ; and then retreated into Westchester. The military officers had discussed the question of burning the city, to prevent it being made a winter-quarters for the British army ; but Congress forbade this extreme measure. Nevertheless, on the 21st of September a fire accidentally broke out in a low tavern near Whitehall Slip, and destroyed 493 houses, obliterating nearly all the North-River side of the city west of Broad Street and Broadway. The British troops believed that the torch had been applied by the Americans, and bayonetted or threw into the flames a number of citizens. At mid-

November, Gen. Howe and 9,000 men stormed the outworks of Fort Washington, and compelled the surrender of that strong fortress, the last American post on Manhattan Island. Thenceforward for over seven years New York lay in the hands of the enemy, a prostrate city under martial law, the chief depot for the soldiers and stores of the invading army, and the place of captivity where their prisoners of war were confined. The Dissenters' churches were turned into hospitals and prisons, and the Middle Dutch Church became a riding school for cavalrymen. The municipal government existed no longer, and about the only commerce was that of the sutlers' shops.

In the East River lay the horrible prison ships in whose disease-infested holds so many American soldiers were confined. It is related that in the *Jersey* alone over

BROADWAY, FROM BOWLING GREEN, IN 1828.

10,000 prisoners of war perished. The American officers and dignitaries were consigned to the new jail (now the Hall of Records). Several of the great sugar houses, including Rhinelander's, near William Street, were also used as prisons for captives from the Continental armies. On the 25th of November, 1783, the rear-guard of Sir Guy Carleton's British army embarked at the Battery. The American advance-guard, composed of light infantry, artillery and the 2d Massachusetts Regiment, marched down the Bowery and Chatham, Queen and Wall Streets to the corner of Broadway and Rector Street. After these came Gen. Washington and Gen. Clinton, the City Council, a group of veteran generals, and other functionaries. A few weeks later, Washington bade farewell to his officers, at Fraunces' Tavern, at the corner of Broad and Pearl Streets.

The first American Congress under the Constitution met in 1789, in the handsome old City Hall, at the corner of Wall and Broad Streets. Here, on the gallery overlooking Wall Street, which was packed with vast and silent crowds, Livingston, the chancellor of the State of New York, administered the oath of office to the first President of the United States, April 30, 1789. For a year thereafter New York was the capital of the Republic (as it had been for five years previously); and the President and Cabinet officers, Congressmen and foreign ambassadors and their families made up a brilliant and stately Court circle. The ruins of the great fires, and the squalor of the British garrison's "canvas town," were replaced by new buildings; the streets were cleared from the rubbish which had for years choked them up; and new shops and warehouses showed tempting arrays of wares. Wall Street, the favorite promenade, was brilliant with richly dressed ladies and hardly less showy gentlemen, and the carriages of the Republican aristocracy crowded Broadway down to the Battery. The finest mansion in the city was built in 1790, from the public funds, for the occupancy of Washington and his successors in the

Presidential office.   Before its completion, the seat of government was moved to
Philadelphia, and so the splendid house with its Ionic-colonnaded front became the
official residence of Governors Clinton and Jay.   It occupied the site of the ancient
fort, and was afterwards replaced by the Bowling-Green block.

The holiday of New Year's had been introduced by the first Dutch colonists on
Manhattan, and their descendants had kept it up faithfully, and with abundant good
cheer.   Washington thus advised a citizen, during one of these receptions :   "The
highly favored situation of New York will, in the process of years, attract numerous
immigrants, who will gradually change its ancient customs and manners ; but, whatever changes take place, never forget the cordial observance of New Year's Day."

The Tammany Society was formed in 1789, as a patriotic national institution,
with a government of a Grand Sachem (chosen from thirteen sachems), a Sagamore,
and a Wiskinskie.   Many Indian forms and ceremonials were adopted ; the months

NORTH BATTERY, AT THE FOOT OF HUBERT STREET.

were "moons"; and the seasons were those of snow, of blossoms, of fruit.   With
a view of conciliating the hostile tribes on the borders, the society took also the
name of Tammany, an Indian chief.   In its early years, some of the most conspicuous and respected of New-Yorkers belonged to this order, which, indeed, did not
become a political party institution until the days of the Jefferson administration.

It was impossible for New York to become the permanent capital of the United
States, because Congress demanded that the Federal District thus dignified should
be ceded to the Nation.   Neither the local nor the State authorities would consent
to this alienation of territory and wealth.   Washington made excursions on Long
Island and elsewhere, in search of an appropriate location, but without success.   His
heart was on the Potomac, where, after a ten years' sojourn at Philadelphia, the
National capital was at last established.

The tract known successively as De Vlackte, the Commons, and City-Hall Park,
in 1785 contained the Alms House and House of Correction, the public gallows, the
Bridewell (on part of the City Hall's site) and the New Jail (now the Hall of
Records).   The present City Hall was begun in 1803, Mayor Edward Livingston

laying the corner-stone. The front and sides were of Massachusetts marble ; but the back, or northern side, was built of red sandstone, because it was thought that the city would never grow to any importance to the northward of the new edifice. As a contemporary writer said, the northern front "would be out of sight to all the world." When this building was finished, in 1812, at a cost of $500,000, it was generally conceded to be the handsomest in the United States.

At the beginning of the century, Broadway had a length of about two miles, paved for little more than half this distance, and lined with comfortable brick houses. Here and there between the houses the view passed down the bay, and out through the Narrows. The homes of the gentry and the rich merchants were along lower Broadway and the Battery, where their occupants could enjoy the beautiful views

CITY HALL AND PARK, AND PARK THEATRE.

and refreshing air of the bay. At little over a mile from the Battery the paving ceased, and Broadway became a rather straggling road, with houses at intervals, and the indications of streets planned for the future. Broad Street in its width recalled the old canal that once flowed down its centre, but had long since vanished. Wall Street possessed many fine residences, and the handsome Federal Hall. The dry-goods marts occupied much of William Street, which afforded a bright spectacle on days favorable for shopping. Most of the other streets were narrow and winding, and lined with small red-brick houses with tiled roofs. On the west side, where the great fire of 1776 had occurred, the streets had been widened and straightened, and provided with brick sidewalks and gutters. The first sidewalk in the city was on Broadway, between Vesey and Murray Streets, constructed of brick and stone, and hardly a yard wide. The numbering of houses began in 1793. Broadway was built up only as far as Anthony Street ; the Bowery Lane, to Broome Street ; the East-River shore, to Rutgers Street ; and the North-River shore, to Harrison Street. Beyond the steep Anthony-Street hill, Broadway plunged sharply into the Canal

3

Street valley, between the Fresh Water Pond and the Lispenard Meadows. At Astor Place, Broadway ceased, its line being crossed by the wall of the Randall farm.

The favorite duelling ground was a lonely grassy glade in the woods of Wee-hawken, high above the Hudson, and allowing glimpses of New York through the surrounding trees. The combatants were rowed across from the city, and clambered up the rocky steep to the scene of their fight. The most mournful event in Ameri-can duelling annals occurred here, July 11, 1804, when the antagonists were Alexander Hamilton, the first Secretary of the Treasury, and founder of the National financial system, and Aaron Burr, Vice-President of the United States. Hamilton had characterized Burr as a "dangerous man," and helped to defeat his political schemes ; and Burr challenged him to mortal combat. Hamilton did not fire at his antagonist, but Burr, with a carefully aimed shot, mortally wounded him ; and he died the next day, in the presence of his wife and seven children. This dreadful encounter closed the practice of duelling in the civilized States of America ; and at the same time put an end to the public career of Burr.

The development of the higher culture in the Empire City received an impetus in 1784, by the re-chartering of the long-closed King's College, under the more republican title of Columbia College. Twenty years later the New-York Histori-cal Society was organized, followed by the College of Physicians and Surgeons in 1807, and the American Academy of Fine Arts in 1808. The education of the children rested in the hands of parochial, charity and private schools until 1806, when a small public school came into existence, from the contributions of wealthy citizens, and small State and city appropriations. The Free School Society in 1809 erected a large brick building on Chatham Street ; and in 1825, six schools were in operation, not as charities, but open to all comers.

New York may be called the cradle of steam navigation, which has completely revolutionized the world's commerce ; for although other localities had seen at an earlier day vessels propelled by steam, yet here occurred the first profitable and successful ventures in this line on a large scale. In 1807 the *Clermont* was built, from the designs of Robert Fulton, the inventor, and with capital furnished by Chancellor Robert R. Livingston ; and in spite of all the evil prognostications of the conservative, she made a triumphant run from New York to Albany in thirty-two hours. As it took the ordinary packets from four to six days to run between the two cities, the rapid success of steam navigation on the Hudson followed as a neces-sity, especially after 1817, when the time of passage was reduced to eighteen hours.

The navigation of Long-Island Sound by steamboats was soon inaugurated by a line opened in 1818 from New York to New Haven, followed by another to New London, and in 1822 by the New-York & Providence line. The advance from the ugly little *Clermont* and her slow and dirty vessels of her class to the magnificent steamboats of modern days was largely due to a young Staten-Island ferryman, Cornelius Vanderbilt, who came to New York in 1829 and established new and im-proved lines on the Hudson and the Sound.

The first steam vessel to dare the storms of ocean was the *Phœnix*, built by Col. John Stevens of Hoboken, in 1807, and a year later sent around from New-York harbor to Philadelphia, by the sea passage. In 1811 Stevens opened between Hoboken and New York the first steam ferry in the world ; and this was followed the next year by Fulton's lines to Jersey City and Brooklyn. The first steam frigate in the world, the *Fulton*, was built from a Congressional appropriation of $320,000, under Robert Fulton's supervision ; and made its successful trial-trip to Sandy

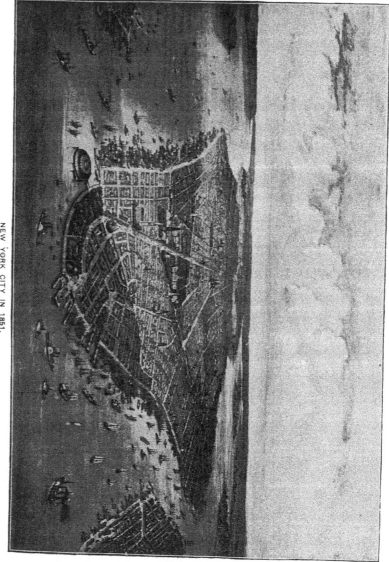

NEW YORK CITY IN 1851.
A REPRODUCTION FROM A LARGE STEEL ENGRAVING.

Hook in 1814.   Transatlantic steam navigation was inaugurated by the *Savannah*, built at New York in 1819 and sent thence to Savannah, Liverpool, Copenhagen, Stockholm and St. Petersburg.   In 1812 Col. Stevens made the plans for a circular iron-clad war-ship, with screw propellers.

About the year 1810 the city began a rapid development to the northward.   The Brevoort estate, between Broadway and the Bowery road and 11th Street ; Henry Spingler's farm, between 14th and 16th Streets, west of the Bowery ; Nicholas Bayard's West Farm, covering 100 acres between Broadway and McDougall Street, and running north from Prince Street ; the Bayard-Hill estate, between Broadway and the Bowery and Broome Street ; the 260-acre domain established by Sir Peter Warren, in the region of Gansevoort and Christopher Streets ; and many other

estates and farms were invaded by the City Commissioners.   Legions of stalwart laborers levelled the hills and filled the hollows ; and new streets were laid out with efficient engineering skill and foresight. Oftentimes the irate landlords assailed the survey-

CORP. THOMPSON'S MADISON COTTAGE, IN 1852.   SITE OF THE FIFTH-AVENUE HOTEL.

ors with dogs, hot water, cabbages and other distressful methods ; but the work went steadily on, especially above Houston Street, whence they laid out the island into parallel numbered cross streets and broad north and south avenues, distinguished by numbers or letters.

When Trinity Church, in 1807, erected St. John's Chapel, in Varick Street, it was regarded as quite beyond civilization, and the parish received much blame for planting their new mission opposite a bulrush swamp, tenanted only by water snakes and frogs.   About the same time, the Lutheran society got into financial straits, and a friend offered to give it four acres of land at the corner of Broadway and Canal Street.   This largess was declined by the church on the ground that the land was not worth the cost of fencing it — which was doubtless true at the time.

The Collect was a broad and placid pond, favored by skaters in winter, and boating parties in summer.   But it lay in the path of the northward advance of the city, and therefore, in 1809, a drainage canal was cut and bordered on either side by shade trees and a pleasant street (afterwards Canal Street).   It was proposed in 1789 to make a public park of this beautiful pond and its shores ; but the scheme came to naught, on the ground that New York would never grow within accessible distance of this lonely region.

The intersection of Leonard and Centre Streets is not far from the centre of the pond, which had a depth of sixty feet.   On the same site now stands the gloomy prison of the Tombs, the abode of so much misery and wickedness.   The Collect was famous as the place where a steamboat with a screw propeller was first tried, in 1796, when John Fitch, its inventor, steamed around the pond several times, in an eighteen-foot propeller.   Among the spectators were Chancellor Livingston and other prominent New-Yorkers.   About this time Oliver Evans aroused considerable popular amusement by saying that "The time will come when people will travel in stages moved by steam engines from one city to another, at fifteen or twenty miles an hour."

When Great Britain declared the ports of Continental Europe to be blockaded, and Napoleon retorted by proclaiming all vessels trading with Great Britain liable to seizure, American shipping suffered grave losses; and President Jefferson (in 1807) ordered all our commercial fleets to remain in our ports, and forbade the shipment of cargoes on foreign vessels.   He believed that warring Europe, thus deprived of American breadstuffs, would hasten to acknowledge our neutral rights.   During this

OLD NEW-YORK POST-OFFICE.   SITE OF THE MUTUAL LIFE-INSURANCE BUILDING, ON NASSAU STREET.

year of interdict the shipping of New York's merchant-princes decayed at their anchorages, the warehouses were closed and abandoned, and the clerks were discharged because there was no work for them.

The War of 1812 broke out in the same year that the City Hall received its finishing touches; and within a few weeks the city had fortified her approaches, and sent to sea 26 privateers, manned by 2,239 bold sailors.   Such a hornet's nest must needs be closed, and so from 1813 until the end of the war the mouth of the harbor was blockaded by tall British ships-of-the-line.   The naval headquarters of the enemy was at Gardiner's Island, east of Long Island, whence their squadrons off Sandy Hook, or blockading New London, could be reinforced or supplied.   In expectation of a dash from the enemy, New York was strongly fortified by the voluntary labor of its citizens, and new lines of defence covered the heights of Brooklyn and Harlem, with forts on the islands and at the Narrows and around Hell Gate.   The city was held by a garrison of 23,000 men, mostly of the State troops.

The first great trunk line of railway finished from New York to the West was the Erie, which ran its trains as far as Dunkirk, on Lake Erie, in 1851.   The line from Albany to Schenectady was opened in 1832, and in 1853 became a part of the newly organized New-York Central, whose rails reached Buffalo a year later.   The Hudson-River Railroad, from New-York to Albany, was opened in 1851, and in 1869 became a part of the New-York Central system.

The horse-railroad, of such incalculable importance in street traffic, was inaugurated in 1832, when the Fourth-Avenue line began its trips, running from Prince

Street as far as Murray Hill. The first street-car ever built was made by John
Stephenson, with compartments, roof seats, and the driver in the roof.

Another valuable modern convenience, illuminating gas, was introduced in 1825,
with pipes traversing Broadway from the Battery to Canal Street.

After the War of 1812, the famous packet lines began their service, the Black-
Ball in 1816 and the Red-Star in 1821, running swift and handsome ships nearly
weekly between New York and Liverpool, and making the run across eastward in
from 15 to 23 days. Depan put four ships on the Havre packet service in 1822;
and Grinnell, Minturn & Co. began to send monthly packets to London in 1823.
After 1840 Low, Griswold & Aspinwall inaugurated the sailing of clipper-ships to
China and California, and their vessels performed the most wonderful feats — as
when the *Flying Cloud* ran from New York to San Francisco, making 433¼ statute

FIVE POINTS IN 1859, VIEW FROM THE CORNER OF NORTH AND LITTLE WATER STREETS.

miles in a single day; or the *Sovereign of the Seas* sailed for 10,000 miles without
tacking or wearing; or the *Dreadnaught* made the passage from Sandy Hook to
Queenstown in nine days and seventeen hours.

The wonderful Erie Canal was built between 1816 and 1825, and became the
most prominent factor in the growth of the Empire City, bringing to her docks the
illimitable products of the Great West (then without railways), and carrying back
much of her vast imports. The telegraph was not then known; and the news of
the opening of the canal was carried in 81 minutes 550 miles from Buffalo to Sandy
Hook by the successive reports of a line of cannon, ten miles apart. A group of
canal boats containing Gov. Clinton and other magnates descended the canal to
Albany, and were thence towed down the Hudson to New York, and out to sea,
escorted by many flag-bedecked vessels and barges. At Sandy Hook, Governor

Clinton emptied into the ocean a keg of Lake-Erie water, and other unique ceremonials were solemnly and decorously performed.

John Jacob Astor, a native of Waldorf, near Heidelberg, came to the New World in 1784, in his twenty-first year, and entered the fur-trade in the Empire City, keeping also a stock of London piano-fortes. He had himself incorporated as the American Fur Company ; bought out the Mackinaw Company and all its forts ; established a line of trading-posts across Oregon ; and developed a rich China trade. This typical merchant lived on the site of the present Astor House, and frequently entertained Irving, Halleck, and other literary men and scholars.

In 1834 occurred the Anti-Abolition riots, in which for the first time the National Guard was called out to restore order ; and a few months later the same potent peace-makers came into service to quell the stone-cutters' riots, and lay under arms on Washington Square for several days.   In December, 1835, a fire in the lower part

VIEW FROM THE SCHOOL-HOUSE IN 42D STREET, BETWEEN SECOND AND THIRD AVENUES, IN 1868.

of the city burned over 13 acres, with 700 buildings and $20,000,000 worth of property, and was stopped only at the wide gaps made by blowing up houses with gunpowder. This portentous calamity showed the need of more water for the growing city ; and the Croton Aqueduct, begun in 1835, delivered water on Manhattan Island in 1842, and was completed in 1845, at a cost of $9,000,000.   The old Manhattan Water Works, whose reservoir stood on Chambers Street, were thus rendered valueless.

The University of the City of New York dates from 1831 ; the *Sun* from 1833 ; the *Herald* from 1835 ; the *Tribune* from 1841 ; the *Times* from 1851 ; and the *World* from 1860.   Other notable achievements of this period were the opening of the Croton Aqueduct in 1842 ; the founding of the Astor Library in 1848 ; and the opening of the World's Fair in the Crystal Palace in 1853.

In 1825 the region north of Astor Place was still devoted to farms and orchards, with a gray old barn on the site of Grace Church, and a powder-house on Union Square.   The fashionable summer evening resort was the Vauxhall Garden, stretching from Broadway to the Bowery, near the present Astor Library, and famous for its trees and flowers, band-music and fire-works, and cakes and ale.   In the triangle where Third Avenue and Fourth Avenue come together, stood the grocery store of

Peter Cooper, where the uptown lads exchanged berries picked in the Bleecker-Street pastures, for taffy and cakes.

Greenwich village occupied the region about the present Greenwich Avenue ; and to the northward, near West 23d Street, the roofs of Chelsea Village peered over the trees. In 1797 the State Prison of Newgate was opened at Greenwich, and served as a terror to evil-doers during full a quarter of a century.

For a number of years after 1825 the vicinity of St. John's Park was the Court end of the city, with the mansions of the Lydigs, Pauldings and other prominent families. In this vicinity, at the foot of Hubert Street, stood the frowning old North Battery, with its empty embrasures.

The old Potter's Field, now known as Washington Square, became fashionable about ten years later ; and here dwelt the Rhinelanders and Johnstons, Griswolds and Boormans, and other well-known families.

The convergence of several streets where Fourth Avenue met the old Bowery road made it necessary to leave there a broad common, which was at times used as the Potter's Field, much of its area being also covered with rude shanties. Not until 1845 was this rugged and filthy field improved into the present Union Square, which was soon surrounded by fine mansions, and up nearly to the time of the War for the Union remained the Belgravia of Manhattan. Only a few houses were to be seen above Union Square in 1845. Gramercy Park was laid out by Samuel B. Ruggles, and presented to the owners of the sixty neighboring lots, to induce the erection of attractive houses here. Where the old Boston Road met the Bloomingdale Road lay another broad area of waste land, in olden times a burial-place for the poor, and from 1806 to 1823 the site of a United-States arsenal. Here the first House of Refuge was founded, in 1825, with six boys and three girls ; and remained until it burned down in 1839. During the mayoralty of James Harper (one of the famous publishers), between 1844 and 1847, this dreary region was cleared and beautified, and became the famous Madison Square. The chief house here in 1852 was the little story-and-a-half cottage of Corp. Thompson, on the site now occupied by the Fifth-Avenue Hotel.

One of the most wonderful of modern inventions, the electric telegraph, was inaugurated by the experiments of Prof. S. F. B. Morse, in the University of the City of New York. A line of telegraph was completed from New York to Philadelphia in 1845 ; to Boston in 1846 ; and to Albany in 1847.

In 1849, Macready, the celebrated English actor, played Macbeth in the Astor-Place Opera House. The populace supposed that Edwin Forrest's ill reception in England, a few years before, had been due to Macready's hostile influence ; and they attacked the Opera House, 20,000 strong, during the play, scattering the police, and breaking the windows with paving stones. The Seventh Regiment cleared the vicinity, after a pitched battle, in which 150 soldiers were severely injured and 70 of the mob.

The commercial and therefore conservative spirit of modern New York naturally held back from the dread hostilities foreshadowed in 1860 ; and by monster petitions and peace societies endeavored to arrest the storm. Mayor Fernando Wood even outlined a plan to make it a free city, like those of mediæval Germany, inviting the trade of the world by nominal duties. But after the first guns were fired, in South Carolina, the spirit of temporizing vanished like a dream, and patriotism and loyalty possessed all classes with full inspiration. Within ten days 8,000 volunteer troops left the city for the South, including the 7th, 6th, 12th and 11th Regiments of militia. In this metropolitan centre also were organized the famous and efficient

THE BLIZZARD OF MARCH 11TH, 12TH, AND 13TH, 1888.
PHOTOGRAPHS TAKEN JUST AFTER THE STORM, BY LANGILL.

societies, the United-States Sanitary Commission and the United-States Christian Commission, and the Union Defense Committee, whose efforts placed 40,000 soldiers under the National colors. New-York City alone sent 116,382 patriotic troops into the field, besides raising scores of millions of dollars for the needs of the Republic.

The terrible Draft Riot of 1863 was caused by popular discontent with the impressment of citizens into the army, a feeling which was intensified by the incendiary editorials of certain Democratic journals, and was not sufficiently discouraged by Gov. Seymour. On July 13th, a mob plundered and burned the provost-marshal's office, at Third Avenue and 46th Street, and then scattered through the city, bent on deeds of rapine and murder. The *Tribune* office was sacked ; the colored Orphan Asylum on Fifth Avenue went up in flames ; the grain-elevators at the Atlantic Docks were burned; and negroes and soldiers were slain or grievously maltreated wherever found. The closed shops, the streets clear of their customary traffic, and even of omnibuses and horse-cars, and many of the houses prepared like fortresses for defence, gave the city a singular and ominous appearance, which was increased by the mad roars of the mob, the clattering of cavalry along the pavement, the roll of volley-firing, and the heavy booming of artillery, sweeping the riotous vermin from the streets. The police behaved with extraordinary valor, but were unable to completely control this vast uprising of foreign-born anarchists, until the arrival of strong military forces, aided by the personal efforts and appeals of the Governor, the Mayor, and Archbishop Hughes. More than 1,000 men were killed and wounded and $2,000,000 of property was destroyed.

The long-continued supremacy of the degraded classes in municipal politics reached its crown of infamy after the close of the War for the Union, when William M. Tweed, a low ward-politician, was elevated to one of the chief offices of the city. In conjunction with other and similar conspirators, he elaborated a shrewd scheme, by which, within a few months, the city was robbed of $20,000,000. The new County Court House alone furnished $7,000,000 of this amount. In 1871, through reason of a disagreement among the municipal officials, the damning documents in the case of " The Ring " passed into the possession of the *New-York Times*, which immediately printed the entire history of this gigantic robbery, and itemized the amounts stolen. The other leading newspapers also came out against the detected thieves, the citizens organized a committee of seventy, and most of the culprits fled to Europe or Canada. Tweed was imprisoned, but escaped to Spain, whence he was returned to the outraged metropolis, and finally died in jail.

The events of later days in New York are familiar to all readers of the newspapers— that is to say, to all Americans. The development of education, of public charities, of artistic and literary culture, of vast works of public utility, have gone forward mightily, and to the great glory of the community. Occasionally, a great financial flurry, like the Black Friday of 1869, or the panic of 1873, threatens to unsettle values and bring ruin to thousands. Now and then a riot occurs, like that of 1871, when 29 policemen and soldiers were killed and wounded, and 104 of their assailants, in the attack of the Irish Catholics on the parading Orangemen. Other years see the rejoicings upon the completion of great public works, like the Park-Avenue improvements, costing $6,000,000, in 1875 ; the blowing-up of Hell Gate, in 1876 ; and the dedication of the East-River Bridge, in 1883.

The year 1886 saw the unveiling of Bartholdi's wonderful statue of " Liberty Enlightening the World," with its attendant civic and National ceremonials. Then also came the trial of the aldermen bribed by persons seeking the franchise of the Broadway Surface Railroad. The same year saw the local Anarchists sent to prison,

WASHINGTON CENTENNIAL EXERCISES IN 1889, AT THE UNITED-STATES SUB-TREASURY.

PHOTOGRAPHED BY JOHNSTON, WHILE THE REV. DR. R. S. STORRS WAS OFFERING PRAYER.

the great street-car strikes, and the twentieth annual encampment of the Grand Army of the Republic.

The most notable event of 1888 was the great blizzard of March 11–13, with its stoppage of transportation, food panic, the forming of an ice-bridge across the East River, and other unseasonable phenomena.

In 1889 the hundredth anniversary of the inauguration of George Washington as President of the United States was celebrated here by a three-days' festival, with a naval review by President Harrison, a march-past of 50,000 soldiers from 21 States, a civic parade of 75,000 persons, and other imposing ceremonies.

In 1890 the Holland Society began to identify interesting historic localities connected with the ancient Dutch settlement of New Amsterdam, and to place near them durable bronze tablets, with explicit inscriptions. In the same year occurred the beginning of the Washington Memorial Arch, erected in Washington Square, to replace a temporary triumphal arch constructed for the preceding year's Washington anniversary. At this time, also, the statue of

THE LOEW BRIDGE, BROADWAY AND FULTON STREET.

Horace Greeley was unveiled. The year was further distinguished by the great conventions here of the mining engineers, and of the manufacturers of iron and steel.

1891 opened luridly with the burning of the Fifth-Avenue Theatre. On the 5th of May occurred the dedication of the grand new Music Hall, founded by Andrew Carnegie. In October the Court of Appeals decided the Tilden Will case in favor of the natural heirs, to the severe loss of the city. The year was further notable as that in which the Metropolitan Museum of Art was first opened to the public on Sundays. In 1891, also, came the visit of Prince George of Greece; and then also occurred the attack of a dynamiter on Russell Sage.

The year 1892 was marked by the deaths of several prominent New-Yorkers : John Jay Knox, on February 9th ; Thomas Sterry Hunt, February 12th ; Gen. G. W. Cullum, February 28th ; Edwards Pierrepont, March 6th ; Roswell Smith, April 19th ; William Astor, April 25th ; Sidney Dillon, June 10th ; Cyrus W. Field, July 12th ; and George William Curtis, August 31st.

On the 7th of February 17 persons were burned alive in the Hotel Royal.

In 1892 the wonderfully successful Actors' Fund Fair was held in Madison-Square Garden, where also occurred, at a later date, the world's convention of the Society of Christian Endeavor. Now also came about the redistricting of the city into thirty Assembly districts, in conformity with the greatly increased population shown by the censuses of 1890. It may be added, that in 1892 occurred the publi-

ON THIS SITE
WILLIAM BRADFORD
APPOINTED PUBLIC PRINTER APRIL 10TH. A. D. 1693
ISSUED NOVEMBER 8, A. D., 1725
THE NEW YORK GAZETTE
THE FIRST NEWSPAPER PRINTED IN NEW YORK

ERECTED BY THE
NEW YORK HISTORICAL SOCIETY
APRIL 10TH. A. D. 1893
IN COMMEMORATION OF THE 200TH ANNIVERSARY OF THE
INTRODUCTION OF PRINTING IN NEW YORK.

Tablet on the Cotton Exchange.

HERE STOOD
THE MIDDLE DUTCH CHURCH
DEDICATED A. D. 1729
MADE A BRITISH MILITARY PRISON 1776
RESTORED 1790
OCCUPIED AS THE UNITED STATES POST OFFICE
1845-1875
TAKEN DOWN 1882.

THIS TABLET IS PLACED HERE BY
THE MUTUAL LIFE INSURANCE COMPANY
OF NEW YORK.

Tablet on the Mutual Life Building, corner of Cedar and Nassau Streets.

THE SITE OF
LIEUT. GOVERNOR DELANCEY'S HOUSE
LATER OF THE "CITY HOTEL".
IT WAS HERE THAT THE "NON-IMPORTATION AGREEMENT"
IN OPPOSITION TO THE "STAMP ACT" WAS SIGNED OCTOBER 31ST, 1765.
THE TAVERN HAD MANY PROPRIETORS BY WHOSE
NAMES IT WAS SUCCESSIVELY CALLED. IT WAS ALSO KNOWN
AS THE "PROVINCE ARMS." THE "CITY ARMS" AND "BURNS'
COFFEE HOUSE" OR "TAVERN".

THIS TABLET IS PLACED HERE BY THE
HOLLAND SOCIETY OF NEW YORK, SEPTEMBER
1890.

Tablet on the Boreel Building, 115 Broadway.

THIS TABLET MARKS THE SITE OF THE
FIRST HABITATIONS OF WHITE MEN
ON THE ISLAND OF MANHATTAN
ADRIAN BLOCK
COMMANDER OF THE "TIGER"
ERECTED HERE FOUR HOUSES OR HUTS
AFTER HIS VESSEL WAS BURNED
NOVEMBER 1613
HE BUILT THE "RESTLESS" THE FIRST VESSEL
MADE BY EUROPEANS IN THIS COUNTRY
THE "RESTLESS" WAS LAUNCHED
IN THE SPRING OF 1614

THIS TABLET IS PLACED HERE BY
THE HOLLAND SOCIETY OF NEW YORK
SEPTEMBER 1890

Tablet at 45 Broadway.

ON THIS CORNER GREW
PETRUS STUYVESANT'S PEAR TREE
RECALLED TO HOLLAND IN 1664
ON HIS RETURN
HE BROUGHT THE PEAR TREE
AND PLANTED IT
AS HIS MEMORIAL
"BY WHICH" SAID HE "MY NAME
MAY BE REMEMBERED"
THE PEAR TREE FLOURISHED
AND BORE FRUIT FOR OVER
TWO HUNDRED YEARS
THIS TABLET IS PLACED HERE BY
THE HOLLAND SOCIETY
OF NEW YORK
SEPTEMBER, 1890

Tablet at Third Avenue and 12th Street.

THE SITE OF FORT AMSTERDAM
BUILT IN 1626
WITHIN THE FORTIFICATIONS
WAS ERECTED THE FIRST
SUBSTANTIAL CHURCH EDIFICE
ON THE ISLAND OF MANHATTAN.
IN 1787 THE FORT
WAS DEMOLISHED
AND THE GOVERNMENT HOUSE
BUILT UPON THIS SPOT.

THIS TABLET IS PLACED HERE BY
THE HOLLAND SOCIETY OF NEW YORK
SEPTEMBER, 1890

Tablet at 4 Bowling Green.

TO COMMEMORATE THE GALLANT AND PATRIOTIC
ACT OF MARINUS WILLETT IN HERE SEIZING
JUNE 6, 1775, FROM BRITISH FORCES THE
MUSKETS WITH WHICH HE ARMED HIS
TROOPS THIS TABLET IS ERECTED BY
THE SOCIETY OF THE SONS OF THE
REVOLUTION, NEW YORK. NOV. 1892.

DANIEL BUTTERFIELD, FLOYD CLARKSON,
MORGAN DIX, JOHN AUSTIN STEVENS,
DAVID WOLFE BISHOP -- COMMITTEE.

Tablet on the Morris Building.

HISTORICAL TABLETS
RECENTLY PLACED IN THE VARIOUSLY DESIGNATED LOCALITIES.

THE SITE OF THE
FIRST DUTCH HOUSE OF ENTERTAINMENT
ON THE ISLAND OF MANHATTAN
LATER THE SITE OF THE OLD STADT HUYS
OR CITY HALL.

THIS TABLET IS PLACED HERE BY
THE HOLLAND SOCIETY OF NEW YORK
SEPTEMBER, 1890

Tablet at 73 Pearl Street, Facing Coenties Slip.

FRAUNCES TAVERN.   TO THIS BUILDING
GENERAL GEORGE WASHINGTON
CAME EVACUATION DAY, NOV. 25, 1783
AND ON THURSDAY, DEC. 4
FOLLOWING HERE TOOK
LEAVE OF THE PRINCIPAL
OFFICERS OF THE ARMY
YET IN SERVICE.

Tablet at corner of Pearl and Broad Sts.

cation and sale of the first edition (of ten thousand copies) of *King's Handbook of New-York City*. The summer of 1892 was memorable by reason of the approach of cholera, from Europe, and the detention of many steamships, with thousands of passengers, by the quarantine authorities. By this efficient vigilance the pestilence was prevented from entering the United States. Nearly all the National Guard belonging in New-York City was sent to Buffalo in 1892 to check the destroying agencies of a strike there ; and other detachments were dispatched to Fire Island, to repress insurrection. This same year, 1892, witnessed the burning of the Metropolitan Opera House, and the magnificent ceremonies at the laying of the corner-stone of the Cathedral of St. John the Divine.

In 1893, when Grover Cleveland, a citizen of New York, was inaugurated President of the United States, the magnificent ceremonies of the day were participated in by thousands of Tammany braves, marching through the streets of Washington. During the same springtime occurred the death of Col. E. F. Shepard, the editor of *The Mail and Express*. In April, 1893, the Duke of Veragna, a lineal descendant of Christopher Columbus, visited New York, as the representative of the Kingdom of Spain to the World's Columbian Exposition. He was welcomed with great society and municipal receptions, and for several days was the most conspicuous personage in the metropolis. He also received the freedom of the city, a distinction conferred not more than half a dozen times in a century. Late in April, in New-York harbor, occurred the most imposing of all the pageants commemorating the discovery of America by Columbus. This was the grand naval review, including the best ships of the American fleet, and squadrons of British, French, Spanish, Russian, Italian, Dutch, Brazilian, and Argentine ships-of-war. This event was virtually the inaugural ceremony of the opening of the World's Columbian Exposition, at Chicago, to which New-Yorkers made most liberal contributions of money, and among the most notable features of which will be the exhibits of the people of New-York City.

Thus pauses, for the time, the record of History. What may be in store for the proud New-World metropolis, who can say? She may be destined to sink beneath the waves that gave her life, like the drowned cities of the Zuyder Zee ; or to be irretrievably shattered by hostile armaments, like Tyre ; or to tranquilly fade away into commercial death, like Venice. Yet such fates can hardly be imagined as awaiting the Empire City of the Western World, now in the full flush of her success and power, and leading in the van of modern life and thought. She has appalling problems to face — the inflowing of half-pauperized foreigners, the menace of the submerged tenth, the evils of municipal misgovernment, the rise of a many-millioned plutocracy, and other serious and perilous questions. But public opinion is awakening on all sides to their consideration, and the grand old city will doubtless meet the strong new troubles with stronger new remedies, just as in the days that are past she has faced and conquered so many other threatening perils.

New York of the Present.

A Comprehensive Outline Description of the Whole City—Area, Population, Wealth, Statistics, Etc.

TO-DAY the City of New York is not only the metropolis of the United States, but in population, in wealth, in influence, in enterprise, in all that best distinguishes modern civilization, it is the rival of the great capitals of the Old World.

The Area actually within the limits of the city includes Manhattan Island, Governor's Island, in New-York Bay ; Blackwell's, Ward's, and Randall's Islands, in the East River ; and a considerable section of the mainland north of the Harlem River, and west of the Bronx. From the Battery, at the southern extremity of Manhattan Island, to the northern line of the city is a distance of sixteen miles. On the island, which is $13\frac{1}{2}$ miles long, the width of the city varies from a few score rods to $2\frac{1}{2}$ miles ; and north of the Harlem its greatest width is $4\frac{1}{2}$ miles. The area of Manhattan Island is nearly 22 square miles, or 14,000 acres ; and with the section on the mainland, the city has a total of $41\frac{1}{2}$ square miles, or 26,500 acres. In the process of growth and annexation New York has absorbed many villages, once its outlying suburbs, and whose memories even now exist in popular local designations, despite the fact that they have become parts of the metropolis. Thus down-town are Greenwich and Chelsea ; farther uptown, in the vicinity of Central Park, Bloomingdale and Yorkville ; above the park, Harlem and Manhattanville ; then Carmansville, Washington Heights and Inwood ; and on the mainland, that was annexed in 1874, are Port Morris, North New York, Claremont, Fairmount, Morrisania, West Farms, Spuyten Duyvil, Mosholu, Williamsbridge, Fordham, Tremont, Mount St. Vincent, Mott Haven and Melrose, and other villages. The insular part of the city is thickly built up and heavily populated, save in certain territories in Harlem, Bloomingdale, Yorkville, and Washington Heights ; but even there building is going forward with rapidity. In the annexed district development has been retarded by the lack of transit facilities, but is now proceeding steadily, and this section promises to become an important residential quarter.

The Population has grown in a phenomenal manner during the last half-century. In 1830, it was 202,000 ; in 1860, 805,000 ; in 1880, 1,206,500. In 1890 the United-States Census gave the city 1,513,501 population ; the Health-Board statistics, 1,631,232 ; and the police enumeration, 1,710,715. In February, 1892, there was a State enumeration that showed a population of 1,800,891. The yearly vote of the city is one vote for every $7\frac{2}{3}$ inhabitants. New York is thus the first city of the United States in population, and that too within a more contracted area than those rivals that come nearest to her in number of inhabitants — Chicago and Philadelphia. The overflow of the city goes out into the surrounding region ; and has built up cities, towns and villages that would scarcely have existence were it not for the activity of Manhattan Island.

PRODUCE EXCHANGE TOWER.　　　　　　　　　　"TRIBUNE."　　　　　　"TIMES."

NEW-YORK CITY.
LOOKING SOUTHWEST FROM THE "WORLD" DOME.

"TIMES." ST. PAUL'S. POST OFFICE. CITY-HALL PARK.

NEW-YORK CITY.

LOOKING WEST FROM THE "WORLD" DOME.

4

Greater New York comprises the city, with its suburban environs in the State of New York. It takes in the City of New York ; the counties of Kings and Rich-mond; the southern portions of the towns of Eastchester and Pelham, in Westchester County ; and Long-Island City, the towns of Newton, Flushing, Jamaica and the westerly portion of the town of Hempstead, in Queens County ; making a total area of 318 square miles, with a population of nearly 3,000,000. A commission to en-quire into the expediency of consolidating this territory into one city was appointed under an act of the New-York State Legislature, in 1890, and has reported in favor of the project. Andrew H. Green, the father of the movement, is also the President of the Commission. Greater New York will thus be the second city of the world, leaving Paris behind ; and still provided with a line of great suburban cities pertaining to New Jersey, and hence isolated from its political life, though united with it socially and industrially.

The Nationalities represented in New York make it the most cosmopolitan city in the world. It has more Irish than Dublin, and more Germans than any German city except Berlin. There are sections almost entirely given over to people of foreign birth or descent, each nationality forming a colony by itself. Thus, we have the French, the German, the Italian, the African, the Chinese, the Hebrew, the Spanish and the Arab colonies. The English-speaking foreigners, as the Irish, the English and the Scotch, have assimilated more readily with the native popula-tion ; and so have the Germans, to a considerable extent. Other nationalities have kept themselves more nearly intact.

The Surroundings of few cities are more remarkable than those of New York. The urban territory and the surrounding country is historic ground. In the lower streets many old houses still stand, or localities are distinguished that recall Rev-olutionary and pre-Revolutionary days ; and on the hills of upper Manhattan, and in the Trans-Val region, modern enterprise has not yet destroyed all the ancient land-marks. Along the west flows the noble Hudson, renowned as one of the world's most beautiful rivers; and on the east, the East River leads into Long-Island Sound. Up and down Long Island are numerous beautiful and historic villages ; and along the south shore of the island extend the great popular summer-resorts, Coney Island, Rockaway Beach, Sheepshead Bay and their rivals. The harbor is one of the largest, safest and most beautiful in the world. A hundred navies could ride at anchor upon its waters. The Lower Bay, almost surrounded by the shores of Long Island, Staten Island and New Jersey, is a magnificent sheet of water. Coming up through the Narrows, between the picturesque shores of Long Island and Staten Island, the view is enchanting ; and the land-locked upper harbor, sheltered by the hills of the two islands and of New Jersey, with the point of Manhattan Island reaching down into it between the two great rivers, the indications of a phe-nomenal commercial energy exhibited on every hand, the Statue of Liberty, and the towering buildings of the city, present a scene never to be forgotten.

The Municipal Administration is conducted mainly by the Mayor and the heads of departments, several of whom are chosen by popular vote, and the others appointed by the Mayor. Municipal legislation is in the hands of the Board of Aldermen, which consists of 32 members, including 29 from Manhattan Island, 2 from beyond the Harlem, and a president elected at large. Previous to 1892 there were only 25 Aldermen.

The City Finances, according to the last report of the Comptroller, for the year ending January 1, 1893, shows the receipts were: From taxes, $33,232,725 ; from other sources, $5,552,856 ; moneys borrowed, $27,665,053. Total receipts,

$66,450,635. The expenditures were by appropriation, $34,732,289, and on special and trust accounts, $30,586,068. The total funded debt was $155,161,974; or, less the amount in the sinking fund, $98,629,567. This debt is bonded at from 2½ to 7 per cent. interest, a considerable part of it being at 2½ and 3 per cent., a handsome testimonial to the credit of the city.

For the year 1893 the final estimate of appropriations allowed amounted to $34,444,155. Of that sum $3,000,000 is provided for by receipts from miscellaneous sources, leaving nearly $35,000,000 to be raised by taxation. Of this amount $4,948,582 was for interest on the city debt; $1,499,021 for the redemption and installments of the principal of the city debt; $3,554,458 for State taxes and State common schools; $3,014,020 for the Department of Public Works; $1,096,455 for the Department of Public Parks; $2,223,425 for the Department of Public Charities and Correction; $5,309,886 for the Police Department; $2,200,000 for the Department of Street-Cleaning; $2,223,134 for the Fire Department; $4,480,448 for the Board of Education; $1,139,890 for Judiciary Salaries; and $1,305,177 for Charitable Institutions.

The Judiciary is partly elected and partly appointed by the Mayor. The elected officials are the seven judges of the Supreme Court, with a salary of $17,500 each; the six judges of the Superior Court, with a salary of $15,000 each; the six judges of the Court of Common Pleas, with a salary of $15,000 each; in the Courts of General Session, one Recorder and three judges, salary, $12,000 each; the six judges of the City Court, with a salary of $10,000 each; in the Surrogate Court, two Surrogates, $15,000 each; in the District Court, eleven justices, $6,000 each; Sheriff, $12,000 and half the fees; and District Attorney, $12,000. The principal appointed officials are fifteen Police Justices, $8,000 each; six Assistant District Attorneys, at $7,500 each; and one Commissioner of Jurors, at $5,000. Legal advice can be secured from 6,000 lawyers.

Political Divisions separate the city into thirty Assembly, eight Senatorial and ten Congressional districts. At the last election, in 1892, 284,984 votes were cast, or twenty per cent. of the total State vote. Within fifteen miles of the New-York City Hall there is a vote of about 500,000, or forty per cent. of the State.

The Police Department numbers 3,906 men, and has a deservedly high reputation for efficiency. The arrests number about 85,000 yearly.

The Fire Department has 1,400 employees, in twelve battalions; and over 200 pieces of apparatus, including 91 steam fire-engines, four water-towers and three fire-boats. There are 1,200 miles of wire and 1,235 boxes for the fire-alarm telegraph. Fire destroys over $4,000,000 of property in this city every year.

The Number of Buildings includes 90,000 dwelling-houses in the city, and 25,000 business-houses, making a total of more than 115,000. Over 1,100 new buildings, valued at more than $13,000,000, are erected yearly. The real-estate valuation for purposes of taxation is $1,464,247,820, which fixes the actual value at over $4,400,000,000. The assessment value of personal property is $321,609,518, making a total of $1,785,857,338. The tax rate is $1.90 per hundred.

The Deaths in 1890 were 40,103, at a rate of 23.51 in a thousand; in 1891, 43,659, or 24.73 in a thousand; and in 1892, 44,329, or 24.26 in a thousand.

Streets, Sewers, Water, Etc.—There are 575 miles of streets; 444 miles of sewers, constructed at a cost of over $22,000,000; 685½ miles of water-mains, and 8,800 hydrants; and 16 public bathing places, used yearly by 4,000,000 bathers. The streets are lighted at night by 26,524 gas-lights and 1,535 electric lights. The city has 144 piers on the North and East Rivers; and 13 public markets.

MURRAY STREET.   CITY HALL.   WARREN STREET.

NEW-YORK CITY.

LOOKING WEST-NORTHWEST FROM THE "WORLD" DOME.

CITY-HALL PARK.   COUNTY COURT-HOUSE.   COURT OF GENERAL SESSIONS.

NEW-YORK CITY.

LOOKING NORTH FROM THE " WORLD " DOME.

The **Public Buildings** belonging to New York include the City Hall, a fine example of the Italian Renaissance architecture ; the County Court-House, an imposing Corinthian structure of white marble, which nominally cost many millions, and is a memorial of the peculations of the notorious Tweed ring ; the Jefferson-Market Court-House, a handsome building of brick and sandstone, in the Italian Gothic style ; the Hall of Records, in City-Hall Park ; the Tombs, a substantial and grim-appearing edifice, in the purest Egyptian style ; the new Court-House, just approaching completion, near the Tombs ; the famous Castle Garden, at the Battery, long used as a receiving station for immigrants ; and many department buildings.   Two other imposing public structures, both works of engineering skill, belong in part or in whole to the city — the East-River Bridge to Brooklyn, and the Washington Bridge, over the Harlem River.

The **Water-Supply** comes from the Croton water-shed, about 30 miles from the city.   Besides natural lakes in that region, there are artificial reservoirs giving a total storage capacity of 17,150,000,000 gallons.   Work now in progress in the construction of new dams will more than double this storage capacity.   The supply is practically unlimited, and with abundant storage facilities 350,000,000 gallons a day would be assured.   Water is brought down to the city by the old aqueduct, which has a carrying capacity of 75,000,000 gallons each day.   The new aqueduct which was opened in 1890 has a carrying capacity of 320,000,000 gallons each day.   It cost over $25,000,000.   In the city proper there are storage and receiving reservoirs that will hold 1,266,000,000 gallons.   The daily consumption is 170,000,000 gallons, and the present storage capacity at the watershed would meet all needs for three months.

The **Militia** constitutes a full brigade of the National Guard of the State. There are seven regiments, two batteries, one cavalry troop, and one signal corps, with 896 officers and 4,268 men.   Besides these there is a Naval Battalion.

Local Traffic is effected by the elevated railroads, horse-cars and cable-cars, and the Fifth-Avenue stage-line.   There are five lines of elevated roads (33 miles), under one management, four running practically the length of Manhattan Island, from the Battery to the Harlem River ; and the fifth extending out into the trans-Harlem district.   There are 17 surface street-car railroad companies, running cars over 42 main lines and branches.   One line across town in Harlem and up Washington Heights (seven miles) has been operated by cable for several years ; and cable-power is about to be substituted for horse-power on Broadway and Third Avenue.

The **Ferries** (with the exception of the East-River Bridge and the several Harlem-River bridges) afford the only means of communication between Manhattan Island and the surrounding localities.   There are 38 ferry lines, including thirteen to Brooklyn, and thirteen to New Jersey.

Steam Railways to the number of 23 serve New York directly.   Only four of these enter the city proper — the New-York Central & Hudson-River, the New-York & Harlem, and the New-York, New-Haven & Hartford, which come into the Grand Central Depot, at 42d Street ; and the New-York & Northern, which has a depot at 155th Street and Eighth Avenue.   The depot of the Long-Island Railroad is at Long-Island City ; and on the New-Jersey side of the Hudson River are the depots of the Pennsylvania, the Baltimore & Ohio, the New-Jersey Central, the Delaware, Lacka-wanna & Western, the Erie, the Lehigh-Valley, the New-Jersey Southern, the Ontario & Western, the West-Shore, and many connecting lines.

Steamboats run from New York to Albany, Troy and other ports on the Hudson River ; to Boston, Newport, Providence, Bridgeport, New Haven, Fall River and other New-England ports ; to Long Branch, Sandy Hook and elsewhere on the

New-Jersey coast ; and to many places on Long Island. There are over thirty such lines, and not fewer than 150 steamboats thus employed, including the palatial boats that are in commission on the Sound routes to Boston, on the Hudson River, and on the summer routes to Sandy Hook and Long Branch. For speed, safety, beauty and elegance of appointments these boats surpass anything in the world.

Coastwise and Ocean Traffic to and from the port of New York reaches enormous proportions. In the trans-Atlantic fleet there are over 120 steamships, belonging to fourteen regular lines to Europe, and lines to Brazil, Central America, the West Indies, Mexico, Venezuela, Trinidad, Newfoundland and other foreign ports, and to the chief Atlantic domestic ports. In the European fleet the great ocean greyhounds are floating palaces that represent the perfection of modern marine architecture. From foreign ports the yearly arrivals of steamships number 3,000, and sailing vessels reach about the same number. From domestic ports there are 1,700 steamships and 14,000 sailing-vessels. The total tonnage of the shipping at this port is 5,000,000 yearly.

Federal Interests of paramount importance are concentrated in New York, which is second only to Washington in this particular. The Custom House, the Assay Office and the Sub-Treasury, all close together on Wall Street, represent the Federal Government financially. Here is the main port of entry for foreign trade for the whole country. The foreign commerce of New York for the last fiscal year amounted to $1,061,000,000, being more than half the total for the United States (which reached $2,010,000,000). The imports at New York reached $576,000,000, including $113,000,000 in coffee, $48,000,000 in sugar and molasses, $37,000,000 in silks, $30,000,000 in woollens, $21,000,000 in cottons, and $19,000,000 each in hides and rubber. The exports of goods reached $462,000,000, mainly in provisions, petroleum, cotton and tobacco.

At the Sub-Treasury the receipts sometimes exceed $1,227,000,000 a year. Enormous quantities of bullion are annually passed through the Assay Office.

The Post Office is the centre for the railway mail service of the Eastern and Middle States, and the distributing point for foreign mail. More than 3,000 men are employed. The United-States Courts hold sessions in the Post-Office building.

Immigration pours a steady tide into the United States through the port of New York. Immigrants were formerly received at Castle Garden, but they are now landed at Ellis Island, where the United-States Government takes charge of them. In the ten years after 1881, the number of immigrants at New York averaged about 380,000 yearly. In 1891 they reached 430,887 ; and in the year closing June 30, 1892, 446,000.

The Military Department of the East has its headquarters here, and the Major-General and his staff reside on Governor's Island. Detachments of troops are in garrison at Fort Hamilton and Fort Wadsworth, which face each other across the Narrows on the Long-Island and Staten-Island shores respectively ; at Fort Schuyler, upon Throgg's Neck, where the East River and Long-Island Sound meet ; and at Willett's Point, on the Long-Island shore, opposite Fort Schuyler. These fortifications would, perhaps, be of small avail against the heaviest modern naval armaments, but the Government is improving the defences at these stations, and projecting new works at Sandy Hook and Coney Island, so that the city and harbor shall have adequate protection in case of war.

The United-States Navy-Yard (virtually a part of New York, although across the East River, in Brooklyn) is the most important naval station in the country; and employs over 2,000 men continually. The dry dock cost over

COURT OF GENERAL SESSIONS.   POLICE COURT.   CENTRE STREET.   "STAATS ZEITUNG."

NEW-YORK CITY.

LOOKING NORTHEAST FROM THE "WORLD" DOME.

"STAATS ZEITUNG." CITY-HALL BRANCH ELEVATED RAILROAD. WILLIAM STREET.

NEW-YORK CITY.

LOOKING EAST-NORTHEAST FROM THE " WORLD " DOME.

$2,000,000, and is unequalled anywhere in the world. The Government property covers 144 acres, and has a mile of water-front. Besides the shops and officers' houses, there are Marine barracks and a naval hospital.

The Wealth concentrated in the hands of residents of New York is almost inconceivable. Many vast fortunes have been made here ; and many enormously wealthy Americans have come here to live and enjoy the fortunes accumulated elsewhere. A recent table of the wealth of New-York's millionaires estimates that at least two New-Yorkers are worth more than $100,000,000 each ; six more have above $50,000,000 each; more than thirty are classed as worth between $20,000,000 and $40,000,000 ; and 325 other citizens are rated at from $2,000,000 to $12,000,000 each.

The Commerce and Finance cannot be adequately measured in words or figures. The aggregate transactions every day reach an amount so stupendous that the figures are beyond comprehension.

The Banks include 47 National banks, with a capital of $50,000,000, and resources of over $500,000,000 ; 47 State banks, with a capital of $18,000,000, and resources of $185,000,000 ; 27 savings-banks, with deposits of $325,000,000, from 800,000 depositors ; and 19 trust-companies, with capital of $20,000,000, or gross assets of $270,000,000.

The Clearing House does a business amounting to from $35,000,000,000 to $50,000,000,000 yearly, and its daily transactions range from $125,000,000 to $250,000,000. Since it commenced in 1853 it has transacted business to the enormous amount of over $1,000,000,000,000,000.

The Stock Exchange has a membership of 1,100 ; and its aggregate transactions amount to many millions of shares a year. The Produce Exchange has 3,000 members ; and the Maritime Exchange, 1,365. There are 2,362 members in the Consolidated Exchange, where often in a single day 75,000 shares of stock are dealt in, and where almost incalculable quantities of petroleum are sold yearly. There are also ninety-six Trade-Associations. In and about Wall Street 289 of the leading railroads of the country have their main or important offices.

The Office Buildings comprise many notable structures. In the down-town business-districts alone, there are several hundred great office-buildings which are hives of industry. Many of them have a business population every day more than equal to the population of a large country village. Such buildings as the Mills, the Equitable, the Havemeyer, the Bennett, the Potter, the Pulitzer, the Times, the Washington, the Columbia, Temple Court, the Western Union, the Postal-Tele-graph-Cable, the Mutual Life, the Jersey Central, the Lackawanna, and a score of others, are notable for their grandeur and solidity and elegant appointments.

The Manufactures in 25,399 factories give employment to over 350,000 people, who make every year $765,000,000 worth of goods, of which clothing, books and papers, cigars and pianos, constitute the largest amounts.

The Publishers of the United States are well represented or located in New-York City, where more books are yearly published than in all the rest of the country combined. There are thirty leading publishing concerns, and others of lesser importance. In periodical publications there is even more activity.

The Papers and Periodicals comprise 43 daily newspapers. Of these, six are German, three Italian, two Bohemian, one Spanish and one French. There are nine semi-weekly papers, 221 weekly, and 48 bi-weekly. The monthly publications lead off with *Harper's Magazine*, the *Century*, *Scribner's*, the *Cosmopolitan*, the *North Ameri-can Review*, and the *Forum*, and run up a list of 394. There are 14 bi-monthlies and

21 quarterlies. All the varied social, religious, literary, political and business interests are served by these periodicals. The most important groups are : Religious, 53; commercial, 15; sporting, 8; art, 5; literary, 64; mechanical, 5; socialist, 2; secret societies, 9; legal, 3; theatrical, 6; scientific, 7; medical, 22; educational, 12; agricultural, 3; and fashions 7. The serial publications include papers in the following languages : German, 58; Spanish, 17; Bohemian, 6; Italian, 5; French, 4; Armenian, 3; Swedish, 3; Portuguese, 2; and Polish, Finnish, Russian, Danish, Slavonic, and Hungarian. There are 14 papers for the Hebrew race.

The Churches own and occupy more than 600 church buildings, valued with their land and foundings at upwards of $75,000,000. They represent every phase of religious belief, and together they have a seating capacity of nearly 300,000. The Protestant Episcopal Church leads, with 103 churches; closely followed by the Roman Catholic, with 85; then come the Presbyterian, with 75; the Methodist-Episcopal, 69; the Baptist, 51; the Jewish, 50; the Reformed Dutch, 32; the Lutheran, 23; the Congregationalist, 11; the Reformed Presbyterian, 5; the African Methodist Episcopal, 6; the United Presbyterian, 6; the Unitarian, 3; the Universalist, 3; and all others, including Swedenborgians, Moravians, etc., 60.

Religious Work in conjunction with the churches is served by many societies and associations. Most prominent among these is the American Bible Society, which, since it started in 1816, has published over 56,000,000 copies of the Bible; has printed the Bible in more than eighty different languages and dialects; has had receipts of nearly $26,000,000; and owns a large building, valued at nearly $500,000. The Young Men's Christian Association is housed in its own building, that cost $500,000, and it occupies a broad field of usefulness in promoting the spiritual, intellectual, social and physical welfare of the community. It supports fourteen branches, of which the most important are the Young Men's Institute, in the Bowery, and the Railroad Branch, which occupies a house on Madison Avenue, built and presented to it by Cornelius Vanderbilt. In local missionary work the New-York City Mission and Tract Society is preëminent, maintaining churches, libraries, missions, gymnasiums, and Sunday-schools. Each of the leading denominations supports one or more missionary societies, publication-houses, and organizations for the propagation of their religious tenets. Three-score missionary societies cover the foreign and home fields.

The Charities (according to a published directory of the charitable and benevolent societies) number more than 700, not including scores of small associations, that never appeal to the public. More than 200 are prominent, and labor unremittingly and effectively in relieving the poor and suffering of every class and nationality. Many of these associations maintain hospitals and homes. Besides all the hospitals, there are a score of homes for the poor, sick and convalescent. Thirty asylums are provided for orphans and destitute children; fifteen asylums for the blind, the insane, the deaf and the crippled; twenty homes for the aged; and numerous temporary refuges for the poor and friendless. Some of these are municipal institutions; and others receive municipal aid. But, aside from civic appropriations, charitable contributions from private sources yearly amount to many millions of dollars. In addition, much is given in the form of permanent endowments and new buildings. The Children's Aid Society alone maintains twenty-two industrial and nine night schools; keeps open six lodging houses; has every year under its charge 37,000 boys and girls; and spends nearly $400,000 annually. Another notable and unique charity is the Fresh-Air Fund, through which poor children are sent into the country every summer.

NEWSBOY'S LODGING-HOUSE.

APPROACH TO BROOKLYN BRIDGE.

NEW-YORK CITY.
LOOKING EAST-SOUTHEAST FROM THE " WORLD " DOME.

BROOKLYN BRIDGE.   FRANKFORT STREET.   HEALY BUILDING.

NEW-YORK CITY.
LOOKING SOUTHEAST FROM THE "WORLD" DOME.

The Charitable and Correctional Institutions of the city are located chiefly on the islands in the East River. Blackwell's Island, 120 acres in extent, has the penitentiary, almshouse, workhouse, charity hospital, hospital for incurables and other institutions. Over 7,000 persons, including criminals, charity patients, officials and attendants live upon the island, which is maintained chiefly by convict labor. A recent proposition that is being favorably entertained looks to the removal of these institutions to a location on the main land, and the transformation of the island into a beautiful public park. On Randall's Island are the Idiot Asylum, the House of Refuge, Nursery, Children's Hospital, and Infants' Hospital and schools. The usual population of the island is between 2,500 and 3,000. On Ward's Island are the Insane Asylum for Males, the Ward's-Island Hospital, the State Emigrant Hospital, and other noble institutions. On Hart's Island is another insane asylum and a branch of the Work-House ; and on North Brother Island is the Riverside hospital for contagious diseases. At Islip, Long Island, is an insane asylum. The city maintains the Bellevue, Emergency, Gouverneur, Harlem, Reception and Fordham hospitals in the city proper. Municipal aid to the amount of nearly $1,250,000 is given for the support of 29 private or State asylums, reformatories and charitable institutions, and altogether the city pays out for these purposes more than $3,300,000 annually.

. **The Hospitals** of New York are not surpassed elsewhere in the world for extent, completeness of appointment, and general excellence of management. The most skilful medical service is at the command of the suffering ; and the reputation of the physicians for skill has travelled even to Europe, so that in recent years European physicians have sent patients across the water to New-York hospitals for treatment in special cases. Particularly is this true of surgery, in which New-York practitioners are without superiors. The leading hospitals are Bellevue, established in 1826, and maintained by the city ; New York, chartered by King George III. of England in 1771, and opened to the public in 1791 ; Roosevelt, opened in 1871, and supported by the endowment of James H. Roosevelt ; St. Luke's (Protestant Episcopal), incorporated in 1850; St. Vincent's (Roman Catholic), 1857 ; Lebanon (Hebrew), 1889; Mount Sinai, opened in 1855; New-York Eye and Ear Infirmary, 1820; New-York Ophthalmic, 1852 ; Presbyterian, 1857; and the Sloane Maternity and Vanderbilt Clinic, endowed by the Vanderbilt family to the amount of $1,000,-000. Other hospitals devoted to special diseases bring the number of these institutions up to nearly seventy. There are dispensaries and infirmaries for the free treatment of the sick in all parts of the city, to the number of over fifty.

The Educational Work of New York is preëminent, and her teaching facilities yearly attract thousands of students from all parts of the country. The public-school system, broad in scope and thorough in instruction, is in charge of a Board of Education composed of 21 commissioners. The number of school buildings is 135, and in these 240,000 children are taught by 4,200 teachers. There are 108 grammar schools, 118 primary schools and departments, 29 evening schools, two colleges, one training school, one nautical school, and 48 corporate schools in reformatories and asylums. The College of the City of New York has a yearly attendance of 1,100 young men ; and the Normal College of 2,800 young women. These two institutions complete the system of public schools.

Advancing beyond the public schools we find educational institutions of higher grade, that in number and in character combine to make New York one of the great university-towns of the world. In the front rank stands Columbia College, one of the five oldest and greatest colleges of the country. With its five departments, Arts, Mines, Law, Political Science, and Medicine, and its Barnard College for Women, it is in effect, as well as in name, a university. Scarcely second to Columbia is the University of the City of New York, which has three well-equipped departments. Both these institutions have had brilliant careers, and the names of scores of men like Barnard, Drisler, Chandler, Quackenbos, Dwight, Morse, Mott, Butler and others, great in various branches of professional attainment, are identified with them. There are 3,000 students yearly instructed in these two universities.

The Union Theological Seminary (Presbyterian), and the Episcopal General Theological Seminary are the next most prominent higher educational institutions. Combined they have a yearly register of over 300 students. To these must be added the medical schools, Bellevue, Physicians and Surgeons, University, Homœopathic, and a dozen like institutions, in special fields. There are several prosperous Catholic colleges, like Manhattan, St. John's, and St. Francis Xavier.

The prominent law-schools are those connected with Columbia College and the University of the City of New York, both unsurpassed in facilities and thoroughness of training; and drawing students from all parts of the world.

Private schools of all grades are numerous. The Cooper Union Schools for free instruction in the sciences, mathematics, art, engraving, telegraphy, and other branches, is one of the grandest philanthropic institutions in existence. Over 4,000 students are taught yearly, most of whom are young tradesmen or mechanics who attend the evening classes. The Trade School is another institution on a large scale for practical instruction in common employments.

The Libraries, special and general, are numerous and large. The Aguilar Free Library and the Free Circulating Library have several branches each; and the Apprentices' Library contains nearly 95,000 volumes. The millions left by the will of Samuel J. Tilden provided a great free library; and even now that the will has been set aside, the generosity of one of the heirs will in the near future make up a part of the loss. The Mercantile Library is the largest circulating library in the city. It contains 245,000 volumes. The Astor Library, richly endowed by the Astor family, with a quarter of a million volumes, mostly valuable for reference rather than for popular reading, is much frequented by students and investigators.

The useful Columbia-College Library has over 160,000 volumes. At the Cooper Union there are 34,000 volumes of a miscellaneous character, and several hundred newspapers and magazines are regularly received. The library of the New-York Historical Society is valuable in Americana. The Lenox Library contains more rare editions of Bibles, Shakespeariana and Americana, and ancient manuscripts than other institutions in this country. It has only a few more than 70,000 volumes, but most of these are priceless in value. The libraries at the City Hall; the Bar Association, 38,000 volumes; the American Institute, 14,000; the New-York Society, 90,000; the Bible Society, 4,000 rare volumes; the Law Institute, 42,000; and the Young Men's Christian Association, 40,000, are useful institutions. There are more than a score others of lesser importance, generally serving the needs of some special class. The libraries attached to the Art Museum and the colleges and seminaries, as Union Theological Seminary (70,000), St. Francis Xavier (25,000), and Manhattan College (17,000), are also note-worthy.

In Art and Architecture, New York leads the country. It is the Mecca towards which artists from all other sections turn. The studios of America's greatest painters, sculptors and designers are here, and the native school of art has always displayed its fullest and most admirable powers in this city. To-day the names of

SHOT TOWER.   SPRUCE AND WILLIAM STREETS.

NEW-YORK CITY.
LOOKING SOUTH FROM THE " WORLD " DOME.

WILLIAM STREET.

PRODUCE EXCHANGE TOWER.

NEW-YORK CITY.

LOOKING SOUTH-SOUTHWEST FROM THE "WORLD" DOME.

such painters as Huntington, Inness, Chase, Millet, Weir, Porter, Parton, Beckwith, J. G. Brown, Blum, Crane, Gay, Moran and Shirlaw, and of such sculptors
as St. Gaudens, Elwell, Ward, Warner, Hartley, and scores of others not less
accomplished, sufficiently uphold the claim of New York to preëminent distinction
in this respect.   The general art taste of the community is revealed on every side,
especially in the local architecture, which has attained to a remarkable degree of
excellence during the last few years.   The Vanderbilt houses, the Stewart mansion,
the Union-League-Club buildings, the Madison-Square Garden, the Metropolitan
Opera House, the Casino, the Carnegie Music Hall, St. Patrick's Cathedral, the
City Hall, the Tribune Building, the Times Building, the World Building, the
Academy of Design, Grace Church, the Produce Exchange, the Mutual-Life and
the Equitable-Insurance buildings, the Imperial, Astor, Savoy, Holland and New
Netherland hotels, the Tiffany house, the new Court House, Trinity Church ; the
record might be continued for pages without exhausting the list of buildings that
give architectural distinction to the city.   The Huntington mansion, the Metropolitan Club House, the Cathedral of St. John the Divine, the New-York *Herald*
and the Manhattan Life buildings, and a score of other residence and business
structures are either projected or in process of erection.   Every conceivable
style and variation of style is represented by admirable examples, Colonial in the
houses of old Greenwich and Chelsea villages, Gothic in Trinity and other churches,
Doric in the Sub-Treasury building, Corinthian in the Court House, Ionic in the
Custom House, Egyptian in the Tombs, Italian Renaissance in the City Hall and
the Produce Exchange, Florentine in the Lenox Library and the W. K. Vanderbilt
house, Moorish in the Tiffany house, the Temple Emanu-El and the Casino, Venetian in the Academy of Design, Byzantine in the German Catholic Church of the
Most Holy Redeemer and St. George's Church, and contemporaneous "Queen
Anne" in the Union-League Club House, and many private residences around about
Central Park.   Nor in this connection can the public statues and memorials be
ignored.   Among them are many admirable examples of art, such as the Farragut
statue, by Augustus St. Gaudens ; the equestrian Washington, by H. K. Browne ;
the Indian Hunter, the Horace Greeley, and the Washington, by J. Q. A. Ward ;
the Union-Square Drinking-Fountain, by Olin Warner ; the Diana, on the Madison-
Square-Garden tower, by Augustus St. Gaudens ; the Still Hunt, by Edward Kemys ;
the Egyptian Obelisk in Central Park ; the Tigress and Young, by Auguste Cain ;
the Washington Memorial Arch, by Stanford White ; the Grant Mausoleum ; and
the magnificent colossal Statue of Liberty, on Bedloe's Island, by Bartholdi.
    The Metropolitan Museum of Art easily stands at the head of institutions of its
character in this country.   It now has treasures valued at over $6,000,000, housed
in a building that has already cost nearly $1,000,000, and is not yet completed.   In
these galleries are many famous pictures presented to the Museum from the Stewart
and other private collections, the Wolfe collection of pictures by modern masters
(valued at half a million), the Marquand old masters, the Di Cesnola collection of
Cypriote antiquities, the E. C. Moore collection of ceramics, the Brayton-Ives Japanese swords, the Marquand, Charvet and Jarves glass, the Stuart and Astor laces,
the Drexel and Brown musical instruments, the Baker Egyptian mummy and
other cloth, the Ward Assyrian antiquities, a remarkably large collection of casts
from the antique, and other valuable and interesting possessions.   The New-York
Historical Society has a valuable collection of portraits of distinguished Americans,
the Durr collection of old Dutch paintings, the Abbott collection of Egyptian
antiquities, the Lenox Nineveh marbles, and other art-treasures second only in extent

and value to the possessions of the Metropolitan Museum. In the Lenox Library there is a precious collection of pictures, including works of most of the great masters of modern times. Recent bequests bring this institution into close rivalry with the Metropolitan Museum and the Historical Society.

The private galleries in New York are not equalled by those in any other American city. The finest collections belong to the Vanderbilts, the Astors, the Belmonts, the Havemeyers, the Rockefellers, H. G. Marquand, J. A. Bostwick, Thomas B. Clarke, C. P. Huntington, Henry Hilton, D. O. Mills, Jay Gould, Morris K. Jesup, J. W. Drexel, Robert Hoe, and many other eminent collectors, who constitute a band of picture lovers and buyers such as no other American community can boast of. The portraits in the Governor's room at the City Hall, and in the Chamber of Commerce, and the Academy of Design's collection of works by its members are interesting. All the leading clubs possess good paintings, and they make exhibitions of these and loaned pictures from time to time. Nearly all the fashionable hotels show fine collections of paintings in their saloons, offices and public rooms. Not much attention has yet been given to art in New-York church interiors. In St. Thomas's, the Church of St. Mary the Virgin, the Church of the Transfiguration, the Church of the Heavenly Rest, Grace Church, St. Patrick's Cathedral and Trinity Church, there are mural paintings, mosaic and sculptured reredoses, statuary and painted windows. A score of art-stores show the best productions of American and European painters, and during the season there are numerous exhibitions. The National Academy of Design has autumn and spring exhibitions ; the Society of American Artists, the Salmagundi Club, the Etching Club, the American Water-Color Society, and other art organizations hold annual exhibitions.

The Parks of New York are commensurate with its great development. Bowling Green was the first public park ; and the fashionable folk dwelt about it in the old Dutch and Colonial times. In the main part of the city the principal reservation for the people is Central Park, one of the handsomest public breathing-places in the world. It contains 840 acres, which have been beautified at an expense of over $15,000,000, with landscape-garden features, statuary, play-grounds and promenades. Part of the park is still left in a state of nature. Morningside Park (of 32 acres) and Riverside Park (of 178 acres), the latter overlooking the Hudson River for nearly three miles, are two of the most beautiful public places in the city. Many smaller squares and parks are generally made attractive with shrubbery and flowers. North of the Harlem River are six parks : The Van Cortlandt, of 1,070 acres ; the Bronx, of 653 acres ; the Crotona, of 135 acres ; St. Mary's, of 25 acres ; Claremont, of 38 acres ; and Pelham-Bay, of 1,740 acres. At present these properties, which cost the city $10,000,000, are unimproved. They are distant from the populated part of the city, but are already much frequented by those who wish a rustic outing in the wild woods and pastures. In time these parks, which are connected by parkways, will form a system that in extent, in natural beauty and in adornment will have no rivals. A new park on the west bank of the Harlem River at Washington Heights is also projected.

Amusements numerous and varied enough to suit all tastes and all purses range in character from the Metropolitan Opera House to the low concert-saloons of the Bowery and Eighth Avenue. The legitimate theatres are thirty-six in number, and at least five others are projected or building. Several of these remain open the year round, comic opera holding the stage throughout the summer months. All of them have a season of at least forty weeks. The Metropolitan Opera-House is the home of German and Italian grand opera, and during the last ten years the productions there have been on a scale of magnificence and musical excellence rivalling the most famous European opera-houses. The receipts for the opera season have amounted to about $200,000 annually, in recent years, leaving a deficiency of $100,-000 to be made good by assessments upon the stockholders, who are the leaders in wealth and society. The Madison-Square Garden, a large and architecturally beautiful structure, has an amphitheatre where horse-shows and dog-shows patronized by fashion are held, and where the circus annually exhibits. In addition, it has a theatre, a restaurant, a roof-garden, a concert-room, and a ball-room. The old Academy of Music, once devoted to grand opera, but now given over to the spectacular drama ; the luxurious Fifth-Avenue ; Palmer's and the Star, both rich with memories of Lester Wallack ; the handsome Casino, where comic opera reigns the year round ; Amberg's and the Thalia, where performances in German only are given ; Daly's, and the Lyceum, with their admirable stock companies ; the handsome Garden Theatre ; the Madison-Square Theatre, with its permanent farce comedy ; these are the most important. In all the legitimate theatres combined there is a seating capacity of nearly 60,000. The dime-museums and other low-priced places will accommodate at least 10,000 more. Even with this total the supply does not exceed the demand. It is estimated that every year there is spent in New York for amusements of this character at least $6,000,000.

In Chickering Hall, Music Hall, the Lenox Lyceum, the Berkeley Lyceum, Hardman Hall and the concert-room of the Metropolitan Opera-House most of the high-class musical entertainments are given. Notable concerts of the year are those by the Philharmonic Society, the Symphony Society, the Oratorio Society, the Boston Symphony Orchestra, the Liederkranz and the Arion Society.

Clubs and Clubmen are legion throughout New-York City. Every conceivable social, political, religious, professional and business interest is concentrated in this manner. A list of the leading clubs in the city would include the names of over fifty, such as the Union League, Manhattan, Union, Metropolitan, Lotus, Century, New-York, St.-Nicholas, Colonial, Aldine, Authors', University, German, Knickerbocker, New-York Athletic, New-York Racquet, Players' and Manhattan Athletic. All these have comfortable homes, and the houses of many are palatial. The purely sporting clubs and associations, such as the American Jockey Club, the American Kennel Club, the Coney-Island Jockey Club, the yacht clubs, the bicycle clubs, and so on down to those of minor importance will number a hundred or more, and there are at least 150 clubs of a miscellaneous character. There are fully 300 clubs of good standing in New York, with a membership of upward of 100,000. Few men of New York do not belong to at least one club, and most of them have membership in several. The desirable clubs are usually full to their extreme limit.

The Hotels, comprising about a thousand of all kinds, include a full hundred excellent hotels, a large proportion of them strictly first-class, with a world-wide reputation. The Fifth-Avenue, Windsor, Gilsey, Hoffman, Imperial, Brunswick, Brevoort, Plaza, Murray-Hill, Buckingham and Astor House are notable. Recent important additions to the list either just completed or building are the Holland House, the Waldorf, the Savoy and the New Netherland.

The Water Ways.

The Harbor and Rivers—Piers and Shipping—Fortifications and Quarantine—Exports and Imports—Oceanic and Coastwise Lines—The Ocean Greyhounds.

THE harbor of New York is perhaps the most interesting in the world, for it has been the portal of a new world and a new life for millions of men and women. It is as beautiful, furthermore, as it is interesting, from the hill-girt gateway of the Narrows up into the broader spaces between Bayonne and Gowanus, with the high blue Orange Mountains crowning the view to the northwest, the rampart-like Palisades frowning down the Hudson, and verdant islands here and there breaking the vivid blue of the bay. On all sides the assembled cities encircle the waters with their masses of buildings, the forests of masts by the waterside, the immense warehouses and factories along the pier-heads, and the spires, domes and towers of the beautiful residence-quarters beyond. At night, the harbor is girded about by myriads of yellow and colored lights and white electric stars, and dotted with the lanterns of vessels in motion or at anchor.

The Lower Bay and its tributary Raritan Bay and Sandy-Hook Bay are formed by a triangular indentation of the coast, between Monmouth County, N. J., Staten Island and Long Island, partly protected from the sea by Sandy Hook and Coney Island, and the long bar and shoals extending between them. The channel is devious and at times difficult, and numerous buoys, beacons and light-houses mark out the path of the inbound ships. At the head of the Lower Bay the maritime route leads through the Narrows, a magnificent water-gate a mile wide, hemmed in between the bold hills of Staten Island and Long Island, and bordered by heavy batteries. Beyond this remarkable portal opens the Upper Bay, or New-York Harbor, an admirable land-locked haven eight miles long and five miles wide, the grand focal point of North-American Atlantic commerce.

The Water-Front of Manhattan Island available for vessels is about 25 miles long, 13 miles being on the North River, 9 on the East River, and the rest on the Harlem River. There are seventy-three piers on the East River, below East 11th Street ; and seventy on the North River, below 12th Street.

On one side of the harbor is the mouth of the magnificent Hudson River, flowing down for 300 miles, from the Adirondack Mountains, navigable for 148 miles to Albany and Troy, and the outlet of the Erie Canal, bringing down immense supplies of grain from the West. On the other side is the entrance to Long-Island Sound, "The Mediterranean of the West," giving an admirable marine route to the ports of New England and the remote East. The strategic position of the city, for purposes of commerce, is one of unapproachable strength and excellence, and has been skillfully availed of by the merchants and public men of this active community ;

and the commerce of the East and the West converges here in immense volume, on the waters of one of the finest American harbors.

The East River is a deep and swift tidal strait twenty miles long, joining New-York harbor, at the Battery, with Long-Island Sound, at Willett's Point. Most of the western shore is formed by New-York City; and the eastern shore includes Brooklyn, and other communes of Long Island. It is the avenue of a vast commerce, and with its many ferry-boats and immense white steamboats flying to and fro presents a pleasantly animated scene. The narrow channel of Hell Gate, near Astoria, was for two and a half centuries a terror to mariners, with its swift eddies and currents, setting over a reef of sharp rocks. Between 1870 and 1885 these ledges were undermined and blown up with nitro-glycerine, by Gen. Newton and a corps of engineers, at a cost of many millions of dollars; and since that time navigation here has been much less perilous.

Harlem River is an arm of East River, seven miles long, partly navigable for small vessels, and connecting near its head with the much-winding Spuyten-Duyvil Creek, a shallow tributary of the Hudson River. These two streams separate Manhattan Island from the mainland, and form the proposed route of the ship-canal between them.

The North River, on the western shore of the great city, preserves a name applied for nearly three centuries to that stretch of the Hudson River extending in front of Manhattan. The old Dutch colonists named the Delaware the *South River,* and the Hudson they called the *North River.* It is a noble straight-channeled reach of deep water, a mile wide and a score of miles long, and gave ample soundings for the *Great Eastern,* as it does now for the *Campania,* the *Spree* and the *New York.*

The lower water-side streets are occupied generally by small irregular buildings, sail-lofts, the haunts of riggers and outfitters, ship-owners and ship-chandlers, mysterious junk shops, and a vast variety of drinking-places, sailors' boarding-houses, and shops for small-wares. Street-railways run along the pier-heads; and a continuous crowded and noisy procession of drays and carts pours up and down the streets, or entangles itself in hopeless blocks, overflowed by tides of objurgations and hearty profanatory expletives.

The Piers and Wharves are for the most part exceedingly irregular and rather unsightly, being of various lengths, and constructed of wood, upon myriads of piles, around and between which the free tides swirl and eddy. Though devoid of the architectural symmetry and structural massiveness of European quays, the water-front of New York is well-fitted for its uses, and has also a singular picturesqueness and diversity of outline and character. Some years ago a well-considered plan was devised and begun, to replace the crazy-looking wharves with a systematic and imposing line of stone piers and docks; but this transformation is a very costly process, and has made but little advance. In 1892 the Legislature passed a bill providing "for the recreation and health of the people of New York by setting aside certain piers along the river-front." The plan involves the construction of very large two-story pavilions on the pier-ends, the lower stories being devoted to commercial purposes, and the high-arched upper floors forming fresh-air gardens, with music and flowers and sea-views, for the pleasure of the people. The piers at Barclay and Perry Streets, on the North River, are being fitted up for this fortunate service; and there are to be four similar roof-gardens on the East-River front.

In going up the North-River side, from the Battery, there is a continual succession of varied and busy scenes, the headquarters of the Coney-Island steamboats; the huge piers of the Pennsylvania Railroad; the trim vessels of the New-Orleans, Boston, and Savannah steamships; the huge white floating palaces of the Sound lines to Fall River and Providence and Norwich; the docks of the Hudson-River lines; the Morgan and Old-Dominion boats; and the resting-places of the unrivalled ocean-greyhounds of the American, Guion, White Star, Cunard and French lines. Along the East River a great space is given up to the large sailing-ships, bringing in cargoes from all parts of the world, and with their lofty masts and long yards interwoven against the sky. Then come the grain-laden canal-boats from the West, hundreds of fruiters from the West Indies, and a line of ferries, above which appear several dry-docks, followed by iron-foundries, lumber-yards, and old steamers laid up in ordinary. Almost every variety of vessel is found in these waters, the brilliant excursion-steamboats, melodious with band-music, and waving with flags and streamers; ark-like canal-boats from the Great Lakes, distended with wheat and corn; the swift Norfolk schooners, redolent of fine tobacco and of early vegetables; oyster-boats from the Connecticut coast, small and pert in outlines and motion; huge full-rigged ships from Calcutta, laden with indigo; sooty steam-barges from the Pennsylvania coal-regions; Nova-Scotia brigs, laden with fine apples and potatoes; heavy old whalers, making port after long Arctic voyages;

UNITED-STATES BARGE OFFICE, BATTERY PLACE.

schooners from the West Indies and Honduras, crammed with tropical fruits; fishermen from the Grand Banks, heroes of the saltest northern seas; Mediterranean merchantmen, with rich cargoes from the Levant; and hundreds of other types, each full of interest and attraction. The loom of the great environing cities, the breadth and life of the confluent waters, the intense and joyous activity of motion, combine to give this cosmopolitan picture an unusual breadth and life.

Space fails to tell of the Barge Office at the Battery, and its customs inspectors and sailors' dispensary; of the natty flotilla of the Battery boatmen; of Ellis Island and its great buildings for the reception of immigrants; of the United-States Navy Yard, at Brooklyn, the chief naval station of the Republic; of the wonderful docks on the Brooklyn side, the home of a universal commerce; and of scores of other interesting scenes which surround the gateway of the New World.

The **Military Defences** of New-York City are formidable, as far as the old style of warfare goes. It remains to be seen how efficient they may be when confront-ing the untried and uncertain naval monsters of the new era; and acting under the support of chains of torpedoes, dynamite guns, and the battle-ships of the new American navy. New mortar-batteries of great power are about to be constructed on Sandy Hook and near Long Island, to command the remote Lower Bay; and Fort Lafayette and other points will be occupied by immense steel turrets.

Fort Wadsworth, the most powerful of the military defences of New York, is a three-tiered casemate work of granite, on the Staten-Island shore of the Narrows. On the heights above stands the heavily-armed Fort Tompkins; and along the chan-nel-side extends a line of water-batteries. From this place a triple fire, water-line and casemate and plunging, could be converged upon a hostile vessel in the narrow channel.

On the Long-Island shore, at the Narrows, opposite Fort Wadsworth, and only a mile distant, glower the heavy stone casemates of Fort Hamilton, on a military reservation of 96 acres. Just off-shore, on an artificial island, stands Fort Lafayette, built in 1812–22, and celebrated as a prison for political captives and disloyal per-sons during the civil war. The inflammable parts of the fort were burned in 1868, and the remaining buildings are used now only for storing ordnance supplies.

Fort Wood, on Bedloe's Island, is a star-shaped work, finished in 1841, and mounted then with seventy guns. The wonderful colossal statue of Liberty Enlight-ening the World rises from a pedestal on the parade-ground.

Willett's Point was fortified in 1862, by the National Government, to close the entrance to the East River from Long-Island Sound. It is the headquarters of the Battalion of Engineers, U. S. A. Across the entrance of the East River looms the ponderous casemated defence of Fort Schuyler, whose construction was begun in 1833.

Governor's Island, within 1,000 feet of the Battery, and six miles inside of the Narrows, is the headquarters of the Military Department of the East, and the usual residence of the commanding general. It is a beautiful island, of 65 acres, with a far-viewing parade-ground, surrounded by fine old trees and the quarters of the officers; an arsenal containing scores of heavy cannon and endless pyramids of cannon-balls; magazines and hospitals; the headquarters of the Military Service Institution, with its library and picture-gallery; and the interesting Military Museum, rich in battle-flags, weapons ancient and modern, and Indian curiosities. The chief defence on Governor's Island is Fort Columbus, a star-shaped stone fort mount-ing 120 guns, and with enclosed barracks for the artillerists. On the point toward the Battery stands Castle Williams, an old-fashioned and picturesque three-story fortress, circular in shape, built between 1808 and 1812.

The **Quarantine Station** defends the port of New York (and with it the entire continent) against the entrance of dangerous and pestilential diseases. The danger of epidemics being brought in by foreign vessels was guarded against as early as 1647; and in 1716 the Council ordered that all West-Indian vessels should be detained at Staten Island. In 1758 the Provincial Legislature enacted laws for the protection of the port in this regard, and established a quarantine station at Bedloe's Island. One of the first measures of the State Legislature, in 1784, was a re-enact-ment of this law. Ten years later, the station was moved to Governor's Island; but the citizens of New York were rather uneasy at having the pest-house so near them. In 1801, therefore, it was again transferred to Tompkinsville, Staten Island, where it remained for more than sixty years. But in the course of time, as Staten Island became thickly settled, its people made serious objections to the continuance of so undesirable a neighbor ; and in 1857 the State Legislature ordered the selection of another site. This was found at Sandy Hook, but the opposition of New Jersey rendered it impossible. The next move appeared in the erection of buildings for the purpose at Seguin's Point, on the south part of Staten Island. The neighboring residents were incensed at the project, and attacked the establishment by night, and set fire to it. This summary process approved itself to the people of Tompkinsville, who also made a night attack upon the existing station, and thoroughly destroyed it. Richmond County was forced to pay for these nocturnal raids, but the result justified the acts, and the State gave up its attempt to establish the quarantine here. In 1859 a commission including Horatio Seymour, John C. Green, and Gov. Patterson adopted the idea of a floating hospital ; and the old steamship *Falcon* entered upon the duty, with an anchorage below the Narrows. In 1866-70 the artificial Swinburne Island was constructed, on the sand-bar of West Bank, and now has rows of hospital wards, a crematory and mortuary, and a dock and break-

BAY AND HARBOR FROM BEDLOE'S ISLAND, ABOUT 1840.

water. Hoffman Island, built in 1868-73, is a quarantine of observation and isolation, for immigrants who have been exposed to dangerous epidemics. The Lower Quarantine is marked by yellow buoys, and has a ship moored for a floating station, where vessels from infected ports are boarded. Their arrival is signalled thence to the main Quarantine Station, six miles above, on Staten Island, from which the proper officials go down to board them. The swift little tug-boat of the station passes the day in rushing from one incoming vessel to another, and the health-officers are kept busy in inspecting their passengers and crews. In a single year 7,600 vessels and 370,000 passengers have been examined here. The New-York quarantine is the most complete, thorough and efficient in the world.

The harbor is guarded from law-breakers, and "wharf-rats," mutineers and rioters, river-thieves and smugglers, as much as possible, by the police of the Thirty-Sixth Precinct, which has jurisdiction over the waters and wharves adjoining the city, along both rivers, and down as far as Robin's Reef. The police headquarters is on the steamboat *Patrol*, and several row-boats are continually moving along the rivers and up into the docks, manned by officers of the law, looking after thieves, fires, lost property, suicides and drowned persons.

The **Exports and Imports** of America find their foremost clearing-houses in this peerless harbor, with its rich adornments of Nature, and improvements and defences of art.   One hundred years ago the total export and import trade of the United States was below $50,000,000 annually.   At present (including specie) it is over $2,000,000,000, of which the imports reach $900,000,000.   The exports of cotton are over $290,000,000; of grain, breadstuffs and provisions, $480,000,000; and of specie, $80,000,000.   The foreign commerce for 1891 and 1892 was the largest in the history of the Nation.   Nearly two-fifths of the exports of the Republic go from New York, which sends out $460,000,000 yearly, to $107,000,000 from New Orleans, $74,000,000 from Baltimore, $70,000,000 from Boston, and $37,-000,000 from Philadelphia.   Two-thirds of the imports to the United States enter at the port of New York.   Less than one-fourth of the trade is under the American flag, which has a tonnage of 1,000,000 in the foreign trade, and 3,700,000 in the coastwise trade, besides 87,000 in the fisheries.   New York owns 2,000 sailing vessels, of 409,000 tons ; 1,000 steamers, of 375,000 tons ; and 900 canal-boats and lighters, of 167,000 tons.

During a single year over 2,000 grain-laden steamships sail from New York, which ships one-third of the American grain and breadstuffs, in spite of its heavy port and storage charges.   The hold is filled with grain in bulk ; the between-decks with grain in bags.   The port has a storage capacity of 26,000,000 bushels, in 22 stationary elevators and 31 floating elevators ; and grain-ships can be loaded at the rate of 458,000 bushels an hour.

New York receives every year over 200 tramp steamships, 136 from transatlantic ports, and the rest from other American harbors.   Many of them come to this great maritime clearing-house for orders, or enter in ballast, seeking cargoes.   These wanderers of the seas have engines of low power, with small consumption of coal, and cross the ocean in from fifteen to twenty days, with cargoes of heavy character, and including all sorts of merchandise.   Here also are seen the singular tank-steam-ships, partly owned by the Standard Oil Company, and carrying over seas from 30,000 to 35,000 barrels of oil, pumped into the hold, which is divided into half-a-dozen or more great tanks.   One of these singular floating reservoirs can be filled with petroleum in twelve hours.   On their return-voyages from Europe the tanks are partly filled with water-ballast.   Vessels of somewhat similar construction are employed in transporting molasses from Cuba.

There are several score of fruit steamers plying between the Central-American and West-Indian ports and New York, bringing bananas and cocoanuts, oranges and pineapples, and mostly sailing under the Norwegian flag.   Between the outer hull of steel and the inner hull of wood opens a considerable space, which is packed with charcoal, for refrigeration.   They have triple-expansion engines, steam steering-gear, and, in many cases, twin-screws, and are built for the trade, with three open decks and separated deck-planks, to ensure free circulation of air, and prevent the fruit from becoming heated.   Their seasons are spring and summer, after which most of them go into the grain and general freighting business to and around Europe.

Before the days of steam, the Atlantic Ocean was traversed by several famous packet-lines, like the Black Star ships of Grimshaw & Co., the Black Ball line of C. H. Marshall & Co., the old Black Stars of Williams & Guion, the packets of the Tapscot Line.   The largest accommodations were for 30 cabin and 20 second-cabin, and a varying number of steerage passengers in a ship, the rates being higher than in the modern steamships.   These ocean racers were built on the finest and most graceful lines, with vast expanses of canvas spread from their towering masts ; and their passages across were of remarkable swiftness.   The *Red Jacket* made the trans-atlantic voyage in 13 days and 1$\frac{25}{60}$ hour; and the *Dreadnaught* in 1860 made the run from New York to the Irish coast in 9 days and 17 hours.   In 1864 the clipper *Adelaide* left New York at the same time as the Cunard steamship *Sidon*, and entered Liverpool before her, in 12$\frac{1}{3}$ days.   At the present time many sailing ships ply to and from the port of New York, and among them are enormous four-masted steel vessels, with a capacity of 6,000 tons of freight.

The science of steam navigation, which has revolutioned modern commerce, changed the aspect of naval warfare, made travel by sea speedy and pleasant, and united the remote places of the earth, had its beginning in the noble harbor of New York.   Various Spanish and German, British and American inventors claimed to

NEW-YORK HARBOR, FROM EAST-RIVER BRIDGE, IN 1893.

have discovered the principles of marine engines, at periods running from the Middle Ages down to the close of the eighteenth century ; but it was reserved for Robert Fulton to practically apply this idea, and to perfect and develop it, so that his fleet of vessels had an immediate economic value for transporting passengers and freight.

This successful demonstration of a great new principle resulted in a rapid spread of the discovered power all over the maritime world.   Fulton's *Clermont* was launched at Jersey City, in 1807, and ascended the Hudson River to Albany. Almost at the same time, John Stevens, of Hoboken, built the *Phœnix*, and sent her around to Philadelphia, the pioneer of all ocean-going steamers.   Following New York's example, the St.-Lawrence River received a steamboat, in 1809 ; the Ohio and Mississippi, in 1811 ; and the Scottish Clyde, in 1812.   The first steamship to cross the ocean was the *Savannah*, built at New York, and equipped with folding paddle-wheels, which were taken out and laid on the deck when not in use.   In

1819 this little 380-ton vessel steamed from Savannah to Liverpool, Cronstadt, and Copenhagen. In 1838 Brunel's steamship *Great Western*, of 1,340 tons, steamed from Bristol, England, to New York, in fifteen days; and the *Sirius* ran across from London and Cork to New York.

In 1850 the Collins Line began its operations, and built up a fleet of five magnificent American steamships — the *Pacific*, *Arctic*, *Adriatic*, *Baltic*, and *Atlantic*, built at a cost of $4,000,000, and operated under a large subsidy from the United-States Government. The first two were lost at sea ; the cost of the voyages far exceeded the receipts ; the subsidy was withdrawn ; and in 1858 the Collins Line ceased to run.

There are now thirty great transatlantic steamship lines between New York and Europe, some of them with several sailings each week. They have eighty-five passenger steamships, bringing to New York yearly nearly 100,000 cabin passengers, four-fifths of whom are returning Americans. Their eastern ports are Liverpool, Southampton, London, Newcastle, Hull, Moville (Londonderry), Queenstown, and Glasgow, in the British Islands ; Havre, Bordeaux, and Boulogne, in France ; Antwerp, Rotterdam, and Amsterdam, in the Low Countries; Copenhagen, in Denmark; Hamburg, Stettin, and Bremen, in Germany ; Christiania and Christiansand, in Scandinavia ; and several Mediterranean ports. The capital embarked in these lines is $500,000,000. The offices of most of the steamship lines are on lower Broadway, or at "Steamship Row," on Bowling Green, where they occupy a block of ancient brick houses once dwelt in by the merchant-princes of New York.

The American Line is the successor of the old Inman Line, which began operations in 1850, under the title of the Liverpool, New-York & Philadelphia Steamship Company. The Inman Line was purchased in 1886 by the International Navigation Company, of Philadelphia ; but it was not until early in 1893 that the company was able to naturalize the two steamships *New York* and *Paris*, and start them running under the flag of the country in which they were actually owned. The ceremonies of transferring the ships to the American flag on the *New York* were appropriately performed on Washington's Birthday by President Harrison, in the presence of the members of his cabinet, and a large gathering of distinguished and representative United-States citizens, invited by the International Navigation Company to witness this most interesting ceremony. The placing of this most magnificent fleet under the Stars and Stripes has attracted an immense patronage from American travellers. Not content with merely changing the flag and name of the line, the management, recognizing the enormous advantages of Southampton as a terminal point in Great Britain over any other available port, started their newly-named service to a new terminus in England. The American Line ships *Paris*, *New York*, *Berlin* and *Chester* now sail every Saturday to Southampton. It will be noticed that, in addition to other changes, the words *City of* in the names of the ships have been dropped. These steamships are so well known to transatlantic travellers that it seems hardly necessary to describe them minutely. The *Paris* has made the fastest westbound transatlantic voyage on record, her time being 5 days, 14 hours and 24 minutes, while her sister-ship, the *New York*, has the honor of holding the record of some of the fastest voyages made to the eastward. These two American steamships are provided with double bottoms, so that the inner skin would keep out the water if the outer one were broken. They have twenty water-tight compartments, separated by solid bulkheads, and fronted by an immensely thick collision-bulkhead, near the bow ; and twin screws, each driven by an independent triple-expansion engine, so that if one becomes disabled, the ship can be brought

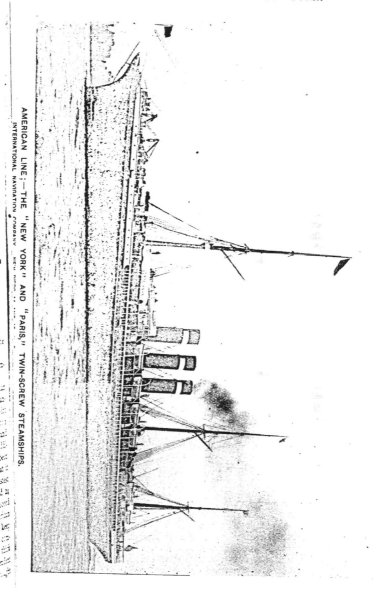

AMERICAN LINE;—THE "NEW YORK" AND "PARIS," TWIN-SCREW STEAMSHIPS.
INTERNATIONAL NAVIGATION COMPANY.

into port with the other engine.   The number of cabin passengers carried by these steamships is limited to the number they can seat at table at one sitting.   All possibility of overcrowding is thereby avoided.   These steamers are each 580 feet long and 59 feet deep, and the extreme breadth is 63¼ feet.   They have a displacement of 10,500 tons each, and 20,000 horse-power.   Each ship carries many of its first-cabin passengers on the promenade and saloon decks, some in suites of sitting-room, bed-room, bath-room and toilet-room, and others in rooms arranged with berths folding up like those in a Pullman car, so that by day the place becomes a pleasant sitting-room.   The other first-class cabins, on the main and upper decks, are of greater size than usual, and elegantly and comfortably furnished.   The dining saloons are spacious rooms of singular beauty and convenience, with high arched ceilings and choice architectural and artistic decorations.   Every device calculated to increase the comfort of passengers has been combined in these splendid ships, which are at once swift, secure and sumptuous, as strong as battle-ships and as luxurious as Belgravia drawing-rooms.   The kitchens are isolated, and ventilated into the funnels.

HELL GATE, FROM GREAT BARN ISLAND, ABOUT 1825.

Hydraulic power is used instead of steam for the daily work of steering, hoisting out supplies, and many other duties ; and its operation is very nearly noiseless.

The rates of first-cabin passage are from $60 to $650, depending on the ship, the season, the number in a state-room, and the location.   All these steamers have spacious state-rooms, ventilated by electric-driven fans and other devices, and containing scientific plumbing and other modern improvements.

The International Navigation Company has contracted with The William Cramp & Sons Ship and Engine-Building Company, of Philadelphia, for the construction of several new steamers of the highest order known to naval architecture, and when this magnificent fleet of modern steamships is afloat, the company will maintain a weekly service to Southampton and a weekly service to Antwerp, calling at Southampton and Boulogne. It is readily appreciated that these two ships, with their promised sisters, among the largest, finest and fastest vessels in the world, are a valuable acquisition to the United-States Navy.

The American Line and the Red Star Line (both of which are owned by the International Navigation Company) land their passengers directly on the company's piers, and thus save them the inconvenience, discomfort and exposure of being transferred by small tenders. American Line and Red Star Line cabin tickets are interchangeable ; the return portion is available by either line, as the passenger may

AMERICAN LINE, NEW PIERS 14 AND 15, NORTH RIVER.

choose. The International Navigation Company has recently acquired the largest and finest pier property in New-York harbor, near the Cortlandt-Street ferry of the Pennsylvania Railroad, and known as New Pier 14, or Washington Pier. They also own New Pier 15. They are rapidly fitting up these piers with a second story, and in the most improved manner ; and New Pier 14 will be in many respects the most commodious pier in the world, with admirable provision for passengers and freight.

The offices of the company are at 6 Bowling Green, New York ; 307 Walnut Street, Philadelphia ; 32 South Clark Street, Chicago ; 3 Cockspur Street, London ; Canute Road, Southampton ; and 22 Kammenstrasse, Antwerp.

The White Star Line (or Oceanic Steam Navigation Company), founded in 1870, sent out in 1875 the *Britannic* and *Germanic*, steamships of a new type, of great length and equipped with powerful compound engines. Fourteen years later, in 1889, the magnificent *Teutonic* and *Majestic* were launched, each of them 582 feet long, and of nearly 10,000 tons displacement. In March, 1891, the *Majestic* crossed from Queenstown to New York in 5 days, 18 hours, and 8 minutes, and the *Teutonic* made the same voyage in 5 days and $16\frac{1}{2}$ hours, the average being $20\frac{1}{3}$ knots an hour, and the swiftest day's run reaching 517 knots. Each of these giants of the sea can carry 1,200 passengers and 2,500 tons of freight ; and each of them cost above $2,000,000. They are built of Siemens-Martin steel, and each is propelled by two independent sets of triple-expansion engines, with manganese bronze propellers. They are minutely divided by athwart-ship and longitudinal bulk-heads, ensuring rigidity, strength and security. There are family and single-berth staterooms, ivory-and-gold Renaissance saloons, smoking-rooms decorated with embossed leather and fine marine paintings, a library-room with well-filled book-cases and luxurious furniture, and many other very comfortable departments. The first-cabin rates are from $80 to $600, depending on the steamship, the season, and the location of the state-room. Among the other vessels of the line are the *Oceanic*, its first boat; the *Belgic, Gaelic* and *Adriatic;* and the *Coptic, Doric* and *Ionic*. All these were built at Belfast, Ireland. The company's dock is at the foot of West 10th Street. The twin-screw steamships *Bovic, Tauric,* and *Nomadic*, and the *Runic* and *Cufic*, are used for freight exclusively, and cross in ten days. In a single voyage, the *Nomadic* has carried 9,591 tons of freight; and the *Cufic* has brought to New York at one time 77,000 boxes of tin-plate.

The **Cunard Line** was established by Samuel Cunard, of Halifax, David McIver, of Liverpool, and George Burns, of Glasgow; and began its voyages in the year 1840. Its official title was the British & North-American Royal Mail Steam Packet Company. The first Cunarders were paddle-wheel vessels, of wood, and bore the names — *Britannia, Acadia, Columbia,* and *Caledonia*. Those four steam-

PECK SLIP, EAST RIVER.

ships carried the mails between Liverpool, Halifax and Boston, for which the company received $400,000 yearly. The mail service has ever since been an important perquisite of the Cunard Company. The fleet was increased by the *Hibernia*, in 1843; the *Cambria*, in 1845; the *America, Niagara, Europa* and *Columbia*, in 1850; the *Asia* and *Africa;* the *Persia*, in 1855; and the *Scotia*, in 1862. The *China*, launched in 1862, was the first iron screw steamship in the Cunard fleet. In 1874, the *Bothnia* and *Scythia* were launched; and in 1881, the *Servia*. In 1884-85, appeared the *Etruria* and *Umbria*, each of over 8,000 tons, and in their day the sovereigns of the seas. The *Campania* and *Lucania* began to run in 1893, and are each of nearly 13,000 tons and 25,000 horse-power, with a length of 625 feet. The Cunard New-York fleet includes the *Campania, Lucania, Etruria, Umbria, Aurania, Gallia, Servia* and *Bothnia*, sailing on Wednesdays and Saturdays for Queenstown and Liverpool. The first-cabin fare from New York to Liverpool is from $60 to $125. The Cunard dock is at Pier 40, N. R., at the foot of Clarkson Street.

Surgeon's Residence.

Landing for Emigrants

Detention Room.

Emigrants Dining Hall.

ELLIS-ISLAND IMMIGRANT STATION, IN NEW-YORK HARBOR.

THE LANDING-PLACE FOR IMMIGRANTS.

6

The Guion Line dates from 1864, when its great new steamships succeeded its line of wooden sailing-packets, established in 1842. The construction of the *Arizona*, in 1879, inaugurated the wonderful rivalry which has since stimulated the ocean lines to increase the size, speed and comfort of their ships. The *Arizona* was of 5,164 tons, and crossed in 7 days and 3½ hours ; and her sister-ship, the *Alaska*, built in 1881, of 6,932 tons, and 11,000 horse-power, made a still better record. These two enormous ships have accommodations for about 1,200 passengers and 2,000 tons of freight each. The other vessels — the *Nevada, Wisconsin*, and *Wyoming* were built at Jarrow, England, between 1868 and 1870, and are smaller. All the Guion boats are of iron, with water-tight compartments. The cabin passage rates vary from $50 to $100, and upward, according to the ship or the location of the berth. The Guion dock is at the foot of Grand Street, Jersey City.

The Anchor Line, founded in 1852, by Thomas Henderson, has on its service between New York and Glasgow, six fine steamships, with weekly sailings. The

SOUTH STREET AND HARBOR, AND JEANNETTEE PARK.

Ethiopia, Devonia, Circassia and *Anchoria* are each of between 4,000 and 5,000 tons. The *Furnessia*, of 6,500 tons, is a fine vessel, with electric lights, water-tight compartments, and a rich furnishing. The *City of Rome*, built in 1881, at Barrow, has a gross tonnage of 8,415, with four masts, three funnels, and a magnificent equipment for passenger accommodation. The Anchor cabin fares from New York to Glasgow are from $50 to $100. The Anchor dock is at Pier 54, N. R., foot of West 24th Street. The route is across to the bold north coast of Ireland ; up Lough Foyle to Moville, where passengers for Londonderry get on a tender ; across the North Channel and the Firth of Clyde ; and up the wonderfully interesting River Clyde for 25 miles to Glasgow. This company also has Mediterranean and Indian services.

The National Line, founded in 1863, runs from New York to Liverpool and London, and has twelve large steamships, once favorite passenger-boats, but now entirely devoted to freighting. In a single trip one of these vessels has carried over 1,000 head of cattle.

The Atlantic Transport Line, running every ten days between New York and London, is also devoted to freight.

The Bristol City Line, at the foot of West 26th Street, and the **Manhanset Line,** for Avonmouth, whose pier is at Jersey City, have a large freight business with Bristol and South Wales, served by weekly steamships on each route. The English coast is also reached by the Hamburg-American and North German Lloyd steamships, calling at Southampton, from or for New York every day or two.

The Allan-State Line, between New York, Londonderry, and Glasgow, was founded in 1872 by a Glasgow company, under the name of the State Line. The New-York fleet includes the Clyde-built steamships *State of California, State of Nebraska,* and *State of Nevada,* strong and comfortable vessels of iron or steel, with saloons amidships, and electric-lighted parlors and sitting-rooms and state-rooms on the main deck. The *California* was built on the Clyde, in 1891, and is 400 feet long, with a tonnage of 4,500, eight water-tight compartments, triple-expansion engines, steel boilers, and accommodations for 1,000 passengers. This line carries large quantities of freight, and is thus able to make very low rates for passengers who are not in a hurry to get across. Its first-cabin rates are $40, or $75 for the trip over and back. The steamships leave the foot of West 21st Street Thursdays. The Allan Line also sends out freight steamships, which bring back passengers.

The Wilson Line owns thirty vessels, with a tonnage of 114,000, mainly devoted to freighting. There are four services from New York, running to Hull, London, Newcastle and Antwerp. The Hull steamships sail from Hoboken (cabin fare, $45), and carry no steerage passengers. The London steamships include several 4,500-ton vessels. They are largely devoted to carrying cattle, and make long and leisurely passages.

The Compagnie Generale Transatlantique, usually known as the "French Line," serves the route between New York and Havre with six fine express mail steamships, *La Touraine, La Bourgogne, La Normandie, La Champagne, La Bretagne* and *La Gascogne.* Each of these vessels can accommodate 1,300 passengers, and carries 2,500 tons of freight. Several of them were built at St. Nazaire, France, by the company; and so also was *La Touraine,* with a tonnage of 10,000, and

NEW-YORK CENTRAL & HUDSON-RIVER RAILROAD COMPANY'S ELEVATOR.

12,000 horse-power, and costing $2,000,000.   She has made the run from Havre to
New York in six days and 8½ hours.   The French Line ships are of steel, with
water-tight compartments and cellular bottoms.   In the latter part of the voyage
the vessels command pleasant views of the Channel Islands and the great naval city
of Cherbourg, and then swing around the French coast to Havre and the mouth of
the Seine.   The pier is No. 42, N. R., at the foot of Morton Street.   The office is
at 3 Bowling Green, Augustin Forget being the general agent for the United States.

The Bordeaux Line, originating in 1880, runs three British-built steamships,
the *Chateau Lafite, Panama* and *Tancarville*, making the voyage in nine days.

The Netherlands-American Line calls at Boulogne-sur-Mer.

The North German Lloyd (Norddeutscher Lloyd) is one of the greatest
steamship companies the world has ever seen, and its flag floats proudly on every
sea.   It was formed in 1856, by Herr H. H. Meier, who amalgamated the shipping
interests of Bremen, and its five maritime companies, into one powerful union.
The steamships *Bremen, New York, Hudson* (afterwards burnt), and *Weser* (afterwards sold) were built at Greenock, and began running in 1858; the *Hansa* came on
in 1861; the *America*, in 1862; the *Hermann*, in 1865, and other steamers in the
fifteen following years, until a great sea fleet was created.   In 1881, the splendid
express steamer *Elbe* began running; in 1882, the *Werra* and *Fulda*; in 1883, the

HOBOKEN FERRY PIER, NORTH RIVER, FOOT OF CHRISTOPHER STREET.

Eider and *Ems;* in 1885, the *Aller;* in 1886, the *Trave* and *Saale;* and in 1888,
the *Lahn.*   All these vessels were built at Glasgow.   The later additions to the
fleet, the *Kaiser Wilhelm II., Spree* and *Havel* were built at Stettin, Germany.
The twelve Lloyd express steamers are of about from 4,500 to 7,000 tons each,
and carry 1,150 passengers and 2,000 tons of freight.   They leave New York
(Hoboken) semi-weekly, crossing in about seven days to Southampton, within two
hours' ride of London; and thence running along the English Channel and the
North Sea to Bremerhaven, which is 1½ hours by railway from Bremen.

The comforts of the Lloyd ships are unexcelled.   The promenade-deck is 200
feet long, and the whole width of the ship, sheltered by awnings, lit by electricity,
and made melodious by the orchestra daily.   A broad stairway leads to the saloon,
of great size, and superbly furnished, with rare carvings, paintings, mirrors, book-
cases, and plush curtains, and perfectly lighted and ventilated.   The saloon is
amidships, and occupies the entire width of the vessel, the sides being taken up by

NORTH GERMAN LLOYD STEAMSHIP COMPANY.

PIERS AT HOBOKEN.   OFFICES AT 2 BOWLING GREEN, NEW YORK

cozy alcoves, with lounges and small tables. The ladies' cabin, in the gallery above, on the upper deck, is richly adorned with paintings, and has many divans and easy chairs. The state-rooms are on the saloon-deck, nearly all outside, of large dimensions, white, airy and comfortable.

The North German Lloyd has 59 ocean steamships, including lines from Bremen to Baltimore, weekly; to Antwerp, Lisbon and Brazil, monthly; to Buenos Ayres and Montevideo, every ten days; to India and China, monthly; to the Australian ports, monthly; and branch lines from Hong Kong to Japan; and from Singapore to Java and Sumatra and the German colony of New Guinea. No other steamship company has so great a tonnage. The general agents are Oelrichs & Co., 2 Bowling Green, New York,—a firm that has existed for almost a century.

The Hamburg-American Packet Company is the oldest German transatlantic line, having been founded as early as the year 1847. Nine years later it sent out its first steam vessel, the predecessor of a magnificent fleet of 54 steamships now owned by the company, and running on sixteen lines, reaching Boston, Baltimore, and Philadelphia, as well as New York, and also plying to the West Indies and the Spanish Main. Safety, speed and comfort are the three prime objects of the line, and it has already forwarded over two million passengers, between the Old World and the New. The Express Service, from New York to Southampton and Hamburg, is served by four of the noblest and most magnificent of the great ocean steamships, the *Fürst Bismarck, Augusta Victoria, Normannia,* and *Columbia.* The two first-named were built at the Vulcan Works, at Stettin, and the others at Govan (Scotland) and Birkenhead. These greyhounds of the sea are constructed of steel and teakwood, with double bottoms and numerous water-tight compartments. They are from 10,000 to 12,000 tons each, with a horse-power of from 13,000 to 16,000, and a speed of from 19 to $20\frac{3}{4}$ knots an hour. The *Fürst Bismarck* has made the run between New York and Southampton in 6 days and $11\frac{3}{4}$ hours, the fastest time between those ports, and the transit between New York and London is made regularly in less than a week by this route. After leaving Southampton, the Express steamships in 24 hours run across the North Sea to Cuxhaven, at the mouth of the River Elbe, whence the passengers are transported to Hamburg by railway. These majestic vessels are among the swiftest plying between America and the Continent of Europe, and their passengers are landed almost in the heart of the Old World. Their safety is increased by powerful turtle-backs at stem and stern, and also by complete twin-screw systems, so that if one engine, boiler, shaft, or screw should be disabled, the ship could be propelled by the other set.

The furnishing of the Hamburg steamships is sumptuous, the saloons having been decorated by eminent European artists. The white and gold furniture of the music-room, the rich damask hangings of the ladies' saloon, the carved dark-wood panels of the main saloon, the great glass cupola, all give the impression of the state apartments in some Old-World palace. The state-rooms are unusually large and airy, some of them arranged in suites, for families.

Besides the Express Service, there is the Regular Service of the Hamburg-American Company, from New York to Hamburg direct, touching at Havre on the return. Its first-cabin fares are from $45 upward. It employs the iron and steel steamships *Bohemia, Dania, Gellert, Gothia, Moravia, Rhætia, Rugia, Russia, Scandia, Slavonia, Suevia, Venetia, Virginia, Wieland,* etc. These great ships are divided into water-tight compartments, and heated by steam, lighted by electricity, and have their state-rooms on the main deck, with abundant light and air. This is a route by which the traveller gets many comforts for comparatively little money.

MAIN SALOON FIRST CABIN.

LADIES RECEPTION ROOM.

FURST BISMARCK.

MUSIC ROOM.

SMOKING ROOM.

HAMBURG-AMERICAN PACKET COMPANY.

PIERS AT HOBOKEN.   OFFICES AT 37 BROADWAY, NEW YORK.

The general office of the Hamburg-American Line is at 37 Broadway, New York, and the docks of the steamships are at Hoboken, with good accommodations for their varied traffic.

The Union Line is operated by the Hamburg-American Packet Company, and maintains the steamships *Sorrento, Marsala, Amalfi,* and *Taormina* on the direct route between New York and Hamburg, taking steerage passengers only.

The Red Star Line is one of the most prominent of the Atlantic steamship lines, running weekly from New York to Antwerp and from Philadelphia to Antwerp, and is owned by the International Navigation Company, the proprietors of the American Line. Although the steamers of this line do not enjoy the reputation of being "ocean greyhounds," they make the voyage between ports in nine or ten days, and compare favorably in this respect with other Continental lines. The steamships *Friesland, Westernland, Noordland, Waesland, Pennland, Rhynland, Belgenland, Switzerland,* etc., are magnificent specimens of naval architecture, and especially constructed for the Atlantic trade. They are not excelled in comfort and safety by any steamers afloat. Their construction is in excess of the rigid requirements of the British Lloyds and Bureau Veritas, under whose inspection they were built. They are very comfortably arranged, with family rooms, dining-rooms on saloon-deck, electric lights, isolated kitchens, saloons artistically decorated with rare woodwork and paintings, perfect ventilating apparatus, and smoking-rooms with tiled floors and mahogany walls. The voyage eastward leads past the Scilly Islands and the Lizard, whence the course is laid up the English Channel, in sight

RED STAR LINE STEAMSHIP "FRIESLAND." OFFICES, 6 BOWLING GREEN.

of Eddystone Rock, the Bill of Portland, the Isle of Wight, Hastings and Dover, with the French coast on the starboard side. Then the steamship heads across the North Sea, passing Dunkirk and Ostend, entering the Scheldt River at Flushing, 47 miles from Antwerp. This port was chosen as the Continental terminal on account of its central geographical position, within a few hours' railway ride of

Paris, Strasburg or Frankfort, and in the very heart of the quaint and fascinating Low Countries, and because it avoided the extremely disagreeable "Channel crossing" which is so dreaded by many experienced travellers. The rates by this line vary from about $50 to $135, according to the season, steamer and location of

RED STAR LINE STEAMSHIP "WESTERNLAND," OFFICES, 6 BOWLING GREEN.

room. The offices of the company are at 6 Bowling Green, New York; 307 Walnut Street, Philadelphia; and 32 South Clark Street, Chicago; the General European Agents are von der Becke & Marsily, 22 Kammenstrasse, Antwerp.

The White Cross Line runs between New York and Antwerp, with the steamships *Hermann* and *De Ruyter*.

The Insular Navigation Company (Empreza Insulana Navegaçao) runs every three weeks from New York to the Azore Islands in nine days (fare, $60), to Madeira (by transfer) in eleven days ($75), and to Lisbon in fifteen days ($90). It is a Portuguese line. The *Vega* and *Peninsular* are finely equipped 4,000-ton steamships.

The Mediterranean Trade is accommodated by several lines, and by many "ocean tramps," bringing to New York yearly 1,500,000 boxes of Sicily oranges and lemons, 600,000 barrels of Spanish grapes, and vast quantities of nuts and dried fruits. Many passengers for Southern Europe and the Levant avail themselves of these routes, which lie far south of the storms and ice of the North Atlantic. There are lines of steamships running monthly from New York by the Mediterranean Sea and Suez Canal to the ports of India, China and Japan. They are usually laden with heavy freights, and bring back valuable cargoes of tea.

The Mediterranean traffic has of late years assumed important proportions, and employs extensive fleets. The recent enterprise of the North German Lloyd and Hamburg-American lines in placing some of their finest vessels on the route from New York to Genoa has been rewarded by large passenger-lists, and this method of entering upon European travel is destined to be increasingly popular. Thus the tourist's land journey begins in the innermost centres of ancient art and civilization.

The Netherlands-American Steam-Navigation Company was founded in 1872, and runs semi-weekly steamers from New York (Hoboken) to Rotterdam or Amsterdam, touching at Boulogne-sur-Mer to land passengers for Paris, four hours' distant by railway. The fleet includes the steamships *Spaarndam, Maasdam, Veendam, Werkendam, Amsterdam, Obdam, Rotterdam, Didam, Dubbeldam, Edam, Schiedam,* and *P. Caland,* the first seven having been built at Belfast, and the next two at Rotterdam (in 1891). The Netherlands steamers are four-masters, with four decks and eight water-tight compartments, and very commodious equipments. They are lighted by electricity and heated by steam, and have commodious and comfortable state-rooms, saloons, smoking-rooms, and other advantages, together with unusually low rates of fare, making this the cheapest of all the Continental lines. The first-cabin rates are from $55 to $70. The route traverses the Atlantic Ocean

NETHERLANDS-AMERICAN LINE STEAMSHIP "SPAARNDAM," OFFICE 39 BROADWAY, PIER IN HOBOKEN.

and the English Channel, with pleasant views of the coasts of England and France and the port of Boulogne, and ascends the River Maas, an arm of the Rhine, fourteen miles, by Vlaardingen and Delfthaven, to Rotterdam. The steamships sailing on Wednesday do not call at this port, but go on to Amsterdam, traversing the costly North-Sea Canal from Ymuiden, about fifteen miles. Either of these great ports has favorable railway communication with Paris, Vienna, Berlin and all other cities of Continental Europe. The magnificent Rhine steamboats start directly from Rotterdam, running to Düsseldorf, Cologne, Bonn, Coblenz, Mayence and Mannheim, which is close to beautiful Heidelberg and the grand old cathedral-cities of Worms and Spires, and within six hours of Switzerland. The Netherlands-American piers are at the foot of 5th Street, in Hoboken; and the offices are at 39 Broadway, in the vicinity of Bowling Green, New York.

The Netherlands-American Line is preferred by many travellers who wish to avoid the discomforts of the Channel passage, and to be landed directly on the Continent, where a comfortable journey by railway will lead them to the great metropolitan cities of Germany, France and Italy, or to the mountain-glories of Switzerland. Although the Netherlands steamships are large and well-equipped, the rates of passage are relatively very moderate, and purchase a high value in good and comfortable accommodations. This is therefore one of the most popular of the prominent Continental lines, and is fully patronized during the seasons of travel by many well-known American and European families.

The **Thingvalla Line** in 1879 began its voyages from New York to Norway and Sweden, with Scandinavian officers and crews and flag, and bearing the mails. The run takes from eleven to twelve days ; and the first-cabin fares are $50 and $60. The *Hekla*, *Thingvalla*, *Norge* and *Island*, make fortnightly sailings from Hoboken to Christiania and Christiansand, in Norway, and Copenhagen, in Denmark.

The **North German Lloyd Mediterranean Service**, inaugurated in 1891, runs about weekly the fast express steamships *Fulda*, *Werra*, *Ems* and *Kaiser Wilhelm II*. They reach Gibraltar in eight days, and thence in less than three days arrive at Genoa, in some cases proceeding to Naples, where connections are made by Lloyd steamers running to Palermo, and also, during the winter season, with special North German Lloyd steamers between Genoa and Alexandria, Egypt. Travellers desiring to reach Italy, Switzerland, the Riviera, Southern France, Sicily, Egypt and the Nile can do so in the shortest possible time, and in the most convenient manner, by these Mediterranean lines of the North German Lloyd Steamship Co. The route from New York to the Mediterranean is on southern latitudes, ensuring comparatively smooth trips and pleasant passages during the winter months, and a corresponding degree of comfort for travellers.

The **Hamburg-American Packet Company's Mediterranean Express Line** runs a fine winter-service of twin-screw express steamers from New York. They cross the Atlantic in less than seven days, and make their first call at Algiers, thus offering a direct means of communication between New York and that celebrated winter-resort. From there they go to the superb bay of Naples, where connection is made for Sicily, Rome and the East. Leaving this port, the Hamburg-American steamship the next day reaches Genoa, convenient to the Riviera, the Italian Lakes, and Switzerland. The Hamburg-American Packet Company also once a year, generally at the beginning of February, sends one of its magnificent twin-screw express steamers from New York on a cruise to the Mediterranean and the Orient, touching at Gibraltar, Genoa, Ajaccio, Alexandria (for Cairo and the Pyramids), Jaffa (for Jerusalem), Smyrna, Constantinople, Athens, Malta, Syracuse, Palermo, Naples and Algiers. The excursion lasts about ten weeks, and embraces the principal places of a region whose every inch of soil abounds with stirring reminiscences of ancient lore and history, in the regions rich with countless treasures of art which surround "the Storied Sea."

The **Anchor Line** also sends steamships every ten days from New York to Gibraltar, Naples, Genoa, Leghorn, Messina and Palermo.

The **Florio Italian Line** sails fortnightly from New York for Gibraltar, Marseilles, Genoa, Naples, Messina and Palermo, connecting with steamships for Egypt, the Black Sea and the West Indies. They take a far southerly course, below the range of ice, fogs and gales.

The **Fabre Line** sends the *Neustria*, *Massilia*, and other steamships from Brooklyn to Naples and Marseilles every two or three weeks.

Peabody's Australasian Line is owned and operated by Henry W. Peabody & Co., of 58 New Street, New York, one of the most important of the large mercantile houses engaged in the foreign commerce of the port of New York. The business of this firm extends to nearly all parts of the globe, but is more especially with Great Britain, Australasia, India, the Philippine Islands, and Yucatan, in all of which countries they have either their own branch houses or regularly established agents. They are also well known, and have extensive dealings in Mexico, Central and South America, the West Indies, and South Africa. It is, however, in connection with the Australian shipping and commission business, which has for a long time been one of the most important mercantile interests of the port of New York, that the firm of Henry W. Peabody & Co. is perhaps best known. In this business, which comprises the purchasing and shipping to the British colonies of Australia and New Zealand of the products of the United States and Canada of every description, Henry W. Peabody & Co. have taken a foremost place since 1859. They established between the United States and Australia the regular line of sailing vessels known as Peabody's Australasian Line, of which the present firm are still the proprietors. In this service Henry W. Peabody & Co. have constantly under charter or loading, in New York, first-class ships, in which they take all freight offering for the various Australian ports.

HENRY W. PEABODY & CO.'S OFFICES, 58 NEW ST.

The Western Seas, to their uttermost ends, are traversed by steamships and sailing vessels, loaded by or for the Empire City.

To the Southern and Gulf coasts, the West Indies, and the Central-American and South-American ports, there are several first-class sea-routes, served by fine vessels, and much used for winter excursions, as well as for freighting. An inexpensive voyage of two or three days conducts the traveller from the snow-bound northern coasts to lands of perennial summer, the lovely semi-tropical Bermudas, the ever-popular Bahamas, the Lesser Antilles, the summerlands of Cuba, Hayti and Jamaica, and the coasts of Mexico and the Spanish Main.

The Red-Cross Steamships *Miranda* and *Portia* visit Halifax, Nova Scotia, and St. John's, Newfoundland (fare, $34; or $60 for the round trip of twelve days). The route lies through Long-Island Sound, and requires fifty hours from New York to Halifax, and an equal time thence to St. John's.

The Mallory Line's Maine and Maritime Provinces Service is maintained by a steamer sailing from Pier 21, E. R., every Saturday afternoon and reaching Bar Harbor Monday morning, Eastport Monday afternoon, and St. John, New Brunswick, Monday evening. C. H. Mallory & Co., at Pier 20, are the agents.

The Maine Steamship Company sends out its swift new 2,000-ton steamships *Manhattan* and *Cottage City* thrice weekly, at 5 P. M., from Pier 38, E. R. (foot of Market Street). During the same night they traverse Long-Island Sound, and the next morning they stop at Cottage City, Martha's Vineyard. Sailing thence eastward through Vineyard Sound, and past lone Nantucket, and up along sandy Cape Cod, the boat reaches Portland at nightfall, 27 hours from New York.

The Metropolitan Line sends its large and powerful freight-steamships thrice weekly, from Pier 11, N. R., to Boston, by the outside passage around Cape Cod.

The Clyde Steamship Company has lines of steamers running between Boston, New York, Philadelphia, Baltimore, Washington, Norfolk, New Berne, Richmond, Troy, Albany, Wilmington, N. C.; Georgetown, S. C.; Charleston, S. C., and Jacksonville, Fla.; and on the St.-John's River between Jacksonville, Palatka and Sanford and intermediate landings; also between New

VESSEL OF HENRY W. PEABODY & CO.'S AUSTRALASIAN LINE.

York and Turks Island, Haiti and Santo Domingo, and other West-India ports. Their line between New York, Charleston, and Jacksonville, comprises the steamers: *Iroquois, Cherokee, Algonquin, Seminole, Yemossee* and *Delaware*, which sail from the company's wharf, Pier 29, E. R., on Mondays, Wednesdays and Fridays.

The Clyde steamships for the far South pass down the beautiful harbor of New York in the glory of the late afternoon, traversing the Narrows, and rounding the lonely Sandy Hook. In about fifty hours they reach the historic city of Charleston, the pride of South Carolina, passing into the harbor by the famous Fort Sumter and Fort Moultrie. Here the vessel sojourns for about eight hours, giving ample opportunity for an inspection of the city, rising undaunted from the ruins of bombardments and earthquakes. From Charleston a short and pleasant voyage outside of the Sea Islands of Carolina leads down to the low semi-tropical coast of Florida, the land of flowers and oranges. The great steamship enters the St.-John's River, and runs up its broad course for 25 miles, to the city of Jacksonville, from which railway or river routes reach all parts of the State. Clyde's St.-John's River Line runs thence southward up this famous river for 193 miles, by Green Cove Springs, Palatka, Astor, Blue Springs, and many other landings, to Sanford, the terminal point of seven railways, and the main distributing point for South Florida. The general office of the Clyde Line is at 5 Bowling Green; and its dock is at Pier 29, E. R., at the foot of Roosevelt Street, under the great Brooklyn Bridge. The steamers of the West-India Line leave from Pier 15, E. R., as advertised.

The Clydes have been active in the building and management of steamships for more than half a century.   Thomas Clyde, the founder of the house, was a co-laborer with John Ericsson, as early as 1837, in introducing the screw-propeller.   He built the steamship *John S. McKim*, the first screw-steamer ever constructed in the United States for commercial purposes, and was one of the originators and owners of the first line of propellers — the Ericsson Line, which to-day has a service between

CLYDE'S STEAMSHIP PIER, AT FOOT OF ROOSEVELT STREET, NEW YORK.

Philadelphia and Baltimore.   The *John S. McKim*, by the way, was a twin-screw ship.   This steamer conveyed Col. Jefferson Davis and his regiment of Mississippi troops from New Orleans to one of the Mexican ports during the Mexican War. Strange to say, it was a Clyde steamship, the *Rebecca Clyde*, which brought President Jefferson Davis, of the Confederacy, a prisoner from Savannah to Fort Monroe, in 1865.   In 1871 the Clydes built for their ship *George W. Clyde*, the first compound engine ever set up in this country, and in 1886 built the first large triple-expansion engines in America.   They were placed in their ship *Cherokee*.   In 1888 the Clydes also built the steamer *Iroquois*, the first steel steamship ever built for commercial purposes in this country.

The Old Dominion Steamship Company has a fleet of eight large steamships, the *Seneca*, 3,000 tons, *Guyandotte* and *Roanoke*, 2,354 tons each, the *Old Dominion*, *Wyanoke*, *Richmond*, and *City of Columbia*.   Their sailings are from the foot of Beach Street, Pier 26, N. R., New York, at 3 P. M., four times a week to Norfolk, Old Point Comfort and Newport News, Va., in 24 hours (fare, $8, including meals and state-room berth); three times a week to Richmond in 36 hours (fare, $9); and thrice a week to West Point, Va.   At Norfolk connection is made with the company's auxiliary steamboat, *New Berne*, running through the sounds.

The Ocean Steamship Company is a favorite route between New York and Georgia, Florida and the Gulf States. Its splendid steamships, *Kansas City, Nacoochee, City of Augusta, City of Birmingham, Chattahoochee* and *Tallahassee* leave New York every Tuesday, Thursday and Saturday, at mid-afternoon, reaching Savannah in from 44 to 55 hours, and connecting there with the Waycross Short Line, the Central Railroad of Georgia, and other routes to the chief points of the Southeastern States. The voyage is full of interest and refreshment, and gives a delightful rest to a tired man or woman, and a marvellous change of climate, from the blue winter ice of the North to the orange-groves and perennial gentleness of the South, or, in summer, from the blazing heats of the Gulf States to the bracing breezes of Yankeeland. The first few hours of the voyage are made charming by the vast and impressive panorama of New-York Bay and the Navesink Highlands, and the last two hours by the ascent of the Savannah River, with its historic for-tresses, tropical jungles and ancient rice and cotton plantations. Between these two landward episodes are forty hours on the open sea, with all its mystery, its rest-

OCEAN STEAMSHIP CO. OF SAVANNAH (SAVANNAH LINE), PIERS 34 AND 35, NORTH RIVER, FOOT OF SPRING AND CANAL STREETS.

fulness, and its invigoration. The Ocean Steamship Line also runs steamships between Boston and Philadelphia and Savannah. It has one of the finest covered piers in New York, at the foot of Canal and Spring Streets, with a handsome and capacious building containing its general offices. The steamships were built on the Delaware River, under the inspection of the highest boards of survey, and are of iron and steel, with triple-expansion engines, and divided into water-tight compartments. Among the fleet are the fastest merchant vessels on the American coasts. The state-rooms are larger than those on the transatlantic steamships, and each has two roomy berths, and is lighted by electric lights. The saloons are finished in

polished satinwood and white mahogany, with rich upholstery, curtains and carpets to match.   There are well-appointed smoking-rooms for the men, on the hur-
ricane-deck.   The promenade-deck is spacious and secure, and affords a capital
place for health-giving walks.   R. L. Walker is the New-York agent of the Ocean
Steamship Company, at New Pier 35, N. R.   The business of the Savannah Line
is so immense that it is necessary to utilize the adjoining pier.

The St.-Augustine Steamship Company sends the *City of St. Augustine*, a
freight-steamer, every three weeks from the foot of Clinton Street to St. Augustine,
Florida.

The Cromwell Steamship Company dispatches a steamer every Wednesday
and Saturday from Pier 9, N. R., New York, to New Orleans direct.   The fleet
includes the largest and finest vessels in this coastwise trade, built of iron, exclusively for this route, and first-class in every respect.   The cabin fare is $35; and
return tickets good for six months cost $60.   This is a six days' voyage, the round
trip, with four days at New Orleans, taking sixteen days.

The Morgan Steamship Line of the Southern Pacific Company, dispatches every Tuesday, Thursday and Saturday from New Pier 25, N. R., one of its
steamships *El Norte*, *El Monte*, *El Sol*, *El Rio*, *El Mar*, *El Sud*, *El Paso*, *Excelsior*
and *El Dorado*, bound for New Orleans.   They are devoted entirely to freighting,
and carry out vast cargoes destined to the Mississippi and Red-River points and to

SOUTHERN PACIFIC CO.'S STEAMSHIP "EL SUD."

Louisiana, Mississippi, Texas, New and Old Mexico, Arizona and the Pacific Coast.
The Morgan Line steamers also run regularly from New Orleans weekly to Port
Tampa, Punta Gorda, Key West and Havana (for passengers and freight); and also
to Bluefields, Nicaragua (passengers and freight); with frequent freight-boats to
Brazos de Santiago, Texas.   The Southern Pacific is also interested in the Occi-
dental and Oriental Steamship Company, running the steamers *Oceanic*, *Gaelic*, and
Belgic from San Francisco to Honolulu (7 days), Yokohama (17 days; fare, $200),

and Hong Kong (25 days; fare, $225). At Yokohama they connect with the Nippon Yusen Kaisha steamers for Hiogo, Nagasaki, and Chinese, Corean and Siberian ports; and at Hong Kong with lines for Chinese ports, Formosa, the Philippines, Java, Australia, Calcutta and Bombay. The New-York offices are at 343 Broadway and 1 Battery Place (Washington Building).

The Mallory Steamship Lines (New-York & Texas Steamship Co.) with their own steamships and connections carry freight and passengers to all points in

MALLORY S. S. LINES. NEW-YORK & TEXAS S. S. CO., PIERS 20 AND 21 EAST RIVER.

Texas, Colorado, Arizona, Utah, New Mexico, California, Mexico, Georgia, Florida, Alabama, etc., and the South and Southwest; and also to Eastport and Bar Harbor, Maine, St. John, N. B., and all points in New Brunswick, Nova Scotia, etc. These lines were established in 1866, and are the only lines of freight and passenger-steamships running "from Maine to Texas." There are three distinct routes — the Texas Route, the Georgia-Florida Route, and the Maine and Maritime Provinces Route. The fleet comprises eleven iron steamships, aggregating 30,772 tons. The most modern of these ships are lighted by electricity, steered by steam-power, and equipped with the most approved appliances for safety and comfort. The saloons are on the hurricane deck, and are lighted from large domes above, as well as from wide windows in the sides. The promenade decks are protected by awnings, and afford a pleasant exercising ground. The state-rooms are large and airy, and eligibly situated on the main and hurricane decks. There are also comfortable and attractive smoking-rooms, and many other conveniences for the sea traveller.

The Texas Service is maintained by semi-weekly sailings every Wednesday and Saturday at 3 P. M., from Pier 20, E. R., to Galveston, Texas, which is reached in six or seven days. During the cotton season in Texas the service is tri-weekly

—Tuesdays, Thursdays and Saturdays. The Saturday boats stop at Key West, Florida, making connection there with the Plant Steamship Line for Havana, which is only ninety miles distant. From Galveston, the chief sea-port of Texas, all parts of the Lone Star State may be visited by railway. There is also a large passenger-travel by the Mallory Line from New York to Galveston, and thence into Colorado and on to the Pacific Coast, or down into Old Mexico.

The Georgia-Florida service is maintained by weekly sailings at 3 P. M. every Friday from Pier 21, E. R., New York, reaching Brunswick, Georgia, in about 62 hours. Brunswick is a fast-growing and very charming city, half buried in live-oak and palmetto groves and Spanish moss, and the coast terminus of the Brunswick & Western Railroad and the East-Tennessee, Virginia & Georgia system. Thence the steamers continue on to Fernandina, on a land-locked harbor inside of Amelia Island, and giving access to all parts of Florida by the Florida Central & Peninsular Railroad.

The Mallory steamships lie at Piers 20 and 21, E. R., close to the Fulton Ferry, where also are the offices of C. H. Mallory & Co., the general agents.

The New-York & Cuba Mail Steamship Company (Ward Line) owns the *Niagara*, *Saratoga*, and *City of Washington*, etc., running from Piers 16 and 17, E. R. (foot of Wall Street), New York, every Wednesday. They reach Havana in from four to five days, connecting with steamers for all parts of the West Indies, and for Mexico and the Spanish Main, England, France and Spain. Ward's Wednesday steamers from New York go to Havana and Matanzas.

Ward's Mexican Line, including the *Yumuri*, *Yucatan*, *Orizaba*, *City of Alexandria*, etc., leaves New York every Saturday, and goes on from Havana to Progreso (the port for Merida, in Yucatan), Vera Cruz (263 miles by rail from Mexico), Tuxpam and Tampico, returning by Campeche, Progreso and Havana. The company's steamer *Manteo* runs between Campeche, Laguna and Frontera. The Wards also send fortnightly the steamships *Cienfuegos* and *Santiago* to Nassau, arriving in three days, and thence running through the Bahama Islands, and around to beautiful old Santiago de Cuba, and 325 miles further to bright modern Cienfuegos. This is a favorite excursion-route in winter, and affords various interesting combination and round tours. The single cabin fares are: From New York to Havana, $35; to Nassau, $40; to Progreso or Vera Cruz, $55; to Santiago, Cienfuegos, Tuxpam or Tampico, $60; to Campeche, $70; to Frontera or Laguna, $75; with steerage at about half these rates. The Ward fleet includes several very handsome and commodious vessels, efficiently managed.

The Compania Trasatlantica is a Spanish mail line, sending steamships every ten days from Pier 10, E. R., New York, to Havana, the voyage taking four days. The steamer sailing on the 20th of each month also goes on to Progreso and Vera Cruz, in Mexico; and the steamer on the 30th goes from Havana to Santiago de Cuba; La Guayra and Puerto Cabello, in Venezuela; Sabanilla, Cartagena, and Colon, in Colombia; and Puerto Limon. At Havana, close connections are made for Spanish ports. The passage-rates (from which 25 per cent. is discounted for excursion-tickets) are: From New York to Havana, first-cabin, $37, second-cabin, $25, steerage, $17; to Progreso, $55, $35 and $20; Vera Cruz, $60, $40 and $25; to Santiago de Cuba, $65, $45 and $30; to La Guayra, $80, $60 and $45; to Cartagena, $93, $72 and $54; to Cadiz, Spain, $190, $145 and $50.

The Quebec Steamship Company has weekly sailings from January to June, and fortnightly the rest of the year, between New York and Bermuda, the fine 2,500-ton iron steamship *Trinidad*, making the voyage in about 50 hours. The fares are $30 for the first cabin, and $20 for the second cabin. The dock is at

FORT WADSWORTH, THE SCHOOL SHIP AND WAR-VESSELS.
VIEWS TAKEN IN NORTH RIVER AND NEW-YORK HARBOR. PHOTOS BY JOHNSTON.

New Pier 47, N. R., at the foot of West 10th Street. The Quebec Line also sends steamers every ten days from New York to St. Croix, St. Kitts, Antigua, Montserrat, Guadaloupe, Dominica, Martinique, St. Lucia and Barbadoes, at fares varying at from $50 to $60. These vessels connect in the Windward Islands with steamships for the other West Indies, and for England and France. The Bermuda Line is much patronized in spring and fall by persons in search of health or respite from bad weather, who find delight in the serene climate of these beautiful coral islands, abounding in flowers and fruits, and one of the impregnable and strongly garrisoned naval stations of the British Empire.

The Atlas Steamship Company owns a favorite line of steamers sailing to the West Indies from Pier 55, N. R., carrying the United-States mails, and offering great inducements to passengers visiting the many interesting ports in the West Indies. Chief among the health-resorts is the British island of Jamaica, renowned for its luxuriant foliage and unequalled facilities for the tourist in the shape of magnificent roads, with good hotels and liveries in every town. The company also has a coastal service sailing regularly around the island, and a trip in one of these steamers, visiting all the ports, cannot be equalled as a yachting voyage in these summer seas. For invalids desiring a winter-resort where they can

ATLAS MAIL LINE TO THE WEST INDIES, PIER 55, NORTH RIVER.

obtain abundant sunlight and an equable temperature, Jamaica offers what cannot be obtained in any other island near the United States. The many mineral springs are wonderful in their cures of neuralgia, gout, rheumatism, etc., and buildings have been erected for the use of invalids visiting the springs. The coffee, tobacco, sugar and banana plantations are well worth a visit, and the fact that many are conducted by American capital renders them doubly attractive. Making Jamaica his headquarters, the tourist can at regular dates embark on the Atlas steamers, and visit Hayti, Costa Rica, and the Spanish Main, whose old towns (bearing the marks and carrying the reminiscences of their Spanish rulers and privateering captains) are full of interest. The spacious and luxurious passenger accommodations offered on these steamers are worthy of note. The saloons and state-rooms are above the main deck, which insures the minimum of motion, perfect ventilation, and freedom from unpleasant smells from holds or engines. The state-rooms are large, well lighted and comfortably furnished ; each room having two berths and a sofa, and electric lights. The company since its formation, twenty years ago, has never lost a life by shipwreck — and being its own insurer offers the best guarantee that every precaution is taken for safe navigation. The company's fleet includes the steamships *Adirondack, Alene, Athos, Alvo, Ailsa, Andes, Alps, Alvena, Claribel, Adula* and *Arden.* These steamers, of from 2,200 to 2,500 tons each, were built on the Clyde and at Belfast, and fill the necessary requirements of the British and American Passenger Acts. The agents of the Atlas Line are Pim, Forwood & Co., at 24 State Street, New York.

The New-York & Porto-Rico Line sails from the Atlantic Dock, Brooklyn, every fortnight, for the famous Spanish island of sugar, coffee, and cotton.

The Trinidad Line has its pier at the Union Stores, Brooklyn, and brings from the far-away British island, under the Venezuelan Andes, large cargoes of tropical products. Its steamboats sail every ten days, carrying cabin passengers.

The Central-American Company sends its steamships *Jason* and *Argonaut* from Atlantic Dock, Brooklyn, fortnightly, to Kingston (Jamaica), Greytown (Nicaragua), Belize, Livingston, Truxillo, and other tropical ports.

The Pacific Mail Steamships sail from the foot of Canal Street, Pier 34, N. R., every ten days, for Colon, connecting there with the Panama Railway for the Pacific Coast. The distance by this route from New York to San Francisco is 5,220 miles ; and the fare is $90, or $40 for forward-cabin passengers. The time is about 25 days. The steamships are the *Columbia, City of Para, Newport* and *Colon.*

The Red "D" Line, at Harbeck Stores, sends out the large American-built iron steamships *Venezuela, Caracas,* and *Philadelphia* every ten days to the chief ports of Venezuela. The fare is $80 ; or $50 for second-class. The steamships are of 2,500 tons burden or more ; and have water-tight compartments, electric lights and bells, large smoking-rooms and social halls, and other comforts. The route leads from New York through the Mona Passage, between San Domingo and Porto Rico ; and at six days out reaches the quaint Dutch island-colony of Curaçoa, 1,763 miles from Sandy Hook. Thence a night's run of 111 miles leads to Puerto Cabello, a busy coffee-port, thirty miles by railway from beautiful Valencia. Another night voyage of seventy miles takes one to La Guayra, celebrated in Kingsley's *Westward Ho,* and twenty-seven miles by an Andes-climbing railway from Caracas, the mountain-girt capital of Venezuela. The smaller Red "D" steamer *Merida* runs regularly over the 214 miles from Curaçoa to Maracaibo, a city of 35,000 Venezuelans, exporting hides, coffee and cocoa, and standing near a great inland sea.

The Red "D" steamers are very comfortable, and well-appointed for travellers ; and they run through seas of remarkable historic interest and picturesque beauty. The legends and traditions of the Spanish Main are of wonderful charm, and when they are studied in connection with the rich tropical scenery of these regions, they acquire a new value.

The general managers of the Red "D" Line are Boulton, Bliss & Dallett, at 135 Front Street, New York, where passages may be obtained, and state-rooms selected.

The Clyde West-India Line sends steamships to Turks Island, Hayti, Puerto Plata, Samana, Sanchez and San-Domingo City.

The Royal Dutch West-Indian Mail Line (Koninklijke West-Indische Maildienst) has the *Prins Willem I.* and five other steamships, leaving New York every three weeks, and running to Port au Prince, $60; Aux Cayes, Jacmel, and Curaçoa, $75; Puerto Cabello, La Guayra, Cumaná, and Carúpano, $80; Trinidad and Demerara, $90; and Paramaribo, $100. From the last port the ships cross the Atlantic to Havre, France, and Amsterdam, Holland.

The Sloman Line runs freight-boats between New York and the Brazilian ports. **Norton's Freighting Vessels** sail to the ports of the River Plate.

Busk & Jevons send occasional vessels down the South-American coast.

The Booth Line sends a monthly steamship to Para and Manaos (on the Amazon River), and another to Para, Maranham and Ceara, with passenger accommodation at from $75 to $125.

The Bays, Rivers and Sounds for more than a hundred miles about New York are traversed by great fleets of passenger-steamers, varying in size from the tiny craft which visit the nearer islands to the immense and magnificent vessels which traverse Long-Island Sound and the Hudson River. No other port in the world has such noble boats as these last mentioned, which, with their superb halls, grand staircases, and spacious dining-rooms, resemble floating hotels of the first-class. In summer an immense passenger and excursion business is done by the suburban steamboats, especially by those running to Coney Island and Rockaway Beach, to Sandy Hook and the coast toward Long Branch, and to the Fishing Banks outside.

The Fall-River Line has its headquarters at the foot of Murray Street, whence in the pleasant season it dispatches at late afternoon two of the vessels of its fleet, the *Puritan, Pilgrim, Plymouth,* or *Providence.* They arrive early the next morning at the Massachusetts port and cotton-manufacturing city of Fall River, whence connecting trains run to Boston in eighty minutes. These are undoubtedly the largest, most magnificent, and most perfectly-equipped vessels in the world, used for interior navigation. They are lighted by electricity, steered by steam, enlivened by orchestral music, and provided with meals *a la carte.* In spring, autumn and winter the Fall-River line sends out but one boat daily.

The Providence Line steamboats leave from Pier 29, N. R., at late afternoon daily (except Sunday), from May to November, and traverse the entire length of the East River, Long-Island Sound, and Narragansett Bay, arriving at six o'clock the next morning at Providence, Rhode Island. Parlor-car trains connecting run to Boston, 42 miles, in 75 minutes; and to Worcester. The *Connecticut* and *Massachusetts* are beautiful vessels, decorated in white and gold, with dining-rooms on the main decks, and fine orchestras.

The Norwich Line steamships *City of Worcester* and *City of Boston* leave Pier 40, N. R., New York, at 5 o'clock, P. M., and run eastward up the Sound to New London, where passengers take the trains at early morning for Boston, Worcester and other New-England cities. This is a very commodious route, served by large and handsome first-class steamboats, and giving easy access to Yankee-land.

The Stonington Line sends a fine steamboat at 5.30 o'clock every afternoon from New Pier 36, N. R., up Long-Island Sound to the quaint little Connecticut port of Stonington, where it connects with swift trains to Boston and other New-England cities. This route is served by the new steel steamers *Maine* and *New Hampshire* and other fine boats; and is especially desirable in winter, or when rough sea-winds make the longer Sound routes uncomfortable.

Other Eastern Lines are those to Saybrook and Hartford, daily, ascending the picturesque Connecticut River; to Bridgeport, the busy manufacturing city on the Connecticut shore; to New Haven, the seat of Yale University; to Stamford, South Norwalk, New Rochelle and Port Chester; and to the towns on the north shore of Long Island, like Sea Cliff and Sands Point, Roslyn and Glen Cove, Sag Harbor and Shelter Island, Southold and Whitestone.

The Hudson-River Day-Line Steamers traverse the most beautiful and interesting river-scenery in the world. Not the Rhine, the Danube, or the Rhone can claim superiority to this glorious stream of the New World, with its cliffs and moun- tain-guards, its legends of centur- ies, and its thronging poetic, liter- ary and artis- tic enrich- ment, made

HUDSON-RIVER STEAMER "NEW YORK."

HUDSON RIVER STEAMER "ALBANY"

HUDSON-RIVER DAY LINE STEAMERS, "NEW YORK" AND "ALBANY," DESBROSSES-STREET PIER, N. R.

still more famous in the Colum- bian year of 1893 by having peaceful- ly floated the great- est aggre- gated naval power ever brought together at any one point in the history of the world. During the pleasant season the great iron steam- boats *Albany* and *New York* leave Desbrosses-Street Pier and 22d Street Pier, N. R., every day (except Sunday) at early morning, and reach Albany at about 6 P. M. They are of about 1,500 tons each, built at Wilmington, Delaware, with over 3,000 horse-power, and a speed of nearly 25 miles an hour. Since these boats are for tourists only, they carry no freight, and are therefore far more comfortable, with broad open spaces, dining-rooms on the main decks, private parlors with bay-windows, and immense grand saloons on the promenade-deck, with almost contin-uous windows. They are finished in hard-wood, furnished with mahogany, carpeted with Axminster, and decorated with choice paintings by Cropsey, Satterlee, Bierstadt and other masters. These are in every respect the finest vessels of their class afloat. The boat touches first at the attractive suburban city of Yonkers. About noon it reaches West Point, amid the magnificent Highlands of the Hudson, where Grant and Sherman, Sheridan and Lee, learned the art of war, and where Scott, Custer and Kilpatrick are buried. A little later, and Newburgh is reached, with its great Washington triumphal arch towering on the hill. Next comes Poughkeepsie, with its famous bridge far overhead. The Catskill Mountains loom grandly in the west, as the steamer goes on, passing innumerable other vessels, of all degrees, and view-ing along the shore scores of quaint old villages and historic country-seats. It is a voyage in Paradise ; and the huge iron steamer itself, being used only as a pleasure-boat, has the lightness, grace and beauty of a royal yacht. A trip on these Hudson-River Day-Line steamers, on a pleasant day, is a joy never to be forgotten after-wards. The general offices are at the Desbrosses-Street Pier, in New-York City.

The Homer Ramsdell Transportation Company's magnificent iron steamers, running between New York and Newburgh, leave New York on week

RAMSDELL LINE TO NEWBURGH : HOMER RAMSDELL TRANSPORTATION CO., FOOT OF FRANKLIN ST., NORTH RIVER.

days at 5 P. M. and on Sundays at 9 A. M., and leave Newburgh every evening in the week at 7 P. M. They stop both ways at Fishkill, Cornwall, Cold Spring, West Point and Cranston's, and on the down trip also at 129th Street. The trip covers the grandest part of the Hudson River. The fare is fifty cents. Besides furnishing the usual accommodations for passengers and freight, special accommodations are pro-vided for horses and perishable freight.

This company is the successor of the firm of J. & T. Powell, who established a line of sloops in 1802. The freighting business was continued by means of sailing vessels until about 1830, when steamboats were first employed. In 1835 Thomas Powell built the steamer *Highlander,* and she was run on the route until 1848, when the barge *Newburgh,* built by Powell, Ramsdell & Co., replaced her; in 1851 the barge *Susquehanna* was built, and ran in connection with the *Newburgh ;* and in 1870 the barge *Charles Spear* was purchased, and with the *Susquehanna* and *Minisink* formed a daily line, each of the boats making two trips a week.

Powell, Ramsdell & Co. were succeeded by Homer Ramsdell & Co. in 1865, and the business was carried on under that name until 1880, when Mr. Ramsdell and his sons (the grandsons of Thomas Powell) formed the present company. In 1886-7 a return was made to the use of steam in the forwarding business, and the barges were replaced by the handsome steel propellers *Newburgh* and *Homer Ramsdell,* which afford to the public express freight accommodations unsurpassed by any other water or railroad line in the country.

The distance between New York and Newburgh is sixty miles, and the wonderful expanse of the Hudson River between the two cities include some of the finest scenery in the world, the tremendous rocky walls of the Palisades, the broad expanses of the Tappan Zee, the legend-crowned villages of Tarrytown and Peekskill, the busy scenes around Haverstraw and Nyack, the palaces of the millionaires about Yonkers and Dobbs Ferry, the magnificent gateway of the Highlands, the State National Guard's camp-ground at Peekskill, the gray old United-States Military Academy at West Point, the far-viewing summer-hotels of Cornwall, and then the venerable and beautiful city of Newburgh, the home-port of the Ramsdell boats. Nearly two centuries ago a band of Lutheran exiles from the devastated Palatinate of the Rhine settled here, under the patronage of Queen Anne ; and since that far-past day the present great, flourishing and enterprising city has grown up on these pleasant hills. The New-York pier of the Homer Ramsdell Transportation Co. is at the foot of Franklin Street, North River.

Other Hudson-River Lines lead to Yonkers, Tivoli, Nyack, Peekskill, Fishkill, Fort Lee, Sing Sing, Tarrytown, etc.

New-Jersey Ports are reached by a fleet of white steamers ploughing the

CENTRAL PARK. THE NEW NETHERLAND. THE SAVOY. THE PLAZA. THE DALHOUSIE.
58TH STREET, LOOKING EAST FROM SIXTH AVENUE.

waves daily to Elizabethport and Keyport, New Brunswick and Bergen Point, Sandy Hook and Red Bank, South Amboy, Perth Amboy, Atlantic Highlands, etc.

The Ferry Boat, as now in use around New York, was designed by Fulton and Stevens, and is remarkably well adapted to its uses, especially with regard to the terminal floating bridges and the spring piles along the slips. The first ferry was established in 1642, by Cornelius Dircksen, from near Peck Slip to Fulton Street, Brooklyn; and for nearly two centuries the transits were made in barges, row-boats or pirogues. From 1814 to 1824 horse-boats were used, being propelled by horses working a wheel by means of a treadmill between twin-boats; and these in turn were succeeded by steam ferry-boats. Scores of these vessels now traverse the waters around the city, carrying the suburbans to and from their work, and are well crowded morning and evening. They are swift, staunch and powerful craft, much more serviceable than they appear; and they make quick and frequent passages, when the fogs and floating ice of winter do not hinder. There are dozens of these routes to Brooklyn and Long-Island City, Jersey City and Hoboken and many other localities, the fare being from one cent upward. On account of their light draft, good speed and great strength, armed New-York ferry-boats were found useful as gun-boats on the Southern rivers, during the civil war; and Capt. Zalinski thinks that they would be valuable adjuncts in the naval defence of the Empire City when armed with pneumatic dynamite guns. Staten Island is reached by large ferryboats running in twenty-five minutes from the Battery to St. George.

FULTON FERRY, FOOT OF FULTON STREET, EAST RIVER.

The waters about New York are traversed by about 400 tow-boats or tugs, equipped with very powerful engines, and competent to pull the heaviest ships, or strings of laden canal-boats. Most of them are below 100 tons each; but the Pennsylvania Railroad twin-screw tugs *Amboy* and *Raritan*, the ocean-tug *Luckenback*, and the mighty drawers of canal-boats — the *Vanderbilt* and the *Oswego* — reach above 250 tons each. Some of these tow-boats have engines of 900 horse-power.

Yachts and Yachting, with an endless number of yachting and boat-clubs, are conspicuous features hereabouts. Nowhere else in the world are there such fleets of white-winged racing boats, flying like huge birds over the harbor and rivers, and swooping away in great bevies up the Sound eastward to Newport. The regattas and cruises of the many local yacht-clubs are events of the liveliest interest, and eager tens of thousands follow them far out to sea, beyond the Scotland Lightship. The patriarch of all these noble maritime amusements is the New-York Yacht Club, the oldest in the United State (founded in 1844), which has in its fleet 200 boats. Many steam-yachts also cruise about Manhattan, varying in magnitude from the puffy little naphtha-launch up to the superb sea-going private steamships of the Vanderbilts, Bennetts, and other rich families.

EAST RIVER --- THE BROOKLYN BRIDGE --- SOUTH STREET.

JEANETTE PARK, COENTIES SLIP, EAST RIVER, LOOKING TOWARD BROOKLYN, SHOWING THE CANAL-BOAT FLEET.

BIRD'S-EYE VIEW FROM WASHINGTON BUILDING, LOOKING SOUTHWEST.

BIRD'S-EYE VIEW FROM WASHINGTON BUILDING LOOKING SOUTHEAST.

Transportation and Transit.

Railroads—Steam, Elevated, Cable, Horse and Electric—Stages, Subterranean Transit, Etc.

THE need of opening communication between New York and the West was recognized as early as the days of Queen Anne, when the first attempt was made in this direction. The Colony appropriated £500 to certain men to open a route from the Hudson River westward, the first section being from Nyack to Sterling Iron-works, over which a road was ordered wide enough for two carriages, with the overhanging boughs of the trees cut away. In 1673 Col. Francis Lovelace, the second British Governor of New York, established a mail-route between New York and Boston. This primitive establishment consisted of a single messenger, who, for the "more speedy intelligence and dispatch of affairs," was ordered to make one round trip each month, with letters and packages. The Puritan town to the eastward having thus been accommodated, in 1729 certain enterprising spirits established a fortnightly line of stages to Philadelphia, the Quaker town to the southward. In the same year (so sure was the march of progress), proposals were issued for a foot post to Albany. In 1793 the running time of the "small, genteel, and easy stage carriages" between New York and Boston was between three and four days, and three trips were made weekly each way. The fare was four-pence a mile.

The subject of intercommunication between the little fringe of settlements along the Atlantic Coast and the great Mississippi-Ohio Valley was one of the most cherished projects of George Washington. As a Provincial military officer, or member of the Virginian House of Delegates, or commander-in-chief of the American armies, or President of the United States, he always kept this theme in view, and in person crossed the Virginian mountains, and examined the valleys of the Potomac and the Mohawk, to find the best route for a canal. He regarded the West ("the flank and rear of the Union," as he called it) as likely to be lured away from the Republic by Great Britain, on the north, or by Spain, on the south. As he remarked : "The Western States hang upon a pivot. The touch of a feather would turn them any way." The crops of the West could not be moved to market, so great was the expense of transportation. To carry a ton of wheat from Buffalo to New York cost $100, where it now costs $1.50. Great arks floated down the Delaware, Susquehanna and Ohio Rivers, laden with produce ; but the voyage was very long, and the returns were uncertain. The first attempt to relieve this blockade was made by building canals, beginning with the one opened in 1802 from the lower Mohawk to Oneida Lake and Lake Ontario. The completion of the Erie Canal, in 1825, revolutionized the commerce of America, and gave New-York City the place of commercial metropolis of the continent. Pennsylvania, Maryland and Virginia attempted to win the West by similar constructions, but their canals reached only to the foot of the Alleghany Mountains. Ohio, Indiana and Illinois built canals connecting the Ohio and Mississippi Rivers with the Great Lakes, at Cleveland, Toledo and Chicago; and by the year 1840, 8,500 miles of canal were in operation.

But a new unifying and civilizing agency was about to enter the world's service. In 1826 the Stockton & Darlington Railway, in England, showed the feasibility of moving trains by steam-power. In 1827 a tramway of three miles was built near Quincy, in Massachusetts, to transport granite from the quarries to tide-water. New York had cut off the Western trade of the other Atlantic ports, by its Erie Canal; and Baltimore hastened to avail itself of the newly discovered mechanism of the rail-

NEW-YORK CENTRAL & HUDSON-RIVER RAILROAD TRACKS ABOVE 98TH STREET.

way, to offset the canal. Accordingly, the Baltimore & Ohio Railroad was chartered in 1827, and began grading in 1828. The first locomotive used in America was the *Stourbridge Lion*, imported from England, and started on the Carbondale & Honesdale Railroad, in 1829. It was too heavy for the unsubstantial rails then in use, and had to be given up. The second locomotive to run in America was called *The Best Friend of Charleston*, and was built at the West-Point Foundry Works, on the Hudson, in 1830. It belonged to the South-Carolina Railroad, which for some years was the longest continuous line in the world. Another locomotive from the same works was placed on the Mohawk & Hudson Railroad, in 1831. In the meantime, the Baltimore & Ohio line had been using horses to draw the trains between Baltimore and Frederick; and had made elaborate experiments to see if the cars could not be propelled by sails.

With all the Atlantic States reaching inland by lines of iron rails, New York also advanced in the same direction, and the result appears in a remarkable system of railways, excelled by none in the world outside.

The New-York Central & Hudson-River Railroad is the only route which runs from New-York harbor to the Great Lakes over the territory of a single State. Its main line, from New York to Buffalo, 441¾ miles, is one of the most perfectly appointed and equipped railways in the world, and for the greater part of its course

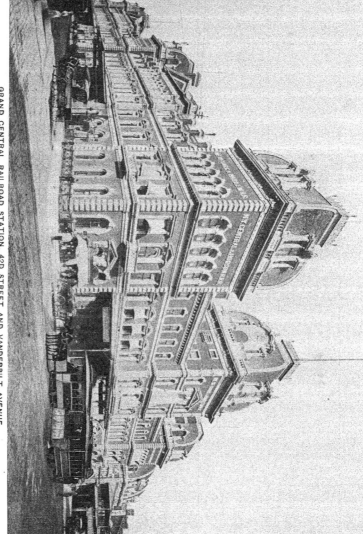

GRAND CENTRAL RAILROAD STATION, 42D STREET AND VANDERBILT AVENUE.

NEW-YORK CENTRAL & HUDSON-RIVER RAILROAD; NEW-YORK & HARLEM RAILROAD; NEW-YORK, NEW-HAVEN & HARTFORD RAILROAD.

RIVERDALE STATION, N. Y. C. & H. R. R. R.

has four parallel tracks, of which two are reserved for passenger trains exclusively. The company controls nearly 5,000 miles of steel-rail track, and has 1,169 locomotives, 1,300 passenger cars, 40,500 freight and other cars, and 136 steamboats and other craft. The sum of $17,000,000 is paid yearly to the 27,000 employees of the company, being more than half of the working expenses of the road. The cost of the road and equipment has exceeded $165,000,000, which is mainly represented by capital stock of $100,000,000, and a funded debt of $65,000,000. In a single year the New-York Central company has carried more than 20,000,000 tons of freight, equalling the movement of nearly 4,000,000,000 tons for one mile; and 22,000,000 passengers. The Grand Central Station on 42d Street, enormous, well-placed and commodious, covers 257,312 square feet, and contains 19 tracks, and the general offices of several railways. Daily 50,000 persons arrive at or depart from this

MOTT-HAVEN STATION, 138TH STREET, NEW-YORK CENTRAL & HUDSON-RIVER RAILROAD.

station, on 245 trains, of 800 cars. The stations at Mott Haven, at Riverdale, and elsewhere are very commodious and highly available. The Central trains (and also those of the routes to New England) traverse Manhattan Island, from the Grand Central Station to the Harlem River, by a series of sunken tracks and viaducts whose construction cost many millions of dollars. Then they follow for over 100 miles the eastern shore of the Hudson River, "the Rhine of America," crossing the inflowing streams on massive bridges, and passing the mountain-promontories by rock tunnels

or broad artificial terraces.   Scores of famous villages and cities and historic localities are passed ; and along the route the magnificent panorama of the Hudson River
and its enwalling mountains and fruitful plains is unrolled before the delighted vision.
Here is the dark line of the Palisades, frowning across the placid Tappan Zee ; the
classic region where the names of Major André, Benedict Arnold, Mad Anthony
Wayne, Hendrick Hudson, Captain Kidd and George Washington are oddly combined with those of the Livingstons and Philipses, with the valorous trumpeter
Anthony Van Corlaer and Jan Peek, and Rambout Van Dam ; the noble Highlands
of the Hudson, the Dunderberg and Anthony's Nose, Storm King and Cro' Nest ;
the historic batteries of West Point, where the art of war was studied for years by
Grant and Sherman, Sheridan and McClellan, Lee and Longstreet ; Newburgh, with
its triumphal arch and Washington's headquarters ; Poughkeepsie, the seat of Vassar
College ; and noble views of the Catskill Mountains, the home of Rip Van Winkle.
At Albany the New-York Central line turns up the great natural highway which
the Mohawk River cut through the Alleghany Mountains ; and for nearly 300 miles

"EMPIRE-STATE EXPRESS," NEW-YORK CENTRAL & HUDSON-RIVER RAILROAD.
FASTEST LONG-DISTANCE TRAIN IN THE WORLD.   PHOTO. BY A. P. YATES, OF SYRACUSE, N. Y.

traverses the grandest railway route in the world, with its continuous four tracks,
side by side.   On this rosary-chain are strung numerous important cities, like Schenectady and Amsterdam, Utica and Rome, Syracuse and Rochester, closing at thronged
and busy Buffalo, "The Queen City of the Lakes."   On the great highway of nature
between New York and Buffalo, some of the most remarkable of railway runs have
been made, crowning the world's record for long-distance rapid transit.   September
14, 1891, a train traversed the stretch of 436 miles between New York and East Buffalo
in 425¾ minutes, making on some sections a speed of 78 miles an hour.   As a result
of this experimental trip, the New-York Central established its Empire-State
Express, which daily makes the run between New York and Buffalo in 8 hours and
40 minutes, an average of over 52 miles an hour.   This is the fastest long-distance
train in the world.

8

At Buffalo the through trains of the New-York Central pass on to the rails of the lines for the farther West, the Lake-Shore, or the Michigan Central.   Some of the finest trains in the world serve this magnificent route to the West, with Wagner drawing-room cars, buffet, smoking, dining, café and library cars, and standard,

MORRISANIA STATION, NEW-YORK CENTRAL & HUDSON-RIVER RAILROAD.

buffet and private-compartment sleeping-cars.   The New-York and Chicago Limited, the Southwestern Limited, the North-Shore Limited, and the Chicago, St. Louis and Cincinnati Express-trains are marvels of comfort and luxury.

The old terminal station of the Hudson-River Railroad, at 30th Street and Tenth Avenue, New York, is mainly used as a freight depot, although passenger trains for all stations on the western side of Manhattan Island, up to Spuyten Duyvil, are still despatched thence.

The northern connections of the Central lines are made mainly at Albany, Troy, Herkimer and Utica, and reach Saratoga and the Adirondacks, both shores of Lake Champlain, Montreal and Ottawa, the Green Mountains of Vermont, and the Thousand Islands of the St. Lawrence.   Myriads of metropolitans every year seek these scenes of vernal beauty for their season of summer rest.

The history of the New-York Central Railroad dates back to the earliest days of the railroad in America.   Its first link was the Mohawk & Hudson, chartered in 1826, and completed in 1831, and afterward re-named the Albany & Schenectady. This was the first railroad in New-York State, and for a long time stationary engines were used on parts of its line.   Another route westward from the Hudson, the Schenectady & Troy, received its charter in 1836, and began operations in 1842. Meanwhile, the Utica & Schenectady had been opened in 1836, and the Syracuse & Utica in 1839; the Auburn & Syracuse in 1838, and the Auburn & Rochester in 1841 ; the Lockport & Niagara-Falls in 1838, and the Attica & Batavia and Tonawanda lines (afterward united as the Buffalo & Rochester) in 1842.   All these and other roads were consolidated under the special law of 1853 into the New-York Central Railroad Company, giving a through route between Albany and Buffalo.

Several other connecting lines were subsequently leased, and then merged into the New-York Central system. The Hudson-River Railroad was chartered in 1846, and opened from New York to East Albany in 1851. In 1869 occurred the consolidation which made up the New-York Central & Hudson-River Railroad.

The New-York & Harlem Railway, operated by the New-York Central, was chartered in 1831. It reached 14th Street in 1832; 32d Street in 1833; York-ville in 1834; Harlem in 1837; Williamsbridge in 1842; White Plains in 1844; Dover Plains in 1848; and Chatham Four Corners in 1852. The line cost $23,-500,000 to build and equip, and is 127 miles long, from New York to Chatham, where it connects with the Boston & Albany Railroad. It was leased in 1873 for 401 years to the New-York Central Company, which pays eight per cent. on the capital stock, and interest on the funded debt. This picturesque route to the north follows the Bronx, Neperhan and Croton Valleys for many miles, through the pleas-ant farming lands of Westchester, Putnam and Dutchess Counties, and near the

SWITCH TOWER CONTROLLING ALL TRAINS ENTERING THE GRAND CENTRAL DEPOT.

Taconic Mountains. Among the charming summer-resorts near the line are Lake Mahopac and the Berkshire Hills, and farther connections lead to the finest scenery of the Green Mountains.

The West-Shore Railroad was organized in 1880, and the following year became possessed of the Jersey-City & Albany line, from Weehawken to Fort Montgomery.   The first through-train between Weehawken and Buffalo was run in 1884, but the road passed into the hands of a receiver during the same year, and in 1885 was sold to a new company, which leased it to the New-York Central & Hudson-River Railroad for 475 years.   The West-Shore route thus became an important and interesting division of the Central system.   It follows the western bank of the Hudson River nearly to Albany, and thence crosses the rich midland counties to Buffalo on a route nearly parallel with that of the New-York Central line.   The West-Shore trains may be reached at the Pennsylvania depot in Jersey City, or at Weehawken (by ferry from Jay Street or West 42d Street).

The Rome, Watertown & Ogdensburg Railroad Co. was organized in 1860 by the amalgamation of the Watertown & Rome Railroad Co. and the Potsdam & Watertown Railroad Co., and has since acquired by consolidation numerous small lines in the northern part of the State, and also, on April 14, 1886, the Utica & Black-River Railroad, which, up to that time, was its chief competitor.   The Rome, Watertown & Ogdensburg Railroad and its leased lines were leased in perpetuity to the New-York Central & Hudson-River Company March 14, 1891.   The New-York Central, appreciating the value of this new acquisition, and its capabilities of becoming the largest and most important tourist traffic route in America, proceeded at once, with its usual enterprise, to raise to Trunk-Line standard that portion of the newly acquired property patronized by summer-travel.   This has been accomplished by hard work and the outlay of a very large sum of money, — nearly $1,000,-000, — in permanent improvements, and relaying the road with heavy steel rails, renewing and reballasting the road-bed, replacing wooden bridges with strong new ones of stone and iron, etc., all of which enables the company to inaugurate a new era in Northern New-York passenger service.   The improvement of the equipment and service has kept pace with the road-bed.   Standard locomotives, capable of hauling the heaviest passenger trains at high speed, have been added to the motive power.   In carrying out the policy of developing summer-travel, by offering every facility, the New-York Central & Hudson-River Railroad has placed in service new fast trains, through from New York and from Buffalo to points on the Rome, Watertown & Ogdensburg Railroad, equipped with new coaches, new Wagner sleeping and drawing-room cars, and buffet smoking and library cars.

The Dunkirk, Allegheny-Valley & Pittsburgh Railroad, from Dunkirk to Titusville, was recently leased by the New-York Central & Hudson-River Railroad.

The Pennsylvania Railroad was incorporated in 1846, and chartered in 1847, to build a line from the Harrisburg and Lancaster route to Pittsburgh or Erie. The State system of transportation, built between 1828 and 1834, at a cost exceeding $14,000,000, consisted of a railway from Philadelphia to Columbia, 82 miles; a canal thence to Hollidaysburg, 172 miles; the Portage Railway, across the Alleghany Mountains to Johnstown, 36 miles; and the railway thence to Pittsburgh, 104 miles.   This route resulted in great benefit to the sections through which it passed, but it was a slow, costly and complicated system, and proved unremunerative to the State.   For years the route between Philadelphia and Columbia was served only by horse-cars, making the transit in nine hours, with relays every twelve miles.   The superior facilities offered by New York and Baltimore threatened to leave Pennsylvania out of the race, as a competitor for Western trade, and therefore local patriotism was highly stimulated to construct a new and first-class route across the State.   The project was advocated by the press and in public meetings; and committees went from house to house asking subscriptions to stock: With the funds thus raised, and under the wise direction of Chief Engineer J. Edgar Thompson, the Pennsylvania

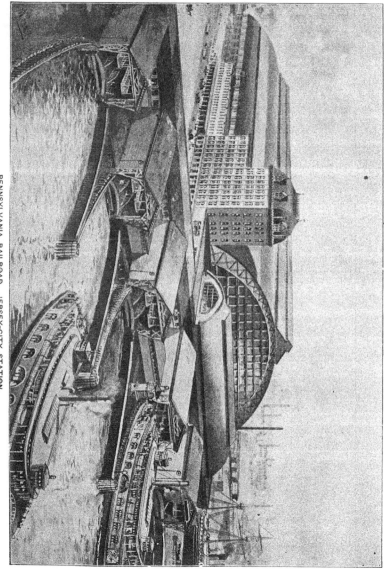

PENNSYLVANIA RAILROAD, JERSEY-CITY STATION.
FERRIES TO DESBROSSES STREET AND TO CORTLANDT STREET, NEW YORK.

Railroad began its construction works in 1847, between Harrisburg and Lewistown ; and in 1854 the entire route, from Philadelphia to Pittsburgh, went into operation. In 1861, after a contest of six years, the company bought the State lines, for $13,570,000. Mr. Thompson held the presidency of the company from 1852 until his death, in 1874, when he was succeeded by Col. Thomas A. Scott, who had been for twenty-four years connected with the company, and had been vice-president since 1860. After constructing its magnificent trunk line across the Keystone State, the company prolonged its routes farther westward by securing control of several lines to the great trade-centres of the West ; gained an admirable entrance to New York by acquiring the United New-Jersey lines ; found an outlet at Baltimore by getting control of the Northern Central Railroad ; completed and opened the Baltimore & Potomac line, to Washington ; and came into possession of numerous minor routes.

The New-Jersey part of the Pennsylvania system includes the plant of the United New-Jersey Railroad and Canal Companies, leased in 1871, for 999 years,

PENNSYLVANIA RAILROAD DEPOT, JERSEY CITY, INTERIOR OF TRAIN-HOUSE.

at a deservedly high rental. This confederacy was formed in 1831, by the practical unification of two companies chartered a year before — the Delaware & Raritan Canal and the Camden & Amboy Railroad, both of which were finished in 1834. Two years later the United Companies got control of the Philadelphia & Trenton line (opened in 1834), and in 1867 they consolidated interests with the line of the New-Jersey Railroad & Transportation Company from New Brunswick to Jersey City. The section from Jersey City to Newark was opened in 1834, and for some years was used only by horse-cars. In 1836 it reached Rahway ; and in 1839 its trains arrived at Philadelphia.

The new passenger station at Jersey City is larger than the Grand Central Depot in New York, and has a length of 653½ feet, with a width of 256 feet, and a height of 112 feet. It is reached from New York by the steam ferry-boats of the com-

PENNSYLVANIA RAILROAD : FREIGHT DEPOT, WEST STREET.

pany, running from Cortlandt Street and Desbrosses Street. The Pennsylvania Railroad has already bridged West Street at their Cortlandt-Street ferry, and is rapidly putting into service a fleet of double-deck ferry-boats, so that eventually passengers will be able to pass from Cortlandt or Desbrosses Streets to the upper decks of the ferry-boats, above the confusion of West Street, and thence on the same level to their trains in the Jersey-City station:

The Southern Pacific Company, one of the greatest transportation systems in the world, has spacious offices in New-York City, whence sails its important

MOTT-HAVEN CANAL.

Morgan Line of steamships for New Orleans.   This efficient link by sea unites
New York with the eastern end of the Southern Pacific Railway system, at New
Orleans, for purposes of freighting goods.   Passengers from New York may go
to New Orleans by the New-York Central or Erie, the Pennsylvania or Baltimore &
Ohio, the Piedmont Air Line or Chesapeake & Ohio, or the Atlantic Coast Line ;
or by the Cromwell steamships every Saturday from New York to New Orleans.
At New Orleans, the quaint old French capital of the Gulf States, begins the renowned Sunset Route, through the lowlands of Louisiana, across the richest and
most populous sections of imperial Texas, up the weird Rio-Grande valley, across
the New-Mexican Sierra Madre, and over the mysterious tropical plateaus of Arizona

SOUTHERN PACIFIC COMPANY -- " MORGAN- LINE," -- PIER 25, NORTH RIVER.

and Southern California.   Northward, along the coast, the line runs by San Francisco, past the wonderful scenery of the Mount-Shasta Alps, to Portland, on the
mighty Columbia River ; and its rails run eastward across the Sierra Nevada to
Ogden, on the Great Salt Lake of Utah.   At San Francisco the line connects with
the sea-route, which penetrate still deeper into the sunset, the Occidental and
Oriental and the Oceanic lines for Hawaii and Japan, New Zealand and Australia,
China and India.   Many travellers also visit Mexico by the Sunset Route, crossing
the Rio Grande at Eagle Pass, or at Laredo or El Paso.

The Southern Pacific Line enjoys peculiar advantages from its connection with
such amazingly rich States as Texas and California, and its close relations with
Mexico and Louisiana.   It is an important and impressive trans-continental route,
first-class in equipment and service, traversing many great cities, and scenery oftentimes unspeakably grand, and for many years a favorite line with veteran travellers
and experts in journeying.   The New-York offices are at 343 Broadway, and at 1
Battery Place, in the Washington Building.

The Reading Railroad System — Lehigh Valley Division — is one of the great lines of travel of America, and well entitled to the appellation, "The Scenic Route." For more than four hundred miles the tracks of its main line, extending from New York to Buffalo, traverse a region rich in natural beauty and in human interest, while the remaining portions of the thousand miles of track, which constitute this single division, penetrate the great mountain ranges and lovely valleys of Pennsylvania, with their wealth of agricultural and mineral resources, and their picturesque scenery. The eastern termini of the Scenic Lehigh Valley Route are at New York and at Philadelphia. In New York the passenger-station is at the foot of Liberty Street, North River, occupied jointly by the Central Railroad of New Jersey and the Reading System. In the new depot in Jersey City, a structure remarkable for its spaciousness and for the convenience and tastefulness of its interior, the tourist may pause to admire the train which is to bear him westward. A feature which strikes him most favorably, and which he will observe wherever he may journey upon the lines of the Reading System, is the complete absence of the smoke, soot and cinders which are attendant upon the use of soft coal, all locomotives being fueled exclusively with clean, hard Pennsylvania anthracite. The coaches are handsome and comfortable, being furnished with the most approved devices for heating, ventilation and lighting. Luxurious drawing-room, dining and sleeping cars complete the equipment of rolling stock. The road is double-tracked, of the most substantial construction, and the track and trains are protected by an improved block system and automatic signals.

Westward from New York the line traverses the most attractive portion of New Jersey, entering the Keystone State and the gateway of the world-famed Lehigh Valley at the city of Easton, picturesquely perched on a group of hills at the confluence of the Lehigh and Delaware Rivers. At the historic town of Bethlehem, 89 miles from New York, the line from the latter city forms a junction with a branch from Philadelphia, which is 56 miles to the southward. The Reading's

READING RAILROAD SYSTEM -- LEHIGH VALLEY DIVISION. DEPOT IN JERSEY CITY.

main passenger-station in Philadelphia is at Market and 12th Streets, in the very centre of the city, almost adjoining the City Hall, and in close proximity to all the chief hotels and places of interest.   It is a magnificent new structure, impressively beautiful in its architectural aspect, and of great size and convenience of arrangement.   The road is elevated through the central portion of the city, and its course hence to Bethlehem lies through a diversified and interesting region of suburban villages and fertile farms.   Beyond Bethlehem there is a chain of thriving industrial towns to interest the man of business, while the æsthetic taste is gratified by a swiftly changing panorama of beautiful scenery.   At Allentown connection is made with another division of the Reading System, reaching Reading, Harrisburg, Gettysburg and other points in the Schuylkill, Lebanon and Cumberland valleys.   As the track follows the graceful curves of the Lehigh River, there flashes into view many a beautiful vista of mountain and valley and stream.   Mauch Chunk, with its encircling peaks, the famous "Switchback" and Glen Onoko require no extended mention.   Glen Summit is a noted summer-resort on the crown of Nescopec Mountain, overlooking the romantic vale of Wyoming.   The cities of Wilkes-Barre, Scranton and Pittston are centres of the coal-producing industry reached by this line.   At Waverly it crosses the line dividing Pennsylvania and New York, and runs through the picturesque lake region, reaching Ithaca, Sheldrake, Cayuga, Geneva and other favorite resorts on Seneca and Cayuga Lakes, and also Clifton Springs.   Rochester is reached by a short branch road diverging from the main line.   At Batavia the trains are divided, some of the cars going to Buffalo and others to Niagara Falls.   Through coaches, parlor, dining and sleeping cars are run to Chicago from New York and from Philadelphia, by way of Buffalo, and also by way of Niagara Falls.   To the latter Mecca of the tourist the "Scenic Lehigh Valley" is a very attractive route, by reason of its picturesque scenery ; and to all classes of travellers the line commends itself by its directness, its promptness, and its general excellence of service.   The principal New-York City ticket office is at 235 Broadway.

WEST STREET, FOOT OF LIBERTY STREET.

The Central Railroad of New Jersey provides transit to many charming residential places in New Jersey.

The commodious depot at Communipaw is reached by ferry from the foot of Liberty Street, North River. In conjunction with the Philadelphia & Reading Railroad this line forms a part of the famous Royal Blue Line from New York to Philadelphia, Baltimore, Washington, and the South and West. It traverses the entire length of the garden-like little State, bringing to the New-York market the products of New Jersey and Pennsylvania. Running westward, it passes through Elizabeth and Easton, Allentown and Mauch Chunk, and the marvellous anthracite coal region between Tamaqua and Scranton, including the whole length of the Valley of Wyoming and the Lehigh Valley. Its suburban service every evening conducts a vast peaceful army of business men from the rush and roar of the metropolis to the flourishing towns and villages of Central New Jersey,—to many towns such as Greenville, Bayonne City, Newark, Elizabethport, Elizabeth, Roselle, Cranford, Westfield, Fanwood, Netherwood, Plainfield, Dunellen, Bound Brook and Somerville.

The three steamers of the Sandy-Hook Route, owned and operated by the Central Railroad Company, include the *Monmouth*, *Sandy Hook* and *St. Johns*, leaving Pier 8, North River, foot of Rector Street, daily and Sunday during the summer season, at frequent intervals, for Atlantic Highlands, connecting there for Highland Beach, Navesink Beach, Normandie, Rumson Beach, Seabright, Low Moor, Galilee, Monmouth Beach, Long Branch, Elberon, Deal Beach, Asbury Park, Ocean Grove, Avon, Bel Mar, Como, Spring Lake, Sea Girt, Manasquan, Brielle and Point Pleasant. This route is one of the most popular in America during the

TRAIN-HOUSE OF THE GRAND CENTRAL STATION, ON 42D STREET.

summer season, when every one tries to escape from the arid streets of the great metropolis, and find the cool breezes which enliven the ocean-shore.

There is also an all-rail route from the foot of Liberty Street, New York, to the above-named coast-resorts, and also to Red Bank, Lakewood, Atlantic City, Tom's River, Bay Side, Barnegat Park, Forked River, Waretown and Barnegat Bay.

The entire coast-line, from Sandy Hook to Barnegat Inlet, is an almost continuous summer-resort, with enormous hotels, colonies of handsome cottages, camp-meeting grounds, and all the other accessories of modern watering-place life. The memories of Grant and Garfield still haunt the bluff of Long Branch; the State troops of New Jersey encamp along the plains of Sea Girt; the light-houses flash across the sea from the Navesink Highlands and Barnegat; the Methodists assemble their devout classes at Asbury Park and Ocean Grove; and the perfume of the pines

CENTRAL BUILDING : CENTRAL RAILROAD OF NEW JERSEY. LIBERTY AND WEST STREETS, NEW YORK.

overflows the sands of Key East. In a way, this strip of wave-beaten coast, in winter "The Graveyard of the Sea," in summer becomes the most popular and delightful suburb of the great city, abounding in piquant varieties of scenery and of humanity.

The Delaware, Lackawanna & Western Railroad had its inception in the little Ligett's-Gap Railroad, down in Pennsylvania, which was incorporated in 1832, and 19 years later became the Lackawanna & Western, running from Scranton northwest to Great Bend. Two years later, upon consolidating with the Delaware & Cobb's-Gap Railroad, it took its present title, although the line did not reach the Delaware River until 1856. A year later, the company leased the Warren Railroad, then just opened from the Delaware River to New Hampton Junction, N. J. Meantime, the Morris & Essex Railroad, chartered in 1835, had been built from Hoboken across the hill-country of northern New Jersey to Phillipsburg, which it reached in 1866; and two years later it was favorably leased to the Delaware, Lackawanna & Western, which thus secured a terminal on New-York harbor. While thus triumphantly planning its route to the seaboard, the company also turned its attention northward and westward, securing the line to Owego and Ithaca in 1855; that to Syracuse and Oswego, in 1869; that to Utica and Richfield Springs in 1870; and that from Binghamton to Buffalo, in 1882. These and other annexed routes and new sections constructed, gave the company its present splendid system, reaching from opposite New York to Lake Ontario and Lake Erie and down through the coal-regions of Pennsylvania to Wilkes-Barre, Scranton and Northumberland. These routes are served by 550 locomotives and 36,000 cars of all kinds. The eastern terminal of the Lackawanna system, at Hoboken, is reached

DELAWARE, LACKAWANNA & WESTERN RAILROAD: DEPOT IN HOBOKEN.

by ferries from Barclay Street and Christopher Street, New York. The through main line from New York to Scranton, Elmira and Buffalo, 409 miles long, is traversed daily by several express-trains, connecting at Buffalo with the routes for the farther West. This Lackawanna route leads to some of the most charming summer-resorts in northern New Jersey, like Lake Hopatcong, Budd's Lake, and Schooley Mountain, and the noble scenery of the Delaware Water Gap and Pocono

Mountains.   The Morris & Essex Division gives access to the most beautiful of all
the suburbs of New York, the villages around the Orange Mountains, the Oranges,
Montclair, Summit, Short Hills, Madison and Morristown, whose pure highland air
and pleasant scenery are widely celebrated.   The suburban traffic on this division
has assumed great proportions, and is yearly increasing, on account of the desire of
New-York business men to keep their families and to spend their own leisure days

ELEVATED RAILROAD NEAR COENTIES SLIP, EAST RIVER.

in the beautiful region of New Jersey, where the climate is of such sovereign salu-
brity that people are sent hither, even by physicians in Europe, as to a sanitarium.
The suburban train-service is kept up to the highest point of efficiency, and affords
the best of facilities, whether one goes northward on the route by Passaic and
Mountain View, or westward by Newark and Orange, Summit and Madison.
Largely on this account, the region of the Orange Mountains, so richly endowed
with landscape-beauty and pastoral charm, has become perhaps the favorite residence-district in the outer suburbs of New York, and presents the aspect of a great
park, adorned with hundreds of pleasant country-seats and dozens of dainty hamlets.

The Delaware, Lackawanna & Western Railroad Building, at William Street and
Exchange Place, completed and opened in 1892, is one of the notable structures of
the financial district.   It measures 85 feet on William Street, and 60 on Exchange
Place, is ten stories in height, and is in the Italian Renaissance style of architecture.
The materials of construction are granite for the foundation and basement, and
Indiana limestone above.   The imposing entrance-arch on Exchange Place is supported on piers of polished granite.   A pleasing effect has been gained by facing the
masonry of the lower two stories, and leaving that of the upper stories rough, as the
blocks of stone came from the quarry.   The building is first-class in all respects.

The Baltimore & Ohio Railroad has a large interest in the Staten-Island
Rapid Transit Railroad and its warehouse and shipping piers on the Bay of New

DELAWARE, LACKAWANNA & WESTERN RAILROAD COMPANY.
GENERAL OFFICES : EXCHANGE PLACE AND WILLIAM STREET.

York, and turns its freight traffic to this terminal, reaching the Arthur-Kill Bridge to Staten Island by its New-York Division, from Cranford, N. J.   From the bridge the cars run over the Staten-Island Rapid Transit Railroad to St. George, whence they are conveyed on floats to the pier at New York.   Passengers for the Baltimore & Ohio routes to the South and West cross the ferry from Liberty Street to the station of the Central Railroad of New Jersey, at Communipaw, and take the vestibuled Pullman trains of the Royal Blue Line for Philadelphia and Baltimore, Pittsburgh and Cincinnati, Chicago and St. Louis.

The New-York, Ontario & Western Railway was organized in 1866, under the name of the New-York & Oswego Midland Railroad, and opened its entire line in 1873, but passed into the hands of receivers the same year, and was afterwards sold and reorganized.   The Ontario & Western owns and leases 500 miles of track, and runs from New York to Oswego, having branches to Scranton, Ellenville, Edmeston, Delhi, Rome and Utica, and a trackage right over the West-Shore road from Cornwall to Weehawken.   Ferries run from Jay Street and West 42d Street to the terminal station at Weehawken, whence for over fifty miles the line follows the Hudson River, with many beautiful episodes of scenery.   From Cornwall it turns westward through the rugged spurs of the Highlands, and beyond Middletown it crosses the Shawangunk Mountains.   After passing Summitville, the line ascends the Delaware Mountains, which are surmounted at Young's Gap, 1,800 feet above the sea.   The Middle Division of the route is celebrated for its picturesque scenery and for its many trout-streams, and great forests abounding in game.   Next come

ELEVATED RAILROAD, AT COENTIES SLIP.   PRODUCE EXCHANGE TOWER.

the picturesque counties of Sullivan and Delaware, in the outer ranges of the Catskill Mountains, and abounding in bright lakes.   After a long run across the hilly farm-lands of Chenango and Madison, the road bends around the broad Oneida Lake for more than a score of miles, and descends the valley to Oswego, one of the chief ports of Lake Ontario.   Connections thence to the northward and westward are offered by the Rome, Watertown & Ogdensburg line, reaching from the St.-Lawrence Valley to Niagara Falls.

The New-York, Lake-Erie & Western Railroad forms one of the grand routes between the Empire City and the West, and, in spite of its many financial vicissitudes, has an enormous business, and controls dozens of tributary lines. The Legislature in 1825 ordered the surveying of a State road through the southern tier of counties, from the Hudson River to Lake Erie ; but the project was soon abandoned as impracticable. In 1832 the New-York & Erie Railroad Company received incorporation, and Col. De Witt Clinton, Jr., reconnoitred its projected route. The company was organized in 1833, and the route was surveyed the next year, by Benjamin Wright, at the cost of the State. New surveys occurred in 1836, and parts of the line were begun. The credit of the State was granted to the amount of several million dollars ; and in 1841 a section of track between Goshen and Piermont went into operation. Nevertheless, a year later the road passed into the hands of a receiver ; and it required subscriptions of $3,000,000 to the stock, by the merchants of New York, to energize the work. At last, on May 14, 1851, the great task was completed, and two trains ran over the entire line, from the Hudson River to Lake Erie, bearing the President of the United States and Daniel Webster, and a great company of notables. It was intended that the Erie line should end at Piermont, on the Hudson, but the directors soon saw that their terminal should be at New York, and therefore they arranged with the Union, Ramapo & Paterson, and Paterson & Jersey-City Railroads, to run trains over their lines from Suffern to Jersey City. The Erie Company owns or leases 800 locomotives, 450 passenger cars, and 42,000 freight and other cars and controls 3,000 miles of track. The Erie station at Pavonia Avenue, Jersey City, is reached by ferries from the foot of Chambers Street and West 23d Street. The line runs out across northern New Jersey to the Delaware Valley, which it follows for nearly 100 miles through a country of great landscape beauty. Then it crosses the mountains to the Susquehanna Valley, and so reaches the cities of the southern tier, and passes on to Dunkirk or Buffalo. There it connects with the main routes to the West and Southwest, the Chicago Express and the St.-Louis Express running through with wonderful speed and security. The Erie also has vestibuled trains to the Pennsylvania coal regions.

CORTLANDT-STREET FERRY, NORTH RIVER.

The Delaware & Hudson Canal Company is a corporation chartered by the State of New York in 1823, mainly to transport coal from the Pennsylvania coal-fields to New York. The canal was begun in 1825 and finished in 1828, and was twice enlarged, first in 1844 and again in 1862, to admit vessels of 150 tons capacity. It extends from Rondout, on the Hudson, to Port Jervis, on the Delaware, 59 miles ; thence 24 miles up the Delaware Valley, to Lackawaxen ; and thence 26 miles to the coal-region at Honesdale. This was one of the most important works of the great era of canal-building, which just preceded the rise of the railways. The capacity of the canal, with its equipments, is about 2,500,000 tons per annum.

The celebrated Gravity Road from Carbondale to Honesdale, over which millions of tons of coal are carried, was begun in 1827 and finished in 1829.

Between 1827 and 1829 the Canal Company built a railway from Honesdale to the coal-mines, and placed thereon the first locomotive that ever ran upon a railroad in the Western hemisphere. This pioneer engine, the *Stourbridge Lion,* was brought across from Liverpool on the packet-ship *John Jay,* in 1829, and passed to Hones-dale, by river to Rondout, and thence by canal. In 1860 the company owned 108 miles of canal and 23 miles of railroad ; in 1870 it leased in perpetuity the Albany & Susquehanna line ; and in 1871 it leased the Rensselaer & Saratoga line and its branches. Subsequently it built a new line along the west side of Lake Champlain, from Whitehall nearly to Montreal, giving a straight route from Albany to the metropolis of Canada and traversing a country of rare beauty and diversity of scenery. Trains run from New-York City to Montreal, 384 miles, without change, in less than 12 hours, reaching Albany over the New-York Central & Hudson-River Railroad. The world-renowned Ausable Chasm is reached from Port Kent, on the Champlain Division.

Apart from its enormous freighting business, in coal and other commodities, the Delaware & Hudson Railroad system has a very large and lucrative tourist and summer-travel business. It affords the best route between New York and other southern points, and Montreal, Ottawa or Quebec, the historic old Canadian capitals ; and also to Lake George and Lake Champlain, with their exquisite scenery of land and water, mountain, island and beach, and the famous Hotel Champlain, at the station of the same name, three miles south of Plattsburg ; to the heart of the Adirondacks, with stages running from its stations to Blue Mountain-Lake, Long Lake, Schroon Lake, and Keene Valley, and by connecting line to Saranac Lake to the remote interior of the Adirondack wilderness, by the Chateaugay Railroad from Plattsburg ; to Ticonderoga, Crown Point, and Plattsburg ; to Saratoga, the queen of summer-resorts ; and to Rutland and other interesting points in southern Vermont. The Delaware & Hudson lines southwestward from Albany reach the famous resorts of Howe's Cave, Sharon Springs, and Cooperstown, on Otsego Lake ; and pass downward to Binghamton, and southward into the valley of Wyoming.

The Delaware & Hudson Canal Company's building is an immense and imposing fire-proof structure, generally known as the Coal and Iron Exchange. It is on Cortlandt Street, at the southeast corner of Church Street. It is not an "Exchange" building, excepting in name ; but it is the property of the Delaware & Hudson Canal Company, for whom it was built in 1874-76, and whose main offices are located therein. Here centres the executive administration of the line, and here is the focal point of its enormous and lucrative coal-trade. The great building was designed by Richard M. Hunt, and to-day is one of the finest office-buildings in the city, having all the modern appliances and conveniences, and being occupied by an interesting group of administrative and executive headquarters.

DELAWARE & HUDSON CANAL COMPANY.
COMPANY'S BUILDING, CALLED "THE COAL AND IRON EXCHANGE," CORTLANDT AND CHURCH STREETS.

DESBROSSES-STREET FERRY AND PASSENGER-STATION, WEST STREET, NORTH RIVER.

The New-York, New-Haven & Hartford Railroad was formed in 1872 by a consolidation of the New-York & New-Haven and the Hartford & New-Haven Companies. The line begins at Woodlawn, N. Y., and runs to Springfield, Mass., 122½ miles, its total trackage, owned and leased, exceeding 900 miles. The com-

A NORTH-RIVER FERRY BOAT.

pany runs its trains from Woodlawn to New York over the Harlem Railroad, by virtue of an agreement made in 1848, the tolls paid to the Harlem being about $1,000 a day. The company owns 200 locomotives and 5,000 cars, and has a first-class road-bed and equipment. The entrance to the great gate-way of land-travel from New-York to New England and the remoter East is the Grand Central Depot, and the only route leads over the rails of the New-York, New-Haven & Hartford line.

All the railway trains between New York and Boston pass over this route, at least as far as New Haven, beyond which they may follow the Springfield Route, the Air Line or the Shore Line. This company also controls the New-Haven &

Northampton line; the Hartford & Connecticut-Valley Railroad; the Naugatuck Railroad, from Stratford Junction to Winsted, Conn. ; the Shore Line, from New Haven to New London, Conn. ; and several other minor lines.

The New-York & New-England Railroad runs from Boston to Fishkill-on-Hudson, N. Y., with branches to Providence, Worcester, Springfield, Norwich, Woonsocket, Pascoag, Rockville, and other Eastern cities. Its trains enter the Grand Central Depot in New-York City by passing over the New-York, New-Haven & Hartford line from Willimantic, or Hartford, Conn. Every day the famous "White Train" leaves New York and Boston at 3 P. M., always making the run between the two cities in exactly 5⅔ hours, with only four stops in the 213 miles. They run between Willimantic and Boston, 86 miles, without a stop. This route is shorter by twenty miles than any other between Boston and New York ; and is served by parlor-cars, dining-cars, royal buffet smoking-cars, and other fine coaches, whose colors of white and gold are very unusual and attractive. The White Train runs by way of Willimantic and the Air Line; and there is also a train leaving New York and Boston at noon, and running by way of Hartford. The New-York and New-

NEW-YORK & NEW ENGLAND RAILROAD : " THE WHITE TRAIN," BETWEEN NEW-YORK AND BOSTON.

England Company also owns the famous Norwich Line of steamboats, between New York and New London, Conn., where it connects with trains for Boston. The route of these lines is so favorable, that it receives a great amount of travel, and will always be a favorite avenue to the eastward. The Washington Night Express runs between Boston and Philadelphia, Baltimore and Washington, by way of the Poughkeepsie Bridge, the Reading system and the Baltimore & Ohio Railroad, giving very good and comfortable facilities for transit between the metropolis of New England and the capital of the Republic.

The New-York & New-England Railroad gives convenient access to many of the most famous cities and towns of Connecticut and the adjacent States, like Danbury, famous for its hats; Waterbury, whose watches are not unknown; Willimantic, where 1,500 operatives make the famous six-cord sewing cotton ; Putnam, with its score of busy mills ; Norwich, on the pleasant hills at the head of the Thames ; New London, always charming as a summer-resort ; and busy groups of manufacturing communities in Rhode Island and Massachusetts. The first-class equipment of the

railway and its efficient and vigilant management give it great value as one of the
foremost avenues leading eastward from New York, and ensure its increasing success
and popularity in the future.

The New-York & Northern Railway has its station at 155th Street and
Eighth Avenue, on the upper part of Manhattan Island, and runs thence northward
54 miles, between the main line and Harlem route of the New-York Central Railroad,
to Brewster, on the Harlem line.   It follows the valley of the Harlem River as far
as Kingsbridge, and thence strikes across Van Cortlandt Park and into Yonkers, to
which it runs many rapid-transit trains daily for the convenience of suburban residents.   Beyond this point it reaches Tarrytown, Sleepy Hollow and Pocantico
Hills, in the region made classic by the genius of Washington Irving.   Farther
north, the line passes near Croton Lake, the great reservoir of the New-York water-
supply ; and Lake Mahopac, a favorite summer-resort among the wooded hills of
Carmel.   At Brewster the route meets the tracks of the Harlem Railroad and the
New-York & New-England Railroad, crossing the latter on its way from Boston to
the Hudson River.   The stretch of 51 miles from High Bridge to Brewster, operated by the Northern Line, belongs to the New-York, Westchester & Putnam Railway, the successor of the New-York & Boston Railroad.   It was opened in 1880,
and is under a fifty years' lease to the Northern line.   Various plans have been
suggested to run through trains from Boston to New York by way of Brewster and
the New-York & Northern, and thus to secure for the New-York & New-England
Company an independent entrance to the metropolis.   The terminal station of the
Northern line is easily reached from lower New York by the Elevated Railroad, on
Sixth Avenue or Ninth Avenue.

The Long Island Railroad for a long time had its eastern terminus at
Hicksville, but in 1844 it reached Greenport ; and the mails between New York and

SOUTH-FERRY STATION--ELEVATED RAILROAD.

Boston were then carried by this route, being transferred by steamboats from Green-
port to the Connecticut shore.   The company was chartered in 1834.   By succes-
sive consolidations and leases the company now controls more than 500 miles of track
on Long Island, including two nearly parallel lines, each about 100 miles long, from
Brooklyn and Long-Island City to Sag Harbor and Greenport.   Branches lead to
Long Beach, Rockaway and Manhattan Beach, on the ocean front ; and to Flushing,
Whitestone, Great Neck, Oyster Bay, Northport and Port Jefferson, on Long-Island
Sound.   This capital system of railways brings to the metropolis the abounding

farm-products of the island, and gives access to the scores of suburban villages and famous seaside resorts. The Hunter's-Point station of the Long-Island Railroad is reached from New York by the ferries from James Slip and East 34th Street.

The New-York and Sea-Beach Railroad connects at Bay Ridge with the boats of the Staten-Island Rapid Transit Company, from the foot of Whitehall Street, the terminus of the elevated roads and the Broadway and Belt-Line surface roads.

ELEVATED RAILROAD AT 110TH STREET AND NINTH AVENUE.

From Bay Ridge it runs down to West Brighton, Coney Island. In 15 minutes, Brooklyn passengers connect with it by the Brooklyn City Elevated Railroad. It is a double-track standard-gauge line, six miles long, opened in 1879.

The Brooklyn, Bath & West-End Railroad, reached by ferry from White-hall to 39th Street, Brooklyn, leads in 6⅔ miles to Coney Island. It was built in 1864; and in 1892 began running to the tide-water ferry-house, by the South-Brooklyn Railroad & Terminal Company's costly new roadway.

The Brooklyn & Brighton-Beach Railroad is a double-track line, 7½ miles long, running from Atlantic Avenue, Brooklyn, to Brighton Beach, across Flatbush.

The Staten-Island Rapid-Transit Railroad is reached by ferry from the foot of Whitehall Street; and gives access to all the important villages on "the American Isle of Wight." The Rapid-Transit Company was chartered in 1880, and in 1886 opened its line from Arrochar to Bowman's Point, opposite Elizabethport. In 1884 it effected a ninety-nine years' lease of the Staten-Island Railroad, chartered in 1851, and seven years later completed from Clifton to Tottenville. The lines of this company have a considerable value as leading from the metropolis to the rising suburban villages on the island. Their chief service, however, is in handling the enormous freight brought by the Baltimore & Ohio Railroad hither, across the Arthur-Kill Bridge, and down to tide-water at St. George and other points.

Local Transit.—The immense population of the metropolis of the New World and the necessity of moving myriads of men daily to and from their place of business, have given rise to many successive problems as to transportation, whose solutions have been of an interesting and ingenious character. The great length of the island, and its separation from the shores on either side by broad and deep tidal estuaries have given the necessary travel thereon a unique character, compelling successive developments of the modes of locomotion.

Stage Coaches were the first means employed for local transits.   Departing at stated and infrequent intervals, and with much fanfare of horns, they ran from the taverns on the lower part of the island, over the Old Boston Post Road and the

FIFTH-AVENUE STAGE AT THE CATHEDRAL.

Bloomingdale Road, to the little embowered hamlets on the north.   These vehicles went through many evolutions, and increased amazingly in numbers, until lower Broadway at times was almost blockaded with their huge and swaying forms. This main artery of the city retained its omnibuses for many years after they had disappeared from the other avenues, and only reliuquished them when the vastly more comfortable street-car system came into use. The modern development of the old-fashioned stage-coach is now seen on Fifth Avenue, which is traversed every few minutes by low-hung stages, beginning their courses at Bleecker Street and running north along the elegant patrician thoroughfare to 86th Street, at the Metropolitan Museum of Art, the last mile or more being alongside Central Park.   Some of these conveyances used in pleasant weather have seats on their roofs, and it is a favorite diversion to ride up the Avenue thereupon, especially in the late afternoon, observing the splendid panorama of architecture and metropolitan life.

Street-Cars.— In the course of time the rattling omnibuses of the provincial era were found ill-adapted to the transportation of the ever-increasing thousands of urban travellers, and ingenious inventors set to work to discover some new method of transit, at once more competent and more comfortable.   This was found in the horse-car, whose idea is a gift from the city of New York to the civilized world, and has been of inestimable benefit to mankind.   Nearly thirty years after their adoption here they were first introduced in Europe by George Francis Train, a citizen of New York, and now they are in constant use in hundreds of cities of Europe, Asia and Oceania, besides American cities and villages from Seattle to Key West.

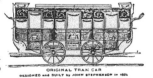

ORIGINAL TRAM CAR
DESIGNED and BUILT by JOHN STEPHENSON in 1831

The New-York & Harlem, the first street-railway in the world, was chartered in 1831, and in 1832 opened its entire line from Prince Street to Harlem Bridge.   The cars were like stage-coaches, balanced on leather springs, and each having three compartments, with side-doors; while overhead sat the driver, moving the brake with his feet.   From this germ has grown up the present immense and efficient street-car system of the Empire City, which is used by millions of passengers and reaches almost every part of the island, with its lines along both water-fronts and up nearly all the north and south avenues and across town at a score of points. It was for a time thought that the introduction of the elevated railways would ruin the business of the street-cars, but this result has not followed, and the surface lines are still as fully employed as ever.

The First & Second Avenue Line runs from Fulton Ferry to the Harlem River, with branches to Worth Street and Broadway and to Astor Place and Broadway, and to the Astoria Ferry.

The Third-Avenue Railroad is one of the ancient street-car lines, its charter dating from 1853. The company has 28 miles of track, from the City Hall to Harlem (130th Street), with branches from Manhattan Street to 125th Street, E. R., and on Tenth Avenue from 125th Street, near Manhattanville, to 186th Street.

The Fourth-Avenue Line runs from the Post Office to the Grand Central Depot, with a branch to the Hunter's-Point Ferry. The Madison-Avenue line runs from the Post Office to Mott Haven.

The Sixth-Avenue Railroad was chartered away back in 1851, and runs from the Astor House (Vesey Street and Broadway) to Central Park. The line properly begins at Canal and Varick Streets, but the track thence to Vesey Street and the branch along Canal Street are owned in common with the Eighth-Avenue Company. The company owns 120 cars and 1,100 horses.

The Seventh-Avenue Line runs from Whitehall to Central Park, and beyond to Washington Heights. It owns 420 cars and 1,200 horses. The cost of construction was $4,500,000.

The Eighth-Avenue Railroad controls 20 miles of track, from Broadway and Vesey Street to the upper part of the island. It was chartered in 1855.

The Ninth-Avenue Line has 16 miles of track, extending from Broadway and Fulton Street to Manhattanville (125th Street). It was chartered in 1859.

The Cross-Town Lines include those on Charlton, Prince and Stanton Streets; from the Hoboken Ferry by Christopher, 8th and 10th Streets to the Greenpoint Ferry; from the 23d-Street Ferry by Grand and Vestry Streets, to the Desbrosses-Street Ferry (to Jersey City); from the Grand-Street Ferry to the Cortlandt-Street Ferry; along 23d Street, from the Erie Ferry to the Greenpoint Ferry; and many others.

The Northern Wards also have numerous street-car lines, reaching Morrisania, Tremont, Fordham, West Farms, Port Morris and other villages north of the Harlem River.

The Broadway Line is one of the latest-built of the street-car routes. It traverses Broadway, from the South Ferry to Central Park, giving admirable facilities for reaching all parts of this grandest thoroughfare of the world. The construction of the line met with a most determined opposition from a great number of citizens, who feared that their favorite commercial avenue would be ruined by the introduction of the rails; and a charter was obtained only after protracted controversies, and resulted in grave municipal complications. But the anticipated annoyances have not been realized, and the line is now one of the most important and useful in the city; and happy was the day for New-Yorkers when the old-fashioned, slow, cumbersome and noisy omnibuses gave way to the swift, quiet and neat horse-cars.

Cable-Cars, so successfully used in many American cities, are about to be introduced in New York on several of the main lines of tramway, and notably on Broadway and Third Avenue, whose routes have been constructed with this modern system of propulsion, so that passengers may be, and are, carried by them for marvelously low fares. The trolley system of electric railways will probably get an entrance into New York in time, although it has been unable to overcome a certain singular prejudice felt here against it, in spite of the success of the trolleys in so many other cities.

The Elevated Railroad is the crowning achievement in solving the problems of rapid transit. By its aid the New-Yorkers fly through the air from end to end of their teeming island at railway speed and in comfortable and well-appointed cars. The simplicity of their structure and the free gift to the companies of the right of way enable these routes to be built at a fraction of the cost of the urban rapid-transit lines in other great cities. Instead of being whirled through the darkness and monotony and poisonous air of almost continuous tunnels (as in London), the New-Yorkers are borne along, swiftly and comfortably, high up above the streets, in view of the wonderful changing panorama of the Empire City, and in a fresh and wholesome atmosphere. A ride on the London Metropolitan Railway is a depressing necessity ; but a flight along the New-York elevated rails is a refreshment.

The movement for elevated railways grew very strong in 1866, and during the following year more than forty plans were submitted to the Legislature. The system of Charles C. Harvey was accepted, and the inventor was allowed to build an experimental track along Greenwich Street from the Battery to 29th Street. If it succeeded Harvey was to have permission to extend the line to the Harlem River,

PASSENGER ELEVATOR AND STATION, ELEVATED RAILROAD, EIGHTH AVENUE AND 118TH STREET.

but if it failed it must be taken down. The system was commenced in 1867, but the means of locomotion then used was a wire rope drawn by a stationary engine. This method was unsuccessful, and the matter lay in abeyance for several years. The company failed in 1870, and was succeeded by the New-York Elevated Railroad Company, which began the use of small locomotives on the tracks. The Manhattan Railway Company was formed in 1875, and in 1879 it leased, for a term of 999 years, the New-York Elevated Railroad and the Metropolitan Elevated Railway, both of which were chartered in 1872 and opened in 1878. The lease was modified in 1884. The New-York line cost $20,500,000 for construction and equipment, and the Metropolitan cost $23,300,000. The Manhattan Company has about 300 locomotives and 1,000 cars, and carries 215,000,000 passengers yearly.

In 1891 the Manhattan Company secured control of the Suburban Rapid-Transit Railroad, running from 129th Street and Third Avenue, in Harlem, and through Mott Haven and Melrose to Central Morrisania (171st Street and Third Avenue).

This system is in process of extension to West Farms, Bronx Park, Fordham and other localities.

The main elevated railway lines are along the East Side, on Second and Third Avenues, two parallel routes from the lower part of Manhattan Island to Harlem ; the Sixth-Avenue line, along the middle of the island ; and the Ninth-Avenue line, nearer the Hudson River, from South Ferry to Central Park and the Harlem River, at West 155th Street. The railways are carried on girders resting upon wrought-iron lattice columns, usually along the line of the curb-stones, and from 37 to 44 feet apart. In some cases each side of the avenue has its elevated track, one for the up-trains, the other for the down-trains. Elsewhere the girders run clear across the narrower streets, and the two tracks are brought close together over the middle

CABLE-CARS ON THE EAST-RIVER BRIDGE, NEW-YORK END.

of the street. On some of the wider and less crowded avenues, the columns and tracks are placed in the middle. The stations are about one-third of a mile apart ; and in the busy hours of the day trains pass them about every minute, drawn by powerful locomotive engines. The crowded junction points of the lines, the stations in mid-air, the swallow-flight of the light trains, the perfect system and discipline of the arrangements, command admiring wonder, and make an especially vivid impression upon foreign visitors. The lofty curving trestles of iron near 110th Street were justly characterized by De Lesseps as one of the most audacious of engineering feats.

Projected Subterranean Transit.—However rapidly the facilities are increased, the needs of the city seem to increase even more rapidly, and the capacity of the elevated lines is already overstrained, especially at certain hours of the day. Consequently, new methods are in process of being worked out, and all possible routes between the Battery and Harlem are being studied by competent engineers.

In the belief that the existing surface and elevated railways occupy as much of the land and air of the city as can properly be used, attention has been directed to subterranean routes, to be bored under Broadway for its entire length. The Rapid-Transit System proposed in 1891 by William E. Worthen, the chief engineer of the commission, provided for a tunnel under Broadway and the Boulevard, from the Battery to Spuyten Duyvil, containing four railway tracks, the outside ones for local trains and the inside ones for express trains, running at forty miles an hour. From 14th Street the East-Side branch diverges up Fourth and Madison Avenues to the Grand Central Depot. The trains were to be run by electric power, and the stations and tunnels ventilated by powerful fans and brightly lighted by electricity. The lines and plan of construction were approved by the Mayor and Common Council. Yet this system failed to be realized, and many new schemes for other routes and methods have since been brought before the Rapid-Transit Commissioners. The tendency seems to be towards more extensive elevated railway services, especially between the Battery and Fort George.

America is the Temple of Liberty, and New York is its Beautiful Gate. Other portals there are : Boston and Baltimore, New Orleans and San Francisco, and many more, but their aggregate of travel and traffic falls below that of this imperial city. In the days of the Cæsars all roads led to Rome ; but in this happier century all routes, by sea or land, converge upon this wonderful harbor. Millions of European immigrants have first touched the land of peace and freedom here ; and armies of travellers in search of pleasure or variety, or along the lines of trade and commerce. Here centre the routes of travel between the rich and prosperous North and the happy and beautiful South, and between earnest New England and her daughter States of the West. Hundreds of thousands of people from all parts of the Republic visit the great city every year for its own sake, because nowhere else are there such abundant facilities for pleasure, for enlightenment, for business. Here, therefore, is the supreme clearing-house for travellers of all kinds, and on all errands.

Along these close converging tracks of steel, each more noble than the Appian Way, hundreds of trains arrive and depart daily, with every variety of traveller, from the Westchester suburban to the New-Zealand globe-trotter. The White Train and other famous convoys fly thence to New England and the remoter East ; the Empire-State Limited and the Erie Flyer to the North and West ; the Royal Blue and the powerful Pennsylvania trains to the West and South ; and scores of other routes have their almost continuous processions of cars, bound for innumerable destinations. Nowhere else in the world is there such a focal point of travel as this.

Another interesting feature in the relation of New-York City to the railway systems of America appears in its overmastering financial control of many of their chief lines. It is hardly possible to construct and equip a new route anywhere without securing some part of the needed capital from this treasure city ; and if the enterprise is promising and feasible there is always plenty of money at hand for the purpose. The little rock-bound cañon of Wall Street has furnished the means to construct thousands of miles of track in all the country between Tampa Bay and Eastport, and between Sonora and Seattle. The great trust-companies of New York are the guardians of incalculable amounts in mortgage-bonds and other obligations, and at their offices many railway companies, both near and far, pay their dividends. The Vanderbilt, Gould, Corbin and other far-reaching systems have their headquarters here, and from this impregnable financial fortress control the destinies of unnumbered myriads of American people.

Thoroughfares and Adornments.

Streets, Avenues, Boulevards, Alleys, Ways, Parks, Squares, Drives, Monuments, Statues, Fountains, Etc.

I N NEW YORK all roads lead not to Rome, but to the Battery. There the
city had its beginning ; and to-day, after three centuries of municipal existence
and of steady expansion northward, the stupendous commercial and financial interests of the metropolis are still in that vicinity. The trains of the elevated railroads
all run to the Battery, and all the principal street-car lines trend in that direction.
Naturally a topographic tour of the city begins at that point.

The Battery was once the court end of the town. Fortifications were erected
here by the first Dutch settlers. Castle Garden was once a fort on a ledge in the

BATTERY PLACE--WASHINGTON BUILDING.   PRODUCE EXCHANGE.

bay, connected by a causeway with the main land. As time wore on, the Castle
became a peaceful summer-garden and a concert-hall. The Lafayette ball was
given there in 1824, and there Jenny Lind, the Swedish Nightingale, made her
American *debut*. From 1855 to 1891 Castle Garden was the immigrant-depot, and
many millions of persons from Europe have passed through its portals on their way
to make homes for themselves in the New World. Now the Garden has changed
character again. It will soon be devoted to a public aquarium, where many varieties of dwellers in the water may be seen. The United-States Revenue Barge-
Office is situated there, on the water-front. Battery Park contains about 21 acres.
It is well kept, with green lawns, flowers and shade-trees, and is a delightfully cool
place in summer time. In colonial days the homes of New-York's wealth and aristocracy looked down upon this lovely spot. Several of the old houses still remain,

but for the most part they have made way for huge warehouses and gigantic office buildings.

Bowling Green, a small triangular plot on the northern confines of Battery Park, is rich with traditions.   Here stood the equestrian statue of King George III. Lord Cornwallis, Lord Howe, Sir Henry Clinton, George Washington, General Gates, Benedict Arnold, Talleyrand and other famous folk lived in this vicinity. Just south of the Green is the site of Fort Amsterdam, built by the Dutch in 1626. The Produce Exchange, the Welles Building, the Standard Oil Company Building, the Washington Building, the Columbia Building and other notable architectural structures now distinguish the locality.

Broadway, which starts from Bowling Green, is one of the longest and grandest business thoroughfares of the world.   It is not always imposing, but it is always

WHITEHALL STREET, LOOKING TOWARDS BROADWAY.   ARMY BUILDING.

interesting ; and in general appearance, variety of scenes and impressive air of business and social activities it has, all in all, no rival on either continent.   It is the main business artery of the city.   On and about it, down-town, are hundreds of great buildings, bee-hives of industry, some of which have a business population equal to that of a country-town.   The street is packed from sunrise to sunset with processions of merchandise, trucks, vehicles and cars, and the sidewalks are crowded with hurrying thousands, all on business intent.   There are few loiterers and few pleasure-seekers in this part of the town.   Financial institutions, shipping interests, the wholesale dry-goods and other branches of business monopolize lower Broadway and the adjacent streets.

At its inception Broadway is dignified with the great buildings that have already been referred to as surrounding Bowling Green ; and the offices of the foreign consuls and the steamship companies and immigrant boarding-houses jostle them.

At every step northward appear tall buildings, the Columbia, Aldrich Court, the Tower, the Consolidated Exchange, the Manhattan Life-Insurance Company, the

PRODUCE EXCHANGE.   STEAMSHIP ROW, BOWLING GREEN.   STATE STREET

Union Trust Company, the United Bank, and others. Opposite Wall Street is Trinity Church and graveyard, breaking the monotony of the busy scene. Once Broadway ended at this point, and meandered beyond as a green country-lane. The

LOWER BROADWAY, LOOKING NORTH, FROM MORRIS STREET TO TRINITY CHURCH.

imposing Equitable Building, extending from Pine to Cedar Streets, stands where in 1646 good old Jan Jansen Damen lived, and shot the bears that prowled about his orchards. More great buildings : the Boreel, the Williamsburg City Fire, the

Mutual Life, the *Evening Post*, the Western Union, the *Mail and Express*, the *Herald*, — and then Broadway reaches Park Row and City-Hall Park. There is St.-Paul's Chapel, its back turned to the great thoroughfare. Opposite is the National Park Bank, and beyond is the famous Astor House, and the Post Office. A little farther on, not on Broadway, but within sight, across City-Hall Park, are

BROADWAY AND FIFTH AVENUE, SOUTH FROM MADISON SQUARE.

the Potter Building, and the newspaper buildings — the *Times*, *Sun*, *Tribune*, *World*, and *Staats-Zeitung*. In the park itself are the City Hall and the Court-House, and just beyond is the Stewart Building. The East-River Bridge terminates at City-Hall Park, in the midst of these noble architectural piles. The Postal-Telegraph-Cable Building, at the corner of Murray Street, and its neighbor, the Home Life-Insurance Building, will be imposing 13 and 14-story structures. The quadrangle formed around the southern end of the City-Hall Park by the newspaper

BROADWAY AND SIXTH AVENUE, NORTH FROM 54TH STREET.

buildings, the City Hall, and the Post Office is, without doubt, the grandest square on the American continent.

From the City Hall northward as far as Grace Church, at 10th Street, wholesale business-houses practically monopolize Broadway. At Duane Street rises the elegant twelve-story building of the Mutual Reserve-Fund Life Association, a splendid fire-proof stone structure. At Leonard Street the New-York Life-Insurance Building attracts attention, and near Lispenard Street is the fine edifice of the Ninth National Bank. Just beyond is Canal Street, in its name a reminder of the time when a canal ran across the island. Farther north are the Metropolitan Hotel

BROADWAY, FROM PARK PLACE TO CHAMBERS STREET.
OPPOSITE CITY-HALL PARK.

10

and Niblo's Theatre, the conspicuous Rouss Building, the Manhattan Savings Institution, the newly remodelled Broadway Central Hotel, the old New-York Hotel, then the Stewart dry-goods emporium, occupying an entire block between Broadway and Fourth Avenue, 9th Street and 10th Street, and then the beautiful Grace Church. At 11th Street is the first-class dry-goods establishment of James McCreery & Co. In this vicinity a literary centre has grown up. The publishing house of D. Appleton & Co. is a few blocks below in Bond Street ; Charles Scribner's Sons, in Broadway, opposite Astor Place ; the Aldine Club and the Astor Library, in Lafayette Place ; the University of the City of New York, in Washington Square ; the Cooper Union and the Mercantile Library, in Astor Place ; the American Book Co., a monopoly of the school-book business ; Wm. Wood & Co., in 10th Street ; the

FOURTEENTH STREET, BETWEEN FIFTH AND SIXTH AVENUES.

United-States Book Co., in 16th Street ; Dodd, Mead & Co., in 19th Street ; and other publishing houses and new and second-hand book-stores are near at hand in all directions.

At 13th Street, leaving the Star Theatre, where for a generation shone the genius of Lester Wallack, Broadway at 14th Street debouches into Union Square, and, deflecting slightly to the west, pursues the rest of its course up-town diagonally across the avenues, instead of parallel to them.

Here is the retail shopping district, from 10th Street to above 23d Street. In Broadway, 14th Street and 23d Street principally, the prominent retail establishments are the wonder and the admiration of all who see them, and in extent and in

MRS. WILLIAM H. VANDERBILT.

WILLIAM D. SLOANE.   MRS. ELLIOTT F. SHEPARD.   WILLIAM K. VANDERBILT.   ST. THOMAS CHURCH.   DR. HALL'S CHURCH.

FIFTH AVENUE, LOOKING NORTH FROM 51st STREET.

SHOWING THE VANDERBILT RESIDENCES, AND ST. THOMAS EPISCOPAL AND THE FIFTH-AVENUE PRESBYTERIAN CHURCHES.

variety of goods they are not surpassed elsewhere in the world.   It has been estimated that the trade in this district annually amounts to over $500,000,000.   A few
play-houses are still found as far south as 14th Street, but the main theatre-region
is in Broadway, or within about a block's distance, between 23d and 42d Streets.
Within that distance — about a mile — are Proctor's 23d-Street Theatre, the Madison-Square Garden, the Garden Theatre, the Madison-Square Theatre, Koster &
Bial's, the Lyceum, the Fifth-Avenue, Herrmann's, Daly's, the Bijou, Palmer's,
the Standard, Harrigan's, the Park, the Casino, the Metropolitan Opera House, the
Manhattan Opera House, the Broadway, and the new Empire Theatre.   Broadway is
also an avenue of great hotels.   Up-town it has the St. Denis, at 11th Street ; the St.
George, at 12th Street ; the Morton, at 14th Street ; the Continental, at 20th Street ;
the Aberdeen and Bancroft, at 21st Street ; the Fifth-Avenue and the Bartholdi, at
23d Street ; the Albemarle, at 24th Street ; the Hoffman, at 25th Street ; the St.
James, at 26th Street ; the Victoria and the Coleman, at 27th Street ; the Gilsey
and the Sturtevant, at 29th Street ; the Grand, at 31st Street ; the Imperial, at 32d
Street ; the Marlborough, at 36th Street ; the Normandie, at 38th Street ; the Oriental, at 39th Street ; the Gedney, at 40th Street ; the Vendome, at 41st Street ; the
St. Cloud and the Metropole, at 42d Street ; the Barrett, at 43d Street ; and the
Gladstone, at 59th Street.

Above 42d Street Broadway yet maintains something of the residential character
that long ago disappeared from it below.   Many large apartment-houses face it as
it nears Central Park, at 59th Street.   There with another turn westward it broadens
out into a wide asphalt-paved thoroughfare, with a shaded parkway in the center,
and is henceforth known as the Boulevard.   It is a long but exceedingly interesting
walk up Broadway from Bowling Green to Central Park — about five miles.

The Boulevard, virtually a continuation of Broadway, beginning at the Park,
goes on for nine miles farther, through the pleasant upper part of the city that is
being rapidly covered with handsome houses, apartment-buildings and churches.   It
passes over the hillside between Riverside Park and Morningside Park, where
Columbia College, the Protestant-Episcopal Cathedral and the Grant Monument are
soon to rise, and down into the ravine at Harlem, and then up again upon historic
Washington Heights, still a region of beautiful country-homes of old New-York
families, and on to the end of the island at Spuyten-Duyvil Creek, by the old Kingsbridge road.   The Boulevard includes two capital roadways, separated by a central
strip of lawns, trees, and flowers.   When finished, it will be one of the most beautiful driveways in the world, traversing, as it does, the remarkably picturesque
region between Central Park and the Hudson River, much of the way over high
ground, commanding beautiful views.

Fifth Avenue is celebrated the world over as the grand residence street of the
aristocratic and wealthy families of the metropolis.   In recent years business has
encroached upon its boundaries, but despite all it still maintains its prestige and its
brilliant character.   There was a time when some people regarded residence in Fifth
Avenue as an indispensable requisite to pre-eminent social recognition.   In recent
years this notion has been decidedly relaxed, and grand residences of prominent
people arise on many of the cross streets immediately out of the avenue, and in Madison Avenue, Park Avenue, around the various squares and parks, in the newly-laid-
out streets, and in other favored localities ; but nevertheless a luxurious residence in
Fifth Avenue is a sort of stamp, or patent of rank.   From Washington Square for
a distance of nearly four miles northward, Fifth Avenue is lined with handsome
residences, club-houses, churches and hotels that give abundant evidence of wealth

THE CHARLES L. TIFFANY RESIDENCE.

MADISON AVENUE, NORTHWEST CORNER OF SEVENTY-SECOND STREET.

1 2 3 0 STREET.   JOHN DWIGHT.   MOUNT MORRIS AVENUE.

MOUNT MORRIS PARK.

and luxurious tastes.   In the lower part of the avenue many of the old New-York
families still hold their mansions, despite the proximity of trade.   Between 14th and
23d Streets, business has almost entirely pushed out residences, and only a few years
will elapse before it will be in full possession of the usurped territory.   The Manhattan Club has gone up-town to 34th Street ; the Lotos is preparing to move ; and
the Union must soon follow.   The *Judge*, the Methodist Book Concern, and the
Mohawk buildings, three large, handsome structures, have been erected recently,
and are prophetic of the transformation now taking place in this part of the avenue.

PARK AVENUE, LOOKING NORTH FROM 55TH STREET.

ST. BARTHOLOMEW'S CHURCH.   MANHATTAN ATHLETIC CLUB.   HOLY TRINITY CHURCH.

MADISON AVENUE, LOOKING NORTH FROM 42D STREET.

PRESBYTERIAN HOSPITAL.   CHARLES F. CLARK   JOHN KING.

MADISON AVENUE, EAST SIDE, BETWEEN 69TH AND 70TH STREETS.

At 23d Street, Fifth Avenue crosses Broadway and makes the western border of Madison Square. From this point northward to 42d Street business is in the ascendant. Many of the private houses that once lined the avenue are gone, and many of those that remain are not used for residences. Art-galleries, book-stores, *bric-à-brac* shops, fashionable millinery and dressmaking establishments, publication offices, clubs and hotels are rapidly making this an aristocratic business street.

Above 42d Street are the palaces of some of New York's millionaires. The Vanderbilt houses are regarded as the finest examples of domestic architecture in the United States. They do not stand entirely alone, however, in respect to beauty. The Stevens house, now owned and occupied by ex-Secretary-of-the-Navy William C. Whitney; the C. P. Huntington mansion, nearly completed; the houses of Robert Goelet, R. F. Cutting, and others add distinction to the mile of avenue between 42d Street and Central Park; and in the same district live, less pretentiously but none the less elegantly, such well-known New York aristocrats as Governor Roswell P. Flower, Darius O. Mills, Henry M. Flagler, Ogden Goelet, Washington E. Conner, Russell Sage, Chauncey M. Depew, and William Rockefeller. Above 59th Street, facing the Park, are other splendid mansions, among them the home of Henry O. Havemeyer, and the Robert L. Stuart house.

Fifth Avenue is the great hotel thoroughfare of the city. In that respect it surpasses even Broadway, its closest rival. It has the Brevoort, at Clinton Place; the Berkeley, at 9th Street; the Lenox, at 12th Street; the Logerot, at 20th Street; the Glenham, at 22d Street; the Fifth-Avenue, at 23d Street; the Brunswick, at 25th Street: the Victoria, at 27th Street; the Holland, at 30th Street; the Cambridge and the Waldorf, at 33d Street; the St. Marc, at 39th Street; the Hamilton

HARLEM VIEW, LOOKING EAST FROM 137TH STREET.

and the Bristol, at 42d Street; the Sherwood, at 44th Street; the Windsor, at 46th Street; the Buckingham, at 50th Street; the Langham, at 52d Street; and the Plaza, Savoy and New Netherland, at 59th Street.

Fifth Avenue is also a street of churches. On it stand Ascension (Episcopal), at 10th Street; the First Presbyterian, at 12th Street; the Collegiate Reformed, at 29th Street; the Brick Presbyterian, at 37th Street; the Jewish Temple Emanu-El, at 43d Street; the Divine Paternity (Universalist), at 45th Street; the Heavenly Rest (Episcopal), near 45th Street; the Collegiate Reformed, at 48th Street; St. Patrick's Cathedral (Roman Catholic), at 50th Street; St. Thomas (Episcopal), at 53d Street; and the Fifth-Avenue Presbyterian, at 55th Street.

Fifth Avenue, moreover, is the main resort of the clubs, nearly all of which have taken possession of old-time residences. Among them are the following: the Union, at 21st Street; Sorosis, near 25th Street; the Reform, at 27th Street; the

JEANNETTE PARK, COENTIES SLIP.

Calumet, at 29th Street; the Knickerbocker, at 32d Street; the Manhattan, at 34th Street; the New-York, at 35th Street; the St.-Nicholas, at 36th Street; the Union League and the Delta Kappa Epsilon, at 39th Street; the Republican, at 40th Street; the Lotos, near 45th Street; the Democratic, near 49th Street; the Seventh-Regiment-Veteran, above 57th Street; the Metropolitan, at 60th Street: and the Progress, at 63d Street.

Among the public and semi-public institutions on Fifth Avenue are: Chickering Hall, Delmonico's, St. Luke's Hospital, the Roman Catholic Orphan Asylum, and the Lenox Library. With its handsome residences, numerous hotels, churches, clubs and other institutions, and with Washington Square at its southern terminus, Madison-Square and the Reservoir in Bryant Park breaking its course, and the 59th-Street Plaza and Central Park illuminating its northern extension, Fifth Avenue is certainly one of the most magnificent thoroughfares of the world.

SOUTH STREET, NORTH FROM THE BATTERY.

Madison Avenue, which, only a block away, runs parallel with Fifth Avenue, contains the Villard Florentine palace, part of which is now the home of Whitelaw Reid, the editor of the *Tribune,* and ex-United-States Minister to France. The Tiffany house, at Madison Avenue and West 72d Street, is one of the most unique and attractive dwelling-houses in America. It was built for and is owned by Charles L. Tiffany, the founder and senior member of the world-famous jewelry house of Tiffany & Co. It was designed by Stanford White, of McKim, Mead & White, and Louis C. Tiffany. The interior was designed by Louis C. Tiffany, son of the owner, who, with other members of the same family, occupies the house. The architecture contains many quaint and delightful features of the old Dutch style; and the lofty and ornate façades and picturesque roof are prominent features of up-town New York. On the same avenue stand other mansions scarcely less notable. Madi. son Avenue, too, might well be termed "the Avenue to the Gods," for imposing shrines of worship, in a greater number than on any other thoroughfare in the city,

EDISON BUILDING.   STOCK EXCHANGE.   WILLS BUILDING.
BROAD STREET, NORTH TO WALL STREET.

of many denominations and many creeds, rise up at every few corners throughout its whole length. At its beginning has just been completed the magnificent white marble edifice of the Metropolitan Life Insurance Company.

Sixth Avenue rivals Broadway, 14th Street and 23d Street in its retail stores. Several of the large dry-goods establishments are there, and hundreds of smaller shops. It contains the Jefferson-Market Court-House at 10th Street; the Greenwich Savings Bank, at 16th Street; the Masonic Hall, at 23d Street; and the Union Dime Savings Institution, at 32d Street; besides which there is little of noteworthy architectural character in the avenue. It has a large resident population, in apartments over stores, and is the main thoroughfare of the Tenderloin District.

Seventh Avenue, extending from Greenwich Avenue to Central Park, is a residence-street for people of moderate means, and has many retail stores. The State Arsenal is at 35th Street; the Osborne Flats, at 52d Street; Tattersall's, at 55th Street; Hotel Grenoble, at 56th Street; Music Hall, at 57th Street; and the Central-Park Apartment-houses, at 59th Street.

West Street and South Street are the water-front thoroughfares, leading from the Battery along the North River and East River respectively. Along the former are the piers of most of the great ocean-steamship lines and of the Hudson-River and Long-Island-Sound boats. Much of the South-American shipping comes

BROAD STREET, SOUTH FROM WALL STREET.

DREXEL BUILDING. MILLS BUILDING. PRODUCE EXCHANGE. STOCK EXCHANGE. WILKS BUILDING

to the East-River front, and sailing vessels predominate there. Near the mouth of the East River, at the Battery, large fleets of canal-boats tie up. The piers on all the river-fronts, with one exception, are wooden or iron structures.

Eighth Avenue is the West-Side cheap thoroughfare. The upper part of the avenue toward 59th Street is respectable, and contains several notable public buildings.

Central Park West is that part of Eighth Avenue that faces Central Park from 59th Street to 110th Street. It is a beautiful street, and is being built up with artistic and expensive private houses and handsome apartment-hotels. The Dakota, the San Remo, the San Carló, and the La Grange, are among the finest houses of their kind in the city. The American Museum of Natural History, in Manhattan Square, and the Cancer Hospital look upon Central Park West.

Wall Street is a short and narrow thoroughfare, but it is second only to Lombard Street, London, in the magnitude, importance and far-reaching influence of its financial operations. Both its sides are lined for about half their length with some of the costliest office and bank buildings in this country ; here, too, are the Sub-Treasury, the Assay Office, and the Custom House. Once the outer wall of the city, surmounted by a stockade, ran where the street now is.   Hence comes the name of the street.   Times have changed since that day when watchful sentinels paced this wall, guarding the little village of New Amsterdam from the Indians and the wild beasts.   Even as late as 1697, when a grant of land was made to Trinity Church, it was described as "in or near to a street without the North Gate of the city, commonly called Broadway."   The Sub-Treasury stands on the site of the first City Hall, afterward called the Federal Hall.

Nassau, Broad and New Streets take a great deal of the overflow of Wall Street.   In Broad Street is the main front of the handsome white-marble building of the Stock Exchange, and several elegant office-buildings — the Mills, the Edison, and the Morris.   In Nassau Street is the Clearing House, and many banks and banking houses.   The majestic Mutual Life-Insurance Building stands on the site of the Middle Dutch Church, which was used for a riding-school by the British soldiers during the Revolution, and was afterwards the New-York Post-Office.   In 1728 the Dutch society bought this land for £575; in 1861 the United-States Government paid the church $200,000 for it; and in 1881 the insurance company bought it for $650,000. It is probably worth now fully $750,000.

Printing-House Square is at the north end of Nassau Street.   The appellation is popular rather than official.   It is an open space, or plaza, at the intersection of Park Row and Nassau and Spruce Streets, abreast of the City-Hall Park; and

WALKER STREET.·· HARRY HOWARD SQUARE.·· CANAL STREET.

is bordered by the offices of the great newspapers.   The statues of Benjamin Franklin and Horace Greeley are appropriately placed as the presiding geniuses of the locality.

Franklin Square is only known and only important because the firm of Harper & Brothers still keep their publishing house there.   A century and less ago this was one of the fashionable quarters of the town.   The old mansions have disappeared, and a tenement-house population and small manufacturing establishments now occupy the land.   The square is pretty well covered over by the network of tracks and depots of the Elevated Railroad.

BROADWAY, FROM THE BROADWAY CENTRAL HOTEL TO GRACE CHURCH.
BOND STREET TO TENTH STREET.

The Bowery is historic ground. In the good old pre-colonial days it was a pleasant country lane, running between the "Boweries" or farms of the worthy Dutch burghers. Its rural character departed years and years ago, and for a long time its name was synonymous with all the worst phases of vice in the slums of the great city. The swaggering "Bowery Boy" tough then ruled the precinct, which was redolent with depravity. In recent years the Bowery has risen from its low estate, and possesses many enterprising business establishments, successful banks,

"CHINATOWN"--MOTT STREET, WEST OF PARK ROW.

and public institutions. A flavor of cheapness from the surrounding tenement region still clings to it, but the decent German and Hebrew elements now chiefly dominate the neighborhood.

The Five Points, once so infamous, was renovated some years ago. Crime and poverty no longer control it. In their place have come mission schools, chapels and manufactories, and industrious working people. New streets and open squares have been laid out by the municipal authorities, and the district is generally improved sanitarily and socially.

Mott, Pell and Doyers Streets and vicinity are now given over to the Chinese. There is a large population in the district just west of the Bowery and Chatham Square. The district is a veritable "Chinatown," with all the filth, immorality and picturesque foreignness which that name implies.

Second Avenue in its southern limits is the great German thoroughfare. A large German population exists to the east of it; and its cafés, gardens and other places of public resort are for people of that nationality. About 10th Street was the farm of Peter Stuyvesant, the last Dutch Governor of New Amsterdam.

Baxter Street is still monopolized by the cheap clothing-dealers, who have made the name of the street famous.

Thompson Street is the centre of one of the largest negro colonies in the city, and has given rise to a very readable book, "The Proceedings of the Thompson-Street Poker Club."

Hanover Square, at the junction of Hanover, Pearl and William Streets, is the centre of the cotton trade, and here, too, is the stately Cotton Exchange. In this locality, in days gone by, lived many of New York's wealthy merchants, and after the French Revolution many notable French *emigrés.* Here is an important station of the Elevated Railroad, greatly utilized by the men connected with the Stock, Cotton and Produce Exchanges.

Lafayette Place, a short street between Astor Place and Great Jones Street, is distinguished as the location of the Mission of the Immaculate Virgin, the Astor Library, the Protestant Episcopal Diocesan House, the DeVinne Press (printers of *The Century Magazine*), and the offices of several publishing concerns and religious societies. In the row of houses opposite the Astor Library, and known as "the Colonnade Row," lived John Jacob Astor and other rich merchants, two generations ago. The north end of the Row is owned and occupied by *The Churchman.*

Astor Place, just north of Lafayette Place, has the Mercantile-Library Building, the Eighth-Street (Jewish) Theatre, and the statue of Samuel S. Cox. In front of the Opera House, which then occupied the present site of Clinton Hall (the Library Building), occurred the "Forrest-Macready riot," in 1849. Astor Place was once a fashionable residence-quarter.

Parks and Squares are generously provided for New-York people. Large public parks and small open squares are scattered about in all districts, especially

MULBERRY BEND, THE ITALIAN QUARTER.

where they can be readily availed of for the children of the poor. Few if any cities of the world now have as great an acreage of parks, and the spirit of the people is steadily favorable to even more such open places, that conduce to the general health

CENTRAL PARK AND FIFTH AVENUE, NORTH FROM 59TH STREET.

and happiness of the community, and this too notwithstanding the high value of every square foot of land in the city.

Central Park is one of the most beautiful and one of the most famous urban parks in the world. It covers the territory between Fifth and Eighth Avenues and 59th and 110th Streets, a tract over 2½ miles long by half a mile wide, including an area of 840 acres. There are about 400 acres of wooded ground, part of which is still in the natural state, while the rest has been improved by the planting of trees, shrubs and vines. There are nine miles of carriage-ways, six miles of bridle-paths, and thirty miles of foot-paths. The Park has been beautified with handsome architecture, landscape gardening, statues and other works of sculpture. There are nineteen entrances, over which it was once proposed to erect imposing arches, a plan that may yet be carried out. Transverse roads from east to west, in open cuts below the level of the Park, accommodate business traffic, which is not allowed within the Park limits. Park-carriages are run for the convenience of visitors. The Park was begun in 1857, during the mayoralty of Fernando Wood; and has cost over $16,500,000, inclusive of maintenance, which has been over $300,000 a year. Frederick Law Olmsted and Calvert Vaux directed the landscape design, and Calvert Vaux and J. W. Mould superintended the architectural features. Washington Irving and George Bancroft Davis were consulting members of the first Park Board, and General Egbert L. Viele was the first engineer. Central Park is twice the size of Regent's Park or Hyde Park, in London; and in the world is exceeded in size only by the Great Park at Windsor, the grounds at Richmond, Phœnix Park in Dublin, the gardens at Versailles, the Bois de Boulogne at Paris, and the Prater in Vienna. None of these equals it in beauty.

Starting from 59th Street, one comes first upon the Ball Ground, a ten-acre plot in the south-west corner, where the boys are privileged to play base-ball and cricket. Near this is the Dairy; and just to the north-east is the Carrousel, with swings for children. Adjoining is the Common, or Green, of sixteen acres, where the sheep

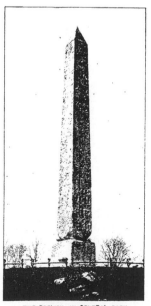

THE OBELISK, IN CENTRAL PARK.

are pastured. On the east side, at Fifth Avenue and 64th Street, is the Menagerie, partly housed in the Arsenal, and partly in pens and wooden houses. There is a large and varied collection of wild animals, elephants, lions, hippopotami, tigers, bears, camels, seals, monkeys and birds. Just to the east of the Green is the Mall, a grand promenade, over 200 feet wide and a third of a mile long, overshadowed by rows of noble elms. Here are many statues; at the southern end, the beautiful Marble Arch, over an underground pathway; and near the middle the Music Pavilion, where concerts are given on Saturday and Sunday afternoons. The goat carriages for the children are kept here; and on the cliff to the left is the arbor, covered with gigantic wisteria vines, that in springtime make a wonderful show of purple blossoms. Close at hand is the Casino, a restaurant for this section. To the north the Mall terminates in the Terrace, the chief architectural feature of the Park.

TERRACE, FOUNTAIN AND LAKE, IN CENTRAL PARK.

There is an Esplanade on the shore of the lake, and the Bethesda Fountain stands there. A central stairway leads down to the Esplanade under the road, beneath which is a tiled hall with arched roof. On either hand outside are other flights of steps. The Terrace is built of a light-brown freestone, with beautiful decorative details, and very intricate carvings of birds and animals.

The Lake covers twenty acres, and is given over to pleasure-boats in the summer and skating in the winter. Beyond the Lake is the Ramble, a spot beautiful with sylvan paths, waterfalls, natural groves, thickets of underbrush and exquisite bits of scenery. Next is the Receiving Reservoir for the city water, and on its margin rises the lofty terrace of the Belvedere, with a picturesque tower fifty feet high, affording a magnificent view of Manhattan Island and all the surrounding country. To the east of the Reservoir are the Obelisk and the Metropolitan Museum of Art; and to the north again, the new Croton Reservoir, which fills nearly the entire width of the Park. At the extreme northern section there is less adornment, but none the less beauty; and, withal, much of historical interest. From Great Hill, with its Carriage Circle, there is a view of Harlem and Washington Heights. Harlem Mere

11

is at the foot of the hill upon which stands the old Block-House ; and McGown's. Pass Tavern is near McGown's Pass, the scene of skirmishes between the British and the Continental troops in 1776.   The North Meadow, a fine grassy lawn of nineteen acres, is largely set apart for tennis-players and picnic-parties.

Other lakes than these already mentioned are the Conservatory Water, where the boys sail little boats ; the Lily Pond, which has a valuable collection of water. lilies, Egyptian lotus and other beautiful flowers ; and the Pond, where swans and

BOAT-HOUSE AND LAKE IN CENTRAL PARK.

other aquatic birds disport themselves. The water area of the Park is : lakes, 43¼ acres ; reservoirs, 143 acres.   The place is much frequented in all seasons of the year.   It is not unusual for 150,000 people to visit it on a single pleasant day in summer ; and 15,000,000 visit it every year.

Riverside Park, next in importance to Central Park, is on the east bank of the Hudson River, extending from 72d Street north to 130th Street, a distance of three miles, with an irregular width, averaging about 500 feet, and an area of 178 acres. That part of it farthest from the river, and known as the Riverside Drive, has been laid out in lawns, driveways and walks, the uneven contour of the land being care-fully preserved.   Throughout the length of this charming thoroughfare, which is on the crest of a hill, there is a wide-sweeping view of the Hudson River and the Jer-sey shore as far north as the Palisades.   On the east line of the Park is Riverside Drive, upon which are built elegant private residences, facing the west ; and this section is becoming one of the favorite places of residence of New-York millionaires, whom the encroachment of trade is driving out of the other districts.   To the west a substantial granite wall borders the Drive, and below this, sloping to the river's edge, is an uneven tract of land as yet unimproved, and abounding in fine old trees. A plan will probably be carried out to fill in the river to the outside pier line for the entire length of the Riverside Park, and raise an embankment above the present level of the New-York Central & Hudson-River Railroad, bridges across the tracks

SCENES AND ORNAMENTAL STRUCTURES.
IN CENTRAL PARK.

STATUES, BUSTS AND ORNAMENTS.
IN CENTRAL PARK.

STATUES AND ORNAMENTAL WORK,
IN CENTRAL PARK.

connecting the embankment with the hillside.   This arrangement would give the
city a water-front park unequalled for beauty elsewhere in the world.   At the northern end of Riverside Park is the tomb of General U. S. Grant.

Morningside Park is a strip of land about 600 feet wide and more than half a
mile long, with an area of 32 acres, extending north and south upon the eastern slope
of Bloomingdale Heights, north of 110th Street and west of Eighth Avenue.   It
overlooks Central Park and Harlem, and commands a view of Washington Heights
and the country to the north and east.   The land at the foot of the hill has been
laid out in a handsome landscape design, and against the face of the cliff has been
constructed a heavy granite wall with projecting bastions and broad stairways leading up to the parapetted promenade on the top.

Madison Square, bounded by Fifth Avenue, Broadway, Madison Avenue, 23d
Street and 26th Street, is the chief popular resort of the central districts.   It covers
nearly seven acres, and in summer is charming with shade-trees and beds of flowers.
The Seward and the Farragut statues are inside the park, and the Worth Monument is at the northern corner.   Here are ornamental and drinking fountains, and

MENAGERIE IN CENTRAL PARK.

in the season beds of beautiful water-lilies.   The Square is much frequented by
prettily dressed children with their nurses, and withal is thoroughly delightful.

Union Square, at Broadway, 14th Street, 17th Street, and Fourth Avenue is 3½
acres in extent.   Here are the Lafayette, the equestrian Washington and the Lincoln
statues, a pretty fountain in the centre, a large drinking fountain surmounted by the
figures of a woman and two children, a small and artistic drinking fountain designed
by Olin T. Warner, a paved plaza on the north bordered by a row of colored gas-
lamps, an ornamental structure and a cottage with a reviewing balcony.   The plaza
is a favored place for large outdoor mass-meetings.

Washington Square has a character peculiar to itself. It is at the lower end of Fifth Avenue, an open space of about nine acres, once the Potter's Field. New-York society, driven successively out of Bowling Green, Bond Street, Bleecker Street and elsewhere down-town, has made a sturdy stand for two generations in Washington Square. The north side is lined by old-fashioned red-brick houses, with white-marble trimmings, in which dwell the Coopers, the Rhinelanders, and other aristocratic families. On the east side is the imposing white-stone castellated structure of the University of the City of New York, hallowed by many associations. The dormitory of this building has for a generation at least been the bachelor home of artists and men of letters, and many a recluse has buried himself from the world in its quiet

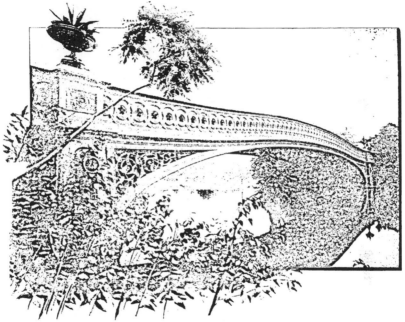

BOW BRIDGE, IN CENTRAL PARK.

precincts. In the next block is the Asbury Methodist Episcopal Church, and the modern Benedict Chambers, principally occupied by artists. On the south side of the Square small shops catering to the neighboring tenement population, have crept in to a considerable extent. Some of the old historic houses remain, and several apartment-buildings. The feature of that side of the Square, however, is the Judson Memorial Baptist Church. On the west side are fine private residences and apartment-hotels. The principal ornament of the Square is the white-marble Washington Memorial Arch, where Fifth Avenue begins. There is a fountain, a statue of Garibaldi, a bust of Alexander-L. Holley, beds of flowers, shade-trees, and hundreds of seats that are generally occupied by poor people from neighboring tenements.

STATUES AND BUSTS.
IN CENTRAL PARK.

THE CAVE, LAKE, OLD FORT, AND ORNAMENTAL STRUCTURES.
IN CENTRAL PARK.

City-Hall Park has been shorn of much of its original dimensions. A century and more ago it was "The Open Field" outside the city limits, and great mass-meetings were held there. Once it was the only park in the city, and the land now

occupied by the Post-Office Building was within its limits twenty-five years ago. The City Hall, the County Court-House, the ancient Hall of Records, and a fire engine-house take up much of the open space of the Park, which has about eight acres. There are two fountains, plenty of shade, and many flower-beds. The asphalt-paved plaza in front of the City Hall is the favorite resort of the fun-loving boot-blacks and newsboys of the neighborhood.

Bryant Park consists of five acres, between Fifth and Sixth Avenues, and 40th and 42d Streets, on the site once occupied by the famous Crystal Palace, which was burned in 1858. On the Fifth-Avenue side is the old Reservoir, from which until 1884 it was

GARIBALDI STATUE, IN WASHINGTON SQUARE.

called Reservoir Park. It preserves the memory of William Cullen Bryant merely in the name, its only statue being a bust of Washington Irving.

East-River Park is on the bluff overlooking the East River, at the foot of 86th Street. Although of limited area, it is very airy, and commands a fine view of the river far up toward Long-Island Sound. It has been fitted up particularly for the comfort of the babies and young children and their mothers, from the adjacent tenements.

High-Bridge Park is the name given to the 23 acres that surround the Reservoir and buildings of the city water-works at the Harlem River and 170th Street.

Manhattan Square, covering about 15 acres, at Central Park West and 77th and 81st Streets, is an annex to Central Park. It is the site of the Museum of Natural History, but the grounds have not been fully laid out nor cared for.

Mount-Morris Park, along Fifth Avenue, from 120th to 124th Street, in Harlem, is over a score of acres in extent. It contains a rocky and well-wooded hill, surrounded with pretty stretches of level land. There is a plaza on top of the hill from which an extensive view is obtained ; and shaded paths, and other natural and artificial adornments make this one of the handsomest of the city's smaller breathing places.

Gramercy Park is a private enclosure of 1½ acres, between 20th and 21st Streets and Third and Fourth Avenues. It is a part of the old Gramercy farm. Looking out upon it are the homes of David Dudley Field, the late Cyrus W. Field, John Bigelow, Hamilton Fish, ex-Mayor Abram S. Hewitt, and other well-known wealthy New-Yorkers. There, too, was the home of the late Samuel J. Tilden ; and next to it is the Players' Club, that Edwin Booth established. In the Gramercy-Park Hotel reside several eminent theatrical and musical artists.

Stuyvesant Square, four acres in extent, on Second Avenue, between 15th and 17th Streets, is a part of the old Stuyvesant farm. Private residences surround it ;

and on the west side rise St. George's Episcopal Church and the Friends' Meeting-House and Seminary. On the east side is the New-York Infirmary for Women and Children. It is an aristocratic neighborhood, but the Square is mostly used by the East-Side tenement dwellers.

Mulberry-Bend Park is a projected new small park between the Bowery, Park Row, Canal, Pearl and Elm Streets. The commission to acquire the property was appointed in 1888, and in 1892 completed its work. The cost of acquiring the property has been about $2,000,000.

The New Park System above the Harlem River has been planned upon magnificent proportions. The lands were selected by a commission, in 1884; and were acquired by the city at a cost of about $9,000,000. There is a fraction over 3,945 acres in the territory, which includes six parks and three parkways. Up to the present time these breathing-places have been left in an absolute state of nature and it is not proposed ever to "improve" them artificially. They are somewhat removed from the popular sections of the city, and mostly frequented by picnic and excursion parties in summer, and skating parties in winter.

Pelham-Bay Park is in Westchester County, outside the city limits. It contains 1,756 acres on the shore of Long-Island Sound, Hunter's Island and Twin Island being included within its limits. The land belonged to the Pell family two centuries ago, and the old manor-house is still standing. Here Ann Hutchinson, fleeing from Puritan persecutions in New England, settled, and was murdered by the Indians. In the Revolution much fighting occurred over all this ground. The Park has a very picturesque shore-line, nearly ten miles long.

Van-Cortlandt Park contains 1,132 acres, and is part of the property once owned by the Van-Cortlandt family. The old family mansion is still preserved, a quaint Dutch building of stone, with terraced lawns commanding views of the Palisades and the Hudson River. There Washington had his headquarters while carrying on operations for the expulsion of the British from New-York City. "Vault Hill" on this property was the burial-place of the Van-Cortlandt family; and "Indian Field" was an aboriginal place of interment, as many graves indicate. There is a large lake, covering sixty acres; and a parade-ground for the city regiments of the National Guard has been laid out, on a level meadow of 120 acres.

ALEXANDER L. HOLLEY BUST, IN WASHINGTON SQUARE.

Bronx Park contains 661 acres, lying on both sides of the Bronx River, a shallow and narrow stream whose picturesqueness has made it a favorite with New-York artists. It is proposed to establish here a botanical garden, like that at Kew.

Crotona Park, 135 acres, lies between Tremont and West Farms, and contains the Bathgate Woods. It commands views of the Palisades and the Brooklyn Bridge.

St.-Mary's Park occupies 25 acres, part of the old Gouverneur-Morris estate, near Morrisania.   It is a pleasant undulating region, with views of river and Sound.

Claremont Park, of 38 acres, is between Inwood and Tremont, beyond the Harlem River.   It is a triangular valley, rich in vegetation.

The Parkways which connect these parks will be handsome roads 600 feet wide. Between Pelham Park and Bronx Park is the Bronx and Pelham Parkway ; between Crotona Park and Bronx Park, the Crotona Parkway ; and between Bronx Park and Van-Cortlandt Park, the Mosholu Parkway.

WASHINGTON IRVING BUST, IN BRYANT PARK.

Other Parks are simply small open places with walks, flowers, shrubbery and seats, and generally less than half an acre in extent.   These are the principal places of the kind : Abingdon, Beach-Street, Boulevard (2), Canal - Street, Christopher - Street, Cooper-Institute, Duane-Street, Five-Points (called Paradise Park), Grand-Street, Jackson, Sixth-Avenue, Cedar, Jeannette, Boston-Road (2), Fulton-Avenue (2), and Tompkins (with 10½ acres).

A new park is to be laid out on the eastern slope of Washington Heights, overlooking the Harlem River, from 155th Street to the bluff at Fort George, a distance of over two miles.

Statues, Busts and Sculpture adorn the parks and public places. There are in the city about fifty portrait-statues and busts and ideal works of sculpture, almost half of which are in Central Park.   Several are very admirable works of art, and on the whole the collection will compare favorably with that in any other American city.

The Washington Memorial Arch had its inception in the celebration in 1889 of the Centennial anniversary of the inauguration of Washington as first President of the United States.   The temporary arch which was part of the street decoration of the occasion spanned Fifth Avenue on the north side of Waverly Place.   The structure, which was designed by Stanford White, the architect, was so generally admired that arrangements were perfected to perpetuate it in white marble.   Now it stands in Washington Square, facing the lower end of Fifth Avenue, fifty feet south of Waverly Place, and spanning the main drive of the Square.   The Arch is the finest structure of its class in this country.   Each of the square piers is 64 feet around, and they are 30 feet apart ; from the ground to the centre of the arch space is 47 feet.   With the frieze, the attic and the coping the structure is 77 feet high. The frieze is carved with a design showing 13 large stars, 42 small stars, and the initial "W" regularly repeated.   American eagles are carved on the two keystones ; in the panels of the piers are bas-relief emblems of war and peace ; and in the spandrils of the arch figures of Victory.   The roof of the arch is ornamented with carved

WASHINGTON MEMORIAL ARCH.

WASHINGTON SQUARE, BEGINNING OF FIFTH AVENUE. JUDSON MEMORIAL CHURCH SHOWS THROUGH THE ARCH.

rosettes in panels.   At the base of the piers are two simple pedestals, on which will be placed symbolical groups of figures.   On the north panel of the attic is this inscription, from Washington's inaugural address: "Let us Raise a Standard to which the Wise and the Honest can repair.   The Event is in the Hands of God."   On the opposite panel is this dedication: "To Commemorate the one-hundredth anniversary of the inauguration of George Washington as the First President of the United States."   Below the frieze and above the centre of the arch are carved the words: "Erected by the People of the City of New York."   The cost of the structure was $128,000, and the amount was raised by popular subscription.   The corner-stone of the arch was laid May 30, 1889; and the main work was completed in April, 1892.

Garibaldi, in bronze, by G. Turini, is in Washington Square.   It was presented to the city by Italians of the United States, and erected in 1888.

Alexander L. Holley is commemorated by a heroic bronze bust, placed upon a simple square column, upon which an inscription states that the memorial was

BRYANT PARK -- SIXTH AVENUE, 41ST TO 42D STREETS.

erected by mechanical engineers of two continents.   The bust is the work of J. Q. A. Ward, and is in Washington Square, where it was unveiled in 1890.

Washington Statues in the city are three in number.   An important one is the colossal bronze statue by J. Q. A. Ward, at the entrance of the Sub-Treasury building in Wall Street, which is on the site of Federal Hall, where Washington took the oath of office as first President of the United States, April 30, 1789.   On the pedestal is the stone upon which Washington stood when he took the oath.   The statue was unveiled November 26, 1883.

Another statue of Washington in the city is a copy of the Houdon statue in the Capitol at Richmond, Virginia, reduced in size.   It stands in Riverside Park, near 88th Street; and was a gift to the city from the children of the public schools.

The Equestrian Washington, the most satisfactory of the Washington statues, is in Union Square.   It is the work of Henry K. Browne.   It is of heroic size, and an excellent piece of sculpture.

Liberty Enlightening the World is probably the best-known statue in the United States.   It stands in New-York Bay, on Bedloe's Island, formerly the place of execution of pirates ; and is one of the most conspicuous objects in view, either from the surrounding shores or from the decks of ocean vessels bound through the Narrows.   It is admired for its magnificent proportions, and by general consent it is admitted to be one of the world's greatest colossi and the largest made in modern times.   The draped female figure, of *repoussé* copper, 151 feet high, is crowned with a diadem, and holds lifted high in the right hand a torch that is lighted by electricity at night.   The left hand clasps close to the body a tablet bearing the inscription "July 4, 1776."   Some of the dimensions of the figure are interesting ; the nose is nearly four feet long, the right fore-finger eight feet long and five feet in circumference; and the head fourteen feet high.   The statue weighs 25 tons ; and the cost (over $200,000) was defrayed by popular subscription in France.   The sculptor Bartholdi, who made the Lafayette statue in Union Square, conceived the idea, and modelled the figure (it is said) from his mother.   The pedestal upon which the statue stands is 155 feet high, a square structure of concrete and granite.   It

MOUNT MORRIS PARK, FIFTH AVENUE, 120TH TO 124TH STREETS.

was designed by Richard M. Hunt, the architect, and erected under the supervision of General Charles P. Stone, engineer.   It cost $250,000, and was paid for by a popular subscription in the United States, the greater part of which was raised by the efforts of *The World.*   Surrounding the island is a sea-wall, and the statue stands on an elevation in the centre of an enclosed space made by the double walls of old Fort Wood.   The statue was unveiled in October, 1886.

Benjamin Franklin, of heroic size, in bronze, keeps watch over the newspapers from his pedestal in Printing-House Square.   The statue was designed by E. Plassman, and was given to the city by Captain Benjamin De Groot, an old New-Yorker. It was unveiled in 1872.

Horace Greeley, in heroic bronze, faces Franklin, seated on an arm-chair on a pedestal at one of the doorways of the Tribune Building, corner of Nassau and Spruce Streets.   The statue was dedicated in 1890, and was paid for principally by the *Tribune* owners.   It is one of the best statues in the city, and is the work of John Q. A. Ward.

WASHINGTON STATUE, ON WALL STREET.

Samuel S. Cox, when a Congressman, be-friended the letter-carriers in National legislation, and they remembered him in a statue that stands in Astor Place, and was dedicated in 1891. It is the work of Miss Louisa Lawson.

William E. Dodge, a bronze by J. Q. A. Ward, was paid for by merchant friends, and erected in 1885 at the junction of Broadway, Sixth Avenue and 35th Street.

Washington Irving's bust, presented to the city in 1866 by Joseph Weiner, is on a pedestal in Bryant Park.

Lafayette, an animated figure, done in bronze, by Bartholdi, stands in Union Square. It was erected in 1876 by French residents of New York, and bears two inscriptions upon its pedestal: "To The City of New York, France, in remembrance of sympathy in time of trial, 1870-71;" and "As soon as I heard of American Independence my heart was enlisted, 1776."

Lincoln is commemorated in a bronze statue which stands as a complement to the equestrian Washington, in Union Square. This fine work of Henry K. Browne was paid for by a popular subscription, and erected in 1868. The martyr President stands in the attitude of addressing an audience, and the angularity and ungracefulness of his figure are expressed with painful exactitude. A low curb of granite surrounds the pedestal, and on this are inscribed Lincoln's famous Gettysburg words, "With Malice Toward None, With Charity For All."

The William H. Seward Statue in Madison Square is from a design by Randolph Rogers. The Secretary of State is represented seated in a chair, beneath which are piles of books, and upon the pedestal is the inscription: "Governor, U.-S. Senator, Secretary of State, U. S." The statue was unveiled in 1876.

The Admiral Farragut Statue in Madison Square is by general consent one of the finest examples of contemporaneous American art in sculpture. It is the work of Augustus St. Gaudens, and a present to the city from the Farragut Memorial Association. The brave admiral is represented as standing on the deck of his vessel, with field glasses in hand, and coat blowing in the breeze. The curving pedestal is decorated with bas-relief female figures, ocean waves, and appropriate bits of marine design.

General Worth is commemorated by a granite obelisk, in the triangle formed by Broadway, Fifth Avenue and 26th Street (Madison Square). On the south face of the plinth is a bronze bas-relief of General Worth on horseback. The east face has the motto, "Ducit Amor Patriæ;" the west face the motto, "Honor to the Brave;" and on the north side is the name and the dates and places of his birth and death. Raised bands are placed at regular

FRANKLIN STATUE, IN PRINTING-HOUSE SQUARE.

LIBERTY ENLIGHTENING THE WORLD.
STATUE, BY BARTHOLDI, ON BEDLOE'S ISLAND, NEW-YORK HARBOR.

GREELEY STATUE, IN PRINTING-HOUSE SQUARE.

intervals about the shaft, and upon these are carved the names of battles with which General Worth's fame was identified. The plot of land on which the monument stands is surrounded by an iron fence ornamented by appropriate military designs, and the shaft also has upon it a bronze coat-of-arms of New-York State and a group of military insignia. The monument was erected by the city in 1857.

Commodore Cornelius Vanderbilt, in bas-relief, is on the façade of the Hudson-Street freight-depot of the New-York Central & Hudson-River Railroad.

Governor Peter Stuyvesant, with his wooden leg most conspicuous, is a wooden statue in front of the Stuyvesant Insurance Company's office, 165 Broadway.

Gutenberg, the father of modern printing, and **Franklin,** America's eminent printer, both modelled by Plassman, adorn the façade of the *Staats-Zeitung* Building, looking out upon Printing-House Square.

Beethoven, in Central Park, is commemorated by a colossal bronze bust on a granite pedestal near the Music Pavilion of the Mall. It is the work of the German sculptor Baerer, and was erected in 1884 by the Männerchor German singing society.

Robert Burns is also on the Mall, in Central Park, a bronze seated figure on a rock, modelled by John Steele, of Edinburgh, and presented to the city in 1880 by Scottish citizens.

Sir Walter Scott, in Central Park, also of bronze, of heroic size, the work of Steele, and a present from resident Scotchmen, is seated opposite the Burns statue, on an Aberdeen-granite pedestal. It was unveiled in 1872.

Fitz-Greene Halleck, in Central Park, of bronze, the work of Wilson MacDonald, is on the Mall. It shows the poet seated in a chair, with note-book and pen in hand. It was erected in 1877.

The Shakespeare Statue, by J. Q. A. Ward, is a standing figure in

COX STATUE, IN ASTOR PLACE.

bronze, at the southern entrance to the Mall, in Central Park. It was unveiled, May 23, 1872, on the 300th anniversary of the great dramatist's birth.

The Indian Hunter, by J. Q. A. Ward, a life-size ideal figure of an Indian, bow and arrow in hand, bending eagerly forward and holding his dog in leash, is just west of the Mall, in Central Park, and is a very spirited and admirable group.

· **The Eagles and Goat** in Central Park is an interesting bronze by the French sculptor Fratin, presented to the city in 1863 by a wealthy resident, Gurdon W. Burnham.

The Bethesda Fountain, the most ambitious work of sculpture in Central Park, stands

DODGE STATUE, AT BROADWAY AND SIXTH AVENUE.

on the Esplanade at the foot of the Terrace, on the shore of the Lake. The design, by Miss Emma Stebbins, the New-York sculptor, represents the angel blessing

JAMES FOUNTAIN, IN UNION SQUARE.

the waters of the Pool of Bethesda. The figure of the winged angel is poised easily upon a mass of rocks from which the water gushes, falling over the edge of the upper basin, which is supported by four figures symbolizing Temperance, Purity, Health and Peace. In her left hand the angel holds a bunch of lilies, flowers of purity, and over her bosom are the cross-bands of the messenger. The basin of the fountain contains lotus, papyrus, Indian water-lilies, and other rare water-plants.

General Simon Bolivar, the Liberator of South America, is represented by an equestrian statue that stands on the west side of Central Park, near 81st Street. It is a replica of the Bolivar statue by R. De La Cora, in Caracas, Venezuela ; and was a present from the South-American Republic to the City of New York in 1884.

WASHINGTON EQUESTRIAN MONUMENT, IN UNION SQUARE.

Daniel Webster is an heroic bronze statue on the West Drive in Central Park, made by Thomas Ball, at a cost of $65,000. Gurdon W. Burnham presented it.

Mazzini, a bronze bust, is on the West Drive of Central Park. It is of heroic size, upon a high pedestal. Turini, the Italian sculptor, made it, and Italian residents of New York, admirers of the great Italian agitator, presented it to the city in 1878.

The Seventh-Regiment Monument is on the West Drive of Central Park, not far from the Webster statue. It represents a citizen soldier at parade rest, leaning on his musket. It was modelled by J. Q. A. Ward, and was erected in 1874, to commemorate the patriotism of those members of the Seventh New-York Regiment who fell in battle during the civil war.

The Falconer, an ideal bronze figure, modelled by George Simonds, stands on a bluff in Central Park. George Kemp presented it to the city in 1872.

Commerce, an allegorical female figure in bronze, of heroic size, is the work of the French sculptor Bosquet. It is in Central Park, near the entrance at Eighth Avenue and 59th Street, and was erected in 1866, a gift from Stephen B. Guion.

Alexander Hamilton, a granite statue in Central Park, stands near the Museum of Art. Ch. Conradts, the sculptor, designed it for the son of Hamilton, John C. Hamilton, who presented it to the city in 1880.

Prof. S. F. B. Morse is honored with a bronze statue, of life-size, modelled by Byron M. Pickett, and erected in 1871 by the Telegraph Operators' Association. It is in Central Park, near the 72d-Street entrance, on Fifth Avenue. Prof. Morse was present at the dedication.

The Pilgrim, an heroic bronze statue on the Grand Drive, in Central Park, was a gift from the New-England Society of New York, in 1885. It is a picturesque and noble statue, by J. Q. A. Ward, to commemorate the landing of the Pilgrims on Plymouth Rock. It represents a strong-faced, alert, and resolute hero, in the quaint English costume of 1620.

The Alexander Von Humboldt bronze bust in Central Park was a gift from the German residents of the city, in 1869. It was designed by Prof. Gustave Blaeser, of Berlin; and stands near Fifth Avenue and 59th Street.

The Thomas Moore bust near the southeastern corner of Central Park, was modelled by Dennis B. Sheehan, and put in place by the Moore memorial committee, in 1880.

LAFAYETTE STATUE, IN UNION SQUARE.

Schiller, the German poet, is remembered in a bronze bust by C. L. Richter, that is set up on a sandstone pedestal in the Ramble, in Central Park. It was the first piece of sculpture to be erected in the Park ; and was presented by German residents, in 1859, less than three years after the Park was begun.

The Still Hunt, in Central Park, by Edward Kemeys, represents a crouching American panther preparing to leap upon its prey. It is on a high ledge near the Obelisk.

The Tigress and Young, a fine bronze group, came from the hand of the French sculptor, Auguste Cain. It stands west of the Terrace in Central Park, and was a gift in 1867 of twelve New-Yorkers.

The Egyptian Obelisk, in Central Park, is one of the most interesting historical relics in the metropolis. It was presented to the city, through the Department of State, in 1877, by the Khedive of Egypt, Ismail Pasha. It was transported to this country under the direction of

LINCOLN STATUE, IN UNION SQUARE.

Lieut.-Com. H. H. Gorringe, U. S. N., at the expense of William H. Vanderbilt. The monolith is of granite, 69 feet high, and weighs 220 tons. It is the sixth in size of the famous obelisks of Egypt, and was erected in the Temple of the Sun, at Heliopolis, 3,500 years ago, by King Thothmes III. The hieroglyphic inscriptions upon it relate the titles of Thothmes, and his illustrious descendant, King Rameses II., who lived 200 years after Thothmes. Until the reign of Tiberius it stood in

SEWARD STATUE, IN MADISON SQUARE.

the Temple of the Sun, and then it was removed to Alexandria, where it remained until it crossed the water to the New World. The obelisk was old in the days of the Roman Empire; antedates the Christian Era by fifteen centuries; looked down upon the land of Egypt before the siege of Troy; and was familiar to Moses and the Israelites in bondage. It now stands on a knoll near the Museum of Art, an impressive reminder of a far-away past. The severities of the American climate may cause the gradual obliteration of the venerable inscriptions on the obelisk, and great care has been taken to protect these annals of the past by covering them with paraffine and other protective materials. Another obelisk, of similar size, stood with this before the Temple of the Sun, and now adorns the Queen-Victoria Embankment, along the Thames, in London. Both were of the rose-red granite of Nubia.

COLUMBUS STATUE, 59TH STREET, BROADWAY AND EIGHTH AVENUE.

The James Fountain, in Union Square, was designed by Adolf Donndorf, of Stuttgart, and dedicated in 1881. It was a gift to the city from D. Willis James. The ornate base, of Swedish granite, supports a beautiful group of a benignant mother and two children, cast in bronze, at Brunswick, Germany.

The Christopher Columbus Monument stands on the Circle, where Eighth Avenue, Broadway, the Boulevard and West 59th Street meet, at the southwestern corner of Central Park. It is a tall column, ornamented with bronze reliefs, anchors, and ships' prows, and crowned with a statue of the great discoverer. One inscription attributes its erection: "By the initiative of *Il Progresso Italo-Americano*, the first Italian daily newspaper in the United States, Cav. Carlo Barsotti, editor and proprietor." . . . . Another inscription reads thus: "To Christopher Columbus, the Italians resident in America.

Scoffed at before, during the voyage menaced, after it chained, as generous as oppressed, to the world he gave a world. Joy and glory never uttered a more thrilling call than that which resounded from the conquered ocean, at sight of the first American island. 'Land! Land!' On the 12th of October, 1892, the fourth centenary of the discovery of America, in imperishable remembrance."

FARRAGUT STATUE, IN MADISON SQUARE.

The John Ericsson Statue, commemorating the illustrious Swedish-
American, whose discoveries in naval
science were of vast importance, was
unveiled April 26, 1893, in the presence
of the international fleet and of many
Swedish gymnastic, singing and social
societies, and military companies. It
was designed by J. S. Hartley, and cast
in bronze by the Gorham Manufacturing
Company ; and stands on a pedestal of
polished Quincy granite, bearing four
historical panels in relief. The statue is
on the Battery, near the Barge Office,
and facing toward Jersey City. It was
erected by an appropriation from the
City of New York. On the base is this
inscription : "John Ericsson. The City
of New York erects this monument to
the memory of a citizen whose genius has
contributed to the greatness of the Republic and to the progress of the world."

ERICSSON STATUE, NEAR BARGE OFFICE, IN BATTERY PARK.

Judge John Watts, Recorder of
the city during the British occupation,
and one of the most sagacious and influential citizens of the older New York, is
commemorated by a noble bronze statue in Trinity Churchyard. It was modelled
by George W. Bissell, and erected by Gen. John Watts de Peyster. The unveiling
took place in 1892. The calm statue looks down on the wild whirl of Broadway.

WORTH MONUMENT, IN MADISON SQUARE.

Archbishop Hughes
stands in bronze, of heroic
size, in the grounds in front
of St. John's College, Fordham. The prelate is represented clad in a silken robe,
addressing an audience.
The statue, which is the
work of W. R. O'Donovan,
is placed on a granite pedestal. It was unveiled in 1891.
Hughes was a poor Irish
immigrant gardener, who
bravely fought his way
through college, and was
made priest in 1825, bishop
in 1838, and archbishop of
New York in 1850. He was
a patriot during the Secession War ; and in 1841
founded the now flourishing
St. John's College.

ARCHBISHOP JOHN HUGHES STATUE, ST. JOHN'S
COLLEGE, FORDHAM.

Regina Sodalium is a statue of the Virgin Mary, at St. John's College, Fordham, erected in 1887, by the students.

Other statues that are contemplated are the equestrian General W. T. Sherman, by Augustus St. Gaudens, to be placed at the Boulevard and West 72d Street; the Nathan Hale, by MacMonnies, to be erected in the City-Hall Park, by the Sons of the Revolution; the Horace Greeley, a gift from the printers of the United States, to be set up at Broadway, Sixth Avenue and 32d Street; the Columbus-Pinzon monument, with gigantic statues, to be erected in Central Park by Spanish residents of the city; J. Q. A. Ward's statue of Roscoe Conkling; and many others, commemorating distinguished citizens, and others.

New York has made a good beginning in adorning her public places with these memorials of the great men of the world. There are many more to be thus honored, among her own sons, as William Cullen Bryant the poet; Robert Fulton, the father of steam navigation; Valentine Mott, the foremost physician of his time; John Jay, the illustrious jurist, and scores of others. Thanks to Ward and St. Gaudens, the statuary work in New York is more worthy and artistic than that of any other American city, and includes some of the choicest memorial work of the present century. The cosmopolitan character of the city is thus illustrated, for the statues include New-Englanders, Virginians and Westerners, Scots, Englishmen and Irishmen, Frenchmen and Italians, Germans and Swedes, Spaniards and Dutchmen, West-Indians and South-Americans, Syrians and Egyptians.

New York is too great in spirit and in appreciation to be confined by provincial preferences. It honors valor, genius, honor, wherever found. Imperial Rome was hospitable to the gods of the world; joyous Paris has welcomed the fine arts to her studios and boulevards; and imperial and joyous New York craves and honors noble men and their memories and achievements.

REGINA SODALIUM STATUE, ST. JOHN'S
COLLEGE, FORDHAM.

Bridges, Tunnels, Sewers, Water, Aqueducts, Reservoirs, Lighting by Gas and Electricity, Telegraphs, Telephones, Etc.

THE exigencies of life in modern municipalities compel the utilization of space overhead and underground; so closely are the people crowded and restricted for room. In New York, the East River and the Harlem River are bridged to allow of quick egress to the surrounding country; and projects are in hand for more bridges and several tunnels across and under the East and North Rivers, and beneath the Narrows from Staten Island to Long Island. Electric-light, telephone and telegraph wires are still suspended from buildings and poles, although many miles of them have already gone into the subways, where it is proposed that all shall follow in due course of time. Beneath the principal streets there is a network of pipes of all descriptions; sewers, water-mains, pneumatic tubes, gas-mains, steam-heating pipes, subways for wires, and, in Broadway, Third Avenue, Tenth Avenue and 125th Street conduits for street-car cables. Beneath sidewalks the abutting property-owners build vaults and sub-cellars, thereby adding valuable room to the establishments above ground. Were it not for all these conveniences overhead and underground, the normal activity of the metropolis would find itself hampered to a serious extent.

The Bridges, aside from the ornamental structures in the parks, comprise fourteen which belong in whole or in part to New York. One is across the East River; and others span the Harlem, connecting Manhattan Island with the mainland.

The East-River Bridge, more popularly known as the Brooklyn Bridge, was erected to meet the pressing necessity for a better means of communication between New York and Brooklyn than was offered by the ferry-boats. In this generation Brooklyn has become essentially a part of the great metropolis in the intimacy of its business and social relations. To a remarkable degree the population of the Long-Island city is made up of those who are employed or who do business on Manhattan Island, and are thus compelled to make the trip twice a day across the East River. It was inconceivable that these two communities would be willing always to remain dependent upon ferriage, which is at times slow and inadequate. As far back as 1819 a civil engineer named Pope published a scientific paper in which he advocated a suspension-bridge across the East River. The same idea was taken up in 1829, when a private corporation was organized, and elaborated plans for a bridge from Brooklyn Heights to Maiden Lane, at an estimated cost of $600,000. In 1849 public agitation of the matter was revived, and the daily newspapers urged that the work be undertaken. John A. Roebling, the successful engineer, had long entertained the idea; and in 1860 at the suggestion of W. C. Kingsley, a wealthy contractor, he publicly outlined his plan. It was not, however, until after the civil war, which had accustomed the public to big undertakings and lavish expenditures, that the scheme was definitely developed.   There were several rival projects ; but Roebling, who had just finished the Cincinnati Suspension-Bridge across the Ohio River, was taken into consultation with Kingsley, Henry C. Murphy and others, and his plans were adopted.   A private company was chartered in which were Roebling, Kingsley, Murphy, John T. Hoffman, S. B. Chittenden, John Roach, Henry E. Pierrepont and others.   This concern was known as the New-York Bridge Company, and work was at once entered upon.   Roebling was chosen Chief Engineer in 1867, and his son, Washington A. Roebling, Assistant Engineer.   The elder Roebling drew the original plans and specifications ; but he died suddenly in 1869, while engaged in the preliminary surveys, before the actual work of construction had begun.

BROOKLYN BRIDGE PROMENADE -- LOOKING TOWARD NEW-YORK.

The son took his father's place ; and, beginning in January, 1870, carried the enterprise through to a successful conclusion, after thirteen years of difficult work. Through exposure and overwork he broke down in health and became an invalid. For ten years, confined to his house on Columbia Heights, Brooklyn, he, with the assistance of his wife, directed the work to the end.   From the window of his sick room he watched the progress of construction through a telescope, day by day, hour by hour, supervising as thoroughly and as efficiently as though he had been on the spot.   It was a wonderful display of indomitable will power and of mechanical genius.   But it was rough sailing sometimes.   In 1874 the Legislature took the enterprise out of the hands of the private corporation that had initiated it, and empowered the twin cities to go ahead with the project, Brooklyn to pay two-thirds and New York one-third of the cost, the control of the bridge during its construc-

EAST RIVER, OR NEW-YORK AND BROOKLYN, BRIDGE.

ACROSS THE EAST RIVER FROM NEW YORK TO BROOKLYN.

tion and afterwards to remain in the same relative proportions in the hands of the authorities of the sister municipalities.   Many unforeseen delays arose, of political as well as of mechanical character.   New problems in engineering had to be met ; experiments made ; and new devices and working machinery invented.   For a time there was much public distrust of the management, which on the New-York side was in the hands of the notorious Tweed ring, and once the work was entirely stopped.   But the municipal plunderers were overthrown before they had succeeded in getting their fingers into the bridge treasury ; the seemingly well-nigh insuperable mechanical difficulties were overcome ; and the bridge was finally completed and opened to general traffic, in May, 1884.   There was a grand military procession, President Arthur and his Cabinet, and Governor Cleveland and his staff, being present. There were speeches by William C. Kingsley, Hon. Abram S. Hewitt, and Rev. Dr. Richard S. Storrs ; the bridge was illuminated, and fireworks were displayed; and the creator of the work, Col. Roebling, watched the proceedings through the faithful telescope at his house, where later in the day the distinguished people who had participated in the celebration went to congratulate him.   The estimate for the construction of the bridge was $8,000,000 ; but owing principally to the amplification of the original plans it cost when completed about $15,000,000.

Statistics of the bridge will be interesting even to the unprofessional reader, for the structure is one of the highest achievements of modern engineering, and ranks as one of the great wonders of the world.   There is a central span across the river 1,595 feet long and 135 feet above high-water mark.   At each end this span springs from a tower, resting upon a caisson.   These foundations are of solid concrete, resting upon rock, 78 feet below the water-level on the New-York side and 45 feet on the Brooklyn side of the river.   The Brooklyn caisson is 168 x 102 feet, and the New-York caisson 172 x 102 feet ; and each caisson contains over 5,000 cubic yards of timber and iron, and over 5,000 cubic feet of concrete, the weight of the caisson being about 7,000 tons, and of the concrete filling 8,000 tons.   At the water-line the towers are 140 x 50 feet, and of solid masonry in the lower part, being hollow the rest of the way up to the bases of the great arches.   The arches, of which there are two in each tower, are 117 feet high, and the capstones are 271 feet above the water.   Travel passes through these arches, the floor of the bridge being across the towers at the bases of the arches.   At their summits the towers are narrowed to 120 x 40 feet.   In the New-York tower are 46,395 cubic yards of masonry, and in the Brooklyn, 38,214 cubic yards.   Behind each tower are the anchorages, 930 feet distant.   They are massive granite structures, each 129 x 119 feet at base, 117 x 104 feet at top, 89 feet high in front and 85 feet in rear.   On each anchorage is an arrangement of iron bars to which the cables are fastened, and an anchor-plate weighing 23 tons.   The four cables upon which the bridge is suspended are bound to the anchor-chains, then pass through 25 feet of masonry, and come out of the walls of the anchorages on the water side, about 80 feet above high-water mark. They are then carried over the tops of the towers and in the middle of the river-span they drop to the level of the roadway, 135 feet above the water.   From these cables hang at regular intervals smaller steel cables that are braced and tied together and that hold the floor beams upon which the bridge proper is laid.   The four large cables are each made of 5,434 galvanized steel oil-coated wires, which are not twisted, but which, lying parallel, are pressed compactly together and then bound tightly with other wires, the whole making a solid cable $15\frac{3}{4}$ inches in diameter. Each cable thus finished is $3,578\frac{1}{2}$ feet long, and has a supporting power of 12,200 tons in the middle of its sag.   The cables were made where they are, and this part

THE WASHINGTON BRIDGE, ACROSS THE HARLEM RIVER.
FROM 181ST STREET AND TENTH AVENUE TO AQUEDUCT AVENUE.

of the work was not begun until June, 1877. Steel wire ropes were stretched between the tops of the towers, and from these were suspended movable platforms for
the workmen. The steel wires were drawn across in place and then bound into a
cable as they hung in mid-air. Between the towers and the anchorages the spans
are also suspended from these cables at a height of from 68 to 119 feet above the
street levels. The New-York approach from the terminus to the anchorage is 1,562

APPROACH TO THE WASHINGTON BRIDGE.

feet in length; and the Brooklyn approach, 971 feet. Heavy-arches of masonry
support these approaches, and the streets are crossed by steel truss-bridges. The
space under these archways is utilized for storage and other business purposes.

The total length of the bridge is 1¼ miles; the width is 85 feet. In New York
the terminus is in Park Row, facing the City-Hall Park, and in Brooklyn at Fulton
and Sands Streets, the terminus of nearly all the elevated and surface railway-lines
in that city. There is an elevated promenade in the middle of the bridge, and seats
are placed at the towers for those who wish to rest and enjoy the view. The fare
for pedestrians was formerly one cent; but the promenade has now been made free,
and consequently the bridge is thronged, especially in hot summer nights and holidays, by those who wish to enjoy the view of the river and harbor and the two
cities, and the refreshing river breezes. On each side of the promenade is a drive
for vehicles, and a railway track, upon which trains are run at intervals of a minute
or less during the entire day. The cars are run by cable from a power-house on the
Brooklyn side. The car-fare is three cents, or ten tickets for 25 cents, and the trip
over is made in about six minutes. During the construction of the bridge twenty
persons were killed by accidents, and many others were injured. Since it was opened
to traffic several notoriety-seekers have jumped from it into the river below. One
of these divers, Stephen Brodie, survived the ordeal. The others were killed. The
bridge has a capacity of 45,000 pedestrians and 1,440 vehicles each hour. It is the
longest suspension-bridge in the world. Bridges not suspension that exceed it in
length are the Maintenon aqueduct of stone, 13,367 feet; the Firth of Forth bridge,
10,321 feet; and the Victoria (over the St.-Lawrence), the Parkersburg (West Va.),
and the St.-Charles (Mo.) iron bridges. The yearly receipts from the bridge
exceed $1,250,000, and the expenses are less than $1,000,000. Over 43,000,000
passengers are carried across every year, and fully 12,000,000 people walk over. As
many as 160,000 passengers have been carried in a single day, but the daily average
is about 120,000.

HIGH BRIDGE (OR "CROTON AQUEDUCT BRIDGE"), ACROSS THE HARLEM RIVER.
AT 175TH STREET AND TENTH AVENUE.

The Washington Bridge across the Harlem River, from 181st Street and Tenth Avenue on Manhattan Island to Aqueduct Avenue on a part of the old Ogden estate on the mainland, is another notable structure.   It connects Washington Heights and the so-called Annexed District, two sections of the city that will in a few years be ranked among its handsomest and most popular residence-quarters.   The bridge was completed in 1889, and cost nearly $2,700,000.   It is a massive structure of granite approaches and piers and iron and steel spans ; and it is much admired for the beauty of its proportions and lines, as well as for its grandeur and substantial character. Its total length, including the span of the bridge proper across the river and the New-York Central Railroad and New-York & Northern tracks on the east bank, the masonry approaches and the arched granite passages, is 2,384 feet.   The east abutment is 342 feet long, with four arched passage-ways of masonry.   The abutment on the west shore is 277 feet long, with three arches.   The two central spans are of steel, and describe beautiful parabolic curves.   They are each 510 feet long, and in the center 135 feet above high-water mark.   Their construction was notable in that it successfully tested a new device in engineering.   The arches were made and placed in position by sections.   One section was firmly anchored in the abutment, and then the next section was sent out on travellers, to be fastened to the extremity of the first, and so on, until the entire space was spanned, when the arches were keyed in the center as stone arches are.   The superstructure is very handsome. With a roadway fifty feet wide, and two pathways each fifteen feet wide, there is abundant accommodation for travel.   There are heavy granite parapets, pierced with loop-holes, polished buttresses, artistic bronze lamp-posts, and many semi-circular niches in the parapet, with low granite steps or seats.   The bridge is one of the most popular places of public resort in the city.   The view from it is superb, taking in the Harlem River to the north and south, the city farther in the distance, the wide sweep of the beautiful Annexed District, even as far as Long-Island Sound to the east, and Fort George, Spuyten Duyvil and Kingsbridge, and the surrounding country to the west and north.

High Bridge spans the Harlem River at 175th Street and Tenth Avenue, a third of a mile below Washington Bridge.   It was built to carry the old Croton Aqueduct across the river and valley at that point, and is 1,460 feet long, from bluff to bluff.   Arches resting upon thirteen solid granite piers support the structure. The crown of the highest arch is 116 feet above high-water mark.   Large cast-iron pipes enclosed in brick masonry convey the water across the bridge.   The structure is not provided with a carriage-way, but there is a wide walk for foot-passengers, who are numerous in summer-time, attracted by the beautiful view, and the enjoyment of the park and picnic grounds at each terminus, and the open country at the eastern end.   On Manhattan Island the water-pipes terminate in the pretty High-Bridge Park, where there is a reservoir, a lofty stand-pipe, a gate-house, and other appurtenances of an important water-station.

The McComb's-Dam Bridge (or Central Bridge), an old wooden draw-bridge, has long existed across the Harlem at the northern terminus of Seventh Avenue.   It has had much local celebrity, for Seventh Avenue, south of the river, and Jerome Avenue, its continuation north of the river, have for a generation constituted the favorite drive for New-Yorkers outside of Central Park.   North of the river the avenue extends to the Jerome-Park racing-track, and thence on to Yonkers; and it is lined with many well-known road-houses.   A new bridge with approaches is now building to take the place of the old one, and this will be, when completed, one of the greatest works of the kind in the world.   It will consist of a viaduct, a bridge, and steel approaches. The viaduct on the west side of the Harlem has been completed. It is in effect an extension of 155th Street from the ridge of Washington Heights on a gentle decline to the river; an ornate steel structure 60 feet wide and 1,602 feet long, with a driveway and two sidewalks. At the Washington-Heights abutment it is 65 feet above the ground, and it crosses above the elevated railroad at Eighth Avenue, with which connection is made by stairways. The bridge will be 731 feet long, and 32 feet above high-water. It consists of an immense swing span, or draw, 400 feet long, resting upon a cylindrical pivot-pier in mid-river; and four fixed spans at the ends. The terminal piers are of masonry, and there are ornamental copings and watch-towers. Two approaches, 50 feet wide, have been arranged at the east end of the bridge. They will consist of steel lattice spans resting upon masonry piers, carrying roadway and sidewalks 50 feet wide, one approach being 350 feet, and the other 1,740 feet long. The total cost of this pontifical improvement will be over $2,000,000. The Department of Public Works has built the viaduct, and the Department of Parks has charge of the construction of the bridge and its approaches.

The New-York Central & Hudson-River Railroad Bridge crosses the Harlem at Park Avenue and 134th Street, a great draw-bridge over which come all trains from New England and Northern New York that enter the Grand Central Station. Work has begun upon a new bridge at this point. It will be a draw-bridge of iron and steel, elevated 24 feet above high-water mark, and it will cost about $500,000. In connection with the bridge, elevated approaches will be constructed, to supersede the present Park-Avenue viaduct for about a mile south of the river, to 106th Street. The approaches will cost about $500,000.

Other Harlem Bridges present no particular points of interest. They include the following-named: At Second Avenue is an iron railway draw-bridge, with a foot-way, intended mainly for the trains of the Suburban Transit and the Harlem-River branch of the New-York, New-Haven & Hartford Railroad. At Third Avenue there is an iron draw-bridge for public travel, resting on stone abutments and iron piers in

THIRD-AVENUE, OR HARLEM, BRIDGE.

the water. It is usually known as Harlem Bridge. At Madison Avenue is an iron draw-bridge for general traffic. At Eighth Avenue is the iron railroad bridge of the New-York & Northern Railroad, by which connection is made with the elevated railroad system of the city proper. At Dyckman Street is an old wooden foot-bridge, that from time out of mind has connected Washington Heights with Ford-ham. At 224th Street, on the plain above Fort George, is the Farmer's Bridge, an antique structure, the name of which sufficiently indicates its purpose. At the junction of the Harlem River and Spuyten-Duyvil Creek, where Kingsbridge Road crosses the water, there is another old bridge. The United-States Government is deepening the creek into a ship-canal, and the old bridge is soon to be torn down and a new structure that will not interfere with navigation will take its place. Where Spuyten-Duyvil Creek empties into the Hudson there is a draw-bridge for the New-York Central & Hudson-River Railroad.

Contemplated Bridges and Tunnels, and those in process of construction, respond to the demand for additional and improved facilities for reaching New Jersey, Long Island and the northern parts and suburbs of the metropolis, a demand created and constantly made more urgent by the overcrowding of Manhattan Island, both in its business and in its residence quarters.

The North-River Bridge is the most important of these undertakings. It will be built by the New-York & New-Jersey Bridge Company, and ground has already been broken for the foundations on both sides. The bridge will be a combined cantilever and suspension structure, with a single river-span of 3,200 feet, two side-spans of 1,000 feet each, and a short span of 300 feet on the New-York side, making a greater length than the present East-River Bridge. The distance above high-water mark will be 150 feet, and at the middle of the structure 193 feet. There will be two main towers, 500 feet high, with bases 120 x 250 feet, extending

HARLEM RIVER AND HARLEM BRIDGE, AT 130TH STREET AND THIRD AVENUE.

about 250 feet below the water to hard rock. On the New-Jersey side the terminus will be at Niles Avenue, Weehawken, and the New-York end will be between 70th and 71st Streets. From the latter point a viaduct 100 feet wide, with four main railroad tracks and three lines of sidings, will run through private property to a point between Eleventh and Twelfth Avenues, and thence down-town to 44th Street. This viaduct, running all the way through the blocks between streets and avenues, will be built of steel and stone. A Grand Union station, modelled after the St. Pancras Station in London, will cover the blocks between Eighth Avenue, Broadway, and 42d and 44th Streets, 400 feet on Broadway and 1,300 feet back to the avenue. Seventh Avenue and 43d Street will be arched over, the grade of the depot being above the street level. The railroad offices will be there, and also a great transferring mail station. The depot will be laid with twenty tracks, and on the bridge there will be six tracks, with room to add four more. The bridge, which it is estimated will cost $40,000,000, is intended for railroad trains exclusively, and not for general traffic. It will give the great railroads which are now compelled to bring passengers and freight by ferry into New-York City a route direct to the heart of the metropolis.

The Citizens' Bridges between New York and Brooklyn will be two in number. Legislation has been granted, and the preliminary work entered upon. Both will be suspension bridges, controlled by one company; and they will cost about $25,-000,000. Both will have a common terminus on the New-York side, between Delancy and Rivington Streets, and from that point connection will be made by elevated structures with the present elevated railroad system. One bridge will extend to Broadway, in Williamsburg, and the other with a long approach to Fulton Street, between Bridge and Little Streets. They are designed to connect the Eastern District of Brooklyn with the central business section of New York. They will be open to general traffic, and the cars that cross them will be run in connection with the Union Elevated Railroad of Brooklyn.

The **Corbin Bridge** has been planned to cross the East River from Long-Island City to a point on the New-York side between 37th and 42d Streets. This will be for cars only, so as to give the Long-Island Railroad entrance into New-York City. A tunnel across the city to the North-River-Bridge Depot, connecting with the Grand Central Station at 42d Street and Fourth Avenue, is also part of this plan. The bridge will

SUBURBAN ELEVATED RAILWAY BRIDGE, AT SECOND AVENUE AND 129TH STREET.

be built of iron and steel, at a cost of $12,000,000. Besides the terminal piers, there will be a mid-river pier, built on Man-of-War Rock. The structure will be 135 feet above high-water mark.

The **Blackwell's-Island Bridge** will extend from 64th Street, New York, to Long-Island City. A company was chartered to construct this bridge in 1867. The project has been recently revived, and work may be begun soon. There will be central piers on Blackwell's Island, abutments in Long-Island City and in New York near 64th Street, and two short river-spans. On the Long-Island side there will be elevated approaches extending nearly two miles inland, and a branch running into Brooklyn. On the New-York side there will be two approaches, one extending to the Grand Central Station at 42d Street, and the other farther north. The bridge will be 150 feet above high-water, and will be for general traffic and for railroad trains. Ground was broken for this great work in 1893.

The **Astoria Suspension Bridge** across the East River, from 90th Street to Astoria, Long Island, has been talked of, and will probably be built in the course of time.

A Tunnel under the Narrows between Staten Island and Brooklyn has been projected. The design is to divert railroad traffic from New Jersey south of Jersey City across Staten Island to Long Island, and eventually thus to make a short route from the coal fields and the West across Long Island and the Sound to New England.

The **Hudson-River Tunnel** has not yet been a fortunate enterprise. It was planned to connect Jersey City with New York for the accommodation of the railroads. Begun in 1874, work was soon suspended, not to be resumed until 1879.

The shafts on the New-York side were begun in 1882, but again for lack of funds all work was stopped in the same year.   In 1887 the work was resumed, only to be suspended in 1892.   At the present time, 1,550 feet have been opened from the New-Jersey shore, and about 550 from the New-York side.   The entire width of the river at that point is 5,600 feet.   The plans provide for a tunnel of elliptical shape, 23½ feet high and 21½ feet wide on the outside, and 18½ feet high and 16½ feet wide inside, to be lined with brick and steel plates, and to rest in blue clay and rock 25 to 50 feet below the river-bed.   In Jersey City the tunnel starts from the foot of 15th Street, and in New York from the foot of Morton Street.   When completed, the New-York terminus will be in the vicinity of Washington Square.

The Park-Avenue Tunnel extends from 49th Street to 106th Street, and through it run all the railway trains that come into the Grand Central Depot.   From 42d Street to the south end of the tunnel the tracks are in the yards of the railroad company, or in open cuts; and these are bridged at the intersecting streets.   The tunnel is brick-arched; is in three parts, separated by walls; and has four tracks and sidings.   The middle of the avenue immediately over the tunnel is laid out in little parkways with green grass, trees and shrubbery, between the streets.   Iron fences enclose these spots, and in them there are openings in the roof of the tunnel by which means ventilation is secured.   The tunnel is owned and operated by the Harlem Railroad Company; and at 106th Street it terminates in a viaduct, which in turn is succeeded by an open cut to the Harlem River.   What is practically an extension of this tunnel goes under Park Avenue from 40th Street to 34th Street.   It is used for horse-cars only, and has several approaches from the street.

The Water-Supply of New York is of the utmost interest.   A little more than fifty years ago the people got their water from private wells, and were very

HARLEM RIVER AND SECOND AVENUE BRIDGE, AT 129TH STREET.

well supplied, for Manhattan Island abounded in springs that gushed out of the living rock, pure and wholesome.   In time, however, this source of supply began to be inadequate, and in 1774 a reservoir was built between Prince and White Streets, east of Broadway.   Into this water was pumped from the wells, and distributed through the city in wooden pipes.   In 1778 a committee of citizens recommended that Rye Pond in Westchester County should be made into a reservoir by building a dam, and that the water should be brought down to a city reservoir through iron pipes, crossing the Harlem River on a bridge.   To this end the Manhattan Water-works were chartered, but the company got no further than to build a reservoir in Chambers

Street, between Broadway and Centre Streets, and to try to support the city with well-water by the plan before attempted. The scheme failed for the second time. Many events served to call attention to the inconvenience and danger resulting from a continuance of this condition of things, and several plans for a better water-supply were brought out from time to time. The great fire of 1834 was a conclusive argument against the folly of longer delay ; and in that year, the Legislature having given the needed authority, a survey of the Croton water-shed was made, and in 1835 the work of constructing reservoirs and an aqueduct was definitely undertaken. The Croton water-shed is about thirty miles north of New-York City, on high land, in a remarkably healthful region. The water is exceptionally good, and is little exposed to contamination, while the flow through thirty miles of conduit to the city has a tendency still further to purify it. Croton Lake is fed by Croton River and other smaller streams, and this was formed into a reservoir, five miles long, by erecting a dam which raised the water forty feet. Then a conduit of brick, stone and cement was built in the shape of a horse-shoe, $8\frac{1}{2}$ feet perpendicular diameter and $7\frac{1}{2}$ feet

PARK AVENUE, NORTH FROM 98TH STREET.   N. Y. C. & H. R. R. R. TRACKS.

horizontal. This conduit begins at Croton Lake, and runs to the Central-Park Reservoir. It crosses 25 streams below grade ; has 16 tunnels from 160 to 1,263 feet long ; and it was designed to carry about 60,000,000 gallons each day. It drew from Croton Lake and other natural and artificial reservoirs, which were then utilized, with a storage capacity of 9,500,000,000 gallons, or about three months' supply for the city. The aqueduct crosses the Harlem River upon the High Bridge, at the city end of which there was built a high-service reservoir, holding 11,000,000 gallons, a tower, and pumping machinery. Thence it goes to the Central-Park reservoirs. On Fifth Avenue, between 40th and 42d Streets, a distributing reservoir with a capacity of 20,000,000 gallons was constructed. The work of providing for this system was completed in 1842. The water was turned on upon July 4th of that year, amid the greatest enthusiasm of the people. There was a military and civic procession, eight miles long, and other forms of celebration in September of the same year. In less than forty years the city had outgrown this means of supply. The aqueduct was forced to the point of carrying nearly 100,000,000 gallons a day, but even that was not sufficient for the needs of the population.   The upper stories of high buildings and even of residences on high land could get no water at all, and the storage capacity of the reservoirs was so limited that a short dry spell always made a water famine imminent.   Public agitation for an increased supply began before the year

1880.   Commissioners were appointed to consider various plans for relief, and they approved of Croton as an ample and pure supply.   An extension of the reservoirs and the construction of a new and improved aqueduct was recommended.   This work was at once entered upon, under the provisions of a special act of the Legislature, passed in 1883, and the metropolis is being provided with a water system that will be unsurpassed in any other city of the world.

The construction of the aqueduct taxed engineering skill and financial management to the utmost.   Unforeseen difficulties were encountered that retarded progress, and the frauds of contractors, who lined parts of the tunnel with thin shells of brick instead of with thick rubble walls, made it necessary to have a great deal of that part of the work done over again.

GATE HOUSE, CROTON AQUEDUCT.
MANHATTAN AVENUE AND 135TH STREET.

But as finally completed the aqueduct is a solid, and will be an enduring achievement.

The total length of the masonry conduit, from Croton Dam to the 135th-Street gate-house, where the tunnel ends, is $30\frac{3}{4}$ miles; from the latter point to the new reservoir in Central Park there are $2\frac{1}{3}$ miles of pipe line, making the total length of 33 miles.   There are 38 shafts, from 28 feet to 350 feet deep, several of them left open to the surface so as to give access to the aqueduct for repairs when needed. The average depth of the tunnel beneath the ground is 170 feet, but at South Yonkers it was built in an open trench for the distance of a half-mile, and also at the Pocantico River and Ardsley it comes to the surface.   At each of these three places there are blow-outs and waste weirs, by which the flow of water can be turned off at any time for the purpose of making repairs and cleansing the aqueduct.   The tunnel begins at Croton Dam, and at its head is a handsome granite gate-house, set in a recess that was blasted for it out of the solid rock, 30 feet below the top of the old dam.   The water flows from the lake through this house into the tunnel, and makes its way to the city by the force of gravity, no pumping being required, as the grade, though light, is continuous to the Harlem River.   The flow is about two miles an hour.   From the Croton Dam to a point a mile above Jerome Park the aqueduct is of horse-shoe form, 13.53 feet high and 13.60 feet wide; then it becomes circular, 12.3 feet in diameter.   At the Harlem River there is a fine piece of engineering in the inverted siphon by which the water is carried under the river to the High-Bridge station.   A circular tube of brick, $10\frac{1}{2}$ feet in diameter, goes down into the river for 1,300 feet; passes under the river-bed, and comes up on the west bank as a shaft 400 feet high.   Through this the water flows and climbs the hill on its way to the gate-house at 135th Street.   At this point the single tunnel ceases, and the water is distributed by pipe lines, eight iron pipes 48 inches in diameter, laid a few feet below the surface and diverging in different directions carrying it.   Four of these pipes go direct to the Central-Park Reservoir, and the others supply the demands of the

Harlem District.   No other tunnel in the world is equal to this in size or in the difficulty of the task that its construction imposed.   The Hoosac Tunnel and the Mt.-Cenis Tunnel are each 5 miles long, and the St.-Gothard Tunnel 9½ miles, as against the 33 miles of this aqueduct, which consumed five years in building.   Of brick-work alone there were 312,258 cubic yards, equal to thirty large 14-story office-buildings.   Material was excavated to the amount of 3,250,000 cubic yards.   The aqueduct was completed and the water turned on in the summer of 1890.   The cost of the construction, exclusive of lands, engineering, superintendence, etc., was $19,612,000, as against the engineers' estimate of $18,957,000.

The new aqueduct has a flowing capacity of 300,000,000 gallons a day.   A reservoir will soon be built on the site of the present Jerome Park, in order to provide for the needs of the growing annexed district.   The aqueduct will keep this reservoir full, and after leaving there will be able to carry 250,000,000 gallons a day down to the Central-Park reservoir, thus allowing 50,000,000 gallons a day for the annexed district, nearly two-thirds as much as the entire city had under the old service. Then the old aqueduct can still be depended upon for at least 75,000,000 gallons a day, and the pipe lines from the Bronx River can bring down 20,000,000 a day.   So it is possible to have a daily supply of at least 350,000,000 gallons.   The present demand is for a little more than 175,000,000 gallons daily.   It has been shown that even in dry weather the Croton-River watershed can be depended upon for fully 250,000,000 gallons a day.

Now that the aqueduct has been completed, the question of storage is engaging the attention of the municipal authorities.   The present storage capacity of the Croton watershed, natural and artificial, is 17,150,-000,000 gallons ; at Croton Lake, 500,000,000 ; Boyd's Corner reservoir, 2,700,000,000 gallons ; Middle Branch, 4,000,000,000 ;   East Branch, 4,500,000,000; Bog Brook, 4,050,000,000 ; Kirk Lake, 500,-000,000 ; Lake Mahopac, 500,000,-000 ; Lake Gilead, 300,000,000 ; and Barrett Pond, 150,000,000 ; total, 17,150,000,000.   Tributary to the above and included in the estimate are the smaller lakes, Gillead, Gleneida and Waccabuc, and White Pond.   The East Branch, which has a depth of 67 feet of water, and the Bog Brook, with a depth of 60 feet, were finished in the summer of 1892.   In addition, three reservoirs are in process of construction, and will be completed

HIGH SERVICE STATION. 98TH STREET, NEAR COLUMBUS AVENUE.

in 1894.   These are Reservoir D on the Western Branch, near Carmel, capacity 10,000,000,000 ; Titicus River, 7,000,000,000 ; and Amawalk Reservoir, on the Muscoot Branch, 7,000,000,000.   Thus the storage capacity will be increased to 40,100,-000,000 gallons.   Still another dam is under way, which is known as the New Croton

Dam, on the Cornell site. The Aqueduct Commissioners have let the contract for this structure, which was begun in the fall of 1892. The dam will be located five miles south of Croton Lake. It will be a wall of solid masonry, 264 feet high and 1,500 feet long, and will cost over $6,000,000. By its construction a reservoir 16 miles long will be erected, with a storage capacity of over 30,000,000,000 gallons. The water thus held will set back and submerge the present Croton Dam 35 feet. Hundreds of farms and houses now in the valley will have to be abandoned, and in 1893 the city authorities began their destruction.

At High Bridge there is a reservoir with a capacity of 10,000,000 gallons, and with two pumping-engines of an aggregate capacity of 10,000,000 gallons a day.

RESERVOIR, FIFTH AVENUE, 40TH AND 42D STREETS.

There can be distributed to high points on the island 20,000,000 gallons a day. In 98th Street, near Columbus Avenue, there is another water-tower and three Worthington high-service engines, with a pumping capacity of 25,000,000 gallons a day. The new retaining reservoir that occupies nearly the entire width of the northern part of Central Park will hold 1,000,000,000 gallons, and the receiving reservoir below it 150,000,000 gallons more. The reservoir at Williamsbridge holds 140,000,000 gallons ; and the distributing reservoir at Fifth Avenue and 42d Street 20,000,000. The new reservoir at Jerome Park will have a capacity of 1,300,000,000 gallons. The total storage capacity at the source of supply and within the city limits by reservoirs completed, building, and arranged for amounts to 84,600,000,000 gallons, sufficient to supply the city at its present rate of demand for two years. It is calculated when all this work is completed the municipal needs will be provided for, for the next fifty or seventy-five years. Water is distributed throughout the city by iron water-mains beneath the street surface. Of these there were on January 1, 1892, 685.48 miles, with 7,129 stop-cocks and 8,752 fire hydrants, and this branch of the water service is being constantly extended. The average daily consumption of water is nearly 100 gallons per capita. Consumers pay for the water, the annual charges ranging from $4 to $18 for each house, with extra rates for special service, and for houses more than fifty feet wide. In hotels, breweries, large office-buildings, manufacturing establishments, stables and other places where water is used in large quantities, meters are put in, and the water is measured and charged for at the rate of one dollar for each thousand cubic feet. A fixed rate is charged to some business establishments. There are 24,264 meters, and they register an annual consumption of over 30,000,000 gallons. The total water revenue from all sources amounted for the year 1891 to $3,375,140. The annual receipts go to pay the interest on the debt, and to the sinking fund, which is intended in time to extinguish the debt.

Lighting the Public Streets in the olden time was a duty imposed upon individual citizens. The first street-lighting was ordained by decree of the corporation in 1697, when it was ordered that every seven householders should unite to pay the expense of burning a candle in a lantern, suspended on a pole from the window of every seventh house on nights when there was no moon. But even this provision was so inadequate that the worthy burghers who were out late at night — that is until 9 or 10 o'clock — continued to carry their own lanterns to dispel the gloom. In 1762 public lamp-posts, with lamps burning oil, were first maintained at city expense, and this method continued down to 1825. Experiments with gas were made as early as 1812, but it was not until 1823 that practical steps were taken to introduce this new illuminating medium. In that year the New-York Gas-Light Company was incorporated, with a capital of $100,000, and given the right to the city south of Canal Street; and in 1825 pipes were first laid down. In 1830 the privilege of supplying gas to the northern part of the island was given to the Manhattan Gas-Light Company, which was incorporated with a capital of $50,000. The people did not take kindly to this innovation. They protested against the use of gas in the streets, for fear of explosions; and many of the old residents would not allow it to be introduced into their houses, holding to what they considered the safer use of oil-lamps and wax-candles. To-day the city is served by seven gas-companies, the Consolidated, Equitable, Standard, New-York Mutual, Central, Northern and Yonkers. The Consolidated is the oldest company, and has 810 miles of gas-mains in the streets. It is the successor of the two original gas companies, combined with several others of later existence. It has a capital stock of $35,430,-000, and seven stations, with an aggregate capacity of 30,000,000 cubic feet a day. Both coal-gas and water-gas is manufactured. The Equitable has 136 miles of mains below 74th Street, and manufactures 6,000,000 cubic feet of water-gas daily. The New-York Mutual, with 123 miles of mains, also manufactures water-gas, supplying the lower half of the city with 4,000,000 cubic feet a day. The Standard principally serves the up-town East-Side with water-gas through 140 miles of mains, at the rate of 4,000,000 cubic feet a day. The Central and the Northern supply the trans-Harlem district with coal-gas, the former with 800,000 cubic feet a day, through 64 miles of mains; and the latter with 250,000 cubic feet a day, through 38 miles of mains. The Yonkers, a suburban company, has 18 miles of mains. In many cases more than one of these companies have mains in the same street. The total miles of gas mains is 1,325, and the total capacity of all the companies is over 45,000,000 cubic feet daily. The Equitable pays an annual franchise fee to the city of over $140,000. There are 540 miles of streets and 69¼ acres of parks and public squares lighted, at a cost varying from $12 to $28 a year for each lamp, according as there is competition or not in the territory lighted, or as the company's charter may have fixed the price.

Electric Lighting of streets costs the city from 40 to 50 cents a night for each lamp. There are six companies, the Brush Electric Illuminating Company, the United-States Illuminating Company, the Thomson-Houston Electric-Light Company, the Mount-Morris Electric-Light Company, the Harlem Lighting Company and the North-River Electric-Light and Power Company. On the first of January, 1893, the city had 26,524 gas lamps, 1,535 electric lights, and at Woodlawn Heights 152 naphtha lamps, at a yearly cost of nearly $800,000.

EDISON ELECTRIC ILLUMINATING CO., 26TH STREET, BETWEEN BROADWAY
AND SIXTH AVENUE.

The Edison Electric Illuminating Company of New York, the general offices of which are at Pearl and Elm Streets, was organized in 1880. It was the first company to supply electricity for incandescent lighting on a commercial basis, and is the largest concern of its class in existence in the world. Its business is the generation and sale of electric currents for all purposes, but especially for incandescent and arc lighting, heat and power. Its principal generating station and general offices are located in the company's building at Pearl and Elm Streets. This new station is planned to be the largest and most efficiently equipped establishment of its kind. When completed, it will have an equipment for generating current equivalent to over 20,000 horse-power. The dynamos are of the multi-polar Edison type of the latest design. The engines are of the marine multi-expansion style, with inverted cylinders, and are connected direct to the dynamos. The boilers are of the extra heavy, water tube safety type, intended for 200 pounds steam pressure, and the whole steam plant is fitted with all the recent economizing devices to be found in marine and stationary engineering practice. The general offices of the Company occupy an upper floor of the building, and are to be very extensive.

The company also operate stations at 255 and 257 Pearl Street, 47 to 51 West 26th Street, and 117 to 119 West 39th Street, and also an annex station in the basement of the Produce-Exchange Building. It is also erecting another station on the premises 118 to 122 West 53d Street. The up-town buildings occupy lots measuring 50 by 100 feet. That at Pearl and Elm Streets, when completed. will cover an area 75 by 200 feet. All the newer buildings are owned by the company, and have been erected for its own use. The company's oldest station, at 255 and 257 Pearl Street, was built under the direct supervision of Thomas A. Edison, in 1882–83, and its successful operation was the real inauguration of incandescent electric lighting as a commercial enterprise. In the few years of the company's existence its business has grown rapidly. The entire plant now supplies current for an equivalent of about 200,000 incandescent lamps. Its operations cover all that portion of the city extending from the Battery to Central Park, included between Third and Eighth Avenues. Current is distributed over this territory by means of over 500 miles of conductors, which occupy 160 miles of underground three-wire conduit. It is led away from the stations to the net-work of "main" conductors by a system of "feeders." From the "main" conductors service wires lead to the premises of the consumers. The station buildings are all constructed on one general plan, and are absolutely fire-proof. A peculiar feature of their design is the placing of the boiler-rooms in the upper stories of the building, in-

EDISON ELECTRIC ILLUMINATING CO., PEARL AND ELM STREETS.

stead of on the ground-floor, while above the boilers are placed large coal-bunkers of 1,000 tons' capacity in the up-town stations and 3,000 tons' capacity in the new Elm-Street station.

The up-town stations are each capable of generating electric current equivalent to 6,000 horse-power, exclusive of the 53d-Street station, which may ultimately have a capacity of possibly 8,000 horse-power. The new Elm-Street station, with its capacity exceeding 20,000 horse-power, will be able to supply current for an equivalent of over 200,000 incandescent lamps, all connected at one time.   Permits to view the stations should be applied for at the general offices.

The Sewer System is on a scale commensurate with the importance of this branch of municipal economy.   As early as 1676 sewers were built on Manhattan Island.   These were simply box-drains of wood or stone, and at first were intended only to relieve low areas of storm water.   Very soon, however, they were built of brick, and connections were made with buildings, so that they could carry off the usual sewage matter.   It was not until 1849 that the character and the method of construction of the sewers were definitely laid down by the municipal authorities. The supervision of the work was then placed in the hands of a city department.   At that time about seventy miles of sewers of a miscellaneous character existed.   They were built four feet in diameter.   Many of these old sewers exist to the present day.   In 1860 the egg-shaped sewer was introduced, with the dimensions of 4 x 3 feet or 4 x 2.8 feet.   In 1865 a Legislative act authorized a general sewerage system. There were then in use 200 miles of sewers, partly of vitrified pipe, which was first laid in 1864.   In 1870 the Department of Public Works was created, and put in charge of the sewers of Manhattan Island.   To the Department of Public Parks were assigned the sewers of the trans-Harlem territory.   Under these arrangements the system has been improved and brought to its present state of efficiency.

The sewage is disposed of by discharging it into tidal water, where it is rendered innocuous by dilution, and by the natural flow of water it is carried away from the city.   Thus the sewers empty into the Harlem, North and East rivers along fifty miles of river-front.   There are about 140 outlets, most of which are at the ends of piers, where swiftly running water takes the sewage immediately and carries it seaward.   The entire city below the Harlem is sewered in the most approved manner, and the work above the Harlem keeps pace with the growth of population there. The city is divided into 26 drainage areas or districts, each of which is practically independent, with its own pipes and mains and outlets.

The sewers are laid in all the principal thoroughfares.   They have all the latest improvements for ventilation and flushing, and some of the pipes are imbedded in concrete.   They are on the system for carrying off sewage and rain-water combined. The average demand made upon them is nearly 100 gallons for each head of population each day, but their capacity is largely in excess of that.   The smallest pipe is 12 inches in diameter.   The largest sewers are in Canal Street, between Washington Street and the North River, 8x16 feet ; in Canal Street between Washington Street and Broadway, 7x10 feet ; and in 110th Street, between Fifth Avenue and the East River, 8x12 feet.   All the main sewers are entered and traversed by workmen for the purpose of cleaning or repairing them.   In 1892, there were 444 miles of sewers and 5,314 receiving-basins.   The total extent of construction in 1891 was over six miles, three-quarters of which was of brick mains.   The maintenance of sewers costs the city yearly $130,000, and the new work completed in 1891 cost over $500,000.

Electric Wires are maintained by the various telegraph, telephone and electriclight companies, and the Police and Fire Departments, strung on poles and attached to roofs.   Formerly there was a vast and intricate net-work of wires over all the city, especially in the business sections ; and the avenues and streets showed a forest of tall poles, many of them carrying several hundred wires.   Even now, despite the development of the subway system, hundreds of poles and thousands of miles of wire are still in mid-air, and over 2,000 miles are attached to the elevated-railroad

BAXTER STREET.
ONE PHASE OF LIFE IN THE METROPOLIS.

structure.   But Broadway, Wall Street, and other main thoroughfares are now void of the erstwhile objectionable poles.

Electrical Subways have been constructed in nearly all the principal streets south of Central Park, and to a lesser extent elsewhere.   They are designed to ac-commodate all the wires that are now hanging overhead.   This municipal undertak-ing is in charge of the Board of Electrical Control.   It had its inception in 1884, when, after nine years of opposition by interested parties, a bill for the purpose of compelling corporations operating electrical conductors to place them underground was passed by the Legislature.   Legal delays hindered the inception of the work ; and, although subways were built, it was not until 1889 that the provisions of the law began to be seriously enforced.   In that year the municipal authorities took upon themselves the task of compelling the companies to use the subways, and to that end they proceeded to cut the wires and chop down the poles in the leading thoroughfares where subways had been built.   Within a year nearly 5,000 poles and 6,000 miles of wire were thus removed, and there were over 12,000 miles of wire placed underground.   Since that time the work of constructing subways and putting the wires into them has progressed without serious interruption.   At present, there are over 200 miles of trench, containing several thousand miles of duct, and this con-struction will accommodate over 100,000 miles of wires.

The Postal Telegraph-Cable Company was organized in 1881, mainly by persons interested in the manufacture of compound steel and copper wire, and of an automatic system of telegraphic transmission.   The theories which led to the con-struction of its original lines were found to be mistaken.   The property was capi-talized upon a basis supposed to be justified by the great earning capacity which the superior construction and the proposed machine transmission were believed to render practicable.   The company was re-organized in 1885 upon the moderate capital of $5,000,000, and, being largely controlled by John W. Mackay, also principal owner of the Commercial cables, was operated in close connection therewith.   The prop-erty now comprises not only the excellent plant of the original Postal Company, but all that was saved from the wreck of the Bankers' & Merchants', and several other smaller telegraph properties, which have been rebuilt and re-equipped, together with new lines of much greater extent than all the original plants above mentioned, cov-ering the South to Savannah, Ga., the Southwest to New Orleans, and the West to Denver, covering the principal points in Kansas and Colorado, and the Northwest, to principal points in Iowa, Nebraska, Wisconsin and Minnesota.   By its connection with the large telegraph system of the Canadian Pacific Railway Company, it reaches the Maritime Provinces — the Dominion of Canada, Manitoba, and British Columbia ; and thence, in connection with the Canadian Pacific Railway, owns an extensive system of new lines, covering the Pacific Coast as far south as San Diego. The whole comprises by far the most extensive, best organized, and most thoroughly equipped system of telegraph that has ever been in competition with the Western Union Telegraph Company and the Anglo-American cables, and the best evidence of its permanence is found in the fact that excellence of service and constant, persistent competition in honorable and not destructive methods, has been its policy from the beginning.   The directors and executive officers of the company are as follows : John W. Mackay, George S. Coe, W. C. Van Horne, J. W. Mackay, Jr., Albert B. Chandler, Charles R. Hosmer, James W. Ellsworth, William H. Baker, Edward C. Platt, John O. Stevens, George G. Ward ; Albert B. Chandler, President and General Manager ; Vice-Presidents, George S. Coe and William H. Baker.

BROADWAY AND DEY STREET.
SHOWING MERCANTILE NATIONAL BANK, WESTERN UNION TELEGRAPH BUILDING, AND "THE MAIL AND EXPRESS."

Its executive officers have for more than four years past been in the Washington Building, No. 1 Broadway, comprising about twenty rooms on the upper floor of that commodious building. The necessity for combining these offices with the main operating rooms, and other departments of the company now occupying widely separated quarters, led to the construction of a building for the company, which is now in process of erection, on Broadway, corner of Murray Street, New York, directly opposite the City Hall, which will be one of the largest and handsomest office-buildings in the country. It will be 14 stories in height, exclusive of basement and cellar, and will rise about 175 feet above the street, with a Broadway front of over 70 feet, a Murray-Street front of 156 feet, and a wing 30 by 50 feet. The first four stories will be built of Indiana limestone, and the upper portion of the building will be of light gray brick, with terra-cotta trimmings. George Edward Harding & Gooch are the architects. The Postal Telegraph and Commercial Cable companies will occupy the eleventh, twelfth, and thirteenth floors, the corner-office of the first floor level with the street, and a portion of the basement and cellar. The rest of the building will be rented.

The Commercial Cable Company was organized in 1884 by John W. Mackay of California, and James Gordon Bennett, proprietor of *The New-York Herald*, for the purpose of establishing permanent competition, and affording an accelerated and reliable service at a moderate tariff, between the Old and New Worlds. Cables were laid during the same year, and business was begun in December, 1884. The company signalized its advent by reducing the cable rates twenty per cent. Its competitors instituted a rate-war by reducing their rates to twelve cents a word, and the Commercial met this by coming down to 25 cents a word, and appealing to the public for support in its fight against monopoly and the excessive rates that had previously existed. From May, 1886, to September, 1888, this rate-war was continued, but was finally compromised by all the companies agreeing to hold to the charge of 25 cents a word. Thus the Commercial Company deserves the credit of bringing about a reduction in rates, fifty per cent. of what they

SECTION OF ATLANTIC CABLE CARRIED IN PROCESSION.

had been, to the lowest figure at which it has been shown that the service can be profitably done. The company has two complete routes to Europe, and the duplex system that is used practically doubles the capacity of the cables. The cables are submarine and underground from the office in New York to Paris and to within 100 miles of London, only that short distance being by overhead wire. The landing-places are at New York, Rockport (Massachusetts), Canso (Nova Scotia), Water-

14   **POSTAL-TELEGRAPH-CABLE COMPANY'S BUILDING.**
BROADWAY AND MURRAY STREET, FACING CITY HALL PARK.

ville (Ireland), Bristol, and Havre.   Nearly 7,000 nautical miles of cable are in operation.   To this company must also be credited the reduction of time in the transmission of messages beneath the Atlantic ; and by the adoption of automatic working, and the introduction of typewriters for taking the messages, a point of excellence in accuracy, speed and reliability never before attained has been reached. It is an interesting bit of history that during the great blizzard of March, 1888, the only means of communication between New-York City and the rest of the world was by the Commercial Cable.   Messages were sent to London, whence they were cabled back to Boston.   The Commercial Cable and the Postal Telegraph Companies are allies, the latter being the land system.   The Directors are : John W. Mackay (President), James Gordon Bennett, George G. Ward (Vice-President and General Manager), George S. Coe, John W. Mackay, Jr., Albert B. Chandler, Sir Donald A. Smith, Wm. C. Van Horne, Charles R. Hosmer, E. C. Platt (Treasurer), Gardiner G. Howland, Richard Irvin, Jr., and Thomas Skinner.

The Western Union Telegraph Company occupies a handsome and well-appointed building in Broadway, corner of Dey Street, and has 137 branch-offices in different parts of the city.   The main building is at present the finest equipped telegraph office in the world.   The company has the largest telegraph system ever established.   It has 21,000 offices and 750,000 miles of wire.   The company leases the two cables of the American Telegraph & Cable Company from Nova Scotia to Penzance, England, which are extended to New-York City direct by the company's own cables ; it also connects with the four cables of the Anglo-American Telegraph Company, Limited, from Valentia, Ireland, to Heart's Content, Newfoundland, and from Brest, France, to St. Pierre, Miquelon ; and with the cable of the Direct United-States Cable Company from Ballinskelligs, Ireland, to Rye Beach, N. H. It has thus the service of seven Atlantic cables, as well as direct connection with the South-American cable at Galveston, Texas ; and messages may be sent from any of its offices to all parts of the world.

Pneumatic tubes extend under Broadway from 23d Street to Dey Street.   They belong to the Western Union Telegraph Company, and through them messages are sent a distance of about $2\frac{1}{2}$ miles.   Similar tubes extend from Dey to Broad Streets.

The American District-Telegraph Company is an adjunct of the Western Union, and does a messenger-service business exclusively.

The Mutual District Messenger Company, with its main offices at Broadway and Grand Street, is the only serious rival of the A. D. T. Company.

The Metropolitan Telephone and Telegraph Company conducts the telephonic communication of New York, and its system comprises eight central offices, upwards of 30,000 miles of underground wire, and about 9,000 subscribers' stations.   The system is in direct communication with those of Brooklyn and the principal towns in New Jersey, and also with that of the Long Distance Telephone Company, whose wires extend through the Eastern States in all directions, so that a New-York subscriber can reach any one of *eighty thousand* other subscribers scattered through New York, the New-England States, Pennsylvania and Ohio.   Of the eight exchanges in New-York City the four more important, viz. : those at Broad Street, Cortlandt Street, Spring Street and 38th Street, are placed in fire-proof buildings of a special type.   There are two reasons why a telephone exchange building should be impregnably fire-proof.   One is the enormous cost of the apparatus, which is equally susceptible to damage by water as by fire, so that a slight fire is as much to be feared as a serious one.   Another is that the crippling of an important exchange would result in heavy loss to the many patrons.   It is not generally known

METROPOLITAN TELEPHONE AND TELEGRAPH COMPANY.
TELEPHONE BUILDING, CORTLANDT STREET, BETWEEN BROADWAY AND CHURCH STREET.

how great the use of the telephone is in large cities.   There are many subscribers in
New York who call for from between 60 and 70 connections a day, while some run
up to as high as 130 a day.   In order, then, to sufficiently protect both its own interests and those of its subscribers, the company has been obliged to design special
telephone buildings, which are at once thoroughly fire-proof and properly adapted,

TELEPHONE OPERATING OR SWITCH-ROOM, ON CORTLANDT ST., METROPOLITAN TELEPHONE AND TELEGRAPH CO.

from roof to basement, to the requirements of a modern telephone central office.
The largest of these new telephonic centres is at 18 Cortlandt Street.   It is a handsome eight-story building, and the only sign of its special vocation is the familiar
blue bell hanging over the entrance.   The cloud of overhead wires formerly inseparable from a telephone exchange is entirely absent, as the wires are all underground.
In the basement of the building is a large department where some 15,000 or 16,000
wires enter from the subways.   These are all encased in heavy lead-covered cables,
from the terminals of which other wires extend up through the building to the eighth
story, the whole of which is occupied by the operating department, or exchange
proper.   Here a huge switchboard extends around three sides of the building in an
unbroken curve about 250 feet long.   This switchboard is the largest of its kind in
the world.   It contains all the most improved devices for metallic circuit working,
and was completed a few years ago at a cost of about $400,000.   It can accommodate
6,000 subscribers' lines, and about 150 operators are required to answer the calls and
facilitate the conversations that are constantly passing through it.   A telephonic
switchboard is the most complicated electro-mechanical device known to science.
This particular one contains more than 260,000 separate electrical instruments, none
of which has less than three wires soldered to it.   Hundreds of miles of fine insulated wire pass through the board and connect the different parts together.   All of
this has to be kept in perfect order, as a single defect may throw more than one
line temporarily out of service.
    The other exchanges referred to are of the same general type as that just
described, differing only in minor details and in switchboard capacity, each district

exchange having accommodation for from 1,200 to 3,600 subscribers' lines. A most interesting feature of the New-York telephone service, is that, practically, the entire system of conductors is under ground. During the past four or five years the Metropolitan Company has expended several million dollars in removing its pole lines and replacing them by costly underground cables. It has put down over 400 separate cables, containing an aggregate of more than 30,000 miles of wire. Underground cables radiate from every central office to points from which groups of subscribers can conveniently be reached. All the exchanges are connected together by several hundred underground wires, and some 500 wires, laid underground the entire distance except across the Bridge, join the various New-York exchanges with the principal exchange in Brooklyn. The wires are made into cables containing generally fifty-one pairs of conductors; these cables are covered with a lead armoring, and are drawn into iron pipes laid under the streets. The adoption of underground cables has been accompanied by so many electrical and mechanical difficulties as to necessitate a complete remodeling of the company's plant. This work has been carried out during the past four years, and is typified by the construction of the

model telephone buildings already described. The Metropolitan Telephone Company employs a staff of about 800 persons; and its pay-roll amounts to over $600,000 a year. The operators, who number about 400, are nearly all girls; they pick up the work very quickly, and give good satisfaction, alike to the company and to the subscribers. At each exchange a suite of rooms, consisting of diningroom, reading and work room, wardrobe and lavatory, are provided for the use of the operators. This department is in charge of a matron, who serves light refreshments and attends to the comfort of the girls generally when they are off duty. An important part of the organization is composed of the technical depart-

METROPOLITAN TELEPHONE AND TELEGRAPH CO., 38TH-STREET BUILDING.

ments that have to do with the construction and equipment of the offices, lines and subscribers' stations, the maintenance of the vast and complicated plant, and the inspection of the many thousands of lines and telephone sets. Each part of the work is done by a special staff, working under a responsible chief, the reins of

METROPOLITAN TELEPHONE AND TELEGRAPH CO., BROAD AND PEARL STREETS.

authority gradually centralizing through the general manager, executive committee, president and board of directors. Accurate record is kept of the work of every individual throughout the entire organization, so that the history of any of the tens of thousands of wires and instruments belonging to the company, and of every transaction connected therewith, is always available. The volume of business done by the company is almost incredible. The average number of telephone connections each day in New York City is about 120,000. Of these, 99 per cent. occur between the hours of 8 A. M. and 6 P. M. A permanent service is kept up at all the offices, but the use of the telephone at night is comparatively slight. The busiest hours of the day are from 11 A. M. to noon, and from 2 to 3 P. M. During those two hours probably nearly one-half of the entire day's business is conducted, and both plant and staff are working at high pressure. An eminent professor of political economy has said that the question of telephone rates was the most difficult problem that had ever been submitted to him, so complicated are the conditions involved. This opinion will be appreciated when it is considered that in a city like New York the entire plant and organization of the telephone system must be designed and arranged to stand the strain of performing almost one-half of the day's work within the short period of two hours. This is a condition of affairs not met with in any other industry.

The American Telephone & Telegraph Company maintains long-distance telephone lines for direct communication with Boston, Philadelphia, Washington, Pittsburgh, Harrisburg and intermediate points, the list altogether embracing 150 important cities and towns. The company has an extensive local service.

Cable Conduits for street-cars are laid underground in Broadway and Seventh Avenue for one line, in 125th Street and Tenth Avenue for another, and in Third Avenue. The conduits are of brick and cement, with iron frames supporting the cable pulleys. On the Broadway route, from the Battery to Central Park, the two conduits with their spurs are nearly twelve miles in length. In Third Avenue there are over sixteen miles of conduit, and in 125th Street and Tenth Avenue ten miles.

The New-York Steam Company supplies steam-power and heat to consumers through pipes laid underground. The company has been in business since 1882, and has fifteen miles of pipe in use in its down-town district, south of Duane Street. Six hundred business consumers and 300 residences are supplied.

Life in the Metropolis.

Hotels, Inns, Cafés, Restaurants, Apartment Houses, Flats, Homes, Tenements, Etc.

WHEN travellers came to the New Netherland settlement in its early days they were entertained at the expense of the Directors of the West India Company. This custom became in time such a burden that in 1642 Director-General Kieft built at the Company's expense a tavern, a quaint stone building near the present Pearl Street and Coenties Slip. This was the first tavern on Manhattan Island, and in later years it became the Stadt Huys. The following year Martin Krigier built and opened Krigier's Tavern, at Bowling Green, and this soon became the fashionable resort for the townspeople as well as for visitors from abroad. This house subsequently became the King's-Arms Tavern, and in Revolutionary days it was the headquarters of General Gage. To the generation of a quarter of a century ago it was the Atlantic Gardens, a popular pleasure-resort.

Many little taverns began to spring up about this time, and Director-General Stuyvesant compelled them to be licensed. In 1676 six wine and four beer taverns were licensed, with permission to sell strong liquors. The rates of charges were regulated as follows : lodging, three and four pence a night ; meals, eight pence and one shilling ; brandy six pence a gill; French wines, fifteen pence a quart ; rum, three pence a gill ; cider, four pence a quart ; beer, three pence a quart ; mum, six pence a quart. There were other restrictions, especially in regard to serving liquor to the Indians. If an Indian was found drunk on the street, the tavern-keeper who sold him the liquor was fined ; and when it could not be discovered which tavern-keeper was guilty, all the residents of the street were mulcted to make up the amount of the fine.

In Revolutionary days there were many public houses, the memory of several of which still remains bright. Fraunce's Tavern was probably the most famous in its day, and is best remembered now. It was originally the homestead of a member of the distinguished De-Lancey family, and was a handsome brick building, erected in 1730, on the corner of Pearl and Broad Streets. It was sold in 1762 to Samuel Fraunce, who opened it as the *Queen Catharine.* It was well patronized, and many receptions, balls and other social gatherings were held in its assembly-hall. There several societies met for their Saturday-night convivialities, and there the Chamber of Commerce had its headquarters for a long time. Washington made his headquarters there ; and in the assembly-room delivered his farewell address to the officers of the Continental Army, in 1783. Burns Coffee-House was also a De-Lancey homestead, standing on Broadway just north of Trinity churchyard, where the Boreel Building now is. It had many different names and many changes of proprie-

tors.   The Sons of Liberty made it their rendezvous, and during the British occupation it was much favored by the military officers.   In 1793 it was torn down, and
the City Hotel put up in its place.

About the same time and later there was the Bull's Head, in Bowery Lane, with
cattle-pens and the public slaughter-house near it.   The old Bowery Theatre, now
the Thalia, occupies its site.   The Merchants' Coffee-House was on the corner of
Water and Wall Streets ; and there were other coffee-houses.   Tea-gardens were
numerous, and opposite the present City-Hall Park was the famous La-Montagne
garden and tavern.   In the country, on the banks of the East River, were several
houses, where turtle feasts, which were important social events, occurred once or
twice a week.   On the North River in Greenwich Village were two very popular
gardens ; and there was the Vauxhall, near Broome Street, in Broadway, once owned
by John Jacob Astor.   Nor was the old Dutch Vauxhall, at the corner of Warren
and Greenwich Streets, forgotten.

Since the nineteenth century came in, the hotel history of New York has been
mainly a record of steady development toward the perfection of luxurious living that
prevails at the present time.   Many of the old hotels remain, although a large
number have gone the way of all things material.   French's Hotel until a few years
ago occupied the site of the Pulitzer Building, and was a popular house of its day,
but it is now well nigh forgotten.   The Golden Eagle Inn was another famous
place.   The building stood until 1893, back of the Broadway Central Hotel.   It
was redolent with memories of old-time theatrical folk and politicians.

Now New York has over one hundred thoroughly good hotels, with a score standing pre-eminently at the head of the list.   There are 250 more of the second and
third class ; and of all grades there are fully 1,000.   Over $150,000,000 in capital
is invested in them.   Of the best of these nearly three-quarters are conducted on
the European plan, but among those on the American plan are several of the most
famous.   Prices in the better American-plan hotels range from $3 to $6 a day for
a single room with board, and almost any figure beyond that for extra accommodations.   At the European-plan houses single rooms are charged at from $1 to $3 a
day ; and again in this case, there are better accommodations for those who want to
pay more.   At all these hotels, of either class, there is every convenience for comfortable living ; and at the best there is nothing to be desired in the way of luxurious
furnishings, charming surroundings, perfect service and exceptional cuisine.   In
these respects several of the leading New-York hotels cannot be surpassed.

Not alone by the travelling public are these establishments patronized.   Many
New-York families make their homes in them the year around, to avoid the
annoyances attendant upon housekeeping, and to secure much more of comfort, luxury and freedom.   It is this assurance of permanent patronage that has done much
to promote the excellence of New-York hotels during the present generation, and
particularly during the last decade.   Several of the best American-plan hotels are
sustained chiefly in this way, and the tendency among many well-to-do people is
more and more toward that style of living.

The great hotel district is between 23d and 59th Streets, and Fourth and Seventh
Avenues.   There are admirable hotels outside those limits, as in Union Square ; in
Broadway, below 14th Street ; and in Fifth Avenue, between 23d Street and Washington Square, and elsewhere ; but they are few in number and are overshadowed
by their modern rivals up-town.   In that territory, which is a little less than two
miles long by a half mile wide, are half of the leading hotels of the metropolis,
and a census of the district would show half of the hotel population living in them.

HOTEL WALDORF.
FIFTH AVENUE, NORTHWEST CORNER OF 33D STREET.

The **Hotel Waldorf** (American and European plans), built by William Waldorf Astor, and opened in 1893, is said to have cost $5,000,000. It has a frontage of 100 feet on Fifth Avenue, and 250 feet on 33d Street; and is twelve stories, or 180 feet high. It is a diversified and picturesque German Renaissance structure, designed by H. J. Hardenbergh, and abounding in loggias, balconies, gables, groups of chimneys, and tiled roofs. One of the chief features is the interior garden court, with fountains and flowers, walls of white terra cotta, frescoes and stained glass. The Empire dining-hall is modelled after the grand *salon* in King Ludwig's palace at Munich, with frescoes, satin hangings, upholstery and marble pillars, all of pale green, and Crowninshield's beautiful frescoes. Among the other rooms are the Marie Antoinette parlor, superbly frescoed by Will H. Low, N. A.; the Turkish smoking-room, with its low divans and ancient Moorish armor; the ball-room, in white and gold, with Louis XIV. decorations; and the café, abounding in carved English oak and leather hangings.

The **Hotel New Netherland** (European plan) is one of New York's newest hotel palaces. It stands as the highest achievement attainable in these times in hotel construction. In situation it is unrivalled, and in furnishings and general equipment it is almost unequalled. In the announcement of the hotel the proprietor claims it is "the most elegant, the safest, the strongest and the most complete hotel palace in the world. Every scientific appliance for ventilating, heating, plumbing and electric lighting. The privacy of a home. The furnishings of a palace. The table of an epicure. Absolutely fire-proof." No one can dispute these claims. It is situated on Fifth Avenue and 59th Street, immediately at the main portal of Central Park. It extends for 100 feet on Fifth Avenue and 125 feet on 59th Street, and rises to the majestic height of 234 feet, the tallest hotel structure in the world, and looms up loftily by the side of the neighboring Plaza and Savoy hotels. It overlooks not only Central Park and the magnificent Fifth Avenue, but all of the main part of New-York City. Built as securely against fire as can be done, its rooms on any floor provide every luxury and convenience that can be furnished by any hotel. Its main floor, with its onyx, mosaic and marble finish, is probably the grandest hotel rotunda on either continent, and from the three floors beneath the street level to the topmost of the seventeen stories above the street the New Netherland is uniformly a complete and perfect structure. It is conducted on the European plan, with restaurants, cafés, and private dining and banquet rooms that are practicably unsurpassable. Its proprietor is Gen. Ferdinand P. Earle, who is one of the most noted of the hotel landlords of modern times.

The **Fifth-Avenue Hotel** (American plan) has borne a conspicuous part in the public life of the metropolis, and has been identified with the most notable local events of the generation, since its opening, in 1859. Both location and management have contributed to this prosperity. The house fronts upon Madison Square, the most charming of the smaller parks of the city, at the junction of Broadway and Fifth Avenue, the two great thoroughfares. It is unequalled in the number and spaciousness of its corridors, halls and public rooms, and the commodious character of its guest-rooms. The proprietors are Hitchcock, Darling & Co.

The **Windsor Hotel** (American plan), seven stories high, substantial, dignified, and inviting in outward appearance, occupies the entire block on Fifth Avenue between 46th and 47th Streets, extending toward Madison Avenue nearly two hundred feet, and overlooking a broad open space in the rear which affords the hotel magnificent light and ventilation. The proprietors are Hawk & Wetherbee.

HOTEL NEW NETHERLAND.
FIFTH AVENUE, NORTHEAST CORNER OF 59TH STREET, AT MAIN ENTRANCE TO CENTRAL PARK.

The Hotel Savoy (American and European plans) is one of the most notable structures in this country. It is a palace of the highest order of art, and in every detail are seen the results of the most perfect workmanship. It is one of the most elegant and comfortable and safest hotels in the world, and occupies a site of remarkable beauty and interest. Even so long ago as 1870 William M. Tweed selected this as the choicest site for a hotel on Manhattan Island; and here he began the construction of the Knickerbocker Hotel. Before the shattering of the Tweed Ring, $250,000 had been spent here on the Titanic foundations of the never-to-be-realized Knickerbocker. The locality, so desirable even in that far-past day, is now simply marvellous in its combination of advantages, with the improvement of rapid transit, the development of Central Park, and the concentration in this immediate vicinity of the wealth, fashion and aristocracy of the Western Hemisphere. To occupy this fine strategic position, looking down on Fifth Avenue and the Plaza, and the main entrance to Central Park, the Hotel Savoy was built, and opened in 1892. It is twelve stories high, and the façades are in the rich efflorescence of Italian Renaissance architecture. This vast structure, with its long fronts on Fifth Avenue and 59th Street, is absolutely fire-proof, being of the steel-framed construction, with every beam and column of steel. The partitions and the arches between the floor-beams are of hard burnt terra-cotta. The walls are of Indiana limestone. The public apartments of the Savoy are of extraordinary interest and beauty. The table-d'hote dining-room, in Greek and Renaissance architecture, is one of the richest in the world, encased with Siena marble and rouge jasper, green and white Killarney marbles, satinwood and white holly, sculptures and frescoes. The breakfast-room is English in style ; the billiard-room is Pompeian ; and the drawing-rooms reproduce the decorative effects of the epochs of Louis XIV., XV. and XVI., and the First Empire. The lobby, main corridor and foyer are finished in Numidian marble, with wonderful sculptured ceilings. There are 135 bath-rooms, with mosaic floors and enamelled tiled walls. The electric plant has a capacity of 6,400 candle-lights, and the fixtures are unsurpassed. The Savoy also has a fine livery, a theatre-ticket office, a celebrated restaurant, and a huge safe, with separate safe-deposit boxes for the free use of guests. Many of the rooms are arranged in suites, with private halls and bath-rooms. The bridal or state suite, on the second floor, looking out over the Plaza, and through the main entrance over Central Park, is one of the most sumptuous and enchanting apartments on either continent. It is a reproduction of the boudoir of Marie Antoinette, in the Trianon Palace, at Versailles. It was occupied in 1893 by the Infanta Eulalia of Spain.

The architect of this vast and imperishable combination of ingenious devices for security and luxury of living was Ralph S. Townsend. The capitalists who built it were Judge P. Henry Dugro and F. Wagner. The men who manage this marvellous caravansary and its army of employees are veterans in the art of hotel-keeping.

Only one block distant is the Elevated Railway, by which in a few minutes the guest can reach the farthest parts of "Down-town ;" and past the Savoy's doors rumble the stages of the Fifth-Avenue line, giving quick access to the swell residence, theatre and shopping districts. And around the great balconies and porticoes of the Savoy sweep the bird-songs and flower-perfumes and fresh airs of the world-renowned Central Park, which has nowhere a rival in beauty. It hardly needs be said that the Savoy cuisine is unsurpassed, in America or Europe ; or that its wines, selected by a *connoisseur* and specially imported, and kept in lonely cellars two stories below the street, are of the very choicest. The house is kept on both the American and European plans, and is now being enlarged.

HOTEL SAVOY.

FIFTH AVENUE, SOUTHEAST CORNER 59TH STREET, OPPOSITE MAIN ENTRANCE TO CENTRAL PARK.

The Plaza Hotel (American and European plans) is one of the most attractive public houses in the wide world, and represents the highest possibilities attained in the art of constructing and keeping great modern caravansaries. Its situation is peculiarly advantageous, in the most delightful and aristocratic residence-quarter in America, almost surrounded by the homes of distinguished families, the architect- ural splendors of the "swellest" club-houses and the most fashionable churches. At its opposite corners are the gorgeous New Netherland and the palatial Savoy hotels. Its front is on the matchless Fifth Avenue, with its unceasing processions of beauty and elegance, on the sidewalks and in the line of carriages, and just at one side opens the main entrance to Central Park, the goal for all fashionable drives. One entire side of the hotel looks down close by on the Park, with its rocky hills, deep thickets, and little ponds, as wild in appearance as a scene deep in the New-Hampshire mountains. In the heart of the great city, and within a few minutes of its finest churches, theatres and art-galleries, you are still on the very verge of the loveliest pleasure-ground in America, with its drives and rambles, its lawns and forests, its statuary and fountains.

The Plaza Hotel to an unusual degree combines beauty and convenience. Ris- ing majestically from the broad asphalt-covered Plaza to the height of eight full stories, in brick and brownstone, diversified but not overladen with terra cotta and polished marble, balconies and cornices, it shows rich and tasteful effects on all sides, and the simple beauty of Italian Renaissance architecture. There is nothing of the narrow-tower effect about this broad-based and dignified structure, but its 500 feet of frontage on three streets suggests comfort, rest and security. This effect is increased by its absolutely fire-proof construction. The ventilating arrangements of the rooms and halls are very ingenious and effective; and the equipment for lighting the house includes one of the finest electrical plants in the country. A large part of the main floor is finished with choice marble mosaic pavements, sil- vered ceilings, enfoliated bronze columns, counters of Mexican onyx, woodwork of mahogany, and fine paintings. Here are the reception-rooms, with their Gobelins tapestries; and the great lounging-room, where ladies and gentlemen meet, amid Persian rugs, dainty tables, rich easy-chairs, costly paintings, and other attractive features. The pink parlor and the blue parlor, facing Fifth Avenue, on the second floor, are furnished in white and gold, with onyx tables, delicately frescoed ceilings, and walls finished *en panel*, in embossed silk drapery in delicate colors. The great dining-room, 80 by 40 feet, has a graceful arched roof, 30 feet high, rich in frescoes and fretted gold; and is finished in dead white and gold, with stained-glass windows and polished oak furniture. The walls are adorned with paintings of the Five Senses, executed in Paris. The Restaurant and Café are beautiful and attractive rooms, of great size, on the 59th-Street side; and the bar-room is equipped with onyx counters and *prima-vera* furniture. The public apartments are adorned with many paintings of the first order, including Pope's life-like pictures of horses, lions and dogs, and Cowles's "Shoshone Falls." There are 400 guest-rooms, most of them *en suite*, and all of them large and airy, with broad corridors laid with heavy red velvet carpets. As it stands, the Plaza Hotel cost more than $3,000,000, and was opened to the public in 1890. The proprietor is F. A. Hammond, for many years a prominent figure among the Bonifaces of America.

On the block below, on Fifth Avenue, at the corner of 57th Street, is the Cornelius Vanderbilt mansion, which in 1893 was so enlarged and remodelled as to make it the rival of any residence on the continent. At the opposite corner of 57th Street is the palatial residence of C. P. Huntington, now approaching completion.

THE PLAZA HOTEL.

FIFTH AVENUE, WEST SIDE, FROM 58TH STREET TO 59TH STREET, AT FIFTH-AVENUE ENTRANCE TO CENTRAL PARK.

Holland House (European plan), at Fifth Avenue and 30th Street, is in some respects the leading hotel of America ; and ranks as the equal of any hotel in the world. Its excellence of construction, its perfection in the furnishings, and its admirable management made the Holland House a marked success from the day of its opening. It has a frontage of 250 feet, on the most noble and aristocratic thoroughfare of the New World, and rises far above the surrounding buildings with impressive and monumental effect. Although so immense and preëminent, the exceeding delicacy of its architectural details, and the fineness of its design, make this one of the most attractive and beautiful secular structures on this avenue of palaces. The architects and designers were George Edward Harding and Gooch; the style is a modification of the Italian Renaissance ; and the material of the walls is a fine gray Indiana limestone. The portico, one of the richest in America, is decorated with admirable stone carvings. The main staircase and corridors are wonderful works of art, in carved Siena marble and bronze. A London magazine recently characterized this as the handsomest staircase of its kind in America. The hotel office, in Italian Renaissance, and encased in Siena marble, contains among its many conveniences an enormous safe, in which are a number of steel safe-deposit boxes for the use of the guests. On the main floor is the Restaurant, with a seating capacity of 300 persons ; the equal in all its details of any room devoted to this purpose in this country. On the same floor is the Café, with its furnishings in the manner of the famous English palace of Holland House ; its exquisite screens of glass, marble and bronze ; and its delicate tones of gray and pale yellow. The Buffet, in a soft yellow and golden brown, has high wainscots of panelled wood. The Foyer, on the parlor floor, is lighted by four immense *torchères*, bearing electric lights, and is furnished in the most attractive style. The Ladies' Reading-room, with pale satin and plush hangings, contains files of newspapers and dainty writing-desks. The drawing-room is in the style of Louis XVI., with its walls covered with salmon-tinted satin damask, embroidered portières, furniture in the Adams and Chippendale styles, and fawn-colored Axminster carpet. The Gilt Room is a reproduction of the famous Gilt Room in the historic Holland House at London, in Elizabethan architecture, with carved wainscotting, quaint heraldic devices, gold-crown ornaments, interesting antique furniture in natural cherry and gold, olden-style fire-places, English parquet floors, Flemish chandeliers, and magnificent plush curtains embroidered with fleur-de-lys. One of the bridal suites is in Louis XV. style, with satin *broché* hangings and furniture, and curtains of Brussels point lace ; and the other is in the style of the First Empire, with upholstering of French tapestry, and curtains of point lace. Each of the 350 rooms is furnished and decorated in a distinctive style. A special feature of each is an electric indicator by which a guest, without waiting for a bell-boy, may signal direct to the office for any of 140 various articles. This indicator, known as the Herzog Teleseme, is in fact one of the great conveniences of Holland House ; it is the most perfect of all signalling systems. It comprises a dial sunk into the wall, and connected by electricity with the office ; upon this dial is printed 140 articles at times needed by travellers, and the guest has only to move the pointer until it points at the desired object, and then press an electric button, whereupon the clerk in the office, thus apprised, will send up, without further instructions or delay, the desired newspaper, or bottle, or food, or servant, or any other needed thing. The rooms have brass bedsteads, red-birch woodwork, Wilton carpets, and the best modern furniture. Holland House is entirely fire-proof, and contains the most perfect sanitary plumbing. Its walls and floor-arches are of porous terra cotta, which is a non-conductor of heat, cold or noise ; and even the heating pipes are encased in asbestos.

HOLLAND HOUSE.
FIFTH AVENUE, SOUTHWEST CORNER OF THIRTIETH STREET.

The floors and stairways are entirely of marble mosaic and cement. All impaired air is sucked out of the building by enormous exhaust air-shafts and a hollow roof-chamber. The house has five noiseless hydraulic elevators, marvels of elegance. The table-ware was made to order, from special designs, and bears the Holland arms. The silverware is of special designs by the Gorham Manufacturing Co. ; the china is Royal Worcester porcelain ; the glass is special English crystal ; and the table-linen was woven to order in Scotland. Holland House is under the proprietor-ship of H. M. Kinsley and Gustav Baumann, famous among American hotel-keepers. They are also proprietors of "Kinsley's," Chicago, a restaurant and catering estab-lishment, known all over the world for its excellent cuisine.

The **Hotel Imperial** (European plan) cost about $2,300,000. Architecturally, it is as admirable as it is conspicuous, being built of light-colored brick, and richly ornamented. The main corridor is in African marble ; the grand staircase is in marble and Mexican onyx ; the ceiling of the corridor is a reproduction from the Vatican, in pale blue and gold ; the dining-room reproduces the boudoir of Marie Antoinette, in gold and white ; the café is in white mahogany, with blue, white and gold ceiling ; the bar-room is in the style of an apartment of a French chateau.

The **Hoffman House** (European plan) is famous the world over for its mag-nificent banquet-hall and its art-gallery, no less than for its cuisine and its general excellence as a hotel. It is on Broadway, between 24th and 25th Streets, and its front takes up nearly the whole block. It has a sightly and beautiful location. The Broadway front of the house dates from 1864 ; and the eight-story fire-proof annex on 25th Street was erected in 1882–85, in Italian Renaissance architecture. The great Banquet Hall of the Hoffman is 60 feet square, with beautiful allegorical paintings. The bar-room contains Bouguereau's painting, "Nymphs and Satyr," Correggio's "Narcissus," Chelmonski's "Russian Mail Carrier," and other price-less paintings and sculptures.

The **Buckingham** (European plan), at Fifth Avenue and 50th Street, opposite St. Patrick's Cathedral, was opened in 1876. It is richly finished within, princi-pally in mahogany and oak. Many families make their homes there, especially those who come from a distance to spend the winter in town. It has the quiet elegance of a refined home. The neighborhood is the most elegant in America.

The **Gilsey House** (European plan) has been a successful establishment for nearly twenty years. The building is a handsome structure of white marble and iron, on the corner of Broadway and 29th Street, in the busy portion of the up-town district. Its guest-chambers are finely appointed, and it attracts the patronage of travellers who are very wealthy and extremely particular, especially army and navy officers, congressmen, coal operators and mine owners, and railroad magnates. The restaurant is famous for its excellence, and has been approved by many lovers of good living. The proprietors of the Gilsey are James H. Breslin & Brother.

The **Hotel Bristol** (American plan) is very favorably situated, at the corner of Fifth Avenue and 42d Street, overlooking the ancient reservoir and Bryant Park, and convenient to the Grand Central Station. It is an aristocratic and elegant house.

The **Hotel Normandie** (European plan), at Broadway and 38th Street, has 200 rooms and an excellent restaurant. All its floors are of iron beams and brick arched work, so that the house is absolutely fire-proof. It is first-class in its appointments. Its architect was W. H. Hume. Gen. Ferdinand P. Earle is the proprietor.

The **St. James** (European plan), at Broadway and 26th Street, under its suc-cessive owners, has been the resort of the better class of sporting men, especially those interested in the turf. Many theatrical stars have been patrons of the house.

The Hotel Grenoble (American and European plans) ranks among the most charming of the public houses of the great metropolis. The situation is very advantageous, either for permanent residents, among those happy families who escape the exasperations of modern housekeeping, or for transient visitors to the city, who find here at once a luxurious and aristocratic home and a locality peculiarly convenient for excursions down-town. The hotel is very favorably placed, and covers the entire block fronting on Seventh Avenue, from 56th Street to 57th Street, its grand façade being 394 feet long and seven stories high, and in attractive architecture. The section reaching to 57th Street is of red brick and Scotch sandstone, and contains exclusively suites of rooms, furnished or unfurnished. The more ornate part of the building, reaching to 56th Street, constructed of Pompeian and buff brick and red and white terra cotta, has a handsome portico. The whole struc-

HOTEL GRENOBLE, SEVENTH AVENUE, FROM 56TH STREET TO 57TH STREET.

ture is adequately equipped as a first-class modern hotel. All visitors are delighted with the beautiful white-and-gold dining-rooms, the spacious and elegant office, the exquisitely equipped café, the white mahogany furniture of the ladies' parlors and reading-room, the wonderful mosaic floorings, the ingenious fire and burglar alarms in every room, the six rapid-running Otis elevators, and the liberal endowment of electric lights. The Grenoble occupies very high land, which helps with the perfect drainage and sanitary conditions to make it an exceptionally healthy house. Only two blocks distant are the unrivalled landscape beauties of Central Park, with its lakes, lawns, woods, crags, and charming drives and rambles. People who want to go down-town will find the Elevated Railway only a block away from the Grenoble; while the Boulevard cars are an equal distance, and the Belt Line two blocks away. The Broadway cable-cars pass the very doors of this hotel. The proprietor of the Grenoble is William Noble, who has large hotel interests elsewhere, especially at Lake George, where he owns the Fort William Henry Hotel.

The Hotel Cambridge (American and European plans) is at the southwestern corner of Fifth Avenue and 33d Street, with its main entrance immediately facing the main entrance of the Waldorf, which is directly across the street. It has a

HOTEL CAMBRIDGE, FIFTH AVENUE AND 33d STREET.

modest exterior, in harmony with the exclusiveness and the quiet elegance of the interior. But it has all of its several floors arranged into the choicest and most desirable apartments for families and travelling parties. It was planned and is conducted as an elegant home for families — many from the North and East making it their winter home ; and many from the South and West occupying a large part of it in the summer. Besides its permanent guests, the Cambridge enjoys a very choice patronage of well-to-do people, who come here for a day, a week, or longer, and prefer this hotel by reason of its quiet elegance, its handsomely furnished apartments, and its exquisite cuisine and service. The hotel is conducted by Henry Walter, who became the proprietor in 1893, after having been the successful proprietor and genial host of the Albemarle Hotel of New York for fifteen years. The Cambridge is most advantageously situated on a high point in America's famous social thoroughfare — the unapproachable Fifth Avenue. In its immediate vicinity are the great theatres, famous clubs, noted churches, and grand public institutions. It is of easy access to surface cars and elevated trains, and past its doors go the Fifth-Avenue stage coaches. The Cambridge is provided with modern improvements, gas and electric lights, elevators, perfect sanitary plumbing, and elegant appointments. Its service is commendable. Its rates range from $5 a day upward, on the American plan ; and from $2 a day upwards on the European plan. During the short period of its present management the Cambridge has become a favorite resort of foreign diplomats, a number of whom may usually be found here. A notable feature of the Cambridge is its quietude, and another is its convenient situation. It is far enough away from Broadway to avoid all its commotions, and yet close enough to enjoy its conveniences. Only one block away is the 33d-Street Elevated Railroad station, which provides rapid transit up-town and down-town, and yet the hotel is entirely apart from it. A short distance away is the Fourth-Avenue tunnel, through which one can reach the Grand Central Station in six minutes, yet no trains can be seen or heard.

The **Park-Avenue Hotel** (American and European plans), on Park (Fourth) Avenue, from 32d to 33d Streets, is one of the greatest of the New-York hotels. It was built by the late A. T. Stewart, with the definite purpose of securing at any cost a house of accommodation that should be fire-proof, comfortable in every way, and in its public rooms magnificent. With his colossal fortune behind it, this project was nobly achieved. Within a year or two the entire building has been improved, refreshed and thoroughly modernized, adding $150,000 to the original cost of $3,000,000. The Park-Avenue is the most obviously and manifestly fire-proof hotel in America. The broad arches overhead in the chambers tell of unin-flammable floors everywhere. It gives one a very restful sense of security to feel thus guaranteed against one of the worst of perils. The chambers are high and airy, well lighted and heated, and supplied with hot and cold water. There are 500 rooms, all newly furnished and decorated. The Park-Avenue is a vast and imposing quadrangular palace, surrounding a spacious courtyard which is beautified with evergreen trees, flowers and fountains, and where the famous Lanzer Orchestra plays exquisite music. All the inside rooms open upon this scene of fairyland, which is especially brilliant under the colored electric lights of evening. The situation is admirable, fronting on the Fourth-Avenue street-car line, not far from

PARK-AVENUE HOTEL, PARK AVENUE, FROM 32D STREET TO 33D STREET.

the Grand Central Station, and only a few minutes' walk from Madison Square or Bryant Park, and two or three squares from the Third and Sixth Avenue Railways, leading everywhere. All the public rooms are floored with mosaic, with bronze and gold reliefs on walls and ceilings, the richest of furniture, and many choice works of art, in paintings and statuary. The Park-Avenue Hotel is under the proprietorship of Wm. H. Earle & Sons, of the well-known Earle family, who are famous in the annals of American hotel development for more than a third of a century.

The **Murray Hill** (American and European plans), on Park Avenue, 40th and 41st Streets, is a great and handsome building of seven stories and ornamental towers, with accommodations for over 500 guests. It is elegantly appointed, and is an establishment of the highest class. Many New-England people sojourn at this very quiet and attractive hostelry, on high ground, near the Grand Central Station, but quite secluded from its noise and uproar.

The **Victoria** (American and European plans), at Fifth Avenue, 27th Street and Broadway, is a high and roomy structure, inclined to exclusiveness in its patronage. The hotel jumped into sudden fame a few years ago, when Grover Cleveland, on his election to the Presidency, made it his headquarters when in New York.

The **Hotel Brunswick** (European plan), eligibly located on Madison Square, at Fifth Avenue and 26th Street, is much favored by English tourists, and is patronized also by the wealthy young men about town. The house has a high reputation for its admirable service and for its restaurant, than which it is claimed by many there is none better in the city. The parades of the Coaching Club start here.

The **Gerlach** (European plan), on West 27th Street, near Sixth Avenue, was built in 1890, by Charles A. Gerlach, its present manager. It is an imposing eleven-story fire-proof house, with elevators, electric lights, sumptuous dining-rooms, and many fine suites. The Gerlach is chiefly for permanent residents, but receives numbers of well-to-do transients, as well, and finds a particularly large and profitable patronage in the winter season.

The **Hotel de Logerot** (European plan), at Fifth Avenue and 18th Street, occupies the grand old Fifth-Avenue mansion of Gurdon W. Burnham, with two others adjoining, refitted and elegantly refurnished for the present use. It is very fashionable and very aristocratic, and the landlord is a genuine nobleman, Richard de Logerot, Marquis de Croisic, who has a good standing in New York's "400."

The **Clarendon** (American and European plans), on Fourth Avenue and 18th Street, is favored by many English people and families, who come to make an extended stay in the city.

The **Everett House** (European plan), in Union Square, at the corner of Fourth Avenue and 17th Street, attracts many professional people, lecturers, authors and actors. Henry M. Stanley has been a frequent guest there. The locality is very convenient for people who wish to be near to the life of the great city, and its manifold amusements and diversion.

The **Brevoort House** (European plan), in Fifth Avenue, near Washington Square, is a quiet and aristocratic hotel that has long been in favor with English tourists. The cuisine of the Brevoort has always been considered one of its attractions. Sam Ward, that prince of epicures and most genial of entertainers, lived there at one time ; and his nephew, F. Marion Crawford, the novelist, describes the house and his uncle's favorite corner in his novel of *Doctor Claudius*.

The **Albemarle** (European plan), on Madison Square, at the junction of Broadway and Fifth Avenue and 24th Street, is a quiet and exclusive place, numbering among its guests many permanent residents and foreigners of distinction.

The Grand Union Hotel (European plan) is located at Fourth Avenue and 42d Street, just across the street from the Grand Central Station. It is architecturally unassuming, but it is very large, its dimensions being 200 by 135 feet. It contains over 500 sleeping-rooms, and does the largest business of any hotel in New York, in respect to the number of guests entertained. The features which first strike the visitor to the hotel are its cleanliness and quaintness, and an air of home comfort which is lacking in many hotels. The walls of the public rooms are covered with paintings, mostly by American artists, of a high order of excellence. There are also a number of examples of foreign schools, purchased by the proprietors at the Paris *Salon.* One of the cafés is devoted to curious old colored prints, and another to prints relating to the early history of New York. Several large rooms on the ground floor are set apart for reading and writing, and are abundantly supplied with stationery, books, papers and illustrated periodicals. This is a popular feature with the travelling public, who appreciate having a comfortable place in which to lounge, read and write. The hotel has the reputation of being one of the most profitable in the country. Simeon Ford, the senior proprietor, having been asked to account for the continued and growing success of the Grand Union, in spite of the building of many new and elegant hotels, said : "In the first place, we have a location which, for transient business, is unique. We are just across the street from the Grand Central Station, and travellers, instead of having to struggle with hackmen and expressmen, can step across to our house, and we deliver their baggage in their rooms in a few minutes, without charge. Then, again, we have a moderate-priced house. We give a nice room for a dollar a day, but, if people want to pay more, we have handsome suites which cost four or five dollars a day. Our food is of the best quality obtainable, and well cooked ; and we don't ask

GRAND UNION HOTEL, FOURTH AVENUE, FROM 41ST STREET TO 42D STREET, OPPOSITE GRAND CENTRAL DEPOT.

enough for it to bankrupt a man.   We are cranks on the subject of cleanliness.   We are eternally scrubbing and mopping.   Then again we are within easy distance of all the best shops and theatres.   But, above all, we attribute our success to the fact that we try to take good care of our guests and make them feel at home, and we try our best to impress upon our employees that we get our living out of the travelling public, and that they are entitled to some consideration, and when our employees do not agree with us on this point we ask them to "seek fresh fields and pastures new."

The St. Denis Hotel (European plan), at Broadway and 11th Street, opposite Grace Church, has for many years been one of the well-known landmarks of the metropolis, and has been celebrated in Howells' works and other choice modern literature.   In 1875 the hotel property was leased by William Taylor, who had served a long apprenticeship with his elder brother, in the famous Taylor's saloon, at Broadway and Franklin Street. This was, perhaps, the most magnificent restaurant ever seen in America.   When Mr. Taylor assumed the charge of the St. Denis, his first work was to reconstruct it ; and this skilful renovation so greatly increased its good fame and patronage that it was found necessary to construct a very large addition.   There are

ST. DENIS HOTEL, BROADWAY AND 11TH STREET.

many points of attractiveness about the hotel, the conveniences and compactness of the office, the quiet and spacious reading-room, the dainty parlors, and the famous Colonial dining-room, a triumph of refined architecture. The whole establishment is pervaded by such an air of home comfort, and is, withal, so convenient to everywhere, that people who once visit it as guests afterwards make it their domicile while in New York. The equipments of the house, as to steam heating, electric lighting, ventilating, and hydraulic elevators, are supplemented by a perfect corps of polite and well-disciplined attendants.

The situation of the St. Denis is exceptionally good, being midway between the up-town residence quarter, and the down-town business quarter, and facing on Broadway, the brightest and most fascinating street in the world. Looking across from the hotel parlors and public rooms, the stranger might fancy himself in some venerable cathedral town of England, for the wide spaces fronting the St. Denis are occupied by the beautiful Gothic edifice of Grace Church and its rectory and connecting buildings, set amid rich velvety lawns. It is a scene full of peaceful and restful suggestions. On the opposite corners are the great retail dry-goods houses of James McCreery & Co., and Hilton, Hughes & Co., the successors of A. T. Stewart & Co. A few minutes' walk above the St. Denis is the brilliant Union Square, and the shopping district extends on all sides. The restaurant of the St. Denis is widely and pleasantly known, as a place where delicious cooking, elegant surroundings and attentive service are combined with very reasonable rates. These recognized facts make the restaurant a favorite resort for shopping parties and many other people of fashion, as well as for the guests of the hotel.

The Broadway cable-cars pass the doors almost every minute, and give quick access to the City Hall or the Battery, and to the up-town squares or Central Park. Within easy walking distance, also, are the 9th-Street and 14th-Street stations of the Third-Avenue and Sixth-Avenue Elevated Railways.

The St. Denis has many points of attraction which may not be found in the great up-town hotels ; and prominent among these is the absolute coziness of its public rooms, which, indeed, do not seem in the least like parts of a hotel, but rather like pleasant nooks in a refined home. Yet there are so many of these charming rooms, for divers uses, that they are never crowded or uncomfortable ; and from their windows one can watch the vast and perpetual human tides flow up and down Broadway, with the cathedralesque gray spires of Grace Church looking calmly down on the busy and brilliant scene.

The Astor House (European plan), on Broadway, Barclay and Vesey Streets, is the leading hotel down-town, and one of the famous houses of the city. For two generations it has been noted, and its solid granite front, nearly opposite the Post Office, makes a conspicuous feature of that part of Broadway. It is an old-fashioned and conservative establishment, substantially furnished, and kept in good style. On the ground floor along the street fronts are stores, but back of the stores opens the great rotunda, which is a much-frequented eating-place for noon-day meals.

The Metropolitan (European plan), at Broadway and Prince Street, is still a favorite with merchants from the South and West. It is near the centre of the wholesale dry-goods district, and is a commodious six-story structure. The dining-room is one of the largest in the city. Niblo's Theatre has an entrance here.

The Morton House (European plan), on 14th Street, has been favored by theatrical folk, who until within a few years made their rendezvous in Union Square.

The Union-Square Hotel (European plan), at Fourth Avenue and 15th Street, has accommodations for 400 guests. It is strictly fire-proof.

The Westminster Hotel (American plan), in a quiet location at Irving Place and 16th Street, is exceedingly convenient to the shopping district and the places of amusement, being but a few steps from Union Square and the rush of Broadway, and a few minutes' walk from Madison Square and Gramercy Park. It enjoys the distinction of being a first-class family and transient hotel, having an apartment-house connected with it. The Westminster is the home of many families of means, who find here quiet elegance and refined conservatism. The hotel was named in honor of the Duke of Westminster, whose coat-of arms appears on its stained windows, stationery and menus. It was a favorite home of Charles Dickens, Christine Nilsson, and Profs. Tyndall, Huxley and Proctor; and has always been much in vogue with English travellers. The dainty drawing-rooms, recently refurnished in the French style; the cream-and-white Colonial dining-room, with its rich-hued curtains, hard-wood floors and rugs; the many commodious guest-rooms, newly carpeted and furnished; and many other attractions, give a quiet distinction to this house. Here also come many native and foreign members of the diplomatic force, drawn thither, perhaps, by the proximity of the house to Gramercy Park, now or formerly the home of statesmen and men of affairs like Hamilton Fish, Samuel J. Tilden, John Bigelow, Cyrus W. Field, David Dudley Field and Abram S. Hewitt.

The Westminster is a remarkable example of an ancient hostelry which has

WESTMINSTER HOTEL, IRVING PLACE AND 16TH STREET, NEAR UNION SQUARE.

never lost its hold upon the public favor, and which is fresher, cleaner, brighter and more modern than scores of hotels erected in New York within five years. Although nestled away in its quiet nook on Irving Place, the Westminster is within two blocks of a station of the Third-Avenue Elevated Railway, whereby the explorer may reach all parts of Manhattan in a trice. The house is practically fire-proof, withal.

The Broadway Central Hotel (American and European plans), at 665 to 675 Broadway, opposite Bond Street, is probably the largest public house in New York, and has accommodated as many as 1,200 guests at one time. On this memorable site La Farge, a sagacious French investor, built the La Farge House, which was opened in 1856. Back of the hotel stood the Tripler Hall, the scene of Jenny Lind's triumphs. The hall was remodelled into Burton's New London Theatre, then the largest in New York; and subsequently into the Winter Garden, where Edwin Booth played *Hamlet* for 100 consecutive nights. In 1869, after La Farge's death and the burning of the Winter Garden, the entire property was acquired by the late E. S. Higgins, the carpet manufacturer, who erected here the most palatial hotel in New York, at first known as the Southern Hotel, and

BROADWAY CENTRAL HOTEL, BROADWAY, OPPOSITE BOND STREET.

afterward as the Grand Central Hotel.   The grand dining-hall occupies the locality made famous by Jenny Lind and Edwin Booth, where Adelina Patti made her first public appearance, and where Rachel met her first American audience.   After making fortunes for several proprietors, the house in 1892 passed into the proprietorship of the Hon. Tilly Haynes, a well-known and public-spirited Massachusetts man, who has made a notable success of the United-States Hotel, at Boston.   The original cost of the Broadway Central was $2,000,000, and nearly a quarter of a million more was spent by Mr. Haynes in thoroughly renovating, refitting, refurnishing and modernizing it up to the times in every regard.   It is a solid and spacious structure, with seven stories above the main floor, and very spacious and comfortable public rooms.   It is admirably protected against fires.   Its cuisine is noted for its excellence.   It is in a singularly interesting part of the city, close to Bleecker Street, the Latin Quarter of New York ; Washington Square, the site of the triumphal arch ; Lafayette and Astor Places, with their libraries, and the centre of the publishers' quarter ; the Bowery, with its picturesque humanity ; and the Cooper Institute. Only a few blocks north is the group of buildings pertaining to Grace Church, one of the handsomest sights in the metropolis.   In front of the hotel flow the vast and impressive human tides of Broadway.   From this central locality one may ride up or down-town by elevated railway or by the cable cars on Broadway, reaching the Battery in 15 minutes, and Madison Square in much less time.   Guests can get rooms here, on the European plan, for from $1 a day upward ; or full board, on the American plan, for from $2.50 a day upward.

   The Hotel Marlborough (American and European plans), on Broadway, from 36th Street to 37th Street, is a solidly built and modern red-brick structure of 400 rooms, perfectly fire-proof, and with a general luxuriousness in all details, broad lobbies, ample billiard-rooms, well-trained servants, and a famous table.

   The Hotel Métropole (European plan), is eligibly placed, at the corner of Broadway and 7th Avenue and 41st Street, and has large and comfortable accommodations.   The building is completely fire-proof.

   The Hotel Vendome (American plan), at Broadway and 41st Street, is largely availed of as a home for families, having many fine suites and a pleasant dining-room.

   The San Remo (European plan) is an immense and imposing edifice, finely situated on the high ground of West 75th Street, and facing on the lawns, woods and waters of Central Park.   The rooms in the San Remo are all in suites.

   The Hotel Beresford (European plan) is a very large new hostelry, fronting on Central Park, at 1 West 81st Street.   It is in a charming section of the city, not far from the American Museum of Natural History.

   Other Noted Hotels might be mentioned, but out of the thousand hotels there are too many worthy of notice to be described in one brief chapter.   The following is merely a partial list of the better class : Grand, Earle's, Gedney, Oriental, Barrett, Madison-Avenue, Wellington, America, Sinclair and Cosmopolitan.

   Nationality in Hotels is represented by several establishments.   The best-known is the Hotel Martin, in University Place, a French house that is also well patronized by Americans, and is of the better class.   Another French hotel is the Hotel Monico, in 18th Street ; and still another, the Hotel Français, in University Place, that, oddly enough, is kept on the American plan.   The Hotel Griffon, in 9th Street, is a French hotel, favored by French and Spanish artists, and musical and literary folk.   Spaniards put up at the Hotel Español, in 14th Street ; and Italians at the Hotel Del Recreo, in Irving Place ; and there are several Spanish and Italian boarding-houses that are practically hotels on a small scale.   On the East Side,

German hotels are numerous, but generally they are no more than lodging-houses above lager-beer saloons and restaurants ; and somewhat similar in character, without the saloon appendage, is a hotel exclusively for colored persons.

Cheap Hotels thrive mainly down town in the business district, or among the tenements. The best of them are respectable, and quite up to the requirements of the class of patronage to which they cater. On the lower West Side there are several large houses of this description, where rooms can be had for 75 cents and sometimes as low as 50 cents a night. They are considerably patronized by marketmen from Long Island and New Jersey, and clerks and porters in the markets and wholesale stores thereabouts, whose business requires them to be on duty for the early marketing before sunrise in the morning. At and around the Battery are houses of about the same class and price as the marketmen's hotels, but designed especially for the accommodation of immigrants, who were a good source of profit when Castle Garden was the immigrant receiving station. In the vicinity of City-Hall Park, where the all-night work of the newspaper offices and the Post Office naturally calls together a large night population, there are other hotels of this description, and several, like the Cosmopolitan and Earle's, that are of a higher grade. These places have but little else than their cheapness to commend them. Most of them are restricted to the accommodation of men only, and are well patronized by poor respectable persons.

Another step, literal as well as metaphorical, brings us to the very cheap hotels that flourish in the Bowery and vicinity, on the East Side, and on West Broadway, South Fifth Avenue, and adjacent streets on the West Side. These establishments are exclusively for men, and in them you will find the apotheosis of misery and vice. Petty thieves, hopeless drunkards, toughs and reprobates of all kinds, loafers and unfortunates whom fate has served unkindly in the struggle for existence congregate there night after night. Only the pencil of a Hogarth or the pen of a Dickens could do justice to this phase of metropolitan life. The general public knows very little about these houses of despair, save as occasionally it may read in the daily newspaper of the death there of some man who was once respected and influential among his fellow citizens, until drink dragged him down to the level of these Bowery dives. The hotel of this class generally has a high-sounding name and much glare of gas-light outside. Within, it is one or two floors or lofts in what was once a business building. Sometimes plain wooden partitions divide the room into many little closets, each with a cot bed ; more frequently the sleeping apartment is a huge dormitory, with a score or more of cots, foul mattresses on the floor, or wooden bunks, with a single old army blanket for the bed-clothing. A single room in the most aristocratic of these places is 25 cents a night, and beds are put down at 10 and 15 cents, and in the very worst of the class at 7 cents. Some of the signs advertise that a hot or cold bath is free to all guests, and at others the price of a night's lodging includes a glass of whiskey. The patronage of these establishments is large, and the proprietors grow rich. In 1892 there were 116 such houses, with accommodations for 14,172 persons.

Restaurants and Cafés are abundant, of all grades, from Delmonico's famous establishment, where it will cost you from $3 upward for a good dinner, to the cheap down-town eating-houses. There are several thousand establishments of this kind, and New York has come to be very much like Paris in respect to patronizing them. For the most part men live so far from their places of business that it is necessary for them to take their luncheons, and often their dinners, away from home, and for much the same reason it is the custom with many people to dine out when they attend the theatres and other places of amusement. More than that, however, thousands of families of all grades in financial means find it more economical and convenient to go to restaurants for their meals than it is to maintain home estab-lishments.   They have all the comforts of home except the kitchen and dining-room-attachment with the consequent care, expense of rent and annoyance of servants. Add to these the army of other folk who live in furnished rooms and take their meals at restaurants, and the thousands of citizens of foreign birth who have brought with them from across the water the ingrained national habit of patronizing cafés, and you have the abundance of restaurants and cafés accounted for.   Nearly all the large hotels have great public restaurants for the accommodation of others than their regular guests.   Every nationality that helps to make up the cosmopolitan charac-ter of New York has its own eating and drinking places.

Delmonico's restaurants are known all over the world.   The name has been a familiar word among the epicures of two continents for nearly three-quarters of

DELMONICO'S :   FIFTH AVENUE, BROADWAY AND 26TH STREET.

a century.   There are two establishments in New York managed by the Del-monicos.   That with which the public of this generation is most familiar occupies the entire building at Broadway, 26th Street and Fifth Avenue.   The gentlemen's Café is on the Broadway side, and the public dining-room looks across Fifth Avenue into Madison Square.   On the floors above are private parlors and dining-rooms, and the elegant banquet and ball room, which is famous as the scene of the Patriarchs' balls, of innumerable brilliant social events, and of nearly all the grand banquets that have been given for a generation.   Many of the belles of the "Four Hundred" have made their *débuts* at Delmonico's.   The place is the social centre of the wealthy and exclusive portion of New York.

The down-town establishment is at Beaver and William Streets, in a handsome eight-story building, erected in 1890.   It stands on the site of the old Beaver-Street

DELMONICO'S.
BEAVER AND WILLIAM STREETS, OPPOSITE THE COTTON EXCHANGE.

House, which was erected in 1836 by Peter and John Delmonico, who were as famous in their day as their successors are now, and established in 1827, not far from this site, the business which has been so successful ever since.   John died in 1843, and Lorenzo Delmonico was admitted to partnership.   In 1848 Peter retired. Lorenzo died in 1881, and his nephew Charles succeeded to the business.   Charles died in January, 1884, and two months later the firm which is now in existence was organized.   The members are Rosa, Lorenzo Crist, Charles Crist and Josephine Crist Delmonico.   The famous Delmonico restaurant at 22 Broad Street was closed in 1893.

The Café Savarin, in the Equitable Building, is one of the most celebrated of dining-rooms. Its ladies' restaurant is a beautiful room, on the main floor.

Roof Restaurants are becoming important features of down-town daily life. The upper parts of the Mills, Central, Equitable and other buildings have them.

Fleischmann's Vienna Model Bakery, Café and Restaurant, at Broadway and 10th Street, attracts many by its specialties in Vienna coffee, bread and ices. There is a plaza in front of the building, provided with a canvas roof and growing vines, where guests may dine in garden-like surroundings during the heated term.

The Dairy Kitchen in 14th Street is a curiosity.   It is an enormous establishment where several thousand people are fed every day.   There is orchestral music day and evening, and much glitter and show.   The prices are moderate, and the food and service correspond.

The Columbia, in 14th Street, with very showy and attractive appointments, and clean and stylish in its service, is a good example of the popular second-class restaurants on a large scale.

Dry-Goods-Store Restaurants.— Several of the large bazaar stores, like Macy's and Hearn's, have restaurants.   These do a large business, and are much to the convenience of shoppers from out of town, who chiefly patronize them.   They are not first-class in cooking or in service.   A peculiar custom distinguishes them from all other restaurants.   Elsewhere prices are wholly in multiples of five cents.   Here, however, prices are in parts of a five-cent standard.   You get a cup of coffee for six cents, and other dishes for seven, nine, thirteen, nineteen and twenty-one cents, and so on.   It is the bargain counter extended to the lunch table, and you always feel that it is bargain-day comestibles that you are getting.

Table d'Hote Dinners are served at several hundred places, from the Murray Hill and Hotel Brunswick down through many grades to the very cheap Bohemian resorts, where a dinner with wine costs 35 cents.   Several restaurants up-town, like the Hotel Hungaria, Martinelli's, Moretti's, and Riccadonna's have more than a local reputation for good cooking.   In the French quarter in the vicinity of Bleecker Street, and elsewhere down town, are several unique and low-priced establishments of this character.

Novelty in Restaurants is in abundant variety.   In the Chinese district are several Chinese restaurants, dirty, foul-smelling and cheaply furnished.   National viands of a mysterious character and national drinks are served at reasonable prices. Those who go slumming take in these restaurants, but they are not often disposed to pay a second visit.   Hebrew restaurants are numerous on the East Side, and even in the wholesale business district.   They make a specialty of serving "strictly Kosher" meat, and many of them are of a very good character.   There is a cheap Japanese restaurant on the East Side, and meals in Japanese style are excellently served at the private Japanese Club.   In East Broadway and vicinity are several Russian restaurants.   Spanish cooking prevails at several places off Park Row.   In

Mulberry Street are Italian restaurants of low order, and in Division Street are Polish eating-places. Of a much higher grade are the restaurants, cafés and summer-gardens in Second Avenue, below 14th Street. They are in effect public club-rooms, where Austrians, Swiss, Hungarians and sometimes Germans spend their evenings. All are liberally supplied with foreign and American periodicals, and they serve odd foreign eatables, and beer, wine and coffee of exceptional quality.

Cheap Restaurants keep company with the cheap hotels in location and in general character. They are feeding-places of the vilest character, where the staple article of food is hash or beans, with bread and butter, and tea or coffee, for 10 cents. Other dishes are at corresponding prices. Sidewalk stands will serve in their respective seasons an oyster, a little fish, an ear of corn or some other simple eatable for a cent; and all the year-round at the St.-Andrew's Coffee-Stands the poor can get a bowl of hot tea or coffee for a cent, and plain food quite as cheap. A tour of these parts of the city will reveal much gastronomic atrocity.

Drinking Saloons exist by the thousand all over the city. Of course, all the hotels have their bar-rooms, and most of the restaurants supply beer, wine or liquors, either with or without food. There are German lager-beer saloons everywhere, wine shops in the Italian and French quarters, "vodka" shops among the Russians, "nomadeo" bars among the Chinese, and liquor saloons on every other corner. The drinking-places are licensed by the Board of Excise Commissioners, and pay fees according to the character of their business. They are under certain restrictions regarding location near a church or school-house, the number permitted in a single block, hours of closing, etc., and they are not permitted to keep open on Sunday. It is almost needless to say that these conditions are continually ignored by the saloon-keepers. There are 9,000 licensed places in the city, and many more that exist in violation of the law. The licensed places pay to the city every year $1,500,000, which goes to the Police Pension Fund, etc. Hundreds of these places are very elegant, with heavy plate and cut glass, rich carved wood, fine frescoes and other decorations, and valuable pictures. Kirk's, at Broadway and 27th Street, and Stewart's, in Warren Street, near Broadway, are particularly famous for their collections of rare oil paintings, the most famous of all being the saloon of the Hoffman House, in 24th Street.

The Private Home Life of the wealthy and middle classes of New-Yorkers is a measure of the prosperity and culture of the community. Evidences of good living multiply on every hand in the handsome buildings and sumptuous interiors.

If old Peter Minuit, the first Governor-General of the Dutch colony in New Netherland, could drop in here to-day he would open his eyes in wonder, and would probably think himself bewitched. He bought all this Manhattan Island from the Indians for $24, which was about ninety cents for one thousand acres. Some of the land is now worth several times $24 per square foot, and the present market value of that original $24 worth of real estate is over $2,500,000,000. Changes in methods of living, in the details of food and shelter, have kept pace with this wonderful development in values of real estate. The men and women of to-day find it difficult in their luxurious, or at least comfortable, houses to realize how their ancestors lived here two centuries and more ago. The first houses were of wood, generally of one story, with two rooms and a high peaked roof, thatched with straw. The chimneys were also of wood, and there was much danger of fire. Furniture was of the rudest description, generally made of rough planks. Wooden platters and pewter spoons prevailed, but there were a few pieces of porcelain in the village, family heirlooms from Holland. Between that way of existence and living in the Vanderbilt mansion

16

or the Plaza Hotel there is a great gulf.   After a time the colonists began to build
their houses of brick, and they bore the date of the building in iron letters.   The
roofs were tiled or shingled, and there was always a weathercock.   Furnishings
were meagre ; sanded instead of carpeted floors, a little solid silver, but more
wooden or pewter ware, stiff-backed chairs and settees and tiled mantles.   Home life
was simple.   Around every house was a garden and pasturage for live stock.   The
mynheer smoked his pipe at the fire-place or under the projecting eaves of his house,
and the good vrouw found her only dissipation in running around the neighborhood
to gossip.   But even as far off as that, a custom was established that has been maintained down to the present time.   All tenants intending to move were compelled by
law to vacate by noon of May 1st.   There is the origin of New York's May moving.
Rents were then $25 to $100 a year.   Think of that in contrast now, with $7,000
for a flat.   Houses were then worth from $200 to $1,000.   Few traces are left of
that old time, but when you come down to the Colonial days, and the early part of
the present century, it is different.   Down-town, where business is in the ascendant,
over on the East Side among the foreign population, in the historic Ninth Ward, in
Greenwich and Chelsea villages, in Washington Square, you find these houses, generally shabby enough, but with an air of gentility even in decay, with their fine old
wrought-iron railings, diamond window-panes, arched doorways, fan-lights and
carved mantels and balustrades; and in the upper part of the island a few old historic
country mansions exist, redolent with memories of the past.   But the domestic life
of New York is no longer in that environment.   Now you cannot buy even an old
house in a decent neighborhood, in the city proper, for less than $10,000, and a
single ordinary lot is worth more than that, even without a house on it.   The
majority of the single private residences are worth from $25,000 to $50,000 each.
Below $25,000 there is not much to be found of a desirable character, and in good
neighborhoods.   Above $50,000 in value come the houses of the millionaires,
occupying several city lots, splendid examples of architecture, and decorated and
furnished at lavish expense.   A list of these homes of the wealthy would number
several hundred that might reasonably be called palaces.   Rents are high, even for
ordinary houses.   It is possible to rent as low as $600 or $800, but either the house
will be old and without modern improvements, or the locality objectionable.   For a
tolerably decent house in the heart of the city from $1,000 to $2,000 must be paid;
and the figure must be increased to $3,000 and upwards if something desirable is
sought.   The West Side above 59th Street has within a few years developed into
the most agreeable residence-quarter.   Rents there are a trifle lower than farther
down-town, while the houses are in every way more attractive architecturally, and
more modern and convenient in arrangement.   In all respects this section of the
metropolis might justly be taken as an example of the perfection of attainment in
the contemporaneous home-life of a great city.   In the country annexed district
across the Harlem, values and rentals are at a lower figure, because municipal
improvements have not yet wholly reached there.

Apartment Houses, it has been said, hold more than half of the middle-class
population of Manhattan Island.   Real estate is so valuable and consequently rents
so high that to occupy a house is quite beyond the reach of a family of ordinary
means, and the suburbs on account of their inaccessibility are out of the question.
Consequently apartments and flats have become a necessity, and a system of living,
originally adopted for that reason, has now become very much of a virtue.   Apart-
ment-life is popular and to a certain extent fashionable.   Even society countenances
it, and a brownstone front is no longer indispensable to at least moderate social

standing. And as for wealthy folk who are not in society, they are taking more and more to apartments. There is a great difference in apartments. You can get one as low as $300 a year, or you can pay as high as $7,000 or even more annually; in the former case you will be the occupant of a flat, but below that rental figure the flats degenerate rapidly into tenements. But even the low-priced flats have much to commend. They have generally five or six small rooms with private hall, bath-room, kitchen-range, freight-elevator for groceries, etc., janitor's service, gas chandeliers, very fair woodwork and wall-paper and often steam-heat. Between $25 and $50 a month rental the difference is chiefly in location, in number of rooms and minor details of finish. A small family with refined tastes and no social ambitions can have an agreeable home of this kind for $50, or possibly $40 a month, the latter figure in Harlem. There are in such flats many comforts that are lacking in houses in the suburbs, and the drawbacks are only contracted quarters, impossibility of privacy, and the chance of annoyance from other tenants. Above $50 a month the apartment may be of seven, eight or nine rooms, handsomely finished, and with much luxurious show in the way of tiled floors, marble wainscot in the public halls, carved over-mantels, stained glass and other fine appointments. In houses where the apartments rent for from $50 upward there are uniformed hall-boys at the public entrance, and when you reach the $1,000 a year figure there will be a passenger elevator and other conveniences. On the West Side are the majority of the medium-priced apartments, renting from $30 to $75 a month, and also several of the highest class houses of the kind. In Harlem the variety and the number is greater, with almost none of the first rank. On the East Side there are more of the low-priced flats, and on Fifth Avenue, Madison Avenue and adjacent streets a few of the best quality.

Most of the handsomest apartment-houses in the city are in the vicinity of Central Park. One of the largest and best, is the Dakota, at Central Park West and 72d Street. It is a many-gabled building in the style of a French chateau, and is elegant in all its appointments. In 59th Street near Seventh Avenue are the Central-Park, or Navarro Flats, which include several independent houses constructed as a single building. Architecturally they are notable with Moorish arches, numerous balconies, grand entrances and highly ornamental façades in the Spanish style. In interior appointments the houses are not surpassed in the world. The structure cost $7,000,000. The different houses in the group are known as the Madrid, Granada, Lisbon, Cordova, Barcelona, Valencia, Salamanca and Tolosa.

Other superior apartment-houses on the West Side in the neighborhood of the Park are the Osborne, Grenoble, Wyoming and Van Corlaer, in Seventh Avenue; the Strathmore, Windsor, Rutland, Albany and Pocantico, in Broadway; the Beresford, San Remo, La Grange, Endicott and Rutledge, in Central Park West; and the Nevada, on the Boulevard. In Madison Avenue are several elegant modern houses of the highest class, with rents up to $2,000 to $4,000 a year, like the Earlscourt, St. Catherine, St. Honore, Hoffman Arms, and Santa Marguerita. In Columbus Avenue are the Brockholst and Greylock; and in Fifth Avenue are the Hamilton and the Knickerbocker. In the central part of the city are the Gramercy. Park, Anglesea, Chelsea, Florence, Westmoreland, Douglas, Beechwood and many others. The Croisic, Benedict, and Alpine are exclusively bachelor apartments.

Lodging and Boarding-Houses afford accommodations for living to a considerable per cent. of the community. High rents have much to do with this, as well as the desire to escape housekeeping cares and the necessities of the thousands of young unmarried people who find employment here away from their family homes.

Most persons of moderate means who hire a house find themselves obliged to rent rooms or to take boarders to help pay expenses, and hundreds go into the business of thus catering to the needs of the homeless, purely as a money-making enterprise. These houses are as widely diverse in character as the people whom they serve. A mechanic or laborer can hire a room for $2 a week, and get board for from $3 to $5 a week ; the wealthy bachelor may pay $25 or more a week for his suite of rooms and as much more for his board. Every individual caprice and purse can find something to suit. Broadly stated, it is not possible to get board and room in a respectable house in a fairly good locality for less than $7 or $8 a week. For that there will be wholesome food, but the room will be a small side-room, or a cramped attic-room, under the roof. For comfortable sleeping quarters with good board, $10 a week is about the lowest figure. Of that amount $4 or $5 a week is reckoned for the board, and the balance for the room-rent. The majority of clerks and others on small salaries bring their expenditure below the $10 limit by sacrificing comforts. These figures can be carried to any extreme that individual taste and means shall dictate.

The Tenements display the lowly side and often the dark side of New-York life. It is not possible to locate the tenement-house population within any closely defined limits. In general, it may be said to hold parts of nearly all the streets below 14th, except a part of the old Ninth Ward, which is distinctively the Native-American section of the city, and in and about Washington Square and lower Fifth Avenue, clinging to the river-front on either side, monopolizing almost entirely the East Side nearly over to Broadway. Above 14th Street on the East Side it is supreme east of Third Avenue as far as the Harlem River, with the exception of a part of lower Second Avenue and a few side-streets here and there. On the West Side it comes from the river-front as far east as Sixth Avenue, with oases of better homes here and there, and this as far north as about 59th Street. The territory above 59th Street to 125th Street has very little of this population. Tenement-houses are as a rule great towering buildings, many of them squalid and in bad repair, and devoid of any but the rudest arrangements for existence. They are packed with human beings. In a single block between Avenue B and Avenue C and 2d and 3d Streets there are over 3,500 residents, and a smaller block on Houston Street contains 3,000 people, which is at the rate of 1,000,000 to the square mile. That section is altogether populated at the rate of 500,000 to the square mile, which is as if the entire population of the city should be crowded into a space less than two miles square.

The picture of life in these quarters repeats what has been so often written of the misery of the poor in great cities. Frequently half a dozen people eat, sleep, and somehow exist in a single room, and tenants who have two or three rooms generally keep boarders besides their own large families. Monthly rents range from $1 a room upward, and $10 a month will sometimes secure a small stuffy apartment of three or four rooms. The landlords of these rookeries become very rich out of the needs of the poor tenants. Most of these old tenement-houses are occupied by immigrants just from Europe. When they have been here a short time they are inclined to seek better quarters in new and improved, although still cheap enough, buildings that are being put up in recent years. But the condition of living is not materially changed ; it is only different in degree of squalor and unhealthfulness.

Of all grades, good, bad and indifferent there were in 1891, according to the report of the Board of Health, 34,967 front and 2,391 rear tenement-houses, containing 1,064,703 persons above five years of age and 106,708 below that age ; about two-thirds of the entire population. In this estimate 150 first-class apartment-houses are not included, but the medium-priced flats and apartments.

The City, County, State and National Government, Offices and Buildings, Courts, Etc.

THE City and County of New York are identical in their boundaries, and were consolidated in their governments by act of the Legislature, April 30, 1874. The Mayor, Aldermen and Commonalty of the City of New York is the name of the corporation representing the city and county. It is a public corporation, and as such its charter is always subject to amendments or alterations by the State Legislature. All local administration of both city and county affairs is in the hands of this corporation. The city has had a corporate existence since the charter for the town of New Amsterdam was granted, in 1657, by Peter Stuyvesant, representing the West India Company and the States-General of Holland. Other charters were granted from time to time afterward, superseding existing ones, and important amendments were made to them. These amendments and all other legislation pertaining to the city were codified in the New-York City Consolidation Act, passed by the Legislature in July, 1882. This act, with later additions, makes a volume of 1,100 pages. Since 1882 the Legislature has passed many laws relating to New-York City, some of which, while not in definite terms amending any of the sections of the Consolidation Act, do so in effect.

General Provisions Pertaining to Departments and Officers provide that a majority of a Board in any department constitutes a quorum to perform and discharge business. No expense can be incurred by any of the boards or officers unless an appropriation for it has previously been made by the Board of Estimate and Apportionment ; and in any year for any purpose the expenditures must not exceed the appropriation. The heads of departments, except in specified cases, appoint and remove chiefs of bureaus (except the Chamberlain) and clerks and employees, without reference to the tenure of office; but the men must be informed of the cause of the proposed removal, and be allowed an opportunity of explanation. In case of removal, a statement showing the cause is filed in the department. The numbers and duties of clerks and other employees, except as is otherwise provided, with the respective salaries, are fixed by the heads of departments, subject to the revision of the Board of Estimate and Apportionment. The heads of departments and the commissions appointed by the Mayor report to him once in three months, and at such other times as he may direct, the reports being published in *The City Record*. They must furnish him at any time such information as he may demand. The heads of departments and of bureaus (except the Police Department) are required to furnish to any tax-payer desiring them true and certified copies of books and accounts upon payment in advance at the rate of five cents for every hundred words. Books, accounts and papers in all departments and bureaus, except the Police Department,

are open at all times to any tax-payer, subject to reasonable rules.   In every department or board there is kept a record of its transactions accessible to the public.
Once a week a brief abstract is made of all transactions, and of all contracts awarded
and entered into for work and materials of every description, along with notices of
appointments and removals from office and changes in salaries ; and these are all
printed in *The City Record*, a publication issued daily at the city's expense, and containing many details as to the municipal life.

The Legislative Department is vested in a Board of Aldermen, including
a President and Vice-President.   Formerly there was a Board of Aldermen, another
of Assistant Aldermen, and another of Councilmen ; and collectively they were
known as the Common Council.   This name still survives, and is applied, semi-
officially, to the Board of Aldermen.

The Board of Aldermen chosen in November, 1892, for a term of two years,
instead of one year, as hitherto, consists of 31 members.   Of these 28 were elected
in that part of the city below the Harlem River ; one in the 23d Ward, and one in
the 24th Ward (on mainland, north of 170th Street).   The President of the Board,
elected at large, is the thirty-first member.   The salary of members is $2,000 a year ;
and that of the President is $3,000.   The Aldermen take office in January succeeding
their election in November.   A majority constitutes a quorum.   The Comptroller, the
Commissioner of Public Works, the Corporation Counsel, and the President of the
Board of Commissioners of each department are entitled to seats in the Board, and to
participate in its discussions, but are not members of the Board nor entitled to vote.
Every legislative act is by resolution or ordinance.   No resolution or ordinance is
passed except by a vote of a majority of all members elected to the Board.   In case
any resolution or ordinance involves the expenditure of money, or the laying of an
assessment, or the lease of real estate or franchise, the votes of three-fourths of the
members are necessary to its passage.   No money can be expended for a celebration,
procession, formal ceremony, reception or entertainment of any kind, unless by the
votes of four-fifths of all the members.   Every resolution or ordinance is presented
to the Mayor for his approval.   He should return it approved or disapproved within
ten days after receiving it, or at the next meeting of the Board after the expiration
of ten days.   It takes effect as if he had approved it, unless he returns it, with his
disapproval in writing, within the specified time.   If disapproved, and again passed
by the votes of at least two-thirds of the members elected, but in no case by a less
vote than is required by its character, it also takes effect.

The Board of Aldermen has power to make, continue, modify and repeal such
ordinances, regulations and resolutions as may be necessary to carry into effect all
the powers vested in the corporation and for the fuller organization and carrying out
of the powers and duties of any department.   It has the power to enforce such ordinances by ordaining penalties in sums not·to exceed $100 for every violation.   It is
part of its duty to regulate the use of the streets, sidewalks and other public places,
especially in regard to traffic, obstructions, openings for gas and water mains and
sewers, paving, grading and cleaning, naming, numbering of houses and other needs.
It regulates the disposition of ashes and garbage, the public cries and noises, the
use of fire-arms, the conduct of places of public amusement, the management of the
markets, the licensing of cartmen, cabmen, junk-dealers, pedlers, intelligence-offices,
etc., and the sale of meats, fruits and vegetables.   Its duties and powers are multifarious.   In general it can exercise authority over everything that pertains to the
domestic economy of the community.   The municipal ordinances of the Board have
all the force of statute law, and are enforced by the police authorities and the courts.

The Board can so far invade the province of legislation that it can establish measures for the suppression of vice and immorality, for restraining and prohibiting certain kinds of business and for preventing the obstruction of the North and East rivers by ships mooring or anchoring in the channels; and the Board can require the public officials to carry into effect its decrees. But there are some things that the Board is especially prohibited from doing. The municipality cannot deprive

PARK PLACE, FROM BROADWAY TO CHURCH STREET.

itself of its legislative power over the streets and their use. Any attempt to do so by contract, either expressed or implied, would not only be revocable at pleasure, but would be null and void. The city has no authority to grant to anyone the right to construct and maintain in the streets a railway for private gain. The Board has no power to appropriate any portion of a street to private use, to the exclusion of the public.

The Executive Department is vested in the Mayor and the heads of the departments. The Mayor is elected at the November general election, for a term of two years, commencing January 1st after his election. His salary is $10,000 per year. It is the duty of the Mayor to communicate to the Board of Aldermen, at least once a year, a general statement of the finances, government and improvements of the city; to recommend to the Board of Aldermen all such measures as he shall deem expedient; to keep himself informed of the doings of the several departments; and generally to perform all such duties as may be required of him by the city ordinances and the laws of the State. The Mayor is a magistrate. He appoints clerks and subordinates to aid him in the discharge of his official duties, and renders every three months to the Board of Aldermen a statement of the expenses and receipts of his office. The aggregate yearly expenditure must not exceed $20,000. He regulates and controls by appointment or license, auctioneers, public exhibitions, immigrant-passenger-agents, solicitors of hotels, etc. He is by virtue of his office one of the Commissioners of Immigration. The Mayor can be removed from office for cause by the Governor of the State.   Formerly the Mayor's appointments were reviewed by the Board of Aldermen.   Now, however, he holds (with a few exceptions) the appointing power entirely independent of that body.

The Finance Department is in charge of the Comptroller, who is elected for three years, and has a salary of $10,000.   The department, which is in many respects the most important and most influential branch of the municipal organization, has control of the fiscal concerns of the corporation, and there all accounts of other departments are subject to inspection and revision.   The Comptroller furnishes to each head of department, weekly, a statement of the unexpended balance of the appropriation available for his department.   There are five bureaus in this department. 1st : For the collection of revenue from rents and interest on bonds and mortgages, and revenue arising from the sale or use of property belonging to or managed by the city, and for the management of the markets.   The chief officer of this bureau is called the Collector of the City Revenue and Superintendent of Markets.   2d : For the collection of taxes ; the chief officer of which is called the Receiver of Taxes. 3d : For the collection of assessments and arrears of taxes and assessments, and of water-rents.   The chief officer is called the Collector of Assessments and Clerk of Arrears.   4th : For auditing, revising and settling all the city's accounts, the auditing bureau, under the supervision of the Comptroller.   The chief officers are two Auditors of Accounts, appointed or removed at the pleasure of the Comptroller. 5th : For receiving all moneys paid into the treasury of the city, and for the paying of money on warrants drawn by the Comptroller and countersigned by the Mayor. The chief officer is called the Chamberlain.   The Comptroller publishes in *The City Record*, two months before the election of charter officers, a full and detailed

CITY-HALL PLACE :   CENTRE, PARK, CHAMBERS AND READE STREETS.

statement of the receipts and expenditures and the cash balances or surplus of the corporation during the year ending the first day of the month in which such publication is made.

The City Chamberlain is appointed by the Mayor for a term of four years.   He gives a bond for $500,000, and has a salary of $25,000 per year, out of which he pays his assistants and clerks.

The Board of Commissioners of the Sinking-Fund is composed of the Mayor, Recorder, Chamberlain, Comptroller, and Chairman of the Finance Committee of the Board of Aldermen. It has power to sell or lease at public auction, or by sealed bids, any city property except wharves or piers.

The Board of Estimate and Apportionment is composed of the Mayor, the Comptroller, the President of the Board of Aldermen, and the President of the Board of Taxes and Assessments. It has meetings at intervals throughout the year, when called by the Mayor. In October and November it makes a provisional estimate of the amounts required to pay the expenses of conducting the public business of the city and county in each department and branch thereof, and of the Board of Education, for the next financial year, and to meet the interest and debt account and taxes due the State. These estimates are scrutinized by the Board of Aldermen, and subsequently revised by the Board of Estimate and Apportionment. They are finally determined late in December, sometimes on the last day, and then they become the appropriations for the ensuing year. The Comptroller prepares and submits to the Board of Aldermen before its yearly meeting a statement setting forth the amounts authorized by law to be raised by tax in that year for city purposes, and also an estimate of the probable amount of receipts of the treasury of the city during the current year from all sources of revenue of the general fund. A summary of the finances of the city is as follows : ˙The entire amount of taxes received by ordinance of the Board of Aldermen for the year 1892 was $33,232,725. ˙ The rate of taxation is about $1.85 per $100, upon a valuation of real and personal estate of over $1,700,000,000, and the rate upon the assessed valuation of the personal estate of such companies as are subject to local taxation thereon, amounting to nearly $80,-000,000, is $1.68 per $100.

The total funded debt of the city and county :

December 31, 1892, was	$155,161,974
Deducting the amount held by the Commissioners of the Sinking Fund as investments, and cash, ...	56,532,407
Left the net funded debt, ...	$ 98,629,567

The general tax rate for 1892 was $1.85 on each $100 of assessed valuation, which is the lowest in thirty years, and lower than the rate in any other large city in the United States. The amount to be raised by taxation in 1892 was $33,725,556, besides which the city has and expends an income of about $3,000,000 a year, from fees, licenses, and other sources. The total assessed valuation of the city, real and personal, is $1,828,264,275, an increase of over $42,000,000 since 1891. Of this amount, $71,306,402 is corporation property, exempt from State taxes, and paying a rate to the city of $1.71 on each $100.

The Department of Public Parks is under the care of the Board of Park Commissioners, four in number, who are appointed by the Mayor, for terms of five years. The President of the Board draws a salary of $5,000 a year. The other members serve without pay. The Board has the care and maintenance of all the parks in the city, and also of certain streets in the vicinity of Central Park, such as Fifth Avenue, Morningside Avenue, and 72d, 110th and 122d Streets. It is assisted by a superintendent, an engineer of construction, and a superintending gardener.

The Police Department is under the charge of the Board of Police. It con_ sists of four persons, known as Police Commissioners of the City of New York. They receive their appointments from the Mayor, and hold their offices (unless sooner removed) for six years, at a salary of $5,000 each. The Board is authorized and empowered to make, adopt and enforce rules and regulations for the government, discipline, administration and disposition of the police department and police force and its members. The police force consists of one superintendent, at a salary of $6,000 ; four inspectors ; captains, not exceeding one to each fifty patrolmen ; sergeants, not exceeding four to each fifty patrolmen ; detective sergeants, not ex-

BROADWAY, LOOKING NORTH FROM BARCLAY STREET.   THE POST OFFICE.

ceeding forty ; surgeons not exceeding fifteen in number ; and patrolmen, etc., making 3,639. The Board of Police appoints all the members, and selects and appoints to perform detective duty as many patrolmen, not exceeding forty, as it deems necessary.

The Department of Public Works is under the charge of the Commissioner of Public Works, who is appointed by the Mayor, and holds his office for four years, at a salary of $8,000. The chief duties of the department pertain to the water-supply ; the altering, opening, paving and lighting of the streets ; and the care of sewers and drainage. These duties are divided among eight bureaus.

The Department of Docks is managed by a board of three commissioners, appointed by the Mayor, each of whom is paid $5,000 a year. The board has control of all the dock property of the city — which is a considerable portion of the entire river-front at the lower end of the city — and makes repairs, improvements, etc.

The Department of Street-Cleaning, the name of which fully describes its mission, is under the control of a single commissioner, whose salary is $6,000 a year. He is appointed by the Mayor. He is assisted by a deputy of his own selection, whose salary is $4,000 a year ; and employs nearly 1,500 sweepers and 500 carts.

The Department of Health is under the charge of the Board of Health, which consists of the President of the Board of Police, the Health-Officer of the Port, and two officers to be called Commissioners of Health, one of whom must be a practising physician. The commissioner who is not a physician is president of the Board. They are appointed by the Mayor, independently of the Board of Aldermen, and, unless sooner removed, hold their offices for six years. The salary of the president is $5,000 a year ; of the other commissioner, $4,000. The authority of the Board extends over the waters of the bay, up to and within the quarantine limits established by law, but not to interfere with the powers and duties of the Commissioners of Quarantine or of the Health-Officer of the Port. The total number of deaths in the city during 1892 was 44,329, or 24.26 to each thousand inhabitants. The number of births registered was 49,447 ; the number of marriages, 16,001. The amount of money expended by the Board yearly exceeds $400,000. The summer corps of physicians inspected in July and August 40,193 tenement-houses ; visited 348,318 families ; and treated 23,834 sick persons. It is the duty of the Board to make quarterly and yearly reports to the Mayor of all its operations. The Mayor can at any time call for a fuller report. The Mayor and one Commissioner from the Department of Health, the Commissioner of Public Works, one delegate from the Bureau of Inspection of Public Buildings, and the Commissioner of the Department of Street-Cleaning are required by law to meet yearly between November 15th and December 30th to consider the subject of tenement and lodging-houses, and to make

POST OFFICE. WORLD, TIMES AND POTTER BUILDINGS. PARK ROW. ANN STREET.

such recommendation in the laws affecting them as they deem best ; and to cause such recommendation to be sent to the Governor of the State, and the Senate and Assembly, yearly, on or before January 15th. They are also to consider the execution of the laws, and recommend to the Board of Health such changes as they deem best. There are two bureaus in the department. The chief officer of one is called the Sanitary Superintendent. He must have been for ten years a practising physician.

He is the chief executive officer of the department. The chief officer of the second bureau is called the Register of Records. In this bureau are recorded, without fees, every birth, marriage and death, and all inquisitions of coroners, which are taken within the city. The Board takes cognizance of the condition of any building, excavation, or premises; of any business pursuit, and of any phase of city life, which may

affect public health, or the healthfulness of the city, and has powers which are virtually absolute to compel changes. The powers of the Board include the supervision of the repairs of buildings, in so far as sanitary condition is concerned; the regulation and control of public markets, in matters affecting cleanliness, ventilation and drainage; and the prevention of the sale of improper arti-

HALL OF RECORDS, OR REGISTER'S HALL, NEAR PARK ROW, IN CITY-HALL PARK

cles; the removal of matter on the public streets which may lead to results dangerous to life or health; the prevention of accidents by which life or health may be endangered; and generally the abating of all nuisances. It is the duty of the owner or person interested in every building or premises, to keep it in such manner that it is not dangerous or prejudicial to life or health. Every person violating or refusing to comply with the provisions of the law in these respects, or with the regulations of the Board, is guilty of a misdemeanor. The Board may remove or cause to be removed, to a place designated by it, any person sick with a contagious, pestilential, or infectious disease; and it has power to provide and pay for the use of such proper places. It may enclose streets and passages, to forbid and prevent all communication with houses or families infected with disease. It may issue a proclamation, declaring every place where there is reason to believe a pestilential, contagious or infectious disease actually exists, to be an infected place within the meaning of the health laws of the State. After such proclamation is issued, all vessels arriving in the port of New York from such infected places, together with their officers and crews, passengers and cargoes, are subject to quarantine for such period as is necessary, and it may regulate or prohibit internal intercourse by land or water with such infected places. It is the duty of the Board to aid in the enforcement of all laws of the State applicable in the city to the preservation of life and the care of health, including the laws relative to cleanliness and the sale of deleterious drugs and foods. It is authorized to require reports from hospitals, prisons, schools, places of amusement, etc. It is to omit no reasonable means for ascertaining the existence and cause of disease, sending such information to health authorities elsewhere, with such suggestions as it may see fit. The Board, the Health-Officer and Quarantine Commissioners are to co-operate to prevent the spread of disease and to ensure the preservation of health. The Board is authorized from time to time to alter, annul or amend the sanitary code. It keeps a general complaint book, in which may be entered by any person in good faith, any complaint of a sanitary nature, giving the names of persons complained of and date of the entry, with suggestion of remedy; and such complaints are to be investigated. It is the duty of all boards and officers having charge of any property controlled by public authority, to report upon and give knowledge of anything affecting sanitary conditions to the Health Board. False reports on these matters from any one required to make reports are misdemeanors. Prompt action in such cases is required of prosecuting officers, and police justices. The Sanitary Code, consisting of 219 sections, is made up of the sanitary ordinances adopted by the Department of Health; and is of profound value in fighting epidemics and other menaces.

The Board of Excise, with rooms at 54 Bond Street, corner of the Bowery, acts under a law of the State, the same that applies in most respects to cities of over 30,000 inhabitants. It is composed of three members, who are appointed by the Mayor, for a term the same as his own, and receive salaries of $5,000 each. The Board issues licenses for the sale of spirituous liquors, wines, ale and beer, to saloons, hotels, restaurants, drug and grocery stores, and collects the license fees therefor. The receipts of the Board for 1892 were $1,523,780. Aside from paying the expenses of the Board, this sum was used as follows: New York Fire-Relief Department, $75,000; police pensions, $307,000; charitable institutions for the support of children committed by magistrates, $667,000; general fund of the city, $350,000.

The Law Department has at its head the Counsel to the Corporation, who receives his appointment from the Mayor, for a term of four years, and draws an annual salary of $12,000. The department has charge of the law business of the corporation and its departments, the management of legal proceedings relating to the laying out of streets, and the preparation of all deeds, leases, contracts and other legal papers connected with any department, and is at all times the legal adviser of the city officials. There are two bureaus in the department, in charge respectively of the Corporation Attorney and the Public Administrator. Certain actions in behalf of the city, such as for the recovery of penalties, etc., are conducted by the Corporation Attorney. The Public Administrator collects and takes charge of the property of persons dying intestate, and is, in effect, a public executor. The District Attorney is the prosecuting officer of the city and county. He is elected by the people for a

JEFFERSON-MARKET POLICE-COURT, SIXTH AND GREENWICH AVENUES.

term of three years, receiving a salary of $12,000 a year. His six assistants, whom he appoints, receive salaries of $7,500 a year each. The Recorder is elected for fourteen years. He receives a salary of $12,000. The City Judge and the Judges of General Sessions are elected for fourteen years, at yearly salaries of $12,000. The Police Justices, fifteen in number, are appointed by the Mayor, at $8,000 a year. The Courts of Special Sessions are held by them, at the Tombs; and there are six police-courts, in various parts of the city.

The Harlem Municipal Building, at the corner of Sylvan Place and 121st Street, is a large building erected in 1891–92, and containing the rooms of the Harlem courts, and the local branches of various municipal departments.   In its imposing architecture and modern equipments it is worthy of this dignity.

The Criminal Court Building, erected in 1891–93, occupies a site alongside the Tombs, with which they are connected by a bridge across the street, connecting the cells and the court-rooms.   The building is in the German-Romanesque style, and the architects were Thom, Wilson & Schaarschmidt.   The wings are crowned by pediments, and adorned with statuary.   The building is of great size, and its internal arrangements are admirably adapted for the serious and solemn purposes for which this temple of justice was erected.   With its brilliant coloring and lofty façades, the court-house forms a striking contrast to the low, dark and massive Tombs.   In it will be held the courts of Oyer and Terminer, General Sessions of the Peace, Special Sessions of the Peace, and one or more police courts; and it provides proper office-accommodations for the judges and clerks of these courts, for juries and grand juries, and for the district attorney and other officers. It occupies the square bounded by White, Franklin, Centre and Elm Streets.

HARLEM MUNICIPAL BUILDING, SYLVAN PLACE AND 121st STREET.

THE CRIMINAL LAW COURTS (UNFINISHED) AND THE TOMBS.
CENTRE STREET, WEST SIDE, FROM FRANKLIN TO LEONARD STREETS.

NINETEENTH-WARD POLICE-COURT, 191 EAST 57TH STREET.

The Department of Public Charities and Correction is under the charge of the Board of Charities and Correction, which consists of three persons known as Commissioners. They are appointed by the Mayor, at a salary of $5,000 each. The department possesses and exercises full and exclusive powers for the government, management, maintenance and direction of the several institutions, buildings, premises and properties belonging to the city, and situated upon Blackwell's, Ward's, Randall's and Hart's Islands; of all places provided for the detention of prisoners (except Ludlow-Street Jail, which is under the Sheriff); and of all hospitals belonging to the city, except such as are conducted by the Department of Health, and especially of the Alms-house and Workhouse; of the nurseries for poor and destitute children on Randall's Island; and of the county lunatic asylum and the lunatic asylum upon Ward's Island; and of the Potter's Field, and especially, also, of the penitentiary and city prison. There is in the department a Bureau of Charities and a Bureau of Correction. The former has charge of matters relating to persons not criminal; the latter of matters relating to criminals. The Board of Public Charities and Correction also maintains on Ward's Island an asylum for inebriates.

The Fire Department is under the exclusive charge of the Board of Fire-Commissioners, consisting of three persons known as Fire-Commissioners. They are appointed by the Mayor and Board of Aldermen, and hold their offices for six years, unless sooner removed. Their salaries are $5,000 each. There are in the department three bureaus. One is charged with the duty of preventing and extinguishing fires, and of protecting property from water used at fires. The principal officer is called the Chief of the Fire-Department. Another bureau is charged with the execution of all laws relating to the storage, sale and use of combustible materials. The principal officer is called the Inspector of Combustibles. Another bureau investigates the origin and cause of fires, under the Fire Marshal.

The Department of Street-Improvements, Twenty-Third and Twenty-Fourth Wards, is in charge of a single commissioner, elected by the people of those wards. Its jurisdiction is north of the Harlem River, and corresponds to that of the Department of Public Works in the rest of the city.

The Department of Taxes and Assessments assesses taxable property, real, personal and corporation, upon which is levied a tax sufficient to meet the expenses of conducting the business of the city and county government in each department, court, etc., including the interest on the City debt, the principal of any stock or bonds that may become due, and the proportion of the State tax for the next fiscal year. It is governed by a Board of three commissioners, appointed by the Mayor for six years each. The salary of the President is $5,000 a year, that of the other members $4,000. The Commissioners are assisted by a Secretary, a Chief Deputy, and 16 Deputy Tax Commissioners; a Board of four Assessors; and a clerical force. The President is by law one of the members of the Board of Estimate and Apportionment, controlling the financial affairs of the city ; and of the Armory Board, charged with the purchase of land and the erection and equipping of armories for the militia. The Board of Assessors apportion the cost of local improvements, and levy it upon the property benefited.

The Department of Buildings has charge of all matters relating to buildings. The Department has full power in passing upon questions of the mode of construction or material to be used in the erection or alteration of any building ; also plumbing and drainage of all buildings; and light and ventilation of tenements; and stairways, fire-escapes and other exits in theatres and other public buildings; with power to make all details of construction conform to the intent and meaning of the law. Its office is at Fourth Avenue and 18th Street.

The Board of Education includes 21 Commissioners appointed by the Mayor, and supervises the free public schools. The office is at 146 Grand Street.

Other Civic Duties are fulfilled by the Commissioners of Accounts, the Aqueduct Commissioners, the Board of Armory Commissioners, the Commissioners of the Harlem-River Bridge, and the Civil-Service Supervisory and Examining Board.

The City Hall has been in its time the finest piece of architecture in the country, but it is surpassed now by many buildings of more imposing structure, if not so classical in their architectural style. It was built between the years 1803 and 1812, at a cost of over $500,000. Its front and east and west sides are of marble, but sandstone was regarded as good enough for the rear, the city being at that time mostly on its front. In 1890 the rear was painted, making all sides uniform in appearance. The city has so outgrown it that many other buildings have to be used for the public offices. An enormous new City Hall, of white marble, is to be built in 1893-95, at a cost exceeding $4,000,000. Richard M. Hunt, Napoleon Le Brun and Wm. R. Ware form the advisory committee of architects. The City-Hall Park, in the very midst of the swarming denizens of the metropolis of the Western Continent, and with its broad sweep of ground, fountain, trees, and plots of grass, forms a redeeming feature to the brick and mortar, granite, marble and asphalt, that rule nearly everywhere else for many square miles on the lower end of Manhattan Island. The park and the City Hall together have been for this century the chief centre and historic place in the city. The Brooklyn Bridge, terminating in such close proximity, has added to the importance of the location. Celebrations of note have made them memorable. October 23, 1812, "The City Hall was like a Sea of Fire" in consequence of Perry's victory on Lake Erie. Here the citizens became wild with enthusiasm on the

LUDLOW-STREET JAIL.   ESSEX-MARKET COURT.

ESSEX-MARKET POLICE-COURT, ESSEX ST. AND ESSEX-MARKET PLACE.

17

opening of the Erie Canal, in 1825, and a correct forecast was made of the future supremacy of the city above all other cities of the Republic. It witnessed the return of Lafayette to this country half a century after its independence was declared, the Republic meantime having taken rank as one of the chief nations of the globe. One of the greatest of modern events, the laying of the Atlantic Cable, was here cele- brated, with a keen appreciation of what it implied to mankind. The sorrows of the Nation have been here expressed, when Lincoln and Grant, the accepted leaders and heroes of the century now nearing its close, were viewed in their inanimate clay by mourning thousands, before going to their final resting places. The interior of the building is made memorable by its relics of the past, and works of art commemora- ting great events and distinguished statesmen. The Governor's Room contains furniture that was used by the first Congress of the United States, held in Federal Hall, in Wall Street. There are two desks used by Washington, one while he was President. There are portraits of Washington, Jefferson, Hamilton, Jay, and Lafay- ette, and busts of Washington and Franklin, by the most distinguished artists of their times. The portraits of many later statesmen adorn the walls.

The Mayors of the City have been elected since the charter was amended in 1830. Previous to that time they were appointed by the Common Council. John Cruger, first president of the Chamber of Commerce, with a distinguished record during the Revolutionary War, was mayor of the city from 1739 to 1744, and again from 1757 to 1766. De Witt Clinton, before becoming governor of the State, and under whose administration the Erie Canal was opened, was mayor for several terms, none succeeding each other. Fernando Wood came into unenviable promi- nence during his second administration, by pursuing a conciliatory policy toward the criminal and corrupt elements of the city. It was during the administration of A. Oakey Hall that the Tweed ring was in full possession of the reins of government, and defiant of public opinion. Its power was broken at the general election in November, 1871. Wm. F. Havemeyer then came a second time to the chair. Tweed soon died in a felon's cell, while some of his companions were sent to prison and others became exiles in foreign lands. Following is a list of mayors with their terms of service since the town has been known by its present name : Thomas Willet, 1665-1667; Thomas Delavall, 1666, 1671, 1678; Cornelis Steenwyck, 668, 1670, 1682, 1683; Matthias Nicolls, 1672; John Lawrence, 1673, 1691; William Dervall, 1695; Nicholas De Meyer, 1676; Stephanus Van Cortlandt, 1677, 1686, 1687; Francis Rombouts, 1679; William Dyer, 1680-1681; Gabriel Min- vielle, 1684; Nicholas Bayard, 1685; Peter de la Noy, 1689-1690; Abraham de Peyster, 1692-1695; William Merritt, 1695-1698; Johannes de Peyster, 1698-1699; David Provoost, 1699-1700; Isaac de Riemer, 1700-1701; Thomas Noell, 1701-1702; Philip French, 1702-1703; William Peartree, 1703-1707; Ebenezer Wilson, 1707-1710; Jacobus Van Cortlandt, 1710-1711-1719-1720; Caleb Heathcote, 1711-1714; John Johnson, 1714-1719; Robert Walters, 1720-1725; Johannes Jansen, 1725-1726; Robert Lurting, 1726-1735; Paul Richards, 1735-1739; John Cruger, 1739-1744; Stephen Bayard, 1744-1747; Edward Holland, 1747; 1757; John Cruger, 1757-1766; Whitehead Hicks, 1766-1776; David Matthews (Tory), 1776-1784; James Duane, 1784-1789; Richard Varick, 1789-1801; Edward Liv- ingston, 1801-1803; DeWitt Clinton, 1803-1807; Marinus Willett, 1807-1808; DeWitt Clinton, 1808-1810; Jacob Radcliff, 1810-1811; DeWitt Clinton, 1811- 1815; John Ferguson, 1815; Jacob Radcliff, 1815-1818; Cadwallader D. Colden, 1818-1821; Stephen Allen, 1821-1824; William Paulding, 1825-1826; Philip Hone, 1826-1827; William Paulding, 1827-1829; Walter Bowne, 1829-1833; Gideon Lee,

THE CITY HALL.

IN CITY-HALL PARK, OPPOSITE MURRAY STREET, BETWEEN BROADWAY AND PARK ROW.

1833-1834 ; Cornelius W. Lawrence, 1834-1837 ; Aaron Clark, 1837-1839 ; Isaac L. Varian, 1839-1841 ; Robert H. Morris, 1841-1844 ; James Harper, 1844-1847 ; William V. Brady, 1847-1848 ; William F. Havemeyer, 1848-49 ; Caleb S. Woodhull, 1849-1851 ; Ambrose C. Kingsland, 1851-1853 ; Jacob A. Westervelt, 1853-1855 ; Fernando Wood, 1855-1858 ; Daniel N. Tiemann, 1858-1860 ; Fernando Wood, 1860-1862 ; George Opdyke, 1862-1864 ; C. Godfrey Gunther, 1864-1866 ; John T. Hoffman, 1866-1868 ; Thomas Coman (acting mayor), 1868 ; A. Oakey Hall, 1869-1870 ; William F. Havemeyer, 1871-1874 ; William H. Wickham, 1875-1876 ; Smith Ely, 1877-1878 ; Edward Cooper, 1879-1880 ; William R. Grace, 1881-1882 ; Franklin Edson, 1883-1884 ; William R. Grace, 1885-1886 ; Abram S. Hewitt, 1887-1888 ; Hugh J. Grant, 1889-1892 ; and Thomas F. Gilroy, 1893-1894.

The Seal of the City had its origin in colonial and Dutch times. The commercial activity at first was in the purchase of furs from the Indians, and nothing was so potent in bringing about a trade as gunpowder, whiskey or flour. The contracting parties were sailors and Indians. Hence we have on the seal a sailor and an Indian, representing the traders, and two beavers and two barrels, representing the articles traded in ; and the windmills of Holland, celebrated in the 17th as well as in the 19th centuries, are represented, and the four arms serve for the quarterings. An eagle surmounts the shield, and in this we have a more modern intimation. The first seal, for New Amsterdam, was granted in 1654, the town having been incorporated the preceding year. For this the seal of the Duke of York was substituted under Governor Nicolls, in 1669, and was continued in use until 1686.

The Courts and Judicial Powers and Proceedings.—The term "City Hall of the City of New York," when used in any law of the State, includes, for all legal purposes, all buildings designated by the Board of Aldermen for the use of the courts or public offices within that part of the city bounded by Chambers Street, Broadway, Park Row, Centre Street, Mail Street and Tryon Row ; but rooms used by any of the courts of the city and county of New York are deemed a part of the City Hall for the purpose of holding a court. The First Judicial District of the State consists of the city of New York. The library of the Law Institute is in the Post-Office Building, under the care and management of the Justices of the Supreme Court of the First Judicial District, who are its trustees. It is open to the public. The Justices of the Supreme and Superior Courts and the Judges of the Court of Common Pleas have power to commit to the Inebriate Asylum, under the control of the Commissioners of Charities and Correction, for a term not to exceed two years, actual inhabitants of the city who are unfit for conducting their own affairs on account of habitual drunkenness. The Circuit and District Courts of the United States are held in the Post-Office Building. The original jurisdiction of the former is in suits arising under the revenue, copyright and patent laws, and in civil law and equity suits between citizens of different States ; its appellate jurisdiction is from the United-States District Court. The latter has jurisdiction in admiralty and maritime cases, in cases where an alien sues on tort in violation of a treaty or the laws of nations, and in suits instituted in the United States by and against foreign consuls. The State courts, — the Supreme Court and the Court of Oyer and Terminer, are held in the County Court-House. The former is the general law and equity court of the State, and the latter is the criminal branch of the same. The appellate branch of the Supreme Court, known as the General Term, passes on appeals from the trial justices of the court, the final appeal being from the General Term to the Court of Appeals, which sits at Albany. The salaries paid the Justices of the First Judicial District are $17,500 each a year, this being $11,500 a year more than is paid to the justices of the other districts of the State, the city and county of New York paying the additional amount. Of the city courts the Court of Common Pleas for the City and County and the Superior Court of the County are courts of record, and each of them has six judges, who are magistrates. The courts have concurrent jurisdiction with the Supreme Court of the State within the city limits. They both hold general terms, final appeals being made to the Court of Appeals. They sit in the County Court-House. The jurisdiction of these courts is about the same ; the former has appellate jurisdiction in cases from the city and district courts, its decisions being final. The salaries paid the judges are $15,000. The City Court, formerly called the Marine Court, sits in the City Hall. It has six Judges, who hold office for six years, with salaries of $10,000 a year each. It is the lowest of the courts of record. It tries actions to the amount of $2,000. It has a limited maritime jurisdiction, and also a general term. The District Courts are inferior civil courts. There are eleven of them, held as follows : First, Chambers Street, corner Centre Street ; 2d, corner of Pearl and Centre Streets ; 3d, 125 Sixth Avenue ; 4th, 30 1st Street ; 5th, 154 Clinton Street ; 6th, 61 Union Place ; 7th, 151 East 57th Street ; 8th, 200 West 22d Street; 9th, 150 East 125th Street ; 10th, 158th Street, corner of Third Avenue; 11th, 919 Eighth Avenue. The Surrogate's Court is held at the County Court-House. It adjudicates in matters pertaining to wills, and administrates matters pertaining to deceased persons. The Court of General Sessions of the Peace is held at 32 Chambers

COURT OF GENERAL SESSIONS, 32 CHAMBERS STREET.

Street by the Recorder, the City Judge and two Judges of the Court of General Sessions, each of whom holds office for fourteen years, at $12,000 a year. Its jurisdiction is similar to that of the Oyer and Terminer. Appeals are to the General Term of the Supreme Court, and finally to the Court of Appeals, except when the judgment is of death, when the appeal is to the Court of Appeals direct.

The Police Courts are inferior criminal courts, having original jurisdiction over minor offenses. Before them are brought, every morning, prisoners arrested and held over night in the police stations and city prisons. Drunkenness, assault and battery, and thieving, are the complaints most frequently dealt with. Nearly all cases in which punishment is inflicted are disposed of by fines or short terms of imprisonment in the city institutions on Blackwell's Island. The police justices have power to examine and hold for trial persons accused of serious crimes. They have great latitude in the exercise of their powers, and much of their work is to adjust minor neighborhood differences, and dispose of petty offenders, without resorting to actual legal proceedings. They are fifteen in number, and are appointed by the Mayor for terms of ten years, at salaries of $8,000 a year. Three police justices, without a jury, constitute the Court of Special Sessions of the Peace. This court has jurisdiction over all misdemeanors, and is held at the Tombs. The locations of the six police courts are as follows : 1st District, the Tombs ; 2d, Jefferson Market ; 3d, 69 Essex Street ; 4th, 57th Street, near Lexington Avenue ; 5th, 121st Street and Sylvan Place (in the Harlem Municipal Building) ; 6th, East 158 Street and Third Avenue, Morrisania.

The County Court-House, adjacent to the City Hall, is in Corinthian architecture, of Massachusetts white marble, and occupies a space of 250 by 150 feet. Kellum was the architect, and was succeeded by Leopold Eidlitz. The original design was noble, but suffered disfigurement by large additions ordered by the city government. It was begun in 1861, but the dome is not yet finished. The Court-House is an inadequate showing for the $10,000,000 it cost the city. Its construction was a basis for a considerable part of the peculations of Tweed and his associates. The new City Hall will enclose this structure on three sides, and probably at no distant date it will be taken down.

The Hall of Records, or Register's Office, is used for courts as well as records. It is the only public building that dates back to the times of the Revolution. Many loyal citizens were imprisoned in it while the British held the city, and it was afterward used as a debtors' prison. It is near Park Row, in City-Hall Park. This historic (but very unattractive) edifice is to be demolished to make room for the new palace of the city government, which will reach within 50 feet of Broadway, Centre Street, and Chambers Street. The Hall was built in 1757, as a suburban prison, on the Boston Road. The patriots confined here in the Revolution suffered inexpressible horrors, and died by thousands.

Jurors.—The Commissioner of Jurors is the judge of the qualifications of petit or trial jurors. He hears and determines claims for exemption. The persons to serve as grand jurors are taken from the lists of petit jurors by a board consisting of the Mayor and certain designated judges of the court. The board meets yearly, on the first Monday in September, and elects one of its number as chairman. Four members comprise a quorum. Not less than 600, nor more than 1,000, are chosen from the lists of persons qualified to serve as petit jurors, to serve as grand jurors of the Courts of Oyer and Terminer and General Sessions, until the next list is prepared. The names on these lists are deposited in a box, and the names of persons to serve as grand and trial jurors are drawn by chance. A grand jury is drawn for every term of the Court of General Sessions, and may be drawn for the Court of Oyer and Terminer. A trial juror is to be not more than seventy years of age, and he is to be the owner, or the husband of a woman who is the owner, of personal property of the value of $250; and he is to be able to read and write the English language understandingly. Certain persons are exempt, as clergymen, physicians, lawyers, teachers, editors, reporters, members of the National Guard, and others. A person trying to escape jury duty by bribery, false statement or illegal means, or one who assists another to do the same, is guilty of a misdemeanor.

The Court of Arbitration.—The Governor nominates and with the consent of the Senate, appoints an arbitrator, to be known as the Arbitrator of the Chamber of Commerce. His salary is fixed and paid by it. In a controversy brought before the arbitrator, the parties to it may each appoint an additional arbitrator if he desires. Upon application of parties interested, contracts, written or oral, are to be interpreted and construed. The parties to any controversy or dispute, arising or

THE COUNTY COURT-HOUSE.
BROADWAY AND CHAMBERS STREET, IN CITY-HALL PARK.

being within the port of New York, or relating thereto in various respects, may voluntarily submit it to the Court of Arbitration. An award being made, an order must, at the instance of either party, be filed at the office of the County Clerk. An award for the payment of money or the delivery of property requires, on request being made, a judgment to be entered. Such judgment has the same force as a judgment of the Superior Court.

The County Officers are elected for three years. The Sheriff of the county is paid a salary of $12,000, and half of the fees paid into the office. There is an under-sheriff, and deputies not to exceed twelve in number. The salary of the County Clerk is $15,000 in full for all services. The salary of the Register is $12,000 a year. There are four coroners, each receiving a salary of $5,000. When a person dies from criminal violence or casualty, or suddenly, when in apparent health, or unattended by a physician, or in prison, or in any unusual or suspicious manner, it is the duty of the coroner to subpœna a coroner's physician, who views the body of the deceased person, or makes an autopsy, as may be required. The testimony of such physician, and of other witnesses, constitutes an inquest. The coroner may call a jury, if he deems it necessary, or if a citizen should so demand. It is the duty of a citizen who may have become aware of the death of a person as here stated, to report such death to a coroner or any police officer, and a person who wilfully neglects this is upon conviction guilty of a misdemeanor. Any person who wilfully disturbs the body or clothing of a person so dying is guilty of a misdemeanor. A coroner is the only officer who has the power to arrest the Sheriff.

The Port Wardens of the Port of New York are nine in number, three of whom are nautical men, appointed by the Governor, with the consent of the Senate. They elect one of their number as president, and one as vice-president. The appointments are for three years. It is the duty of the Board, or some of them, on being notified, to go aboard of any vessel to examine the condition and stowage of the cargo, and if there are any goods damaged to seek the cause, and to enter the same upon the books of the office. The members of the Board are exclusive surveyors of any vessel that has been wrecked, or is deemed unfit to proceed to sea. They are to specify what damage has occurred, and record in the books of the office full and particular accounts of surveys made on vessels; and they are judges of repairs necessary to make vessels seaworthy again. They have exclusive powers over the survey of vessels and their cargoes arriving in the port of New York in distress.

Quarantine for the protection of the public health is provided for by the laws of the State for the port of New York. The Quarantine establishment consists of warehouses, anchorage for vessels, hospitals, a boarding station, crematory, and residences for officers and men. The Health-Officer is appointed by the Governor and Senate for four years. He receives a salary of $12,500 a year. He appoints and dismisses at pleasure two Assistant Health Officers. There are three Commissioners of Quarantine, at a yearly salary of $2,500 each, who, with the Mayors of New York and Brooklyn, constitute a board that erects hospitals, docks, etc., and has care of the Quarantine property. On Swinburne and Hoffman Islands, in the Lower Bay, fifteen miles from the city, and between Staten Island and Sandy Hook, are the chief hospitals. Persons from infected ships are taken there. Vessels from non-infected ports are boarded from Clifton by the Health-Officer and his assistants.

Pilots and Pilotage.—The Board of Commissioners of Pilots consists of five persons, each holding his office for two years. Three are elected by the Chamber of Commerce, and two by the presidents and vice-presidents of the marine-insurance companies of the city, composing the Board of Underwriters. The commissioners license for such time as they think proper as many Sandy-Hook pilots as they deem necessary, for the port of New York. Candidates are subject to examination pertaining to the duties to be performed by them, and are required to give bonds in two sureties, not exceeding $500 each, for the faithful performance of their duties. Pilots

for the safe pilotage of vessels through the channel of the East River, known as Hell-Gate pilots, are appointed by the Governor with the consent of the Senate, on recommendation of the Board of Port-Wardens of New York. This board makes the rules and regulations under which they act.

The Post Office is the chief architectural representative of the Federal Government in the city. It occupies a specially favored site — the lower end of what was once the triangular City-Hall Park. More people daily come in view of it than of any other building in the city. In its rear it has the City Hall and park, and the

THE UNITED-STATES POST OFFICE, BROADWAY, PARK ROW AND MAIL STREET.

western terminus of the East-River Bridge ; and close to it are the two great thoroughfares, Broadway and Park Row.   A dozen streets converge towards it ; the great newspaper offices with their newer architecture tower over it ; and the elevated cars and the street-cars carry hundred of thousands of people daily past it, or pour them out near by.   At night the spaces around it are illuminated with almost the brilliancy of day.   Here the heart-throb of the city is more than anywhere else evident.   The building was no doubt designed to reflect the power and dignity of the Federal Government.   Its cost was $10,000,000, including the furniture.   The architecture is Doric and Renaissance.   It extends 340 feet on Broadway, 340 feet on Park Row, and 290 feet on Mail Street, facing the park.   It is made of a light-colored granite.   Its height is five stories.   The United-States Circuit and District Courts here hold their sessions.   In handling the mail of New-York City, 1,561 clerks and 1,175 letter-carriers are employed.   The Post-Office receipts for the fiscal year ending June 30, 1892, were $6,783,202.   The expenditures reached $2,568,-700, leaving a net revenue of $4,214,502.   There are 18 branch post-office stations, 20 sub-stations, 100 agencies for the sale of postage stamps, and 1,770 street letter-boxes, attached to lamp-posts, and located in hotels, clubs, and large business buildings.

The Postmaster of New York is Charles Willoughby Dayton, appointed by President Cleveland in 1893, to succeed Cornelius Van Cott, appointed by President Harrison in 1889.   His predecessor was Henry G. Pearson, appointed by President Garfield, in 1881.   Thomas L. James was postmaster during President Hayes's administration, and went into President Garfield's cabinet as Postmaster-General, in 1881.

The Bureau of Animal Industry, at 18 Broadway, is under the Department of Agriculture of the United-States Government.   The duties are the inspection of all live animals intended for export to Europe.   The exportation of cattle exceeds that of all other animals.   The special object of the office is to detect cases of pleuro-pneumonia and other contagious diseases in animals.   The veterinary inspector of the port has a corps of assistants at the stock-yards.   The inspection of the cattle-carrying steamers comes within the jurisdiction of the office.   All cattle exported are tagged, showing the sources of shipment.   There are offices in Brooklyn, Jersey City and many other points, for detecting the contagious diseases of animals.

The New-York State Fish-Commission, consisting of five members, is appointed by the Governor.   It has its chief office at 83 Fulton Street.   Its object is to disseminate the fry of food-fish in public waters throughout the State.   There are five hatcheries for the propagation of the fry from the eggs of the female fish.   They are as follows :   The Adirondack, Saranac P. O. ;   Franklin County ; Cold Springs P. O., Long Island ;   Fulton Chain, Old Forge P. O. ;   Sacandaga, Newton Corners ; Chautauqua, Caledonia P. O.   There is a shell-fish department, for the surveying and granting of franchises to the holders of oyster grounds.

The United-States Immigrant Bureau, on Ellis Island, New-York Harbor, is under the charge of the Commissioner of Immigration and a staff of officers.   The principal function of this bureau is to inspect and examine arriving immigrants ; and to see that the provisions of the laws forbidding the landing of certain prohibited classes, namely : convicts, lunatics, idiots, paupers, persons likely to become public charges, or suffering with contagious or loathsome diseases, contract laborers, and polygamists, are carried out.   All immigrants are landed at Ellis Island, which covers an area of 6 acres.   For the twelvemonth ending June 30, 1892, the immigration was 445,987, including 81,592 from Germany, 60,233 from Austria-Hungary, 59,205 from Russia, 58,687 from Italy, and 47,635 from Sweden and Norway.

·The General Culture·

Educational Institutions—Universities, Colleges, Academies, Seminaries and Public, Private and Parochial Schools and Kindergartens.

THE ancient history and traditions of New York, its immense increase and conservation of wealth, and the gathering here of the brightest men and women in the Republic, combine with many other causes to make of the Empire City one of the foremost educational centres of the Western World. This leadership is not dependent upon any single institution, or any special line of study, or any individual group of influences. Besides its two universities, which stand among the foremost exponents of the German system, it has schools of medicine, theology, law, art, and music second to none in efficiency and value of results. Students in New York work and play with equal and intense zest, as the merchants of the city do, for the electric air of Manhattan allows no place or time for bucolic stagnation. In the great libraries and art-galleries, museums and hospitals, the scholar finds numberless object-lessons, and extends the bounds of his observation far beyond his text-books.

The first schoolmaster in New Amsterdam was Adam Roelandsen, who enjoyed a monopoly of teaching the round-faced little Dutch children. After a time this pioneer of pedagogues fell into ill repute, so that his pupils all departed, and he was forced to earn a scanty living by taking in washing. Not even as a launderer was he permitted to dwell in the New World, for in 1646 he was publicly flogged and banished from the country. A year before this exile began, Adrien Jansen Van Olfendam opened a school, and met with good success, his price for a year's tuition being two beaver-skins. This lucrative business stimulated Jan Stevenson to open another school in 1648.

Four years later, in response to the earnest appeals of Captain-General Stuyvesant, the first public school was founded, to teach reading and writing and the knowledge and fear of God. The teachers were, successively, Dr. La Montagne, William Verstius, Harmen Van Hoboken and Evert Pietersen, who received $14.50 a month, besides $50 a year for board. In 1658 the burghers erected a new school-house, and the West India Company sent over the learned Dr. Curtius, who founded here a flourishing Latin school, using his spare time in practising as a physician. After his return to Holland the academy was conducted by Dominie Ægidius Luyck, the private tutor of the Director's children.

The Free Public Schools of New York are remarkably efficient, and have received many commendations from competent authorities. They number more than 300, including about 100 each of primary and grammar schools, 48 corporate schools, and 29 evening schools. The enrolment of pupils is in the vicinity of 240,000, and the average daily attendance exceeds 160,000. There are 4,200 teachers; and the expense of the schools to the city is $5,000,000 a year. The children learn their letters in the lower primary schools, and thence advance, after rigid and careful examinations, through the various grades of the grammar schools, studying the English branches, drawing, vocal music, and (if desired) French and German. All such as may desire a higher education, and have passed the examinations, are provided

GRAMMAR SCHOOL NO. 94, AMSTERDAM AVENUE AND 68TH STREET.

with collegiate instruction, free of cost; the boys in the College of the City of New York, and the girls in the Normal College. In the evening schools, education is given to 22,000 young people who are obliged to support themselves by working during the day. The discipline in all the public schools is stringent and rigid, and teaches the desirability of system and subordination. There are 40 manual training schools, with 430 teachers and 20,000 pupils, doing an admirable and efficient practical work.

Children between eight and fourteen years of age are compelled by law to attend school; and a group of twelve agents of truancy continually look up the delinquents, and enforce the statute. The more vicious and incorrigible truants are sent to reformatories. Since this efficient organization has been at work, many thousands of loitering and unemployed children have been placed in school; and the number of children arrested by the police for crimes or under suspicion has dwindled from 1,200 to 500 yearly. The public property used for school purposes exceeds $15,000,000 in value. A department of public instruction for teachers is attached to the American Museum of Natural History, with series of lectures on subjects illustrated by the vast collections of that institution.

The College of the City of New York was established in 1848, under the name of the Free Academy, and in 1866 received its present name, and the powers and privileges of a college. Instruction and the use of text-books and apparatus are free to young men of New-York City. There are three courses of study, classical, scientific and mechanical, each of five years' duration; and a two years' post-graduate course in civil engineering. The rather picturesque buildings of the college are at Lexington Avenue and 23d Street, and contain valuable collections and apparatus, a large work-shop, and a library of 28,000 selected volumes. There are about 40 professors and tutors, and 1,100 students. The college costs the city $160,000 a year, and stands in the place of the usual city high school, although its range of studies is much higher than that followed in high schools.

The Normal College For Women occupies a great building, which with its grounds takes up the block bounded by Park and Lexington Avenues, and East 68th and 69th Streets. The building was erected at a cost of nearly $500,000, and contains a spacious hall, three lecture-rooms and thirty recitation rooms. About 2,800 students are at work in the college and the adjacent kindergarten and primary training departments. More than 5,000 graduates have gone out from this institution, and eighty per cent. of them have become teachers in the public schools. The Normal College costs the city $100,000 a year, and is widely renowned for the perfect discipline maintained among its students.

The Board of Education, at 146 Grand Street, is the supervising legislative body, and is made up of 21 Commissioners appointed by the Mayor, who also appoints three inspectors in each school district, while the Board names five trustees in each ward.

The Universities. — The beginnings of the movement for liberal education in New York appeared in 1703, and funds were raised for the purpose soon afterward by legislative authority. The two great institutions for higher education in New-York City, Columbia College and the University of the City of New York, pursue mainly the continental European methods. They have relatively little under-graduate work, their strong efforts being in the direction of higher academic study and special professional work. Of their 3,000 students fewer than one-fifth are under-graduates, but more than one-fourth are graduates of other colleges. Like other first-class metro-

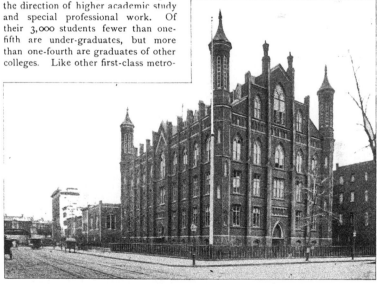

COLLEGE OF THE CITY OF NEW YORK, LEXINGTON AVENUE AND EAST 23D STREET.

politan universities, they are constrained to maintain their graduate departments at the highest rate of efficiency; while their magnificent professional schools could almost carry the entire organizations if needed. In these regards, they differ from nearly all other American universities, which mainly seek to house and train many young under-graduates, and whose professional schools fail to meet their

cost. They have no dormitories, and from this cause college associations and inti-
macies, as generally understood, are little known. There has been considerable discussion, but very little probability, of uniting Columbia and the University of New
York under the same roof, each to retain somewhat of its own corporate existence,
traditions and special work, and both to co-operate in a unified higher education.
Some form of federation may in time be adopted.

Columbia College is the lineal successor to King's College, which was chartered in 1754, with the Archbishop of Canterbury and a number of prominent gentle-

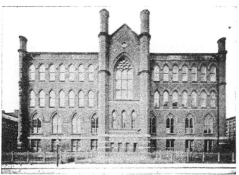

NORMAL COLLEGE, TRAINING DEPARTMENT.

men of England and New
York as governors. The
first president was the Rev
Dr. Samuel Johnson, of Connecticut, who convened the
earliest college class, numbering eight young men, in
the vestry-room of Trinity
Church. Trinity was the
most efficient friend of the
new institution, and granted
to it lands now of enormous
value. A handsome stone
building, one side of a projected quadrangle overlooking the Hudson River, was
opened in 1760. After a
time Dr. Johnson sought rest, feeling the weight of years ; and the Archbishop of
Canterbury sent over the Rev. Myles Cooper, a fellow of Queen's College, Oxford,
to succeed him, in 1763. Dr. Cooper was an ardent loyalist, and wrote strongly
against the growing sentiment of American independence, until finally a mob
attacked his lodgings in the college, and he escaped with difficulty to England, in
1775. During the Revolution the library and apparatus were scattered, and the
college building served as a military hospital. Among the young men who had been
educated here were Alexander Hamilton, John Jay, Gouverneur Morris, Robert R.
Livingston, and other leading patriots of New York.

When the war ceased, and the city restored her waste places, this institution was
revived, under the more appropriate name of Columbia College. Among its students
were De Witt Clinton and John Randolph of Roanoke. From 1784 to 1787 Columbia was officially styled a university, with projected faculties of Arts, Divinity, Medicine and Law, although it had but 40 students. The president from 1787 to 1800
was William Samuel Johnson, a son of the first president, and withal a friend of the
famous Dr. Samuel Johnson, of England, and a United-States Senator from Connecticut. From him the administration passed nominally to Benjamin Moore,
Bishop of New York. The presidencies of William Harris (1811–29), William Alexander Duer (1829-42), and Nathaniel F. Moore (1842–49) followed thereafter. The
presidency of Charles King extended from 1849 to 1864, and witnessed the removal
of the college from College Place to its present location, the founding of the Law
School and the planning of the School of Mines, and the nominal addition of the
Medical Department. The presidency of Dr. F. A. P. Barnard lasted from 1864 to
1889, during which period the college prospered greatly. In 1890 the Hon. Seth
Low, a graduate of the college, and a well-known political reformer and business

NORMAL COLLEGE.
PARK AND LEXINGTON AVENUES, EAST 68TH AND EAST 69TH STREETS.

man, and ex-mayor of Brooklyn, was elected president.   The college chairs have been occupied by such men as Anthon and Drisler, in the classics ; Adrain, Anderson and Van Amringe, in mathematics ; Chandler, in chemistry ; McVickar, in political economy ; Boyesen, in the Germanic languages ; and many other illustrious scholars in various departments.

In 1801 Dr. David Hosack, of the Medical School, bought for a botanical garden the domain called Elgin, which the State purchased from him and gave to the college in 1814, to replace a township of land granted long before, and lost when Vermont (in which it lay) became a State.   Elgin covered nearly the domain included between Fifth and Sixth Avenues and 47th and 51st Streets, then nearly four miles from the city, but now in its very heart.   When the delightful green and the venerable sycamores of the original site on College Place had become only a little oasis in a great roaring world of commercial activity, the college resolved to move to its uptown estate, and plans for a noble group of buildings were prepared by Upjohn, the famous Gothic architect.   Pending their erection, Columbia bought and occupied the old Deaf and Dumb Asylum and grounds ; and there it still remains, for the civil war of 1861–65 put an end to its ambitious scheme of building.   The Elgin estate is of enormous value, and yields large revenues to the college.

The college buildings form almost a double quadrangle, covering the block between Madison and Fourth Avenues and 49th and 50th Streets, with handsome and commodious brick buildings, in collegiate Gothic architecture.   The library is a noble hall, with a triple-arched roof on iron trusses ; 160,000 volumes, arranged by subjects ; long lines of tables for readers ; and an admirable system of service.   Seven hundred serial publications are kept on file in the reading-room.   In one of the stack-houses is the precious Torrey Herbarium, with its 60,000 volumes ; and the astronomical observatory occupies the tower.

COLUMBIA COLLEGE, SCHOOL OF ARTS,
MADISON AVENUE AND EAST 50TH STREET.

Columbia has developed into a great and powerful university, with 226 professors and officers and 1,630 students.   Its college under-graduate department is relatively small, the main strength being given to the professional and advanced schools.   There are no dormitories, or other institutions for residence.   Plans are being actively developed to augment the already large endowments, and to move the university to a new site, covering $17\frac{1}{2}$ acres, at Bloomingdale, near the inchoate Protestant-Episcopal Cathedral.   The land has already been purchased ; and Charles F. McKim, Charles C. Haight and Richard M. Hunt, the eminent architects, are serving as a commission to lay out the new site.

The University faculties of Law, Medicine, Mines, Political Science, Philosophy, and Pure Science, taken together, constitute the University, offering advanced study and investigation in private or municipal law; medicine and surgery; mathematics and pure and applied science; history, economics and public law; and philosophy, philology and letters. Columbia has an extensive system of co-operation, by which it confers benefits upon others and obtains for its own students increased opportunities. This system embraces Barnard College, the Teachers College, the Union Theological Seminary, Cooper Union, the Metropolitan Museum of Art, and the American Museum of Natural History.

The School of Arts occupies the range of buildings along Madison Avenue, and has nearly 50 professors and instructors and 300 students.

The School of Mines was founded in 1864, and ten years later occupied the costly new building erected for its use. Among the earlier professors were Gen. F. I. Vinton, Thomas Egleston, Charles F. Chandler (now Dean of the school), and

John S. Newberry, the latter of whom brought hither his unrivalled geological and palæontological collections. The seven courses are: Mining engineering, civil engineering, electrical engineering, metallurgy, geology and palæontology, analytical and applied chemistry, and architecture; and the students are given practical instruction in geodesy, mining, metal-

COLUMBIA COLLEGE: LIBRARY AND OPEN QUADRANGLE,
MADISON AVENUE AND 49TH STREET.

working and other departments. There are also three graduate courses, of two years each, in electrical engineering, sanitary engineering, and special courses. The department of architecture, under the charge of Prof. William R. Ware, is the foremost architectural school in America, and has a large number of enthusiastic students, under competent and careful instruction.

The School of Law, of which Professor William A. Keener is Dean, was organized in 1858 under the direction of Professor Theodore W. Dwight, and is recognized as one of the leading law-schools of the country. It has a three years' course of study in private and public law, leading to the degree of LL. B. It has a staff of ten instructors, with 315 students. The famous commentaries of Chancellor Kent are an outgrowth of lectures delivered by him at Columbia.

The School of Political Science, an outgrowth of the School of Law, was founded in 1880, under Prof. John W. Burgess, "to prepare young men for the duties of public life." It has already won a high measure of success, in teaching constitutional history and law, history of political theories, political economy and social science, Roman law and comparative jurisprudence, administrative law, international law and history.

18

   The School of Philosophy was founded in 1890, for advanced courses in philosophy, philology and letters.

   The School of Pure Science, an outgrowth of the School of Mines, began in 1892, for advanced courses in pure (as distinguished from applied) science.

   The College of Physicians and Surgeons, the medical department of Columbia College, was chartered in 1807; and six years later, the School of Medicine of the college, which dated from 1767, united with it. In 1860 this college became nominally a department of Columbia, and in 1891 became an integral part of it. In 1884 William H. Vanderbilt presented $500,000 to the college, which with this gift

purchased land and erected a building at 59th Street, near 10th Avenue. A few months later Mr. Vanderbilt's daughter, Mrs. William D. Sloane, and her husband gave $250,000 for the erection of the Sloane Maternity Hospital, under the control of the college; and still later Mr. Vanderbilt's four sons gave $250,000 for the

COLLEGE OF PHYSICIANS AND SURGEONS, 437 WEST 59TH STREET.

construction of the Vanderbilt Clinic and Dispensary. The college has 50 instructors and 570 students. It is equipped with electric lights, Worthington pumps, etc.

   Barnard College, at 343 Madison Avenue, has professors appointed by the President of Columbia. It is practically a section of Columbia, with the same entrance examinations, the use of the same extensive library, and the receipt of the same degrees. Here women may secure an education identical in quality and official recognition with that given to men. Founded in 1889, it was named for the late President of Columbia College. It has its own botanical and chemical laboratories. Its 85 students are mainly New-York girls, whose parents prefer that their daughters should live at home during their college education.

NEW-YORK TRADE-SCHOOL, FIRST AVENUE, 67TH AND 68TH STREETS.

The University of the City of New York was planned in 1829 and 1830, in several meetings of public-spirited merchants and professional men, and incorporated in 1831. The idea was to offset Episcopalian and conservative Columbia with an undenominational modern university. Until 1883 a part of the Council was elected by the City Legislature, and it was forbidden that any religious denomination should have a majority in the Council. John Taylor Johnston and Charles Butler, recent Presidents of the Council, have served in it respectively forty-six years and fifty-six

UNIVERSITY OF THE CITY OF NEW YORK, WASHINGTON SQUARE, EAST, AND WAVERLY PLACE.

years. The property of the University, all of which has come from gifts and bequests, amounts to about $2,000,000. The University building, on Washington Square, erected in 1832-35, is a conspicuous structure of light-colored limestone, in Gothic architecture, and contains the Council-room, with its many portraits of distinguished members of the Council, and the class-rooms and laboratories, museum and observatory of the Department of Arts and Science. In ancient days many famous authors, artists and scholars dwelt in this noble building, where Prof. S. F. B. Morse discovered the recording telegraph, Dr. John William Draper made the first photographs from the human face, and Theodore Winthrop wrote *Cecil Dreme.* The University has about 100 professors and instructors and 1,330 students. The Chancellors have been Drs. James Matthews, Theodore Frelinghuysen, Gardiner Spring, Isaac Ferris, Howard Crosby, John Hall and Henry M. MacCracken.

In 1891-92 the University took an important step, in purchasing for $300,000, a new site, intended in particular for the College of Arts and Philosophy, the technological schools, and the Graduate Seminary. The School of Law, the School of Pedagogy, and part of the Graduate Seminary work will remain upon Washington Square, where a new building will be erected, of which probably seven or eight stories will be rented for business purposes, while two or three stories will be reserved for the schools named, and for University offices, and popular lectures. The Medical School will continue as at present. The new site is an elevated plateau of twenty acres, accessible by railway in less than twenty minutes from 42d Street. It is to be known as "University Heights," and is admirably adapted to University purposes.

The Department of Arts and Science dates from 1832, and for over half a century consisted of a college on the approved American plan, with from 100 to 150 students. University College now has twenty-six professors and lecturers, and its classical and scientific courses lead respectively to the degrees of Bachelor of Art and Bachelor of Science. Among its professors have been the Drapers, Vethake, McIlvaine and Robinson; John Torrey, the botanist; Tayler Lewis, the philologist; George Bush, the commentator; Nordheimer, the Hebraist; Henry P. Tappan, the philosopher; Davies and Loomis, the mathematicians, and S. F. B. Morse, the inventor.

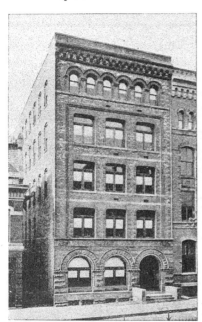

LOOMIS LABORATORY, UNIVERSITY MEDICAL COLLEGE, 414 EAST 26TH STREET.

The School of Civil Engineering and **the School of Chemistry,** two well conducted institutions for technical training, are controlled by the Faculty of Arts and Science, which also conducts

The School of Pedagogy, founded in 1890, to give higher training to teachers, in psychology and ethics, the theory and practice of pedagogy, and the history, classics and systems of education. There are 260 students in the school.

The Graduate Seminary, founded in 1886, receives candidates for the degrees of Master of Arts or Science, and Doctor of Philosophy. Over 100 graduate students are in attendance, and thirty special courses are provided.

The Department of Law, with its under-graduate and graduate schools, has its lecture-room and library in the fine old University building. The foundation of this faculty was carefully planned in the year 1835, by the Hon. B. F. Butler, then Attorney-General of the United States. The council of the University adopted his plans, and Mr. Butler accepted the office of Senior Professor. The Law school was soon suspended, and again opened in 1858; but it is only during the past few years that it has advanced to a prominent rank. As Prof. Stoddard remarks, in that period "it has changed its character from a school of law forms to a school of jurisprudence;" and develops at once the systematic study of statute law and the observation of professional methods of research and practice. The Dean and Senior Professor is Austin Abbott, LL. D.; and there are three other professors and six lecturers. The course js of two years, with several advanced courses in the graduate year. There are 240 students (nearly half of them college graduates), including also ten women. The Graduate Law School was opened in 1891, with 40 pupils, and requires the completion of five subjects for the degree of Master of Laws. The University also gives popular courses of lectures on law, in particular to business women, every winter. This lectureship is endowed by the Women's Legal Education Society.

Theology is not taught by the University ; but in 1890 an alliance was formed with the Union Theological Seminary, by which students of either institution are admitted under easy conditions to the libraries and lecture-courses of the other. Also, the graduates of Union Seminary may receive the degree of Bachelor of Divinity.

The Faculty of Medicine (University Medical College), founded in 1841, numbered among its earlier members Drs. Valentine Mott, Bedford, Post, Draper, and Paine. Its buildings are on 26th Street, near the East River, fronting Bellevue Hospital, and near the ferry-entrance to the great city charities. They consist of the central edifice, which includes the offices, with the lecture-room and amphitheatre, either of which seats 500 students ; the west wing, in which are the Dispensary, and eight "section rooms" ; and the east wing, to which the anonymous giver of $100,000 for its erection attached the name of the Loomis Laboratory, after the senior professor. Its five floors contain the five laboratories of Materia Medica, Physics, Chemistry, Physiology, Biology and Pathology. There are 23 professors, and 35 lecturers. Three winter courses, each comprising eight months' study, are required for the degree of M. D. The University Medical College has 640 students, of whom 30 came from Canada, 30 from Russia, and many others from Central and South America, and other countries. Among its 6,000 graduates have been many illustrious physicians and scientists.

UNIVERSITY MEDICAL COLLEGE, 410 EAST 26TH STREET.

The Medical Schools bring wide renown to the great metropolis for their magnitude and their very unusual opportunities for imparting a practical education. Many of the foremost of American physicians live in New York, and here also are brought thousands of patients requiring the care of the most skillful specialists. The notable museums, libraries and scientific societies also afford rich stimulus to the student, and tend to elevate more and more the spirit of the profession. Here occur the meetings of the laryngological, dermatological, clinical, microscopical, medico-historical, medico-legal, neurological, obstetrical, medico-chirurgical, surgical, pathological, ophthalmological, therapeutical and other cognate societies. Here also are held the fortnightly meetings of the

POST-GRADUATE MEDICAL SCHOOL AND HOSPITAL, 226 EAST 20TH STREET.

New-York Academy of Medicine, which dates from 1847, and has for nearly half a century studied how best to promote the public health, to raise the standard of medical education, to advance the honor of the profession, and to cultivate the science of medicine. The Academy maintains a library of more than 50,000 volumes, which is open to the people all day long ; and it also subscribes for and keeps on file all the current medical periodicals and monographs, showing the latest results of professional research in all countries. Students are able to live in New York at an expense not exceeding that attending life at other educational centres, and also find more frequent opportunities for partial self-support. They are broadened by the myriad influences of the metropolitan city, and may become in a sense citizens of the world, while preparing for the arduous professional life before them. If their opportunities and advantages are fully availed of, they will enter upon the practice of the healing art with a better equipment of special and general knowledge than can usually be acquired by students in the quiet cloisters of secluded rural colleges.

The noted medical schools of Columbia College and the University have been hereinbefore described.

Bellevue-Hospital Medical College owes its inception to the construction of an amphitheatre for clinical lectures at Bellevue Hospital, in 1849, followed eight years later by the erection of a pathological building. The college began its work in 1861, with lectures on military surgery, a theme of vital interest at that time ; and has since developed into one of the leading medical schools of America, under the lead of men like Mott, Flint, Hammond and Doremus. The institution occupies a part of the grounds of Bellevue Hospital, at the foot of East 26th Street, and close to the East River. The contiguity of the great public hospital, with the numberless opportunities there afforded for obtaining a practical knowledge of both the duties and the resources of the medical profession, places it in the power of the Bellevue students to enter upon their life-duties competent to meet intelligently every emergency. Almost every physical ill which they may encounter in future practice comes under their observation here, and also the most modern scientific and skilful means of relief, as given by sagacious physicians. The hospital clinics afford object-lessons in every variety of disease requiring indoor treatment ; and the Bureau of Medical and Surgical Relief for the Outdoor Poor at its clinics illustrates the best treatments in minor surgery, and of commoner and less grave diseases, especially in disorders of children. The bureau was organized and elaborated by the Faculty of the college, and has been of immense service to the poor, whose profound respect for the skill of the attendants is justly deserved. Over 40,000 patients are treated here every year. The college has graduated upwards of 4,000 doctors. It has 35 instructors and 550 students (60 of whom are foreigners, mainly from Canada and the West Indies). A recent addition to the college buildings is the Carnegie Laboratory, a five-story building containing three general laboratories and a large auditorium. The President of the college is William T. Lusk, M. D.

The New-York Post-Graduate Hospital and Medical School has a plain and substantial brick building at 226 20th Street, near Second Avenue. This institution dates from 1882, and is intended to give practising physicians opportunities to see and study the newest discoveries in medical and surgical science. Its clinics diffuse the freshest knowledge.

The New-York Homœopathic Medical College and Hospital received its charter in 1861, and has been very successful. Its building, at 63d Street and Avenue A, is well equipped for the curriculum of lectures, clinics, and demonstrations, which extend over a period of three years. The Dean is Timothy Field Allen, M. D., LL. D., with whom serves a body of 28 instructors. The pupils number 130.

The New-York College of Dentistry, chartered in 1865 and opened in 1866, is at 23d Street and Third Avenue, and has 40 instructors and 250 students. The dean is Dr. Frank Abbott. It educates students in the scientific and chirur-gical requirements of the science, with series of lectures on operative and mechan-ical dentistry, and daily practice and demonstration at operations in the chair, and careful laboratory practice.

The College of Pharmacy of the City of New York was founded in 1829, and gives instruction in chemistry, materia medica, botany, pharmacognosy, pharmacy, physiology, and physics, by afternoon lectures, quizzes, and laboratory work. The buildings, on West 68th Street, near Ninth Avenue, contain valuable museums and apparatus, spacious laboratories and lecture-room, and the largest phar-maceutical library in America. The course includes thirty hours a week, for two years; and converts druggists' apprentices into thoroughly equipped and scientific pharmacists, fitted to understand and compound all manner of medicines. There are 400 students, including about a dozen foreigners. The president is Samuel W. Fairchild.

The Women's Medical College of the New-York Infirmary for Women and Children was chartered in 1865, as an outgrowth of a dispensary which was founded in 1854, and the hospital which was added thereto in 1857. The sessions of the college are held in a handsome and commodious new building on Stuyvesant Square, near the Infirmary. There are 30 professors and instructors, and about 90 students (including 16 foreigners), the course covering three years. Dr. Emily Blackwell is the Dean.

N.-Y. COLLEGE OF DENTISTRY, 205 EAST 23D STREET NEAR THIRD AVENUE.

The New-York Medical College and Hospital for Women dates from 1863, and has about 40 students in homœopathic medicine, at 213 West 54th Street.

The Eclectic Medical College of the City of New York, founded in 1865, is composed of 21 instructors and 80 students. It is at 239 East 14th Street.

The School of Ophthalmology and Otology is connected with the New-York Ophthalmic Hospital (201 East 23d Street), and gives a complete course of study in diseases of the eye, ear and throat.

COLLEGE OF PHARMACY, 209 EAST 23d STREET.
(OCCUPIED UNTIL 1893)

Nurses' Training-Schools.— Large hospitals find their best development in large cities ; and among their most valuable agencies are their corps of trained nurses. Conversely, the training-schools for nurses must be intimately associated with hospitals, where the students may daily observe the practical workings of their profession. There are over 300 pupils in the nurses' training-schools connected with the Charity, the Bellevue, the New-York and St. Luke's Hospitals. One of the largest of these is the one connected with the New-York Hospital, where 60 pupils are enrolled.

The D. O. Mills Training-School for Male Nurses occupies a substantial brick building erected in 1888 in the Bellevue-Hospital grounds, at the foot of East 26th Street. It is arranged and fitted up as a home for the nurses during their two-years' course of study, which is on the same lines as that of the Training-School for Female Nurses, nearly opposite. Two classes have been graduated from the school, and there are now 54 inmates, all of whom serve in the male wards of the hospital. It is a generous educational charity, founded by Darius O. Mills.

The Columbia College of Midwifery, 242 West 33d Street, is another manifestation of the healing art. It was incorporated in 1883. Connected with it is the Dispensary for Diseases of Women.

The College of Midwifery of the City of New York was organized in 1883, and in 1884 became connected with the Nurses' Training-School of the Woman's Infirmary and Maternity Home, 247 West 49th Street.

The New-York College of Massage, also at 247 West 49th Street, was organized in 1884.

The New-York College of Fine Forces, at 4 West 14th Street, was chartered in 1887. It teaches chromopathy, mind cure, patho-mechanism, magnetic massage, and solar magnetics. E. D. Babbitt, M. D., is dean.

Veterinary Colleges and Hospitals have arisen from the vast investments in American live-stock, the annual losses of millions of dollars by contagious diseases, the need of scientific inspection of meat and milk, and the ruin caused by quack horse-doctors. With its organized Veterinary Society of graduates, its two veterinary colleges and its two hospitals, New York is one of the foremost educational centres as to the arts of healing domestic animals. The students are taught the theory and practice of veterinary medicine, anatomy (with dissections) and surgery, pathology and obstetrics, therapeutics and microscopy, ophthalmology, and bacteriology; with scientific care, and abundant illustrations and experiments.

The New-York College of Veterinary Surgeons and School of Comparative Medicine, chartered in 1857, is at 332 East 27th Street. It has ten professors and four lecturers; and over 100 students, attending lectures on equine anatomy, bovine pathology, horse-shoeing, and many connected subjects. Many of its graduates are appointed veterinary surgeons for the United-States Army. The hospital of the college affords opportunities of observing the diseases of domestic animals, and their treatment, and also of witnessing surgical operations. The President is Dr. William T. White.

The American Veterinary College dates from 1875; and has its home at 141 West 54th Street, where the American Veterinary Hospital receives and treats disabled horses and dogs, admitting patients at all hours. The President is Dr. A. Liautard; and there are 16 instructors and 130 students.

Religious Instruction.—The Empire City has long been recognized as an admirable drill-ground for students in the fields of religion and philanthropy. Here are thousands of the most formidable heathen in the world, whose condition demands amelioration; and other thousands of earnest and devoted Christians, always studying and practicing methods of beneficence. Many of the foremost clergymen in the Republic occupy pulpits here; and the headquarters and conventions of various denominations seek this great metropolitan focus. Large opportunities are also afforded for students to support themselves in mission-work, teaching and parochial assistance.

D. O. MILLS TRAINING SCHOOL FOR MALE NURSES, 431 EAST 26TH STREET.

The General Theological Seminary of The Protestant Episcopal Church was established by the General Convention in 1817; it began instructions in 1819; and was incorporated in 1822. Since that date, it has graduated 1,200 men, of whom 34 have become bishops. It is governed by a Board of Trustees, composed of the Bishops of the Church, the Dean, 25 appointees of the House of Deputies of the General Convention, and 25 men elected by former contributing dioceses. There are twelve professors and instructors, and 131 students in holy orders. Ninety of these are college-graduates, including seven from colleges in Sweden, and others from colleges in Canada, Persia and Turkey. Tuition is free, to properly accredited candidates. There are rooms for 117 students

in the seminary; and each of these pays $225 a year for the room and its care, coal
and gas, and board.   The buildings are on Chelsea Square, between 20th and 21st
Streets and Ninth and Tenth Avenues.   In 1880 the square was occupied only by two
grim old stone edifices ; but since that date there has been erected a series of handsome brick and stone buildings, in collegiate Gothic architecture.   The Memorial
Chapel of the Good Shepherd has a melodious chime ; a reredos of exquisitely carved

UNION THEOLOGICAL SEMINARY, PARK AVENUE, FROM 69TH TO 70TH STREETS.

alabaster, adorned with the Good Shepherd and eight Evangelists and Apostles, in
statuary marble; and ten storied windows of English stained glass.   The beautiful
Hobart Hall contains the library of 23,000 volumes, with an open timber roof, and
many interesting portraits.   The velvety green lawns and the groups of shrubbery
between the buildings and the extent and massive construction, and the quiet dignity
of the seminary buildings make a charming oasis of verdure and peace in the vast
whirl of the city's secular life.

The **Union Theological Seminary** occupies a range of handsome buildings
on Lenox Hill, along Park Avenue, between 69th and 70th Streets.   This location
was occupied in 1884 ; and the buildings form a quadrangle, and include offices and
lecture-rooms, library, chapel and gymnasium, museum and reading-room, and
many furnished chambers for the students.   The library, containing 70,000 volumes
and 50,000 pamphlets, was built up on the basis of the library of Leander Van Ess.
The seminary was founded in 1836.   Since 1857 the Directors have made a yearly
report to the General Assembly, though now the institution is not under ecclesiastical control.   Its officers give their assent to the standards of the Presbyterian
Church ; but the seminary is open to students from any Christian denomination.
There are 13 members of the Faculty, and 150 students.   Among the professors are

GENERAL THEOLOGICAL SEMINARY OF THE PROTESTANT EPISCOPAL CHURCH.

CHELSEA SQUARE, NINTH AND TENTH AVENUES, 20TH AND 21ST STREETS.

Thomas S. Hastings (President), George L. Prentiss, Philip Schaff, Marvin R. Vincent, Charles A. Briggs and Francis Brown. The seminary has endowed instructorships in vocal culture, elocution and sacred music ; and lectureships in the evidences of Christianity, the relations of the Bible to science, and hygienic instruction. The course of study covers three years. The recent trial of Dr. Briggs on doctrinal points profoundly affected Union Seminary.

The Jewish Theological Seminary, founded in 1886, in 1892 occupied the handsome residence at 736 Lexington Avenue ; and has three preceptors and

fifteen students. The course lasts nine years, and educates young Hebrews to be rabbis or teachers. The seminary is maintained chiefly by the New-York, Philadelphia and Baltimore synagogues. The president of the Faculty is Dr. Sabato Morais.

MANHATTAN COLLEGE, BOULEVARD AND WEST 131ST STREET.

The New-York Missionary Training College aims to prepare persons devoid of an elaborate liberal education, for city and foreign missionaries and evangelists, by spiritual and scriptural studies of the Bible and theology, and a practical and experimental training. The college, a fire-proof five-story building at 690 Eighth Avenue, is occupied by the men-students. Berachah Home, at 250 West 44th Street, and the annex at 453 West 47th Street, are for the women. The course is three years in length. There are about a dozen instructors and 200 students, of whom 90 are women. A score come from Canada, and there are others from Scotland, England, Germany, Switzerland, Russia, India, Japan and Hayti.

The New-York Deaconess Home and Training-School of the Methodist Episcopal Church, at 241 West 14th Street, has about a score of inmates, studying the Bible, elementary medicine, hygiene, nursing and other requisites for the sisterhood of service among the poor and the sick. Graduates of the school become probationers, and these become uniform deaconesses, devoted entirely to Christian labor with the wandering and sorrowing, the poor and the orphan, the sick and the dying.

The International Medical Missionary Training Institute is at 118 East 45th Street, with a ladies' branch at 121 East 45th Street.

St. John's College was founded in 1841 by Archbishop John Hughes, on the famous old Rose-Hill estate at Fordham, and its first President was John McCloskey, who became the first American Cardinal. In 1846 the college passed into the hands of the Jesuits, who have ever since controlled its destinies with singular ability and devotion, preparing many young men for high achievements. St. John's has several massive and imposing stone buildings, looking out on a broad lawn, which is adorned with a bronze statue of Archbishop Hughes. The college conducts three courses of study, collegiate, academic and scientific, and about 350 students are engaged therein. The surrounding country and the St. John's estate are very picturesque and attractive, and the avenues of ancient elms add beauty to the grounds.

The College of St. Francis Xavier is a Jesuit institution, opened in 1847 and chartered in 1861, and now having twenty instructors and over 300 collegiate students. Its handsome and imposing buildings are at 39 to 59 West 15th Street and 30 to 50 West 16th Street, near Sixth Avenue. The library contains 25,000 volumes, and the museum and herbarium have large and valuable collections.

ST. FRANCIS XAVIER CHURCH AND COLLEGE, ROMAN CATHOLIC.   36 WEST 16TH STREET, BETWEEN FIFTH AND SIXTH AVENUES.

Manhattan College is another great Catholic institution.   Its stately buildings overlook Manhattanville and many leagues of the Hudson River and the Palisades.   It was founded by the Brothers of the Christian Schools in 1853, and received
a charter in 1863.   It has twenty-two instructors and 300 students, one-third of
whom are collegiate.   It possesses a fine library and museum.

The Academy of the Sacred Heart is at Manhattanville (130th Street and
St.-Nicholas Avenue), where it occupies a group of stone buildings in a pleasant

CONVENT OF THE SACRED HEART, ST. NICHOLAS AVENUE AND 130TH STREET.

park of lawns and groves.   It has about 250 students, mostly boarders, cared for
by the Ladies of the Sacred Heart, who also conduct a large day-school at 49 West
17th Street, and a boarding and day academy at 533 Madison Avenue.

The Academy of Mount St. Vincent, under the care of the Sisters of
Charity, is just above Riverdale, on the banks of the Hudson River.   Near the
academy stands the stone castle of Font Hill, built by Edwin Forrest for his home,
and now a part of the religious institution, whose domain covers sixty-three acres.
The 200 girls studying here wear blue uniform dresses, and French is the language
spoken.   The property of this academy is valued at nearly $1,000,000.

St.-Louis College, at 224 West 58th Street, has 75 pupils.   It was founded in
1869, by Rev. Père Ronay, for Catholic boys of refined families.

The La-Salle Academy, at 44 and 46 2d Street, has 130 pupils, under the
care of the Christian Brothers.

The Holy-Cross Academy, is at 343 West 42d Street.   It has 250 girl-
students.

St. Catharine's Convent is at Madison Avenue and East 81st Street.

St. Vincent Ferrers Convent, at Lexington Avenue and East 65th Street,
has fine buildings, and a capable body of teachers.

Catholic Parochial Schools, with large and costly buildings and appliances,
are numerous.

The Catholic Private Schools, of which there are a dozen of a high order,
are for Catholic children.   Among them are the Ursuline and Villa Maria Academies, the Holy Rosary, St. Augustine's and St. Cecilia's.

Trinity-Church Schools include a group of interesting Episcopal institutions,
such as the parochial school for boys, on Trinity Place ; the girls' school of St.

Paul's on Church Street ; and the night schools for men and women. The industrial schools of the parish teach sewing to more than 2,000 women ; and the Sisters
of St. Mary conduct a training-school for girls to learn household service.

The St. John Baptist and St. Mary's Schools are private institutions for
girls, at 231 East 17th Street and 8 East 46th Street. St. Mary's (founded in 1867)
has 160 girls, under the Sisters of St. Mary. It is an expensive and efficient school.

The Riverside School, at 152 West 103d Street. is an Episcopal private
school, with 100 pupils.

The Friends' Seminary, at 226 East 16th Street, has 125 students.

St. Matthew's Academy, at 156 Elizabeth Street, is attended chiefly by
children of the Evangelical Lutherans.

The Society for Ethical Culture was founded in 1888 for the study and practical teaching of the science of ethics, based on purely humanitarian grounds as distinguished from the theological basis of Christian ethics. Prof. Felix Adler has
long been prominently identified with the society, of which he was one of the
founders. Religious services are held every Sunday at Chickering Hall, corner of
Fifth Avenue and West 18th Street, and the society is actively engaged in benevolent work. It is about to erect a half-million-dollar building up town.

Art Education.—New York is the foremost of American cities in regard to
art, and its public galleries, private collections, and sales galleries are of more than
continental reputation, and in-
clude many noble works, both
of the old masters and of the
best modern schools. It is
therefore natural that several
well-attended art-schools have
grown up amid such surroundings. Even the public schools
teach drawing to all their
pupils ; and several famous
artists admit to their studios
promising students. The
American Academy of Fine
Arts was founded in 1802,
mainly by merchants, and
opened its collections to art-
students in 1825. But the
policy was narrow and churl-
ish ; and in the same year the
students withdrew and, under
S. F. B. Morse and A. B.
Durand, formed the New-York
Drawing Association.

**The National Academy
of Design,** whose art-schools

ACADEMY OF THE SACRED HEART, 49 WEST 17TH ST., NEAR SIXTH AVE.

occupy a part of the Venetian palace at Fourth Avenue and 23d Street, grew out of
the New-York Drawing Association. The schools are open both to men and women,
in morning, afternoon and evening sessions. There are classes in sketching, and
drawing from antique statuary and living figures, with lectures on perspective,
anatomy, and composition. The pupils average 250.

The **Metropolitan Museum of Art** has art-schools which give careful technical instruction in free-hand and mechanical drawing, designing, painting, modelling,
architecture, and other branches.   A travelling scholarship has lately been endowed,
to enable competent male students in painting to have the benefit of European
instruction also.

The **Art-Students' League of New York,** founded in 1875, is in its elegant
new building at 215 West 57th Street ; and has day and evening classes of men and

MOUNT ST. VINCENT ACADEMY, RIVERDALE, BEYOND THE HARLEM RIVER.

women studying portraiture, composition, sketching, modelling, and drawing and
modelling from sculptures or from live models.   Among the students here have been
Church, Remington, De Thulstrup, Howard Pyle, and other well-known men.   Among
the instructors are Beckwith, Mowbray, Weir, Chase, St. Gaudens and Kenyon Cox.

The **Gotham Art Students** are at 17 Bond Street.

The **Harlem Art Association,** at 149 East 125th Street, affords art instruction for the residents of upper New York.

The **Society of Decorative Art,** at 28 East 21st Street, has classes in fine
needle-work, china-painting, fan-painting, water-colors, and other branches of art ;
and aims to thoroughly train women, each in one kind of decorative work.

The **School of Industrial Art and Technical Design for Women,**
founded in 1881 by Mrs. Florence E. Cory, is at 134 Fifth Avenue, and successfully
teaches designing for carpets, wall-paper, cretonne, calico, silk, linen, portières,
carved and inlaid work, stained glass, lace, decorated cards, china, and all industrial
art manufactures.

The **American Art School** (A. L. Blanchard's), at 326 Fifth Avenue, near
33d Street, was established in 1879, and teaches drawing and all branches of
painting, and especially tapestry painting.

The **New-York Institute for Artist-Artisans,** at 140 West 23d Street, is a
school founded in 1888 by eminent firms, citizens and artists to develop distinctive
American art and artisanship combined, and to popularize art and make it vital, domestic and national.   A *N.-Y. Times* editorial says, " It is by all odds the best, most democratic, most thorough and promising art-school in the country.   It is leading the van in
industrial art-education."   There are departments in Illustration, Painting, Sculpture,

Architecture, Textiles, Wall-paper, Ceramics, Wood-carving, Metal and Jewelry work. The terms are $50 a year, with a few prize-scholarships. John Ward Stimson, previously so successful at the Metropolitan Museum, is the educational director.

The Woman's Art-School in the Cooper Union maintains classes in painting, oil-color, drawing from the antique and from life, photo-color, photo-crayon, painting porcelain photographs, pen and ink drawing, retouching negatives, designing for silks and windows, and preparation for teaching art. It is intended to supply to women of taste and capacity, from anywhere, a free education in some one professional branch of art, in morning and afternoon classes. The night school of art has over 1,000 pupils in cast-drawing, form-drawing, decorative designing, ornamental drawing, rudimental drawing, modelling in clay, perspective drawing, mechanical drawing and architectural drawing. The students are instructed by able artists, like Gifford and Weir, and are provided with lectures on various branches of art. Over 400 persons study in the Woman's Art-School, and a still larger number in the night school, and there are always many more applicants than can be received. These Cooper-Union schools are among the very foremost enlightening influences in America, and have disseminated practical æsthetic ideas for many years.

Music Instruction is well provided in New-York City, for here is the musical centre of the Union, and all musicians depend mainly upon the New-York verdict. Here the German, English and Italian operas are presented as nowhere else in America, and the great musical societies render the best oratorio and orchestral compositions. Music is taught in the public schools; and by hundreds of private teachers throughout the city.

ST. CATHERINE'S CONVENT, MADISON AVENUE AND EAST 81ST STREET.

The Metropolitan College of Music was founded in 1886, as a vocal school, and in 1891 received incorporation as a college. It occupies many rooms, at Nos. 19 and 21 East 14th Street; and has 20 professors, among whom are Dudley Buck, Harry Rowe Shelley, R. H. Woodman and other well-known musicians.

19

The New-York College of Music was founded in 1878, and has more than a score of instructors and 700 pupils. The handsome building at 128-130 East 58th Street was erected for the college, and has a commodious concert-hall. Among the instructors are Alex. Lambert, Mme Fursch-Madi and Walter Damrosch.

The New-York Conservatory of Music is at 5 East 14th Street.

The German Conservatory of Music is at 7 West 42d Street.

The Liederkranz Schools are free for instruction in vocal music for young men and women, in the Liederkranz building, on East 58th Street.

Industrial and Scientific Training is accomplished through numerous important institutions, like the Hebrew Technical School, with its 140 students; the manual-training department of the College of the City of New York; and the Workingman's School, of the United Relief Works of the Society for Ethical Culture, at 109 West 54th Street, in which Felix Adler is interested.

MOUNT SINAI HOSPITAL.   CHURCH OF THE DOMINICAN FATHERS.   ST. VINCENT FERRERS CONVENT.   65TH STREET.
ST. VINCENT FERRERS CONVENT, LEXINGTON AVENUE AND EAST 65TH STREET.

The Cooper Union, one of the greatest popular educators in America, occupies a seven-story brown-stone building, covering the block at the intersection of Seventh Street and the Bowery, and Third and Fourth Avenues. One of its chief features is the Free Night School of Science, giving a thorough instruction in mathematics, and mechanics, in a five-years' course. The night schools of science and art have over 3,000 students, most of whom work at their trades during the day. The pupils must be fifteen years old, and acquainted with the rudiments of education. The Union costs $50,000 a year, which is derived from the rentals of stores in the building and from the income of the endowment. Among its interesting features are the library of 32,000 volumes; the reading-room, with 500 magazines and newspapers on file, and visited by 600,000 persons yearly; the evening Elocution Class, with 150 attendants; the Literary Class, with 200 debaters and declaimers; the free Saturday-evening lectures, by celebrated scholars and scientists; the free class in

Stenography and Type-writing, numbering 40 women ; the Free School of Telegraphy for women, with 40 women ; and the Woman's Art-School.

Peter Cooper was born when New York contained **27,000** inhabitants, and
reached only to Chambers Street ; when there was not a free school in the city ; and
in the first presidency of George Washington.   He died in 1883.   He was a plain
and practical man, and a successful inventor and manufacturer ; and a million dollars
of his wealth was devoted to the construction and endowment of the Cooper Union,
"dedicated to Science, to make life intelligent, and to Art, to make life beautiful."

Columbia Grammar School, on 51st Street, near Madison Avenue, was founded
in 1764, as a Preparatory Department of Columbia College, and was transferred by
the trustees to the entire control of the late Dr. Charles Anthon.   It is a first-class
private school, with 20 instructors, and fine school-rooms and gymnasium.

COOPER UNION, IN JUNE, 1893, JUNCTION OF THE BOWERY, THIRD AND FOURTH AVENUE AND 7TH STREET.

The New-York Trade-School, at First Avenue, 67th and 68th Streets,
was founded by Col. Richard T. Auchmuty, in 1881, to enable young men to learn
certain trades, and to give young men already in those trades an opportunity to improve themselves.   This school covers nearly an acre of ground, and is attended
yearly by 600 young men, from all parts of the United States and Canada.   Connected with the school is a lodging house, accommodating 100 young men, where
well-furnished rooms are rented at a moderate cost.   The average age of the young
men in the day classes is 19 ; those in the evening classes are younger.   Until the
present year the New-York Trade-School has been supported as well as managed
by Col. Auchmuty, but recently it has received an endowment of $500,000 from
J. Pierpont Morgan.   The workshops at the school are always open to visitors.   The
pupils are taught by skilful mechanics the right ways of working, and also why work

should be done in a certain way, by thorough, direct and friendly methods.   The classes in Bricklaying have erected several great buildings.   The evening classes work three evenings in each week.   The classes in Plumbing, under the careful supervision of the Master Plumbers' Association, have a shop 37 by 115 feet in area, perfectly

BARON HIRSCH FUND TRADE-SCHOOLS, 225 EAST NINTH STREET.

equipped.   The classes in Carpentry have built some of the Trade-School edifices, in admirable style. The classes in House, Sign and Fresco Painting are supervised by the Master Painters' and Decorators' Association, and have a wide reputation.   The classes in Stone-cutting, Blacksmith's Work, Printing and Plastering, are all of great efficiency and service.

The Nautical School is a very interesting department of education, intended to prepare boys for service in the American merchant-marine.   It numbers about 80 lads, between 16 and 20 years old, who are under the care of United-States naval officers, the entire institution being governed by the city Board of Education.   The school occupies the old war-ship *St. Mary's,* sometimes at the foot of East 28th Street, or anchored in the harbor, and every year making long practice cruises to Europe or the islands of the Atlantic.   Besides the usual English branches, the lads are taught orally and practically in making knots and splices ; the names and uses of rigging and sails, bending and loosing, reefing and furling ; the management and steering of boats, by rowing, sculling or sailing ; the compass, boxing and steering, and taking bearings ; heaving the lead and marking log and lead lines ; swimming and floating ; and many other details needful for sea-life.   There is a post-graduate course, fitting students for the position of mates. All instruction is free, as the *St. Mary's* is practically one of the New-York public schools.   It is in no sense a reformatory, and only willing and well-accredited boys are admitted.

Webb's Academy and Home for Shipbuilders was planned and built by William H. Webb, an eminent New-York shipbuilder, and incorporated in 1889. It was opened in 1893, to serve a double purpose : As a home for infirm and unfortunate shipbuilders, and their wives, and as a school for young Americans who desire to learn how to build ships and marine engines, and have no money to pay for skilled instruction.   The tuition includes all the details of shipbuilding and marine engineering, theoretical and practical ; and the students are boarded and taught free of cost.   The stately tall-towered building is in handsome Renaissance architecture, and stands in a park of thirteen acres, on Fordham Heights, overlooking the Harlem River.   Besides its dormitories and parlors, library and hospital, it has spacious draughting-rooms and an immense laying-out room.

The Teachers College, the first established in America, offers courses in pedagogy, and gives opportunity for studying children from the kindergarten to the end of the high school, and also for observation and practice in teaching. It has students from eighteen States, including many experienced teachers and college graduates. Its aim is to bring modern life and the modern school more into touch with each other, and to train teachers able to accomplish this result by teaching in accordance with the principles of the new education. In 1892 the college received a gift of a valuable building site on Morningside Heights, adjoining the future site of Columbia College, and entered upon the work of raising a building fund of $700,000. In 1893 a permanent charter was granted, the name being changed from New-York College for the Training of Teachers, by which it had been known since

HOLY CROSS PAROCHIAL SCHOOL, 240 WEST 43D STREET.

its foundation in 1889, to Teachers College; and an alliance was formed with Columbia College by which its students, whether men or women, may become candidates for the degrees of A. B., A. M., and Ph. D., given by Columbia College, and the students of Columbia College may pursue courses in the Teachers College leading to such degrees. An especial feature of the work in its new quarters will be the Mechanics-Arts Building, than which no more commodious edifice for a similar purpose exists. There are 34 officers and several hundred students. The college occupies the old Union Seminary, at 9 University Place, pending the completion of the new structures on Morningside Heights.

Commercial Colleges have attained a high rank as educational institutions. It is natural that this great metropolitan centre of commercial activities, the chief port of entry and clearing-house of the continent, should have thousands of students of business forms and principles.   For many years the commercial colleges of New York have been fitting great numbers of young people for practical service in the counting-rooms and offices of the city, and preparing them to become expert accountants and book-keepers in positions of trust and responsibility. The standard of commercial honor is higher in New York than in London or Paris, and among most of its business men their word is as good as their bond.   In the normal condition of affairs here, apart from the infrequent panic of a financial crisis or the fever of speculation, the rectitude of the commercial spirit follows the lines of absolute truth.   Much of this nobility in the life of trade came from the grand old merchants of the early days of New York, who held honor as high and stainless as the members of any learned or military profession have ever done.   Much of it also is derived from the teachings of the business colleges of the city, where the sentiments of exactness and precision are taught step by step with those of vigilance and enterprise.

Packard's Business College and School of Stenography is one of the institutions of New York.   It was located in the then new building of the Cooper Institute in 1858, where it remained five years, then removing to more spacious

PACKARD'S BUSINESS COLLEGE, NORTHEAST CORNER 23D STREET AND FOURTH AVENUE.

quarters in the Mortimer Building, corner of 22d Street and Broadway, where it stayed seven years, when, in 1870, it occupied the entire fourth story of the Methodist Building — now McCreery's — at the corner of Broadway and 11th Street.   In 1887 it took possession of its present admirable quarters, at the corner of 23d Street and Fourth Avenue, occupying the entire upper part of the building formerly held by the College of Physicians and Surgeons. The notable fact of this institution is its hold upon its students, which comes from its individualizing system of instruction and government. The .Packard boys and girls are never reckoned *en masse*, but have unusual opportunities to impress their individuality upon their teachers, as they afterwards have upon the world. While being thoroughly educated for business — that is, for clerkships of all kinds — they are also educated for citizenship. While bookkeeping, arithmetic, penmanship and phonography are the principal technical studies of the school, especial care is given to the study of English, commercial law, civil

PARISH SCHOOL, CHURCH OF OUR LADY OF MT. CARMEL.
445 EAST 115TH STREET.

WORKINGMEN'S SCHOOL, SOCIETY FOR ETHICAL CULTURE,
109 WEST 54TH STREET.

government, and questions of public interest. One of the constant exercises of the school is public speaking, which receives intelligent and discriminating attention, and constitutes a charming feature of the course of training. During the past thirty-five years many thousands of graduates have been sent out of this school, and are holding important places in the foremost enterprises of the city. Among its constituents are merchants, bankers, legislators, lawyers, ministers, and physicians, and among its friends and patrons many of the most eminent men of the country. Its proprietor and president, S. S. Packard, is a recognized leader in his line of work, having given more time and achieved a fuller measure of success in it than any other man. He is, in fact, the pioneer business-college man, and the man whose impress is most firmly fixed upon that specialty of education represented by the business college. Through Mr. Packard's efforts, mainly, has been carried forward the Business Education Exhibit at the World's Fair, which will undoubtedly form a remarkable spectacular effect, and in impressiveness will lead the educational exhibits of the great Exposition.   In short, the Packard College, while being a marked feature of the great metropolis, is a recognized American institution.

Physical Culture is given much consideration.   Among the great gymnasiums of the city are those of the New-York Athletic Club, at 55th Street and Sixth Avenue ; the Racquet and Tennis Club, at 27 West 43d Street ; the Young Men's Christian Association, at 23d Street and Fourth Avenue, and at Mott Haven ; and the Berkeley Ladies' Athletic Association, on 44th Street, near Fifth Avenue.   The Turnverein conducts a school for 1,000 children, between the ages of six and fifteen,

DICKEL'S RIDING ACADEMY, 124 TO 136 WEST 56TH STREET.

in which, besides the usual studies, the young people are taught in calisthenics and other branches of gymnastics.

Dickel's Riding Academy, at 124 to 136 West 56th Street, is the most famous of the excellent schools of equestrianism which abound in the vicinity of Central Park ; and is also the oldest institution of this kind in the city.   From the very first Dickel's has enjoyed the patronage of the best families of New York, and therefore it has long since acquired a social *prestige* of great value.   The riding takes place in a spacious, airy and well-ventilated hall, floored with tan-bark, and bordered at either end with large galleries.   Every evening there is a considerable assemblage of patrician equestrians, who ride to music, while their friends enter-tain themselves in the galleries, and watch the brilliant sight.   Instruction is given under the personal supervision of Charles W. Dickel, and begins with the teaching of persons entirely unacquainted with riding, imparting to them confidence, gracefulness and strength in the saddle. Even the most timid and fearful girls, who at first have to be held onto the saddles, in a short time acquire a notable mastery over their steeds, and are able to enjoy the long gallops in Central Park. The academy also teaches the most difficult achievements in rough field riding, including proficiency in leaping and other delights of experienced horsemen. At certain hours the ring is set apart for the use of Troop A, N. G., S. N. Y., which is so celebrated for its splendid equestrianism. It is natural that this exercise-ground of the best families should be guarded against unworthy intruders, and no one can be admitted to the classes without satisfactory introduction or references. The hall of the ring is of attractive and appropriate architecture, with a fine Louvre roof, for copious air and light, and ingenious truss-supports. On one side are a great number of lockers and dressing-rooms, from which the equestrian issues fully equipped, from spurs to

INTERIOR OF DICKEL'S RIDING ACADEMY, 124 TO 136 WEST 56TH STREET.

riding-hat and gloves. The academy is under the proprietorship of Dickel & Kroehle, both well-known in the world of horse-lovers.

Other Riding Schools are mostly near Central Park, whose roads and bridle-paths afford fine opportunities for equestrian practice and exercise. Durland's, near the Eighth-Avenue entrance to the Park, at the Grand Circle, is one of the largest equestrian schools in the world. Other riding academies are the Boulevard, at 60th Street; the Central Park, at 58th Street and Seventh Avenue; the Belmont, on 124th Street; the West End, at 139 West 125th Street; and Antony's, at 90th Street and Fifth Avenue. These institutions have well-equipped riding-rings and saddle-horses, with competent teachers, and some of the evening classes are inspired by pleasant music.

Dancing Schools are numerous and varied, where this graceful art is taught to thousands of young people. Among the foremost terpsichorean academies is Dodsworth's, whose patrons come from the select circles of the city, and are instructed in all the most modern forms of dancing.

Rutgers Female College, at 56 West 55th Street, was founded by Chancellor Ferris, in 1838, and for many years held a very high rank. After it lost its fine buildings on Fifth Avenue, the institution declined; but of late many influential friends have risen to sustain it. Rutgers now has sixteen instructors. The president is George W. Samson, D. D., and the lady principal is Mrs. James T. Hoyt.

Fencing Classes are taught by Prof. H. Armand Jacoby, at the New-York Athletic Club, and at 75 West 44th Street (Prof. Jacoby is also the instructor of Troop

A); M. Gouspy, at the Racquet and Tennis Club; Frederick and Heins, at the Turnverein; M. Regis Senac; and several other masters of swordsmanship.

The New-York Institution for the Instruction of the Deaf and Dumb, on Washington Heights, opened in 1818, as a free school for residents of the State, has 16 instructors and over 300 pupils, including many in articulation and auricular perception; trade-schools, with in-

NEW-YORK INSTITUTION FOR THE INSTRUCTION OF THE DEAF AND DUMB, ELEVENTH AVENUE, NEAR 162D STREET.

structors for the several branches; and a department for technical and applied art.

The Institution for the Improved Instruction of Deaf Mutes, on Lexington Avenue, between 67th and 68th Streets, has 20 instructors and 200 pupils. It was founded in 1867, and teaches the oral method, by articulation and lip-reading, not using the deaf and dumb alphabet. The building is an attractive one; and near it stands the four-story fire-proof structure of the Technical Training Department and Art-Studio, metal-working, wood-working, natural philosophy and art-studios, each having one full floor. The children are also taught sewing, cooking, dress-making and other useful avocations; and a kindergarten is provided.

St. Joseph's Institute for the Improved Instruction of Deaf Mutes, at Fordham, has commodious modern buildings, and an industrial department.

The New-York Institution for the Blind, at 34th Street and Ninth Avenue, is another beneficence of far-reaching value, founded in 1831, and now occupied by 30 instructors and 240 pupils. Here the unfortunate who have lost or never seen the light of day are educated in literature and in the essentials of a sound musical-education, and also in piano-tuning and other useful avocations, with a view to becoming happy and self-supporting members of society. The library contains over 3,000 volumes, many of them in raised letters. Since its origin, upwards of 1,500 persons have been instructed here, a number of whom have attained success and distinction in the business and profes-

INSTITUTION FOR THE IMPROVED INSTRUCTION OF DEAF MUTES, LEXINGTON AVENUE, EAST 67TH AND EAST 68TH STREETS.

sioual walks of life. The school has been the source of many original improvements in the methods and appliances used in educating the blind, the latest and most important of which is the New-York Point System of Tangible Writing and Printing, for literature, music and mathematics.

Private Schools, Seminaries and Academies in great numbers are found scattered throughout New-York City, giving every variety of education, and largely patronized by the well-to-do families of the city.

The American Academy of the Dramatic Arts, 19 and 21 West 44th Street, is the principal training school for the professional theatrical stage in this country. The

NEW-YORK INSTITUTION FOR THE BLIND, NINTH AVENUE AND 34TH STREET.

faculty numbers twenty prominent professionals. This academy was founded in 1884 under the name of The Lyceum Theatre School of Acting. It was the first and only institution of its kind in this country. Since 1884 nearly 300 students have graduated from the American Academy of the Dramatic Arts, and most of them are playing in various theatrical companies. Its president is Franklin H. Sargent. In 1892 it moved to the Berkeley Lyceum, on West 44th Street, where it utilizes the beautiful theatre, besides class and rehearsal-rooms.

The Berkeley School has a magnificent new fire-proof building, at 18 to 24 West 44th Street, with a front of Indiana limestone and Roman brick, in Ionic architecture. On the ground floor is the armory and gymnasium, occupying 85 by 100 feet. The first floor contains a library, large dining-room, offices and reception-rooms. The library and hall are embellished with four superb memorial windows. On the second and third floors are the school and class-rooms ; and the upper floors

contain a studio and a laboratory, with dormitories for twenty students. The main halls and toilet-rooms are wainscoted in marble and floored with mosaic. The building is heated by hot water, with inlets for fresh air upon every floor and in every room. An original system of ventilation is employed, by which the vitiated air is drawn from every room through a smoothly-masoned flue, to a chamber on the fifth floor, opening from which to the outside air is a Blackman propeller-fan run by an electric motor, which can change the air in the entire building in four minutes. The athletic grounds of the school, known as the Berkeley Oval, comprise ten acres, with thirty tennis courts, a quarter-mile running track, and a straight-away 220 yards running track, together with a boat-house and thirty boats upon the Harlem River. The Oval is 130 feet above the

BERKELEY SCHOOL, 20 WEST 44TH STREET, NEAR FIFTH AVENUE.

level of the Harlem River, and affords a superb view of the Harlem and Hudson valleys. The Berkeley School has made an enviable reputation as a preparatory school, and has sent nearly 200 boys to the leading colleges within twelve years, 90 per cent. of them going to Harvard, Yale, Columbia and Princeton, where their scholarship has attested the thoroughness of their preparation. The systematic physical instruction afforded, together with the discipline and proficiency acquired by the students in the military drill, have been no small factors in the success which the school has obtained. The school was founded by the present head master, John S. White, LL. D., a graduate of the Boston public schools and of Harvard University, Class of 1870, where he took the first classical honors. The Berkeley School has 30 instructors and 300 students.

Collegiate School, a private school for boys, at 241 and 243 West 77th Street, has a continuous history running back to the early settlement of the Island of Manhattan by the Dutch. The first school-master was an official of the Dutch West India Company, with Wouter Van Twiller, in 1633. This is, therefore, the oldest school now in existence in America. The new building, occupied in the fall of 1892, adjoins the new Collegiate Church on West-End Avenue. The school has classical, scientific and commercial studies, and military drill. There are twelve teachers in the Primary, Intermediate and Senior departments. Many boys are prepared here for college. The head master is Lemuel C. Mygatt, A. M.

Weingart Institute, at 22 and 24 East 91st Street, between Madison Avenue and Fifth Avenue, is a select day and boarding school, with kindergarten, under the direction of S. Weingart. It occupies two handsome and commodious four-story buildings on the highest and healthiest ground in the city, and within half a block of Central Park. One building is devoted to school purposes entirely, and the other is the residence of the principal and the boarding pupils. The ground-floor is occupied by a spacious gymnasium, equipped with the most approved modern appliances. Both buildings are well adapted to their educational uses, and are fitted up in a thorough and efficient manner. The grades of the school are kindergarten, primary, intermediate, junior and senior, the latter department preparing for the leading colleges and scientific schools. All the English branches are taught by competent American teachers. As a large portion of the pupils are of Germanic origin, the German language forms a regular part of the course. The Weingart Institute was founded in 1882, on 55th Street ; and the thorough intellectual, physical and moral training it gives its pupils has caused its continual growth and prosperity.

The Lenox Institute, founded in 1888, at 334 and 336 Lenox Avenue, is practically a German gymnasium, or college preparatory school, with business, primary and kindergarten classes also. It has men teachers, and boy and girl pupils.

The Hebrew Free School Association, founded in 1864, has four large schools and 3,200 students, with daily sessions from 4 to 6 P. M. (except Fridays and Saturdays). The pupils also attend the public schools.

The Baron Hirsch Fund, established by a wealthy Berlin banker, and with headquarters at 45 Broadway, conducts a series of day and night schools for children and adults of the Russian and Roumanian Hebrew race, to teach them to become good citizens, giving instruction in trades, and in American elementary studies. It also furnishes tools to mechanics ; loans small sums to deserving persons ; and endeavors to prevent the Hebrews from congregating in the cities.

Other well-known institutions include the following : The Columbia Grammar School, at 34 and 36 East 51st Street, near Columbia College, a preparatory school for all colleges and scientific schools ; Dr. Sachs's Collegiate Institute, at 38 and 116 West 59th Street, fronting on Central Park ; William Freeland's admirable and efficient Harvard School, 578 Fifth Avenue, corner of 47th Street, fits many lads for the leading colleges. Still others are the Barnard School for boys, at 119 West 125th Street, with 120 pupils ; Callisen's School for boys, 131 West 43d Street ; Morse's English and Classical School for boys, 423 Madison Avenue ; Dr. Chapin's Collegiate School for boys, 721 Madison Avenue ; Cutler's Private School for boys, 20 West 43d Street ; the Dwight School for boys, 1479 Broadway ; the Irving School for boys, 20 West 59th Street ; Halsey's Collegiate School for boys, 34 West 40th Street ; Lyon's Classical School for boys, 6 East 47th Street ; McMullen's Private School for boys, 521 West 161st Street ; Richard's School for boys, 1475 Broadway ; the University Grammar-School for boys, 1473 Broadway ; the West-End

Avenue School for boys, 208 West-End Avenue ; the Woodbridge School for boys, 32 East 45th Street ; Madame Ruel's Boarding and Day School for girls, 26 East 56th Street ; the Brearley School for girls, 6 East 45th Street ; the Classical School for girls, 1961 Madison Avenue ; the Misses Ely's School for girls, Riverside Drive, near 85th Street ; the Comstock School for girls, 32 West 40th Street ; the English and French Schools for girls, 148 Madison Avenue and 55 West 47th Street ; Miss Perrin's Girl's School, 244 Lenox Avenue ; the Van Norman Institute for girls, 2 West 71st Street ; Mrs. Weil's School for girls, 711 Madison Avenue ; Misses Peebles and Thompson's School for Young Ladies, 32 East 57th Street ; Rev. C. K. Gardner's School for Young Ladies, 601 Fifth Avenue ; the Misses Grahams' School for Young Ladies, 63 Fifth Avenue ; Miss Anna C. Brackett's School, 9 West 39th Street ; Miss Emily A. Ward's Riverside School, 50 West 104th Street ; and the Heidenfeld Institute, for both sexes, 824 Lexington Avenue.

A commanding advantage which New York has over other American cities, for purposes of education, is its massed treasures of art, literature and humanity. The Astor, Lenox and Mercantile Libraries, and other great collections of books ; the Metropolitan Museum and several other very rich collections in art ; the American Museum of Natural History ; the moving life of the parks and avenues, architecture in every form, philanthropy organized to benefit millions, oratory and dramatic art, consecration and self-sacrifice — almost every form of civic and social life may be observed and entered into, in the proud metropolis of the New World. The contemplation of these manifold phases makes versatile men and women.

Cooking Schools, wherein is taught the art of preparing and cooking food to the best advantage, comprise several well-equipped institutions, ranging from the simple cooking-classes of the charity schools to the scientific academies.

The New-York Cooking School, in the United Charities Building, elevates the poor by free lessons in plain cooking, marketing, nurses' cooking, etc., and has nearly 1,000 pupils yearly. A large dining-room is attached.

Maillard's New-York Chocolate School is at 114 West 25th Street, where free lessons are given on Monday, Wednesday and Friday afternoons, from October to June, in the art of making a cup of chocolate or cocoa.

Kindergartens and other peculiar schools show the imperial beneficence of New York. Here have been instituted great numbers of schools for the dependent and defective classes. The New-York Kindergarten Association has opened numerous schools for the very young children in the tenement-house districts.

The Children's Aid Society conducts 22 admirable day and night industrial schools, and 14 kindergartens. The 15,000 poor Italians in New York are aided by three industrial schools in Leonard, Sullivan and Crosby Streets, where more than 1,200 children and adults are taught in ordinary studies and in carpentry, cooking, sewing, etc. Similar schools are maintained in the Five-Points Mission House, with cooking classes and other practical features. The House of Industry, at 155 Worth Street, teaches type-setting, carpentry, and other industries, to about 300 children ; and has a well appointed kindergarten. St. Joseph's Home, on Great Jones Street, is an enormous Catholic mission, with industrial and other schools attached. The Catholic Protectory has large trade-schools for boys, and sewing-schools for girls.

Besides these, are the great reform schools, like the New-York Juvenile Asylum, founded in 1851, with 70 instructors and 1,100 pupils ; the House of Refuge, on Randall's Island, founded in 1825, with 50 instructors and 1,000 pupils ; and the New-York Catholic Protectory, with 50 instructors and 1,500 pupils. These enormous schools are liberally conducted, and accomplish inestimable good.

The Higher Culture

Art Museums and Galleries, Scientific, Literary, Musical and Kindred Institutions, Societies and Organizations.

IN THE interest of the United States the New-Yorkers never rest. They are at work unceasingly, in order that they may give to the Americans all the types of beauty and of elegance. Even the least lavish among them — those who do not buy miniatures, vignettes of the eighteenth century, art-objects of Japan — pay cheerfully for perfection, the price of which is fabulous. In their estimate of value, it is not the actual worth, but the art truer than truth, that counts.

Elsewhere there are skies, fields, plains, forests, brooks under dark leaves, delicious corners of shade ; but in New York, there are flowers that are living jewels made of light. In New York, myriads of periwinkles, forget-me-nots, rose-bushes and geraniums, uniformly embroidered on miles of lawn, are as if cut out of an endless cloth, regularly woven and inexhaustible.

Elsewhere there are Queens, Princesses, great ladies, and peasants ; but in New York there are women prodigiously dressed, young and beautiful — not only because they are, but because they wish to be young and beautiful — and representing plastically the ideal of thoughts human.

Elsewhere intelligent men read journals, books, scientific pamphlets, everything ; and in comparison with New-Yorkers, most of whom are too busy to read, are little informed and provincial, because ideas are in New York in the air that one breathes. In London and Paris, the only cities in the world that New York might not surpass in higher culture if it ceased to labor, art-galleries, literary, scientific and artistic societies, museums, are in the charge of the government.

The Metropolitan Museum of Art, in Central Park, near Fifth Avenue and 82d Street, in a stone and brick building on the site formerly called Deer Park, was formed as the result of a meeting instigated chiefly by the art-committee of the Union League, in October, 1869, wholly in reliance upon the public spirit of New-Yorkers. It was incorporated in 1870, and soon thereafter purchased a collection of pictures, which it exhibited, together with loaned objects of art, in a leased building at 681 Fifth Avenue. In 1873, before its lease had expired, it rented the Douglas mansion, 126 West 14th Street ; having in 1872 purchased from General L. P. di Cesnola the antiquities unearthed by him in Cyprus. Gifts were received, in money and objects of art, with members' subscriptions, and an offer from the Park Commissioners to furnish a building in the Park if the museum should be transferred thither. In 1871 the Legislature had passed an act authorizing the Department of Public Parks to erect a building for the purposes of a museum, and to enter into an agreement for its occupancy by the Metropolitan Museum of Art. The first portion of the proposed building was finished and inaugurated in 1880. By the agreement just mentioned the museum was opened to the public without charge four days in the week. The second, or south, wing of the building was completed and occupied in 1889 ; the third is now in progress. In 1890 petitions were circulated in the city requesting that the museum be opened to the public on Sundays without charge. The Trustees complied, at the cost of large pecuniary sacrifices, and submitting to an inevitable deficit. Out of 751,856 visitors in 1892, 246,988 came on Sundays. This loss has been in part made up by increased appropriations from the city.

INTERIOR OF THE METROPOLITAN MUSEUM OF ART.

The Cyprus collection has no parallel anywhere for extent and value. It comprises stone sculptures, sarcophagi, inscriptions, alabastra, ivories, lamps, pottery, terra-cotta statuettes, bronzes, glass, gems, jewelry and other objects in gold and silver ; Assyrian, Egyptian, Phœnician, Greek and Roman in character, and of dates from the earliest times to later than the Christian era; many of its objects and classes of objects are unique. The museum's collection of glass was increased by a purchase from Charvet by Henry G. Marquand, and by him presented to the Museum ; also a later collection presented by J. J. Jarves ; making the entire collection of glass the most valuable known. There are magnificent collections of Babylonian, Assyrian, and other ancient cylinders, seals and inscribed clay tablets ; Egyptian, Greek, Roman, Indian and American antiquities, the last in gold and silver, as well as pottery and stone; modern sculptures and bronzes; the Huntington collection of memorials of Washington, Franklin and Lafayette ; the E. C. Moore collection of ancient terra-cotta statuettes, ancient and modern glass, Oriental enamelled and other pottery, and objects of art in metal, ivory, etc.; the Coles collection of tapestries and vases; the Lazarus collection of miniatures, enamels, jewelry and fans; the Drexel collection of objects of art in gold and silver ; the C. W. King collection of ancient gems, purchased and presented to the museum by John Taylor Johnston ; the collection of Oriental porcelain purchased from S. P. Avery ; the Japanese swords from the Ives collection ; the unique collection of musical instruments of all nations, presented by Mrs. John Crosby Brown, with a smaller collection presented by J. W. Drexel ; the Baker and other collections of ancient textile fabrics from the Fayoum, in Egypt ; the pictures, gold medals and other objects commemorative of the laying of the Atlantic Cable, presented by the late Cyrus W. Field ; the models of inventions by the late Captain John Ericsson, presented by George H. Robinson ; the reproductions of ivory carvings, exhibiting the mediæval continuance of the art ; the collec-

METROPOLITAN MUSEUM OF ART.
CENTRAL PARK, NEAR FIFTH AVENUE AND 82D STREET.

20

tion of Renaissance iron work, the Della Robbia altar-piece, the metallic reproductions of gold and silver objects in the imperial Russian museums, all presented by Henry G. Marquand; the McCullum, Stuart and Astor laces; the collection of architectural casts, made from a fund bequeathed by the late Levi H. Willard, amounting to $100,000; the sculptural casts, presented by H. G. Marquand; and the beginning of a series of casts, purchased by subscription, intended to illustrate progressive art from the earliest examples to the later Christian; drawings by the old masters, collected by Count Maggiori of Bologna, Signor Marietta, Professor Angelini and Dr. Guastala, purchased and presented by Cornelius Vanderbilt; with another smaller but equally fine collection presented by Mrs. Cephas G. Thompson; a large collection of paintings by old Dutch and Flemish masters; another exceedingly important and valuable collection of paintings by old masters and painters of the English school, presented by Henry G. Marquand; the noble galleries of modern paintings bequeathed by the late Catharine Lorillard Wolfe; other galleries of masterpieces by modern artists, including the most famous works of Rosa Bonheur (presented by Cornelius Vanderbilt) and Meissonier (presented by Henry Hilton). The Metropolitan Museum of Art would be a museum of the first class even if it were limited to any one of the collections that it includes; but its symmetry and extent are as remarkable as its rapid growth, especially when we reflect that its creation and increase are due wholly to private enterprise. Besides the advantages furnished to artists, artisans and art-students in copying and designing from its collections, the museum has also, during the greater period of its existence, maintained an institution called the Art-Schools, in which the fine arts and decorative arts, in their chief branches, are taught, and lectures on art are given. In coöperation with Columbia College an arrangement has been made, under which the College provides for the delivery of lectures on art during each winter season, at the Museum, and the Museum supplies the illustrative material for the lectures. These plans will have much effect in developing art-taste in New York.

The American Museum of Natural History, in Central Park (77th Street and Eighth Avenue), was incorporated in 1869, for the purpose of establishing and maintaining in New-York City a museum and library of natural history. The first president was John David Wolfe, who was succeeded by Robert L. Stuart, now both deceased. The present officers are: Morris K. Jesup, President; James M. Constable and D. Jackson Steward, Vice-Presidents; Charles Lanier, Treasurer; John H. Winser, Secretary and Assistant Treasurer; and William Wallace, Superintendent of Buildings.

The museum held its first exhibition in the old arsenal, where the Verreaux collection of natural-history specimens, the Elliot collection of North-American birds, and the entire museum of Prince Maximilian of Neuwied were displayed. It was not until June, 1874, that the corner-stone of the first building in Manhattan Square was laid. A new portion has recently been added which greatly strengthens the effect of the architectural design — a not very pronounced tendency to the Romanesque. The building proper is of brick, with a front of red granite from New Brunswick and Canada. The imposing and ornamental entrance is of Massachusetts granite. The seven arches resting on short polished pillars of stone make a commanding and dignified front. The structure is so designed that it can be extended to occupy the whole of Manhattan Square, which has been set aside for that purpose; wings will be added as the collections require them, and the liberality of the city allows. The plans are now ready for the addition of another wing, to provide the much needed additional space for the exhibit of material now stored in the

AMERICAN MUSEUM OF NATURAL HISTORY.
CENTRAL PARK WEST, BETWEEN WEST 77TH AND WEST 81ST STREETS.

building.   The expenses are paid by the city, by the board of trustees, and by sub-scriptions.   In birds, mammals, insects, fossils, minerals, shells, and implements of the aborigines of our own and foreign lands, the collections are extremely rich and note-worthy ; the library on many subjects is unequaled by any other in the country. The collections of woods and building stones of the United States, presented by Morris K. Jesup, are far the most extensive and valuable in America and, possibly, in the world.   Most conspicuous in the other departments are :   The American gems and gem minerals, exhibited at the Paris Exposition by Tiffany & Co. (these brilliant and precious stones were purchased for and presented to the museum by J. Pierpont Morgan, one of the trustees); the collection of Prof. James Hall, the State Geologist ; the Spang collection of minerals ; the Jay collection of shells, pre-sented to the museum by Catherine L. Wolfe ; the D. J. Steward collection of shells ; and a series of specimens on Mammalian Palaeontology, the result of original research and investigation under the direction of Prof. H. F. Osborn.   Prominent in the department of Ethnology and Archæology are the collections of Lieut. Emmons, H. R. Bishop, Jones, Terry, and Sturgis ; the celebrated collection of jade objects made by George F. Kunz ; the Harry Edwards collection of entomo-logical specimens ; and the private collection of Andrew E. Douglass.

The different departments of the institution are designated as :

Public Instruction — Prof. Albert S. Bickmore, Curator.

Geology, Mineralogy, Conchology, and Marine Invertebrate Zoology — Prof. R. P. Whitfield, Curator.

Mammalogy, Ornithology, Herpitology, Ichthyology — Prof. J. A. Allen, Curator.

Mammalian Palaeontology — Prof. Henry Fairfield Osborn, Curator.

Archaeology and Ethnology — James Terry, Curator.

Taxidermy — Jenness Richardson, Taxidermist.

Entomology — William Beutenmuller, Curator.

Library — Anthony Woodward, Ph. D., Librarian.

Every object, however small, is labeled with its scientific and common appella-tion, its description, and its history.   The catalogues record the investigations, the researches and the studies of ages.   The trustees encourage the use of the halls and study-rooms for the holding of receptions, exhibitions and business meetings of the different scientific societies of the city and country.   The aim of the institution is to establish a post-graduate university of natural science, that shall be as complete in all its appointments as any similar institution in London or Paris.

The National Academy of Design, at the northwest corner of 23d Street and Fourth Avenue, was formed in 1826, of the New-York Drawing Association, and is the American Ecole des Beaux-arts, the American equivalent of the Royal Academy and of the Salon.   In its act of incorporation, passed April 5, 1828, are the names of Samuel F. B. Morse, Henry Inman, Thomas S. Cummings, John L. Morton, Asher B. Durand, Charles Ingham, Frederick S. Agate and Thomas Cole. It has in its list of students names of the most eminent artists.   The schools directed by the Academicians, instructed by the ablest professors, are opened the first Monday in October and closed in the middle of May.   The instruction is free. There are composition classes, costume classes, sketching classes from casts, from the living model, draped and undraped, painting classes, lectures, prizes to deserv-ing students, and exhibitions of works by artists.   The students have access to the books of an art library, the value of which is inestimable.   The spring and autumn exhibitions of the National Academy of Design introduce the work of American artists to the critics and to the public.

The Academy building, designed by P. B. Wight, is of white and dark marble, in the beautiful Venetian Gothic architecture. It has a double stairway to the main entrance, with massive balustrades. The building was paid for by public subscriptions. There are about 100 Academicians and 50 Associates.

The American Water-Color Society, at 52 East 23d Street, founded in 1866, makes a very popular yearly exhibition at the National Academy of Design of the works of painters in water-colors, members of the society and others, and awards the William T. Evans prize of $500 to the painter of the picture adjudged by a vote of the society to be the most meritorious of the exhibition. The society has 100 members.

The Kit-Kat Club, at 20 West 59th Street, founded in 1881, and incorporated in 1884, is a working club of artists. There are classes three times a week, at

NATIONAL ACADEMY OF DESIGN, FOURTH AVENUE AND 23D STREET.   LYCEUM THEATRE.

night, without professors. The members criticise the work of each other. There are informal receptions called smoking parties, and annual exhibitions of *tableaux vivants*.

The New-York Etching Club is at 49 West 22d Street. Its catalogues contain an etching and a portrait of every member of the club, and short essays on the art of the etcher. There are about 50 members.

The Society of American Artists, at 215 West 57th Street, was founded in 1877, by artists dissatisfied with the National Academy of Design. Several Academicians are members, and one, W. M. Chase, is President of the society. Its purposes are the same as those of the National Academy of Design. It has brilliant May exhibitions, well-contested prizes, a large membership, and Parisian artistic ideals. Among the members are Abbey, Beckwith, Blashfield, Bridgman, Appleton Brown, Chase, Church, Duveneck, Cox, Gay, Gifford, LaFarge, Millet, Pearce, Picknell, St. Gaudens, Vedder, Vinton, and Weir.

The Art-Students' League, at 215 West 57th Street, was organized in 1875, and incorporated in 1878.   There, every day, are life, portrait, sketch, modelling, composition and costume classes.   There are frequent lectures, art-receptions and exhibitions.   There are a dozen class-rooms in the Fine-Arts Building.

The Architectural League of New York, at 215 West 57th Street, was organized in 1881.   It has monthly meetings, lectures and dinners, an annual exhibition and banquet (in December) and prizes.   Its president is Russell Sturgis ; and the membership is large and influential, including St. Gaudens, Ward, McKim, Tiffany, Ware, Upjohn, Renwick, Rich, Port, Bruce Price, Le Brun, Hunt, Gibson, Robertson and other well-known men.

The American Fine-Arts Society was formed in 1889, by a combination of the Society of American Artists, the Architectural League of New York, and the

Art-Students' League of New York, for the purpose of erecting a building for their home, and for a headquarters of the graphic arts in New York. They jointly own and occupy the exquisite building erected by them, at a cost of $400,000, at 215 West 57th Street, between Broadway and Seventh Avenue. The architect was Henry J. Hardenbergh ; and the façade reproduces that of the house of Francis I. in Paris. The materials are pink granite and Indiana limestone. The building was finished in 1892. The large Vanderbilt gallery valued at $100,000 was presented to the

AMERICAN FINE-ARTS BUILDING, 215 WEST 57TH STREET.

society by George W. Vanderbilt ; and together with the South Gallery, forms an admirable place in which to display pictures to the best effect.

The Associated Artists, at 115 East 23d Street, is a corporation founded by Mrs. Candace Wheeler, its President, to paint ceilings and decorative panels, and for the manufacture of artistic patterns in silk, and artistic prints in cotton.   It has done a great work in the elevation of textile industry, and its goods have been

largely copied, even by European manufacturers. The embroideries and needle-
woven tapestries which have come from this society, having been worked under
Mrs. Wheeler's supervision, are
widely celebrated for their beauty.
The business is managed and run
by women.

Other Art Organizations
include the Society of Painters in
Pastels, with its yearly exhibi-
tions ; the New-York Water-
Color Society, which was organ-
ized in 1890 ; the Art Guild, the
Salmagundi, the Artists' Fund
Society and others.

**The New-York Institute
for Artist-Artisans,** at 140
West 23d Street, founded in 1881,
and directed by John Ward Stimson, former director of the Metropolitan Museum of Art Schools,
is a training school for all the
arts, kept constantly in touch
with the various trade guilds and
associations. The arts are taught
in their application to various
branches of trade. The school
is under the patronage of influential men and women of the city,

ASSOCIATED ARTISTS, 115 EAST 23D STREET.

and interests every person who cares for the progress of American industrial art.

The Cooper-Union Free Night Schools of Science and Art, at the
Cooper Institute, are open to all applicants at least fifteen years of age, whether they
are or are not residents of the city. In the scientific department are taught mathematics, chemistry, astronomy, electrical measurements, mechanics, mechanical
drawings. In the art department are taught mechanical, architectural, perspective,
cast, form, ornamental, figure and rudimental drawing, decorative designing and
modelling in clay. There are lectures, exhibitions, prizes and diplomas.

The Cooper-Union Woman's Art-School, at the Cooper Institute, is open
to all applicants at least sixteen and not over thirty-five years of age. There are
classes in oil-painting, life and cast drawing, designing and normal drawing, pen
and ink illustration, crayon photograph, lectures on art and on anatomy, exhibitions, diplomas. There are supplementary afternoon classes for women who study
art as an accomplishment, or have the means to pay for tuition.

The Society of Decorative Art, at 28 East 21st Street, incorporated in 1878,
exhibits and sells art-work of women, pottery, china, tiles, plaques, embroideries,
hangings, curtains, book-cases, cabinets, table and other house linen, articles for
wardrobes of infants, panels for cabinet work, painting on silk for screens, panels
and fans, decorated bills of fare, and works of like description. A subscriber of
$100 may nominate a pupil for one year in any of the free classes taught by the
society. A subscriber of $10 may place one pupil unable to pay for tuition in the
china, water-color or fan-painting classes, for five free lessons. A subscriber of $5

may nominate one pupil for six free lessons in art needlework, the pupil's ability to be determined by the first two lessons. The society charges 10 per cent. commission on its sales, and it sells nothing that its committees have not approved.

The Exchange for Women's Work, at 329 Fifth Avenue, is devoted to the sale of artistic articles, mainly made by poor gentlewomen, and often of great beauty and originality of design.

The Municipal Art Society was organized in 1893, for the development of a higher art taste in the city, and a purer sentiment in its monuments, parks and public buildings, and for the appropriate decoration of public places with works of sculpture, painting, mosaic or stained glass. Foremost artists are enrolled in this most commendable organization, which has a semi-official relation to the municipal government. The President is Richard M. Hunt. The Executive Committee includes three architects : E. H. Kendall, W. B. Bigelow, and Henry J. Hardenbergh ; three artists : E. H. Blashfield, Will H. Low, and George W. Maynard ; three sculptors : Augustus St. Gaudens, J. Q. A. Ward, and Olin L. Warner ; and three laymen : August Belmont, J. Armstrong Chanler, and W. T. Evans.

The Art Stores of the American Art Association, 6 East 23d Street ; of Moore, in West 17th Street ; of Thomas B. Clarke, 4 East 34th Street ; of S. P. Avery, Jr., W. C. Baumgarten & Co., Boussod, Valadon & Co., Cottier & Co., L. Christ Delmonico, Durand Ruel Brothers, H. J. Duveen & Co., Knoedler & Co., Reichard & Co., Herman Schaus and A. W. Conover (successors of Wm. Schaus), and Sypher & Co., in Fifth Avenue ; of H. B. Herts & Co., Frank Hegger, Tiffany & Co., and Wunderlich, on Broadway ; of Frederick Keppel, Wernicke and many others, have in their books records of private collections only a little less interesting than their wares, to the public of New York. But these records are sealed. It is not by them that one may know what treasures are hidden behind many severe, ordinary, uninviting brownstone fronts of New-York houses. However, they may be known, for many of these treasures appear at loan exhibitions frequently. When known, they are not difficult of access.

Everybody in New York is interested in the industrial phase of the arts, if one may judge by the attraction which the shop-windows have for the crowds, the increasing taste for beauty being displayed everywhere, the popularity of exhibitions of handicraft, and the interest displayed to learn the value, the history, and the names of buyers of works of art.

The Private Art Collections of New York include those of Mrs. Astor, Samuel P. Avery, Heber R. Bishop, James B. Colgate, R. L. Cutting, Charles A. Dana, W. B. Dinsmore, Henry Hilton, C. P. Huntington, G. G. Haven, Henry G. Marquand, J. Pierpont Morgan, Levi P. Morton, Darius O. Mills, Oswald Ottendorfer, J. W. Pinchot, Charles Stewart Smith, Mrs. Paran Stevens, Mrs. W. H. Vanderbilt, Cornelius Vanderbilt, W. K. Vanderbilt and C. F. Woerishoffer. The most valuable collection is the one formed by William H. Vanderbilt. Not one is limited to paintings. Samuel P. Avery has paintings, bronzes of Barye, and the greatest private collection of etchings extant ; Heber R. Bishop has an unsurpassable collection of jades ; Charles A. Dana, of vases of china ; and Henry G. Marquand has classified in appropriately designed rooms, Persian, Japanese, Arabic and Hispano-Moresque, the most valuable antique tapestry, porcelain arms and art-objects. The value of the private art-collections in New York is calculated at $8,000,000. In 1885 the paintings collected by George I. Seney, 285 in number, brought $650,000. Meissonier's "1807," presented by Henry Hilton to the Metropolitan Museum of Art, cost the late Alexander T. Stewart $67,000. The portrait

BIRD'S-EYE VIEW OF FIFTH AVENUE.

NORTH OF 51ST STREET.

by Rembrandt, which Henry G. Marquand bought from the Marquis of Lansdowne and presented to the Metropolitan Museum of Art, cost $25,000 and expenses. The paintings shown at one of the annual receptions of the Union League were insured for $400,000. In 1883 a loan collection of paintings and various objects of art at the National Academy of Design was insured for more than $1,000,000. The sales at one exhibition of the National Academy of Design aggregated $40,000. Mr. Drewry, secretary of the Kit-Kat Club, and art-editor of the American Press Association, estimates at 4,000 the number of professional artists in New York. Among these are the foremost painters and sculptors of America, enriching the Empire City with the art of Paris, the statuary of Athens, the architecture of Italy.

The Fifth-Avenue Art-Galleries are famous all over the continent, wherever there are *connoisseurs* and lovers of the best works of art. They occupy a building

admirably designed for the purpose, at 366 and 368 Fifth Avenue, between the houses of the Manhattan Club and the New-York Club. This perfectly planned structure was erected expressly for the purpose, by the Caswell estate, after plans wrought out by the late Henry O. Avery, the well-known architect. The upper floor, only one flight from the street, is occupied by the commodious and well-lighted galleries in which Samuel P. Avery, Jr., displays constantly the choicest works of European and American art. Mr. Avery has devoted himself to this business for over twenty years, and makes annual visits to Europe to give commissions to celebrated artists, and to purchase the choicest paintings at the great art-centres. In these unrivalled

FIFTH-AVENUE ART GALLERIES, 366 AND 368 FIFTH AVENUE.

galleries may be seen examples of almost all the best-known painters of Europe and America, exquisite French landscapes, *genre* pictures, brilliant marines, and all the wide range of modern art. The patrician mansions of New York secure their choicest pictures here, and many a hamlet among the New-England hills or on the limitless Western prairies has been enriched by paintings from this magnetic centre of art. The works exhibited and sold here have been selected with the finest and most highly-trained æsthetic taste, and are the crown-jewels of each year's studios and *salons*. The Avery galleries are lighted from above, with broad sky-lights; and what may be called the domestic effect of pictures is shown also in the contiguous private rooms, where the paintings are exhibited in the side-lights from windows.

Ortgies & Co., the best-known and longest-established art-auctioneers in New York, occupy the great galleries on the ground-floor of the Fifth-Avenue Art-Galleries building, extending around to 35th Street. These galleries have 5,000 square feet of hanging space, and 5,300 square feet of floor area, with perfect overhead lighting. They were specially designed for the exhibition and sale by auction of paintings, sculptures, books, *bric-à-brac*, engravings, etc. During the past twenty years this firm has conducted nearly thirty picture-sales, each of which brought over $30,000, at least seven bringing over $100,000 each. Among these were the collections of John Taylor Johnston, $328,286; Albert Spencer, $284,025; and J. F. Kensett, $137,944. At times of these great sales, or when unique collections of porcelains and other artistic property are offered, the galleries are crowded with the very flower of metropolitan society. The firm is made up of John Ortgies and Robert Somerville, with Samuel P. Avery, Jr., as special partner.

Frank Hegger's Photographic Depot, at 152 Broadway, is the best-known and most popular establishment of its kind in America. The spacious store is a

HEGGER'S ART ESTABLISHMENT, 152 BROADWAY, NEAR LIBERTY STREET.

magazine packed with everything that is choice in water-colors, etchings, engravings, photographs of every possible description, and unmounted views from all parts of the globe. "If you can't get them at Hegger's, you can't get them in this country," is a well-deserved compliment and literally true. Hegger's is always abreast with the time, and the selections which continually replenish his stock are made with the taste and judgment of a man of travel and a knowledge of the best one sees as a traveller. It is a case of a man fitted by every natural inclination and gift to his vocation, and who has become conspicuous among us by the natural development and vast public utility of his business. The absence of the Hegger establishment from New York would leave an aching void to the eyes of thousands to whom his show-windows and port-folios are a perpetual source of intellectual refreshment and æsthetical delight. The Broadway sidewalk is often blockaded by the throng attracted by his ever freshly renewed and ever novel and interesting displays, and brokers and business men, hot with the fever of mid-day business, break suddenly away from their drive for gain to " run in and see what Hegger has new," and jostle grave divines and college professors in their investigations of the huge sample books.

The Tiffany Glass and Decorating Company of New York.— It is without doubt evident to every careful observer that a strong artistic taste is rapidly developing among us, and that the American people are ultimately destined to become deeply imbued with an unprecedented love for all forms of material beauty,

architectural, pictorial and decorative. The phenomenal growth and expansion of the Tiffany Glass and Decorating Company, of 333–341 Fourth Avenue, are sufficient evidence of this fact, as such an organization could not exist without a large clientage of art-loving people. Take the subject alone of colored glass windows, and it is in the memory of all that only a

TIFFANY GLASS AND DECORATING COMPANY, FOURTH AVENUE AND 25TH STREET.

few years ago most Americans were contented with imported windows, or with poor imitations made here. In both cases the windows were but copies of mediæval work, seldom equalling the originals, and never showing an advance, either in artistic qualities or improvement of method, or even mechanical skill, over the windows of the Middle Ages. All this is now a thing of the past. To-day America leads the world in the making of colored glass windows ; a result brought about mainly through the investigations and experiments of Louis C. Tiffany, an artist of rare ability, having a most exquisite appreciation of color values and their relations, one to another. He intuitively took up the subject where the mediævalist left off, viz.: The study and the unfolding of the inherent properties of the glass to their fullest extent, both in color and in texture, in order to obtain in the glass itself light and shade, through depth and irregularity of color, in union with inequality of surface, in that way hoping to avoid the dullness, opacity and thinness which invariably accompany the use of paint, and are marked characteristics of European glass-work.

Moreover, he endeavored to obtain effects in this obstinate material which were hitherto deemed impossible. Among other things he introduced the use of opalescent glass. He softened the hard lead lines by plating glass over glass, and he developed the mosaic system of work, substituting it for glass-painting.

BEETHOVEN MÆNNERCHOR, 210 FIFTH STREET.

In a word, he originated a system of work which requires the strictest attention of the artist, a method founded on the most perfect practice of the mosaic system, an artistic method *par excellence.* The result is that a Tiffany window made by the company that bears his name is indeed a thing of beauty, and for which the demand is growing from day to day, and so fast, that the company is compelled to carry constantly in stock over a hundred tons of glass in the raw state, and employ a large corps of artists exclusively for this branch of its business. Just as the Glass Department has grown, in the same way every other one has developed, until in the studios of the company all forms of artistic handicraft are found. Churches, houses, hotels and theatres are decorated and furnished throughout. In fact, both domestic and ecclesiastical work of every description is undertaken by the company. The demand for its work has been so great that an increase of capital became a necessity, and the company now has a paid-up cash capital of $400,000. The artistic department is under the immediate direction of Louis C. Tiffany; the general management is under the care of Pringle Mitchell; while the Board of Direction is composed of a number of well-known men, viz.: John C. Platt, John DuFais, Henry W. de Forest, George Holmes, Von Beck Canfield and J. A. Holzer.

Music in New York has shown a remarkable and vigorous development. This city knew all Wagner before Paris accepted *Lohengrin.* It has capital orchestras, choral societies, music clubs, conservatories, professors, lectures by musical experts, and exquisite private performances.

The Philharmonic Society, organized in 1842 by Uriah C. Hill, a violinist,

NEW-YORK MÆNNERCHOR, 203 EAST 56TH STREET.

native of New York, who had studied with Spohr at Cassel, is composed of professional orchestra players and a non-professional president. It gave at the first concert, December 7, 1842, the Symphony in C Minor of Beethoven, which seemed far above the faculty of appreciation of a public so little educated musically as the public of New York was then ; but it had a high aim and never faltered. It led the public taste. In 1867 the membership was increased to 100 players. At that time Carl Bergman was its conductor, and remained in office until 1876. Dr. Leopold Damrosch was conductor, 1876-77 ; Theodore Thomas, 1877-1878 ; Adolph Neuendorff, 1878-79 ; Theodore Thomas, 1878-91 ; and Anton Seidl.

The Symphony Society was organized in 1880 by Dr. Leopold Damrosch. Its Symphony Orchestra, the only permanent one in New York, is directed by Walter Damrosch. Its concerts are brilliant social events.

The Oratorio Society, organized in 1873, is under the skilful direction of Walter Damrosch. Its predecessors in the place that it occupies were the Church

Music Association, the Mendelssohn Union and the Harmonic Society. Like the Harmonic Society, it gives every year during Christmas week a performance of the *Messiah.* It has given and continues to give, with perfect art, works like Bach's *Passion Music,* Berlioz's *Messe des Morts,* Handel's *Judas Maccabeus,* Haydn's *Creation* and *Seasons,* Schumann's *Paradise and the Peri,* Liszt's *Christus,* Grell's *Missa Solemnis,* and the cantatas of Dr. Damrosch.

The Mendelssohn Glee Club was organized in 1865 by Joseph Mosenthal, a violinist, a pupil of Spohr, and a native of Cassel, who became an influential organist of the Episcopal Church in

LIEDERKRANZ, 58TH STREET, BETWEEN LEXINGTON AND FOURTH AVENUES.

New York, and resigned from Calvary Church not to yield to a fashionable craze for boy choirs. The club gives concerts invariably excellent.

The Manuscript Society, organized in 1889 for the performance in public of unpublished works of American composers, has for president Gerritt Smith.

The Musurgia, devoted exclusively to part songs for men's voices, is under the direction of William R. Chapman, who also directs the Rubenstein (part songs for women) and Metropolitan Musical Societies, for the study of music.

Orpheons, of Swiss and French, are represented by several organizations.

Church Choral Societies, which Trinity Church encouraged so effectively when New York had no other music than the music of churches, have been organized in various sections.

The **New-York Maennerchor,** founded in 1870, in 1887 erected its spacious and handsome building on 56th Street.

Maennerchors and Saengerbunde, mainly Germans, are numerous.

The **Deutscher Liederkranz,** at the north side of East 58th Street, between Park and Lexington Avenues, gave to New York the fervor of German lyrism. It was organized in 1847, and incorporated in 1860, and it has steadily given, in concerts, in cantatas, in courses of instruction that have powerful influence, the best works of the German composers. It has admirably produced works like Mozart's *Requiem,* Liszt's *Prometheus,* and Mendelssohn's *Walpurgisnacht.* Its membership is composed of active members who are musicians or students in the perfect school of vocal music provided by the club, and others to whom the seductive social features only of the club have appealed. Its membership includes 1,200 Germans and German-Americans, 200 Hebrew-Americans, and 100 Americans of British origin. There are female choruses. The conductor is Heinrich Zöllner, of Cologne, whom the club called to New York in 1890. The festivals of the Liederkranz, especially the annual Carnival, are thoroughly artistic. The club-house of the Liederkranz is a large brownstone building in the style of the German Renaissance. The president is William Steinway.

ARION SOCIETY, PARK AVENUE AND EAST 59TH STREET.

The **Arion Society,** with its home at the corner of Park Avenue and 59th Street, was organized by fourteen seceding members of the Liederkranz in 1854. They gave their first concert in the Apollo Rooms, at Broadway and Canal Street ; produced an operetta *Mordgrunbruck,* in 1855 ; another, *Der Gang Zum Eisenham-mer,* in 1856 ; furnished the choruses in the first Wagner opera performed in America, *Tannhäuser,* August 27, 1859 ; performed *Der Freischutz* in 1869 ; and gave brilliant Carnival meetings and masquerade balls that are still maintained. In 1871, the Arion brought Dr. Leopold Damrosch from Breslau. In 1870, it occupied 19 and 21 St. Mark's Place, and in 1887 it entered its present beautiful palace. It is, unlike the Liederkranz, almost exclusively German. It has no chorus of mixed voices. It gives concerts, balls, and operettas in the large hall on the third floor of its graceful building. The lower story is of Berea sandstone, the rest of buff brick and terra cotta. The style is early Italian Renaissance. The groups of heroic size at the roof are Arion on a huge shell borne by dolphins accompanied by Tritons on the Park-Avenue side, and Prince Carnival with Terpsichore and the Genius of Music on the 59th-Street side.

The Music Hall, founded by Andrew Carnegie, at the corner of 57th Street and Seventh Avenue, has a main hall or auditorium for concerts, smaller rooms for chamber music, studios, rehearsals, fairs, and a gymnasium. The building, opened in May, 1891, is of mottled brick and terra cotta, in the style of the Venetian Renaissance. The house decoration is of pale salmon color, produced by a stencilling of white on a background of old rose. Music Hall is the home of the Oratorio Society. The Symphony and other societies play there.

The Lenox Lyceum, on Madison Avenue, near 59th Street, on the site of the Old Panorama, has the most beautiful but not the best in acoustics of the New-York music halls. The stage is under a shell-shaped building. The façade is of colored marbles. The style is early Italian Renaissance. The building was opened in January, 1890, and is fitted for concerts, fairs, banquets, balls and other festivals.

Semi-Artistic Societies and Scientific Organizations find in New York their great headquarters on the Western Hemisphere, and their collections and proceedings win the attention of the world.

The New-York Historical Society, at 170 Second Avenue, southeast corner of 11th Street, founded in 1804, incorporated in 1809, has a library of 100,000 volumes of reference, in large collections of scarce pamphlets, maps, newspapers, manuscripts, paintings and engravings, records of every phase in the progress of New York. Egbert Benson, DeWitt Clinton, William Linn, Samuel Miller, John N. Abeel, John M. Mason, David Hosack, Anthony Bleecker, Samuel Bayard, Peter G. Stuyvesant and John Pintard were its founders ; and it never lacked the liberality, the public spirit, the influence and the labor of men like these. John Pintard gave paintings, books and manuscripts ; James Lenox, marbles of Nineveh ; Luman Reed, Thomas J. Bryan, Louis Durr, the New-York Gallery of Fine Arts and the American Art Union, paintings, books and statuary. The home of the society was in the City Hall from 1804 to 1809, in the Government House from 1809 to 1816, in the New-York Institution from 1816 to 1832, in Remsen's Building in Broadway from 1832 to 1837, in the Stuyvesant Institute from 1837 to 1841, in the

New-York University from 1841 to 1857. It could not be predicted in 1857, when the society took possession of its present edifice, that in less than half a century the rooms would be over-crowded. They are a solid mass of books and paintings and statuary and antiquities. In the Department of Antiquities, the larger collections consist of the celebrated Abbott Collection of Egyptian Antiquities, purchased for the institution in 1859 ; the Nineveh Sculptures ; and a considerable collection of relics of the American aborigines. The Gallery of Art includes 835 paintings and 63 pieces of sculpture. Here, in addition to the society's early collection of paintings and sculpture, is the largest and most important gal-

AMERICAN INSTITUTE HALL, 1079 THIRD AVENUE, BETWEEN
63D AND 64TH STREETS.

lery of historical portraits in the country, together with the original water-colors, 474 in number, prepared by Audubon for his work on Natural History; the famous Bryan Gallery of Old Masters, presented to the society by the late Thomas J. Bryan in 1867; and the extensive Durr Collection, presented in 1881. The society is to érect a new building on a site which it has purchased, facing Central Park and the Museum of Natural History, on Central Park West, between 76th and 77th Streets. It will have a fire-proof building for its invaluable library, gallery and museum, and a large hall for meetings and lectures.

The American Institute, for the promotion of domestic industry, at 111 to 115 West 38th Street, gives every year in the fall, for two months, in the large building on Third Avenue, between 63d and 64th Streets, an exhibition of the latest inventions for advancing commerce, agriculture, manufactures and the arts. It awards premiums and certificates of merit, and publishes reports of its proceedings. Its library, of 15,000 volumes, interesting to scientific men, is freely opened to all the members and friends of the Institute. The American Institute was founded in 1828, and now has 2,000 members. The Polytechnic Association, Farmers' Club, and Photographic Section of the Institute hold frequent public meetings, lectures, and discussions.

The American Geographical Society, at 11 West 29th Street, founded in 1852 and chartered in 1854, had for its first President the historian George Bancroft. It has a library of 25,000 volumes, an extensive collection of 8,000 maps, a treasury of valuable information not easily accessible elsewhere, and here well classified. It gives lectures by famous travellers and geographers, and issues a quarterly bulletin. Its privileges and advantages are for its 1,500 members, whose annual dues are $10.

The New-York Academy of Sciences was founded in 1817, under the name of the Lyceum of Natural History, which was changed in 1876.

AMERICAN GEOGRAPHICAL SOCIETY, 11 WEST 29TH STREET.

It began in 1824 the publication of *Annals,* and in 1881 of *Transactions,* wherein its labors are recorded. It has a valuable library of 8,000 volumes; and meetings Monday evenings in Hamilton Hall of Columbia College. It has 300 members. Prof. John S. Newberry is President.

The American Society of Civil Engineers, founded in 1852, has an active membership of about 1,600, composed of engineers of good standing, and at least ten years' experience. Its house, at 127 East 23d Street, contains a large lecture hall, a library of 17,000 volumes — the finest and most comprehensive library on civil engineering in the country — and various other apartments. There are meetings of the society twice a month at its house, and an annual convention, which is held in the larger cities in rotation. The *Transactions* of the society are published monthly, and make two large volumes a year. The President is William Metcalf; the Secretary, Francis Collingwood; and the Treasurer, John Bogart.

21

The American Society of Mechanical Engineers, organized in 1880, with 40 members, now has on its membership roll the names of 1,600 mechanical engineers of good standing. Among the honorary members are Prof. Francis Reuleux of

AMERICAN SOCIETY OF MECHANICAL ENGINEERS.
12 WEST 31st STREET.

Berlin, and Sir Henry Bessemer of England. There are two stated meetings of the organization a year — the annual meeting in November, which is held in a large hall in the society's house at 12 West 31st Street, and an annual convention in the spring, which may meet in any city. The society has a free public library, purely technical, of about 4,000 volumes. The *Transactions* of the society are published yearly, in a volume of about 1,000 pages. The President is Eckley B. Coxe, of Drifton, Pa.; the Secretary, Prof. Frederick R. Hutton of Columbia College; and the Treasurer, William H. Wiley.

The American Institute of Mining Engineers, founded in 1871, numbers 2,000 members, including also metallurgists and chemists, many of them foreigners. It usually has three meetings a year, in different cities, and the proceedings are published. The secretary is R. W. Raymond, 13 Burling Slip.

The American Numismatic and Archæological Society of New York has frequent meetings in its rooms at the Academy of Medicine Building, 17 West 43d Street. It was founded in 1858, and has 225 members. The cabinets contain 8,000 coins and medals; and the library is the finest collection of numismatic books in America.

The American Ethnological Society was organized in 1842, by Albert Gallatin, John R. Bartlett, George Folsom, A. I. Cotheal, Francis L. Hawks, Theodore Dwight, Jr., Edward Robinson, Charles Welford, W. W. Turner, Henry R. Schoolcraft, A. W. Bradford, John L. Stephens, and Frederic Catherwood. Its first president was the Hon. Albert Gallatin, followed by the Rev. Dr. Edward Robinson, the Hon. George Folsom, and Dr. John Torrey. Its objects are the prosecution of inquiries into the origin, progress, and characteristics of the various races of men, especially into the origin and history of the aboriginal American nations, and the phenomena connected therewith; the diversity of languages, the remains of ancient art, and traces of ancient civilization in Mexico, Central America, and Peru; the arts, sciences and mythology of the American nations; and the earthworks and other monuments of the United States. Besides its resident membership, the society has numerous corresponding members in different countries. It has published three volumes of ethnological contributions, and gathered a considerable library and many ancient relics, which are deposited in the American Museum of Natural History, where its regular meetings are held. The officers are: President, Alex. I. Cotheal; Corresponding Secretary, A. S. Bickmore; Recording Secretary, Rev. Dr. Browne; Librarian, Anthony Woodward.

The New-York Genealogical and Biographical Society, incorporated in 1869, designs to procure and perpetuate whatever may relate to genealogy and biography, particularly of families and persons associated with the State of New York. Its library and hall, at the Berkeley Lyceum, 23 West 44th Street, are open to members and to others introduced by them. Gen. James Grant Wilson is the president. Meetings are held on the second and fourth Fridays of each month, excepting in July, August and September. *The New-York Genealogical and Biographical Record,* now in its 24th volume, is published under its supervision. The society has also published, as its first volume of collections, "Marriages from 1639 to 1801 in the Reformed Dutch Church, New York." Other volumes will follow, the intention being to print correctly the Record of the Reformed Dutch Church in New Amsterdam and New York.

The American Chemical Society, organized in 1876, has meetings in December and August, in various cities, and includes nearly all the leading American and many foreign chemists. It has published many valuable papers and journals. The New-York Section meets monthly at the University, on Washington Square.

The New-York Mathematical Society is of a national character. Among its 250 members are the prominent mathematicians in America. The meetings are held at Columbia College, on the first Saturday of each month. The society's *Bulletin* is the only journal in the English language devoted to historical and critical mathematical work. The officers are: President, Dr. Emory McClintock; Vice-President, Prof. Henry B. Fine; Secretary, Dr. Thomas S. Fiske; Treasurer, Harold Jacoby; Librarian, Prof. D. A. Murray; other members of the Council, Prof. Thomas Craig, Prof. W. Woolsey Johnson, Prof. J. E. Oliver, Prof. J. K. Rees, and Prof. J. H. Van Amringe.

The American Microscopical Society devotes itself to a study of microscopy, histology, optics, and kindred works. It was founded in 1865, and five years later was incorporated. It holds fortnightly meetings at 12 East 22d Street.

Other learned bodies are: Academy of Anthropology, in the Cooper Union; American Metrological Society on 49th Street, near Madison Avenue; New-York Horticultural Society, 26 West 28th Street; New-York Public Health Association, 12 West 31st Street; Electric Club, 17 East 21st Street; Sorosis, a society of women; and the Archæological Institute.

Debating and other Societies; clubs of authors, artists, newspaper men; informal meetings in modest rooms of lovers of poetry, worshippers of the beautiful, searchers of light and truth, merchants who are art-lovers; artists who are not Bohemians; exalted dilettantism, are contributors to the greatness of New York as active, as indefatigable as its famous men of business. The rapid growth of a high civic pride in New York is largely attributed to these agencies of enlightenment, stimulating among the people a municipal self-respect almost equal to that of Athens, or Florence, or Chicago.

The Fowler & Wells Company is a scientific institution that has a world-wide reputation. For nearly sixty years its founders and owners have maintained an office in the city of New York, and have been the recognized leaders in the phrenological, physiological and hygienic sciences, and for half a century they have been the main educators in these branches of useful study. They are classed in a business way as phrenologists and publishers, but they might well be called a scientific and educational institution. They occupy the building at 27 East 21st Street, near

Broadway, where is carried on the work inaugurated by Orson S. Fowler and Lorenzo N. Fowler in 1835. These men were the first in America to give the science of phrenology a practical value by making special delineations of character. They began work in a small way, but steadily increased its scope. In 1843 they were joined by Samuel R. Wells, who subsequently married Charlotte Fowler, the sister of his partners. In course of time both the Fowlers withdrew from the house. Orson, who was one of the most famous phrenologists of the world, died in 1887. Lorenzo still practices his profession in London. Mr. Wells conducted the business of the original house until his death, in 1875, and his widow, Charlotte F. Wells, assumed the management until 1884. Then the Fowler & Wells Company was incorporated, with Charlotte Fowler Wells, President; Nelson Sizer, Vice-President and phrenological examiner; Dr. H. S. Drayton, Secretary and general editor of the company's publications; and Albert Turner, Treasurer and business manager.

FOWLER & WELLS CO. AND AMERICAN INSTITUTE OF PHRENOLOGY, 27 EAST 21ST STREET, NEAR BROADWAY.

The company publishes *The Phrenological Journal*, of which the ninety-fifth volume has just been completed, a number of serial publications, and a large list of standard works on phrenology, physiognomy, ethnology, physiology, psychology and hygiene. It has handsome business offices and spacious editorial rooms, lecture-rooms and phrenological parlors, where examinations are made and charts given daily, indicating choice of pursuits, means of culture, etc. An outgrowth of the business of the concern is the American Institute of Phrenology, which was incorporated as an educational institution in 1866. Among the original incorporators were Horace Greeley, Rev. Dr. Samuel Osgood, Judge Amos Dean, Henry Dexter, Samuel R. Wells, Lester A. Roberts, Edward P. Fowler, M. D., and Nelson-Sizer. Each year, beginning on the first Tuesday in September, a course of instruction in practical phrenology is given by a corps of experts, under the direction of Prof. Sizer, the President of the Institute. An interesting feature in the lecture-room of the Fowler & Wells Company's building is a large collection of casts of the heads of people who have been prominent in various ways in past years; also, skulls from many nations and tribes, as well as animal crania, illustrative of phrenology, and constituting a free public museum, and material for instruction in the institute.

The Literary Culture.

Libraries and Reading Rooms. Public, Club, Society and Private.

THE libraries of New York are nearly perfect. They have not only quantity and quality; they have availability. In this respect they are easily in advance of those of the great cities of Europe. There books accumulate, while librarians, literary men whom the government has rewarded with sinecures, study special works, or write on special subjects. The American business education has admirably mingled book-lore, literary tact and commercial order in the formation and management of libraries. Here books are classified, catalogued, inventoried, better than was ever imagined. If the treasures be not as rich as in countries that have lived ages, the service of such treasures as there are is quicker, surer and more gratifying. At the Bibliothèque Nationale one may obtain any books, but the process is slow, and at the end of it one is in a doubt that may not be solved, for there is no way of telling if the books obtained were not less valuable than others obtainable. The libraries of New York are without secrets.

The Astor Library, on the east side of Lafayette Place, is an ideal public library of works of reference. As it has no artificial light, the building must be closed at sunset. As it has a perfect system of classification, book catalogues, card catalogues, and the quickest and ablest of librarians and assistants, its hours count double. There are not all the treasures of the British Museum and the Bibliothèque Nationale, but the fact is not easily discovered. "He gives twice who gives quickly," says the ancient proverb. The Astor Library gives quickly. Suggested by Washington Irving and Dr. J. C. Cogswell to John Jacob Astor, the library was founded by virtue of a codicil of Mr. Astor's will, which bequeathed for the purpose $400,000. It was incorporated January 1, 1849. The trustees were Washington Irving, William B. Astor, Dr. Cogswell, and others. Then there were 20,000 volumes, the cost of which had been $27,000. In 1854 the library was opened to the public. In 1859 William B. Astor, son of the founder, built a second hall in Lafayette Place, and gave, in all, $550,000. In 1864 Dr. Cogswell made a printed catalogue of the library, which then numbered 100,000 volumes. In 1881 John Jacob Astor, grandson of the founder, erected the third hall of the library, his gifts exceeding $800,000.

The building, of brownstone, has 200 feet of front and 100 feet of depth. The exterior is graceful, the interior is as bright as a house of glass. The entrance is through a Pompeian vestibule, bordered with pedestals of colored marble, on which are busts in white marble, sculptured by a Florentine artist, of the great and wise men of ancient Greece and Rome. There is a wide stairway to the Middle Hall, where are the librarians and the catalogues, tables for women, a department for students of patents, alcoves for special students, and in glass-covered cases curious autographs, specimens of missals, books of hours, early typography and marvels of the art of book binding. The south building is the hall of science and art ; the north building is that of history and philosophy. There are 90 alcoves ; each alcove has 20 presses ; each press has 7 shelves, with a capacity for 175 volumes.

ASTOR LIBRARY, LAFAYETTE PLACE, BETWEEN ASTOR PLACE AND GREAT JONES STREET.

The ground floor, yet unused for books, may hold 250,000 volumes. There, in the south room, used by the trustees for their meetings, is a collection of paintings, presented to the library by William Waldorf Astor, comprising works of Saintin, Madrazo, Toulmouche, Knaus, Gifford, Leroux, Muller, Meissonier, Schreyer, Berne-Bellecour and Lefebvre. There are marble busts of John Jacob Astor, Dr. Cogswell and Washington Irving ; a portrait of William B. Astor, by Eastman Johnson ; of Alexander Hamilton, by Huntington ; of Daniel Lord, by Hicks ; and of Fitz-Greene Halleck, by Prof. S. F. B. Morse. This collection is open to the public every Wednesday. Frederick Saunders is the chief librarian.

The Astor Library contains 250,000 books and 15,000 pamphlets. Each year the library has more than 50,000 readers, reading nearly 200,000 books, besides 8,000 visitors to the alcoves. The trustees are the Mayor, *ex-officio*, Hamilton Fish, Dr. T. M. Markoe (president), Prof. Henry Drisler (secretary), J. L. Cadwalader, Rt. Rev. H. C. Potter, S. V. R. Cruger, Robbins Little (superintendent), Stephen H. Olin, Edward King (treasurer) and Charles H. Russell. This is the foremost American library in mathematics, Egyptology, South American and Mexican history, and Orientalia. It is a free reference library, open all day, and affording a delightful retreat for scholars.

The Lenox Library, on Fifth Avenue, between 70th and 71st Streets, is a curiosity of the world. It is the library of a bibliophilist, made public. The gift of James Lenox, a retired merchant of New York, who loved books immeasurably, it was incorporated January 20, 1870. It was the private collection of Mr. Lenox, a mysterious, fabulously beautiful and valuable collection, guarded in a house which was a fortress; it became a public collection, as free as the trees in the Central Park. Mr. Lenox would not show his books to his friends; braved public opinion by refusing to let Prescott consult his Mexican manuscripts; barred the great book-binder, Matthews, between two doors of a vestibule, that he might neither quit nor catch a glimpse of the sacred library room; and at one stroke, in the gravest deliberation, gave his treasures to the world. He named nine trustees, including himself; gave the land, the books, and funds for a building; and in 1875 the Lenox Library was a dream realized. The building is of white stone, a solid and graceful structure, with two projecting wings. The entrance is by two massive gateways, a court, wide stairs, and a vestibule laid in tiles of white marble, between walls skirted with a dove-colored marble base. The stairs to the upper stories are of stone, and have balustrades in iron scroll-work. The rooms have vaulted ceilings, the walls priceless paintings, the cases for books inestimable works. There are missals, Bibles, incunabula, Americana, master-pieces of ancient and modern literature in original editions, curiosities of printing that most book-lovers have heard of and never seen elsewhere. There are autographs, ceramics, glassware. There are paintings by Landseer, Gainsborough, Bierstadt, Turner, Ruysdael, Peale, Delaroche, Stuart, Reynolds, Munkacsy. There are marble busts of great sculptors. There are the marvelous Drexel musical

LENOX LIBRARY, FIFTH AVENUE, 70TH AND 71ST STREETS.

library, and the Robert Lenox Kennedy collection. There are the admirable books of the R. L. Stuart legacy, and those of Evert A. Duyckinck. The number of volumes exceeds 70,000. The library is open, free, from 10 to 5, except in July, August and September. The architect of the building was Richard M. Hunt.

The Mercantile Library is at the junction of 8th Street, Astor Place and Lafayette Place, on the sixth and seventh floors of a substantial building of buff brick and red sandstone, erected by the trustees of the library and the Clinton-Hall Association. It is a reference library and a circulating library for members, whose annual dues are $5. Works of art and other costly publications must remain in the library rooms as books of reference, but standard, instructive, popular, historical and scientific books are kept in circulation. The library was founded November 9, 1820, by clerks of merchants. In 1821, in one room at 49 Fulton Street, it had 150 members and 700 volumes. In 1826, in the building of Harper & Brothers, in Cliff Street, it had 6,000 volumes. In 1828 the merchants, made enthusiastic by the achievement of the clerks, organ-

MERCANTILE LIBRARY, ASTOR PLACE, 8TH STREET AND LAFAYETTE PLACE.

ized the Clinton-Hall Association for the purpose of giving a building to the library. This association, in 1830, erected the first Clinton Hall, on the corner of Nassau and Beekman Streets, where Temple Court now stands, In 1854 the association and its books were removed to the Astor-Place Opera-House, which had been re-modelled for the purpose. In 1891 the historic opera-house was taken down, and in its place was built the present Clinton Hall. The library rooms have shelf space for 475,000 volumes. There are 50,000 volumes in the department of works of reference, and 245,000 in the entire library. The librarian is W. T. Peoples.

The New-York Society Library is the oldest in the city. It was at first the Public Library, founded in 1700 during the administration of the Earl of Bellomont; augmented in 1729 with the library presented to the Society for the Propagation of the Gospel in Foreign Parts, by Dr. Millington, Rector of Newington, England; and until 1754 in the inefficient charge of the corporation of the city. Then several citizens united with it their private libraries, and placed the entire collection, which they called the City Library, in the charge of trustees. In 1772 George III. granted a charter to the trustees, in the name of the "New-York Society Library." The establishment is still the property of a corporation, the shares in which have a market value, but any person may, with the approbation of the Board of Trustees, become a member of the corporation and be entitled to one right in the library for every sum of $25 paid to the treasurer. There are yearly dues on all shares, except the free shares. The amount has been increased at various times since 1819, when it was $4. Now the maximum is $10. These annual dues may be commuted by the payment of $125 for the annual payment of $10, $75 for the annual payment of $6, and $50 for the annual payment of $4, on the respective rights subject to these payments. Until 1795 the library was in the City Hall, and it was in reality the first Library of Congress. Then a building, large and remarkable for its time, was erected especially for the library in Nassau Street, opposite the Middle Dutch Church. In 1836 this building was sold. The books were removed to the rooms of the Mechanics' Society, in Chambers Street, and remained there until 1840, when a new building of the library, at the corner of Broadway and Leonard Street, was finished. In 1853 this edifice was sold, and the books were kept in the Bible House until 1856, when the present library building, at 67 University Place, was finished. In 1793 there were 5,000 volumes; in 1813, 13,000; in 1825, 16,000; in 1838, 25,000 volumes. There are at present 90,000 volumes. Many valuable gifts have been made to the library. The most notable one was made by Mrs. Sarah H. Green, a gift of $50,000 from the estate of her husband, John C. Green. The income is used for the purchase of books, one half of which circulate among the members. The other half are costly illustrated works and are placed in a department called the "John C. Green Alcove." The librarian is Wentworth S. Butler. He

was appointed in 1856, and is the sixth incumbent since 1793. A list of persons holding rights in the Society Library includes nearly all of the most ancient and wealthy families of the city.

The Free Library of the General Society of Mechanics and Tradesmen (formerly the Apprentices' Library), at 18 East 16th Street, circulates its books, without charge, among persons approved by the General Society of Mechanics and Tradesmen. This society, founded in 1785 for the relief of widows and orphans, gave free instruction to apprentices, when there were no free schools. When its exclusive benevolence in that respect was a little impaired by the establishing of

NEW-YORK SOCIETY LIBRARY, 67 UNIVERSITY PLACE.

public schools, the society began to circulate freely the books of its library. The library was formed in 1820, in rooms of the Free-School Building. In 1821 it was in the society's building in Chambers Street; in 1832, in a building in Crosby Street, extending to 472 Broadway. The present building was adapted to library purposes in 1878. In the cases on the walls are interesting relics, old books, deeds, flags, the

APPRENTICES' LIBRARY, 18 EAST 16TH STREET.

skull (yellow as ivory) of a famous pirate, an iron key of the Bastile, old newspapers and playbills. There are 95,000 volumes, having a yearly circulation of 250,000, absolutely free, with the exceptions of books of the De Milt bequest, the charge for which is trivial. William Wood, who originated the idea of forming the Apprentices' Library of New York, established the one in Boston. He also signed the first call for a meeting which resulted in the establishment of the Mercantile Library. J. Schwartz is the librarian.

The New-York Historical Society maintains, at 170 Second Avenue, an establishment that is at once a library, an art-gallery and a museum. It has been in existence since 1804. There are in the library 100,000 books, 2,700 bound volumes of newspapers and large collections of pamphlets and manuscripts. On American history and genealogy a vast quantity of information is available. The art-gallery contains many works of the earliest American artists, such as Benjamin West, the Peales, Stuart, Trumbull and Durand, and also a large number of paintings by old Italian masters. The Abbott collection of Egyptian antiquities, the Lenox collection of Assyrian sculptures, rare and curious medals and coins and specimens of Mexican and Indian antiquities constitute the museum. The establishment is open daily excepting Sundays and the month of August. Admission may be had by means of an introduction by a member of the society.

The Young Men's Christian Association Library occupies a rectangle in the magnificent building of the Association, at the southwest corner of 23d Street and Fourth Avenue. There are three tiers of books, on three sides. The books in the upper tiers are reached by winding stairways and balconies. William Niblo bequeathed $150,000 to the Association for the purchase of books and the support of the library. In 1870 there were 3,500 volumes; there are at present 42,000. The northern end of the room is occupied by the librarian, Reuben B. Poole, and his assistants. He has classified the library in accordance with the Dewey decimal system and Cutter's dictionary catalogue. The library is varied and valuable. It has 43 early-printed Bibles which antedate 1700, including the Koburger Bible of 1477, Luther's Bible of 1541, the Bishop's Bible of 1568, and one in French of the eighteenth century, bound in marvellous covers of mosaic leather. A relic of great interest is a musical manuscript of the thirteenth century, containing the Ambrosian ritual for the entire year. The manuscript is decorated with brilliant miniatures and initial letters. It has an autotype of the Codex-Alexandrinus, a printed fac-simile of the Frederico-Augustanus Codex, and a photographic fac-simile of the Codex-Vaticanus (1889-90). It has many works on art useful to architects and decorators, and representative works in different languages. The collected portraits number about 17,000, including one unique collection of 8,000, in 35 volumes, formed mainly by John Percival, Earl of Egmont, A. D. 1 to 1736. This library is almost the only one that is open evenings and holidays. The hours are from 8.30 A. M. to 10 P. M.

Membership in the Association includes the privileges of the library ; and all reputable persons, male or female, are admitted to its use, whether members or not.

The Cooper-Union Library, in the Cooper Institute, is one result of the work of the six intelligent, benevolent and public-spirited trustees, to whom Peter Cooper deeded in fee simple, on April 29, 1859, an extensive property, with the injunction that it, "together with the appurtenances and the rents, issues, income and profits thereof, shall be forever devoted to the instruction and improvement of the inhabitants of the United States, in practical science and art." There are 34,000 bound volumes, besides 471 newspapers and periodicals on file, and a complete set of the Patent-Office reports. All are accessible to the public every day, including a part of Sunday. There were last year 1,650 readers daily.

The Maimonides Library, 203 East 57th Street, corner of Third Avenue, was founded by District Grand Lodge No. 1 of the Order of B'uai B'rith, in accordance with its law that commands intellectual advancement. It contains about 40,000 volumes. The library is general in character and contents. Its departments of political and social science and education are very full. Special interest is devoted also to Jewish literature. There are books written by Jews and other writers on Judaic topics, in all languages, besides books in every branch of knowl-

HISTORICAL SOCIETY.   BAPTIST TABERNACLE.
NEW-YORK HISTORICAL SOCIETY, SECOND AVENUE AND EAST 11TH STREET.

edge. The library is easily accessible to the public every day except Saturdays and Jewish holidays. The librarian is Max Cohen.

The Free Circulating Library has four library buildings, situated at 49 Bond Street, 135 Second Avenue, 226 West 42d Street and 251 West 13th Street, and a distributing station at 1943 Madison Avenue, near 125th Street. The library was incorporated March 15, 1880, and re-incorporated under special charter April 18, 1884. Its object is clearly defined in its title. In March, 1880, it occu_pied two rented rooms at 36 Bond Street, and circulated 1,004 volumes. In May,

NEW-YORK FREE CIRCULATING LIBRARY,
251 WEST 13TH STREET.

1883, it had a new library building at 49 Bond Street, and then gave circulation to 6,983 volumes. It has a special Woman's Fund, founded in 1882, for the employment of women and the purchase of books. In 1884 Oswald Ottendorfer founded the Second-Avenue Branch, in the centre of the German district. It is called the Ottendorfer Library, and is maintained with the aid of a special fund of $10,000 and of frequent contributions of the founder. In 1887 Miss Catherine Wolfe Bruce founded the 42d-Street Branch, and gave $30,000 for its maintenance. The building was opened in 1888. It is called the George Bruce Memorial Library. The 13th-Street Branch, founded by George W. Vanderbilt, was opened July 6, 1888. The ten founders who contributed $5,000 or more each, were John Jacob Astor, Miss Catherine Wolfe Bruce, Andrew Carnegie, Mrs. Benjamin H. Field, Julius Hallgarten, Henry G. Marquand, Oswald Ottendorfer, Jacob H. Schiff, George W. Vanderbilt and Mrs. C. F. Woerishoffer.

There were also 22 patrons, each of whom gave $1,000 ; 80 life-members, each contributing $200 ; 62 associate members, paying $25 a year ; and 154 annual members, at $10 a year each. The city government grants to the library from $10,000 to $15,000 a year, in accordance with the State Legislative Act of 1886, to encourage the growth of free public libraries. The library has 65,000 volumes, and a yearly circulation of 500,000. The cost of distribution per volume is smaller than in the great libraries of Boston, Chicago or Baltimore.

The Columbia-College Library, at 41 East 49th Street, has 160,000 volumes, beside the libraries of the Huguenot Society, the New-York Academy of Science, and Townsend's Civil-War Record. The Avery Architectural Library has 9,000 volumes, richly illustrated, on architecture, decoration and the allied arts. Over 900 different serials are currently received. The library includes all the standard works of reference indispensable to students, the costly classics, the masterpieces of literature, the scientific works and books of law. The library is open day and evening, to students and scholars. George H. Baker is librarian.

The Law Libraries include the noble collection of the Law Institute, in the Post-Office Building ; the 41,000 volumes of the Bar Association's Library, at 7 West 29th Street, between Broadway and Fifth Avenue ; and the admirable and extensive collections of the law-schools of Columbia College and the University. The Harlem Law Library, on West 125th Street, near Lenox Avenue, is for reference. The Law Library of the Equitable Life-Assurance Society, at 120 Broadway, is intended for the use of the officers of the society, the tenants of the building, and members of the Lawyers' Club. It has 14,000 volumes.

Theological Libraries of great value are found at Union Theological Seminary (70,000 volumes) and the General Theological Seminary (23,000 volumes), including several special collections of historical interest. There is also one in the Methodist Book-Concern building.

Medical Libraries.—The Mott Memorial Library, at 64 Madison Avenue, has 3,000 medical and surgical books, mainly collected by Dr. Valentine Mott, and free to medical students and physicians. The library of the New-York Academy of Medicine (50,000 volumes) is at 17 West 43d Street ; that of the New-York Hospital (25,000 volumes), 6 West 16th Street, founded in 1796, and open free daily. The great medical schools have very extensive and valuable libraries.

Special Libraries include those of the American Numismatic and Archæological Society (6,000 books and pamphlets), at 17 West 43d Street ; the American Geographical Society (25,000 volumes and 8,000 maps), at 11 West 29th Street ; the Gaelic Society (1,200 volumes), at 17 West 28th Street ; the New York Genealogical and Biographical Society (2,500 volumes), at 19 West 44th Street ; the American Institute Library (14,000 volumes), at 113 West 38th Street ; the Museum of Natural History Library (27,000 volumes), in Central Park West ; the American Society of Civil Engineers (17,000 volumes), at 127 East 23d Street ; and the American Society of Mechanical Engineers (5,000 volumes), at 12 West 31st Street. There is a Free Circulating Library for the Blind at 296 Ninth Avenue.

The Produce Exchange and the Maritime Exchange have good libraries for their members.

The Masonic Library is at Sixth Avenue and 23d Street ; and the Odd Fellows' Library is at 2374 Park Avenue.

The Young Women's Christian Association, at 7 East 15th Street, has a library of 13,000 volumes ; and there are other libraries for women at 19 Clinton Street, and 16 Clinton Place.

Seamen's Libraries are provided by benevolent persons, to be carried away on ships for the diver-

MOTT MEMORIAL FREE MEDICAL LIBRARY, 64 MADISON AVENUE, NEAR EAST 27TH STREET.

sion and solace of the mariners. The headquarters of this work of the Seamen's Loan Libraries is at 76 Wall Street, under the care of the American Seamen's Friend Society. The Protestant Episcopal Mission Society Library for seamen is at 21 Coenties Slip ; the Seamen's Library, at 34 Pike Street ; the New-York Port Society Library, at 46 Catherine Street.

Miscellaneous Libraries include the First-Ward, at 135 Greenwich Street ; the Broome-Street ; the Five-Points Mission at 63 Park Street ; the Benjamin Townsend, at the foot of East 26th Street ; the Children's, at 590 Seventh Avenue ;

the Harlem, at 2,238 Third Avenue; St. Mark's Memorial, at 228 East 10th Street; Washington-Heights, at Amsterdam Avenue and 156th Street; St. Barnabas, at 38 Bleecker Street; the Lorraine, at 41 West 31st Street.

The Aguilar Free Library was established in 1886, and has departments at 197 East Broadway, 721 Lexington Avenue, and 624 East 5th Street.

The libraries of clubs like the University, Century, Lotos and Press Clubs have invaluable standard and reference books. The Grolier Club has an inimitable collection of books about books; the Players' Club, a valuable collection of books about the drama; the Aldine Club is forming a collection of books about book-making.

The Private Libraries of Robert Hoe, missals, manuscripts and general literature; of William Loring Andrews, typographical curiosities, New-York City relics and books bound by Roger Payne; of Samuel P. Avery, master-pieces of bookbinding; of George Beach de Forest, Elzevirs, books with vignettes of the eighteenth century, books with original illustrations; of C. Jolly-Bavoillot, Romanticists of France; of Marshall Lefferts, Americana; of C. B. Foote, works by modern English and American authors; of Rush C. Hawkins, first books printed everywhere, Incunabula; of Beverly Chew, works of the Elizabethan era; are easily accessible to serious students.

Three hundred members of the Grolier Club are men who have formed libraries. Every literary, artistic or simply social circle has its library. In New York where men have the distinctive business air of the ancient Venetian merchants, the fate of a man in search of a fortune may not be enviable, but the fate of a man in search of knowledge is the fate of a favorite of the gods.

FIFTH AVENUE, LOOKING NORTH FROM 42D STREET.

Shrines of Worship·

Cathedrals, Churches, Synagogues and Other Places of
Religious Worship and Work.

NEARLY all religious creeds are represented in New York. The ecclesiastical
annals of the city form a most interesting chapter in its history, and the
churches have played an important part all through its development. Earnest men
have filled its pulpits. Many of its charitable, educational and reformatory institutions owe their origin to the labors of the clergy, nobly seconded by zealous laymen.

The multiplication of churches has kept a fairly even pace with the increase in
population. From 1638 to 1697 the Reformed Dutch Church was the only place of
worship. The coming of the British in 1664 gave the Church of England a foothold
on the island, and in 1697 its first house of worship was erected, on the site of the
modern Trinity. From 1697 to 1770 the number of churches increased but slowly,
and in the latter year fifteen ecclesiastical edifices sufficed for the ten different denominations. The outbreak of the Revolution temporarily suspended all thoughts
of church extension, and it was not until the coming of more peaceful times that the
churches began to multiply. In 1845 there were 245 houses of worship in the city.
Now there are 600, with nearly an equal number of Sunday-schools. The average
attendance is 150,000. These 600 churches, representing nearly all religious faiths,
and many styles of architecture, provide sittings for nearly half a million worshippers, and, with the land on which they stand, have a valuation of $75,000,000.
Their yearly disbursements, including salaries, amount to $5,000,000. The com-
bined membership of all the religious societies of the city, including Protestant,
Catholic and Hebrew organizations, is not far from 700,000, not quite one-half the
total population. This includes, however, the large claims made by the Catholic
Church, whose method of including baptized infants, as well as adults, in estimating
church-membership, differs wholly from that of the Protestant Church.

The religious history of New York is remarkably free from the bitter persecutions that characterized the early history of many of the other colonies. The early
Dutch settlers were a kindly and tolerant folk, in the main, and the English had
not been long in possession of the Province when the outbreak and successful issue
of the War of Independence gave liberty of conscience and faith to all religious
opinions. The early law, forbidding the holding of public worship other than
that allowed by the authorities, never very strictly enforced, and easily evaded ; the
brief imprisonment of a few Quaker refugees from Massachusetts ; the hanging of
a Roman Catholic for alleged complicity in the Negro Riot of 1741, with the added
accusation of being a Catholic priest ; a Baptist and a Presbyterian clergyman
imprisoned for brief periods, and a Lutheran minister forbidden to preach in the
Province — these form the scanty annals of religious persecution.

The churches have shared in the northward migration of the citizens. The early edifices were in the extreme southern portion of the island ; but when the city began its journey to the north, they began to desert the old historic sites, and seek new ones in the up-town districts, leaving scarcely a score in their old locations. To-day the finest of the city's churches stand where forty years ago were green fields and the pleasant country-seats of the magnates of the city.

The Collegiate Reformed Protestant Dutch Church was the first ecclesiastical organization in New York. In 1628 the Rev. Jonas Michaelius reached the "Island of Manhattas," and immediately organized a church, with the worthy Director Minuit as one of the elders. The meetings were held in the loft of a horse-mill until 1633, when a small wooden church was built in Broad Street. In the same year the Rev. Everardus Bogardus came over from Holland, with Adam

COLLEGIATE CHURCH, 5TH AVENUE AND WEST 48TH STREET.

Roelandsen, a schoolmaster, who opened the first church-school in America, the latter still in existence as the Collegiate Grammar School. In 1642 a small stone church was erected within the walls of Fort Amsterdam, and called St. Nicholas, in honor of the patron saint of Manhattan, and here for half a century the early Dutch settlers met for worship. The first Dutch church outside the walls of the fort was built in 1693 in Garden Street (now Exchange Place). The Old Middle Church was built in 1729, in Nassau Street, and the North Church in 1769, in William Street. For nearly a century and a half these three churches, forming but one parish, then and now called the Collegiate Reformed Protestant Dutch Church (although the name does not appear upon the records, and has no legal authority), were the only Reformed Dutch churches in the city.

The Collegiate Church received a royal charter from King William III. in 1696 ; and now has four churches and as many mission chapels, all under the control of a central body called the Consistory, composed of the ministers of the four congregations, with twelve elders and twelve deacons, chosen from the congregations. During the 264 years of its existence the church has had twelve different houses of worship and thirty-one ministers, many of the latter widely known for eloquence and commanding influence, including John Henry Livingston, William Linn (who was chaplain of the first Congress of the United States), Jacob Brodhead,

Philip Milledoler, John Knox, Thomas De Witt, Joseph T. Duryea, William Ormiston, and Thomas E. Vermilye.

The consistory of the parish meets monthly, in the consistory-room of the church at 48th Street; and the congregations, besides holding their own communion services, join in the reception of the Lord's Supper once yearly, in the church at 29th Street. The parish has 2,146 communicants. The Reformed Dutch churches in the city number 22, besides several missions and chapels. Of these, the four churches mentioned as under the control of the consistory of the Collegiate Church constitute, technically, a single parish, as is the case in the Episcopal Church with Trinity and its chapels. These four are at Second Avenue and 7th Street; at Fifth Avenue and 29th Street; at Fifth Avenue and 48th Street, and at West-End Avenue and 77th Street. The senior minister of the Collegiate Church is the Rev. Talbot W. Chambers, S. T. D., LL. D., and as such he has a general oversight of the whole parish.

MIDDLE COLLEGIATE CHURCH, SECOND AVENUE AND 7TH STREET.

The Middle Collegiate Church built its first shrine in 1729, on Nassau Street, on the site now occupied by the Mutual Life-Insurance Company. Its second church, from 1839 to 1887, was in Lafayette Place. In 1891-92 a third edifice was erected, at Second Avenue and 7th Street, to hold a site for religious worship well down-town. It is a handsome structure in the Gothic style of architecture, built of limestone, with a graceful spire. The pulpit is an object famous among old New-Yorkers, having originally been in the church in Lafayette Place. It is of pure statuary marble. The windows are of stained glass, made by the Tiffany Glass and Decorating Co.; and present a unique and very brilliant feature by reason of receiving their illumination, day and night, from electric lights behind the glass. The subjects of the windows are from the life of Christ, after designs by Heinrich Hoffmann of Dresden. The minister in charge of the Middle Church is the Rev. John Hutchins. In connection with this church is a hand-

22

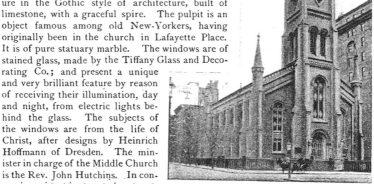

COLLEGIATE CHURCH, FIFTH AVENUE AND WEST 29TH STREET.

some Church House, facing on 7th Street, and thoroughly equipped with reading-rooms, gymnasium, and all the appliances for aggressive modern church work.

The **Marble Collegiate Church,** at Fifth Avenue and 29th Street (popularly known as "the Marble Church"), is a massive marble building, erected in 1851 – 1854, in a simple type of Gothic architecture. The large auditorium is attractively decorated, and contains a triple organ, with electric wires connecting the different parts. The old bell which hung in the belfry of one of the Collegiate churches stands at the left of the entrance, bearing an inscription stating that it was cast in Amsterdam in 1768. A special feature of the church is its work among the apartment-houses and large hotels in the vicinity, and its courtesy to strangers is famous. The Rev. Dr. David James Burrell is the minister in charge, with two assistants.

The **Fifth-Avenue Collegiate Church,** at Fifth Avenue and 48th Street, is a strikingly beautiful edifice, of Newark sandstone, in the decorated Gothic architec-

COLLEGIATE REFORMED CHURCH, AT WEST-END AVENUE AND 77TH STREET.

ture of the fourteenth century, with a lofty spire, flying buttresses, numerous gables, and a colonnaded entrance-porch on the avenue. A flying buttress on the northern corner supports a small spire, which adds to the symmetry of the front. The interior has a lofty groined roof, resting upon exquisitely carved stone and marble pillars. The organ-gallery is picturesque, and the walls are delicately tinted. The church was dedicated in 1872. The minister in charge, Dr. Edward B. Coe, is one of the most esteemed preachers in the city.

The **West-End Avenue Collegiate Church,** at West-End Avenue and 77th Street, was built in 1891 – 92, after designs by R. W. Gibson ; and is a large and imposing structure in quaint Flemish architecture, with decorated crow-step gables and many pinnacles, and ornate dormer-windows in the roof. The interior is decorated in old ivory effects and harmonious tints of orange. Dark cross-beams under the roof carry out the Flemish idea. Pillars of Tennessee marble support the arches. The pulpit and choir-stalls are elaborately carved ; and the communion-table is copied from that in Leonardo de Vinci's picture of "The Last Supper." The minister in charge is the Rev. Henry Evertson Cobb.

The Fulton-Street Prayer-Meeting is the outcome of a missionary enterprise of the Collegiate Reformed Church, and the meetings have been held in the Consistory building, at 113 Fulton Street, since they were begun, in 1857, with no deviation from the original plan, which was "to give merchants, mechanics, clerks, strangers and business men generally, an opportunity to stop and call upon God amid the daily perplexities incident to their respective avocations." The meetings are held daily, at noon, and continue for one hour, but the visitor is at liberty to leave at any time. When the desire is expressed, prayer is offered for individual needs and perplexities, and the meetings have been a source of comfort and encouragement to thousands.

The First Collegiate Reformed Church of Harlem began with the election of John LaMontagne as deacon, in the year 1660, when Harlem was a venturesome journey from the little burgh of New Amsterdam. For the long period of 105 years the good burghers of Harlem were compelled to depend upon their "Vorleser," or reader, and the help of neighboring clergymen, for their Sunday instruction in the Scriptures. Good old Dominie Selyns occasionally used to ride over to the little settlement on the Harlem from his Brooklyn charge, in the days of Peter Stuyvesant ; and later, Dominies Drisius and Niewenhuysen came now and then from the lower end of the island for a Sunday service ; but it was not until just before the outbreak of the Revolution that a minister was settled over the church, Rev. Martinius Schoonmaker, who has had eight successors. The present church, a plain building with pillared front, on 121st Street, near Third Avenue, was dedicated in 1835. Its minister is Rev. Dr. Joachim Elmendorf.

The Second Collegiate Reformed Church of Harlem has its beautiful Gothic house of worship at 267 Lenox Avenue, at the corner of 123d Street. Rev. W. J. Harsha is the pastor.

SECOND COLLEGIATE REFORMED CHURCH OF HARLEM, LENOX AVENUE AND WEST 123D STREET.

The South Reformed Dutch Church, at Madison Avenue and East 38th Street, is one of the oldest ecclesiastical organizations in the city. Its earlier history, previous to the year 1812, is connected with that of the Collegiate Church, of which it formed a part. The first South Church, erected in Garden Street, in 1693, was a solid and substantial building, with an imposing belfry and round-arched windows. The old church was torn down in 1807, to make room for a larger building, destroyed by fire in 1835. Previous to this, in 1812, the South Church had become independent of the North and Middle Collegiate Churches, and assumed the title of "The Ministers, Elders and Deacons of the Reformed Protestant Dutch Church in Garden Street in the City of New

York," which is still the legal title of the society.   Differences of opinion regarding the advisability of rebuilding on the old site led to the formation of a new society, which built the church now owned by the Asbury Methodists, in Washington Square, while the old society erected a church in Murray Street, followed in

SOUTH REFORMED DUTCH CHURCH, MADISON AVENUE
AND 38TH STREET.

1849 by a larger and more imposing building on Fifth Avenue.   This was sold in 1890, and the present Gothic stone church, formerly Zion Episcopal Church, was purchased and re-decorated.   The large memorial window in the west end, representing the Nativity, Baptism and Resurrection of Our Lord, is the work of the Tiffany Company.   The first minister of the South Church after its separation from the Collegiate Church was Dr. James M. Matthews, who became Chancellor of the University of the City of New York in 1834.   The Rev. Roderick Terry, D. D., is now in charge, and the parish is prospering.

The **Madison-Avenue Reformed Church,** at the corner of 57th Street, an imposing Gothic brownstone building, was erected in 1870.   The society, formerly known as the Northwest Reformed Church, was organized in 1808, and worshipped in a church on Franklin Street until 1854, when it moved to a more eligible location on East 23d Street.   The Madison-Avenue Church has a seating capacity of 1,000, and with its galleries, groined roof and picturesque arrangement of round arches, the interior is extremely attractive and commodious.   The minister is Rev. Dr. Abbott E. Kittredge.

The **Thirty-Fourth Street Reformed Dutch Church,** at 307 West 34th Street, was organized in 1823, and its first church was a modest brick structure at Broome and Greene Streets.   Under the ministerial care of Dr. Jacob Brodhead and Dr. Samuel A. Van Vranken it attracted large and fashionable congregations. Dr. Brodhead was one of the most eloquent preachers of his day, and Dr. Van Vranken possessed pulpit talents of a high order.   Later, the ministerial charge was assumed by the Rev. Dr. George H. Fisher and the Rev. Henry V. Voorhees, both noted preachers.   In 1860 the present large Gothic church was built.   It is of brick, with yellow stone front and double towers, and the interior is plain and comfortable, with free pews and a very sweet-toned organ.   Previous to the building of the new church, the members of the Livingston Reformed Church, then worshipping in a hall on 33d Street, united with the 34th-Street parish, adding materially to its strength and influence.   The minister is the Rev. Dr. Peter Stryker, a writer, lecturer, and active worker in the temperance cause.

The Bloomingdale Reformed Church is at 68th Street, where it crosses the Boulevard. It is one of the most impressive and stately of all the churches in this region, and has a noble Gothic spire. The Rev. Madison C. Peters is the pastor.

Trinity Church is the chief edifice of the Protestant Episcopal Church, which maintains the prestige that it secured as the State Church two centuries ago, and in wealth and influence easily distances all rivals. Bishop Henry C. Potter is at the head of the diocese, and the Church is ministered to by men of wide fame. It has churches for Englishmen, Frenchmen, Italians, Germans, Africans, Chinese, and Spaniards; and for soldiers, seamen, deaf-mutes, and prisoners.

MADISON-AVENUE REFORMED CHURCH, MADISON AVENUE AND EAST 57TH STREET.

Trinity Church is the second oldest religious organization in the city proper. It was organized under the provisions of an Act passed by the Colonial Assembly of 1693, but the royal charter establishing the Parish of Trinity Church was not granted until 1697. The services of the Church of England had been introduced immediately after the arrival of the British fleet in 1664, and were held in old St. Nicholas Church, within the Fort, until March, 1697, when a small wooden building was opened on the site of the present Trinity Church. This stood unchanged for nearly forty years, when it was virtually rebuilt. The close of the Revolution left the Episcopalians, many of whom had remained loyal to King and Parliament, in small favor with the patriots; but with the restoration of order came wiser counsels. The ritual was revised by omitting the obnoxious prayer for the King, and with the consecration of the first American bishops in 1784, and the General Convention in 1785, which organized the Protestant Episcopal Church in the States of America, officially declared to be loyal to the new government, came the beginning of a growth that has made that church the most powerful Protestant denomination in New York. St. George's and

BLOOMINGDALE REFORMED CHURCH, BOULEVARD AND WEST 68TH STREET.

St. Mark's remained the only other Episcopal churches in the city until 1794, when the increasing population necessitated a second parish, and Christ Church was organized. As the population has increased, other parishes have been formed, and new churches erected; and there are now 84 Episcopal churches and chapels in the city, with 35,000 communicants, and a vast network of parochial charities. Trinity still remains the wealthiest single church corporation in the United States. Most of its annual income of half a million dollars comes from what remains, after many generous gifts, of the royal grant of the Queen's Farm, made in 1705, and comprising a large tract of land along the North River, between Christopher and Vesey Streets, now in the heart of the business part of the city. This property is valued at $9,000,000. At the outbreak of the Revolution Trinity was closed for a time, owing to the persistent refusal of the clergy to omit the prayer for the King. It was re-opened after the British occupation, only to be destroyed a few days later in the great fire of 1776. The second church was built in 1788, on the same site on Broadway, opposite the head of Wall Street. The third, that is to say, the present Trinity Church, was finished in 1846, from the designs of Richard Upjohn. It is a stately Gothic edifice, with an exquisite sharply pointed ornate spire, rising to a height of 284 feet, and carrying a melodious chime of bells. On either side is a quiet graveyard, with many interesting memorials of men and women of the past. The interior is lofty and spacious, with a groined roof borne aloft by sandstone columns. The pews are of carved oak. The chancel is enriched by a fine altar and reredos of white Caen stone, with mosaics and cameos, a memorial to William B. Astor from his sons. Of the many benefactions of Trinity, from its early gift of a communion-service and an altar-cloth to a church at Rye, down to the present time, none has been of greater service to the city than the numerous chapels which she has erected and still maintains. The first was St. George's, now an independent parish, opened in 1753, and endowed by Trinity with a generous gift of over a quarter of a million dollars; then came St. Paul's, in 1766; St. John's, in 1807; Trinity Chapel, in 1856; St. Chrysostom's, in 1869; St. Augustine's, in 1877; and St. Agnes' and St. Luke's, in 1892. Trinity has over 6,000 communicants. The music in this church is famous for its beauty, a full cathedral service being sung every Sunday morning, with a full choral vesper service later in the day.

Of the large income enjoyed by Trinity not a cent is hoarded. The expenses of keeping up the estate; the support of the chapels; the large yearly grants to twenty-four parishes; the payment of taxes and assessments; and the maintenance of the several parochial schools and other parish charities exhaust the yearly income. Of the former rectors of Trinity three have been made bishops of the Church, and one was banished from the State for his royalist proclivities, and became bishop of Nova Scotia. The Rev. Dr. Morgan Dix is the rector of the parish.

St. Paul's Chapel is the oldest church edifice now remaining in the city, and the oldest of the chapels of Trinity Parish. It stands in its ancient location at the corner of Broadway and Vesey Street, Vesey being the name of the first rector of the mother church. It was built in 1764-66, before the troublous times of the War of Independence, and with its simple but impressive architecture of the style of a century and a half ago; its exquisite spire, recalling one of Sir Christopher Wren's, standing where seemingly it ought not, on what is now the rear end of the building; and its quiet God's Acre surrounding it, it is one of the picturesque features of lower Broadway. The spacious interior is interesting, not so much for its architectural or decorative beauties (of which indeed it makes but scanty show), as for its old-fashioned look, and the hints it gives of the simple taste and moderate ideas of

TRINITY CHURCH -- PROTESTANT EPISCOPAL.
BROADWAY, BETWEEN RECTOR AND THAMES STREETS, AT THE HEAD OF WALL STREET.

splendor which belonged to the men of the past. Many interesting events have taken place within St. Paul's, but none surpass in impressiveness the solemn service of thanksgiving there, which Washington and the civic authorities attended in simple state, after the inauguration ceremonies in 1789 of the first President of the United States, in the old City Hall, hard by. The centennial anniversary thereof was celebrated within these walls in 1889. A tablet in the rear wall of the chapel, facing Broadway, commemorates the bravery of General Richard Montgomery, the hero of Quebec; and in the churchyard are monuments to Emmet, the Irish patriot; George Frederick Cooke, and others. The Rev. Dr. James Mulchahey is in charge. The music is rendered by a double quartette and a chorus choir of 27 voices.

St. John's Chapel, on Varick Street, was built by Trinity Parish, between 1803 and 1807, in a region then just beginning to be fashionable for homes. It is a quaint and venerable edifice, surrounded by factories and tenements, and the only church within a great area. The front presents a high Corinthian porch, supported by four massive columns of sandstone. The church-yard, in effect like a diminutive park, with trees and shrubbery, lies on either side. The position which St. John's occupies makes it a conspicuous as well as a picturesque object, as seen from the Sixth-Avenue Elevated Railroad, just below Canal Street. Its quaint hewn-oak spire, with a tower clock, rises above the surrounding buildings, 214½ feet high. The Rev. Philip A. H. Brown is in charge. The music is famous.

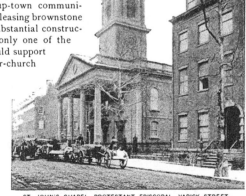

ST. JOHN'S CHAPEL, PROTESTANT EPISCOPAL, VARICK STREET.

Trinity Chapel, on 25th Street, near Broadway, was erected in 1851-56 by Old Trinity, for the accommodation of the up-town communicants of the parish. It is a pleasing brownstone Gothic edifice, of the most substantial construction; and is probably the only one of the chapels of Trinity which could support itself if the aid of the mother-church were withdrawn. The plans of the building were designed by Richard Upjohn, and the interior is peculiar in being simply a lofty nave, with arcades along the sides to indicate the position of the aisles, if they had not been omitted. This causes the building to seem very long and narrow; but the great height of the walls and the open roof make an impressive and satisfactory interior. The spacious chancel ends in an apse of seven bays, and paintings fill the tympanums of the sanctuary. The interior is chastely decorated, the corbel pillars in the nave being ornamented with gold leaf. The reredos is of Caen stone and alabaster. Adjacent to the church are the vestry-room and the parish-school building. The Rev. Dr. Swope was a long time in charge of Trinity Chapel, which is now ministered to by the Rev. Dr. William H. Vibbert. The music at the chapel is under the direction of Dr. Walter B. Gilbert, organist and choir-master, and is largely of modern forms.

ST. PAUL'S CHAPEL--PROTESTANT EPISCOPAL.
BROADWAY AND CHURCH STREET, FROM FULTON STREET TO VESEY STREET.

St. Chrysostom's Chapel, at the corner of Seventh Avenue and West 39th Street, is a commodious Gothic edifice, of brownstone, equipped with auxiliary schools and mission and guild rooms. It dates from 1869, and is a power for good in a crowded poor district. Rev. T. H. Sill is the clergyman.

St. Augustine's Chapel is one of the striking architectural features of the city.

TRINITY CHAPEL, PROTESTANT EPISCOPAL, WEST 25TH STREET, BETWEEN BROADWAY AND SIXTH AVENUE.

One of the chapels of Old Trinity, erected in 1876-77 in East Houston Street, between the Bowery and Second Avenue, it stands in the most densely populated part of New York, and, according to the *London Times,* of the whole world. The church cure is a region where all grades of poverty, and almost all forms of vice abound. The buildings consist of the chapel proper and the Mission House. The former, entered through a broad archway with tiled walls and floor, and timbered ceiling, is cruciform, with an open Gothic roof and richly decorated in warm colors. It is handsomely and completely furnished, and seats nearly a thousand. The font is a Caen monolith, and the black iron lectern and oaken altar, placed in Trinity Church at its consecration, are fine specimens of the ecclesiastical art of that period. In the west transept Roger's statue of 'Isaac' is seen. There are four services on Sunday, the spire cross being illuminated at all night services. The bell is one of the oldest in the country, having been made in 1700, and given in 1704 by the Bishop of London to the first English parish-church in New York. The Mission House contains a large hall, rooms for the day and night-schools, guild-rooms, a music-room, and various offices. Besides the Sunday-

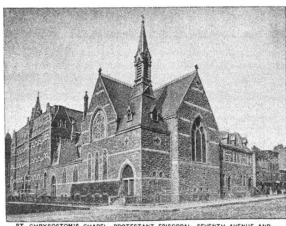

ST. CHRYSOSTOM'S CHAPEL, PROTESTANT EPISCOPAL, SEVENTH AVENUE AND WEST 39TH STREET.

school, that occupies twenty different rooms, ten of which are in the basement of the chapel proper, there are a day-school for boys, a night-school for young men and women, a sewing-school with dressmaking and millinery classes, a house-school for teaching girls all kinds of housework, the parish cooking-school, and a number of

guilds and societies. The Rev. Dr. Arthur C. Kimber is in charge, with three assistants.

St. Cornelius' Chapel, on Governor's Island, is maintained by Trinity Church, under an arrangement with the War Department, for army officers and soldiers who may desire to attend divine services; and for baptisms, burials, weddings and other ceremonials in the garrison.

St. Agnes' Chapel, near the Boulevard, on West 92d Street, is the newest and most magnificent of Trinity's chapels. Its cost was about $800,000, and it was opened for public services in 1892. St. Agnes' is a cruciform Romanesque building, of striking design and treatment. The main front is of brownstone, flanked and crowned by plain granite walls. The lower stage is occupied by a portal of three deep and heavily-moulded arches. The upper stage is pierced by a large arched window, and the intervening frieze is decorated with emblems of the four Evangelists. The tower is a straight

ST. AUGUSTINE'S CHAPEL, PROTESTANT EPISCOPAL,
107 EAST HOUSTON STREET.

shaft of granite, with belts of brownstone; and the belfry stage is ornamented with arches and spandrils of the same material. A large square lantern rises above the roof-line, at the intersection of the nave and transepts, and forms the dominating feature of the exterior. The interior treatment is elaborate and costly, the richest effects centering in the aspidal chancel, which has a massive rail of white marble, filled with rich inlaid work in green marble. The same material is used in the construction of the pulpit, lectern and altar. The ceiling has a background of gold, upon which are painted in rich colors heroic figures of the Apostles, each bearing an emblem. In the centre is a large representation of Christ, the Triumphant

King, seated upon a throne.   The walls of the chancel are broken by window
openings, arches communicating with the vestries, and recesses backed with glass
mosaics, having ornamental work in relief.   The beautiful Morning Chapel is on
the west side, opening into the transept and nave by two large archways.   In the
rear of the church are the parish-house and the rectory.   The chapel seats about
1,200 people.   All the interior decorative work, including the windows, was done
by the Tiffany Glass and Decorating Company.   The architect was William A.
Potter.   The minister in charge is the Rev. Dr. Edward A. Bradley.   The grounds
surrounding St. Agnes' are effectively adorned with lawns, trees and shrubs.

   Grace Church, on Broadway, near 10th Street, is, with the exception of
Trinity, the wealthiest Episcopal corporation in New York.   The parish was organized in 1808, and the first church stood at the corner of Broadway and Rector
Street, then a fine residen-
tial quarter.   The present
location was selected in

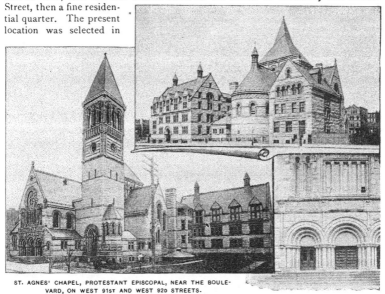

ST. AGNES' CHAPEL, PROTESTANT EPISCOPAL, NEAR THE BOULE-
VARD, ON WEST 91ST AND WEST 92D STREETS.

1844, and was thought to be very far up-town.   The graceful white limestone church,
in the Decorated Gothic style, is one of the architectural features of Broadway, and
its spire, once of wood, but now of marble, is one of the most exquisite in the city.
The group of buildings belonging to Grace Church comprises the rectory, on the
north, connected with the church by Grace House, erected in 1880 by Miss Catherine L. Wolfe, and containing the vestry and clergy-rooms, library and reading-
room ; the Chantry, adjoining the church on the south, also the gift of Miss Wolfe ;
and Grace Memorial House, in the rear, on Fourth Avenue, erected by the Hon.
Levi P. Morton in 1880 in memory of his wife, and used as a day-nursery for small
children.   Grace Chapel, at 132 East 14th Street, was erected by the parish in
1876 to replace the former chapel, built in 1852, and destroyed by fire in 1872.
Grace-House-by-the-Sea, at Far Rockaway, Long Island, was opened in 1883 as a

GRACE CHURCH — PROTESTANT EPISCOPAL.
BROADWAY, NEAR 10TH STREET, AT THE HEAD OF LOWER BROADWAY.

summer home for poor women from tenement houses.   Liberal support is given to this and the many other parochial charities, and generous contributions are made to aid benevolent work outside the parish limits.   The architect of Grace Church was James Renwick.

Few if any of the churches surpass Grace in beauty of interior design and decoration.   It is impressive and magnificent.   In the eastern end a large chancel window, the gift of Miss Wolfe (as are also the altar and the lofty reredos), is filled with English stained glass.   The groined roof of the nave is supported by graceful columns ; and the clere-story and side windows contain some of the finest examples of the glass-worker's art.   A beautiful memorial porch forms the entrance ; and the chime of bells in the belfry rivals that of Trinity in sweetness.   Grace has long been

GRACE MEMORIAL HOUSE, FOURTH AVENUE, NEAR 10TH
STREET, IN REAR OF GRACE CHURCH.

noted for fashionable weddings.   The Bishop of New York, the Rt. Rev. Henry C. Potter, was long rector of the parish.   He was succeeded in 1883 by the Rev. Dr. William R. Huntington.

Christ Church was the second parish of the Episcopal Church organized in New York, dating back to 1794, when a church was built on Ann Street.   Here a goodly congregation soon gathered, under the Rev. John Pillmore, one of the first Wesleyan itinerants sent over from England, who labored for a time with the brethren of the John-Street Church, but later joined the Episcopalians.   The parish grew rapidly, and in 1823 its former accommodations became too straitened for its needs, and a larger church was built on Worth Street, where the parish remained in peace and prosperity until it migrated up-town in 1854, building and occupying the present St. Ann's Church on West 18th Street.   In 1859 a church at Fifth Avenue and 35th Street was purchased from the Baptists, and here again the parish rested and throve for more than thirty years.   In 1890 Christ Church removed to its present site, at the corner of 71st Street and the Boulevard.   The architect was C. C. Haight.   Among the prominent rectors of the parish have been Dr. F. C. Ewer, the founder of the ritualistic church of St. Ignatius ; the Rev. Hugh Miller Thompson, a preacher of nervous and picturesque force ; and Dr. William McVickar.   Dr. J. S. Shipman has been the rector for sixteen years.

St. George's Church began its independent existence in 1812.   The first church, a chapel of Trinity, was built in 1752, at Beekman and Cliff Streets.   The more modern building, erected in 1845, is a graceful brownstone structure, in the Gothic style, and a prominent landmark on the East Side, in Stuyvesant Square.   Formerly it had two noble spires, but they became weakened, as the result of a fire.   They were taken down, and have never been replaced.   For many years the

Rev. Dr. Stephen H. Tyng, the elder, was rector, and his sturdy preaching brought the church well to the front in the Episcopal body. The Rev. Dr. William S. Rainsford became rector in 1881, and since then many changes and improvements have been made in the working methods of the parish; which is one of the most active in the city, and the largest in the country, having 2,600 communicants. One of the most important of its parochial agencies is St. George's Memorial House, adjoining the church. It was erected in 1888, the gift of J. Pierpont Morgan, in memory of Mr. and Mrs. Charles Tracy. It is built of red sandstone, and contains schoolrooms, club-rooms, clergy-rooms, gymnasium, library and reading-room, and is the centre of much philanthropic work among the poorer classes in the neighborhood.

ST. MARK'S CHURCH, PROTESTANT EPISCOPAL, STUYVESANT STREET AND SECOND AVENUE.

St. Mark's Church was organized in 1791. The present church at Second Avenue and 10th Street was cousecrated in 1829, and is one of the few survivors of the old colonial style of ecclesiastical architecture, with lofty pillared porch and a sharply tapering steeple. The interior preserves its olden quaintness, and is pleasingly decorated. Many memorial tablets adorn the walls; and on the east side of the outer wall, an ancient stone bears

CHURCH OF THE HEAVENLY REST, PROTESTANT EPISCOPAL, FIFTH AVENUE, ABOVE 45TH STREET.

ST. GEORGE'S CHURCH, PROTESTANT EPISCOPAL, STUYVESANT SQUARE AND EAST 16TH STREET.

witness to the fact that Governor Petrus Stuyvesant lies buried in the vault below. When the doughty Dutch Captain-General retired from office, after the surrender of the province to the English, he withdrew to his "Bouwerie," or farm, in the vicinity of the present Stuyvesant Square, then two miles from the centre of the city. He built a small chapel adjoining his manor-house, and here the Rev. Henry Soleyns was wont to preach on Sunday afternoons. In a vault underneath the chapel the Governor was laid to rest, after his death in 1682, to be followed, in 1691, by Henry Sloughter, the English royal governor, and still later, by Daniel Tompkins, an early governor of the State.   At one time the Methodists held meetings in the chapel, commonly called the "Two-Mile-Stone Meeting House," from its distance from the centre of the city.   It was taken down in 1793, and the offer of Petrus Stuyvesant, a descend-ant of the Governor, to present the ground and 800 pounds in money to Trinity for a church, was accepted.   The church was built in the years 1795-99, and long bore the name of "St. Mark's in the Bowery."   It is still the spiritual home of many descendants of the old families.   The Rev. Dr. J. H. Rylance is the rector.

The Church of the Heavenly Rest, at 551 Fifth Avenue, was built through the efforts of Dr. Robert S. Howland, then rector of the Church of the Holy Apos-tles.   The parish originated in services held in the hall of Rutgers Female College, in 1865.   The narrow front of the church, ornamental in design and surmounted by angelic

figures, gives little promise of the spaciousness of the interior, which is cruciform in shape, and contains some of the finest wood-carving and stained-glass windows in the country.   Polished marble pillars support the roof; the walls are richly frescoed and adorned with beautiful paintings; and Ary Scheffer's *Christus Consolator* forms the altar-piece.   The entire effect of the interior is one of ex-treme and satisfying richness, re-finement, beauty and peace.   The Church of the Heavenly Rest is one of the fashionable shrines of the city, and the wealth of its members is shown in their liberal support of public and parochial charities.   The rector is the Rev. Dr. D. Parker Morgan.

St. Thomas's Church, at Fifth Avenue and 53d Street, was organized in 1823; and its first church stood at Broadway and Houston Street, then a rural sub-urb.   The parish attained to a high degree of prosperity under

ST. GEORGE'S MEMORIAL HOUSE, 207 EAST 16TH STREET, IN REAR OF ST. GEORGE'S CHURCH.

the rectorship of Dr. Francis L. Hawks, but as early as 1843 the need of a location farther up-town began to be felt, and in 1870 the present magnificent edifice was opened for worship.   The church is one of the most imposing architectural features of the city, and was regarded by the architect, Upjohn, as the masterpiece of his long career as a church architect.   The church and the adjoining rectory are built of brownstone, in the Gothic style ; and, with the grounds and furnishings, represent a value of nearly one million dollars.   The interior is one of the finest in the city, with monolithic columns supporting the nave, a central dome at the intersection of the nave and transept, an apsidal chancel adorned with a series of cartoons by LaFarge, and a reredos in old gold by St. Gaudens, representing the Adoration of the Cross by cherubs and angels.   The chancel is flanked by shallower recesses, in which is built

PROTESTANT EPISCOPAL CHURCH EDIFICES.

23   ST. LUKE'S.   ST. MICHAEL'S.   ST. THOMAS'.   ZION AND ST. TIMOTHY.   ST. MARY THE VIRGIN.

the great organ, in two parts, for a double choir, whose rendering of church music is famous throughout the country.   The entire decoration of the chancel, including the costly works of LaFarge and St. Gaudens, is a memorial from Charles H. Housman to his mother ; and to his generosity the church also owes the angelic figures with musical instruments, after Fra Angelico, by LaFarge, which form the decorations above the organ.   Other memorials are the chime of bells in the tower, rivalling those of Trinity in sweetness, the cross surmounting it, and many stained-glass windows and other fittings of the interior.   While St. Thomas's is a church for the wealthy, it is by no means neglectful of the claims of the poorer classes.   In addition to its numerous benevolent societies, it maintains St. Thomas's Chapel, on 60th Street ; a German mission ; and St. Thomas's House, in the rear of the chapel, erected in 1872 by Hon. and Mrs. Roswell P. Flower as a memorial to their son, Henry Keep Flower.   The rectors of St. Thomas have been : Rev. Cornelius R. Duffie ; Rev. Dr. George Upfold, later bishop of Indiana ; Rev. Henry J. White-house, some time bishop of Illinois ; Rev. Dr. Edmund Neville ; Rev. Dr. William F. Morgan ; and the present incumbent, Rev. Dr. John W. Brown.

St. James's Church grew out of a chapel-at-ease erected in 1810 at 69th Street and Park Avenue, for the convenience of those New-York families whose country-

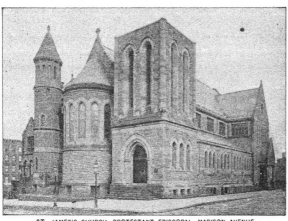

seats were in the vicinity of Hamilton Square (now Lenox Hill). This was succeeded by an edifice erected in 1869 on the north side of 72d Street, between Lexington and Third Avenues,— the present church having been built in 1884 at the northeast corner of Madison Avenue and 71st Street. It is an imposing Gothic building; designed to have a lofty

ST. JAMES'S CHURCH, PROTESTANT EPISCOPAL, MADISON AVENUE
AND EAST 71st STREET.

tower in the Florentine style.   It has an apsidal chancel at the side of the tower ; a smaller round tower ; and a loggia, with bold projections, forming with the two gables a very beautiful and picturesque effect.   The interior is extremely pleasing. A tower-room, with a notable stairway, opens upon the chancel, which is very deep, with two arches and an apsidal sanctuary.   At the east end is a large gallery.   The interior finish is oak, and the entire scheme of decoration is chaste and harmonious. There is a vested choir ; and the building contains two choir-rooms, a large parish-room, a library, a guild-room, and a kitchen.   In the tower are three large brass tablets, having representations of the two former buildings of the parish, and inscribed with the names of former vestrymen.   The rector, the Rev. Dr. Cornelius B. Smith, began his work in 1867.

St. Luke's Church, at Convent Avenue and 141st Street, is an impressive Romanesque brownstone church, designed by R. H. Robertson, and opened in 1892. It cost $275,000. It occupies very high ground, on Washington Heights; and the rectory is the old mansion of Alexander Hamilton, known as "The Grange." Old St. Luke's, at 483 Hudson Street, was built in 1821, in Green-

ST. LUKE'S CHURCH, PROTESTANT EPISCOPAL, AND ALEXANDER HAMILTON'S "THE GRANGE," CONVENT AVENUE AND 141ST STREET.

wich Village, and in 1892 became a chapel of Trinity Parish. It is in a densely settled part of the city, and is supported as a mission. When it was sold to Trinity, the records and traditions of the parish were transferred to the new and magnificent church on Washington Heights. The Rev. Dr. Isaac H. Tuttle, rector of old St. Luke's for 42 years, is now rector emeritus of the migrated parish; and the Rev. Dr. John T. Patey is the active rector.

Calvary Church was built in 1837, on Fourth proved to be too far up-

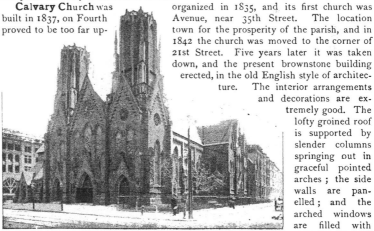

CALVARY CHURCH, PROTESTANT EPISCOPAL, FOURTH AVENUE AND EAST 21st STREET.

organized in 1835, and its first church was Avenue, near 35th Street. The location town for the prosperity of the parish, and in 1842 the church was moved to the corner of 21st Street. Five years later it was taken down, and the present brownstone building erected, in the old English style of architecture. The interior arrangements and decorations are extremely good. The lofty groined roof is supported by slender columns springing out in graceful pointed arches; the side walls are panelled; and the arched windows are filled with richly colored

glass. Calvary has long been one of the leading Episcopal parishes, and with Cal.
vary Chapel and the Galilee Rescue Mission on East 23d Street, and a goodly number of parochial charities, it is the centre of much beneficent activity. There are
1,600 communicants. The rector is the Rev. Dr. H. Y. Satterlee. The congregational singing at Calvary is very fine, trained singers being scattered throughout the
congregation. The new building which is to be occupied by the Church Missions
House is slowly rising into view, on Fourth Avenue, just north of Calvary Church.

The Church of the Ascension, at Fifth Avenue and 10th Street, is an
attractive brownstone edifice, erected in 1840. Its founder was Dr. Manton Eastburn, afterwards bishop of Massachusetts; who was succeeded by Dr. Gregory
T. Bedell, afterwards bishop of Ohio ; Dr. John Cotton Smith ; and Dr. E. Winchester Donald, who in 1892 succeeded Phillips Brooks as rector of Trinity Church,
in Boston. In 1888-89 the church was beautified by a new chancel, furnished by
Stanford White, and adorned with angel figures by St. Gaudens, mosaics by Maitland Armstrong, a richly carved memorial pulpit and walls of Siena marble. Above
these is the largest ecclesiastical painting in America, representing the Ascension.

ST. ANDREW'S CHURCH, PROTESTANT EPISCOPAL, FIFTH
AVENUE AND EAST 127TH STREET.

This magnificent picture was the work
of John LaFarge, and took two years
to execute, its cost having been $30,-
000. It was the gift of the Misses
Rhinelander. The parish has been
widely known for its generous gifts,
including a hall at the Theological
School near Alexandria, Va.; a hall
and church for Kenyon College, at
Gambier, Ohio ; and the Church of the
Ascension, at Ipswich, Mass.

St. Andrew's Church was organized in 1829, and built its first ecclesiastical home during the following year.
The early growth of the parish was
feeble, owing to its remote situation,
far up-town ; and it was not until the
year 1873 that the need of large accommodations became sufficiently urgent
to cause the erection of a more spacious church, which remained in use until the
opening of the present edifice, in 1889, at Fifth Avenue and 127th Street. The
exterior is picturesque in appearance, with a stately corner tower carrying a sweet
chime of bells, gabled entrances, and a pleasing roof-line. The interior is churchly
and impressive in the best sense, with lofty nave, lower side aisles, transepts, baptistery and apsidal chancel. Slender shafts, surmounted by a clere-story pierced with
many windows, and spanned by graceful pointed arches, support the lofty arched
roof. Two narrow lancet windows light the chancel, and between them is a large
painting of *The Call of St. Andrew,* the patron-saint of the church. The chancel
and transepts open out into smaller spaces through pointed arches, adding greatly
to the perspective effect. The color scheme is in terra cotta, relieved by lighter
lines on the faces of the arched ribs of the roof. The first rector of the parish was
the Rev. George L. Hinton. Later incumbents have been the Rev. Dr. James R.
Bailey, who withdrew to join the Roman Catholic Church, and became Archbishop
of Baltimore ; the Rev. Dr. Francis Lobdell ; and the present rector, the Rev. Dr.

George R. Van De Water, one of the strongest preachers and leading organizers in the city. The communicant list numbers 1,500 ; and St. Andrew's is noted for the variety and liberality of its gifts.

The Church of the Holy Communion, at Sixth Avenue and 20th Street, was erected in 1846 by Mrs. Anna C. Rogers, in obedience to the dying request of her husband, that "a church might be built, to the glory of God, where rich and poor might meet together." Mrs. Rogers's brother, Dr. William A. Muhlenberg, the founder of St. Luke's Hospital, became the first rector. It was a free church from the beginning, and the first in the country to establish early communions, weekly celebrations, daily prayers, and a boy choir, and the first to organize a sisterhood. The group of buildings includes the church and rectory, in brownstone, after designs by Upjohn ; a Sisters' House ; a home for aged women ; and other edifices. The church is cruciform in shape, and the interior is plain but churchly in its decorations. The Rev. Dr. Henry Mottet is rector.

The Church of the Transfiguration, at 5 East 29th Street, is better known as "The Little Church around the Corner," from the fact that its rector once

CHURCH OF THE TRANSFIGURATION (THE LITTLE CHURCH AROUND THE CORNER), PROTESTANT EPISCOPAL, EAST 29TH STREET. BETWEEN FIFTH AND MADISON AVENUES.

read the funeral service of the Church over the body of an actor, after a neighboring clergyman had refused, telling the friends of the deceased to go to "the little church around the corner." This simple incident has made the church an object of affectionate regard to the whole dramatic profession, many of whom have shown their interest in a substantial manner. The parish was organized in 1849 by the present rector, Dr. George H. Houghton, and early in the following year a part of the rambling but picturesque church was erected. The building has grown by degrees, as need arose and funds were forthcoming, and is now a long low structure, with a single transept and many beautiful and costly decorations. The church has 600 communicants, and is recognized as a very earnest body of communicants. Services are conducted three times a day throughout the year. The rectory adjoins the church. There is a Transfiguration Chapel on West 69th Street, between the Boulevard and Columbus Avenue.

St. Ann's Church is engaged in an interesting field of work among the deaf-mutes, in whose behalf the parish was organized by the rector emeritus, the Rev. Dr. Thomas Gallaudet, in 1852. For several years the services were held in the chapel of the University of the City of New York and the lecture-room of the New-York Historical Society. The church, on 18th Street, near Fifth Avenue, was purchased in 1859. The main interest attaching to the parish is its peculiar field of work among the deaf-mutes, of whom there are more than 100 among the

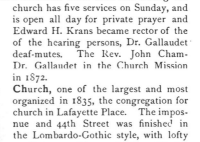

communicants. This free
two on every other day, and
meditation. The Rev. Dr.
parish in 1892, being pastor
devoting his energies to the
berlain is a co-laborer with
to Deaf-Mutes, incorporated
St. Bartholomew's
fashionable in the city, was
many years worshipping in a
ing building at Madison Ave-
1876. It is a fine example of
decorated front and a cam-
terior is handsomely treated
granite columns, carrying a

church has five services on Sunday, and
is open all day for private prayer and
Edward H. Krans became rector of the
of the hearing persons, Dr. Gallaudet
deaf-mutes. The Rev. John Cham-
Dr. Gallaudet in the Church Mission
in 1872.

Church, one of the largest and most
organized in 1835, the congregation for
church in Lafayette Place. The impos-
nue and 44th Street was finished in
the Lombardo-Gothic style, with lofty
panile tower with open belfry. The in-
in polychrome. Polished Scotch
triforium gallery and a clere-story,
support the lofty nave roof, and
all the appointments bespeak
the wealth of the congregation. The rector is the
Rev. Dr. David H.
Greer. Aside from
the usual benevolent
and missionary activi-
ties of a well-organ-
ized parish, there is St.
Bartholomew's Parish
House, on East 42d
Street, near Third
Avenue, erected in
1891, the gift of Mrs.
William H. Vander-
bilt and Cornelius
Vanderbilt. It is a
costly stone and brick

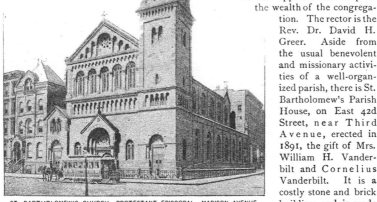

ST. BARTHOLOMEW'S CHURCH, PROTESTANT EPISCOPAL, MADISON AVENUE
AND EAST 44TH STREET.

building, and is made
the centre of an im-

portant religious and humane work among the poor of the East Side.

All Souls' Church, at Madison Avenue and 66th Street, is one of the most attractive Episcopal temples in the city, and is the home of the parish ministered to by the Rev. Dr. R. Heber Newton, the somewhat iconoclastic preacher. The parish was organized in 1859, and early in 1861 its first edifice, on West 48th Street, was consecrated as a memorial to the Rev. Dr. Henry Anthon. In 1890 the parish bought the property of the Church of the Holy Spirit, selling its former place of worship, and taking possession of the beautiful stone church which it now occupies. The building is in the Romanesque style, with a massive tower and an imposing front on Madison Avenue; and the interior is quaint and attractive, with richly tinted walls and a series of fine paintings on the rear wall of the chancel.

The Church of Zion and St. Timothy was formed in 1890 by the union of the two Episcopal parishes of Zion and St. Timothy,

ALL SOULS' CHURCH, PROTESTANT EPISCOPAL, MADISON AVENUE AND EAST 66TH STREET.

the latter having an organization dating back to 1853, while the former was formed in 1810, when the English Lutheran Church Zion conformed to the Episcopal Church.

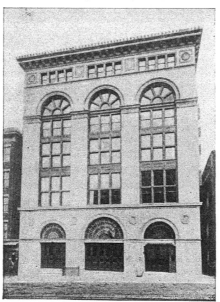

ST. BARTHOLOMEW'S PARISH HOUSE, 205 EAST 42D STREET.

The new Church of Zion and St. Timothy, at 332 West 57th Street, was erected in 1891. It is early Gothic in design, treated in a simple and massive manner, and with an avoidance of carving and minute detail, in order to bring the design within the rightful use of brick and stone, the latter being employed only when needed to strengthen the walls. A massive tower, with strongly marked pier-braces at the corners, is placed in the north of the main front, the plainness and severity of the latter being relieved by the staircase pinnacle and the deeply recessed doors and windows. On the 57th-Street elevation three sharply pointed gables relieve the monotony and give character to the design. The same simplicity of treatment marks the interior. The level of the sanctuary is several feet above the choir floor, giving greater dignity to altar and reredos, and the use of the customary chancel-arch has been avoided. The roof and side walls are on the same lines as those of the nave, but greatly enriched by extra braces in the open timber-work of the roof. A system of double trusses, supported by clustered stone columns at the four transept angles, divides the nave from the aisles and chancel, giving an appearance of greater length to the interior. The roofs are constructed entirely in open timber-work, in natural hard pine, colored to suit the expression of the interior, the walls of which are finished in red brick, relieved by gray brick in wide bands. Connected with the church there is a large parish-house, of similar construction. The combined parish is in charge of the Rev. Henry Lubeck, with the former rector of Zion Church, Dr. Charles C. Tiffany, as rector emeritus.

The Church of the Holy Trinity, at Madison Avenue and East 42d Street, was erected in 1873. It is near the Grand Central Depot, and its variegated brick and ivy-covered walls and lofty corner tower make it a conspicuous object. The parish was founded in 1864, by the younger Stephen H. Tyng, and the result of his early labors was a remarkable growth in many directions. In 1888 the Rev. E. Walpole Warren, an English "missioner," was called to the rectorship. He has introduced many new agencies for increasing the effectiveness of the parish. Holy Trinity has always been marked by the co-operation of its laymen, the practical character of its preaching, and its adherence to the "evangelical" school of churchmanship. It has a specially commendable boy choir. The parish has 840 communicants, with nearly a score of societies.

The Church of St. Mary the Virgin, at 228 West 45th Street, is the most ritualistic of the Episcopal churches of New York, with a daily celebration, an elaborate ceremonial, and all the usages of the advanced Anglo-Catholic school. The parish was organized in 1868, and the church was opened in 1870. It is a small Gothic building, and the interior is chiefly notable for its white marble altar, tabernacle and altar-screen; the hanging sanctuary lamps, and the sculptured figures of Christ,

CHURCH OF THE HOLY TRINITY, PROTESTANT EPISCOPAL, MADISON AVENUE AND EAST 42D STREET.

the Virgin and St. John; and of St. Paul (as founder of the British Church), on the pulpit. The Sunday and festal services are largely choral, and of the most elaborate and beautiful character. The parish is active in good work among the poor, supporting mission-house, schools, guilds, and other agencies for charitable work. The Rev. Thomas McKee Brown is rector and founder; and the church has 600 communicants, lovers of good deeds as well as æsthetic forms.

The Church of the Incarnation, at Madison Avenue and East 35th Street, is a modern Gothic temple, in a pleasant residence-quarter. The Rev. Dr. Arthur Brooks is the rector ; and the Rev. Newton Perkins has charge of the Chapel of the Reconciliation, at 246 East 31st Street. The church is a picturesque structure, built of dark sandstone, with many buttresses, a quaint entrance porch on the Madison-Avenue front, and a solid-looking square tower, at the corner nearest the intersection of the street and avenue. The spire was carried in 1892, after remaining thirty years incomplete, to its present height, as seen in the illustration. The front of the church is literally covered with ivy. It grows thickly around the bases of the buttresses at the side of the building, quite concealing the size of the church, which is one of the largest in the city.

All Angels' Church, at the corner of West-End Avenue and West 81st Street, was built in 1890. The society came into existence about the middle of the century, and had its first building in what is now Central Park. It occupies a corner-lot of 100 by 102 feet, and is 140 feet long, the builders having adopted the shrewd device of placing it diagonally. Dr. Charles F. Hoffman is the rector, and Rev. S. DeLancey Townsend, associate rector.

The Church of Holy Trinity, at Lenox Avenue and 122d Street, Harlem, is one of the recently erected Episcopal shrines. The building was consecrated in 1888, and is Italian Gothic in style, and substantially constructed of rough-faced Indiana limestone, with brownstone trimmings. A massive tower with long, narrow openings surmounts the main entrance on 122d Street, and the long frontage on Lenox Avenue is agreeably diversified by

CHURCH OF THE INCARNATION, PROTESTANT EPISCOPAL, MADISON AVENUE AND EAST 35TH STREET.

two gables and a small spire, breaking the monotony of the roof-line. The main feature of the spacious interior, which has a seating capacity of 1,200, and is cruciform in shape, with lofty arched roof, is the chancel, which is extremely decorative in its treatment. An oaken communion table, surrounded by the chancel rail, occupies the centre, and the Bishop's chair is behind it. The walls are finished in polished variegated marble, above which the effect of small galleries is produced by arched openings. There are two transept galleries, and the walls are decorated in terra cotta and buff. On the first floor of the Lenox-Avenue side are the parish parlors, and above them, the Sunday-school rooms. The parish was organized in 1868, and the Rev. William N. McVickar became the first rector. He was succeeded in 1884 by Dr. Randolph H. McKim, during whose term of office the parish grew rapidly, establishing in 1884 Holy Trinity Chapel and Holy Trinity Mission House and Day Nursery, on East 112th Street. The first church was built in 1870, on Fifth Avenue, at the corner of 125th Street. Under its successive rectors, Holy Trinity has enjoyed a continually increasing measure of prosperity, culminating in the present beautiful edifice, and a communicant list of 1,000. The Rev. Dr. C. D'Witt Bridgman is rector. The architect was William A. Potter.

St. Michael's Church, at Amsterdam Avenue and 99th Street, is one of the five picturesque and impressive ecclesiastical buildings which the Episcopalians have recently erected in the upper part of the city. St. Michael's parish was organized in 1807, the first church having been built the previous year. The second church was erected in 1854, and for many years the parish had but a feeble growth, owing to its situation far up-town. But in recent years the city has stretched out in this direction, and the increase in population has brought increasing prosperity, together with the need of larger accommodations. The pres-

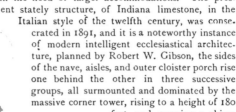

ent stately structure, of Indiana limestone, in the Italian style of the twelfth century, was conse- crated in 1891, and it is a noteworthy instance of modern intelligent ecclesiastical architec- ture, planned by Robert W. Gibson, the sides of the nave, aisles, and outer cloister porch rise one behind the other in three successive groups, all surmounted and dominated by the massive corner tower, rising to a height of 180 feet, and carrying a chime of bells. The windows and arcades are round-arched. The interior, in the shape of a Latin cross, is spacious and impressive. Massive square columns separate nave from aisles, and sup- port the lofty roof, which is panelled in wood. The wide round arches have ornamental faces, and the side walls are treated in terra cotta. The windows are filled with cathedral glass, and there are two

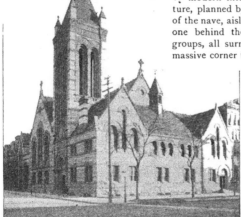

CHURCH OF THE HOLY TRINITY, PROTESTANT EPISCOPAL, LENOX AVENUE AND WEST 122D STREET.

large windows in the transepts. The church has sittings for 1,600 people. The total cost of the building, which is the crowning success of the 48 years' toiling of the rector, the Rev. Dr. T. M. Peters, in the upper part of the city, was nearly $200,000.

The Cathedral of St. John the Divine.— In 1885 the authorities of the Episcopal Church in the Diocese of New York began to agitate the subject of a cathedral, worthy of the increasing growth of the Church, and for a centre of its numerous religious and charitable activities. The result of the preliminary meetings and the public agitation of the subject was the receipt of subscriptions sufficient to warrant the purchase, at $850,000, of an eligible site between 110th and 113th Streets and Morningside and Tenth Avenues, then occupied by the Leake and Watts Orphan Asylum. Designs were then invited from the leading architects of the world; and after careful examination of the plans submitted, four were chosen for a second competition. Those of Heins & LaFarge were finally accepted, as a basis for beginning the work, the details of which will be determined as it proceeds. The

CATHEDRAL OF ST. JOHN THE DIVINE. (PROTESTANT EPISCOPAL.)
MORNINGSIDE PARK.

corner-stone was laid on St. John's Day, December 17, 1892, by Bishop Potter. In the amended drawings the ground-plan has the shape of a cross, the arms of which are formed by the nave and transepts and chancel, with central and side aisles. The gen-eral exterior design is that of a group of seven towers; two at the west front; a large central tower or lantern over the crossing of the transepts and nave; and four smaller flanking towers at the angles of the cross. There are to be entrances in each of these flanking towers, as well as in those on the west. The central tower alone is crowned by a spire, which is to dominate the group. Around the chancel will be seven apsidal chapels, each capable of seating 150 persons; and a high arcaded balustrade will crown the cornices of the side-aisles, whose buttresses will

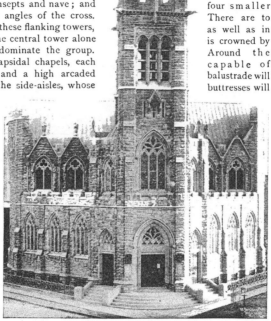

ALL ANGELS' CHURCH, PROTESTANT EPISCOPAL, WEST-END AVENUE AND WEST 81st STREET.

be surmounted by figures of angels with folded wings. The cathedral will face towards the west, and the chapels will appear to rise abruptly from the retaining wall of Morningside Park.

The principal dimensions of the cathedral, as proposed, are as follows: Total length outside, 520 feet. Width across the front, 192 feet; across the transepts, 290 feet. Width of the front towers, 57 feet, and their height 248 feet. The width of the four flanking towers will be 43 feet, and their height 158 feet. The total exterior diameter of the central tower is to be 116, and its interior diameter 96 feet, with a height of 253 feet for the vaulting, and 445 feet from the floor of the cathedral to the top of the cross. The chancel will have a depth of 120 feet, and the nave will be 60 feet in width, with a length of 180 feet and a height of 105 feet, while the front gable will tower aloft to the height of 164 feet. The building will be constructed in the most substantial manner, and its total cost will probably reach $6,900,000 or more, of which it is proposed to expend $200,000 yearly until the construction is completed. As seen from the streets of Harlem the spire of the cathedral will appear higher than that of the Cologne Cathedral, and with the exception of Ulm Minster and the Eiffel Tower, it will be the highest structure in the world when measured from the street-level. Years will elapse before its completion, but when finished the Cathedral of St. John the Divine will be the noblest ecclesiastical building in America, rivalling the grand cathedrals of England and the Continent.

The First Presbyterian Church is the oldest local society of that denomina-‧ tion. It was formed in 1717, and the early meetings were held in the City Hall. In 1719 the famous Wall-Street Church was opened, and here George Whitefield preached in 1740. The church now occupied by the parish, on Fifth Avenue, between West 11th and 12th Streets, was erected in 1845. It is a rich Gothic structure, of graceful and stately proportions, and with a dignified and spacious interior. The first pastor was James Anderson, a Scotch clergyman, installed in 1717. Dr. John Rodgers, "the Father of Presbyterianism" in New York, was

another early minister. Dr. Howard Duffield is now in charge.

The Presbyterians began their services in 1706, with private meetings at the houses of a few families of Presbyterian sympathies. In 1707 the Rev. Francis McKemie preached to a small congregation in a private house, and baptized a child. He was arrested by order of Lord Cornbury and thrown into prison, but was soon released. From 1719 to 1809 there was but one Presbyterian church, the Wall-Street, with the church in Beekman Street, erected in 1768, and that in Rutgers Street, built in 1797, as Collegiate charges. The Collegiate relation was dissolved in 1809. The Presbyterian churches of the city are divided among the Presbyterians proper, the Reformed Presbyterians and the United Presbyterians. The first is much the strongest, having 53 churches, while the others have

FIRST PRESBYTERIAN CHURCH, FIFTH AVENUE, BETWEEN 11TH AND 12TH STREETS.

but five each. The Presbyterian Church is to New York what Congregationalism is to New England, a strong and aggressive religious force. It has 30,000 members.

The Scotch Presbyterian Church, recently on 14th Street, was organized in 1756 by a party of seceders from the old Wall-Street Church, under the name of the First Associate Reformed Church. The chief cause of the formation of the new society was difference of opinion regarding the use of musical instruments in the church. The first pastor was the Rev. John Mason, a Scottish clergyman, and the first church stood on Cedar Street. In 1837 the congregation removed to a church on Grand Street ; and in 1853 the church on West 14th Street was opened. Rev. Dr. David G. Wylie is the pastor. The church in 1893 occupied a new edifice, at 96th Street and Central Park West.

The Brick Presbyterian Church, at Fifth Avenue and 37th Street, one of the most important Presbyterian churches in the city, was erected in 1858, supplanting the old Brick Church, which had stood since 1767 on the corner of Beekman and

BRICK MEETING-HOUSE, PARK ROW, NASSAU AND BEEKMAN STREETS, IN 1800.

Nassau Streets. The new church is a partial reproduction in brick and brownstone of the older edifice, on a much larger scale ; and its interior, recently redecorated by La-Farge, is very attractive. The parish was formed by members of the First Presbyterian Church, and for forty-two years the two branches continued their organic connection, with one session and the same trustees. The first pastor was the famous Dr. John Rodgers. He was succeeded in 1810 by the Rev. Dr. Gardiner Spring, who remained in office for sixty-two years. The Rev. Dr. Wm. G. T. Shedd, late of Union Theological Seminary, was one of his colleagues. The present pastor, the Rev. Dr. Henry Van Dyke, was installed in 1883, and his ability as a pulpit orator has attracted a large and representative congregation. Its Christianity is simple, practical, and non-sectarian.

The Fifth-Avenue Presbyterian Church was organized in 1808, and its first church was erected on Cedar Street in that year. The Rev. John Brodhead Romeyn became the first pastor, retaining his connection with the parish until his death, in 1825. In common with all the earlier churches, the Cedar-Street parish made several removals farther up-town ; in 1834, to Duane Street ; in 1852, to its first Fifth-Avenue church, at the corner of 19th Street, when the corporate name was changed to the present title ; and again, in 1875, to its present location, at the corner of 55th Street. It is an ornate Gothic structure of imposing proportions, and the interior differs widely from the traditional simplicity

BRICK PRESBYTERIAN CHURCH, NORTHWEST CORNER OF FIFTH AVENUE AND 37TH STREET.

and plainness of the older Presbyterian churches. There is an abundance of rich coloring and elaborate carving ; light woods are effectively used in the panelling of the walls ; and the floor slopes gradually down from the entrance to the pulpit, giving something of the effect of a public hall. The pastor, Rev. John Hall, D. D., LL. D., was installed November 3, 1867. The church is foremost, probably, in its gifts to missionary and benevolent work in the Presbyterian denomination, if not in the United States ; and occupies a position of noble prominence among the Christian societies of the world.

The **University-Place Presbyterian Church** was organized in 1845, by a colony from the older Duane-Street Church. The present substantial stone church,

on University Place, at the corner of East 10th Street, was erected in 1844 by private subscription. In 1870 the congregation received a large and important addition to its numbers from the Mercer-Street Church, which, after a prosperous existence since 1835, had been so greatly weakened by the building of up-town churches that it was compelled to sell its place of worship to the Church of the Strangers, and unite with the University-Place congregation. Thus strengthened and invigorated, the parish has enjoyed continued prosperity. The Rev. Dr. George Alexander is pastor.

The **West Presbyterian Church** was organized in 1829, with eighteen members, and its first house of worship was erected on Carmine Street, in 1832. There, for many years, the congregation grew and prospered. The present ecclesiastical structure, on West 42d Street, near Sixth Avenue, was erected in 1862. It is a noble example of the decorative Gothic style, with lofty roof and gabled entrance and tapering spire. The auditorium, seating 1,200, is striking and attractive. Four broad

FIFTH-AVENUE PRESBYTERIAN CHURCH, FIFTH AVENUE AND 55TH STREET.

and sweeping arches span the interior, one at either side and end, crossing near their spring from the gallery floor. The large round arch at the pulpit end is supported by massive pillars of polished stone, and roomy galleries sweep in a circle around three sides of the auditorium. A large chapel and spacious parish-rooms are con-nected with the church. Under the care of the Rev. Dr. John R. Paxton, one of the best-known preachers in the city, the West Church has gathered a large and fashionable congregation, with a goodly record of practical charities.

The **Fourth-Avenue Presbyterian Church**, at 286 Fourth Avenue, corner of 22d Street, was long in charge of the Rev. Dr. Howard Crosby, so well known as a reformer and earnest worker in the temperance cause. The church was built in 1856, and Dr. Crosby, in virtue of his prominence in public affairs, as well as his solid merits as a pulpit orator, attracted a large and influential congregation. The Fourth-Avenue Church became one of the most noted in the city, active in reform movements and greatly given to practical Christian work among the poor and wretched. The church is substantially built, after the Gothic manner, and has an attractive interior, but its chief claim to public notice is its goodly record in the past. It adjoins the 23d-Street Branch of the Young Men's Christian Association, and a view of the church is shown elsewhere with the Association Building.

The **Madison-Square Presbyterian Church**, at Madison Avenue and 24th Street, was organized in 1853, in response to the growing demand for churches in

MADISON-SQUARE PRESBYTERIAN CHURCH, MADISON AVENUE AND 24TH STREET.

what was then the up-town portion of the city. Its original membership was drawn mainly from the Central Presbyterian Church, in Broome Street, and the Rev. Dr. William Adams left the pastorate of the Central Church to assume that of the new organization. Public worship was begun in the chapel of the Union Theological Seminary; and subsequently the services were held in Hope Chapel, on Broadway, until the present building was ready for occupancy, in December, 1854. The church is built of brownstone, in a simple style of Gothic architecture; and contains, besides the auditorium, which has a seating capacity of 1,200, a large Sunday-school room and lecture-room. In November, 1873, after a long and fruitful pastorate of more than twenty years, Dr. Adams tendered his resignation, in order to assume the duties of the Presidency of the Union Theological Seminary. In 1875 the Rev. Dr. William Tucker was installed as pastor. He resigned in 1879, to assume the chair of sacred rhetoric in Andover Theological Seminary. The present pastor, the Rev. Dr. Charles H. Parkhurst, was installed in 1880. The history of the church has been a record of continuous progress, and its present membership is nearly 800. A mission Sunday-school, started in 1858, has gradually grown into the Adams Memorial Church, at 211 East 30th Street, which is now ecclesiastically independent, **and** dependent financially only in a slight degree. The resources of the parent church, no longer required in this direction, are now devoted to the maintenance of the Mission and Church House at 30th Street and Third Avenue, where there is being carried on a variety of religious and humane work.

The Church of the Covenant was founded in 1860 by the Rev. Dr. George L. Prentiss, in the interest of the New School of Liberal Presbyterians. For some time the services were held in the chapel of the Home for the Friendless, in East 23d Street. The church was formally organized in 1862, and the graceful stone building at Park Avenue and 35th Street was dedicated in 1865. Few of the more modern structures surpass it in beauty of design, spaciousness and attractiveness. Dr. J. H. McIlvaine is the pastor.

ADAMS MEMORIAL CHURCH, PRESBYTERIAN, 211 EAST 30TH STREET.

The Westminster Presbyterian Church, at 210 West 23d Street, has 500 members. Its commodious stone edifice, near Seventh Avenue, has recently been extensively improved ; and it is hoped that the church will long maintain this valuable down-town position. The pastor is Dr. Robert F. Sample, well known as a preacher and author.

The Madison-Avenue Presbyterian Church was organized in 1844, and in 1871 took possession of the Gothic building which had been erected at Madison Avenue and 53d Street, to meet the need of a Presbyterian church in that vicinity.

It is a lofty brownstone structure, in the simple Gothic style so much affected in the ecclesiastical architecture of the middle of the present century, which was largely imitative in character. The large auditorium, seating near'y 1,600, is decorated in neutral tints. The church has enjoyed the services

CHURCH OF THE COVENANT, PRESBYTERIAN, PARK AVENUE AND 35TH STREET.

24

WESTMINSTER PRESBYTERIAN CHURCH,
210 WEST 23D STREET.

of a succession of powerful preachers. Under the pastorate of the Rev. Dr. Charles L. Thompson it has become one of the most influential of the Presbyterian churches in the city. In 1892 it was converted into a People's Church, with free pews, and a variety of educational, philanthropic and religious enterprises.

The Central Presbyterian Church, at 220 West 57th Street, was built in 1878. It is a large and sightly stone structure, with tower and pinnacles, and a spacious auditorium, decorated with light colors. The society was formed by the Rev. William Patton, who in 1820 began preaching to a handful of people in a school-room on Mulberry Street. A church was built on Broome Street in 1821. Dr. Patton continued with the parish until 1834, building up a strong and zealous congregation of nearly 1,000 members. During all its changes of location and ministers the church has prospered, becoming one of the prominent Presbyterian societies. Its pastor is Rev. Dr. W. Merle Smith.

The Phillips Presbyterian Church, at Madison Avenue and East 73d Street, built in 1858, is a lofty brick edifice in the Gothic style of architecture. The auditorium is nearly square, with arched ceiling and pleasing decorative work on the walls. The organ occupies an elevated position at the east end of the church and is flanked on either side by two small galleries. The parish was formed in 1844, and its church, erected by the generous gifts of James Lenox, stood in East 15th Street. Rev. Dr. George L. Spining is the pastor.

The Park Presbyterian Church, at 86th Street and Amsterdam Avenue, was founded in 1853, and called the 84th-Street Presbyterian Church. Francis L. Patton, President of Princeton University, was pastor for awhile. In 1879 the present pastor, Rev. Anson P. Atterbury, took charge. In 1882 a new location was purchased; and two years later the society moved into the new building. The church is prospering greatly.

The West-End Presbyterian Church, at Amsterdam Avenue and 105th Street, is an example of the rapid multiplication of new and beautiful church edifices in the upper part of the city. The church was organized in 1888, and for two years worshipped in its attractive chapel in the

CENTRAL PRESBYTERIAN CHURCH.
220 WEST 57TH STREET.

CHURCH OF THE PURITANS, PRESBYTERIAN, 15 WEST 130TH STREET.

rear of the church, pending the completion of the latter. The corner-stone was laid June 22, 1891. The church is constructed of yellow pressed brick, with ornamental line work, in the Romanesque style, and presents an extremely picturesque external appearance, with its stately corner tower and highly decorated round-arch entrances on the avenue. The auditorium is spacious and tastefully decorated, and a large gallery extends around three sides. The Rev. Dr. John Balcom Shaw is the pastor.

The Church of the Puritans, at 15 West 130th Street, near Fifth Avenue, is one of the leading churches of Harlem, and has grown with great prosperity and vigor. It was organized in 1872, as the Second Presbyterian Church of Harlem. The present name arose from the generosity of the Rev. Dr. George B. Cheever, who gave to the new church the funds resulting from the sale of the lease of the Church of the Puritans in Union Square, which had for long years a national reputation from the character of its people and the public spirit and ability of Dr. Cheever. This noble gift of about $87,000 was coupled with the condition that the Harlem church should adopt the name of the older society. One of the finest church buildings in New York was then erected and fully paid for, by the aid of the Church Extension Committee of the New-York Presbytery and the self-sacrificing offerings of its members. The church is Gothic in architecture, and beautifully decorated, in simple and elegant taste, much of the carved

PARK PRESBYTERIAN CHURCH, AMSTERDAM AVENUE AND WEST 86TH STREET.

woodwork and plaster-work having been designed and executed by Rev. Dr. Edward L. Clark, the pastor for more than twenty years, until 1893. The church has steadily advanced in a noble and liberal spirit of Christian love and charity. It has partaken of the wide influence of the church after which it was named, and has been a power for righteousness in the great community of Harlem.

The Washington-Heights Presbyterian Church, at 155th Street and Amsterdam Avenue, was built in 1860. The Rev. Dr. Charles A. Stoddard was its pastor for 25 years, during which time the church was built and paid for. He resigned to become editor of the *New-York Observer.* The Rev. Dr. John C. Bliss is the present pastor. Isaac L. Peet, LL. D., of the Deaf and Dumb Institution, the officers of the Juvenile Asylum and the Colored

WASHINGTON-HEIGHTS PRESBYTERIAN CHURCH, AMSTERDAM AVENUE AND WEST 155TH STREET.

Orphan Asylum, Shepherd Knapp, William A. Wheelock, F. N. DuBois and many others, have been, or are, members of this congregation. The building occupies ground which once formed part of the estate of Audubon, the naturalist, and over which the battle of Harlem Heights was fought ; and some mementoes of this battle were found in digging for foundations. The church is free from debt, and is in a prosperous and healthy condition. It is a landmark in this locality.

RUTGERS RIVERSIDE PRESBYTERIAN CHURCH, BOULEVARD AND 73D STREET.

The Rutgers Riverside Presbyterian Church dates back to 1798, when this and the Brick and Wall-Street societies formed the three collegiate Presbyterian churches of New York. Milledoler, McClellan, McCauley and Krebs were its early pastors. The handsome church on Madison Avenue pertained to the Madison-Avenue society, which united with the Rutgers. In 1888 the church was sold to the Freemasons. This famous old society is now flourishing amain, in its beautiful new home at the Boulevard and 73d Street. The Rev. Dr. R. R. Booth is the pastor.

The Riverdale Presbyterian Church was organized in 1863, and the present church-building, a very pretty Gothic structure, designed by Renwick, was completed the same year. The first pastor was Rev. Dr. George M. Boynton. He was followed in 1867 by Rev. Dr. H. H. Stebbins, in 1874 by Rev. Charles H. Burr, and in 1879 by Rev. William R. Lord. Rev. Ira S. Dodd was installed in 1883, and is the present pastor. For many years the Riverdale Church has maintained a mission at Spuyten Duyvil. In 1889 a beautiful new chapel, called, after the old one, the Edgehill Chapel, was completed at Spuyten Duyvil, where it is the only house of worship. The evening service of the church is now held there.

There is also a flourishing Sunday-school and Society of Christian Endeavor at Spuyten Duyvil. The morning service is held at the church at Riverdale. The Riverdale Church is the most northerly in the New-York Presbytery. The gray stone church and parsonage are among the most picturesque and beautiful in suburban New York.

The First Reformed Presbyterian Church, at 123 West Twelfth Street, was opened in 1849. The society, organized in 1797, was the first Reformed Presbyterian organization in America. The early meetings were held in school-rooms, shops and other humble places, until the building of a small church in Chambers Street, in 1801. In 1845 the Union Presbyterian Church on Prince Street was purchased. For nearly three-quarters of a century the church had but two pastors, Dr. Alexander McLeod and his son, Rev. John Niel McLeod, who labored faithfully for this devoted

FIRST METHODIST PLACE OF WORSHIP IN NEW YORK, 120 WILLIAM STREET.

flock. Later pastors have been Wm. Wylie, 1874; J. M. Stephens, 1887; and James D. Steele, Ph. D., the present incumbent, installed in 1891.

The John-Street Methodist-Episcopal Church, the first organized society of that denomination in America, was formed by Philip Embury in 1766, with four or five members. The meetings were held in Embury's house, and later in a rigging loft on William Street, until 1768, when a stone church, 60 feet long and 42 in width, was built in John Street, and called Wesley Chapel. The exterior walls of the church were covered with blue plaster, and for some years the interior was left unfinished, the only means of ascent to the galleries being by means of ladders. At that period in the colonial history no public services could be performed in churches except such as were established by law, and a fire-place and chimney were among

JOHN-STREET METHODIST-EPISCOPAL CHURCH,
44 JOHN STREET.

the internal fittings of the building, in order that it might legally be regarded as a private dwelling. A second church was erected on the same site in 1817; and in 1841 the third and present structure was built, somewhat smaller than the earlier building, with two brick houses, one on each side, as a source of income. The external appearance of the church, which is Doric in its style, is simple and plain, and the interior is devoid of any striking features. The only relics of the old John-Street Church which have been preserved are its venerable clock, the gift of John Wesley, and its library. The site of the church, 44 John Street, has been called "the cradle of American Methodism." The John-Street Church has been the mother of many churches. It has long been the Mecca of American Methodists.

Its pastor is the Rev. F. G. Howell. The Methodist-Episcopal Church was formally organized in America in 1773. In 1817 there were five churches of that denomination in New York : the John-Street ; the Forsyth-Street, consecrated in 1789 ; the Duane-Street, in 1797 ; the Two-Mile-Stone (now Seventh-Street) ; and the Allen-Street. The denomination now ranks among the foremost in the city, with 57 churches and 14,000 members.

The Seventh-Street Methodist-Episcopal Church was formed in 1786 by the Rev. William Veloe, a zealous local preacher from the John-Street Church. The earlier meetings were held in a private residence,

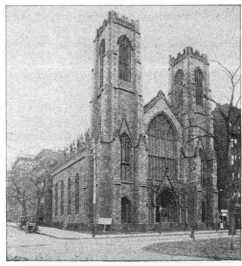

ASBURY METHODIST-EPISCOPAL CHURCH, WASHINGTON SQUARE
AND WASHINGTON PLACE.

and were known as the "Two - Mile - Stone Meetings." Later the Village Academy on the Bowery was used for the meetings, and here Bishop Asbury preached. The first church edifice was erected in 1818, near the Academy, and became known as the Bowery Village Church. The building was soon removed to 7th Street, near Second Avenue, and here the tumult of a long revival so troubled the wealthy families who had colonized St. Mark's Place, that they gladly offered to give two lots near Third Avenue and other considerations to have the church removed. The offer was accepted, and the church was moved to the present site. The more modern edifice was erected in 1836, and is a plain brick structure of

MADISON-AVENUE CHURCH, METHODIST-EPISCOPAL, MADISON AVENUE AND EAST 60TH STREET.

the Grecian temple style, with large columns at the front. The chief interest of the church is its age. The pastor is the Rev. J. V. Saunders.

The Asbury Methodist-Episcopal Church, at the corner of Washington Square East and Washington Place, is a rich old society, with an average Sunday congregation of fewer than a hundred, owing to the general occupation of the vicinity

ST. ANDREW'S METHODIST-EPISCOPAL CHURCH, WEST 11TH STREET, NEAR COLUMBUS AVENUE.

by foreigners. Its two towers are familiar features in the picturesque environment of Washington Square. In 1893 its members joined the Washington-Place M. E. Church.

The Madison-Avenue Methodist-Episcopal Church, an impressive brownstone building in the Romanesque style, at Madison

SWEDISH METHODIST-EPISCOPAL CHURCH, LEXINGTON
AVENUE AND EAST 52D STREET.

Avenue and East 60th Street, was built in 1882. Its most striking external features are the graceful tower and the pleasing variation of its lines. The auditorium is large and tastefully decorated. This was General Grant's spiritual home during his last years; and the large and fashionable congregation sustains many practical and beneficent charities.

St. Andrew's Methodist-Episcopal Church, on 76th Street, near Columbus Avenue, has grown out of a prayer-meeting held 25 years ago, on West 69th Street, by Townsend H. Harrington. Under the auspices of the New-York City Sunday-School and Missionary Society it began, in 1882, to occupy a neat stone chapel at West 71st Street, near Columbus Avenue. The present church was com-pleted and dedicated June 8, 1890. It is in the early Romanesque style, the front being of Indiana limestone; and is one of the hand-somest Methodist churches in the city. Be-sides the church, there is a chapel and parsonage. The interior is novel and charming as a place of worship, and has several exquisite stained-glass windows; and the whole is admirably lighted and venti-lated.

The Swedish Methodist-Episcopal **Church** is a plain and spacious structure at the corner of Lexington Avenue and East 52d Street, and has a large and devout constituency among the Scandina-vians of the city.

Calvary Metho-dist-Episcopal Church is said to have the largest congrega-tion of any church of that denomination in the city, although it is of recent formation, the organization having been effected in 1883. In 1887 a commodious brick edifice was built at the corner of Seventh Avenue and 129th

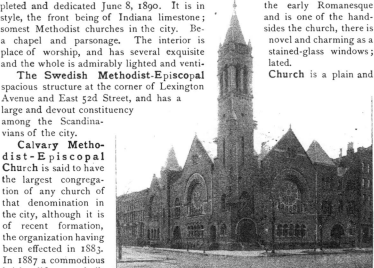

CALVARY METHODIST-EPISCOPAL CHURCH, SEVENTH AVENUE AND
WEST 129TH STREET.

Street, under the pastorate of Rev. F. M. North, D. D., and largely through the generosity of the late J. B. Cornell. In 1890, in the pastorate of Rev. James R. Day, D. D., this edifice was more than doubled in its seating capacity, and is now the largest Protestant church auditorium in the city. The church is Romanesque in style, with a massive tower, impressive from its size but not strikingly picturesque in treatment. It is attractively furnished and decorated, and abundantly lighted from three large Catharine-wheel windows and numerous smaller ones, and from a beautiful stained-glass opening in the flat panelled ceiling. A spacious gallery, with graceful horseshoe curve, accommodating 800 people, sweeps around three sides of the auditorium, and there is a feeling of roominess and light which adds to the general attractiveness. A large lecture-room and several Sunday-school rooms are connected with the church. The pastor is the Rev. Dr. James R. Day.

The Park-Avenue Methodist-Episcopal Church is at the corner of Park Avenue and 86th Street, near Central Park. It is an ancient society, dating its origin from about the year 1836, when its little congregation of five members began to meet in a chamber over a grocery store. Then for a time it held meetings at the house of Gilbert Bates, at Third Avenue and 84th Street; and afterwards it bought the church of the Bowery Village, and re- erected it at Third Avenue and 86th Street. This little band of wor- shippers retained its connection with the Harlem Mission until after the great revival of 1842, when it became inde- pendent. Its new church on the old site was dedicated by Bishop Janes, in 1859; and in 1884 its pres- ent handsome brownstone church was dedicated by Bish- op Warren. Under the place where the preacher stands are several of the great tim- bers shaped by Philip Em- bury, and used in the origi- nal John-Street Church, and afterwards in the Bowery Church. The society has now 600 members, and is flourishing nobly, under the ministration of the Rev. Fer- dinand C. Iglehart.

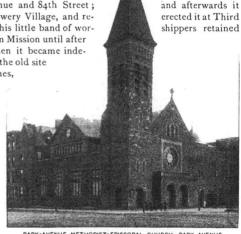

PARK-AVENUE METHODIST-EPISCOPAL CHURCH, PARK AVENUE AND 86TH STREET.

St. James' Methodist-Episcopal Church, at Madison Avenue and 126th Street, is a noble outgrowth of the historic Harlem Mission. Its early meetings were held at John James's house, on 125th Street, between Third Avenue and Lex- ington Avenue; in a store on Third Avenue; in 1831 in the Academy on 120th Street, between Second and Third Avenues; and in its church built in 1834 on 125th Street between Third and Fourth Avenues. In 1869 the society bought land at its present site; and in 1870 Bishop Janes laid the corner-stone of the present fine brownstone church, which was dedicated in 1871, at which time the society received the name of St. James's. This handsome and attractive edifice is adjoined by a chapel and a parsonage. The society has over 700 members. Its pastor is the Rev. Jacob E. Price, D. D.

The First Baptist Church was formed in 1762, by the reorganization of the Gold-Street congregation, and under the zealous ministry of the Rev. John Gano, which lasted through the Revolutionary era, when the people were scattered, and the church became a stable. A larger stone church was opened in 1802; followed by a still

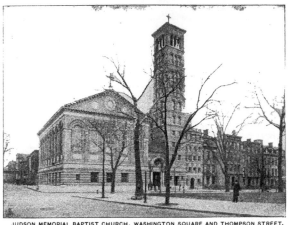

JUDSON MEMORIAL BAPTIST CHURCH, WASHINGTON SQUARE AND THOMPSON STREET.

more spacious temple, at Broome and Elizabeth Streets, in 1842. In 1871 the great Gothic church at Park Avenue and 39th Street was dedicated; and when the encroachments of trade made this locality undesirable, the property was sold, in 1890, and the society occupied the brick chapel on West 81st Street. The First Church has had but nine pastors, in 131 years; and among them were the Rev. John Gano, the patriotic Revolutionary chaplain, who offered the prayer of thanksgiving at Newburgh; the Rev. Dr. Spencer H. Cone, long-time President of the American and Foreign Bible Society and the American Bible Union, and one of the leaders in the re-translation of the Scriptures; and Rev. Dr. Thomas B. Anderson, pastor from 1862 to 1878, a genial, scholarly and eloquent divine. The Rev. Isaac M. Haldeman became pastor in 1884. The new edifice of the First Baptist Church on 81st Street, between West-End Avenue and the Boulevard, is an architectural gem, and has but few superiors in the metropolis.

The Baptists began work in New York before 1669; and their first preacher, William Wickenden of Rhode Island, was imprisoned for several months. The first church, founded in 1712, died in 1720; and its successor, founded in 1745, advanced but slowly, holding worship for some years in a rigging-loft in Horse and

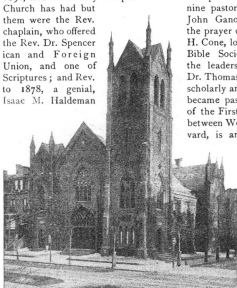

ST. JAMES METHODIST-EPISCOPAL CHURCH, MADISON AVENUE.

Cart Lane (now William Street). In 1760 the society built a small stone church on Gold Street. The city now has 44 Baptist churches, with 14,000 members, who support many commendable institutions.

The Judson Memorial Baptist Church, on Washington Square, succeeds the old Berean Baptist Church, organized in 1838, and formerly worshipping in Downing Street. The imposing group of buildings in Washington Square was completed in 1892, at a cost of $450,000, as a memorial to the Rev. Dr. Adoniram Judson, the first American foreign missionary. The main building, Greco-Romanesque in style, is a handsome structure of ornate buff brick, with a conspicuous tall square tower, surmounted by a cross which at night is illuminated by electricity. It contains a beautiful auditorium, with massive columns and marble wainscoting, and

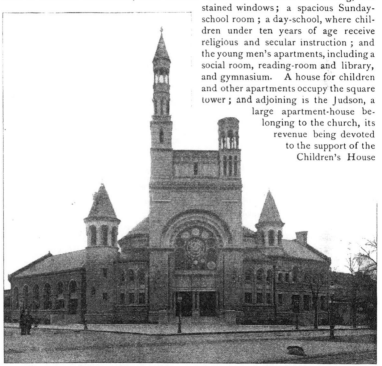

stained windows; a spacious Sunday-school room ; a day-school, where children under ten years of age receive religious and secular instruction ; and the young men's apartments, including a social room, reading-room and library, and gymnasium. A house for children and other apartments occupy the square tower ; and adjoining is the Judson, a large apartment-house belonging to the church, its revenue being devoted to the support of the Children's House

FIRST BAPTIST CHURCH, BOULEVARD AND WEST 79TH STREET.

and other philanthropic activities. The excellent music is rendered by a chorus choir of 100 young persons. The work of the church is mainly among the crowded population of the neighborhood, which is rapidly increasing, owing to the replacement of small old-fashioned dwellings by tall apartment-houses, holding from twelve to sixteen families each. The Rev. Dr. Edward Judson is pastor. The architects were McKim, Mead & White.

Baptist Church of the Epiphany, Madison Avenue and 64th Street, is the home of a strong religious organization. It is one of the oldest Baptist societies in the city, with a history running back in unbroken succession to the year 1791, when a few members of the Second Baptist Church organized the Fayette-Street Baptist society, and in 1795 erected a small wooden meeting-house, on the corner of Oliver and Henry Streets. There the congregation remained until 1860, when a new church was built in 33d Street. Still later, a larger and finer church was occupied, on 53d Street, but a troublesome lawsuit led to the dispossession of the congregation, and the erection of the present brownstone Gothic edifice in 1882. The Madison-Avenue front is quite imposing, with its lofty gable and double towers. The attractively decorated auditorium has a high open roof, and seats about 1,000.

BAPTIST CHURCH OF THE EPIPHANY, MADISON AVENUE AND EAST 64TH STREET.

Calvary Church is one of the strongest Baptist congregations, as its ecclesiastical home is one of the finest. The parish was organized in 1846; its first pastor and many of its members coming from the old Stanton-Street Baptist Church. Its first place of worship was Hope Chapel, on Broadway; but so great was the success of the work, under the Rev. Dr. John Dowling, that in 1854 a large brownstone edifice was erected on 23d Street. One of the noted pastors of the church was the Rev. Dr. Gillette, who acted as the spiritual adviser to the conspirators who murdered President Lincoln. The present pastor is the Rev. Dr. Robert S. MacArthur, one of the most eloquent preachers in the city. The church was erected in 1883. It occupies a commanding position on West 57th Street, near Seventh Avenue, and close by the new Music Hall. It is Gothic in style, substantially built of Albion red sandstone and Lockport stone; and with its tall steeple, smaller tower, and long extended front it makes an imposing show. Above the central doors is a magnificent Catharine-wheel window, twenty feet in diameter, filled with richly stained and jewelled glass. The interior appointments are beautiful and complete. The main auditorium, sloping down from the entrance toward the pulpit, has a seating capacity of nearly 1,500, and is abundantly lighted by many windows of richly colored glass, some of them being memorials. In the centre of the lofty ceiling is a large lantern, whose central part is carried up into a dome, with sides and top filled with painted glass, producing a very rich effect. Galleries, in a horseshoe curve, are carried around three sides of the auditorium, and behind the imposing bronze pulpit and over the baptistery, a triplet of richly carved panels with central medallions form an effective background. The organ is one of the largest and finest in the city, containing 41 speaking registers, divided among three manuals. On the east of the auditorium is a beautiful chapel for special services. The membership is over 1,900, and the parish is the centre of much religious and humane work, one of its adjuncts being a mission on 68th Street, near the Boulevard, which is doing a valuable work in that vicinity.

The North Baptist Church, at 234 West 11th Street, was erected in 1882, to replace the church on Christopher Street, which had been built in 1828. It is an attractive Gothic building, with a large and pleasant auditorium. The society was organized in 1827, with twelve members, and the early meetings were held in the school-house on Amos (now West 10th) Street. The congregation afterwards removed to the old Green-wich-Village Watch-house, where the Rev. Jacob H. Bronner began a long and successful pastorate. Rev. John J. Bronner, the present pastor, was installed in 1869.

Trinity Baptist Church was founded in 1866 by Dr. J. Stanford Holme, who began preaching in a small hall on West 52d Street. A large congregation was soon gathered, and in 1870 the church of the Eleventh Presbyterian society, at 141 East 55th Street, was purchased, and here the congregation has remained and prospered.

The Baptist Tabernacle, at 166 Second Avenue, adjoining the Historical Society, was formed in 1839 by members of the older Mulberry-Street Church. In 1850 the church left Mulberry Street, and erected the present Gothic edifice during

CALVARY BAPTIST CHURCH, 57TH STREET, BETWEEN SIXTH AND SEVENTH AVENUES.

Dr. Edward Lathrop's pastorate. In 1886 the present pastor, Dr. D. C. Potter, remodelled the interior, making it an amphitheatre. He also added the large parish-house adjoining. The church has important missions and country houses, and one of the largest and finest organs in the city. The late Dr. A. C. Kendrick and Dr. Wayland Hoyt were among its pastors.

The Madison-Avenue Baptist Church is another of the leading societies of this denomination. It was organized in 1839, as the Rose-Hill Baptist Church. Its first meeting-house, on Lexington Avenue, is now occupied by the Moravian Brethren. The substantial stone edifice at Madison Avenue and East 31st Street was erected in 1858. The large auditorium, seating nearly 1,200, is tastefully decorated. Dr. Henry M. Saunders is the pastor.

MADISON-AVENUE BAPTIST CHURCH, MADISON AVENUE
AND EAST 31ST STREET.

The Fifth-Avenue Baptist Church, at 6 West 46th Street, was erected in 1861. It is a plain brown-stone building, with a large and taste-fully decorated auditorium. Its pulpit was acceptably filled for forty years by Dr. Thomas Armitage, who resigned in 1888. The society was organized in 1841, and before the removal to 46th Street it worshipped in a church on Norfolk Street. Because of its prominent and wealthy members, it is regarded as one of the foremost Baptist congregations of New York.

St. Matthew's Church, at 354 Broome Street, is the oldest Lutheran society in the city. In 1841 the church in Walker Street was purchased from the English Lutherans, and in 1868 the church in Broome Street was bought from the Baptists, and has ever since remained the ecclesiastical house of the German Lutherans in its vicinity.

The Lutherans were early comers to New York. They first attempted to hold services in 1653, about the time of the Indian massacres at Pavonia and Hoboken; but Governor Stuyvesant issued a proclamation, the first in New York against freedom of conscience, forbidding the people to assemble for any public service contrary to that of the Reformed Church.

He was rebuked by the Dutch West India Company for his intolerance, and the Rev. Ernestus Goetwater was sent out from Holland to organize a Lutheran church. But he was igno-miniously sent back, and the members were heavily fined. According to the old Dutch records, still extant, and in the custody of this church, the congregation again sought recognition in 1656, but it was again re-fused. The Lutheran Church was formally recognized by the English Governor, Rich-ard Nicolls. The document bears date 1664. Their first church-edifice stood near where now Bowling Green

FIFTH-AVENUE BAPTIST CHURCH, 6 WEST 46TH STREET.

is. According to an order of the Dutch, who had again taken possession of the island, it was razed to the ground, with many other buildings, because it was deemed an obstacle to a proper defence in case of an attack. But the government paid the congregation 45 guilders in cash, and gave it a new plot of ground to build on. The documents bearing on this transaction bear the signatures of A. Colve, Governor, and N. Bayard, Secretary. The property which the government gave in lieu of the former ground and church is designated as "No. 5, west of Broadway, between the property of George Cobbet and the City-wall"; date, "May 22, 1674." It was four rods square. Up to 1749 the services were held entirely in the Dutch language, although the Germans preponderated as eight to one. From that time the Germans demanded services in their own tongue. When this was refused, they separated, and organized as the Lutheran German Christ Church, and bought an old brewery on what is now Cliff Street. In 1767 they built the "Swamp Church," at the corner of Frankfort and William Streets. In the year 1789 the two congregations united again, under the name "United German Lutheran Churches in the City of New York." In the year 1866 their name was changed by an act of the Legislature to "German Evangelical Lutheran Church of St. Matthew." The pastor of this venerable and historic church is the Rev. J. H. Sicker.

ST. JAMES' LUTHERAN CHURCH, MADISON AVENUE AND EAST 73D STREET.

St. James' Lutheran Church, at Madison Avenue and East 73d Street, is the home of the first English Lutheran congregation organized in the city. The society was formed in 1827, and its first church, the gift of Pierre Lorillard, was in Orange Street. Following the constant up-town movement, it has made three removals; in 1843 to Mulberry Street; then to Stuyvesant Square; and in 1890 to its present location. The church is an excellent example of the Gothic Romanesque. It is built of pink Milford stone, with brownstone trimmings. A portico, with a balcony and carved pillars, surmounted by a stone cross, forms the Madison-Avenue entrance. Stone pillars with embossed capitals separate the nave from the aisles, and lofty Gothic arches span the chancel and transepts. The richly decorated chancel, with a beautiful marble altar; the great rose window on Madison Avenue, representing Christ in glory; the baptismal font, modelled after Thorwaldsen's Angel of Baptism, in the Copenhagen Cathedral; and other works of art, make the interior attractive. All the interior decorations and the memorial window are the work of the Tiffany Company. The Rev. Dr. J. B. Remensnyder is the pastor.

The **Evangelical Lutheran Church of the Holy Trinity**, at 47 West 21st Street, was organized in 1868 by a few members of St. James's Church, to provide an English service for the Lutheran residents of the West Side.   The Rev. G. F. Krotel, then pastor of St. Mark's Lutheran Church, in Philadelphia, accepted a call to the pastorate ; and the Reformed Dutch Church, formerly the scene of the ministry of the celebrated Dr. Bethune, was leased, and named the Church of the Holy Trinity, in memory of the original Trinity Lutheran Church, built on Manhattan Island two hundred years before.   During the 25 years of its history it has grown to be the largest English Lutheran congregation in the city, and has contributed liberally to general church work.   The building has recently been re-decorated. Dr. Krotel still retains his position as pastor.

St. **Peter's Lutheran Church**, at Lexington Avenue and East 46th Street, is a sombre struc- ture in appearance, with its high gable, fronting on the avenue, and its severe square tower rising from the centre of the front.   The society was organized in the year 1862, and has been pros- pered.   The Rev. Dr. E. F. Moldenke is the pastor.

The **Gusta-** vus **Adolphus Church** (or Svenska Lutherska Gustaf Adolf Kyrkan, as it is called in the Swedish tongue), is in East 22d Street, near Third Avenue.   It is attended by a consider- able number of Swedish people, and the affairs of the congregation are in a flourishing condition.

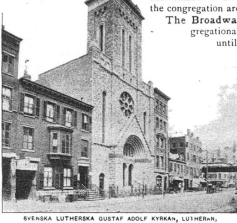

SVENSKA LUTHERSKA GUSTAF ADOLF KYRKAN, LUTHERAN, 22D STREET, NEAR THIRD AVENUE.

The **Broadway Tabernacle Church** (Con- gregational) was organized in 1840, and until 1857 worshipped in the Taber- nacle built in 1836, by an earlier Congregational soci- ety, on Broadway, between Leonard and Worth Streets. During the long pastorate of Dr. Joseph P. Thompson, a great anti-slavery preacher and worker, many stirring scenes were enacted within its walls.   The present church, a large Perpendicular Gothic building of stone, at Sixth Avenue and 34th Street, was completed in 1859, and re- modelled in 1872.   The Rev. Dr. William M. Taylor was pastor from 1872 to 1892.   The Rev. Dr. Henry A. Stimson became pastor in 1893.

The first Congregational minister to hold services in the city was the Rev. John Townley, about 1804, and a Congregational church was formed in 1805. Its first building was erected in Elizabeth Street, in 1809, but after a few years of fruitless struggle, under a heavy debt, it was sold to the Asbury colored Methodists, and the congregation disbanded.   An Independent Congregational church was organized in 1817, but in 1821 it was united with the Presbyterians.   Other organizations were made later, but the strength of the closely related Presbyterian denomination has acted unfavorably upon the growth of New-England Congregationalism in New York, and there are only seven churches in the city.

All Souls' Church, at 245 Fourth Avenue, was the first Unitarian organization in New York. The society was incorporated in 1819, as the "First Congregational Church of New York," from the outcome of a few services held by William Ellery Channing. Edward Everett preached at the dedication of the church, in Chambers Street, in 1820. The Rev. Henry Ware, Jr., was the first pastor, and his successor was Dr. Henry W. Bellows, the President of the Sanitary Commission during the war. The present church was erected in 1855 by J. Wray Mould, the famous and eccentric architect. It is of brick, trimmed with Caen stone, in the form of a Greek cross, and was the first experiment made in this country toward a Byzantine

BROADWAY TABERNACLE, CONGREGATIONAL, SIXTH AVENUE AND WEST 34TH STREET.

style of architecture, though the remarkable tower drawn in the original design was never completed. The full-length bronze bas-relief of Dr. Henry W. Bellows, by Augustus St. Gaudens, is considered one of his best works. It can be seen by ringing the bell at the north door. The entrance-porch is effective in treatment, and the large auditorium is unobstructed by pillars. A central lantern rises above the roof, and

2 5   ALL SOULS' UNITARIAN CHURCH, FOURTH AVENUE AND EAST 20TH STREET.

the transepts are spanned by lofty round arches.   A large parish-house adjoins the church.   Rev. Theodore C. Williams is the pastor.   All Souls' was the church of the poet Bryant and of Peter Cooper, and among its present attendants are Joseph H. Choate, Dorman B. Eaton and Daniel H. Chamberlain.

The Church of the Messiah is a well-proportioned brownstone building in the Gothic style, with a large and attractive interior.   The parish was formed in 1825 by a few members of the older Chambers-Street society.   The first church, in Prince Street, was destroyed by fire in 1837; and two years later another was built on Broadway, near Washington Square, and called the Church of the Messiah.   In 1867 the present church was erected, at the corner of Park Avenue and East 34th Street.   Orville Dewey was once pastor of the church, which is now in charge of the Rev. Dr. Robert Collyer.

The Lenox-Avenue Unitarian Church, the youngest Unitarian society in New York, has a handsome new building at Lenox Avenue and 121st Street.   Rev. Merle St. Croix Wright is pastor.

The Church of the Divine Paternity is the strongest Universalist congregation. The building is a brownstone Gothic edifice at Fifth Avenue and 45th Street, and dates from 1865. The society was formed in 1839, and the first church stood in Elizabeth Street, running through to the Bowery, between Hester and Canal Streets. In 1845 the society moved to more commodious quarters, in Murray Street, just west of Broadway.   In 1848 a third building was erected, on Broadway, between Prince

CHURCH OF THE MESSIAH, UNITARIAN, PARK AVENUE AND EAST 34TH STREET.

and Spring Streets; and here, under the Rev. Dr. Edward H. Chapin, the parish increased rapidly in strength and influence.   The Rev. Charles H. Eaton is the present pastor.

The society was the fourth Universalist organization in the city.   Towards the close of the last century the Rev. John Murray and other preachers of Universalism held services, and induced several prominent members of the John-Street Methodist Church to unite in the "Society of United Christian Friends of New York," formed in 1796. The next year a small church was built, in Vandewater Street, and Edward Mitchell was installed as pastor. He was an eloquent preacher, and in 1818 a large brick church was erected in Duane Street. Mr. Mitchell died soon afterward; and the congregation disbanded. A second society was organized in 1824. There are now three Universalist churches in New York.

The Church of The Strangers, at 299 Mercer Street, was purchased by Commodore Vanderbilt in 1870, and presented to the Rev. Dr. Charles F. Deems, as a token of interest in his work. Dr. Deems, who had been a Methodist-Episcopal clergyman, in North Carolina, came to the city in 1866, and began to preach in the chapel of the University of New York. His practical and independent presentation of the truths of Christianity attracted large audiences, and in 1868 a church was organized and called The Church of The Strangers, on account of its special field of work among sojourners in the city. It has no organic connection with any of the denominations, and remains faithful to its original work, which is a source of great blessing to the strangers within our gates.

The Broome-Street Taber-nacle, at 395 Broome Street, is a station of the New-York City Mission and Tract Society, and the centre of an important work among the 60,000 English-speaking people in its vicinity, for whom there is no other Protestant church. It is a substantial brick building, with a large auditorium, a reading-room and library, a gymnasium, and numerous smaller rooms. The Lodging-House Missionary Society carries on an aggressive missionary work in the lodging-houses in the vicinity of the Tabernacle, and numerous other societies are actively engaged in philanthropic work, resulting in great good in this populous district. The minister in charge is the Rev. C. H. Tyndall.

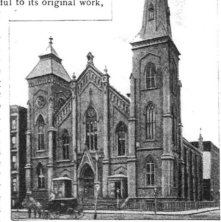

CHURCH OF THE DIVINE PATERNITY, UNIVERSALIST, FIFTH AVENUE AND WEST 45TH STREET.

The Church of the New Jerusalem, at 114 East 35th Street, a substantial stone building in the Doric style, was erected in 1859. The founder of the New Church (often called Swedenborgian) in New York was Edward Riley, who came from England in 1805. The society was organized in 1816, with the name of The Association of the City of New York for the Dissemination of the Heavenly Doctrines of the New Jerusalem; and in 1821 a small church in Pearl Street was purchased, and the Rev. Charles I. Doughty installed as pastor. The Pearl-Street church was sold to the Zion Baptist society in 1838, and the services were held in various places until the erection of the 35th-Street building; and this, and a mission at 356 West 44th Street, and a German church on Chrystie Street, are the only New-Church places of worship in the city. Rev. Samuel S. Seward is pastor.

CHURCH OF THE STRANGERS, 299 MERCER STREET.

The Church of the Disciples of Christ, at 323 West 56th Street, a substantial brick building in the Gothic style, was erected in 1883, and is the spiritual home of the oldest local congregation of that denomination. Its pastor is the Rev. Dr. B. B. Tyler. At different periods in its history the society has worshipped in halls and churches on Hubert, Greene, 17th and West 28th Streets, and it has grown and increased with gratifying certainty.

The Disciples date from about the year 1827. Their purpose is to unite Christians in a visible fellowship on the basis of Primitive Christianity, as described in the New Testament — its creed — its ordinances — its life. They number nearly 1,000,-000. Their greatest strength is in the West and South, where they are known as "Christians," or "Christian Church." They are sometimes called "Campbellites" (which name, however, they repudiate), from Alexander Campbell, one of their early preachers. There are three churches of Disciples in New York.

The Catholic Apostolic Church is a handsome structure, at 417 West 57th Street. The congregation was organized in 1850, and the early services were held in a small room in the University of the City of New York. About 1855 a church was purchased in West 16th Street. This was sold to the French Presbyterian society in 1886, when the present edifice was opened. The Catholic Apostolic people are better known as

CHURCH OF THE NEW JERUSALEM, SWEDENBORGIAN, 114 EAST 35TH STREET.

BROOME-STREET TABERNACLE, BROOME STREET AND CENTER MARKET STREET.

Irvingites, from the Rev. Edward Irving, a Scottish clergyman, who is popularly regarded as the founder of the movement. (This name they themselves repudiate.) One of the distinctive features of the sect is a return to apostolic methods and principles; another is "the preparation of the church as a body for the coming and kingdom of the Lord." Daily services are held at 6 A. M. and 5 P. M., and the Holy Communion is celebrated every Sunday morning. There are about 400 members. The church building was planned by F. H. Kimball. There is also a small German congregation.

The Swedish Evangelical Bethesda Church, at 240 East 45th Street and on 127th Street, supports three missionaries in China and three in Kongo, Africa. The church was organized in 1878, by a few members of the Swedish Lutheran Church, who left that body by reason of differences of opinion on matters of doctrine and discipline. There are 300 members. The pastor is the Rev. Professor K. Erixon.

The Reading-Room and Church for Seamen is a picturesque structure at the corner of Houston and West Streets, in the midst of the busy North-River traffic district. It is maintained by the Society for Promoting the Gospel among Seamen.

The Friends' Meeting-House, on Stuyvesant Square, a plain but substantial brick building, with a large schoolhouse connected, was erected in 1860, and is one of the two Quaker places of worship in the city, the other being an equally plain building with a brownstone front, on Gramercy Park. The first Quakers came to New Amsterdam in 1657, fugitives from New England, and received but scanty welcome from Peter Stuyvesant, who arrested two of the women for

READING-ROOM AND CHURCH FOR SEAMEN, HOUSTON AND WEST STREETS.

preaching in the streets.   One of the men, Robert Hodgson, was arrested at Hempstead, Long Island, whither he had gone intending to preach, and haled before Gov.
Stuyvesant, who used him harshly until Mrs. Bayard, the Governor's sister, prevailed
upon him to allow the unwelcome visitor to depart in peace.   The first meeting-
house was built in Little Green Street in 1700, and in 1775 a second was erected in
Pearl Street.   After the great schism of 1827, the Orthodox Friends built a third
meeting-house in Henry Street, leaving the Hicksite party in possession of the
others.   Later, these were sold, and the two now in use were erected.

   The First Moravian Church, at Lexington Avenue and 30th Street, is the
fourth edifice occupied by this congregation since the corner-stone of its first church

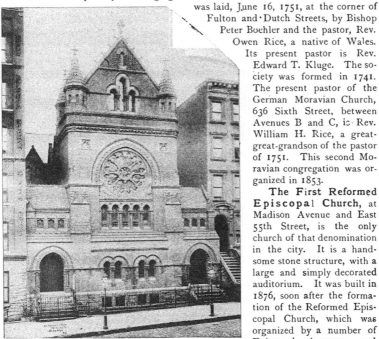

was laid, June 16, 1751, at the corner of
Fulton and Dutch Streets, by Bishop
Peter Boehler and the pastor, Rev.
Owen Rice, a native of Wales.
Its present pastor is Rev.
Edward T. Kluge.   The so-
ciety was formed in 1741.
The present pastor of the
German Moravian Church,
636 Sixth Street, between
Avenues B and C, is Rev.
William H. Rice, a great-
great-grandson of the pastor
of 1751.   This second Mo-
ravian congregation was or-
ganized in 1853.

   **The First Reformed
Episcopal Church,** at
Madison Avenue and East
55th Street, is the only
church of that denomination
in the city.   It is a handsome stone structure, with a
large and simply decorated
auditorium.   It was built in
1876, soon after the formation of the Reformed Episcopal Church, which was
organized by a number of
Episcopal clergymen and
laymen, under the leader-

CATHOLIC APOSTOLIC CHURCH, WEST 57TH STREET, BETWEEN
NINTH AND TENTH AVENUES.

ship of Bishop G. D. Cummins, who objected to what they considered the Roman-
izing tendencies of the Prayer Book.   Rev. Dr. William T. Sabine, a former Episcopal clergyman, is in charge of the parish.

   The Hebrew-Christian Church, the first of its kind in America, began in
1882 with its present pastor, the Rev. Jacob Freshman, a converted Jew, who had
resolved to devote himself to evangelizing the Hebrews of New York.   For some
time the meetings were held in a small room in the Cooper-Union building, and in
the lecture-room of the Fourth-Avenue Presbyterian Church ; but in the year 1885 a
private house, at 17 St. Mark's Place, was purchased and fitted up for the work.   The

audience-room, seating about 150, and lighted by stained-glass windows, is on the ground floor, while the remaining rooms are used by the missionary for various purposes connected with the work, which has met with a fair degree of success.

St. Patrick's Cathedral is the head of the great Archdiocese of New York. Roman Catholics visited Man-

FRIENDS' CHURCH AND SEMINARY, STUYVESANT SQUARE, EAST 16TH STREET, CORNER OF RUTHERFORD PLACE.

hattan Island as early as 1629, but when Father Isaac Jogues, the first priest to visit the island, came here in 1643, after his escape from the Mohawks, he found only two of his co-religionists. Jesuit fathers labored here at intervals between 1683 and 1785, when the first congregation was formed. Severe laws were enacted against the Catholics, but with no serious results, until the execution of John Ury for alleged participation in the Negro Riot of 1741, and on suspicion of being a Catholic priest. Governor Dongan was an ardent Catholic, as was his royal master, King James, and during his administration, in the closing years of the seventeenth century, a number of Catholic families of repute settled in the city, and a college was founded. In

FIRST REFORMED EPISCOPAL CHURCH, MADISON AVENUE AND EAST 55TH STREET.

1785 Sieur de St. Jean de Crevecœur, the French consul, and three others were incorporated as the Trustees of the Roman Catholic Church in the City of New York, and from that time the Church has steadily grown in numbers and power, largely through the immense foreign immigration. There are 83 Catholic churches and a long list of homes, asylums and schools. There are 400,000 Roman Catholics in the city, and besides the churches for English-speaking persons, there are others for Germans, Italians, Frenchmen, Canadians, Bohemians, Syrians, Afro-Americans, Poles and other nationalities.

St. Patrick's Cathedral, on 5th Avenue, between 50th and 51st Streets, is one of the grandest ecclesiastical buildings in the country, and has cost the greatest sum of money. It was projected by Archbishop Hughes, in 1850, and soon afterward the plans were drawn, by James Renwick, the architect of Grace Church. The corner-stone was laid in 1858, and the Cathedral was opened in 1879.. The building is now nearly completed, according to the original plans, only the Lady Chapel remaining to be constructed.   The style of the architecture is the Decorated Gothic of the thirteenth century, of which the cathedrals of Rheims and Cologne are examples ; and, with the mansion of the archbishop and the rector's residence, it occupies the entire block bounded by Fifth and Madison Avenues, and 50th and 51st Streets.   It is built of white marble, and its leading dimensions are : Length, 322 feet ; breadth, including chapels, 120 feet ; breadth of nave and choir, 97 feet ; length of transepts, 172 feet ; height of nave, 100 feet ; height of aisles, 54 feet.   The principal front, on

ARCHBISHOP'S AND RECTOR'S RESIDENCES.

ST. PATRICK'S CATHEDRAL, ROMAN CATHOLIC, MADISON-AVENUE AND 51ST-STREET SIDES.

Fifth Avenue, consists of a central gable, 156 feet in height, flanked by twin spires, 328 feet high.   The grand portal is richly decorated, and buttresses, pinnacles and carved ornamentation abound in rich profusion.

The interior is particularly impressive.   Massive clustered marble columns support the lofty groined roof ; the organ-gallery in the nave, between the towers, has a richly moulded front and ceiling ; and a magnificent rose window, 26 feet in diameter, filled with costly glass, dominates the western end, and forms a fitting pendant to the high altar in the sanctuary, in the eastern end.   The altar was made in Italy of purest Carrara marble, and its front is inlaid with alabaster and precious stones.   The lower front is divided into niches and panels ; the former containing statues of the four Evangelists, and the latter presenting in bas-reliefs the Last Supper, the Carrying of the Cross, the Agony, and the Betrayal.   The tabernacle,

ST. PATRICK'S CATHEDRAL, ROMAN CATHOLIC.
FIFTH AVENUE, 50TH AND 51ST STREETS.

ARCHBISHOP'S RESIDENCE, ST. PATRICK'S CATHEDRAL,
MADISON AVENUE AND 50TH STREET.

above the altar, was carved in France, and its three niches contain statues of Our Lord, St. Peter, and St. Paul. The altar of the Blessed Virgin, at the eastern end of the north aisle, is made of French stone, delicately sculptured in panels, on which are carved scenes connected with the life of Christ. At the eastern end of the south aisle is the bronze altar of the Sacred Heart, with four statues, representing the sacrifices of the old dispensation and, in the central niche, Jesus holding a chalice. The columns on each side, surmounted by statues of St. Peter and St. Paul, were the gift of Pope Pius IX. West of the sacristy is the elaborate bronze altar of St. Joseph, and in a side chapel is the altar of the Holy Family, above which hangs a fine painting of the Holy Family, by Costazzini. The Cathedral is seated for 2,600 people, and nearly as many more can be accommodated in the aisles. The interior is lighted by 70 windows, the majority being memorial windows made in Chartres, France, at a cost of over $100,000. The total cost of the building has been not far from $3,000,000, and $500,000 will be necessary to complete it.

St. Peter's Church, at Barclay and Church Streets, is the oldest Roman Catholic organization in the city. The first church, a brick building, 48 feet wide and 81 feet long, was erected in 1786, and torn down in 1836, when the present stone church in the Ionic style was erected in its place. The interior is spacious, and contains a fine marble altar. The ceiling is frescoed, and there are 12 large stained-glass windows.

St. Patrick's Church is the oldest existing Catholic church-building in the city. It was built in 1815, at Mott and Prince Streets, and until the opening of St. Patrick's Cathedral, in 1879, it was the cathedral church of the See of

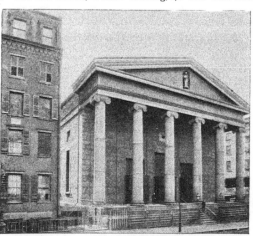

ST. PETER'S CHURCH, ROMAN CATHOLIC, BARCLAY AND CHURCH STREETS.

ST. PATRICK'S CATHEDRAL, ROMAN CATHOLIC.
THE HIGH ALTAR IN THE SANCTUARY, AT THE EASTERN END.

ST. PATRICK'S CHURCH, ROMAN CATHOLIC. MOTT AND
PRINCE STREETS.

New York. In earlier days the massive Gothic building, with its richly decorated auditorium, was one of the sights of the city ; but with the departure of the Archbishop it lost much of its ancient fame, and is now merely the parish-church of the Catholics who live in the neighborhood.

The Church of St. Benedict the Moor is an impressive classic building, at 210 Bleecker Street, in one of the ancient and crowded quarters of the city. The congregation is mainly composed of colored people.

St. Stephen's Roman Catholic Church was organized in 1850, and a portion of the large Italian Renaissance building, on 28th Street, between Third and Lexington Avenues, was opened in 1855. This was enlarged and richly decorated in 1865. It extends through to 29th Street. It is cruciform in shape, and the interior is extremely beautiful. Above each of the transept galleries are large rose-windows, and the side windows of the nave are filled with richly stained glass. A fine painting of the Crucifixion surmounts a lofty marble altar in the sanctuary. The beautiful high altar and the two rich side altars cost $40,000. St. Stephen's has long been one of the fashionable Catholic churches, and for many years its choir has been acknowledged as one of the finest in the country. The Rev. Dr. J. W. Cummings founded this church, and Dr. Edward McGlynn held the pastorate from 1866 until 1887. During his term of office a large Orphans' House and an Industrial School for girls were built. Father Colton is now the rector.

The church property extends through the whole block from 28th Street to 29th Street.

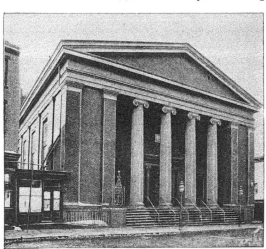

CHURCH OF ST. BENEDICT THE MOOR, ROMAN CATHOLIC,
210 BLEECKER STREET.

St. Francis Xavier's Church, at 36 West 16th Street, near Sixth Avenue, was erected in 1882, and is in charge of the Jesuit Fathers. It is a massive stone structure in the Roman Basilica style, and is constructed in the substantial manner which characterizes the work of the Jesuits. A lofty porch, with massive stone pillars, and a vestibule, both with vaulted stone ceilings, give entrance to one of the grandest church interiors in the city. The church is cruciform in shape; and the lofty vaulted and richly decorated ceiling of the nave is supported by stone columns carrying a triforium gallery, pierced with round-arched openings. The prevailing tone of the decorations gives an effect of luminosity, and there is a profusion of ornamentation in relief. The high altar is a costly marble structure, and on either side of the sanctuary stand the altars of the Blessed Virgin and St. Joseph. In the transepts are the altars of St. Aloysius and the Sacred Heart, all in marble, with statues and carvings. The walls are filled with large paintings of Scriptural scenes. Twelve hundred electric lights have been placed in the church, which is illustrated on page 285. On this site stood the old church of the same name, founded in 1847. The Infanta Eulalia of Spain visited St. Francis Xavier's in 1893.

The Church of St. Paul the Apostle, at Ninth Avenue and 59th Street, is one of the greatest Catholic churches in the city, second only to the Cathedral in size and magnificence. It is in charge of the Paulist Fathers, a missionary order founded in 1858 by the late Very Rev. Isaac Hecker, who, with four other converts from Protestantism, began a remarkable series of missions throughout the United States. The community then established has since increased to twenty-five priests and sixteen theological students. The Paulist Fathers devote all the time they can spare from the missions to the preparation and spread of Catholic literature. In connection with the great Church of St. Paul they have a large convent and school-house, and lately built a printing-house, from which they issue their monthly publications, *The Catholic World, The Young Catholic,* calendars, sermons, tracts, etc. The cornerstone of the first church was laid in 1859, and of the present church in 1876, while the solemn opening took place in 1885. It is the second largest church edi-

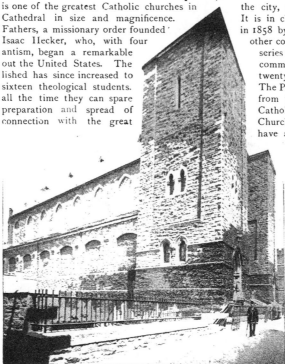

CHURCH OF ST. PAUL THE APOSTLE, ROMAN CATHOLIC, NINTH AVENUE AND WEST 59TH STREET.

fice in the country, being 284 feet long and 132 feet wide. The walls are constructed of rough stone, and there is very little attempt at mere ornament, the
architect aiming to obtain simplicity and dignity by the size and massiveness of the
building, correctness of detail and harmonious grouping. The main façade, on
Ninth Avenue, approached by a double flight of granite steps, is 134 feet wide,
with a central compartment flanked by two towers 38 feet square, and with a total
height of 300 feet when the spires are built. The style of architecture is the
Thirteenth-Century Gothic, adapted to meet the special needs of the Fathers. The
spacious and impressive interior, with its side aisles and passages, has a seating
capacity of nearly 5,000. The lofty nave arches are carried by columns of polished
Syracuse limestone, four feet in diameter, alternately round and octagonal, with
carved caps and moulded bases over each arch ; the tracery windows of the clere-
story give ample light from above, leaving a large
expanse of wall space for
effective decorative work.
The windows, twenty-seven
feet in length and twelve in

ACADEMY OF THE HOLY CROSS FOR YOUNG LADIES, AND CHURCH OF THE HOLY CROSS, ROMAN CATHOLIC,
335-343 WEST 42D STREET.

width, are of the finest workmanship. Those in the sanctuary represent the
Queen of Angels surrounded by hundreds of angels in the centre, and flanked on
either side by the four great archangels, all in adoration of the Blessed Sacrament on
the altar. These were made in Munich. The fourteen tracery windows in the nave,
the work of the American artist LaFarge, are unrivalled for richness of color. The
sanctuary floor is well elevated above that of the nave, and contains the high altar,
of variegated marble, with a lofty baldichino, whose canopied roof is supported by
polished columns of Numidian marble. The great organ stands behind the high altar,
and on each side are the stalls for the choir and the dignitaries of the Church. On
the left of the sanctuary, at the head of the south aisle, is the altar of the Blessed
Virgin, constructed of Siena marble and beautiful Mexican onyx, and surmounted

by a lofty canopy, beneath which is a large marble statue of the Virgin. At the head of the north aisle is the altar of St. Joseph, similar in treatment, with a marble statue of the saint. At the end of the south aisle, and near the entrance, is a beautiful baptistery, with marble font, enclosed by a substantial marble rail. In the side chapels of the same aisle are altars of St. Agnes, The Annunciation and St. Justinus the Martyr. The side chapels of the north aisle contain the altars of the Sacred Heart, St. Catharine of Genoa and St. Patrick. The total cost of all the altars was not far from $50,000, and of the whole church $500,000. The magnitude of the interior is best shown by a few figures : The length of the nave and chancel is 257 feet, the width 60 feet, and the height 96 feet, while the aisles have

ST. CECILIA'S CHURCH, ROMAN CATHOLIC, EAST 106TH STREET, NEAR LEXINGTON AVENUE.

a combined width of 50 feet, giving an auditorium of immense size and striking and impressive perspective effect. The impression of immense space, height and solitude of the interior is increased by the treatment of the ceiling, which is painted a deep blue and studded with stars. It is concave in form, and the stars and constellations which thickly stud its surface are arranged from exact maps made by one of the Paulist Fathers, to represent their positions on January 25, 1885, the festival of the conversion of St. Paul, the patron-saint of the church. The decoration of the church is in the hands of the well-known artist LaFarge, and looks its best when lighted at night. The Annunciation altar has a fine copy of the Michael Angelo at Bruges ; and St. Justinus' altar has a bronze reredos, by James Kelly. Here, every Sunday evening, can be heard the best congregational singing of English hymns in New York. The singing at the other regular services is done by a surpliced choir of 100 men and boys. The group of buildings of which St. Paul's is the centre forms one of the strongest fortresses of Catholicism in New York.

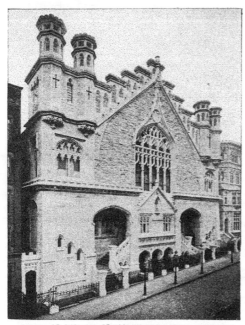

CHURCH OF OUR LADY OF GOOD COUNSEL, ROMAN CATHOLIC,
236 EAST 90TH STREET.

The Church of Our Lady of Good Counsel, at 236 East 90th Street, is one of the youngest of the Catholic churches. The building, a handsome structure in the decorated Gothic style of architecture, with a front of Rutland marble, was completed in 1892, and dedicated on September 18th. There are two entrance-porches recessed into the front of the church, with steps which turn toward each other and unite in an outer lobby, which is screened from view by the front main wall. There are a number of handsome stained-glass windows, which were made in Munich. The high altar of marble came from Venice, and four smaller altars were made in the quarries of Carrara. Five paintings, over the high altar, are the work of Sig. Rossi, a prize-winner of the Paris Salon. The parish is a new one, established in 1886, and the corner-stone of the church was laid in May of that year. Rev. William J. O'Kelly is the rector, and he has four assistants.

Other Interesting Catholic Churches are St. Andrew's, away down-town, at City-Hall Place and Duane Street ; St. Bernard's, a noble Gothic building on West 14th Street ; the Holy Cross, on West 42d Street ; and St. Cecilia's, on East 106th Street.

The B'Nai Jeshurun, "Children of Jeshurun," is the oldest Anglo-German Hebrew congregation in the city. It was founded in 1825 by a few German and Polish Jews, who left the Spanish synagogue on Mill Street, and adopted the Polish or German ritual, in place of the Portuguese, in use in the former congregation. The early meetings were held in a small hall in White Street, but in 1826 the former Presbyterian Church in Elm Street

ST. ANDREW'S CHURCH, ROMAN CATHOLIC, DUANE
STREET AND CITY-HALL PLACE.

was purchased and remodelled. In 1850 a large synagogue was erected on Greene Street, followed in 1866 by a second in West 34th Street. In 1885 the large and impressive edifice on Madison Avenue, near East 65th Street, was erected, at a cost of $200,000. It is built of stone and pressed brick, in the Spanish-Moresque style, with twin towers, and an imposing façade. The audi-

ST. BERNARD'S CHURCH, ROMAN CATHOLIC, 332 WEST 14TH STREET.

torium is decorated in white and gold, and harmonizes with the Moorish exterior. Its seating capacity is 1,200, and the congregation is the leading orthodox Hebrew

TEMPLE EMANU-EL, HEBREW, FIFTH AVENUE AND 43D STREET.

body in the city, holding conservatively to the old Mosaic standards, and paying little regard to the changeful spirit of the nineteenth century. Dr. Henry S. Jacobs is the Rabbi; and Rev. Stephen S. Wise the junior minister.

The Jews were early settlers in Manhattan, and in 1695 there were twenty Hebrew families in the city; but their petition for permission to establish a place of worship was refused by the Provincial authorities. A Jewish congregation was formed early in the last century, and in 1729 the first synagogue was opened, in Mill Street, near Beaver. The Crosby-Street Synagogue was a spacious and elegant building. With the rapid increase in the Jewish population, others have been erected, and there are now 47 synagogues and temples, some of them magnificent edifices, and many charitable institutions, well-supported by the Jewish people.

The Temple Emanu-El, at Fifth Avenue and East 43d Street, is one of the finest and most costly synagogues in the world. The congregation was formed in 1845, as a reformed Hebrew society. It was "a day of small things" with the infant congregation for some years, and the earlier meetings were held in the Grand-Street court-room. In 1850 a church on Chrystie Street, which had been deserted by its Christian congregation, was purchased and remodelled. The first Rabbi was the Rev. Dr. Leon Merzbacher, one of the early Jewish reformers. In 1856 the Baptist church on East 12th Street was secured for the congregation, and here they remained until 1868, when their modern magnificent temple was completed, at a cost of nearly $600,000. Like all the finer Jewish synagogues of the city, it is Moorish in design and decoration, with twin towers and an impressive front on

TEMPLE BETH-EL, HEBREW, FIFTH AVENUE AND 76TH STREET, OPPOSITE CENTRAL PARK.

Fifth Avenue. The auditorium will seat nearly 2,000 people. The decorations are of the most elaborate character, conceived and carried out in the Moorish manner, with massive columns spanned by the peculiar Saracenic arch, a lofty clere-story, and a fine pulpit and ark. Leopold Eidlitz was the architect. The Rev. Dr. Samuel Adler, father of Felix Adler, was long the Rabbi of the congregation, which is one of the most liberal in the city, as it was the first established; and it is now the only one maintaining regular Sunday services, in addition to the usual Saturday service. Its music is celebrated for stateliness and brilliancy, and very effectively accompanies the impressive ritual of the ancient Hebrew Church. The present Rabbis are the Rev. Drs. Gustav Gottheil and Joseph Silverman.

The Temple Beth-El, at Fifth Avenue and 76th Street, is one of the costliest and most imposing religious buildings in the city. It is constructed of Indiana limestone, and its architectural features show a blending of the Byzantine and Moorish styles. Its front is 102 feet long on Fifth Avenue, and it extends back 150 feet on 76th Street. The land and building cost $750,000. The main entrance takes the form of a massive arch, with a screen of columns and small arches, and richly foliated bronze gates. The dome is enriched with lines of gilded ribbing. The main audience-hall has a lofty arched ceiling and galleries surmounted by large round arches. Beneath the great arch at the eastern end is an apsidal recess, containing the organ-loft, pulpit and shrine, the latter a magnificent structure of onyx

SHAARAI TEPHILA SYNAGOGUE, HEBREW, 127 WEST 44TH STREET.

columns and arches with capitals of gold, all richly decorated. The Congregation Beth-El was formed in 1874 by the union of the Congregations Anshi-Chesed and Adas-Jeshurun, the former being the first German Jewish congregation in the country, dating back to 1828. The Adas-Jeshurun Congregation, under the ministry of the Rev. Dr. D. Einhorn, became the leading Jewish reformed synagogue, and when the Beth-El Congregation was formed, it worshiped in the Lexington-Avenue synagogue until the Temple Beth-El was completed in 1891. Under Dr. Einhorn's successor, the Rev. Dr. K. Kohler, the reforming tendencies of the congregation have steadily strengthened, and it is now the leading exponent of modern liberal Judaism.

The Shaarai Tephila, "Gates of Prayer," at 127 West 44th Street, was erected in 1865. It is a magnificent building in a modified Moorish style of architecture, of Newark freestone, with trimmings of Dorchester stone. The spacious interior, seating 1,200, is richly decorated in contrasting colors. Four slender iron

AHAVATH CHESED SYNAGOGUE, HEBREW, LEXINGTON AVENUE AND EAST 64TH STREET.

TEMPLE SHEARITH ISRAEL, HEBREW, 5 WEST 19TH STREET,
NEAR FIFTH AVENUE.

columns support the roof on transverse and longitudinal arches, and all the interior fittings are of the most costly character. Above the richly inlaid and carved ark or shrine is a large rose window. The synagogue cost $200,000. The congregation was formed in 1845 by members of the Elm-Street Synagogue. The Rabbi is the Rev. Dr. F. de Sola Mendes.

The Rodoph Sholom, "Followers of Peace," organized in 1842, and formerly worshipping in Clinton Street, now owns the former Beth-El Synagogue, erected in 1873 at a cost of $250,000. It stands at Lexington Avenue and 63d Street, and is a lofty stone building in the Spanish-Moresque style. The interior is elaborately decorated in the Oriental manner prevailing among the Jewish synagogues. The congregation is large and influential. The Rabbi is the Rev. Aaron Wise.

The Ahavath Chesed, "Neighborly Love," was founded in 1850 by some of the moderate reform Hebrews. For some years it occupied a former Christian church on Avenue C. The stately synagogue, at 652 Lexington Avenue, was erected in 1872. It is built of stone, in the Moorish style, and the front has five elevations; a central one for the main entrance, with a tower and a stairway wing on each side. The towers are 122 feet high, square at the base, changing to octagons near the top, and crowned by gilded metal cupolas. The interior is very beautiful, with arabesque decorations and graceful Moorish arches and tall pillars. The Rabbi is the Rev. Alexander Kohut.

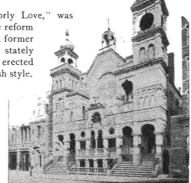

CONGREGATION SICHRON EPHRAIM, HEBREW, EAST.
67TH STREET, NEAR THIRD AVENUE.   . .

The **Temple Shearith Israel**, in West 19th Street, close to Fifth Avenue, is one of those structures of unfamiliar appearance which makes New York cosmopolitan in architecture. The front presents the appearance of two very high stories, each with its capital supported by double columns. The entrance is broad and high, and the windows are capped with semi-circular arches. The temple is surmounted by a Moorish dome, which is prominent for a considerable distance. The Temple Shearith Israel looms high over the houses of West 19th Street, with its classic front and ponderous dome.

The congregation, which is of the orthodox type, and is composed mainly of English-speaking Hebrews, is in a sense an offshoot from a very old Portuguese congregation of Newport, R. I., and as such it claims to be the oldest Jewish congregation now existing in New York. Rev. H. Pereira Mendes is the Rabbi, and Rev. Abraham H. Niets assistant.

The **Sichron Ephraim** synagogue, on East 67th Street, near Third Avenue, is a handsome piece of Saracenic architecture, with a North-African sentiment in its tall and unique tower and the arcades along its front.

The synagogue was built in 1890, by Jonas Weil, a wealthy Hebrew, and a new congregation was organized from the orthodox Hebrews residing in the vicinity. A portion of the work of the organization is the mainte-

BETH ISRAEL BIKUR CHOLIM, HEBREW, LEXINGTON AVENUE AND
EAST 72D STREET.

nance of a religious school, which holds sessions on Tuesday and Thursday afternoons and Sunday forenoons. Rev. Dr. Bernard Drachman is the Rabbi.

The **Beth Israel Bikur Cholim** synagogue, in a fine neighborhood, at Lexington Avenue and 72d Street, is a spacious and commodious temple, with a rich and vivid interior. The society was formed in 1859, by the union of the Congregation Beth Israel and the Society Bikur Cholim; and worshipped in White Street and then in Chrystie Street until 1887, when it joined the great up-town movement of the churches. It is one of the foremost of the orthodox Jewish congregations. The Rabbi is Herman Lustig.

Other forms of worship abound in the great metropolis, in many sects, and with hundreds of societies, conclaves, missions and chapels. There are Christian

Israelites, Reformed Catholics, German Evangelicals, True Dutch Reformed, Christian Scientists, and many others.

The Greek Church holds its services at 340 West 53d Street, for the members of the large Greek colony. The Rev. Paisius Ferendinos is archimandrite.

The First Society of Spiritualists, the only organized Spiritualistic society in the city, holds weekly meetings in Music Hall, on West 57th Street. "Seances" and meetings of the Spiritualists are also held in private houses.

.Mahommedanism is being preached to the New-Yorkers by Mohammed Webb, a native of this city, and longtime a consul in the East Indies. He is supplied with large funds, by wealthy Moslems of Bombay and Allahabad, and lectures and distributes Mohammedan literature.

The Chinese Joss House occupies the upper floor of a building at 10 Mott Street. It is a small room containing the shrine, before which lights are kept constantly burning. The shrine is a magnificent specimen of Chinese carved work.

Religious Societies and Associations, devoted to the advancement of the cause of religion, in charities, preaching, literature, and many other ways, abound throughout this great city.

The magnificent system of the Catholic hierarchy is exemplified here in a perfect manner, and all the vast interests connected with the Papal Church are governed with the precision and security of an ancient province of Rome.

The Church Missions' House, at Fourth Avenue and East 27th Street, is one of the noblest of the new buildings of the year 1893. The architects are R. W. Gibson and Edward J. N. Stent, and the style is a very rich and unusual variety of the Flemish, with clustered columns, pinnacles and statues. The lower part is of rock-faced granite, and the rest of the building of Indiana limestone, with a steel frame. The land and struc-

CHINESE JOSS HOUSE, 16 MOTT STREET.

ture cost $420,000. Its central gable is crowned by a statue of Faith. This edifice is not a diocesan affair, but pertains to the whole American Church, by whose free-will offerings it was erected. Here are to be the headquarters of the Domestic and Foreign Missionary Society and other great Episcopal associations.

The Domestic and Foreign Missionary Society of the Protestant Episcopal Church in the United States of America, at 22 Bible House, was founded in 1820 and incorporated in 1846. It supports 21 bishops and gives stipends to 1,200 missionaries; and has missions, orphanages, hospitals, schools and colleges in Africa, China, Japan, Greece and Hayti; also among the negroes and Indians. It supports many lay-readers and women-workers. This society is the established agency of the entire American Episcopal Church, and is under the direction of the General Convention. It disburses $600,000 yearly.

The Diocesan House, 29 Lafayette Place, was opened in 1888, as a See House for the Episcopal Church in the Diocese of New York. The house originally belonged to Miss Catherine L. Wolfe, the munificent benefactor of the Metropolitan Museum of Art and of Grace Church; and was given by her for its present purpose. Extensive alterations were made in the original building, and the Diocesan House is now an ecclesiastical-looking edifice, conveniently arranged for the purpose for which it is intended, containing the offices of the Bishop of the Diocese, Arch-deacon of New York, Presiding Bishop of the Episcopal Church, Standing Committee of the Diocese, Secretary of the House of Bishops, a large reception-room, a reading-room, sleeping-rooms for the members of the Clergy Club, and a large hall, called Ho-

bart Hall, in memory of the great bishop of that name, in which is kept the Diocesan library.

The New-York Protestant Episcopal City Mission Society was founded in 1830, and chartered in 1833 "to preach the Gospel to the poor, and to relieve the unfortunate." Acting under its charter, the society led the way in the establishment of free churches for the middle and poorer classes of the city population. Later, when this need no longer existed, it inaugurated a mission work among the public institutions of the city and adjacent islands, and out of this work have grown many of the best benevolent institutions of the city, such as the House of Mercy; St. Barnabas' House; the Midnight Mission; the New-York Infant Asylum; the Sheltering Arms; the House of Rest for Consumptives; and many others. The so-

CHURCH MISSION HOUSE, PROTESTANT EPISCOPAL, FOURTH AVENUE AND 22D STREET.

ciety now employs eleven clergymen, two lay-readers, and women visitors in its work at its mission stations, the city jails, hospitals and courts. The missions of the society are St. Ambrose Chapel, on Thompson Street; the Rescue Mission, on Mott Street; St. Barnabas' Chapel, mission-house and schools, on Mulberry Street; and three chapels. The yearly expenditure is about $50,000. The Mission-House is at 38 Bleecker Street, where there is a free reading-room for males.

The Protestant Episcopal Church Missionary Society for Seamen in the City and Port of New York, at 77 Houston Street, was founded in 1841. It supports three chapels, as many reading-rooms, and a sailors' home. Every Episcopal Church in the city is required to make a yearly contribution for this society.

The Presbyterian House, at Fifth Avenue and 12th Street, was the former residence of the Lenox family, and the scene of many notable events in the social history of the city.   This stately old mansion now contains the Home and Foreign Mission Board rooms, the Board of Church Erection, the Woman's Boards, and other great Presbyterian societies.   It was virtually a gift from the Lenox family.

The Board of Foreign Missions of the Presbyterian Church, at the Presbyterian House, 53 Fifth Avenue, was established in 1834, and received its charter in 1862.   The Foreign Board sustains missions in China, India, Siam, Japan, Korea, Africa, Central America, Brazil, Chile, Columbia, Mexico, Syria, Persia, and among the Chinese and Japanese in the United States, expending $1,000,000 yearly.

DIOCESAN HOUSE, EPISCOPAL CHURCH, 29 LAFAYETTE PLACE.

The Board of Home Missions of the Presbyterian Church, U. S. A., began its work in 1802, and received its present charter in 1872.   It employs about 2,100 missionaries and teachers, in nearly every State and territory of the Union, including Alaska, maintaining missions among foreign populations, Indians, Mexicans, Mormons, Alaskans and mountain-whites.   Its yearly appropriations are $950,000.

The Methodist Mission House is a noble stone and brick building, eight stories high, erected in 1889, at a cost of $1,000,000. It contains the offices and salesroom of the Publishing Agents, the press-rooms, composing-rooms and bindery, where thousands of books and pamphlets are manufactured yearly; the offices of the missionary society; a large chapel; the library; Board-room; Bishop's room; and a number of private offices.   A picture will be found in another chapter.

The Methodist Book Concern, at Fifth Avenue and 20th Street, is the eldest auxiliary of American Methodism.   It was established in 1779, when the Rev. John Dickins was appointed book steward, and began publishing books for the Methodist Church, with a borrowed capital of $600.   The first New-York office of the Concern was in Church Street.   Later the business was transferred to Mulberry Street ; still later to Broadway and 11th Street; and then to Fifth Avenue and 20th Street.   The profits of the Concern are used for the support of old and disabled ministers, widows and orphans, and during the century of its existence it has paid the Methodist Church for these purposes more than $1,500,000.

The New-York City Church Extension and Missionary Society of the Methodist Episcopal Church was chartered in 1866 to plant and support Sunday-schools, churches and missions in the city of New York.   It extends financial aid to 23 churches and missions, at an annual expense of $40,000.

The **Reformed Church Building,** at 25 East 22d Street, contains the Boards of Domestic Missions, of Foreign Missions, of Publication, of Education, and the Women's Committees of Foreign and Domestic Missions. Here also is a large assembly-room for the special use of the clergy.

The **Board of Domestic Missions of the Reformed Church in America,** at 25 East 22d Street, was formed in 1832 to promote the extension of the Reformed Dutch Church in America. At present the Board aids 115 missionary pastors, and supplies ministers to 170 churches and missions, at a yearly expense of $65,000.

The **Board of Foreign Missions of the Reformed Church in America,** at 25 East 22d Street, was organized in 1837. It has missions in China, India and Japan, where it maintains 66 missionaries and 325 native assistants. About $110,000 are disbursed yearly.

The **New-York City Baptist Mission Society,** in the United Charities Building, at Fourth Avenue and 22d Street, was founded in 1870, and re-organized

PRESBYTERIAN HOUSE, FIFTH AVENUE AND EAST 12TH STREET.

in 1891, to sustain missions in the lower part of the city; to establish new churches in the upper part; to preach the gospel to the foreign populations; to circulate religious and denominational literature; to promote Baptist educational work; to provide for the training of Sunday-school teachers, and other Christian workers; and to conduct various charities in connection with churches and missions.

The **Bible House,** owned by the American Bible Society, is a great brick edifice covering the whole block bounded by Third and Fourth Avenues and Astor Place and Ninth Street. It is six stories high and has an open court in the centre. The original cost of the property was about $300,000, provided for by special contributions, so that not a dollar of the ordinary benevolent contributions to the society was used in the purchase of the lot or the erection of the building. It contains the offices, library, and publishing departments of the society, and is the local head-quarters of the following societies: American Sunday-School Union; American

Home-Missionary Society; Congregational Church Building Society; American Missionary Association; American Board of Commissioners for Foreign Missions; Domestic and Foreign Missionary Society of the Protestant Episcopal Church; American Church Building Fund Commission; New-York Sabbath Committee; New-York Bible Society; Christian Aid to Employment Society; National Women's Christian Temperance Union; Women's Union Missionary Society; Willard Tract Repository; the *Christian Herald,* and a number of other religious publications.

The American Bible Society was organized in the City of New York in May, 1816, by delegates from 35 local Bible societies which had been previously formed in various portions of the United States.   Its constitution declares that its sole object is to encourage a wider circulation of the Holy Scriptures without note or comment.   Its field is the world.   Its founders expressed the purpose to extend its operations to other countries, whether Christian, Mohammedan or Pagan.   It is an unsectarian institution.   Its 36 elected managers are identified with various branches of the Christian Church, while its affairs are conducted without denominational bias or control.   It is also a benevolent institution.   Its founders and their successors have always aimed by all wise methods to place the Holy Scriptures within the reach of all.   Its publications are in no case sold at a profit.   Those who can may buy them at the mere cost of manufacture, while those who cannot are supplied without price.   The total receipts of the Society to March 31, 1893, were $26,546,248, but over eleven millions of this amount were received in payment of books sold at cost or less than cost.   This aggregate also includes over $4,500,000 received from legacies.   The Society has aided in the translation, printing or distribution of the Scriptures in 95 languages and dialects.   The total number of volumes issued to April, 1893, was 56,926,771.   The issues of the past five years are equal to those of the first forty years of the Society's operations.   The Society has four times conducted a general Bible supply of the United States.   The entire distribution of the Scriptures in the fourth re-supply was 8,146,808 volumes, in 27 different languages. Besides these special efforts the Society has constantly supplied the Scriptures to seamen, the immigrants, the freedmen, the soldiers, the inmates of humane and criminal institutions, and to mission churches and Sabbath-schools.   The foreign work is conducted directly by its own agents and colporteurs, and indirectly through the foreign missionary societies of the various Christian denominations in the United States, or through the Bible societies established in other lands.   There are six special agencies on the Western Continent — LaPlata, Peru, Venezuela, Brazil, Mexico and Cuba.   During the ten years ending March 31, 1893, 538,237 volumes were sent from the Bible House to Latin America, including Cuba.   There are five special agencies on the Eastern Continents, — the Levant, Persia, China, Siam, and Japan and Korea.   The Scriptures are circulated in the Levant Agency in about thirty languages, and the total issues for 35 years to December 31, 1892, amount to 1,306,814 copies.   Over 2,500,000 copies have been circulated in China since 1876. The Society's work is helped by buying and circulating its publications; by commending the Scriptures to others; by coöperating with the auxiliary Bible societies; by donations to the Society for its benevolent work.   During the 77 years of the Society's history eleven persons have held the office of president — the first being the Hon. Elias Boudinot, LL.D., and the present being the Hon. Enoch L. Fancher, LL.D.   The Rev. Edward W. Gilman, D.D.; Alexander McLean, D.D.; and Albert S. Hunt, D. D., are the corresponding secretaries.   William Foulke is treasurer, and Caleb T. Rowe is general agent.   The noble work of the American Bible Society has helped to shed God's light on all lands, heathen or Christian.

THE BIBLE HOUSE OF THE AMERICAN BIBLE SOCIETY.
THIRD AND FOURTH AVENUES, FROM 8TH TO 9TH STREETS, OPPOSITE ASTOR PLACE.

The New-York Bible Society was organized in 1823, and incorporated in 1866, as an auxiliary of the American Bible Society, to distribute copies of the Bible in the city and harbor of New York, and to raise funds in aid of the former society. Its office is in the Bible House. During 1891 it distributed nearly 100,000 copies of the Bible.

The New-York Sabbath Committee, 31 Bible House, was formed in 1857, by prominent laymen of different denominations, to protect and promote the observance of Sunday, by securing and enforcing just and wise Sunday laws, and by cultivating a sound public sentiment by documents, addresses and the press. The committee was incorporated in 1884. It has exerted a wide influence over our land, and a number of its documents have been reprinted in Europe.

The New-York City Mission and Tract Society, in the United Charities Building, was established in 1827 and incorporated in 1866. It is the leading

FOURTH-AVENUE PRESBYTERIAN CHURCH.   ASSOCIATION HALL.   23D STREET.

YOUNG MEN'S CHRISTIAN ASSOCIATION, 23D STREET AND FOURTH AVENUE.

city missionary society, and its field of work is New York below 14th Street. It sustains six mission stations, five Sunday-schools and sixty missionaries, at a yearly expense of $70,000. It is entirely undenominational.

The American Home Missionary Society, at 34 Bible House, was organized in 1826 and incorporated in 1871, "to assist congregations unable to support the Gospel ministry, and to send the Gospel and the means of Christian education to the destitute within the United States." It is the home missionary society of Congregationalism, and now employs 2,000 missionaries, expending yearly not far from $700,000 in its religious and educational work.

The American Tract Society, at 150 Nassau Street, was organized in 1825 for the publication and circulation of religious literature. It is undenominational,

FIFTH AVENUE ON A SUNDAY MORNING.
LOOKING NORTH FROM THE CATHEDRAL.

and has issued more than 8,000 distinct publications, books, tracts, wall-rolls, etc., including supplies for immigrants in many languages. The work is carried on largely through colporteurs, of whom there are now 174 working in different States. It has published thousands of books and tracts at foreign mission-stations. The society expends over $300,000 yearly.

The American Seamen's Friend Society was established in 1828 to promote the spiritual and temporal welfare of seamen. It supports missionaries and homes in numerous home and foreign ports, and provides loan libraries for ships, besides rendering aid to suffering and needy seamen. Its annual expenditures are about $40,000 ; and it has an office at 76 Wall Street.

The Society for Promoting the Gospel Among Seamen in the Port of New York is better known as the New-York Port Society. It was founded in 1818, and its headquarters

HARLEM BRANCH, YOUNG MEN'S CHRISTIAN ASSOCIATION, 5 WEST 125TH STREET.

are at 46 Catharine Street, where it maintains the Mariner's Church, a library and a reading-room at a yearly cost of $16,000.

The Salvation Army has been working here for nearly ten years, and now has 500 officers and soldiers in the city. The National headquarters of the Army are at 111 Reade Street. There are large "barracks" where nightly and Sunday meetings are held, at 122 West 14th Street, 14 Fourth Avenue, 39th Street and Sixth Avenue, 232 East 125th Street, West 11th and Bleecker Streets, 153 East 72d Street, and 340 East 8th Street. There is a large Food and Shelter Depot, and three Slum Posts, a Slum Crèche, and a Rescue Home for fallen women. The Army is doing energetic and blessed work in its hearty fashion among classes of people who most need help.

The Young Men's Christian Association was organized in 1852, for the mental, social, physical, and spiritual improvement of young men. The main Association Building, at Fourth Avenue and East 23d Street, is a large stone edifice built in 1869, at a cost of

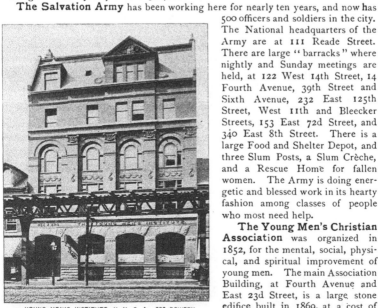

YOUNG MEN'S INSTITUTE, Y. M. C. A., 222 BOWERY.

GERMAN BRANCH, Y. M. C. A., 140 AND 142 SECOND AVENUE, NEAR 9TH STREET.

$500,000. It contains reception-room, parlors, reading-room, a lecture and concert hall, seating 1,300 people, a smaller lecture-room, numerous class-rooms, a library of 42,000 volumes, a gymnasium, bowling-alleys and baths. To aid in its work among the young men of the city, the Association has established fourteen branches in different sections, and employs the endeavors of 81 young men in superintending its work. Seven fully equipped gymnasiums, in charge of competent men, afford facilities for physical culture. The well-stocked libraries, containing over 60,000 volumes ; the various reading-rooms, where more than 1,000 newspapers, magazines and reviews are kept on file ; and the class-room instruction in 23 different lines of practical study, provide mental food for the studious-minded. Frequent religious meetings, Bible-classes, and public addresses minister to the spiritual needs of the members and their friends ; while the social element is fostered by frequent entertainments, lectures and receptions. The total membership of the various branches is 7,200, and the average daily attendance for 1892 was nearly 4,000. A prominent feature of the Association work is aiding deserving young men to obtain situations ; and recently a Students' Movement has been organized, to maintain religious meetings and Bible-classes in the colleges in the city. The general offices of the Association are at 40 East 23d Street, just west of the main Association Building, which is now designated as the 23d-Street branch. It was made a branch in 1887, and is the centre of local Association work, and of many kindly and civilizing influences.

The Bowery Branch, 153 Bowery, was organized in 1872, to aid young men out of employment and in temporary destitution, with free meals and beds.

The Harlem Branch, formed in 1868, has an attractive building, at 5 West 125th Street, containing a reading-room, parlor, library, gymnasium, entertainment hall and class-rooms.

RAILROAD BRANCH, Y. M. C. A., MADISON AVENUE AND 45TH STREET.

The East 86th-Street Branch was organized in 1884, and occupies two buildings at 153 and 155 East 86th Street, with a well-equipped gymnasium, bowling alleys, lecture-hall and bath-rooms.   The buildings also contain a reading-room, library, parlor, reception-room, bicycle room and junior department rooms.

The Young Men's Institute, at 222 Bowery, is a branch of the Young Men's Christian Association, and was built in 1885, at a cost of $150,000.   The building is in the style of the English Renaissance, with a frontage of 50 feet on the Bowery, and a depth of 96 feet.   The first story is trimmed with Nova-Scotia sandstone, and special prominence is given to the entrance vestibule.   An impression of height is conveyed by the gables and the mansard roof, on which has been constructed a flooring for summer-evening meetings and entertainments.   There are six stories in the front and two in the rear, and the interior is conveniently divided.   On the ground floor, at the right of the spacious vestibule of tiled brick and oak, is the large reception-room, attractively finished and furnished, with a wide-mouthed fireplace and cushioned-seats.   A well-equipped gymnasium is in the rear of the

YOUNG WOMEN'S CHRISTIAN ASSOCIATION, 7 EAST 15TH STREET, NEAR FIFTH AVENUE.

reception-room ; and beneath are the bowling-alleys, locker-rooms, and baths.   The second story contains a large reading-room and the library, finished in mahogany, a lecture-hall, and other rooms. On the third story are several large class and committee rooms, finished in cherry, and connected with each other by sliding doors. Several large class-rooms and the secretary's private room occupy the fourth story, and on the fifth floor there are private bath-rooms, a large class-room and the janitor's apartments.   The object of the Institute is to provide for the physical, intellectual and spiritual welfare of the young men living in its vicinity.   Its membership is over 600, with an average daily attendance of 200.   There are classes in technical studies ; and summer outings.

The German Branch, on Second Avenue, was organized in 1881 for work among the East-Side Germans, by whom it is greatly appreciated.

The French Branch, at 114 West 21st, was formed in 1889; and it offers the attractions of a reading-room, library, gymnasium, restaurant, employment bureau and parlor to the great numbers of French-speaking young men in its vicinity.

The Washington-Heights Branch, on 155th Street, near the Boulevard, furnishes a reading-room, library, parlors, gymnasium and bowling-alley.

The Railroad Branch was organized in 1875, and occupies the beautiful and elegantly equipped Railroad Men's Building, erected for it in 1887 by Cornelius Vanderbilt, at a cost of $75,000. The building is on Madison Avenue and 45th Street. It is unique in many respects, and is the outgrowth of Mr. Vanderhilt's desire to provide the employees of the railroads which enter the Grand Central station with a modern club-house, suited to their needs. It contains a reading-room, a library of 7,000 volumes, social rooms, a gymnasium, bowling-alleys, sleeping-rooms, and a lunch-room.

The West-72d-Street Branch was organized in 1889, and provides a reading-room, library, sleeping-rooms and lunch-room at the round-house of the New-York Central & Hudson-River Railroad.

The Association Boat House is on the Harlem River; and the athletic grounds are at Mott Haven.

The Young Women's Christian Association was founded in 1870, and incorporated in 1873, to aid self-supporting young women by providing special training in such industries as are adapted to them ; to assist them to obtain employment; and to provide opportunities for self-culture. The building of the Association is at 7 East 15th Street, and contains a library of 20,000 volumes, a reading-room, and numerous class-rooms. A Bible-class and social meetings are features of the work ; and there is an employment bureau, a board directory, and free classes in type-writing, stenography, physical culture, needle-work and art, and a salesroom for

APPRENTICES' LIBRARY.

MARGARET LOUISA HOME OF THE Y. W. C. A., 14 EAST 16TH STREET.

the work of consignors. The Association conducts a seaside cottage. There is a branch at 1509 Broadway, with classes in cooking, millinery and physical culture.

The Margaret Louisa Home of the Young Women's Christian Association is at 14 and 16 East 16th Street, communicating with the main building of the Association. It is a beautiful six-story structure, designed by R. H. Robertson, in the Romanesque style, fire-proof, and everywhere abounding in light and air. The main floor has the parlors, offices and restaurant ; and four floors above are occupied by 78 chambers, with 104 beds. This institution is for Protestant self-supporting women, with references, as a safe and very comfortable temporary home, at moderate rates of board. The building was erected (at a cost exceeding $200,000)

27

and presented to the Association by Mrs. Elliott F. Shepard, the oldest daughter of Cornelius Vanderbilt. At the laying of the corner-stone in December, 1889, the services were conducted by the Rev. Drs. John Hall and W. R. Huntington, and Hon. Chauncey M. Depew. The home was opened to the public January 19, 1891.

The Hebrew Institute, dedicated in 1891, at East Broadway and Jefferson Street, is a noble fire-proof building, 87 by 92 feet, and five stories high. The lower part is occupied by an entertainment and lecture hall, seating 710 persons ; the first floor, by kindergarten and industrial-school rooms ; the second and third floors, by ten class-rooms, and the Aguilar Free Library and Y. M. H. A. reading-room ; the top floor, by a gymnasium, lockers and baths, a cooking-room and the manual training workshop ; and the paved roof by a summer-garden.

The Young Men's Hebrew Association was founded in 1873 to advance the moral, social, intellectual and religious welfare of Hebrew young men. It adopts the general methods of the Young Men's Christian Association, and occupies the building at 721 Lexington Avenue, with a branch at East Broadway and Jefferson Street.

HEBREW INSTITUTE, EAST BROADWAY AND JEFFERSON STREET.

The Young Women's Hebrew Association, at 721 Lexington Avenue, and at the Hebrew Institute, corner of Jefferson Street and East Broadway, was founded in 1888. The rooms are open for conversation, games and dancing for members, as well as for instruction. Entertainments of a musical and literary character are frequently given for members and their friends. During the summer of 1891 the association opened a summer-home for working girls at Sea Cliff, Long Island, at nominal rates.

It is difficult to estimate the enormous continual outlay of money, talent and toil in the behalf of religious work on Manhattan Island, and especially among the poor and degraded classes, who stand most in need of elevation and up-building. Certainly the religious people of the city do not withhold from giving most liberally, not only of their funds, but also (and of greater importance) of their own individual and personal efforts. The splendid churches from the Battery to Harlem River have all been erected by voluntary contributions, and the immense cost of their maintenance is similarly borne. In like manner, continuous streams of money are flowing through the treasuries of the great missionary and philanthropic societies, to do good all over the wide world. However sordid some aspects of New York may appear, it has much of the heroic, the beautiful and the noble. This, however, is not much in evidence, in obedience to the injunction of the Divine Teacher, and its benevolent activities are conducted quietly, in the secret shadow of humility.

Charity and Benevolence.

Institutions and Associations for the Poor and Unfortunate—Homes, Asylums, and Temporary Relief.

THE many public and private organized charities of the city are bewildering in their variety and all-comprehensive in their work. The useful *New-York Charities Directory*, published yearly by the Charity Organization Society, summarizes the benevolent resources of the city as follows : Public charities, 28 ; for temporary relief, 83 ; for special relief, 51 ; for foreigners' relief, 26 ; for permanent relief, 67 ; for medical relief, 101 ; for defectives, 16 ; reformatory, 16 ; miscellaneous, 232 ; making a grand total of nearly 700 charitable and benevolent institutions.

The Commissioners of Public Charities and Correction, three Commissioners appointed by the Mayor, have charge of the charitable and correctional institutions, and receive all applications for relief, or admission to the hospitals, etc. The office is at 66 Third Avenue. The yearly appropriations exceed $2,000,000.

The United Charities Building, at the corner of Fourth Avenue and 22d Street, was erected and presented jointly to the Charity Organization Society, the Children's Aid Society, the Association for Improving the Condition of the Poor, and the New-York City Mission and Tract Society, by the munificence of John S. Kennedy, and with the expectation that many other charities of the city will be gathered under its roof, and that their efficiency and economy will be promoted thereby. It is a magnificent seven-story fire-proof edifice, erected in 1891-93, at a cost exceeding $700,000. The lower stories are of granite, and those above are of stone and brick, leading up to a noble tiled roof. The architects were R. H. Robertson and Rowe & Baker. Besides the offices of the four great unsectarian societies, the building contains a beautiful little hall, commodious bath-rooms for the Children's Aid Society, safe-deposit vaults for archives, a library of books about charities, the New-York Cooking School's restaurant, four studios, and many fine offices.

The Charity Organization Society of the City of New York, in the United Charities Building, was inaugurated in 1882, to secure the concurrent action of the various public and private charities of the city, and to act as a source of information on all matters relating to benevolent work. It aims to raise the needy above want, to prevent begging and imposition, to diminish pauperism, to encourage thrift, self-dependence and industry, and to aid the poor by teaching and enabling them to help themselves. At the main office a central registry is kept of all applicants for, and recipients of, charitable relief, with a record of all that is known of their past history. To this registry more than 500 churches and societies and upwards of 1,000 private families contribute information concerning their beneficiaries. To systematize the work, the city is divided into districts, in charge of local committees for investigation and relief. The society bestows no alms from its own funds, but obtains

the needed relief from the proper existing sources.   Its affairs are controlled by a
Central Council, and in addition to its regular work it maintains a Penny Provi-
dent Fund, a Laundry and a Wood-yard.   The society publishes monthly *The
Charities Review*, discussing social and economic questions.

The New-York Association for Improving the Condition of the Poor,
in the United Charities Building, organized in 1843 and incorporated in 1848, aims
by systematic and scientific management to improve the condition of the working

UNITED CHARITIES BUILDING, FOURTH AVENUE, NORTHEAST CORNER OF 22D STREET.

classes, and to elevate their physical state.   Its plan is to promote whatever tends
to the permanent improvement of the condition of the working people ; to uplift
their home-life and habits ; to improve the sanitary condition of their dwellings ;
to supply baths in convenient localities, and at small cost ; to provide fresh-air benefits for those who cannot supply such for themselves ; and whenever the necessity
arises, to get relief for the destitute and deserving, making employment its basis.   It
further endeavors to prevent indiscriminate and duplicate almsgiving ; to secure
the community from imposture ; and to reduce pauperism by ascertaining and recti-
fying its accidental causes.   It is controlled by a board of managers and executive
committee, and supported by voluntary contributions.   It is non-sectarian in character,
and recognizes no distinction of race or nationality.   It supports the People's Baths,
at 9 Centre Market Place, where baths at any temperature can be had the year round
for five cents.   It maintains a Harlem Branch ; and covers the entire city.   It conducts six branches of work, registration, relief, sewing, sanitary, fresh-air and public
baths.   It has the co-operation of the responsible charitable agencies of the city.

In 1891 there were 37,626 beneficiaries ; 17,518 aided by the Fresh-Air department ; 19,000 bathers at the People's Baths ; and 906 aided by work. There were 16,051 visits to and for the poor ; and the sum of $44,333 was disbursed.

Trinity Church Association, at 209 Fulton Street, was organized in 1879, and incorporated in 1887, to carry on general charitable work in the lower part of the city. It maintains the Trinity Mission House, at 209 and 211 Fulton Street, as headquarters for work among the poor, where they may apply for relief ; a kindergarten for young children ; a kitchen-garden, where 25 little girls receive instruction in general housework ; a Down-Town Relief Bureau ; a Provident Dispensary ; a Sea-side Home for Children, near Islip, L. I., and a Training-School for young girls in household work. The yearly expenditures are about $10,000.

DEPARTMENT OF PUBLIC CHARITIES AND CORRECTION; THIRD AVENUE AND EAST 11TH STREET.

The Down-Town Relief Bureau, at 209 Fulton Street, was founded in 1882 for general out-door relief work among the poor in the lower wards of the city. It is supported by Trinity-Church Association and by voluntary contributions. Five thousand applicants were aided in 1892, at an expense of $35,000.

The Society of St. Vincent De Paul in the City of New York was organized in 1835, and chartered in 1872. Its leading objects are the cultivation of the Christian life ; the visitation of the poor and sick ; educational work among children ; and general charitable work. Nearly all the local Catholic churches have separate conferences of the society, each confining its work to the limits of its own parish. There are upwards of fifty local conferences, all under the jurisdiction of the Particular Council of New York, which holds monthly meetings at the Cathedral School-house, 111 East 50th Street.

The University Settlement Society was formed for the purpose of bringing men of education and refinement into closer relations with the laboring classes of the city, for mutual instruction and benefit. It aims to establish "Settlements" in the tenement-house districts, where college men interested in the work may live, and mingle with their poor neighbors, on terms of perfect equality, somewhat after the plan of the famous Toynbee Hall, in London. It maintains the Neighborhood Guild, at 26 Delancey Street, which includes kindergartens, a gymnasium, boys' and girls' clubs, a reading-room and circulating library, penny-provident bank, concerts, and lectures, besides dancing, cooking, sewing, singing and other classes. It has organized the Tenth-Ward Social Reform Club, to establish public baths, laundries, kitchens, lavatories, parks, co-operative stores, sick benefit societies, etc.

The College Settlement, at 95 Rivington Street, was established by women college-graduates, in 1889. The residents, with outside helpers, conduct clubs for women, boys and girls; classes in cooking, millinery, dressmaking, embroidery, kitchen-garden, wood-carving, drawing, singing, literature and municipal government; a library and reading-room; a penny-provident fund; and a kindergarten.

The League of Theosophical Workers, organized in 1891, with head-quarters at 144 Madison Avenue, is a central exchange, through which individual members of the Theosophical Society and branches work so that better results may be accomplished. The objects of the League are to relieve the sufferings of mankind, physical, mental and moral. The means employed are general, mainly through the propaganda of the science of Theosophy and of the doctrine of the universal brotherhood of man. Cases of charity are given such attention as the funds of the League permit, but the means employed tend more especially to the eradication of the cause of evil and sorrow than to the alleviation of physical effects.

The Five-Points House of Industry is one of the best-known charitable institutions of the country. It has had a long and glorious history. For many years the Five Points of New York, the meeting-place of Baxter, Worth and Park Streets,

FIVE-POINTS HOUSE OF INDUSTRY, 155 WORTH STREET, OPPOSITE PARADISE PARK.

bore an evil name and fame throughout the world. Dickens wandered into its dens of iniquity in 1841, and described its horrors. With a few dilapidated wooden buildings, thickly peopled with human beings of every age, color and condition, it was an abode of atrocious crime and vice, avoided by peaceful citizens, and regarded with anxiety by the police. As early as 1830 earnest Christian efforts were made to regenerate this degraded neighborhood. A mission was started on Baxter Street, and a day-school opened, mainly under the auspices of the Central and Spring-Street Presbyterian Churches. No very promising results followed. In the spring of 1850 the Rev. Lewis Morris Pease, a Methodist clergyman, was commissioned by the Conference to open a mission at the Five Points, under the guidance of the Ladies' Home Missionary Society of the Methodist Episcopal Church. Differences of opinion regarding the best methods of work soon caused a separation between the society and Mr. Pease, who immediately, on his own responsibility, leased a number of houses, and opened the Five-Points Home. His success was so great that generous gifts were made for the extension and support of the work, and in 1854 a board of trustees was formed, and the Home incorporated as the Five-Points House of Industry. In its early years the work of the Home was largely among the abandoned women of the neighborhood, but of late it has labored mainly among the children. A commodious brick building was erected in 1856 ; and here, with additions, the work has been successfully carried on. Over 40,000 inmates have been received in school, and provided with homes, sent to their friends, or placed in other institutions. The leading features of the work are the preservation of children from crime and destitution ; and the providing for them of homes, support, and religious and secular education. The institution also boards children of poor parents at merely nominal rates ; shelters women while they are seeking work as servants ; and affords temporary relief to destitute families in its neighborhood. Over 700 were sheltered in the Home during 1892, while 1,023 pupils received instruction in the day-schools. The infirmary and free dispensary gives free treatment to 1,600 cases yearly, and a lay missionary is constantly employed among the poor and destitute classes in the vicinity. The yearly expenses average $40,000, and are met by voluntary contributions and grants from the public funds. Morris K. Jesup is president of the Board of Trustees ; and William F. Barnard is the superintendent of the Home.

The Five-Points Mission, at 63 Park Street, was organized in 1850, by the Ladies' Home-Missionary Society of the Methodist-Episcopal Church. The work at the Five Points was begun in a former dram-shop at the corner of Cross and Little Water Streets. The need of larger accommodations led to the purchase, in 1852, of that lazar-house of crime, the Old Brewery, in Park Street, which, built long before the city extended to the vicinity, had been for many years the resort of thieves and murderers, and the scene of many

FIVE-POINTS MISSION, 63 PARK STREET, OPPOSITE PARADISE PARK.

horrible crimes. This nest of iniquity was speedily demolished, and its place was filled by a group of buildings, comprising a chapel, parsonage, school-house, bathing-rooms, dining-rooms, etc., and tenements for poor families. This Mission has been a potent factor in the regeneration of the entire neighborhood, its chief object being so to educate children as to make them capable of self-support. The work is both religious and philanthropic. There is much missionary work done among the poor of this part of the city ; and the Mission also provides for the physical welfare of many children and adults. It has in successful operation the Boys' and Girls' Shoe-Club; the Cooking-School for Girls; the Day-School, in which 600 pupils are enrolled; the Free Library and Reading Room for men and boys; the Fresh-Air Fund; and the Girls' Sewing-School. Over 6,000 individuals and 600 families were assisted during 1892; and nearly 100,000 dinners were served to hungry mouths. Church and Sunday-school services are held regularly. A much larger evangelistic and school building, with modern appliances, is about to be erected here.

The Bowery Mission and Young Men's Home, at 105 Bowery, was founded in 1880, for aggressive Christian work among the young men living in that locality, in which there are only two Protestant churches for an English-speaking population of 30,000. The work has been uniformly successful, over 300,000 young men having attended the evening meetings, many of whom have been reclaimed from evil lives. There are evening and Sunday religious meetings; a reading-room and library; and a lodging-house, where 125 persons can be boarded at a low rate. A distinctive feature of the work is the visitation of the lodging-houses in the neighborhood, of which there are sixty, crowded nightly with young men.

The Old Jerry McAuley Water-Street Mission, at 316 Water Street, was established in 1872 by Jerry McAuley, at one time a convict in the State Prison

OLD BREWERY, SITE OF THE FIVE-POINTS MISSION.

at Sing Sing, and afterwards a no-torious river-thief about New York. He was converted in prison by Orville Gardner, the converted pugilist, and reclaimed in 1868, at a little prayer-meeting at Franklin Smith's house. This change of heart was of profound benefit to thousands of outcasts, and in 1872 McAuley opened the Water-Street Mission, which has become famous for the good it has accomplished among the fallen men and women of the Fourth Ward, thousands of whom have been transformed into useful members of society by its work. The original mission, which occupied a former dance-house, was replaced in 1876 by the present well-arranged building. Services are held nightly, and substantial aid is extended to those who desire to lead better lives. The work is entirely among the degraded ones of a district teeming with crime, and presents many interesting features. The yearly expenses of the Mission, which are met by voluntary contributions, are $6,000. S. H. Hadley is superintendent.

The Cremorne Mission, at 104 West 32d Street, was opened in 1882 by Jerry McAuley, for rescue work among the fallen and inebriate men and women of the West Side. It occupies a part of the building once known as the Cremorne Garden, a notorious resort in its day. There is no home in connection with the Mission, its work consisting mainly of nightly religious services of a revival character. Many converts have been made and much good accomplished in the last ten years.

Scores of societies have been organized for the protection and endearment of children, and they have done a mighty work in alleviating the sufferings of the little ones, born to misery in the dives of the great metropolis.

The New-York Society for the Prevention of Cruelty to Children,
the first of its kind in the world, was organized in 1875, under the provisions of the general law of that year, providing for the institution of such societies in the different counties of the State. Its objects are the prevention of cruelty to children, and the enforcement by all lawful means of the laws relating to, or in anywise affecting, children, and the care of children pending investigations. All magistrates, constables, sheriffs and police officers are required by law to aid the society in its work, which has been a source of incalculable benefit to the poor waifs of the city, too often at the mercy of hard

THE NEW-YORK SOCIETY FOR THE PREVENTION OF CRUELTY TO CHILDREN, FOURTH AVENUE AND 23D STREET.

and cruel taskmasters or depraved parents. The society is governed by a board of directors, who elect the members ; these are of three classes — regular, honorary and life members. A life membership costs $100 ; regular members pay $5 yearly ; and honorary members are those who have been active in aiding the work of the society. The offices and reception-rooms for children are at 297 Fourth Avenue, corner of East 23d Street. Elbridge T. Gerry is the President ; Dallas B. Pratt, Treasurer ; and E. Fellows Jenkins, Superintendent.

NEW-YORK INFANT ASYLUM, AMSTERDAM AVENUE AND WEST 61st STREET.

The New-York Infant Asylum was founded in 1865, and chartered in 1871, for the protection, care and medical treatment of young unmarried women during their confinement, needy mothers and their infants, and foundlings. The asylum, at Amsterdam Avenue and 61st Street, is a large and well-appointed building; and there is an efficient staff of attendants and nurses. During 1892, 1,400 inmates were cared for, at an expense of $100,000. The institution has a country home and nursery at Mount Vernon, N. Y., to which poor mothers and children are sent during the summer months.

The New-York Foundling Hospital was incorporated in 1869, and until 1891 it was known as the Foundling Asylum of the Sisters of Charity. The Asylum comprises a group of buildings at 175 East 68th Street, with accommodations for 700 children and 300 adults; and is fitted up in a most complete and thorough manner. Its objects are the reception, care and education of foundlings and abandoned children, who are brought up in the Christian faith; the influencing of the mothers to lead useful and honest lives; and obtaining homes in the West for indentured children. Mothers who are willing to act as nurses are admitted with their infants. Nearly 1,400 infants are cared for yearly at their homes by the Outdoor Department. In connection with the Asylum, and under the same management, there is a Chil-

NEW-YORK FOUNDLING ASYLUM, 175 EAST 68TH STREET, NEAR THIRD AVENUE.

dren's Hospital, for the inmates of the institution; a Maternity Hospital; and a Day Nursery and Kindergarten School. There is also an annex at Spuyten Duyvil, accommodating 150 children. The yearly expenses reach $300,000.

St. Joseph's Day Nursery of the City of New York, at 473 West 57th Street, was incorporated in 1890. It receives and cares for during the day the children of working-women, irrespective of color or creed. The children receive kindergarten instruction, and have two meals daily. The average daily attendance is 50. Here also is a free employment bureau for domestic help.

The Bartholdi Creche, at 105 East 22d Street, was founded in 1886, and incorporated in 1890. During the summer months it maintains a seaside cottage at Randall's Island for poor mothers with sick infants and children under 12, who are unable to leave the city for a prolonged stay at any of the more distant seaside homes. A trained nurse and assistant are constantly in attendance, and cots and hammocks, pure milk, tea and coffee are provided. A ferry is maintained at the foot of East 120th Street for all who hold tickets, which are issued free of charge by the Charity Organization Society, the dispensaries, and other similar institutions. About 3,000 women and children are received each year.

The "Little Mothers'" Aid Society, at 305 East 17th Street, was founded in 1890 to furnish summer-day excursions for little girls compelled to take charge of younger children while their parents are at work, and who, therefore, cannot receive the benefit of other fresh-air charities. During the winter it provides entertainments, and classes in cooking and sewing, and supplies clothing and other necessities to the deserving.

The Tribune Fresh-Air Fund was established in 1877 by the Rev. Willard Parsons, sixty children having been sent out into the country for a brief stay during the

CHILDREN'S AID SOCIETY, CENTRAL OFFICE,
24 ST. MARK'S PLACE.

year. In 1878 the cause was championed by the *Evening Post*, and in 1882 the Fund was transferred to the *New-York Tribune*, which has had charge of the work since that time. The children are selected by Christian workers among the poor in New York, Brooklyn and Jersey City, and are given a fortnight's stay in the sweet peacefulness and healthfulness of farm-houses, far away in the green and sunlit

CHILDREN'S AID SOCIETY: NEWSBOYS' LODGING-HOUSE.
9 DUANE STREET, CORNER OF WILLIAM STREET.

open country, where they are received, not as boarders, but as guests, generous readers of the *Tribune* paying all transportation expenses. There are no office expenses, and all the receipts are used for the benefit of poor children. During 1892 nearly 15,000 children were aided by this charity, at an expense of $28,000. Since 1877, 110,000 children have been sent into the country, and over $280,000 has been contributed for the work. Besides the children sent for long sojourns among the fields and woods, 85,000 have been given shorter outings in the country, usually of a day or so.

St. John's Guild was organized in 1866 by twelve gentlemen, who had been touched by the sight of the sufferings and privations of the thousands of New-York's tenement-house children, of whom a recent census of the Board

CHILDREN'S AID SOCIETY : BOYS' LODGING-HOUSE.
SEVENTH AVENUE AND 32D STREET.

of Health shows more than 160,000 under the age of five, with as many more between five and fifteen. The city had made no adequate provision for healthful out-door exercise for these little dwellers in the crowded tenement-houses, and the death-rate among them was appalling. St. John's Guild is organized for the express purpose of assisting sick children and their mothers, by trips down the harbor in the Floating Hospital Barge, and by food and nursing at the Seaside Hospital on Staten Island. As many as five trips a week are made during the summer, and over 30,000 mothers and children receive the benefits of invigorating sea breezes. At the Seaside Hospital, 1,000 children and more than 500 weary mothers yearly are admitted and tenderly cared for. Since the organization of the Guild over half a million sick children and mothers have had the benefit of excursions down the

bay. The Guild has a membership of 700 representative citizens, and is a favorite channel of beneficences. It embodies and exemplifies the true spirit and method of charitable effort, and is conspicuous for its application of the most careful business system and practice to every department of its work. The trustees have recently inaugurated a new feature in the work of ministering to the vast multitude of poor children, by opening the first of a series of small hospitals for children, which they hope to establish in the centres of densely populated districts. The new hospital, opened in 1892, is on West 61st Street, near Amsterdam Avenue. Others will follow as soon as the necessary funds are forthcoming, and will alleviate much of the harshness of life for the unfortunate children of the poor.

CHILDREN'S AID SOCIETY : EAST-SIDE BOYS' LODGING-HOUSE AND
INDUSTRIAL SCHOOL, 287 EAST BROADWAY.

The **Children's Aid Society,** one of the most helpful charities, was organized in 1853 by the late Charles Loring Brace and a few other gentlemen, who had been engaged in teaching some of the little arabs of the streets. The society was incorporated in 1856, "for the education of the poor, by gathering children who attend no schools into its industrial schools, caring and providing for children in lodging-houses, and procuring homes for them in the rural districts and in the West." In 1892 35,659 children were cared for, of whom nearly 3,000 were provided with homes. The offices of the society are at 24 St. Mark's Place. As supplementary to its work it maintains : The East-Side Mission, a fragrant charity, whose work is to distribute flowers daily during the summer months among the sick and poor ;

Free Reading-Rooms for Young Men, in Sullivan and 44th Streets; the Health Home at West Coney Island, comprising cottages and dormitories where mothers with sick children are given a grateful outing; the Sick Children's Mission, at 287 East Broadway, with a staff of ten physicians and four nurses, who visit the sick poor at their homes and supply free medical attendance, medicine and food for sick children, of whom 1,500 are treated yearly; a Summer Home at Bath Beach, Long Island, where over 4,000 tenement-house children are given a week's outing by the seaside each year; six lodging-houses, five for boys and one for girls, in which, during 1892, over 6,000 boys and girls were fed and sheltered; and twenty-two industrial and ten night schools, in which 12,000 children

CHILDREN'S AID SOCIETY : LODGING-HOUSE AND INDUSTRIAL SCHOOL FOR CRIPPLED BOYS, SECOND AVENUE AND 44TH STREET.

were taught and partly fed and partly clothed during 1892. One of the industrial schools is located in each of the lodging-houses for boys, and the two branches of the work are very closely interwoven. The lodging-house for girls is at 307 East 12th Street. Those for boys are at 9 Duane Street, 295 East 8th Street, 287 East Broadway, Second Avenue and East 44th Street, and Seventh Avenue and West 32d Street. A special feature of the Second-Avenue establishment is the industrial instruction for crippled boys. An adjunct is a brush-shop, in which a dozen crippled boys are employed, and 150 are at work pending permanent employment. The Children's Aid Society has found homes for 80,000 children, many of whom are educated and influential men and women. They become adopted children of the farmers, in field-work and house-work, and are loved and cared for and educated.

The **Leake and Watts Orphan House,** one of the most benevolent in design and meritorious in mission of all the city charities, was incorporated in 1831 as a free home for full orphans between the ages of three and twelve years, in destitute circumstances.   This graceful charity owes its origin to the benevolence of John G. Leake, a wealthy New-York lawyer, who died in the early part of the century, leaving his large fortune to Robert Watts, the son of an old friend, on condition that he should assume the name of Leake.   In case of a failure to comply with this provision, or of the death without heirs of the testator, the estate was to be applied to the founding of an orphan asylum.   After a long lawsuit, it was decided that Mr. Leake had left no direct heirs, and that Robert Watts could inherit the property.   He, however, died before he could comply with the condition mentioned in the will, and the estate passed into the hands of a board of trustees, who obtained a charter for an asylum under the name of the Leake and Watts Orphan Home.   In 1843 they erected buildings in 113th Street.   Here the institution cared for homeless and friendless orphans, educating them and, at the age of fourteen, obtaining Christian homes for them.   In 1886 the estate was sold to the trustees of the Cathedral of St. John the Divine, for a building site, and the pleasant and spacious home now occupied was built at Ludlow, near the northern boundary of the city.

The **Roman Catholic Orphan Asylum** was founded in 1825, and incorporated in 1852, superseding an older society called the Roman Catholic Benevolent Society, which received its charter in 1817.   The original location of the asylum was on Prince Street, but in 1851 the present asylum for boys at Fifth Avenue and 51st Street was completed.   It is one of the largest and best-equipped orphan asylums in the country, and has accommodations for 500 lads. An additional wing is being built as a trade-school, and will accommodate 200 more boys. The girls' asylum was completed in 1890, and is

ROMAN CATHOLIC ORPHAN ASYLUM (BOYS), FIFTH AVENUE AND 51st STREET.

of the same substantial character as that of the boys, but somewhat larger, accommodating 800 girls.   In both the boys' and girls' departments provision is made for the religious, moral and technical instruction of the inmates.   The work is carried on with a thoroughness which is characteristic of the Catholic Church.   The new and admirable building on Madison Avenue was completed in 1893.

St. Joseph's Orphan Asylum in the City of New York, at 89th Street and Avenue A, was founded in 1858, and incorporated in 1859, for the support of orphans, half-orphans and homeless and neglected children of German parentage, who are cared for until they are sixteen years old, or until homes or occupations could be provided.   The home is a large building, accommodating 750 inmates, and costing $65,000 a year.   It is in charge of the Sisters of Notre Dame.

The Orphans' Home and Asylum of the Protestant Episcopal Church in the City of New York, one of the most important charities of its class, was founded in 1851, at the request of a few ladies connected with St. Paul's Chapel, to whom a child had been entrusted by a dying father, with the injunction that it should be brought up in the faith of the Protestant Episcopal Church. The asylum was incorporated in 1859, for the care, support and religious training of orphans and half-orphans, who are received between the ages of three and eight, and may be retained

ORPHANS' HOME AND ASYLUM OF THE PROTESTANT EPISCOPAL CHURCH, LEXINGTON AVENUE AND EAST 49TH STREET.

— the boys until they are twelve, and the girls until they are fourteen, when homes are provided for them. In common with other kindred institutions, religious, moral, intellectual and technical instruction is imparted to the inmates, the aim being to fit them to become useful and upright members of society. The smaller children are kept at the summer-home during the warm months, and the older ones enjoy vacations there. The home, at Lexington Avenue and East 49th Street, has accommodations for 150 inmates. A new home is greatly desired. The yearly expenses are $27,000, and there is an endowment fund of $212,000.

The Orphan Asylum Society in the City of New York is the oldest and one of the best-endowed institutions of its class in the country. It was founded in March, 1806, to minister to the wants of the parentless children of the community, and train them up in the paths of virtue. The work was begun in a small way by leasing a house in Greenwich Village. The act of incorporation came in 1807, and in the following year a suitable building was erected, not far from the first temporary quarters. A desirable location on Riverside Drive and West 73d Street was secured in 1835, and a large building was immediately erected, with accommodations for 250 children. The location is a charming one, overlooking the Hudson, and the grounds are attractively laid out. Orphans not above ten years of age are admitted to the home, and given thorough moral, mental and manual training, until they reach the age of fourteen, when Christian homes are obtained for them. The home is usually taxed to the utmost of its capacity. It

ORPHAN ASYLUM SOCIETY, RIVERSIDE DRIVE AND WEST 73D STREET.

is free and unsectarian.   Its yearly expenses are $32,000, two-thirds of which are
met by the income from invested funds.

The Eighth-Ward Mission was established in 1877, and maintains a home
at Charlton Street, where orphan boys too old to be retained in other institutions,
and unable to support themselves, are cared for and educated, and assisted in their
efforts to obtain permanent employment.   The Mission also supports an industrial
school, where young girls are taught sewing and other household work ; and the
Brown Memorial Home, at Sing-Sing-on-the-Hudson, a summer home for boys.

The Society for the Relief of Half-Orphan and Destitute Children
in the City of New York was organized in 1835 and incorporated in 1837.   Protestant children of both sexes, between the ages of four and ten, are received and
properly cared for at a charge of $4 a month.   Until 1890 the home was in West
10th Street.   Then it was removed to a more desirable location on Manhattan
Avenue, between 104th and 105th Streets, where a building had been erected for it.
It has 200 inmates ; and the work is similar in character and scope to that of other
orphan asylums, the object being the intellectual and moral training of the bereaved
children of working people until homes can be provided for them.

The American Female Guardian Society and Home for the Friendless
was founded in 1834, "to protect, befriend and train to virtue and usefulness those for
whom no one seemed to have a thought or pity."   For a number of years the work was carried on entirely by w o m e n, with great energy, fearlessness and success.   In 1846 a successful appeal was made to the public for funds sufficient to b u i l d a Home for the Friendless, and in 1848 a substantial and convenient house was erected at 32 East 30th S t r e e t. There is a Home C h a p e l, fronting on East 29th Street.   Here homeless girls, and boys not over eleven years of age, are received and cared for until they can be placed in Christian. h o m e s.   Besides the Home, the society supports a Home - School

AMERICAN FEMALE GUARDIAN SOCIETY AND HOME FOR THE FRIENDLESS,
HOME CHAPEL, 29 EAST 29TH STREET AND 82 EAST 30TH STREET.

in East 29th Street, and twelve industrial schools, where the children of poor parents
are clothed and taught.   The work is supported by voluntary subscription and by a
yearly grant from the public-school fund.   In 1892 there were 450 inmates in the
Home, and 5,832 pupils in the schools.   The yearly expenses are $130,000.

The Sheltering Arms, one of the graceful charities for "The children in the midst," in which New York so generously abounds, was founded in 1864 by the Rev. Dr. T. M. Peters, then and now rector of St. Michael's Church, for the reception and care of homeless and destitute children, between five and twelve years of age, for whom no other institution in the city made provision. Here the blind, the deaf and dumb, the crippled and the incurables, are received and tenderly cared for until they are old enough to enter other suitable institutions. For six years this charity occupied a house given to it, rent free, by the founder, but in 1870 it removed to more roomy quarters at Amsterdam Avenue and 129th Street, where

SHELTERING ARMS, AMSTERDAM AVENUE AND WEST 129TH STREET.

ample accommodations for 200 waifs are provided. Whole orphans and infants are not received, and the children are not surrendered to the institution, but are held subject to the order of the parents or other relatives, being sent to the public schools and trained to household and other work. The yearly expenses are $17,000, and there is an endowment fund of $100,000.

The Children's Fold is a charity organized in 1867 to provide homes for homeless children between the ages of four and ten. They receive religious training, and education in the public schools. There are three families; two for boys, in Westchester County, and the other for girls, on 155th Street. The three homes have nearly 200 inmates, and each is in charge of its own "house-mother," with a general superintendent in charge of all. The yearly expenses are $17,000.

The Howard Mission and Home for Little Wanderers, known far and wide for the extent and value of its work, received its charter in 1864. Its purpose is to aid poor, neglected and helpless children, and worthy families among the very poor, by providing food, clothing, shelter and Christian love and sympathy, expressed in all practical ways. The homes of poor widows or disabled fathers are kept together by relief ; the sick are relieved ; and children are educated and kept, and at last placed in selected Christian families. The Mission has relieved more than 150,000 persons. It is purely unsectarian. The Mission-House and Home is at 225 East 11th Street, quite accessible to a region of squalor, wretchedness, vice and poverty, which provides many clients for the care of the officers of the mission.

St. Christopher's Home, formerly at Riverside Drive and West 112th Street, and now at Ingleside, near Dobbs Ferry, is under the patronage of the Methodist Episcopal Church. It was founded in 1882 as a home for destitute and orphan Protestant children between the ages of two and ten years. About 100 inmates are received yearly, who are taught some useful occupation to enable them to obtain self-supporting employment. Admission is free to those whose parents or friends are unable to contribute to their support.

28

The United Relief Works of the Society for Ethical Culture is an organization chartered by the Legislature for charitable and educational purposes, and entirely unsectarian in character. It was founded in 1879 ; for the last eleven years its quarters have been at 109 West 54th Street. It maintains the Working-man's School, comprising a Kindergarten ; a fully graded school (for children from six to fourteen years of age) based on the kindergarten principle, and a Normal Class for the training of kindergartners ; a Fresh-Air Fund, and a District Nursing Department. The annual expenses are $28,000.

The Children's Charitable Union was organized in 1877 to establish and maintain kindergartens for destitute young children, and to educate young women as kindergarten teachers. The school of the Union is at 70 Avenue D, where 75 poor children are taught daily and are fed at noon. The expenses are met by private charity.

The Asylum of St. Vincent de Paul is a large and well-arranged house at 215 West 39th Street. The institution was incorporated in 1868 for the reception,

ST. VINCENT DE PAUL'S ASYLUM, 215 WEST 39TH STREET.

care and religious and secular education of destitute and unprotected orphans of both sexes, preferably of French birth or parentage, over four years old. It is in charge of the Roman Catholic Sisters "Marianites of the Holy Cross," and is connected with the Church of St. Vincent de Paul. There are about 250 inmates, for whom a fresh-air fund provides seaside trips in summer. It is supported by voluntary contributions, and grants from the public funds. The architect was W. H. Hume.

The Dominican Convent of Our Lady of the Rosary, also known as the House of Our Lady of the Rosary, is at 329 East 63d Street. It was established in 1880 by the Sisters of St. Dominic, for religious, charitable, educational and reformatory work among young girls. Homeless and destitute girls between the ages of 2½ and 14 are admitted free, educated, and trained in the Catholic faith ; and when 16 years of age, provided with good homes. The convent educates nearly 500 girls yearly, at an expense of $60,000, which is partly met by a grant from the public funds.

The New-York Catholic Protectory was incorporated in 1863, to care for destitute Catholic children of the following classes ; 1st, children under fourteen years old, entrusted to it for care or protection ; 2d, those between the ages of seven and fourteen, who may be committed to its charge by magistrates as idle, truant, vicious or homeless ; 3d, those of the same age transferred from other institutions by the Commissioners of Public Charities and Correction. The protectories proper are at Westchester, N. Y., and the office and House of Reception are at 415 Broome Street. The Boys' Protectory is in charge of the Brothers of the Christian Schools, and the inmates are educated and taught useful trades. The Girls' Protectory is in charge of the Sisters of Charity, who educate the girls, and teach them housework and other industrial employment. This is one of the largest institutions of its class in the country, and cares for over 3,000 children yearly. The annual expenses, of $425,000, are met by grants from the public funds, voluntary contributions, and the sale of articles made by the inmates.

The Mission of the Immaculate Virgin, which occupies a large brick build-ing at Lafayette Place and Great Jones Street, was incorporated in 1870 as a home for destitute boys under 16 years of age, who receive secular and religious educa-tion, and are taught habits of industry and self-reliance. Newsboys, bootblacks, and other youthful workers who are able to pay, are allowed meals and lodgings at $2 a week, and in every case of destitution meals and lodg-ings are given free. The in-stitution is in charge of St. Joseph's Union, a Catholic benevolent society. There is a country branch, at Mount Loretto, Staten Island, to which invalid inmates of the home are sent for an outing in the summer months. The Mission usually has in its care 2,000 boys, many of whom obtain situations through its employment bureau. The institution receives a large yearly grant from the public funds.

St. Joseph's Indus-trial Home for Destitute Children was established in 1868 by the Sisters of Mercy,

MISSION OF THE IMMACULATE VIRGIN AND ST. JOSEPH'S UNION, LAFAYETTE PLACE AND GREAT JONES STREET.

as a branch of the Institute of Mercy. The home is at the corner of Madison Avenue and 81st Street, and has accommodations for 750 children. It affords a home and an industrial education to destitute young girls of good character, and also receives children over three years of age, who may be committed to its charge by a magistrate. In connection with the parent-house there is the Institution of Mercy, at Tarrytown, delightfully situated amid charming rural scenery.

St. Ann's Home for Destitute Children, at Avenue A and East 90th Street, is a Catholic charity, founded in 1879, for the care and education of destitute chil-dren over two years of age, who may be entrusted to it by parents or guardians, or committed by a magistrate. The Home is a large and cheerful edifice, with accom-modations for nearly 300 inmates. It is in charge of the Sisters of the Good Shep-herd, who receive the suffering regardless of creed, and give them a happy and com-fortable home, in the mournful absence of their parents.

The **House of the Holy Family**, at 136 Second Avenue, was founded by the Rt. Rev. Mgr. Preston, formerly Vicar-General of the Archdiocese and Domestic Prelate to His Holiness Leo XIII., and was incorporated in 1870. The interior

administration was entrusted to the Sisters of the Divine Compassion. The work is the rescue, care and education of vagrant and tempted children and young girls, who are there trained and educated morally, intellectually and industrially. The House receives 500 inmates annually, and provides homes and occupation for deserving members when they wish to leave. The Sisters also conduct the House of Nazareth, at White Plains, for the care of young children still innocent, but who have been rescued from impending evil.

Many associations have been formed for the education, defence and relief of women, from the young girls just looking out upon life, up to the venerable grand-dames almost ready to pass away.

HOUSE OF THE HOLY FAMILY, 136 SECOND AVENUE.

The **Ladies' Christian Union** of the City of New York was organized in 1859 to promote the moral, temporal and religious welfare of women, particularly self-supporting young women, by providing them with home-like boarding-houses. The society maintains two homes : The Young Women's Home, at 27 Washington Square North, where nearly 100 respectable working-girls, other than house-servants, are lodged and boarded, at from $3 to $6 a week ; and The Branch Home, at 308 Second Avenue, where the same privilege is given to 40 self-supporting girls and women.

The **Working Women's Protective Union** was formed in 1863, to protect working women against the exactions and oppressions of unscrupulous employers. In every possible way the Union seeks to stand between the female wage-earner and the employer who would defraud her of her scanty wage. It also aids the same class in their efforts to obtain employment, and maintains a library at its office, 19 Clinton Place. Household servants are not included in its clients.

The **Working Girls' Vacation Society,** at 222 West 38th Street, was founded in 1883 to provide a two weeks' vacation for respectable unmarried working-girls who have satisfactory recommendations and a physician's statement that a vacation is needed. Railroad fares and board are provided, at the nominal rate of $1.50 a week. The society also pays the fares of working-girls to their friends in the country, and gives frequent day excursions in New-York harbor. Applications are made through clergymen, city missionaries or the Charity Organization Society. In 1892 776 girls were sent into the country for two weeks, 73 fares paid, and over 5,000 Glen-Island excursion-tickets furnished.

The **Female Assistance Society** was organized in 1813 for the relief of poor women in sickness. It has no house or home for its beneficiaries, and does its work by house-to-house visitation of those who apply for aid.

The **Society for the Employment and Relief of Poor Women** was founded, in 1844, to supply work at remunerative prices to poor women able and willing to work, who, having young children, or from sickness, are unable to leave their homes to obtain employment. About 100 applicants are aided yearly by the society, which has a repository at 146 East 16th Street, and an office at 104 East 20th Street.

The House and School of Industry, at 120 West 16th Street, was founded in 1851, to relieve poor women by furnishing them with plain and fine sewing, at living prices. Instruction in needle-work is also given to large classes of young girls. The yearly number of beneficiaries is about 125. The Home has a very attractive and comfortable brick building.

St. Mary's Lodging-House for Sheltering Respectable Girls, at 143 West 14th Street, was founded in 1877 by the "Friends of the Homeless," for the comfort and protection of respectable young women in search of work, who are given the comforts of a pleasant home free of cost, until they are able to support themselves. The object of the Home is to protect its inmates from the numerous temptations that beset unemployed girls in all large cities. Nearly 2,000 young women were received in 1892.

HOUSE AND SCHOOL OF INDUSTRY, 120 WEST 16TH STREET.

The Institution of Mercy, on 81st Street, between Madison and Fourth Avenues, was opened in 1848, for the care and protection of destitute young women of good character, whom it trains in some useful pursuit, and assists in securing employment. About 400 young women are aided yearly by this charity, which is in charge of the Sisters of Mercy.

The New-York Female Asylum for Lying-In Women, at 139 Second Avenue, was incorporated in 1827, to provide free accommodation and medical attendance during confinement, to respectable indigent married women. It also gives the same aid to similar cases at their homes, and trains wet nurses for their profession.

St. Barnabas' House, at 304 Mulberry Street, is one of the numerous noble charities of the Episcopal City Missionary Society. It was established in 1865, as a temporary refuge for destitute and homeless women and those recently discharged from hospitals, cured, but needing rest ; and a temporary home for destitute and homeless children. In connection with the House, and as auxiliary to its work of relief, there is a dispensary ; a free day-nursery ; an employment society for women ; a fresh-air fund ; a free library ; an industrial school, where needle-work is taught ; and a chapel where frequent religious services are held. During 1892 nearly 1,300 women and children were aided, 82,000 meals supplied to hungry applicants, and 18,630 lodgings given to the homeless.

The Isaac T. Hopper Home, at 110 Second Avenue, was opened in 1845 by the Women's Prison Association to assist liberated female prisoners with advice and encouragement; to provide them with a home and work; and to watch over them during the transition from prison-life to freedom. The aims of the manage. ment of the Home, which was named in memory of Isaac T. Hopper, the founder of the Women's Prison Association, are to prevent the recently liberated prisoners from falling back to their former evil courses, and to make an upright life easier for them. The privileges of the institution are free to the inmates, of whom there are about fifty.

The Riverside Rest Association, at 310 East 26th Street, provides a temporary home for friendless women who have been discharged from the public institutions on Blackwell's Island, and, so far as possible, procures work for them. It also cares for women who are addicted to drink, or victims of the opium habit, or immoral, and transfers them to the suitable institution for each case. The association was founded in 1887, and the Home has accommodations for 30 inmates.

The unfortunate women of the town, who are numbered here by legions, also have pitying hands outstretched to help them.

The New-York Magdalen Asylum was established in 1833 by the New-York Magdalen Society as a home for fallen women. It was the first American charity of its class. For twenty years it occupied a building on West 25th Street, but in 1850 the large brick building on 88th Street, between Madison and Fifth Avenues, was erected. In 1893 it occupied a new building, at the foot of 139th Street and North River. The asylum accommodates 125 inmates, and every effort is made to reclaim them by kindly treatment and also by teaching them different kinds of work, so that they may support themselves honestly.

The House of Mercy is a Protestant Episcopal home for fallen women, pleasantly located at Inwood-on-the-Hudson (at 206th Street). It originated in 1850, in the Christian labors of Mrs. Wm. Richmond, the wife of the then rector of St. Michael's, in aid of the abandoned women who found no hand outstretched to help them. Her labors resulted in the purchase of a suitable building at the foot of 86th Street, in 1856. The work was there carried on until 1891, when the present quarters were secured. The south wing, known as St. Agnes Hall, is devoted exclusively to the moral and industrial training of young girls between twelve and eighteen years of age. The rest of the edifice is devoted to the work among the older inmates. The House of Mercy is in charge of the Sisters of St. Mary, and a regular chaplain is provided. •Legacies, donations and grants from the public funds are relied on to meet the expenses.

The House of the Good Shepherd, at the foot of East 90th Street, was founded in 1857 by five nuns of the Order of Our Lady of the Good Shepherd of Angers, a Catholic sisterhood founded in France as long ago as 1661, by Père Eudes. It is a house of refuge for fallen women and girls who desire to reform. Although founded and maintained by members of the Catholic communion, the privileges of the institution are free to all, regardless of creed, and there is kindly treatment of all who apply for help and shelter. The inmates are allowed to remain until a thorough reformation is effected, when permanent homes are secured, or employment is found for them. The House of the Good Shepherd is the largest of its kind in the city, having accommodation for 500 inmates, and it has been the means of restoring hundreds of Magdalens to industrious, useful and respectable lives.

St. Joseph's Night Refuge was founded in 1891 by the Friends of the Home-less. The Refuge is in the rear of 143 West 14th Street, and is open to all home-less women, no questions being asked or references required. There are 100 beds. Yearly, over 3,500 wandering women received shelter; and 7,000 meals are given to poor people in the neighborhood. In connection with the Refuge there is a laundry and sewing-room, where employment is given to inmates willing to work.

The Midnight Mission, at 208 West 46th Street, was opened in 1866, for the reclamation of fallen women, who are here given homes, and, if found worthy, aided in obtaining permanent homes or employment. It is in the charge of the Sisterhood of St. John Baptist, an order of the Protestant Episcopal Church.

The Florence Crittenton Mission for Fallen Women was established, in 1883, by Charles M. Crittenton, in memory of his little daughter Florence, and has

since been maintained by him, mainly at his own expense. The Mission is at 21 and 23 Bleecker Street, in the imme-diate vicinity of Mott Street and the Bowery, and finds its work ready to its hand. Its purpose is to reclaim the fallen women of the neighborhood, by providing them with lodging and food until they are strong enough to go out to work for themselves, and by Gospel meetings, which are held nightly until midnight. Many fallen women and dissolute men have been reclaimed here. The nightly services are quite interesting, and often bring out some heart-breaking experiences.

The Margaret Strachan Home and Mission, at 103 and 105 West 27th Street, is the outcome of a ven-ture of faith begun in 1883 by Mar-garet Strachan, a poor seamstress. Her daily walks to and from her work brought her in contact with the licen-tiousness then rife in the vicinity of

FLORENCE CRITTENTON MISSION, 21 BLEECKER STREET.

27th Street, and she resolved to devote her life to the work of rescuing the fallen women in that part of the city. She rented a house; hung out a rude sign, bearing the legend, "Faith Home," and began the work, which she continued until her death, in 1887. She succeeded in interesting some of her patrons. The work increased to such an extent that the adjoining house was rented, and in 1887 both houses were purchased by the Mission, which was incorporated in that year. After the death of the founder the name was changed to the Margaret Strachan Home, and the work has been continued with remarkable success. The lower story of one of the houses is fitted up as a chapel, and Gospel-meetings are held there every night for the inmates, of whom there are about thirty. In the other house there are two pleasant parlors, and the sleeping-rooms are above, in both houses. The Home and Mission engages the attention and care of a number of wealthy ladies.

The Wetmore Home and several other institutions of similar character are actively engaged in the work of relieving the bitter distress of the social outcasts.

Invalids' Homes and the distress of incurables have aroused the pity of thousands, who have banded themselves together into societies to alleviate the woes thus seen.   One of the best of these is the Montefiore Home, described farther on.

The Home for Incurables, at Third Avenue and 182d Street, near Fordham, is one of those useful but mournful charities made necessary by the incurable nature of many diseases.   Its pleasant and well-ventilated buildings stand in a park of twelve acres, surrounded by shade-trees.   It was incorporated in 1866, and receives incurables of the better class at a charge of $7 a week.   There are 180 beds, one-third of them free.   The yearly expenses of $55,000 are met by voluntary contributions and the income of an endowment fund.

The House of the Holy Comforter Free Church Home for Incurables is well named, for if any are in sorest need of comfort it is the unfortunate for whom this home stands open.   The house is one of the numerous beneficent charities of the Protestant Episcopal Church, and was founded in 1880 to provide a free home for the care of destitute Protestant women and children of the better class suffering

HOME FOR THE RELIEF OF THE DESTITUTE BLIND, AMSTERDAM AVENUE AND WEST 104TH STREET.

from incurable diseases.   All patients are received on a three-months' trial and tenderly cared for by the Sisters of the Annunciation of the Blessed Virgin Mary, who are in charge of the work.   The house is at 149 Second Avenue, and the work involves the yearly expenditure of $7,000.

The New-York Home for Convalescents, at 433 West 118th Street, was opened in 1878 to afford gratuitous temporary care, employment and other assistance to worthy Protestant poor people, discharged as cured from the hospitals, but not yet able to resume their usual occupations.   This very necessary charity receives 300 inmates yearly, and is supported by private munificence.

The Lazarus Guild of the New-York Skin and Cancer Hospital was formed in 1891, to provide clothing, old linen and sick-room delicacies for the patients, as well as to raise funds for the endowment of free beds in the hospital.

The Society for the Relief of the Destitute Blind of the City of New York and vicinity, founded in 1869, maintains a house for the indigent and friendless blind of both sexes, at 104th Street and Amsterdam Avenue, with privileges free to those unable to pay ; and at $10 a month to others.   Employment at fair wages is given to those able to work at mattress-making, re-seating chairs and all kinds of

knitting-work. During 1892 the expenditures were $9,000, and 150 inmates were received.

The Sisters of Bon Secours, whose convent is at 1195 Lexington Avenue, devote their lives to the nursing of sick persons at their own homes. A number of these saintly nuns are consecrated to work for the sick poor, amid their surroundings of deprivation and destitution. Sister Eulalie de Barcelona is the Superior.

Homes for the Aged. — There are half - a - dozen comfort-

SISTERS OF BON SECOURS, LEXINGTON AVENUE AND 81ST STREET.

able and well-maintained homes for aged women, as well as for aged couples, and for men and women suffering from friendlessness and penury.

The Association for the Relief of Respectable, Aged, Indigent Females is one of the oldest of the city's charitable institutions. It charter runs back to 1814, a time when there was no other refuge than the poor-house for those gentle. women who, having in their youth known better things, had in their old age fallen upon evil days.   The society had no suitable home for its pensioners until 1833, when

a subscription list was opened, which John Jacob Astor headed with $5,000. Petrus Stuyvesant gave three lots of land in East 20th Street, and here the Asylum was erected, in 1838, followed in 1845 by a second building for the Infirmary. The asylum is now located on Amsterdam Avenue, at 104th

ASSOCIATION FOR THE RELIEF OF RESPECTABLE, AGED, INDIGENT FEMALES, AMSTERDAM AVENUE AND WEST 104TH STREET.

PRESBYTERIAN HOME FOR AGED WOMEN, 47 EAST 73D STREET.

Street, and here aged indigent gentlewomen find a pleasant and congenial home, as their faces turn toward the setting sun. Gentlewomen over sixty years of age are admitted on payment of $200 and the surrender of any property they may possess at their death. In addition to the regular inmates of the Home, the society supports a number of outside pensioners, at a total yearly expense of $56,000.

The Presbyterian Home for Aged Women, at 47 East 73d Street, was established in 1866, at the instance of a few ladies, to provide a refuge for aged and indigent female members of the local Presbyterian and Reformed Churches. Applicants for admission must be over 65 years old, and must pay a small weekly sum for board, in return for which they are given a pleasant home and tender care. Fifty inmates can be accommodated. The yearly expenses are met by contribution.

St. Luke's Home for Indigent Christian Females originated in an application made to the Rev. Dr. Tuttle, Rector of St. Luke's Church, by an aged woman for a place in which to spend her declining years. The good rector was compelled to refuse, as there was then no such home in the city. "But," said he, "please God, there soon will be"; and he immediately set about providing one, with such success that a house was soon leased and fitted up. In 1852 a house was opened, and in 1854, after an appeal to the leading city parishes, a building adjoining St. Luke's Church, in Hudson Street, was purchased. The present cheerful and commo-

ST. JOSEPH'S HOME FOR THE AGED, 207-215 WEST 15TH STREET.

dious house, at Madison Avenue and 89th Street, was built in 1870, and here the declining years of 65 good women are made pleasant and happy. The Home is open for the communicants of any of the Protestant Episcopal churches in the city which contribute to its support. The applicant must be 50 years of age, and must surrender any property she may possess, and pay an entrance-fee of $300.

The Peabody Home for Aged and Indigent Women was founded in 1874 by the Peabody Home and Reform Association, as a free and unsectarian home for poor but worthy women, who must be over 65 years, and in destitute circumstances. The home is pleasantly located on Boston Road, West Farms, and cares for 25 inmates, at a yearly expense of $5,000.

St. Joseph's Home for the Aged is an enormous building at 207-215 West 15th Street. This great charity was founded in 1868, and is under the charge of the Sisters of Charity of St. Vincent de Paul. It is entirely for the comfort of aged women; and has 350 inmates, of whom 100 pay according to ability.

The Home for Old Men and Aged Couples, a charity of the Protestant Episcopal Church, was incorporated in 1872, for members of the classes indicated, who are communicants of the Episcopal Church. The Home is at 487 Hudson Street, and here aged married couples are allowed to dwell comfortably together during their closing years.

The Home for the Aged of the Little Sisters of the Poor of the City of New York was incorporated in 1871, to provide a home for old persons

HOME FOR THE AGED, LITTLE SISTERS OF THE POOR, 207 EAST 70TH STREET.

of both sexes, irrespective of religion and belief. They must be over 60 years old, and destitute. There are two homes in the city; one at 207 East 70th Street, for applicants from the East Side; and another at 135 West 106th Street, for those from the West Side. The two homes give gratuitous care to nearly 500 inmates. They are in charge of the Little Sisters of the Poor, a Catholic charitable order instituted a quarter of a century ago, in France, by a poor priest and two working-girls.

The Methodist Episcopal Church Home of New-York City, a large brick edifice at the corner of Amsterdam Avenue and 93d Street, was incorporated in

HOME FOR THE AGED, LITTLE SISTERS OF THE POOR, COLUMBUS AVENUE AND WEST 106TH STREET.

1850 to provide a refuge for the aged and infirm destitute members of the Methodist Church. Applicants must have been members of that denomination for at least ten years, the last five in connection with one of the local churches. They must be of sound mind. No entrance fee is charged, but all property must be surrendered to the Home, which supplies clothing, employment and medical and other necessary care. One hundred and twenty-five aged and infirm pensioners are cared for in the institution.

The Baptist Home for Aged and Infirm Persons was established in 1869 by the Ladies' Home Society of the Baptist churches of the city of New York, as an abiding-place for aged, destitute or infirm members of the Baptist churches. Applicants for admission must have been members of one of the Baptist city churches for at least five years, must be recommended by the pastor and deacons of the church to which they belong, and must pay an admission-fee of $100 each ; in return for which they receive a home, clothing, medical attendance and religious privileges. The home has about 100 inmates, who are cared for at a yearly expense of $15,000. It is in charge of a board of managers. The building stands on 68th Street, between Park and Lexington Avenues.

The Samaritan Home for the Aged of the City of New York was incorporated in 1867, in order to relieve the crowded condition of other similar institutions.

METHODIST EPISCOPAL CHURCH HOME, AMSTERDAM AVENUE AND WEST 93D STREET.

The first building stood on West 37th Street. The cheerful and commodious home at 414 West 22d Street was opened in 1870. The object of the institution is to provide a haven of rest for aged Protestants of either sex, over 65 years of age, on payment of an admission-fee of $250. Forty-five inmates are provided for, and there is an endowment fund of $40,000. The affairs of the Home are in charge of a board of managers.

The **Chapin Home for the Aged and Infirm,** at 151 East 66th Street, was opened in 1869 as a home for aged and infirm persons of both sexes, in reduced circumstances, who must be recommended by the board of managers. An applicant must be over 65 years old, and must pay an admission fee of $300, a physician's examination fee of $5, and a burial fee of $50, and surrender all property in possession at the time of admission. There are 70 inmates; and an invested fund of $60,000.

The **Isabella Heimath,** corner of Amsterdam Avenue and 190th Street, was established in 1875, by the late Mrs. Anna Ottendorfer, at Astoria, as a home for indigent old women. The institution on its completion in 1889 was presented by

ISABELLA HEIMATH, AMSTERDAM AVENUE AND 190TH STREET.

Oswald Ottendorfer to a society incorporated under the title Isabella Heimath. It is for the maintenance and care of the aged and the sick, without regard to creed, sex or nationality, comprising a home for the care of indigent persons — of at least sixty years of age — unable to support themselves, and without relatives to support them; and a hospital for chronic invalids without means. Consumptives, or patients suffering from infectious diseases, epileptics, idiots, and those requiring constant personal attendance, cannot be admitted. There is a convalescent ward, in which convalescents who need rest after an acute disease or a surgical operation are admitted for a limited time. The admission to all departments is gratuitous. There are 176 beds. The hospital is equipped with Worthington pumps, electric lights, and other conveniences and safe-guards.

Many avocations and trades, as confederated in modern times, have established extensive charitable agencies for their own people, when fallen on unhappy days, and have also made provision for helping their young people.

The Actors' Fund of America, at 12 West 28th Street, was incorporated in 1882 for the relief of needy actors and other persons connected with the stage. Its active founder was A. M. Palmer, who has constantly been its president. Its funds are derived from membership dues, and the proceeds of the annual benefit perform-ance held in many theatres throughout the country. During 1892 over 400 persons were relieved, at an expense of $28,000. In 1892 a grand fair held in Madison-Square Garden netted nearly $200,000 for the fund.

The General Society of Mechanics and Tradesmen, at 18 East 16th Street, is one of the oldest local organizations. It was founded in 1785 for the general improvement of mechanics and tradesmen. It has a large membership ; is in a flourishing condition ; and has become a valued friend to the young men and women who avail themselves of its many privileges. Its leading features are the Free Library, at 18 East 16th Street, a public circulating library, founded in 1820 ; the mechanics' schools, furnishing free instruction in stenography, type-writing, and mechanical and free-hand drawing to worthy young men and women ; courses of free lectures every winter ; and free scholarships in the New-York Trade Schools. It supports its indigent members, and pensions the widows and orphans of deceased members.

The New-York Society for the Relief of Widows and Orphans of Medical Men was formed in 1842 to render aid to the needy widows and orphans of deceased members. In special cases, other near relatives, who had been depend-ent upon the deceased, are aided. Twelve widows and four orphans received assist-ance in 1892, at an outlay of $4,000.

The Exempt Firemen's Benevolent Fund, at 174 Canal Street, was founded in 1791, under the name of the Fire Department Fund, by a few members of the old volunteer force, at a convivial meeting. A charter was obtained in 1798, providing for the maintenance and increase of the fund. For many years the beneficiaries were few in number, and a large surplus accumulated. This was lost in the great fire of 1835, which ruined the fire-insurance companies in which it had been invested. The citizens, however, contributed $24,000 ; and when the volunteer system was super-seded by the paid Fire Department, in 1865, the fund was placed in charge of the Association of Exempt Firemen, which had been formed in 1841. At that time the fund amounted to $90,000. Now it is nearly $200,000, and the income is expended for the benefit of indigent and disabled firemen, or their widows or children. The Fire Department has a fund amounting to nearly $500,000, the income of which is used in the same manner.

The maritime class, the sailors who go down to the sea in ships, are admirably protected by charitable funds, mainly of their own institution.

The Sailors' Snug Harbor, at New Brighton, Staten Island, was established in 1801, by Captain Robert Richard Randall, who bequeathed to it considerable tracts of city real estate, now of enormous value. The asylum buildings are very extensive, and the grounds contain 180 acres, attractively laid out. The Snug Har-bor is a home for aged, infirm and superannuated sailors, who must be native-born, or, in case of those of foreign birth, must produce documentary evidence that they have served at least five years in vessels flying the American flag. The home is in charge of a board of trustees, and there is ample accommodation for 1,000 inmates. The institution has a yearly income of over $300,000, and is self-supporting.

Webb's Home for shipbuilders, now approaching completion, on Fordham Heights, palatial, endowed with millions, is intended partly for a home for aged and destitute master-shipbuilders and their wives.

The Marine Society of the City of New York, in the State of New York, at 19 Whitehall Street, was incorporated as early as 1770, for the improvement of maritime knowledge, and the relief of indigent members who are or have been masters of ships, or their widows or orphans. It is supported by voluntary contributions and membership dues. It aids nearly 50 widows yearly.

The Home for Seamen's Children was founded in 1846 by the Society for the Relief of the Destitute Children of Seamen. It is pleasantly located at West New Brighton, Staten Island, and about 130 children are cared for and educated yearly. No one is received for a shorter period than a year; and a small weekly payment is required from parents who are able to contribute to the support of their children. The inmates, unless claimed by friends or guardians, are retained in the home until fourteen years of age, when suitable homes are obtained for them.

The Mariners' Family Asylum of the Port of New York, the only institution of its kind in the United States, was incorporated in 1854, as a home for the destitute sick or infirm mothers, wives, widows, sisters or daughters of seamen of the port of New York. Applicants must be over 60 years of age, and pay an admission fee of $100. The asylum is located at Stapleton, Staten Island, and about $5,000 is spent yearly in caring for the fifty pensioners.

The Seamen's Christian Association, at 665 Washington Street, was founded in 1888, and maintains a chapel, reading and writing room for seamen and boatmen, where religious and moral entertainment is provided for them. The "Rest" is open daily from 2 P. M. until 10 P. M., and here "Jack" may always find a hearty welcome. Religious services are held every evening.

Foreign Relief Societies.— An interesting manifestation of charity is in its application to various races from abroad. The great network of Jewish philanthropies is entirely built up and maintained from the abounding wealth and liberality of the Hebrew-American population. On the other hand, the African asylums, and the beneficent works done among the Chinese, the Italians and certain other immigrant colonies are maintained at the cost of the older population of the city. Among these fraternal groups are: The Italian Benevolent Society, founded in 1857; the German Mission-House Association, 1867; the Spanish Benevolent Society, in 1882; the Norwegian Relief Society, in 1883; the Hungarian Association, in 1884; the Jewish Immigrants' Protective Society, in 1885; the Polish Benevolent Society; and the Greek Benevolent Society, in 1891.

St. George's Society, at 7 Battery Place, was established in 1786, succeeding an older society with similar aims, which had existed before the Revolution. It was incorporated in 1838. Its object is to afford relief and advice to indigent natives of England and the British Colonies, or to their wives, widows or children, in the cities of New York and Brooklyn. Its income can be expended only in charity. The persons eligible to membership are: natives of England or any of its dependencies, and their sons and grandsons, and British officers and their sons, wherever born.

St. Andrew's Society of the State of New York was founded in 1756 and incorporated in 1826. It is one of the oldest existing benevolent societies in the country. Its objects are the promotion of social and friendly intercourse among the natives of Scotland and their connections and descendants in the city and vicinity, and the relief of such as may be indigent. If employment cannot be found for the industrious poor in the city, the society pays their passage to any other place where

work may be offered.   In 1892 2,300 persons received assistance.   The society has
a permanent fund of about $75,000 ; and 450 members.   Its main office is in the
United Charities Building, with a branch at 287 East Broadway.

St. David's Society, at 21 University Place, was founded in 1835, and incorporated in 1846, for the relief of needy Welsh people.   Welshmen and their descendants, and persons married to Welsh women, are eligible to membership.

The Irish Emigrant Society, at 51 Chambers Street and 29 Reade Street,
was founded in 1841, and incorporated in 1844, to afford advice, protection and
relief to needy Irish immigrants.   It is an outgrowth of the Social Benevolent Society
of the Friendly Sons of St. Patrick, the successor of the Friendly Brothers of St.
Patrick, which existed previous to the Revolution.   The Society of the Friendly

Sons of St. Patrick was organized in 1784, and became very
active in extending aid to indigent natives of Ireland in the
city, especially in aiding newly
arrived immigrants in obtaining
employment.   Since the founding of the Emigrant Society it
has turned its activity in other
directions.

**La Societe Francaise de
Bienfaisance** (French Benevolent Society) was organized in
1809, and incorporated in 1819,
to assist needy Frenchmen by
providing medical advice, medicines, food, clothing, money,
and temporary shelter for those
in need or sickness.   It depends
entirely on the generosity of the

SWISS BENEVOLENT SOCIETY, 108 SECOND AVENUE.   public for its yearly expenses,

which average $20,000.   The society maintains a relief bureau, bureau of immigra-
tion, night refuge, dispensary, hospital and home, at 320 West 34th Street.

The Young Women's Home Society of the French Evangelical Church
in the City of New York, at 341 West 30th Street, was organized in 1888 and incorporated in 1890, to provide unemployed governesses, teachers and domestics of
French birth with homes and board.   It also supplies needy applicants with clothing, money and medical attendance, and procures employment for them.   The
Home furnishes rooms and board for 24 inmates, at a cost of $4 a week each.
Nearly 1,000 worthy cases are assisted yearly, at a cost of $7,000.

The Belgian Society of Benevolence, at 135 Duane Street, was incorporated in 1871, for the relief of indigent Belgians and their descendants.   Its funds
are derived from private subscriptions largely from the natives of the Low Countries.

The Swiss Benevolent Society, the title of which indicates the scope of its
work, maintains a home at 108 Second Avenue, where needy natives of Switzerland
are cared for.

The Leo House for German Catholic Immigrants is for the protection
and care of recently-landed German Catholic immigrants, who are aided by advice,
financial assistance in extreme cases, and in all other possible ways.   The society in

charge was incorporated in 1889. The House itself, at 6 State Street, is one of the few old-time mansions that have survived all the changes of the modern city. It was for many years the home of James Watson, the first president of the New-England Society of New York, and in its parlors that society was founded.

The Mission of Our Lady of the Rosary, at Castle Garden (7 State Street), receives yearly over 4,000 young immigrant girls, and cares for them until they meet their friends, procure work, or proceed on their journeys. It has neither State nor municipal aid, and is supported through the generosity of the charitable. The Rev. M. Callaghan is director.

The Lutheran Pilgrim House, at 8 State Street, was opened in 1885, for benevolent and humane work among the poorer classes of German Lutheran

LUTHERAN PILGRIM HOUSE.   MISSION OF OUR LADY OF THE ROSARY.   LEO IMMIGRANT HOUSE.
MISSION AND EMIGRANT HOUSES, ON STATE STREET.

immigrants, for whom a lodging-house, temporary employment, advice, and all other needful assistance is provided. The House is supported by the Lutheran churches.

The Evangelical Aid Society for the Spanish Work of New York and Brooklyn, at 1345 Lexington Avenue, was founded in 1886 to carry the Gospel to the Spanish-speaking people in their own language, to provide missionaries to visit them in their houses, to relieve the sick and help the poor, and to establish Sunday and industrial schools.

St. Bartholomew's Chinese Guild, at 23 St. Mark's Place, was founded in 1889 for the improvement, spiritual elevation and religious training of the Chinese. It renders legal aid to its beneficiaries, and cares for the sick and dying in the city and vicinity. There are nearly 700 members, who have the privileges of a reading-room, library and gymnasium, and receive instruction in the manual arts. The guild is supported by St. Bartholomew's Episcopal Church and by its membership dues.

29

The Colored Orphan Asylum and Association for the benefit of colored children, in the city of New York, is due to the earnest labors of two ladies, Miss Anna H. Shotwell and Miss Murray, who in 1836 began to work in behalf of the neglected colored children of the city. As the result of their labors, at a time when the negro was generally regarded as nothing more than the white man's chattel, the Association for the Benefit of the Colored Orphans was formed, the

first of its kind in the country, and a small house on 12th Street was purchased. The association was incorporated in 1838, and in 1842, after repeated appeals to the Common Council, a grant was obtained of twenty-two lots of land on Fifth Avenue, and a suitable building was erected. This was destroyed in the

COLORED ORPHAN ASYLUM, WEST 143D STREET, NEAR TENTH AVENUE.

Draft Riot of 1863, in spite of heroic efforts to save it. Instead of rebuilding on the old site, the managers secured a location on West 143d Street, between Tenth Avenue and the Boulevard, and the present home was erected. With the passing away of the old prejudice against the negro the institution has steadily gained in the confidence and good will of the community. Colored orphans of both sexes, between the ages of two and ten years, are received and gratuitously provided for, except in cases where the children are intrusted to the society by parents or guardians, when a nominal fee of seventy-five cents a week is charged. All the inmates are instructed in home industries, and at the age of twelve indentured into families or at trades. The leading design of the home is not merely to rescue from poverty, and minister to the physical comforts and necessities of those committed to its care, but to elevate the character, develop the faculties and impart a knowledge of religious and moral obligations and duties. About 350 children are cared for. The expenses are met by private subscriptions and grants from the public school fund.

The Colored Home and Hospital of the city of New York originated in 1839, in the labors of a few women, who sought to alleviate the condition of the indigent colored population. In 1845 the society was incorporated and $10,000 was secured from the State, for a suitable structure. The group of buildings, at 65th Street and First Avenue, was erected in 1849, and comprises the home, a chapel, a hospital for general diseases, and a lying-in hospital. The privileges of the home are free to all indigent colored residents of the city, and are open to non-residents upon the payment of a fixed sum quarterly. The Commissioners of Public Charities have the right to place in the institution adult destitute, infirm, sick and incurable colored persons of either sex, for whose support partial provision is made from the public funds.

The New-York Colored Mission, at 135 West 30th Street, was founded in 1871 for the religious, moral and social elevation of the colored people in the city. It seeks to attain its purpose by means of frequent religious services, by Sunday-school instruction, by its free employment office, reading-room and library, and by the zealous labors of a missionary, who visits the sick and poor, and gives relief in food and clothing and other necessaries. It also has a lodging-room, where colored women can obtain lodgings at nominal rates. Nearly 6,000 lodgings are furnished yearly. A sewing-school for women and young girls is also in successful operation. The yearly expenses are $5,000, and are met by private contributions.

The United Hebrew Charities of the City of New York, at 128 Second Avenue, was formed in 1874 by the union of the Hebrew Benevolent and Orphan Asylum Society ; the Hebrew Benevolent Fuel Society ; the Hebrew Relief Society ; the Congregation Darech Amuno Free Burial Fund Society, and the Ladies' Hebrew Lying-in Society. Its objects are to afford relief of all kinds to worthy Hebrews, and by co-operation to prevent fraud. The city is divided into districts, with visitors and physicians attached to each district ; the sick are visited in their homes ; immigrants from Europe and other places are aided ; and the worthy Hebrew poor are assisted in many ways. In 1892 nearly 40,000 persons were aided ; situations were obtained for 5,000 applicants ; and 20,600 lodgings and 64,000 meals were furnished.

The Hebrew Benevolent and Orphan Society of New York was incorporated in 1822, and reincorporated in 1860. It maintains a large asylum, one of the best appointed in the country, at Amsterdam Avenue and 136th Street, where

Hebrew orphans and indigent boys and girls are sheltered and educated. The building has a capacity of 1,000. The origin of the society is touching. Many years ago a Hebrew soldier of the Revolution lay dying in the City Hospital, and expressed a desire to see some of his co-

HEBREW BENEVOLENT ORPHAN ASYLUM, AMSTERDAM AVENUE AND WEST 136TH STREET.

religionists, a number of whom visited him. Becoming interested in the suffering soldier, they collected a small fund, and after his death, they found themselves in possession of $300, which was made a nucleus of the larger sum with which the asylum was founded. Wm. H. Hume designed the present building.

The Home for Aged and Infirm Hebrews of the City of New York, at West 105th Street, near Columbus Avenue, was opened in 1848, and incorporated in 1872. Aged and infirm Hebrew New-Yorkers, of either sex, over sixty years of age, are received here and given a home in their declining years. About 160 are cared for yearly, at an expense of $30,000.

The Hebrew Sheltering Guardian Society of New York was formed in 1879, to found and maintain an asylum where Jewish infants, orphans, half-orphans and deserted children, not admitted into other institutions, might be received, cared

for and educated until they could be provided with homes or permanent employ.
ment.   The asylum buildings are at Eleventh Avenue and 151st Street, for infants
and grown-up boys, and at the Boulevard and 150th Street, for girls.   In addi.
tion to its regular work, the institution gives temporary employment, food and
shelter to former inmates out of employment, and furnishes meals to poor persons
and children not connected with the asylum.   The yearly expenses are $60,000.

The Montefiore Home for Chronic Invalids, at the Boulevard and West
138th Street, a useful Hebrew charity, was established in 1884, to afford shelter in

MONTEFIORE HOME FOR CHRONIC INVALIDS, BOULEVARD AND WEST 138TH STREET.

sickness to such invalid residents as, by reason of incurable disease, are unable to
obtain treatment at other institutions.   Incurables of both sexes, discharged from
the city hospitals, are received and cared for, irrespective of their religious belief.
The families of the patients are also relieved, when deprived of the labor of the
breadwinner, from the income of the Julius Hallgarten Fund.   There is also a Discharged Patients' and Climatic Cure Fund, the income of which is used to send
improved patients to Vineland, N. J., or to Colorado, for a few months' change of
air and scene.   In 1892 this charity cared for 300 inmates and over 200 out-door
patients, at a cost of $73,000.

The Ladies' Deborah Nursery and Child's Protectory was founded in
1878, for the reception, care and education of destitute Hebrew children from four
to fourteen years old, who may be committed to its keeping by magistrates.   The
buildings are at 95 East Broadway, for boys, and East 162d Street, near Eagle
Avenue, for girls.   The inmates are cared for and instructed in some trade or household work until they are able to support themselves.   The average number received
yearly is 375.

The Aguilar Aid Society was founded in 1890 to assist the up-town Jewish
poor on the East Side with fuel, clothing, groceries, and in special cases money, and
also to provide Passover supplies to those unable to purchase them.

The Hebrew Sheltering Home, 210 Madison Avenue, was opened in 1889,
to aid Hebrew immigrants by furnishing free temporary lodgings and food, and
assistance in obtaining employment.   During 1892 4,000 immigrants were assisted.

The Young Women's Hebrew Association, 721 Lexington Avenue and
206 East Broadway, was founded in 1888 to advance the cause of Judaism, to promote culture among women, and to improve the moral and intellectual welfare of

girls of over fourteen years, and of women of the laboring and immigrant classes. Lessons are given in the domestic arts, cooking, physical culture, dressmaking, etc., mainly to Russian immigrants, who are also taught the rudiments of English.

Miscellaneous Charitable Societies abound on every side, and quite defy classification. A few of them may be mentioned, almost at random, in order to exhibit the wide sweep of metropolitan kindliness.

The New-York Fruit and Flower Mission, at 104 East 20th Street, was founded in 1870. It distributes flowers, fruits and delicacies among the sick in hospitals, asylums and tenement-houses, and sends Christmas greetings to sick children in houses and hospitals.

The New-York Bible and Fruit Mission to the Public Hospitals is an important local charity, organized in 1876 for work among the sick in public hospitals. Weekly visits are made to all the hospitals in charge of the Department of Public Charities and Correction, and flowers, food, fruit and reading-matter are distributed to the patients. The institution is also engaged in useful philanthropic work among the poor, and labors to reform criminals and inebriates. The Mission Building at 416 to 422 East 26th Street contains a chapel, where services are held every evening ; a coffee-house and restaurant, where meals and tickets for food are sold at moderate prices ; a lodging-house for men, which furnishes lodgings and baths at low rates ; a broom factory, which gives employment to men out of work, convalescents from the hospitals, and discharged convicts ; a reading-room and circulating library ; and a sewing-school for young girls.

HOME FOR AGED AND INFIRM HEBREWS, 125 WEST 105TH STREET, NEAR COLUMBUS AVENUE.

Other branches of the mission work are the Penny Provident Fund, the Fresh-Air Fund, and the Loan-Relief Bureau. During 1892 85,000 meals were furnished at the coffee-house ; 33,000 men were registered at the lodging-house ; and the sum of $2,200 was paid out in wages at the broom factory.

The Christmas Letter Mission, was organized in Europe in 1871, and in the United States in 1881. It is a charming charity, formed to distribute Christmas messages of consolation and encouragement among the inmates of hospitals, prisons and other similar institutions. These messages are written by friends of the movement. In 1892 nearly 2,500 letters of Christmas greeting were distributed among the inmates of the local institutions, and over 35,000 in the United States.

The Island Mission for Cheering the Lives of the Poor and Sick, at 102 Waverly Place, is an unsectarian charity, formed in 1887, to brighten and cheer the lives of the inmates of the public charitable institutions by means of pictures, books and entertainments, and by providing the ordinary comforts of life for the aged, infirm and insane. It is supported entirely by private charity.

The Hospital Book and Newspaper Society, at 21 University Place, is a department of the State Charities Aid Association. It was formed in 1874, and its mission is to receive and distribute gratuitously among the inmates of the local hospitals and asylums, books, newspapers and other reading matter. Nearly 60,000 books and papers are distributed yearly.

The Needlework Guild of America, New-York Branch, was founded in 1891 to provide new and suitable garments for the inmates of the local hospitals, homes and other charities, and to unite all who are interested in that special field of charitable work. The guild has no office, but does its work privately, by house-to-house meetings among the members.

The Ladies' Fuel and Aid Society, at 199 Henry Street, was incorporated in 1888. It distributes coal, provisions, clothing and other necessaries of life to the worthy and suffering of any class or creed, assists in obtaining employment, and renders any other assistance thought to be wise and good. In 1893, 2,325 families were aided. Other fuel and aid societies are : The Hebrew Benevolent Fuel Society (1869), the Earle Guild (1876), and the East-Side Ladies' Aid Society (1889).

The New-England Society in the City of New York, at 76 Wall Street, was organized in 1805, as a charitable and literary association. It had but a feeble growth for many years, but after the opening of the Erie Canal, in 1825, many New-Englanders settled in the city, and infused new life into the society, which has for many years been a flourishing and popular institution. There is a committee on charity, which distributes the money voted by the board of officers to the benefi-ciaries, who are the widows and orphans of deceased members. The society has 1,500 members. Daniel G. Rollins is its President ; and L. P. Hubbard, Secretary.

The Penny-Provident Fund of the Charity Organization Society was established in 1889, to inculcate habits of providence and thrift among the poor, by supplying them with facilities for small savings, such as the savings-banks do not afford. The plan is similar to that of the English Postal Savings System. Deposits of one cent and upwards are received and receipted for by stamps attached by a Stamp-Card, given to each depositor. As soon as a sufficient amount has been deposited in this small way, the depositors are encouraged to open accounts in some savings-bank. Over 210 local stamp-stations have been established in various parts of the city, and more than 60,000 persons have made deposits, varying from one cent to larger sums. The central office is at Fourth Avenue and 22d Street.

The Christian Aid to Employment Society, at 50 Bible House, was incor-porated in 1888, to assist worthy men and women to suitable employment. No worthy applicant is refused aid because of inability to pay a fee. A small charge is made to employers for services rendered.

The German Legal Aid Society, at 35 Nassau Street, was incorporated in 1876, to render free legal advice and aid to persons too poor to employ a lawyer. It has aided over 50,000 persons, and has collected for claimants over $350,000. Formerly the work was confined to Germans, but it is now international in char-acter, and distributes its benefits to all applicants.

The Ladies' Union Relief Association was formed in 1865 for the care and relief of sick and disabled soldiers and their families, and of the widows and orphans of those who fell in the War of the Rebellion. Its work at present consists mainly in obtaining pensions for those entitled to them, and in granting out-door relief, not exceeding $10 a month, to those who have claims upon the National Soldiers' Home at Washington. It is managed by a board of women trustees.

The International Telegraph Christian Association, American Branch, was founded in 1890, to promote religion and Christian fellowship in telegraph offices. The parent organization is of English origin. The American Branch has already established six Junior branches in different parts of the city, where messenger and telegraph boys under sixteen years of age receive moral, social and physical benefits ; and a Senior Branch for letter-carriers. The address of the General Local Secretary is 70 West 36th Street.

The Tenement-House Chapter of the King's Daughters and Sons, Madison Street, was organized in 1892 to bring the members of the Order into personal relation with the dwellers in tenement-houses, whose moral and physical elevation is the principal aim of the organization. In cases of special need, such aid as seems best suited to each case is given ; and nursing, sick-room comforts and food are supplied to the sick. A valuable fresh-air work is done among the children during the summer months. The headquarters of the King's Daughters are at 158 West 23d Street, in the former home of David M. Morrison.

KING'S DAUGHTERS, 158 WEST 23D STREET.

The Ladies' Mission of the Protestant Episcopal Church of the Public Institutions of the City of New York was incorporated in 1862. The membership is composed of charitably inclined women of the Episcopal Church, who are willing to devote a portion of their time to visiting the inmates of the numerous local public institutions, including special prison-work on Blackwell's Island. During 1892 over 25,000 visits were made by the members of the mission.

The Guild of St. Elizabeth, at 440 West 23d Street, was organized in 1876 to minister to the sick and poor in the public institutions at Bellevue Hospital, and on Blackwell's, Ward's, Hart's and Randall's Islands.

The Istituto Italiano (Italian Home) is a charitable organization, founded in 1889 by Gian Paolo Riva, the Italian Consul-General, and other prominent Italian residents, to maintain a hospital and to give advice to Italian immigrants, disseminate information among them, and promote their welfare in various ways. It has occupied its present quarters, at 179 Second Avenue, near East 11th Street, since February, 1891. Its work has been comparatively limited because of lack of funds. Giovanni Starace is president.

The New-York Society for Parks and Playgrounds for Children, at Room 7, 36 Union Square, was founded in 1891 to supply fresh air, sunshine and healthful recreation to as many as possible of the 400,000 children crowded into the stuffy tenement-houses of the city. The first playground started by the society, at Second Avenue and 92d Street, accommodates 500 children, at an expense of only

ITALIAN INSTITUTE AND ITALIAN HOME, 179 SECOND
AVENUE, BETWEEN EAST 11TH AND EAST 12TH STS.

$5 a day. It is proposed to open other similar grounds, provided with swings, see-saws, wagons, wheelbarrows, shovels, heaps of sand and jumping-ropes as rapidly as funds are forthcoming. The economy of the work is such that all this can be provided at an outlay of one cent a day for each child in attendance, and the value of the work is out of all proportion to its cost. The expenses are met by voluntary contributions.

Many Old-time Charities of New-York City have in recent years wisely removed their establishments into the neighboring country, where, amid verdurous forests, lapsing waves and pure sweet breezes, their unhappy patrons may find some better chance of recovery and sanity. Thus on the shores of the Hudson, and overlooking the blue sea from Long Island and Staten Island, now stand many asylums formerly poisoned by the stenches and oaths of the down-town slums. The latest to move out of the city was the Babies' Shelter of the Church of the Holy Communion, which has been removed to St. Johnland, the Church Industrial community on Long Island.

The heroic attacks of Grace, St. Bartholomew's, Trinity, Judson Memorial, and other churches and secular bodies are continuously delivered against the powers of the slums, and with marked effect. The University and College Settlements, encamped in the heart of the "Suicide Ward," or the "Typhus Ward," where over 60,000 people are packed into 110 acres, are to erect a grand building, to be a centre of regenerative influences. Thousands of active philanthropists are daily saving New York from the poison of its depraved and degraded humanity and the venom of pauperized peasant immigration, by a self-imposed round of brave and self-denying and fragrant charities. Although this city is a sink into which pour the crime and poverty of all countries, the efforts of its philanthropic societies have resulted in a perceptible diminution of crime, especially among boys and girls, and therefore in an incalculable saving to the community — and to Humanity.

LEAGUE OF THEOSOPHICAL WORKERS, 144 MADISON AVENUE.
BETWEEN 31ST AND 32D STREET.

The Sanitary Organizations.

Board of Health and Health Statistics—Hospitals and Dispensaries—The Morgue—Curative Institutions—Insane, Inebriate and other Asylums.

THE general sanitary condition of New York is fairly good, in view of the many unfavorable conditions necessarily prevailing in all large cities. The average annual death-rate of about 25 in 1,000, while somewhat higher than that of most American and many foreign cities, is not abnormally high, when the large yearly influx of immigrants, the crowded condition of the tenement-houses, and the number of patients from other cities, who come here for treatment in the hospitals, are taken into consideration. The average yearly number of deaths is not far from 40,000, fully 8,000 of which occur in the numerous public and private institutions, and about 25,000 in houses containing three or more families. One drawback to a satisfactory sanitary status is the difficulty of keeping the many miles of streets in a cleanly condition, a trouble which is not so strongly felt in smaller cities. Strenuous efforts are made by the Street Department to improve the condition of the streets, and to remove all these menaces to the public health.

The Board of Health controls the sanitary affairs of the city. In its present form it was established in 1873. It consists of the President of the Board of Police, the Health Officer of the Port, and two Commissioners, one of whom must have been a practising physician for five years previous to his appointment. The Commissioners hold office for six years, and are appointed by the Mayor, independent of the Board of Aldermen. A large corps of medical inspectors is constantly employed in the cure and prevention of disease, in the inspection of houses, and for the enforcement of the health-laws and the sanitary code. There is also a night service of such physicians and surgeons as are willing to undertake the work, who answer all night-calls that may be sent to them from the different police-stations; a vaccinating corps; a disinfecting corps; and an organization of meat and milk inspectors; all of which are potent factors in promoting the general healthfulness of the city. The Board also has charge of the Reception Hospital, at the foot of East 16th Street, built in 1885 for the temporary care of contagious cases while awaiting transportation to the Riverside Hospital, on North Brother Island, which was erected in 1884 for the treatment of such contagious diseases as cannot well be isolated at home, as well as similar cases from Quarantine; and the Willard Parker Hospital, at the foot of East 16th Street, opened in 1884 for cases of scarlet fever and diphtheria.

The Quarantine Service is administered by three Commissioners of Quarantine appointed by the Governor for three years, and a Health Officer, for two years. The Commissioners are authorized by law to make all needful regulations for the examination and (when necessary) the detention of all incoming vessels. The State of New York furnishes residences for the Health Officer and his three assistants, at the boarding station at Fort Wadsworth, Staten Island. These officials are obliged to board every vessel subject to quarantine or visitation, immediately after her arrival at the boarding station ; to ascertain the sanitary condition of the vessel and all its passengers by strict examination ; to send all sick passengers to the Quarantine Hospital ; and to determine what persons and vessels are to be detained in Quarantine. The property of the Department comprises the Hospital Ship, used as a residence for the deputy health officer and a boarding station for all vessels arriving from infected ports ; Swinburne Island, on which is the hospital for contagious diseases ; Hoffman Island, used for the detention and purification of well persons arriving in infected vessels ; the Crematory, on Swinburne Island ; the upper boarding station at Fort Wadsworth, Staten Island ; and a steamer for daily communication between all points of the Quarantine establishment.

Hospitals are more numerous in New York than in any other city on the continent. There are nearly eighty of these "inns on the highway of life where suffering humanity finds alleviation and sympathy," and many of them are among the largest and most magnificent buildings in the city. The newer ones are built of warm red brick, and fitted with the latest and most efficient heating and ventilating apparatus. There is no kind of bodily suffering that may not find skillful treatment and kindly nursing in one or the other of these healing homes, where the most eminent physicians and surgeons give freely of their time and skill to the inmates. The wealthy patient may command all the luxuries a fine private home could give, and the poor man unable to pay may enjoy comforts impossible to him in his

BELLEVUE HOSPITAL, FIRST AVENUE, EAST 26TH STREET, AND EAST RIVER.

own narrow dwelling. Fully 100,000 patients are treated yearly in these curative institutions, more than three-quarters of them without any payment for the care and skill which restore them to health or smooth the pathway to the grave ; and the death-rate is less than eight per cent. Nearly all the larger hospitals have an ambulance service in constant readiness to answer calls for help, and some have training-schools, where nurses are taught the duties of their calling, and trained in those kindly ministrations which often are more potent factors in the patient's restoration to health than all the skill of the physician.

Bellevue Hospital is a great charity institution. It receives gratuitously the sick poor of the city. The first stone of the original building was laid in 1811, and in 1816 it was opened as a hospital, almshouse and penitentiary, under the direction of the Common Council. At that time the medical staff consisted of one visiting and two young resident physicians. In 1826 the Hospital and Almshouse were separated; and in 1848 the Bellevue grounds were divided, a large part sold to private purchasers, and the convicts and paupers sent to Blackwell's Island. In 1849 the Common Council was superseded by a board of ten governors, who in 1860 gave place to the Commissioners of Public Charities and Correction, who now have charge of the Hospital. Until 1849 the members of the hospital staff were appointed by the Common Council, but in that year the present system of appointment after a rigid competitive examination was inaugurated. At that time the Junior, Senior and House Services were each of six months' duration ; the service was divided into four medical and two surgical divisions ; and the physicians rotated, serving three months on

STURGIS SURGICAL PAVILION, BELLEVUE HOSPITAL, FOOT OF EAST 26TH STREET.

the male, and three months on the female side. In 1866 this service was rearranged into four medical and four surgical divisions, each having male and female sections, while the physicians no longer rotated. This method is still in force, but the number of wards has increased to forty, with 768 beds, making Bellevue one of the largest institutions of its kind in the world.

The entrance to the hospital grounds, comprising 4½ acres, lying between East River and First Avenue, is on 26th Street, through an arched gateway built in 1885. Immediately to the left of the entrance gate is the Marquand Pavilion, a one-story brick building erected in 1877 by Frederick and Henry Gurdon Marquand in memory of their brother, Josiah P. Marquand, who died from the effects of an operation. It is a medical ward for women and children, and contains 18 beds for adults and 16 for children. Nearly opposite, on the right, is the Insane Pavilion, a low brick building erected in 1879 by the city for people who become insane. It accommodates 25 patients, who are kept five days to allow of communication with their friends, and arrangements for their transfer to suitable institutions. The one-story brick pavilion to the north is the Sturgis Surgical Pavilion, built in 1879 by Mrs.

William H. Osborne in memory of her father. Immediately opposite is the long
stone building of the old almshouse, four stories in height, which forms the centre
of the hospital. The long prison-like structure comprises a central division, with
side wings, giving a total length of 350 feet. The buildings, including the northeast wing, built in 1855, have external balconies and staircases for each story, affording ample means of escape in case of fire, and also space for exercise. The central
portion of the building contains the reception-room, store-room, Warden's office,
the library, the consulting-room, and a notable operating-room, the largest in the
country, with a seating capacity of 1,000. In the rear, on First Avenue, is the
Townsend Cottage, where cases of uterine tumors are received. This building, and
the adjoining chapel and library, were erected in 1888 by Mrs. R. H. L. Townsend
as a thank-offering for recovery from sickness. An Alcoholic Pavilion was built in
1892, for the reception of male and female patients suffering from the improper use
of stimulants. Since 1873 a superior grade of nurses has been obtained from the
Training-School for Nurses. The immediate care of the hospital is entrusted to a
medical board, appointed by the Commissioners of Public Charities and Correction,
and comprising three consulting and twelve visiting surgeons, three consulting and
sixteen visiting physicians. The House Staff includes four physicians and four
surgeons, and three assistants to each, none of whom receives any other compensation
for his services than suitable accommodations and a small yearly allowance for board.

The exceptionally large number of patients, averaging 14,000 yearly, has made
the hospital one of the most valuable in the country for the study of diseases of every
kind. This exceptional condition led in 1861 to the founding of the Bellevue-Hospital Medical College, one of the leading schools of medicine and surgery in the
country, occupying a building in the hospital grounds, on East 26th Street.

The free dispensary service of the hospital, one of its most valuable features, was
established in 1866, and treats 100,000 patients yearly, besides the large number of

cases which are sent to different hospitals. The Ambulance Service is an im-
portant feature in the work
of the hospital, as may be
seen from the fact that nearly
5,000 calls are answered
yearly.

Under the same man-
agement as Bellevue are
the Adult, Children's and
Infants' Hospitals and the
Idiot and Epileptic Asylum
on Randall's Island ; the
Emergency Hospital, at 223

GOUVERNEUR HOSPITAL, GOUVERNEUR SLIP AND FRONT STREET.   East 26th Street ; the Gouv-
erneur Hospital ; the Harlem Hospital, at 533 East 120th Street ; the Hart's
Island Hospital for the reception of convalescents ; the Fordham Reception
Hospital, at Fordham, N. Y.; the Insane Asylum for Males and the Ward's Island
Hospital ; and on Blackwell's Island the Charity and Convalescent Hospitals, Female
Insane Asylum, the Hospital for Incurables, and the Paralytic and Alms-House
Hospitals, mostly large stone buildings, with a combined capacity of fully 5,000
beds, forming the largest group of associated charities under one management in

the world, a proof of the liberality of New-York City in caring for its sick and afflicted poor. In fact, the public and the private medical institutions indicate New York's intelligence as well as its generosity.

The Morgue, on the Bellevue-Hospital grounds, is a one-story building of 62 by 83 feet, containing an office, autopsy-room, room for refrigerator, and two special rooms where the remains of the deceased are laid out, that friends may view the bodies, or hold religious services previous to their burial. It was opened in 1866, and contained at that time four marble tables. A corpse remains in the Morgue for 72 hours, more or less, according to condition and weather, and if not identified it is removed to the City Cemetery, on Hart's Island, for interment. The clothing is preserved for six months, and if not then identified it is destroyed. All bodies are photographed, and the photographs are carefully preserved as a possible means of future identification. There are usually from three to five bodies awaiting identification, and the sight is anything but a pleasant one. The number of bodies received here exceeds 4,000, the average being from 175 to 235 yearly. The number of bodies received here annually, from all sources, averages about 8,000, including Morgue cases proper (the unknown dead).

The Gouverneur Hospital, at Gouverneur Slip and East River, is an emergency hospital, in charge of the Department of Public Charities and Correction. It occupies the old Gouverneur-Market building, and was established in 1885.

The Charity Hospital, on Blackwell's Island, was opened in 1852 for the city's indigent sick. The original wooden building was destroyed by fire in 1865, and a large granite edifice was opened in 1870. It is four stories high, and extends across the southern end of the island. With the outlying pavilions of the maternity, epileptic and nervous wards it contains 1,000 beds. There are thirteen male and twelve female wards. The number of patients received yearly is 6,800. The medical and surgical staff comprises twenty-four physicians and a large number of attendants. In 1886 a training-school for female nurses was opened in the castellated stone building erected in 1872 for a small-pox hospital. A training-school for male nurses was established in 1887, and these schools have done much to improve the quality of the nursing in the hospital.

The Ward's-Island Hospital, on Ward's Island, was opened in 1876, for the treatment of all classes of diseases, both male and female. It is under the Commissioners of Public Charities and Correction.

The New-York City Asylums for the Insane on Blackwell's, Ward's and Hart's Islands, and at the City Farm at Central Islip, are in charge of the Commissioners of Public Charities and Correction. The buildings are of enormous extent ; and upwards of 6,000 patients are cared for at one time, at a cost of $800,000 annually. The accommodations are inadequate, and many plans for relieving the crowded condition of the asylums have been proposed. Those now in progress are the use of the large building on Ward's Island, formerly occupied for the uses of the State Commissioners of Immigration (but long since abandoned), the removal of all the insane to Ward's Island and Central Islip, Long Island, and the expenditure of $1,500,000 in new buildings. Several unsuccessful attempts have been made to transfer the city insane to the care of the State, which has a uniform system of hospitals, where it is claimed the patients would receive better care. Passes to visit the asylums may be obtained from their heads, or from William Blake, 66 Third Avenue. The general medical superintendent is Dr. A. E. MacDonald.

The New-York City Asylum for the Insane, on Blackwell's Island, was opened in 1848, and is now used for women only. The buildings occupy extensive grounds on the northern end of the island, and have accommodations for about 1,300 patients. The main building is a four-story granite structure, and contains the office, rooms for the house staff, and eight wards for patients. In each ward there is a large sitting-room for the inmates, and all the wards open into a spacious central rotunda. In 1881 a stone building, accommodating 500 patients, was erected at the southern end of the grounds, for acute cases ; and in 1892 a brick building was opened for chronic cases. There are also ten wooden pavilions, one brick pavilion, a laundry, bath-house, superintendent's residence, and a Roman Catholic chapel on the grounds. The amusement building contains a large hall with a stage and piano, where dances and entertainments are given frequently for the amusement of the patients, and a work-room where mats, brushes, rugs, carpets, and fancy articles are made by the inmates. The patients are kept without restraint, and every possible effort is made to ameliorate their condition, by allotting them some occupation to employ their minds. Twice a day they are given an hour's exercise in the grounds, in charge of the attendants ; and once a week they are given baths, under the supervision of the resident woman-physician. About 2,500 patients are received yearly ; and the daily census averages nearly 1,900. Dr. E. C. Dent is medical superintendent.

The New-York City Asylum for the Insane, on Ward's Island, has been used for male patients only. It is a large brick building, with towers and turrets, and has trimmings of Ohio freestone, presenting a fine architectural appearance. It was opened in 1871, and accommodates, with out-lying buildings, over 2,200 patients. The number of admissions during the past year was 750, and the total

NEW-YORK CITY ASYLUM FOR THE INSANE (WOMEN), BLACKWELL'S ISLAND.

number under treatment for the year was 2,498. The asylum has a resident medical staff of sixteen physicians. The general treatment is that in vogue in advanced and progressive asylums ; and all patients capable of appreciating them are provided with occupation and amusements. Dr. W. A. Macy is medical superintendent.

The New-York City Asylum for the Insane, on Hart's Island, was opened in 1878, for the reception and care of chronic cases of female insane. The buildings comprise a number of pavilions. In 1886 the former Hart's-Island Hospital was discontinued, and the pavilions utilized for insane of both sexes. There are accommodations for about 1,000 patients. Dr. G. A. Smith is medical superintendent.

The New-York Hospital is the oldest local institution of its class. As early as 1770 a number of public-spirited citizens contributed for the erection of a hospital in the city, and a charter was obtained from the Provincial authorities in the following year. Considerable sums of money were contributed in England, and the Provincial Legislature made a grant of $2,000 a year for twenty years towards its support. The corner-stone of the first building was laid in 1775, and when nearly completed the structure was destroyed by fire, entailing a loss of $35,000. The Legislature made a grant of $20,000 for its rebuilding, and the work was

NEW-YORK CITY ASYLUM FOR THE INSANE (MEN), WARD'S ISLAND.

begun. The building was nearly completed again, when the outbreak of the Revolution turned men's thoughts into other directions. The unfinished building was occupied by the British and Hessian soldiers as a barrack and hospital, and it was not until January, 1791, that it was in a proper condition to receive patients. Eighteen sick persons were then admitted. The original buildings were near Broadway, between Worth and Duane Streets. In 1869 they were torn down, and a new structure was erected on West 15th Street, between Fifth and Sixth Avenues. This was opened for the reception of patients in March, 1877. The hospital has been liberally aided by the State. In addition to the grants already mentioned, a grant of $10,000 a year-was made in 1792, which was increased to $20,000 in 1795, and still further increased to $25,000 in the following year. The Bloomingdale Asylum for the Insane, opened in 1821, is a branch of the New-York Hospital. In 1799 an arrangement was entered into with the United-States Treasury Department whereby the hospital was to receive a stipulated sum for the care of sick and disabled seamen. Under its present administration it is a general hospital for the reception and care of both pay and free patients, the latter constituting nearly 80 per cent. of the 5,200 patients taken yearly. Private patients are received and treated at varying rates, the price in the general wards being $7 a week, and for private rooms from $15 to $35 a week. The New-York Hospital's many advantages have made it one of the best schools of medicine and surgery in the country, and no pains are spared to render it valuable to students by furnishing every possible facility for the study and treatment of disease. Clinics are regularly given in cases arising in the practice of the house, to which students from all the local medical colleges are admitted. As early as 1796 a library was founded for the use of physicians and students, and it now numbers upward of 19,000 volumes. In 1840 a pathological cabinet, now one of the most important in the city, was begun, and has grown into a large collection of specimens of morbid anatomy, casts, drawings, etc., embracing nearly 3,000 specimens. A training-school for nurses was opened in 1877, which has graduated over

200 nurses.   The new building, opened in 1877, is said to be one of the most luxu-riously appointed hospitals in the world.   It is seven stories high, with a mansard roof, and has accommodations for 200 patients, with their attendants.   Stone, iron and red brick form the constructive materials, and the building is as nearly fire-proof as is possible to the builder's art.   In the rear, on West 16th Street, is the venerable Thorn mansion, an old-time structure, used as an administration building for the executive offices of the hospital ; and a handsome brick building, completed in 1891, and occupied by the library, the pathological museum and the training-school for nurses.   The hospital is heated by steam, and artificial ventilation is

NEW-YORK HOSPITAL, WEST 15TH STREET, NEAR FIFTH AVENUE.

secured by means of a large fan, which forces a current of fresh air through the wards and cor-ridors.   The kit-chens and laundries are in the upper stories, above the wards.   An unusual and pleasing feature of the hospital is the solarium, a large room on the upper story of the administration building, covered with a canopy of translucent glass, filled with plants and flowers, fount-ains and aquaria, a sunny and healthful resting-place for convalescents.   On other stories are the large operating and autopsy rooms, the general wards, pri-vate apartments for

pay patients, and the offices.   The corporation is controlled by a board of twenty-six Governors.   Besides the hospital proper it supports the Bloomingdale Insane Asylum ; the House of Relief, or Emergency Hospital, at 160 Chambers Street, where 2,000 cases of accidents are received yearly ; and a dispensary, where upwards of 20,000 patients are annually given free treatment and advice.   The ambulance services re-spond to more than 4,000 calls yearly, and are of great service in many emergencies. During 1892 the total number of patients in all departments of the hospital was 38,118, and the grand total since its foundation is 577,630.   The former site of the hospital is covered by substantial iron-front buildings, occupied by a number of the strongest houses in the dry-goods trade.   Merritt Trimble (president of the Bank for Savings) is president of the hospital ; and George P. Ludlam is superintendent.

BLOOMINGDALE ASYLUM FOR THE INSANE.

VARIOUS BUILDINGS IN THE ASYLUM GROUNDS AT BOULEVARD, WEST 117TH AND WEST 120TH STREETS.

30

The **Bloomingdale Asylum** was occupied by the insane patients of the New-York Hospital in 1821, when what is now known as the "main building" was opened. The asylum is substantially built of brick and stone, and has long occupied a commanding site on Harlem Heights, at the Boulevard and 117th Street, over-looking the Hudson and surrounding country. For many years no better location could have been found. The rapid growth of the city in that vicinity has made a change of location desirable, and the land and buildings have been sold to Columbia College. Bloomingdale will remove in 1894 to new and imposing structures at White Plains, N. Y. About 450 patients are received yearly, who are divided into classes, according to the nature of their mental aberration; and suitable methods of treatment are adopted for each class, the so-called moral method being largely employed, supplemented by the best-known scientific and medical treatment; harsh measures and all unnecessary confinement being strictly prohibited. The asylum has some free beds, but most of the patients are required to pay, in proportion to their ability; and thus a quiet hospital has been provided, for those of moderate means, as well as the rich, who are suffering from mental disease, where they can be assured of kind and skilful treatment. During 1892, 442 patients were treated, of whom 144 were new cases. During the year 43 patients were discharged as cured; 36 as improved; 18 as unimproved; and 38 died. The accommodations for the insane having become inadequate at the New-York Hospital, the Governors applied to the Legislature in 1815 for aid to construct new buildings elsewhere, and a grant was given them for that purpose of $10,000 yearly, to date from 1816 to 1857. Accordingly, in 1816 a plot of ground was purchased at Bloomingdale Heights, then seven miles from the city, and buildings were erected thereon and completed in 1821.

The **Roosevelt Hospital**, at 59th Street and Ninth Avenue, was referred to in 1874 by an eminent English surgeon as "Without exception the most complete medical charity in every respect" that he had ever seen. It owes its existence to the princely bequest of .James H. Roosevelt, who, dying in 1863, left his whole estate "for the establishment, in the City of New York, of a hospital for the reception and relief of sick and diseased persons, and for its permanent endowment." The amount received from the bequest was a little more than $1,000,000; and, after long and careful consideration, the nine trustees under the will decided to adopt the pavilion plan. The corner-stone was laid October 29, 1869; and the hospital was formally opened November 2, 1871. The cost of the grounds, which embrace the entire block lying between Ninth and Tenth Avenues and 58th and 59th Streets, and the build-ings constructed thereon up to 1893, together with their equipment, amounted to about $1,200,000. The original design was for a central administration building, with two pavilions on each side for patients and their attendants, to be connected with the administration building by covered corridors, and yet so far apart from each other as to secure light and ventilation for all. The money at the disposal of the trustees did not admit of the execution of the entire plan. The buildings con-structed comprise the following: 1st. The administration building, in the centre of the block facing on 59th Street, a four-story brick edifice containing the offices, examining room, apothecary's department, staff dining-room, etc., on the first floor; on the second floor, the private apartments of the superintendent, a reception-room for the trustees, a medical-board room, and an amphitheatre for clinical instruction, etc.; on the third floor, a few rooms for private patients; and on the fourth floor, two surgical wards — one for women, and the other for children. 2d. In the rear of this, facing on 58th Street, is a building used for kitchen, laundry, store-rooms, sewing-room, linen-room, and dining and sleeping-rooms for out-ward help; while in the basement, and running east, are the boiler-room, engine-rooms, fan-room, and various agencies for heating and ventilating all the buildings. 3d. East of the administration building, and fronting on 59th Street, is the Medical Pavilion, a four-story structure, with wards on each floor for patients, as well as living quarters for members of the house staff and nurses. 4th. East of the Medical Pavilion is the Surgical Pavilion, containing a ward for 36 male patients, with rooms for members of the house staff and male nurses. 5th. East of the Surgical Pavilion is the new Syms Operating Theatre, built through the liberality of William J. Syms, who left $350,000 for the purpose of construction, equipment and maintenance. Of that amount $150,000 is reserved for maintenance. It is believed to be the best-appointed operating building in this or any other country. The exterior is of brick, with granite trimmings, and built in the most substantial manner. The main amphitheatre occupies the centre, and is semi-circular in shape, with abruptly rising seats, to allow an unobstructed view of the operating table from all parts of the room. In the basement are the janitor's apartments, the engine-room, and

ROOSEVELT HOSPITAL AND SYMS OPERATING THEATRE, NINTH AVENUE AND WEST 59TH STREET.

the fan-room for ventilating. The first story contains, besides the amphitheatre, a special operating room, an operating room for septic cases, a private reception-room, a reception-room for patients, an examining room, two etherizing rooms, a photographic room, a microscopic room, a bandage-preparation room, a bandage-storage room, an instrument-washing room, and the instrument room. The floors are of mosaic tile, and in many cases the walls are wainscoted in marble. On the second floor, south front, are four rooms for the reception of patients after operation, and on the floor above that six other rooms for nurses, etc. 6th. There is also the small and perfectly appointed McLane Operating Room, opened in 1890, the gift of Dr. James W. McLane, the President of the College of Physicians and Surgeons, in memory of his son, James W. McLane, Jr., and designed solely for the use of the gynæcological service. 7th. Adjoining the administration building on the west is the Out-Patient Department, which received over 83,000 visits during 1892, of patients who were cared for there without taxing the ward accommodations of the hospital.   There are 180 beds for patients in the hospital. 8th.   The dead-house and ambulance stable are in a separate building.   Fourteen beds have been endowed in the Roosevelt Hospital, in the sum of $5,000 each.   In 1892 2,788 patients were treated, of whom 1,159 were discharged as cured, 948 improved, 210 not improved, and 307 died, leaving 164 under treatment.   During the same period 3,768 patients were treated in the accident room who were not detained for ward treatment, and the calls of the ambulance during the year numbered 1,905. From the opening of the hospital to the beginning of 1893, 39,104 patients had been treated, 34,741 of them gratuitously, so that the institution well deserves its name of a great free hospital, whose charity is bounded only by its ability to care for those who seek its aid.

The Presbyterian Hospital in the City of New-York comprises an imposing group of brick buildings, occupying the entire block between Madison and Park Avenues, and extending from 70th Street to 71st Street.   The group comprises the operating pavilion, erected in 1892 ; the administration building, completed in 1872 ; the dispensary, opened in 1888 ; the chapel, pathological department, and an isolating pavilion, erected in 1889 ; two surgical pavilions and a surgical administration building, opened in 1890 ; and the laundry ; all constructed of pressed brick, and connected by corridors, as at the Roosevelt Hospital.   The Presbyterian Hospital was founded in 1868, and the first buildings were opened in 1872, on land given by James Lenox, who took a deep interest in the work.   In 1889 most of the original buildings were destroyed by fire, and as a result the entire scheme was re-arranged, with a view to secure greater efficiency, convenience and economy.   The new edifices embody the latest and best methods of hospital construction, and are admirably adapted to their purpose.   The operating pavilion, administration building and dispensary are on 70th Street.   In the rear of the latter, on Madison Avenue, is the chapel, and near it the isolating pavilion.   On 71st Street are the large medical and surgical pavilions and a surgical administration building, with a second surgical pavilion on Park Avenue.   These pavilions provide 22 wards, having 330 beds, with a possible increase to 450, and numerous other rooms for a great variety of purposes, such as reception-rooms, parlors, dining-rooms, doctors' parlors, and consultation rooms; 22 private rooms, for paying patients; press-rooms, drying-rooms, pantries, dormitories, solaria, etc.   The buildings are entirely fire-proof, being constructed of masonry and iron throughout; and the system of ventilation is as perfect as could be devised ; the great factor in the system being the lofty dispensary tower on Madison Avenue, which has at its base a large battery of steam-driven fans.   The tower and the fans open into an immense underground duct, connecting by smaller branches with all the hospital buildings, except the Isolating Pavilion and the Pathological Department, which have independent systems of ventilation.   While the foul air is drawn from the buildings by these great fans, fresh air, taken from a considerable height above the ground, is forced into them by other fans, thus ensuring a constant current of pure air in all the wards.   The heating and plumbing arrangements are of the most approved pattern, and the comfort of the patients is still farther secured by the ample lighting facilities of the wards, which are 16 feet in height, and painted in delicate tones of color.   The Children's Ward, with its long rows of dainty cribs, is especially attractive.   One noteworthy feature of the interior arrangement is the provision of rooms for cases where death must speedily ensue, thus freeing the wards from the depressing effects of death-bed scenes.   The new operating pavilion has three halls for surgical operations, each with a series of adjoining rooms, that add much to the comfort, completeness and success of the best surgical work. The amphitheatre seats 100 persons, and is abundantly lighted by a ceiling light and three great side-lights. The wainscoting and floors are of marble. The smaller operating rooms afford facilities for operations where retirement is essential to success and spectators are undesirable. The pathological department is fully equipped with the best modern appliances ; and the new dispensary building, a lofty hall 100 feet in length, lighted by three-story windows, and surrounded by doctors' rooms, provided with every convenience for the treatment of patients, is a model of its class. The buildings represent an outlay closely approaching $1,200,000. Everything that the best medical and surgical skill can suggest, and the lavish expenditure of money can secure, is done for the relief of the patients. While the hospital is largely supported by members of the Presbyterian and Reformed Churches, it is entirely undenominational in its work, less than ten per cent. of the patients being Presbyterians, and over fifty per cent. being Roman Catholics. Of the 3,300 patients cared for yearly over 3,200 are treated gratuitously ; and scarcely more

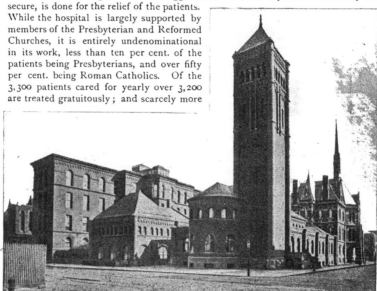

PRESBYTERIAN HOSPITAL, MADISON AVENUE AND EAST 70TH STREET.

than $3,000 is received from pay patients. The dispensary treats upwards of 70,000 patients yearly, and dispenses about 22,000 prescriptions, while the ambulance service answers 1,500 calls. The entire plant is lighted by both gas and electricity, the latter light permitting surgical operations under ether to be performed with safety night or day. The hospital is also equipped with powerful Worthington pumps.

The Mount-Sinai Hospital was originally known as "The Jews' Hospital in the City of New York." It was founded in 1852 by a number of benevolent Hebrews, headed by Sampson Simson, who gave a lot of land on 28th Street. It was opened in 1855, and remained in the first location until 1872, when it took possession of its group of buildings on Lexington Avenue, extending from 66th Street to 67th Street. The land is leased from the city for ninety-nine years, at a nominal rental of $1 a year.   Brick and stone form the constructive materials.   The group comprises three five-story buildings, connected by closed corridors.   Like most other so-called private hospitals, Mount Sinai has two grand divisions — the medical and

the surgical — each having four wards; a gynæcological department, classed as surgical; and a children's ward. It has also an eye and ear department, to which six rooms, each containing two beds, are allotted. These are on the first floor of the administration building, on Lexington Avenue.   On the same floor are the

MOUNT-SINAI HOSPITAL, LEXINGTON AVENUE, EAST 66TH AND 67TH STREETS.

directors' room, the offices of the superintendent and the admitting physician, a sitting-room and a library containing 2,000 volumes.   The remaining floors are given up to private rooms, those of the house staff and the superintendent, the synagogue and operating rooms.   The wards for women and children occupy the northern wing, on 67th Street ; and the men's wards are in the southern wing.   The arrangement is alike for all the wards, each containing from 20 to 25 beds, ranged along the sides of the room.   All the wards are kept scrupulously clean, and abundantly lighted and ventilated.   In the rear of the administration building is the isolation-house for contagious cases, the laundry building, and the morgue.   In summer the intervening court-yard forms a pleasant lounging-place for convalescent patients.   The kitchen and dining-rooms are in the basement of the main building.

Just across the way, in 67th Street, is the Dispensary Building, erected in 1890, at a cost exceeding $125,000.   It is connected with the hospital by a warm and well-lighted tunnel under the street, and is thoroughly fire-proof.   The first story of the front is of Belleville stone, and the remaining five stories are of salmon pressed brick and terra cotta.   On the right is the entrance to the free dispensary, which, with its reception-rooms and smaller operating and examination rooms, occupies the first two stories of the building.   There are eye, ear, throat, venereal and general departments. The last annual report shows that over 70,000 patients were treated, and upwards of · 58,000 prescriptions dispensed, in most cases free of cost.   On the left side of the building is an entrance to the rooms of the Ladies' Auxiliary Society and the Training School for Nurses, which occupy the upper stories.   The Ladies' Auxiliary Society is an important factor in the work of the hospital. · It was established in 1872, and finds an ample field of work in providing clothes and bedding for the unfortunate sick and needy.   The Training-School for Nurses was opened in 1881, and has graduated many well-trained nurses.

Although Mount-Sinai was founded and is sustained by benevolent Hebrews, it does not limit its ministrations to members of that faith, but admits patients of all nationalities and creeds. About eight per cent. of the patients are Russian Jews; and of the 3,000 cases yearly admitted, ninety per cent. are free patients. Mount-Sinai receives a larger proportion of the annual Hospital-Sunday collection than any other of the local institutions, as its percentage of free patients is the largest. Unlike most of the other local hospitals, Mount-Sinai makes only provision for clinical instruction for a limited number of students, but devotes all its energies to the care of its inmates, seeking to make its work educational only to the limits of the house staff, and medical students and practicing physicians and surgeons who are invited to be present at operations. This was the first hospital in the city to admit women to membership on its house staff, and although none are now serving, their absence is not due to any change in the rules, but because the young men have stood the highest in the rigid competitive examinations required of all applicants for positions. Women are still on the general staff, but they have charge of a division in the children's department, in the dispensary. The administration of the hospital is under the control of a board of directors, elected by the members. Besides directing all expenditures of money, and regulating the general policy of the institution, they have the appoint-

ment of the medical and surgical staff, all the members of which serve without pay, for the term of two years. The hospital accommodates 220 patients, including those in private rooms, who pay from $12 to $40 a week, and have whatever advantages come from isolation and an abundance of room. The report for 1892 shows the number of applications for admission to have been 5,669; number of patients treated, 3,159; number of consultations in the dispensary, 91,449; number of prescriptions in the dispensary, 74,883; total amount of receipts, $127,230; amount of expenditures, $109,689; permanent fund, $179,500; number of members and patrons, 4,016. Of the 3,159 patients admitted during 1892 1,679 were discharged as cured, 851 as improved, 156 as unimproved, 20 were sent to other institutions, and 247 died in the hospital.

MOUNT-SINAI HOSPITAL DISPENSARY AND NURSES' HOME, 151 EAST 67TH STREET, NEAR LEXINGTON AVENUE.

St. Luke's Hospital, at Fifth Avenue and 54th Street, holds a unique place among the local hospitals, as it is not merely a hospital, but also a religious house. The superintendent is a clergyman of the Protestant Episcopal Church; the central feature of the building is a large chapel; and the services of the Church are recited daily in the wards. While maintaining the highest standard of scientific work, it is the most home-like of the local hospitals, and the relations between patients, physicians and nurses are as nearly as possible the same as would obtain in private families under like conditions. The beginnings were made in 1846, when Rev. Dr. William A. Muhlenberg, then rector of the Church of the Holy Com. munion, took up a collection of $30 for the work. In 1850 an appeal to the public

ST. LUKE'S HOSPITAL, FIFTH AVENUE AND WEST 54TH STREET.

resulted in the formation of a corporation and in subscriptions amounting to $100,000. In 1854 the Sisters of the Holy Communion opened an infirmary, in a house on Sixth Avenue, where upwards of 200 patients had been treated when the work was transferred to the newly erected St. Luke's, in 1858. The building fronts on West 54th Street, and faces south, with a length of nearly 300 feet. Its general plan is that of an oblong parallelogram, with wings at each end, and a central chapel flanked by two towers. The building stands well back from the street, with a large lawn intervening, and is constructed of brick, painted a modest drab. The chapel is well lighted and ventilated. There are nine wards for medical and surgical cases, including three wards for consumptives. All acute, curable and non-contagious cases are received, and treated free, if necessary. There are 224 beds. To the extent of accommodation, no patient whose disease is suitable for treatment is turned away because unable to pay for board. Over 2,000 patients are treated yearly, at an expense of about $100,000. In connection with the hospital there is a training-school for nurses, established in 1888. The popularity of St. Luke's has been such as to make larger accommodations necessary, and the trustees have recently purchased a spacious tract of land on 113th Street, near the proposed Cathedral of St. John the Divine, where they will erect magnificent new buildings.

The corner-stone of the new St. Luke's Hospital was laid May 6, 1893, in the presence of the trustees of St. Luke's, of Columbia College, of the Teachers College and of the Cathedral, the medical staff of the hospital, the bishops of New York and of Long. Island, and a large body of vested clergy. The site to be occupied by the new hospital extends from 113th Street to 114th Street, and from Morningside Avenue to Amsterdam Avenue, with the principal front on 113th Street, adjacent to the grounds of the Cathedral. The new hospital is to be com-

ST. LUKE'S HOSPITAL, NOW BUILDING ON WEST 113TH STREET, NEAR MORNINGSIDE PARK.

posed of nine semi-detached buildings, four facing on each street, and with the lofty administration building in the centre. The architect is Ernest Flagg. The amount of money invested, when the entire establishment is completed, will be in excess of $2,000,000. The buildings will be five stories high, and thoroughly fire-proof and fitted with every modern appliance. The administration or central building is named in honor of Dr. Muhlenberg, and the pavilions to be built at first bear the names of Minturn, Norrie, and Vanderbilt, benefactors of the hospital. Other pavilions will be built as the money is furnished and the necessities of the work require. Although St. Luke's was founded by the Episcopal Church, and is practically a religious house of that denomination, it is entirely unsectarian in the range of its benefactions. Up to October 18, 1892, 36,050 patients had been treated in its wards, and of these 38½ per cent. were Episcopalians, 33 per cent. were Protestants of other sects, and 27½ per cent. were Roman Catholics.

Lebanon Hospital was organized in 1889 and incorporated in 1891. It purchased the building formerly occupied by the Ursuline Convent, at 150th Street and Westchester Avenue, and very thoroughly remodelled and reconstructed it so that it might be suited for the purpose in mind. It is not only a hospital, but a convalescent home, and is intended for the worthy poor who need fresh air, rest and medical care. There are beds for 500 patients, besides ample and commodious offices for the general departments of the institution. It was founded by benevolent Hebrews, but there is

NEW-YORK OPHTHALMIC HOSPITAL, THIRD AVENUE AND EAST 23D STREET.

nothing of a sectarian character about the Lebanon Hospital, which is open to all sufferers, without distinction as to their race or creed. The president is Jonas Weil.

National Hospitals have been established in several localities, by the foreign colonies residing in New York, for the benefit of their sick and unfortunate members and compatriots. These institutions serve a most kindly and worthy purpose in taking care of the weary immigrants, often thrown upon our shores almost in destitution, exhausted by the long sea-voyage, devastated by home-sickness, and almost ready to succumb. The Chinese Hospital, for the moon-eyed Celestials of New York, is in the neighboring city of Brooklyn, and draws its support from philanthropic Americans. It is for the reception, care and maintenance of, and the giving of medical and surgical advice exclusively to, Chinese afflicted with maladies or physical injuries or weaknesses, deformities or infirmities, excepting contagious diseases. The French Hospital, at 320 and 322 West 34th Street, receives about 500 sick poor French people yearly, giving the indigent free treatment. This fine charity is conducted by the French Benevolent Society. The Norwegian Relief Society maintains the Norwegian Deaconess Home and Hospital, with 30 beds. It has

LEBANON HOSPITAL, WESTCHESTER AVENUE AND 150TH STREET.

lately been removed from East 57th Street to Brooklyn. The Swiss Home, at 108 Second Avenue, gives medical attention to Swiss who are without means. The strong local societies of Scots, Irishmen, Englishmen, Welshmen, Hollanders, Spaniards, Russians, Belgians, Poles, Hungarians and other foreigners have provision for looking out for their sick and injured fellow-countrymen, mainly by the aid of the great city hospitals. The Germans, however, have two or three finely equipped establishments (as described elsewhere); and the tide of Italian immigration of late years pouring through this port has caused the erection of two hospitals entirely for people of this nationality, taking care of above 2,000 patients yearly. The best facilities, care and attention, however, are provided at the great public hospitals, and as there are no restrictions as to race or creed, these noble institutions are wide open to our impecunious European and Asiatic guests.

St. Vincent's Hospital of the City of New York, at 195 West 11th Street, was founded in 1849, and for some years occupied a house in West 13th Street. In 1857 the building of the Catholic Half-Orphan Asylum in West 11th Street was secured. The work of the hospital increased to such an extent that a large four-story brick building was erected in 1882, at the corner of West 12th Street and Seventh Avenue, giving the hospital accommodations for nearly 200 patients. The Sisters of Charity of St. Vincent de Paul, a Roman Catholic order instituted in

France in 1633, have charge of the hospital, which, since its foundation, has received and treated upwards of 50,000 cases, the average number now admitted being nearly 2,500. No charge is made to persons unable to pay for treatment, and these form a majority. The hospital has an ambulance service which answers upwards of 2,000 calls yearly. Although a Catholic institution, patients are admitted without regard to their religious belief, and St. Vincent's occupies a prominent position among the local hospitals.

The Hahnemann Hospital of the City of New York is a general hospital for the reception of such free and pay patients, not suffering from incurable or chronic diseases, as may desire to be treated by homœopathic methods. It was chartered in 1875, two older institutions, the New-York Homœopathic Surgical Hospital, incorporated in 1872, and the New-York Homœopathic Hospital for women and children, incorporated in 1848, uniting under the name of the Hahnemann Hospital. The substantial four-story brick and stone building on Park Avenue, between 67th and 68th Streets, was erected in 1878, and has accommodations for about seventy patients. There are four well-lighted and pleasant wards, one each for men and children, and two for women, besides an endowed room for firemen, containing three beds; one for saleswomen, containing two beds; one for policemen, containing one bed; and the Anthony Dey room, with one bed. In 1887 the Ovariotomy Cottage was erected on the grounds, and in 1891 the Dispensary was opened. In addition to its free beds, the hospital provides a quiet and comfortable home for the sick and suffering of all classes under homœopathic treatment; and persons requiring surgical operations, or taken ill with any disease not contagious, can be received and obtain the best medical and surgical treatment and skilled nursing, their comfort and sensibilities being always considered and secured. Private patients pay at rates varying from $18 to $40 a week. A gift of $5,000 endows a bed in perpetuity; one of $3,000 during the donor's lifetime; and the same amount endows a bed in perpetuity in the Children's Ward, a cheery apartment containing beds and cribs for the little ones. About 2,000 patients are treated yearly. The managers contemplate the erection of a maternity hospital and the establishment of a training-school for nurses.

St. Francis Hospital, at 605 to 617 5th Street is a general hospital for the gra-

HAHNEMANN HOSPITAL, PARK AVENUE, BETWEEN EAST 67TH AND 68TH STREETS.

tuitous treatment of the poorer classes. It was opened in 1865, and is in charge of the Roman Catholic order of the Sisters of the Poor of St. Francis. No contagious or incurable cases are admitted, but all others are received and treated without charge, when unable to pay. There are 240 beds; and about 2,700 patients are admitted yearly.

GERMAN HOSPITAL, PARK AVENUE AND EAST 77TH STREET.

The German Hospital and Dispensary of the City of New York, at Park Avenue and 77th Street, was incorporated in 1861. Patients of every nationality, color and creed are received, and treated gratuitously, when they are unable to pay. Private patients are charged from $15 to $35 a week. There are 165 beds. Upwards of 2,500 patients are treated yearly, a large proportion of them being free patients. The dispensary department was opened in 1884, and gives free treatment and advice to nearly 30,000 cases yearly. A nominal fee of ten cents is charged to those who are able to pay. The annual expenses of the hospital and dispensary are met by voluntary subscriptions, and the interest of an endowment fund of $170,000.

The Manhattan Dispensary and Hospital is a brick building at Amsterdam Avenue and 131st Street. The dispensary was opened in 1862, and treats about 8,000 patients yearly. The hospital was opened in 1884, and contains seventy beds. Medical and surgical treatment is given free to patients who are unable to pay for relief, and pay patients are charged from $7 to $35 a week. Upwards of 600 cases are cared for yearly.

MANHATTAN HOSPITAL, AMSTERDAM AVENUE AND WEST 131ST STREET.

St. Elizabeth's Hospital, at 225 West 31st Street, is in charge of the Sisters of the Third Order of St. Francis of Assisium. It was founded in 1870; and all persons in need of surgical or medical aid, except contagious, insane and violent cases, are admitted, and treated by their own physicians when desired. The charges vary from $8 to $35 a week, and there are 90 beds.

·The New-York Post-Graduate Medical School and Hospital, at Second Avenue and East 20th Street, a school for clinical instruction to practitioners of medicine, was opened in 1882 for the treatment of general diseases. Patients who are able to pay are charged from $7 to $20 a week; and no contagious or chronic cases are admitted. There are women's wards, men's wards, orthopædic wards for children, and an entire building for babies' wards. The hospital has 114 beds, and upwards of 800 new patients are admitted yearly. The directors are building a fine six-story fire-proof structure for the school and hospital, at Second Avenue and 20th Street. During the year 502 physicians attended the school.

The Christopher Columbus Hospital is at 41 East 12th Street. It was opened in 1890, for the free medical and surgical treatment of both sexes; and receives all classes of patients, except those suffering from contagious diseases. It is in charge of the Catholic Salesian Sisters of the Sacred Heart of Jesus.

St. Mark's Hospital of New-York City is at 177 Second Avenue. It was incorporated in 1890, and receives general charity and pay patients. Private cases pay from $15 to $50 a week, and have the privilege of selecting their own physicians. The hospital is small, treating 600 patients yearly. It numbers among its staff physicians of national repute.

St. Joseph's Hospital was opened in 1882, by the Sisters of the Poor of St. Francis, for the reception and care of consumptives, and a limited number of other chronic and incurable diseases which cannot be properly treated in other hospitals. But no acute diseases, affections of the mind and nervous system (such as insanity, idiocy and epilepsy), chronic surgical diseases, cases of deform-

ST. JOSEPH'S HOSPITAL, BROOK AND ST. ANN'S AVENUES, EAST 143D AND 144TH STREETS.

ity or aged persons are admitted. The building occupies the entire block between East 143d and 144th Streets and Brook and St. Ann's Avenues, and is well adapted for its purpose, everything possible in the way of improved sanitary conditions, pleasant surroundings and skilled medical treatment, being provided to alleviate the sufferings of the patients. St. Joseph's is one of the handsomest of the New-York hospital buildings, and is favorably placed in the open country, not far from St. Mary's Park, beyond the Harlem River. There are 300 beds; and admission is free to the poor, without regard to nationality, creed or color.

The Seton Hospital for Consumptives, on the Spuyten-Duyvil heights, is a magnificent Italian Renaissance structure of brick, built in 1892-93, at a cost of $300,000, for 250 patients. Its minutest details have been arranged by the most eminent specialists, and this is the best hospital for consumptives in the world. It is conducted by the Sisters of Charity.

The Beth-Israel Hospital Association was incorporated in 1890. It maintains a free hospital and dispensary at 206 East Broadway and 195 Division Street. The hospital contains 50 beds; and the dispensary treats yearly 12,000 patients.

The Flower Surgical Hospital was opened in 1890, by the authorities of the New-York Homœopathic College, on Avenue A, between East 63d and East 64th Streets.   Surgical cases only are taken here, and 200 cases are received annually.   The dispensary averages 25,000 free prescriptions yearly.

The Sloane Maternity Hospital, at the corner of Tenth Avenue and 59th Street, has been pronounced by many home and foreign physicians to be a model lying-in hospital.   It was erected in 1886 and 1887 by William D. Sloane, whose wife, a daughter of the late William H. Vanderbilt, endowed the institution by making all its beds free in perpetuity.   It is built of brick, with mouldings of granite and terra cotta, and its construction is fire-proof throughout.   The flooring of the halls and the wainscoting of the stairways are of white marble ; the wards and operating rooms are floored with white vitrified tiles.   In the basement are the laundry, kitchen, servants' dining-room, coil chamber, and fan for warming and ventilation ; a bath-room, where newly admitted patients are thoroughly cleansed before going to the wards ; and a locker-room for the safe-keeping of the clothing worn by patients on admission to the hospital.   On the first floor are the rooms of the house-physician, the assistant house-physician, and the matron ; a reception-room, a din-

THE WOMAN'S HOSPITAL IN THE STATE OF NEW YORK, PARK AVENUE AND EAST 50TH STREET.

ing-room for the house staff, the manager's room, and a large examination room. The second floor contains three wards with 20 beds, a delivery-room, sleeping-rooms for the nurses, the drug-room, and a dining-room.   On the third floor there are five wards, containing 25 beds, a delivery-room, the apartment of the principal of the training-school for nurses, two isolating rooms, and sleeping-rooms for the ward-nurses.   The total number of beds is 45.   In the attic are the rooms of the house-servants.   The lying-in wards are used in rotation.   Each one, having been occupied by five patients, is thoroughly cleansed and the furniture washed with a solution of carbolic acid.   Each of the delivery-rooms contains a table of special design, and the high character of the service is shown by the fact that in 2,500 cases, many of them emergency cases brought to the hospital in ambulances, only 13 deaths are recorded. The hospital is in charge of the College of Physicians and Surgeons, which is the Medical Department of Columbia College.

The Woman's Hospital in the State of New York, the first of its class established in the world, was founded in 1854 by Dr. J. Marion Sims, at that time the leading expert in female diseases in the world, and the discoverer of a new method of treatment, which has revolutionized the prac-

SLOANE MATERNITY HOSPITAL, TENTH AVENUE AND WEST 59TH STREET.

tice of medical surgery as applied to female complaints. The institution began its work in 1855, in a house built for a private residence, on Madison Avenue. The hospital was incorporated in 1857, and in 1866 it was removed to 50th Street, between Lexington and Park Avenues, where two commodious brick buildings have been erected, with accommodations for 150 patients, and completely equipped with

NEW-YORK INFIRMARY FOR WOMEN AND CHILDREN, 5 LIVINGSTON PLACE, OPP. STUYVESANT SQUARE.

all necessary conveniences for the treatment of this class of complaints. Each county in the State is entitled to one free bed, and the medical and surgical attendance is gratuitous. At the Dispensary 1,500 outdoor patients receive treatment yearly. The yearly expenses, met by voluntary subscriptions and the income of an endowment fund of $152,000, are about $70,000.

The New-York Infirmary for Women and Children, on Stuyvesant Square (East), near 16th Street, was founded in 1854 by Drs. Elizabeth and Emily Blackwell, who were the pioneers among women physicians. It is the only hospital in the city (except the Homœopathic Hospital) where women and children can be treated by women physicians. Its doors are open to all classes for medical or surgical treatment. The present hospital accommodates 65 patients, and additions soon to be made will double its capacity.

During 1892 341 patients were treated, and of this number more than half were free. The dispensary, where over 28,000 patients received free treatment during the

NEW-YORK DISPENSARY FOR WOMEN AND CHILDREN, 15TH STREET AND LIVINGSTON PLACE.

year, occupies the first floor of the college building, 321 East 15th Street. The Woman's Medical College of the New-York Infirmary moved into its present commodious building, corner of Stuyvesant Square and 15th Street, in 1890. Twenty-one students graduated in 1892. The Training School for Nurses was united in 1891 with the New-Haven Training School, the nurses from the latter school coming to the Infirmary for obstetrical and gynæcological training. The Nurses' Home is at 327 East 15th Street.

The Nursery and Child's Hospital in the City of New York was opened as a day-nursery in 1854, largely through the instrumentality of Mrs. Cornelius DuBois. The original location was in St. Mark's Place ; and in 1857 a hospital was added as a necessary adjunct of the work, and the institution became incorporated under its present name. In 1855 a substantial brick building, 119 feet by 60 feet, with two wings, was erected on the present site, at Lexington Avenue and 51st Street. In 1863 a foundling asylum was built, but for four years it was used as a soldiers' home, for the reception and care of sick and wounded soldiers. In 1867 the building reverted to the institution, and has since been used as a lying-in hospital. A new three-story brick building, erected in 1888 in memory of Miss Mary A. DuBois, for many years a directress of the institution, contains the wards and offices of the corporation. Upwards of 600 mothers and 1,000 children are received yearly and cared for, at an expense of $100,000, which is met by voluntary subscriptions.

The New-York Medical College and Hospital for Women, at 213 West 54th Street, was founded

NURSERY AND CHILD'S HOSPITAL, LEXINGTON AVENUE AND EAST 51st STREET.

in 1863. The treatment is homœopathic, and the aim is to provide a
hospital for self-supporting young
women, whose only home is the
boarding-house, where, when over-
taken by sickness, they may receive
skilful treatment from physicians of
their own sex at a moderate cost,
or free of expense when necessary.
The larger part of the service, both
in the hospital and dispensary, is
gratuitous, and a steadily increasing demand for the services of
women physicians in the treatment
of women and children has made
the present leased building inadequate, and a larger structure is

NEW-YORK MEDICAL COLLEGE AND HOSPITAL FOR WOMEN,
213 WEST 54TH STREET.

contemplated to meet the needs of the work. The building now occupied has
accommodations for thirty patients. During 1891 174 cases were treated, with only
six deaths. During the same period, at the dispensary, upwards of 1,500 patients
were treated and 5,000 prescriptions dispensed. This is the only local homœopathic
hospital where women physicians are exclusively employed, and the maternity ward
shows the remarkable record of but one mother lost in thirty years.

 St. Mary's Free Hospital for Children, at 407 West 34th Street, was organized in 1870 and incorporated in 1887, for the medical and surgical treatment of
children between the ages of two and fourteen years. It is in charge of the Sisterhood of St. Mary, a Protest-
ant Episcopal order, and
accommodates 70 patients.
The yearly expenses are
about $14,000, and upwards
of 400 cases are treated
yearly. In connection with
the hospital, there is a free dispensary for children, where
5,000 suffering children are
treated yearly; the Noyes
Memorial House, at Peeks-
kill, N. Y., for patients who
have been treated in the
Hospital, and whose diseases
assume an incurable form;
and a Summer Branch House,
at Rockaway Beach, Long
Island, for convalescent children.

 **The Laura Franklin
Free Hospital** in the City of
New York, at 19 East 111th
Street, a three-story brick

ST. MARY'S FREE HOSPITAL FOR CHILDREN, 407 WEST 34TH STREET.

31

LAURA FRANKLIN FREE HOSPITAL FOR CHILDREN,
19 EAST 111TH STREET.

building, was opened in 1886 for the free medical and surgical homœopathic treatment of children between two and twelve years of age. It is in charge of the Sisters of St. Mary, a Protestant Episcopal order. It accommodates fifty patients, and is supported by voluntary subscriptions.

St. Andrew's Convalescent Hospital, at 213 East 17th Street, was opened in 1886 for the reception and care of women and girls over 15 years of age, of good character, and in need of rest, nursing and medical treatment. All cases, except those suffering from nervous or contagious diseases, are admitted free. There are twelve beds. The hospital is in charge of the Sisterhood of St. John the Baptist, a Protestant Episcopal order founded at Clewer, England, in 1851.

The Yorkville Dispensary and Hospital in the City of New York, at 1307 Lexington Avenue, was incorporated in 1886, to maintain an out-door service for the treatment of women and children. It is also a maternity charity, furnishing medical and nursing attendance to poor women during confinement. As yet it has no accommodations for in-patients, but confines its work to out-door relief. It is supported by voluntary subscriptions.

The New-York Mothers' Home of the Sisters of Misericorde, at 523 to 537 East 86th Street, was incorporated in 1888, to provide and maintain maternity hospitals and children's asylums in the State of New York. At present the society maintains a maternity hospital, for destitute women and young unmarried girls, hitherto respectable, about to become mothers. There are accommodations for 125 free and 30 pay patients, with private rooms. During 1892 206 women and 167 children were cared for, at an expense of $12,000.

The Babies' Hospital of the City of New York, at 657 Lexington Avenue, was incorporated in 1887, for the care of poor sick children under two years of age. It has accommodations for 30 babies ; and in 1891 expended upwards of $13,000 in its work. In connection with the hospital there is a dispensary for children ; a country branch, at Oceanic, N. J. ; and a training-school for children's nurses, where young girls of good character, over 18 years of age, are taught the management and training of sick and well children.

The Lying-in Hospital of the City of New York was founded in 1798. A suitable building was procured on Cedar Street ; and Robert Lenox, Dr. David Hosack, and other leading citizens were appointed managers. It soon became evident that the funds of the society were insufficient to meet the expenses, and an arrangement was made with the New-York Hospital by which that institution should receive the income of the funds, on condition that the governors should provide a lying-in ward. This arrangement continued until 1827, when the lying-in asylum was reorganized, and began an independent work. The society has no home or hospital for its beneficiaries, but renders assistance to them in their houses.

The Ladies' Hebrew Lying-In Society, at 58 St. Mark's Place, is a branch of the United Hebrew Charities. It was incorporated in 1877, and cares for poor Hebrew mothers during confinement, and supplies medical aid, food, nurses and clothing to all deserving cases. The yearly disbursements are about $2,000.

The New-York Eye and Ear Infirmary, at 218 Second Avenue, was the first institution opened in the city for the treatment of diseases of the eye and ear. The work was begun in 1820, by two young physicians, Edward Delafield and J. Kearney

BABIES' HOSPITAL, 657 LEXINGTON AVENUE, CORNER EAST 55TH STREET.

Rogers, who leased two small rooms in a house on Chatham Street, and announced their readiness to treat all eye and ear diseases. Within seven months over 400 patients were treated, and many cases of partial blindness were cured. As a result of the first year's work, a society known as the New-York Eye Infirmary was organized, in 1821 ; and in 1824 the old Marine Hospital of the New-York Hospital was leased. This was occupied until 1845, when a house in Mercer Street was purchased and fitted up for the use of the society. In 1854 an appeal to the Legislature

and the public resulted in a grant and subscription amounting to $30,000, which was used in the erection of a commodious building on Second Avenue. In 1890 the corner-stone of a new and larger building was laid, and in the following year a hospital wing containing 70 beds was opened for the free treatment of patients. An average of 700 patients are received yearly. The dispensary department gives advice and treatment to 60,000 cases annually.

The New-York Ophthalmic Hospital, at Third Avenue and East 23d Street, is a hospital for the treat-

NEW-YORK EYE AND EAR INFIRMARY, SECOND AVE. AND EAST 13TH ST.

ment of diseases of the eye, ear and throat, and a college affording clinical instruc-tion in the diverse forms of these diseases. It was incorporated in 1852, and after many years of useful work, in cramped and insufficient quarters, the present four-story brick building was erected, in 1871, at a cost of $100,000, the gift of Mrs. Emma A. Keep. It is conveniently arranged for its purpose, and contains reception and operating rooms for out-door patients, numerous wards and private rooms for those whose cases require a prolonged stay at the hospital, and two large contagious wards, entirely isolated from the other patients. The hospital is free to those unable to pay for the service of a physician, the directors and surgeons serving without com-pensation, and it is one of the great charities deserving of confidence and support. It is the only institution in the country authorized by law to confer the degree of Surgeon of the Eye and Ear upon properly qualified students, and the steady growth of its work is shown by the fact that while only 830 patients were treated during the first year of its existence, in 1890 it treated over 13,000 cases, received 400 resident patients, and issued more than 53,000 prescriptions. The large visiting and consulting staff comprises many eminent specialists, and the institution enjoys an enviable reputation for its skilful treatment of the difficult diseases of which it makes a specialty.

The **Manhattan Eye and Ear Hospital** was chartered in 1869, and occupies a substantial brick building at 103 Park Avenue, corner of 41st Street. It is supported

by voluntary contribu-tions, and is intended solely for the treatment of those who cannot pay for medical aid. Besides the ophthalmic and aural departments there is one for nervous diseases, and one for throat diseases; and an isolated ward for the treatment of conta-gious diseases of the eye. Upwards of 13,000 cases are treated yearly. The administration is in the hands of a board of directors; and the

MANHATTAN EYE AND EAR HOSPITAL, PARK AVENUE AND EAST 41ST STREET.

medical staff is composed of many of the best-known physicians and surgeons of the city, who give freely of their time and skill for the relief of the unfortunate. The work has already outgrown the accommodations, and to relieve the pressure upon the day clinics, as well as to meet the wants of those unable to leave their work during the day, night clinics have been established in some of the departments; and the directors are contemplating the enlargement of the building so as to increase the usefulness of the institution, which has long been recognized as one of the best of its class. The hospital has an endowment fund of $80,000; the C. R. Agnew Memorial Fund of $12,000; and seven endowed beds.

The **New York Ophthalmic and Aural Institute**, at 46 East 12th Street, was opened in 1869 as a dispensary and hospital for the treatment of diseases of the eye and ear, and a school of ophthalmology and otology. Patients unable to pay are, so far as the resources of the institute will permit, received, provided for, and treated in the hospital without charge. Dispensary patients (about 8,000 a year) are treated gratuitously. The Institute leases the building it now occupies, and in 1891 treated nearly 400 in the hospital, where 160 cataracts were successfully extracted. About one-third of the patients receive free treatment.

The New-Amsterdam Eye and Ear Hospital, at 212 West 38th Street, a substantial brick building, was opened in 1888 for the treatment of eye and ear diseases. There are also nose and throat departments. It is supported by voluntary subscriptions. Seventy patients are treated yearly; and 175 operations are made; while the dispensary department gives free treatment to upwards of 2,000 needy applicants.

The New-York Cancer Hospital, at Central Park West and 106th Street, was founded in 1884, for the treatment of all sufferers from cancer, whose condition

NEW-YORK CANCER HOSPITAL, CENTRAL PARK WEST AND 106TH STREET.

promises any hope of cure or relief. The building is of recent construction; replete with all the modern improvements and appliances; and has 130 beds. About 600 new patients are admitted yearly, two-thirds being free. The charges for pay patients vary from $7 to $30 a week; and the yearly expenses are nearly $40,000.

The New-York Skin and Cancer Hospital, at 243 East 34th Street, was incorporated in 1883, for the free treatment and care of the poor afflicted with cancer and skin diseases. It has accommodations for 100 patients, and maintains a country branch hospital for chronic cases at Fordham Heights, a dispensary for the free examination and treatment of the poor, and the Guild of St. Lazarus, which assists in providing necessary clothing, sick-room comforts and delicacies for the inmates of the hospital.

The Metropolitan Throat Hospital, at 351 West 34th Street, was incorporated in 1874. It affords free treatment to those who are unable to pay special fees for all affections of the nose and throat. The institution is unsectarian, is supported entirely by voluntary contributions, and treats 1,000 cases yearly, aside from the much larger number of those who simply make visits for treatment.

The New-York Society for the Relief of the Ruptured and Crippled began its work in a small way in 1863, in a building on Second Avenue. Its found. ing was due to Dr. James Knight, whose long medical experience among the poor had convinced him of the need of some provision for the gratuitous treatment of cases of hernia and deformity. The rapid increase of the work soon made large accom-

NEW-YORK SOCIETY FOR THE RELIEF OF THE RUPTURED AND
CRIPPLED, LEXINGTON AVENUE AND EAST 42d STREET.

modations necessary ; and in 1867 a hospital was opened at the corner of 42d Street and Lexington Avenue. It is an ornamental structure of brick and stone, five stories in height, with accom- modations for 200 inmates, most of whom receive gratui- tous treatment, the annual expenses of $50,000 being met by an appropriation from the city, private sub- scriptions, and a grant from the Hospital Sunday-Fund. Upwards of 9,000 cases are yearly treated in the hospital and out-door department, the large majority receiving ad- vice, apparatus and treat- ment free of charge.

The New-York Or- thopedic Dispensary and Hospital, at 126 East 59th Street, was established in 1866. It receives and treats destitute persons suffering from diseases and deformi- ties of the spine and joints, infantile paralysis, bow-legs, club-foot and similar ailments, besides such cases as can not get proper treatment at home.

St. Bartholomew's Hospital and Dispensary, at 300 West 36th Street, was organized in 1888, for the gratuitous treatment of the poor suffering from skin and certain other diseases. Over 600 patients are treated yearly at the Dispensary. Although managed by Episcopalians, the hospital is unsectarian in character.

The New-York Pasteur Institute, at 1 West 97th Street, the first one of its class in America, was opened in 1890 for the anti-hydrophobic treatment of rabies according to the method of M. Pasteur. Its founder was Dr. Paul Gibier, a pupil of Prof. Pasteur. Since the opening of the Institute, 2,000 patients have been received, of whom 1,200 have been sent back, after having their injuries properly dressed, it having been demonstrated that the animals attacking them were not mad. In the remaining 300 cases the anti-hydrophobic treatment was resorted to, with a loss of only three patients. In all cases patients unable to pay for treatment have been inoculated and cared for free of charge. In 1893 the Institute occupied the Central-Park Sanatorium, at Central Park West and 97th Street, a six-story fire- proof building, admirably equipped.

The New-York Christian Home for Intemperate Men was established in 1877 to rescue victims of intemperance and the opium habit by bodily rest, mental repose, religious influence, and freedom from annoyance, irritation or temptation. No drugs or nostrums are used, but every possible means is employed to divert the minds of the patients and to keep them happily occupied. The Home, at 1175 Madison Avenue, has accommodations for 75 inmates. None is received for a stay of less than five weeks. During 1892, of the 247 inmates received, 188 professed conversion, and of these 143 remained steadfast. The refuge of the Home is free to residents of the city who are unable to pay; and otherwise the rates vary from $8 to $20 a week, according to the room selected. The yearly expenses are about $22,000, and there is an endowment fund of $50,000.

The Vanderbilt Clinic was opened in 1888 as a free dispensary for the poor. It is in charge of a board of five managers, but allied with the College of Physicians and Surgeons; and stands on land belonging to the college, at the corner of 60th Street and Amsterdam Avenue. It is a large three-story brick building, similar in design to the Sloane Maternity Hospital; and was erected and endowed by the four sons of the late William H. Vanderbilt, who gave the money for the purchase of the half block on which the College of Physicians and Surgeons, the Sloane Maternity Hospital and the Vanderbilt Clinic now stand, and with which the college buildings were erected. Besides its dispensary department, where nearly 125,000 patients received free treatment and advice during 1892, the building contains numerous small rooms for the direct practical teaching of diagnosis and treatment to the students of the college, and a theatre for clinical lectures which accommodates an audience of 400. Although of recent foundation, the Vanderbilt Clinic has already become an important medical institution.

The New-York City Dispensary, at White and Centre Streets, was established in 1791 on Tryon Street, afterward Tryon Row, which extended along the north-eastern side of the City-Hall Park, between Chambers and Chatham Streets. In 1796 the Dispensary was incorporated by the Legislature, and in 1805 it was united with the "Kinepox Institution," which had been established in 1803 for vaccinating the poor with cow-pox instead of small-pox. In 1828 the three-story brick building now in use was opened. Dur-

INFIRMARY OF FIVE-POINTS HOUSE OF INDUSTRY, 155 WORTH STREET.

ing the cholera season of 1832 it is said that the Dispensary physicians "were found in every part of the widely extended city, stopping, as far as they were able, the ravages of the plague." The institution treats 50,000 patients yearly, at a cost of $25,000. Since its foundation, dispensaries of many kinds have been established throughout the city, and are doing a noble work in relieving suffering humanity.

The **Infirmary of the Five-Points House of Industry**, at 155 Worth Street, is maintained by the charitable organization from which it takes its name. It treats 2,000 patients yearly. Two stories were added to the building in 1892.

The **Church Hospital and Dispensary** of the Protestant Episcopal Church was organized and incorporated in 1892 to concentrate and centralize Church medical work upon the most modern scientific medical principles, to provide a visiting staff, and to give special care to the worthy poor who are averse to receiving medical aid from a public clinic.

The **German Dispensary** was opened in 1857, and has been of vast benefit to the population of the crowded German quarter and to the poor of New York in general.

OTTENDORFER FREE LIBRARY.   GERMAN DISPENSARY.   LYING-IN-HOSPITAL.
THE GERMAN DISPENSARY, 137 SECOND AVENUE, BETWEEN 8TH AND 9TH STREETS.

The present handsome and commodious building at 137 Second Avenue was erected in 1883 by Mrs. Anna Ottendorfer. It contains a medical library of about 5,000 volumes.

The **Northern Dispensary** was founded in 1827. It is at Christopher Street and Waverly Place, and furnished medical and surgical aid to over 1,000,000 indigent persons. It is supported by voluntary gifts.

The **Good-Samaritan Dispensary** (formerly the Eastern Dispensary, opened in 1832), at 75 Essex Street, was opened in 1891. Upwards of 1,250,000 patients have been aided, and 160,000 cases receive treatment yearly, the number of prescriptions dispensed being about 110,000.

The **DeMilt Dispensary** occupies a building at 23d Street and Second Avenue. It was opened in 1851, and its service includes the district lying between 14th and 40th Streets and Sixth Avenue and the East River. It treats upwards of 30,000 cases yearly and dispenses nearly 70,000 prescriptions. It has cared for nearly 1,000,000 patients and given out 2,000,000 prescriptions.

The **Northeastern Dispensary**, at 222 East 59th Street, was founded in 1862. It is a large medical and surgical relief institution, treating 22,000 cases yearly, and dispensing upwards of 60,000 prescriptions.

The Harlem Dispensary, at Fourth Avenue and 125th Street, was opened in 1868. The district comprises that part of the city north of 100th Street and east of Eighth Avenue. Upwards of 7,000 cases are treated yearly.

The German Poliklinik, 78 Seventh Street, is managed mostly by German physicians, for the poor in the vicinity. It was opened in 1883, and affords medical relief to 15,000 patients yearly.

Other Local Dispensaries, aside from those mentioned above and those connected with the hospitals, include the West-Side German, opened in 1872; the Dispensary of the Trinity-Church Association, 1880; the Dispensary of St. Chrysostom's Chapel, 1880; the New-York Dispensary for Diseases of the Skin, 1869; the Homœopathic Dispensary, 1870; the Northwestern Dispensary, 1852; the Yorkville Dispensary, 1887; and the Eclectic Dispensary, at 239 East 14th Street. Each of these is of notable service in the locality which it covers.

The New-York Training-School for Nurses was founded in 1873, for the instruction of intelligent women in hospital and private nursing. It was the first school for nurses opened in this country, and was the outgrowth of a desire on the part of a few charitable and public-spirited women to elevate the standard of nursing in the Bellevue and other public hospitals. Previous to the opening of the school the male and female nurses in Bellevue Hospital had been the product of chance, physical misfortune, and practical politics, and the service left very much to be desired. The first class was graduated in 1875, and consisted of six well-trained nurses, most of whom entered upon their duties in Bellevue. The work of the school has been such as to elevate the nursing service in all the local hospitals, and the graduates have in many instances been called upon to establish similar schools in other cities, and even in Italy, China and Japan. When the school was opened, in 1873, only five applicants presented themselves, but such has been the growth of the work that 1,500 applications for admission are now received yearly, and the school always has its full quota of 68 students. The requirements are exacting. The candidates must be from 25 to 35 years of age, and physically and mentally fitted for their calling. At the expiration of a short probationary period, those who have proved satisfactory are engaged for a two-years' course of theoretical and practical training, which includes lectures by eminent physicians and surgeons and actual service in the wards of Bellevue. The school building is at 426 East 26th Street, opposite the entrance to Bellevue. It is a four-story brick

ECLECTIC DISPENSARY AND ITALIAN INDEPENDENT CLUB,
237 AND 239 EAST 14TH STREET.

structure, and was built in 1887 by Mrs. William H. Osborne. It contains a kitchen, parlor, dining-room, library, lecture rooms and sleeping apartments for the nurses. The distinctive garb of the nurses is blue and white seersucker, with a white apron and cap and linen collar. Over 400 nurses have been graduated.

The D. O. Mills Training-School for Male Nurses occupies a substantial brick building, erected in 1888 in the Bellevue-Hospital grounds, at the foot of East 26th Street.   It is arranged and fitted up as a home for the nurses during their two-years' course of study, which is on the same lines as that of the training-school for female nurses, nearly opposite.   Several classes have been graduated from the school, and there are now fifty-seven inmates, all of whom serve in the male wards of the hospital.   It is a generous charity, founded by Darius O. Mills.

The New-York Post-Graduate Medical School Training-School for Nurses, at 163 East 36th Street, was founded in 1885 for the instruction and training of hospital and private nurses.   It has graduated upwards of 250 nurses.

The New-York County Medical Society, at 19 West 43d Street, is the oldest local organization of doctors.   It was established in 1806 "to aid in regulating the practice of physic and surgery, and to contribute to the diffusion of true science, and particularly the knowledge of the healing art."   It is authorized to examine students in medicine, and to grant diplomas to such as are duly qualified.

The New-York Medical and Surgical Society was founded in 1834 for the discussion of professional topics.   The membership is limited to thirty-two, and the meetings are held at the residences of the members.

The New-York Academy of Medicine, at 119 West 43d Street, was established in 1847, and incorporated in 1851, for the cultivation of the science of medicine ; the advancement of the profession ; the elevation of the standard of medical education and the promotion of the public health.   It is a large and important organization, and has sections in pediatrics, obstetrics and gynæcology, the theory and practice of medicine ; neurology, orthopedic surgery, materia medica and therapeutics ; laryngology and rhinology, surgery, ophthalmology and otology, and public health and hygiene.   The fine Academy building was opened in 1890.   It is Romanesque in style and ornate in treatment, and contains numerous meeting and reception-rooms and a large medical library, which is open to the public.   The Academy is one of the leading institutions of its kind in America, and its membership includes many eminent physicians and surgeons.   It has a library of 50,000 volumes.

NEW-YORK ACADEMY OF MEDICINE, 19 WEST 43D STREET.

The Scientific Meeting of German Physicians was established in 1857, for the exhibition and study of interesting pathological specimens, and the report and discussion of notable medical and surgical cases.   It has a membership of about 90 ; and the monthly meetings are held at 110 West 34th Street.

The Medico-Chirurgical Society of German Physicians meets bimonthly at 411 Sixth Avenue.   It was organized in 1860, for "the cultivation of medical science and the promotion of the honor and interest of the profession."

The **Medico-Historical Society** was founded in 1864, for the preservation and publication of interesting and valuable facts regarding the medical history of the city. Among its other valuable publications mention may be made of its yearly Medical Directory, which contains valuable information and statistics relating to the many local benevolent and medical institutions.

The **New-York Ophthalmological Society** was organized in 1864, for the improvement of its members in ophthalmic and aural studies. There are thirty members; and the meetings are held bi-monthly at the members' houses.

The **Medico-Legal Society** was founded in 1866, and incorporated in 1868, for the study and advancement of the science of medical jurisprudence. The membership comprises regular practitioners of the medical and legal professions in good standing, leading scientists, and eminent literary men, 1,000 in number.

The **New-York Dermatological Society** was formed in 1869, for the study and investigation of the causes of skin diseases, the best curative methods, and all subjects connected with dermatology.

The **New-York Neurological Society** meets monthly at 17 West 43d Street, for the advancement of the science of medicine in all its relations to the nervous system. It was established in 1872, and has 75 members.

The **American Laryngological Association** was

VANDERBILT CLINIC, CORNER 60TH STREET AND AMSTERDAM AVENUE.

founded in 1878, for the study of diseases of the throat. Its headquarters are at 20 West 31st Street.

The **New-York Clinical Society** is devoted to the consideration of medical and surgical topics in their clinical and therapeutical aspects. The membership is limited to twenty, and monthly meetings are held at the houses of the members.

The **New-York Surgical Society** holds bi-monthly meetings at the New-York Hospital, for the discussion of interesting surgical cases occurring in the hospital practice. It was founded in 1879.

Other Medical Societies are the American Microscopical Society of the City of New York, founded in 1865; the New-York Medical Union, 1865; the Harlem Medical Association, 1869; the Yorkville Medical Association, 1870; the Association for the Advancement of the Medical Education of Women, 1874; the New-York Therapeutical Society, 1877; the Materia Medica Society, 1881; the Practitioners' Society of New-York, 1882; the Society of Medical Jurisprudence, 1883; the Manhattan Medical and Surgical Society, 1883; the Lenox Medical and Surgical Society, 1885; and the Hospital Graduates' Club, 1886. Most of these societies hold meetings at stated times, and discuss important topics.

Convalescent Homes have been established in many of the pleasant places near New York, for invalids to recover in. Among these are All Saints' Convalescent Homes for men and boys, at Oak Summit, Ruhberg and Farmingdale; the Fresh-Air and Convalescent Home, at Summit, N. J.; the New-York Home for Convalescents, at 433 East 118th Street; and others of like nature.

The Sanitary Aid Society, at 94 Division Street, was incorporated in 1885. It investigates evasions and violations of existing sanitary laws, prosecutes the offenders, and endeavors to educate public opinion on this important subject. It maintains the Model Lodging-House and Dormitories, at 94 Division Street, where a bed and bath, with access to a reading-room and library, are supplied to sober single men at a nominal cost. The house has 140 beds, and lodgings are furnished to 50,000 applicants yearly.

The Ladies' Health Protective Association, of New York, at 27 Beekman Place, was organized in 1884, to protect the health of the people of the City of New York by taking such action as may be necessary to secure the enforcement of existing sanitary laws and regulations, also calling the attention of the authorities to any violations thereof, and procuring the amendment of such laws and regulations when necessary.

DEMILT DISPENSARY, SECOND AVENUE AND 23D STREET.

The Hospital Saturday and Sunday Association at 79 Fourth Avenue, was founded in 1879, to get funds for the local hospitals, by collections in the churches, etc. In 1892 $60,000 were distributed among the hospitals.

The New-York Diet-Kitchen Association was incorporated in 1873, to provide the destitute sick with nourishing food, free of cost, upon a written requisition of any of the house and visiting physicians of the local dispensaries. It supports five diet-kitchens, in various parts of the city, and assists 15,000 persons yearly.

The American Veterinary College Hospital, at 139 West 54th Street, was opened in 1886 for the reception and care of animals needing treatment. Upwards of 3,000 domestic animals are treated yearly. In the dispensary horses and other animals belonging to the poor are treated free of charge. Since its opening over 7,000 animals have been received, and upwards of 2,500 operations performed.

The New-York College of Veterinary Surgeons has a large and efficient hospital for domestic animals, at 332 East 27th Street.

Reformatories
—and—
Corrections.

The Police Courts, Prisons, House of Refuge, Penitentiary, Work-House, House of Correction, Etc.

THE prevention, detection and punishment of crime and, when possible, the reformation of the criminal, form important features in the municipal activity of New York. All arrested persons are taken to the nearest station-house, and thence at the earliest possible moment they are brought before one of the six police-courts, where they are charged with specified offences and committed, bailed or discharged, according to the nature of the evidence against them.

The Police-Courts have original jurisdiction over minor offences. They are held at the Tombs, Jefferson-Market Court-House, Essex-Market Court-House, Yorkville, Harlem and Morrisania. Drunkenness, assault and battery, and thieving make the bulk of the work. Nearly all the convictions are disposed of by fines, or by short terms of imprisonment in the city institutions on Blackwell's Island. The courts have power to examine prisoners accused of serious crimes, and to hold them for trial in the higher courts. In fact, they have an extended jurisdiction and a wide latitude in the exercise of their powers. They stand next to the common people, and their province is not only to punish offences, but it is even more to correct abuses and to adjust family and neighborhood differences. For these reasons, the justices, who are appointed by the Mayor, are not often members of the legal fraternity. They are men of practical sense and experience in the every-day affairs of life, and that they have knowledge of the character, the foibles and the needs of the people with whom they come most in contact is regarded as more important than that they have legal lore. They hold office for ten years, and have salaries of $8,000 a year.

The Tombs, at Franklin and Centre Streets, is a large granite building, occupying an entire block. It is the city prison; and covers the site of the pre-Revolutionary gibbet, which was planted on a small island in the Collect Pond. The most notable execution on the island was that of seven negro slaves, in 1741, for alleged complicity in the negro riot of that year. The Collect Pond was a small sheet of water, separated from the river by a strip of marsh-land. The early experiments of John Fitch in steamboat navigation were made in 1796, on the pond. It was filled in 1817. The Tombs was built in 1840, and some of its granite stones came from the old Bridewell, erected in City-Hall Park about 1735, and torn down in 1838. The building is a pure specimen of Egyptian architecture; and it is deplorable that its really noble proportions are dwarfed by its location in a low hollow. The name arose from its gloomy and funereal appearance and associations. It appears as a single lofty story, with windows extending to the cornice. The main entrance is on Centre Street, through a lofty porch, supported by massive stone columns. Projecting entrances and columns vary the somewhat monotonous appearance of the sides of the building. The Tombs Police-court is on the right of the entrance, and the Court of Special Sessions is on the left. The latter is connected with the prison in the rear by a bridge, known as the "Bridge of Sighs," from the fact that condemned prisoners are led across it, after conviction. The entrance to the prison proper is on Franklin Street, through a locked and barred grating. The warden's office is on the left of the entrance ; and a short hallway leads the visitor to the cells, 300 in number. These are arranged in tiers, one above the other, with a corridor for each tier. In addition to the old granite building, two smaller prisons of yellow brick were erected in 1885, to relieve the crowded condition of the Tombs. Criminals awaiting trial in the Special Sessions or Tombs Police courts are detained here, as well as those accused or convicted of more serious crimes. Executions formerly took place in the central courtyard, but since the introduction of electrocution, all executions occur at the State prisons at Sing Sing and Auburn. The Tombs prison is in charge of the Department of Public Charities and Correction. The yearly number of committals is about 25,000.

The Jefferson-Market Prison is a minor city prison, virtually a branch of the Tombs, and an adjunct of the Jefferson-Market Police-Court. There is such a prison attached to each of the police-courts, for the temporary detention of persons accused of or convicted of crime. The Jefferson-Market Police-Court and prison, and the market from which they take their name, occupy different portions of a unique and handsome brick structure of irregular shape and considerable architectural beauty, at Sixth Avenue, Greenwich Avenue and West 10th Street. It was built in 1868. One of its features is a tall tower, on the northeast corner, in which is a clock with an illuminated dial.

The Ludlow-Street Jail is a large brick building in the rear of the Essex Market, extending from Ludlow Street to Essex Street. It was built in 1868, and is used for the safe-keeping of persons arrested under writs issued to the Sheriff of the

County of New York, who has charge of the jail. Those who have violated the United-States laws are also confined there, the Government paying a stipulated daily sum for each prisoner. Sheriff's prisoners who are willing and able to pay for the privilege are allowed superior accommodations, and the system has led to many abuses, which the Legislature has often attempted to correct. Persons arrested for debt were formerly confined here, but the practice is now done away with, as contrary to the Federal laws. A debtors' prison was built in 1735, on the City Commons, near the present City

LUDLOW-STREET JAIL, LUDLOW AND ESSEX STREETS.

Hall. During the Revolution it was used as a prison by the British, and in 1840 it was converted into the present Hall of Records, which is thus the oldest public building in the city, and the only Revolutionary prison remaining in the country. It is a low brownstone building, in the Doric style ; and stands near the entrance to the East-River Bridge.

THE TOMBS. THE PLACE OF DETENTION FOR CRIMINALS AWAITING TRIAL.
FRANKLIN, CENTRE, LEONARD AND ELM STREETS.

Blackwell's Island, purchased by the city in 1828, for $50,000, is a long, narrow island in the East River, extending northward 1½ miles, from opposite East 50th Street to East 84th Street, and containing about 120 acres. It is the principal one of the group of islands upon which are most of the public reformatory and correctional and many of the charitable institutions for which New York is famous. Upon it stand the Charity Hospital, the Penitentiary, Alms-House, Hospital for Incurables, Work-House, Asylum for the Insane, and other institutions. Most of the buildings are of granite, of imposing size, and built after the turretted and battlemented designs of feudal times. They have all been erected by convict labor, as was also the sea-wall surrounding the island. The name of the island commemorates Robert Blackwell. He married the daughter of Captain John Manning, who in 1673 surrendered New York to the Dutch. After his disgrace, Manning retired to his farm on Blackwell's Island, then known as Hog Island; and after his death it became the property of his daughter. It remained in the Blackwell family for many years. The old Blackwell homestead, a low rambling wooden house, built nearly 125 years

THE PENITENTIARY, BLACKWELL'S ISLAND.

ago, still stands, and is used as the residence of the warden of the Alms-House. The warden of the Penitentiary occupies a picturesque stone cottage, standing on an elevated plateau, just north of the Penitentiary. The island contains much fertile land, and gardening and farming are carried ôn by the convicts. The population is about 7,000 persons, all in care of the Commissioners of Public Charities and Correction, from whom permits to visit the island must be obtained. The island-ferry leaves the foot of East 26th Street twice daily.

The Penitentiary on Blackwell's Island is a stone building, 600 feet long, with a long projecting wing on the north. The main building was erected in 1832, and the northern wing in 1858. The material used in its construction was the grey stone from the island quarries. It is four stories in height, castellated in design, and contains 800 cells, arranged back to back, in tiers, in the center of the building. A broad area runs entirely around each block of cells; and each tier is reached by a corridor. Persons convicted of misdemeanors are confined here, and the number of prisoners averages nearly 1,000 a day. Over 3,000 offenders are received yearly, of whom 400 are women. Each of the cells bears a card, giving the inmate's name, age, crime, date of conviction, term of sentence, and religion. All inmates are compelled to follow some trade or occupation. Stone-cutting in the quarries on the island, and mason-work on the buildings which the city is constantly erecting, furnish employment to a large number ; others are employed in the rough work of the

SCENES ON BLACKWELL'S ISLAND.

THE ALMS-HOUSE CHAPEL, OLD BLACKWELL RESIDENCE, AND OTHER BUILDINGS.

32

Department of Public Charities and Correction ; and still others work at the various trades which they followed before their incarceration. Most of the women prisoners are employed in sewing, or as cleaners in the female department. Each cell contains two canvas bunks, and all are kept freshly whitewashed and scrupulously clean. Solitary confinement is not practised, except as a punishment for insubordination ; and in spite of the fact that the inmates of the Penitentiary are to be seen at work all day in various parts of the island, and with a seemingly insufficient guard, escapes are almost unknown, only one prisoner having got away in ten years. This immunity from escapes is due to the exceptionally strong natural safeguards afforded by the insular position of the institution, and the tremendously swift flow of the tide in the river, which makes it possible to guard nearly 1,000 criminals with fewer than 20 guards and about 35 keepers. To this same fact, as well as to the open-air life of the prisoners, is due the exceptionally healthy condition of the inmates.

As early as 1796 the Legislature provided for two State prisons, one at Albany, and one in New-York City. The first Newgate Prison, in Greenwich Village, was

WORK-HOUSE, BLACKWELL'S ISLAND.

opened in 1797, but it soon became crowded, and in 1816 the Penitentiary was built, on the East-River shore at Bellevue. In 1848 the Bellevue grounds were divided, and the convicts were removed to Blackwell's Island.

The Work-House, on Blackwell's Island, was built in 1852, to take the place of an older building which had been erected early in the century in the Bellevue grounds, on East 23d Street, where portions of the massive stone walls are still to be seen. The Bellevue grounds once extended from East 23d Street to East 27th Street, and from the river to Third Avenue, but in 1848 they were divided, and the larger portion sold for business purposes and dwellings. The Work-House is of granite, three stories in height, and comprises a long wing running north and south, and two cross wings, running east and west. The main building is about 600 feet long, and contains 221 cells, arranged in tiers against the side walls, and separated by a broad hallway. The cells are large, airy and well-lighted, and the entire building is kept immaculately neat. The offices are in the west wing ; and the kitchen in the east wing. The Work-House is intended to be an institution for the punishment of the large class of petty criminals, always abounding in large cities. Most of the

BLACKWELL'S ISLAND INSTITUTIONS.

THE CHARITY HOSPITAL, PENITENTIARY WORKSHOPS, AND CHURCHES.

22,000 inmates yearly committed to the institution belong to the class known as "drunks." Many of them are old offenders, who have become almost permanent residents. Some of the inmates are daily drafted to perform household and other duties in the other public institutions controlled by the Commissioners of Public Charities and Correction. Those who remain at the Work-House are kept busily engaged in some useful occupation — much of the clothing, bedding, etc., used in the other institutions being made here. The average daily number of inmates is about 1,900, and about the same number are furnished to other institutions. The terms of commitment range from five days to one year, the majority of committals being for short periods, for drunkenness or disorderly conduct. Chief among the reformatory methods adopted at the institution are the Protestant and Roman Catholic religious services. The large percentage of short-term sentences makes the Work-House a house of detention, rather than a house of correction, or reformation. Destitute persons not criminals are committed to this cheerless abode upon their own application to the Commissioners.

The Branch Work-House, at Hart's Island, occupies a number of buildings formerly belonging to the Hart's-Island Hospital, which was given up in 1887. It is intended to relieve the overcrowding of the main Work-House, and it receives yearly about 2,500 prisoners.

The Alms-House, on Blackwell's Island, was built, in 1846, by convict labor, from the granite of the island quarries. The original buildings were two in number — one on the south for women, and one on the north for men. They are similar in design and treatment, and, with the later additions, they afford accommodations for 2,000 of the city's paupers. The grounds of the Alms-House occupy the central portion of the island, and contain about a dozen buildings, including the five now occupied by the Alms-House proper, the two older stone buildings, and three brick structures erected in 1889–91; the Alms-House hospital for women, a number of wooden buildings, opened in 1881; the hospital for incurables, opened in 1866; the pretty little Episcopal Chapel of the Good Shepherd, erected in 1888 by George Bliss as a memorial; the old Blackwell mansion; the Alms-House Hospital, for men; and other buildings used for various purposes connected with the management of the institution. There is a large reading-room in the basement of the chapel; and much active religious work is done among the inmates by the Episcopal City Mission Society, the Roman Catholics, and numerous charitable guilds. Over 3,000 paupers are annually received and cared for, and in their pleasant island-home they are more comfortably situated than are thousands of the dwellers in the crowded tenement-houses of the city. The first alms-house was built in 1734, on the Commons, now City-Hall Park, alongside the Bridewell. It was of stone, two stories high, and served also as a house of correction and a calaboose for unruly slaves. A new building, on the same site, was opened in 1795, just after the breaking out of an epidemic of yellow fever in the city, and for some time it was used as a hospital for the victims of the fever. In 1816 a large building was opened on the Bellevue grounds, which was occupied by the hospital and the almshouse until 1828, when they were separated, and in 1846 the paupers were removed to Blackwell's Island.

Randall's Island, near the union of the East River and Harlem River, comprises about 100 acres. Located upon it are the House of Refuge, the Idiot Asylum, Nursery, Children's and Infant's Hospitals, schools, and other charities provided for destitute children. Passes to visit the city institutions may be obtained from the Commissioners of Public Charities and Correction, but are not needed at the House of Refuge, which is open daily until 4 P. M.

The House of Refuge, on Randall's Island, was erected in 1854, and is a reform school for juvenile delinquents of both sexes. It is in charge of the Society for the Reformation of Juvenile Delinquents, the oldest organization of its class in the country. It was founded in 1817, as the "Society for the Prevention of Pauperism;" and one of its first important works was the investigation of the prison systems of England and the United States. In 1823 it was merged into the Society for the Reformation of Juvenile Delinquents. The first House of Refuge was opened in 1825, in the old barracks on Madison Square. In 1839 the Refuge was removed to the Bellevue grounds, at East 23d Street and East River, where it remained until the Randall's Island location was occupied, in 1854. The grounds of the institution are on the southern end of the island, and comprise a tract of 37½ acres, upon which numerous buildings have been erected from time to time, to meet the needs of the work. They are of brick, in the Italian style of architecture. The two

FEMALE ALMS-HOUSE, BLACKWELL'S ISLAND.

main buildings are nearly 1,000 feet in length, and will accommodate 1,000 inmates. Children brought before police magistrates for misdemeanors are committed to the institution. The yearly number of committals approaches 400. The boys and girls are kept apart. They are taught useful trades, and are instructed in the common English branches. The secretary is Evert J. Wendell.

The Prison Association of New York, at 135 East 15th Street, was founded in 1846 to improve the penal system, to better the condition of prisoners, and to aid reformed convicts after their discharge. Daily visits are made to the Tombs and the police-courts, and all needful aid is given to those prisoners who are deemed worthy. The association has been instrumental in introducing many reforms in prison management. In 1888 it founded the United-States Press Bureau, to give employment to deserving ex-convicts in the collection and sale of newspaper clippings.

The New-York Juvenile Asylum, at 176th Street and Amsterdam Avenue, was incorporated in 1851 as a reformatory home for truant and disobedient children, committed by magistrates or surrendered by parents or friends. The asylum is a large stone building, with accommodations for 1,000 inmates, who receive moral, mental, and industrial training, and are provided with homes when they reach a suitable age.   Truant and disobedient children between the ages of 7 and 14 years, belonging in the city, are received; and the institution draws $110 from the city treasury for each child supported during the year.   This amount is supplemented by a grant from the public school funds and by private gifts.   The thoroughness of the work is shown by the fact that of the many children who have been placed in western homes, not more than five per cent. have proved to be incorrigible or guilty of serious misconduct.   There is also a House of Reception at 106 West 27th Street, where the children are kept for a few weeks before being sent to the asylum.

The Wetmore Home for Fallen and Friendless Girls, at 49 Washington Square, was founded in 1865, with the late Apollos R. Wetmore as president, to protect young girls against temptation, and to rescue them when they have been led astray.   Mr. Wetmore took a warm interest in the work, and upon his death, in 1881, the present building was purchased, and named the Wetmore Home, in his

NEW-YORK JUVENILE ASYLUM, AMSTERDAM AVENUE AND 176TH STREET.

memory.   Since the opening of the institution over 3,000 young women and girls have been admitted to its shelter.   Instruction is given in housework and sewing, and the inmates are aided in procuring employment.

The American Society for the Prevention of Cruelty to Animals, at 10 East 22d Street, is one of the most widely known of the many civilizing influences of the city.   It was founded in 1866, by the late Henry Bergh, who remained its President until his death in 1888.   The first laws for the prevention of cruelty to animals were enacted in 1866, and have been amended by successive legislatures until they are the best of their kind in existence.   Nearly every State and Territory has adopted similar laws, with societies to enforce them, and which are in communication with the parent institution.   The headquarters are open perpetually. Thousands of complaints are received yearly of cruelty to animals, all of which are thoroughly investigated, and the evils remedied.   No animal is too insignificant for attention.   The society has ambulances for the removal of disabled animals; a patrol service for rendering first aid to injured and sick animals; and a force of uniformed officers, who have authority to arrest and prosecute offenders found violating any of the humane statutes of the State. By numerous publications and the work of sixty affiliated societies, it has developed a strong public sentiment; and the good work it has accomplished to mitigate and prevent suffering to animals is incalculable. Its monthly official journal is called *Our Animal Friends.* The Society has prosecuted 17,000 cruelists; suspended over 50,000 animals from labor by reason of disabilities; humanely destroyed 34,000 horses and other animals, injured or diseased past recovery; and removed 6,000 disabled horses in ambulances. The President, John P. Haines, has been connected with the organization for many years, and under his guidance the humane work has been greatly extended.

The New-York Society for the Suppression of Vice, at 41 Park Row, was incorporated by the Legislature of the State of New York in 1873, through the efforts of Anthony Comstock, its secretary, aided by a few public-spirited citizens. Its object is the enforcement of all laws for the suppression of obscene literature, pictures, and articles for indecent and immoral use, including gambling in its various forms, lotteries, and pool-selling. It seeks the defence of public morals by preventing the dissemination and seed-sowing of criminal influences. Through the efforts of this society five acts were passed in 1873 by Congress prohibiting the importation into this country, or the dissemination by mail, or in provinces under the exclusive jurisdiction of the United States, of obscene books, pictures or articles. Through its efforts stringent laws were enacted the same year in New-York State, and since then in various other States. Branch organizations have been established in New England and the Southern and Western States. Nearly 2,000 arrests have been made, and 45 tons of obscene matter and 17 tons of gambling material and paraphernalia have been seized and destroyed. Upon persons convicted, 324

SOCIETY FOR THE PREVENTION OF CRUELTY TO ANIMALS, FOURTH AVENUE AND EAST 22D STREET. *

years' imprisonment and more than $120,000 of fines have been imposed. The annual expenses are about $10,000, which are met by voluntary contributions. Through the efforts of this society stringent laws were enacted by Congress in 1889 prohibiting "green-goods" swindlers and other fraudulent devices from using the mails.

The Society for the Prevention of Crime, with spacious and commodious offices at 923 Broadway, was organized in 1877 and incorporated in 1878. Its special and peculiar mission is the attempt to remove the sources and causes of crime, by the enforcement of existing laws and the enactment of new ones, and by arousing public opinion, more particularly regarding the excise laws, gambling, and public nuisances in general. Under the direction of its former President, the late Rev. Dr. Howard Crosby, the society accomplished a vast amount of work, and incurred a corresponding degree of hostility from those upon whom the laws have no other restraining

* Taken down in 1892, to make room for new Episcopal Church Missions House.

power than that due to the fear of detection and punishment.   The society employs a number of agents to detect violations of the law.   The present President, the Rev. Dr. Charles H. Parkhurst, is well known as the author of the crusade against the brothels and gambling-houses of the city, as a result of which the Grand Jury in 1892 found a sweeping indictment against the Police Department.

The Home of Industry and Refuge for Discharged Convicts was founded in 1879, and incorporated in 1882.   Its object as stated in the articles of incorporation is "To do good to the souls and bodies of men," but its labors are confined to the criminal class.   A small house at 305 Water Street was secured for the initial stages of the work, and after several removals they located in 1891 in a large and commodious building of their own at 224 West 63d Street.   Since its start, 3,000 ex-convicts have been received into the "Home," 1,400 of whom have obtained employment. The yearly expenses are $8,000, of which fully one-fourth is earned by the inmates, chiefly at broom-making.   The yearly average of inmates is 40.   Gifts are greatly needed to pay indebtedness existing.

HOME OF INDUSTRY AND REFUGE FOR DISCHARGED CONVICTS,
224 WEST 63D STREET.

The National Christian League for the Promotion of Social Purity, at 33 East 22d Street, was organized in 1886, and secured by special act of Congress in 1889 a National charter.   Its aims are to elevate public opinion regarding the nature and claims of social purity, with its equal obligation upon men and women ; to enlist and organize the efforts of Christians in protective, reformatory, educational and legislative work ; and to supply employment and furnish advice and various forms of aid to girls and women in need.   The League holds two meetings a month.   At these meetings papers are read, taking up any department of the subject, after which discussion follows.   The work is done specially through ten committees.

The Society for the Purification of the Italian Quarters may be classed as among the reformatory organizations of the city, since its work is the important one of driving disorderly houses and disreputable people from the Italian quarters of the city.   It was organized in 1890, and, in addition to the work outlined above, it endeavors to do away with the crowded condition of the Italian tenement-houses.

The Lunacy Law Reform and Anti-Kidnapping League, at 10 East 14th Street, was founded in 1890 to protect sane persons against unjust and unlawful imprisonment in insane asylums and hospitals, and to secure humane treatment and the protection of their legal and constitutional rights to those suffering from insanity. Legal and medical advice is freely given to all deserving applicants.

Final Resting Places.

Cemeteries, Burial-Places, Crematories, Church-Yards and Vaults, Tombs, Etc.

IN AND about New York are some of the most beautiful and most interesting resting-places of the dead in the world. With all the demands of high-pressure civilization the needs of the dying and the dead have been most sacredly cared for. Great and small, there are nearly fifty cemeteries in the city, or in the immediate vicinity, that are used for the interment of the dead. A reasonable estimate gives the population of these burial-places at nearly, if not quite, 3,000,000, and that number is added to at the rate of 40,000 a year. By a law of 1830 interments were prohibited within the city limits below Canal Street, except by special permit, and the tendency in recent years has been strong toward closing altogether the city cemeteries, and using only those that are in the suburbs, or far removed from the thickly settled wards. Forgotten God's Acres still exist in various parts of the city, mostly down-town, where they are crowded by tenement-houses and towering warehouses and manufactories. The history of New York in this respect shows a constant record of the pushing the dead out of place by the living. Some of these old places still remain in part, but a far greater number have disappeared altogether. Only the established and powerful corporations of Trinity and a few other churches have been able to resist the demands of modern life and business for the ground once sacred to the dead. Hundreds of acres, now covered by huge buildings or converted into public thoroughfares, were at some time burial-places; over ninety of which have thus existed, and passed away. Of most of them even the location has been forgotten by this generation.

There was a burial-ground around the old Middle Dutch Meeting-House, on the site of the Mutual Life-Insurance Company, in Nassau Street, between Cedar and Liberty Streets; another in John Street, adjoining the John-Street Methodist Church; others in Maiden Lane, in Frankfort Street, and near Burling Slip. On the site of the Stewart Building, corner of Broadway and Chambers Street, and where is now the City-Hall Park, was a negro burying-ground; in 1770 hundreds of negroes who died in the small-pox epidemic were buried there. The old Potter's Field was on the site of the present Washington Square, then far out in the country. Where now are asphalt walks, flowers, fountains, the Washington Arch, and aristocratic homes, the poor were once buried by the thousands in nameless graves. Afterward the Potter's Field was where Madison Square is.

The old Jewish Cemetery on the New Bowery, at Chatham Square, dates back more than a century and a half. A wealthy Portuguese Jew, Louis Gomez, gave a large tract of land for that purpose in 1729. The cemetery was in high esteem for a century, but then it began to be shorn of its proportions for new buildings and streets.   Now only a small strip of land remains, containing a hundred tombs, with illegible inscriptions and many unknown dead.

When this cemetery became unfashionable many of the bodies were removed to a larger and handsomer place far out of the city, in the green fields, where it was thought that they would remain forever undisturbed.   To-day what is left of that once beautiful place of the dead is a few feet of land in 21st Street, just west of Sixth Avenue, hemmed in by a huge dry-goods store and other buildings, and shut in from public gaze by a high brick wall on the street side.   A few tomb-stones remain, and that is all.

On 11th Street, just to the east of Sixth Avenue, in a little triangular plot, shut in by the walls of adjoining buildings, is all that is left of what was once a large

MARBLE CEMETERY, A HIDDEN GOD'S ACRE, BETWEEN THE BOWERY, SECOND AVENUE, 2D AND 3D STREETS.

cemetery.   The place is overrun with a wild growth of shrubs and vines, and one little pyramidal monument is all that tells the story of what has been.   In 85th Street, near Fourth Avenue; in Ninth Avenue, where old Chelsea village once was; in Mott Street, about St. Patrick's Roman Catholic Church ; and in several localities in Harlem, there are cemeteries that have fallen into neglect and that must soon pass out of existence.

Trinity Churchyard, surrounding Trinity Church, on Broadway, opposite Wall Street, is to the antiquary and the student of local history a most interesting burial-place.   Some of the gravestones date back nearly 300 years, and they constitute in their names an index-book to the leading families of the metropolis for nearly two centuries.   The churchyard is a quiet and attractive spot, immediately at the head of the financial district of the American continent, with the whirl of the money market and the uproar of traffic about it night and day.   On one side is Broadway, thronged from morning to night with hurrying crowds of men and teams, and on the other side the cars of the Elevated Railroad rattle noisily by. But within there are the greensward and the stately old trees, reminders of the time when all this country hereabouts was fair orchard or pasture land. The sparrows twitter cheerfully about in the trees or on the ground, and New York's illustrious dead rest there, undisturbed by the traffic or the birds, sleeping their last sleep. The dead are placed in vaults underground, and flat slabs set into the green grass or into the slabs of the

paved walks indicate the locations. You literally walk above the dead wherever you go, and under your feet are names of once prominent families that have long since been forgotten, as well as of those that are still bright in civic annals. Here are the Laights, the Bronsons, the Ogdens, the Lispenards, the Bleeckers, the Livingstons, the Apthorpes, the Hoffmans, and so on.

At the left, as you enter the churchyard, is the last resting-place of the naval hero Captain Lawrence, of the *Chesapeake*. On a rectangular base of red sandstone is a sarcophagus of like material, upon one end of which is carved the side of a war-vessel with protruding guns, and on the opposite end a wreath and anchor. The base bears this inscription : "The Heroick Commander of the *Chesapeake*, whose remains are deposited here, expressed with his expiring breath his devotion to his country." Neither the fury of battle, the anguish of a mortal wound, nor the horrors of approaching death could subdue his gallant spirit. His dying words were 'Don't Give Up the Ship.'" An iron fence encloses the Captain-Lawrence tomb, within which is also interred his wife.

In the south part of the yard is the tomb of Alexander Hamilton, a rectangular sarcophagus of white stone, with urns at the four corners, and a stunted pyramid surmounting it. On

MARTYRS' MONUMENT, TRINITY CHURCHYARD.

the base there is an inscription, now nearly obliterated by the ravages of the weather, reciting the history and the virtues of the great statesman and financier. At the foot of this monument, beneath a slab, simply inscribed, are the remains of Hamilton's devoted wife. By a curious coincidence, near the Hamilton monument is a slab marking the final resting-place of Matthew L. Davis, who was Aaron Burr's intimate friend and biographer, and Burr's companion on that fateful morning when Burr and Hamilton met in the duel at Weehawken, whence Hamilton was brought away dying.

Near the southwest corner of the church is the tomb of Albert Gallatin, a red sandstone sarcophagus, with a slanting ribbed top and a frieze of leaves cut in bas-relief. Gallatin and his wife are interred there. Just east of the Gallatin tomb is the Livingston vault, in which are the remains of Robert Fulton, the inventor of the steamboat. In the immediate vicinity, beneath a slab in the pavement marked Anthony Lispenard Bleecker, are five generations of the old Bleecker family. Near the Rector-Street railing are the remains of Bishop Benjamin Moore, second Bishop of New York, and President of Columbia College. On the west slope, in the south part of the yard, in a vault built in 1738, is buried the third Earl of Stirling, the Scottish nobleman who gave up a coronet to fight for freedom in the New World, and who was Washington's trusted and valued friend. Over in the middle of the north side, an old slab, broken and moss-covered, shows where is buried Benjamin Faneuil, father of Peter Faneuil, of Boston fame. One of the quaintest headstones in the churchyard is that at the grave of William Bradford, the friend and companion of William Penn, the first printer in the United States outside of Boston, the first newspaper publisher and paper-maker, and the father of book-binding and copperplate engraving in this country. The inscription on his tomb-stone reads : "Here lies the body of William Bradford, Printer, who departed this life May 23, 1752, aged 92 years. He was born in Leicester, in Old England, in 1660, and came over to America in 1682 before the city of Philadelphia was laid out. He was Printer to this Government for upwards of fifty years ; and being quite worn out with old age and labors, he left this mortal State in the lively Hopes of a blessed Immortality.

> " Reader reflect how soon you'll
> quit this Stage.
> You'll find but few attain to
> such an age.
> Life's full of Pain : Lo Here's a
> Place of Rest !
> Prepare to meet your God : then
> you are blest."

Another interesting stone stands at the grave of Sydney Breese, a wealthy New-York merchant and a witty society man, whose name still lives in the fame of one of his descendants, Professor S. F. Breese Morse, inventor of the telegraph. The stone bears the curious inscription :

> " Sydney Breese, June 19, 1767. Made by himself.
> Ha, Sydney, Sydney !
> Lyest thou Here ?
> I Here Lye
> 'Till Time is flown
> To Its Eternity."

The most conspicuous monument in the churchyard is that erected thirty years ago by the Trinity-Church corporation in memory of the soldiers of the American Revolution who died in the prison-pens during the occupation of the city by the British. The monument faces Pine Street, and was built at a time when there was talk of extending Pine Street through the churchyard, from Broadway to Church Street and the desecration was thus forever prevented. The ashes of the patriot soldiers repose in undistinguishable graves about this monument. The memorial is a square structure of red sandstone in Gothic style, to harmonize with the neighboring church building. Above the base there is a high arched canopy with open sides, the four corners of which terminate in ornamental finials, and a tall spire stands up from the centre. On each of the four gables of the roof is a group of thirteen stars. This is the inscription on the east or Broadway face of the base : "Sacred to the memory of those good and brave men who died whilst imprisoned in this city for their devotion to the cause of American Independence."

Among other interesting things in Trinity churchyard are the Bronson head-stone, curiously carved with winged cherubs, a border of leaves and a group consisting of an hour-glass, crossed thigh-bones, a corpse and a skeleton, emblems of mortality ; the slab that covers the remains of Charlotte Temple, whose name, by a peculiar coincidence, was erroneously associated with a fictitious sad story in one of the romances of New York's early life ; the Watts family vault, that, marked by a single slab, contains the ashes of the gallant General Phil. Kearny ; the tomb of Francis Lewis, one of the signers of the Declaration of Independence ; of General John Lamb, a famous Liberty Boy ; of Lieut.-Governor and Chief-Justice James De Lancey ; and of the De Peysters, Crommelins and other Huguenot families.

St. Paul's Churchyard, in Broadway, between Vesey and Fulton Streets, and extending back to the Trinity Building in Church Street, is hardly less interesting than Trinity, to which it is, in fact, an adjunct. It is not as old, but it contains many honored and distinguished dead. On the Broadway side are three notable monuments, all of them curiously enough to men of Irish birth. In the Broadway wall of the chapel is a memorial tablet to General Richard Montgomery, who fell at Quebec. There is a pedestal with an urn upon it, and trees and palms and military insignia surrounding. On the tablet is the inscription. The memorial was erected by Congress in 1776 ; and the remains of the gallant Irish-American were brought from Quebec at the expense of the city of New York, and with pomp and ceremony placed in a vault directly beneath the tablet. To the south of the church is the monument to Thomas Addis Emmett the Irish patriot of '98, who died November 14, 1827. It is a granite obelisk, upon the east face of which, near the top in bas-relief, is a bust of Emmett, and below a group showing an urn, clasped hands and an eagle. The north face has an inscription in English, giving the facts of Emmett's life, and on the opposite face is the same inscription cut in Celtic characters.

THOMAS A. EMMETT MONUMENT, ST. PAUL'S CHURCHYARD.

Upon the west face on a sunken tablet is the inscription "40° 10′ 12″ N. 71° 05′ 21.5″ W. L. G." To the north of the church is the monument to Dr. William J. MacNevin, who, an Irish refugee of '98, came to New York and attained eminence as a physician, chemist and medical instructor. The monument that com-memorates him is a square pedestal, surmounted by a pyramidal shaft. Both base and shaft are decorated with elaborate floral designs. The pedestal has inscrip-tions in Latin, in English and in Celtic. On the east face of the shaft is a bas-relief bust of Dr. MacNeven, an eagle and an urn, and a draped harp with clasped hands

MEMORIAL TABLET TO MAJOR-GENERAL RICHARD MONTGOMERY, ST. PAUL'S CHAPEL.

beneath it. The monument to George Frederick Cooke, the actor, is near the centre of the grounds to the west of the church. It is a low, square marble pedestal, on a double base, and sur-mounted by an urn, with the repre-sentation of flames flashing upward from its mouth. The pedestal bears this motto

" Three kingdoms proclaim his birth :
Both hemispheres pronounce his worth."

Inscriptions on the four sides of the pedestal record that the monument was erected by Edmund Kean, and successively repaired by Charles Kean, Edward A. Sothern and Edwin Booth.

Not far from the Cooke monument is the Bechet tomb, a large square structure of stone, overrun with climb-ing vines. There reposes Colonel Etienne Marie Bechet, the Sieur de Rochefontaine, who served under Count Rochambeau in our Revolutionary War; and with him are his wife and other members of the family. Within the church is a tablet in memory of Sir John Temple, the first Consul-General of England to the United States. The tablet is in the form of a rectangular base, bearing an inscription, and surmounted by a pyramid, upon the face of which are carved an urn and the Temple coat-of-arms. Other distinguished persons have been buried in St. Paul's churchyard; members of the Somerindyke, Ogden, Rhinelander, Onderdonk, Van Ameringe, Bogert and other families; John Dixey, R. A., an Irish sculptor; Captain Baron de Rabenau, a Hessian officer; Major John Lucas, of the Georgia line; Major Job Sumner of the Massachusetts line; Lieut.-Col. Beverly Robinson; Philip Blum, who was sailing-master of Commodore McDonough's flag-ship *Saratoga* at the battle of Lake Champlain; Colonel Thomas Barclay, the first British Consul to New-York City; Anthony Van Dam; John Wells, whose bust is in the church; and many other American patriots and British officers.

The New-York City Marble Cemetery is on 2d Street, between First and Second Avenues, in a thickly settled tenement district. When it was first opened, it was a fashionable burial-place, but now it is little in favor, save by a few old families. It is about half the length and half the depth of the block. On the street side is a high iron fence. Opposite is a tall brick wall, shutting out the tenement-yards, and at both ends the abutting houses look down upon the plot. The ground is devoted entirely to vaults underground, and interments are still permitted, under restrictions. The place is well kept, but is laid out in severe style. Half a dozen parallel gravel walks run the length of it. Between the walks are narrow strips of sodded ground in which at regular intervals lie the gray slabs that cover the entrances to the vaults. President James Monroe was buried in a vault here, but his remains were subsequently removed to Richmond, Va., for permanent interment. John Ericsson, the inventor and builder of the famous war-vessel *Monitor*, whose remains were finally sent to his native land, Sweden, on board a United-States war-ship, rested for a time in the Marble Cemetery. There

NEW-YORK CITY MARBLE CEMETERY, 20 STREET, BETWEEN FIRST AND SECOND AVENUES.

are several monuments historically interesting, noticeably one to Stephen Allen, once Mayor of New-York City; and the names of Lenox, Lewis, Ogden, Varian, Webb, Oothout, Hyslop, Kip, Van Alen and other old families appear.

There is another little cemetery, hidden in the centre of the block bounded by the Bowery, Second Avenue, and 2d and 3d Streets, which belongs to the same corporation. It is sometimes called the New-York Marble Cemetery, and is distinguished from the other by the omission of the word "City" from the title. It is scarcely half an acre in extent, and it cannot be seen from either street or avenue. The entrance is through an iron gate and a heavy wooden door on Second Avenue, near 2d Street. Even this is kept closed constantly, and, so far as appear-auces go, it might be the entrance to the adjoining house.

St. Mark's Churchyard is also a record of the past. It is at the corner of Stuyvesant Street and Second Avenue, even now an aristocratic neighborhood, and formerly more so. Here was once the farm of old Peter Stuyvesant. Near by he lived, and on the site of St. Mark's he built a chapel, over two centuries ago, and when he died he was buried therein. When the chapel made way for St. Mark's the body of Stuyvesant was removed and placed in a vault beneath the walls of the new building. On the east side of the church is a massive red sandstone block, held in place by iron clamps. This marks the Stuyvesant tomb, and it bears this inscription: "In this vault lies buried Petrus Stuyvesant, late Captain-General and Governor-in-Chief of Amsterdam in New Netherlands, now called New York, and the Dutch West India Islands, died in A. D. 1671-2, aged 80 years."

In the churchyard are buried Colonel Sloughter, one of the English Colonial governors; Daniel D. Tompkins, an early governor of the State of New York; Nathaniel Prime, an old-time merchant; and Philip Hone, one of the most courtly and most distinguished of the mayors of New-York City; and there, too, are the family vaults of Nicholas Fish, P. P. Goelet, David Wolfe, Frederick Gebhard, Abraham Iselin, Peter M. Suydam, Abraham Schemerhorn, R. S. Livingston and others. It was from a vault in this yard that the body of A. T. Stewart was stolen by grave-robbers.

MEMORIAL TABLET TO
PETRUS STUYVESANT,
ST. MARK'S CHURCH,
SECOND AVENUE AND
STUYVESANT STREET.

St. Luke's Churchyard, in Hudson Street, near Christopher, is another place of the dead, with only the inscribed tablets on the surface to indicate the vaults below. There are several hundred vaults here, but no interments are now made in them.

St. John's Burying-Ground, connected with St. John's Chapel of Trinity Church, is between Hudson, Leroy and Clarkson Streets. It was established about sixty years ago; and more than 10,000 bodies are interred in it, for the most part (it would appear) people of the middle and poorer classes, although some well-known folk were laid at rest here. Christopher P. Collis, the friend of Robert Fulton, and the projector of the Croton water-system, was buried there. The ground contains the body of William E. Burton, the famous comedian, and of Naomi, the wife of Thomas Hamblin, a famous actor and manager of Burton's time. A quaint monument is that erected by Engine Company 13 to Eugene Underhill and Frederick A. Ward, who were killed while on duty in 1834. It is a sarcophagus, surmounted by a stone coffin, upon the top of which is a fireman's cap, a torch and a trumpet. Most of the monuments and stones are in a dilapidated condition. The burial-ground is a picturesque place in summer time, with its fine old shade-trees. There has been talk of the city taking it for a park, which is much needed in that tenement-house district.

TRINITY CHURCH.
BROADWAY, OPPOSITE WALL STREET.

Trinity-Church Cemetery is at Washington Heights, on Tenth Avenue, be-tween 153d and 155th Streets. It contains fifteen acres, and was opened for the burial of Trinity parishioners, sixty years ago, when intra-mural interments were forbidden. The location is sightly, on an eminence overlooking the country round about, and the Hudson River to the west, the grounds extending to the river. A handsome granite wall with frequent columns, supporting an ornamental iron fence, surrounds the property. Spacious gateways give ingress to it, and on the corner of Tenth Avenue and 153d Street there is a pretty Queen-Anne lodge with the offices. The grounds are divided into two parts by the Boulevard, a broad public thorough-fare, the grade of which is below the level of the cemetery hill. An iron suspension-

STATUE OF JUDGE JOHN WATTS, TRINITY CHURCHYARD.

bridge, with Gothic sand-stone archways at either end, spans the avenue and con-nects the two parts of the cemetery. The grounds are well laid out with paths and roadways, and trees and shrubs are abundant. There is little floral decoration ex-cept on private lots. Many prominent New-York fami-lies bury their dead here. The tombs or headstones bear such well-known names as Astor, Hargous, Schief-felin, Sayre, Delafield, Gal-latin, Dix, Furniss, Harsen, Wilmerding, Livingston, and De Peyster. There are few mausoleums, those of Stephen Storm and Garritt Storm, large Gothic redstone structures near the south-east entrance, being the most conspicuous. Most of the tombs and vaults are in the western section. There the hillside slopes steeply to-ward the Hudson River, and offers peculiar advantages.

The tombs are built underground, on the side hill, and have ornamental granite or sandstone façades. There are several hundred homes of the dead of this description. The Astor lot is a smooth stretch of unbroken greensward, entirely concealing from view the vault underneath. In the centre of the plot is a plain marble shaft, with the inscription, "Astor Vault." In this vault are the remains of the original John Jacob Astor, and his wife. Elsewhere rest Audubon, the world-renowned ornitholo-gist ; Fernando Wood, longtime Mayor of New York ; Robert B. Minturn, the eminent merchant ; Madame Jumel, the friend of Washington ; Gen. John A. Dix ; and other famous persons. The Albert-Gallatin tomb is the largest in America, having eighty marble catacombs. Trinity-Church Cemetery contains 10,000 bodies.

Woodlawn Cemetery is the most important modern place of burial within the city limits. It is in the Twenty-Fourth Ward, about twelve miles from the City Hall; and is reached easily by trains over the New-York & Harlem Railroad from the Grand Central Depot. The railway tracks border the cemetery on one side, and the station is a few steps from the main entrance. Trains run every half-hour during the day, and there are also special funeral trains. The cemetery has an area of 396 acres. Within a few years it has become the fashionable burial-place of New-York millionaire families. The grounds are on an eminence, with gently sloping sides, and an uneven surface, that is capable of many fine landscape and other effects. Woodlawn ranks among the most notable of American cemeteries in the beauty of its adornments, as well as in the richness of its monumental work. Its present predominating feature is the group of mausoleums, erected by wealthy New-Yorkers of this generation, including some quite notable structures. Woodlawn is destined to be

SUSPENSION BRIDGE, TRINITY-CHURCH CEMETERY, ELEVENTH AVENUE AND 155TH STREET.

preëminent in this particular. It surpasses every other place of burial in the country in the number, the beauty and the value of these imposing houses of the dead. The mausoleums cost from $10,000 upwards.

Jay Gould was one of the first to build a mausoleum at Woodlawn. It was put up about ten years ago. It stands alone on a high hill; a cold gray granite structure, like a Greek temple. It was built and designed by H. Q. French of New York. There are heavy bronze doors of artistic workmanship, and at the end of the building opposite to the door is a handsome stained-glass window. Mr. Gould's wife is interred here. Not far from the Gould mausoleum is that of Henry Clews, the banker; a simple Greek temple of rough gray granite, with bronze door and stained-glass windows. It stands near a little lake upon whose shores are the mausoleums of Maurice B. Flynn, the Matthiesons, George L. Lorillard, H. H. Cook, G. A. Osgood, Peter C. Baker, Peter F. Meyer, and others, and the lots of Cornelius Vanderbilt, Joseph H. Choate, the eminent lawyer, Washington E. Conner, and others. Truly, this is a neighborhood of plutocrats. On the Vanderbilt lot is only a marble tree-stump with straggling vines carved upon it. The Lorillard mausoleum is a large and ornate structure of rough white marble, with door-frames of finished Siena marble, and cornices and columns of finished white marble. Even more elaborate is the Matthieson mausoleum, imposing in size, and built of colored marble and granite, with much decoration in buttresses, carved work and moulding finials, and crosses on the gables of the roof, and many stained-glass windows. On the Austin Corbin lot is a plain block of granite. Sidney Dillon's lot is marked by an elaborately carved Runic cross.   The monument in the Sloane lot is a showy creation of highly polished rich red marble, consisting of a rectang_ ular pedestal upon which is a column with a square base, and a conical shaft sur_ mounted with an elaborate finial.   On the sides of the base are the names of the Sloane brothers, William Sloane, John Sloane, Henry T. Sloane and Thomas C. Sloane.

Probably the most costly, as it is the most elaborate Woodlawn monument, is that belonging to Henry M. Flagler, the Standard-Oil millionaire.   It is a massive granite cylinder, surmounted by a dome, upon the apex of which is a cross, standing

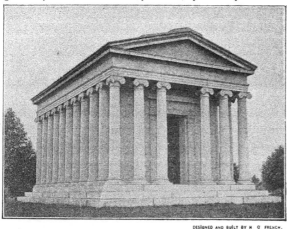

DESIGNED AND BUILT BY H G FRENCH.
JAY GOULD'S MAUSOLEUM, AT WOODLAWN CEMETERY.

upon a circular granite platform. It is covered in nearly every part with the most delicate carvings and traceries.   On opposite sides of the shaft are four sunken panels, framed with light columns, and arched over with semi-circular porticoes of carved granite. Scripture texts are carved on these panels, and the name Flagler is in raised letters upon the base of the shaft.   The monument stands on an eminence that makes it the most conspicuous object in this part of the cemetery.   The mausoleum that holds the remains of the millionaire Daniel B. Fayerweather is also notable.   It is near the Flagler monument, and almost equally conspicuous.   The material used in its construction is a dull red granite, with polished columns upholding the portico, on the pediment of which is a bronze wreath and crossed palms.   The bronze door has a beautiful figure of an angel with opened wings.   The main part of the building is oval in shape, with tessellated floor, vaulted roof and four stained-glass windows.   Other mausoleums are the Butterfield and Falconer, a heavy Egyptian structure of granite ; the Cossitt, the J. M. Randell, the Ladew and the Tilt.   There are nearly a hundred of these costly structures in Woodlawn.   Illustrious dead are not lacking in this cemetery.   Admiral Farragut is here, sleeping at the foot of a simple monument.   Just a broken mast of marble it is, standing on a square pedestal and draped at the top.   Around the base of the mast are flags, swords and other insignia of naval warfare, and the arms of the United States.   The only inscriptions are :

" Erected by his wife and son.
David Glasgow Farragut.
First Admiral in the United-States Navy.
Born July 5, 1801.
Died Aug. 14, 1870."

WOODLAWN CEMETERY.
WOODLAWN STATION, NEW-YORK AND HARLEM RAILROAD.

And another to Virginia D. Farragut, his wife. Within a stone's throw of the Farragut monument is the grave of another naval hero, De Long, of the ill-fated Arctic expedition. With him repose his four brave companions, without a monument.

Another part of the cemetery, on the brow of the hill, overlooking to the eastward the grassy slope that extends to the railroad, a quarter of a mile away, is also much in favor. Here are many tombs built into the side of the hill, with handsome marble or granite entrances, as well as mausoleums, which are the independent structures most popular at Woodlawn. Not far from the cemetery entrance on this eminence Collis P. Huntington is erecting a mausoleum that in size and cost will be one of the most notable structures of its kind in the world. With its approaches its cost exceeds $300,000. It was designed and erected by Robert Caterson, who

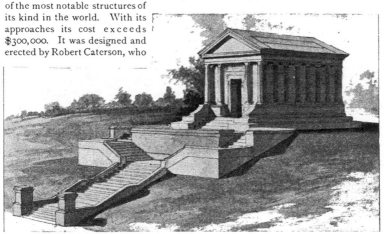

C. P. HUNTINGTON MAUSOLEUM, WOODLAWN CEMETERY.   BUILT BY ROBERT CATERSON.

has placed upwards of 500 monuments and mausoleums in Woodlawn. Near by is the mausoleum of Marshall O. Roberts, a Gothic structure of granite, with polished red marble columns ; and also the granite tomb of William E. Dodge.

The monument of Dr. Leopold Damrosch, the eminent musical conductor, is very artistic. It is a seated granite figure of Music, of heroic size, with one arm outstretched over the grave. Upon the low pedestal is the word " Damrosch," and a bronze scroll has the inscription " Erected by the Oratorio, Arion and Symphony Societies of New York, A. D. 1888." The inscription upon the headstone is " Leopold Damrosch. Born Oct. 22, 1832. Died Feb. 15, 1885." Another artistic monument is that of Auguste Pottier, a granite pedestal with a bronze bas-relief portrait-bust in a medallion, and an exquisite draped figure of Grief, with bowed head and drooping hands, seated upon it.

Rev. Dr. Howard Crosby is buried here. Over his grave is a plain granite shaft, in summer-time covered with a thick mass of ivy and woodbine. On the shaft is the inscription " Howard Crosby. Born Feb. 27, 1826. Died Mar. 29, 1891." On the headstone is the same inscription, with the text, " Well done, good and faithful servant. Enter thou into the joy of thy Lord." A massive granite sarcophagus, with a palette and brushes, encircled by a laurel wreath, marks the grave of Frank Leslie. Other monuments are those of Edward C. Moore, a large, dark-colored boulder covered with vines, and marked "Family of E. C. M.;" of Spencer C. Stokes, the famous circus-rider, over whose grave is the marble statue of his favorite horse ; of Julius, Count Seyssee d'Aix ; of Horace F. Clark, an Aberdeen-granite tomb upon a polished granite platform ; and of the Wheeler family, a rough boulder, with a large bronze bas-relief of a boy reclining in the grass on the front. The Havemeyers, James Law, Judge Whiting, Rev. Dr. John Hall, Edward A. Hammond and ex-Secretary of the Navy William C. Whitney own lots in Woodlawn. The offices are at 20 East 23d Street, and the Comptroller is Caleb B. Knevals.

The **Green-Wood Cemetery,** in Brooklyn, is the largest and handsomest in the vicinity of New York, and is one of the famous cemeteries of the world. It comprises 474 acres, which have been beautified with well-kept avenues, neat paths, and flowers, shrubbery and other adjuncts of landscape-gardening. The cemetery was

WOODLAWN CEMETERY, WOODLAWN STATION, NEW-YORK AND HARLEM RAILROAD, 24TH WARD.

opened in 1840, and over 270,000 interments have been made in it. The place is reached from New York easily by the Hamilton Ferry, or by the Elevated Railroad at the Brooklyn terminus of the East-River Bridge. Thousands of monuments, statues and other ornamental structures have been set up in the grounds. Most prominent are the northern entrance building, with its beautiful statuary groups, representing scenes from the life of the Saviour, and the monuments to Horace Greeley, James Gordon Bennett, Louis Bonard, John Matthews, the Brown brothers, S. F. B. Morse, Harry Howard, Miss Mary M. Danser, Miss Charlotte Canda, Captain John Correja and A. S. Scribner, the Pilots', the Soldiers' and the Firemen's monuments and the bronze statue of DeWitt Clinton. Its New-York offices are in the Standard Oil Company's Building, at 26 Broadway.

Mount Hope Cemetery, at Mount Hope, on the New-York & Northern Railway, just beyond the city of Yonkers, six miles to the north of the limits of New York, and one mile east of the Hudson River, is in Westchester County, and on old maps it is designated as Odell's. St. Luke's Episcopal Church of New-York has purchased a large plot, and to it have been removed many remains originally interred in St. Luke's churchyard, in Hudson Street. The Chapel of St. Augustine, of Trinity Parish, has also purchased a plot. The New-York Typographical Union No. 6 owns a lot. Dion Boucicault, the dramatist, is buried here.

Kensico Cemetery is located on the Harlem Division of the New-York Central & Hudson-River Railroad, about fifteen miles from the city limits of New York. The natural beauty of Kensico, in the midst of an elevated and extended plateau, with picturesque and historic surroundings and many other natural advantages, makes it most desirable for the purpose for which it has been selected. The new stone depot, of Queen-Anne style, costly and perfect in all its appointments and exclusively used for cemetery purposes, forms an entrance to this most interesting and beautiful Necropolis. Visitors are at once most favorably impressed by the thoughtful consideration displayed for their comfort.

The public receiving tomb, built of stone and granite, contains 178 marble catacombs, with a most perfect system for their interior ventilation ; the floors are of mosaic, the windows of stained glass ; the inner walls are lined with pyrolith, repre-

KENSICO CEMETERY, SHOWING KENSICO-CEMETERY STATION.

senting pure white marble. In front of this tomb is a large fountain, and the grounds near by are reserved for a garden. The artistic treatment of this building and its surroundings has made it a most beautiful and attractive spot.

All drives, roads and avenues are built on stone foundations. The cemetery will be enclosed by a stone wall placed on deep culverts and laid in the best cement. In the laying out of this place of burial an equal regard has been displayed to convenience, completeness of arrangements, and beauty of effect ; the winding drives diversifying the scene and breaking the monotony of the ordinary graveground.

It is the purpose of the founders and managers of Kensico Cemetery, having secured the largest tract of land used for this purpose, to make it one of the most beautiful of American burial-places, and, therefore, recognized leading architects and landscape gardeners have been given the work of planning the buildings and laying out the grounds. Among the attractions soon to be added are a chapel and conservatory. This group of buildings will be placed near the entrance, and will offer greater conveniences than can be secured in any of the other large cemeteries. A

KENSICO CEMETERY.

CEMETERY AT KENSICO STATION ON HARLEM RAILROAD. OFFICE NO. 16 EAST 42D STREET, NEW YORK.

number of expensive mausoleums and monuments, costing from $3,000 to $25,000, have been ordered, and will be erected within the next twelve months.

Kensico Cemetery has been liberally patronized by New-Yorkers. Among the names of some of the lot proprietors are Gardner Wetherbee, of the Windsor Hotel; ex-Gov. Lounsbury, of Connecticut ; Jas. F. Sutton, President of the American Art Gallery ; Hon. C. M. Depew, President of the New-York Central Railroad ; Samuel I. Knight, President of the Acme Paper & Stationery Co. ; F. S. Winston, M. D., of the Mutual Life-Insurance Co. ; Allen S.. Apgar, Cashier of the Mer. chants' Exchange National Bank ; W. P. Howell, Austin Hall, Edward Kearny, Samuel Shethar, M. D. Middleberger, W. H. Webb, Wm. E. Dodge Stokes, John A. Post, F. E. Ransom, S. S. Darling, John J. Devoe Estate, Thos. D. Husted, E. H. Miller Estate, J. O. Miller, and Henry II. Landon.

Other Cemeteries outside the city limits are the principal last resting-places of the people of New York. For the most part these are on Long Island and in New Jersey. The greater number of them are located in the town of Newtown, on the outskirts of Brooklyn and Long Island City. This village has become a real city of the dead. It contains twenty-four cemeteries, with a total acreage of 2,000. There is a population of about 1,800 in the town, and over 1,400,000 dead are buried there, or nearly 800 dead to every living person in the village.

Calvary Cemetery is the principal burial-ground in Newtown. It is the place of interment for the Roman Catholic diocese of New York, and belongs to St. Patrick's Cathedral. There are about 200 acres in the cemetery, which is in two sections, and was opened in 1848. Over 750.000 have been buried there. It is very crowded, and the dead are buried three, four and five in a single grave.

The Lutheran Cemetery in Newtown comes next to Calvary in number of interments, 250,000 — and exceeds it in extent, which is 400 acres. It is a German cemetery, controlled by Lutherans. Severe simplicity characterizes the place.

Evergreen Cemetery, in Newtown, also has about 400 acres, and has received 100,000 bodies since it was opened in 1851. It contains a soldiers' monument.

Cypress-Hills Cemetery, in Newtown, has 400 acres, and 133,000 bodies. The National plot for soldiers killed during the civil war is here, and also the lots of the New-York policemen and the New-York Press Club.

Other Cemeteries in Newtown are Salem Field, Ahawath Chesed, Washington, Macpelah, Mount Nebo and Union, Jewish places of burial; and Maple Grove, Linden, Mt. Olivet, St. John's, St. Michael's and Holy Cross. Sleepy Hollow, at Tarrytown ; New-York Bay, on the New-Jersey shore, and Rockland, in Rockland County, are cemeteries in which New-York people are interested to a degree.

Fresh-Pond Crematory is also in Newtown. The building is in the form of a Grecian temple, with an ornamental marble front. A large apartment is in connection with the retort. The body is subjected to a heat of 2,700 degrees Farenheit, and when the process of incineration is complete, the ashes are deposited in ornamental urns.

The Huguenot Graveyard on Staten Island contains the Vanderbilt mausoleum. It is a handsome marble structure, with many buttresses and angles, and two marble domes, for light and ventilation. With one exception, all the dead of the family are buried here. The mausoleum cost more than $100,000.

The Potter's Field is the city cemetery on Hart's Island. Only a soldiers' monument is there. Annually the interments of unknown and paupers are about 2,000.

Defense and Protection

The Police and Fire Departments; Detectives and Fire Patrol;
The National Guard; United-States Army and
Navy Stations and Forts.

LIFE and property in the metropolis are substantially guarded against the criminal elements of society, the mishaps incidental to all large communities, and the possible invasion of foreign foes. In its police, firemen and National Guard the city has a brave army of defenders, whose efficiency has been proven on many occasions such as try men's souls. Not secondary in importance to these, even if less evident in every-day life, are the detachments of the regular army of the United States, in the harbor defences that are maintained by the Federal Government.

The Police Department, in general efficiency, discipline and morality, is conceded to be "one of the finest" in the world. In one form or another, it is over 250 years old. As early as 1624, under Peter Minuit, the first Director-General of the Dutch West India Company at New Netherland, when there was a population of only 270, the police force consisted of one important officer called the Schout Fiscal, a sort of sheriff and attorney-general. Under Wouter Van Twiller, in 1632, a penal system was established; and there is a record, in the time of Director-General William Kieft, in 1638, of jails and a gibbet, and severe penalties for many offenses. In 1643 a burgher guard, the first of which there is any record, was created. Among the regulations for this guard were these:

"If any one, of the burgher guard, shall take the name of God in vain, he shall forfeit for the first offense, 10 stivers; for the second, 20 stivers; and for the third time, 30 stivers.

"Whosoever comes fuddled or intoxicated on guard shall for each offense pay 20 stivers; whosoever is absent from his watch without lawful reason shall forfeit 50 stivers."

With the advent of Peter Stuyvesant in 1647 a more systematic order of affairs than had heretofore prevailed was established. The city of New Amsterdam was incorporated in 1652, and a year later the machinery of the municipality was put into operation. The Schout Fiscal was still the important officer whose business it was to see that the people did not break the laws, and he was assisted at night by the burgher watch. In October, 1658, a permanent paid "rattle watch" of eight men was appointed, to patrol the city by night; and in 1655 Dirk Van Schelluyne was appointed by the Burgomasters the first High Constable of New Amsterdam. Ludowyck Post was made Captain to the Burgher Provost, as a sort of inspector, to see that the rounds were regularly made.

When the English came into possession of the city, in 1664, the same method of policing remained in operation, but in 1674 the police force was increased to 16 members; and in 1675 to four corporalships of seven persons each. In 1684 the yearly cost of the city watch was £150. Probably the first uniformed policemen were the four bellmen, appointed in 1693. It was ordered by a vote of the Common Council that each one should be provided with "a coat of ye citty livery, with a badge of ye citty arms, shoes and stockings, and charge itt to ye account of ye citty." This system was continued far into the next century, with occasional changes in the character of the force, constables and watchmen dividing the duty. In 1710 the cost of the force was £277, 4s. In 1731 the first watch-house was built, near the corner of Wall and Broad Streets. In 1735 the force was increased to ten watchmen and two constables. About this time, too, a bridewell and debtors' prison were built, near the present City Hall.

The Revolution and the occupation of the city by the British brought about the subordination of the civil to the military power. But after the war there was a return to the old system of constables for day duty, and watchmen with bells, hourglasses, lanterns and staves, for night patrol. With the beginning of the century there was a force consisting of two captains, two deputies, and 72 men, maintained at a cost of $21,000 a year. In 1838 a law was passed, creating a force to consist of a superintendent, 12 captains, 34 assistant captains, 132 sergeants and 784 watchmen, half the men to be on duty every alternate night. The force was made up of citizens, who were occupied in private pursuits during the day time. They wore heavy firemen's hats of leather, highly varnished ; and from this circumstance they received the nick-name "Old Leather-Heads." At one time they wore copper shields, and thence comes the word "copper," and its abbreviation, "cop," as applied to the policemen of to-day.

Down to this time the old system established by the first Dutch settlers had practically continued, with only immaterial change. In 1840, George W. Matsell, the founder of the modern police system of the city, was appointed one of the four police justices. Shortly after his appointment, James Harper was elected mayor, and immediately organized a police force on the English model, adopting the English dress and the "M. P." on the coat-collar, an imitation of English customs which gave great offense to the "Native Americans." In 1844 the State Legislature passed an act establishing the police department of New-York City. This act abolished the old watch department, and divided the seventeen wards of the city into separate patrol districts, with a station-house, captain and sergeant for each precinct. Justice Matsell was appointed chief of the department, which included over 900 officers.

In 1857 the police forces of New York, Westchester, Kings and Richmond Counties were consolidated under the name of the Metropolitan Police, governed by a board of seven commissioners, including the mayors of New York and Brooklyn, and commanded by a Superintendent. In 1870 the Metropolitan District was abolished, so far as New York was concerned, and in its place the Police Department of the City of New York was created, and placed in charge of four commissioners. The Commissioners are appointed by the Mayor for terms of six years, and receive yearly salaries of $5,000 each. The chief executive officer is the Superintendent, who is appointed by the Commissioners, and serves for an indefinite period, at a yearly salary of $6,000. Next in rank are four inspectors, who are each paid $3,500 a year ; then 38 captains, at $2,750 ; 15 police surgeons, at $2,250 ; 40 detective-sergeants, at $2,000 ; 167 sergeants of police, at $2,000 ; 178 roundsmen, at $1,300 ; 3,379 patrolmen, at from $1,000 to $1,200 ; and 82 doormen, who are paid $1,000. There are also 20 police matrons, who look after the welfare of arrested women. The Commissioners have absolute power of appointment, but are limited in their range of selection for all the offices by the civil-service laws. Neither they nor anybody else can.

dismiss any member excepting for cause. All candidates for positions on the force are compelled to pass examinations regarding their physical, mental and moral qualifications ; and all the higher officers are required to give bonds for the satis-factory performance of their duties. The appropriations for the Police Department in 1893 were $5,309,886.

There are 38 precincts in the city, with separate station-houses, connected with the central office in Mulberry Street by special telegraph and telephone services. Each precinct is in charge of a captain and several sergeants. The force in one pre-cinct is known as the Harbor Police, and watches the river fronts from the steamboat *Patrol.* In addition, there are squads assigned to duty at the six police courts, at the Central Office, for sanitary in-spection, and for special detective service, under the direction of an in-spector ; and during the entire year there is a Steamboat Squad, whose particular duty is to look after the piers, wharves, ferries, steamship lines, and pleasure-boats gener-ally. The department has a patrol-wagon ser-vice, for emergency duty in carrying the men quickly and in force to any spot where they may be suddenly needed. The force in-cludes a considerable number of mounted

POLICE HEADQUARTERS, 300 MULBERRY STREET, NEAR BLEECKER STREET.

men, most of whom are employed in the trans-Harlem part of the city, a large portion of which is as yet essentially a country district. The control of the local election machinery is also entirely in the hands of the department, the Com-missioners having the appointment of the chief of the bureau of elections (who supervises all the election machinery), the inspectors of election, and the poll clerks, and the selection of polling-places, while patrolmen protect the ballot-boxes and take charge of the returns. After twenty years of service each man is entitled to ask to be placed on the retired list, and to an annual pension propor-tioned to his rank. Each of the 38 precinct station-houses has a jail connected with it, for the temporary detention of prisoners, and the yearly number of arrests is about 85,000, nearly one third of which are for intoxication, and one sixth for disorderly conduct.

The property-clerk retains in his possession all lost or stolen property, recovered by the police, until it is satisfactorily identified and claimed by the owners. The value of the property so recovered and restored yearly is nearly $1,000,000.

There are about 85,000 arrests a year. The first quarterly report for 1892 shows that 20,231 arrests were made, one-quarter being of women. Most of these arrests were for intoxication, disorderly conduct, larceny and assault. Lodgings were pro-vided for 45,000 indigent persons; 415 lost children were recovered; 1,972 sick, injured or destitute persons cared for; 38 rescued from drowning; and 723 fires were reported.

Connected with the force during the last half century have been several superin-tendents and inspectors who have had more than local renown. Among them have been George W. Matsell, J. A. Kennedy, John Jourdan, J. J. Kelso, George W. Walling, George W. Dilks, and in the present day William Murray and Thomas

POLICE BOAT "PATROL," PIER A, NORTH RIVER.

Byrnes. The last named is now the Superintendent. The department is continually subjected to a great deal of adverse criticism from those who think that crime is not sufficiently repressed. Nevertheless the fact remains that according to statistics no other city of equal size in the world is less afflicted by the criminal class. There has been a radical change for the better during the last ten or fifteen years, and vice is now kept in control to a gratifying degree. In many emergencies the police have shown their courage and their devotion to duty. Notably was this the case during the Draft Riots, when for a week, day and night, they fought bloodthirsty mobs and helped to save the city from dire disaster. The yearly parade of the department is an event of considerable importance. A good showing is made by the force, and the moral effect of the display is not inconsiderable.

Police Headquarters is between Houston and Bleecker Streets, with the main entrance on Mulberry Street, but extending through the entire block to Mott Street. It is a large building, not particularly handsome, with a marble front. The interior is plain, and there are not many modern conveniences, for the building was put up many years ago. It contains the offices of the Board, the Superintendent, the Chief Inspector and other inspectors, and various others. Special telegraph-wires keep headquarters in immediate communication with all branches of the service in every part of the city.

The Detective Bureau, connected with the Police Department, is practically the creation of Thomas Byrnes, who was placed at the head of the detectives as Chief Inspector in 1880, retaining that position until his promotion to the Superintendency in 1892. It was not, however, until 1882 that the bureau was created, and it was a year later before it was definitely organized. Since then it has developed a wonderful efficiency. As an inspector, Byrnes acquired the reputation of being one of the foremost detectives of the world ; and the corps which he trained is now regarded as equal in cleverness and courage to that of any European or American capital. There are 40 detectives in the Bureau, and 24 patrolmen, all under charge of Inspector William W. McLaughlin. Until April, 1892, there was a ward detective system, which consisted of 44 patrolmen, assigned to duty in special territories, and to a considerable extent independent of the Central Office. Upon the accession of

320 PRECINCT (MOUNTED) POLICE STATION, AMSTERDAM AVENUE AND WEST 152D STREET.

Superintendent Byrnes to the head of the Department, this corps was reorganized more directly under the control of the Superintendent and Chief Inspector.

The Rogues' Gallery is in connection with the Detective Bureau. It is a large collection of photographs of criminals, kept for purposes of record and identification. There is also a museum which contains many interesting relics, principally implements with which notorious crimes have been committed. To those who have a morbid curiosity this is one of the most fascinating museums in the city, but it is not open to the general public. Not the least important of Inspector Byrnes' achievements was one that is little heard of, save in financial circles. At the outset of his career he turned his attention to the neighborhood of Wall Street, where thieves had run riot for years, to the dismay of the monied interests there. He established in that locality a special detective bureau, to which some of the best men in the service have been permanently assigned. They maintain a rigid supervision of that part of the city, not merely for the detection of crime, but, what is more important, for its prevention. Well-known "crooks" who are found there, are either arrested summarily, or are escorted out of the financial district. The territory is absolutely forbidden ground to the known dishonest fraternity. Even a reformed criminal, no matter what his present standing may be, dares not go into Wall Street, in broad daylight on legitimate business, without first securing a permit, and then submitting to detective espionage from the time he enters until he leaves the precinct. The result of this system is that professional thievery has been almost entirely driven out, and notwithstanding the temptations offered by the almost limitless wealth, property is as safe there, as in any other part of the city.

The Police-Department Pension Fund is kept up from donations, excise receipts, and various official sources. The total receipts of this fund for 1892 was

$522,847, and the disbursements were $509,498.   Members of the force are retired on half pay, on their own request, after twenty years of service, on attaining to sixty years of age, and for disabilities.   The widows and orphans of deceased policemen are also cared for.   In 1893 the beneficiaries of this fund are 695 ex-officers, and 421 widows and orphans, a total of 1,116.   Among the distinguished pensioners are ex-Superintendent William Murray, who was retired in 1892 ; ex-Chief-Inspector Henry V. Steers ; and ex-Inspector George W. Dilks.   Ex-Superintendent George W. Walling, who died in 1891, drew a pension for many years.

Private Detective Agencies are numerous.   The uprightness of many of them is questionable, but the principal ones are honest, reliable and capable.   There are more than a score of such establishments, employing several hundred men and women in work of a private character that does not well fall within the legitimate scope of the public officers.   The leading agencies of this kind are Pinkerton's, Drummond's, Fuller's, Meehan's, and Wilkinson's.   Several of these make a point of refusing all business pertaining to marital affairs, but there is a small army of less scrupulous detectives, who live mainly upon divorce cases.

Private Watchmen are employed by many individuals and corporations, and they make all told an army of several thousand men.   Nearly all the large mercantile and banking houses and manufactories have these employees, and buildings in process of erection, which number over a thousand a year, are thus protected.   There are some unusual phases of this system of private protection.   Maiden Lane, the headquarters of the jewelry trade, is guarded at night by a regularly organized company of watchmen, supported by the Jewelers' Association.   There is a captain and several men.   The district is patrolled throughout the night, and every store is entered and inspected several times between dark and daylight.

Many of the millionaires in recent years have felt constrained to secure private protection for themselves, their families and their property, since they have become the point of attack for "cranks."   Several well-known men have stalwart body guards.   But more particularly do the millionaires have their mansions thus guarded, day and night.   In upper Fifth Avenue and vicinity there are some two-score watchmen thus employed by Gould, Sage, the Vanderbilts, the Rockefellers, the Astors, and others of their class.   These watchmen are strong and brave men, several of them ex-policemen.   They are well armed ; and by night they practically constitute a subsidiary police force for that part of the town.

The Park Police is an independent body, under the control of the Park Commissioners, for the policing of the parks and the streets that come under the care of that department.   The handsome gray uniforms are familiar sights to the frequenters of the pleasure-grounds.   It is a well-drilled and efficient body of men, who have lived down the derisive designation of "sparrow cops," originally given to them because of the place and the character of their duties.   Many of them are mounted, and one of their most frequent, most dangerous and most valuable services to the public is the saving of life by stopping runaway horses in the parks.   The force consists of one captain, one surgeon, nine sergeants, 17 roundsmen, 247 patrolmen, 10 doormen and 14 minor employees, a total of 299.   The headquarters of the force is in the Arsenal Building, in Central Park, where 170 men are stationed.   Other parks ·in the city south of the Harlem, to the number of 21, are patrolled by about 82 men, while the seven new parks, north of the Harlem, have only 23 officers.

Protection against Fire. — In the good old days of the Dutch West India Company, when the population of New Netherland was only a few hundred, the duty of protecting the little community from fire was imposed upon every house.

holder. Chimneys were looked after by a warden, and owners were compelled to keep them clean and to pay fines if fires broke out. The fire apparatus consisted of leathern buckets, which every family was compelled to possess ; a few fire hooks and poles and seven or eight ladders ; and the department included the entire community. After a while the first fire-company was organized, a night patrol of eight men, and the apparatus consisted of 250 fire-buckets, 12 ladders, and hooks and poles brought over from Holland. In 1731 a room was fitted up in the City Hall, and in it were placed two hand fire-engines, imported from England. Five years later the first engine-house was built in Broad Street, and Jacobus Tink was paid £10 a year to keep the apparatus in order. In 1737 a regular Fire Department of 25 men was organized.

At the beginning of this century the Department was in charge of an engineer, who had full control of all fire matters. There were five wardens, to inspect buildings and to keep order at fires; and several engine-houses, with hand-engines that were operated by volunteer companies. Great dependence was still placed upon the old hooks, ladders and buckets, that were kept ready for service in the basement of the City Hall.

Those were exciting times with men who "ran wid der machine." Rivalry existed between the different volunteer companies, and free fights sometimes occurred at the fires. The companies went deep into politics, and many men found in a fire-company the stepping-stone to political preferment. "Big Six"

MT. SINAI NURSES' HOME.   FIRE DEPARTMENT.   JEWISH SYNAGOGUE.
FIRE DEPARTMENT, 67TH STREET, NEAR THIRD AVENUE.

was a famous engine and company in its day, and thence William M. Tweed graduated to be "boss" of the city.

The Fire Department is governed by a board of three Commissioners, appointed by the Mayor, each with a salary of $5,000 a year. Under them comes a Chief, salary, $5,000. Then there are two Deputy Chiefs, each salaried at $3,500, and 12 Battalion Chiefs, each at $2,750. In all the branches of the department there are 1,400 men. The department has three marine engines, or

34

ENGINE HOUSE No. 7.   CHAMBERS AND CENTRE STREETS.

fireboats, for service on the water front, 91 steam-engines, 100 hose-carriages, 38 hook-and-ladder trucks, 4 water-towers, 5 chemical engines, 136 chemical fire-extinguishers, 3 hand-engines, and 55 other pieces of apparatus. Additions are being constantly made to this apparatus. The force is divided into 79 companies, and uses 300 horses and 200,000 feet of hose. All the most improved appliances for putting out fires and for saving life are in use. The new water-tower and the new fireboat are not surpassed by anything of their kind in the world. The firemen are brave, hardy and proficient. They are splendidly drilled, especially in life-saving manœuvres, and they frequently display heroism that calls out public applause and wins the medals of honor that are given for the decoration of the deserving. The department maintains an extensive repair-shop ; and a training-school where new horses are taught in the peculiar requirements of their work, until in intelligence and expertness they are second only to their human associates.

On the principle that an ounce of prevention is worth a pound of cure, the prevention of fires is looked after by a Bureau of Combustibles. Another bureau, with the Fire Marshal at its head, investigates the origin and causes of fires, and also the losses, with a particular purpose of detecting and suppressing incendiarism. Until April, 1892, the bureau for the inspection of old buildings and also those in process of erection, so as to insure an observance of the laws relating to exits, fire-escapes, strength of walls and floors, and other details for the protection of life, was for many years connected with the Fire Department. The Legislature of 1892 made it a department distinct by itself, with a Commissioner appointed by the Mayor at its head. The appropriation for the Fire Department for 1893 was $2,223,134.

There are about 4,000 fires every year, with an estimated loss of $4,000,000.

The Fire-Alarm Telegraph is one of the most valuable features of the general outfit for extinguishing fires. A system of independent telegraph-wires covering the entire city is maintained, in charge of a superintendent of telegraph. There are over 1,200 miles of wire ; and 1,235 alarm-boxes, keys to which are held by all policemen and firemen, and are also placed in the houses or the places of business of reputable citizens. There are also in use many keyless alarm-boxes, through which alarms are rung in by merely opening the door and pulling a hook.

The Insurance Patrol co-operates with the Fire Department, but in the special interests

ENGINE NO. 15 AND HOOK-AND-LADDER HOUSE.
OLD SLIP, NEAR FRONT STREET.

of the combined insurance companies, who support it through the Board of Fire-Underwriters. The corps was organized in 1835, when there was an epidemic of incendiary fires. The Patrol has saved millions of dollars by its vigilance in detecting and extinguishing incipient fires. But its most important service is in saving goods, which it does by removing them from burning buildings, or by covering them with rubber and oiled sheets, as a protection from water, dirt and cinders. The Patrol is provided with wagons and an equipment designed for its special work.

The National Guard stationed in the city constitutes the entire First Brigade, Brigadier-General Louis Fitzgerald, commanding. The organizations are two batteries of artillery ; the First, Capt. Louis Wendel, 88 men ; and the Second, Capt. David Wilson, 81 men ; one Troop of Cavalry, Capt. Charles F. Roe, 105 men ; one Signal Corps, Capt. E. B. Ives, 32 men ; and seven regiments of infantry : the Seventh, Col. Daniel Appleton, 1,046 men ; the Eighth, Col. George D. Scott, 500 men ; the Ninth, Col. William Seward, 607 men ; the Twelfth, Col. Herman Dowd, 606 men ; the Twenty-Second, Col. John T. Camp, 716 men ; the Sixty-Ninth, Col. James Cavanagh, 827 men ; and the Seventy-First, Col. Francis V. Greene, 545 men. The First Brigade numbers 5,164 officers and men. The Naval Battalion, Lieut.-Com. J. W. Miller, 350 men, is an independent organization.

The citizen soldiers are enlisted for five years. They are required to go into camp on the State Camp-ground at Peekskill for a week every other summer, and to drill regularly in the armories during the winter. The regiments are provided with armories by the city, and with arms, equipments and munitions of war by the State. The members receive pay for duty when called out by the commander-in-chief — the Governor — for parade or military service.

Armory accommodations for the militia have not always been adequate to the necessities of the service. In years gone by there were small armories down-town, in what is now the business part of the city, and the old castellated structure in Central Park, now used for the menagerie, was the arsenal a quarter of a century ago. The Tompkins-Market Armory is the only important building of the old times that is now left, and that is very soon to make way for a more modern structure. The need of new armories was pressed closely to the attention of the authorities as far back as 1880, and in 1883 the Legislature created an Armory Commission, consisting of the Mayor, the Commissioner of Public Works and the Brigadier-General of the First Brigade. In 1886 this law was amended so as to make the Commission consist of the Mayor, the President of the Board of Taxes and Assessments, the Commissioner of Public Works and the two senior officers of the First Brigade. This Commission has full power to condemn land and to erect armory buildings, expending such amounts of money as it alone may consider advisable. Under the provisions cf this law the Eighth, Twelfth and Twenty-Second Regiments have been provided with armories that are not surpassed anywhere in the United States for architectural beauty and practical military usefulness, while the Ninth, Sixty-Ninth and Seventy-First Regiments will, in a short time, be equally as well established.

In the early days every man was prepared to aid in the public defence. The Burgher Companies were paraded four times a year, and in 1686 were organized as a Regiment of Foot, under Col. Nicholas Bayard. The regiment and the independent companies were broken up in 1775, when many of their members entered the Continental army. In 1786 the militia was re-established, and in New-York City were raised Isaac Stoutenburg's First Regiment, Morris Lewis's Second Regiment, Aaron Burr's Third Regiment, Richard Varick's Fourth Regiment, and Sebastian Bauman's New-York City Regiment of Artillery.

The Seventh Regiment, the pride of New York, with its membership based upon character, and its superb discipline, has a noble history. It is an outgrowth of the New-York City Regiment of Artillery, organized in 1786, as a successor to Lamb's Artillery Regiment, so famous in the Revolutionary War. The first four companies, practically, of the Seventh Regiment were organized in 1806, when British frigates were blockading New York, and firing upon all passing vessels. Patriotism and a desire to defend the city led hundreds of young men to enter the ranks. The four new companies were attached to the Battalion of Artillery, which was entitled the Third Regiment in 1807, and in 1812 was re-numbered the Eleventh. Twice during the War of 1812 the regiment was enrolled for terms of several months in the United-States service, and garrisoned the forts defending New York. In 1824 the four companies left the regiment, and became an independent battalion of infantry, adopting the name The Battalion of National Guards, in honor of Lafayette, commander of the National Guard of France, who was then in New York. This title belonged to the Twenty-Seventh (7th) Regiment alone from 1824 until 1862, when the Legislature adopted it for the entire State militia. The gray uniform was selected for the new battalion, which was the first American militia force to wear gray. Prosper M. Wetmore became commander in 1825, and a year later the battalion became the Twenty-Seventh Regiment of Artillery. The standard was presented by Mayor Philip Hone, in front of the City Hall, and was of red silk, bearing the regimental arms. A State flag, of blue silk, was added soon afterwards. The re-organization of the militia, in 1847, brought about a change in the title of the regiment, which was thereafter known as the Seventh. The history of the regiment, its campaigns and reviews, achievements and purposes, fill a huge thousand-page illustrated history, written by its long-time commander, Col. Emmons Clark. In every emergency the Seventh has been prompt and patriotic in serving the public welfare. When the Astor-Place riot against Macready, the English actor, occurred, in 1849, and the police force of 300 men was overmatched, the Seventh dispersed the mob of 20,000 with powder, ball and bayonet, killing many of the rioters. Seventy of its own men were disabled. In 1861 the regiment gave its services to the cause of the Union, and made a memorable march from Annapolis to the defence of the Federal capital. It was sent three times to the front, and took a strong hand in suppressing the Draft Riots. The regiment furnished 660 officers to the regular and volunteer armies against the Disunionists in 1861-65. In the Orange Riots of 1871, in the Railroad Strike troubles of 1877, and on other occasions the Seventh has proved its courage, its ability and its patriotism.

The armory of the Seventh Regiment was built before the municipality took this work upon itself. The land is owned by the city, and constitutes the entire block between Park and Lexington Avenues and 66th and 67th Streets. The armory was erected with funds raised by public subscription, a regimental fair and other entertainments, the total cost, including decorating and furnishing, being about $650,000. The corner-stone was laid in October, 1877, and the armory was first occupied in September, 1880. Col. Emmons Clark planned and supervised the erection of the building. The armory consists of the Administration Building, which occupies the entire Park-Avenue front of 200 feet, and the drill-room, 200 x 300 feet. It is built of Philadelphia red brick, with granite trimmings, in the Italian style of architecture, and is a substantial and handsome structure, with a genuine military air about it. The Administration Building is three stories high. A handsome central tower, with open belfry, and square solid-appearing towers at the two corners add to the impressiveness of the facade. The entrance is at the second story, reached by a flight of granite steps. Here, under an archway, is a massive bronze gate, over which is a bronze tablet showing the regimental coat of arms. Farther under the arched recess is a solid oak, iron-studded door, opening into the main hall. The basement of the building has thick granite walls with narrow defensible windows. In this basement is a rifle range, 300 feet long, and storage, toilet and heating arrangements. On the upper floors are ten company rooms, six squad drill-rooms, and other rooms for the colonel, the adjutant, the field and staff, the Board of Officers, the non-commissioned officers, and reception, library and reading-rooms, gymnasium, veterans' quarters, and memorials. All these rooms are beautifully decorated and elegantly furnished. In the hall there are bronze tablets, recording the history of the Armory. The library and reading-rooms are handsomely finished in hard woods and wrought

SEVENTH REGIMENT ARMORY. 66TH AND 67TH STREETS, PARK AND LEXINGTON AVENUES.

iron, and the decorations and furnishings are of a pronounced military character. The unique iron chandeliers and basket lights, the antique fire-place and mantel, the quaint frieze, the paneled ceiling, and even the chairs, tables and standing lamps make an artistic ensemble that is wholly delightful. Among the art-treasures of the Armory are portraits of Washington, by Rembrandt Peale; of Colonels Abram Duryea, Marshall Lefferts, Vermilye and Emmons Clark, and of many other officers and distinguished former members of the regiment; paintings of the Seventh in camp and on the march, by S. R. Gifford and Thomas Nast; a large bronze statue of Mercury; a bronze reproduction of Bartholdi's statue of Liberty; and a plaster cast of Ward's Central-Park statue of the Seventh-Regiment soldier. The drill-room is a fine spacious hall, roofed by a single arch at a great height. At one end are glass cases for the arms, and on the sides are platforms and galleries, with seats for spectators. At the east end is the exit, through an arched doorway, closed with thick oaken doors and a heavy iron gate, directly on a level with Lexington Avenue.

The Eighth Regiment is the successor of the battalion of artillery formed in 1786; changed into the Third Regiment in 1807, and then to the Eighth Regiment in 1847. It entered the National service three times during the Secession War; and lost many men at the battle of Bull Run. The Eighth-Regiment Armory occupies nearly an entire block, between Park and Madison Avenues and 94th and 95th Streets.

EIGHTH REGIMENT ARMORY.   PARK AVENUE, FROM 94TH TO 95TH STREET.

There is an administration building, fronting on Park Avenue, and a drill-hall in the rear, 200 feet square and 85 feet high in the clear. The front of the building is a wide gable, deeply recessed between two great towers, 50 feet in diameter and 125 feet high. The lower story between the towers is occupied by a terrace, the front wall of which is pierced by an entrance leading directly to the main drill-hall. The terrace has an area of 33 x 90 feet and can be used for drill purposes. In the sub-basement is the rifle range, with six targets; and in the terrace basement is a squad drill-room. In the 94th-Street tower the first story is fitted up as a reception-room; and in the corresponding room of the 95th-Street tower is the Board of Officers' room. These rooms are 47 feet in diameter, and 21 feet high. In the same story, in the gable, are the library, reading-room and officers' quarters, substantially furnished. The companies have the entire second floor of the building. Here are ten meeting-rooms, measuring about 23 by 33 feet, and 18 feet high, plainly furnished with desks and chairs. On the third floor are 12 rooms, besides the quarters for the band and drum-corps. The fourth floor in the 94th-Street tower has been fitted up as a gymnasium; and in the 95th-Street tower on the same floor, is the regimental club-room. The block upon which this armory stands measures 61,430 square feet, but this includes an unoccupied space on Madison Avenue. The total cost of the land was $350,000, and of the building $330,000. An armory for the Cavalry Troop A will soon be built on the Madison-Avenue part of the block.

The Ninth Regiment can be traced back to 1812. In 1848 it was re-organized, as an Irish regiment, and disbanded a few years later. In 1859 it was again re-formed. In 1861 the Ninth was ignored when the State sent her quota of troops to defend the Union ; but the entire command went to Washington, independently, and was sworn into the United-States service (837 strong), for three years' service. During this period the Ninth had 2,278 members, and lost 684 in dead and wounded, mainly in the Wilderness, at Antietam, Fredericksburg, the second Bull Run, and Gettysburg. In the National service it was known as the 83d New-York Volunteers. Between 1870 and 1872 James Fisk, Jr., was colonel of the Ninth. The armory, being built by the city in 1893, at a cost of $300,000, occupies most of the square between 14th and 15th Streets and Sixth and Seventh Avenues, the land alone having cost $422,000. It is a massive brick and stone structure, with a vast drill-room, administration and company-rooms, and a rifle-gallery.

The Twelfth Regiment, organized in 1847, has had an honorable record for performing duty with its companion organizations in suppressing local riots. It served with distinction in the Army of the Potomac during the Civil War. The armory of the Twelfth, on Columbus Avenue, from 61st to 62d Street, was the first building to be constructed under the Armory Law. It was completed and occupied in 1887, and was dedi- cated on April 27th, the twenty-sixth anniversary of the departure of the regi- ment for the front in the Civil War. The building is a castellated structure in the Norman style of archi- tecture, and has a solid fortress-like character, with its mediæval bastions, machicolations and narrow

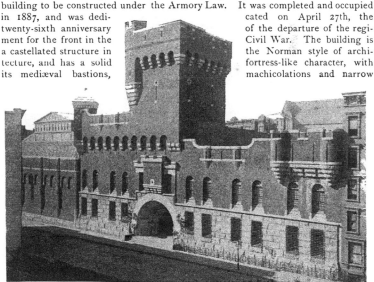

TWELFTH REGIMENT ARMORY.   61ST STREET, NEAR COLUMBUS AVENUE.

slits in corbelled galleries, and grille-work at the windows. At each street corner are flanking towers, with loop-holes and arrangements for howitzers, or Gatling guns, on the top. Around the entire roof is a paved promenade, protected by a parapet with many loop-holes, constituting a valuable defensive position. Brick and granite are the materials used in construction. The building measures 200 by 300 feet, and cost about $300,000, with $208,000 additional for the land. In the administration building there are the usual company, officers' and reception-rooms, library and gymnasium.   The salmon-tinted walls, solid brick fire-places and wrought-iron work in gas fixtures and railings are wholly artistic, and in harmony with the character of the building.   There is a rifle-range, with eight targets ; and the drill-room is a great high-roofed hall, 300 by 175 feet.

The **Twenty-Second Regiment** dates from 1861 and had two terms of service at the front during the Secession War.   Its new armory, occupied in 1890, occupies the square between 67th and 68th Streets, Columbus Avenue and the Boulevard. The land cost $265,000, and the building $280,000.   It is a granite-trimmed brick fortress, in the general style of the fifteenth century.   It is, to an exceptional degree, a defensive structure, with re-entering angles, loop-holes for cannon and musketry, a bastion for heavy guns on the northwest corner, a machicolated parapet, and a sally-port and portcullis.   The main entrance on the Boulevard will allow the free

TWENTY-SECOND REGIMENT ARMORY.   BOULEVARD, 67TH TO 68TH STREETS.

passage of batteries and cavalry.   The main building contains the offices, library, etc., a handsome reception-room, two stories high, kitchen, gymnasium and mess-room on the third floor, and a hospital and medical department in the tower.   The rifle-range, 300 by 25 feet, is in the basement.   The drill-room is 235 by 175 feet, with a high arched roof and large central skylight.   On the north side of this room are ten company locker rooms, for uniforms and arms ; and above these are ten company parlors, nicely furnished and with galleries, each capable of seating 50 persons.   The armory was erected from designs of Captain John P. Leo, a member of the regiment.   The building was completed and occupied in 1890.

The **Sixty-Ninth Regiment** was organized in 1852, and has always been made up mainly of Irishmen.   In 1860 it refused to obey the orders of the commander-in-chief, to parade in the procession reviewed by the Prince of Wales.   The next year it entered the United-States service, and lost at the battle of Bull Run alone 192 men, including Colonel Michael Corcoran, who was captured by the rebels. Many of its members enlisted in the Sixty-Ninth New-York Volunteers, which lost 412 men, dead, and 765, wounded, in its three years of service.   The Sixty-Ninth Militia, recruited again to full ranks, served also three months in the defence of

Washington in 1862; in the Pennsylvania campaign of 1863, and three months in the New York harbor forts in 1864. It also furnished most of the membership of the One Hundred and Eighty-Second New-York Volunteers, which lost 385 men in the field. The armory is in the Tompkins-Market building, on Third Avenue, 6th and 7th Streets. The building, which is of iron, of composite architecture, measuring 225 by 135 feet, was erected in 1860 for the Seventh Regiment. In the basement are drill-rooms. On the first floor are markets; on the second floor, ten company rooms and offices; and on the third floor, a drill-room. The building is inadequate, and measures have been taken to tear it down and erect a new armory in its place. The land alone is valued at $898,000, of which the city already owns $500,000 worth. The area is 57,900 square feet, and the new armory will cost over $300,000.

The Seventy-First Regiment was organized in 1852, and has rendered the State very active and valuable service. It was among the troops that saved Washington from the rebels, in 1861; and lost 62 men at the battle of Bull Run.

In 1862 the regiment served another three months under the National colors, on the Potomac; and at the end thereof, a large number of its members formed the

SEVENTY-FIRST REGIMENT ARMORY. FOURTH AVENUE, FROM 32D TO 33D STREET.

nucleus of the well-known One Hundred and Twenty-Fourth New-York Volunteers — the Orange Blossoms — which lost 567 men in the field, nearly half of them at Chancellorsville. The new armory of the Seventy-First on Park Avenue, at 33d and 34th Streets, was designed by J. R. Thomas, its corner-stone laid in 1892, and is to be finished in 1894, at a cost (including the land) of nearly $900,000. In this armory will be the Brigade Headquarters, the Signal Corps, and the Second Battery, all of which are now in leased armories.

Troop A, the only cavalry organization in the brigade, includes many of the foremost young society men of New York. It is an outcome of the First Hussars, and was mustered in in 1889. Captain Roe is an old West-Pointer, and served twenty years in the U.-S. Cavalry on the Plains. It is a very serviceable command of finely-trained riders, and did good service in the Buffalo campaign of 1892, and as Governor Flower's escort at the Presidential Inauguration in 1893. It is the largest cavalry troop in America, and has a long waiting-list. It occupies a leased building at 136 West 56th Street. Its permanent armory, designed by J. R. Thomas, is to be erected on Madison Avenue, from 94th Street to 95th Street, adjoining and harmonizing with the Eighth Regiment Armory. Land and building will have cost $240,000. The riding ring will be 200 x 100 feet ; and there will be stables for 105 horses, rifle-ranges, saddle-rooms, and many other departments. Upstairs will be the rooms for dismounted drill, and the company parlors, kitchen, etc.

The First Battery has its armory at 340 West 44th Street, in leased quarters. It is largely made up of German volunteers.

The Second Battery was organized in 1832, as Washington Gray Troop, Horse Artillery, then in the Third and after 1847 in the Eighth Regiment, with which it saw service in Pennsylvania and Virginia. From 1867 it served as cavalry until 1879, when it became Battery E, and three years later received its present name.

The State Arsenal, at Seventh Avenue and 35th Street, is a big turreted building, of gray stone and brick. It is the oldest of all the military structures in the city, save the old arsenal in Central Park. In appearance it is much like a fortress — and this is augmented by the half-dozen field pieces which are parked in the little strip of grass which skirts the sides of the building next the street and avenue. The Arsenal is a storehouse for the State's munitions of war, and the headquarters of the Ordnance and Quartermaster's Departments of the National Guard.

NEW-YORK STATE ARSENAL. SEVENTH AVENUE AND 35TH STREET.

The Naval Militia of the State of New York was authorized in 1889, and the First Naval Battalion of New-York City was mustered into service in 1891, and cruised with the United-States Squadron of Evolution in 1891 and 1892. Its armory is on the United-States line-of-battle ship *New Hampshire*, at the foot of East 28th Street, E. R. The Naval Militia bears the same relation to the United States Navy that the State National Guard does to the regular army. Every summer there is a week or more of practical service and naval instruction on a Government war-ship, with naval officers in charge. The battalion numbers 350 men.

U.-S. LINE-OF-BATTLE SHIP "NEW HAMPSHIRE," HEADQUARTERS OF THE NAVAL BATTALION, EAST RIVER, AT THE FOOT OF EAST 28TH STREET.

The United-States Military Headquarters of the Department of the East are on Governor's Island, in upper New-York Bay, half a mile from the Battery. Major-General Oliver O. Howard is in command. This department covers all the country east of the Mississippi River, excepting Illinois, Michigan and Wisconsin. The troops near New York are three batteries of the First Artillery, at Fort Columbus ; four batteries of the First Artillery, at Fort Hamilton ; two batteries of the Second Artillery, at Fort Schuyler ; three batteries of the First Artillery, at Fort Wadsworth ; and one company of the Sixth Infantry at Fort Wood.

FIRE-BOAT "NEW-YORKER," AT CASTLE-GARDEN BULKHEAD.

Governor's Island was shunned by the early Dutch settlers of New Netherland, but Lord Cornbury, an English colonial governor, preëmpted it and built thereon a mansion, and laid out a race-track.   After the British had been driven out of the city, Governor Clinton took the island, and leased it to a Dr. Price, who proceeded to pull down the earthworks that had been thrown up by the British and the patriot troops, and to put up a hotel and make the place a public pleasure-resort.   With the danger of war with England again threatening, the island was turned over to the Federal Government, which has since remained in possession.   The island, which is egg-shaped, with a circumference of a little more than a mile, contains 85 acres. It is very handsome, with its fortifications, barracks and other buildings, fine trees and stretches of grass.   At the northern end are piles of cannon-balls, large guns and other ordnance.   Near the center of the island is Fort Columbus, with its star-shaped embankments.   Within it are barracks and magazines of stone and brick, and guns are mounted on the ramparts.   On the land side, the fort is entered across a moat, with a draw-bridge, and through an archway of stone, above which is a relief group of military insignia : a bundle of fasces and a liberty-cap, a mortar, a cannon, shells, an eagle and a flag.   Conspicuous on the north point of the island is Castle Williams, which was completed in 1811 ; a stone fort with three tiers of casemates and an abundant armament.   At the opposite end of the island is the small triangular South Battery, two magazines, and munitions of war.   The center of the island is elevated thirty feet above high-water mark and laid out as a parade-ground and a handsome park, with band-stand, brick walks, trees, flowers and shrubbery.   A score or more of pretty houses, the residences of the officers, surround this park ; and hereabouts and elsewhere on the island are the offices, a chapel, library, billiard-room, laundries, work-shops, store, the rooms of the Military Service Institution, and a museum, in which are battle flags, mementoes of Washington, Sheridan and others ; and many Indian trophies.

Fort Hamilton, a fortified military post, is situated on the southwest shore of Long Island, on the Narrows, 2½ miles from the county-town of New Utrecht, and adjoining the village of Fort Hamilton.   It is a stone casemated structure.   There are 150 acres in the reservation, over 50 acres having only within the last year been acquired.   This new ground is on the southeast side, adjoining the old reservation, towards Bath and facing Gravesend Bay, and was acquired with a view of extending the fortifications along the water-front.   The corner-stone of the post was laid June 11, 1825 ; and the works were first garrisoned by troops November 1, 1831.

Fort Lafayette became familiar to the public during the Civil War as a prison for political captives.   It is at the entrance to the Narrows, on an artificial island, built upon a ledge, and is overlooked by Fort Hamilton.   In appearance the fort is a large circular brick building, and its guns used to command the channel.   The name originally selected for it when it was begun, in 1812, was Fort Diamond, but as it was first occupied about the time of Lafayette's famous visit to this country, the name was then changed.   The interior was damaged by fire in 1868 ; and the place is now used for the storage of ordnance, and for experiments in torpedoes and other appliances.

Fort Wadsworth is a triple casemated fortification of granite.   The Government reservation, to which as a whole the name applies, is 100 acres of precipitous land on Staten Island, commanding the entrance to the harbor through the Narrows.   It is in all respects, a perfect position for a fort, and could be easily made impregnable against any force approaching by sea.   The crest of the hill is 140 feet above high-water mark, and there is Fort Tompkins, with a heavy armament.   Below, is Fort Wadsworth, proper ; and on the water's edge are Battery Hudson and a continuous line of other fortifications. The Narrows at this point are only a mile wide, and the passage is completely commanded by the cross fire of Fort Wadsworth and Fort Hamilton.

Fort Schuyler is on Throgg's Neck, near the western end of Long-Island Sound, where its tide and that of the East River meet. The Government reservation consists of 54 acres. The fort is a casemated fortress of gneiss, with extensive earthworks. It was first garrisoned in 1861, and during the war was the site of the McDougal Government Hospital. Opposite, across the river, is Willett's Point, with fortifications, a station of the Engineer Corps of the United-States Army. These two fortresses command the approach to New-York City, by the way of Long-Island Sound. A little further north is David's Island, a depot for the reception of United-States recruits.

Fort Wood is the double star-shaped fortress on Bedloe's Island, enclosing the site of the Statue of Liberty. The fort was built in 1841, and was a strong structure in its day. It is partly dismantled, and though the walls are in excellent condition, they would offer little protection against heavy modern artillery.

Harbor Defences on a large scale have, in recent years, been projected by the National Government. These include the acquisition of territory at Sandy Hook, Coney Island, Staten Island, adjoining Fort Wadsworth, and Long Island, adjoining Fort Hamilton. The plan is to mount batteries of powerful modern guns on embankments, on lifts, on disappearing carriages and in steel turrets, and to establish lines of torpedoes under water, thus effectually barring the harbor entrance. These works have been steadily in progress for a number of years.

UNITED-STATES ARMY BUILDING. WHITEHALL, PEARL AND WATER STREETS.

The United-States Army Building is on Whitehall Street, at the corner of Pearl Street, near the Produce Exchange. It is a large square building of imposing proportions, eight stories high, and occupying the whole block. It covers the site of the old Produce Exchange. The two lower stories are of granite, and with the barricaded entrances and narrow windows give the place the general air of a fortification. The upper stories are of red brick, and the offices, which are arranged on the four sides of a large central opening are light and airy. Over the main street entrance is a

flag, carved in stone, with the motto "This we defend," and the same design and
motto is engraved on the glass of the doors inside.   In this building are grouped
nearly all the principal offices of army administration stationed in New-York City,
such as those of the Quartermaster's, Subsistence, Medical, Engineer, Pay and
Recruiting departments.   There are recruiting-offices in Park Row and in Abington
Square, from which recruits are sent to David's Island.

The Navy Yard, although on the Brooklyn side of the East River, plays a
very important part in the defenses of New York.   It is situated on Wallabout Bay,
and with all its appurtenances covers 145 acres.   There are officers' quarters,
store-houses, marine barracks, machine-shops, two dry-docks, one of them the
finest in the world, built at a cost of over $2,000,000, and the United-States Naval

CASTLE WILLIAMS, GOVERNOR'S ISLAND.

Hospital, with a fine library and museum.   The yard is the principal naval station
of the Republic, and is in charge of a Commodore, with about 2,000 men constantly
employed.   One or more naval vessels are generally to be found here.   In case of
war the yard would become a most important depot for naval supplies.   It occupies
a position unequalled in advantages for projecting naval movements in Atlantic
waters.   During the War of the Revolution the *Jersey* and other British prison-
hulks were stationed here, and more than ten thousand patriots, who miserably
died in confinement, were buried in the neighborhood.

The United-States Pension Office is at 396 Canal Street, just west of West
Broadway.   Only two offices in the country—that of Indianapolis, Ind., and that
of Columbus, O., exceed this in the magnitude of business transaction.   The
names of about 60,000 pensioners are on the books, and of these about 17,000 are
paid in person, while the remaining 43,000, residing in different parts of the
country, and even in foreign lands, have their payments forwarded to them.   The
office pays out over $2,500,000 every quarter.   The disbursing agent is Col. Frank
C. Loveland.

Clubs and Social Associations, Secret and Friendship Organizations.

THE clubs of New York at first were in taverns. To Old Tom's came the poets ; at the Pewter Mug, the politicians planned. William Niblo, who afterward owned a garden and playhouse on Broadway, near Prince Street, and bequeathed a fortune to the Young Men's Christian Association, that it might form a library, kept the Bank Coffee-House, where assembled the politicians in office. A French noble-man, a refugee, Jerome Cressac de Villagrand, kept, in College Place, a hotel where Fitz-Greene Halleck, manager of Astor's business in Vesey Street and in Prince Street, received Prince Louis Napoleon. In 1824 James Fenimore Cooper lived at 3 Beach Street, and founded, with Halleck, Bryant, Chancellor Kent, Francis and Verplanck, the Bread and Cheese Club. When the club received great men from abroad, or entertained Irving, it hired Washington Hall, at the corner of Chambers Street and Broadway, for a whole evening. In 1836 the Hone Club, named after Mayor Philip Hone, gave dinners at the houses of the members, at the expense of every member in turn. The Hone Club never failed to have a dinner when Daniel Webster was in town. Since then many clubs have been founded and dissolved that shall not be forgotten. Among them were the Bohemians, who met at Pfaff's, and who, although they were real and not pretentious or masquerading Philistines, made that man Pfaff wealthy; the Arcadians, who had a costly club-house, and were too exclusively artistic ; the Fellowcraft Club, which was vain enough to exclude Mecænas ; and the Tile Club, the enchanting adventures of which on land and afloat have been recorded with pen and pencil.

At the present day, the club-life of New York is a prominent and interesting feature of the metropolitan cosmorama. Besides a great number of local and special fraternities and organizations, there are at least 300 social clubs in the city, affording to their members a vast variety of luxuries and delights, outside the sometime worried precincts of home. The greater clubs, like the Union League and Manhattan, have incomes of not far from $1,000 a day each, throughout the year, the Manhattan much exceeding that figure. Perhaps a third of this amount comes from members' dues ; and the rest is received from the dining-rooms, from the sale of liquors and cigars, and from lodgings and billiards. These enormous expenses and receipts give an idea of the extension of club-life, and the wealth and freedom of its devotees. Nearly all the great clubs are around or above Madison Square, and Fifth Avenue is their favorite street, and contains some of their best houses.

The Union Club, on Fifth Avenue, at the northwest corner of 21st Street, was organized in 1836. The President is Clarence A. Seward. The entrance-fee is $300; the yearly dues are $75. With the sanction of the House Committee the Secretary may invite to the privileges of the club Ministers Plenipotentiary and

UNION CLUB, FIFTH AVENUE AND 21ST STREET.

strangers of distinction. It was the first club, in the modern sense, organized in this city. The founders met at the Athenæum, and limited the membership to 600 persons. They were the Beekmans, Kings, Schuylers, Livingstons, Stuyvesants, Griswolds, Van Burens, the Astors and other patrician leaders. There are now 1,500 members; they are the patricians of to-day. The first club-house of the Union was at 343 Broadway; the second at 376 Broadway, a large and handsome dwelling owned by William B. Astor; the third at 691 Broadway, opposite Great Jones Street, the property of the Kernochans; the fourth is the present brownstone palace, the property of the Union Club, dedicated as its club-house in the year 1855.

The **Union League Club**, at the northeast corner of Fifth Avenue and 39th Street, was organized in 1863, and incorporated in 1865, "to discountenance disloyalty to the United States, and for the promotion of good government, and the elevation of American citizenship."

UNION LEAGUE CLUB, FIFTH AVENUE AND 39TH STREET.

The President is Gen. Horace Porter. The entrance-fee is $300; the yearly dues are $75. The founders of the Union League Club were members of the United-States Sanitary Commission. Its Presidents have been Robert B. Minturn, Jonathan Sturges, Charles H. Marshall, John Jay, Jackson S. Shultz, William J. Hoppin, Joseph H. Choate, George Cabot Ward, Hamilton Fish, William M. Evarts, and Chauncey M. Depew. Its library is regarded as the most valuable of club-libraries. Its art-gallery is superb. The interior decorations of its stately building are by La-Farge and Tiffany. The Union League Club has a standing political committee, of strong Republican proclivities. The membership of the club includes 1,700 gentlemen. The club-house was erected for the Union League, at a cost of $400,000, and is a magnificent specimen of Queen-Anne architecture, with admirable interior arrangements and a famous oak-panelled dining-room.

The **Manhattan Club**, at the northwest corner of Fifth Avenue and 34th Street, was organized in 1865, and re-organized in 1877, "to advance Democratic principles, to promote social intercourse among its members, and to provide them with the conveniences of a club-house." The home of the club was at the southwest corner of Fifth Avenue and 15th Street, until 1891, when it purchased the white marble mansion built for A. T. Stewart. The President is Frederic R. Coudert. The entrance-fee

MANHATTAN CLUB, FIFTH AVENUE AND WEST 34TH STREET.

is $250; the half-yearly dues are $37.50. The Manhattan has one of the largest, most commodious, and most beautiful club-houses in the world, and is celebrated, moreover, for its delicious cuisine. Nearly all of the club's thousand members belong to the Democratic party, some of whose most important councils and receptions are held in this marble palace.

The **Metropolitan Club** is building a house at the corner of Fifth Avenue and 60th Street, on a site formerly owned by the Duchess of Marlborough. It is a noble palace of white marble, with halls of Numidian marble. The architects are McKim, Mead & White. A feature of this club, organized February 20, 1891, by members of the Union Club, is to be a ladies' annex. The entrance-fee is $300; the annual dues are $100 for resident members, and $50 for non-residents. The president is J. Pierpont Morgan. The club already has the favor of so many men of great wealth that it is known as the Millionaires' Club. It has 800 members.

The **New-York Club**, on Fifth avenue, at the southwest corner of 35th Street, was organized in 1845, and incorporated in 1874. The president is James H. Parker. The entrance-fee is $100; the yearly dues are $75. For non-resident
35

NEW-YORK CLUB, FIFTH AVENUE AND 35TH STREET.

members the entrance-fee is $50; the yearly dues are $37.50. The club-house is the Caswell house, the former home of the University Club, remodelled into a graceful building of the Queen-Anne style. The club was originally housed in Chambers Street, opposite the Court-House. It moved to the corner of Broadway and Walker Street, to 737 Broadway, to 558 Broadway, to 620 Broadway, to Astor Place and Broadway, to 15th Street and Fifth Avenue, to Madison Square, opposite the Worth monument, and in 1887 to its present building.

The Knickerbocker Club is at 319 Fifth Avenue, in a brick building with brownstone trimmings at the bay windows on the avenue and the entrance on 32d Street. It was organized in 1871, of descendants of original settlers of New York; of "Knickerbockers," elected by a Board of Governors. The entrance-fee is $300; the yearly dues are $100. Visitors are admitted for six months and three months by ballot of the Board of Governors.

The St.-Nicholas Club, at 386 Fifth Avenue, is formed of descendants of residents, prior to 1785, of the city or State of New York. Its object is social, and to collect and preserve information respecting the early history and settlement of the city and State of New York. The President is James W. Beekman. The admission-fee is $100. The yearly dues are $75 for resident and $37.50 for non-resident members. The social object of the club is predominant.

The Calumet Club, at 267 Fifth Avenue, a large brick building with brown-stone

KNICKERBOCKER CLUB, FIFTH AVENUE AND 32D STREET.

trimmings and bay windows on the avenue, and entrance on 29th Street, was organized in 1879, and incorporated in 1891. The members are elected by the Governing Committee. The initiation-fee is $200; and the yearly dues are $65 for resident and $35 for non-resident members. The Calumet is a club for the men whom the limit of membership and the long waiting list keep out of the Union.

The **Gotham** Club, at 651 Madison Avenue, was organized and incorporated in 1887. The initiation fee is $100; the yearly dues are $80. Its object is to promote sociability among its members. The club is composed entirely of members of the most refined and wealthiest Hebrew families. It is a very exclusive club, and until recently the membership has been limited to 100, the limit now being raised to 200. The new club-house, at Madison Avenue and 60th Street, is centrally located and elegantly furnished.

ST.-NICHOLAS CLUB, 386 FIFTH AVENUE.

The **New** Club, at 747 and 749 Fifth Avenue, was organized and incorporated in 1889. The initiation-fee is $100; the yearly dues are $100 for resident and $50 for non-resident members.

The **Fulton** Club, at 81-83 Fulton Street, in the Market and Fulton Bank Building, was organized and incorporated in 1889. The initiation fee is $100; the yearly dues are $50 for resident and $25 for non-resident members.

The **West-End** Club, at 134 West 72d Street, was organized and incorporated in 1889. The initiation fee is $100; the yearly dues are $50.

The **Authors'** Club, organized in 1882, and incorporated in February, 1887, is formed of authors of published books proper to literature, and writers holding a recognized place in distinctively literary work. The entrance-fee is $25; the yearly dues are $20. New members are elected by a committee. Frank D. Sherman is secretary of the club. To obtain funds for a house the members have written stories

CALUMET CLUB, FIFTH AVENUE AND EAST 29TH STREET.

sketches, and poems, to fill a large and sumptuous volume, which the club will publish in a limited edition of 251 copies. Every article will be signed by its author, with pen and ink, in every copy of the book. The subscription-price is $100 a copy. The manuscripts will be bound up and sold to the highest bidder.

The Century Club, at 7 West 43d Street, was organized in 1847, and incor.
porated in 1857, to promote the advancement of art and literature.   It was called
the Century, because the number of members was limited to a hundred.   There are

CENTURY CLUB, 7 WEST 43d STREET, NEAR FIFTH AVENUE.

at least 900 members at present.   The building agreeably recalls the palatial English
club-houses.   The style is Italian Renaissance.   The basement is of light stone, the
superstructure of cream-colored brick.   The contrast between the severity of the
lower stories and the ornateness and plasticity of the superstructure, between the
tall and massive archway of the main entrance and the rich and graceful loggia, is
enchanting.   The President is Daniel Huntington.   The members are authors,
artists, and amateurs of literature and the fine arts.   The entrance-fee is $150 ; the
yearly dues are $50.   An art-gallery, an art-library, a Twelfth-Night revelry,
wherein the greatest artists and men of letters are sublime jesters, and a superb disregard for the money standard of value, are the distinctive traits of the Century Club.   Its incorporators were Gulian C. Verplanck, William Cullen Bryant, Charles M. Leupp, Asher B. Durand, John F. Kensett, William Kemble and William H. Appleton.

HARLEM CLUB, LENOX AVENUE AND 123d STREET.

The Harlem Club, at Lenox Avenue and 123d Street, was organized in 1879, and incorporated in 1886. The initiation-fee is $50; the annual dues are $40. The handsome club-house was designed by Lamb & Rich. There are nearly 800 members.

The Lotos Club, at 556 Fifth Avenue, was organized in 1870, and incorporated in 1873, "to promote social intercourse among journalists, artists, and members of the musical and dramatic professions, and representatives, amateurs and friends of literature, science and fine arts." The Lotos is celebrated for its charming receptions and art-exhibitions. It has 650 members. The initiation-fee is $100;

LOTOS CLUB, 556 FIFTH AVENUE, NEAR 45TH STREET.

the yearly dues are $60 for resident and $25 for non-resident members. Whitelaw Reid was formerly the President. The President now is Frank R. Lawrence. The new club-house is from plans by William H. Hume.

The University Club, at Madison Square and East 26th Street, was incorporated in 1865, for "the promotion of literature and art, by establishing and maintaining a library, reading-room and gallery of art, and by such other means as shall be expedient for such purpose." The members are graduates of colléges or universities, where a residence of three years is required; distinguished men who have received honorary degrees; and graduates of the United-States Military Academy and the United-States Naval Academy. The President is James W. Alexander. The building is the property of Lawrence Jerome's daughter, Lady Randolph Churchill.

The Colonial Club, at the southwest corner of 72d Street and Sherman Square, near Washington's headquar-

UNIVERSITY CLUB, MADISON AVENUE AND 26TH STREET.

COLONIAL CLUB, BOULEVARD AND 72D STREET.

ters, and in the center of a circle of Revolutionary sites—whence the name Colonial Club—was organized in April, and incorporated in May, 1889. The building, of gray limestone to the second story, of gray brick with white terra cotta trimmings from there to the top story (which is entirely of terra cotta)—is colonial in its style of architecture and colonial in its interior decorations. There are a drawing-room, sitting-room, smoking-room, billiard-room, ball-room, dining-room, and bowling alley. The roof is flat, paved with brick, and surrounded by a high stone balustrade. Members are elected by the Trustees. The entrance-fee is $100; the yearly dues are $50. Ladies are accorded privileges at this club, an entrance being provided for them on 72d Street.

The Germans have several very fine social clubs, besides their numerous musical and athletic organizations, press-club, etc.

The Harmonie Club, at 45 West 42d Street, is the most homelike in jealous regard for privacy of clubs. An ancient and honored institution of the German colony of New York, an aristocratic club, with the characteristic that the members attend it with their wives, if they please, reputed to be

HARMONIE CLUB, 45 WEST 42D STREET.

very wealthy, and one of the most delightful of social circles, it seldom permits itself to appear in the printed newspapers.

The Progress Club, at Fifth Avenue and 63d Street, was organized in 1864, and incorporated in 1865. It transacts its business and keeps its records in the English language. "The members, however, shall be privileged to use the German language at all meetings of the club." It is composed entirely of Hebrews. The initiation-fee is $100; the yearly dues are $100. The president is David Wile. The club building, in the style of the Italian Renaissance, was inaugurated in March, 1890.

PROGRESS CLUB, FIFTH AVENUE AND EAST 63D STREET.

The Deutscherverein, or German Club, has been in existence since 1842, although its charter dates from March 20, 1871. It is a social organization, limited in its membership to Germans and those who speak German. For many years its club-house was at 13 West 24th Street. In 1890 it erected a handsome building at 112 West 59th Street, which it now occupies. It is five stories in height, of Indiana limestone, in the Renaissance style of architecture, and occupies three city lots. The membership is about 250, but for its numerical strength the club is one of the richest in the city. The initiation-fee is $100, and the annual dues $75. Charles Unger is the President, and Otto Hofmann Secretary.

The Freund-Schaft Society, at Park Avenue and 72d Street, was organized in 1879. The initiation-fee is $100; yearly dues, $100. The club-house cost $560,000, and has a superb white ball-room.

The Fidelio Club was organized in 1870, and incorporated in 1887. It designs only to

FREUNDSCHAFT SOCIETY, PARK AVENUE AND 72D STREET.

FIDELIO CLUB, 110 EAST 59TH STREET.

promote social intercourse among its members. Its membership is under no close restriction. The club-house that it occupies is a handsome building, of brick, in the Moresque style of architecture, four stories in height. It occupies two city lots at 110 East 59th Street, near Park Avenue, adjoining the Arion Club. There are about 250 members. Sol. M. Rothenheim is the president, Sam. Louisson the secretary, and Ben. Hamburger the treasurer.

There are numerous important literary and artistic social organizations, besides the Century, the Authors', and the Lotos.

The Lambs' Club, at 8 West 29th Street, was organized in 1874, and incorporated in 1877, for "the social intercourse of members of the dramatic and musical professions with men of the world, and the giving of entertainments for mutual amusement and instruction." The admission-fee is $50 for lay members, and $25 for professional and non-resident members; the yearly dues are $50 for resident, and $25 for non-resident and professional members.

The Salmagundi Club, at 40 West 22d Street, was organized in 1871, and incorporated in 1880, for "the promotion of social intercourse among artists, and the advancement of art." It is made up of painters, draughtsmen, sculptors, and crayon artists. The President is C. Y. Turner. The initiation-fee is $20 ; the yearly dues are $20.

The St.-Anthony Club is a local organization of members of the Delta Psi college fraternity. Its mission is social, and its membership is limited to post-graduate members of some chapter of the fraternity. It has a modest club-house at 29 East 28th Street, near Madison Avenue, which was extensively remodelled in 1892. It is of brick, relieved with stone, and it occupies a single lot. Valentine Mott is the president, Frederick A. Potts the secretary, and Lyman R. Colt the treasurer.

The Quill Club, at 22 West 23d Street, was organized in 1890 for "the promotion of fellowship and interchange of views on questions in the domains of religion, morals, philosophy, and sociology," formed of believers in the Christian religion, members of one of the learned professions or engaged in literature. The initiation-fee is $3; yearly dues are $15.

ST.-ANTHONY CLUB, 28TH STREET, BETWEEN MADISON AND FOURTH AVENUES.

The **Grolier Club,** at 29 East 32d
Street, was organized in 1884, and incorporated in 1888, for "the literary
study and promotion of the arts pertaining to the production of books."
The building is small and graceful,
and in the style of the Renaissance.
The club takes its name from Jean
Grolier, a great French book-lover of
the Renaissance. It occasionally publishes books that are models of typography, and not for sale excepting to
members, and several times yearly exhibits works of art and arranges lectures germane to its purposes, to which
the public is admitted by a member's
card. The initiation-fees are $50 and
$25. It has 350 members. Beverley
Chew is President.

The **Cosmos Club,** at 98 Fifth
Avenue, was organized in 1885, "for
the promotion of knowledge and social
intercourse among its members and
their families." Members must have
read Humboldt's *Cosmos.* The initiation-fee is $100; the yearly dues are
$50 for resident and $25 for non-resident members.

The **Shakespeare Society of
New York,** organized and incorpo-
rated in 1885, is formed of students of
Shakespearean and Elizabethan litera-

GROLIER CLUB, 29 EAST 32D STREET.

ture. The President is Appleton Morgan. The initiation-fee is $25; the annual
dues are $5. The Bankside Shakespeare, in 20 volumes, with addenda, besides
original works of reference, were published under the auspices of the society; which
for a time published the magazine, *Shakespeareana.* J. O. Halliwell-Phillips
bequeathed to it his wood-blocks and electros. The society meets at Hamilton Hall,
Columbia College. Its secretary is Wm. H. Fleming, 74 Franklin Street.

The **Holland Society of New York** was organized and incorporated in
1885, "to collect and preserve the history of the settlement of New York and elsewhere in America by the Dutch; to collect documents, perpetuate the memory of
Dutch ancestors, promote social intercourse, gather a library, and publish a history
of the Dutch in America." It is formed of descendants in the male line only of
Dutchmen, Dutch settlers, or Dutch citizens in America prior to 1675. Members
are elected by Trustees. The President is J. William Beekman. The initiation-fee
is $5; the yearly dues are $5. There are 1,000 members.

The **Players,** at 16 Gramercy Park, organized in 1887, incorporated in 1888.
"Its particular business and objects are the promotion of social intercourse between
the representative members of the Dramatic profession, and of the kindred professions of Literature, Painting, Sculpture and Music, and the Patrons of the Arts;

THE PLAYERS, 16 GRAMERCY PARK.

the creation of a library relating especially to the history of the American Stage, and the preservation of pictures, bills of the play, photographs and curiosities connected with such history." The club-house, the gift of Edwin Booth to the society, is filled with paintings and engravings, scarce books, and relics of the stage. Members are elected by Trustees. The President was the late Edwin Booth. The Vice-President is Augustin Daly ; the Secretary, Laurence Hutton ; the Chairman of the House Committee, A. M. Palmer.

The **Aldine Club**, at 20 Lafayette Place, organized and incorporated in 1889, is formed of printers, publishers, authors and artists. The President is Frank R. Stockton. The initiation-fee is $100 for resident, and $50 for non-resident members ; the yearly dues are $50 for resident, and $25 for non-resident members. The club-house was formally opened February 12, 1890, with an exhibition of portraits, photographs, and manuscripts of American authors. Exhibitions, dinners, meetings at which celebrated writers of stories and celebrated speakers tell anecdotes and recollections of men and events, are Aldine traits.

The **New-York Press Club**, at 120 Nassau Street, was organized in 1872, and incorporated in 1874, for benevolent and social purposes. The initiation fee is $10 ; the yearly dues are $10. A congenial dinner and monthly informal receptions of prominent artists, musicians and players, are distinctive features of the Press Club. The membership is 700, making the largest organization of newspaper and literary men in the world. It has a good reference library ; and also a reading-room, with files of all the prominent American newspapers, periodicals and magazines.

The local societies of college men include, besides the University Club, the following :

The **Union-College Alumni Association** was organized in 1888 for "social intercourse and mutual acquaintance and the promotion of the best interests of Union College." It is formed of persons who have attended the college for a year.

ALDINE CLUB, 20 LAFAYETTE PLACE.

The Yale Alumni Association of New York aims "to increase the acquaintance among Yale graduates, to facilitate the entrance of young graduates into active life, and to promote the interests of the University." It is formed of Yale graduates. The President is Henry E. Howland.

The Delta Phi Club, at 56 East 49th Street, was organized in 1884, and is formed of graduate members of the *Δ Φ* college fraternity. The President is T. J. Oakley Rhinelander.

The Delta Kappa Epsilon Club, at 435 Fifth Avenue, was formed in 1885, and is made up of 500 graduate members of the *Δ KE* fraternity. The President is Hon. Calvin S. Brice.

The Zeta Psi Club, at 45 West 32d Street, was organized in 1882, and incorporated in 1886, by graduate members of the *Z Ψ* college fraternity. The President is Austen G. Fox.

The Sigma Phi Club, at 9 East 27th Street, incorporated in 1887, is formed of graduate members of the *Σ Φ* college fraternity. The President is Daniel Butterfield. The yearly dues are $5 for non-resident and $20 for resident members.

The Psi Upsilon Club, at 33 West 42d Street, was organized and incorporated in 1886, by graduates of the *Ψ Υ* college fraternity. The President is Dr. George Henry Fox. The initiation-fee is $15; the yearly dues are $25 for resident and $10 for non-resident members.

The Delta Upsilon Club, at 142 West 48th Street, organized and incorporated in 1887, is formed of graduates of the *Δ Υ* college fraternity. The initiation-fee is $10; the yearly dues are $20 for resident and $5 for non-resident members.

The Alpha Delta Phi Club, at 226 Madison Avenue, organized and incorporated in 1890, is formed of graduate members of the *A Δ Φ* college fraternity. The President is Joseph H. Choate. The initiation-fee is $25 for resident and $10 for non-resident members.

PSI UPSILON CLUB, 33 WEST 42D STREET.

NEW-YORK PRESS CLUB, 120 NASSAU STREET.

HARVARD CLUB, 11 WEST 22D STREET.

The Harvard Club of New York City, at 11 West 22d Street, was organized in 1865, and incorporated in 1887, "to advance the interests of the University, and to promote social intercourse among the alumni resident in New York and vicinity." It is formed of graduates of Harvard elected by the club. The president is Edward King, '53 ; the Treasurer, Frederic Cromwell, '63 ; the Secretary, Evert Jansen Wendell, '82. The annual Harvard-Club dinner assembles, at Delmonico's, in February, many eminent persons. A new building is to be erected on West 44th Street, near Fifth Avenue.

The Congregational, Universalist and Unitarian denominations each has a powerful central club.

The Catholic Club of New York, at 120 West 59th Street, was organized in 1871, and incorporated in 1873, to advance Catholic interests, to encourage the study of Catholic literature, and for the moral and intellectual improvement of its members. The first story and basement of the building are of rustic stone, the upper stories of Roman brick and terra cotta. The style is early Italian Renaissance. The library occupies the third story. It is one of the best Catholic libraries in the United States. The President is Charles V. Fornes ; Vice-President, Joseph F. Daly.

The Church Club was organized in 1887, "to promote the study of the history and the doctrines of the Church, and to stimulate the efforts of Churchmen for her welfare and for the maintenance of the faith." It is formed of baptized laymen of the Episcopal Church. The President is George Zabriskie.

The Clergy Club, at 29 Lafayette Place, organized in 1888, is a social and literary club of the Protestant Episcopal clergy. The President is Bishop Potter.

The Xavier Club is a powerful organization of Roman Catholic gentlemen, with a fine club-house, at 29 West 16th Street. It is many-sided in its activities and aims.

XAVIER CLUB, 29 WEST 16TH STREET.

The Association of the Bar of the City of New York, at 7 West 29th Street, was organized in the year 1870, and incorporated in 1871, "for the purpose of maintaining the honor and dignity of the profession of the law, of cultivating social relations among its members, and increasing its usefulness in promoting the due administration of justice." The presidents have been William M. Evarts, 1870 to 1879; Stephen P. Nash, 1880 and 1881; Francis N. Bangs, 1882 and 1883; James C. Carter, 1884 and 1885; William Allen Butler, 1886 and 1887; Joseph H. Choate, 1888 and 1889; Frederic R. Coudert, 1890 and 1891; and Wheeler H. Peckham. The initiation-fee is $50; the yearly dues are $40. The club-house, wid-

ASSOCIATION OF THE BAR OF THE CITY OF NEW YORK,
7 WEST 29TH STREET, NEAR FIFTH AVENUE.

ened by the addition of a new building, is filled with oil-paintings of eminent lawyers, and engraved portraits of famous judges, and contains the most famous law-library in America. The association has standing committees on amendment of the law, to watch all proposed changes in the law, and propose such amendments as in their opinion should be recommended; the judiciary, to observe the practical working of the judicial system, and to entertain and examine projects for change or reform in the system, and recommend such action as they deem expedient; grievances, to investigate charges against members of the Bar, whether or not they are members of the association; and judicial nominations, to pass upon the qualifications for judicial office of candidates nominated by political parties.

The Lawyers' Club, at 120 Broadway, was incorporated in 1887, to provide a meeting-place, lunch-room, and library for members. The President is William Allen Butler. Jr. Members are elected by a Governing Committee. There is a special dining-room for women.

The clubs of business men include many strong organizations.

The Electric Club, at 17 East 22d Street, was organized in 1885, and incorporated in 1887. It is formed of persons interested in electrical science and industry, and officers of the Army and Navy of the United States. The initiation-fee is $40 for active and $20 for associate members; the annual dues are $40 for active and $20 for associate members. The club-house contains a museum of electrical works.

The Insurance Club, at 52 Cedar Street, is formed of persons engaged in the insurance business. It was incorporated in 1891. The President is James A. Silvey. The admission-fee is $20; the yearly dues are $24 for resident and $12 for non-resident members.

DOWN-TOWN ASSOCIATION, 60 PINE STREET.

The Down-Town Association, at 60 Pine Street, was organized and incorporated in April, 1860, to afford "facilities and accommodations for social intercourse, dining and meeting during intervals of business." The President is Samuel D. Babcock. The entrance-fee is $150 for resident and $75 for non-resident members; the yearly dues are $50 for resident and $25 for non-resident members. The club-house is elegant and handsomely appointed.

The Merchants' Club, at 108 Leonard Street, was incorporated in 1871, "to promote social intercourse among the members thereof, and to provide for them a pleasant place of common resort for entertainment and improvement." Its locality makes it an ideal place of dining for business men of the dry-goods district. The initiation-fee is $100; the yearly subscription is $75. Members are elected by the Board of Directors.

The Merchants' Central Club, at 29 Wooster Street, was organized and incorporated in July, 1886, "to promote social intercourse among the members, and to provide for them a pleasant place of common resort for entertainment." The entrance-fee is $75; the yearly dues are $50. Visitors introduced by members obtain the privileges of the club-house for $10 a month.

The Building-Trades' Club, at 117 East 23d Street, was organized in 1889, "to maintain a club-house furnished with all the requirements for the advancement of social enjoyment and encouragement of friendly intercourse between the members thereof, and to advocate the establishment of uniformity of action upon general principles, among those concerned in the erection and construction of buildings." It is formed of "employers in any legitimate business connected with the erection or furnishing of a building." The initiation-fee is $25; the yearly dues are $20 for resident, and $10 for non-resident members.

The Importers' and Traders' Club, at 13 Cedar Street, was organized in 1891, "to promote a more enlarged and friendly intercourse between merchants and business men and united action in all matters of common interest." The entrance-fee is $35; the yearly dues are $50.

The Engineers' Club, at 10 West 29th Street, although of recent origin (incorporated in 1888), has had a steady and constant advance as to the number and

MERCHANTS' CLUB, 108 LEONARD STREET.

standing of its members equalled by but few of the many New-York clubs. While its aims are purely social, it has in its membership engineers whose accomplished work at home and abroad has made them famous. The engineer is ever a thoughtful man, bearing about with him the heavy responsibilities of his undertakings, but here, more than elsewhere, he for the time being lays them aside for social good fellowship. The membership is 600. The president is J. F. Holloway, who is consulting engineer of the corporation of Henry R. Worthington, steam-pump manufacturers. The treasurer is Addison C. Rand, of the Rand Drill Co.; and the secretary is David Williams, publisher of *The Iron Age.*

ENGINEERS' CLUB, 10 WEST 29TH STREET.

There are many clubs devoted to Americans of foreign origin or antecedents, besides the great German social clubs, the Arion and Liederkranz and other musical societies, and the Turn-verein and other special organizations. Almost every nationality is thus represented, and even the Japanese have their bright little club.

St. George's Club is made up entirely of Englishmen, and dates its origin from 1891.

The New-York Caledonian Club, at 8 and 10 Horatio Street, was organized in 1856, and incorporated in 1861, for "the preservation of the ancient literature and costume, and the encouragement and practice of the ancient games, of Scotland." It is formed of Scotchmen and sons of Scottish parents. The Chief is William Hogg. The initiation-fee is $5; the yearly dues are $3. The annual fall games, at

NEW-YORK CALEDONIAN CLUB, 8 AND 10 HORATIO STREET.

Jones's Wood, are distinguished for their athletic feats, and the assemblage of Scots from all over America. The Caledonian built its own brick and stone club-house.

St. Patrick's Club, Morton House, was organized in 1884 for "social intercourse among Irishmen, their descendants, and all those friendly to the Irish people." The president is Edward E. McCall. The yearly dues are $10. The club has an annual banquet, on March 17th.

The New-York Swiss Club, at 80 Clinton Place, was organized in 1882, for social and literary intercourse among the Swiss residents of New York and its environs. The President is J. J. Metzger. The yearly dues are $10.

Other interesting societies are those formed by men from other States, now dwelling in the Empire City.

The New-England Society, the first of the kind in America, was founded in 1805, by Watson and Woolsey, Lawrence and Dwight, Wolcott and Winthrop, and other New-England-born New-Yorkers. It is for New-Englanders and their descendants, and to promote friendship, charity and mutual assistance ; and for literary purposes. The membership is 1,542; and the society's productive fund of $92,000 pays annuities to the widows and children of deceased members; if in need.

The Ohio Society of New York, at 236 Fifth Avenue, was organized in 1886, and incorporated in 1888, "to cultivate social intercourse among its members and to promote their best interests." It is formed of natives of Ohio, sons of natives of Ohio, and persons who have lived for seven years in Ohio. The President is William L. Strong. The initiation fee is $20 for resident and $10 for non-resident members ; the yearly dues are $15 for resident and $10 for non-resident members.

The New-York Southern Society, at 18 and 20 West 25th Street, was organized in 1886, "to promote friendly relations among Southern men resident in New-York City, and to cherish and perpetuate the memories and traditions of the Southern people." It is formed of persons of Southern ancestry, or who resided in the South twenty years prior to 1884. The initiation-fee is $50 for resident and $10 for non-resident members ; the yearly dues are $30 for resident and $10 for non-resident members.

Among the clubs of military men are :—

The United Service Club, at 16 West 31st Street. It was organized and incorporated in 1889, of commissioned officers or ex-officers of the Army, Navy, and National Guard, and graduates of the U.-S. Military and Naval Academies. The President is Brig.-Gen. G. H. McKibben. The initiation-fee is $25 ; the yearly dues are $20. The membership is nearly 800.

The Old Guard of the City of New York, at the northwest corner of Fifth Avenue and 14th Street, was organized as the Light Guard

UNITED SERVICE CLUB, 16 WEST 31ST STREET.

in 1826, and as the City Guard in 1833, and reorganized and incorporated as the Old Guard in 1868. It is a military company, governed as the National Guard, but formed as a club "to afford pecuniary relief to indigent or reduced members and their widows and children ; and to promote social union and fellowship." Members are over 30 years of age, and duly qualified by military service. The initiation-fee is $25 ; the yearly dues are

$30. The President is the Major of the Guard, Thomas E. Sloan. The yearly Old-Guard ball, in January, is a brilliant social festival.

The **Seventh Regiment Veteran Club**, at 756 Fifth Avenue, was organized and incorporated in 1889, and formed of veterans of the Seventh Regiment, N. G., S. N. Y., officers of the Army and Navy and Marine Corps, and active members of the Seventh Regiment. The initiation-fee is $25 ; the yearly dues are $35. The President is Locke W. Winchester.

The **Society of the War of 1812,** was incorporated in 1892, "to inculcate love of country and to perpetuate the memory of the glorious dead and of the soldiers of 1812." The President is Morgan Dix, S. T. D., D. C. L.

The **Grand Army of the Re**public, a secret order, membership in which is open to any Federal soldier or sailor who served honorably during the Civil War, is very strong in this city, although the headquarters of the department of New York are at Albany. There are 55 posts in New-York City, of which the best-known are Phil-Kearny Post 8, which meets at 117 West 23d Street; Abraham-Lincoln, 13, at 54 Union Square ; George G. Meade 38, at 501 Hudson Street ; Farragut 75, at the Boulevard and 74th Street ; George-Washington 103, at Hotel Brunswick; John-A.-Dix 135, at 33 Union Square ; Lafayette 140, at Masonic Temple ; and Phil-Sheridan 233, at 1591 Second Avenue. The membership of the order in this city is not far from 8,000. Two officers of the Department-Commander's staff come from this city. They are the Junior Vice-Commander, William F. Kirchner, of L.-Aspinwall Post 600, and the Senior Aide-de-Camp, L. C. Bartlett, of Lafayette Post 140. There is in the city a permanent relief and memorial committee, chosen from the different posts, with headquarters in the basement of the City Hall. The officers of this committee are David S. Brown, of James-Munroe Post 607, chairman; N. W. Day, of John-A.-Dix Post 135, treasurer; E. J. Atkinson, of Horace-B.-Claflin Post 578, recording secretary.

The **Military Order of the Loyal Legion of the United States** is an organization composed of men who held commissions in the army or navy, regular or volunteer, during the Civil War. The headquarters of the Commandery of the State of New York are in the Morse Building, 140 Nassau Street. The organization has regular meetings on the first Wednesdays in February, April, May, October and December, at Delmonico's. Gen. Wager Swayne is the Commander.

Political Clubs are numbered by the score, in all grades of organization and society. The van of the Democratic line is led by the magnificent Manhattan Club ; and the Republican columns are marshalled by the sagacious leaders of the Union League Club.

The **Tammany Society,** or Columbian Order, has a large brick building on East 14th Street, with a spacious public hall. This organization was formed in 1789, as a benevolent society, with many queer observances and titles borrowed from the Indians. Even yet the two classes of its members are known as Braves and Sachems, and other aboriginal titles diversify the roll of officers. The membership is almost identical with that of

The **Tammany Hall General Committee,** which is allowed by the society to occupy its building. This is the most powerful and the most skilfully organized political organization in the world, and practically holds the headship of the Democratic party in the city of New York, besides being a power in State and National politics. The General Committee is composed of 1,100 members ; and each election-district has its local committee. The organization of the entire Tammany mechanism is so perfect and so efficient that it will probably control the city for an indefinite period.

36

TAMMANY HALL, 14TH STREET, BETWEEN IRVING PLACE AND THIRD AVENUE.

The **Democratic Club of the City of New York,** at 617 Fifth Avenue, was organized in 1852, and incorporated in 1890, "to foster, disseminate, and give effect to Democratic principles." The President is John II. V. Arnold. The initiation-fee is $25; the yearly dues are $25 for resident members.

The **Sagamore Club,** at 21 West 124th Street, incorporated in 1889, is formed of persons Democratic in politics. The entrance-fee is $10; the yearly dues are $10.

The **Iroquois Club,** at 4 West 13th Street, was organized and incorporated in 1889. It is formed of persons Democratic in politics. The initiation-fee is $25; the yearly dues are $13.

The **West-Side Democratic Club,** at 59 West 96th Street, was incorporated in 1892, for the promotion of Democratic political ideas and the protection and secure develop-

ment of West-Side property. The initiation-fee is $10; the yearly dues are $12.

The **Harlem Democratic Club,** at 15 East 125th Street, was organized in 1882, "to foster and disseminate Democratic principles." The initiation-fee is $10; the yearly dues are $20.

The **New-York Free-Trade Club,** whose secretary's office is at 365 Canal Street, was incorporated in 1878, for the "formation of a public opinion that will secure Congressional action toward freedom of commercial intercourse, otherwise abolition or a reduction of the tariff." The President is D. H. Chamberlain.

The **Lincoln Club of New York,** at 56 Clinton Place, was organized in 1870, and incorporated in 1871, of persons who are residents of the city, citizens of the United States, and Republicans in politics. The President is Cornelius Van Cott, postmaster of the city of New York. The initiation-fee is $25; the yearly dues are $24.

SAGAMORE CLUB, 21 WEST 124TH STREET.

The Republican Club, at 450 Fifth Avenue, was organized in 1879, and incorporated in 1886, "to advocate, promote and maintain the principles of the Republican party." The President is James A. Blanchard. The initiation-fee is $50 for resident and $25 for non-resident members.

The Harlem Republican Club, at 145-147 West 125th Street, was organized in 1887, and incorporated in 1888, "to advocate and maintain the principles of Republicanism as enunciated by the party." The initiation-fee is $10; the yearly dues are $12 for resident and $6 for non-resident members.

The William H. Seward Club, was organized in 1888, and incorporated in 1890, "to honor and perpetuate the memory of William H. Seward, and to collect and preserve in the

REPUBLICAN CLUB, 450 FIFTH AVENUE.

archives of the club everything appertaining to his public and private life ; and to advocate and maintain the principles of the Republican party." The President is William M. Evarts.

The City Reform Club, at 677 Fifth Avenue, is a non-partisan municipal organization, founded in 1882. Its objects are to promote honesty and efficiency in municipal affairs, and to secure honest elections, and to issue publications upon these subjects, and an annual record of the members of the Legislature, in book form. It makes a specialty of securing and preserving information bearing upon all these subjects, which information is imparted to those wishing to use it for proper purposes. The club has a small active and large subscribing membership.

The Commonwealth Club was organized in 1886, for the discussion of political and economical questions at monthly dinners. The members are com-

REFORM CLUB, FIFTH AVENUE AND 27TH STREET.

mitted to the principles of civil-service reform, and assert the right of individual action in politics. The Chairman of the Executive Committee is Hon. Carl Schurz. The initiation-fee is $5 ; the yearly dues are $3.

The Reform Club, at the corner of Fifth Avenue and 27th Street, has a brick building with brownstone trimmings at the bay windows on the avenue and the entrance on the street, widened by the addition of a new building on the street. It was organized in 1888 "to promote honest, efficient and economical government." The President is Chas. S. Fairchild. The initiation fee is $25 ; the yearly dues are $40 for resident, and $10 for non-resident members.

The City Club, at 677 Fifth Avenue, was organized in 1892, as an "anti-bad-city-government club." The object of the club is to purify the government of that city, and render it efficient, and it has already made itself felt in various directions. The President is James C. Carter. There are 650 members.

The City Improvement Society was organized in 1892. Its objects are : To promote the improvement and beautifying of the city, and to assist and stimulate the authorities in enforcing the laws relating to such subjects. The headquarters is at 126 East 23d Street.

The Athletic Clubs of New York include some of the famous record-breakers of the world, and have spacious, beautiful and admirably arranged houses. The Berkeley, Caledonian, Y. M. C. A., West - Side, Olympic and other societies give much attention to athletics, and there are several capital private gymnasiums. The grounds of the New - York Base - Ball Club ("The Giants") are at Eighth Avenue and 157th Street.

The Manhattan Athletic Club, at the southeast corner of Madison Avenue and 45th Street, was organized in 1877, and incorporated in 1878, "for the encouragement of athletic exercises and games, and to promote physical cul-

MANHATTAN ATHLETIC CLUB, MADISON AVENUE AND 45TH STREET.

ture and social intercourse among its members. The magnificent iron and stone club-house is said to be the finest and most costly of its kind in the world, and exemplifies the Renaissance style, with a little of Flamboyant Gothic. It has a swimming-tank in the basement, a concert-hall and a roof-garden, besides the complete appurtenances of a perfect athletic and perfect social club. The club has an eight years' lease of Manhattan Field, which is said to be the finest athletic plant on the globe. In 1892-93 the club became financially embarrassed, and its great club-house was closed, and with the contents sold at auction.

The New-York Athletic Club, at West 55th Street and Sixth Avenue, was organized in 1868, and incorporated in 1870, for "the promotion of amateur athletics, physical culture and the encouragement of all manner of sport." The President is August Bel-mont. The initiation-fee is $100; the yearly dues are $50 for resident members, $20 for resident athletic, and $10 for non-resident athletic members. The magnificent four-story brick club-house has bowling-alleys, baths and a swimming-tank in the basement; dining-rooms, parlors and reading-rooms on the first floor; 1,100 lockers on the second floor, and boxing and dressing-rooms; a rubber running-track around the grand gymnasium on the fourth floor, beside the admirable equipments. Travers Island, near New Rochelle, is the property of the club, and contains a country club-

NEW-YORK ATHLETIC CLUB, SIXTH AVENUE AND WEST 55TH STREET.

house, boat-houses, a track and athletic field. The cycle department of the club is at 26 West 60th Street. The membership of the N. Y. A. C. is 3,000.

The University Athletic Club, at 55 West 26th Street, in the building formerly occupied by the Racquet Club, was organized and incorporated in 1891, "to furnish athletic facilities for its members, and to cultivate a love for athletic sports in the amateur spirit, without a trace of professionalism." Members must be graduates of colleges where at least three years of residence and study are required. The President is George A. Adee. The yearly dues are $50 for resident and $25 for non-resident members.

The Actors' Amateur Athletic Association of America, at 43 West 28th Street, was organized in 1889, and incorporated in 1890, for the "encouragement of athletic sports among actors, and for social purposes." The initiation-fee is $25; the yearly dues are $12. It is usually called the Five A's.

The Pastime Athletic Club, at 66th Street and East River, was organized in 1877, and incorporated in 1891, "to encourage all out and in-door exercises, and to promote the social interests of its members." The initiation-fee is $3.

The Racquet and Tennis Club, at 27 West 43d Street, stands "for the encouragement of all manly sports among its members." The President is Isaac Townsend. The initiation-fee is $100 ; the yearly dues are $75 for resident and $40 for non-resident members. The club-house is of Long-meadow stone, in the Romanesque style. The second story has the racquet-courts, the third the gymnasium, and the fourth the tennis-courts ; and there are all the appurtenances of a delightful social club.

RACQUET AND TENNIS CLUB, WEST 43D STREET.

The Central Turn-Verein was organized and incorporated in 1886 for physical culture. The initiation-fee is $5 ; the yearly dues are $9 for active and $12 for passive members. The President is Dr. H. A. C. Anderson.

CENTRAL TURN-VEREIN, 211 EAST 67TH STREET.

The Central Turn-Verein had a magnificent new German Renaissance building, modern and fire-proof, extending from 205 to 217 East 67th Street, near Third Avenue, six stories high, and covering a ground-area of 175 by 104 feet. It cost in the vicinity of $800,000. Among the interior equipments were admirable rooms for swimming, shooting, fencing, bowling, and schools ; a huge gymnasium, with all kinds of apparatus ; a library and reading-room ; meeting-rooms, a restaurant, a theatre, and the largest ball-room in the city. The society found it impossible to pay the interest on the mortgage, and in 1893 it vacated the building, which became the property of Jacob Ruppert.

The New-York Turn-Verein, at 66 and 68 East 4th Street, was organized in 1849, and incorporated in 1857 "for mental and physical education and for the relief of members in case of sickness or distress." Members must be citizens of the United States. The initiation-fee is $5.

Yachting is one of the most popular amusements of a New-York summer, and there are more than a score of clubs here.

The patriarch of these is the famous old New-York Yacht Club; and the American Yacht Club, with its splendid fleet of steam-yachts, is also of great interest.

The New-York Yacht-Club is the foremost and the oldest yachting organization in the country. It was organized in 1844, and incorporated in 1865. Its club-house is at 67 Madison Avenue, New York; its general rendezvous, off Bay Ridge, just inside the Narrows; its racing-course, from Bay Ridge to Sandy-Hook Bay, and thence to Sandy-Hook light-ship, and return. Its membership-roll includes the best-known amateur sailors and yacht-owners in the East. Its fleet numbers nearly 300 steam and sailing vessels, many of which are famous for speed or cruising qualities. One of the principal yachting events of the year is the annual cruise of the New-York Yacht Club, which begins early in August, and

NEW-YORK TURN-VEREIN, 66 AND 68 EAST 4TH STREET.

extends generally to Marblehead, Mass., with calls of some length at Newport and Martha's Vineyard. It lasts for two weeks or more. The club is the custodian of the famous " America Cup," and under its auspices have been sailed all the international races, in which English yachtsmen have attempted to win the cup. The entrance-fee is $100; the yearly dues $25. The officers of the club are Edwin D. Morgan, Commodore; V. S. Oddie, Secretary; Frank W. J. Hurst, Treasurer.

The American Yacht-Club has its principal rendezvous and club-home at Milton Point, on Long-Island Sound, some distance beyond the city limits, but it is distinctively a New-York organization, and its business meetings are held in the city. Jay Gould, George Gould, Washington E. Conner, the Vanderbilts, the Aspinwalls, and other owners of palatial pleasure-craft, are among the members. The officers are

SEAWANHAKA CORINTHIAN YACHT CLUB, 7 EAST 32D STREET.

Frank R. Lawrence, Commodore; Thomas L. Scoville, Secretary, and George W. Hall, Treasurer.

The Seawanhaka Corinthian Yacht Club, at 7 East 32d Street, was organized in 1871, and incorporated in 1887, to encourage its members "in becoming proficient in navigation, in the personal management, control and handling of their yachts; and in all matters pertaining to seamanship." The club has a very handsome and commodious house at Oyster Bay, L. I. The initiation-fee is $50; the yearly dues are $50.

The Columbia Yacht Club, at 86th Street and the Hudson River, was organized in 1867, and incorporated in 1869 and 1885. The initiation-fee is $5; the annual dues are $12.

The **Audubon Yacht Club** was organized in 1890. The initiation-fee is $5, the annual dues are $6. Grounds have been procured for a new club-house, at the foot of West 147th Street.

The boat-clubs include the Bloomingdale, Walhalla, Gramercy, Friendship and others, and the following named :

The **Knickerbocker Canoe Club**, at the foot of West 152d Street, Hudson River, was organized in 1880, and incorporated in 1884, "to promote canoeing, sailing and racing." The initiation-fee is $20 ; the yearly dues are $12 for active and $5 for associate members. The New-York Canoe Club has its house at Stapleton, Staten Island.

The **Atalanta Boat Club** was organized in 1848, and incorporated in 1866, "to improve, encourage and perpetuate the healthful exercise of rowing, and to promote the cultivation of social intercourse among its members." The club has a boat-house on the Harlem, and on the Passaic River.

The **Dauntless Rowing Club**, at 147th Street and Lenox Avenue, was organized in 1863, and incorporated in 1880, for "the promotion of rowing, athletics and social intercourse." The initiation-fee is $10 ; the yearly dues are $24.

The **Nassau Boat Club**, at East 132d Street and the Harlem River, was organized in 1867, and incorporated in 1868. The initiation-fee is $10 ; the yearly dues are $25.

The **Nonpareil Rowing Club**, at 132d Street and the Harlem River, was organized in 1874 for aquatic and athletic sports. The initiation-fee is $20 ; the yearly dues are $15.

The **Union Boat Club**, at 140th Street and the Harlem River, was organized in 1878, and incorporated in 1882. Members must be Christians. The initiation-fee is $20 ; the yearly dues are $12.

The **Waverley Boat Club**, at 156th Street and the Hudson River, was organized in 1859. The initiation-fee is $10 ; the yearly dues are $12.

The **Metropolitan Rowing Club**, on the Harlem River, was organized in 1880. The initiation-fee is $10 ; the yearly dues are $18.

The **Wyanoke Boat Club**, at East 132d Street and the Harlem River, was organized in 1878, and incorporated in 1885. The initiation-fee is $10 ; the yearly dues are $15.

RIDING CLUB.   DICKEL'S RIDING ACADEMY.   TROOP A.

RIDING CLUB AND TROOP A ARMORY, 130 WEST 56TH STREET.

The **Wheelmen's Clubs,** besides the New-York, Citizens' and Harlem, are :

The **Manhattan Bicycle Club,** organized in 1887, and incorporated in 1888, "to promote cycling as a pastime and pleasure," formed of persons eligible to member-

ship in the League of American Wheelmen, and amateurs as defined by the
L. A. W. rules. The yearly dues are
$24 for resident, and $6 for non-resident members.

The Gotham Wheelmen, at 54
East 79th Street, was organized and
incorporated in 1890, "for the promotion of cycling as a pastime, and for
social intercourse among its members."
The initiation-fee is $5 for men, and
$10 for women ; the yearly dues are
$18 for resident, and $9 for non-resident members.

The Riverside Wheelmen, at
232 West 104th Street, incorporated in
1889, exclude professionals under the
L. A. W. rules, and members of other
bicycle clubs. The initiation-fee is
$5 ; the yearly dues are $24 for resident, and $6 for non-resident members.

Among the clubs of lovers of equestrian exercise are :

The New-York Riding Club,
at Durland's Academy, Central Park
West, organized in 1873, incorporated
in 1883, for improvement in the art of
riding. The initiation-fee is $100; the
yearly dues are $50.

Boys' Clubs are conducted by humane gentlemen who provide meeting
rooms in various localities, and occasional outings for about 20,000 poor boys.
They conduce to keep boys out of mis-
chief by furnishing them amusement.

Shooting Clubs, besides the
Amateur Rifle Club, and the St. Nicholas Gun Club, includes :

The Deutsch-Amerikanische

DEUTSCH-AMERIKANISCHE SCHUETZEN GESELLSCHAFT,
12 ST. MARK'S PLACE, NEAR THIRD AVENUE.

Schuetzen Gesellschaft, the central organization of the German shooting-clubs
in New York and the adjacent cities, the ranges and shooting-grounds of which are
mainly on the western end of Long Island, to the south and east of Brooklyn. It
has a fine club-house at 12 St. Mark's Place, near Third Avenue, which contains,
besides the usual club-apartments, a large hall for social assemblies.

The Washington-Heights Gun Club, at Fort-Washington Hotel, was
organized in 1878 "to perpetuate the use of the rifle and shot-gun in the city of
New York and vicinity." The initiation-fee is $5 ; the yearly dues are $12.

The city also has clubs for fishing, bowling, racquet, tennis, cricket, base-ball,
and other active amusements, besides others devoted to the more sedentary amusements of chess, whist and the like.

The Fencers' Club, at 8 West 28th Street, was organized in 1883 for the encouragement of fencing in the United States. The President is Charles de Kay. The initiation-fee is $50; the yearly dues are $30 for resident and $15 for non-resident members.

There are societies devoted to the English beagle, the fox terrier, the mastiff, and the spaniel; and to Jersey cattle. The Westminster Kennel Club, the American and Long-Island Jockey Clubs, and the Monmouth-Park Association, and many other societies of this class are very useful in their way.

Among the clubs of women are these:

Sorosis, at 212 Fifth Avenue, was organized in 1868, for "the promotion of agreeable and useful relations among women of literary, artistic and scientific tastes; the discussion and dissemination of principles and facts which promise to exert a salutary influence on women and on society." Dr. Jennie de la H. Lozier is President. The initiation-fee is $25; the yearly dues are $5.

The Meridian Club, at the Fifth-Avenue Hotel, was organized in 1886, to discuss social, economical and literary topics for men and women only, limited in number to thirty. Every member may bring guests, but all are committed to secrecy about the proceedings at meetings. There are no fixed dues; members are assessed for actual expenses. The Secretary is Mrs. Rossiter Johnson.

The Berkeley Ladies' Athletic Club, at 23 West 44th Street, was organized in 1890, "for the promotion of physical culture, the encouragement of athletic sports and the increase of means of recreation for women." The President is Mrs.

MASONIC TEMPLE, 23D STREET AND SIXTH AVENUE.

Arthur Brooks. The initiation-fee is $25; the yearly dues are $40 for resident and $25 for non-resident members.

The Women's Press Club was organized in 1890 by women engaged in literary and art work. The President is Jennie June Croly. The club has about 150 members, including many well-known writers.

The Ladies' New-York Club, at 28 East 22d Street, was organized in 1889. The admission fee is $20 ; the yearly dues are $30.

An unclassified club is :—

The Thirteen Club, incorporated in 1882, "to combat superstitious beliefs," especially the one relative to the presence of thirteen persons at one table at dinner. The club exerts itself to prevent the choice of Friday for sentences of criminals, makes of 13 a favorite number, publishes essays, speeches, and reports of its meetings, and is doubtless one of the most persistently advertised clubs in New York. The dues are trivial. The expenses of the monthly dinners are assessed on the members present.

Secret and Mutual Benefit Societies number more than a hundred organizations.

The Masonic Temple, at the northeast corner of Sixth Avenue and 23d Street, is a granite building, the portico of which has coupled Doric columns of bronze. The building was erected and is owned by the fraternity of Free and Accepted Masons of the State of New York. The corner-stone was laid June 8, 1870, and the building dedicated June 2, 1875. Ninety lodges meet regularly

SCOTTISH RITE HALL, MADISON AVENUE AND 29TH STREET.

in the building, and the Grand Lodge meets there annually on the first Tuesday in June. In addition, a number of Chapters of Royal Arch Masons, Councils of Royal and Select Masters, Commanderies of Knights Templar, and Chapters of the Order of the Eastern Star, meet there regularly. The Temple contains a valuable Masonic library and museum. The architect of this fine building was Napoleon Le Brun. Here are halls modeled after Gothic cathedrals, or classic temples, or Egyptian tombs, in wonderful and interesting architectural forms, shadowing forth the occult symbolism of the Masonic order, and richly and appropriately decorated. There are scores of minor lodges, meeting in halls all over the city, and exemplifying the mysteries and the charities for which they are famous.

Scottish Rite Hall, at Madison Avenue and 29th Street, was formerly the Rutgers Presbyterian Church. The building was purchased in 1888, for the Scottish Rite bodies, who confer the 32d degree in Masonry. Mecca Temple, of the ancient Arabic order Nobles of the Mystic Shrine, also meets here. There is the original jewel of the Mystic Shrine, which was presented to W. J. Florence at Cairo, in Egypt. In a valuable collection of photographs which the Lodges preserve is material for an interesting biographical record.

The Odd Fellows enumerate more than 150 lodges in New York City, and their lodges meet in almost every part of the metropolis, advancing the cause and the purposes of the order. The head-quarters are at 853 Broadway. The German Odd Fellows have a handsome and commodious building at 69 St. Mark's Place.

Other Secret Societies are the Knights of Pythias, at 254 Broadway; the Good Templars, 167 Chambers Street; the Order of United Americans, 20 Second Avenue; the Knights of Honor, 38 Park Row; the Elks, 115 West 23d Street; and the American Legion of Honor, 268 West 34th Street.

Other Clubs and Associations, difficult of classification, include the following:

Aschenbroedel Verein, at 146 East 86th Street, was founded in 1860, for the purpose of the promotion of good music and good fellowship among its members. The entrance-fee is $45. It includes the representative German musicians of New York and vicinity, other musicians being admitted as associate members. In November, 1892, the club occupied its handsome new house, on 86th Street, near Lexington Avenue, and close to Central Park. It has 700 members, besides associates. The club-house contains a Kneipe (or German Inn), assembly and reception rooms, and a commodious hall, seating 1,000 persons.

The Coaching Club was organized with the purpose of promoting four-horse driving in the United States. It was organized in 1875, and has between 40 and 50 members, the initation-fee being $75, and the yearly

GERMAN ODD FELLOWS HALL, 69 ST. MARK'S PLACE.

dues $35. William Jay is the president and J. R. Roosevelt the vice-president. The membership includes only persons of large wealth and high social standing, and the parades of the club, which are held in Central Park, are very brilliant events and command much attention. The movement which has been set in operation by the Coaching Club has obtained a considerable vogue among the rich youth of America.

The Riding Club is the largest in the United States of its kind, and has the largest club-house in the world devoted to riding. It is a fine four-story brick edifice, sumptuously equipped and furnished, and with a riding-ring attached, more than a hundred feet square, and stables for 300 horses. This interesting group of buildings is on the square between Fifth Avenue and Madison Avenue and 58th and 59th streets. The club limit is 500 members, all of them men, although their women relatives have extensive apartments reserved for their use in the clubhouse, and continually avail themselves of the privileges of the riding ring. The initiation-fee is $200, and the yearly dues $100. In its earliest period this association was known as the Gentlemen's Riding Club, but when it was incorporated, in 1883, the present name was assumed. There are many other clubs in the city having the same purpose, but this is the most fashionable.

Le Cercle Francais de l'Harmonie, which has its house at 26 West 24th Street, is one of the most interesting of the New-York City clubs. It is peculiarly a French institution, and no other language except that of France is allowed in the club-house. The exclusiveness found among the membership is not exceeded in its way by that

ASCHENBROEDEL VEREIN, 146 EAST 86TH ST.

RIDING CLUB, 58TH STREET, NORTH SIDE, BETWEEN FIFTH AND MADISON AVENUES.

which appears in the Union Club or the Knickerbocker, and nearly all the 400 members are well-known persons of means and cultivation in the French colony of New York.

The Tenderloin Club, organized in 1889, whose house is at 114 West 32d Street, is a singular and interesting organization of nearly 500 journalists, actors, and other men with vivacious Bohemian proclivities. In winter it gives many entertainments.

The Arion Society, whose club-house is illustrated in another chapter, is the largest social organization in the United States pertaining to the German people. It occupies the costly and beautiful building at the corner of Park Avenue and 59th Street. The Arion has 1,500 members. The initation-fee is $25, and the annual dues $30. The original purpose of the Arion was to develop the art of singing and instrumental music, both secular and sacred, and to organize and foster these noble arts in the heart of the great German-speaking population. This design has by no means been lost sight of, and the Arion chorus of 200 admirably trained voices is celebrated for its fine work. But, apart from this artistic development, the society maintains a fascinating series of musical carnivals. Since the business and most of the social amenities of the Arion are conducted in German, it results that there are very few persons in the society who are not of the Teutonic race.

Various Other Clubs and Societies comprise an infinity of debating societies, reading clubs, music clubs, amateur dramatic clubs, clubs of cooks, and clubs of vegetarians. There are even clubs of club-haters, for the New-Yorkers lack the capacity not to form clubs and cults. When they are agnostics they hire a hall which becomes a temple where Voltaire and Paine are worshipped; when they are club-haters, they must meet and form variations of an Anti-Club Club.

In this Paris of the New World, the tendency is to social life, to fraternal union, to manifold forms of confederation. There is little opportunity here for ascetic seclusion, or for withdrawal from the brightening attrition of humanity. There is also little inclination for such separation. The air of the metropolis is full of mercurial activities, and gregariousness becomes inevitable. Hence the multiplication of clubs, or places for the reunion of kindred spirits, of brothers in art, literature, music, war's alarms, athletics, and religious efforts, as well as in the pleasures of sociability.

CATHOLIC CLUB, 120 WEST 59TH STREET, OPPOSITE CENTRAL PARK.

The clubs of New York, like those of London, have plenty of gossips, and their windows are favorite places from which to watch the world's passing show, and to comment upon its actors. But among these great associations of gentlemen scandals are almost unknown, and a general serenity pervades their fraternal halls.

Amusement Places.

AMONG all the cities of America New York stands first in the strength and scope of its interest in the drama. There is good reason, too, for claiming first position in the world, for, aside from its purely local enterprises, New York is distinctly a metropolis in the dramatic field. It is the great clearing-house and out-fitting depot for the theatrical enterprises of the entire continent. In this respect it is a city of greater importance than London, Paris, Berlin or Vienna. As many new plays are produced in New York in a season as are brought forward in London or Paris. Occasionally four, five and even six new plays are put on at different theatres on a single Monday night. Then, too, New York is the only city in the world in which the music drama, or grand opera, is maintained as a permanent insti-tution without assistance from a public or royal treasury.

In its business phase the drama is of great importance in New York. There are in the city thirty-four houses at which regular dramatic or operatic performances are given, with the accessories of stage scenery and drop curtains, and at which no other inducements than the regular performances are held out to patrons. Four new theatres, all of the first class, are either in process of construction, or have been planned to that degree of certainty that makes it safe to predict their erection within a year. Including as theatres all houses which have more or less distinctly defined claims to the title, and at which variety or vaudeville performances are given, the number in the city of New York is about fifty. The people of the city and its visi-tors pay upward of $5,000,000 a year for theatrical amusement. There is printed in any one of several of its leading newspapers, in a year, as much matter, critical, descriptive and narrative, concerning plays and players, as would make a volume of perhaps twice the size of this "King's Handbook." The theatrical managers pay to the proprietors of the newspapers about $400,000 each year for advertising space. Several hundred reputable actors and actresses find permanent employment in New York. Many thousands regard this city as their home, and every year return to it to secure their employment for the following season. All America looks to New York for its dramatic entertainment. Nearly all the large theatrical companies which travel over the continent are organized, drilled and fitted out here. Eight or ten men, whose desks are located within a circle of a radius of a quarter of a mile, allot, six months or a year in advance, the main part of the theatrical amuse-ment to nearly every city and town in America for a whole season. In the business aspect of the drama New York is the first city in America. The purely artistic aspect is inseparable from the business phase.

Dramatic history in New York began more than a century and a half ago. Col. T. Allston Brown, who has written extensively on the history of American theatres for the New York *Clipper*, and who is recognized as an authority on the subject, avers that the first dramatic performance ever seen in America was given in New York during the last week in September, 1732. A group of actors who came from England formed the nucleus of a company, in which there were also a number of amateurs, and an upper room in some building which cannot be definitely located served them for a theatre. The company gave three performances a week for about a month, and then disbanded. It re-assembled in December of the same year and held together for a short time. *The Recruiting Officer* was one of the plays presented in those early days.

The first play-house erected as such in New York was the Nassau-Street Theatre, and its site was on the east side of Nassau Street — then called Kip — between John Street and Maiden Lane. It was a wooden building, and it belonged to the estate of the Hon. Rip Van Dam. It was opened on March 5, 1750. Kean and Murray were the managers, and the play for the first night was *Richard III*. There were performances twice a week, and the season lasted for five months. This house gave place to a new one, built in 1753, by Lewis and William Hallem, the one a manager, the other an actor; but in a few years the new house was converted into a church for the use of the German Calvinists. The building was torn down in 1765.

One David Douglass built, in 1761, a theatre at Nassau and Beekman Streets, where Temple Court now stands, at which, on November 26th of that year, *Hamlet* was presented for the first time in America. It is interesting to know that the cost of this play-house was $1,625, and yet it was a theatre of fair proportion, for the dimensions are given as 90 by 40 feet. This establishment was very nearly demolished by a mob which assembled to express disapproval of the Stamp Act, in 1764.

The John-Street Theatre, erected in 1767, and opened on December 7th, was the first of the really famous play-houses of New York. Its location was on the north side of John Street, six doors from Broadway. It was the leading theatre, and at times the only one, for thirty-one years. Good work in the cause of the drama was done on its stage, for among the plays brought forward were *The Beaux' Stratagem, Richard III., Hamlet, Cymbeline, The Busy-Body, A Clandestine Marriage, Romeo and Juliet, Othello, Jane Shaw* and *The Merchant of Venice.* There is a popular supposition that this theatre was the first one built in New York. This arises from the fact that President Washington attended performances on various occasions, and thus gave the house a prominence which none of its predecessors ever enjoyed. The John-Street Theatre was pulled down in 1798.

The Park Theatre, which was located on Park Row, at what is now numbered 21 to 25, was built by a stock corporation, and was opened January 29, 1798. With this opening the real history of the drama, or rather that of its most important period, began. For fifty years the Park Theatre was the prominent play-house of New York. It occupied a position similar to that filled by Wallack's Theatre twenty years ago. At the outset there were four performances a week, but very soon afterward the house was open every secular night. John E. Harwood, who was as popular in his time as was ever Lester Wallack, played there in 1803. George Frederick Cooke, the great tragedian, made his American debut at the Park, November 21, 1810, in *Richard III.* James W. Wallack made his first appearance in America in *Macbeth* at this house, September 7, 1818. Junius Brutus Booth made his first appearance October 5, 1821, also in *Richard III.* During the season of 1825–26 actors of such prominence as W. A. Conway, Edmund Kean, and Edwin Forrest played upon its stage; and the Kean riot, so-called, occurred in the vicinity of the theatre, November 14, 1825. The first performance of Italian opera in America was given at the Park, November 29, 1825. The opera was *Il Barbiere di Seviglia.* The company was brought here by Sig. Garcia, the father of the singer who afterward became famous under the name of Malibran. Edwin Forrest played his first star engagement at the Park, beginning October 17, 1829. *Rip Van Winkle,* which made J. H. Hackett as popular during the early days of the century as it has made Joseph Jefferson in the later days, was produced April 29, 1830. The Ravels, Charles and Fanny Kemble, Charles Kean, and Tyrone Power were among the artists seen on the stage in 1832 and 1833. Ellen Tree, who afterward became Mrs. Charles Kean, appeared as *Rosalind* on December 12, 1836. James E. Murdock made his first appearance in 1838 as *Benedick* in *Much Ado About Nothing.* Fanny Ellsler introduced the ballet in America, May 14, 1840. She danced a *pas seule* called *La Craco-Vienne,* and aroused the indignation of all the clergymen and church-going people in the city. The theatre was burned, May 25, 1820. It was rebuilt, and opened a year afterward ; and was again destroyed by fire December 16, 1848. It was never again rebuilt, but in after years its name was given to theatres in other localities. There is a reminiscence of the ancient play-house, however, in Theatre Alley, the narrow passage which runs from Beekman Street to Ann Street, in the rear of the buildings on Park Row.

Two buildings only, Castle Garden and the Bowery Theatre, remain in existence to-day as landmarks of the drama of the first half of the century, although a third (Niblo's) brings down to the present generation something of the prestige of its predecessor, which was burned.

Castle Garden, the picturesque structure at the southern extremity of New-York City, is the oldest. It was erected by the General Government in 1807, and its site was then 300 yards from the main land. A portion of Battery Park is made

CASTLE GARDEN, BATTERY PARK, AS IT IS.

land, occupying the intervening space. The structure was known as Castle Clinton in the early days, and, as its name indicates, it was a fortress. The necessity for its existence as a means of defence passed away in time, and in 1822 the structure was ceded to New-York City. Two years later it was leased to private individuals as a place of amusement, and its floor was laid out elaborately as an in-door garden. Many pieces of statuary, the work of famous sculptors, were placed in it. A stage was erected at the north side, concerts were given at intervals, and refreshments were sold in the audience. Six thousand people easily found room for amusement and recreation, and on various occasions as many as 10,000 people were in the gar-

37

den at one time.   Col. Richard French (afterward well-known as the proprietor of French's Hotel) became the manager in 1839, and thereafter the place became more distinctly a play-house.   Various dramatic companies occupied the place, and for several years, succeeding 1847, Castle Garden was distinctively the home of grand opera.   The Havana Opera Company began a season August 8, 1847, and sung such operas as *Ernani, Norma* and *La Sonnambula*.   Signor Arditi, whom all musical people now know as Patti's conductor, was the musical director, and Signorina Detusco was the prima-donna.   Max Maretzek, a famous impresario, gave opera in Castle Garden for several seasons.   The one event, however, which has made Castle Garden famous as a place of amusement was the appearance of Jenny Lind in concert, on September 11, 1850, under the management of P. T. Barnum. What Patti is to-day, and has been for twenty years, in the musical world, Jenny Lind was forty years ago.   The enterprising manager had engaged her for a concert tour of America, at figures which were then considered fabulous, but Jenny Lind's personal prestige was so well supplemented by Manager Barnum's methods of advertising that the singer's first appearance in concert was regarded by musical people of the day as the event of a life-time.   Fabulous prices were paid for seats, and a tradesman of the time (Genin, the hatter) made a business reputation, which lasted for many years, by buying the first choice of seats for $225.   Jenny Lind gave four concerts at Castle Garden in the fall of 1850.   Another event of importance in the old fort was a grand dramatic festival which was held on September 6, 1852, to celebrate what was then erroneously considered the 100th anniversary of the first theatrical performance in America.

Castle Garden's history as a theatre ended in May, 1855, and the building was turned into a depot for the reception of immigrants.   A fire on May 23, 1870, destroyed the interior, but the walls remained intact, and the structure was re-built. When the General Government assumed the care of the immigrants, two years ago, the reception depot was transferred to the Barge-office, and Castle Garden shortly afterward passed into the control of the Department of Public Parks of New-York City.   It has been used occasionally for great popular concerts, and recently has been the rendezvous of the New-York State Naval Reserve.   The Park Commissioners have determined to turn the place into a grand aquarium.   A large tank, fifty feet in diameter and about five feet deep, is to be built in the center of the floor, and around this will be arranged, in a circle, six other pools, somewhat smaller. All these will be filled with very large fish.   Around the walls will be arranged two rows of smaller tanks, one above the other, numbering about 150 in all, in which every form of marine life, both animal and vegetable, will be exhibited.   It is intended to make the aquarium an educational fully as much as an amusement establishment.

The Old Bowery Theatre was second only in interest and prestige to the Park Theatre.   Its site was on the west side of the Bowery, just below Canal Street. It was built in 1826, and opened in October 23d of that year.   It was the first theatre in New York to be lighted by gas.   For many years Thomas S. Hamblin, who did greater work in the interest of the drama than any man of his time, was the manager.   The house was the scene of Edwin Forrest's first appearance as a tragedian, on November, 1826 ; of Malibran's last appearance in America, October 28, 1827 ; of Charlotte Cushman's debut as *Lady Macbeth*, September 13, 1836 ; and of the first grand production of *London Assurance*, May 16, 1842.   The theatre was destroyed by fire four times.   First on May 26, 1828, when it was rebuilt and re-opened in ninety days.   It was destroyed again September 22, 1836 ; for the third time, February 8, 1838 ; and last on April 25, 1845.   It retained the name Bowery until 1879, when it was re-christened the Thalia. This theatre is the second of the two landmarks mentioned.

Burton's Chambers-Street Theatre, another old play-house, was famous mainly because of the name of its manager, William E. Burton, a popular comedian who had been identified prominently both as actor and manager, with a number of other theatres. It was originally known as Palmo's Opera-House, and was opened February 4, 1844, for a season of grand opera. It was occupied by Christy's Minstrels during the summer of 1846, and was leased by Burton July 10, 1848. Some years later it passed into the hands of Harry Watkins and E. L. Davenport, and was then known as the American Theatre. In 1857 it was leased to the Federal Government, and occupied for offices. The site of the building is now occupied by the American News Company's establishment, having been sold to that company, January 29, 1876.

Barnum's Museum is a title which is familiar to theatre-goers even of the present day. The nucleus was Scudder's American Museum, which was originally opened in 1810, on Chambers Street, where the Court-House now stands. It was bought by Phineas T. Barnum in 1841, and the equipment of curiosities and objects of interest was removed to Broadway and Ann Streets, the site of the *New-York Herald* Building. As a museum simply, the new establishment was not successful, but Mr. Barnum opened as accessory thereto his famous "Moral Lecture Room," which was purely and simply a theatre ; and the joint establishment, comprising both museum and theatre, became very profitable. It was here that Charles S. Stratton, who became famous as General Tom Thumb, made his first appearance, in December, 1842. As a theatre, Barnum's Museum ranked with the first of the day for twenty years or more. It was fired on November 25, 1864, by an incendiary, but the flames were extinguished, after serious damage had been done. The establishment was destroyed by fire July 13, 1865. The name Barnum was then transferred to a building at 539 and 541 Broadway, which previously had been known as the Chinese Rooms. The establishment was re-fitted and opened September 6, 1865, as Barnum and Van Amburgh's Museum and Menagerie, with a dramatic company and a large collection of curiosities. Fire followed Mr. Barnum, however, for this place was burned, March 3, 1868. Again Barnum transferred his name and prestige to an establishment on the south side of 14th Street, opposite the Academy, which had been previously known as the Hippotheatron and Lent's Circus. But this establishment, too, was burned, on December 24, 1872. Since then, the name and prestige of Barnum have been attached to a travelling amusement enterprise, billed all over the world as "The Greatest Show on Earth," which has had for its temporary New-York home, each season, the Madison-Square Garden.

The Astor-Place Opera-House, which was opened November 22, 1847, was for a number of years the home of grand opera. Sanquirico and Patti were the managers at the outset, and Max Maretzek conducted operas there for several seasons. The place was best known, however, because of the fierce Macready riot, which occurred on May 9, 1849. This was the forcible expression of the intense dislike of a certain class of New-York people toward Macready, the famous English actor, because of their belief that he was responsible for the ill-treatment of Edwin Forrest in London a few years previous. The house was re-christened the New-York Theatre in 1852, and two years later was sold to the Mercantile Library Association, and remodelled and re-opened as Clinton Hall. In 1890 the old building was torn down, and the fine new Clinton Hall and Mercantile Library building arose on its site.

Tripler Hall, which was on Broadway, nearly opposite Bond Street, was built to serve for Jenny Lind's debut, and it was because it was not finished in time that the famous singer made her debut at Castle Garden.   Tripler Hall was the scene of the first appearance in public of Adelina Patti, on September 22, 1853.   Patti was then a child of ten years, and Max Maretzek, who was the manager, is authority for the statement that the price of her services was a hatful of candy.   The house was burned on January 8, 1854.   It was re-built, and re-opened on September 18th, as the New-York Theatre and Metropolitan Opera-House, and as such was the scene of Rachel's first appearance in America, September 3, 1855.   The house was re-fitted and re-christened in December as Laura Keene's Varieties ; and in September, 1856, was called Burton's New Theatre.   Still later, it was known as the Winter Garden, and in August, 1864, it passed into the control of William Stuart, Edwin Booth and John S. Clarke.   A performance of *Julius Cæsar*, given November 25, 1864, is of historical interest, in that Junius Brutus Booth, Edwin Booth and John Wilkes Booth were in the cast.   It was at this house that the famous 100-night run of *Hamlet* occurred.   It began November 26, 1864.   The house was destroyed by fire March 23, 1867.

Brougham's Lyceum Theatre, which was on Broadway, near Broome Street, was opened December 23, 1850, and passed under the management of James W. Wallack a few years later, and was re-christened Wallack's Lyceum.   This was the first Wallack's Theatre, and the one dear to the hearts of the older theatre-goers.   It was a successful establishment from the outset.   Lester Wallack's name appeared as such for the first time, October 30, 1859.   Previous to that date he had appeared under the name of John Lester.   The Wallacks retired from this house in 1861, and transferred their prestige and name to a new theatre at Broadway and 13th Street, now known as the Star Theatre.   The old house was finally torn down in 1869.

Franconi's Hippodrome is well remembered by many New-York people.   It was built by a syndicate of eight American showmen, among them Avery Smith, Richard Sands, and Seth B. Howe, as a permanent home for a Roman circus and chariot races, such as have been made popular in recent years by P. T. Barnum and his associates.   Its site is now occupied by the Fifth-Avenue Hotel.   Before the days of the Hippodrome there was on the spot a famous road-house called the Madison Cottage, kept by Corporal Thompson, which was very popular with horsemen.   The Hippodrome was of brick, two stories high, and 700 feet in circumference.   There was a roof over the auditorium only.   The arena, which was in the center, was uncovered.   The opening, on May 2, 1853, was a brilliant event.   About 4,000 people were present, and many of them had paid high prices for their tickets.   For two seasons the Hippodrome was in high favor.   Then it gave way to the Fifth-Avenue Hotel.

The Crystal Palace was a unique structure, modelled after the Crystal Palace of London, but much more beautiful as an architectural work.   It occupied the plot of ground at Sixth Avenue, 40th and 42d Streets, now known as Bryant Park.   It covered five acres of ground.   The building was two stories in height ; the lower one octagonal in form, the upper one in the shape of a Greek cross.   The central portion rose to a dome, 148 feet from the ground, and there were eight towers, 70 feet high, at the angles of the octagon.   There was an entrance, 47 feet wide, on each street.   The style of architecture was Moorish and Byzantine.   Strictly speaking, there were no walls.   The roof was supported by iron columns, and the spaces between them was closed in with glass.   Hence the name of the edifice.   The dedication of the place as an industrial exhibition hall, on July 14, 1853, occasioned a grand public demonstration.   There were present President Franklin Pierce, Secretary of War Jefferson Davis, Secretary of the Treasury James Guthrie, Attorney-General Caleb Cushing, many United-States Senators, army officers, the governors of several States, prominent foreigners, and about 20,000 people. Several of the

THE CRYSTAL PALACE OF 1853, IN BRYANT PARK.

annual fairs of the American Institute were held at the Crystal Palace. The edifice was burned on October 5, 1858. The land was owned by the city of New York, and it was turned into a park. It is advocated by some people, especially through the New York *Herald*, that this is the proper site for a new city hall.

Laura Keene's Varieties was a title attached to half a dozen different theatres during the period from 1850 to 1870. But the best-known house was that which was opened on Broadway, just above Houston Street, November 18, 1856, and which was soon afterward re-christened Laura Keene's New Theatre. Joseph Jefferson, already a good and well-known actor, came prominently to the front during the years 1857 and 1858. *Our American Cousin*, a play afterwards made famous the country over by E. A. Sothern, was first produced October 18, 1858, and Jefferson played the part of Asa Trenchard. *The Colleen Bawn*, one of the best of Dion Boucicault's Irish plays, was presented for the first time March 29, 1860. Laura Keene retired in 1863, and John Duff, who then became the manager, re-opened the house as Mrs. John Wood's Olympic Theatre. Mrs. Wood retired in 1866. Afterward the house had a checkered career, and finally became a variety theatre. It was demolished in 1880.

The Broadway Athenæum was the title given by A. T. Stewart to a theatre, built out of a church, which stood on Broadway, opposite Waverly Place. It was opened January 23, 1865. Lucy Rushton, Lewis Baker and Mark Smith, the Worrell Sisters, and Josh Hart were in control at various times during the following eight years. Augustin Daly leased the house soon after the burning of the first Fifth-Avenue Theatre, and opened it January 21, 1873, as Daly's New Fifth-Avenue Theatre. A year later it was known as Fox's Broadway Theatre, but it is best remembered by play-goers of to-day as Harrigan & Hart's New Theatre Comique. It was the house at which *The Mulligan Guards Ball* and others of Edward Harrigan's earlier plays were produced. Harrigan & Hart took possession on October 29, 1881. The house was burned December 23, 1884. Three years later the quaint structure known as The Old London Streets was built. It was an attempt to reproduce a fragment of ancient London, and to combine it with nineteenth-century retail shop-keeping; but it was not a success. The place has been tenantless for some time.

Booth's Theatre, at Sixth Avenue and 23d Street, was one of the leading play-houses of the city for fourteen years. It was built of granite, in the Renaissance style of architecture, and occupied a plot of ground measuring 184 feet on 23d Street and 76 on Sixth Avenue. The seating capacity was about 1,800. It was opened February 3, 1869, with Edwin Booth as manager, and with such artists as Mary McVicker, Edwin Adams, Fanny Morant, Mark Smith, Kate Bateman, W. E. Sheridan and Agnes Booth as members of the company. Among the significant performances given here were those of *A Winter's Tale,* April 25, 1871 ; *Man O'Airlee*—its first in America—June 5th ; *Julius Cæsar,* with Edwin Booth, Lawrence Barrett, F. C. Bangs, D. W. Waller and Bella Pateman, in the cast, December 5th ; Adelaide Neilson's first appearance in America as Juliet, November 18, 1872 ; George Rignold's production of *Henry V.,* February 8, 1875 ; and Sarah Bernhardt's American debut in *Adrienne,* November 8, 1880. J. B. Booth, Jr., succeeded his brother as manager in 1873; Jarrett & Palmer followed in 1874 ; James C. Duff, in 1878 ; and then, after several quick changes, Henry E. Abbey became the manager, April 12, 1879. John Stetson succeeded him, August 31, 1881, and he held the house until it was permanently closed, April 30, 1883. The site is now occupied by a large business block.

The Park Theatre, a title which became famous down-town, reappeared April 13, 1874, over the door of a new play-house on Broadway, between 21st Street and 22d Street. William Stuart was the manager, and Charles Fechter stage-manager. The construction had been begun by Dion Boucicault in 1873, but he lost control of the house, through business complications. It was at this theatre that the French opera *Giroflé-Girofla* was sung for the first time in New York, February 4, 1875 ; and its stage was the scene on December 18th of the same year of the debut of ex-Mayor A. Oakey Hall in his own play, *The Crucible.* Henry E. Abbey became the manager, November 27, 1876. The house was burned late in the afternoon of October 30, 1882, the day on which Mrs. Langtry was to have made her American debut on its stage. It was never rebuilt.

Other Play-Houses by scores have risen and passed out of existence during the present century. For example, the Chatham-Street Garden and Theatre, on Chatham Street, between Duane and Pearl, was a formidable rival to the old Park Theatre during the period from 1821 to 1823. Henry Wallack was at one time the manager, and the elder Booth, the stage-manager. The National Theatre, at Leonard and Church Streets, was in existence from 1833 to 1841. During a part of that time it was the home of Italian opera, and for the latter portion it was under the management of William E. Burton. The Franklin Theatre, in Chatham Street (now Park Row), was opened in 1835, and remained in existence for 19 years. William Rufus Blake, a comedian contemporary with Burton, was stage-director in its early days. Mitchell's Olympic Theatre, at 442 Broadway, contemporary with the Franklin, was also the scene of some of the best work of Burton and Blake. The old Broadway Theatre, which stood on Broadway, between Pearl and Worth Streets, was opened in 1847, and continued as a play-house, under various names, for twelve years. At this house Edwin Forrest and W. C. Macready won their greatest laurels. The Wallacks also played there in its early days. C. W. Couldock, who has been on the stage in this country almost constantly for forty-three years, made his American debut there, October 8, 1849 ; and E. L. Davenport played *Hamlet* on its stage for the first time in New York, February 19, 1855.

Theatre Fires have caused fearful losses to the theatrical interest of New York. Thirty-seven theatres have been burned during the past century. This is the record :

Rickett's Circus and Greenwich-Street Theatre, burned December 17, 1799; Park Theatre, May 25, 1820; again, December 16, 1848; Vauxhall Garden, August 30, 1808; Bowery Theatre, May 24, 1828, September 22, 1836, February 18, 1838, and April 25, 1845; Lafayette, April 11, 1829; Mount-Pitt Circus, August 5, 1829; National Theatre, September 23, 1839; again, May 28, 1841; Niblo's, September 18, 1846; again, May 6, 1872; White's Melodeon, May 20, 1849; Wood's Opera-House, December 20, 1854; Tripler Hall, January 8, 1854; Crystal Palace, October 5, 1858; Barnum's Museum, July 13, 1865; Barnum's at Broadway and Spring Street, March 3, 1868; Barnum's at 14th Street, December 24, 1872; Butler's American Theatre, February 15, 1866; Academy of Music, May 21, 1866; New Bowery Theatre, December 18, 1866; Winter Garden, March 23, 1867; Theatre Comique, December 4, 1868; Mechanics' Hall, April 8, 1868; Kelly and Leon's, November 28, 1872; Daly's Fifth-Avenue, January, 1873; Tony Pastor's, at 585 Broadway, December 28, 1876; Abbey's Park, October 30, 1882; Windsor, November 29, 1883; Standard, December 14, 1883, Harrigan & Hart's Theatre Comique, December 23, 1884; Union-Square, February 28, 1888; Fifth Avenue, January 2, 1891; and the Metropolitan Opera-House, August 27, 1892.

Theatrical Construction at present is governed by very stringent building laws, which have been enacted from time to time, and which were revised in 1887. Some of the important provisions are, that there shall be an open court or alley on

MADISON-SQUARE GARDEN, FOURTH-AVENUE PORTICO AND 26TH-STREET FRONT.

each side of a theatre, providing of course that the side wall is not also the street wall; that extra doors shall open upon the courts; that there shall be outside stair-ways of iron, leading to the galleries; that the proscenium-wall shall extend from the foundation to and through the roof, and, with a fire-curtain, shall constitute a fire-proof boundary ; that the roof of the stage shall be fitted with skylights, arranged to fly open automatically when released by the cutting of cords on the stage, in order that the direction of the draught shall be away from the auditorium ; that there shall be, at suitable points on each floor, fire-extinguishers and a supply of fire-hose, con-nected to pipes leading from a large tank on the roof ; that all floors and partitions shall be constructed of iron and masonry ; and that diagrams of each floor, showing all the exits, shall be printed in the programmes.   Plans of new theatres are subjected to the closest scrutiny in the Department of the Inspection of Buildings ; and the structures themselves are examined rigidly before permits to open the doors are issued.   A fireman in uniform, a regular member of the department, is detailed to every theatre at every performance.   His post is on the stage, and it is his duty, not only to act as fireman in case of fire, but also to watch for and report to the depart-ment any proceeding which may tend to increase the risk of a blaze.   As a matter of fact, it may be said, for the comfort of timid people, that the theatres built since 1887 are as nearly fire-proof as scientific construction and the exclusion of burnable material can make them.

· **The Places of Amusement** in 1892 in New York include three — the Madison-Square Garden, the Metropolitan Opera House, and the Music Hall — which are of special prominence because of their magnitude as buildings and of their breadth of purpose.   All are comparatively new.   Each of them requires · the expenditure of enormous sums of money, and each stands alone in its field.

The Madison-Square Garden is, in magnitude, the most important of the three.   It is the largest building in America devoted entirely to amusements.   It occupies the entire block bounded by Madison and Fourth Avenues and 26th and 27th Streets.   It is 465 feet long and 200 feet wide, and its walls rise to a height of 65 feet.   Architecturally it is a magnificent structure, because of the simplicity of the construction and the absence of trifling details in the ornamentation.   The style is in the Renaissance, and the materials buff brick and terra-cotta.   The roof is flat, or nearly so, but the sky-lines are broken by a colonnade which rises above the roof at the Madison-Avenue end and extends along either side for 100 feet; by six open cupolas, with semi-spherical domes, which rise above the colonnade ; by two towers at the Fourth-Avenue corners ; and by a magnificent square tower which rises from the 26th-Street side, with its lines unbroken for 249 feet, and then in a series of open cupolas, decreasing in diameter, on the smallest and topmost of which is poised a figure of Diana, of heroic size, the crown of whose head is 332 feet from the side-walk.   Along the Madison-Avenue end, and extending along either side for a distance of 150 feet, there is an open arcade, which covers the side-walk, and the roof of which rests upon pillars of polished granite and piers of brick.   The top of the arcade is laid out as a promenade.   The main entrance to the building is at the Madison-Avenue end, through a triple doorway, and above it is the most promi-nent feature of exterior decoration, an elaborate arch in terra-cotta, set in relief into the wall.   From the entrance a lobby 100 feet long and 23 feet wide leads to a foyer, and this opens into the amphitheatre, which is the main feature of the build-ing.   This grand hall is 300 feet long, 200 feet wide, and 59 feet in height to the bottom of the girders.   In the centre is the arena floor, 268 feet long and 122 feet wide, with parallel straight sides and semi-circular ends, and from this floor rise the box-tiers and rows upon rows of seats, extending back to the walls.   No· attempt has been made at decoration, other than to leave all the construction open to view and to paint the columns, roof, girders, etc., a light buff tint ; and the beauty of·the

MADISON-SQUARE GARDEN.
MADISON SQUARE, MADISON AND FOURTH AVENUES, AND WEST 26TH AND WEST 27TH STREETS.

interior resides in the simplicity and the light and graceful appearance of the con-struction. Above the arena seats there is a balcony, which extends around the amphitheatre, and still above is a promenade, which is 20 feet wide in its narrowest part. Properly speaking, there is no stage, but when one is required it is con-structed at the eastern end, either in front of the boxes or in the space gained by removing a number of them. There are 110 arena boxes around the edges of the floor, 52 in the first tier, 26 in the second, and 26 in the third, these tiers being dis-posed at either end of the amphitheatre. With the floor left open, for a perform-ance like that of a circus, for example, there are seats for 5,000 people. With the floor occupied by chairs, as for concerts, leaving space either in the centre or at the eastern end for a band stand, the seating capacity is 9,000, and there is standing room for many thousands more. On the opening night, June 16, 1890, with a con-cert by Edward Strauss's orchestra and two grand ballets as attractions, there were present 17,000 people, and that ample provision for exit had been made was shown in the fact that the amphitheatre was vacated after the performance in 4½ minutes. There are ten exits, and all of them, save that on Fourth Avenue, are on inclines, without stairs. Besides the usual means of ventilation, there is a movable sky-light, the area of which is one-half that of the roof. When this is moved aside the people in the amphitheatre are virtually, in so far as fresh air is concerned, out of doors. The whole building is thoroughly equipped with Worthington pumps. Since the opening the amphitheatre has been in use for gigantic musical and social under-takings, circus performances, horse and dog shows, bicycle tournaments and other sporting events. During the week of May 2–7, 1892, the Actors'-Fund Fair was held in it. The entire floor was laid out as a miniature village of one street in the midst of a plain. The buildings were models of famous theatres of ancient London and older New York, and the architecture and picturesque local color of several centuries and of places far distant from each other were cleverly brought into har-mony. On the evenings of May 10 and 12, and the afternoon of May 14, 1892, Adelina Patti sang, in association with other distinguished soloists, a chorus of 1,000 volunteers and a grand orchestra, to three of the largest audiences ever assem-bled at concerts. As the price of seats was set at popular figures the audiences were composed for the most part of people who had never heard Patti sing, and on each occasion the enthusiasm rose almost to the point of hysteria. At the after-noon concert Patti's managers and agents were compelled to rescue her almost by force from the chorus people, who paid homage to her so vigorously as seriously to frighten her.

In the Madison-Avenue and 26th-Street corner of the building there is, on the first floor, a café 115 feet long and 70 feet wide. Above it is a concert-hall, elabo-rately decorated in white and gold, with two balconies, the lower of which is divided into 36 open boxes. The seating capacity is 1,100. Opening from the lower bal-cony there is an assembly, or dining-hall, 69 by 32 feet ; and connected therewith is a kitchen equipment, sufficiently large to provide for 2,000 people. Above the Madison-Avenue end of the building there is a roof-garden, 200 by 80 feet, with a small stage or band-stand. This was opened for the first time on May 30, 1892, and it is estimated that 3,500 people were present. The roof-garden is reached by two principal stairways, 10 feet wide, and a third of lesser dimensions, as well as by two elevators of large carrying capacity. One of the elevators runs to the top of the main tower, 249 feet from the ground, and from this level there is a stairway, by means of which visitors may ascend to the topmost cupola, just below the feet of Diana. The view of New York and the surrounding country which is had from the top of the Madison-Square-Garden tower is one that cannot be seen from any other point, and is paralleled only by that from the dome of the Pulitzer Building, $2\frac{1}{4}$ miles farther down-town. Manhattan Island, North River, East River, and broad sections of Long Island and New Jersey, are at the feet of the visitors. The building is lighted in every part by electricity. There is a complete plant of engines, dynamos, etc., in the basement, and about 6,800 incandescent lamps are in use. Some hundreds are disposed about the roof, the roof-garden, cupolas and main tower, and around the figure of Diana. When the edifice is fully illuminated at night, it presents a spectacle the beauty of which is unsurpassed. It becomes an object of great interest, and can be seen from thousands of points of view in New York and vicinity.

The cost of the Madison-Square-Garden building was about \$3,000,000. It is owned by the Madison-Square-Garden Company, among the stock-holders of which are J. Pierpont Morgan, James T. Woodward, Charles Lanier, Alfred B. Darling, Hiram Hitchcock, Darius O. Mills, Charles Crocker, and Adolph Ladenburg. William F. Wharton is the manager.

The site of the building was occupied for nearly twenty years by the older Madison-Square Garden, which was the abandoned passenger-station of the New-York Central & Hudson-River Railroad, remodelled. It was at one time called Gilmore's Garden, because of a series of popular concerts, given under the direction of the famous band-master, P. S. Gilmore.

The Garden Theatre is a portion of the Madison-Square Garden structure, although the management is distinct. It is in the Madison-Avenue and 27th-Street corner, and occupies a space 115 feet long and 70 wide. The entrance is at the extreme corner, through a lobby and foyer, which together occupy the entire front of the theatre. The auditorium, with eight boxes, a balcony, and a gallery, has a seating capacity of about 1,200. The interior gives one the impression of costliness in the construction and decoration, for the bases of the box tiers, and the heavy columns which form the frames of the outer proscenium arch, are of onyx. The walls are hung with silk, in tints of light yellow and cream. The stage is 39 feet deep and 70 feet wide. The Garden Theatre was opened to the public on September 27, 1890, with the production of the farcical comedy entitled *Dr. Bill.* The most significant production that has ever been made on its stage was that of the comic opera, *La Cigale,* which ran nearly all the season of 1891-92. The house is under the management of T. Henry French, and comic operas are the principal attractions.

The Metropolitan Opera-House, which occupies the whole block bounded by Broadway, Seventh Avenue and 39th and 40th Streets, was perhaps the second establishment of importance on the continent. In some sense it may be considered the first, as it was the only permanent home of grand opera. It was built by a corporation, composed largely of men who were unable, several years ago, to secure boxes at the Academy of Music, which was then the only opera-house in the city. The cost was about \$1,500,000. The building is of buff brick, stone and iron, in the Italian Renaissance style of architecture. The exterior dimensions are : on Broadway, 205 feet ; 39th Street, 284 feet ; Seventh Avenue, 197 feet ; 40th Street, 229 feet. Each of the Broadway corners, occupying a space of about seventy feet square, rises to a height of seven stories. The lower floors are occupied, one by the Bank of New Amsterdam, and the other as a restaurant. The second story of the 39th-Street corner is one of a suite of assembly-rooms. The upper stories of both corners are laid out in apartments for dwellings. The intervening section on Broadway is carried to a height of full four stories, and, is devoted to the purposes of the Opera-House, and to such other apartments as will increase the convenience of the establishment for balls and extensive social functions. The main auditorium occupies the geographical centre of the block. It is reached from the front, through a vestibule 65 by 35 feet, and from either side, through vestibules which are 33 feet wide, and 70 and 50 feet in length, respectively. All three vesti-bules open into a semi-circular corridor, which extends around the auditorium to the proscenium-wall on either side. The box tiers and upper circles are approached by a magnificent double stairway, which rises from either side of the front vestibule and joins in a single stairway above the first tier, and by four other stairways lead-ing from the side vestibules. Within, the auditorium is surrounded by two tiers of boxes, and three balconies, making in all five galleries. There are 73 boxes in the two tiers, and twelve below the first tier, near the stage, six on either side, on a level with the main floor. There are 584 seats in the parquet, 750 in the balcony and dress-circle, and 930 in the gallery ; the total seating capacity, including the boxes, is 3,500. The tone of the decoration is in old gold. There are figures repre-senting The Chorus and The Ballet, on the pilasters at the sides of the curtain opening ; and above the middle of the arch, there is an allegory, with Apollo as the central figure. Statues of the Muses are placed in niches at either side. Strictly speaking, there is no proscenium. The great curtain opening is 48 by 50 feet. The stage, which is the largest in the country, is 101 feet wide, 90 feet deep, and 150 feet high, to the roof. As a consequence, the scenic outfits are made on a gigantic scale. On either side of the stage, facing 39th and 40th Streets respectively, are large apartments which are used as executive offices. Above the vestibules and the three entrances, are assembly-rooms, parlors, retiring-rooms, toilet-rooms, and other accessory apartments. A feature of the stage is a fine organ, which has ten speaking stops and 661 pipes. It occupies a position next to the proscenium wall on the south side, twenty feet above the stage floor.· The key-box is at the left end of the orchestra space and the action is electric. The house was thought to be fire-proof. The partitions are all of masonry ; the floors of iron beams and brick arches ; and the roof of iron and brick. The Opera-House was opened October 22, 1883, with a performance of *Faust* in Italian. Henry E. Abbey was the manager, and Italo Campanini and Christine Nilsson were the prin-cipals of the cast. Mr. Abbey's management ended for the time being in the spring following. In the fall of 1884 a season of German opera was begun, under the management of Edmund C. Stanton, acting in the interests of the stockholders, and with Leopold Damrosch as Musical Director. The giving of German opera was an experiment in those days, but it was so successful, especially in an artistic sense, that a similar policy was pursued for the six years following. During that period, all Wagner's operas (excepting *Parsifal*) were produced in magnificent style, some of them for the first time in America. In the spring of 1891 the stockholders decided to set aside German opera for the time being, and contracted with Henry E. Abbey for a season of Italian and French opera, to be given during the winter of 1891 and 1892. A fire destroyed the interior of this supposed fire-proof opera-house on August 27, 1892. New York will continue to have one of the great opera-houses of the world, for a newly formed company of wealthy and influential citizens is now rebuilding the burnt-out auditorium. Among these men are George G. Haven, Adrian Iselin, Elbridge T. Gerry, Edward Cooper, J. Pierpont Morgan, S. D. Babcock, S. P. Wetmore, Perry Belmont, D. O. Mills, Henry Clews, W. C. Whitney, John Jacob Astor, and Cornelius, Frederick and W. K. Vanderbilt. The fact that the Opera-House has not been financially profitable is offset by the benefit derived by the people from the musical culture developed here.

METROPOLITAN · OPERA-HOUSE.
BROADWAY, SEVENTH AVENUE, 39TH AND 40TH STREETS.

Music Hall, at the southeast corner of Seventh Avenue and 57th Street, is the next in magnitude of the principal establishments to which reference has been made.   It was built by a corporation known as the Music-Hall Company, of the stock of which Andrew Carnegie owns about nine-tenths.   The material of construction is brick and terra cotta.   The architecture is simple, but rich.   The 57th-Street front is a modification of the modern Renaissance.   The centre of the façade, a space 80 feet broad, is divided into a series of five arches, which serve collectively as the main entrance.   Above these is a similar series which extends through two stories ; and still above, a series of small double arches, which extends to the main cornice. Still above is a plain roof, of the style known as the Mansard.   The appearance presented by the exterior is one of dignity, rather than of beauty.   In so far as the arrangement of wall-openings indicates, the building is of six stories, but the floor lines are irregularly placed, and only a small portion of the edifice conforms to that arrangement.   The principal feature of the building is the grand concert-hall, which occupies the main part of the ground-floor. . It is a magnificent auditorium, with seats for 3,000 people, and standing room for 1,000 more.   The entrance leads to a vestibule 70 feet long, the ceiling of which is a semi-circular vault, 25 feet high. The vestibule opens into a spacious corridor, which extends around three sides of the hall, and from both angles of which broad stairways lead to the box tiers, dress-circle and balcony.   The parquet floor, which of itself seats over 1,000 persons, has nine exits to the corridor, and the latter and the main vestibule have doors opening upon the three streets.   The upper circles do not extend to the proscenium-wall, but terminate at points on the side-walls farther and farther back as they rise.   This arrangement brings the ceiling into view, and (it is claimed) improves the acoustic properties.   The decorations are in ivory and gold, relieved with tints of old rose.   The stage is an integral part of the hall, and has no theatrical equipment, the hall having been designed purely for concerts and lectures.   The hall is lighted by electricity.   The incandescent lamps are so disposed in the cornices and decorative work that very few of them are in sight of any one in the audience.   The effect of lighting is something like that of sunlight coming over one's shoulder.   In the basement below the grand hall, and having a separate entrance on 57th Street, is Recital Hall, the seating capacity of which is 1,200.   These two large halls are so connected by stairways and ante-rooms that they may easily be transformed into a ball-room and banquet-hall for use on a great social occasion.   Connected with Recital Hall is an extensive kitchen. Above the latter, on the street level, is a dining-room.   On the second story there is a grand drawing-room ; on the third, a chamber music hall, with seating capacity of 450 ; on the fourth, a chapter-room, so-called, which sometimes serves the purpose of an additional chamber music room, and on the fifth, still another hall of similar size.   The roof-story is laid out in offices and music studios, which are very conveniently arranged for the purposes of instruction or recital, or other kindred uses.   There are in the building numbers of parlors, retiring rooms, cloak-rooms, and the like ; and the entire edifice is so arranged that the different portions may be used for the special purposes for which they were planned, with complete isolation, or all may be thrown into connection for a grand social event, as easily as the apartments in a private residence.   A grand musical festival, which was begun on May 5, 1891, and lasted five days, was the dedicating event in Music Hall, although Recital Hall had then been in service for some weeks.   The festival was carried out jointly by the Symphony and Oratorio Societies, with the assistance of a boys' choir of 100 voices, and eighteen prominent solo singers, among whom were Frau Antonia Mielke, Mlle. Clementine de Vere, Frau Marie Ritter-Goetze, Sig. Italo

Campanini, Herr Theodor Reichmann and Herr Emil Fischer. Walter Damrosch was the director, and he was assisted by P. Tschaikowsky, an eminent Russian composer, who led the orchestra in the interpretation of a number of his own compositions.

The building of Music Hall was largely in the nature of an experiment, and experience has shown that extensive alterations will be necessary to make it a thoroughly available property. Plans have been perfected, therefore, for rebuilding, which will involve an expense nearly equal to the first cost. The corner-lot on

CARNEGIE MUSIC HALL, SEVENTH AVENUE, SOUTHEAST CORNER OF 57TH STREET.

56th Street has been purchased, and it is intended to extend the building over it; to continue the edifice several stories higher; and to provide a large number of studios and offices. When these changes shall have been made, Music Hall will be one of the foremost centres of culture and elegance in the Empire City, and the home of art and melody.

The Casino is one of the picturesque buildings in New-York City. It stands on the southeast corner of Broadway and 39th Street, and is a fine illustration of the Arabesque or Moorish style of architecture. The materials are terra cotta, brick and sandstone. As viewed from the corner diagonally opposite, it presents a round tower, surmounted by a Moorish dome, at the street angle; a curved overhanging gallery at the upper story on the 39th-Street side; and an open colonnade, which rises above the roof on the Broadway front. The dimensions of the building are 144 by 107 feet. The interior architecture corresponds with the exterior appearance. The auditorium, which is in the second story, and is reached by means of a wide marble stairway from a spacious lobby on the 39th-Street side, is decorated in plastic materials, of which asbestos forms a considerable part.   Everywhere is seen the low horse-shoe arch, the semi-spherical dome, the low colonnade, and the lattice work, which are characteristic of Moorish architecture.   The seating capacity is about 2,000.   There are 16 boxes, a balcony, and (in place of the usual gallery) a buffet floor, virtually an open smoking-room, with the performance in view.   The stage is 40 feet wide, and 32 feet deep.   A feature of the Casino is its roof-garden, where in hot weather one may partake of refreshments, and listen to the orchestral music. The garden, tower and overhanging balcony are brilliantly lighted with electricity at night.   The Casino was built and is owned by the New-York Concert Company, and was intended as a concert-hall, but from the outset until recently it has been a permanent home for comic opera.   It was opened October 22, 1882, with a perform- ance of *The Queen's Lace Handkerchief.*   Its most famous production was that of *Erminie,* which in several runs has been performed upwards of 1,000 times.   In the fall of 1892 the proprietors of the Casino abandoned the field of comic opera, rearranged the auditorium and stage of the house, and turned it into a concert-hall of the English type.   The manager is Rudolph Aronson.

Palmer's Theatre, at Broadway and 30th Street, is often spoken of as the leading theatre in America ; partly because it is the play-house with which the name of Lester Wallack was most recently associated, and partly because of the prestige of the present manager, Albert M. Palmer, who had achieved distinct success at the

PALMER'S THEATRE (AS IT IS), BROADWAY, NORTHEAST CORNER OF 30TH STREET.

Union-Square and Madison-Square Theatres before he took charge of this house. This prestige is also made evident by the fact that Mr. Palmer has been president of the Actors' Fund ever since it was founded.   The theatre was built by Lester Wallack and Theodore Moss, and opened January 4, 1882, with a performance of *School for Scandal*, with John Gilbert, Harry Edwards, Osmond Tearle, Gerald Eyre, Rose Coghlan, Mme. Ponisi and Stella Boniface in the cast. Mrs. Langtry made her debut in America on its stage in *An Unequal Match*, November 6, 1882. Lester Wallack retired from the management early in 1887, and during the season of 1887-88 the affairs of the house were conducted by Henry E. Abbey. Mr. Palmer took possession as manager in September, 1888. Theodore Moss is now the owner. The engagement of Mary Anderson, her last in this city; the production of *Antony and Cleopatra*, by Mrs. James Brown Potter; and the engagement of the Coquelin-Hading Company were the principal events of Mr. Palmer's first season; the productions of *Samson*, by Salvini, the famous Italian tragedian, and of *Richard III.*, by Richard Mansfield, were significant occurrences of his second. E. S. Willard, an English actor of great ability, occupied the stage during the third; and Mr. Palmer's own stock-company furnished the attractions during the fourth, which ended April 30, 1892. In the summer, Palmer's Theatre is given over to comic opera.

PALMER'S THEATRE (WHEN COMPLETED), BROADWAY AND WEST 30TH STREET.

The house has a frontage of 92 feet on Broadway, and of 150 feet on West 30th Street. The auditorium stands back from both streets, and is skirted by a portion of the projected lofty and magnificent edifice, which is now completed for two stories only. The entrance lobby and main foyer on the first story, and a grand foyer on the second, which is reached by two wide stairways, occupy the Broadway front for the full width of the theatre proper, which is 75 feet. There is a side entrance, used principally by people who arrive in carriages, on 30th Street. The rest of the incomplete building fronting on both streets, is devoted to stores and business offices. The auditorium is handsomely decorated in dark tints, relieved with gold. There are seats in the parquet, balcony, gallery and boxes for 1,200 people. The stage measures 70 by 35 feet, and is entered from 30th Street. Palmer's Theatre may invariably be depended on as worthy of the best and most fastidious patronage.

Daly's Theatre occupies the centre of the block on the west side of Broadway, between 29th and 30th Streets. Its front is an unpretentious brick building, of three stories and a Mansard roof, the single feature of which is a portico which covers the entrance to a lobby, twenty-five feet wide. The lobby leads, by succeeding stairways of half a dozen steps each, into a foyer, which is nearly as large as the

38

auditorium into which it opens. The auditorium is richly decorated, dark red and gold being the prevailing tints. There are eight boxes, a balcony and a gallery, and the seating capacity is about 1,400. The stage is very large, and the accessory building in the rear for dressing-rooms and scenery unusually spacious. An addition extending at right angles to 29th Street was built in 1892. Daly's Theatre is the home of the most famous stock-company in America, a company which, with Ada Rehan as the leading lady, has won repeated triumphs in London, Paris and Berlin. The productions are mainly Shakespeare's comedies and plays adapted by Augustin Daly from German or French sources. A peculiarity of the business management is that a person who purchases a seat in advance does not receive the conventional theatre-ticket, but simply a strip of paper, bearing upon its face two numbers, which are meaningless, apparently, but which prove to the attachés of the house the right of the holder to enter the theatre at a specific performance, and to seats which are designated upon a coupon, which is given to him at the gate. This method was adopted to put an end to ticket speculation. As the strip of paper bears no evidence on its face that it is a theatre-ticket, it is not salable. Daly's Theatre was opened as Banvard's Museum, in 1867, and during the succeeding twelve years it was variously known as Wood's Museum and Metropolitan Theatre, Wood's Museum and Menagerie, and the Broadway Theatre. In its early days it was both a museum and a play-house, and in the early 70's it was the home of burlesque. Augustin Daly took possession, remodelled it, and gave it its present name in 1879. The house was again remodelled in 1891.

The Empire Theatre is a new play-house, on 40th Street, near Broadway, on which is the main entrance. It was built by Hayman and Sanger, and leased for a term of ten years by Charles Frohman and Rich & Harris. Work upon the foundation was begun on May 1, 1892. The theatre proper is 100 feet square, and seats 1,050 people. Charles Frohman's stock company has occupied the stage. The theatre is in the style of the First Empire. The top story on Broadway is of terra cotta, the next two of pressed Roman brick, and the two lower stories of Indiana limestone. The auditorium is frescoed in crimson and gold, and lighted by clusters of electric lights. The interior is rich, quiet and restful. The Empire is not a large theatre, but is one of the most comfortable and luxurious in the country.

The Manhattan Opera House is on West 34th Street, between Broadway and Seventh Avenue. This also is one of the new theatres, having been erected by Oscar Hammerstein, in 1892–93, for the purposes of opera. The entrance is one of the finest in New York, and conducts to a splendid auditorium, seating 2,500 persons. There are 72 boxes ; and the great gallery seats 2,500 persons.

The American Theatre, at the southeastern corner of Eighth Avenue and West 42d Street, was opened for the first time in 1893, and attained immediate popularity. It has a very rich and attractive interior, beautifully decorated and adorned. The auditorium seats 1,800 persons. The stage is of unusual size, and elaborately equipped with machinery, to facilitate the spectacular productions which the theatre gives. The manager of the American is T. Henry French.

Abbey's Theatre, the newest of the great places of amusement in which New York delights, combines in its construction and decoration all the comforts and beauties of the last decade of the nineteenth century. It was finished in 1893. The situation of the building is peculiarly favorable, in the heart of the theatre district, at the corner of Broadway and 38th Street, and adjoining the Casino. The long and successful experience of Mr. Abbey as a manager ensures for this establishment a prominent and worthy place among the most notable theatres of New York and of the world.

BROADWAY AND 40TH STREET, SHOWING EMPIRE THEATRE AND ORIENTAL HOTEL.

EIGHTH AVENUE AND 42D STREET. SHOWING AMERICAN THEATRE.

The Lyceum Theatre, a parlor play-house, is on the west side of Fourth Avenue, between 23d and 24th Streets. The building is 50 feet wide and 125 feet deep. The first floor is devoted to an entrance lobby, business offices, cloak and smoking rooms, and stage dressing-rooms. The theatre proper is on the second floor. The auditorium is decorated in dark colors. There are four boxes and a balcony, and the seating capacity is 700. The stage is $47\frac{1}{2}$ feet wide and 50 feet deep. The house is owned by the New-York Theatre Company, a corporation of which Brent Good is the president and Daniel Frohman manager. The theatre was opened in April, 1885, with a production of Steele Mackaye's play *Dakolar*. Helen Dauvray and her company gave the performances for the seasons of 1885–6 and 1886–7, and the Lyceum-Theatre stock-company was organized in November, 1886. The policy of the management is to present modern society dramas of English and American authorship. During the season of 1893–4 the house will be devoted to the seventh annual appearance of E. H. Sothern and the seventh annual season of the Lyceum-Theatre stock-company.

The Fifth-Avenue Theatre is the fourth play-house that has borne that name. It is on the north side of West 28th Street, a few feet from Broadway ; on the site of its namesake, which was burned on January 2, 1891. It is one of the handsomest theatres in the country. The 28th-Street front, which is the broadside of the building, is in the style of the Italian Renaissance, very elaborate in the detail of its ornamentation, in which free use has been made of the emblems of the drama. An architectural feature of this front is a 'handsome portico, which covers a portion of the sidewalk, and serves as a commodious fire-escape. All of the windows are filled with stained glass. There are two principal entrances, one of which is sheltered by the portico, and opens into the main foyer, an apartment 40 feet long and 15 feet wide, and from which a wide marble stairway leads to the upper boxes and balcony. The other entrance is through a lobby 50 feet long and 12 feet wide, which leads from Broadway to the rear of the orchestra. The floors of the foyer and lobby are laid in white marble, and the walls are divided into panels by pilasters and columns of Mycenian marble. In the auditorium the decorations are in tint, grading from a dark crimson to pink, with ornamentations in ivory and gold. The distinctive architectural feature is the great semi-spherical dome of steel and tiles, silver and blue in tints, around the base of which extends a series of panels, containing figures of the Muses. There are eight boxes, a balcony and a gallery, both of which extend well forward, and the seating capacity is 1,400. The auditorium is 68 feet wide and 64 feet deep, and the height of the dome is 65 feet. The stage is 80 by 35 feet. The Fifth-Avenue Theatre was built by the executors of the Peter-Gilsey estate, and is leased to Manager Henry C. Miner. It was opened on May 28, 1892, with a production of the comic opera, *The Robber of the Rhine*. Its predecessor was built by the Gilsey estate in 1873, on the site of a building which was opened October 16, 1868, as Apollo Hall, and was variously known as Newcomb's Hall and the St. James Theatre, and used for concert and minstrel performances. Augustin Daly became manager December 3, 1873, and named the new house the Fifth-Avenue. During his tenancy of four years he gained fame but lost money. Succeeding managers were Stephen Fiske, Daniel H. Harkins, John H. Haverly, John Stetson, Eugene Tompkins and Henry C. Miner. The house was the scene of Mary Anderson's New-York debut, November 12, 1877 ; of Modjeska's New-York debut, December 22, 1877 ; of the first authorized performance in America of Gilbert and Sullivan's famous opera, *The Mikado*, September 24, 1885 ; and of Mrs. James Brown Potter's debut, October 31, 1887. At the time of the fire the attraction was Fanny Davenport's production of Sardou's *Cleopatra*.

Hoyt's Madison-Square Theatre is a handsome play-house on the south side of West 24th Street, near Broadway. The front of the main building, fifty feet wide, is of granite, and there is an extension of brick, which contains the entrance-lobby, dressing-rooms and offices. The auditorium is finished in carved mahogany and other rare woods, and is one of the handsomest in the city. The seating capacity is 800. A peculiarity of the stage is that it consists of two platforms, like the roof and floor of an elevator, one thirty-five feet above the other. Either platform is brought to the proper level at will, by means of counter-weights. This peculiarity

enables the management to furnish elaborate and solid scenic settings, without necessitating any waits between the acts. The theatre was built in 1879 and 1880, by the Mallory brothers, for Steele Mackaye, and was opened on February 4, 1880, with the production of *Hazel Kirke*, which had a run of about 456 performances. Mackaye's tenancy was short. Daniel Frohman succeeded him as manager. Albert M. Palmer took possession, as a partner of the Mallorys, on September 1, 1884, and organized a stock-company for the house. Hoyt & Thomas (Charles H. Hoyt and Charles W. Thomas) succeeded as managers on September 15, 1891, and produced Hoyt's farcical comedy, *A Trip to Chinatown.* This piece had a run of about a year. Both the managers are young men, and have been singularly successful. They began in

HOYT'S MADISON-SQUARE THEATRE, 24TH STREET, NEAR BROADWAY.

the spring of 1884. The site of this theatre was occupied in 1865 by Christy's Minstrel Hall. This building was later leased and remodelled by James Fisk, and opened January 5, 1869, as Brougham's Theatre. It was rechristened the Fifth-Avenue Theatre, April 5th following, and leased to Augustin Daly. It was the first of the four different theatres which have borne that name. It was the scene of the first performance in America of *Frou Frou*, on January 15, 1870, and of Clara Morris's New-York debut, on September 30th of the same year. It was burned on January 1, 1873. It was rebuilt in 1877, and opened on December 10th as Fifth-Avenue Hall. and was so known until rebuilt by the Mallorys.

Harrigan's Theatre occupies a plot of ground 75 by 100 feet, on the north side of West 35th Street, east of Sixth Avenue.   The front is in the Italian Renaissance style, of buff brick and terra cotta.   The auditorium is decorated in tints of ivory, with gold ornamentation.   There are seats in the orchestra, six boxes, a balcony and a gallery, for about 800 people.   The theatre was built by Edward Harrigan, well-known both as an actor and as a writer of Irish comedies.   It was opened December 29, 1890, with the production of Mr. Harrigan's play, *Reilly and the 400.*

The Broadway Theatre, one of the largest in the city, is at Broadway, 41st Street and Seventh Avenue.   It is 92 feet wide on Broadway, and has an average depth of 160 feet.   The front, of Anderson pressed brick, five stories high, presents an imposing appearance.   The entrance is through a spacious arch, the crown of which reaches through the second story.   The lobby, 24 by 18 feet, opens into a foyer, 72½ by 15 feet, from either end of which an iron stairway leads to the balcony. The decorations are Romanesque, in dull colors, varying from maroon to antique pink.   Most of the incandescent lamps by which the house is lighted are so placed in the ceiling, proscenium-arch and decorations as to appear like stars.   There are seats for 700 people on the orchestra-floor ; and the capacity of ten boxes, the balcony and the gallery bring the total up to 1,776.   The stage is 75 feet wide and 48 feet deep.   The house was built by the Broadway-Theatre Company, consisting of Elliot Zborowski, T. Henry French and Frank W. Sanger ; and was opened on March 3, 1888, with a production of *La Tosca* by Fanny Davenport.   Mr. Sanger managed the house up to the present season of 1892-93, when he sold out and was succeeded by Mr. French.   The house is devoted to comic opera, the Francis Wilson and De Wolf Hopper companies alternating in possession of the stage during the regular seasons.   The site of the Broadway was occupied from May, 1880, until the construction of the new theatre was begun, in 1887, by a building erected by Zborowski, Rudolph Aronson and others as a concert-hall, and variously known as the Metropolitan Concert-Hall, Metropolitan Casino, Alcazar, Cosmopolitan Theatre, and Skating-Rink.   It was the scene not only of musical and dramatic performances, but also of sporting events.

The Bijou Theatre, distinctively the home of farce comedy, or variety farce, is a little play-house on the west side of Broadway, between 30th and 31st Streets. It is long and narrow, the width of the building being only 40 feet, while the depth of the auditorium is sufficient for thirty rows of seats.   The seating capacity of the orchestra, balcony, gallery and eight boxes, is about 1,400.   The stage is 38 by 37 feet.   The house, which is owned by Edward F. James, was built on leasehold title by Miles & Barton, and was opened in the fall of 1883, Edward E. Rice having charge of the performances.   Its fame rests upon the long run of the burlesque *Adonis*, with Henry E. Dixey in the principal role, which held the stage from October, 1884, to the spring of 1886.   Alexander Herrmann succeeded Miles & Barton as lessee in 1887, and transferred his lease to J. Wesley Rosenquest, the present manager, a year later.   Travelling companies give the performances.   There was on the site previous to Miles & Barton's tenancy a theatre, which had been remodelled from Jerry Thomas's saloon, a place of considerable publicity twenty years ago, and which was variously known as the Theatre Brighton, the St.-James Theatre and the Bijou Opera House.   The last manager, in 1881-82, was John A. McCaull, who produced a number of comic operas, among them *The Snake-Charmer*, in the performance of which Lillian Russell came prominently before the public, and was received with continuous and enthusiastic applause.

Proctor's Theatre, at 141 West 23d Street, is a picturesque structure, unique in that it is an example of the peculiarly sombre but pleasing Flemish style of architecture. It has a frontage of 75 feet, and a depth of 137½ feet, with an extension 25 feet wide, which runs to 24th Street. The material is brick set in dark cement. The building stands a few feet back from the sidewalk line, and the intervening space is covered by a closed porch with a tiled roof. The entrance lobby is of the full width of the building, and has a wide stairway at either end, leading to the upper circles. There are twelve boxes, a balcony and a gallery, besides the orchestra floor, and the seating capacity is 1,717. The decorations are in soft tints of grey-

blue, on the ceiling, running into red and old gold on the walls. The scenery is handled from the main floor by means of a system of counter-weights. Proctor's Theatre was built and is owned by Alfred B. Darling, senior partner of the firm of Hitchcock, Darling & Co., of the Fifth-Avenue Hotel; and it is leased for twenty years to Frederick P. Proctor. It is absolutely fireproof. The architect was H. Edwards-Ficken. It was opened on March 5, 1888, with a production of *The County Fair.* Its site was once occupied by the 79th-Regiment Armory, which in 1882 was converted by Salmi Morse into a "Temple," in which he proposed to present a Passion Play. A dress rehearsal was actually

PROCTOR'S THEATRE, 141 WEST 23D STREET, NEAR SIXTH AVENUE.

held on February 16, 1883, but Mr. Morse was enjoined from giving a performance. Then the place was known as the Twenty-third-Street Theatre, and had several managers, among whom was Max Strakosch. Then it was rechristened the Twenty-third-Street Tabernacle and used for religious meetings. It was the place in which Munkacsy's painting of *Christ before Pilate* was exhibited, in 1886.

Proctor's Theatre is now devoted to amusement for women and children, and is conducted as a woman's club, with colored boys and girls as uniformed pages and waiting maids. The performance, on the lines of the French family vaudeville Theatre, begins at 10.30 A. M., and continues until 10.30 at night.

The **Standard Theatre**, a combination house, so called, in that its stage is occupied by traveling companies, is geographically speaking, on Sixth Avenue, between 32d and 33d Streets, but by law that portion of what apparently should be the west side of Sixth Avenue is declared to be Broadway. Legally, therefore, the location of the Standard is at 1287 Broadway. The front is 75 feet wide, and six stories high, and is built of brick, painted white. The house has a seating capacity of 1,200, and a large stage. The auditorium is decorated in conventional style, with little attempt at artistic effect. There are eight boxes, a balcony and a gallery. The performances given at the Standard are usually of a high grade. The original Standard was built in 1873, and opened by Josh Hart, as the Eagle Theatre. It was leased and re-named the Standard by William Henderson, in 1875 ; and was burned December 14, 1883. John Duff was the first manager of the present house. The present manager, James M. Hill, took possession in January, 1890. The most significant performances of recent years were those of Sarah Bernhardt and her company, in November, 1891.

The **Park Theatre**, the second to bear the name since the final destruction of the historic house on Park Row, is at the northwest corner of Broadway and 35th Street. It was built in 1883, partly of the material taken from Booth's Theatre when that house was demolished. The owners are Hyde & Behman, of Brooklyn. It was occupied by Edward Harrigan's company from 1885 to 1890, and the plays presented were the Irish comedies written by that author-actor. William M. Dunlevy was the manager from September 1, 1890, until May, 1892, and ran it as a combination house, with variety farces as the attractions. The house is now a variety theatre, managed by the owners. The seating capacity is 1,800 ; and the stage is quite large.

Herrmann's Theatre is on Broadway, between 28th and 29th Streets. The façade is of galvanized zinc, indented with arches of vari-colored glass, which gives, when lighted, a brilliant effect. The lobby is of tessellated marble and prismatic glass. The theatre is toned in terra cotta, cream and old gold, and is carpeted in color harmonizing. The stage is 43 x 28 feet, surmounted by an oil-painting over the proscenium arch representing the apotheosis of Music. The theatre was originally opened as the San-Francisco Minstrel Hall, in 1873. It was afterward known as the Comedy Theatre, and from 1886 to 1890 as Dockstader's Minstrel House. Herrmann, the magician, under a lease from the Gilsey estate, remodelled and practically rebuilt the theatre, enlarging it and beautifying it. Under his management the house was opened October 4, 1890.

The **Star Theatre**, at Broadway and 13th Street, is the Wallack's Theatre best remembered as such by theatre-goers of the present generation. It was there that the name Wallack gained its brightest laurels. It was opened September 25, 1861, with James W. Wallack, Sr., as manager ; but he never appeared on its stage ; and to all intents John Lester Wallack was the manager as well as the leading actor from the outset. During twenty years there were in the company such actors as Charles Fisher, John Sefton, Mark Smith, John Gilbert, James Williamson, E. L. Davenport, J. H. Stoddard, Harry Montague, Dion Boucicault, Charles Coghlan, Fanny Morant, Rose Eytinge, Katherine Rogers and Rose Coghlan. Among the plays presented were standard old comedies and the best of the works of contemporaneous English dramatists. The house and the company were famous for the general excellence of the productions, rather than for the brilliancy of particular events. The name Wallack's Theatre disappeared in 1881, and for a time the house was known as the Germania Theatre. In 1883, it was rechristened the Star. Theodore Moss, Wallack's old business-partner, has been the manager for many years.

BROADWAY AND 28TH STREET, SHOWING FIFTH-AVENUE THEATRE, GILSEY BUILDING, AND HERRMANN'S THEATRE.

BROADWAY AND 39TH STREET, SHOWING CASINO THEATRE, ABBEY'S THEATRE, AND HOTEL NORMANDIE.

He remodelled the interior of the house in 1883, and again in 1889. Of late, it has been considered a first-class combination house, and its stage has been occupied by the best travelling stars and companies. The building is 75 feet wide and 148 feet deep. The stage is 48 by 45 feet, and the seating capacity of the auditorium is 1,600.

The **Union-Square Theatre,** on 14th Street, facing the Square from which it derives its name, is the successor of the original Union-Square, which was built by Sheridan Shook, and opened as a variety-house September 11, 1871. Albert M. Palmer became Mr. Shook's partner and the responsible manager September 17, 1872, and during the eleven years succeeding made the house famous by the production of such plays as *The Two Orphans,* Sardou's *Agnes, Led Astray, Miss Multon, The Danicheffs, A Celebrated Case, The Banker's Daughter* and *A Parisian Romance,* each of which had a long run. The Union-Square Theatre stock-company was considered second only to that of Wallack's Theatre. James W. Collier succeeded as manager in 1883, and James M. Hill as lessee and manager in 1886. The house was burned February 28, 1888, and was rebuilt by the Cortlandt-Palmer estate, the owner of the land, and reopened by Hill March 27, 1889. Since then it has been a first-class combination house. Greenwall & Pierson are now the managers, having taken Hill's lease May 14, 1892. The new Union-Square Theatre is entered from 14th Street through a main lobby, 49 by 33 feet. The auditorium, with its orchestra, balcony and gallery and eight boxes, will accommodate 1,300 people. The decorations are in ivory and gold. The stage, 55 by 33 feet, is entered by a passage-way which leads from Fourth Avenue.

The **Fourteenth-Street Theatre,** on 14th Street, west of Sixth Avenue, was built in 1866, and opened on May 26th as the Theatre Français, under the management of Guegnet & Drivet. Jacob Grau became the lessee on August 25th, and under his management Ristori made her first appearance in America, September 20, 1866, in *Medea. La Grande Duchesse* was first presented here in its entirety in French September 24, 1867, and *La Belle Hélène* was first performed, with Tostee in the title role, September 24, 1867. Charles Fechter purchased and rebuilt the house in 1871, renaming it the Lyceum, but lost control of it through financial embarrassment. W. L. Mauser, J. H. McVicker, James M. Hill, John H. Haverly (who gave his own name to the house), Samuel Colville, Bartley Campbell and Colville & Gilmore were managers in succession. Mr. Colville, who gave the house its present name, died in 1886, and J. Wesley Rosenquest, the present manager, purchased various conflicting interests in the lease November 1, 1886. The Fourteenth-Street Theatre is a first-class combination house, in which plays slightly melodramatic or sensational are the principal attraction. The front is unique, in that it presents the appearance of two very high stories with a double portico, supported by columns, and a permanent canopy which extends over the sidewalk. The entrance lobby is shallow, and opens directly upon the auditorium. There are eight boxes, a balcony and a gallery, and the seating capacity is 1,600. The stage is 73 by 45 feet, with an extension 14 feet wide, which runs through the block to 15th Street. The building is owned by the estate of Marshall O. Roberts.

The **Irving-Place Theatre** (formerly Amberg's), the German play-house, is at the southwest corner of 15th Street and Irving Place. It is a picturesque structure, of the Spanish-Moresque style of architecture, constructed of mottled yellow and dark red brick, with terra-cotta trimmings. The building is 75 by 125 feet. The auditorium is reached through two shallow lobbies, from Irving Place. The decorations and hangings are of a deep red tint. There are ten boxes, a balcony and a gallery ; and the seating capacity is 1,250. The stage is 70 feet wide and 40 deep. The theatre was opened December 1, 1888, and since then has been the home of Amberg's stock-company, a double organization, suited to both dramatic and operatic performances. An interesting event in the history of the house was the appearance there of the Muenchener Company, on November 5, 1890. The theatre occupies the site of Irving Hall, which was opened on December 20, 1860, for balls, lectures and concerts, and which was famous for many years as the rendezvous of one faction of the local Democratic party, to which it gave its name.

The Grand Opera-House, at the northwest corner of Eighth Avenue and West 23d Street, is in some respects the most imposing in appearance of the older theatres. The front building, through which there is a wide entrance from either street to a common lobby, is six stories in height, and is built of marble. The theatre proper stands parallel to and back from 23d Street. A striking feature seen on entering is the grand foyer, the largest in any theatre in the city, open in part to the roof. A stairway of unusual width leads to the balcony. The auditorium has seats in the orchestra, balcony, gallery and boxes for 2,000 people, and standing room for 1,500 more. It is magnificent in its outlines and proportions, but the decorations are sombre. The stage, one of the largest in New York, is eighty feet wide and seventy feet deep, and the green-room is much the most extensive in the city. The house was built by Samuel N. Pike, the builder of Pike's Opera-House, in Cincinnati ; and was opened January 9, 1868, as Pike's Opera-House, with a performance of *Il Trovatore*, given under the direction of Max Strakosch. James Fisk and Jay Gould purchased the house in March, 1869, but Gould's name was withdrawn from the enterprise on March 31st. Fisk gave the theatre its present name, and made it famous by his grand spectacular and ballet productions, such as that of *The Tempest*, with which he began his career as manager, and of *Twelve Temptations*, on February 7, 1870. After Fisk's death Mr. Gould purchased the property, and for several seasons, under various lessees and managers, grand opera in Italian, spectacles and extensive dramatic productions were seen on its stage. Pauline Lucca made her first appearance there, October 6, 1873, and Ilma di Murska first sang in America the following night. For ten years the Grand Opera-House has been a second-class combination house, so classed because the price of the best seat is one dollar. Joseph H. Tooker, Poole & Donnelly and Henry E. Abbey succeeded each other as managers. T. Henry French, the present lessee, took possession November 23, 1885.

The Academy of Music occupies a plot of ground 117 by 204 feet, at the northeast corner of 14th Street and Irving Place. It is an imposing building in its outlines, rather than in architecture. The original Academy was built in 1854, by a corporation, as a permanent home for Italian opera. It was opened on October 2d of that year, with a performance of *Norma*, by the Grisi and Mario Company. It was burned on May 22, 1866 ; and the present Academy, built on the same site, was opened in February, 1868. Max Maretzek, Jacob Grau, Max and Maurice Strakosch, Bernard Ullman, Leonard Grover, Carl Anschutz, and James H. Mapleson were among the managers who conducted seasons of grand opera during the years from 1854 to 1887. As an opera-house, however, it could not endure the opposition of the newer and more fashionable Metropolitan ; and the Academy Company sold it to William P. Dinsmore on April 27, 1887. It was purchased by Gilmore & Tompkins, November 28, 1887 ; and since then has been a dramatic house, famous only by virtue of the run of *The Old Homestead*, which began August 30, 1888, and ended in May, 1891. In 1893 the main attraction was *The Black Crook.* All the boxes of opera days, save the twelve under the proscenium arch, were removed five years ago, and the auditorium is arranged in the ordinary fashion. It has a seating capacity of 2,700. The stage is 73 feet wide and 49 deep, with an extension a third as large, which runs towards 15th Street.

Niblo's Theatre, on the east side of Broadway, between Prince and Houston Streets, with an entrance through the Metropolitan-Hotel building, occupies the site of the Columbia Garden, which was opened as a summer-night place of amuse. ment in 1823. Niblo's Theatre, disconnected from the garden, was built by William Niblo, and opened on May 19, 1843. It was burned on September 18, 1846 ; rebuilt, and opened January 30, 1849 ; burned again May 6, 1872 ; and rebuilt and opened on November 30, 1872. At various times it has been the home of grand opera, of the spectacle and ballet, and of the drama. Henrietta Sontag made her first appearance in America there January 10, 1853. William Niblo retired in May, 1861, and for a short period, subsequent to January 7, 1862, the stage was occupied by the Wallack-Jarrett-Davenport Company, consisting of James W. Wallack, E. L. Davenport, Tom Placide, and other prominent actors of the time. An event which brought the house to the attention of the whole country was the production of the spectacle *The Black Crook,* on September 12, 1866. There were 475 performers and auxiliaries, and the ballet was led by Marie Bonfanti, Rita Sangalli and Betty Rigl. *The Black-Crook* was the most violently abused play of the time. Clergymen preached against it, and good people denounced it, because of the presumed immorality of the display of the female figure. But the production popularized the ballet, and the piece has been revived many times since, and always successfully. For many years Niblo's has been a second-class house, with spectacles and melodramas as attractions. The property is owned by the estate of A. T. Stewart, Edward Gilmore was the lessee from 1885 to 1892. In July, 1892, he was succeeded by Alexander Comstock, who made old Niblo's a low-priced house. The auditorium is 82 by 75 feet. Its seating capacity is 2,000. The stage is 75 by 62 feet, and the entrance thereto is on Crosby Street.

The People's Theatre, at 199, 201 and 203 Bowery, is a dramatic house, of which Henry C. Miner is both owner and manager. The house stands a little back from the street, and is entered by a wide lobby. There are seats in the orchestra, balcony, gallery and boxes for 1,400 people. The theatre, which was opened September 3, 1883, was built on the site of Tony Pastor's Opera-House, a variety theatre, at which Pastor first appeared in 1865. It was originally opened as Hoym's Theatre, in 1858.

The Windsor Theatre is at 45 Bowery. The house will accommodate 2,000 people. It was built on the site of the first Windsor Theatre, which was burned November 29, 1883; and was opened February 8, 1886. It was built by a company of Germans, and was originally opened as the Stadt Theatre, September 6, 1864. Frank B. Murtha ran it as a combination house for a long time. In 1893, Isidore Lindemann, Sigmund Magulesko and Joseph Levy leased the house until May, 1897, for the production of Hebrew and German operas and Sunday sacred concerts.

The Thalia Theatre, at 46 Bowery, was thus christened by Gustave Amberg, who became manager, with Mathilde Cottrelly as stage directress, September 11, 1879. It is (or rather was) the Bowery Theatre, the history of which has been told. German plays and operas were the attractions until 1888, when Amberg sub-leased the house to H. R. Jacobs for a year. A company of Hebrew actors gave performances in their own tongue at the Thalia during the season of 1889-90. Then it was closed for a year, and during the season of 1891–92 it was open for performance in German, under the management of the Rosenfeld Brothers.

The Third-Avenue Theatre, at Third Avenue and East 31st Street, is a so-called "Cheap-price" house, at which the attractions are melodramas and sensational plays. It is the headquarters theatre of H. R. Jacobs' chain of popular play-houses, which extends through many cities. It was built in 1875, by J. S. Berger.

The Eighth-Street Theatre, at 145 8th Street, is devoted to performances in Hebrew, given by native actors. The manager is Leonard Hangan. The building was once St. Ann's Roman Catholic Church; and was turned into a variety theatre by Jac. Aberle, in 1879.

The Roumania Opera-House, at 104 Bowery, is another play-house devoted to the Hebrew drama. It is a small establishment, and is not open continuously.

Tony Pastor's Theatre, is a little play-house in the Tammany-Hall building, on the north side of 14th Street, near Third Avenue. The attractions are invariably of the variety order. It was partly burned on June 6, 1888, and was rebuilt thereafter. The house was originally opened in 1868, as Dan Bryant's Minstrel Hall, and was afterward known as the Germania Theatre.

Koster and Bial's Concert Hall, at 115 West 23d Street, is a high-class vaudeville theatre and a beer-garden. The entertainments are of the vaudeville or variety order, like those given at the Alhambra in London, and the Eldorado in Paris, with a burlesque to lead the programme, and are given without the use of a curtain. The property is owned by Alfred B. Darling, who is also the owner of Proctor's Theatre, and is one of the senior proprietors of the Fifth-Avenue Hotel.

The Eden Musee, at 55 West 23d Street is primarily a museum of wax groups, some of which are meritorious as works of art. Secondarily it is a concert-hall and variety house. The establishment is 75 feet wide on 23d Street, and runs through the block to 24th Street, on which it has a frontage of 50 feet.

Miner's Bowery Theatre is a variety house, at 169 Bowery. The entertainments given are of a reputable sort, but boisterous.

The London Theatre is a variety house at 235 Bowery.

Miner's Eighth-Avenue Theatre, at 312 Eighth Avenue, furnishes variety entertainment for the West Side of the City.

The Harlem Opera-House is the principal theatre of the up-town section of the city. It is a handsome structure, at 207 West 125th Street, occupying three city lots, each of 25 feet frontage on that street and four on 126th Street. There are really two buildings, one on each street. That on 125th Street contains the entrance and lobby of the theatre, and also a music-hall 100 by 75 feet. The theatre proper stands broadside to 126th Street, and is entered through an arcade, 130 feet long and from 20 to 40 feet wide. The auditorium is handsomely decorated, blue being the prevailing tint. There are seats in the orchestra, balcony, gallery and boxes for 1,800 people. The stage is 70 by 40 feet. The house was built and is owned by the manager, Oscar Hammerstein. It was opened September 30, 1889. It is a first-class combination house.

The Columbus Theatre, at 114 East 125th Street, is also owned and managed by Oscar Hammerstein. The building is 200 by 100 feet, and runs through to 124th Street. It has a seating capacity of 2,000 people. The stage is 76 by 40 feet. It is a combination house. It was opened October 11, 1890.

The Olympic Theatre, built in 1882, at 130th Street and Third Avenue, is a small variety house, which was devoted to dramatic performances previous to the opening of the Harlem Opera-House.

The Theatre Comique is on the south side of 125th Street, near Third Avenue. It is a small variety house. It was remodelled from a skating-rink in 1888.

The Falls of Niagara is a cycloramic painting, exhibited in a circular iron building at the southeast corner of 19th Street and Fourth Avenue. The painting itself is 50 feet high and 400 feet long, with the ends joined to complete the circle. It is a very faithful reproduction on canvas, by Phillipotteaux, of a bird's-eye view of Niagara Falls and the surrounding country. The building was devoted for several years to the display of a similar painting of the battle of Gettysburg.

The Lyceum Opera-House, at 160 East 34th Street, near Lexington Avenue, is mainly used for balls, receptions, concerts, literary entertainments, fairs, banquets, conventions, commencements, weddings, and similar events. It is a handsome and elaborately decorated hall, with boxes, balcony and stalls. W. W. Astor is its owner.

Terrace Garden and Lexington Opera-House are two names by which an establishment which extends from East 58th Street to East 59th Street, near Lexington Avenue, is known. It consists of a theatre, fronting on 58th Street, a ball-room and an open-air garden. Properly speaking, the first title applies to the entire establishment, and the second to the theatre only. Performances of comic opera in German are given in the theater, and concerts in the garden in the summer, and both theatre and ball-room are used for social affairs in winter. The place is greatly in favor among the Germans. During the summer of 1892 the interior of the theatre was repaired and re-decorated, and an addition to the building, extending to 58th Street, was erected. This provided another ball-room, four Masonic lodge rooms, and space for enlarging the restaurant connected with the garden. Michael Heumann is proprietor and manager.

BERKELEY LYCEUM.   BREARLEY SCHOOL.
BERKELEY LYCEUM, 23 WEST 44TH STREET, NEAR FIFTH AVENUE.

The Berkeley Lyceum is a theatre originally built for amateurs by the Berkeley-Lyceum Company. It is at 19 and 21 West 44th Street, near Fifth Avenue. The auditorium will accommodate 500 people, and the stage measures 30 feet by 30. The house was opened February 27, 1888. It is now the home of the American Academy of the Dramatic Arts, at the head of which is Franklin H. Sargent.

The Lenox Lyceum is a large hall, suitable for concerts, at Madison Avenue and 59th Street. The floor is circular in form, 135 feet in diameter. It is surrounded by a tier of 57 boxes and a balcony, and the total seating capacity is 2,300. The decorations are in ivory white, blue and gold. There is a concert platform simply, and above it there is an immense sounding board. Banquet and drawing-rooms make the establishment suitable for social affairs. The Lenox Lyceum was opened on January 2, 1890, with a concert by the Theodore Thomas Orchestra.

Steinway Hall, on the north side of East 14th Street, between Union Square and Irving Place, was erected in 1866, and opened on October 31st of that year with a concert at which Madame Parepa, Brignoli, and Ferranti sang ; and S. B. Mills played the first concerto of Schumann in A minor. Theodore Thomas conducted the orchestra. For about 25 years Steinway Hall, so to say, has been the cradle of classical music in this country ; every prominent orchestral organization has been heard within its walls, and so have the most eminent vocalists and instrumentalists, an enumeration of whom may prove of interest.

Pianists : Anton Rubinstein, Rafael Joseffy, Leopold De Meyer, S. B. Mills, William Mason, Theo. Ritter, Franz Rummel, Moriz Rosenthal, Carl Baermann, Ferd. Von Inten, Carl Wolfsohn, Annette Essipoff, Anna Mehlig, Adele Aus Der Ohe, Marie Krebs, B. Boeckelmann, J. H. Bonawitz, F. Boscovitz, Teresa Carreno, Edward Dannreuther, Cecilia Gaul, Mme. Arabella Goddard, Robert Goldbeck, Emil Guion, Robert Heller, Max Liebling, S. Liebling, Lina Luckhardt, Arthur Napoleon, Willie B. Pape, Alfred H. Pease, Max Pinner, D. Pruckner, Madeline Schiller, Alida Topp, Jean Vogt.

STEINWAY HALL, 109-111 EAST 14TH STREET, NEAR FOURTH AVENUE.

Violinists : Maurice Dengremont, Henry Schradieck, Henri Wieniawski, Henri Vieuxtemps, Ole Bull, August Wilhelmj, Pablo de Sarasate, Carl Rosa, Camilla Urso, Wenzel Kopta, F. J. Prume, Ovide Musin, Edward Mollenhauer, Maud Powell, Bernhard Listemann, Franz Kneisel, Richard Arnold, S. E. Jacobsohn, Joseph Mosenthal, Hermann Brandt, Emile Sauret, Leopold Lichtenberg, Alfred Vivien, Fritz Kreisler, Edward Remenyi, Nahan Franko, Jeanne Franko, Madge Wickham, Nettie Carpenter, Dora Becker, M. Van Gelder, Franz Wilczeck, Max Bendix.

Violoncellists: Frederick Bergner, Carl Werner, Joseph Diehm, Louis Lubeck, Gaetano Braga, A. Hekking, Fred. Mollenhauer, Wilhelm Mueller, Louis Blumenberg, Adolphe Fischer, Victor Herbert, Fritz Giese, Rudolph Hennig.

Sopranos: Adelina Patti, Parepa Rosa, Carlotta Patti, Anna de la Grange, Gazzaniga, Marie Roze, Minnie Hauk, Eugenie Pappenheim, Louisa Cappiani, Teresa Parodi, Lilian Norton (Nordica), Ilma di Murska, Caroline Richings, Emma Juch, Etelka Gerster, Christine Nilsson, Bertha Johanssen, Anna Bishop, Lilli Lehmann, Clara Louise Kellogg, Isabella McCullough, Mme. Ambre, Alwina Valleria, Emma Albani, Marcella Sembrich, Amalie Materna, Emmy Fursch-Madi.

Contraltos: D'Angri, Scalchi, Zelie Trebelli, Antoinette Sterling, Lena Little, Adelaide Phillips, Zelda Seguin, Jennie Kempton, Annie Louise Cary, Krebs-Michalesi, Antonia Henne, Kate Morensi, Mrs. Patey, Anna Drasdil, Marie Gramm, Anna de Belocca, Emily Winant, Anna Lankow, Mme. Lablache, Marianne Brandt.

Tenors: Massimiliani, Campanini, Ravelli, Theodore Wachtel, W. Candidus, Achille Errani, P. Brignoli, Le Franc, Ernest Perring, Theo. Habelmann, Paul Kalisch, Christian Fritsch, Wm. Courtney, Theo. J. Toedt, Jos. Maas, Ernesto Nicolini, Anton Schott, Albert Niemann.

Baritones: Bellini, Fossati, Ferranti, Ardavani, J. R. Thomas, Galassi, Tagliapietra, Victor Maurel, Del Puente, Charles Santley, Georg Henschel, Harrison Millard, Max Treumann, Jacob Muller, N. Verger, Theodor Reichmann.

Bassos: Carl Formes, Susini, Ronconi, Coletti, Myron W. Whitney, Joseph Weinlich, Joseph Herrmann, Conrad Behrens, L. G. Gottschalk, Max Heinrich, Joseph Jamet, Franz Remmertz.

Organists: George F. Bristow, George W. Morgan, S. E. Warren, Dudley Buck.

Conductors: Carl Bergmann, Luigi Arditi, Theodore Thomas, Leopold Damrosch, Wilhelm Gericke, Frederick Louis Ritter, Carl Anschutz, Anton Seidl, Max Spicker, Frank Van der Stucken, Gotthold Carlberg, W. E. Dietrich, Max Maretzek, Franz Abt, Agr. Paur, Reinhard Schmelz, Adolph Neuendorff, Arthur Claassen, Arthur Nikisch, Walter Damrosch.

Other Halls.— Chickering Hall, at Fifth Avenue and 18th Street; Hardman Hall, at Fifth Avenue and 19th Street; Behr Hall, at 81 Fifth Avenue; Steck Hall, at 11 East 14th Street; and Mason & Hamlin Hall, at 158 Fifth Avenue, are used mainly for concerts and recitals. Sherry's Hall, at 402 Fifth Avenue, and Jaegar Hall, at Madison Avenue and 59th Street, are in favor for social events, banquets, and balls of considerable importance. Lyric Hall, at 723 Sixth Avenue, Adelphi Hall, at 201 West 52d Street, and Koster & Bial's upper halls, at 115 West 23d Street, are social rallying-places of lesser importance. Cooper-Union Hall, upper and lower, at Third Avenue and 8th Street, and Grand Opera-House Hall, at Eighth Avenue and 23d Street are much in use for political and public meetings, as well as for other gatherings. The titles of Masonic Hall, at Sixth Avenue and 23d Street, and Scottish Rite Hall at Madison Avenue and 29th Street, indicate their main purposes. The Young Men's Christian Association Hall, at Fourth Avenue and 23d Street, is in use for religious meetings, concerts, lectures and semi-religious or instructive entertainments. Clarendon Hall, at 114 East 13th Street, and Arlington Hall, at 21 St. Mark's Place, are meeting-places for trades-organizations. The first-named is in occasional use for dramatic performances in French. Neilson Hall, on 15th Street, near Irving Place, is available for miscellaneous use. Pythagoras Hall, 134 Canal Street, is used by the Knights of Labor. Hotz Assembly-rooms, 263 Bowery, Military Hall, 193 Bowery, Germania Assembly Room, 291 Bowery, are used for social and political gatherings.

Journalism and Publishing.

Newspapers and Periodicals, Book, Music and Other Publishing.

NEW YORK has not a complete file of its first newspaper, the *Gazette*, printed from 1725 to 1741, by William Bradford, but it guards jealously the *Weekly Journal*, printed from 1733 to 1746, by John Peter Zenger, who was arrested and tried for libel against the government of the New-York colony in 1735, and acquitted by jurors anxious to keep inviolate the liberty of the press. In 1743 Bradford's *Gazette* had a successor in the *New-York Gazette* or *Weekly Post-Boy*, published by James Parker. It lasted until 1773. In 1746 and 1747 Henry De Forest published the *Evening Post*. In 1752 the *Independent Reflector*, a literary journal founded by James Parker, and the *Mercury*, founded by Hugh Gaine, made their first appearance. The former lasted until 1754, and the latter until 1783. In 1753 William Wenman began the publication of the *Pacquet*, which lasted until 1767. In 1761 and 1762 Samuel Farley published the *American Chronicle*. In 1766 John Holt published *The New-York Journal*, or *General Advertiser ;* in 1787 the paper was sold to Thomas Greenleaf, who changed its name to *The Argus*, or *Greenleaf's New Daily Advertiser*, and published semi-weekly *Greenleaf's New-York Journal and Patriotic Register*. These papers were sold in 1800 to James Cheetham, who continued their publication—under the name of *The American Citizen* for the daily, and *The American Watchman* for the semi-weekly—until 1810. In 1766 A. and J. Robertson published the *Chronicle* and removed to Albany. In 1773 appeared Rivington's *New-York Gazetteer* or *The Connecticut, New Jersey, Hudson's River and Quebec Weekly Advertiser ;* in 1775 the publication was suspended ; in 1777 it was resumed as *Rivington's New-York Loyal Gazette*, and the name was changed to *Royal Gazette* a short time before its suspension, in 1783. In 1775 John Anderson's *Constitutional Gazette* was born and died. In 1776 Samuel Loudon published the *New-York Packet* and the *American Advertiser*, and during the war removed to Fishkill. In 1776 appeared for three months *John Englishman in Defence of the English Constitution*. The publishers were Parker & Wyman. After the Revolution there were the *New-York Daily Advertiser*, founded in 1785 by Francis Childs & Co. ; the *Independent Journal*, founded in 1787, wherein appeared the first of the essays in favor of the Constitution, afterward united in book-form under the title of *The Federalist ;* the *Gazette*, founded in 1788, and absorbed in 1840 by the *Journal of Commerce ;* the *United-States Gazette*, founded in 1789 by John Fenno, and removed with the National capital to Philadelphia in 1790 ; the *Minerva*, founded in 1793 by Noah Webster, and merged with *The Commercial Advertiser*, the most ancient of the New-York city papers extant.

In 1816 there were the *Mercantile Advertiser*, of Ramsey Crooks, with a circulation of 2,250 copies ; the *Gazette*, 1,750 ; the *Evening Post*, 1,600 ; the *Commercial*

39

Advertiser, 1,200; the *Courier*, 920; the *Columbian*, 825; the *National Advocate*, 875. In 1826 appeared *Noah's New-York National Advocate*, the name of which was enjoined, and changed to the *New-York Enquirer*, merged with the *Courier* in 1839. In 1823 Woodworth, author of the popular *Old Oaken Bucket*, edited the *Weekly Mirror*, which became *The Mirror*, with George P. Morris and Nathaniel P. Willis. In 1822 appeared *The Albion*, an organ of English opinion. Of course it failed at once. In 1825 appeared the first Sunday newspaper, the *Sunday Courier*. In 1832 James Gordon Bennett founded the *Globe*, and it failed. In 1848 the *Journal of Commerce*, the *Courier and Enquirer*, the *Tribune*, the *Herald*, the *Sun* and the *Express* united in the formation of the Associated Press, the object of which, immediately attained, was to put an end to extravagant rivalry for news, and to obtain service very much better. There are at present the Associated Press, the United Press, the American Press Association, the International Telegram Company, the Dalziel Cable News Company, and several city press syndicates, serving 735 daily and periodical papers. There are printed in German, 51 papers; in Spanish, 9; in Italian, 4; in French, 4; in Swedish, 2; in Bohemian, 5; in Hungarian, 1; in Armenian, 1. There are 160 trade-papers; 16 art-papers; 39 scientific papers; and 10 sporting papers.

There are many powerful religious papers published in New York, and circulated all over the continent. Among these *The Churchman*, the great organ of the Episcopal Church; *The Freeman's Journal*, *The Tablet*, and five other Roman Catholic papers, besides the scholarly magazine, *The Catholic World;* *The American Hebrew*, and seven other Jewish papers; *The Examiner*, founded by the Baptists away back in 1823; *The Observer* and *The Evangelist*, powerful Presbyterian weeklies; the widely circulated *Christian Advocate*, known to all Methodists; *The Christian Intelligencer*, the organ of the Reformed Church; *The Independent*, *The . Outlook*, and *The Christian Herald*, evangelical and literary, and edited with great ability; and many other denominational papers.

The Commercial Advertiser, founded in 1797, edited by John A. Cockerill, Republican in politics, is an evening paper, containing illustrations that startling news or curious news evoke. In its later history, a Republican paper, under the management of Hugh Hastings; an ardent advocate of the Cleveland administration, and with a distinctive artistic aim, under the management of Henry Marquand; it was until recently impartial in politics. Although the oldest New-York paper, it is also one of the brightest, and has gained greatly in circulation since 1890.

The Evening Post is almost coeval with the nineteenth century, its first number having appeared on the 16th of November, 1801. The purpose of its establishment was to afford an organ for the Federalist party, and Alexander Hamilton and a number of his political friends, men then very prominent in National affairs, were the founders of the paper. The editor-in-chief for the first twenty years was William Coleman, at one time the law-partner of Aaron Burr. In 1826 William Cullen Bryant became one of the editors, and assumed full control two years later. While he was in Europe, between 1834 and 1836, the *Evening Post* was edited by William Leggett, who vigorously denounced the subjection of Abolitionists to mob-law, and demanded the right of free speech for all Americans, on all topics. The paper fought heroically for these principles, but lost ground, and Bryant was obliged to return, and renew its popularity. In Jackson's administration the *Evening Post* won wide recognition by its opposition to the United-States Bank, and its advocacy of free trade. In 1881, three years after his death, the paper changed hands, and was edited by Carl Schurz, ex-Senator and ex-Secretary of the Interior. Upon Mr. Schurz's withdrawal, his colleagues, Horace White and Edwin L. Godkin, continued

"THE EVENING POST" AND "THE NATION," EVENING POST BUILDING.
BROADWAY, SOUTHEAST CORNER OF FULTON STREET.

the editorial management.   The *Evening Post* Building, at Broadway and Fulton Street, was one of the first of the large office-buildings to be erected in New York.

In politics the *Evening Post* is absolutely independent.   It is constant in its opposition to high protection, and continually exposes what it considers the fallacies of that doctrine.   It stands in general for the political principles represented by Grover Cleveland, economy in National administration, tariff-reform, civil-service reform, the industrial development of the United States, and unity, reciprocity and broadening trade with other nations.   In its news, as well as in its editorial columns, it is dignified, straightforward and accurate, publishing all the news of the day, but eschewing sensationalism.

The lofty and impressive building of the *Evening Post* is crowded with important offices and the headquarters of many important enterprises, occupying, as it does, a favorable position just between the district of the great business exchanges and that of the newspapers, and close to the Post Office and the City Hall.   At this notable strategic point, Broadway, the noblest street of the world, is crossed by the ever-busy Fulton Street, which runs from the Washington Market, on the North River, to the Fulton Market and the ferry to Brooklyn, on the East River.   At this intersection is one of the best points for offices in the city, and the *Evening Post* Building occupies it with fine effect.

The Journal of Commerce and Commercial Bulletin is a consolidation (in 1893) of the *Commercial Bulletin*, founded in 1865, and the *Journal of Commerce*, founded in 1827.   It is absolutely faithful to its title.   Containing the market reports in detail, and intended as a guide for men of business, it is found in offices and stores, and not in the hands of newsboys.   Its editorials treat all questions of public interest with fairness and candor, and are widely copied at home and abroad. Its market, stock, crop and other reports are among its special features.

The Courrier des Etats-Unis, founded in 1828, is edited by H. P. Sampers and Leon Meunier, printed in French, Republican in French politics, Democratic in American politics.   One of its founders was Charles Lasalle, a French compositor, who worked at the case in New York with Horace Greeley.   The paper contains all the news cabled to other papers from Paris, an editorial article, a feuilleton or serial story, local news in brief, and reprints from the French journals.

The Sun was founded in 1833 by a Yankee job-printer named Benjamin H. Day, as a penny paper; and on the 3d of September he issued the first number. In 1835 it printed Locke's celebrated "Moon Hoax."   In 1838 it passed into the hands of the Beach family, who ran it for thirty years, except during an interval of about a year, in 1861, when it was owned by a religious enthusiast, and published as a theological daily.   It was smart enough in its early days, but for the last quarter of a century it has been a work of genius.   The Sun Printing and Publishing Association became the owners, and Charles A. Dana the editor, in 1868.   The publication and editorial rooms were transferred to their present location at the corner of Park Row and Frankfort Street, the old Tammany-Hall structure; then lofty and imposing, but now a seemingly small and insignificant brick building, with mansard windows, quite dwarfed by the tall edifices between which it stands. Instantly the *Sun* became "the *Sun* that shines for all."   It was a journal of broad and human symmetry, enthusiastic, patriotic, vigorous, and full of convictions of which it had the courage.   It was too learned to be pedantic; it was too sincere to be commonplace.   It was and is a model.   The *Sun* gives the news without useless ornaments, but with words that paint.   "If you see it in the *Sun* it is so."   The *Sun's* prose is good sound Anglo-Saxon.   Its editorial writers know how to say the

" THE SUN," NASSAU AND FRANKFORT STREETS.

things that they wish to say, as they wish to say them. Its bright young men do not report occurrences that they have not seen, nor report everything they hear. Its correspondents know that it would be folly to try to make it print banalities, and those who have hugged that fond delusion have been speedily dissuaded. The *Sun* is the wit, humor, science and art of New York expressed. If its owners build for it a new domicile, to be emblematic it must be marvelous. It is not surprising that the most daring, novel and seductive of plans for an architectural masterpiece of thirty-two stories has come to the *Sun*, by the design of its business manager, W. M. Laffan.

The **New-Yorker Staats-Zeitung**, founded in 1834, and edited by Oswald Ottendorfer, is independent in politics. It occupies in Tryon Row its own granite building. Printed in German, severely classic in tone, filled with notes of the Fatherland, besides all the American news, it is an influential journal in Berlin by reflection of its German-American authority. The Staats-Zeitung Building is at the junction of Centre Street and Park Row.

The Herald, founded in 1835 by James Gordon Bennett, is independent in politics. It is against everything that savors of the wrong. It aims to give news, not to explain or interpret them. It paid the expenses of Stanley, who found Livingston ; it has fitted out expeditions to the North Pole ; it has a reputation wherever there are readers of news. It is unique. It defies criticism. Its building, on Broadway at the corner of Ann Street, was formerly the site of Barnum's Museum. The paper is more famous than Barnum ; Barnum was more ambitious for literary, scientific, political and social authority. It could, if it wished, be a tyrant in art, letters and politics, but it does not wish. It is deliberately that its editorial page is weak. It is a newspaper, simply, perfectly. To have the faintest suspicion that the *Herald* might suppress or amend any bit of news for any reason, political, literary, social or artistic, is not to understand the *Herald*. That is the secret of its success.

The Herald is now erecting, on the immense block bounded by Broadway and Sixth Avenue, 35th and 36th Streets, a magnificent Italian Renaissance building, richly adorned with marble, with arcades of polished granite columns, press-rooms

PRINTING-HOUSE SQUARE IN 1868.

separated from Broadway only by plate-glass, and an enormous clock with a deep-toned bell. This noble structure, abounding in reminiscences of the palaces of Venice, Verona and Padua, is to be used exclusively by the *Herald*. Its architects are McKim, Mead & White, who constructed the gorgeous Madison-Square Garden.

The Mail and Express is pre-eminently a leading evening newspaper of New York. It is "newsy," in the professional sense of the word, in that its record of the day's events is comprehensive, and is carried down to the latest possible moment. Its editorial page is dignified and scholarly. Its political faith is Republican, and it is a leader in expressing the opinion of the party. As its name suggests, the *Mail and Express* is a consolidation of two newspapers. The New-York *Evening Express* was established in 1839, and for many years it was edited by James and Erastus Brooks. The New-York *Evening Mail*, an evening daily paper, was started about 1869. The consolidation of the two into one great newspaper was effected by the late Cyrus W. Field. He purchased the *Mail* in 1880, and the *Express* two years

THE "MAIL AND EXPRESS" BUILDING.
BROADWAY, SOUTHWEST CORNER OF FULTON STREET ; OPPOSITE ST. PAUL'S CHURCHYARD.

later. The combined establishment was purchased by the late Col. Elliott F. Shepard, in March, 1888, and since then the paper has made long strides.

It is the only evening paper that has a franchise in the New-York Associated Press. The new *Mail and Express* Building, on Broadway and St. Paul's Church-yard, is one of the most elaborate newspaper establishments in the country. It is **T**-shaped in form, thus, **T**. Its Broadway front measures 25 feet, and its depth 100 feet. The St. Paul's Churchyard front is 77 feet, and the depth of that section of the **T** is 90 feet. There are eleven stories, and the highest point is 211 feet above the curb. The building is a handsome illustration of the French Renaissance (Henry the Second) style of architecture, designed by Carrère & Hastings. Four large figures, allegorically representing the four continents, adorn the lower story of the Broadway façade. The material is Indiana limestone throughout, with steel construction. The newspaper establishment occupies the basement for mechanical purposes, the first story as a business office, and the tenth and eleventh stories for editorial departments and the composing-room. The new Hoe presses in the new building are capable of printing 98,000 papers an hour. The motive powers for the machinery and the Otis elevators are electricity and steam.

"THE SUN" AND "THE TRIBUNE."

Col. Shepard imprinted his strong and fearless personality upon all departments of the paper, making it clean, pure and sweet, and at the same time bright and enterprising. The super-abundant space devoted by some journals to minute and wire-drawn records of crime, the successive rounds of a prize fight, the gory details of a murder, is avoided in the *Mail and Express*, which devotes its space to the best and most interesting general news of the day, to careful accounts of philanthropic, charitable, religious and educational movements, and to the leading and happiest events in social life. This sweetness and light in one of New-York's greatest secular dailies is the result of Col. Shepard's firm and faithful policy, and stands as a monument to his finished life.

The New-York Tribune, founded by Horace Greeley in 1841, and conducted by him until he was nominated for President of the United States, in 1872, has been almost constantly, since the birth of the Republican party, its organ and counselor. Aside from politics it represents the best elements in the National character and life. It was foremost in the struggle for free men and free speech, and foremost in the fight for National unity. It is brilliant at times, forceful and telling usually, dignified and scholarly always. Its influence upon its readers has not been surpassed by any other American newspaper. It speaks in pure, clean-cut English. Graduates from its editorial room take high rank in journalism. Since December, 1872 (with the exception of the period when Mr. Reid was abroad, and during

FIFTH AVENUE, LOOKING NORTH FROM 40TH STREET.

BROADWAY, SIXTH AVENUE AND 35TH STREET, SHOWING "HERALD" BUILDING AND DODGE STATUE.

1892), the *Tribune* has been conducted by Whitelaw Reid, United-States Minister to France for three years, beginning in 1889, and the Republican nominee for Vice-President in 1892. The *Tribune* Building, an eleven-story edifice at Nassau and Spruce Streets, facing Printing-House Square, and the pioneer of the great newspaper office-buildings in New York, was erected during the early years of Mr. Reid's administration. It is the greatest newspaper centre in the United States, for more than 6,000 journals, mostly Western and Southern, have their New-York representatives in the *Tribune* Building. The great bulk of the stock of the *Tribune* Association is owned by Whitelaw Reid, Darius O. Mills and Ogden Mills. Ogden Mills is the President of the corporation.

The New-Yorker Zeitung, founded in 1845, is independent in German and American politics, and is printed in the German language.

L'Eco d'Italia was founded in 1849 by political refugees, companions of Garibaldi. It is monarchical and anti-clerical in Italian politics, and independent in American politics; and is one of the most influential and largely circulated Italian journals in the United States.

The New-York Times, founded in 1851 by George Jones and Henry J. Raymond, is Democratic in politics. The recent death of Mr. Jones has, in the unanimous expression of respect and admiration for him and his work that it evoked, made familiar a valuable lesson. In this age, called materialistic, wherein mere apparent success is said to be accepted as a test of worth, this great newspaper has an inspiring, elevated ideal, and is a journal of scholars, artists, lovers of truth, country and humanity. It is absolutely sincere. It fears nothing, because it looks at truth in the face. Monsters of corruption have come to life, and the *Times* has destroyed them with its arrows of light. The Tweed rule undone; the relinquishment of great financial advantages in favor of popular welfare; the abandonment of a great patronage for a question of principle; acts of the *Times* most frequently quoted in records of the services of the Press in America, are only better-known instances of its value. In science, in literature, in art, in matters theological and social, the *Times* is a guide as conscientious as in politics. The old home of the *Times* was replaced in 1889 by the present *Times* Building, of which David H. King, Jr., was the builder. The substitution was accomplished as by enchantment. The offices of the newspaper were not removed. The conventionally designed old building disappeared as scenes are shifted in plays. The crowds that passed by Printing-House Square saw an infinity of workmen by day and by night, and were perpetually surprised by their work. The corner-stone of the new building was laid, privately, June 7, 1888. The building is an architectural treasure. There are fifteen stories, two of which are below the pavement. The architect, George B. Post, accomplished a masterpiece of the Romanesque style, that is becoming national. Discreet, moderate, bold, vigorous, perfect in every detail of ornamentation, in moldings, in capitals, in gargoyles; so beautiful that it charms the naive and the refined, the ignorant and the most learned in art; the *Times* Building is the *New-York Time* expressed in stone. In April, 1893, the *Times* was purchased of its former owner by the *New-York Times* Publishing Co., a stock company organized by Charles R Miller and George F. Spinney, who for many years had been respectively Editor in-Chief and Managing Editor of the paper, Mr. Miller still retaining his position as Editor-in-Chief, and Mr. Spinney becoming the publisher and business manager The new management has put fresh life and greater energy into the paper; it ha been expended and improved on every department, and as a wide-awake Democrati newspaper now occupies a leading position.

NASSAU STREET. "THE TIMES." PARK ROW. POST OFFICE. HALL OF RECORDS.

The World was founded in June, 1860, as a religious journal. In 1861 it absorbed the *Courier and Enquirer.* Later, The Albany Regency, Thurlow Weed, August Belmont, Samuel L. M. Barlow and others, were said to be its owners. In 1869 it became the property of Manton Marble. After varied fortunes it fell under an editor who was bound to Jay Gould and devoted to the aristocracy of England. When its redemption seemed hopeless, it was purchased by Joseph Pulitzer. He signed this inaugural announcement :

"The entire *World* newspaper property has been purchased by the undersigned, and will from this day be under different management, — different in men, measures and methods, — different in purpose, policy and principle, — different in objects and interests, — different in sympathies and convictions, — different in head and heart. Performance is better than promise. Exuberant assurances are cheap. I make none. I simply refer the public to the new *World* itself, which henceforth shall be the daily evidence of its own growing improvement, with forty-eight daily witnesses in its forty-eight columns.

"There is room in this great and growing city for a journal that is not only cheap but bright, not only bright but large, not only large but truly Democratic, — dedicated to the cause of the people rather than that of purse-potentates, — devoted more to the news of the New than the Old World, — that will expose all fraud and sham, fight all public evils and abuses, — that will serve and battle for the people with all earnest sincerity. In that cause and for that end solely the new *World* is hereby enlisted, and committed to the attention of the intelligent public."

This was a decade ago. Then, in 1883, the daily average circulation of the *World* was 33,521 ; weekly, 234,648 ; yearly total, 12,235,238. In 1892 the daily average circulation was 380,499 ; total, 139,262,685. In 1883 the *World* printed 86,577 advertisements ; in 1892, 890,975. In 1892 the *World* used 37,562 rolls of white paper, weighing 26,973,252 pounds, and forming 473,018,836 four-page sheets ; set 90,927 columns of type, formed of 568,316,999 ems, that involved the handling of 1,278,713,247 pieces of type. On Sunday, May 7, 1893, the *World* celebrated the tenth anniversary of Mr. Pulitzer's ownership of the paper by publishing an edition of 400,000 hundred-page papers — the largest newspaper ever printed, using 303 tons of white paper and $47\frac{1}{2}$ tons of ink. If the elder Dumas could make an electoral canvass with no other platform than the gratitude of the men whom the mere mechanical production of his works had benefited, what might not the editor and proprietor of the *World* expect from a similar platform ?

When, in October, 1889, on the site formerly occupied by French's Hotel, the corner-stone of the Pulitzer Building was laid, Joseph Pulitzer wrote :

"God grant that this structure be the enduring home of a newspaper, forever unsatisfied with merely printing news — forever fighting every form of Wrong — forever Independent — forever advancing in Enlightenment and Progress — forever wedded to truly Democratic ideas — forever aspiring to be a Moral Force — forever rising to a higher plane of perfection as a Public Institution.

"God grant that the *World* may forever strive toward the Highest Ideals — be both a daily schoolhouse and a daily forum, both a daily teacher and a daily tribune, an instrument of Justice, a terror to crime, an aid to education, an exponent of true Americanism.

"Let it ever be remembered that this edifice owes its existence to the public ; that its architect is popular favor; that its moral corner-stone is love of Liberty and Justice ; that its every stone comes from the people and represents public approval for public services rendered.

THE "WORLD" BUILDING--PARK ROW AND FRANKFORT STREET.
AS SEEN FROM BROADWAY, ACROSS CITY-HALL PARK.

"God forbid that the vast army following the standard of the *World* should in this, or in future generations, ever find it faithless to those ideas and moral principles to which alone it owes its life, and without which I would rather have it perish."

The Pulitzer Building, the home of the *World*, erected in 1889-90, is the tallest office-building in the world, reaching 309 feet from sidewalk to lantern, or 375½ feet from the foundation to the top of the flagstaff. It has a huge skeleton of iron and steel, sustaining its 26 stories ; an impressive dome ; and a perfect modern equipment, electric lights, Worthington pumps, etc.

The News, founded in 1867, is edited by Benjamin Wood ; Democratic in politics. A small evening paper, giving the news in a popular form, it contains, in the supplement of its Sunday edition, information invaluable to persons who have not the time or the opportunity to read books. Its offices are in a five-story brick building in Park Row.

The Evening Telegram was founded in 1867, by James Gordon Bennett. It is independent in politics ; having no other purpose than to give the news of the day, which it does, in a most piquant manner.

The City Record, founded in 1873, is the official municipal journal, printing only city advertisements and minutes of the several departments of the city government. It is supervised by William J. K. Kenny.

Las Novedades, founded in 1876, edited by J. G. Garcia, is independent in politics. It is printed in Spanish, with all the important news of Spain, its colonies and South-American descendants, of whose interests in this country it is the champion.

Il Progreso Italo-Americano, founded in 1879, edited by Carlo Barsotti, is conservative in Italian, independent in American politics. It is printed in Italian, and has a reflected influence at the Quirinal.

New-York Herold, founded in 1879, is the evening edition, printed in German, of the *Zeitung.* It is independent in politics.

New-Yorker Tages-Nachrichten, founded in 1870, edited by Benjamin Wood, is Democratic in politics. It is the German edition of the *News.*

New-Yorker Volks-Zeitung, founded in 1878, is independent in politics. Printed in German, it expresses the theories and aims of the German Socialists.

The Morning Journal, founded in 1882, edited by Albert Pulitzer as a one-cent paper, is independent in politics. It was organized with practically no capital but energy. Its leading motive was to amuse, while instructing. It was painstaking, brilliant, ingenious. At first it was printed on presses of the *Tribune.* It became gradually a wealthy, popular, distinctive newspaper.

The Evening World, founded in 1887, edited by Joseph Pulitzer, Democratic in politics, is a popular newspaper.

The Evening Sun, founded in 1887, edited by Charles A. Dana, Democratic in politics, is also a popular newspaper.

The Press was founded in 1887. Republican in politics, it is especially devoted to tariff problems. It quickly attained its aim, to rival the Democrats in the field, which they occupied entirely, of penny popular newspapers. It is an exceedingly influential Republican newspaper, with a daily circulation of over 100,000 copies. Its editorial and business offices are in the Potter Building.

Hlas Lindu, founded in 1886, edited by John Korinek, is printed in Bohemian.

New-Yorské Listy, founded in 1875, is printed in Bohemian. The Bohemian population in New York supports two Bohemian newspapers.

Das Morgen Journal, founded in 1890 by Albert Pulitzer, is Democratic. It is the counterpart in German of the *Morning Journal,* and has a Sunday edition.

NEW-YORK HERALD BUILDING, BROADWAY AND ANN STREET.

NEW-YORK HERALD BUILDING (IN CONSTRUCTION), BROADWAY AND 35TH STREET.

CITY HALL. "WORLD." "SUN." "JOURNAL." "TRIBUNE." "TIMES." POTTER BUILDING. "PRESS." TEMPLE COURT. POST OFFICE.

CITY-HALL PARK, FROM BROADWAY TO PARK ROW.

THE DAILY PAPERS AND PROMINENT BUILDINGS OF NEWSPAPER ROW.

40

The Morning Advertiser was founded in 1891 by Col. John A. Cockerill, with the distinctive aim of furnishing in brief, without attempting to be entertaining in a literary sense, to busy people the news of the day.   It is Republican.

The Recorder, founded in 1891, Republican in politics, is edited and managed by George W. Turner, one of the most energetic workers ever connected with a daily paper.   It is one of the marvels of journalism, and has one of the best equipped plants in the city.   The *Recorder* Building is an eight-story brick edifice, at 15 Spruce Street, probably the first time a newspaper has ever put up its own building in the second year of its existence.   It is occupied solely by the *Recorder.*

Daily America, a straight Democratic newspaper, with special features on Wall Street, the drama, racing, and all legitimate sports.   It was founded in 1893, by George II. Dickinson, and is a paper for busy men.

The Daily Mercury is a Democratic morning one-cent paper, founded in 1893 by the company which has published the *Sunday Mercury* since 1839.

There are daily legal, financial, sporting and other papers.

Harper's Weekly, illustrated, was founded in 1856.   It is independent in politics; and forms a pictorial history of the period in which we live, with admirable literary and artistic features.   It is rightly called "A Journal of Civilization."

Harper's Bazaar, illustrated, founded in 1868, is a paper particularly devoted to fashions, home management, the progress of women, and art and literature.

Harper's Young People, illustrated, founded in 1879, is a paper for boys and girls.   It abounds in stories and pictures, and articles on games, needle-work, boat-building, drawing, and other practical themes made attractive to boys and girls.

Frank Leslie's Illustrated Newspaper, founded in 1853, is Republican in politics.   It affords a picturesque chronicle of the events of the day.

Frank Leslie's Illustrirte Zeitung, founded in 1855, and Republican in politics, is printed in the German language.

The New-York Dramatic News was founded in 1874, by C. A. Byrnes, and has long been edited by Leander Richardson.   It is devoted to critical reviews of theatrical performances, and news about actors, plays and managers.

The Dramatic Mirror, established in 1879, is under the editorial charge of Harrison Grey Fiske.   It is published every Tuesday, and has a very large circulation among persons interested in theatrical news of all kinds.

The Critic, founded in 1881, is edited by Jeannette L. and Joseph B. Gilder. It is probably the leading literary and critical paper in America, and has achieved a commanding success with its learned and scholarly book-reviews and its always entertaining news of authors and new publications.

The Ledger, founded by Robert Bonner in 1844, is a family story-paper.

Forest and Stream, founded in 1871, is a paper devoted to outdoor life.

The Spirit of the Times, founded in 1831, is a foremost sporting paper.

The Clipper, founded in 1853, is authority on sporting and theatrical events.

Puck was founded in 1876, by Joseph Keppler and Adolph Schwarzmann, as a German comic paper.   Six months later an English edition of *Puck* was started, with H. C. Bunner as editor, and has attained a tremendous success.   It is an independent journal, with many colored cartoons of a comical character.

Judge, founded in 1881, a satirical paper, with illustrations in colors, is Republican in politics, and wages a merry war against the Democrats.

Life, founded in 1883, is a satirical journal, illustrated; independent in politics. Its pictures are of the most refined and dainty character, and aptly illustrate social foibles and political phases.   They are illuminated also by charmingly witty text.

The Churchman, at 47 Lafayette Place, was established in 1844. It is the leading, largest and most widely circulated weekly paper in the Protestant Episcopal Church. The full significance of this is not entirely in the statistics, which show that there are 532,230 communicants in the Protestant Episcopal Church, 300,000 of whom are residents of the New-England and Middle States. These communicants are the wealthy and intelligent people in every community. To be agreeable to them a journal must be excellent. It must be as *The Churchman* is. The only denominational paper regularly illustrated, it is illustrated with exquisite taste. Having to reflect not only the artistic life of its readers, but their religious life, the beautiful ideals of their faith, it is written by scholars, by men of letters in the truest sense. The editor is the Rev. Dr. George S. Mallory, formerly professor of English literature in Trinity College. The business manager is Marshall H. Mallory. They knew well at the outset the difficulties and the possibilities of their task. Before them several men of undoubted ability had lost fortunes. A paper, founded

EPISCOPAL DIOCESAN HOUSE   COLONNADE ROW.   "THE CHURCHMAN."

"THE CHURCHMAN," 47 LAFAYETTE PLACE, OPPOSITE ASTOR LIBRARY.

in 1831, and wearing the name which they chose, had made a brave effort, and died, giving way to *The Church Journal;* but the Messrs. Mallory had the strength of the faithful and the confidence of genius. They made a success of *The Church-man.* In 1878 it absorbed *The Church Journal.* Since then *The Churchman* has been more than a success. It is an accepted power. The paper is printed with a jealous regard for typographical beauty and accuracy. It is published in magazine form, and makes an annual record of 2,500 pages, every phase of which is a phase of Christian thought, admirably expressed. The owners of this "most distinctively religious of journals" have purchased for its offices one of the Colonnade Buildings, in Lafayette Place, formerly the residences of New York's most eminent citizens, and the brilliant centre of New York's intellectual supremacy. It is immediately opposite the Astor Library, and near the Episcopal Diocesan House, which is the first building on the left of the Colonnade Row, in the picture on preceding page.

The New-York Observer, the oldest religious newspaper in America, has for seventy years occupied a noble and glorious position as a defender of the faith and a recorder of the news of the churches and of the world. *The Observer* was established in 1823, by Sidney E. and Richard C. Morse ; and for many years was published at the corner of Nassau and Beekman Streets, on the site of the Morse Building, erected by the sons of the founders of the paper. In 1840 Samuel Irenæus Prime became editor of *The Observer*, and retained this position until his death, in 1885. His brother, E. D. G. Prime, was connected with the paper from 1853 to 1890. In 1859 Charles Augustus Stoddard, pastor of the Washington-Heights Presbyterian Church, and son-in-law of Irenæus Prime, became associate editor of *The Observer;* and Wendell Prime, the son of Irenæus, in 1878. The Prime brothers bought the paper from the Morse brothers ; and it now belongs to the children of Irenæus, and is managed by his son-in-law. The offices were established at 37 Park Row, on the site of the original Brick Church, from 1859 to 1881, when the building was burned, with the loss of several lives. When the new Potter Building was erected, on the same site, *The Observer* returned to its former place, at 37 and 38 Park Row, where it still abides. Under its firm, harmonious and progressive editorial administration, *The Observer* has continued steadfast to the ideals of its founders ; and is now, as it was in the early days, a wholesome, conservative and interesting family newspaper, always supporting the things which are right and good, defending the principles of Christian truth, and presenting an admirable record of the world's news, as seen from a religious standpoint. Its files present the fullest and most accurate religious history of the world, and are continually consulted for facts and figures. When the Southern States seceded, the paper lost 10,000 subscribers in a single day ; but it survived this amazing mischance by the same inherent strength which has carried it through the disasters of fire and panic and ecclesiastical disturbances. At the present time, with a larger corps of editors than ever before, and with unexcelled facilities, it has more subscribers than at any previous time in its history, and has no rival as an invaluable, instructing, and entertaining repository of the events and opinions of the day, in their bearings upon the American Republic and the Christian Church.

The Nation is published every week, at Broadway and Fulton Street. Its writers include some of the foremost specialists in science, art, public affairs, and literary criticism. The *Nation* is an independent weekly review of literature, science, art and politics, with a serial commentary on the most important American and foreign events, special and occasional correspondence, and thoroughly competent criticism of the latest developments of literature, science, art, music and the drama. The two hundred contributors who prepare this feast for the scholar and the thinker include the foremost names in literature and thought. The *Nation* has been pronounced by the *Saturday Review* to be "on the intellectual level of the best European periodicals." In 1881 it became the property of the owners of the *Evening Post*, and maintains an allied yet original existence.

The Home Journal, founded in 1846, edited by Morris Phillips, is a newspaper of literature, art and society, with abundant news of pleasure-resorts.

NEW-YORK OBSERVER.
REDUCED FAC SIMILE OF THE FIRST NUMBER OF THE FIRST RELIGIOUS PAPER.

The Christian Advocate, the official organ of the Methodist Episcopal Church, is issued weekly from the headquarters of the Church in New-York City, known as the Methodist Book Concern. This large and prosperous establishment (located on the corner of Fifth Avenue and 20th Street) is managed for the Church by two ministers, who are called Agents, and who are elected by the General Conference of the Church quadrennially. Rev. Sanford Hunt, D. D., and Rev. Homer Eaton, D. D., are the present heads of the house, and conduct its business under the title of Hunt & Eaton. This ably conducted church newspaper has for its editor-in. chief Rev. James M. Buckley, D. D., one of the brightest and clearest minds in the membership of the great Church ; a man also of amazing industry and wonderful mental resources. He is assisted in the conduct of the " Great Official " by a com. pany of able contributors, and the general managing editorship is in the hands of Rev. W. H. Depuy, D. D., who was the editor-in-chief of the People's Encyclo. pædia, which was published so successfully by the Methodist Book Concern. *The Christian Advocate* was established in September, 1826 ; and during the sixty-seven

FRANKLIN SQUARE AND THE HARPERS' PUBLISHING HOUSE.

years of its history has been under careful management, and has been kept in touch with the progress of humanity on all religious and philanthropic lines. The advertising department is under the business management of William Baldwin. The Advertisements are subject to the supervision of the editor. Medical advertisements are not admitted, except when well known to have exceptional merit. Advertisements are declined also in which the name of any bishop or minister is used as an endorsement of the article advertised. No advertiser is permitted to use a picture of his face, and no financial advertisement is admitted offering a higher rate of interest than 8% to investors. The discriminating care shown in its general business management has gained the confidence of its subscribers and readers, which necessarily is of decided advantage to its advertisers.

Bradstreet's, founded in 1879, is a paper for men of business. It is the foremost journal of its class in America. It is published by the Bradstreet Company, and reaches all parts of the world.

"THE CHRISTIAN ADVOCATE," METHODIST BOOK CONCERN AND MISSION HOUSE,
FIFTH AVENUE, SOUTHWEST CORNER OF 20TH STREET.

The Christian Herald is a leading weekly religious illustrated journal. Probably no publication in the history of religious journalism in America can point to so successful a record. Established in 1878, it speedily took rank as a publication of influence; but it was not until 1890, when it passed under the control of its present proprietor, Dr. Louis Klopsch of New York, that it attained the splendid success which has since crowned its career. One of the first steps taken by the new management was to secure the Rev. T. DeWitt Talmage, D.D., as editor, and the powerful Gospel sermons of this preëminent American divine were supplemented by the rich pulpit utterances of Pastor Spurgeon of London,

THE BIBLE HOUSE, AND OFFICES OF " THE CHRISTIAN HERALD. "

Rev. Dr. R. S. McArthur of New York, Rev. Dr. A. J. Gordon of Boston, and other preachers of world-wide eminence. *The Christian Herald* was enlarged and greatly improved, and to-day mechanically, artistically, and in point of circulation and practical Christian teaching it leads the entire religious weekly press. Its press-rooms and bindery, in the De Vinne Building, are equipped with the latest and most improved machinery for printing and folding; and its business offices, Rooms 91 to 98 in the Bible House, occupy the largest space of any tenants in the building next to the Bible Society itself. Absolutely undenominational, *The Christian Herald* appeals to the moral and spiritual interests of Christians everywhere. Pastors find in its models a powerful aid to sermon-making ; Sunday-school teachers draw inspiration from it ; workers in every branch of Christian service find it a valuable help and encouragement. With its half million readers, in every State of the Union, it has an influence possessed by no other weekly religious newspaper. In the field of charity and philanthropy *The Christian Herald* has performed distinguished service. For years it has supported a missionary in the Southwest, where he has been the means of founding many Sunday-schools and chapels, and it also supported two evangelists in the East for several successive seasons. It conducted, at its own cost, the famous winter series of evangelistic services in the New-York Academy of Music, a few years ago, when many hundreds of conversions occurred. In the summer of 1892 it raised a fund of $40,000, with which it purchased a cargo of breadstuffs for the starving peasants of Russia. It cashed, free of charge, the checks of army pensioners (aggregating half a million dollars), to keep them from the degrading contact of the saloons. In one year it distributed among its readers 150,000 beautiful genuine Oxford Teachers' Bibles, as free gifts. In a multitude of other ways its influence is exerted for the good of the deserving; and object-lessons in Christian helpfulness are furnished to a circle of readers whose members are found in every country of the globe.

The Dry Goods Economist, the leading dry-goods paper in the world, enjoys the further distinction of being the oldest trade journal in existence, having been established in 1846. It was published for many years under the name of *United-States Economist and Dry Goods Reporter*, which was abridged to its present title. The scope of the paper comprises everything pertaining to the origination and distribution of textile fabrics, excepting only the mechanical processes of their production. The evolution of styles, weaves, colors and fashions abroad and at home, the

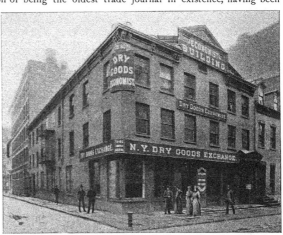

"DRY GOODS ECONOMIST" AND NEW-YORK DRY GOODS EXCHANGE,
78 AND 80 WALKER STREET.

problems of importation, transportation, and the whole machinery of distribution receive its constant attention. Commercial methods and abuses form a staple of discussion in its columns, while the practical operations of merchandise, purchasing, stock-keeping, advertising, window dressing and store management are each in its own department regularly elucidated. The staff of the *Dry Goods Economist* is unique in trade journalism, approaching probably more nearly than that of any publication to the organization of a great daily. This staff is distributed throughout the textile centres of the United States, Great Britain and Continental Europe, and is composed of expert specialists, so that its reports, statistics and opinions upon the subjects within its scope are regarded as authoritative not only in America, where it is the *vade mecum* of dry goods men in every State and territory, but also throughout Europe, where it is widely circulated. From its prominence as the recognized organ of our largest group of allied industries, its influence extends to matters of finance, and of legislation affecting textile industries. By reason of its unequalled hold upon the jobbing and retail merchants, the *Dry Goods Economist* has become the recognized sign-board of the dry-goods trade, and in its advertising pages will be found the timely announcements of the great textile establishments. The paper is distinguished for the extent and elegance of its special issues at the opening of the trade seasons, which are models of editorial and artistic excellence. The home of the paper is in the *Economist* Building, close to Broadway, on Walker Street, which marks the longitudinal centre of the metropolitan dry-goods district, and contains

" INSURANCE MONITOR;" 137 BROADWAY.

the New-York Dry-Goods Exchange. The paper is published weekly by the Textile Publishing Co., Charles T. Root, President ; Max Jaegerhuber, Treasurer ; Henry R. Elliot, Secretary.

The Insurance Monitor, published by C. C. Hine, at 137 Broadway, is one of the oldest trade journals in America, and the oldest in its particular line of service. It has been published continuously since March, 1853, — upwards of 40 years, — and during this time has not only recorded but has been influential in every important move that has helped to develop the insurance business in all of its many branches. In size of page it has remained virtually the same from the start, but in number of pages it has run up from 8 pages to a regular 48 pages, and occasional 80 pages, — in one year (1871–72) having issued 1,078 pages. In name it was at first *The Monitor;* then *The Insurance Monitor and Commercial Register;* later *The Insurance Monitor and Wall Street Review;* and since 1869 simply *Insurance Monitor.* Its first owner was T. Jones, Jr.; and since 1868, — a full quarter of a century, — it has been owned and edited by C. C. Hine, who has done more than any one else to elevate and maintain the character of insurance journalism. Its mission has been well executed, and in its columns has been disseminated and perpetuated all that is worthy of notice, technically, critically and practically, in every matter pertaining to all the various branches of insurance. The *Insurance Monitor* has not only watched and chronicled, but it has taken such part as an active journal would naturally take in the promulgation and advancement of insurance business. And then, too, under Mr. Hine's editorship the whole insurance fraternity, from the east to the west and from the north to the south, have learned to respect the clean, honest and trustworthy columns of the *Insurance Monitor.*

Other Weekly Publications include legal, financial and innumerable others.

The Monthly Publications cover every conceivable topic. There are magazines devoted to homœopathy, obstetrics, veterinary science, cutaneous diseases, microscopy, phrenology, ophthalmology ; to telegraphy, electricity, water works ;

to home-decoration, music, cabinet-making, penmanship ; to insurance, banking, and investments ; to dogs, bees, poultry, and horses.

The grocers have their magazines here, and so have the hair-dressers, the railroad men, the booksellers, the engineers, the photographers, the gas-men, the wine-merchants, the carpet-dealers, the printers, the stationers, the plumbers, the apothe-

"JUDGE" BUILDING, THE HOME OF FRANK LESLIE'S PUBLICATIONS, FIFTH AVENUE AND 16TH STREET.

caries, the paper-makers, the brewers, the bottlers, the exporters, the silk-makers, the tailors, the bankers, the blacksmiths, the wheelwrights, the woodworkers, the stenographers, the builders, the cloak-makers, the confectioners, the clothiers, expressmen, millers, hatters, furriers, jewellers, cooks, newsdealers, milliners, car_ builders, sailors, teachers, travellers, and many other classes of the great American people.

Harper's New Monthly Magazine was founded in 1850, and now enjoys an enormous circulation all over the world. H. M. Alden is the editor; and among the writers for departments have been Curtis, Warner, Howells, Aldrich, Mitchell, and other foremost leaders in American literature. The illustrations are the finest work of the best artists, and richly illuminate the magazine.

The Century Magazine, whose first editor was Dr. J. G. Holland, is now edited by Richard Watson Gilder, and published by the Century Company, of which the late Roswell Smith was longtime President. It is international in its character and circulation, and has an enormous circulation, running far beyond 100,000. The literary and artistic character of *The Century* cannot be surpassed.

Scribner's Magazine was founded in 1887, and has been edited, ever since that date, by E. L. Burlingame. It is a brilliantly illustrated modern periodical, treating vigorously of themes of present interest, with articles from the best writers.

The Cosmopolitan, founded in 1885, and edited by James Brisben Walker, is a handsome illustrated magazine, absolutely *fin du siècle* in its range of subjects and manner of treatment, and reaching a vast constituency of readers.

The North American Review, founded in 1815, is edited by Lloyd Brice. The most venerable publication of the kind in the Western World, it discusses the leading problems of the day, giving the views of the foremost authorities.

The Forum, founded in 1886, is edited by Walter H. Page. It is a monthly review of the uppermost topics of the time, in essays by well-known writers.

The Art Amateur, founded in 1879, is owned and edited by Montague Marks; and has been of great avail in the development of American art.

The Art-Interchange dates its origin from the year 1864, and has choice illustrations, and articles on modern painting, etching, engraving and similar themes.

The Catholic World, founded in 1840, and edited by Rev. W. D. Hughes, is published by the Paulist Fathers, and has a wide circulation among cultivated Roman Catholics. It is purely literary in tone, and has many able contributors.

Outing is an attractive illustrated magazine, devoted to descriptions of out-door life, fresh, breezy and exhilarating. It was founded by W. B. Howland, at Chatham, N. Y., and, after being transferred to Boston for a few years, became a New-York institution.

Godey's Magazine is one of the most venerable of American periodicals. It was founded at Philadelphia in 1830, and recently moved to New York, where it has developed into a brilliant and progressive modern magazine.

McClure's Magazine, founded in 1893, is a small-priced illustrated periodical, with contributions from the most illustrious authors, on the most interesting subjects. It is published by S. S. McClure, of newspaper "syndicate" fame.

The Magazine of American History, founded in 1877, is occupied by illustrated articles on historical themes. It was long edited by the late Martha J. Lamb.

The Popular Science Monthly, founded in 1872, and edited by Prof. W. J. Youmans, is devoted to papers by competent writers on the latest phases of sciences.

St. Nicholas, founded in 1873, edited by Mary Mapes Dodge; for boys and girls; illustrated. This is the best magazine for young people ever published.

In the years between 1833 and 1872 more than a hundred papers, periodical and daily, were founded and suspended. In the two decades since 1872, there was a still greater number. The new processes of engraving illustrations tempted many newspaper minds, but in the struggle for life the fittest survived.

COLUMBIA BUILDING.   BROADWAY.   CONSOLIDATED EXCHANGE.

TRINITY CHURCH.   MANHATTAN LIFE BUILDING.   STANDARD OIL BUILDING

LOWER BROADWAY.

LOOKING NORTH FROM BOWLING GREEN.

PUCK BUILDING,
EAST HOUSTON AND MULBERRY STREETS.

Fire and Marine Insurance·

Offices and Companies for Assuming Losses by Fires and Transit, and Fire and Marine Underwriters' Associations.

IN 1759 the "Old Insurance Office," open from noon to one o'clock and from six to eight o'clock in the evening every day, and the "New-York Insurance Office," the former at the Coffee-House, under charge of Kefeltas & Sharpe, the latter in an adjoining building, under charge of Anthony Van Dam, gave marine insurance to merchants, secured by subscriptions of underwriters. In 1778, as the destruction of vessels by American privateers had increased the risk of navigation, a "New Insurance Office" was opened at the Coffee-House. Vessels or their cargoes were then in a primitive manner protected ; but if buildings were burned, their value to the owners of them was lost, unless they circulated subscription-papers, as did the owner of a wooden building in Barclay Street, destroyed by fire in November, 1796. He said to the public : "Citizens are all dependent, the one upon the other. Relieve the distress of a sinking brother, and he, and not he only, will bless you."

In 1770 as the "Philadelphia Contributionship for the Insurance of Houses from Loss by Fire" had eighteen years of life and prosperity, a member of the Chamber of Commerce in New York proposed the formation of a similar Contributionship ; but not until 1787 was incorporated, under the name of "Mutual Assurance Company," the first New-York fire-insurance company.

In 1798 a charter was granted to Nicholas Low and others, with corporate powers, in the name of "United Insurance Company in the city of New York," enabling them "the better to carry on and extend the business of maritime insurance and of insurance upon houses, goods and lives, which were the useful purpose of their institution." The "Mutual Assurance Company" was renewed and incorporated — it had been organized in 1787, under a deed of settlement, by its secretary, John Pintard, according to the English custom. In 1809 the company was reorganized, with a capital stock ; in 1846, its name was changed to "Knickerbocker Fire-Insurance Company" ; and in 1890 it was dissolved. One of its policies of 1798 is framed in the Fire Patrol Office. In 1798 a third company was incorporated, "The New-York Insurance Company for Maritime Insurance, Houses, Goods and Lives." It had a capital, in shares of $50 each, not to exceed $500,000 ; and its charter expired in 1809.

In 1801 the first exclusively marine stock company in New York, the "Marine Insurance Company," was organized, with a capital of $250,000. Then came a revision of contracts, a classification of hazards, and a re-arrangement of rates, made necessary by extension of business and provoked by experience. The "Eagle Insurance Company," incorporated in 1806, issued this tariff :—

"Hazards of the first class, brick or stone buildings, with slate, tile or metal roofs, and non-hazardous goods therein, 25 per cent. Hazards of the fourth class, wooden buildings, non-hazardous goods therein, and hazardous goods in third class, 75 to 100 per cent."

In 1830 there were in New York eight marine companies, with an aggregate capital of $3,050,000 ; and twenty-five fire companies, with an aggregate capital of $7,800,000. In 1835 there were twenty-six fire companies ; and twenty-three of them were thrown into bankruptcy by the fire which destroyed, on the night of December 16, 529 stores and 41 other buildings situated south of Wall Street, the business centre of the city. Then followed the wise law by which fire companies are prohibited from engaging in the affairs of life-insurance, banking and trust companies; and other companies may not accumulate functions, but are chartered for specific purposes, life or marine or other insurance, or banking. Then came the repeal of an act passed in 1829, by which foreign companies were excluded from the State of New York. Then forms of policies, conditions of insurance, classifications, the entire system of fire and marine insurance acquired the precision, the exactness of the present time. With Massachusetts, New York began to shape insurance legislation and methods for the whole country. In 1845 a second conflagration in the business center of New York destroyed property valued at $6,000,000. In 1846 an association of city underwriters, formed for mutual protection, convened in New York a national meeting of underwriters. Of this meeting, and of two others, in 1849 and 1850, came in 1866 the National Board of Fire-Underwriters, by which the advantages obtained in New York were made applicable to the whole country.

In 1859 the Insurance Department of the State of New York was organized. In 1864, for the first time, all the insurance companies were required by law to make and file annual statements. From this period, the complete historical and financial chronicles of insurance may be easily compiled. They are in the reports made to the State Assembly by the Superintendent of the Insurance Department. In 1860 the premium receipts of the New-York stock fire companies were $7,000,000 ; in 1863, after two years of civil war, they were $10,000,000 ; in 1865 they were $20,000,-000. In 1860 the premium receipts of the marine companies were $14,000,000 ; and in 1863 they were $18,000,000. In 1871 the Chicago fire, in 1872 the Boston fire, ruined the Astor, Beekman, Corn-Exchange, Excelsior, Humboldt, Market, New-Amsterdam, North-American, Washington, Yonkers, New-York and other insurance companies, some of which were afterward reorganized. In thirty years the Insurance Department noted the withdrawal of eighty-three fire and ten marine insurance companies.

The Board of Fire-Underwriters is an evolution of the "Salamander Society," a combination of insurance officers organized in 1819 to 1826, transformed frequently, and incorporated under its present title in 1867. It guides insurance legislation ; guards or advises the Superintendent of Buildings, the Fire-Commissioners and the Fire-Marshal ; maintains the Fire-Patrol, with the aid of a legislative enactment that it created ; and usually commands a tariff of rates of premium to be charged by all underwriters on metropolitan risks. It has, at present, an executive committee of forty members. Its standing committees are on Finance, Fire-Patrol, Laws and Legislation, Surveys, Police and Origin of Fires, Arbitration, Patents, Membership, and Water Supply. It adopted in 1886 a standard fire-insurance policy, the form of which is desirable.

The Fire-Patrol is an organization of the Board of Fire-Underwriters, and was a condition of its charter, "to provide a patrol of men, and a competent person to act as superintendent, to discover and prevent fires, with suitable apparatus to save and preserve property or life at and after a fire ; and the better to enable them so to act with promptness and efficiency, full power is given to such superintendent and to such patrol to enter any building on fire, or which may be exposed to or in danger of taking fire from other burning buildings, at once proceed to protect and endeavor to save the property therein, and to remove such property, or any part thereof, from the ruins after a fire." For the maintenance of this patrol the Board of Fire-Underwriters obtained the passage of an act obliging all insurance companies doing business in New York to pay two per cent. of their city premium receipts semi-annually, as a tax.

The Fire-Patrol existed long before this act, but in a different form. In 1835 the city association of fire-insurance companies paid $1,000 a year to a Fire-Police of four men ; in 1839 it employed forty members or past members of the Volunteer Fire-Department as patrolmen at night in the Fifth Fire (the mercantile) District. In 1845 water-proof covers for merchandise, in 1851 covers for roofs and sky-lights, in 1864 a steam pumping-engine for drying cellars, were adopted ; but the service was practically, like the contributions of the insurance companies for the expenses, voluntary. The last statistical record, the record of 1891, of the present well-equipped and well-paid Fire-Patrol, shows that during the year 1891 it attended to 2,091 fire-alarms, performed $2,228\frac{18}{10}$ hours of service, spread 9,819 covers, and cared for property the total insurance on which was $29,897,649, and the total loss $5,252,659. The Fire-Patrol stations are : No. 1, 41 Murray Street, 42 officers and men ; No. 2, 31 Great Jones Street, 40 officers and men ; No. 3, 104 West 30th Street, 29 officers and men ; No. 4, 113 East 90th Street, 14 officers and men ; and No. 5, 307 West 121st Street, 14 officers and men. Abram C. Hull is the superintendent. Wm. M. Randall, an old volunteer fireman and underwriter, has long occupied the office of Secretary to the Fire-Patrol committee.

The Insurance Companies of to-day represent an enormous accumulation of assets for the payment of losses by fire and the elements. There were $63,947,365 in assets of New-York joint-stock companies ; $112,072,902 in assets of joint-stock companies of other States ; $2,637,562 in assets of mutual companies ; and $56,324,823 in assets of foreign companies, invested in the fire-insurance business in New York, at the date of the report to the Insurance Department, December 31, 1892.

FIREMEN AT WORK IN 1800.

The history of the following companies is the main history of the fire-insurance business in New York in its best aspects:

The New-York Bowery Fire-Insurance Company, at 124 Bowery and 168 Broadway, was incorporated April 24, 1833. It commenced business September 21, 1833, and at the end of a year had gross assets amounting to $322,818. Its paid-up cash capital was then $290,318. January 1, 1892, its paid-up cash capital was $300,000, and the amount of its gross assets $548,719, invested as follows: New-York City stock, $150,000; railroad bonds, $76,565; stocks, $204,733; loans on bond and mortgage, $16,200; call loans on collateral security, $3,700; interest accrued, $4,623; premiums in course of collection, not over ninety days due, $90,532; cash in bank and office, $1,654; re-insurance due from other companies on losses, $711. It has a net surplus of $70,521 over all its liabilities, including the capital stock and the reserve-fund for re-insurance, making a surplus

NEW-YORK BOWERY FIRE-INSURANCE COMPANY, BOWERY AND GRAND STREET.

to policy-holders of $370,521. It has paid in losses by fire, since its organization, $4,772,457. It passed, without imperilling its constant financial solidity, through the conflagrations of 1835, 1845, 1871, and 1872, by which hundreds of companies were thrown into bankruptcy. Its President is Henry Silberhorn, its Vice-President is Charles A. Blauvelt, its Secretary is J. Frank Patterson, New-Yorkers, long and faithful servants of the company, as were before them Geo. G. Taylor, William Hibbard, Peter Pinckney, James Lovett, and the first President, Benjamin M. Brown. The Directors are: Thompson Pinckney, William P. Woodcock, 2d, Henry Silberhorn, John Wilkin, Gurdon G. Brinckerhoff, Helmuth Kranich, Charles A. Blauvelt, Henry B. Pye, Herman F. Kanenbley, George W. Silberhorn, J. Frank Patterson, James E. Morris, Edwin Van Houten, O. J. Wiggins, Benjamin T. Rhoads, Jr. Personally acquainted with every phase of the company's experience, the officers and Board of Directors merit the confidence that the record of the New-York Bowery Fire-Insurance Company and its financial statement command.

The company has its agencies scattered throughout the United States, but it seeks to do only the most conservative class of business, moderate lines and well distributed. The New-York Bowery is virtually, with a single exception, the oldest of the New-York fire-insurance companies, for, while some have taken the names and succeeded to the business of older companies, they were either re-organized or decapitalized after the great fires of 1835, or 1871 and 1872.

The Greenwich Insurance Company, of New York, the principal offices of which are in the company's own five-story stone-front building at 161 Broadway, has been uninterruptedly and successfully in business nearly sixty years. It was organized in 1834. Timothy Whittemore was its first President and held that office 25 years. Samuel C. Harriot was President for 31 years. Joseph Torrey was Secretary 13 years. James Harrison was Secretary 23 years. Mason A. Stone was Secretary 19 years. Such tenures of office indicate an unusual conservatism of policy and security of operation, and must inevitably inspire confidence in the Greenwich Insurance Company as a strong and secure financial corporation.

The value of property destroyed by fire in the United States in 1891 was $143,764,967, an amount larger than the yearly cost of the public schools of America, larger than the payments to pensioners, larger than the value of the National bank notes in circulation, larger than the aggregate yearly cost of the War and Navy Departments, larger than the coining value of the gold and silver mined in the United States yearly. It is to save the people from the appalling consequences of such losses, unrelieved, that the Greenwich and its sister companies are perpetually active.

An institution that has paid nearly $10,-000,000 for fire-losses and dividends, as the Greenwich has, without a single failure or delay in over half a century of extremely active business, is certainly a firm support to lean upon.

Its capital stock is $200,000; and its net surplus January 1, 1891, was nearly $400,000; making, with its capital, a net surplus, so far as concerns policy-holders, of $595,000. It owns real estate to the value of $170,000, and its available assets amount to about $1,600,000. The Greenwich has had an honorable career. It has paid losses amounting to nearly $7,000,000, since it began business ; and it has paid to its stockholders in cash dividends over $2,000,000,

THE GREENWICH INSURANCE COMPANY, 161 BROADWAY, BETWEEN LIBERTY AND CORTLAND.

and has never failed to pay a semi-annual dividend in every year since organization. Its business at its home office in the city of New York is very large, only two of the 140 companies doing business in the city receiving as large a volume of premiums on New-York City business as the Greenwich. The directors of the company own more than 25 per cent. of its stock. The present President, Mason A. Stone, has been an officer of the corporation for 21 years, having been chosen Assistant-Secretary in 1871 and Secretary in 1872. Associated with him, as a Board of Directors, are William H. S. Elting, Quentin McAdam, Solomon W. Albro, James A. Roosevelt, George Gordon, Allen S. Apgar, Augustus C. Brown, William P. Douglas, Samuel W. Harriot, William Brookfield, Alexander T. Van Nest, John L. Riker, Robert B. Suckley, Isaac G. Johnson, Joseph P. Puels, Ebenezer Bailey and J. Lynch Montgomery. Walter B. Ward and William Adams are Assistant-Secretaries. The Greenwich has its agencies in most of the chief cities of this country. Its policies are sought for by the best business men of the whole country, and the fire-insurance agents and brokers everywhere never hesitate to recommend to their patrons the insurance protection afforded by the Greenwich Insurance Company.

The Citizens' Insurance Company, at 156 Broadway, was incorporated April 28, 1836, as the "Williamsburgh Fire-Insurance Company" of Williamsburgh, N. Y., now the Eastern District of Brooklyn; changed in name to "Citizens' Fire-Insurance Company," and in location to

Brooklyn, in 1849; and amended in title to "Citizens' Insurance Company" simply, in 1865. It had in 1849 a capital of $105,000, and gross assets amounting to $131,143. In a quarter of a century, after the great fires of Chicago and Boston had thrown into bankruptcy a hundred insurance companies, and crippled and almost ruined many others, the Citizens' Insurance Company had a capital of $300,000 and gross assets amounting to $843,802. This in spite of the fact that the great fires of Chicago and Boston had multiplied by eight its annual average of losses by fire. At present the Citizens' Insurance Company has a capital of $300,000, and gross assets amounting to $1,081,041. It has a net surplus over all its liabilities and the reserve fund for re-insurance, of $228,150. It has paid for losses, since its organization, $6,355,398, about fifty per cent. of its premium receipts, a smaller proportion of loss than the statistics of the fire-insurance business concede. The Citizens' Insurance Company has had in its entire history three Presidents: Daniel Burtnett, until 1859; James M.

CITIZENS' INSURANCE COMPANY, 156 BROADWAY.

McLean, until 1886; and Edward A. Walton, until the present time. Mr. McLean was Secretary during the entire period that Mr. Burtnett was President, and was in the service of the company for 39 years. Mr. Walton was Secretary until 1881, and from that year Vice-President until 1886, when he became President, and has been in the service of the company for 43 years. The Vice-President is George H. McLean, a well-known and esteemed New-Yorker, son of the former President of the company, and in its service for a decade. The Secretary is Frank M. Parker, a prominent citizen of Newark, N. J., and a servant of the company in every department for a quarter of a century. Thus the Citizens' Insurance Company has the advantage of a management intimately allied with every phase of its experience — an experience which begins with the first years of fire-insurance in this country. The Directors are : Wm. J. Valentine, capitalist ; Edward Schell, President Manhattan Savings Institution ; Amos F. Eno, real estate ; John D. Jones, President Atlantic Mutual Insurance Co. ; Edward A. Walton, President ; De Witt C. Hays, President Manhattan Company Bank ; Edward King, President Union Trust Co. ; George H. McLean, Vice-President ; James W. Smith, President Consolidated Gas Co. ; George F. Baker, President First National Bank ; Garret A. Hobart, lawyer ;

ATLANTIC MUTUAL INSURANCE COMPANY, WALL AND WILLIAM STREETS.

William Barbour, President Barbour Brothers Thread Co. ; and H. B. Stokes, President Manhattan Life-Insurance Co. It is allied with the "Hanover" in the operations of the New-York Underwriters' Agency in the South and West.

The Atlantic Mutual Insurance Company was incorporated in 1842 as a mutual insurance company, without capital other than the sum of $100,000, which was borrowed as a temporary convenience, and which was returned within two years. Since its organization, the premiums received from dealers on risks terminated amount to $186,730,564. The losses paid to dealers on risks insured have been $107,981,322. The certificates of profits issued to dealers have amounted to $66,147,580, of which there have been redeemed in cash $59,135,560, and the cash paid for interest on certificates amounts to $14,020,573.

Its main business is the insuring of vessels and their cargoes, as well as inland transportation risks.   Since its incorporation in 1842 it has done a great service to the commercial interests of New York, by reason of its absolute protection to the property of the owners of vessels, the importers and exporters, by making insurance in their interests.   Its gross assets exceed $12,250,000, as may be seen in the detailed statement.   Perhaps some conception of the insurance it grants can be obtained from the statement that its annual premium receipts alone exceed $5,000,000. This company is a wholly mutual organization, and for this reason it is a semi-public institution.   All the profits of the company revert to the insured, and are divided yearly upon the premiums terminated during the year, thereby reducing the cost of insurance.   These dividends are paid in interest-bearing certificates known as " scrip," which are in time redeemed by the company.   Provision is made for issuing policies by which the losses are payable in England.

January 1, 1893, the company's assets amounted to $12,485,685, and in 1892 its gross premiums aggregated $5,162,393, while the losses paid amounted to $1,466,-178, and return of premiums and expenses, $738,617.   The company owns ·its own office-building on Wall Street, at the corner of William Street.   Its plain and sub-stantial appearance indicates the solid conservative corporation whose offices it con-tains.   When it was built, in 1852, it was the finest office-building on Wall Street, but now it is overshadowed by many superb structures, so that it seems to be a con-spicuous landmark of two generations ago.   European countries boast of long records of officers of their great corporations, and the civil-service advocates make great claims for the advancement of men in various positions, but the Atlantic Mutual In-surance Company has a record in this particular hardly equalled on either continent. Its President, John D. Jones, has been continuously an officer almost coeval with the history of the company for 50 years, first as its Secretary, and for the past 37 years as its President.   Its Vice-President, W. H. H. Moore, has been connected with the company for 37 years ; the Second Vice-President, A. A. Raven, for 40 years ; the Secretary, Joseph H. Chapman, for 38 years ; four óf those holding im-portant positions have been connected with the company for 40 years and over ; and many of its trustees, the leading influential men of New York, have served on the Board continuously for more than a quarter of a century.   The peculiar constitution and methods of the Atlantic Mutual have made it an interesting study for insurance experts, as well as an invincible tower of strength to all shipowners who can avail themselves of its splendid defence.

The Niagara Fire-Insurance Company owns and occupies its own six-story stone-front building at 135 and 137 Broadway.   It was incorporated December 29, 1849, and commenced business August 1, 1850, with a paid-up cash capital of $200,-000.   In 1864 it had paid the equivalent of its capital more than twice in dividends, and more than twice in losses, and yet accumulated a large surplus.   The capital was increased to $1,000,000 in 1864.   In 1871 came the Chicago fire, which destroyed property to the value of $200,000,000, ruined 68 companies and forced 24 to assess their stockholders.   The next year came thé Boston fire, which destroyed property to the value of $73,500,000, and ruined several other companies. The Niagara paid at once every claim, and reduced its capital to $500,000.   There was not a moment of hesitation in its affairs.   The company wished to prove, and it proved, that it was ready for any emergency.   Its progress in twenty years has been constant.   The assets, which were $1,264,538 at the end of 1872, were at the end of 1891, $2,723,185.   The total liabilities, actual and contingent, including the re-insurance fund, are $1,902,401.   The company has a surplus, as regards policy-holders, of $820,784. Its business is excellent; its investments sacrifice speculative profits in favor of absolute security; its management is celebrated for its carefulness.

The officers of the company are personally allied with every phase of its history. The earlier Presidents have been W. B. Bend, in 1850; Jonathan D. Steele, in 1852; Henry A. Howe, in 1871, and Peter Notman, in 1880. The President is Thos. F. Goodrich, who became connected with the company in 1880 as Secretary, and was made Vice-President in 1884, and President in 1893. The Secretaries are George C. Howe, who has been with the company since he was fifteen years of age, and Charles H. Post, who has been with the company over five years.

NIAGARA FIRE-INSURANCE COMPANY, 135 AND 137 BROADWAY.

The Niagara Fire-Insurance Company, in 1892, consummated the arrangements by which it takes charge of the American business of the Caledonian Fire-Insurance Company of Scotland, the officers of the Niagara Fire-Insurance Company being the American managers for that famous old Scottish organization.

The Hanover Fire-Insurance Company of New York, the principal office of which is at present in the Mutual Life-Insurance Company's Building at 40 Nassau Street, was incorporated April 6, 1852, and commenced business April 16th, with John N. Wyckoff as its first president, and a cash capital of $150,000. This was increased to $200,000 in 1857, and to $400,000 in 1863; and reduced to $250,000 after the losses by the Boston fire, in 1872, which ruined so many companies, had been paid; increased within four months to $400,000, in 1873; and to $500,000 in 1875, by a stock dividend of $100,000. The cash capital is now $1,000,000, and the gross assets are $2,600,990. The amount is made up of real estate, $250,000; United-States bonds, $111,025; bonds and mortgages, first liens on improved real-estate in New York and Brooklyn, $23,000; State and city bonds, $485,000; loans on call, $51,600; cash in banks and in office, $95,412; railroad first-mortgage bonds, $770,778; bank and trust companies' stocks, $92,715; railroad, gas and telegraph companies' stocks, $538,262; premiums in hands of agents, in course of transmission, and uncollected office premiums, $172,194; accrued interest, $11,002. The Hanover Fire-Insurance Company has a net surplus over its capital, liabilities and re-insurance reserve of $403,089. It has never passed a dividend, and has paid 450 per cent. to stockholders in its forty-one years of life. It has paid to policy-holders for losses by fire in that period $13,943,180. Its losses by the great fires in Chicago (1871) and Boston (1872) were over a quarter of a million dollars each.

The President is I. Remsen Lane, who has been connected with the company for thirty years, and began service with it as a clerk. Vice-President and Secretary Charles L. Roe, Assistant-Secretary Charles A. Shaw, and General Agent of the Eastern Department, Thomas James, have all been identified with the company for a long series of years. It is allied with the "Citizens'" in the operations of the New-York Underwriters' Agency in the South and West.

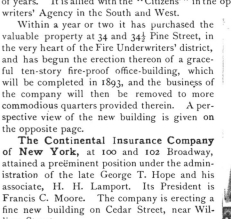

Within a year or two it has purchased the valuable property at 34 and 34½ Pine Street, in the very heart of the Fire Underwriters' district, and has begun the erection thereon of a graceful ten-story fire-proof office-building, which will be completed in 1893, and the business of the company will then be removed to more commodious quarters provided therein. A perspective view of the new building is given on the opposite page.

The Continental Insurance Company of New York, at 100 and 102 Broadway, attained a preëminent position under the administration of the late George T. Hope and his associate, H. H. Lamport. Its President is Francis C. Moore. The company is erecting a fine new building on Cedar Street, near William Street.

42D STREET, WEST FROM FOURTH AVENUE.

HANOVER FIRE-INSURANCE COMPANY OF NEW YORK.
PINE STREET, BETWEEN NASSAU AND WILLIAM STREETS.

The Home Insurance Company of New York is, with a single exception, the greatest of all the fire-insurance companies of America. The Home was organ-ized April 13, 1853, and has had over forty years of success and steady growth. From the start it has been a national institution, seeking its patronage from every nook and corner of the whole country, and the traditions and experiences of the agency business might readily be written within the records of this company. It

HOME INSURANCE COMPANY, 117 AND 119 BROADWAY.

was the pioneer New-York company to enter the agency business, and, jointly with a few of the oldest Hartford companies, it was the founder of the whole business of fire-underwriting through agencies. It started with a cash capital of $500,000, at that time considered an enormous amount for a fire-insurance company. It has since been increased — in 1858, to $600,000; in 1859, to $1,000,000; in 1864, to $2,000,000; in 1870, to $2,500,000; and in 1875, to $3,000,000, at which it still remains, equalled by only one other American company. Its gross assets, which exceed $9,000,000, are also equalled by only one other company. It has passed through all the great fires of the last forty years, and after the Chicago fire its stockholders almost spontaneously paid in $1,500,000, to more than make good its impairment of capital, so as to leave the Home richer in assets and stronger in reputation than ever before. At the beginning of the year 1893 its gross assets were $9,328,754, which included its great reserve premium fund of $4,225,113, besides a net surplus over its capital of $3,000,000, and all liabilities, of $1,279,239. It had also set aside $637,255 for unpaid losses, and $187,147 for other items. A glance at its detailed statement shows conclusively that its enormous assets are judi-ciously invested, with a keen provision for any extraordinary demand that may come up in any emergency. Its officers are men of ripe experience, several having been identified with the company since its beginning. Its President is Daniel A. Heald. The Vice-Presidents are John H. Washburn and Elbridge G. Snow ; the Secretaries, William L. Bigelow and Thomas B. Greene ; and the Assistant-Secretaries are Henry J. Ferris and Areunah M. Burtis ; altogether forming a coterie of fire-under-writers that commands the respect of the whole profession ; and the Board of Directors includes a most distinguished body of New-York business men. The company's New-York offices for sixteen years were at 135 Broadway, but at the completion of the Boreel Building, in 1879, at 117 and 119 Broadway, it took possession of its present offices, the main floor being one of the largest and grandest offices on this continent. In Chicago the " Home " built, in 1885–86, and still owns, one of the best of those gigantic and admirable office-buildings for which the Western metropolis is famous. The Home Insurance Company has its ramifications everywhere, and its corps of reporting agents would make an army of about 3,500 men. Founded, built up, and conducted on the broadest, most progressive, and most generous lines, the " Home " is an institution that, in its field, brings the utmost credit to the American metropolis.

The Rutgers Fire-Insurance Company, on Chatham Square, at the junction of Park Row, Mott and Worth Streets, was incorporated October 3d, and commenced business October 10, 1853. " Are you insured ? " For thirty-nine years the New-Yorkers have read and heard this startling question of the Rutgers. " Are you insured ? Rutgers Fire-Insurance Company," on the signboard in front of its plain, unpretentious building, on its policies, bills, letter-paper, cards ; in the flames that made the sky red ; in the alarm-bells of the City Hall in the days when firemen were volunteers. Are you insured ? It is like a cry of conscience. In over forty years there were many who did not heed it ; there were many who heeded it partly, insuring in other companies, some of which failed, some of which were ruined by the fire in Chicago, some of which were burned out of life in Boston, and some perhaps by injudicious management, but the Rutgers never desisted a moment. Are you insured ? The most intelligent New-

RUTGERS FIRE-INSURANCE CO., PARK ROW, WORTH AND MOTT STREETS.

Yorkers have always understood. It is not everything to have a policy of insurance ; is it a policy of the Rutgers? The company began with a capital of $200,000. It has paid nearly six times the amount of its capital in dividends to its stockholders ; it has paid $1,400,000 to its policy-holders for losses ; it has contributed handsomely to the business supremacy of New York ; but it has its capital of $200,000 intact, and a net surplus of $134,576 over all its liabilities, including its reserve-fund for re-insurance, Are you insured? The President of the Rutgers from 1853 until 1866 was Hon. Isaac O. Barker, an eminent New-Yorker, and President of the Board of Aldermen. At his death, Edward B. Fellows, who had been Secretary since the first day of the company's existence, and one of its originators, became President. It was principally by his influence that the office of Fire-Marshal was created in 1854. He has had a share in every labor for the improvement of New York within the lines of the fire-insurance business. The present officers are : E. B. Fellows, President ; D. H. McAlpin, Vice-President ; H. C. Kreiser, Secretary ; Wm. Peet, Attorney ; Lewis S. Watkins, Surveyor ; and Geo. F. Burger, Agency Department. The Directors are William Peet, Jacob Miller, Edgar M. Crawford, Thomas H. Brown, Geo. Williamson, Henry Silberhorn, Oscar Purdy, William M. Cole, David H. McAlpin, Edward B. Fellows, James L. Stewart, David Mahany, Seth P. Squire, Thos. H. Dolan, Joseph Haight, Henry Demarest, Elwood B. Mingay, George F. Coddington, Geo. W. Quackenboss, and James Y. Watkins. The Rutgers has never changed. If the members of its Board of Directors who have died should return they would find the table at which they sat, familiar furniture, well-known office surroundings. The Rutgers has improved with age ; every decade has made it stronger and stronger. Its funds are wisely invested, its affairs are managed with economy and ability.

The American Fire-Insurance Company, at 146 Broadway, was incorporated in 1857. In 1860 its assets were $269,671 ; in 1870 they were $743,405 ; in 1880 they were $1,044,604. The first of January, 1892, they were $1,685,083. In 1868 the American was one of 95 New-York-State insurance companies ; in 1870, one of 96 ; in 1880, one of 78 ; in 1891, one of 41. It has staying qualities unsurpassed by any other company. Its first President was James M. Halsted, who remained in office until his death, in 1888. Its present President came into the service of the company in 1862, was Assistant-Secretary in 1866, afterward Secretary, Vice-President in 1887, and naturally succeeded James M. Halsted. Its first Secretary was Frederick W. Downer, until 1865 ; its second, Thomas L. Thornell, until 1880 ; its third, David Adee, now President, then assisted by William H. Crolius, now Secretary, for 27 years in the company's service. The Assistant-Secretary, Charles P. Peirce, was cashier for 20 years, and has been an employee of the company for 25 years. The Agency Manager, Silas P. Wood, has also been connected with the company for a number of years. Few companies anywhere have their experience more intimately allied with their officers. Few have made better use of their opportunities. The American passed without injury through the conflagrations of Boston and Chicago, and despite the depression in business of later years, from which so many strong institutions have suffered, has accumulated a surplus, over unearned premiums and other liabilities, amounting to $642,167. Prompt in its adjustment of losses, and zealous in the interest of its policy-holders, the American unites all the qualities that command implicit confidence. Its capital is $400,000 ; its re-insurance reserve, $792,552 ; its gross liabilities, $1,042,915, and its gross assets $1,685,083.

The Williamsburgh City Fire-Insurance Company, organized in 1853, owns the tall and graceful brick-and-stone building at the northeast corner of

AMERICAN FIRE-INSURANCE COMPANY.
MUTUAL LIFE BUILDING, BROADWAY AND LIBERTY STREET.

Broadway and Liberty Street, a model office-building, erected on a site formerly occupied by houses of the Jumel estate. The structure is equipped with Worthington pumps, electric lights, and other modern conveniences.

The German American Insurance Company, at 115 Broadway, was organized March 7, 1872, by merchants, among whom were some of the most eminent dry-goods men of the city. It has a capital of $1,000,-000, and gross assets amounting to $5,879,208, thus invested: United-States, New-York City, and Brooklyn city bonds, $1,410,988; St. Louis, Portland, Ore., Atlanta and Nashville city bonds, $213,500; railroad bonds, $1,590,107; railroad stocks, $1,497,931; New-York City bank stocks, $121,365; New-York City gas-companies' stocks, $140,250; Standard Oil Trust stock, $84,500; Western Union Telegraph Company stock, $83,750; cash in banks, trust-companies

GERMAN AMERICAN INSURANCE COMPANY, 115 BROADWAY.

CANAL, VESTRY, AND VARICK STREETS, SHOWING ST. JOHN'S CHURCH.

WILLIAMSBURG CITY FIRE-INSURANCE COMPANY.
BROADWAY AND LIBERTY STREET.

and office, and with department managers, $420,775 ; premiums in course of collec-tion and accrued interest, $316,044. Above all its liabilities and reserve-fund for re-insurance it has a surplus of $2,255,389. The President of the company is E. Oelbermann, the head of one of the wealthiest and greatest of American importing houses ; the Vice-President is John W. Murray, an old and experienced fire-under-writer, who was Secretary at the organization ; the Second Vice-President and Secre-tary is James A. Silvey ; the Third Vice-President is George T. Patterson ; the Assistant-Secretaries of the Agency Department are W. S. Newell and P. E. Rasor. In its Board of Directors, in its managing officers, in the character of its investments, the German-American Insurance Company is excellent. In the just pride with which it is regarded as an institution of New York, the share of praise to be divided between its sound financial and skilful underwriting departments could not easily be figured. It started at the time of the great Chicago and Boston fires, with a paid-up capital of immense magnitude, and its career has been steadily and remarkably successful.

The Western Department of the German-American has its headquarters at Chicago, under Eugene Cary, Manager, and Rogers Porter, Assistant-Manager. The Pacific Department is managed by George H. Tyson, General Agent, at San Francisco.

The New-York Underwriters' Agency, formerly at 34 Nassau Street and now at 135 Broadway, is under the management of Alexander Stoddart. It is formed of the Hanover Fire-Insurance Company and of the Citizens' (Fire) Insur-ance Company, and issues by its agents throughout the South and West a single policy representing assets amounting to $3,632,371, and a net surplus over all liabilities of $683,588. It represents the combined strength and integrity of two fire-insurance companies which promptly paid every cent of their losses by the conflagrations which destroyed the business districts of Chicago and Boston, and ruined hundreds of insurance companies. It has its own independent record, the

NEW-YORK UNDERWRITERS' AGENCY ; ALEXANDER STODDART, GENERAL AGENT.

record of an organization as distinct as either of the companies that form it. With the public and with all the prominent fire-insurance agents of the country the name of the New-York Underwriters' Agency is a synonym for correct business methods. Its agents are its firm friends, and it carefully guards their interests. It is equitable in its adjustments of losses, it is prompt in meeting its obligations, it is an honor and an advantage to every agent by whom it is represented, for its policy of insurance is a guarantee of absolute safety. There is no institution with which the interests of the people of the West and South are more closely allied.

Mr. Stoddart was the originator of the plan, since quite often followed, of utilizing the combined assets of two or more companies by means of issuing a single policy to the insured; thus giving to the insured far greater security, and affording to the companies a minimum of cost in securing and carrying on the business. The general offices of the New-York Underwriters' Agency were in the Mutual Life-Insurance Building on Nassau Street ever since that magnificent building was completed until 1893. Sketches of the Citizens' and the Hanover Fire-Insurance companies appear elsewhere in this chapter.

The Mutual Fire-Insurance Company, in the City of New York, commenced business June 19, 1882, with a cash fund of $200,000, contributed by about two hundred of the leading business houses of New York, Philadelphia and Boston. At the end of the fiscal year, June 30, 1883, its cash assets amounted to $317,988;

and on January 1, 1893, the cash assets were $1,284,656. From its organization to January 1, 1893, it has received $6,464,315 net premiums, and paid losses amounting to $3,662,715, and paid cash dividends to its policy-holders of over $1,000,000. This company makes a specialty of writing large lines on selected and protected risks, in fact, this was the fundamental idea upon which the company was organized. It is in fact a business men's institution, organized and conducted by business men in their mutual interests for the prevention and indemnification of fires and fire losses. The financial standing of every applicant and the peculiar hazard of each risk are carefully scrutinized, and when they are found satisfactory, a policy for the maximum amount is written. This company has organized a system of frequent and thorough examination of all risks taken, for the purpose of discovering the particular fire hazards and the means of overcoming them. The Mutual Fire was the first company to apply a system of regular and rigid inspection of mercantile risks, and while claiming no original ideas with regard to preventing fires, yet good work has been done in securing improvements and removing dangers.

MUTUAL FIRE-INSURANCE CO., 49 CEDAR STREET.

42

Its main offices are in the handsome and graceful eleven-story Stokes Building, at 45, 47 and 49 Cedar Street, on the north side between William Street and Nassau Street.

The Mutual Fire-Insurance Co.'s policies are sought for by the largest and most conservative business houses everywhere.

The financial condition of the company on January 1, 1893, was as follows : assets, $1,284,656 ; liabilities, $557,321 ; surplus to policy-holders, $727,335. The present officers of the company are : Joseph C. Hatié, President ; Oscar R. Meyer,

CUSTOM HOUSE.   ATLANTIC MUTUAL.
WILLIAM STREET : LOOKING TOWARDS EXCHANGE PLACE FROM WALL STREET, AND SHOWING SITE FOR PROPOSED BUILDING OF NORTH BRITISH & MERCANTILE INSURANCE CO.

Vice-President ; and James W. Durbrow, Secretary.

The Trustees of the Mutual Fire-Insurance Company for 1893-1894 are : O. R. Meyer, Joseph Fox, John Dickson, A. F. Troescher, Otto Von Hein, Aaron Carter, Emil Calman, W. E. Lowe, R. A. Loewenthal, C. S. Braisted, J. C. Hatié, D. W. Crouse, William Eggert, Ed. Barr, John R. Waters, David Calman, Samson Lachman, Nathan D. Bill, J. Spencer Turner, Henry Morgenthau, and S. M. Milliken.

The North British and Mercantile Insurance Company of London and Edinburgh dated its beginning to 1809, and has a record of fourscore and four years, having few equals among insurance companies. Of the American fire companies there are only half a dozen so old as this company. It had its origin and grew slowly and strongly on Scottish soil, for originally it was the North British of Edinburgh, and continued as such for over half a century, until 1861, when it was united with the Mercantile Insurance Company of London, under the present corporate name. In the past 32 years the company has extended its business into eleven different countries, and stands in the front rank of the great insurance corporations of the world. In the United States alone the company had, on January 1, 1893, cash assets of $3,453,-004 ; a reserve for unearned premiums, $1,929,077 ; a reserve for unpaid losses, $339,961 ; a reserve for all other liabilities, $88,641 ; and a net surplus of $1,095,-324. In this country its income on fire premiums was nearly $2,500,000 in 1892 ; and since 1866, when it entered this country, it has received in the United States over $39,000,000 in premiums. It has paid out for fire-losses here over $25,000,000, including $2,330,000 in the Chicago fire of 1871, and $750,000 in the Boston fire of 1872. Twenty years ago it had about 225 agents in this country ; now it has over 3,500. At home and abroad it has eminent men at the head of all its different departments. Its President is the Duke of Roxburghe ; its Vice-President, the Duke of Sutherland ; and the Directory is of notable strength. The Manager is G. H. Burnett, at London. The Manager for the United States is Sam. P. Blagden, who became Assistant-Manager in 1869, Associate-Manager in 1870, one of the two Managers in 1876, and sole Manager in 1887. The Assistant-Manager is William A. Francis, who has held this position since 1888. The General Agent is E. T. Campbell ; and the Secretary in New York is H. M. Jackson. The Pacific Department of the company is in San Francisco, under the management of Tom C. Grant, General Agent. In principal cities of the East and Middle West the company has established branch-offices, in charge of resident secretaries, and thus the company secures immediate local supervision over its business. The United-States Branch has a Board of Directors composed of Solon Humphreys, of E. D. Morgan & Co. ; H. W. Barnes ; Jacob Wendell ; David Dows, Jr. ; Charles H. Coster, of Drexel, Morgan & Co. ; Charles Ezra White ; and William Waldorf Astor. The company has lately bought the southwest corner of William Street and Exchange Place, and will soon begin the erection of a fine office-building.

BROADWAY AND ASTOR PLACE, LOOKING SOUTHWARD ON BROADWAY.

The Northern Assurance Company, of London, England, whose principal United-States office is at 38 Pine Street, New York, was organized in 1836, and commenced business the same year. Its head-offices are in London, England, and in Aberdeen, Scotland. One of the largest and strongest among the older British companies, it does business in all the civilized portions of the world, and is noted for its careful and successful management. The marvellous growth of the company appears in the record of its fire-premiums, which were $4,500, in 1836; $14,500, in 1840; $19,000, in 1845; $40,000, in 1850; $276,500, in 1855; $607,000, in 1860; $820,000, in 1865; $1,068,000, in 1870; $1,756,500, in 1875; $2,223,-000, in 1880; $2,886,500, in 1885; and $3,553,810, in 1892. In Great Britain the company does a fire and life-insurance business. In the United States its business is restricted to fire-insurance only. Its United-States assets, December 31, 1892, were $1,653,232; unpaid losses, unearned premiums, and all actual and contingent liabilities, $1,155,318. The company has, specially deposited with the Insurance Departments of the several States, and with trustees in New York, securities to the value of $1,364,692, none of which it may withdraw or remove while it has any existing liability in the United States. Since its organization the company has received in fire-premiums alone, $64,-496,666; and paid in fire-losses alone, $37,954,407. It is represented in nearly all the States, cities, principal towns and villages of the United States and Canada. Its territory in the United States is divided into four departments: The New-York, Middle-States and Southern Department, the head-office of which is at 38 Pine Street, New York, and the Manager, George W. Babb, Jr.; the New-England Department, the head-office of which is at 27 Kilby Street, Boston, and the Manager, Howard S. Wheelock; the Western Department, the head-office of which is at 226 La Salle Street,

NORTHERN ASSURANCE CO. OF LONDON, 38 PINE STREET.

Chicago, and the Managers, William D. Crooke and Warren F. Goodwin ; and the Pacific-Coast Department, the head-office of which is in San Francisco, and the Manager, George F. Grant. The growth of the company has been steady and uninterrupted. It has established a fire fund, co-extensive with its net surplus, to meet extraordinary conflagrations. No conflagration which can be considered possible could retard for a single hour the operations of the Northern Assurance Company. Its accommodations to its policy-holders, and its equitable and prompt adjustment of losses, have made it popular with its customers and agents. Its vast resources furnish certain indemnity. The cut on preceding page represents the Northern's graceful stone building, completed in 1889, and entirely occupied for its own use. It is at the heart of the "insurance district."

The Imperial Insurance Company, Limited, of London, England, is one of those old and staunch foreign corporations which have become an absolute necessity for the protection of losses against fire in this country. The Imperial is over ninety years old, having been instituted in 1803. It is, with a single exception, the largest purely fire-insurance company in Great Britain ; and, without any exceptions, it has the largest net surplus of any English insurance company doing a fire business. At home it is esteemed as one of the strongest and most successful of the insurance corporations. In this country, since its establishment in 1868, when it opened its office in New York, it has made a record which places the United-States branch on an equal footing with the best American companies. In this country its gross assets are $1,854,882, which includes the reserve of $964,666 for unearned premiums, $128,625 for unsettled losses, and $41,165 for all other claims, leaving a net surplus in the United States of $720,425. It has paid the colossal sum of $64,000,000 for losses.

THE IMPERIAL INSURANCE CO., LD., OF LONDON, 31, 33 AND 35 PINE STREET.

The General Manager of the company is Edward Cozens-Smith, who has been at the head of the company's affairs for over twenty years. The managers of the Metropolitan District of the Imperial are J. J. Courtney and John R. McCay, a firm composed of two experienced and energetic underwriters. Mr. Courtney has been connected with the Imperial for twenty-eight years, eighteen of which were spent at the company's head-offices in London, and during the last ten years he has been the company's resident-secretary in this country. Mr. McCay has been the representative of the Phenix Insurance Company of Hartford, with which company he made a record as a most efficient underwriter. Besides having the management of the Metropolitan District for the Imperial, they have the management of the old Phenix of Hartford, one of the staunchest of the American insurance companies, and also of the Lion Insurance Company of England, another of the great English fire corporations. Their offices are in the Imperial Building, at 31 and 33 Pine Street, a six-story, marble-front, office-building owned by the Imperial Insurance Company, and well situated in what is regarded now as the insurance district. John J. Swainson, for ten years connected with the London offices, has been appointed resident-secretary at New York. The trustees of the Imperial in the United States are Thomas Maitland, of the time-honored banking house of Maitland, Phelps & Co., of New York ; Col. Josiah II. Benton, Jr., of Boston ; and John C. Paige, the resident-manager of the company in Boston. The Imperial has its representatives in every nook and corner of the United States, and also throughout the civilized world.

The Liverpool, London and Globe Insurance Company is one of the greatest insurance corporations in the world. It was founded in 1836, as the Liverpool Insurance Co. ; acknowledged its success at the British metropolis by taking the title of the Liverpool and London Insurance Co., in 1848 ; and in 1864 acquired the business and title of the Globe Insurance Co. In 1848 it opened an American business, which has already paid over $56,000,000 in fire-losses, and accumulated a surplus of $3,000,000. In the Chicago and Boston fires the company lost $4,670,000, and paid every cent of it. Its fine office-building is **L** shaped and fronts on two streets — Pine and William.

Other New-York Fire-Insurance Companies are : the Eagle Fire, Peter Cooper, Farragut, United-States, Manufacturers' and Builders', North-River, Stuyvesant, Westchester, Alliance, Commonwealth, Empire City, Exchange, Germania, Globe, Guardian, Hamilton, New-York, Pacific, People's, and Standard.

There are a number of New-York companies in process of liquidation ; the rates or premiums generally being too low, and the commissions and compulsory expenses too high, for the smaller companies to earn the dividends expected by their stockholders. But the general record of the well-managed fire-insurance companies shows a profitable business.

English insurance corporations have become an important part of the insurance business of this country. Many foreign corporations have established their American branches in this city, and thereby practically become local institutions. The Liverpool and London and Globe, the Royal, the Sun, the Imperial, the London and Lancashire, the Lancashire, the Guardian, the Northern, and the Commercial Union, own their own office-buildings ; and the North British & Mercantile is about to build a fine office-building. The American branches of some of these companies have assets in this country which place these branches on a level with the strongest American companies.

Life Insurance.

Companies for Protection of Widows, Orphans and Others, and
for Providing Incomes in Advanced Age, Etc., and
Life-Insurance Associations.

IN 1769 the Proprietaries of the Province of Pennsylvania obtained charters in
Pennsylvania, New York and New Jersey for the "Corporation for the Relief of
the Widows and Children of Clergymen of the Communion of the Church of England in America." In 1797 the Legislature of Pennsylvania authorized a division of
the funds among the three States. In 1798 the Legislature of New York recognized
the New-York branch as "The Corporation for the Relief of the Widows and Children of Clergymen of the Protestant Episcopal Church in the State of New York."
In 1798 the "United Insurance Company" and the "New-York Insurance Company
for Maritime Insurance" were chartered, to insure lives as well as vessels, houses
and goods ; but their life-insurance privilege was unused. The "Union," chartered
in 1818 to do a marine and life insurance business, and the "New-York Mechanics'
Life-Insurance and Coal Company," incorporated in 1812, "with power to make
insurance upon lives or in any way depending upon lives, to grant annuities and to
open, find out, discover and work coal-beds," issued only an insignificant number of
life-policies. In 1830 the "New-York Life-Insurance and Trust Company" was
chartered. It had a capital of $1,000,000, and thirty trustees, among whom were
Van Rensselaer, Verplanck, Bloodgood, Lenox, and Lorillard ; but in nine years it
had issued only 1,821 policies, 694 of which were in force, for $2,451,958, at the
end of 1839. In 1841 the Nautilus Insurance Company and an existing marine corporation, the New-York Mutual Insurance Company, were chartered, with power to
combine fire, life and marine business. The Nautilus did no business until 1845.
In 1849 its name was changed to the New-York Life-Insurance Company. In 1842
the Mutual Life-Insurance Company was chartered. It began business in February,
1843, and thus won the honor of being the first mutual life-insurance company of
New York. The New-York Life-Insurance and Trust Company and all other life-
corporations previously formed in New York had been proprietary. The Mutual
and the Nautilus made a new era. In nineteen months the Mutual had issued 796
policies, as follows : merchants and clerks, 396; brokers, 37 ; officers of incorporated companies, 34 ; lawyers, 46 ; clergymen, 30 ; physicians, 26 ; mechanics, 36 ;
manufacturers, 25 ; college-professors and students, 26 ; army and navy officers, 116 ;
and farmers, 24. It had received nearly $90,000.

In 1851 all the life-companies doing business in New York· were required by
the New-York deposit law, passed in April, to deposit with the comptroller of the
State, within ten months, $100,000, in two installments. Other States adopted
retaliatory measures against the companies of New York, until the law was modified

in 1853, when outside companies were allowed to make the required deposits in their own States. In 1856 the New-York State comptroller published the statements of eleven American companies, with total assets of $18,804,303. In 1859 the first National meeting of life-underwriters was convened, at the Astor House, in New York. Vital statistics, extra rates, renewal of lapsed policies, and State legislation received then careful consideration. In 1861 the Insurance Departments of New York and Massachusetts were agreed in a doctrine that the standing of each company, for State purposes, must be judged from its present status and its past receipts and expenditures, although they differed in the method of testing net valuation. Without precedent or aid from England, they made perfect the system of State supervision. In 1859 the life-insurance companies of New York had assets amounting to $10,000,000, only $770,000 of which was invested in stocks or bonds of any description. In 1863, when the war was at its height, they had assets amounting to $17,000,000, and one-third and more of the amount, $7,000,000, was invested with patriotic purpose in securities of the United States. They took the life-risks of the war with similar public spirit. Their policies increased by over 7,000 during 1862, while in 1861 the increase was only 1,300. After the war the increase was constant until 1869, when it fell to 123,631, from 136,454 in 1868. In 1876 the number of life-insurance companies authorized to transact business in New York was decreased by 25, but the remaining 45 companies had a larger volume of business than the 70 companies of 1870. At present there are 31 insurance companies authorized to transact business in New York. Their assets amount to $903,-734,557, and $538,938,478 of that sum, much more than half, is the property of New-York companies. The New-York companies have an aggregate surplus as regards policy-holders of $69,232,669, the companies of other States of $44,827,-851. The receipts for 1892 of the New-York companies were $139,903,917 ; of the companies of other States, $83,121,081. The disbursements for 1892 of all the companies were, for claims, $72,576,867 ; for lapsed, surrendered and purchased policies, $15,658,759 ; for dividends to policy-holders, $14,386,195 ; for dividends to stock-holders, $602,783 ; for commissions, $24,451,161 ; for salaries, medical fees and employees, $10,140,167 ; miscellaneous, $15,074,403 ; a total of $152,-890,333. The sum of $102,621,821 was paid to policy-holders. The cost of management, including dividends to stock-holders, was $50,268,512.

The history of life-insurance is best told in the records of the following companies :

The Mutual Life-Insurance Company is on Nassau Street, between Liberty and Cedar Streets. Its beautiful building, of granite and Indiana stone, is located on the site formerly occupied by the Post-Office, originally the Middle Dutch Church. It also owns the splendid white marble office-building at 140 to 146 Broadway, where its business offices were formerly located, before its removal to the present building. This corporation leads the life-insurance business of the United States, by which the life-insurance business of the world is led. The Mutual Life-Insurance Company, incorporated April 12, 1842, by 36 merchants, waited until $1,000,000 of insurance had been subscribed ; until one-half of the amount that it had taken a proprietary company nine years to accumulate had been pledged ; and the first day of February, 1843, opened the first mutual life-insurance office in New York. Its cash receipts that day were $109.50 ; its cash receipts in nineteen months were $90,000. Its chronicles have the splendor of Oriental tales, but every phase of them has a realistic element of arduous labor and incessant watchfulness. Professor Charles Gill was appointed actuary of the company in 1849. He was

C.W.Clinton, Arct.

MUTUAL LIFE-INSURANCE COMPANY OF NEW YORK.
NASSAU, LIBERTY AND CEDAR STREETS.

famous as a teacher of mathematics, and had been from the age of 17 a constant contributor to mathematical works.   He compiled the first distinctively American system of rates and tables.   His formulæ embraced every question that could then be foreseen in the company's experience.   Frederick S. Winston became President in 1852.   In 1856 a board of examiners reported :   "This institution, in the method of its administration, was never so judicious ; in the principles of its transactions, never so sound ; or in the general conduct of its affairs, never so safe and prosperous, as at the present moment."   To mention the fact that subsequent boards of examiners repeated variations of the same report is unnecessary.   The vital statistics of the United States were made for the Mutual Life-Insurance Company by Dr. Wynne ; and they were universally accepted as the most valuable work on the subject in America.   The Mutual Life-Insurance Company compiled a mortuary table of its experience, and in 1868 it was published, under the name of the *American Experience*, and adopted by New York as the legal standard of the State.   In 1872 commutation and other extensive tables were published, based on the Mutual Life Experience.   In 1876 the company issued its *Mortality Report*, the standard authority on all questions relating to the laws of American insured lives. Financial ability was never less characteristic of the company than mathematical precision.   Always, as at present, it adhered to a rigid cash basis ; confined its contracts to insurance and annuities upon life ; made its investments at home with regard to safety and not speculative rates of interest ; and won advantages by merit, not by purchase.   It is ideally a policy-holders' company.   The original terms of the charter required the application of all dividends to the purchase of a paid-up policy, and they were modified that the assured might convert his dividend into an annuity, or to the payment of an annual premium.   Dividends were declared quinquennially from 1848 to 1863.   In 1866 a triennial dividend of nearly $3,000,000 was credited.   Since 1867, every year has produced an annual dividend, ranging in amounts from $2,500,000 to $5,000,000.   In 1850 the company had in assets $1,000,000 ; in 1863, $10,000,000 ; in 1876, $78,000,000.   Its assets at present are $175,084,-157, the exclusive property of the holders of 246,650 policies.   The Mutual Life-Insurance Company has received for premiums in 50 years, $454,550,997 ; in interest, $128,645,568.   It has paid to members, for claims by death, $130,069,-209 ; for endowments, $32,176,665 ; for dividends, $85,653,562 ; and for surrendered policies, $98,092,465.   It has 246,650 policies now in force, insuring $745,-780,083.   There is no other institution of its kind rivalling it in financial magnitude ; and there is no institution with which the interests of Americans are more closely allied than with the Mutual Life-Insurance Company.   Its president is Richard A. McCurdy ; and its Board of Trustees is composed of men whose names are synonymous with financial wisdom, integrity and greatness.

The New-York Life-Insurance Company, which divides with the Mutual Life the honor of being the only purely mutual life-insurance companies in New-York State, owns and occupies a handsome white marble edifice at 346 and 348 Broadway, corner of Leonard Street.   The site is a familiar one with old New-Yorkers, having been formerly occupied by the Society Library.   The present building, erected in 1868–70, is 60 by 172 feet, and five stories in height above the basement.   When first built, it had only three stories, but the now universally-used Otis passenger-elevator was first introduced into this building, and resulted in the adding of two new stories.   These five stories are now all required for the company's use, so vast has its business become, while the basement and sub-cellar are occupied by the Manhattan Safe-Deposit & Storage Company and the Farragut Fire-Insurance

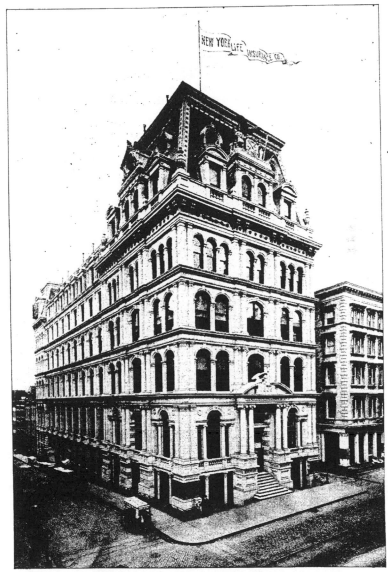

NEW-YORK LIFE-INSURANCE COMPANY.
346 AND 348 BROADWAY, SOUTHEAST CORNER OF LEONARD STREET.

Company. The location is an ideal one for all purposes, being open on three sides to light and air ; and to accommodate the company's increasing business, the building will be extended along Leonard Street to Elm Street. The New-York Life was organized in 1845 ; and after 48 years' business, during which time it has paid to its members over $169,000,000, it holds as security for contracts now in force $137,-499,199. Of this vast amount nearly $17,000,000 is surplus, according to the legal standard of the State of New York. During 1892 the company was thoroughly examined by the New-York Insurance Department, the examination covering a period of nearly six months, and requiring the services of over fifty men. The present statement of the company's condition is therefore officially certified, after careful valuation of each item that enters into its assets and liabilities. The Superintendent of Insurance, in his report for 1892 (page 39), refers to President John A. McCall's expressed determination to conduct the company as "a company of the policy-holder, by the policy-holder, and for the policy-holder," and adds : "Under an administration which thus broadly announces the fundamental principle that is to control its policy for the future, this company now enters the forty-eighth year of an honorable business career. "

The New-York Life has borne an honorable and a leading part in the reforms which have simplified and made more valuable the policy contract. It was the first company, and for many years the only company, to omit from its policies the clause making them void in case of suicide. It was the first company to recognize the policy-holder's right to paid-up insurance, in case of a discontinuance in the payment of premiums, by originating and introducing, in 1860, the first non-forfeitable policies. It was the first company to attach to its policies a copy of the application upon which the contract is based. The company has recently (June, 1892) begun the issue of a contract containing no restrictions whatever as to occupation, residence, travel, habits of life, or manner of death. Its "Accumulation Policy" contains but one condition ; viz., that the premiums be paid as agreed. If the insured pays the premiums the company agrees to pay the policy. The New-York Life-Insurance Company is one of the dozen great financial corporations of the world. It carries policies of insurance amounting to almost $700,000,000. The endowment business of this company exceeds that of any other, and its annuity business is as great almost as that of all other American companies combined. The New-York Life owns large fire-proof office-buildings in New York, Kansas City, Omaha, Minneapolis and St. Paul, and in Paris, Berlin and Vienna.

The Manhattan Life-Insurance Company is one of the staunchest and most highly esteemed of the fiduciary institutions, not only of New-York City, but of the whole country, and it will soon occupy its new and gigantic edifice, which is to be one of the most notable structures on this continent. The company was incorporated in 1850, and issued its first policy on August 1st of that year, from its office at 108 Broadway, at the corner of Pine Street. Fifteen years later it moved to 156 and 158 Broadway, into what was then an important building on Broadway, but which to-day appears simply as a graceful white marble structure, with a lower story of iron and Doric columns. Its new building is to be erected at 64, 66 and 68 Broadway. It will be nominally 16 stories high, but in fact it will be 19 stories on Broadway and 17 stories on New Street, and will be surmounted by a tower which would make the total structure equivalent to 20 stories in height. Even its stately neighbors, such as the Standard Oil Co. Building, the Columbia Building, Aldrich Court, the Consolidated Stock and Petroleum Exchange, the Union Trust Co., and the tall and graceful spire of Trinity Church will be well shaded by this new

KIMBALL & G. KRAMER THOMPSON ARCHTS.

THE MANHATTAN LIFE-INSURANCE COMPANY OF NEW YORK.
64 AND 66 BROADWAY (NOW BUILDING), BETWEEN WALL STREET AND EXCHANGE PLACE.

imposing Manhattan Life Building. An idea of its façade can be had from the illustration on the preceding page. Its height from the sidewalk on Broadway to the foot of the flagstaff will be about 350 feet. The size of the building will be 67 x 125 feet, and indicates a feat in building construction heretofore unknown. It is to be supported on piers sunk to the solid rock, 55 feet below Broadway ; the method of sinking being by means of caissons operated by the pneumatic process. The building will contain about 160 offices, exclusive of the company's quarters, which will occupy the sixth and seventh floors. The Broadway front will be of Indiana limestone. The structure throughout will be absolutely fire-proof. The style of architecture adopted is the Italian Renaissance, enriched in keeping with the best examples of that style. Francis II. Kimball and G. Kramer Thompson, architects, have charge of the entire construction and supervision of the work.

The Manhattan Life has an admirable record of growth, size, rank and stability, of which its new building will be emblematic. In its first year its assets were $108,500 ; in 1865 they were $2,619,691 ; at present they are $13,293,778. In its first year it paid to policy-holders $1,000 ; in 1865 it paid to them $285,175 ; in December, 1891, it had paid to them an aggregate of $31,935,138. If the total amount paid to policy-holders up to December, 1891, be added to the assets then held for their protection, the sum exceeds the premiums received from them by $5,058,056, showing a gain to policy-holders of 12.7%. A similar computation shows the gain of the policy-holders in all the other New-York State companies other than the Manhattan Life as only 3.8%. In 1893 it has over $61,000,000 of insurance in force, none of which was acquired by re-insurance of unsuccessful companies. The New-York Insurance Reports for 1892 showed for the Manhattan an increase in assets, increase in insurance in force, increase in surplus, increase in new insurance written, increase in interest, increase in premiums, increase in all the facilities and ramifications of the company. All the faculties of the company are used solely in the interest of its policy-holders. It was the first company to introduce the non-forfeiture system. It was the first company to adopt the indisputable policy to guarantee payment in spite of errors, omissions, and mis-statements in the assured's application. It was the first company to issue the most progressive policy of the age — a simple, clear, direct form of contract which everybody may understand, wherein there is not an equivocal word. It pays all claims promptly. Litigation is something exceptionally rare in its records. The Manhattan Life desires nothing but the interest of its policy-holders. It is sound, economical, just and liberal. Its Survivorship Dividend Policy is incontestable, non-forfeitable and payable at sight ; contains no suicide nor intemperance clauses ; grants absolute freedom of travel and residence ; and is free from all technicalities. The agents of the Manhattan Life-Insurance Company are a representative body of men, and are to be found in every city of any importance in the country. In Philadelphia the company owns one of the finest office-buildings in that city.

Its presidents have been : Alonzo A. Alvard, form 1850 to 1854 ; Nathan D. Morgan, from 1854 to 1861 ; Henry Stokes, from 1861 to 1888 ; and James M. McLean, from 1888 to 1890. The president is Henry B. Stokes, who has been in the service of the company for about thirty years. The vice-president is Jacob L. Halsey, who has been in the service of the company from its inception. The second vice-president, H. Y. Wemple ; the secretary, W. C. Frazee ; and the assistant secretary, J. H. Giffin, Jr., are also old and faithful servants of the company, familiar with every phase of its experience. Its Board of Directors include the following well-known names : Edw. Schell, Henry Van Schaick, Jno. H. Wat-

THE EQUITABLE LIFE-ASSURANCE SOCIETY OF THE UNITED STATES.
BROADWAY, BETWEEN PINE AND CEDAR STREETS.

son, Henry B. Stokes, O. G. Walbridge, D. H. McAlpin, W. J. Valentine, E. A. Walton, Geo. W. Quintard, Geo. H. McLean, Robert S. Green, Artemas H. Holmes, Henry B. Peirce, E. F. Del Bondio, Wm. H. Oakley, Jas. O. Hoyt, Benj. F. Tracy, Philip Bissinger, Thos. F. Oakes, Hyman Blum, Jno. W. Hunter, P. Van Zandt Lane, Jacob Naylor, Jas. Stokes, H. Y. Wemple, John King, DeWitt C. Hays, N. F. Palmer, Jr., S. H. Smith, Jacob L. Halsey, Walter C. Stokes, C. D. Wood, Benj. Griffen, and Andrew Mills.

The United-States Life-Insurance Company, in Elbridge T. Gerry's vermilion iron-front building, at Broadway and Warren Street, was organized in 1850. Its assets amount to $6,889,712, invested in United-States bonds, in bonds and mortgages, and real estate. It has a surplus, as regards policy-holders, over all its liabilities, including the reserve-fund for outstanding policies, of $611,405. In 1881 its assets were $4,994,670; now they are $6,889,212; its annual income was $809,918, now it is $1,495,629; the number of its policies in force was 9,508; now it is 17,944; its total amount insured was $16,671,328; now it is $43,730,853. In ten years the company attained an increase of $1,743,318 in assets, and $24,492,798 in insurance in force. Its new insurance in 1888 amounted to $6,335,666; in 1889, to $8,463,625; in 1890, to $11,955,157; in 1891, to $14,101,654; in 1892, to $14,001,695. It paid in 1892 for death claims, endowments and surrendered policies, $688,570. The President is George H. Burford; the Secretary is C. P. Fraleigh, since 1875; the Assistant-Secretary, A. Wheelwright; the Actuary, William T. Standen; the Cashier, Arthur C. Perry; the Medical Director, John P. Munn. J. S. Gaffney is Superintendent of Agencies. Its Finance Committee comprises: George G. Williams, the President of the Chemical National Bank; Julius Catlin, the dry-goods merchant; John J. Tucker, the builder; and E. H. Perkins, Jr., the President of the Importers' and Traders' National Bank.

The Equitable Life-Assurance Society of the United States is one of the foremost life-insurance corporations of the world. Its policies include a variety of forms, tontines, indemnity bonds, annuities and others. The society was organized in 1859. It has done much to liberalize the policy contract, and to make insurance popular. The Equitable Building in New York, erected by the society in 1872, and enlarged in 1887, contains the main offices. It is one of the largest and most substantial commercial buildings in the world. It fills the block bounded by Broadway and Cedar, Pine and Nassau Streets, save two small corners on Nassau Street, and covers about an acre of ground. The architectural treatment of the exterior gives the impression that it is of five very high stories, with an immense Mansard roof, the cornice of each story being supported by a colonnade. Really, the number of stories is twice as many, as each space is divided by a floor line. The material is granite, and the building gives an impression of solidity in a greater degree than does any other in the city. The Broadway entrance, which is through a high semi-circular arch, leads into one of the finest rotundas in America, the sides of which are outlined by rows of marble columns, with onyx capitals, upholding an entablature of red granite and an arched roof of stained glass. The offices of the society on the second floor are perhaps the most costly business headquarters in the country. The view from the roof of the building includes the city, harbor and suburbs, and is one of the great attractions to strangers. Along the roof, in several towers, are the apartments of the superintendent of the building and the offices of the local forecast officials of the Department of Agriculture's Bureau for Meteorological Observations, popularly known as the " Weather Bureau." The building is equipped with Worthington pumps and Otis elevators.

The Germania Life-Insurance Company, at 20 Nassau Street, commenced business in 1860. In 32 years it paid for claims by death, $15,534,697; for matured endowments, $3,312,808; for annuities, $213,467; for dividends and surrendered policies, $9,023,487; a total of payments to policy-holders of $28,084,459. At the same time, it accumulated assets to the amount of $17,744,263, invested in bonds and mortgages on real-estate and domestic and foreign State, city and railroad bonds. It has a surplus as regards policy-holders of $1,230,288 over all its liabilities, including the reserve fund, computed at four per cent. for outstanding policies. If this reserve-fund be computed on a 4½ per cent. basis this ample extraordinary surplus even reaches the figure of $2,041,215. The total amount of insurance outstanding on the company's books is $66,061,867. The economical and successful administration of the company's affairs is evident from a number of comparative exhibits compiled from official records. One, prepared by C. C. Iline, is a recapitulation of American life-insurance for ten years. It shows that the growth of the Germania was the most healthful, the increase during those ten years being: in assets, $7,217,501; in annual income, of $1,664,268; in number of policies in force, 13,989; in amount insured, $25,424,060. The increase in the assets and income bears a larger proportion to the increase in amount insured than in any other company. Another exhibit shows that the company paid to policy-holders and holds for future payments $2,575,996 more than it received in premiums. There

GERMANIA LIFE-INSURANCE COMPANY, NASSAU AND CEDAR STREETS.

is a third exhibit, issued in three parts, showing that its income from investments averaged during the last five years $751,097; and that the total amount of its expenses was $611,941, an excess of investment income over expenses of nineteen per cent.; that in many companies the expenses exceeded the investment income; that the ratio of its expenses to its assets was 3.97 per cent., much smaller than in other

43

companies ; and that the proportion of assets to each $1,000 of insurance in force is much larger than in the other companies.   The company offers in its Dividend Tontine Policies a contract of insurance as simple in form, as liberal in character, and as productive of good results as any that can be devised.   After one year from their date, these policies are incontestable, free from restrictions, a simple promise to pay the amount assured when due.   After three years, they are non-forfeitable.

HOME LIFE-INSURANCE COMPANY, 254 BROADWAY.
(OLD OFFICES, TAKEN DOWN IN 1892.)

The officers of the company are as follows : Hugo Wesendonck, President ; Cornelius Doremus, Vice-President ; Hubert Cillis, Secretary and Actuary ; and Gustav Meidt, Assistant-Secretary.

The Home Life-Insurance Company of New York was organized in 1860 by a party of Brooklyn capitalists, whose names are connected with the financial and commercial growth of that city during the last 35 years. It has always been managed on the most conservative lines, and while in point of size it does not attain the prominence reached by many other companies, yet it stands without a peer in solidity and strength.   With assets of over $8,000,000, it has an absolute surplus of over $1,500,000.   It issues all forms of life and endowment insurance and annuity bonds. In June, 1892, the company commenced the erection of a new building on their lot on Broadway, near the corner of Murray Street, on the site immediately adjoining on the north the building owned and occupied by the company for many years.   In order to secure the best results, from an architectural as well as a business standpoint, the company instituted a competition in which the highest architectural talent was represented ; the decision being left to Prof. William R. Ware, of Columbia College, the eminent expert in this line.   The result was a most noteworthy set of designs, from which was selected that of Napoleon LeBrun & Sons.   The building was to have had a frontage on Broadway of 30½ feet ; and its construction was rapidly pushed until the early part of 1893, when the company purchased 25 feet additional on Broadway, from the Merchants' Exchange National Bank, thus acquiring a total frontage for their new building of 55 feet.   The original elevation has been altered to cover the entire lot, and shows a building of 14 stories, surmounted by a high gable, the terminating finial of which will be 256 feet above the sidewalk.   The first story of the new building will have a ceiling height of 18½ feet, and will be arranged for counting-rooms or banking purposes.   The second story, to be used as the general offices of the company, will be 23½ feet in height on the Broadway front, and will have main and mezzanine floors in the rear.   The depth of the building will be 107½ feet, and it will abut against the L of

HOME LIFE-INSURANCE CO. OF NEW YORK.
BROADWAY, WEST SIDE, BETWEEN MURRAY AND WARREN STREETS, OPPOSITE CITY-HALL PARK.

the Postal-Telegraph-Cable Company's building.   As will be seen from the accompanying illustration, the style of building is the severest kind of early Italian Renaissance, most effective in its purity and simplicity.   The structure will be absolutely fire-proof, and thoroughly equipped with all the modern appliances of office-buildings.   The material for the front is of white marble, bringing out in exquisite detail the carvings, which are merely suggested in the accompanying

PRODUCE EXCHANGE.   BOWLING GREEN.   STEAMSHIP ROW.
BROADWAY AT ITS BEGINNING.

elevation.   In view of the most fortunate location of this building, fronting as it does on the City-Hall Park, it has the advantage of being so situated that its artistic merit is conspicuous, which is rarely the case in our city streets.

The officers of the Home Life-Insurance Company are George H. Ripley, President ; George E. Ide, Vice-President ; Ellis W. Gladwin, Secretary ; and William A. Marshall, Actuary.   Its agents are at all important points throughout the country.

The Washington Life-Insurance Company was organized in 1860, and has enjoyed a third of a century of gradual and healthy development.   It is one of the soundest and most popular corporations of its class in the city.   It is unique in the character of its investments, which include only the soundest and most available securities, seven-eighths of them being in bonds and mortgages.   No other American company has so large a percentage of its assets in non-fluctuating real-estate securities.   Since the stability, strength and value of a company is measured justly by the character of its assets, the standing of the Washington Life will be seen to be in the very highest rank.   Nor does the company seize all the new business that offers, since it prefers to accept only such classes of risks as may safely provide reserves and strengthen assets.   Since 1880, the Washington Life has more than doubled its assets, its income, and its insurance in force.   The great principle followed from the first is to give absolute protection to policy-holders, and to secure this end, the company has made its investments in carefully selected loans on American real-estate (in New-York City and vicinity), avoiding foreign securities and bank or corporation stocks. It has now assets of over $12,500,000, and insurance in force amounting to above $50,000,000, and has paid to policy-holders more than $22,000,000 in cash since organization. With the largest proportion of bond and mortgage investments; a comprehensive yet simple and concise policy contract; non-forfeitable policies and immediate settlement of claims; residence, travel and occupation unrestricted after two years; with loans on policies to assist the owners to keep them in force; there is no organization that better fills the conditions of a first-class life-insurance company than the Washington Life of New York. Its President, William A. Brewer, Jr., was its first Actuary; its Vice-President, William

Haxtun, was its Secretary in 1869; and its second Vice-President, E. S. French, who is also the Superintendent of Agencies, has been connected with the company more than a score of years. Cyrus Munn has been its Assistant-Secretary almost from the date of the company's incorporation. The Actuary is Israel C. Pierson, Ph. D., Secretary of the Actuarial Society of America. The Directors include: W. A. Brewer, Jr., Wm. Haxtun, George N. Lawrence, Levi P. Morton, Merritt Trimble, George A. Robbins, James Thomson, Chas. H. Ludington, Robert Bowne, Francis Speir, Frederic R. Coudert, Benjamin Haxtun, Edwin H. Mead, Henry F. Hitch, Chas. P. Britton, Francis G. Adams, David Thomson, Harold A. Sanderson, Roland G. Mitchell, Randolph F. Purdy, George M. Hard, John Hopson, Jr., and Henry S. Harper.

The **Metropolitan Life-Insurance Company,** the leading industrial life-insurance company in America, issues life-insurance policies on the ordinary plans, with special advantages that have always been praised; but its originality is in its Industrial system. This is utility itself; family insurance, accessible to everybody; indemnity

THE WASHINGTON LIFE-INSURANCE COMPANY, COAL AND IRON EXCHANGE, 21 CORTLANDT STREET.

for loss of life of all persons, of both sexes, of all ages, from two years to seventy years; endowment policies that the least disposed to thrift may buy; the practical application of life-insurance in the most valuable way; that is, for those who being the least able to pay for it are most in need of it. There are other industrial companies, but the Metropolitan eclipses them all. · It has assets exceeding $18,000,000, a net capital and surplus over all liabilities, actual and contingent, including the re-insurance fund and special reserve, amounting to more than

$4,000,000. It has in force 3,000,000 policies, a larger number than the total number insured by all the other life-insurance companies (excepting industrial) of the United States combined. Its agents make a weekly call for premiums, the average amount of which is ten cents on every policy-holder. Its death-claims, which are paid immediately after notice of death is received, are 150 a day in number, and $10 a minute every minute of the year in amount. The list of persons in its service contains 8,000 names. And these figures are increasing. They gained over 1891 in 1892 in premium receipts, $1,683,704; in total income, $1,884,315; in assets $2,845,775. During 1892, the company issued, on an average, each working day, 3,737 policies, wrote new insurance of $422,000, paid claims to the amount of $16,016, and added to its assets $9,410. The management is intelligent, careful, economical, devoted to the interests of the policy-holders. The officers are : John R. Hegeman, President ; Haley Fiske, Vice-President ; George II. Gaston, Second Vice-President and Secretary ; J. J. Thompson, Cashier and Assistant Secretary ; James M. Craig, Actuary ; Stewart L. Woodford, Counsel ; and Thomas II. Willard, M. D., Chief Medical Examiner. The company was organized in 1866 ; occupied since 1876 its own large white-marble building in Park Place, at the southwest corner of Church Street ; and in May, 1893, moved to its present magnificent home office-building. Its cost was in the neighborhood of $3,000,000 ; and its height is ten stories. Situated on Madison Square, at the northeast corner of 23d Street and Madison Avenue, it has 125 feet of width on the avenue and 145 on the street. Its style is early Italian Renaissance, in pure white marble, beautifully carved. The main entrance is on Madison Avenue, by a corridor 18 feet in width, and lined with marbles, beautifully decorated, to an interior court 40 feet square, covered by a stained glass dome, paved in mosaic, 75 feet in height, lined with delicately decorated marble and onyx ; having in its centre a grand marble and bronze stairway leading to the second story. The Board room, 28 feet in height, and the rooms of the officers are trimmed in wood-work of San-Domingo mahogany. The main office is 30 feet in height, and surrounded at the mezzanine floor with a tall and graceful gallery. All the offices are lit by windows facing on the street, the square or the court. There are four elevators. All the machinery, heating apparatus and dynamos are in duplicate. The architects are Napoleon LeBrun & Sons, and the builder is Jer. T. Smith. The building is a fine contribution to the architecture of the century, for which the Metropolitan Life-Insurance Company has the gratitude of all art-lovers. It covers one of the most conspicuous sites in the city, and its height makes it clearly visible across the whole of Madison Square, while its grandeur makes it a superb ornament to the lovely park which it faces. In course of time many notable buildings are likely to border Madison Square, but it is not likely that any of them will surpass the Metropolitan. The peculiar province of the Metropolitan Life-Insurance Company, providing insurance as it does mainly for the working or industrial class of people, makes it an exceptionally praiseworthy institution ; while its solidity and magnitude places it as unexceptionably trustworthy. Its system of small weekly payments gives the opportunity to every man, however moderate his income, to provide for his family in the event of his death.

The Provident Savings Life-Assurance Society, at 29 Broadway, was organized in 1875 with an idea of genius, by Sheppard Homans, who had been for twenty years one of the most prominent and successful of actuaries. Maintaining that investments and endowments which constitute the enormous reserve-deposits of the old companies have no necessary connection with insurance, but rather lessen its security by adding unnecessarily the hazards of banking to the hazards of insurance

METROPOLITAN LIFE-INSURANCE COMPANY.
METROPOLITAN LIFE BUILDING : MADISON SQUARE, 23D STREET AND MADISON AVENUE.

proper, he so organized the Provident Savings that it gives certain indemnity in return for premiums that provide for every item of mortality, expense and margin, but do not require in addition large and unnecessary overpayments or deposits, the care and investment of which are hazardous to companies and expensive to policy-holders. This is secured under several forms of low-priced policies, each of which has some especial point of merit, while all are models of fairness and equity in the conditions of the contract, and of brevity and clearness in phraseology. The Provident Savings issues investment-policies, twenty-year insurance-bonds, and limited-payment life-policies, wherein the investment is guaranteed as well as the insurance, whether the assured lives or dies. If he lives, he receives the full benefit of his investment, with surplus. If he dies, his investment is paid to his family or estate, in addition to his insurance. The Provident Savings gives insurance and investment under one policy, but treats them separately. There is no loss to the assured in case of either life or death; there is no penalty for his dying imposed on his heirs; there is no risk of his losing his insurance because he may not always be able to pay for investment. The Provident Savings does not estimate; it guarantees. It is careful in the selection of risks, liberal to policy-holders, economical in management. It has paid to January 1, 1893, for death claims to beneficiaries under its renewable term policies, the sum of $3,843,074, at a total cost for premiums of - $297,065. The ordinary whole-life premiums would have been $764,496. Thus the Provident Savings has given to its policy-holders nearly three times as much in death benefits as they would have obtained

THE PROVIDENT SAVINGS LIFE-ASSURANCE SOCIETY, COLUMBIA BUILDING, BROADWAY AND MORRIS STREET.

for the same amount of premiums in ordinary life insurance. Its financial success would be incredible if the elements of it were not easy to define. The Provident Savings has more than $200 of assets to each $100 of liability. Its President from the beginning has been Sheppard Homans, its founder. The Vice-President is Joseph H. Parsons. The Secretary is William E. Stevens. The Manager of the Agency Department is Charles E. Willard.

The Mutual Reserve Fund Life Association, in the Mutual Reserve Building, at Broadway and Duane Street, is the largest purely mutual natural-premium life association in the world. Its membership is over **70,000.** Its yearly

MUTUAL RESERVE FUND LIFE ASSOCIATION.
MUTUAL RESERVE BUILDING, BROADWAY, NORTHWEST CORNER OF DUANE STREET.

interest income exceeds $125,000. Its bi-monthly income exceeds $600,000. Its Reserve Fund now approaches $3,500,000. It has paid in death claims about $16,000,000. The amount of insurance that it has in force exceeds $250,000,000. Founded in 1881, with the deliberate object to furnish life-insurance at cost, in spite of formidable opposition it accumulated in a dozen years, assets amounting to nearly $5,000,000, and an Emergency Fund, a Cash Reserve deposited with the Central Trust Company as Trustee, periodically returnable to persistent members, amounting to $3,449,326. January 1, 1893, it had a net surplus of $3,048,202 over all its liabilities, including the net present value of its policies in force. These figures as they appear in the certificate signed by the President of the Central Trust Company in vouchers of easy access to everybody, are magnificent as pearls of a necklace, the string of which is undone. Re-united, they have an amazing splendor. Tested, they are perfect. The Mutual Reserve Fund Life Association's figures were examined and found correct, the company was investigated in all its details and endorsed — by the Insurance Department of New York in 1885 ; by the Insurance Department of Ohio in 1886 ; by the Insurance Department of Michigan in 1886 ; by the Insurance Department of Wisconsin in 1887 ; by the Insurance Department of Minnesota in 1887 ; by the Insurance Department of Rhode Island in 1887 ; by the insurance Department of Missouri in 1888 ; by the Insurance Department of Colorado in 1889 ; by the Insurance Department of West Virginia in 1889 ; by the Insurance Department of North Dakota in 1891 ; by the late Hon. Elizur Wright, ex-Insurance Commissioner of Massachusetts, and the Mentor of life-insurance, in 1883 ; by Price, Waterhouse & Co., Chartered Accountants, of England, in 1889. The Association has no secrets. Everything it does it tells. Its rates at age of entry average about 50 per cent. less than those of the old-system companies, and yet they provide for an average death-loss considerably in excess of the American Experience Table of mortality. It provides for an excessive death-rate, by its interest income and reserve accumulation, and it has never lost a dollar of principal or interest on its highly profitable investments. Yet it gives in detailed lists, of which there is no other example, the complete record of all its investments. It knows every avenue to success, and lights it without fear of imitators. Its policies are unrestricted as to travel, occupation or residence, incontestable and indisputable after three years, participating in the profits and yet not involving any personal liability for membership in the Association. Its management is so wise and economical that its expenses have averaged but $3.22 per $1,000, whereas the expenses of the old-system companies averaged $8.26 per $1,000. It is self-regulating, as its liabilities in income in premiums and interest cannot but meet its death-losses and expenses. It is a creation of genius. Its President is its founder, E. B. Harper. The Mutual Reserve Building at the northwest corner of Broadway aud Duane Street, as can be seen from the view shown on the preceding page, is one of the finest office-buildings in the city. In addition to providing suitable offices for the great organization, the building is expected to return to the Association a satisfactory income for the investment. Thus the Mutual Reserve Fund Life Association, after contributing its magnificent record to the business.glory of New York, is contributing a masterpiece of architecture to its artistic aspect. It was designed and constructed by William H. Hume, one of the foremost of American architects. The marvellous success of the Association is due almost entirely to the rare ability and indomitable energy of its President, E. B. Harper, who, having unbounded faith in the wisdom of its plan, has pushed the business of the company with such vigor as is seldom known in any line of work.

Miscellaneous Insurance

Providing Against All Kinds of Accidents, Explosions, Broken
Plate Glass, Dishonest Employees, and for Furnishing Legal and Fidelity Bonds.

TWENTY years ago the insurance companies were devoted almost exclusively to the indemnifying of losses caused by fires, by the loss of life, or by personal injuries. To-day they seem to cover the entire range of casualties, fatalities and possibilities. A new scheme for some kind of insurance is devised almost yearly, and variations of the older forms of insurance are constantly being introduced.

The Fidelity and Casualty Company of New York, at 140 to 146 Broadway, was organized in 1879, to transact a general fidelity business, and introduced the system into the United States. There was at the time, in business in New York, the Knickerbocker Casualty Company, organized in 1876, with a charter so liberal that it could adopt the fidelity idea, and make of it an additional branch. The founders of the Fidelity and Casualty, realizing that the growth of fidelity insurance in this country would be slow, purchased the charter of the Knickerbocker Casualty and its business, and re-organized their company. The capital, which was originally $100,000, was increased to $250,000. The company furnishes indemnity in several branches of insurance : Fidelity, Accident, Plate Glass, Steam Boiler, Elevator, Employers', Landlords' and Common Carriers' Liability. The company was built up under the presidency of the late William M. Richards, whose successor is George F. Seward.

The American Surety Company of New York, in the Guernsey Building, 160 Broadway, organized in 1884, transacts only surety business. It has a capital of $2,000,000, and is the only company organized in the United States devoted exclusively to acting as surety on bonds and undertakings required in judicial proceedings ; for administrators, executors and guardians ; for contractors, and for persons holding positions of pecuniary responsibility. Its Fidelity Department furnishes bonds required of officers and employees of banks, corporations and associations, and employees in Federal, State and city offices. Its Law Department issues three classes of bonds : Judicial, which embraces security required in appeal, arrest, attachment, capias, indemnity to sheriff, injunction, land damage, replevin, maritime libel ; Fiduciary, which includes bonds for the fidelity of administrators, committee of lunatic, conservators, curators, executors, guardians, guardians *ad litem*, trustees ; Commercial, under which bonds are required by assignees, common carriers, for demurrage, receivers, warehousemen, elevators, and surety on bids and contracts. William L. Trenholm is President.

The Metropolitan Plate-Glass Insurance Company, at 66 Liberty Street, was organized in 1874, to do exclusively plate-glass insurance against accidental breakage. Its capital is $100,000. The President is Henry Harteau.

The American Casualty Insurance and Security Company, although legally a Maryland corporation, with head offices at Baltimore, is virtually a New-York institution, for its stock is chiefly owned here; the majority of its directors reside here; its executive offices are here, and so are the offices of its general agents and managers. The New-York offices are at 44 Pine Street.

This notably progressive company was formed in 1890, the charter having been drawn by Robert Sewell, of New York. The company deals in employees' insurance. It insures against liability under claims for injuries or death caused to persons other than employees on the premises of the insured. Its insurances are accompanied with systematic inspections by experts. It takes risks on steam boilers, paying for damages to property in case of explosions, and also paying for injuries to persons so caused, whether fatal or otherwise. The company inspects the boilers under its care thoroughly and systematically, and at regular periods. It also insures against loss by water, in case of the leakage of sprinklers or the breakage of their heads; and inspects these equipments regularly. The Employees' Contribution Insurance Policy, written in the names of employers, guarantees to their workmen, if injured, half-wages and doctors' bills for fifty weeks, and in case of death from accident six months' full pay, with doctors' bills and funeral expenses. The employers assess their workmen a few cents a week, with which to pay the policies. The company also insures individuals against all kinds of accidents, at very low rates. The President is William E. Midgley; the Vice-Presidents, Edward Austen and Robert Sewell; the Secretary, John J. Jackson, with George H. Morand and John W. Pulis as Assistant-Secretaries. The General Managers are Beecher, Schenck & Co., a corporation composed chiefly of Col. H. B. Beecher, V. R. Schenck, John W. Taylor, and H. W. Beecher. Col. H. B. Beecher is a son of the eminent preacher, the late Henry Ward Beecher. The success of the company appears from the fact that in three years it has paid all expenses and losses, besides $250,000 in dividends to its stockholders, and has assets of $2,600,000, a reserve of $1,200,000, and a surplus to policy-holders of $1,100,000. It has paid over $1,500,-000 in losses under its policy. In New York the offices occupy three spacious floors, and several scores of clerks are employed.

AMERICAN CASUALTY INSURANCE AND SECURITY COMPANY, 44 PINE STREET.

The Preferred Mutual Accident Association, at 203 Broadway, was incorporated in 1885 for the purpose of insuring, at a fixed rate of premium, only the persons classed as preferred risks by all experts in accident insurance. The idea was original, and, like all original ideas, found adverse critics; but it is triumphant, and everybody recognizes now that only bad managers could have made it otherwise. Preferred risks naturally believe that their interests are safer with an association excluding extra and special hazards than with one which makes the admission of them simply dependent on higher premium payments. The Preferred Mutual had, at the end of 1885, 1,427 policies in force, insuring $7,135,000; and assets amounting to $4,624. It progressed steadily, until, at the end of 1892, it had 31,281 policies in force, insuring over $270,000,000; and assets amounting to $173,000. The Association has a net surplus of $113,843 over all its liabilities. And every one of its risks is preferred. It has paid in losses $366,984. It gained in 1891, 42 per cent. of the entire increase of amount of insurance in 35 mutual accident companies. It has paid in claims, for each $1 received in premiums, 52 cents, which is six cents more than the proportion of the Travelers; but its proportionate amount used for expenses for each $1,000 of insurance was $3.10 less. It issues for an annual premium of $16 a $10,000 combination policy, covering all injuries by accident, to the extent of $5,000 for death by accident; $5,000 for loss of hands or feet; $5,000 for loss of hand and foot; $5,000 for loss of both eyes; $2,500 for permanent total disability; $650 for loss of one eye; $25 per week for temporary total disability. If the injuries be received "in consequence of the wrecking or disablement of any regular passenger conveyance propelled by steam, electricity or cable," while the injured shall be riding therein, the Association, under the same combination policy, will pay $10,000 for death by accident, and amounts proportionately larger for the other contingencies. The Preferred has recently been reincorporated as a joint-stock company, with a paid-up capital and surplus of $250,000, and will continue to insure preferred risks only. In 1894 its offices will be in the beautiful building now being erected at 257 Broadway. The President is Phineas C. Lounsbury, Ex-Governor of Connecticut; the Treasurer is Allen S. Apgar; the Secretary is Kimball C. Atwood.

PREFERRED MUTUAL ACCIDENT ASSOCIATION, 257 BROADWAY.
(BUILDINGS NOW BEING REPLACED BY TWO ELEGANT 13-STORY EDIFICES.)

The Lawyers' Title Insurance Company of New York, at 120 Broadway, and Franklin Trust Company Building, Brooklyn, particularly recommends itself to real-estate investors and dealers by the following features :—1. The safety of its method of examining titles. The examination is by well-known lawyers of ability and experience. 2. The publication of the amount of all losses paid, and of all claims pending against it. This enables the public to judge intelligently of its management. The more careful the examination of the titles to be insured, the fewer should be the losses. 3. Its continuation of the custom of furnishing abstracts of titles and searches, giving to purchaser and mortgagee full information as to the facts of his title, in addition to his policy of title insurance. 4. The strength of its method of insurance, the elements of which are : method of examination; review of examination by the law department of the company ; examination of doubtful questions by committee of counsel ; rejection of titles admitted to be defective ; large capital ; and professional character of its managers. 5. The universal acceptance of its policies by individuals, trustees, and corporations. The United-States Government is among its assured. There is very grave doubt whether an individual trustee or corporation has the right to take title on purchase or mortgage on a policy of title insurance only, without risk of personal liability. But there is no doubt that an individual trustee or corporation has a right to take title on purchase or mortgage on the opinion of his own counsel, approved by this company, and with its policy of title insurance, and that by so doing he secures the greatest possible security, and incurs no risk of personal liability. 6. The ready means of access, through its bureau of investment, to the principal individuals, estates and corporations having money to lend on bond and mortgage. 7. The particular advantages offered to parties selling tracts of land in parcels, because of the above features, and because of the terms of its contracts made in such cases. 8. The peculiar advantages offered by its methods to builders and brokers.

The company commenced business July 18, 1887. Its capital and surplus on January 1, 1893, amounted to $1,500,000. It holds further security in aid of liability, of the value of $425,000. It has a permanent guarantee-fund, invested, as required by law, in bond and mortgage, United-States, State, city or county bonds, amounting to $750,000. It had no losses on policies in 1892. Its total losses since the organization of the company amount to $3,144.

Edwin W. Coggeshall is the President and General Manager ; Charles E. Strong, First Vice-President ; David B. Ogden, Second Vice-President ; William P. Dixon, Secretary ; John Duer, Treasurer. The directors are : Edwin W. Coggeshall, William Allen Butler, William P. Dixon, John Duer, Henry E. Howland, John T. Lockman, J. Lawrence Marcellus, David B. Ogden, John H. Riker, Charles E. Strong, Herbert B. Turner, James M. Varnum, and John Webber.

The Committee of Counsel are John W. Pirsson, Chairman ; E. Ellery Anderson, of Anderson & Man ; Charles Coudert, of Coudert Bros. ; William G. Choate, of Shipman, Larocque & Choate ; Frederic de P. Foster ; Joseph H. Gray, of Owen, Gray & Sturges ; Myer S. Isaacs, of M. S. & I. S. Isaacs, Lecturer on Real-Estate Law, N. Y. University Law School ; Theo. F. Jackson, of Jackson & Burr ; Benjamin F. Lee, of Lee & Lee, late Professor of Real Estate and Equity Jurisprudence, Columbia College Law School ; J. Lawrence Marcellus ; David B. Ogden, of Parsons, Shepard & Ogden ; Thomas L. Ogden, of Ogden & Beekman ; J. Evarts Tracy, of Evarts, Choate & Beaman ; George Waddington, and Sidney Ward.

The Lawyers' Title Insurance Company will soon move into more commodious offices in its own building, which it is now erecting, with fronts on both Liberty

- THE LAWYERS' TITLE INSURANCE COMPANY, OF NEW YORK.
LAWYERS' TITLE BUILDING, MAIDEN LANE, SOUTH SIDE, BETWEEN NASSAU AND WILLIAM STREETS.

Street and Maiden Lane, extending through the whole block between Nassau and William Streets.   It will be the most conspicuous office-building in this vicinity, thoroughly fire-proof, a fine specimen of artistic office architecture, designed by C. C. Haight, and built by David H. King, Jr. Its height will be 12 stories, and it will provide accommodations for many noted firms and corporations.

The Mercantile Credit Guarantee Company of New York, at 291 Broadway, has a capital of $250,000, with $100,000 deposited with the Insurance Department at Albany.   It was the first credit guarantee company organized under the Insurance Department of the State of New York.   It issues its policies of insurance to merchants and others, guaranteeing them from excessive or unexpected loss by the failures of customers.   The merchant first stands an agreed percentage on his yearly sales, equal to the usual yearly loss, and in turn is absolutely indemnified against all losses in excess thereof arising from failures.   The contracts may be made for varying times and amounts, and are thoroughly equitable in their terms and conditions.   The payments for credit insurance then take their place among the fixed charges of the business, and the merchant, covered and secured against losses in business, gains

THE MERCANTILE CREDIT GUARANTEE COMPANY,
291 BROADWAY.

greatly in comfort and peace of mind. Thus also larger lines may be sold without peril, when otherwise the limitations of a small capital would render it inadvisable, and more extensive credits may be given, when circumstances warrant.   The company does not interfere with the conduct of the business in any way, since it has made its terms and conditions before the assumption of the contract.   This is as important and vital a field, in its way, as either fire or life or marine insurance, and at no distant time will come into general use among merchants.   W. M. Deen is President ; James R. Pitcher, Vice-President ; Jas. E. Granniss, Treasurer ; C. Vincent Smith, Secretary.   The counsel are Hon. A. J. Dittenhoefer and Peet, Smith & Murray.   The directors are James E. Granniss, W. H. Male, Siegmund J. Bach, James R. Pitcher, E. C. Converse, G. Gunby Jordan, Leopold Herzig, J. W. Hinkley, W. M. Deen and C. Vincent Smith.

The United-States Mutual Accident Association was founded in 1877, for insurance against accidents.   The rates are determined by a pro-rata cost of the losses and expenses.   The record shows that since its organization to January 1, 1893, it paid 26,029 losses, amounting to $2,998,539, of which $444,739 was in 1892.   The offices are at 322 and 324 Broadway.   The President is Charles B. Peet.

The German-American Real-Estate Title Guarantee Company, at 34 Nassau Street, was organized in 1885, with a paid-in cash capital of $500,000, to afford protection to purchasers of real estate.   It supersedes the old system, which requires a re-examination of title, with its consequent delays and costs, at every transfer of real property.   Andrew L. Soulard is President.

BIRD'S-EYE VIEW FROM THE WASHINGTON BUILDING.
LOOKING NORTHWEST.

44

LLOYDS PLATE-GLASS INSURANCE COMPANY,
WILLIAM AND CEDAR STREETS.

The **Lloyds Plate-Glass Insurance Company,** at 63 William Street, organized in 1875, insures plate-glass against loss by breakage through accident. Its capital is $250,000. James G. Beemer was its President until 1893, when he was succeeded by William T. Woods, its former Secretary.

The **New-York Plate-Glass Insurance Company** began business in 1891. The capital is $100,000. Its offices are at 24 Pine Street.

The **Lawyers' Surety Company** began April 1, 1892, to issue bonds or policies of indemnity. Its capital is $500,000. Its President is Joel B. Erhardt, and its Vice-President, James E. Granniss.

The **United-States Guarantee Company** was organized in 1890. Its capital is $250,000. It issues bonds of indemnity against losses by unfaithful officers and employees. It is closely allied to the Guarantee Company of North America, a Canadian institution doing the same line of insurance.

Its offices are in Trinity Building. Its President is Edward Rawlings.

From the accounts of these great representative companies, it will be seen that the mutual protection of insurance has been extended over many departments.

GUERNSEY BUILDING, 160 BROADWAY.

Financial Institutions.

United-States Treasury and Assay Offices, Clearing-House,
National and State Banks, Bankers, Brokers, Etc.

THE financial centre of the United States is at the lower end of Manhattan
Island. The influence of New York in this respect, indeed, extends over the
entire Western hemisphere. It yields the supremacy among the great money-markets
of the world to London alone. The prediction is often made that before many
decades the preëminence in the monetary affairs of civilized countries will be transferred from the banks of the Thames to the banks of the Hudson. This involves
no stretch of the imagination. The steady and magnificent growth of New York's
financial power and importance points to such a result. Whatever fresh triumphs in
this field the future has in store for the metropolis of the Western World, it already
presents one of the greatest combinations of accumulated wealth, banking capital,
organized credit, corporate power, and speculative activity which civilization can
offer.

Historical facts afford the best explanation both of the rise of financial New York
to its present proud position, and of the organization which furnishes facilities for
the exercise of its supremacy. Another chapter of this work furnishes an exposition
of the workings of the system by which New York fills the economic function of a
general clearing-house for the whole United States, and is the central mart in which
the wholesale business of the entire country is ultimately settled. The attainment
of this pre-eminence, however, was a matter of slow progress. Physical and geographical factors gave New York an advantage over her sister cities in the race.
Nevertheless the acquisition of a preponderating share of the country's foreign commerce, and the ensuing process by which she became and continues the great money-
market, were largely the results of that mingled enterprise and conservatism which
has distinguished New-York's merchants, bankers and capitalists.

At the close of the Revolutionary War, New York, like the other seaboard cities,
was mainly a local centre. The close of the struggle for independence and the revival
of commerce and industry rendered financial organization a necessity to the country.
Philadelphia, then the most prosperous of American towns, possessed the first bank
(1781) organized in the country, and there the original Bank of the United States,
chartered by Congress in 1790, had its principal office. The institution of an incorporated bank in New York dates from 1784, and the first beginnings of the
present New-York Stock Exchange were in 1792. In 1800, when the country had
for ten years enjoyed a settled government under the Federal Constitution, New York
possessed two State banks, besides a branch of the Bank of the United States, with
an aggregate capital of about $3,000,000. Even at that early day, the path of for-
eign commerce which she was to travel with such success was clearly marked out.

The revenue of the Government from customs collected at New York in 1800 was $2,373,000, against $1,300,000 at Philadelphia, and an equal amount at Boston. A traveller of that day declared that Philadelphia was the London of America, but that New York was its Liverpool. The Embargo and the War of 1812, with the interruption of commerce, and the disorganization of the currency which followed, interfered somewhat with the financial development of New York. Its banks and wealthy citizens gave effective support to the Government during the struggle. John Jacob Astor, whose fortune gained in the fur-trade made him the leading capitalist of the city, became a large subscriber to the Government loan of that period. The peace of 1815 found New York with augmented banking facilities, and with increased energies on the part of her merchants and business men. In 1816 the banking capital employed was about $10,000,000, and the collections of Government revenue at New York in that year were nearly $15,000,000. Speculation, too, was stimulated by the war, and the regular organization of the New-York Stock Exchange dates from 1817.

The completion of the Erie Canal in 1825 marks the close of the preliminary period in New York's financial history. From that moment her leadership was no

MANHATTAN.   MERCHANTS.   NORTH AMERICA.   AMERICA.   NEW YORK.

WALL STREET, NORTH SIDE, NEAR WILLIAM STREET, IN 1860.

longer a matter of doubt. The introduction of steamboat navigation had some years before given her a decisive advantage over every rival, through the possession of waterways affording easy communication with a considerable portion of the country. As soon as an avenue was opened between the Hudson and the Lakes, the products of the rapidly growing West began to pour into the lap of New York, for distribution to other seaboard points or for shipment to Europe, while an increased percentage of the country's imports passed through and paid toll at the same gateway, This predominance in foreign commerce naturally brought with it a virtual monopoly

WALL STREET, FROM THE ASSAY OFFICE TO TRINITY CHURCH.

of the foreign exchanges of the country, that is to say, the collection of the amounts which foreign countries pay for our products and the settlements for foreign products imported into the United States.

New York's financial expansion on the line of foreign commerce was not without set-backs. The most noteworthy of these was the panic of 1837, when the culmination of a period of general speculation, reckless financiering and inflation in banknote circulation resulted in a crash which shook the whole country. The banks of New-York City generally suspended specie payments in May, 1837, and did not resume them for about a year. Trying as this experience was, it resulted in one great advantage to New York. In 1838 the State of New York enacted the celebrated law known as the "Free Banking Act." This statute established the principle that banking was a business in which all citizens might under proper regulations freely engage, and did away with the restrictions and abuses connected with the grant of special legislative charters. It also declared that bank-notes must be based upon Government or State bonds or other tangible security ; placed the banks under more direct supervision by the authorities ; and generally surrounded the banking business with needed safeguards. Its principles were adopted by several other States, and furnished the model ou which the National Banking Act was subsequently drawn. Under this salutary law, and during the period of recuperation which followed the panic, some of the strongest of the present financial institutions of New York were organized. It may also be noted that the refusal of the Government to renew the charter of the second Bank of the United States, and the subsequent failure of that institution had a noteworthy influence in favor of New York. The chief offices of both the earlier Bank of the United States (1791–1811) and the second institution (1816–1836) were in Philadelphia, and the downfall of the latter institution ended all claim on the part of the Quaker City to financial rivalry with New York.

Between the panic of 1837 and the outbreak of the civil war the moneyed power of New York kept pace with the material expansion of the country. The introduction of the ocean steamship and the steam railroad gave a powerful impetus to the commerce of the city ; and the California excitement and gold discoveries opened up a trade which brought the product of the new mines to the vaults of the New York banks. Three important financial institutions originated in this period ; the United-States Sub-Treasury, in 1846 ; and the New-York Clearing-House Association

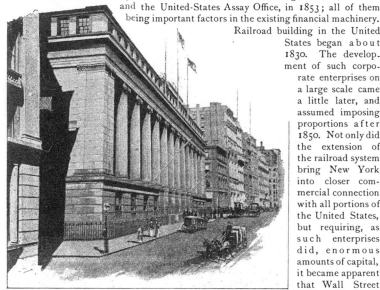

and the United-States Assay Office, in 1853 ; all of them being important factors in the existing financial machinery. Railroad building in the United States began about 1830. The development of such corporate enterprises on a large scale came a little later, and assumed imposing proportions after 1850. Not only did the extension of the railroad system bring New York into closer commercial connection with all portions of the United States, but requiring, as such enterprises did, enormous amounts of capital, it became apparent that Wall Street

WALL STREET, SOUTH SIDE, FROM THE CUSTOM HOUSE TO BROAD STREET.   was the sole money-market of the land which possessed the means or the facilities with which the great mass of securities created in such operations could be floated, i. e., placed before the American and foreign investing public. A necessary consequence of this was the augmentation of speculation in the bonds and stocks of the railroad and other great corporations thus created, and the Stock Exchange of New York then assumed that importance as an economic factor which has never departed from it. In the closing years of the decade, 1850–60, the banks of New York were over 50 in number, and represented a capital of upwards of $65,000,000, their deposits being about $80,000,000, and their circulation between $7,000,000 and $8,000,000. Over-expansion and over-trading, the usual accompaniments of a period of intense national development, led, however, by natural steps to another panic, that of 1857. "Runs" on banks, a suspension of specie payments lasting from October 15th to December 14th of that year, a depreciation of speculative values, and a crop of failures followed by a stagnation of business were the results. The recovery of confidence was, however, in this case more rapid than usual.

The outbreak of the civil war seemed to fall with destructive effect upon financial New York. It shook to its foundations under the blow, then rallied, devoting its whole strength and energy to supporting the credit of the Nation in that life-and-death struggle. Specie payments were suspended in December, 1860, and the Associated Banks at once formed a loan committee to facilitate action on behalf of the Government. Large amounts were advanced by the banks to the Treasury, on the security of Treasury notes and bonds, and more than once the banks responded to the appeal of the Secretary of the Treasury for aid at critical times during the contest. New York furnished the great market for the Government loans, and such operations coupled with the inflation of the currency and the business activity which the war engendered made Wall Street the scene of the most excited speculation that the modern world has probably ever witnessed. As the seat of the country's principal custom-house, where duties on imports were payable to the Government in specie, and the chief mart for foreign exchange, New York became at once the market in which the gold value of the National currency was measured and adjusted. The eyes of the whole country during these anxious years were fixed upon the "Gold Room," near Wall Street, in which the transactions in specie were conducted, the price of gold rising and falling on every turn of the war or change in the financial prospects of the country.

The National Banking Act of July, 1865, had an important influence in strengthcuing the position of New York as the financial centre of the country. It might be said that it really recognized and gave the force of law to existing facts. By the provisions of this famous Act, New York was made the depository for the banking reserves of the whole country. The National banks of New-York City must maintain a reserve in cash of 25 per cent. against their deposits ; but the banks of the other chief cities may deposit one-half of their similar cash reserves with National banks in New York. This provision results in the accumulation in New York of a large proportion of the surplus funds of the whole country, for the purpose of earning interest, while it also creates at New York a large financial reservoir from which when trade is active money can flow to all parts of the land. Some years ago Boston, Chicago and other cities were also made depositories, but without changing the tendeney of banks to deposit in New York. As illustrating this, it is estimated that of the $535,000,000 deposits held by the Associated Banks in June, 1892, no less than $240,000,000 was money of country banks deposited in New-York institutions. A majority of the banks of this city accepted charters under the National Banking Act, though there are some noteworthy exceptions; and the system has always found decided approval and support from New York's financial interests.

The close of the civil war found the United States with a superabundance of energy, which it was equally ready to turn in the direction of National development or exaggerated speculation. New York stood as the great financial mart, prepared both to furnish the organized capital which would build the railroads and establish the industries, and to afford the facilities for the speculative activity into which the country was anxious to throw itself. The latter was indeed an incident to the first tendency. Yet it obscured the substantial progress of the republic, and created a false impression of the economic functions which New York exercised as the point at which the whole financial system focused. Great railroads like the lines to the Pacific were constructed ; other systems, like the Pennsylvania and the New-York Central, were created by consolidation of smaller lines ; industries of all kinds were established ; and commerce reached unheard-of proportions. Cornelius Vanderbilt effected the great operations which made his name famous, and Jay Gould appeared as the boldest manipulator of stocks and corporations Wall Street had ever seen. The maintenance of the National credit during the war, and the energy and success with which the Government and people entered upon the unprecedented task of paying off a National debt rising into the billions, had an exceedingly stimulating effect upon the investment of foreign capital in American securities and enterprises. The historic banking dynasties of Europe, like the Rothschilds and Barings, had long been represented in New York. In fact, transactions in foreign exchange were, as they still are, mainly conducted through private banking-houses of large means, more or less directly connected or in correspondence with private or incorporated banks in the great cities of Europe. The augmented flow of the Old World's capital to this country increased the number and importance of such concerns, which, by their dealings in exchange (estimated at from fifteen to twenty billion dollars yearly), the great holdings of our securities they represent, and the enormous amounts of foreign money which through them are employed in buying investments, or loaned directly in the New-York money-market, are most important factors in the financial organization of the metropolis and of the country. These houses also issue letters of credit for travellers and commercial representatives, available through their correspondents in every city of Europe or indeed of the civilized world. The completion of the Atlantic Cable brought a closer union of interests between the New-York and foreign markets. To-day business messages are often transmitted from Wall Street to London and an answer returned in less than ten minutes, and enormous transactions are closed by this medium.

The mingled attractions of social and business life have of recent years tended to an increasing extent to draw to New York from all parts of the country successful men with accumulated means. Their wealth is added to the aggregate which gives New York its financial power, and their ability finds scope in the vast enterprises, financial, railroad and industrial, which are centred here. The great corporations of the land, too, find it necessary to manage their affairs from financial headquarters here, and with few exceptions the executive offices or fiscal agencies of the leading railroads are in New York, where their dividends and the interest on their bonds are paid, where their financial arrangements for raising capital must be concluded, and where the investments and speculation in their securities are conducted. · The latest additions to the great corporations of the United States—the industrial combinations—have followed the example. The Standard Oil Trust Organization, probably the strongest and most extended association of capital in the world, is entrenched in a lofty granite block on lower Broadway, and most of the great industrial trusts or corporations, such as the American Sugar-Refining Company, the American Cotton Seed-Oil Company and the National Lead Company, have their executive headquarters in New York's financial district.

If any decided change has taken place since the close of the war in the tendencies of financial New York, it has been the steady growth of conservatism which has accompanied the increase of its wealth and influence. Some severe lessons were needed to bring this about. The rampant speculation of 1866 and the succeeding years ran its course, culminating in a mad attempt to corner the supply of gold. September 24, 1869, "Black Friday," as it was called, was one of the most trying days in the history of Wall Street. Indeed, it necessitated the closing of the Stock Exchange for a short time, so that losses could be ascertained, and the solvent be separated from the ruined. A commercial and financial panic in 1873 was the result of general over-expansion. On this occasion, however, the Associated Banks of New York faced the stringency of money and the threatened disorganization of business throughout the country, and, uniting their credit and resources, issued Clearing-House certificates by which those of their own number temporarily endangered were carried through. The same method was successfully adopted in 1884, and again in the panic of 1890, when the failure of the great house of Baring Brothers & Co., in London, regarded then as second only to the Bank of England, brought dismay to the entire financial world.

The Financial Organization of New York is a complex one. It is composed of many separate elements, working to some extent in particular channels, yet all coöperating and mutually dependent upon each other for the smooth operation of the great machine. The Sub-Treasury of the United States is intimately connected with the great banks by which the flow of wealth through every commercial vein and artery of a great nation is regulated. The foreign banking-houses serve as the connecting links between the financial systems of the Old World and the New World. While the great trust-companies of New York are both banking institutions of enormous power, and are also the fiduciary connections between corporate organizations and the investing and money-saving public, the stock exchanges are the marts, in which the investing power of the country is brought into juxtaposition with its great enterprises, besides furnishing the facilities by which speculation in securities (which, if it is an evil, is also a necessity) is conducted. Private bankers and brokers innumerable deal in water, gas and electric lighting, telephone, telegraph, street-railway and other classes of securities, and in commercial paper. All these and other agencies which it is impossible to enumerate constitute that complicated machine — the New-York money-market — which fixes the value and supply of capital of the entire country.

The Sub-Treasury of the United States at New York is one of the most conspicuous buildings in Wall Street. It stands at the corner of Nassau Street, facing Broad Street, and extends through to Pine Street. Its Greek façade, graced by eight lofty Doric columns, surmounts a massive flight of steps extending the width of the building, the effect being dignified if not graceful. Midway the steps are broken by the pedestal on which stands Ward's heroic-sized bronze statue of Washington. This work of art was unveiled November 26, 1883, the day following Evacuation Day. Imbedded in the pedestal, immediately in front of the statue, is a slab of red sandstone bearing an inscription, stating that standing upon that identical stone, then forming part of the balcony of Federal Hall, and in the same place it now occupies, George Washington took the oath of office as the first President of the United States, April 30, 1789. An inscription on the side of the pedestal commemorates the fact that the statue was erected by voluntary subscriptions, under the auspices of the Chamber of Commerce. In 1889 the chief centennial celebration exercises took place on these steps.

The site of the Sub-Treasury was originally occupied by the City Hall of New York. The building was altered and repaired in 1789 for the use of the first Congress under the Constitution, and became the scene of the first inauguration. Hence it was known as the Federal Hall, though the seat of Congress was soon removed to Philadelphia, and finally to Washington. The building was acquired by the Government, to be used as the Custom House, and was demolished in 1834, when the construction of the present edifice was begun. It was completed in 1841, and remained the Custom House until 1862, when that establishment was removed to its present quarters in the old Merchants' Exchange building, and the Sub-Treasury took possession. The Act of Congress establishing the Sub-Treasury system was passed August 6, 1846, and Ex-Gov. William C. Bouck was in that year appointed the first Assistant Treasurer of the United States at New York.   The establishment was at first located in the adjacent building, now occupied by the Assay Office.

The interior of the edifice is mainly occupied by a large rotunda, with desks and railings like those of a bank, for the transaction of business with the public.   At the sides and at either end are smaller apartments occupying two stories, furnishing offices for the Assistant Treasurer and staff.   Below are massive vaults, in which the coin and notes entrusted to the Sub-Treasury are stored under constant guard.

The Assistant Treasurer of the United States at New York occupies one of the most responsible positions in the financial service of the country.   Besides being the

UNITED-STATES SUB-TREASURY, WALL AND NASSAU STREETS.

custodian of immense sums of Government money, and having the care of the largest receipts and disbursements it makes through any one agency, he is the representative of the Treasury Department at the financial centre, and is the direct channel through which the Secretary at Washington is kept in touch with the money-market.   The office is a Presidential appointment, and the incumbent is required to furnish a bond of $400,000 for the faithful performance of his duties.   The post has been filled by several men famous in political and financial history, among them John A. Dix, John J. Cisco, John A. Stewart (now President of the United-States Trust Company), Gen. Thomas Hillhouse (now President of the Metropolitan Trust Company), Charles J. Folger, Thomas C. Acton (now President of the Bank of New Amsterdam), Charles J. Canda, Alexander McCue, and Ellis H. Roberts (now President of the Franklin National Bank).   The present incumbent is Conrad N. Jordan, formerly Treasurer of the United States.   The Cashier is Maurice L. Muhleman.

It is estimated that the New-York Sub-Treasury conducts fully two-thirds of the direct money dealings of the Government with the public. In the year ending June 30, 1891, the total fiscal movement of the office was $2,800,000,000, and the actual cash handled in the same period was $1,900,000,000. It receives the money paid into the New-York Custom House, as well as from postmasters and other Government officers. The interest on the Government debt is paid in checks drawn upon it, together with about three-fifths of all the money disbursed to pensioners and for miscellaneous Government payments of all kinds. The employees of all the local Government offices are paid through it, and accounts with a majority of all the disbursing officers of the Government are kept here. It receives and redeems mutilated paper money from the banks of the city, and exchanges gold and silver coin for notes. It is the agency through which transfers of money are made between the various sub-treasurers and National-bank depositories in other cities and local banks. The amount of coin and currency stored in its vaults varies, having at one time (1888) reached the total of $225,000,000. At present, the amount is upwards of $135,000,000, of which about $60,000,000 is gold and $30,000,000 is in silver dollars. In former times as much as $100,000,000 in gold bars had accumulated at one time in the vaults, awaiting either delivery to depositories or shipment on orders from Washington to the mints.

In addition to its ordinary transactions, the Sub-Treasury has at different times proved a useful and efficient ally of the Department, in carrying out its financial plans, notably in the refunding operations so successfully accomplished, and in the resumption of specie payments. In these, as well as in other important measures, the office has demonstrated its capability to meet unforeseen exigencies, and with but slight changes in its machinery, to handle great amounts, in securities, as well as money, with the utmost accuracy and promptness. It is believed that never in the history of any government have such vast sums been received and disbursed, through a single agency, with so little friction, and so small a percentage of loss.

The United-States Assay Office at New York is a branch of the Mint. It occupies the building on Wall Street adjoining the Sub-Treasury. This edifice was built in 1823, for the New-York branch of the Bank of the United States, and is the oldest building on Wall Street. After the failure of that institution it was occupied by two banks, finally passing into the possession of the Government, and on the establishment of the Assay Office at New York in 1853 was converted to its present use. Dr. John Torrey, the famous botanist and chemist, was appointed the first assayer, and Hon. John Butterworth was appointed the first superintendent. A large building was erected in the rear for refining operations. Complaint that the acid fumes from the parting of bullion annoyed the occupants of neighboring private property resulted in 1891 in increasing the height of the lofty brick chimney at the rear of the building. The addition, though successful in its object, cannot be styled an architectural adornment. Nearly the whole of the building is occupied for the assaying, parting and refining of gold and silver. The precious metals, in the form of crude bullion, bars, old jewelry, coin, etc., are received at the office, and turned out in the form of bars, bearing the Government stamp certifying to their weight and fineness. The greater part of the work is executed for private parties, who deposit bullion with the office for that purpose, a small charge fixed by law being imposed for the service. Gold bars or gold coin are returned for gold deposits, and silver bars only for silver. The gold bars manufactured here vary in value from $100 to $8,000, and the silver bars from five ounces to 1,500 ounces. The office accepts no amounts of either gold or silver of less than $100 in value. During the year ending June 30, 1891, the bullion deposited for treatment at the

ASSAY OFFICE, 30 WALL STREET.

Assay Office amounted to $32,615,334 in gold, and $5,523,392 in silver; the total deposits since its establishment aggregating $806,013,626 in gold, and $132,038,089 in silver. Andrew Mason, who has been connected with the Assay Office since its establishment, has been its Superintendent since 1883. The other chief officers are Herbert G. Torrey (son of the late Dr. John Torrey), Assayer; and Benjamin T. Martin, Melter and Refiner. Visitors are admitted between 10.30 A. M. and 2.30 P. M., to witness the interesting processes of dealing with the precious metals, which are carried on here.

The Banks, National and State, are the most important portion of the mechanism by which New York controls the finances of the country. They represent an accumulation of capital, assets and deposits almost without parallel in the civilized world. Their influence is, however, multiplied by their wide-reaching connections. Nearly every bank and banker in the United States maintains a correspondence with and keeps an account at some New-York bank. In this way New York serves as the centre at which every thread in the complicated web of organized credit meets, and through their own organization — the Clearing-House Association — they complete the connection and supply the apparatus by which the larger proportion of the wholesale business of the country effects its settlements. The rise of the great financial institutions of the city has already been outlined. It remains, however, to indicate the present status of the metropolitan banks, and in particular instances to supply the interesting details in regard to the history and progress of some of the more prominent among them. There are in New York at present 49 National banks, with a combined capital (as per the last statement to the Comptroller of the Currency) of $49,810,000. Their aggregated surplus and undivided profits are $59,948,759; their total resources, $572,758,212; their deposits, $456,522,627, and their circulation $6,103,443. The State banks in the city number 46. Their aggregate capital (as per the latest report of the Superintendent of the Banking Department) is $17,672,700, their surplus and undivided profits $15,883,242, their total resources $154,633,244, and their deposits $120,787,185.

The New-York Clearing House Association, or, as it is called, "The Associated Banks," is the most important piece of financial mechanism in the country, if not in the world. It is a voluntary organization of 64 banks of New York and the Assistant Treasurer of the United States, for effecting in one place the daily exchanges between the Associated Banks, and the payment of the balances resulting therefrom. It occupies the brownstone building at the northwest corner of Nassau and Pine Streets, in the heart of the banking quarter. The upper floors contain the large apartment in which the daily clearings are carried out, with accommodations for the clerks employed by the Association itself. The Clearing House is not an incorporated body, and its property is held by trustees representing the collective ownership by the members of the Association. Prior to the formation of this Association, each bank would accumulate notes, drafts and checks drawn upon some or all of the other city banks. The bank "runner" (an important and busy functionary in early days) would take these drafts, visit each of the other banks on which they were drawn, and collect the respective amounts in cash. This system was evidently suited only for a primitive stage of business. It involved endless friction and unnecessary waste of time, and obliged banks to keep on hand more money than was actually available. Under it, each bank, after paying the drafts and checks drawn on it held and presented by other banks, and collecting the drafts on other banks which it had received, had either received a net balance of cash due to it or paid out a net balance. It was not strange that as the banking business of New York began to assume colossal proportions, and the amount of the exchanges between the banks grew to millions daily, some means should be sought to simplify these trans-actions by a process of off-setting debits and credits, and merely paying balances. At first, a custom arose for the bank "runners" to effect partial settlements by exchanging their mutual collections, and a system of weekly settlements between banks on Fridays was also essayed. This, however, was productive only of confusion and danger. A clearing house had been formed by London bankers as early as 1775, on something like ex-isting lines; and in 1841 . Albert Gallatin, then the Nestor of American finan-ciers, recommended the regu-lar settlement of exchanges between banks. A decade, however, elapsed before the many suggestions on the sub-ject took effect, and on October 11, 1853, after much consultation between bank officials, the New-York Clearing House Association came into existence as an experimental organization. Its success was almost in-stantaneous, and on June 6, 1854, the written constitu-tion, which in substance still governs the organization, was adopted. The first place occupied by the Clearing

CLEARING HOUSE, NASSAU AND PINE STREETS.

House was the basement of 14 Wall Street. Subsequently 82 Broadway was used ; and in 1858 it moved to the upper floors of the building of the Bank of New York, at William and Wall Streets. The present building was purchased by the Association and first occupied in 1875. Thomas Tileston, then President of the

Phenix Bank, was the first Chairman of the Clearing House, and George D. Lyman its first manager.

The workings of the Clearing House are eminently simple. Each bank represented in the Association despatches to the Clearing House, every morning, two clerks, who convey with them all the checks and drafts drawn on other members that have been deposited in the bank. Each member has a number, those of original members according to seniority of organization, the others according to their admission to the Clearing House. At 10 o'clock in the morning the clearing clerks of the various banks take their allotted places behind a great circular desk in the large hall of the Clearing House. Their assistants stand outside the desk carrying trays containing the drafts on the other banks, bundled and arranged in order. At a signal from the rostrum, the assistant clerks commence to make the circuit of the room, stopping at each settling clerk in rotation, and handing in the exchanges on each bank, until they have completed the circle and returned to the clearing clerk of their own bank. The settling clerks on entering the Clearing House knew the amount of their credit items, and the operation just described has informed them of the debits, that is, the exchanges of other banks on their own. In spite of the large number of clerks engaged in the clearing, perfect order is maintained, and the clerks themselves are generally experts. A very few minutes suffices for balances to be struck, which determine which banks are on the whole of their exchanges debtors and which are creditors. This is announced by the Clearing House official who presides, and nothing remains to be done but for the debtor banks to send to the Clearing House by 1.30 P. M. the amount in cash of the balances against them, and for the creditor banks at the same hour to draw the amounts due them. A vast amount of business is thus transacted without friction, delay or unnecessary waste of any kind. As a typical example, on the morning of January 17, 1893, the total exchanges at the Clearing House were $216,885,053, and the balances $8,521,844. That is, the latter amount settled the whole mass of transactions represented by the former figures. In the year 1892 the total clearings were $36,662,469,201.55; and the aggregate of its transactions from its formation to December 31, 1892, reaches the formidable figures of $1,041,209,050,209.

The affairs of the Association are controlled by meetings of the Presidents of all the constituent banks, though immediate powers are exercised by the chairman and Clearing House Committee, who are elected annually. A new member is admitted only on application, and examination of its affairs by the Committee, which must pronounce that the intended member is "sound." It is also not uncommon for the Committee to make an examination of the affairs of any member which has fallen under suspicion. Some members also act as clearing agents for other banks not members of the Association. In 1891 the Association adopted more stringent regulations in regard thereto, and the institutions which clear through members must now also submit to an examination as to "soundness" by the Committee.

The Clearing House is not merely a mechanical device for the settlement of bank-exchanges. That is its main function, but it also supplies the formal organization which enables the New-York banks to act unitedly in time of emergency. The Clearing House as a body was often and successfully appealed to on behalf of the Government during the trying times of the war. It also during the panics of 1873 and 1884, and again in 1890, stayed the progress of financial distrust by the issue of "Clearing House Certificates" against the deposit of approved securities by the banks with the Committee, and the acceptance by the members of the Association of these certificates in settlement of Clearing House balances. Another important function is the issue every Saturday of the weekly statement showing the averages for the week of the several items of loans, specie, legal tenders, deposits and circulation of all the members. The "Bank statement," as it is known, determines the extent to which the Associated Banks are above or under the 25 per cent. reserve to secure deposits which is required of National banks by law. No other financial document, not even the statement of the Bank of England, has an equal influence in determining the course of the money-market. During the panic of 1893 the Association supported the interior banks by issuing Clearing-House loan certificates. The President is George G. Williams, President of the Chemical National Bank ; and the Clearing House Committee is composed of Edward H. Perkins, Jr., President Importers' and Traders' National Bank, Chairman ; J. Edward Simmons, President Fourth National Bank ; Henry W. Cannon, President Chase National Bank ; Frederick D. Tappen, President Gallatin National Bank ; and William A. Nash, President Corn Exchange Bank. William A. Camp, whose service dated from 1857 as Assistant Manager and from 1864 as Manager, resigned in 1892, retiring upon half-pay, and was succeeded by Wm. Sherer, W. J. Gilpin succeeding the latter as Assistant Manager.

The American Bankers' Association is an organization of National and State banks, trust-companies, and private bankers. Its object is to promote the welfare of banking interests, and to secure unity of action in regard to legislation and other matters affecting banks and bankers. The institution was formed in 1876, the late Charles B. Hall (then President of the Boston National Bank of Boston) being its president, and the late James Buell (at the time President of the Importers' and Traders' National Bank of New York) being its secretary. Its permanent office is at 2 Wall Street and 90 Broadway. It has a membership comprising nearly every important banking institution in the country. The annual meetings of the Association, which it holds at different cities by rotation, furnish occasion for the discussion of subjects of importance to banking interests. The officers are, President, William H. Rhawn, President National Bank of the Republic, of Philadelphia ; First Vice-President, M. M. White, President Fourth National Bank, of Cincinnati ; Chairman of the Executive Council, E. H. Pullen, Vice-President National Bank of the Republic, of New York ; Treasurer, George F. Baker, President First National Bank, of New York ; Secretary, Henry W. Ford, 90 Broadway.

The Bank of New York, National Banking Association, is not only the oldest financial institution of the city, but one of the three oldest in the United States. It was founded in 1784 by leading New-York business men, who on the close of the Revolutionary War found pressing need for the facilities of a well-conducted bank. The Bank of North America, at Philadelphia, incorporated by Congress in 1781, was the only bank then existing in this country, and the formation of the Massachusetts Bank, of Boston, dates from 1784, the same year as the Bank of New York. These three institutions have acted as each others' correspondents for more than a century. Alexander Hamilton took a leading part in the foundation of the Bank of New York. His hand traced the constitution, and he was one of the first Board of Directors, his associates including Robert Brown, Comfort Sands, Thomas Randall, Nicholas Low and Isaac Roosevelt. Gen. Alexander McDougall was the first President, and William Seaton the first Cashier. The bank began business in the Walton mansion (demolished in 1881), which stood on Pearl Street, opposite Harper & Brothers' establishment. In 1788 it was removed to 11 Hanover Square, a house occupying part of the site of the former Cotton Exchange. In 1796 it purchased the premises at the corner of Wall and William Streets, where the bank still remains. A new building with the necessary vaults was at once erected on this lot.

This edifice was demolished in 1857, and the present brownstone and brick edifice was built.   This handsome structure (one of the first fire-proof buildings in the city) was originally four stories high, but has been increased by successive imposi-tions to seven stories.   The basement is utilized for safe-deposit vaults.   The his-tory of the Bank of New York is an epitome of the financial and commercial pro-gress of the city, State and Nation for more than a century.   This record has been preserved and set forth in a volume entitled "The History of the Bank of New York," compiled on its centennial anniversary, in 1884.   The bank has always pre-served its place among the foremost institutions of the country, in point of success and stability as well as age, and its management has invariably been recruited from the ranks of the leading business men of New York.   Among its earlier presidents were

BANK OF NEW YORK, N. B. A., WALL AND WILLIAM STREETS.

Jeremiah Wadsworth, Isaac Roosevelt, Gulian Verplanck, Herman Le Roy and Matthias Clarkson, and of more recent date John Oouth-out and Charles P. Lev-erich, the latter being prominent in the finan-cial negotiations by which the Government, during the Civil War, received effective support from the banks and financial interests of New York.   Many distin-guished men have had business relations with the bank, Talleyrand and Aaron Burr (checks signed by them are still preserved at the bank) being of the number. The stock of some of the original subscribers has been inherited by, and is still owned by, their descendants, and it is a remarkable circumstance in its history that the bank has never passed a dividend, except in 1837, when it was obliged to do so by law.   In 1864 it became a National bank, but as a special distinction retained its original title, adding thereto the words "National Banking Association."   The net deposits exceed $15,000,000. The officers are :   Ebenezer S. Mason, President ;   Richard B. Ferris, Vice-Presi-dent ; Charles Olney, Cashier ; and E. T. Hulst, Assistant-Cashier.   The Board of Directors is composed of James M. Constable, Franklin Edson, Charles B. Leverich, George H. Byrd, James Moir, Gustav Amsinck, Anson W. Hard, H. B. Laidlaw, Darius O. Mills, Eugene Kelly, John L. Riker, J. Kennedy Tod and E. S. Mason.

GALLATIN BANK. THOMPSON BUILDING.   MANHATTAN BANK.   MERCHANTS' BANK.   BANK OF AMERICA

WALL STREET, NORTH SIDE, FROM WILLIAM TO NASSAU STREETS.
32 TO 46 WALL STREET.

45

The Manhattan Company, virtually the second oldest bank in the city, is an institution with a history.   In this case there is a dash of romance.   The charter of the corporation was granted by the State Legislature in 1799, for the purpose of introducing pure water into the city.   This, however, veiled another object.   The Bank of New York controlled by Hamilton and the Federalists was then the only chartered institution in the city.   Its managers opposed the establishment of any rival, and were able to prevent it.   Leading members of the Republican (we should now say Democratic) party wished to found a bank, and called Aaron Burr to their assistance.   Burr engrafted, in an apparently innocent measure incorporating a company to supply the city with water, a clause providing that its surplus capital might be employed in any transactions not inconsistent with the laws of the State.   The bill, of course, passed, and it was found too late that the power establishing a bank had been conferred.   A capital of $2,000,000 was at once provided, and the Manhattan Company's Bank began its long and successful career.   The ostensible object of the company was, however, fulfilled ; and excavations in the older streets of New York still bring to light decaying pieces of wooden pipes, which were laid by it, and used to supply the city prior to the introduction of Croton water.   The latter event ended its usefulness in this respect, though the company still maintains a dilapidated tank, near Centre Street, by which it purports to be prepared to fulfill the purpose of its charter.   Banking, however, has been its chief business, and it has always been one of the most prominent banking concerns of New York.   Its place of business since the first decade of the century has been at 40 Wall Street, the old building having been replaced in 1883 by the Merchants' and Manhattan Building.

The Merchants' National Bank is the third of the New-York banks in point of antiquity.   It was founded in 1803, by leading merchants, who maintained that political influences were permitted to affect the conduct of the two local banks which then existed, as well as that of the Branch Bank of the United States.   The original subscription-list, still preserved at the bank, embraces many names of families prominent in the commercial and social life of early New York.   Among the original stockholders were Gilbert Aspinwall, Josiah Ogden Hoffman, Jordan Mott, Abraham R. Lawrence, Judge Daniel D. Tompkins, Charles L. Camman, C. C. Roosevelt, Col. Nicholas Fish, and John Peter DeLancy.   Oliver Wolcott, who had succeeded Hamilton as Secretary of the United-States Treasury, was the first President of the bank.   He resigned a few years later to become Governor of Connecticut.   The first Board of Directors included Isaac Bronson, Henry J. Wyckoff, John Hone, and John Swartwout.   The bank from its inception ninety years ago has occupied premises on the same site, at 42 Wall Street, where its business is now conducted.   The private house originally converted to this purpose gave way to a granite structure of Grecian architecture, with two massive stone pillars.   It was long one of the landmarks of Wall Street, but was in its turn demolished in 1883 to make room for the splendid "Merchants' and Manhattan Building."   Its original capital was $1,200,000, which was increased later to $3,000,000, and finally reduced to $2,000,000.   The late Alexander T. Stewart had been for years, and was at the time of his death, a member of the board.   The history of the bank has not been eventful.   It is a record of conservative management, weathering with success all the financial storms of nearly a century.   The late Jacob D. Vermilye, who in length of service was the dean of New-York bank presidents, was succeeded in the presidency in 1891 by Robert M. Gallaway.   The Cashier of the Merchants' Bank, Cornelius V. Banta, has been connected with the institution 45 years, and enjoys the distinction of the longest service of any bank cashier on Wall

ATLANTIC MUTUAL.   UNITED STATES TRUST CO.   UNITED STATES NATIONAL BANK.   METROPOLITAN TRUST CO.

WALL STREET, SOUTH SIDE, FROM WILLIAM TO NASSAU STREETS.
37 TO 51 WALL STREET.

Street.   The directors include John A. Stewart, of the United-States Trust Company ; Henry Sheldon ; E. A. Brinckerhoff ; Charles S. Smith, President of the Chamber of Commerce ; Jacob Wendell ; W. G. Vermilye ; Gustav H. Schwab, of Oelrichs & Co.; Donald Mackay, of Vermilye & Co.; and Charles D. Dickey, Jr., of Brown Brothers & Co.

The Mechanics' National Bank, the fourth oldest of the banks of New-York City, was organized in 1810, chiefly through the influence of the General Society of Mechanics and Tradesmen ; to accommodate the members of which, its capital of $2,000,000 was divided into shares of $25 each.   For a number of years the society was prominent in the bank's affairs, and has never severed its connection ; being still the holder of the stock originally subscribed, and has one of the many accounts that have stood upon its books for 83 years.   The banking-house, until two years ago, was one of the landmarks of Wall Street.   The original quarters were in a remodelled three-story dwelling-house, which was at one time occupied by Alexander Hamilton.   The present magnificent nine-story granite edifice, one of the finest on Wall Street, is the third building erected by the bank upon its property.

Among its noted presidents were John Slidell, Jacob Lorillard, Shepherd Knapp and Benjamin B. Sherman.   In 1854, the original charter expiring, the bank was re-organized as a State bank, becoming a National bank in 1865.   The original capital of $2,000,000 remains the same, but a stately surplus of $2,000,000 has been added.   Its gross assets exceed $15,000,000, and the deposits of $11,000,000 are almost wholly from individuals, manufacturers and mercantile houses.   The officers are Horace Everett Garth, President, who became associated with the bank in 1883 ; Alexander E. Orr, Vice-President ; William Sharp, Jr., Cashier ; and Granville W. Garth, Assistant-Cashier.

The Board of Directors, from the time of organization, has been composed of men foremost in financial circles, and at present consists of Horace Everett Garth, Alexander E. Orr, Henry F. Spaulding, Henry E. Nesmith, William B. Kendall, Charles H. Isham, Lowell Lincoln, Henry Hentz, Eckstein Norton, Charles M. Pratt, Henry Talmadge, John Sinclair, William L. Trenholm, and William Sharp, Jr.

The Bank of America has occupied, for more than eighty years, the site at the northwest corner of Wall and William Streets, on which now stands its lofty and admirable granite building.   The old Winthrop mansion stood on this corner, and was leased when the bank was chartered by the State in 1812, and used as its banking-house.   In 1831 the bank purchased this property, and in 1835 erected a building which, for upwards of fifty years, was a conspicuous object in Wall Street. It was of Greek architecture, Corinthian period, and furnished quarters only for the bank.   In 1888-89 the present Bank of America building took its place, covering the old site and twenty-five feet additional frontage, purchased from the Bank of North America.   This imposing building supplies office-room for a number of corporations and private bankers, besides the bank's own exceedingly spacious and elegant banking apartments on the main floor.   The Bank of America ranks as fifth in age among the city banks.   It was founded at a time when the expiration of the charter of the first Bank of the United States opened the way for the development of State banks.   Its first directors and stockholders were recruited from among those interested in the Bank of the United States, and it attracted much of the capital and business of that institution.   The charter provided for a capital of $6,000,-000, and required the bank to pay the State $600,000, and to loan it $2,000,000. Oliver Wolcott, ex-Secretary of the Treasury, was the first president ; and the original Board of Directors were Oliver Wolcott, William Bayard, Arthur Smith, George

MECHANICS' NATIONAL BANK.
31 AND 33 WALL STREET, BETWEEN BROAD AND WILLIAM STREETS.

Griswold, Thomas Buckley, Abraham Barker, Theodorus Bailey, John T. Lawrence, John T. Champlin, John De Peyster, Philip Hone, Preserved Fish, Stephen Whitney, Archibald Gracie, Patrick G. Hildreth, Elisha Leavenworth, Josiah Ogden Hoffman, and Henry Post, Jr.

The War of 1812, and the financial troubles of that era, prevented the development of the business of the bank upon the lines originally intended, and the provisions of the charter of 1812 were modified, the modifications including a reduction in the amount of the authorized capital and in the amounts to be paid and loaned the State. The bank, however, prospered, and ranked, as it still does, among the most respected and successful institutions of the country. For a long time it was the local depository of the National funds, and from October 3, 1854 (upon which date, at the first annual meeting of the New-York Clearing House Association, the Bank of America was chosen as depository), until the old building was removed in 1888, its vaults were used for the deposit of gold coin by the Associated Banks, the Bank of America issuing its certificates for the coin deposited; hence it is sometimes spoken of as the "Bank of the Clearing-House." At one time nearly $50,000,000 in gold was in its custody.

A notable fact in the bank's history is the unbroken record it enjoys of having under all circumstances paid its circulating notes in gold, even in the face of more than one general suspension of specie payments. No holder of a Bank of America note has ever had his demand for payment of the note in gold refused. The Bank of America is the most prominent and influential bank now doing business under a State charter. Its capital of $3,000,000 is reinforced by a surplus in excess of $2,000,000; and its deposits approach $20,000,000. The Board of Directors includes Samuel Thorne, George A. Crocker, David S. Egleston, J. Harsen Rhoades, Augustus D. Juilliard, Oliver Harriman, Frederic P. Olcott, George G. Haven, William H. Perkins, James N. Jarvie, and Dallas B. Pratt. The officers of the bank are William H. Perkins, President; Frederic P. Olcott, Vice-President; Walter M. Bennet, Assistant Cashier; and John Sage, Assistant Cashier.

The National City Bank of New York, one of the oldest, largest, and most conservative banks in the country, was incorporated in 1812, with a capital of $800,000, which was increased in 1853 to $1,000,000. Its capital, surplus and undivided profits exceed $3,500,000, and its deposits range from $15,000,000 to $18,000,000. The bank is situated at 52 Wall Street, where it has had its office since it first commenced business, the present building being the second one on the same site occupied by it. The building which it first occupied had been previously used by the New-York branch of the first Bank of the United States, the stock of the latter having been received in payment for subscriptions to the stock of the City Bank. The first president of the bank was Samuel Osgood, who had been Naval Officer of the port; and the first Board of Directors comprised Abraham Bloodgood, Ichabod Prall, William Irving, Samuel Tooker and William Cutting. G. B. Vroom was its first cashier. Moses Taylor became its president in 1856; and the energy, ability and integrity, which long made him one of the foremost and most conspicuous merchants and business men of New York, characterized his administration of the bank and contributed largely to its increased prosperity. He died in 1882; and was succeeded in the presidency by his son-in-law, Percy R. Pyne, who resigned in 1891, when James Stillman, of the well-known firm of Woodward & Stillman, cotton merchants, was elected President. The other officers of the bank are David Palmer, Cashier, and Gilson S. Whitson, Assistant Cashier. The present Board of Directors consists of George W. Campbell, Cleveland H. Dodge (of.

BANK OF AMERICA.
WALL STREET, NORTHWEST CORNER OF WILLIAM STREET.

Phelps, Dodge & Co.), Hon. William Walter Phelps, Percy R. Pyne, Roswell G. Rolston (President of the Farmers' Loan & Trust Company), Samuel Sloan (President of the Delaware, Lackawanna & Western Railroad Company), James Stillman, Henry A. C. Taylor and Lawrence Turnure.

The Tradesmens National Bank, on Broadway, at the northwest corner of Reade Street, is one of the most conspicuous institutions of the Dry-Goods

District. Its lofty six - story white - marble building, which it owns, and of which it occupies the lower part, was built in 1860 as its permanent home. Its upper floors are occupied by corporations and for offices of professional men. Its value as a piece of real estate has advanced to a marvellous extent since it was bought by the bank thirty - three years ago. The bank has a long history, having been organized in 1823 under a State charter, and is the eighth oldest existing bank of New-York City. It was originally located in the vicinity of Chatham Square.

TRADESMENS NATIONAL BANK, BROADWAY, NORTHWEST CORNER OF READE STREET.

The most famous of its early presidents was Preserved Fish, one of the most active merchants and bankers of his time in this city. In 1865 the Tradesmens organized as a National bank, and it is a noteworthy fact that since that date it has paid in dividends upon its stock no less than $2,250,000, and is regarded among capitalists as a safe dividend-paying stock. The surplus is nearly $210,000; the total resources approach $5,000,000; and the deposits exceed $4,000,000, an increase in the year 1892 of nearly $2,000,000. Under its present management it has materially developed its business, and has become the New-York correspondent of a large number of banks throughout the West and South. Tradition and inclination, however, have kept the management of the Tradesmens closely with the conservative policy of legitimate banking business. The Board of Directors consists of George Starr, capitalist; Elliot L. Butler, of Belt, Butler & Co., wool; Julius Kaufmann, of Smith & Kaufmann, manufacturers of ribbons; Henry

NATIONAL CITY BANK OF NEW YORK.
52 WALL STREET, NORTH SIDE, BETWEEN PEARL AND WILLIAM STREETS.

Campbell, of Martin & Campbell, wholesale grocers; F. S. M. Blun, of F. S. M. Blun & Co., corset supplies; James R. Pitcher, General Manager of the United-States Mutual Accident Association; Joseph T. Low, of Joseph T. Low & Co., commission dry-goods; Thomas B. Kent, President of Holmes, Booth & Haydens, brass manufacturers; John A. Tweedy, of Lee, Tweedy & Co., dry-goods importers; and Henry C. Berlin, President of Berlin & Jones Envelope Company. The officers of the bank are James E. Granniss, President, who is identified with numerous local institutions; Logan C. Murray, Vice-President, formerly President of the United-States National Bank; and Oliver F. Berry, Cashier, who has been connected with the Tradesmens Bank for a score of years.

The Chemical National Bank is a famous corporation. Its stock commands a greater price in proportion to its par value than any other bank stock. It has the greatest surplus and undivided profits, with a single exception, of any bank in the country. It has the largest amount of individual deposits. It pays the largest percentage of dividends on its par value of any corporation of any kind. The Chemical Bank originated in 1824, being organized under a State charter as "The Chemical Manufacturing Company," with banking privileges. The name was determined by the fact that some of the leading men in the enterprise were connected with the drug trade. The charter expired in 1844, when its line of deposits was $600,000. A new bank took its place, with a capital of $300,000, and on February 26, 1844, the business of the Chemical Manufacturing Company was taken over by the Chemical Bank. John Q. Jones, the first President, remained in that office till 1878. Its enormous individual deposits exceed $23,000,000, and are secured without the payment of a particle of interest. Its first dividend was paid in 1849, five years after its reorganization, being at the rate of 12 per cent., which was increased to 18 and then to 24 per cent., advancing in 1863 to 36 per cent., in 1867 to 60 per cent., in 1872 to 100 per cent., and in 1888 to 150 per cent. per annum. The shares of the bank based on $100 par value have sold as high as $4,980 each, the quotations varying from that sum to $4,600 a share.

CHEMICAL NATIONAL BANK, 270 BROADWAY, NEAR CHAMBERS STREET.

The Chemical's first banking-house was on Broadway, opposite St. Paul's Chapel, occupying part of the site of the present Park Bank. In 1850 it moved to and occupied its present site at 270 Broadway. George G. Williams entered the service of the old Chemical Manufacturing Company in 1841, became Cashier in 1855, and President in 1878. William J. Quinlan, Jr., the Cashier, has filled that office since 1878. The Directors are George G. Williams, James A. Roosevelt, Frederic W. Stevens, Robert Goelet, and William J. Quinlan, Jr.

The Merchants' Exchange National Bank occupies some of the finest and most commodious banking quarters in the city. They are in the grand new edifice at 257 Broadway, an exceptionally choice location, directly opposite the City Hall and the City-Hall Park, and covering the site of Alexander T. Stewart's first store, where the bank has been located about thirty years. The Merchants' Exchange Bank stands among the oldest of the financial institutions of this city. It was organized under a State charter in 1829, and commenced business, September 7, 1831, at the corner of Greenwich and Dey Streets. When it began business, there were only sixteen other local banks in existence : the Bank of New York, the Manhattan, the Merchants', the Mechanics', the Union, the Bank of America, the Phenix, the City, the North-River, the Chemical, the Fulton, the Tradesmens, the Mechanics' and Traders', the Butchers' and Drovers', the Greenwich, and the Branch Bank of the United States. Besides these, the New-York Dry-Dock Company and the Delaware & Hudson Canal Company were chartered with bank privileges. There were only two savings-banks, the Bank for Savings and the Seamen's. There were no trust-companies, and the total banking capital was quite small compared with the amount now invested. The Merchants' Exchange Bank was founded by leading merchants, and its name indicates its intended and actual character as a bank for merchants. Its first President was Peter Stagg, the shipping merchant. The President now is the Hon. Phineas C. Lounsbury, ex-Governor of Connecticut, who became President in 1888, and brought to the bank the support of an extensive and influential connection. The first Cashier was William M. Vermilye, who afterwards became a member of the banking house of Vermilye & Co. The Vice-President and Cashier is Allen S. Apgar, who has been connected with the bank for 27 years. He was elected Cashier in 1869, and Vice-President in 1890, both of which offices he still

MERCHANTS' EXCHANGE NATIONAL BANK,
257 BROADWAY.

(TAKEN DOWN IN 1893 TO MAKE ROOM FOR THE NEW EDIFICE.)

retains. He became connected with the bank after he had been honorably discharged from the United-States Navy, in which he had served as Paymaster for three years of the late war. He is generally regarded as one of the most industrious and efficient bank officials in the city. The Board of Directors includes : Robert Seaman, of the Iron Clad Manufacturing Company ; Jesse W. Powers, capitalist ; Allen S. Apgar, Vice-President ; Joseph Thomson, real estate ; Alfred M. Hoyt, capitalist, and Vice-President of the Produce Exchange ; Phineas C. Lounsbury, President ; James G. Powers, of James G. Powers & Company, grocers ; Alfred J. Taylor, lawyer ;

E. Christian Körner, wholesale grocer ; Lucius H. Bigelow, publisher ; John H. Hanan, of Hanan & Son, shoes ; Isaac G. Johnson, of the Spuyten-Duyvil Foundry ; Timothy L. Woodruff, President of the Maltine Manufacturing Company ; Lyman Brown, wholesale drugs ; and the Rev. Sanford Hunt, D. D., of the Methodist Book Concern.

In 1865 it became a National bank, and in 1888 its capital was reduced to $600,-000, by returning $400,000 to the shareholders. Under the present management the bank has steadily prospered. It has total resources of about $6,250,000 ; deposits exceeding $5,000,000 ; surplus and undivided profits of $200,000 ; and its shares on a par value of $100 are quoted at $135 or more. The business of the Merchants' Exchange National Bank is not merely local but extends throughout the Union.

The Gallatin National Bank commemorates by its name the connection with the institution of the illustrious financier and statesman, Albert Gallatin. It was organized in 1829, under the name of the "National Bank of New York." John Jacob Astor was interested in the matter, and as the original capital of $1,000,000 was not fully subscribed, he proposed its reduction to $750,000, and offered to complete that sum provided that he could name the bank's president. The offer was accepted, and Astor nominated Gallatin, who, having served as Senator from Pennsylvania, as Secretary of the Treasury in the Jefferson and Madison administrations, as a negotiator of the Treaty of Ghent, and as Minister to France, had retired to private life. Albert Gallatin remained at the head of the bank until 1838, when being eighty years of age, he resigned. He was succeeded by his son, James Gallatin, whose presidency lasted for thirty years, during which time he ranked as a leader in the banking business of New York, and the institution under his management enjoyed great prosperity. The change of name from the "National Bank of New York" to the present title occurred in 1865, when the bank accepted a charter under the National Banking Law, which rendered an undesirable confusion of names possible. The selection of the present title was quite natural, the bank from its foundation having been identified with the name of Gallatin. James Gallatin resigned in 1868, and some years afterwards died abroad. His successor, Frederick D. Tappen, had then been 17 years in the service of the institution, and during the 25 years that have since elapsed he has ably maintained its record for success and conservatism. He has taken a prominent part in the counsels of the Clearing House Association, being now its Chairman, and is actively identified with many public interests in New York. The bank began business at 36 Wall Street, this lot being purchased for $12,000, while the building then erected cost $14,000. In 1856 a new banking-house was built on the same site. In 1887 the adjoining lot was bought by the Gallatin from the dissolved Union Bank, for $400,000 ; and on the site thus provided the present stately nine-story redstone edifice, called by its name, was erected, and here are its commodious banking rooms. It is unsurpassed in elegance as well as in practicability. It was built and is owned jointly by the Gallatin Bank and by Adrian Iselin, the undivided half interest of the former being set down at a value of $500,000. The first dividend was paid nine months after the bank's organization, and it has never since passed a dividend. A surplus of over $1,500,000 has been accumulated, and its shares sell for $320. Large amounts of its stock have been permanently held by the families of original stockholders. This is shown in the composition of its Board of Directors, which includes Frederic W. Stevens and Alexander H. Stevens (grandsons of Albert Gallatin), William Waldorf Astor, W. Emlen Roosevelt, Adrian Iselin, Jr., Thomas Denny and Henry I. Barbey. The Cashier is Arthur W. Sherman. The Gallatin ranks among the strongest, most enterprising and most secure of banks.

GALLATIN NATIONAL BANK.
36 WALL STREET, BETWEEN NASSAU AND WILLIAM STREETS, ADJOINING ASSAY OFFICE.

BROOKLYN BRIDGE, EAST FROM UNITED STATES ARMY BUILDING.

NORTHEAST FROM UNITED STATES ARMY BUILDING, SHOWING EAST RIVER AND BROOKLYN.

BATTERY PARK, ELEVATED RAILROADS AT SOUTH AND STATEN ISLAND FERRIES, AND BARGE OFFICE.

CASTLE GARDEN, FROM BATTERY PLACE.

The National Butchers' and Drovers' Bank is a time-honored institution, founded in 1830, taking its name from the fact that its originators were in the cattle and butchering trades, which in New York's early days centred at the famous Bull's Head, in the Bowery. For many years its chief business was drawn from this class of patrons. Its banking-house was first established in the Bowery, near Broome Street, and after moving to 128 Bowery (the site of the present Bowery Savings-Bank), the bank in 1832 purchased an adjacent lot, 124 Bowery, at the corner of Grand Street, and erected the dignified old-fashioned granite bank and office-building which has since been its home. Col. Nicholas Fish was the first President. His successor, Benjamin M. Brown, became the first President of the Bowery Savings Bank. That great institution in fact was founded by the Directors of the

NATIONAL BUTCHERS' AND DROVERS' BANK, BOWERY AND GRAND STREET.

Butchers' and Drovers' Bank, and its organization was effected in the latter's Board Room. It is still the neighbor and a depositor of the bank. The early history of the bank was prosperous. It became a National bank in 1865. Its capital is $300,000. It has a net surplus and undivided profits of over $309,000; total resources of $2,700,000; and a deposit line of over $2,000,000. The latter figures represent almost entirely individual and mercantile deposits, the policy of the bank being the conservative one of confining its business to the strictly commercial branches of banking. Since organizing as a National bank its average dividends have been nine per cent. per annum, and $190 is quoted for its shares. Gurdon G. Brincker-hoff, the President, entered the bank's service in 1853, was elected Cashier in 1866, and became its head in 1879. The Cashier, William H. Chase, dates his connection with it from 1856, and was elected to his present post in 1879. The Directors of the bank are: George W. Quintard, Henry Silberhorn, Henry Hofheimer,

Gurdon G. Brinckerhoff, William H. Chase, John Wilkin, John A. Delanoy, Jr., Edward Schell, and Max Danziger. E. G. Tucker is Assistant Cashier. The bank has a diversified clientage among the business interests of an important district.

The Seventh National Bank, at Broadway and John Street, is the successor of the Seventh-Ward Bank, established in 1833, in East Broadway. For many years the bank was at Pearl Street and Burling Slip. It had among its directors at one time three mayors of New York, Walter Browne, also President of the bank, Daniel P. Tiemann, and Abram S. Hewitt. George Montague, now President of the Second National Bank, was for many years President of the Seventh National. The Directors are: John

SEVENTH NATIONAL BANK, BROADWAY AND JOHN STREET.

McAnerney, President; James Hall, of Cooper, Hewitt & Co.; Henry A. Rogers, railroad supplies; H. Duncan Wood, banker; Henry R. Beekman, of Ogden & Beekman; Alfred Wagstaff, of John Anderson & Co., tobacco; Charles H. Pine, President Ansonia National Bank; Hugh Kelly, commission merchant; Patrick Farrelly, President American News Co.; Charles Siedler, late of Lorillard & Co.; Daniel F. Cooney, iron merchant; and J. Preston McAnerney. George W. Adams is Cashier.

The National Bank of Commerce in New York has an importance of more than local character. Its capital of $5,000,000, coupled with its surplus, undivided profits and contingent fund aggregating $8,600,000, give it a strong position among American banks, for it is one of the ten banks having the largest combined capital and surplus in this country. It was founded in 1839, with a capital of $10,000,000, afterwards reduced to the present amount. The first President was Samuel Ward, and its original Directors included such famous names in New York's mercantile history as Robert B. Minturn, James Brown, Robert Ray, Jonathan Sturges and Stephen Whitney. John A. Stevens, its second President during a long incumbency, was one of the most eminent members of the banking profession in New York. The bank first occupied (jointly with the Bank of the State of New York) the old building of the Bank of the United States (now the Assay Office), in Wall Street. This was sold to the Government in 1853, and temporary quarters were sought at Broad Street and Exchange Place, while the present white marble building at the northwest corner of Nassau and Cedar Streets was in course of erection. The Bank of Commerce settled permanently in this dignified structure in 1857, the only changes since that time being the addition of a sixth story, affording additional offices for rental.

46

The eminent position of the Bank of Commerce has been maintained ever since its foundation. It, however, attained additional prominence by the patriotic attitude of its management toward the Government during the civil war, and the lead which the institution took in supporting the contest for the Union. It became a National bank in 1865, though this action was attended by exceptional circumstances. Secretary of the Treasury Chase was anxious that the institution should accept a National charter. The management and stockholders, however, hesitated, on account of the provisions of the National Bank Act making shareholders liable

for the value of their stock, and an equal amount in addition. To fit this case a clause was introduced in the Act, providing that shareholders of National banks with at least $5,000,000 capital and a surplus of 40 per cent. thereof should be exempt from double liability. The Bank of Commerce, with one exception, is the only bank in the country which meets both these conditions. The fact that its shareholders are accordingly liable for its debts only to the extent of their stock gives its shares a decided preference as an investment for executors, trustees and others in a fiduciary position. A vigorous management of its affairs has contributed to maintain its leading position. This was illus-

NATIONAL BANK OF COMMERCE, NASSAU AND CEDAR STREETS.

trated in the panic of 1890, when the officers of the Bank of Commerce championed the issue of the Clearing House certificates, which arrested the panic and saved weak institutions from failure. In fact, although in no need whatever of such assistance, it took out $500,000 of the certificates simply as an example and encouragement to other banks which actually required help. The late Richard King, the President of the bank since 1882, was on his decease in 1891 succeeded by W. W. Sherman, whose connection with it dates from 1858, and who had been its Cashier for ten years. J. Pierpont Morgan is Vice-President ; William C. Duvall, Cashier ; and Neilson Olcott, Assistant Cashier. The Directors are W. W. Sherman, J. Pierpont Morgan, of Drexel, Morgan & Co., William Libbey, Frederick Sturges, Charles Lanier, Charles H. Russell, Alexander E. Orr, John S. Kennedy, and Woodbury Langdon.

The Mercantile National Bank, at 191 Broadway, corner of Dey Street, is an illustration of the development under vigorous and efficient management of a small institution into one of large proportions. The bank is a comparatively old one. It was organized as a State institution in 1850, the Bank of Ithaca, New York, itself a concern of some antiquity, being practically transferred to New-York City, and Ithaca capitalists were largely identified with the original Mercantile Bank. William B. Douglas was the first President, and among the prominent Directors were Isaac N. Phelps, Josiah B. Williams, Charies P. Burdett and William W. and Edward S. Esty of Ithaca. The present building was erected by the bank in 1862. In 1865 it became a National bank under the existing designation. The real importance of the institution, however, dates from 1881. At that time its business and deposits had from several causes fallen off, and its surplus was practically exhausted. The late George W. Perkins, a banker of unusual ability and experience, then holding the position of Cashier of the Hanover National Bank, saw in the condition of the Mercantile the opportunity to create it anew on a strong basis. He accepted the presidency ; invited Mr. St. John from the extensive sugar-refiners, Havemeyers & Elder, into the cashiership ; reorganized its directory; they together extended its busi ness connections with great rapidity, and laid the foundation of the confidence and sound prosperity which it still maintains under its present able administration. Successful as Mr. Perkins's labors were, they nevertheless undermined his health, causing his praetical retirement in less than a year, and his death in 1883. His talent for organization was well shown in the choice of his chief assistant, William P. St. John, as Cashier,

MERCANTILE NATIONAL BANK, BROADWAY AND DEY STREET.

who in 1883 became President ; a position he still holds.   Frederick B. Schenck, who at first filled the post of Assistant Cashier, has been Cashier of the institution since 1883.   The Mercantile National has a Surplus Fund of $1,000,000, in addition to its capital of $1,000,000.   Its deposits average over $10,000,000, a large part of which is from National and State banks, which attests the extent of its connections and correspondence throughout the Union.   Semi-annual dividends of six per cent. a year are paid on the stock, for which the market price is $235.   William P. St. John is known throughout the country as an original and forcible writer on financial topics.   The Board of Directors consists of William P. St. John, President ; William C. Browning, clothing ; Charles T. Barney, capitalist ; John E. Borne, oils ; Charles L. Colby, railroads ; George W. Crossman, coffee ; Emanuel Lehman, cotton ; Seth M. Milliken, dry goods ; James E. Nichols, wholesale grocer ; George H. Sargent, hardware ; Charles M. Vail, butter ; Isaac Wallach, men's furnishing goods ; James M. Wentz, dry goods ; Richard II. Williams, coal ; and Frederick B. Schenck, Cashier.

The National Bank of the Republic of New York is one of the most widely-known institutions in the country.   It was established in 1851 as a State bank, and was noted at first for the large extent of its connections throughout the South.   Its first President, G. B. Lamar, was a Southern man, with great influence in that section.   The first Cashier of the bank was Henry F. Vail.   The bank purchased in 1851, for $110,000, the lot at the corner of Wall Street and Broadway, which now as then is considered the most valuable piece of ground in the country, and long occupied it with its banking-house.   This site, however, with two additional lots, is now occupied by the magnificent nine-storied United Bank Building, erected in 1880, in which the Bank of the Republic is the owner of an undivided half, and where its commodious quarters are now located.   The cost of the land and building was $1,300,000, and it is understood that an offer of $2,250,000 has been refused for it.   It accepted a charter under the National Bank Act in 1864, though the most remarkable growth of the institution dates from less than a decade ago.   The late Hon. John Jay Knox, after 22 years of service in the financial department of the Government, and twelve years as Comptroller of the Currency, became the President of the bank in 1884.   Under his administration the deposits rose from $4,800,000 to over $15,500,000, and the total assets of the bank from $7,000,000 to $18,000,000.   The connection of the bank as correspondent of out-of-town institutions is very large, and it takes a position as one of the most influential in New York.   On Mr. Knox's death, in 1892, Oliver S. Carter, for four years the Vice-President, succeeded to the presidency.   He is the senior partner of the great tea-importing house of Carter, Macy & Co., and one of the most highly esteemed of business men.   Eugene H. Pullen, whose connection with the bank dates for 32 years, and who was long its Cashier, became Vice-President.   The Board of Directors of the National Bank of the Republic is composed of a careful body of experienced men, of large means and influence.   They include the following : George B. Carhart, Oliver S. Carter, Sumner R. Stone, D. H. McAlpin, William H. Tillinghast, Charles R. Flint, A. H. Wilder, James S. Warren, William Barbour, James A. Blair, George C. Rand and Eugene H. Pullen.   Charles H. Stout, who has been connected for some years with the bank, is the Cashier, and W. B. T. Keyser is the Assistant Cashier.

The Importers' and Traders' National Bank, at the corner of Broadway and Murray Street, is prominent for the number and magnitude of its mercantile accounts.   Its deposits are about $26,000,000, and its surplus $5,600,000.

NATIONAL BANK OF THE REPUBLIC.
UNITED BANK BUILDING, WALL STREET AND BROADWAY.

The Hanover National Bank, one of the soundest and most energetic of the banks of the United States, was organized in 1851, and was originally located in Hanover Square, at the corner of Pearl Street, then a centre of the shipping and importing trades. Isaac Otis and Chas. M. Livingston were its first President and Cashier respectively. The original capital of $1,000,000 has remained unchanged. The bank received a National charter in 1865. In 1877 it moved to its present central location, at the southwest corner of Nassau and Pine Streets. Through all varying business and financial conditions since the Hanover was established, it has maintained an unvarying reputation for stability. A feature of its policy has been the maintenance of a large cash reserve. At the present time its total resources are $27,137,080; and it holds no less than $5,114,000 in specie, and $510,665 in legal tenders, a total of more than 25 per cent. of its deposits. In periods of financial pressure this policy has been of inestimable value, not only to its own dealers but to the entire business community. During the panic of 1890, as in former emergencies of a similar nature, no customer of the Hanover was refused prompt accommodation, a record of which there are few examples. From its inception the bank has been identified with the importing interests, and dealings in foreign exchange constitute

HANOVER NATIONAL BANK, NASSAU AND PINE STREETS.

a prominent portion of its business. It is a duly authorized State depository, and embraces among its depositors and customers many large and influential railroad and other corporations. The growth of its connection as correspondent and depository for out-of-town banking institutions has also been remarkable. Success as well as conservatism has signalized its management. The $100 shares of the bank sell for over $330 each, and it now pays ten per cent. per annum on its stock, having paid during its existence dividends to the amount of $2,750,000, besides accumulating a surplus and undivided profits of about $2,000,000. James T. Woodward is the President of the Hanover, his associates in the management and the Board of Directors, which is a decidedly representative body, being Vernon H. Brown, agent of the Cunard Steamship Line; Sigourney W. Fay, of Wendell, Fay & Co.; Martin S. Fechheimer, of Fechheimer, Fishel & Company; Mitchell N. Packard, of Packard, Thomas & Co., Vice-President; William Rockefeller, President of the Standard Oil Company; James Stillman, of Woodward & Stillman, and President of the National City Bank; Elijah P. Smith, of Woodward,

MARKET AND FULTON NATIONAL BANK.
FULTON STREET, NORTHWEST CORNER OF GOLD STREET.

Baldwin & Co., Isidor Straus, of L. Straus & Sons; James M. Donald, Cashier; and William Halls, Jr., Assistant Cashier.

The Market and Fulton National Bank denotes, in its title, the union of the Market Bank, founded in 1852, and the Fulton Bank, organized in 1824. The consolidation took place on December 20, 1887, when the Market National Bank (its National charter dating from 1864) increased its capital of $500,000 to $750,-000, giving the stockholders of the Fulton the privilege of subscribing for the amount of the increase, and changed its name to the present title. The banking-house of the Fulton was at Fulton and Pearl Streets, and the Market had in 1854 established itself at Beekman and Pearl Streets. By their union, the two institutions, which drew their custom from the same busy and opulent section of the town, formed one large bank. In 1888, at the northwest corner of Fulton and Gold Streets, the massive bank and office building occupied by the Market and Fulton since May, 1889, was erected at a cost of about $500,000. This edifice is an architectural ornament to that section of the city. On its upper floor is the Fulton Club. Robert Bayles has been President of the Market Bank ever since 1863. Alexander Gilbert, who became Cashier in the same year, is the senior Cashier of New York.

The National Shoe and Leather Bank was founded by merchants identified with the leather trade of New York. It organized under the State law in

NATIONAL SHOE AND LEATHER BANK, 271 BROADWAY,
SOUTHWEST CORNER OF CHAMBERS STREET.

1853; and its original place of business was at the corner of William and John Streets. Loring Andrews, a merchant prominent and successful in the leather business, was its first President, being succeeded by William H. Cary. Each of these presidencies lasted for about a year. The third President was Andrew Varick Stout, chosen in 1855, and unanimously re-elected yearly thereafter until and including January, 1883, thus serving the bank as its President for 28 consecutive years. In 1855 the bank moved to 271 Broadway, at the southwest corner of Chambers Street, on which site a white marble bank and office building, valued at a quarter of a million, was erected for its use. This was replaced in 1893 by one of the most noticeable business structures in lower Broadway. It is 11 stories high. It is across the street from the County Court-House, which stands in City-Hall Park. In 1865 it became a National bank, the capital remaining at $500,000 until the month of July, 1893, when it was increased to $1,000,000. Its prosperity has been steady and uniform, and it has attracted and retained a custom recruited from the hardware and numerous other conservative lines of trade which are located in its vicinity, its management including representatives of such interests, in addition to prominent and wealthy capitalists. Its surplus and undivided profits amount to nearly $300,-000, and its total resources are $5,400,000, the aggregate line of deposits reaching $4,500,000. The $100 par value of shares of the bank are quoted at $160. John M. Crane, the President of the National Shoe and Leather Bank, is in length of service one of the oldest bank officials in the city, having entered the service of the bank in the very year of its formation, becoming afterwards its Cashier, and later assuming the place of its chief executive. George L. Pease is the Vice-President, and William D. Van Vleck the Cashier. The present Board of Directors of the National Shoe and Leather Bank is composed of the following representative gentlemen : William Sulzbacher, of Sulzbacher, Gitterman & Wedeles, woolen importers ; Thomas Russell, thread ; Theodore M. Ives, thread ; John M. Crane, President National Shoe and Leather Bank ; George L. Pease, of the Bocrum & Pease Co. ; Joseph S. Stout, banker (son of its former president) ; Alonzo Slote, of Treadwell & Slote, clothing ; Moritz Josephthal ; Felix Campbell, iron pipe ; John R. Hegeman, President Metropolitan Life-Insurance Co. ; and John H. Graham, hardware.

For forty years the time-tried and thoroughly tested Shoe and Leather Bank has pursued its quiet, conservative and successful career ; always securing its full share of business, earning and paying its expected dividends, and accumulating a creditable surplus. While making no special effort to obtain accounts from banks and bankers, it has on its books a very fine line of accounts from financial institutions throughout the country ; looked out for with as much care and satisfaction as at any bank in the city ; no officers having had longer experience than those of the National Shoe and Leather Bank.

The Corn Exchange Bank is one of the most famous of the financial institutions of New-York City. It was founded in February, 1853, by a number of members of the old Corn Exchange, then at the corner of Broad and South Streets, which was the predecessor of the New-York Produce Exchange. The first President was Edward W. Dunham, whose administration lasted from 1853 to 1872. He was succeeded by William A. Falls, who retained the presidency until 1883, when he was succeeded by William A. Nash, the present incumbent. Among the original directors were David Dows, Nathaniel T. Hubbard, Jacob B. Herrick, Nathaniel H. Wolfe, Thomas C. Durant, Effingham Townsend, and Alexander H. Grant. The original capital of the bank was $500,000, and this was increased in 1854 to $1,000,000. At first, the offices were at the head of Coenties Slip, and subsequently they were transferred to the site of the present Cotton Exchange. In 1855 they occupied the other corner of William and Beaver Streets, where they have since remained. The Corn Exchange was the first bank to lend on warehouse receipts, a practice which has since been adopted by all banks. Its business now, as in the beginning, is largely with the grain, provision, cotton and coffee trades, and with the foremost houses in these standard lines of commerce the bank has always been a favorite depository. It has therefore developed in power collaterally with the tremendous expansion of those departments of business, at once helping them and being helped by them, until now its influence is continental in its scope. President Nash began his financial career in 1855, and for many years has been a member of the Clearing House Committee, having also served as its Chairman. The Directors of the Bank are : Wm. Harman Brown, of the famous family of bankers ; David Bingham, of the New-York Produce Exchange ; Thomas T. Barr (Vice-President), President of the Nassau National Bank, of Brooklyn ; Wm. A. Nash (President) ; M. B. Fielding, cotton merchant, formerly President of the Cotton Exchange ; Thomas A. McIntyre, a prominent grain commission merchant, of the Produce Exchange ; James N. Platt, of Platt & Bowers, lawyers ; Howland Davis, of Blake Bros. & Co. ; David Dows, Jr., son of one of the original directors and founders ; Alexander T. VanNest, the well-known capitalist ; Wm. W. Rossiter, President of the New-York Terminal Warehouse Co. ; Clarence H. Kelsey, Presi. dent of the Title Guarantee & Trust Co.; and Leonard J. Busby, of Holt & Co. The Cashier is Loftin Love ; and the Assistant-Cashier is Wm. E. Williams.   The

Corn Exchange Bank has nearly $10,000,000 in deposits, and surplus and profits exceeding $1,300,000. Its resources are about $12,000,-000. It is now erecting a magnificent eleven-story building, from plans by R. H. Robertson, of absolutely fire-proof construction, with iron columns, steel girders and floor-beams, terra-cotta floor arches, partitions and wall furring. The outer walls of the lower two stories are of red granite, and those of the nine stories above are of

CORN EXCHANGE BANK (FORMER BUILDING), WILLIAM AND BEAVER STREETS.

buff Indiana stone, with polished red granite columns on the upper stories, and a copper cornice.   The bank will occupy the spacious main floor, and all the other stories are to be leased as offices, etc.   The building has three swift elevators, a full steam plant for heating and electric lighting, safety-vaults for tenants, and admirable facilities for light and ventilation.   It is one of the newest and most perfect office-buildings in New York ; and is very convenient to the great exchanges and wholesale districts in the lower portions of the city.   During the period between the demolition of its old building and the completion of the new one on its site, the Corn Exchange Bank occupies offices on the main floor of the Morris Building, at Broad and Beaver Streets.

The completion of this immense and elegant structure on the northwestern corner of Beaver and William Streets, a locality already so interesting with the historic memories and traditions of nearly three centuries, will add greatly to this

CORN EXCHANGE BANK OF NEW YORK.
WILLIAM STREET, NORTHWEST CORNER OF BEAVER STREET, BETWEEN THE COTTON AND PRODUCE EXCHANGES.

focal point of vast and beneficent financial forces. The advance of the Corn Exchange Bank has been largely along lines of its own discovery, and has been singularly steady, successful and fortunate ; until now the institution occupies a position of unchallengeable primacy in its department.

The National Park Bank of New York is the largest bank in the United States, and stands not only preëminent among the banks of New York, but indeed among those of the entire country. It has now, and for a long time has maintained, the largest aggregate deposits, resources, and business of any American bank, its influence extending to every portion of the United States. In fact, the banking connections of the National Park Bank are not confined to this country, but among the hundreds of banks and bankers who act as its correspondents, and of which it is the New-York agent and depository, are a number in Canada, Mexico, and other countries. In addition, the relations of the bank with commercial, manufacturing and corporate interests, as well as with bankers and capitalists, furnish a volume of business unequalled in the history of American banking. A perfect organization, exceptional facilities for the transaction of every class of business, an uninterrupted record of success, and a management in which experience, energy and conservatism predominate, are the foundations upon which this prosperity has been established. The name of the bank recalls to former generations of New-Yorkers the Park which surrounds the City Hall. The charter dates from 1856, the bank being established in that year at the corner of Beekman Street and Theatre Alley, where Temple Court now stands. Reuben W. Howes and Charles A. Macy were the first President and Cashier, respectively. The original capital of $2,000,000 has remained unchanged, and a surplus of more than $3,000,000 has been added to it. In 1865 it became a National bank, and in 1866 it purchased the premises at 214 and 216 Broadway, opposite St. Paul's, and built thereon the dignified marble building, of fire-proof construction, which has since been its home. This site had been at one time occupied by the Chemical Bank. The upper portions are divided into offices, the tenants of which include prominent firms and corporations, notably the Illinois Central Railroad Company. The entire first floor is occupied by the bank, the rotunda in the rear being a stately apartment decorated in white and gold. Its proportions are ample for its 125 employees, the largest number engaged in any New-York banking institution. The treasure-vault in the bank is one of the strongest in the world, and contains from $10,000,000 to $15,000,000 in specie and notes. Beneath the banking-room is a great safe-deposit vault, the entrance to which is through the bank, and which is conducted as one of its departments. In safety and convenience it compares with any in New York, and scarcely a safe among its hundreds is unrented.

The character of the management is shown by the prominence and high standing of the Board of Directors, which consists of Eugene Kelly, Ebenezer K. Wright, Joseph T. Moore, Stuyvesant Fish, George S. Hart, Charles Sternbach, Charles Scribner, Edward C. Hoyt, Edward E. Poor, W. Rockhill Potts, August Belmont, Richard Delafield, Francis R. Appleton, John Jacob Astor and George S. Hickok. Ebenezer K. Wright became its President in 1890, having entered the bank in 1859 as teller's assistant, rising through the various grades to the post of Cashier in 1876, Director in 1878, and Vice-President in 1889. The Vice-Presidents are : Stuyvesant Fish, President of the Illinois Central Railroad Company, and Edward E. Poor, senior partner of the great dry-goods house of Denny, Poor & Co. The Cashier, George S. Hickok, and the Assistant-Cashier, Edward J. Baldwin, have each a record of many years' service in the bank.

THE NATIONAL PARK BANK OF NEW YORK.
214 BROADWAY, BETWEEN FULTON AND ANN STREETS, OPPOSITE ST. PAUL'S CHAPEL.

EAST FROM MADISON-SQUARE GARDEN TOWER.

WEST FROM MADISON-SQUARE GARDEN TOWER.

NORTH FROM MADISON-SQUARE GARDEN TOWER.

SOUTH FROM MADISON-SQUARE GARDEN TOWER.

The Central National Bank is the largest and strongest banking institution of the dry-goods district of New York. It has enjoyed this distinction almost from its organization in 1863, when it temporarily occupied the building at the southeast corner of Broadway and Pearl Street, and subsequently the white marble building on the opposite corner, in which it has since been comfortably housed, and which it afterwards bought. It is situated in the heart of the dry-goods district, where it has a large business. William A. Wheelock was its President for fifteen years, resigning in 1882, when William M. Bliss became President. The present chief executive of the Central National, Col. William L. Strong, who was elected Vice-President in 1882 and President in 1888, maintains the traditions of this strong line of predeces-

sors. A merchant of long experience and successful record, and identified with many of the city's financial, social, and political institutions, with personal prominence and wide influence in the dry-goods and allied trades, he presides over a Board of Directors representing the strongest elements among the textile interests. The Directors are: William A. Wheelock, William M. Bliss, Simon Bernheimer, James W. Smith, William L. Strong, Edward C. Sampson, James H. Dunham, Edwin Langdon,

CENTRAL NATIONAL BANK, BROADWAY AND PEARL STREET.

Woodbury Langdon, John Claflin, and John A. McCall. Edwin Langdon, the Vice-President of the bank, has been in its service since 1865, rising through all the grades to his present post, having been elected thereto in 1889. Charles S. Young, for many years Paying Teller, is now the Cashier of the bank. The Central is among the "two-figure" institutions, its total resources and deposits exceeding $13,000,000. The character of its business, however, merits attention, for it is one of the largest and strongest banks in the country, based mainly upon a mercantile connection and custom. The collection and correspondence of the Central National with "outside" banks are, of course, considerable, and its deposits from this source, as well as from business and corporate interests other than the dry-goods trade, are elements in its prosperity. The capital of the Central is $2,000,000, its surplus and undivided profits $553,515, and its aggregate resources are over $16,000,000. Its aggregate deposits, now $14,000,000, represent 1,200 depositors ; and during the current year the bank paid checks aggregating more than $560,000,000. The conservative character of its business, and the confidence which the mercantile community feels in the Central's position, are such that at times of financial disturbance and uncertainty, when bank deposits tend to shrink, those of this institution usually show a positive increase. There are very few financial institutions of which this can be said.

The Second National Bank occupies one of the busiest, most frequented, and most conspicuous corners in New York. It is at the intersection of Broadway, Fifth Avenue and 23d Street. At this point, the southwestern corner of Madison Square, the business life and the social life of the metropolis meet. Forty years ago the site was occupied by a roadside hostelry, which, when the steady northward march of improvement reached 23d Street, gave place to the Fifth-Avenue Hotel building. In 1863 the Second National Bank was organized and took possession of its present suite of offices, and there it has since remained. The original capital of $300,000 remains unchanged, a surplus of $450,000 having accumulated in addition. On December 31, 1875, an extra dividend of 100 per cent. was declared, and paid to the stockholders. The first president of the institution, Henry A. Hurlbut, is

BEGINNING OF MADISON SQUARE. SECOND NATIONAL BANK.
SECOND NATIONAL BANK, 23D STREET, FIFTH AVENUE AND BROADWAY, IN FIFTH-AVENUE HOTEL.

47

still a member of its Board of Directors. George Montague, its President since 1884, is one of the well-known and experienced bankers of New York. The Board of Directors is a strong and conservative one, representing both up-town business and investing wealth, and down-town banking interests as well. It consists of Amos R. Eno, who built and still owns the Fifth-Avenue Hotel; Henry A. Hurlbut, Alfred B. Darling, John L. Riker, William C. Brewster, Wm. P. St. John, George Montague, Charles B. Fosdick, George Sherman, Welcome G. Hitchcock, and John W. Aitken. The Second National Bank was a pioneer in its field. Its organizers were the earliest to perceive that not only did the large mercantile interests of all kinds concentrating in the central up-town portion of New York demand banking facilities, but that the same section of the city was the abode of wealthy citizens not actively engaged in business, who would furnish an unusually desirable clientile for such an institution. In 1869, Joseph S. Case, then its paying teller, now its Cashier, observed that the latter class included many women; and he was the first to suggest that the bank should provide special accommodations for women customers. A parlor, with windows at teller's and bookkeeper's desks for their use, was accordingly provided, and has become very popular — so popular that several banks have introduced the same feature. The bank's deposits amount to $6,000,000, and its gross assets upwards of $7,000,000. The Fifth-Avenue Safe-Deposit Company occupies with its well-arranged fire and burglar proof vaults the basement immediately beneath the bank, the entrance thereto being through the banking-rooms of the Second National Bank. The safeguards it affords are largely patronized by the latter's dealers, as well as by the community around Madison Square.

The First National Bank, at Broadway and Wall Street, was organized under the National law in 1863. It acquired renown by its management of United-States Government loans. In the refunding operations of 1879 it was the principal agent of the Treasury, placing $500,000,000 of bonds. Its business is largely as reserve agent for National banks throughout the country, and its deposits from that line are the greatest in the United States, as is also its surplus, which is over $7,000,000. George F. Baker is its President.

The Ninth National Bank of the City of New York was organized in 1864, its first President being Joseph U. Orvis; and its first offices were established at the corner of Broadway and Franklin Street. The location of the bank was favorable to the development of a large connection in the dry-goods and allied trades. In 1871 the imposing marble building at 407 and 409 Broadway, between Walker and Lispenard Streets, was built and occupied by the institution. It covers a lot 50 feet wide by 102 feet deep, and is one of the most spacious and best-arranged banking-houses in the city. This property has a much greater value than it is carried at on the books of the bank, and yields upwards of 7 per cent. as an investment. The capital of the bank is $750,000, and its surplus and profits $350,000. John K. Cilley, a merchant of large experience and conservative judgment, was elected President in November, 1891; and since then the bank's deposits have steadily increased, and the market value of the stock has shown a very large advance. While its mercantile accounts, embracing, as they do, a great variety of trades, form the most important part of the bank's business, it possesses also an extensive and desirable correspondence among banks and business houses all over the country, enabling it to extend superior collection facilities to its customers. The Directors are John K. Cilley, President; Albert C. Hall, of Alvah Hall & Co., umbrellas; Haskell A. Searle, of Searle, Dailey & Co., straw goods; William E. Tefft, of Tefft, Weller & Co., dry goods; Augustus F. Libbey, of H. J. Libbey & Co., commission dry

NINTH NATIONAL BANK.
407, 409 AND 411 BROADWAY, BETWEEN WALKER AND LISPENARD STREETS.

goods ; Ernest Werner, of Joseph & Werner, commission woolens ; William E. Iselin, of William Iselin & Co., importers dry goods ; Addison C. Rand, President of the Rand Drill Co. ; and Hiram H. Nazro, Cashier. Mr. Nazro has been connected with the bank ever since it was organized in 1864, and has been Cashier since 1873.

The Bank of the Metropolis is a flourishing outgrowth of the movement of business to the up-town section of New York.   Union Square, where its banking

house is established, was thirty years ago a fashionable residence-district. To-day it is surrounded by some of the largest retail business houses in New York, and important manufacturing and wholesale industries are plentiful in the neighborhood.   The magnitude of these interests is attested by the success of this prosperous institution, the business of which is derived from their requirements, and which is conducted in a manner to attract the custom and support of the dry-goods, furniture, jewelry and other classes of merchants whose places of business are in the vicinity.   The bank was organized in 1871, and commenced operations in June of that year.   The first President was W. A. Kissam

BANK OF THE METROPOLIS, 29 UNION SQUARE, WEST, SOUTHWEST CORNER OF 16TH STREET.

(who died in the same year), and the original place of business was 31 Union Square. A removal to 17 Union Square followed six years later, and in 1888 the bank took the more commodious quarters at 29 Union Square, which it now occupies.   Robert Schell, the President, who has held the position steadily for twenty years, was formerly a well-known jewelry merchant in Maiden Lane. William B. Isham, the Vice-President (since 1885), was prominent in the leather trade ; and the Cashier, Theodore Rogers, has occupied the same position since the formation of the bank.   The Board of Directors is a remarkably strong body, comprising representatives of houses which are known not only in New York but throughout the United States.   They are Charles L. Tiffany, of Tiffany & Company ; Hon. Samuel Sloan, President of the Delaware, Lackawanna & Western Railroad ; Robert Schell, the President ; Joseph Park, of Park & Tilford ; William Steinway, of Steinway & Sons ; William B. Isham, capitalist ; W. D. Sloane, of W. & J. Sloane ; and Hicks Arnold, of Arnold, Constable & Co.   The bank has a deposit line of nearly $7,000,000 ; and a surplus of $700,000 has been accumulated on the capital of $300,000.   Its shares have a market value of over $400 each.

An institution of such solidity and enterprise, and with such widely and favorably known officers and directors, is of great benefit to business in the up-town district.

The Seaboard National Bank, located at 18 Broadway, is less than a decade old, but from its organization it has steadily risen to the highest position among the banks of this city, in the extent of its business, and the sound yet enterprising character of its management ; and it has passed, in volume of business and deposits, some fifty banks of this city which were well established before this bank was organized.   During the panics of 1884 and 1890 this bank relied entirely upon its own resources, not accepting the assistance of the New-York Clearing House Association, which was offered to all banks that were members of the Association, and was freely used by many of the strongest.   It has been the practice of the bank never to charge its depositors more than the legal rate of interest, no matter what the ruling rate in the market, so that in a time of stringency in the money market its depositors have had every assistance which the bank was able to extend, which fact has been greatly appreciated by them, as shown by the steady increase of its deposits, which, during the last five years, have increased at the rate of one million dollars per annum.   The bank is also represented in the management of the New-York Clearing House Association, one of its officers being a member of one of the most important committees, necessitating the examination of all banks applying for membership to the Association.   The varied interests of its depositors are duly represented in its Board of Directors, and contribute to its business, which covers all departments of trade. The bank has an extended connection with, and line of deposits from, leading banks and bankers in other cities, a large corporation custom, and many accounts among large mercantile firms and individuals.   It is also a depository for the United States, the State of New York, and the City of New York, and is officially designated for the same purpose by the Produce, Cotton, and Coffee Exchanges of New York.   Promptness, accuracy and a spirit to accommodate its depositors, of whatever class, is the rule of its management ; and this to a large extent explains its remarkable progress in establishing, in less than ten years, a business represented by more than eight millions of resources, and a line of

SEABOARD NATIONAL BANK, 18 BROADWAY.

deposits of $7,500,000, in addition to a surplus of $250,000, to its capital of $500,-
000. The shares of the bank sell at $176 each, on a par value of $100, and pay
dividends of six per cent. per annum.

Its Board of Directors is notably strong. It consists of Samuel G. Bayne, President; Stuart G. Nelson, Vice-President; Alex. E. Orr, of David Dows & Co.,
produce merchants; Edward V. Loew, President of the Manufacturers' & Builders'
Fire-Insurance Co.; Samuel T. Hubbard, Jr., of Hubbard, Price & Co., cotton
merchants; George Milmine, of Milmine, Bodman & Co., produce merchants;
Henry Thompson, President of the Broadway and Seventh-Avenue Railroad; William A. Ross, of William A. Ross & Brother, merchants; Daniel O'Day, President
of the People's Bank, Buffalo; Joseph Seep, of the Standard Oil Co.; and T.
Wistar Brown, Vice-President of the Provident Life and Trust Co., Philadelphia.
John F. Thompson is the Cashier. The Seaboard National Bank is situated at the
lower end of Broadway, facing the historic Bowling Green; within a stone's throw
of the Produce and other exchanges.

The Mount Morris Bank is the representative financial institution of the
growing quarter of New York which now occupies the former suburb of Harlem.
The increase of population in that district following the introduction of rapid transit was accompanied by the development of business interests both commercial and
manufacturing. To supply the needed banking facilities the Mount Morris Bank
was organized, in December, 1880, under a State charter. For three years it
occupied the premises 133 East 125th Street; but in 1883, the present
handsome building, at the corner of 125th Street and Park Avenue, was
built by the bank, at a cost of $300,000 for land and
improvements, and has thenceforth been its home.
The fact that the $100 shares of the bank sell
for $300 each, is an evidence of the wisdom of
its organizers, as well as of the soundness of
its management. Although the accumulation
of surplus and profits of over $330,000 has
more than doubled the capital of $250,000,
and a line of deposits aggregating over
$2,800,000 are even more significant, it
should be remembered too
that this is the result of
legitimate banking in its
strictest sense. These results are attributable to the
effective management which
the bank has enjoyed since
its organization. The only
change that has occurred in
its officers was the election
of Joseph M. De Veau, who
is now its President, as
successor to Alexander

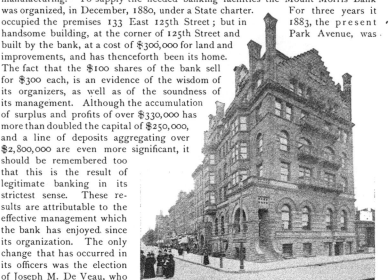

MOUNT MORRIS BANK, 125TH STREET AND PARK AVENUE.

Ketchum, its first head. Thomas W. Robinson has been Cashier since its formation.
The Directors are Joseph M. De Veau, C. C. Baldwin, George B. Robinson, David
L. Evans, Thomas W. Robinson, C. O. Hubbell, Jesse G. Keys, W. Morton Grin-
nell, William H. Payne, Waldo P. Clement, Lucien P. Warner, and Levi P. Morton.

The Bank of New Amsterdam, at Broadway and 39th Street, was founded as recently as the year 1887, by some of the most prominent financial men in the city. They believed that a new up-town bank would pay well, if conducted on a liberal scale, and that a board of directors including men whose experience and integrity were everywhere known would attract considerable business. These prognostications were correct, and the bank has enjoyed the confidence of the community, and has prospered greatly. It collects coupons, dividends and interest free of charge ; loans money on securities ; buys or sells stocks or bonds for investment ; issues letters of credit ; and has a special department for ladies. The deposits on July 1, 1888, were $532,000 ; July 1, 1889, $917,000 ; July 1, 1890, $1,398,000 ; July 1,

1891, $1,418,000 ; July 1, 1892, $1,739,000 ; January 6, 1893, $2,001,000. The capital is $250,000, and the surplus has reached $147,000. Thomas C. Acton, formerly Assistant-Treasurer of the United States, is President ; Frank Tilford, of Park & Tilford, Vice-President ; and Nelson J. H. Edge (formerly of the old Merchants' Bank), Cashier. The Directors are : Thos. C. Acton, Samuel D. Babcock, J. S. Barnes, Frank Curtiss, Thos. Denny, Robert Goelet, G. G. Haven, R. V. Lewis, Geo. W. Loss,

BANK OF NEW AMSTERDAM, METROPOLITAN OPERA HOUSE, BROADWAY AND 39TH STREET.

Jas. A. Roosevelt, John L. Riker, Elihu Root, John A. Stewart, G. H. Scribner, Jesse Seligman, Louis Stern, F. D. Tappen, Jno. T. Terry, and Frank Tilford.

Hamilton Bank is named in honor of Alexander Hamilton, the statesman and financier of the Revolution, whose home was not far distant from the bank's building, whose district was familiar ground to Hamilton. The bank was organized on January 12, 1888, and on the same day the Bank of Harlem was organized. On May 10, 1892, both banks consolidated under the name of the Hamilton Bank of New-York City, and soon afterward took possession of the present commodious and well-appointed banking-rooms on the main floor of the imposing Hamilton Bank Building, 213, 215 and 217 West 125th Street, — the main thoroughfare of Harlem, — between Seventh and Eighth Avenues. The bank was organized to meet the demands for banking facilities in the northwestern part of the city. At the time of consolidation David F. Porter, who had been President of the Bank of Harlem, was chosen President, a position he still retains. In the Board of Directors are many names of prominent New-York business men and financiers who have residences or business interests in this up-town district. The Directors are : David F. Porter, President of the Hamilton Bank ; Charles B. Fosdick, President of the Hide and

Leather National Bank ; William P. St. John, President of the Mercantile National Bank ; David M. Williams ; Emanuel Lauer ; John J. Fowler ; Lucien C. Warner ; William S. Gray ; John J. Sperry ; Julius W. Tieman ; James Rogers ; Joseph Milbank ; John J. Lapham ; Isaac A. Hopper ; Henry Morgenthau ; Cyrus Clark ; Louis Strasburger ; Frederick B. Schenck ; and Welcome T. Alexander. The Vice-President is William S. Gray and the Cashier is Edwin S. Schenck.

HAMILTON BANK, 215 WEST 125TH STREET, NEAR SEVENTH AVENUE.

The prosperity of the bank is shown by its present condition. Its capital is $200,000; its deposits, which are almost wholly individual accounts, already approach one million dollars ; so that its gross assets range from $1,100,000 upwards. A general banking business is transacted, collections are made, and Bills of Exchange are issued. A portion of the banking-room is arranged for the special accommodation of ladies, who form an important line of the patrons of the Hamilton Bank, and the lower floor is to be fitted up with a modern safe-deposit vault. President Porter is one of the Rapid-Transit Commissioners.

The **Nineteenth Ward Bank** is one of the up-town banks that has made a noteworthy success. · It was organized in 1884, with a capital of $100,000, to meet the needs of its populous district. The way it has served its constituency is shown in the fact that its deposits approach $1,500,000, an unusually large line for a bank of its age and its capital, particularly so for a bank depending mainly on a local constituency in an up-town district. In addition to its capital, it has a surplus and undivided profits of about $70,000, and altogether its total resources amount to about $1,700,000. The market value of its stock ranges in the neighborhood of $200 a share, and on the books of the bank it is worth over $170 a share ; but it is not on the market.

The Nineteenth Ward Bank Building is on Third Avenue, at the northeast corner of 57th Street ; and besides the bank's quarters it is occupied for real estate, insurance, and other offices ; by the Maimonides Library ; and for numerous lodge and society rooms.

The officers of the bank are Samuel H. Rathbone, President ; Martin B. Brown, Vice-President ; James B. Story, Cashier ; and Louis H. Holloway, Assistant-Cashier.

The Directors include Matthew Baird, builder and contractor ; Martin B. Brown, printer and stationer ; Richard A. Cunningham, contractor ; Myer Hellman, banker ; John P. Kane, of Canda & Kane, builders' and masons' materials ; Joseph J. Kittel, capitalist ; Julien L. Myers, retired ; Robert C. Rathbone, of R. C. Rathbone & Son, underwriters ; Samuel H. Rathbone, President ; George P. Sheldon, President of the Phenix Insurance Company ; Richard K. Sheldon, Treasurer of the American Casualty Insurance and Security Company ; and James B. Story, Cashier. The Board of Directors represent a group of successful, energetic business men, who

NINETEENTH WARD BANK, THIRD AVENUE AND 57TH STREET.

take pride in the welfare of the bank and are active in building up its success. A majority of them were incorporators of the bank, and have ever since remained among its directors.

The East Side Bank accommodates a very densely settled part of the city. Its present quarters are in the new seven-story building at 135 Grand Street. They are well equipped, their vaults containing specially constructed Corliss burglar-proof safes. The bank was organized in October, 1888, and until August, 1893, was located at 459 Grand Street. It has enjoyed a quiet, steady growth. Its authorized capital is $500,000 ; its paid-in capital is $100,000 ; and its surplus is $40,000. It is a duly appointed depository for the State of New York. It does a general banking business and gives special consideration to the needs of its local constituency. Thomas R. Manners was one of its incorporators, and has been the President from the beginning. John Byrns is Vice-President ; William B. Nivin,

THE EAST SIDE BANK, 135 GRAND STREET, BETWEEN ELM AND
CROSBY STREETS.

Cashier; and E. A. Henderson, Assistant-Cashier. The Directors are Walter Luttgen, of August Belmont & Co.; John Byrns, plumber; G. Wessels, of The Wessels Co.; Abraham Stern, attorney; John Overbeck, capitalist; Francis Halpin, Assistant-Cashier of the Chemical National Bank; Emmanuel J. Meyers, of Hahn & Meyers, attorneys; Thomas S. Ollive, of the New-York Biscuit Co.; Jacob Horowitz, jeweler; Martin Simons, broker; Samuel Cohn, of S. Cohn & Bro., shoes; and Thomas R. Manners, President.

An institution favored by the financial support and counsel of such a board of officers must be a tower of strength in the business community, rising above the transient perils of monetary panics.

SKATING IN THE PARK.

The Plaza Bank has its banking house opening into one of the grandest plazas or squares in the world; and it is situated in the line of those magnificent churches, superb residences, famous clubs, and Aladdin-like hotels that combine to make Fifth Avenue the unrivalled residence-thoroughfare of any country. The bank's new quarters are on Fifth Avenue, at the southeast corner of 58th Street, and starting directly from its corner begins the Plaza, upon which face the Plaza, the New Netherland and the Savoy hotels, and from which opens the main entrance to Central Park. Surrounded by palatial residences of many of New York's wealthiest and best-known citizens, this is indeed an ideal situation for a bank to serve an aristocratic constituency, and those business houses that of necessity congregate close to such a locality. The bank building is part of the Mason-Jones block of residences. It was remodelled for the Plaza Bank by Richard Howland Hunt. The upper floors have been rented by the bank to the Seventh-Regiment Veteran Club.

The Plaza Bank was started not only to serve such a constituency, but its constituents were to a great extent identified with its organization, as is shown by the following list of original stockholders, which includes a peculiarly representative group of noted New-York names: A. Newbold Morris, Wm. H. Tillinghast, T. C. Eastman, Woodbury G. Langdon, Morris K. Jesup, Benj. H. Bristow, Wm. C. Brewster, D. S. Hammond, Wm. Ottmann, Wm. Rockefeller, Bishop Henry C. Potter, John J. Astor, F. A. Hammond, H. O. Havemeyer, Linda F. Mower, Sol Friend, Simon H. Stern, Roderick J. Kennedy, John L. Riker, B. Beinecke, Wm. D. Sloane, Wm. C. Whitney, Col. Wm. L. Strong, Addison Cammack, Dr. T. Gaillard Thomas, Obed Wheeler, Dr. Wm. M. Polk, James Morris, Joseph Park, John B. Reynolds, Josiah M. Fiske, W. E. Damon, David Aaron, C. DeSilver, Theodore Wheeler, Wm. Kraus, Geo. C. Park, Richard M. Hunt, Joseph Larocque, David Wolfe Bishop, Horace L. Hotchkiss, Ferdinand P. Earle, Wm. B. Wheeler, Gardner Wetherbee, Henry G. Marquand, Wm. M. Fliess, Mrs. Seth Low, C. P. Huntington, Judge P. H. Dugro, C. M.

PLAZA BANK, FIFTH AVENUE, SOUTHEAST CORNER OF 58TH STREET.

McGhee, W. McMaster Mills, Max Naumburg, Elkan Naumburg, Chas. L. Tiffany, and Mrs. Lucy Fayerweather.

The Board of Directors likewise includes names well known throughout the country : A. Newbold Morris, Wm. L. Strong, Obed Wheeler, John J. Astor, Joseph Larocque, D. S. Hammond, Wm. C. Whitney, Addison Cammack, Wm. Ottmann, David Aaron, B. Beinecke, Wm. C. Brewster, Woodbury G. Langdon, Benj. H. Bristow, Wm. II. Tillinghast, Joseph Park, Josiah M. Fiske, John L. Riker, and Ferdinand P. Earle. The officers, who have been the same since the bank began business in 1891, are William C. Brewster, President ; Woodbury G. Langdon, Vice-President ; and W. McMaster Mills, Cashier.

The Sherman Bank, although one of the newest of New-York's financial institutions, starts out under such auspices as to give it a good position among the solid and progressive banks of the

SHERMAN BANK, BROADWAY, NORTHEAST CORNER OF 18TH STREET.

city. Its name commemorates one of America's greatest generals and noblest and most beloved patriots, General William T. Sherman ; and is also suggestive of another name equally honored by Americans, Senator John Sherman, who, besides being one of the greatest statesmen, has been almost without a peer in his knowledge of financial matters. Moreover, it calls to mind the revolutionary patriot and statesman, Roger Sherman, a signer of the Declaration of Independence, all together indicating that the name "Sherman" is peculiarly appropriate for a great American banking institution. The bank's quarters, elegant, spacious, and admirably arranged, are in the handsome McIntyre Building, on Broadway, at the corner of 18th Street, today one of the most frequented and thickly settled neighborhoods of the city. Its capital of $200,000 is re-inforced by a surplus of $100,000. Although it began business on June 16, 1892, it immediately obtained a large line of deposits, which were attracted to it from the business people and residents of the vicinity, and from a number of firms and corporations interested in the bank or drawn to it by its list of officers and stockholders, which comprises a thoroughly representative body of New-York business men. The officers are Charles E. Bulkley, President ; Henry D. Northrop, Cashier ; both veterans in banking circles. The Directors are William J. Arkell, of *Judge* and *Frank Leslie's;* Charles E. Bulkley, President of the Whiting Mfg. Co. ; Jacob D. Butler, builder and real estate ; William Crawford, of Simpson, Crawford & Simpson ; George C. Flint, President of the G. C. Flint Company ; Louis C. Fuller, President of the Electric Cutlery Co. ; George B. Jacques, of Jacques & Marcus ; George P. Johnson, Treasurer of the New-York Biscuit Co., and New-York Manager of the Diamond Match Co. ; Ewen McIntyre ; John McLoughlin (Vice-President), of McLoughlin Bros. ; Ludwig Nissen, diamond importer ; Henry D. Northrop, Cashier ; James H. Parker, President of the United-States National Bank ; Douglass R. Satterlee ; George P. Sheldon, President of the Phenix Insurance Company ; William R. Smith, of Worthington, Smith & Co. ; Benjamin B. Van Derveer, of the Tenney Company ; and Lucien C. Warner. The banking rooms of the Sherman Bank are among the most elegant in the city ; and were specially designed for the best working facilities for the bank's officers and clerks, and the most satisfactory accommodations of the customers. There are entirely separate quarters for the lady patrons, and special rooms for customers who wish to look over private papers or have a secluded place for conferences.

The Franklin National Bank began business March 27, 1893, under promising conditions. With a capital of $200,000, and a surplus of $50,000, and immediate deposits of considerable amount, it had sufficient resources to command the confidence and patronage of its constituency. Its location, too, is in one of the most populous and energetic sections of the city, where the industries and trades are especially diversified. Its bank building is at the corner of Greenwich and

FRANKLIN NATIONAL BANK, GREENWICH AND DEY STREETS.

Dey Streets, midway between Broadway and the North River, in the premises formerly occupied by the North-River Bank, a building especially constructed for banking purposes. Its President is the Hon. Ellis H. Roberts, who for four years past has been the Assistant-Treasurer of the United States at New York, a position which can be filled only by a man of unquestioned ability in finance and of extreme conservatism and exceptional integrity. The Vice-President is Charles F. James, and the Cashier is Nathan D. Daboll. The Board of Directors includes Joseph Beckel, C. S. Brainerd, John Byrne, Philip Carpenter, E. M. Cutler, Brent Good, Wm. James, Hugo Josephy, Charles H. Parsons, William C. Roberts, Arthur W. Talcott, Dillon C. Willoughby, Charles F. James, N. D. Daboll and Ellis H. Roberts. The measure of success thus far secured promises that the bank is to be one of the strong and prosperous institutions of the city.

The **Foreign Banking** Houses of New York form an important and useful part in the financial machinery of the country, and no account of the organization of wealth and commerce in the great city would be complete without a description of their functions, and a reference to some of the leading firms in this line which, in wealth, influence, and volume of business, rival the largest of incorporated financial institutions. The banking business of Europe, it is well known, is more largely conducted as a matter of private enterprise than is the case here ; and great firms like the Rothschilds, with their branches and connections in every city of Europe, are powers of the first magnitude in the world of money, ranking, it is fair to say, even with the Banks of England and of France. The private financial houses of Wall Street are the extension of this system to the United States, and through the connection which they maintain with the bankers of London, Paris, Berlin, and other cities, constitute the link which binds together the financial systems of the two hemispheres. The most important of their duties is furnishing the facilities for payment of debts incurred in Europe, or *vice versa*. These bankers are the purchasers of the drafts which American shippers draw upon foreign buyers of their products, and on the other hand the drafts which they draw upon their correspondents abroad, when sold to our importers, are the medium through which our payments for foreign commodities are settled. This constitutes the country's foreign-exchange market, which business, being entirely concentrated at New York, forms one of the city's strongest titles to its financial supremacy. The magnitude of these transactions is seldom duly appreciated. Yet it is estimated by competent authorities that the volume of transactions which the foreign banking-houses of New York perform in the course of a year, including purchases of commercial drafts, sales of their own bills on European cities, or the issuance of letters of credit to merchants and travellers, foot up not less than $20,000,000,000. Another important function performed by these banking-houses is the representation in this country of the investment of foreign capital in American securities. Through their agency great amounts of stocks and bonds of our railroads and other corporations are placed abroad, and the representation of these holdings being generally confided to such interests, they are very important factors in the general conduct of railroad affairs. The direct representation of corporations in the money market is a hardly less important branch of their usefulness. Large companies desirous to effect loans on these bonds almost invariably offer the transaction through private bankers, and usually through those with foreign connections. Their services are also applied for when it becomes necessary to adjust the affairs of corporations by means of the now familiar process of re-organization. Great wealth, conservatism, and ability are their distinguishing features, and they are, therefore, the representatives of the investing public on both sides of the ocean. Most of their houses are connected through membership of one or more of their partners with the Stock and various other Exchanges, and furnish by the operations which they carry on therein for their foreign clients a large portion of the activity of those institutions.

Drexel, Morgan & Co. enjoy the distinction of being the most noted financial house in Wall Street, that is to say, in America. Their establishment occupies the whole floor of the white marble Drexel Building, at the southeast corner of Broad and Wall Streets, directly facing the Sub-Treasury and Assay Office. This building was erected in 1872 for the firm, the lot having cost the then unheard-of sum of $1,000,000. The firm is of distinctively American origin, having been formed in July, 1871, by a union of forces of Drexel & Co., of Philadelphia, one of the oldest and richest of American banking houses, and the great interest and power representative sented by Junius S. Morgan of London (the partner of the late George Peabody), and his son, J. Pierpont Morgan. The latter, with Anthony J. Drexel of Philadelphia, are now the heads of the establishment, the Philadelphia house of Drexel & Co., Drexel, Harjes & Co., in Paris, and J. S. Morgan & Co., of London, being closely connected. The firm is rated, from point of capital, in the tens of millions, and in individual wealth at a fabulous amount. It does a large banking business, and is one of the leading drawers of foreign exchange. Its preëminence, however, is due to successful participation in some of the greatest financial operations in connection with the placing of railroad loans, or the re-organization of bankrupt or involved corporations, the West Shore and the Reading properties being the most conspicuous instances of the latter. The firm exercises a supremacy unique in the history of American financial affairs.

Maitland, Phelps & Co., merchants and bankers, at 22 and 24 Exchange Place, have a history which runs back over a period of nearly a hundred years. The

house was established in 1796 by James Lenox, an ancestor of the late Robert Lenox of New York, and William Maitland, under the firm name of Jas. Lenox & Wm. Maitland. In 1812 Robert Maitland of Virginia, and afterwards David S. Kennedy were taken in, and the firm became Lenox, Maitland & Co., and then Kennedy & Maitland, and later Maitland, Kennedy & Co., and Maitland, Comrie & Co. The business of the house under the present style of Maitland, Phelps & Co. was begun on the 1st of January, 1847, and has continued under this name up to the present time. Royal Phelps, than whom no man was perhaps better or more favorably known in this city, during his time and generation, was the senior partner of the firm from 1847 until his death, which occurred July 30, 1884. With him were associated Robert Gordon and Benjamin F. Butler (both of whom retired from the firm in 1883), also George Coppell and Thomas Maitland.

MAITLAND, PHELPS & CO., EXCHANGE PLACE, BETWEEN WILLIAM AND HANOVER STREETS.

Mr. Phelps was succeeded as senior partner by Mr. Coppell. On the 30th of June, 1892, Mr. Maitland, having taken up his residence in England, retired from the firm. The partners now are George Coppell, Gerald L. Hoyt and Dallas B. Pratt. The merchandise business of the firm, which is a commission business, is with Mexico, South America, Cuba, etc., and besides this they do a general domestic and foreign banking business, issuing Letters of Credit and drawing exchange on London and Paris ; and are financial agents for a number of large railroad and other corporations.

This part of Exchange Place is quite interesting.   Intermingled with great modern buildings are still left a number which give one some idea of New York of the past generation.   The Maitland, Phelps & Co. Building, so long occupied by this historic firm, has as its neighbor on the east the dignified Post Building, and on the west side the elegant new structure of the Delaware, Lackawanna & Western Railroad.   Immediately across the street is the solid granite United-States Custom House, which is connected with the Maitland, Phelps & Co. Building by a bridge, the upper floors of this building being partly utilized by the National Government. Wall Street is but a stone's throw distant.   At the next corner above, the North British & Mercantile Insurance Co., of London and Edinburgh, are about to erect a grand modern office structure, while in the same block with Maitland, Phelps & Co. is the Farmers' Loan & Trust Co. Building.

Brown Bros. & Co., at 59 Wall Street, is an American firm which has long occupied a distinguished and honorable position in the financial world.   The term, "Brown's rate," applied to the quotations current for foreign exchange, is the standard authority for the operations of that market.   The house originated in Baltimore, where Alexander Brown, a linen merchant, who came to this country in 1798, afterward embarked in the banking business.   Sons of the founder of the house established branches in Liverpool and other cities, James Brown coming to New York in 1826, originating the house which now exists here.   James Brown, who died in 1877, was one of the most prominent bankers and financiers of New York.   The prominence of the firm dates from 1837, when panic convulsed the United States, and American credit abroad threatened to collapse.   The London houses of the Brown family had, or were responsible for, immense amounts of bills of American drawers, which were affected by these events.   They deposited securities with the Bank of England, made a loan which enabled them to protect every bill bearing their name, paid off the loan within six months, and rendered a service to American credit which should never be forgotten.   The London house is Brown, Shipley & Co., the Baltimore establishment still being Alexander Brown & Sons.

August Belmont & Co. are the American representatives of the Rothschild family of bankers.   The house was founded in 1837 by August Belmont, Sr., a German by birth, who was for fifty years one of the most prominent financiers of New York, and who, in addition, identified himself socially and politically with the interests of his adopted country and city, serving as United-States Minister to the Hague, and taking an active part in municipal and national politics.   The firm has always occupied a leading and dignified position, not only as drawers of exchange, but as the representatives of vast foreign-investment interests in American railroad and other corporations, their European connections extending to every city of importance abroad.   The present head of the house is August Belmont, the son of the founder (who is also chairman of the Louisville & Nashville Railroad), the banking establishment being in the Nassau-Street wing of the Equitable Building.

Morton, Bliss & Co. is a banking house, especially noted, as its senior member, the Hon. Levi P. Morton, was the Vice-President of the United States during the Harrison administration in 1889–93.   Their banking rooms are in the Mutual Life Insurance Co.'s Building on Nassau Street, at the corner of Cedar Street.

Other Prominent Bankers include Eugene Kelly & Co.; Baring, Magoun & Co.; Ladenburg, Thalmann & Co.; Blair & Co.; Winslow, Lanier & Co.; James G. King's Sons; Blake Brothers & Co.; J. & W. Seligman & Co.; Heidelbach, Ickelheimer & Co.; John Munroe & Co.; H. B. Hollins & Co., and many others.

Fiduciary Institutions.

Trust and Investment Companies, Savings-Banks, Safe-Deposit Companies, Etc.

IN NO particular is New York's position as the centre of the National wealth and financial power more distinctly emphasized than by the multiplicity and strength of its institutions of a fiduciary character. It is unsurpassed in the facilities which are thus afforded in the care and administration of individual rights and possessions, or the exercise of those powers, which, in a less highly developed stage of commercial and financial prosperity, are committed to individual trustees. The great savings-banks are among the proudest indications of the city's preëminence and wealth, representing, as they do, the accumulations of her toilers for more than three generations. The financial trust companies are, in their numbers, and the magnitude, extent, and variety of the functions that they exercise, unsurpassed by similar bodies at any of the world's capitals. Nor does any other city possess or offer such unequalled facilities for the safe-keeping of evidences of values as those which are presented by the numerous public safe-deposit vaults of New York. All of these different classes of institutions, with others of a somewhat similar character, find full employment, and are in fact being steadily multiplied. This is explained by the fact that, to a large extent, they deal with the wealth, not of New York alone, but of the whole country. It should, however, be noted as a primary fact that, in each instance, such organizations demand the exercise, not only of the highest order of financial talent, but must in their entire administration present a degree of experience, personal responsibility and fidelity, which it is safe to say that New York alone could supply. The corporations of the class to which attention is now directed are not alone enormous and successful, but they are in the highest degree evidences of the reputation and character of New York's business men, merchants and capitalists, who furnish their officers and trustees. It is safe to say that nowhere in the civilized world is such a mass of wealth belonging to others entrusted to the care and management of organized bodies of such a nature, and that nowhere else can greater fidelity and success be found, in the exercise of such functions.

The Trust Companies constitute one of the most important parts of New York's financial mechanism. They originated from an appreciation of the fact that individual responsibility in positions of a fiduciary character is often attended by more or less danger. The administration of personal or other property is a task demanding both responsibility and integrity. The possessor of these qualities is not always desirous of assuming such duties, and the disastrous effects of errors of judgment, no less than of absolute wrong-doing, in such cases is proverbial. The substitution in such matters, for the individual, of a permanent corporation, having a financial responsibility which could not be affected by the contingencies of individual

48

fortunes, possessing an administration calculated to execute precisely that class of business, and moreover representing in its management the collective talent of the highest business and social elements, could not fail to commend itself as a valuable expedient to a community in which the accumulation of wealth proceeded at so rapid a rate. The governing idea in the earlier corporations of the class formed in New York was that they should primarily act as executors, administrators, guardians of estates of minors, or committees of the property under testamentary provisions or by order of the courts, and as trustees for the administration of property under appointment by individuals or legal authority. At the same time it was intended that by this means secure depositories should be provided for funds involved in litigation, and for the great variety of real and personal property which the courts are accustomed to order in safe custody awaiting the decision of suits. These still continue to be leading functions of the financial trust companies. In fact, the preference for the services of such institutions in matters of that class has of late years increased. Great estates are administered by them under such commissions, and vast sums of money and large amounts of real or personal property are constantly put in their charge by the courts, the moderate commissions and charges which trust companies make for such services amounting, nevertheless, to a large aggregate return. Many other functions, however, soon annexed themselves to those of a semi-legal character, for the performance of which trust companies were originally created. The receipt of money on deposit and the payment of interest thereon is a feature in which these institutions supplement the work of the banks. At the same time many trust companies receive current deposits subject to check, and conduct a business in its essential features similar to that of a bank. The care of property, the investment of funds, and the collection of rents and interest are other important branches of their business, in which there is a growing demand for such service. One of the most important, useful and profitable features of these concerns is the relation which they occupy between railroad and industrial companies and the public, in the capacity of holders of stocks and bonds. The great progress of the United States has been largely the work of corporations, and the money with which its railroads have been built and its industries established has largely come from corporate borrowings on mortgages of property and franchises securing issues of bonds, thus facilitating the division of immense transactions into amounts which could be distributed among a multitude of investors. From an early date the trust companies of New-York City assumed the important position of trustees under such corporate mortgages. In nearly every instance obligations of this character are payable, principal and interest, in this city, and it is usually a leading trust company which is selected to act in the capacity of a fiscal agent for corporations. As a consequence of this, in cases of default upon railroad or other obligations, the trust companies of New York appear as the plaintiffs in foreclosure suits in various parts of the country ; and when reorganizations of corporations are necessary they are invariably designated by the parties in interest as the depositories of securities and the intermediaries through which the transactions are completed. Municipal indebtedness, as is natural, follows the course of corporation borrowings in the great money-market of the land, and various States, counties and cities which obtain money on these bond issues are usually represented in New York by a trust company. Another very important duty of the trustee remains to be mentioned. This is the registration of transfers of corporate stocks. The New-York Stock Exchange, as a check upon the fidelity of the officials of companies whose securities are dealt in in the stock market, requires that such certificate issues shall be countersigned by a trust company as guarantee.

Until within a recent date the formation of trust companies was in this State a matter of special legislative enactment. The charters of the older organizations therefore differ. The oldest dates back to 1822, and the next to 1830. In both instances the original organization was coupled with a plan for an insurance business. Indeed, to this day the granting of annuities is retained as a feature of some organizations. Most of the companies are formed under special charters, though in 1887 the Legislature passed a general law for their organization and administration.

THE TRUST COMPANIES OF ·NEW-YORK CITY.

FIGURES GIVEN UNDER DATE OF JANUARY 1, 1893.

NAME.	LOCATION.	CAPITAL.	GR. ASSETS.	PRESIDENT.	SECRETARY.
Atlantic..........	39 William,	$500,000	$6,997,000	Wm. H. Male,	J. S. Suydam.
Central	54 Wall,	1,000,000	27,304,000	F. P. Olcott,	C. H. P. Babcock.
Continental......	18 Wall,	500,000	2,691,000	Otto T. Bannard,	M. S. Decker.
Farmers' Loan...	22 William,	1,000,000	30,689,000	R. G. Rolston,	E. S. Marston.
Holland..........	33 Nassau,	500,000	2,674,000	J. D. Vermeule,	J. B. Van Woert.
Knickerbocker...	234 Fifth Ave.	750,000	6,861,000	J. P. Townsend,	F. L. Eldridge.
Manhattan.......	1 Nassau,	1,000,000	4,951,000	J. I. Waterbury,	A. T. French.
Mercantile.......	120 Br'dway,	2,000,000	28,576,000	Louis Fitzgerald,	H. C. Deming.
Metropolitan.....	37 Wall,	1,000,000	9,842,000	T. Hillhouse,	Beverly Chew.
N. Y. Guaranty & Indemnity.	59 Cedar,	2,000,000	14,206,000	Edwin Packard,	H. A. Murray.
N.Y. Life Insurance & Trust.	52 Wall,	1,000,000	26,987,000	Henry Parish,	Henry Parish, Jr.
N.Y. Security & Trust	46 Wall,	1,000,000	8,027,000	C. S. Fairchild,	J. L. Lamson.
Real Estate Loan	30 Nassau	500,000	2,935,000	H. C. Swords,	H. W. Reighley.
State.............	32 Wall,	1,000,000	8,403,000	Andrew Mills,	J. Q. Adams.
Title Guarantee..	55 Liberty,	2,000,000	3,830,000	C. H. Kelsey,	L. V. Bright.
Union............	80 Broadway,	1,000,000	36,099,000	Edward King,	A. W. Kelley.
U. S. Transfer & Exchange .	1 Nassau,	200,000	432,000	J. I. Waterbury,	C. H. Smith.
United States....	45 Wall,	2,000,000	48,607,000	J. A. Stewart,	H. L. Thornell.
Washington......	280 Br'dway,	500,000	4,481,000	D. M. Morrison,	F. H. Page.
Totals, 19 Co's.		$19,450,000	$267,595,000		

The New-York Life-Insurance & Trust Company, at 52 Wall Street, is virtually the oldest of all the trust companies. It is one of the most interesting of the great financial institutions of America, both on account of its antiquity, and its curiously specialized line of business. It was chartered in the year 1830, and therefore became the earliest life-insurance company in the State of New York, and the pioneer of that wonderful group of insurance companies whose business and resources are now of such enormous proportions. Its originator and first President was William Bard, an enthusiast in the then new field of life-insurance, and for many years a widely known and respected authority on all matters connected therewith, being succeeded January 1, 1843, by Stephen Allen, who had also a notable reputation in political life. June 3, 1845, John R. Townsend became President, and was succeeded April 18, 1846, by David Thompson, during whose long and prosperous rule the company began to develop its present position of power. In 1871 the presidency was conferred upon Henry Parish, under whose administration of nearly a quarter of a century vast progress has been made.

The New-York Life-Insurance & Trust Company is now the foremost corporation in the world in the management of private trusts, such as come from wills, deeds of trust and similar documents.   It avoids railroad and corporation trusts, and thus escapes the perils attendant upon wide-spread financial convulsions.   The business in life-insurance, once so important a feature, has been largely reduced, this reduc-

CORNER-STONE OF UNITED-STATES BRANCH BANK, IN DIRECTORS' ROOM OF NEW-YORK LIFE-INSURANCE AND TRUST CO.

tion having begun soon after the year 1840, when the great mutual companies came into existence. In this regard, its history resembles those of the two other famous corporations which arose about the same time, and are still in existence, — the Massachusetts Hospital Life-Insurance Company and the Pennsylvania Company for Insurance on Lives and Granting Annuities.

The company's building stands on the site of the United-States Branch Bank which was erected in 1797, and bought in 1830 by the City Bank, from which the New-York Life-Insurance and Trust Company purchased half the estate. A new building was erected here in 1838, and replaced in 1867 by still another, which was largely extended in 1888. The original corner-stone of the United-States B r a n c h Bank, with its long inscription, is sacredly preserved in the Directors' room.

The company does not take mercantile deposits, but receives and allows interest on deposits from executors, trustees, treasurers of religious and benevolent societies, and lawyers and other persons acting in a fiduciary capacity.   Its annuity business has been kept up, and shows a continuous enlargement.   Aside from its large and profitable investments in State stocks, in railroad bonds of the highest grade, in bonds and mortgages, etc., the company always keeps several million dollars in cash in its impregnable vaults, so as to be at all times superior to the shocks which agitate "the street."   The conservative policy of the present administration is proven successful by the market-price of the stock, which is between $600 and $700 per share, on an original par value of $100.   The permanence of this prosperous policy is ensured by the method of electing the officers, which is done, not by the stockholders, but by the trustees, who thus stand as a self-perpetuating body. By its charter, the officers must be citizens of New York.   Henry Parish is President; Walter Kerr, Second Vice-President; Henry Parish, Jr., Secretary; George M. Corning, Assistant-Secretary.   The trustees are: William W. Astor, Edmund L. Baylies, Frederic Bronson, George S. Bowdoin, S. Van Rensselaer Cruger, William E. Dodge, Stuyvesant Fish, Robert Goelet, Henry C. Hulbert, C. O'Donnell Iselin, James P. Kernochan, H. Van Rensselaer Kennedy, George A. Robbins, James A. Roosevelt, W. Emlen Roosevelt, Wm. C. Schermerhorn, Frederic W. Stevens, Charles E. Strong, Charles F. Southmayd, Rutherford Stuyvesant, Hewlett Scudder, Ludlow Thomas, Charles G. Thompson, H. A. C. Taylor, and Henry Parish.

TRINITY CHURCH.   NEW-YORK LIFE-INSURANCE & TRUST CO.

NEW-YORK LIFE-INSURANCE & TRUST CO.
52 WALL STREET, NORTH SIDE, THREE DOORS EAST OF WILLIAM STREET.

The United-States Trust Company is one of the oldest trust companies in the State of New York. It is also the largest and greatest trust company on the American continent, having by far the greatest amount of assets. It is in the front rank of all fiduciary institutions. Its capital of $2,000,000, surplus of $8,000,000, deposits of $42,000,000, and gross assets of $52,000,000 render it one of the most important institutions of any kind. It was organized in 1853, under a charter with liberal powers, to act as trustee, executor, and guardian, and as a legal depository of money. Joseph Lawrence was the first president, the company occupying quarters in the Manhattan Company's old building, and moving afterwards to the Bank of New-York Building, and then to the building, at 49 and 51 Wall Street, which it owned jointly with the Atlantic Mutual Insurance Company. In 1888 the company purchased the lots at 45 and 47 Wall Street, and erected thereon a noble granite bank and office-building, in the Romanesque style, which is one of the grandest and most elegant buildings in this country. The apartment which the company occupies with its offices on the first floor is unsurpassed in size, appointments and convenience. The head of the company, John A. Stewart, was its Secretary at the start. He resigned to become Assistant-Treasurer of the United States, and in 1865 returned to the company as its President. The Vice-President is George Bliss; the Second Vice-President, James S. Clark; and the Secretary, Henry L. Thornell. The Assistant-Secretary is Louis G. Hampton. The Board of Trustees is a body which represents to the fullest extent the wealth and stability of New York. It comprises: Daniel D. Lord, Samuel Sloan, James Low, William Walter Phelps, D. Willis James, John A. Stewart, Erastus Corning, John Harsen Rhoades, Anson Phelps Stokes, George Bliss, William Libbey, John Crosby Brown, Edward Cooper, W. Bayard Cutting, Charles S. Smith, Frank Lyman, Wm. Rockefeller, Alexander E. Orr, William H. Macy, Jr., Wm. D. Sloane, Gustav H. Schwab, George F. Vietor, Wm. Waldorf Astor, and James Stillman. The business of the United-States Trust Company is of the most extensive and varied character. It is often selected by the courts to act as depository for funds in litigation. It has the care of many large estates, and is the guardian of minors. It is trustee for the bondholders of numerous railroad and other corporations, and acts as transfer agent and registrar of company stocks. It allows interest on deposits, which may be withdrawn at any time, subject to five days' notice of payment. The property in its hands as executor, trustee, etc., is kept wholly apart from its general business; and it holds in the trustee department property to a very large amount.

Financial operations of such magnitude certify to the wonderful discipline and efficiency of the New-York methods of monetary business, and the probity and sagacity of the men and institutions administering these enormous trusts.

The Union Trust Company of New York, one of the greatest fiduciary institutions in the world, and one of the older trust companies of New-York City, was organized in 1864. For nearly twenty years the company occupied offices at 73 Broadway, on the corner of Rector Street, in the building now owned by O. B. Potter, in which the crank attempted to blow up Russell Sage with dynamite, just after the Union Trust Company had moved away. In 1890 the company purchased the property at 80 Broadway, having a front of 73 feet on Broadway, just opposite the head of Rector Street, and running 110 feet to New Street. On this there has been erected one of the stateliest of modern office-buildings, at a cost of $1,000,000, the company itself occupying the spacious first floor, which in the simple elegance of its appointments is without a rival among bankers' apartments in New York. The company is authorized to act as executor,

UNITED-STATES TRUST COMPANY OF NEW-YORK.
45 AND 47 WALL STREET, SOUTH SIDE, BETWEEN BROAD AND WILLIAM STREETS.

administrator, guardian or trustee, and is a legal depository for trust monies, and a trustee for corporation mortgages and transfer agent and registrar of stocks. The management of estates and care of real estate and the collection and remittance of rents therefrom is a specialty ; while in its new burglar and fire-proof vaults it makes ample provision for the safe-keeping of deposits of securities, on which it collects and remits income. It allows interest on deposits which can be withdrawn on five days' notice, and also opens current accounts with depositors subject to check, and allows interest on daily balances. In the exercise of these different functions the company has developed a business of immense magnitude. Its total resources are now $35,-044,000, and the surplus has grown to over $4,000,000, the capital being $1,000,000. It pays 20 per cent. annual dividends on its stock, which is quoted at $800 per share. Edward King, formerly President of the New-York Stock Exchange, is the President of the Union Trust Company. He is one of the most highly esteemed of New-York financiers, a graduate of Harvard University, the honored President of the Harvard Club, and identified with scores of New-York financial, commercial, social and educational bodies. Cornelius D. Wood and James H. Ogilvie are its Vice-Presidents ; Augustus W. Kelley, Secretary ; and J. V. B. Thayer, Assistant Secretary. The Trustees of the institution are a representative body of bankers and capitalists of the highest standing. The Executive Committee of the Board consists of William Whitewright, George G. Williams, Edward Schell, E. B. Wesley, George C. Magoun, James T. Woodward, D. C. Hays, and C. D. Wood.

The Knickerbocker Trust Company, occupying the building at 234 Fifth Avenue, at the corner of 27th Street, and having branch-offices at 3 Nassau Street and 18 Wall Street, is an exemplification of the fact that enormous and increasing business and investment interests are concentrated in the up-town portion of New-York. This institution was formed in 1884, by prominent capitalists, who perceived that the facilities afforded by a strong organization of this kind would obtain the support of an influential monied class, the real-estate owners and investors of the residence-quarter of New York. The results have more than answered this expectation. The company's progress has been

KNICKERBOCKER TRUST CO., 234 FIFTH AVENUE, CORNER OF 27TH STREET.

UNION TRUST COMPANY OF NEW YORK.
80 BROADWAY, OPPOSITE RECTOR STREET, BETWEEN WALL STREET AND EXCHANGE PLACE.

brilliant and substantial. It has a capital of $750,000, and an accumulated surplus of $350,000. Its total deposits are $5,650,000, and its resources $6,770,000. It has attracted by conservative management a clientage of the most desirable character, and is in every way equipped to carry on all the branches of business which its charter authorizes, including the functions of executor, administrator, guardian, receiver, registrar, and transfer and financial agent for corporations and municipalities, and to accept any trusts in conformity with law. It allows interest on time deposits, and receives current deposits subject to check ; and issues letters of credit for travellers available throughout the world. It has occupied the commodious offices at the corner of 27th Street and Fifth Avenue since its organization ; and rents safe-deposit boxes in the fire and burglar proof vaults which have been built for that purpose. The company is an exception in maintaining a down-town branch-office, which is rendered necessary by the extent of its corporation, investment and loan business. The officers of the Knickerbocker are : John P. Townsend, President ; Charles T. Barney, Vice-President ; Joseph T. Brown, Second Vice-President ; Frederick L. Eldridge, Secretary ; and J. Henry Townsend, Assistant-Secretary. The Board of Directors is a body of unusually prominent and strong capitalists, financiers and business men, being composed of : Joseph S. Auerbach, of Lowrey, Stone & Auerbach ; Harry B. Hollins, of H. B. Hollins & Co.; Jacob Hays ; Charles T. Barney ; A. Foster Higgins, of Higgins, Cox & Barrett ; Robert G. Remsen ; Henry W. T. Mali, of Henry W. T. Mali & Co.; Andrew H. Sands ; James H. Breslin, proprietor of the Gilsey House ; Gen. George J. Magee, President of the Fall-Brook Coal Co.; I. Townsend Burden, President of the Port-Henry Iron Ore Co.; John S. Tilney ; Hon. E. V. Loew, ex-Comptroller of the city of New York ; Henry F. Dimock, President of the Metropolitan Steamship Co.; John P. Townsend, President of the Knickerbocker Trust Co.; Charles F. Watson ; David H. King, Jr.; Frederick G. Bourne, President of the Singer Manufacturing Co.; Robert Maclay, President of the Knickerbocker Ice Co.; C. Lawrence Perkins ; Edward Wood, President of the Bowery Savings Bank ; Wm. H. Beadleston, of Beadleston & Woerz ; Alfred L. White, of William A. White & Sons ; and Charles R. Flint, Treasurer United-States Rubber Co.

The Central Trust Company of New York, at 54 Wall Street, is appropriately housed in an imposing brick and granite building, erected in 1887 at a cost of about $1,000,000. The organization of this important institution dates from 1875, its charter having been granted in 1873. The company was formed at a period when the expansion of corporation and investing interests at New York demanded additional facilities such as it affords. Henry F. Spaulding was its first president, and, up to the time it removed to its own edifice, it occupied the basement of 14 Nassau Street, and subsequently the first floor of the Clearing-House Building, at 15 Nassau Street, corner of Pine. The company exercises all the functions allotted to such institutions. It allows interest on deposits, is a legal depository for Court monies, is authorized to act as Executor, Guardian or in other positions of trust, and as Registrar or Transfer Agent of Stocks and Bonds, and as Trustee for railroad and other mortgages. The organization is the custodian of large trust-funds, and represents many important estates. Its business in connection with railroad companies is one of the most extensive in the country, and it has been the fiscal agent and depository of securities in some of the most important railroad re-organizations of recent years. In this department Frederic P. Olcott (who has held the office of president for over eleven years) is a recognized authority, being consulted in the most difficult transactions involving the rights of investors. The other officers are George Sherman,

CENTRAL TRUST COMPANY OF NEW YORK.
54 WALL STREET, OPPOSITE THE CUSTOM HOUSE.

First Vice-President; E. Francis Hyde, Second Vice-President; C. H. P. Babcock, Secretary; and B. G. Mitchell, Assistant-Secretary. The Executive Committee, which is representative of the trustees of the institution, is composed, in addition to the President, of Samuel D. Babcock, Charles Lanier, John S. Kennedy, Cornelius N. Bliss, Adrian Iselin, Jr., Samuel Thorne, A. D. Juilliard, and Charles G. Landon. The capital and surplus of the company amount to over $6,000,000; the deposits to $20,800,000; and the gross assets to $27,300,000. The stock of the Central Trust Company sells for the highest price ever paid for the stock of any trust company in this country, and probably in the world.

The Metropolitan Trust Company was chartered by a special act of the State Legislature, in 1881. Its powers are of an ample character, including, among other provisions, authority to act as depository for the funds of individuals, estates, or corporations, as agent for the payment of bonds and coupons, as trustee of corporation mortgages, and as transfer agent and registrar. The act incorporating this company has been made the model of subsequent State legislation in regard to the formation of trust companies. The institution at its inception occupied quarters in Pine Street, and then migrated to a banking-room in the Wall-Street wing of the Mills Building. In 1889 it purchased the seven-story brick and brownstone building at 37 and 39 Wall Street, and occupies the first floor with its large and increasing business. Gen. Thomas Hillhouse, ex-Assistant-Treasurer of the United States at New York, has been its president since its foundation. Frederick D. Tappen is Vice-President; Charles M. Jesup, Second Vice-President; Beverly Chew, Secretary; and Geo. D. Coaney, Assistant-Secretary. The Board of Trustees includes: A. Gracie King, of James G. King's Sons; D. O. Mills; Frederick D. Tappen, President Gallatin National Bank, New York; Morris K. Jesup; John T. Terry, of E. D. Morgan & Company; Walter T. Hatch, of W. T. Hatch & Sons; C. P. Huntington, Vice-Presi-

METROPOLITAN TRUST CO., 37 WALL STREET.

dent Central Pacific Railroad ; Bradley Martin ; Dudley Olcott, President Mechanics' & Farmers' Bank of Albany, N. Y. ; Heber R. Bishop ; George A. Hardin, Justice New-York Supreme Court, Little Falls, N. Y. ; J. Howard King, President Albany Savings Bank, Albany, N. Y. ; Joseph Ogden ; Henry B. Plant, President Southern Express Company ; Edward B. Judson, President First National Bank, Syracuse, N. Y.; Thomas Hillhouse, late Assistant-Treasurer of the United States ; William A. Slater, of Norwich, Conn.; John W. Ellis ; W. H. Tillinghast ; Robert Hoe, of Robert Hoe & Company ; W. L. Bull, of Edward Sweet & Company ; and George Henry Warren. The institution is now in its eleventh year of successful existence, with a paid-up capital of $1,000,000 ; an earned surplus of over $900,000 ; deposits aggregating $9,000,000 ; and total resources aggregating over $10,000,000.

The Manhattan Trust Company was chartered in 1888, and is to-day one of the strongest and most active financial institutions in the United States. The company is authorized to act as executor, administrator, guardian, receiver and trustee ; as fiscal and transfer agent ; and as registrar of stocks and bonds. The company offers to executors and trustees of estates, and to religious and benevolent institutions, exceptional facilities for the transaction of their business. Deposits received are subject to check at sight, payable through the New-York Clearing-House. In every department the company has developed its resources and increased

WALL STREET.   MANHATTAN TRUST CO   SUB-TREASURY.

MANHATTAN TRUST CO., WALL STREET, CORNER OF NASSAU STREET.

its annual volume of business. It has a paid-up capital stock of $1,000,000, and has accumulated a surplus fund of over a quarter of a million, with assets amounting to upwards of $5,000,000. The company has been designated by the New-York-State Banking Department as depository for the reserve of State Banks, and is also a Court Depository for the State of New York.

John I. Waterbury, President of the company, has been identified with the corporation since its organization, and succeeded Francis O. French, who died in March, 1893. Mr. Waterbury is also a Director of the Old Colony Trust Company of Boston, and of the Lawyers' Surety Company of New York, and is also President of the Security Corporation. John Kean, Jr., the Vice-President, is also President of the National State Bank of Elizabeth, N. J., and other institutions. Amos T. French is Second Vice-President; and C. H. Smith, Assistant-Secretary. The Directors for 1893 are August Belmont, of August Belmont & Co.; R. J. Cross, of Morton, Bliss & Co.; T. Jefferson Coolidge, Jr., President of the Old Colony Trust Company, Boston; John Kean, Jr., President of the National State Bank, Elizabeth; Hon. H. O. Northcote, London, England; E. D. Randolph, President of the Continental National Bank; John N. A. Griswold, Esq.; Jas. O. Sheldon; H. W. Cannon, President of the Chase National Bank; Henry L. Higginson, of Lee, Higginson & Co., Boston; C. C. Baldwin; A. S. Rosenbaum; R. T. Wilson; John R. Ford; and John I. Waterbury. The Executive Committee is composed of H. W. Cannon, August Belmont, John R. Ford, Jas. O. Sheldon, John Kean, Jr., John I. Waterbury, R. J. Cross, and Henry L. Higginson. The Manhattan Trust Company Building, at the corner of Wall and Nassau Streets, New-York City, is one of the most conspicuous buildings in the financial centre of New York, and is one of the most desirable and valuable in the metropolis. It is opposite the United-States Sub-Treasury, at the strategic financial heart of the republic, and amid the great metropolitan banks and trust companies.

The Washington Trust Company was organized in 1889, by a number of prominent capitalists and business men identified with the opulent and varied interests which occupy the busy district adjacent to the City-Hall Park. The offices of the company are established in a convenient and roomy suite in the great marble building, once A. T. Stewart's gigantic wholesale dry-goods establishment, and now remodelled into a most notable office structure, and known as the Stewart Building, at 280 Broadway. The organization was effected under the general law, and is authorized to act as trustee for individuals and corporations, and as a legal depository for Court and trust funds, as well as to receive deposits, to issue interest-bearing certificates, and to serve as agent for estates and individuals. The management and connections of the institution, no less than its admirable location, have been favorable to the rapid development of a profitable and conservative business in all of its diversified functions. Many important trusts have been committed to its care, its proximity to the Courts rendering it particularly useful in instances where a fiduciary agent is required in connection with litigation or proceedings before the Surrogate. Its capital is $500,000, and the surplus and undivided profits now amount to about $400,000. Its deposits are over $4,000,000 ; and the total resources of the institution (included in which are $500,000 in New-York City bonds and other securities of an immediately available character) foot up no less than $5,000,000. The Board of Trustees of the company embraces the following names, representing conservative strength, all of whom are well known in New York, a number of them having a National reputation : Charles F. Clark, David M. Morrison, Charles H. Russell, Geo. H. Prentiss, Joel F. Freeman, L. T. Powell, George

THE WASHINGTON TRUST COMPANY, STEWART BUILDING, 260 BROADWAY.

L. Pease, Wm. Henry Hall, Geo. E. Hamlin, P. C. Lounsbury, Seth E. Thomas, Lucius K. Wilmerding, Joseph C. Baldwin, George Austin Morrison, John F. Anderson, Jr., E. C. Homans, William Lummis, Charles A. Johnson, John R. Hegeman, and William Whiting. David M. Morrison, its President, comes from a banking family, his father for two generations having been President of the Manhattan Company Bank. Charles F. Clark, the Vice-President, is known throughout the mercantile world as the President of the Bradstreet Mercantile Agency, whose ramifications extend over three continents. William Lummis, well-known in financial circles, and ex-Vice-President of the New-York Stock Exchange, is Second Vice-President ; Francis H. Page, Secretary ; and M. S. Lott, Assistant-Secretary.

The State Trust Company, at 36 Wall Street, was organized as recently as 1889, under the general laws of the State, with full powers to transact all business usual to fiduciary institutions of this character. Its success from the very first gives promise of a gigantic institution in the near future.

The State Trust Company, although one of the younger fiduciary institutions, being but three years old, has developed into one of the larger and stauncher of the trust companies, having a capital of $1,000,000, a surplus of $814,692, and gross assets of $9,664,202, which includes deposits of almost $8,000,000. Its stock, on a par of $100 a share, sells at about $275 a share. It pays semi-annual dividends, at the rate of six per cent. a year. The reason for The State Trust Company's success is readily found in its able management. Its first President was Willis S. Paine, for many years the Bank

Superintendent of the State of New York ; and its Secretary, John Quincy Adams, was the former Chief Bank-Examiner.   Its Board of Trustees includes : Willis S. Paine ; Henry H. Cook, capitalist ; Charles R. Flint, of Flint & Company, shipown- ers; William L. Trenholm, ex-Comptroller of the Currency, and President of the American Surety Company ; William B. Kendall, of the Bigelow Carpet Company ; Walter S. Johnston, President Spanish-American Light and Power Company ; Joseph N. Hallock, proprietor of the *Christian at Work ;* Percival Knauth, of Knauth, Nachod & Kuhne, bankers ; Edwin A. McAlpin, of McAlpin & Company, tobacco ; Andrew Mills, late President of the Dry-Dock Savings Institution ; William A. Nash, President of the Corn-Exchange Bank ; George Foster Peabody, of Spencer, Trask & Company, bankers ; J. D. Probst, of J. D. Probst & Company, bankers ; Henry Steers, President of the Eleventh-Ward Bank ; George W. Quintard, proprietor of the Quintard Iron Works ; Forrest H. Parker, President New-York Produce Exchange Bank ; Charles Scribner, of Charles Scribner's Sons, publishers ; William Steinway, of Steinway & Sons, pianos ;   Charles L. Tiffany, of Tiffany & Company, jewellers ; Ebenezer K. Wright, President of the National Park Bank ; William H. Van Kleeck ; George W. White, President of the Mechanics' Bank of Brooklyn ; John Q. Adams ; and Francis S. Bangs, of Bangs, Stetson, Tracy & MacVeagh.   Andrew Mills is the President, and W. L. Trenholm and William Steinway are the Vice-Presi- dents.   The trust company's quar- ters are in the Gallatin National Bank Building, at 36 Wall Street. The State Trust Company is au- thorized to act as executor, admin- istrator, trustee, guardian, re- ceiver, and in all other fiduciary ca- pacities, and to serve as transfer agent and regis- trar of incorpo- rated companies. It allows interest on long and short time deposits and accounts, and does all that pertains to a general trust company's busi- ness.

TRINITY CHURCH.   TREASURY   ASSAY OFFICE.   STATE TRUST CO.
THE STATE TRUST COMPANY, 36 WALL STREET; ADJOINING ASSAY OFFICE.

The New-York Guaranty & Indemnity Company, at the northeast corner of Cedar and Nassau Streets, in the magnificent Mutual Life Building, has a capital of $2,000,000 and a surplus of $1,000,000. It transacts a general banking and trust-company business, and with continuous success solicits the accounts of corporations, firms and individuals. In addition to its special charter privileges, this com-

pany possesses all the powers of trust companies under the New-York banking laws; acts as trustee for corporations, firms and individuals, as executor or administrator of estates, and as a legal depository of trust funds. It allows interest on deposits. It enjoys exceptional privileges by reason of its special charter, which was granted over twenty years ago. Its present business was not begun, however, until 1891; and yet its current statement shows an amazing and unparalleled success in so short a time. Its first offices were, as now, in the Mutual Life Building, at 59 Cedar Street; and now it has added to these the northeast corner of Nassau and Cedar Streets. The New-York Guaranty & Indemnity Company is one of the powerful financial institutions which have concentrated much of the capital of America in the Empire city, and there wisely and profitably administered it. Its officers are: Edwin Packard, President; Adrian Iselin, Jr., Vice-President; George R. Turnbull, Second Vice-President; Henry A. Murray, Treasurer and Secretary; J. Nelson Borland, Assistant-

NEW-YORK GUARANTY AND INDEMNITY COMPANY, MUTUAL LIFE BUILDING, NASSAU AND CEDAR STREETS.

Secretary. The Directors — one of the most distinguished Boards in the financial world — comprise: Samuel D. Babcock, George F. Baker, Frederic Cromwell, Walter R. Gillette, Robert Goelet, George Griswold Haven, Oliver Harriman, R. Somers Hayes, Charles R. Henderson, Adrian Iselin, Jr., Augustus D. Juilliard, James N. Jarvie, Richard A. McCurdy, Alexander E. Orr, Edwin Packard, Henry H. Rogers, Henry W. Smith, H. McK. Twombly, Frederick W. Vanderbilt, William C. Whitney and J. Hood Wright.

The Continental Trust Company of the City of New York, at 18 Wall Street, was formed in 1890, under the General Act of the State providing for such institutions. Its founders are among the most conservative and substantial business men and financiers of New York, and the powers granted it under the law are of a very comprehensive character, embracing authority to act as trustee for individuals or corporations, or as executor or guardian, to receive deposits of money, and to become the depository of Court funds, with additional provisions which complète its ability to act in a fiduciary capacity. The management and care of estates is a prominent feature of its functions, and it receives accounts of individuals, firms,

corporations and estates, allowing interest on deposits, checks on the company being paid through the Clearing House. The capital is $500,000, and the surplus and undivided profits exceed $350,000. Its management is of a character to command confidence and respect ; and is composed of Otto T. Bannard, President; William Alexander Smith, first Vice-President; Gordon Macdonald, second Vice-President ; and Maurice S. Decker, Secretary. The trustees of the institution embrace an array of names widely known in the financial and business world, being composed of : Robert Olyphant, Alfred M. Hoyt, John C. Havemeyer, Gordon Norrie, Hugh N. Camp, William Jay, James C. Parrish, Robert S. Holt, Henry M. Taber, William H. Wisner, A. Lanfear Norrie, Oliver Harriman, Jr., William F. Cochran, Giraud Foster, Robert W. de Forest, Otto

THE CONTINENTAL TRUST COMPANY, 18 WALL STREET,
BETWEEN BROADWAY AND NASSAU STREET.

T. Bannard, William Alexander Smith, Gordon Macdonald, and Walter Jennings. The location of the banking quarters of the Continental Trust Company is in the very midst of the financial activity of the Metropolis. Its building is immediately opposite the Wall-Street entrance to the Stock Exchange, a minute's walk from the Sub-Treasury and the Assay Office. Interest is allowed on deposits, computed on daily balances subject to check ; and the deposits may be withdrawn at pleasure. The checks drawn on the company are paid through the New-York Clearing House. It is enabled to offer all the advantages usual to any regularly organized trust company.

The Farmers' Loan & Trust Company, 16, 18, 20 and 22 William Street, New York, R. G. Rolston, President; W. D. Searls, Vice-President; William H. Leupp, Second Vice-President; E. S. Marston, Secretary; Samuel Sloan, Jr., Assistant-Secretary. Directors: Samuel Sloan, William Waldorf Astor, William Remsen, Henry Hentz, Thomas Rutter, D. O. Mills, James Stillman, Wm. H. Wisner, James Roosevelt, E. R. Bacon, Charles L. Colby, A. C. Cheney, M. Taylor Pyne, Percy R. Pyne, Isaac Bell, Alex. T. Van Nest, Wm. Walter Phelps, R. L. Cutting, Edward R. Bell, C. H. Thompson, James Neilson, H. Van Rensselaer Kennedy, Robt. C. Boyd, Henry A. C. Taylor, Robert F. Ballantine, Franklin D. Locke, R. G. Rolston. Capital, $1,000,000; surplus, $4,000,000.

THE FARMERS' LOAN & TRUST COMPANY, BEAVER AND WILLIAM STREETS.

Savings-Banks in the United States date from 1816, when a voluntary organization for that purpose was formed at Philadelphia. In 1817 Massachusetts granted a charter for such an institution, and Maryland in 1818. In the succeeding year several States authorized their institution, New York among the number, the Bank for Savings in New York, now one of the greatest savings-banks of the world, dating from that year. With the growth of the city, and the increase of its industrial population, the spirit of philanthropy which has always distinguished the business men and financiers of New York prompted the creation of additional facilities of this character. Legislative charters of a special character were required until 1874, when the State Constitution of New York was amended by requiring the charters of all savings-banks to conform to a general law, and prohibiting the organization of these institutions with a share capital. In accordance with this, the Legislature in 1875 repealed all special privileges contained in savings-bank charters, and enacted a general law for their regulation. Under this law (which has contributed greatly to the prosperity of the savings-banks of New-York City) trustees are prohibited from deriving any benefit, direct or indirect, from their offices, except as officers whose duties are constantly at the bank, nor can they borrow any of the bank's funds. The banks are confined, with respect to investments, to United-States Government obligations, bonds of the State of New York, or any county or municipality thereof, bonds of any State which has not defaulted in payment of interest for ten years, or in mortgages on real estate in New York, worth twice the amount loaned, but not to exceed sixty-five per cent. of the amount of deposits. Where such loans are on unimproved real estate the amount is restricted to forty per cent. of actual value. The aggregate amount of an individual deposit is limited to $3,000, in any one bank ; and the rate of interest paid on deposits may not exceed five per cent., though after the bank's surplus exceeded fifteen per cent. of the deposits extra dividends may be declared. This law merely codifies the principles upon which, from an early date, the success of the great savings-institutions of New York was based. It is a noteworthy fact that the members of the Society of Friends took a leading part in the establishment of the savings-banks, and that the philanthropic tenets which distinguished that sect had a powerful impulse in moulding their policy. Service as a trustee of any of the large savings-banks has been considered an honor by the leading merchants and bankers of the metropolis, and the magnificent results and unshaken confidence which are presented in this field represent an enormous aggregate of arduous duty, unselfishly performed for the benefit of the whole community by its most prominent members. And, furthermore, the savings-banks of New-York City, with their deposits of $340,000,000, and their resources of nearly $50,000,000 in excess of that amount, point to another moral. While every class in the community is represented among the depositors, the industrious working class predominates. No city in the country supplies such numbers of toilers, and the 1,600,000 depositors in New-York State savings-banks are a convincing proof that the thrift and economy which go far to make good citizens have a hold upon the bone and sinew of the great city.

The Bank for Savings in the City of New York is the oldest savings-bank in the State of New York, and one of the oldest in the country. It is the second savings-bank in America, in the amount of deposits, and also the second in number of depositors. It was founded in 1819, the philanthropic objects of its originators, as quaintly stated, being "to cherish meritorious industry, to encourage frugality and retrenchment, and to promote the welfare of families, the cause of morality and the good order of society." The institution was given by the city the use of a room in one of the buildings which then occupied the Broadway and

Chambers-Street corner of the City-Hall Park. William Bayard was the first President, and James Eastburn, Secretary. Among the original trustees were Henry Eckford, De Witt Clinton, Cadwalader Colden, Peter A. Jay, Brockholst Livingston, Richard Varick, Thomas Eddy, Najah Taylor, John Pintard, and Gilbert Aspinwall. The gentlemen who gratuitously gave their services at first received deposits personally on certain evenings of the week only, it being recorded of the initial session on July 3, 1819, that "the trustees had the satisfaction of receiving the sum of $2,809." At the end of 1819 the deposits had risen to $150,000. A regular place of business was established at 43 Chambers Street in 1825; and in 1845 it removed to 107 Chambers Street; and finally, as population moved northward, the bank in 1856

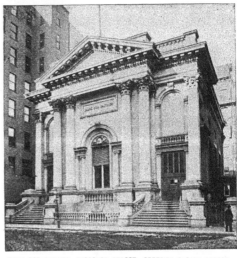

BANK FOR SAVINGS, BLEECKER STREET, OPPOSITE CROSBY STREET.

erected the old-fashioned but characteristically imposing structure, in Grecian architecture, which it still occupies, at 67 Bleecker Street, just east of Broadway, and at the northern terminus of Crosby Street. The familiar name by which the present generation of New-Yorkers know it is the "Bleecker-Street Savings-Bank." During its 74 years of existence it has had 645,000 depositors, and received altogether $239,000,000 in deposits, paying thereon $43,000,000 in interest. The present depositors number 117,000, with $47,130,000 to their credit, the total assets, including $1,200,000 cash, and a surplus of over $3,500,000, being over $52,000,000. The full history of this venerable institution would recall the names of a multitude of the foremost business men of the city whose services have been cheerfully given for the benefit of its depositors. Among its presidents were John Pintard, Philip Hone, Najah Taylor, Marshall S. Bidwell, John C. Green, and Robert Lenox Kennedy. The present officers are Merritt Trimble, President; James A. Roosevelt, second Vice-President; Robert S. Holt, Secretary; and William G. White, Comptroller. The Board of Trustees is composed of: Frederick D. Tappen, John J. Tucker, Adrian Iselin, John E. Parsons, John Crosby Brown, Robert S. Holt, Alfred W. Spear, George M. Miller, Alfred M. Hoyt, Orlando B. Potter, James A. Roosevelt, Thomas Hillhouse, Merritt Trimble, William A. Hoe, William L. Andrews, Frederic W. Stevens, John M. Dodd, Jr., Charles A. Sherman, Henry W. de Forest, W. Irving Clark, William J. Riker, Charles S. Brown, and William W. Appleton. The Bank for Savings has bought a new site at the corner of Fourth Avenue and 22d Street; and is at work on the erection of a banking-house especially designed to accommodate its large and increasing business.

The Seamen's Bank for Savings, founded in 1829, and occupying its own substantial and specially constructed building at 74 and 76 Wall Street, at the north-west corner of Pearl Street, is the second oldest institution of the kind in New York. The philanthropic object of its organizers was to provide a safe and advantageous deposit for the sea-faring community. This object has never been lost sight of, and though its facilities have from the first been open to the public it still continues to receive considerable deposits from officers and seamen in the naval and merchant service. Since its organization, it has received total deposits of $210,000,000, and has paid in interest thereon over $27,000,000. The amount due its depositors at present is $31,535,293, and its assets are $35,220,680. The first President was Najah Taylor, who was succeeded in 1834 by Benjamin Strong. Peletiah Perit in turn assumed the office in 1851 ; William H. Macy in 1863; and George F. Thomae in 1867. William H. Macy was again elected in 1872, and was succeeded in 1887 by its present President, William C. Sturges. Daniel Barnes is Cashier, and Silvanus F. Jenkins is Treasurer. The Board of Trustees has always represented the commerce of New York, and many leading merchants have cheerfully given their time and labor to the care of the seamen's affairs. The present Board consists of William C. Sturges, President ; William A. Booth, E. H. R. Lyman, and Horace

SEAMEN'S BANK FOR SAVINGS, WALL AND PEARL STREETS.

Gray, Vice-Presidents ; John H. Boynton, Secretary ; Ambrose Snow, Emerson Coleman, James R. Taylor, W. H. H. Moore, William de Groot, George H. Macy, John D. Wing, Vernon H. Brown, Frederick Sturges, J. W. Frothingham, George C. Magoun, David S. Egleston, William H. Phillips, and William H. Macy, Jr.

All classes of the community avail themselves of the facilities afforded them by this famous old savings-bank, to deposit their earnings in a safe place, at fair interest, and ready for use at any emergency. In this way, and on account of the existence and conservation of such institutions, habits of thrift and foresight are developed among the people, to the vast advantage of the general community, and the stability of the institutions of modern civilization.

The Greenwich Savings-Bank is one of the oldest and most solid fiduciary institutions in the country. It was founded in 1833, and has an untarnished record for sixty years. Its first home was at 10 Carmine Street, in Greenwich Village ; thence it moved to Sixth Avenue and 4th Street ; and thence to Sixth Avenue and Waverly Place, where it remained for many years. In 1892 the bank erected at the corner of Sixth Avenue and 16th Street a magnificent and fire-proof Italian Renaissance building, designed by R. W. Gibson. This building, architecturally one of the finest in the city, is constructed of white Worcester granite, rock-faced for the walls and smooth-cut for decorative work, adorned with pilasters, pediments and turrets. The interior is a noble hall, 150 by 50 feet in area, and 60 feet high, with coupled columns, domed ceiling, counters and wainscots of red Numidian marble, Roman mosaic floors, and other artistic decorations. The whole of the structure is devoted to the uses of the bank, none of it being rented for other purposes. The

GREENWICH SAVINGS-BANK, SIXTH AVENUE, SOUTHEAST CORNER OF 16TH STREET.

deposits of the Greenwich Savings-Bank amount to $24,730,632, from 51,487 depositors, and it has a surplus of $3,727,036. Over $12,000,000 of its funds are invested on bond and mortgage secured by real-estate in New-York City.

The officers are John Harsen Rhoades, President ; William Remsen, First Vice-President ; John S. McLean, Second Vice-President ; and James Quinlan, Treasurer. The Trustees are John S. Dickerson, William Remsen, John Harsen Rhoades, Samuel B. Van Dusen, John A. Stewart, Lowell Lincoln, Charles P. Daly, John S. McLean, Edward Oothout, Joseph H. Gray, John Wilson, Charles A. Davison, J. B. M. Grosvenor, Julius Catlin, William Moir, George Bliss, Arthur B. Graves,

Edward N. Tailer, John L. Riker, Leonard D. White, Geo. W. Smith, Francis H. Leggett, A. S. Frissell, William T. Wardwell, Charles S. Smith, David M. Morrison, Benjamin O. Chisolm, Warren N. Goddard, James Quinlan, John Downey, George G. Haven, and A. G. Agnew.

The Bowery Savings-Bank enjoys the distinction of having the greatest amount of assets, a total of about $53,000,000, of any financial institution in this country. Of this sum, about $48,000,000 are the deposits of 107,000 depositors, and a profit and loss account of over $5,000,000. The bank was chartered in 1834, and among its incorporators were many well-known New-York names. It has been a fiduciary institution of the highest order; it has taken care of the savings of the poorer classes, and has earned for them all that their small accumulations could safely return. Its presidents have been: Benjamin M. Brown, David Cotheal, James Mills, Thomas Jere-miah, Samuel T. Brown, Henry Lyles, Jr., and Edward Wood, who has been President since 1880. Its Board of Trustees, always a representative body of New York's best citizens, includes the following: Edward Wood, President; John P. Townsend, First Vice-President; Robert M. Field, Second Vice-President; John D. Hicks, Robert Haydock, Henry Barrow, Henry Lyles, Jr., Richard A. Storrs, Aaron Field, Edward Hincken, Wm. H. S. Wood, Timothy H. Porter, Enoch Ketcham, William H. Parsons, William H. Hurlbut, William V. Brokaw, Samuel H. Seaman, Edward C. Sampson, Wm. H. Beadleston, James W. Cromwell, John J. Sinclair, Joseph B. Lockwood, William Dowd, George

BOWERY SAVINGS BANK, BOWERY, NEAR GRAND STREET.

Montague, George M. Olcott, Charles Griffen, Alexander T. Van Nest, David S. Taber, Washington Wilson, Isaac S. Platt, Eugene Underhill, George E. Hicks, John W. Cochrane, Octavius D. Baldwin, George H. Robinson, George Jeremiah, Robert Maclay, William L. Vennard, Henry C. Berlin, John F. Scott, Charles E. Bigelow, A. Blanchard Dominick, and C. Lawrence Perkins.

Its Secretaries have been: Giles H. Coggeshall, who was elected in 1836, and served until 1885; and Robert Leonard, his successor, who had been Assistant Secretary from 1859 until 1885. The bank has always occupied the premises on the Bowery, just north of Grand Street, to which it extends by an **L**. It is erecting a bank building that will furnish more suitable accommodations.

The **Dry-Dock Savings Institution** dates its organization from 1848, at which period the ship-building trade was a leading industry of New York. The old dry-dock at the foot of East 10th Street, East River, was a centre in the district devoted to shipbuilding, and its name was adopted when a number of gentlemen principally interested in that business established this institution to encourage thrift and prudence among their workmen. The bank was first located at 530 East 4th Street. In 1859 it purchased a building at 339 and 341 East 4th Street. In 1872 the

DRY-DOCK SAVINGS INSTITUTION, 341 AND 343 BOWERY, CORNER OF 3D STREET.

site at 341 and 343 Bowery was purchased, and the present building (valued at $250,000) was erected, and occupied in 1875. It was then one of the finest buildings in the country for its purpose, and is to-day an admirable structure. At the present time the institution has total assets of over $19,500,000, with deposits of $17,929,209, and a surplus of $1,668,763. Since its establishment 236,-982 accounts have been opened, the deposits have aggregated $119,000,000, and $12,200,000 has been paid for interest on deposits. The success which has attended the "Dry Dock" is largely the result of the exceptional management which it has always enjoyed. The first President of the bank was Schureman Halsted; and in 1854 Andrew Mills, a leading ship-joiner, who had been identified with the institution from the start, became its head, and remained in the position until 1879. Charles Curtiss served in the same capacity until 1888, when Andrew Mills (second of that name, and son of the former President), who had served as Treasurer and Secretary from 1877, was elected to the Presidency, which he resigned in 1893, to become President of the State Trust Company. John Tiebout is now President. Samuel P. Patterson, a trustee since 1848, and David J. Taff, elected a trustee in 1857, are Vice-Presidents; and the Secretary is Charles Miehling, who entered the service in 1865, and was appointed Paying Teller in 1873, and to his present post in 1888. The Board of Trustees still represents the shipbuilding interests. The Board consists, in addition to the officers, of Jesse J. Davis, Andrew Mills, Richard L. Larremore, Stephen M. Wright, Guy Culgin, Sidney W. Hopkins, Robert J. Wright, Henry E. Crampton, M. D., Abner B. Mills, Charles E. Pell, George B. Rhoads, Frederick Zittel, Henry C. Perley, John A. Tackaberry, Charles T. Galloway, Arthur T. J. Rice and William H. Hollister.

The Institution for the Savings of Merchants' Clerks, at 20 Union Square, is the fifth in age of the local savings-banks, and is one of the most highly esteemed fiduciary institutions of New York. Incorporated in 1848, it has had a dignifiedly quiet and uniformly steady growth ever since. As its name implies, it was founded to encourage the clerks of business men to take care of their earnings. Its inception was due to members of the Chamber of Commerce, who enlisted with them members of the Mercantile Library Association, and for a long period these two organizations in a degree designated the trustees of the savings institution. All through its history the prime object of the bank has been adhered to, although its depositors include thousands of men, women and children who can hardly be classed as clerks. The bank has had but five presidents, James G. King, Moses H. Grinnell, A. Gracie King, Joseph W. Patterson, and Col. Andrew Warner. Col. Warner has been connected with the bank for 38 consecutive years, first in 1854 as Cashier, afterwards in 1855 as Cashier and Secretary, and later in 1881 as President. He has a notable record in connection with institutions, from his years of service as Corresponding Secretary of the American Art Union; 47 years as Secretary of the New-York Historical Society; 40 years as manager of the House of Refuge; 30 years as Governor and

Treasurer of the Lying-in Hospital; and now in his 86th year taking an active interest in many public institutions. Among the treasurers of the institution have been Merritt Trimble, President of the Bank for Savings, on Bleecker Street, who was a trustee here for fifteen years; and George G. Williams, the President of the Chemical National Bank, who while a clerk in the Chemical Bank became almost the first depositor in this savings-bank, on the day of its opening

INSTITUTION FOR SAVINGS OF MERCHANTS' CLERKS, 20 UNION SQUARE, CORNER 15TH STREET.

in 1848, and has continued as a depositor ever since, still retaining his original passbook, which was No. 10, in marked contrast with over 75,000 issued since. The bank's earliest quarters were in the old Clinton Hall, at the corner of Beekman and Nassau Streets. Later they were at 516 Broadway, opposite the old St. Nicholas Hotel; and in 1868 the present Union-Square property was bought and remodelled to its uses. The bank statement of January 1, 1892, shows gross assets of $6,402,861; deposits of $5,822,960; and a surplus of $579,901. It has over 13,000 open accounts. Its officers are: Andrew Warner, President; James M. Constable and George A. Robbins, Vice-Presidents; George G. Williams, Treasurer; and William T. Lawrence, Secretary and Cashier.

The Emigrant Industrial Savings-Bank was incorporated by an Act of the Legislature of the State of New York, passed April 10, 1850, and it opened for business in the month of October following. The idea of establishing the bank originated in the Board of Trustees of the Irish Emigrant Society, which was established many years previous, for the purpose of assisting and protecting the Irish emigrants landing at the port of New York. Many of these strangers brought some money with them, and it was desirable to teach others thrift and industry ; it was, therefore, deemed an absolute necessity to provide some place for the safe-keeping of the means of these poor people, which would be under the guidance and influence of the officers of the Irish Emigrant Society, and of the Commissioners of Emigration.

At that time Gregory Dillon and Andrew Carrigan were members of the society, and the latter, and Gulian C. Verplanck, were Commissioners of Emigration ; they

procured the charter from the Legislature and established the bank, Mr. Dillon becoming its first President, and Mr. Carrigan its Comptroller, and they associated with them in the direction, Robert B. Minturn, William Watson, Terence Donnelly, John P. Nesmith, Felix Ingoldsby, and about a dozen others, all old merchants of New York.

The bank was successful. For the first two or three years these gentlemen not only gave their services gratis, but they each contributed their pro-rata of expenses, until the business of the bank had become self-supporting. It fulfilled its mission, took good care of the money of the emigrants, and by degrees its business widened until it became a cosmopolitan institution, having dealings with people of all countries. It has been scarcely forty-two years in existence, yet its assets to-day amount to the enormous sum of more than $45,000,000, including its surplus fund of over $4,000,000. The amount of its deposits is upward of $41,000,000. The bank owns and occupies, at 49 and 51

EMIGRANT INDUSTRIAL SAVINGS-BANK, 49 AND 51 CHAMBERS STREET. Chambers Street, the handsomest savings-bank room in this city, and one of the most valuable savings-bank buildings in the country. The building is of granite, eight stories high, with an entrance through an arch of polished granite. The main banking-room, 50 feet wide, extends the full depth of the building, from Chambers Street to Reade Street. The present officers and trustees are : James McMahon, President ; James Olwell, first Vice-President ; Bryan Lawrence, second Vice-President ; James Rorke, Secretary ; Eugene Kelly, Robert J. Hoguet, James R. Floyd, Henry Amy, Arthur Leary, John C. McCarthy, P. H. Leonard, John D. Keiley, Jr., Eugene Kelly, Jr., John Good, Louis V. O'Donohue, Charles V. Fornes, James G. Johnson, John Crane, and John A. McCall.

The **Manhattan Savings Institution** has its banking-rooms on the ground floor of its own stately eight-story sandstone front building, at 644 and 646 Broadway, corner of Bleecker Street, completed for its use in 1890, at a cost of over half a million dollars. This structure replaced another

which had been erected in 1863, the bank having in 1867 purchased this site and moved thither from its original quarters at 648 Broadway. The incorporation of the institution dates from 1851, when it was formed by such leading citizens as Augustus Schell, James Harper, E. D. Morgan (afterwards Governor of New York), Henry Stokes and A. A. Alvord. Ambrose C. Kingsland, ex-Mayor of New York, was the first President. The institution has a history of steady growth and of the confidence to which the high standing of its management entitles it. The deposits from its inception to 1892 amounted to $92,764,119. The amount due depositors January 1, 1893, is $8,565,545, the assets representing a cost or par value of $9,733,932, and a market value of over $10,000,000. Edward

MANHATTAN SAVINGS INSTITUTION, BROADWAY AND BLEECKER STREET.

Schell, its President, has been a trustee nearly forty years, ever since 1854, and was elected to his present office in 1876. The Vice-Presidents, Robert G. Remsen and Joseph Bird, have been identified with the bank for many years ; the Secretary, Frank G. Stiles, has a record of 32 years spent in its service ; and George H. Pearsall, the Assistant-Secretary, has been connected with the institution since 1865. The Board of Trustees, in which the officers are also included, consists of : Henry M. Taber, John H. Watson, P. Van Zandt Lane, E. A. Walton, William J. Valentine, DeWitt

C. Hays, Edward King, H. B. Stokes, George Blagden, John D. Jones, George
H. McLean, William H. Oakley, S. R. Lesher, James W. Smith, J. William
Beekman and Philip Schuyler.

The **Union Dime Savings Institution** was organized in the year 1859, and
commenced business in a small building at the corner of Canal and Varick Streets.
It was designed to receive smaller deposits than were ordinarily accepted, and was
the first to assume the name "Dime." Its founders, who were all loyal supporters
of our National Government, then assailed by internal foes, emphasized their patriotism by adding to its name the word "Union." From the first the
policy of welcoming the small depositor, and extending to him the same
courtesy and accom- modating spirit that was shown to the one who
brought a larger sum, proved successful, and the bank grew steadily.
The trustees further evinced their faith in
American institutions by investing largely in
United-States bonds, which proved a very
profitable course. In 1866 the
bank, having reached a prominent
position among the savings-banks
of the city, found larger accommodations necessary for its business, and erected the commodious
building at Canal and Laight
Streets, now used for the
United-States Pension
Agency. Ten years later,
it was deemed advisable to
make another move, and to
follow the march of the population in the "up-town"
direction. A plot was purchased at the junction of
Broadway, Sixth Avenue and
32d Street, where was erected
the magnificent white marble

UNION DIME SAVINGS INSTITUTION, BROADWAY, SIXTH AVENUE
AND 32D STREET.

structure still occupied for its business. There is certainly no finer site on Manhattan Island for the purpose, and it is accessible by numerous public conveyances. The bank is now the custodian of over $14,000,000, in deposits ranging from
a single dime to the maximum allowed by law. Its depositors number 57,000
persons, of all classes, races and ages. It is still noted for the promptness and
courtesy with which business is transacted, and is visited by many officers of
kindred institutions from a distance, who have heard of its beautiful building and of
the perfection of its methods. The presidents of the institution from its organization have been: E. V. Haughwout, John McLean, Napoleon J. Haines, John W.
Britton, Silas B. Dutcher, Gardner S. Chapin, recently deceased, who was an officer
of the bank from its foundation, and who received the first deposit ever made, and
Charles E. Sprague, the present incumbent. The other officers are Channing M.
Britton and James S. Herrman, Vice-Presidents; George N. Birdsall, Treasurer;
and Francis M. Leake, Secretary. The savings-banks of New-York City, during
the great panic of 1893, showed remarkable caution and conservatism, and most
other savings-banks followed their example.

Other Savings-Banks include the American, Fifth Avenue and 42d; Broadway, 4 Park Place; Citizens', 56 Bowery; Dollar, 2771 Third Avenue; East River, 3 Chambers; Excelsior, Sixth Avenue and 23d; Franklin, 656 Eighth Avenue; German, 100 East 14th; Harlem, 2281 Third Avenue; Irving, 96 Warren; Metropolitan, 1 Third Avenue; New York, 81 Eighth Avenue; North River, 266 West 34th; Twelfth Ward, 271 West 125th; United States, 1048 Third Avenue; and West Side, 56 Sixth Avenue.

Safe Deposit Companies include several gigantic institutions organized solely to provide as nearly absolute protection as human ingenuity can devise. There is the Safe Deposit Co., 140 Broadway; the Mercantile Safe Deposit Co., 120 Broadway; the Bankers' Safe Deposit Co., 2 Wall Street; the Manhattan Safe Deposit Co., 344 Broadway; the American Safe Deposit Co., 42d and Fifth Avenue; the Fifth Avenue Safe Deposit Co., 23d and Fifth Avenue; the Garfield Safe Deposit Co., 23d and Sixth Avenue, etc.

The Fifth-Avenue Safe Deposit Company, under the Fifth-Avenue Hotel, is the representative up-town institution of its class. It occupies spacious vaults at the northwest corner of 23d Street and Fifth Avenue, the entrance being through the

Second National Bank, with which it is closely allied, though maintaining a separate organization. Being in the heart of the residence-quarter, it has a clientage composed of people of means, and is also found to be exceedingly useful by visitors to New York residing in the hotels in that neighborhood, who desire a place of deposit, for securities or other valuables. The company's vault contains 2,500 safes and compartments, and is constructed in the most secure modern methods, being completely burglar-proof, and is in addition guarded in the most thorough manner. W. C. Brewster is President; George Montague, Treasurer; and D. C. Silleck, Superintendent.

FIFTH AVENUE, NORTH FROM 29TH STREET, COLLEGIATE CHURCH AND HOLLAND HOUSE.

Financial and Commercial Associations.

The Custom House, Chamber of Commerce, the Stock, the
Produce, the Cotton and Other Exchanges, the Board
of Trade, Mercantile and Other Agencies,
Markets and Warehouses.

THE commercial preëminence enjoyed by New York has been so continuous and uniform that it would be useless to speculate as to the probability of anything like rivalry from another member of the sisterhood of American cities. Commercial New York will be understood to include the territory within a dozen miles of the City Hall, with a population of 3,000,000 people, something less than five per cent. of the total number of inhabitants of the United States. The volume of the whole traffic of the first city of the continent with reference to the aggregate of like transactions throughout the United States, as well as the volume of business at other of the more important centres, may best be gauged by a comparison of totals of bank clearings. As the composition of "bank clearings" is not generally understood, a brief explanation may show how totals of clearings at various cities enable one to furnish comparisons of the relative volume of wholesale business. General wholesale dealings, whether interstate, inter-municipal, international or others in wheat, iron, cotton or wool, the products thereof, in shoes, clothing, hats, or the thousand and one other articles of trade are almost exclusively paid for (ultimately) by checks and drafts, or bills of exchange, which are mailed or otherwise sent by purchasers to consigners. In the ordinary course of business these are deposited in banks for collection, though, of course, but seldom in banks at which such paper is finally payable. Before the day of clearing houses, these instruments of exchange had to be mailed for collection to banks on which they were drawn, but now, when nearly all important banks throughout the country have balances at banks in New-York City, practically final settlements of "country bank" checks and drafts may be made at the metropolis. By this it is meant that the thousands of checks and drafts received at New York and deposited daily, may be paid there through correspondent banks. The story of the New-York Clearing House is given in detail in another chapter, and its daily adjustment of bank-accounts, including practically all checks and drafts upon the New-York City banks, nearly represents a settlement of transactions of all kinds, and thus furnishes a tangible measure of New-York's wholesale trade.

When it is understood that there are nearly seventy cities in the United States having bank clearing houses, it becomes apparent how useful their annual totals may be as a means of comparing relative volumes of wholesale transactions. But in order to confine the bank clearing totals at New-York City as nearly as practicable to dealings in actual commodities, it is necessary to eliminate the proportion due to trading in securities at the Stock Exchange, which proportion (of the daily or yearly clearings) is reached by regarding two and a half times the total actual value of transaction in shares and bonds as the aggregate, based on the estimated average number of times securities.

From analysis of bank clearings totals covering 1885, a year of special depression, following the panic in 1884, the period of expansion during 1890, and restricted commercial and industrial enterprise in 1891, one may find material for comparing New-York City's traffic, although in order to extend the comparison, totals for other of the more important business centres are appended :

BANK CLEARINGS TOTALS.	1885.	1890.	1891.
New-York City, excluding Wall Street, . .	$14,452,200,000	$27,514,447,000	$24,218,704,000
Boston, ...	3,483,100,000	5,130,878,000	4,753,840,000
Chicago, ...	2,318,500,000	4,093,145,000	4,456,885,000
Philadelphia, ...	2,374,400,000	3,710,248,000	3,296,852,000
St. Louis, ...	759,100,000	1,118,573,000	1,139,599,000
San Francisco, ...	562,300,000	851,066,000	892,426,000
Baltimore, ...	581,900,000	753,093,000	735,714,000
Pittsburgh, ...	356,100,000	786,694,000	679,062,000
Other cities reported, ...	2,506,460,000	6,082,397,000	6,011,875,000
Grand Totals,	$27,394,060,000	$50,040,541,000	$46,184,957,000

As shown by the foregoing, it is apparent that New-York City's aggregate of foreign and domestic distributive trade amounted to about 52 per cent. of the grand total of such traffic throughout the country in 1885, a period of greatly restricted

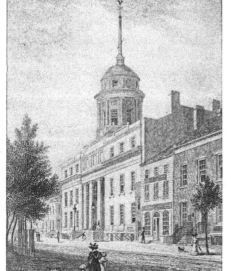

THE OLD MERCHANTS' EXCHANGE ON WALL STREET.

trading ; to about 55 per cent. in 1890, a year of more active business ; and to 52 per cent. in 1891, during which period there was a falling off in the volume of general business.

By comparing totals at the larger cities it is found that whereas New-York's aggregate was only four times as large as Boston's in 1885, six years later it was more than five times as large. But Chicago's trade has grown more rapidly than that of Boston, for its clearings total, which was only 16 per cent. of that of New York in 1885, amounted to nearly 19 per cent. of the aggregate at the metropolis in 1891. Carrying the comparison farther, one finds that while Philadelphia furnished a total less than one-sixth as large as New York in 1885, it gave one proportionately smaller six years later, being not quite one-seventh. The clearings at St. Louis in 1885 were much smaller than those previously specified, only 5 per cent. of those at the metropolis, and while they increased fully 50 per cent. within six years, yet in 1891 they amounted to only 4.7 per cent. of those of New-York City. By the combined clearings at cities other than New York, the latter's commercial dominance becomes even more conspicuous, for the aggregate of totals at Boston, Chicago, Philadelphia, St. Louis, San Francisco, Baltimore and Pittsburgh is found to have amounted to only 72 per cent. of the total at New York in 1885, and to only 66 per cent. in 1891. It remains to be stated that all wholesale business does not, of course, come in contact with clearing-house banks throughout the country, though undoubtedly a very large proportion of it does; just how large a share it is not necessary to discuss within the limits of this chapter. It is generally believed by students of clearing statistics that the proportion of the general trade of the country accounted for by them is so large that they may, with discriminating use, be fairly taken as indices of the volume of trade current.

New York's foreign trade, in comparison with that of other cities, is a matter of Government record, and gives that city a long lead over the six or seven which rank next as to values of exports and imports. This is shown by the appended condensed exhibit from the Treasury-Department records.

VALUE OF EXPORTS OF MERCHANDISE AND PRODUCE, FOREIGN AND DOMESTIC.

	Year Ending June 30.	1870	1880	1890	1891	Per Cent. 1891.
1	New York . . .	$196,614,746	$392,560,090	$348,051,791	$346,528,847	39.2
2	New Orleans, . .	107,586,952	90,442,019	108,126,891	109,106,687	12 3
3	Boston, ...	14,126,429	59,238,341	71,201,944	77,020,081	8.7
4	Baltimore, . . .	14,510,733	76,245,870	73,983,693	64,412,247	7.2
5	San Francisco, . .	13,991,781	32,358,929	36,876,091	40,168,771	4.5
6	Galveston, . . .	14,873,732	16,749,889	24,446,831	33,772,005	3 8
7	Philadelphia, . .	16,927,610	49,649,693	37,410,683	33,674,355	3.8
8	Savannah, . . .	29,749,058	23,992,364	30,884,451	33,506,426	3.8
	All Other, . . .	62,982,595	94,401,463	126,846,309	146,291,391	16.5
	Total U. S., . . .	471,363,636	835,638,658	857,828,684	884,480,810	100

VALUE OF MERCHANDISE IMPORTED AT LEADING CITIES.

	Year Ending June 30.	1870	1880	1890	1891	Per Cent. 1891.
1	New York, . . .	$281,048.813	$459,937,153	$516,426,693	$537,786,007	63.6
2	Boston, ...	47,484,060	68,503,136	62,876,666	71,212,614	8.4
3	Philadelphia, . .	14,483,211	35,944,500	53,936,315	59,427,890	7.0
4	San Francisco, . .	15,982,549	35,221,751	48,751,223	50,943,299	6.0
5	Baltimore, . . .	19,512,468	19,945,989	13,140,203	20,555,687	2.4
6	New Orleans, . .	14,377,471	10,611,353	14,658,163	20,267,060	2.4
7	Chicago, ...	735,894	847,935	13,590,124	15,303,373	1.8
	All Other, . . .	42,333,942	36,942,029	65,931,022	69,420,266	8.2
	Total U. S., . . .	435,958,408	667,954,746	789,310,409	844,916,196	100

The comparison of bank clearings together with reports of foreign trade at several of the more important cities of the country indicate that a little less than one-half of the total value of the aggregate imports and exports to and from the United States pass through New York annually, while that city controls so much larger a proportion of domestic trade that its share of the business of the country of all kinds amounts to more than one-half of the grand total.

The Custom House occupies a square bounded by Wall, William and Hanover Streets and Exchange Place. The building is a venerable pile of Quincy granite, with an appropriate air of impressive solidity about it. Originally, it was the Merchants' Exchange. It is 200 by 160 feet on the ground plan, and 77 feet high, and is a fair example of Doric architecture. In the centre is the rotunda, with an
50

CUSTOM HOUSE, WALL STREET, HANOVER TO WILLIAM.

imposing dome supported upon marble columns. The building and ground cost $1,800,000. The Government business has outgrown the accommodations, and a new Custom House, or this one enlarged, is greatly needed.

The Customs business is supervised by the Collector of the Port, the Naval Officer, the Surveyor of the Port, and the Appraiser of the Port. There are 50 steamship lines running vessels to this port, all of them from foreign countries, and bringing goods subject to duty. Most of these lines have piers of their own. There are 69 corporations and firms of warehouse and transportation companies bonded for the storage and transportation of appraised merchandise, the transportation companies taking goods to 42 interior places of entry and to all places in Canada.

The amount of tariff duties collected here during the fiscal year ending June 30, 1892, was $120,732,614, out of a total of all tariff duties collected by the Government of $177,452,964, the percentage being 68 4-100. The cost of collection at New York was .0216 per cent. The Custom House has 1,700 employees.

The United-States Bonded Warehouses comprise the following seven classes : 1. Owned or leased by the United States ; 2. In sole occupancy of an importer for goods imported by himself ; 3. In occupancy of persons engaged in storage business, used solely for warehouse goods, and approved by the Secretary of the Treasury ; 4. Yards covered or uncovered, and used solely for bulky articles ; 5. Bins or parts of buildings for imported grain ; 6. Warehouses exclusively for the manufacture of medicines, cosmetics, and the like ; 7. Warehouses for smelting and refining imported ores and crude metals intended to be exported in a refined but unmanufactured state.

These warehouses are located on the North and East Rivers, New York, and in Jersey City, Hoboken and Brooklyn. The legal rates of storage and labor in the care of imported merchandise deposited in the United-States private bonded warehouses are regulated and arranged by a joint committee appointed by the Chamber of Commerce, the Collector of the Port, and the proprietors of the warehouses, and are approved by the Secretary of the Treasury. Under the Collector there are divisions of the business as follows ; each one with its special officers : General Administration, Marine, Entry of Merchandise, Warehousing and Withdrawals, Cashier, Bonded Goods and Warehouses, Public Stores, Liquidations, Drawbacks, Law, Disbursements and Auditing. The Naval Department, under charge of the

Naval Officer, is divided into six divisions, as follows : Entry, Drawbacks, Navigation, Liquidation, Warehouse, Auditors. The Surveyor's Department is presided over by the Surveyor, and has divisions as follows : Custom House, Barge Office, and Weighers and Gaugers. There are districts and offices in number as follows : North River, 15 ; East River, 12 ; Brooklyn, 18 ; Hoboken, 4 ; Jersey City, 4 ; and Staten Island, 1. There are seven Weighers' districts and Weighers. In the Appraisers' Department, presided over by the Appraiser of the Port, there are ten divisions, each in charge of an Assistant Appraiser. The United-States General Appraisers' Board consists of nine Appraisers, of whom there are three generally in New York. Their duties are to reappraise merchandise ; individually to hear and determine questions as to the dutiable value of merchandise on appeal from appraisers ; collectively, in boards of three, to review, on appeal, the undivided action above mentioned, and to decide questions as to classification of merchandise, etc., on protests against assessments of duty made by the Collector. The Appraiser's offices and sample stores are located on Washington Street, nearly two miles distant from the Custom House.

The New-York Chamber of Commerce was first convened on April 5, 1768. The original corporators were twenty merchants, who declared themselves to be "sensible that numberless inestimable benefits have occurred to mankind from commerce ; that they are, in proportion to their greater or less application of it, more or less opulent and potent in all countries ; and that the enlargement of trade will both increase the volume of real estate as well as the opulence of our said colony " and other communities. They obtained from King George, through Lieutenant-Governor Cadwallader Colden, March 13, 1770, the charter under which they operated until the convulsions of war suspended their meetings. The Chamber was re-incorporated April 13, 1784, by the passage of an Act of the New-York Legislature, confirming its rights and privileges. Both charters convey the ordinary rights of corporations and the power, subject to constitutional and statute law, "to carry into execution, encourage and promote by just and lawful ways and means, such measures as will tend to promote and extend just and lawful commerce ;" and also to provide for, at their discretion, such members as may be reduced to poverty, and to aid their widows and children. The proceedings of the Chamber of Commerce at first related to materials, instruments, tare, weight and inspection of the provision-trade ; the relative values of New-York, New-Jersey and Pennsylvania paper money, to bills of exchange, fire and marine insurance, collection, brokerage, fisheries, etc. The Chamber was re-organized April 20, 1784, by the forty incorporators under the new charter, with John Alsop as president. Since then, the career of the corporation, under consecutive amendments to its charter, has been one of patriotism and beneficence. It took and has held prominence in the affairs of the city, and has included among its members the most important citizens, from its establishment to the present. Its first President was John Cruger, who was a prominent merchant and ship-owner, a trusted representative of the Crown, and a chosen representative of the people. He was Mayor of the city for ten consecutive years, and checked the growing insolence of British officers. For seven years he was leader of the Long Assembly, to whose courageous patriotism the union of the colonies and the vindication of American liberties were largely due. He was Speaker of the last Colonial Assembly, from 1768 to 1775, when its functions passed to the Council of Safety, and subsequently to a Provincial Congress.

In 1786 the Chamber of Commerce first suggested the construction of the Erie Canal, a work that in later years was to be a foundation of much of New York's wonderful prosperity. In 1784, on its petition, the Legislature ordered that duties should be levied under a specific instead of an *ad-valorem* tariff, a system of which the Chamber has since been the consistent advocate. All questions affecting domestic and foreign commerce and the prosperity of the city, State and Nation at large are within the province of the Chamber to investigate, discuss and act upon. In a speech at a recent dinner of the Chamber its President, Charles S. Smith, said : "No matter which of the great parties hold for the time being the reins of government, this Association was bound by its traditions and precedents, in all matters of State and National legislative relations to commerce and industry, to promote good laws, to amend imperfect, and to defeat bad ones. In the matter of relief to sufferers by famine, fire or flood, more than $2,000,000 in charity has passed through the hands of our treasurer for these commendable objects within the last quarter of a century."

Courtesies are especially extended by the Chamber to distinguished foreign guests. Its annual dinners are marked events in metropolitan life, on account of the expressions upon public questions there made, members of the President's Cabinet often speaking on the vital issues of the hour. The membership is limited to 1,000. It has the largest and finest gallery of portraits of men connected with the commerce of the country to be found in the United States. The rooms of the Chamber are in the Mutual Life Building, at 34 Nassau Street.

The New-York Stock Exchange is without question one of the most important commercial and financial bodies in the world. The economic usefulness of the Stock Exchange, and the true reason for its growth and present prosperity, is that it furnishes the facilities by which a regular and constant market for the securities of great corporations of the country is maintained, a market never without buyers or sellers, and one in which quotations can be obtained without difficulty or delay. The internal development of the country has been mainly the work of capital associated in corporate form. Without a ready market for the immense mass of shares and bonds that are created in this way, money would not be so freely invested in railroads and other undertakings. The Stock Exchange is the mechanism that supplies this, and the speculation, which the unthinking regard as its sole object, is really only an incident to its useful functions. But whatever view may be taken of the subject, the institution under consideration is certainly a power in the land, and an element of prime importance in maintaining the commercial and financial supremacy of New York.

The Renaissance façade of the Stock-Exchange building rises on Broad Street, a few doors from Wall Street. The lot it occupies is irregular in shape, extending through to New Street, and has a narrow wing with an entrance on Wall Street. The executive offices occupy the Broad-Street side, and nearly the whole interior of the building is given up to the large hall or Board room in which the transactions of the Exchange are carried on. This apartment is **T**-shaped, being 141 to 145 feet in its greatest dimensions, while the ceiling (decorated in arabesque, with large skylights for light and ventilation) is from 60 to 80 feet above the floor. The total area of the room is nearly 14,000 square feet. A gallery reached from the Wall-Street entrance extends around three sides, from which spectators who are admitted between 10 A. M. and 3 P. M. (the hours during which the Board is in session) may look down upon probably the busiest scene in the world. A railing, with openings at intervals, surrounds the outer edge of the room, and leaves a narrow space for clerks and subscribers, who for a payment of $100 per annum obtain certain privileges. The floor within the railing is sacred to the members of the Exchange and the uniformed attendants. On the New-Street side is a lofty rostrum for the Chairman, who with a blow of the gavel calls the Exchange to order, opens and closes its sessions, and makes announcement of admissions, deaths, failures, or other formal communications. At intervals throughout the floor are ornamental iron posts bearing the names of some particular stock, as "New-York Central," "Lackawanna," and so on. Every portion of the room in fact is given over to some particular security, and transactions between the brokers must be made, in what is technically called the proper "crowd," openly, in the presence of other brokers who may desire to trade in the stock in question. Formal rules govern the trading. The first bid or offer made has priority, until accepted or displaced by a higher bid or lower offer. Other regulations prohibiting fictitious or "washed" quotations. And the strictest rule of all is, that a commission of 1-8 of 1 per cent. on the par value must be charged for buying or selling securities. Originally, the whole list of stocks dealt in was "called" from the rostrum several times a day, and bids and offers were thus ex- changed. Business, however, soon overflowed into the intervals between the "calls," and in 1875 the system was abandoned. A formal call of the bond list still occurs daily in one of the upper rooms of the Exchange, though trading in bonds goes on continuously in one portion of the room. As rapidly as transactions are made, the amounts and prices are taken by attendants who stand by each "crowd" to telegraph operators, whose boxes are at several places in the room. They are at once transmitted to the quotation companies connected with the Exchange, and in a few seconds the prices are carried by the "stock ticker" into the brokers' offices and banks, and to other cities. The "ticker," or stock instrument, is a printing telegraph, and records on a narrow "tape," or strip of paper, cabalistic signs, such as S T 83—— N P P R 500——54 1-4—— E 27 5-8 3-4, which to the initiated mean that 100 shares of Chicago, Milwaukee & St. Paul Railway has sold at $83 a share; that 500 shares of Northern Pacific Preferred stock have just brought $54.25 each; and that Erie shares are offered at $27.75, with $27.62½ bid. Two concerns supply this service, one

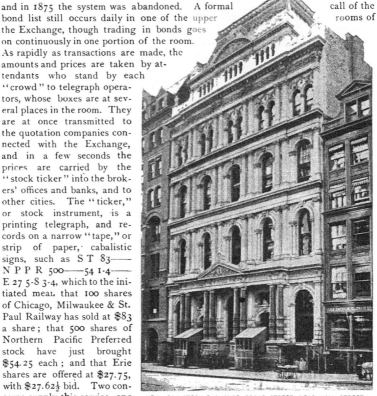

NEW-YORK STOCK EXCHANGE, BROAD STREET, NEAR WALL STREET.

the New-York Quotation Company, being controlled by the Stock Exchange itself; the other, the Gold & Stock Telegraph Co., is operated by the Western Union Telegraph Company. The celerity and accuracy with which the quotations of the New-York Stock Exchange's immense dealings are thus transmitted and made public are without parallel in the world. Much ingenuity has been expended by the Exchange in a partly unsuccessful endeavor to prevent the quotations from being used by the class of concerns known as "bucket-shops," which are simply places where gambling on the course of stock-market prices is carried on, and where many young men have suffered ruinous losses, in betting on the turn of the market. The daily dealings on this Exchange are printed in the great newspapers throughout the country.

The history of the New-York Stock Exchange is parallel to that of New York's financial development. Its centenary was celebrated on May 17, 1892. One hundred years previous to that day 24 brokers of New York met under a cotton-wood tree opposite 60 Wall Street, and signed a still extant agreement regarding rates of commission. This organization was somewhat indefinite, though meetings were held irregularly at the Tontine Coffee-House, at Wall and Water Streets. Not until 1817 was a formal organization of the Stock Exchange effected on the present lines. The first meeting-place of the Board was in the Merchants' Exchange (now the Custom House). In 1853 it moved to the corner of Beaver and Wall Streets; and finally in 1865 took possession of the edifice which by additions and alterations has become its present building. In 1869 the members of a rival body called the "Open Board of Brokers" were absorbed. In 1879, after the closing of the "Gold Board" (the Exchange in which during the war dealings and speculations in gold were conducted, and which after August, 1865, had its quarters on New Street, next to the Stock Exchange) its building was taken in and used to extend the premises pertaining to the Stock Exchange.

The Stock Exchange is a voluntary association. It is not even incorporated. The membership now is 1,100. Memberships, called technically "seats" pass by sale and transfer from a member, or his legal representative, in case of decease. Seats sold about ten years ago for $34,000, the highest price on record. The present value is $20,000 each. A purchaser of a seat must, however, be approved by the Committee on Admissions. The immense business between the members of the Exchange being entirely by word of mouth, and dependent upon personal veracity and honor, a careful investigation is made of all applicants for admission. Disputes in fact are very rare, and as a rule nowhere in the world is good faith and honorable dealing better observed than between the members of the New-York Stock Exchange. A member's seat is in event of failure responsible for his debts to other members. The annual dues are $50, and an assessment of $10 is levied on members for each death, this sum maintaining a gratuity fund, from which a life-insurance of $10,000 is paid to the family of a deceased member. A majority of the members are associated with some banking or brokerage firm as partners, the houses thus having representatives on the Exchange. Many brokers, however, do business for others, in executing orders; and there is a small but influential class who speculate for themselves and are known as "room traders."

The internal government of the Exchange is vested in a President, Secretary, Treasurer, and a Governing Committee of forty members, ten of the latter being chosen each year. The present officials of the Exchange are: F. K. Sturgis, President; R. H. Thomas, Vice-President; D. C. Hays, Treasurer; and George W. Ely, Secretary.

NEW-YORK STOCK EXCHANGE. INTERIOR OF THE MAIN FLOOR.
BROAD, WALL AND NEW STREETS.

On May 17, 1892, the Stock Exchange celebrated its one hundredth anniversary by adopting a system of "clearing" (offsetting mutual debits and credits between its members) in the leading active stocks traded in on the Board. This system, which is in use on all the great exchanges of Europe, involves for the Stock Exchange the same economy of time and money that the bank clearing house does for the banks. As yet only a limited number of the most active stocks are dealt in under this plan. The balance of the share list and the dealing in bonds is still conducted under the old method of actual deliveries. All stocks or bonds purchased on the Stock Exchange, except in the case of those subject to the clearing plan, still must be delivered to and paid for by the brokers who purchase them before 2.15 P. M. of the succeeding day. The extent of the business transacted on the New-York Stock Exchange is shown by the fact that the aggregate amount of railroad and other shares "listed" and open to dealings between its members does not fall short of $20,000,-000,000 in par value. In 1891 the recorded transactions aggregated 66,000,000 shares, of an estimated value of nearly $4,000,000,000. In 1882 the total was 113,-000,000 shares, valued at $7,000,000,000. The largest transaction for any day in the history of the Exchange was February 11, 1892, when 1,441,000 shares of stocks changed hands.

The business transacted on the Exchange has developed a peculiar slang which almost rises to the dignity of a technical language. The client of a brokerage house is its "customer." An outsider unversed in the ways of speculation, and apt to lose his money, is a "lamb;" and the deposit he makes with his brokers as security for his dealings (usually ten per cent. on the par value of stocks bought or sold for speculative account) is "margin." The operators who buy stock in expectation of a rise in prices are "bulls," and are "long" of the market; and those who sell them in anticipation of buying them back at lower figures are "bears," and are "short" that is, they have borrowed the stocks they sold for delivery, and have to "cover" or buy them back to complete their transaction. When prices advance and the bears have to protect their contracts by buying at advancing figures they are said to "climb" for stocks, while if the bulls encounter a decline in values, and are obliged to sacrifice their holdings to avoid or mitigate losses, it is called "liquidation," or a "shake-out." A decline is also known as a "slump," and when it immediately follows an advance it is a "reaction," an advance coming on the heels of a decline being a "rally." A declining market is "weak," and its converse "strong;" while an undecided but active trading is "feverish," and a time when the public comes in and buys stocks recklessly, causing prices to advance rapidly, is a "boom." "Puts," "calls" and "straddles" are contracts issued by leading operators, agreeing for a consideration to receive a stipulated number of specified shares at a given price, to deliver the same at a stipulated figure, or to do either. They are all so-called "privileges," and are dealt in by a class of "privilege dealers," or "curbstone brokers," so-called because their transactions are often concluded in the streets adjoining the Exchange, New Street being the favorite place with these dealers.

The Consolidated Stock and Petroleum Exchange of New York is an outgrowth of the consolidation of several bodies dealing in mining shares and in petroleum certificates, in which some years ago an active speculation was maintained. The last of these consolidations was effected in 1885, when the present name was adopted, and the membership limited to 2,000 members. In their early days the various mining and petroleum boards were in a measure allies of the Stock Exchange, but the resolution to add trading in railroad shares and bonds to their functions made them the avowed rivals of the more ancient institution. In spite of the more or less open opposition of this powerful enemy, the Consolidated Board has continued to flourish, and is often the scene of trading which in its magnitude and activity approaches to that witnessed on the older board. The amalgamated minor boards at first occupied quarters at Exchange Place and Broadway; but in 1887–88, the institution erected on three lots, covering 58, 60 and 62 Broadway, the splendid edifice which is known by its name. The building fronts on Broadway, Exchange Place and New Street. The Board-room is 132 feet long by 90 feet wide, and gives 11,000 square feet of floor, being exceedingly well lighted. The basement and upper floors supply offices for rental, besides the committee-rooms and administrative offices of the Exchange. The business of the Consolidated Exchange is similar to that of the Stock Exchange. It gives attention to trading in both petroleum and mining shares, but in both cases the markets are by no means what they were a few years ago. Dealings in general stocks and bonds occupy the attention of its members, who are largely recruited from active young Wall-Street men, to whom the high price of Stock-Exchange seats is a prohibitory tariff. It, however, embraces in its membership many operators of experience, and brokerage firms of high standing are attached to it. It is a noteworthy fact that

during the speculation panic that followed the Baring Brothers' collapse in 1890 the Consolidated did a large business without a single failure of any importance among its members. This may be partly ascribed to the stock-clearing house system in the adoption of which for its stock transactions the institution was a pioneer in New York. Under this system, which has been in successful operation since the Exchange commenced to make stock-trading a part of its business, it is possible for a broker or brokerage firm to carry out large transactions with a moderate employment of capital. It is noticeable that in spite of the avowed hostility of the Stock Exchange toward the Consolidated, sons

CONSOLIDATED STOCK AND PETROLEUM EXCHANGE, BROADWAY AND EXCHANGE PLACE.

and other relatives of the former's members are found in the latter institution, and a number of prominent brokers in the elder board graduated from the ranks of the younger. The present value of seats in the Consolidated is upward of $200, though in times of active speculation they have sold for several times that sum, and would doubtless do so again were Wall Street again visited by a "boom." It should be noted that a membership involves a life-insurance feature, the family of a deceased member receiving $8,000 from a gratuity fund maintained by an assessment of $10 on each member for every death that occurs.

The affairs of the Consolidated are conducted by a governing committee of 42 members. Its president is a salaried officer, and assumes considerable responsibility in its executive management. Charles George Wilson (who is also President of the Board of Health of the city) has been at the head of the Consolidated since 1884, and has filled the post with great success. The other officers of the Exchange are : Thomas L. Watson, First Vice-President ; R. A. Chesebrough, Second Vice-President ; John Stanton, Treasurer ; Rudolph Huben, Secretary ; W. H. Lewis, Assistant Secretary ; and A. W. Peters, Chairman. The extent of the business of the Exchange is shown by the fact that the stock clearances through its clearing-house organization in 1891 aggregated 77,235,000 shares of stock and 47,500,000 barrels of oil certificates, the transactions in bonds in the same period being for $30,800,-000 par value. The mining stocks dealt in footed up 2,050,000 shares.

The Mechanics' and Traders' Exchange of the City of New York, at 289 Fourth Avenue, was organized in 1834, and incorporated in 1863. It is composed of employers whose business is connected with the construction or finishing of buildings. The purposes are to provide suitable rooms for daily meetings ; to establish a more general and good understanding, and just and equitable principles in all business transactions with each other ; and to acquire, preserve and disseminate valuable business information. The membership is 300. There is a daily attendance of about 100, between the hours of 12 and 3. Certificates of membership are transferable. The expenses are annually assessed upon the certificates.

The New-York Produce Exchange is a corporation that has held its present name since 1868, when it was changed by act of the State Legislature from the New-York Commercial Association, which had its origin in 1861. There were two other corporations that figured as its forerunners — the Produce-Exchange-Building Company and the Corn Exchange. The latter was incorporated in 1853. There are records of merchants and traders meeting for mutual advantage on Manhattan Island as far back as the time of Governor Peter Stuyvesant, who established in 1648 weekly Monday markets, on the very site of the present mammoth structure at Broadway and Beaver Street. The building now occupied was begun May 1, 1881, and finished May 1, 1884. The cost, with land and furniture, was $3,178,645. It is one of the largest and finest structures of its kind in the world. It is 307 feet long and 150 feet wide, and with its tower and terrace covers 53,779 square feet. From the sidewalk to the roof is 116 feet ; to the coping of the tower, 225 feet ; and to the top of the flag-staff, 306 feet. The main hall is on the second floor. It is 220 by 144 feet, with heights of $47\frac{1}{2}$ feet to the ceiling and 60 feet to the skylight. The building is of brick, terra cotta, and granite, in the modified Italian Renaissance architecture. It contains 12,000,000 bricks, fifteen miles of iron girders, $1\frac{3}{4}$ miles of columns, 2,061 tons of terra cotta, $7\frac{1}{2}$ acres of flooring, more than 2,000 windows, and nearly 1,000 doors. Four thousand separate drawings were required in its construction. The nine hydraulic elevators carry an average of 27,500 people daily, or 11,250,000 every year. The building is equipped with powerful Worthington pumps.

NEW-YORK PRODUCE EXCHANGE.
WHITEHALL, BEAVER AND STONE STREETS, FRONTING BOWLING GREEN.

The income from 190 rented offices and from special privileges is over $260,000 a year, and returns about six per cent. net on the entire investment.   When the bonded debt is liquidated, the Exchange will enjoy a net income of about $200,000 a year, which may be applied to the reduction of either dues or to gratuity assessments.   The charter expresses the purpose of the corporation, viz., to inculcate just and equitable principles in trade; to establish and maintain uniformity in commercial usages; to acquire, preserve and disseminate valuable business information ; to adjust controversies and misunderstandings between persons engaged in business ; and to make provision for the widows and children of deceased members.   The membership is limited to 3,000.   The initiation-fee at the time of limiting the membership was $2,500, but certificates of membership are transferable, and have varied in price from

PRODUCE EXCHANGE, INTERIOR OF MAIN FLOOR.

$700 to $4,700.   The charter permits the ownership of property to the extent of $5,000,000.   The affairs of the corporation are controlled by a president, vice-president, treasurer and twelve managers, who together constitute the Board of Management.   The president appoints, with the approval of the Board, a standing committee for each of the trades, to which all disputes arising in it may be referred for arbitration, at a cost of $15 to $25 to the losing party.   The expenses of the Exchange are defrayed by assessments of $25 annually on each certificate of membership.   An Arbitration Committee of five members hears and decides disputes between parties who bind themselves to acquiesce in its decision.   Any controversy which might be the subject of an action at law or in equity, excepting claims to real estate, is within the jurisdiction of the Committee.   Judgments of the Supreme Court of the City of New York may be rendered upon these awards.   The Exchange rooms are open for business from 9 A. M. to 4 P. M., with a half-holiday after 12 M. on Saturday.

Warehouse receipts of provisions are for 250 barrels, containing an average of 200 pounds.   On the arrival at the city of cereals they are probed by a hollow iron sampling-rod, whose valve opens to admit the grain as the rod is thrust into the hatches of a vessel, or the interior of a car, and closes so as to retain the sample when it is drawn out.   This process repeated several times by responsible inspectors in different parts of a car or boat load, secures reliable samples, which are placed in boxes on the Exchange tables.   The system of grading grain now in vogue enables the Western buyer, who has accumulated as much grain in his warehouse as he wishes to carry, and who knows daily and almost hourly the market prices in New York, to telegraph to any broker, and through him to sell for future delivery the amount and grade of wheat he may have on hand.   He then ships it so that it may

WASHINGTON MARKET, WASHINGTON AND WEST STREETS, BETWEEN FULTON AND VESEY STREETS.

arrive in time to fulfil his contract.   Dealing in futures accompanies very largely the present system of handling grain.   The various grain ware-houses and elevators have a collective capacity of 30,000,000 bushels, and are conveniently approached by ocean vessels, and have customary shipping facilities.   The precision with which the business is conducted is shown by the fact that wheat has 29 grades ; corn, 13 ; oats, 12 ; rye, 3 ; barley, 16 ; peas, 3.   Unmerchantable grain is not graded at all.   The facility with which sales for future delivery are made has enormously augmented the volume of trade.   Foreign merchants avail themselves of it to provide for prospective needs of different markets.   It gives the farmer a ready home-market for his products, and affords the traders the opportunity of selling at a reasonable profit, and at a moment's notice, and to deliver at option within specified times.   The wheat-pit is the chief point of the future and speculative trading.   Wheat, corn and oats are sold in quantities of 5,000 bushels, and multiples.   There are special committees, in control of inspectors and their assistants, and regulating other affairs, on flour, distilled spirits, naval stores, petroleum, National transit certificates, oils, lighterage, butter, cheese, hops and maritime affairs.   This is the largest exchange in the world, in point of membership.   It has a gratuity-fund of about

$1,000,000, and each subscribing member pays $3 on the death of any other member. The heirs of a deceased member receive about $10,000. The average daily business handled by the Exchange exceeds $15,000,000. The greater part of the farm-products exported are handled here ; and the dealings on the New-York Produce Exchange profoundly influence the agricultural population of this continent, the results of whose work, at sunrise and mid-day and evening, are finally marketed here.

The United States Brewers' Association, at 109 East 15th Street, in the building formerly occupied by the Century Club, was organized and held its first convention in New York in November, 1862. As the immediate cause of the organization,

BREWERS' EXCHANGE, 109 EAST 15TH STREET.

it is stated that the brewers felt it to be their duty to assist to the extent of their ability in bringing to the treasury of the United States the full share of tax-burdens justly due from their industry. It is chartered by the Legislature of New York. Its members number about 1,000, distributed throughout the United States. It seeks the protection of its industry from prohibitory and unduly stringent laws, and coöperates with the Government in the execution of the laws pertaining to malt liquors. It is contended by the Association that the industry it represents is in the interest of temperance and morality, as its effect is to diminish the consumption of intoxicating liquors. Henry Claussen, Jr., at its 25th annual convention, said : "Nobody ever heard of a 'beer-ring' organized to baffle the efforts of the revenue officials at every stage ; on the contrary, the official records of the Treasury Department contain ample testimony that every official act of your Association, so far as it is related to the revenue, was conceived in the spirit of patriotism and with a design of aiding the Government. During the first three or four years after the enactment of the Revenue law of July, 1862, the brewing interest generally did not respond as promptly as it should have done to the demands made upon it by our country's necessity. Your Association deplored this deeply, but the remedy was beyond their power. When the Government, in 1865, took measures to correct the defects of the law, and to prevent infractions, your Association at once took the initiative in regard to the brewing industry, by sending a commission of three of its members to Europe, to inquire into the excise systems of Great Britain, France and Germany, and to report to the United-States Special Revenue Commission the results of their labor. Have we not reason enough, gentlemen, to be proud of the history of our Association, when we reflect upon the single fact that the report of this commission was not only adopted by the Revenue Commission, but also approved by a majority of the National law-makers, and made to serve as a basis for the new law, the principal features of which are enforced even to-day?"

The American Shipmasters' Association, at 37 William Street, was incorporated in 1863, to collect and disseminate information upon subjects of marine or commercial interest; to encourage and advance worthy and well-qualified commanders and other officers of vessels in the mercantile service; to ascertain and certify the qualifications of such persons as shall apply to be recommended as commanders or officers; and to promote the security of life and property on the seas. It has agents and surveyors at seaports throughout the world. The subscribers are public and Government officers and marine insurance and other companies throughout the world. The work it does and the information it disseminates are similar to those of the Lloyds of Great Britain. Its *Record of American Shipping* is a volume that has been issued annually since 1867, and is published with the approvals of the Boards of Marine Underwriters of New York, Boston and San Francisco.

The New-York Cotton Exchange was organized with 100 members, August 15, 1870, and incorporated April 8, 1871. The building now owned by it extends 116 feet on William Street, 87 feet on Beaver Street, and 89 feet on Hanover Square. Its height is seven stories. Its construction began September 11, 1883; the corner-stone was laid February 25, 1884; and it was occupied April 30, 1885. The cost, including ground, furniture, etc., was about $1,000,-000. The rent of the offices in the building pays a handsome return on the investment. The property, affairs and business are under the direction of a president, vice-president, treasurer, and fifteen managers, who together constitute the Board of Managers. The purposes of the Association are to adjust controversies between members; establish just and equitable principles in commerce; maintain uniformity in rule and procedure; adopt classification standards; acquire and disseminate useful information relating to the cotton interests; to decrease local business risks; and to increase and facilitate the cotton trade. For these purposes an Adjudication Committee of five persons, not members of the Board of Managers, is annually balloted for by the Board, and thus appointed to decide any controversies between members, which might be the subject of actions at law or in equity, save as regards real

NEW-YORK COTTON EXCHANGE, BEAVER AND WILLIAM STREETS.

estate. Judgments of the Supreme Court are rendered upon such awards made pursuant to such submission. Certificates of membership may be transferred by members to members elect. The initiation fee is $10,000 and the annual dues not in excess of $50. Trading is done in cotton—"spot," "to arrive," "free on board," "in transit," and for "future delivery." A gratuity fund to heirs in case of the death of a member is made up of an assessment not exceeding $12.50 upon every

COTTON EXCHANGE, INTERIOR OF MAIN FLOOR.

membership, at the death of any member; and is collectible under the regulations that apply to annual dues. As a gratuity-fund it is not subject to will, pledge or mortgage. The Committee on Classification, salaried and wholly at the service of the corporation, consists of five recognized expert members of the Exchange, of whom three, drawn by lot, act upon each appeal. The Committee on Quotations on Spot cotton, at 2 P. M., by a majority vote of its seven members present, establishes the market quotation for the time being of Middling Upland cotton. Relative differences of valuation between the grades are determined by the Revision of Quotations Committee. The Committee on Quotations of Futures determines and reports every morning the tone and price of the contract market, for transmission by cable to Europe. Under the inspection system in vogue, with warehouse and inspection certificates in hand, the buyer may borrow money at the bank on these as security. The classification of cotton extends into 33 different grades, which are marvellous to the uninitiated, but simple enough to the practical experts. More than 400,000 bales have been stored in New York at one time. Negotiable warehouse receipts are issued for cotton in store. Delivery of Spot cotton and cotton on contract is guarded by regulations assuring the equity and faithfulness of all parties. Commissions on sale of cotton contracts are paid for by buyer and seller both, at the rate of 12½ cents a bale, when the transaction is not for members of the Exchange. Seven and a half and two and a half cents respectively are the rates for members whose offices are more and less than half a mile from the Exchange, and one cent a bale when one member merely buys or sells for another. In case of time contracts of cotton, either party has the right to call for margins as the variations of the market may warrant. Such margins must be kept good. The hours for business are from 10 A. M. to 3 P. M.; on Mondays between June 1st and October 1st, from 11 A. M. to 3 P. M.; on Saturdays, from 10 A. M. to 12 M. Trading or offering to trade for future delivery of cotton after these hours is punishment by fine, suspension, or expulsion.

All such contracts not made in prescribed hours are invalid. Non-resident visitors and representatives of absent members may be admitted to the floor, but not to trade thereon. Futures are seldom traded in beyond a period of twelve months; more frequently they are for six or eight and often for four months ahead. The largest total of dealings for delivery are for one or two months from date. Agents from New York buy largely from planters on their estates. Direct connection exists between producers and agents on the Exchange. The latter are instructed by clients to sell on time contracts, which are fulfilled by shipments of cotton as the terms of the contract may direct. Future contracts within twelve months are always seller options as to day

TOMPKINS MARKET, THIRD AVENUE, 6TH TO 7TH STREETS.

of month for delivery. Business, as a rule, is heaviest during the months of November and December. Contracts may be bought in or sold out as the interests of the parties may determine. Manufacturing firms and corporations in this country use the future market constantly as a hedge. Orders from Great Britain and the continent of Europe arrive every morning.

The Maritime Association of the Port of New York was organized in 1873, and incorporated in 1874, by special act of the New-York Legislature, to furnish its members with current maritime, mercantile and monetary information in advance of publication; and to promote the maritime interests of the Port of New York. Its membership is about 1,300, comprised of individuals in every business connected with shipping. Among its most active members are marine underwriters. Through it they receive the promptest possible reports of disasters and marine miscellany. The membership embraces all the local companies of underwriters, several of Boston and Philadelphia, and the resident representatives of foreign Lloyds. The scope has been extended beyond the marine department, and now includes financial, mercantile and miscellaneous intelligence; and general business facilities have been added to such a degree that the distinctively shipping interest is now considerably outnumbered. Its usefulness extends beyond New York, the membership including

51

residents of Boston, Philadelphia and other cities.   The executive officers conduct
the details, under direction of an Executive Committee of three, which meets weekly.
This committee reports monthly to a Board of Directors, consisting of fifteen members elected annually ; and the Board, in turn, reports to the Association at the end
of each year.   Members' dues are annually assessed upon the estimated revenue and
expense.   The by-laws allow a range of $15 to $30 for dues, but they have never
exceeded $25 a year.   No attempt is made to accumulate a fund.   New members
purchase the certificate of a deceased or retiring member, entitling the holder to
one card of admission, for his own use only.   The rooms of the Association are
designated the Maritime Exchange, and are in the Produce-Exchange Building, at
Broadway and Beaver Street.   The nominal "change" hours are at 11.30 A. M. and
3 P. M., but there is a general flow of attendance throughout the day, the daily
admissions reaching about 2,500.   It has hundreds of skilful correspondents in every
quarter of the globe, making liberal expenditures for the speediest ways of communication.   It controls lines of special telegraph, by which it reports the approach of
every sail or steam craft from the time it is sighted off Long Island or Sandy Hook.
Its reading-room contains files of newspapers of the principal ports of the world.
Its library is rich in charts and manuals of commercial importance.   Its museum of
commercial specimens and curiosities is a valuable source of instruction.   The Arbitration Committee is empowered by the legislative charter to decide commercial
controversies between the members of the Association and any other person desiring

OYSTER MARKET, WEST STREET, FOOT OF PERRY STREET, NORTH RIVER.

its services, touching any matters in dispute, except titles to real estate in fee or
for life, and its decisions have equal force with the judgments of the Supreme
Court.

   The New-York Board of Trade and Transportation was organized in
September, 1873, and incorporated in 1875.   The name at first was the New-York
Cheap Transportation Association ; and it was changed to the present style in
July, 1877.   The Board is located in the Mail and Express Building at 203
Broadway, and has a membership of 800 firms.   The initiation-fee is $5, and
the annual dues $15.   Its objects are to promote the trade, commerce and manu-
factures of the United States, and especially of the State and city of New York ; to
preserve and circulate valuable and useful information relating thereto ; to study the

workings of the system of transportation, upon which commercial prosperity so largely depends ; to support and promote, or oppose, legislative or other measures affecting these interests ; to facilitate, by arbitration, the adjustments of differences, controversies and misunderstandings between its members and others ; and to advocate such other principles and projects, and do such other things as may conduce to the prosperity and commercial supremacy of the city, State and Nation. Any person, firm or corporation interested in these objects is eligible to membership. The management of the business and property is entrusted to a board of 36 Managing Directors, with whom may be associated for the considerations of public questions, others nominated by affiliated associations. The officers are president, three vice-presidents, secretary and treasurer. The Directors appoint the following standing committees : Executive, Finance, Terminal Facilities, Arbitration and Claims, Railway Transportation, Ocean Transportation, Canal Transportation, and Legislation. The Directors meet monthly, and all members are invited to attend and take part in the discussion of public questions, and vote thereon. It was chiefly through the action of this organization, with the coöperation of the Chamber of Commerce, that the investigation was made into the management of railroads by the Hepburn Senate Committee of the New-York Legislature. The voluminous report, of about 6,000 pages, enlightened the public mind regarding railroads, and brought to light abuses, some of which have been corrected ; and the investigation is now generally recognized to have been an important public service. Many trade and transportation subjects have been elucidated by the Board's discussions. The Board has

been influential in canal improvement, elevator construction, naval militia, opposing unlimited silver coinage and inequitable taxation, and in cases before the Interstate Commerce Commission.

The New-York Mercantile Exchange was organized under the title of the Butter and Cheese Exchange, in 1873. Its objects are declared in its charter to be : to foster trade ; to protect it against unjust or unlawful exactions ; to reform abuses ; to diffuse accurate and reliable information ; to settle differences between members ; to promote among them good fellowship and a more enlarged and friendly intercourse ; and to make provision for the widows and orphans of deceased members. The present spacious and handsome brick and granite five-story building owned by the Exchange, at the corner of Hudson and Harrison Streets, was first occupied April 7, 1886. It has an Exchange-Room, on the second floor,

MERCANTILE EXCHANGE,
HUDSON AND HARRISON STREETS.

seventy feet square and thirty feet high. Fifty offices not used by the Exchange are rented. The Exchange has a membership of 740. The articles mostly dealt in are butter, cheese and eggs. Change hours begin at 10 A. M. There are regular calls for bids, and offerings on the articles mentioned. There is comparatively no speculation, the transactions being bona-fide spot sales. On some days sales are made of 10,000 or 11,000 cases of eggs, containing thirty dozen eggs to the case. $15,000 worth of eggs have been sold within an hour.   Certificates of membership have varied in price from $20 to $400.   The price at which they were originally sold was $25.   The

FULTON MARKET, BEEKMAN, SOUTH AND FULTON STREETS.

annual dues are $15.   Its charter enables it to hold property to the extent of $500,000.

The Coffee Exchange of the City of New York was incorporated originally in 1881, and was re-incorporated by special act of the New-York Legislature in 1885.   The purposes are to provide and maintain a suitable place for the purchase and sale of coffee ; to adjust controversies between its members ; to inculcate and establish just and equitable principles in trade, and uniformity of rules and usages; to adopt standard classifications ; to acquire and disseminate useful business information ; and to promote the trade of the city of New York.   The standard coffee dealt in is called Exchange Standard, No. 7, Low Ordinary.   There are nine types, from prime to good common.   There are warehouses, licensed by the Exchange, for storing the coffee.   Speculation at times is very active, and the fluctuations are great.   The latter have been as much as 12 cents a pound a year.   The Exchange owns property worth about $200,000.   The number of members is 312.   The nominal value of membership is $1,000 ; but certificates of membership have varied in price from $300 to $1,400.   Annual dues are $35.   Change hours are from 11 to 3.   New York, Havre and Hamburg are the principal coffee-markets of the world, and take the lead in making prices.   The leading coffee firms are represented in the membership.   The board-room and offices are at 53 Beaver Street.

The Building-Material Exchange of the City of New York, occupying the floor of the Real-Estate Exchange from 2 to 4 P. M., was incorporated April 27, 1882, to acquire, preserve and disseminate valuable information relating to the building-material interests of the city and surrounding cities, to produce uniformity and certainty in the customs and usages of trade, to settle differences between its members, to diffuse accurate and reliable information among its members

FULTON FISH MARKET, PIERS 22 AND 23, EAST RIVER.

as to the standing of merchants, and to promote an enlarged and friendly intercourse. Any reputable person connected with the business of manufacturing of or dealing in materials used in the construction of buildings is eligible to become a member. The initiation-fee is $100 ; and the annual dues not in excess of $20. The membership is over 300.

The Real-Estate Exchange and Auction-Room, Limited, at 59 to 65 Liberty Street, was incorporated in 1883, under the Limited Liability Act of 1875 of the State of New York. It owns the building occupied by it, which extends for 90 feet on Liberty Street and 90 feet on Liberty Place. It receives an income from rents, exclusive of the auction-room, of about $34,000 a year. The Exchange and auction-room occupies the street floor. It is a centre for dealings in real estate and selling real-estate securities at auction. It lets out stands to auctioneers, and furnishes a general meeting-room for real-estate dealers and brokers. It adjusts controversies and misunderstandings between members ; and furnishes valuable information by collecting statistics in regard to real-estate and building matters, and preparing and keeping files of maps and other records relating to real estate and allied subjects. It obtains and files information and all legislative acts pertaining to the City and State

REAL-ESTATE EXCHANGE, 59 TO 65 LIBERTY STREET.

governments, reports of the various commissioners on taxation, street and other improvements, and awards and assessments affecting realty in the city of New York and vicinity. The capital stock of the company is $500,000, divided in 5,000 shares of $100 each. The membership is 600. The business conducted by its members amounts to about $50,000,000 a year, in sales of real estate by auction, and $50,000,000 a year in private sales between members.

The Real Estate Auctioneers' Association of the City of New York was organized December 23, 1890, by real-estate auctioneers for mutual protection. Its objects are the general welfare of the real-estate auction business ; promoting and facilitating the sale of real-estate and other properties, at auction and otherwise ; the support and advocacy of every movement tending to elevate the real-estate business ; and to inspire a feeling of confidence and mutual reliance between owners of realty, auctioneers and brokers. It commenced business May 1, 1892, at the Real-Estate Sale-Room, at 111 Broadway. Its membership embraces nearly all the local real-estate auctioneers. Legal sales, authorized by the courts of the city and county of New York, are held in the rooms of the association, and conducted under its auspices. The initiation fee is $100 ; the yearly dues $10. Its rooms are in the basement of the Trinity Building, adjoining Trinity Churchyard.

The New York Lumber-Trade Association, with its office at 18 Broadway, was incorporated November 8, 1886. Its objects are to foster trade and commerce, to reform abuses in trade, to protect trade and commerce from unjust and unlawful exactions, to diffuse accurate and reliable information among its members as to the standing of merchants, to acquire, preserve and disseminate valuable information regarding the lumber interests of this and surrounding cities, to produce uniformity in the customs and usages of trade, to settle differences between its members, to establish rules for inspection, and to promote a more large and friendly intercourse between merchants. The membership embraces nearly every firm in the Metropolitan District, including New York, Brooklyn, Long-Island City, Jersey City, Hoboken, and Bergen Point. The special interest now shown in the Association dates from the spring and summer of 1891, when under regulations and boycott from the Lumber-Handlers' and Truck-Drivers' Association, commencing on May 4th, the lumber-dealers united against the movement, and in a great measure closed their yards until June 24th, causing great embarrassment to the building and other trades. The victory of the Lumber Association was complete over the Union men.

The New-York Fruit Exchange, at 78 Park Place, was incorporated May 1, 1885, under the name of the Foreign Fruit Exchange. It is a bureau of statistics of the trade, and a place for the interchange of views of members. The cost of membership is $50, and the annual dues $25. Its membership is 150.

The Hop-Dealers' Exchange, at 45 Pearl Street, was organized in 1890. The object is to facilitate trading in hops, and to gather and disseminate statistics.

The New-York Dry-Goods Exchange was incorporated in April, 1893, and begins under auspicious conditions. It occupies commodious quarters at 78 and 80 Walker Street, in the *Dry-Goods Economist* Building, just a short distance east of Broadway, and within a few minutes' walk from all the great dry-goods houses. It is on the street floor, and has been thoroughly furnished with desks, sample tables, and telephone, telegraph, messenger, typewriter and kindred services, private conference rooms, etc. It was organized to help the out-of-town dry-goods merchant in the purchase of dry goods and in the transaction of his New-York business. Its members, consequently, are out-of-town dry-goods houses who buy in New York, and utilize the Exchange as their sole or partial New-York headquarters. Here, too, they attend to their correspondence, especial facilities being provided for this purpose. By co-operation among themselves, and by means of the special concessions enjoyed by the Exchange, the members are enabled to buy and ship goods to the greatest advantage. The Exchange is also a general dry-goods centre, where buyers meet sellers, a bureau of dry-goods information, and a sample-room maintaining a large collection of samples of current goods in the various dry-goods lines. It is the pioneer Dry-Goods Exchange, and the only institution of its kind in the United States at the present writing. The membership dues are $100 per annum. There is no initiation fee. Its president is Charles T. Root, who, as proprietor of the *Dry-Goods Economist,* has been for a number of years directly interested in all Dry Goods and kindred interests. The secretary is Charles G. Phillips. In the course of time this new Exchange will no doubt become of great usefulness and influence in its important field. Plans are being considered which may lead to the erection of a Dry-Goods Exchange Building for a general headquarters.

Kindred Organizations are noticed in other chapters, such as the American Bankers' Association, the Clearing House, the Underwriters' Association, etc. There are many concerns styled exchanges or boards of trade which are mainly private agencies for making collections and issuing reports on mercantile credits.

THE "FARMERS'" AND THE "WEST WASHINGTON" MARKETS.
WEST STREET, FROM GANSEVOORT TO LITTLE WEST 12TH STREET.

The **Public Markets** yield the city, in rentals and fees, over $300,000 yearly. Each occupant hires space and builds his own stand.   Leases for stands are revocable at the pleasure of the Comptroller of the city at the end of any week.   Rentals are paid every two weeks.   The clerk of the markets and his assistant visit the markets every day to see that the rules and regulations are properly carried out.   A force of from fifty to sixty sweepers and cartmen keep the markets clean, at a cost of $40,000 a year.   The government of the markets is by the City Comptroller.

Washington Market occupies the square between Fulton and Vesey Streets and Washington and West Streets, close to the North River.   If you add together

OLD CLINTON MARKET, WEST AND CANAL STREETS.

the traffics of all the other markets, the sum will not equal that of this enormous mart, which is flanked for squares on either side by the shops and booths of unnumbered merchants.   The great provision district surrounding the market may almost be called the food-centre of the country — so rich the variety, so vast the quantity, of its wares.   On Saturday mornings and evenings, and on the eves of the great festivals, the market is a scene of wonderful animation and interest, crowded by myriads of purchasers, amid the flaring of oil torches, the shouts of the venders, the strange commingled smells of the fruits and meats, and countless other oddities. Meats are sold here at wholesale and retail, and foreign and domestic fruits may be seen in apparently inexhaustible piles.

Fulton Market, at the foot of Fulton Street, dates from the year 1821.   A large conflagration having swept away the buildings on this site, the farmers and marketmen earnestly petitioned that the locality should be taken for a market, and the *Long-Island Star* and other newspapers advocated this measure.   At the present time, the market covers the entire square lying between Fulton and Beekman, Front and South Streets, and has a famous display of comestibles.   Just across the street, and partly overhanging the East River, is the Fulton Fish Market, one of the most interesting localities of the kind in America.

Catharine Market was established in 1786, and named after the wife of Capt. Harman Rutgers, whose mansion stood near by.   Here in old times the negro-slaves from Long Island used to engage in dancing matches with the New-Jersey negroes, the Islanders wearing their hair in plaits bound with tea-lead, and the others having cues covered with dried eel-skin.   In those days the butchers had no carts ; and their patrons, even of the better classes, agreed with Dr. Samuel L. Mitchell that "the man who was ashamed to carry home his dinner from market, did not deserve any."   The fish-market here was for many years the best in America, liberally replenished from the skiffs down the bay and out on the Sound.

West Washington Market, at the foot of West 12th Street, is the landing-place of hundreds of vessels laden with fruit and vegetables, coming from the Southern ports, Bermuda and the West Indies, including during the season 75,000 baskets of peaches daily, and proportionate quantities of potatoes, melons, etc. Here also is the chief wholesale oyster market of the city, where a long pier is bordered by many barges, upon which are the stores of the dealers.

ESSEX MARKET, GRAND AND ESSEX STREETS.

On the other side is the Gansevoort Market, an immense paved area where a thousand market wagons may stand, while the farmers are selling their wares therefrom. The rustic dealers reach the market before midnight, driving in from Long Island, New Jersey, or other agricultural country, and sleep on their wagons until their commerce begins.

Essex Market dates from 1818, when it was founded for the mechanics of the Tenth Ward, and has been rebuilt several times. The steep, rocky hills of this locality long since vanished, and have been replaced by solid blocks of buildings, in the crowded district about the intersection of Essex and Grand Streets.

Centre Market is a ruinous old barrack, in Centre Street, between Grand and Broome Streets. Here may be found the most brilliant and fragrant flowers.

CENTRE MARKET, GRAND AND CENTRE STREETS.

Other Markets are Jefferson, at Greenwich Avenue and Sixth Avenue; Tompkins, on Third Avenue, between 6th and 7th Streets; Union, at Houston and 2d Streets and Avenue D; Clinton, at Spring, Canal, West and Washington Streets; and Central, on East 42d Street, near Park Avenue.

The Manhattan Storage and Warehouse Company owns two of the most notable structures in the city. These are two large and grand warehouses, constructed in an extraordinary manner, especially for the safe-keeping of furniture, trunks, valuables and personal property of every description. One of the warehouses looms up conspicuously near the Grand Central Station, and occupies the entire block on Lexington Avenue, between 41st and 42d Streets. The other, completed in 1892, is of still more striking architecture, and occupies the entire block on Seventh Avenue between 52d and 53d Streets. These buildings may be truthfully described as absolutely fire-proof. Large, massive, substantial, constructed of brick and stone, concrete and iron, they are conceded by all experts who have examined them to be indestructible depositories. Years were devoted to their construction. Each one consists of sections which are separate storage buildings under one roof, having no connection with each other except by the central court. These sections are separated from each other by solid brick walls, from 36 inches to 28 inches thick. Their floors and ceilings are made with cement and concrete arches, formed so as to entirely envelope the rolled-iron floor-beams. All these floors rest upon the heavy division walls, and no cast-iron or other columns are used to support them. Elevators capable of lifting a loaded van weighing 20,000 pounds ascend from the central court to the various floors. The van is drawn upon the elevator and sent up. When it reaches the floor to which it is destined, it is unloaded, and the goods are placed in storage, with only one handling. The engines working these elevators

MANHATTAN STORAGE AND WAREHOUSE CO., 42D STREET AND LEXINGTON AVENUE.

are located in the cellar under the central court. The steam boilers are in vaults under the avenues. These magnificent fire-proof warehouses receive on storage at the lowest current rates, household furniture, oil paintings, engravings, bronzes, statuary, porcelains, heir-looms, plate glass, mirrors, books, *bric-à-brac*, silver-ware, trunks of clothing, pianos, organs, wines, business papers, account-books, and anything else which the owner may desire to be thoroughly secure. The absolutely fire-proof construction of these buildings makes insurance almost unnecessary, but, if desired, it can be effected at the minimum rate. Rooms are rented by the month, at prices varying with the size, from $4 a month and upwards. The company will pack, box and ship furniture, etc., to any part of the world, for which purpose it employs skilled workmen. It will have carpets taken up, cleaned, moth-proofed, and packed for storage. It will also have carpets refitted and laid in houses and apartments. The company owns a large number of furniture and trucking vans built expressly for its business. It uses its own horses, drivers and helpers in the removal of the contents of dwelling-houses, or other prop-erty. A safe-deposit department is in each ware-house, entirely devoted to that purpose. It has large, airy and fine apart-ments for renters of safes to hold interviews, con-duct conversations, examine securities, etc.

MANHATTAN STORAGE AND WAREHOUSE CO., SEVENTH AVENUE, 52D TO 53D STREETS.

Tattersalls (of New York) Limited, — agents : Messrs. Tattersall, London, England, — is one of the most interesting of the many agencies of exchange and sale. New York has been steadily growing in favor as a mart for the highest grade of horses, and the famous sales which have taken place here have included many thousands of valuable harness and saddle horses, usually above the average in quality, and commanding exceptionally good prices.   Under such conditions it is of great importance that sellers and buyers should be brought together under the most favorable circumstances, and this desirable result has been achieved by the institution of Tattersalls, whose building, at 55th Street and Seventh Avenue, is one of the most nearly perfect ever devised for the purpose.   The New-York Tattersalls has already won such an extensive and favorable reputation that it is employed by almost every influential breeder and owner of valuable blooded stock in the country to manage their sales.   It has the advantage of practically unlimited capital, broad experience and admitted ability, and combines with these valuable traits an unquestionable practical knowledge, and a thorough attention to all the details connected with this peculiar and interesting industry.   Tattersalls (of New York) Limited, is the only house in the world connected with the famous Tattersalls in England, and is the only one authorized to use the name.   It has many advantages which could not be found in connection with any purely local institution.   The repository on Seventh Avenue is visited not only by buyers and sellers and lovers of horses, but by many others who are interested to see how a model institution of this kind is carried on, and to observe the wonderful improvements which have been made in the business it represents.   In the details of the building there are many points of interest and suggestiveness.   The sales are largely attended by ladies — frequently the élite of New-York society — who attend without escort, which speaks volumes

TATTERSALLS (OF NEW YORK) LIMITED -- EXTERIOR -- SEVENTH AVENUE AND 55TH STREET.

for the character of the establishment. Sometimes exciting episodes take place, as when horses of famous lineage or achievements are offered for disposal, and scores of the innermost of New-York's exclusives open a spirited bidding.

The entire business is under the active direction of William Easton, Managing Director, who has had a long experience in this branch of industry, to whom is due all the credit of the present successful undertaking, and who has done so much for years past in the interest of owners and breeders of race-horses. In the apt words of a writer in a recent number of *The Spirit of the Times,* the truth of the adage, "nothing succeeds like success," was never more thoroughly shown than in the great work accomplished by William Easton, genial gentleman, man of the world, and consummate master of the art of saying the right thing at the right time, whatever the company, and whatever the occasion. That Mr. Easton labored long and untiringly to attain to his present high rank among the world's few great auctioneers is to his credit ; and if now success succeeds success without apparent effort on his part, let it be remembered that he who planted the twig has earned the right to enjoy the fruit of the tree.

The business of this great company is not confined to New York, but has branched out to Chicago, where a building has been erected larger than that of the New-York Madison-Square Garden. Some idea of the magnitude of this building can be gained when it is mentioned that the same is let at a rental of four thousand dollars a week, for show purposes. The company has also established itself in Cleveland, O., and in Lexington, Ky., where a splendid new building has been erected. Altogether the company has over a million dollars invested in its different establishments.

The *New-York Herald* says of Tattersalls, "People like to go to Tattersalls, not only because of the admirable order and comfort of the place, but also because its reputation for straightforward agency between buyer and seller is firmly established. The attractive interior, easy seats and well-conducted café make it a pleasant place to visit even though one does not intend to buy."

TATTERSALLS (OF NEW YORK) LIMITED -- INTERIOR -- SEVENTH AVENUE AND 55TH STREET.

The Terminal Warehouse Company has, by the erection of its splendid Central Stores at Eleventh Avenue and North River and West 27th and 28th Streets, simplified the problems of storage, shipping, and trans-shipping. The structures occupy the entire block, extending to the water's edge, and consist of 25 storage-buildings, adjoining each other, so that in general appearance they form one vast edifice, 700 feet long, 200 wide, and seven stories high, with cellars under them all. These are the only stores in New York at which railway cars, steamships and trucks are in close communication. The tracks of the New-York Central & Hudson-River Railroad run into the buildings, and there is deep water at the piers at the end.

The cellars are particularly adapted for the storage of wines, liquors, gums and rubber. One store is set apart for cold storage. Any temperature above the zero point is produced by artificial means. Another store, kept at

NEW-YORK CENTRAL & HUDSON-RIVER RAILROAD FREIGHT DEPOT ON HUDSON STREET.

low temperature, is devoted to the storage of furs, rugs and robes. Four others are United-States bonded warehouses. The rest are for general storage purposes. The Central Stores were erected in 1891. The Terminal Warehouse Company also owns the Rossiter Stores, at West 59th and 60th Streets and the North River. Its capital stock is $800,000. The President is William W. Rossiter ; and the Secretary, Barent H. Lane ; and the trustees are, besides the President, H. Walter Webb, W. R. Grace, John E. Searles, B. Aymar Sands, James Stillman and C. W. Hogan.

The Bradstreet Company has achieved a wonderful work in relation to mercantile credit. Society studies into peoples' genealogies and characters ; the Church examines their creeds and practices ; and the mercantile world keenly scrutinizes their methods and responsibility. If these last-named are worthy to establish credit, they must be reported by human action and personal judgment. The Bradstreet Company is practically a clearing-house for all classes of information concerning mercantile affairs and mercantile credit, originated by and intended for business men throughout the world. Its information is obtained from a vast number of sources, competent, trustworthy, and ramifying everywhere, and in such close and confidential touch with The Bradstreet Company that the result is an immense array of digested facts as to business men, containing the detailed histories of more than 1,500,000 firms and individuals in active trade, at home and abroad:

CENTRAL STORES, TERMINAL WAREHOUSE COMPANY.
ELEVENTH AVENUE, NORTH RIVER, 27TH AND 28TH STREETS.

The object of search is the absolute truth as to each mercantile credit, and this is attained by a consensus of many impartial reports from honorable local observers, who also note each passing change, and the advance or falling back of the firm or the individual. With these facts in view, business may be done with intelligence, and thereby with the reasonable assurance of success, and encouragement for the enlargement of enterprise and the development of trade.

The massive quarto volumes of more than 2,300 pages, which it publishes four times in every year, contain the estimated worth and recognized credit, business and address of more than a million of subjects, besides much other valuable information. Bradstreet's offices nearly compass the earth. That its mighty mission has been fulfilled with fidelity as to facts, conservatism as to judgment, and conscientiousness as to details, is proven by a record which challenges the attention and commands the respect of every person who has sought information through its channels or availed himself of its facilities for the investigation of personal credits. The Bradstreet Company is the oldest, and financially the strongest, organization of its kind working in the one interest and under one management. It has wider ramifications, with greater investment of capital, and expending more money every year for the collection and dissemination of information than any similar institution in the world. It has long been recognized and practically endorsed by the highest local courts in the United States.

" BRADSTREET'S," 279, 281 AND 283 BROADWAY, NEAR CHAMBERS STREET.

This company publishes, under the name of *Bradstreet's*, a sixteen-page weekly newspaper, which covers the condition of the crops and markets ; and, dealing as it does, with the news of commerce, finance and manufactures, *Bradstreet's* occupies a unique place. It is impartial and unbiased, and is quoted the world over as an authority. An active department of this company's business is the Bradstreet's bindery, which ranks with the most famous binderies of Paris and London.

The Bradstreet Company has been an important factor in the development of the world's commerce for more than forty years, but its pre-eminence began in 1876, under the presidency of Charles F. Clark. The executive and New-York offices are at 279, 281 and 283 Broadway.

Architectural Features.

Development in Architecture; Notable Office Buildings and Business Blocks.

THE Hollanders, who are so humorously described by Washington Irving in his *History of New York*, would gaze in wonder and amazement, if they were brought back to Mother Earth, at the magnificent edifices which now exist on the island where they once lived. In their day business was transacted, for the most part, in one and two-story buildings; and even as late as a century ago it was customary for men of affairs to carry on their occupations on the first floor, and live on the floor above. When men became opulent, the three-story building made its appearance, the extra story being very generally in the shape of an attic, where the servants and younger members of the household slept, and where old furniture and wearing apparel were stored away. Later on, four-story houses made their appearance, and of these many examples, dating back to the early part of the present century, are still to be found in the lower part of the city. Some of these still remain untouched by the hand of commerce, but they have for the most part succumbed to the inexorable demands of business. In many cases they have been demolished, to make way for larger and finer structures.

It was not until after the civil war that the five-story building made its appearance to any extent. The population of New York then began to increase enormously, and when the higher buildings came, they appeared in the form of flats and tenements. With the crowding of population in the lower wards came a demand for higher structures. This eventuated in the introduction of the elevator, which has revolutionized the construction of buildings in New York, as it has in other cities.

It was the elevator, and that alone, that made possible the enormously high office-buildings that are to be seen in the great business centres of New York to-day. When the seven-story office-building made its appearance, nearly a quarter of a century ago, the popular belief was that the limit in high construction had been reached. But we have since seen scores of eight-story buildings erected, and to-day there are other scores of ten-story buildings in the metropolis. At least a dozen exceed eleven stories in height; some are as high as fifteen and sixteen stories, and *The Sun* has planned a building for its own uses, to be 32 stories high. An important factor in the construction of high office and other buildings in recent years has been the introduction of fire-proofing material. This has made it safe for tenants to occupy the upper stories. Indeed, it is an axiom among real-estate brokers that the upper stories rent most quickly, and at high figures, because the light and ventilation are better than on the lower floors. Another important factor is the introduction, during recent years, of the method of building known as iron or steel skeleton construc-

52

BUSSING HOMESTEAD.   FROM PHOTO BY MISS CATHARINE WEED BARNES.

tion. It was customary with architects, until within three or four years, to draw plans whereby walls of immense thickness were run from the foundation to the roof, to support the general structure. These walls were in some cases required by the Building Department to be three feet or more in thickness at the base, according to the height of the building; so that, under such conditions, the owner of a single lot, no matter how valuable the ground, was unable to put up a very high building, as the two side-walls would take up a space equal to about one-quarter the width of his entire lot, hence, the values of single lots down-town were kept in check by the impossibility of erecting very high structures on them, which consequently decreased their earning power.

The system of iron skeleton construction, however, effected a remarkable change. By its use the thickness of walls was considerably reduced, thus giving a larger floor space. Architects and builders were enabled to plan and erect buildings as high as twelve and thirteen stories on lots from twenty to thirty feet wide, as is noticeable in the Columbia, the Havemeyer, the Home Life and other office-buildings. By this system of construction, iron and steel columns are carried up from foundation to roof, and then covered in

RIVERSIDE DRIVE, CORNER OF 108TH STREET.   RESIDENCE OF SAMUEL G. BAYNE.

with bricks. Thus a carrying capacity equal to that of walls of much greater thickness is produced. When it is considered that unimproved property in the great office section of New-York City has sold as high as $330 per square foot (equivalent to $825,000 per lot of 25 by 100), it will readily be seen that iron skeleton construction will have a very important bearing upon the office-building of the future. A prominent architect says that in a twelve-story building covering two New-York City lots of 25 by 100 feet each, the saving in floor-space effected by means of this new construction amounts to thousands of square feet.

As the office-building has increased in height and size, so has it advanced in the style of its appointments. The modern elevator, with its handsome wrought-iron wall inclosure and its quick speed, has made the former elevator antiquated. Where wood was universally applied, the costliest marbles are now used for stairs, wainscotings and other parts of the interior. Light and ventilation, the lack of which was the bane of the old five-story structures, are now considered all important ; while the toilet arrangements in the modern office-buildings are superior to anything dreamed of a quarter-of-century ago, and are the delight of the tenant, as much as of the sanitary expert and the plumber. Then where woodwork is used for trimming, it is of the finest hardwoods : mahogany, ash, oak, sycamore and bird's-eye maple have replaced the pine and soft lumber used in the older buildings. The architecture of the office-building has also improved. As recently as 1870 the vast majority of such structures displayed plain fronts. Now they illustrate the skill, taste and creative talents of architects, artists, artisans and builders. In this direction New York has made gigantic strides in late years. No metropolis in the civilized world shows such an aggregation of magnificent office-buildings, in the same small area of territory, as are to be found between the Battery and City-Hall Park. Some great office-buildings are being erected up-town.

In the city of New York there are a score of architects whose work has earned for them an international reputation. Then there are hundreds of others whose work is steadily improving the character of the whole city.

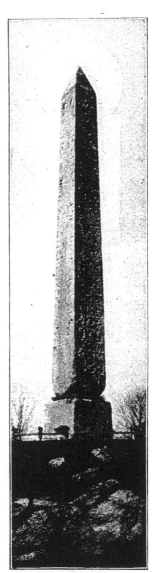

EGYPTIAN OBELISK, CENTRAL PARK.

The **Washington Building** is one of the finest and largest office-buildings in America.   It occupies an historic spot, and also has one of the most conspicuous locations possible, at the foot of Broadway, overlooking Battery Park and the harbor. The location, too, is picturesque and beautiful.   Castle Garden is a few hundred yards away, across the park ; and, since the immigrants are no longer to be landed there, it is to be used as an aquarium.   The Statue of Liberty is seen in the middle distance, and up and down the North and East Rivers and around the Battery there is a never-ending panorama of all sorts of ocean and harbor craft in full view.   From the top of the building the course of the Atlantic "liner" may be easily followed through the Narrows and the lower bay, and out past Sandy Hook.   It faces the Produce Exchange, across Bowling Green.

There was a market stand on the site of the Washington Building in 1656.   The first newspaper issued in New York was printed in the vicinity, in 1693.   It was called *The New-York Gazette,* and it was half as big as a sheet of foolscap.   In 1745 Archibald Kennedy, the eleventh Earl of Cassilis, built a handsome and imposing house, of English model, on the lower portion of the site.   It had a fine entrance, with a carved doorway.   In this house the twelfth Earl of Cassilis was born.   In later years it was occupied by Nathaniel Prime ; and about thirty-five years ago it was converted into a hotel, known as the Washington Hotel.   Adjoining the house, and on land which is a portion of the site of the Washington Building, another handsome residence was built in 1750 by John Watts.   When large entertainments were given by the family in either house, the two buildings were connected by

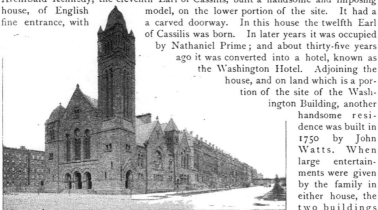

WEST 86TH STREET, EAST OF AMSTERDAM AVENUE.

a bridge in the rear and were thrown into one.   Broad piazzas overlooked the gardens, which extended down to the river front.

The Washington Building was erected by the Washington Building Company, which was organized by Cyrus W. Field, "the father of the Atlantic Cable," and of which he was for a considerable time the principal owner.   It was completed in 1884.   It covers 17,000 square feet of land ; is thirteen stories in height ; and is fire-proof.   The ball of the flag-pole on the dome is higher than the torch of the Statue of Liberty.   The material is brick, with sandstone trimmings and ornamentation.   The architectural treatment of the exterior is pleasing.   The great surface of either front is broken up by arched window-caps, so that no long monotonous lines meet the eye.   The roof is of the Mansard style, two stories in height, and is surmounted by two low towers, one of circular form, on the Battery side, and one of rectangular form, on the Broadway side.   The building contains 348 offices, reached by means of six large elevators.   The tenants and their employees number about 1,500 people.   The officers of the Washington Building Company are : President, T. E. Stillman ; Secretary and Treasurer, William Shillaber.

WASHiNGTON BUILDING.
BROADWAY, BATTERY PLACE AND BATTERY PARK.

The Mills Building, named for the owner, Darius O. Mills, is one of the best known office-buildings on this continent. It is said to be the most costly office-building owned by any individual — its reputed cost being about $3,000,000. At the time of its erection it far outranked any similar structure, and to-day it is seldom equalled. It is exceptionally fortunate in its situation to show off its architectural effects. Its main front is on Broad Street — a street actually broad in fact as well as in name. It has two other street fronts, one on Wall Street, and the other on Exchange Place; the three fronts having distinct entrances, all of which lead into the grand rotunda which leads especially from the Broad-Street entrance. Its Broad-Street side is opposite the main entrance to The Stock Exchange; the Wall-Street entrance is opposite the United-States Sub-Treasury building; and the Exchange-Place entrance is within a stone's throw of the Custom House. It is eleven stories high, and covers about 23,000 square feet of surface area, taking in 11 to 23 Broad

HARLEM RIVER, HIGH BRIDGE AND WASHINGTON BRIDGE, AND THE WATER TOWER.

Street and 35 Wall Street. It has seven excellent elevators. Its tenants number about 800, among them many railroad and other corporations, and some of the most important banking and brokerage houses in "The Street." On the lower floor, on Broad Street, is the St.-Nicholas Bank, and on the eleventh floor, above the offices, is a restaurant. The great feature of the Mills Building, architecturally, is its large open court, which gives admirable light to all its offices. It almost dwarfs the Drexel-Morgan Building, which it adjoins, and which, scarcely a decade ago, was considered one of the finest office-buildings in Wall-Street. Mr. Mills is one of the Californian magnates who came to New York many years ago. He also owns one of the finest buildings in San Francisco, which was completed in 1893, and is also known as the "Mills Building." He is identified with a large number of the greatest of New York's financial, commercial and other institutions. The erection of the Mills Building enhanced the value of all Broad-Street real estate.

MILLS BUILDING.
BROAD STREET, WALL STREET AND EXCHANGE PLACE.

The Potter Building is one of the tallest of the range of office-buildings around Printing-House Square and City-Hall Park, and is of an extraordinary height. It is admirably situated, with its superb frontage of 96 feet on Park Row, 90 feet on Nassau Street, and 150 feet on Beekman Street. It is eleven stories high, and was the first building in the midst of the great newspaper section to be erected to such a height. The Potter Building possesses two unusual features, from a con-structive point of view : first, it was the first building erected in this city which was ornamented elaborately with terra cotta ; second, it was the first in its locality which had its iron-work and stone-work covered with hollow brick, so that the iron and stone are not ex- posed to view or to heat from fire. It is also one of the most sub- stantially constructed and absolutely fire-proof among the office buildings in the metropolis. The owner, ex-Congressman Orlando B. Potter, who is a very large real-estate proprietor, erected it as an investment, and so ordered its construction that it would endure, practically, forever. Mr. Potter has his offices on the eleventh floor. The build-

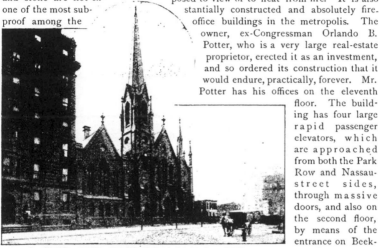

ing has four large rapid passenger elevators, which are approached from both the Park Row and Nassau-street sides, through massive doors, and also on the second floor, by means of the entrance on Beek-man Street. There

WEST 57TH STREET, BETWEEN SEVENTH AND EIGHTH AVENUES.

are 200 offices in the building, including those of several newspaper and periodical publishers, insurance and other companies, lawyers and professional men ; and the tremendous energies concentrated here are felt far and wide.

Among the tenants are *The Press*, the penny Republican newspaper which claims a daily circulation of over 100,000 ; the *New-York Observer*, the first and oldest religious paper ; Otis Brothers & Co., the foremost passenger-elevator builders ; and the Mutual Reserve Fund Life Association, the leading assessment insurance com-pany of the world.

The Potter Building is immediately across the street from the Post Office and the Park-Row front faces City-Hall Park. It is in full view from Broadway. It is within a minute's walk of the Brooklyn Bridge and the Elevated Railroad, and is hedged in on all sides by the daily newspapers. No office building has a choicer location. It is one of the groups of buildings that is forming around the City-Hall Park the grandest architectural square in America.

The really noble proportions of the Potter Building, and the impressive character of its architecture, make of it one of the great and illustrious monuments of commer-cial success in the Empire City. In time, the City-Hall Park will be surrounded with such buildings, the centre of incalculable activities.

POTTER BUILDING.
PARK ROW, NASSAU AND BEEKMAN STREETS.

The Havemeyer Building, on Cortlandt, Church and Dey Streets, is a majestic pile of architecture and pertains to Theodore A. Havemeyer, of the well-known Havemeyer family, whose names are indelibly connected with the sugar industry of this country. It is one of the most perfect office-buildings in existence, and in a location remarkably convenient and central. The structure is fifteen stories high, and the exterior being mainly of a light-colored high-grade Anderson brick, it is a conspicuous feature of lower New York. It is entirely fire-proof, being constructed of stone and brick, steel and wrought-iron, terra cotta and glass. Each floor has its own service of light and heat, water service and mail-chutes ; and all the floors are reached by seven first-class Otis hydraulic elevators. From the roof, which is sheltered by an awning in summer, one overlooks a vast area of Manhattan, the harbor, North River, Staten Island, the Palisades, the Orange Mountains, etc. With three sides free and open to the light and air, the Havemeyer Building has no inside or dark rooms, and its hundreds of tenants enjoy bright, comfortable and cheery offices. The service of janitors, watchmen and other employees of the building is organized with almost military precision, and gives the busy workers in the offices the maximum of security and comfort. The building was designed by George B. Post, and is under the command and direction of William B. Duncan, Jr. The occupants include many eminent business firms and corporations.

ALDRICH COURT, 41 TO 45 BROADWAY, 17 TO 21 TRINITY PLACE.

THE HAVEMEYER BUILDING.
CHURCH STREET, EAST SIDE, FROM DEY TO CORTLANDT STREETS.

The Scott & Bowne Building is one of the most conspicuous structures recently erected in the business portion of New-York City, and occupies a convenient location at the corner of Pearl, New Chambers and Rose Streets. This section has recently taken a rapid stride, and a number of fine large buildings are replacing the old-fashioned houses. This massive twelve-story building, of fire-proof construction, is of high-grade brick, with stone trimmings. It is the home of Scott's Emulsion of Cod-Liver Oil, which is now known the world over, and has become a household preparation. The Scott & Bowne Building is the most complete one for light manufacturing purposes in the city. It is supplied with steam power, electric lights, freight and passenger elevators, and, in fact, every modern convenience that is of advantage to the business man of to-day. The history of the business enterprise which resulted in the erection of the Scott & Bowne Building can be told in a few words. Scott & Bowne acquired among the medical profession the reputation of making the best emulsion of cod-liver oil in the world, and as Scott's Emulsion possesses other qual- ities also that are beneficial to health, it has found a ready market. The active growth of the business has been within the last ten years, dur- ing which time the development has been phenom- enal. Scott's Emulsion is sold throughout four continents, and gives employ- ment to a small army of men.

The Jef- **ferson Market Court House,** on Sixth and Green- wich Avenues, is one of the unique speci- mens of architecture, and especially attracts the atten- tion of those who ride on the Sixth-Avenue Elevated Railroad. The edifice is in the Italian Gothic style of architecture, and is much admired for its unusual pic- turesqueness. Withers was the architect. One of the district courts for petty actions is held here ; and also one of the police courts.

COLUMBIA BUILDING, BROADWAY, MORRIS STREET AND TRINITY PLACE.

SCOTT & BOWNE BUILDING.
ROSE, PEARL AND NEW CHAMBERS STREETS.

The **Morse Building**, at the northeast corner of Nassau and Beekman Streets, is a striking illustration of the architectural beauty of brick and terra cotta. It is a solid, handsome structure, nine stories in height, with a frontage of 85 feet on Nassau Street and 69 feet on Beekman Street. The entrance is on Nassau Street, through a noble semi-circular arch, supported by massive pillars. The windows are deep-set, in brick and terra cotta ornamental work, and the front of the building is divided into three façades by ornamental pilasters. There are semi-circular or flattened curved arches over all the openings. The heavy cornice is of terra cotta, and the roof is covered with tiling of the same material. The floors are constructed of iron beams, supported at both ends on brick-work, and filled in with fire-proof arches. The partitions are also fire-proof. An iron stairway, with marble and slate treads, occupies the center of the building. Immense water tanks, of a total capacity of 4,500 gallons, supplied by Worthington steam-pumps, are at all times connected with fire-hydrants on each floor. Two Otis hydraulic elevators convey visitors to the upper floors, and there is a separate hoisting apparatus for safes and furniture.

ST. PETER'S LUTHERAN CHURCH, LEXINGTON AVENUE AND EAST 46TH STREET.

Steam heat is supplied, but there are also open fire-places in nearly all the rooms. The boiler and smoke-stack are outside of the building, and excessive heat in summer is avoided. The structure is finished in oak, wrought in tasteful designs. The hall floors are of Spanish tiling; those of the offices, of yellow pine. The hardware is bronze. The windows are glazed. with plate glass. The offices are occupied for the most part by lawyers and the agents of manufacturing corporations. The Morse Building was erected, in 1879, by Sidney E. and G. Livingstone Morse, and they and their architects, Silliman & Farnsworth, were influenced in their choice of material by the fact that in the great Boston and Chicago fires brick proved to be the best resistant of heat. The building is now the property of Nathaniel Niles, who purchased it as an investment in 1892. It is considered absolutely fire-proof. Seldom are any of its offices vacant. The location is exceptionally good, being near the Post Office and City-Hall Park, the Third-Avenue Elevated Railroad Station, and the Brooklyn Bridge. Its surrounding buildings on the other three corners are the Vanderbilt Building, Temple Court and the Potter Building.

Temple Court, owned by Eugene Kelly, is a fine office structure, at the southwest corner of Beekman and Nassau Streets. On its site stood the first Clinton Hall. Here, too, was started the National Park Bank.

MORSE BUILDING.
NASSAU STREET, NORTHEAST CORNER OF BEEKMAN STREET.

WEATHER BUREAU -- OBSERVATION STATION, EQUITABLE BUILDING.

Other Notable Office-Buildings are illustrated and described in the insurance, bank and railroad chapters, in connection with the corporations which occupy them. There are also many great and splendid office-buildings like Aldrich Court, Mortimer Building, J. Monroe Taylor Building, Morris Building, Hays Building, Bennett Building, Columbia Building, Wilks Building, etc.

Modern Domestic Architecture, in some of its most interesting developments, is to be seen in upper New-York, in the newer residential quarters, occupied by well-to-do city merchants. Especially is this the case on the West Side, between Central Park and the Hudson River, a region of considerable natural beauty, and sufficiently elevated to be very healthful. Here the usual monotony of long city blocks has been diversified by many skilful devices of the metropolitan architects, revealing the results of careful technical study and wide travel and observation. On these long streets, running from the park to the river, are many picturesquely diversified façades, with suggestions of the Elizabethan, the Gothic, the Romanesque, or a noticeable Nuremberg or Italian feeling, or a pleasing touch of old Flemish or Dutch sentiment. An interesting feature of dwelling architecture has reached a definite and gratifying result in the unique blocks of "King Model Houses," designed and constructed by the famous builder, David H. King, Jr. When the West Side is finished it will be one of the most diversified and agreeable residence quarters in the world. The newer streets also show a pleasing variety of materials used in construction, the dull brownstone or plain brick of former days being now relieved by Caen stone, creamy Ohio sandstone, the many varieties, odd

ARLINGTON HALL, 21 ST. MARK'S PLACE.

TEMPLE COURT.
BEEKMAN STREET, SOUTHWEST CORNER OF NASSAU STREET.

shapes, and peculiar colors of pressed brick and terra cotta, and by fine wrought-iron work. The new churches in upper New York are also of high value from an artistic and æsthetic standpoint, and give a needed distinction to the growing wards.

The American Institute of Architects was formed at New York, in 1836, when there were but about a dozen properly trained architects in the United States.

CENTRAL MARKET, SEVENTH AVENUE AND 48TH STREET.

These met in session in New York, and formed the American Institution of Architects, the predecessor of the present American Institute of Architects, which was chartered in New York in 1857. Ten years later it was found expedient to re-organize the Institute into a group of Chapters, one in New York, and others at Philadelphia, Chicago, Cincinnati, Boston, and other cities. The quarters of the Institute, and of the New-York Chapter, are in a fire-proof building. The presidents of the Institute have been : Richard Upjohn, architect of Trinity Church, from 1867 to 1876 ;

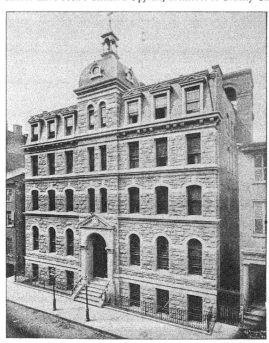

ST. ANTHONY'S MONASTERY, ON THOMPSON STREET, NEAR BLEECKER.

Thomas U. Walter, architect of the United-States Capitol, from 1876 to 1887 ; and Richard M. Hunt. The secretaries have been : R. M. Hunt, Henry Van Brunt, J. W. Ritch, Charles D. Gambrill, F. C. Withers, Russell Sturgis, P. B. Wight, Carl Pfeiffer, A. J. Bloor, C. F. McKim, H. M. Congdon, and Geo. C. Mason, Jr.

New York has always been prominent in the architectural history of America, from its fearless enterprise, vast wealth, and metropolitan position. The foremost architectural school of America is that pertaining to Columbia College, whose Avery Architectural Library, together with the richly endowed Architectural Depart-

BENNETT BUILDiNG.
NASSAU, FULTON AND ANN STREETS.

ment of the Metropolitan Museum, afford admirable opportunities for studies in this noble and beautiful phase of art.

The grand openings made by Union Square, Madison Square, and the triangles or squares formed by the swinging of Broadway diagonally across the island, and then intersecting the main avenues, afford fine opportunities for architectural display which are fast being improved.

Marc Eidlitz & Son, with offices at 487 and 489 Fifth Avenue, and yards and stables at 308 and 310 East 59th Street, is one of the oldest and most favorably known building concerns, having been established in 1854. Its original head was Marc Eidlitz, a man of such energy and diligence that, while still young, contracts involving great responsibility were entrusted to him, and the efficiency with which these were fulfilled soon secured for him an extended list of clients, including many well-known families. Having thus early secured this *clientèle*, the firm has never been obliged to do speculative or the cheaper grade of contract work, and has always taken the stand that thoroughness of construction and attention to detail are not consistent with cheapness. After carrying on the business alone successfully for thirty years, Marc Eidlitz admitted his son, Otto M., to partnership, in 1884; and in 1888, although retaining his interest in the firm, he practically retired, to accept the presidency of the Germania Bank. At the time of his death, in 1892, he was also

president of the Building Trades Club; and had been from its founding a director of the National Association of Builders, representing New-York City in the directorate. He was a warm friend of the working classes, and through his untiring efforts much has been accomplished toward the prevention of strikes and the establishment of a system of arbitration between the mason-builders and the unions of their employees. This system has been in successful operation since 1885. The business is now administered by Otto M. Eidlitz, a civil engineer by profession and education, who has supervised most of the heavy structures erected by the firm. He is assisted by

MARC EIDLITZ & SON, 487 AND 489 FIFTH AVENUE.

his brother, Robert James Eidlitz, an architect, from the Royal Polytechnic, Berlin.

Besides scores of other buildings, the firm points with pride to the following unparalleled list: The Broadway Tabernacle, Church of the Incarnation, Temple Emanu-El, St. Thomas' Church and Parish House, at Mamaroneck; St. Gabriel's Church and Rectory, at New Rochelle; St. George's Clergy House, Home of the Sisters of Bon Secours, the principal buildings of the Presbyterian Hospital, St. Vincent's Hospital, German Hospital, Woman's Hospital, St. Francis Hospital,

THE WESTERN ELECTRIC BUILDING.
GREENWICH AND THAMES STREETS.

German Dispensary, New-York Eye and Ear Infirmary, Isabella Heimath, Loomis Laboratory, Lancashire and Eagle Fire-Insurance Companies' buildings, Gallatin National Bank, National Shoe & Leather Bank, Seamen's Savings Bank, Bank for Savings, Metropolitan Opera House, Eden Musée, Steinway Hall, new part of Astor Library, Deutscher-Verein and Harmonie-Society Club-houses, Astor Building, Schermerhorn Building, Roosevelt Building, Black Building, Western Electric Building, Manhattan Storage and Warehouse Company's Building, and the stores of Arnold, Constable & Co., Lord & Taylor, Le Boutillier Bros., Mitchell Vance Co., Park & Tilford, Scott & Bowne, and others.   Also the residences of Ogden Goelet, Isaac Stern, Robert L. Stuart, J. Pierpont Morgan, Peter Doelger, and Charles Moran; James M. Constable, at Mamaroneck; and Adrian Iselin, Jr., at New Rochelle.

Jer. T. Smith, recently at 11 Pine Street, but now in his own newly erected building on 23d Street, at the beginning of Madison Avenue, and just opposite his recent great masterpiece, the Metropolitan Life Building, — has for many years been known as one of the leading builders and contractors of the Empire City. In mastering all the problems of this difficult art he has shown wonderful aptitude and skill, and his structures stand as permanent witnesses of high attainment.   He was prominently engaged in the construction of the United-States Post-Office, at New York; and of the hardly less enormous structure owned and occupied by the Equitable Life Assurance Society.   He constructed the National Park Bank build-

JER. T. SMITH, AND MENLO PARK CERAMIC WORKS, 23D STREET, OPPOSITE MADISON AVENUE.

ing, on Broadway, near Fulton Street; the Drexel Building and the Leather Manufacturers' Bank, at the corner of Wall and Broad Streets; the Market and Fulton Bank, at Fulton and Gold Streets; the H. B. Claflin storehouses, and many other mercantile structures.   Many other notable works in this line have been carried through successfully by this well-known builder, whose latest conspicuous construction was the building of the Metropolitan Life-Insurance Company, on Madison Square.

Jer. T. Smith is also known as the owner and developer of the Menlo Park

JEFFERSON-MARKET POLICE COURT.
SIXTH AVENUE, WEST SIDE, FROM GREENWICH AVENUE TO 10TH STREET.

Ceramic Works, founded in 1888, with their manufactory at Menlo Park, New Jersey, and their offices and ware-rooms at 16 East 23d Street, New York. These works produce a new kind of tiling and wainscoting, and similar goods, of peculiar beauty, and endowed with special merits in various ways. No less than 90,000 square feet of this material were used in the Metropolitan Life Building. The beautiful vestibule and loggia of William Rockefeller's residence at Tarrytown were finished with modelled faience resembling carved onyx; and the same rich material adorns the vestibule of George M. Olcott's house, on Brooklyn Heights. The works are now also producing modelled faience mantels, in various colorings, and of much beauty. This valuable new ceramic ware has been received with great favor by many architects and builders, and at times the capacity of the works is tasked to the utmost. For many purposes connected with the constructive arts the products of the Menlo Park Works are of unrivalled merit, and command a steadily increasing sale.

FOURTH AVENUE AND MURRAY HILL HOTEL, FROM GRAND CENTRAL STATION.

The successive eras of New-York architecture have left but little individual impress upon the city. The Dutch and colonial edifices, memorials of vanished civilizations, have vanished before the spirit of change, and left almost no trace behind. The brownstone and iron-front period is still much in evidence, by its surviving structures, but these, too, are passing away, and with them the reason for John Ruskin's reproaches for Manhattan architecture. New York rebuilds itself every decade, and the city of the twentieth century will be one of the world's wonders. It may not be classical in its outward look, and it surely will lack the uniformity of the Parisian boulevards, but for comfort, health and security, and for perfect business efficiency and domestic comfort, the buildings of the Empire City will have no rivals in all the world.

THE BOWERY.
LOOKING NORTH FROM CANAL STREET.

MORTIMER BUILDING.
WALL STREET, SOUTH SIDE, CORNER OF NEW STREET.

Notable Retail Establishments.

Interesting and Prominent Retail Concerns, Nearly all Being Unquestioned Leading Houses in Their Respective Lines.

ALL AMERICA goes to New York for its shopping, when it can. Here you can find the perfection of everything, from the brightest of cambric needles and the most delicious of crumpets, up to the bridal *trousseau* for a daughter of the Winthrops or the Washingtons, or a line of ocean-steamships with their entire outfit. Humanity enjoys seeing the products of mankind, and the shops of New York, the resplendent lines of retail stores sweeping around Union and Madison Squares and along the intervening and branching streets, these are always fascinating, alluring, irresistible. What cannot be found here, is not to be found in any shopping district anywhere. The brightness of Broadway, the vivacity of lower Fifth Avenue, the sparkle of 23d Street, are made up of the splendid temptations of the shop windows, and the groups of charming people who linger about them spell-bound. Ill fares the rural or provincial purse whose owner ventures before these attractive windows, extending for miles on miles, ever diversified and varied ; a perfect kaleidoscope of silks and velvets, laces and jewels, rich books and music, paintings and statuary, rifles and racquets, confections and amber-like bottles, *cloisonnée* and cut-glass, everything imaginable for use or luxury, massed in perfect affluence, and displayed in the most attractive way possible. What are the Parisian boulevards, or even Regent Street, to this magnificent panorama of mercantile display, reaching from the Washington Arch to Bryant Park? In harmony with the growth of the city from the simple Dutch village, the tastes and requirements of a cosmopolitan population of about 3,000,000 people who reside within or around the present city, have developed so that they demand and seem to be able and willing to pay for the best of everything that can be produced in this or any other country.

It should be borne in mind that the great and famous places of business, as a rule, are the best places to do shopping : their immense establishments offering the greatest varieties, the best of service, the most reliable goods, and withal a responsibility that is a consideration to the stranger buying in a strange city.

The houses mentioned in this book have been selected with especial care ; the aim of the publisher being to insert notices only of establishments which are known to be absolutely of the highest rank in their respective lines.

Arnold, Constable & Company's dry-goods establishment is one of the oldest and best-known in the United States. It is one of the business houses which bring credit to the mercantile world of this country. Its record for conservative enterprise, extreme integrity, and unquestioned reliability stands untarnished.

The firm occupies a huge and magnificent storehouse, covering very nearly an acre of ground, fronting on Broadway and Fifth Avenue ; it also covers the whole of 19th Street, between these two great arteries of the city ; then by an extension through to 18th Street, it commands an entrance to that street, and secures for the firm one of the best-lighted and best-ventilated buildings in the city, which occupies more than half of the big city block. The building is seven stories in height, is of iron, marble and brick, and the newer portions are fire-proof. It is one of the prominent features of business architecture in the up-town section.

The house of Arnold, Constable & Co. was founded by A. Arnold, in 1827, nearly three generations ago. He began business just west of the corner of Canal and Mercer Streets, and in course of time removed to larger quarters on Canal Street, three doors east of Mercer Street, gradually purchasing all of the lots bounded by Canal, Mercer and Howard Streets, with a frontage of 75 feet on Canal Street, and 100 feet on Howard Street. He built for the firm in 1857 a store then celebrated for the attention paid to its light, and to all the wants of a growing business. Here the panic of 1857 passed over them, leaving them still anxious to enlarge their trade. Ten years later, the growth of the city northward warned Mr. Arnold that the retail trade would soon leave Canal Street. After first purchasing on Union Square, he determined to locate on Broadway and 19th Street; and purchased of Mr. Hoyt the ground on which part of their retail store now stands, and which was then covered with two-story-and-a-half brick buildings. Moving their retail business into their new quarters in 1869, the transfer had hardly been accomplished when it was discovered that more room was a necessity. Two stories were added to the original building, and an extension fifty feet wide was erected on 19th Street. Then came a demand for more room for the wholesale department, which was still located on Canal Street, and, notwithstanding most of the great hotels were below Bond Street, it was determined to re-unite the business under one roof, and to purchase the property on Fifth Avenue surrounded by the dwellings of the Belmonts, Parishes, Marshall O. Roberts, and dozens of New York's wealthiest families. This was accomplished in 1877, just half a century after the business had been started in Canal Street. A. Arnold died before the building was completed ; and James M. Constable, who had been taken into partnership in 1842, became the senior member, and still continues at the head of the firm, which now consists of James M. Constable, Frederick A. Constable, and Hicks Arnold, a nephew of the founder of the house. It is one of the few dry-goods stores which have not been converted into a "Bazaar." The business is divided into three principal divisions : dry-goods, carpets, and upholstery. The first floor of the big retail store is devoted to the display of silks, dress goods, laces, hosiery, linens, flannels, etc. The second floor is alloted to ladies' and children's garments, furs, dresses, shawls, and mourning goods. Upholstery, carpets, and Oriental rugs occupy the third, fourth and fifth floors. The display on all these floors is a veritable art exhibit, made possible by the extensive foreign connections of the firm, and the large staff of buyers in the employ of the house, who are constantly seeking in every corner of the globe for novelties. The sixth and seventh floors are used for manufacturing purposes. The 18th-Street extension is a portion of the retail store, and the two lower stories open into the main building through broad arches. The upper stories of the 18th-Street building are assigned to the manufacturing departments. The wholesale section of the business is located in the Fifth-Avenue part of the building, with the general offices on the second floor ; and a large stock of goods is stored in the firm's warehouse at Ninth Avenue and 16th Street. Arnold, Constable & Co. are known all over the country. Their travelling salesmen visit every section. Their Paris house is at 21 Rue d' Hauteville ; their Lyons house, at 8 Quai St. Clair.

ARNOLD, CONSTABLE & CO.'S DRY-GOODS ESTABLISHMENT.
BROADWAY, 19TH STREET AND FIFTH AVENUE.

The Gorham Manufacturing Company, at the northwest corner of Broadway and 19th Street, makes of its silverware and ecclesiastical metal work a perpetual exhibition of American art.   There is not a lover of colors, gems, or graceful forms that it may not vividly impress.   The four corners of Broadway and 19th Street are all specially notable : on one corner is the ancient dwelling-house of the Goelet family, which is, with its surrounding grounds, a curious spectacle of Broadway ; on another, the palatial carpet warehouse of W. & J. Sloane ; on another, the great dry-goods house of Arnold, Constable & Co. ; and on the other, the grand establishment of the Gorham Company, the finest in its line in the world.

The Gorham factory is at Elmwood, Providence, R. I., in model buildings, covering five and a half acres, comprising offices, a library and a museum, besides an infinity of rooms that the silver enters in the form of blocks called bricks and quits in the form of exquisite objects of art encased in artistic boxes.   There are made the designs, which are original as well for the slight edge ornament of a card case as for Cluny, Medici, Fontainebleau and Nuremberg spoons that demand a patent.   There are made beside masterpieces of silversmiths, memorial brasses, mural tablets, altar railings, busts, statuettes, reliefs, plaques, in bronze ; and ornaments of chapels and cathedrals.

In New York, for more than a quarter of a century, all these marvels of handicraft that the government of France rewarded with its highest award at the Exposition Universelle of 1889 have been famous.   In New York the mark of the Gorham Manufacturing Company has the authority which the ancient official poinçon has in France.   It is the mark of objects of art indisputably perfect.   Their form is gracefulness itself ; their decoration has impeccable tact and taste.   They are works of artists, made for the view and touch of artists.   In the warerooms, from the glass-covered cases where they are displayed, come a gaiety, a harmony of forms and colors that enchant.   On the first floor, at the right as one enters, is the silver-plated ware which is exclusively tableware.   At the rear are the large pieces — the magnificent punch bowls, carved in representation of vine leaves, grapes, Bacchanals, or nymphs and satyrs, or sculptured with arabesques in relief, or colored, as engravings and etchings are colored, with hatches, in admirable pictures of sea and shells ; silver and silver-gilt mounted crystals and cut-glass ; loving-cups ; presentation and memorial works.   At the left are the goblets, the tea sets, the coffee sets, the toilet sets, the silver-mounted glassware, porcelain and faience.   The shelves are of mahogany, glass and mirrors, the boxes are of leather, silk, velvet and plush. In the cases which, placed at right angles with the shelves on the walls, form compartments, and in the cases in the middle of the room, are clocks, watches, jewelry, table sets, silver fashioned for every conceivable use, designed for great celebrations and festivals, desk ornaments, favors for the German, trifles that have required marvels of ingenuity, skill and artistic feeling.   Here are princely gifts accessible to every purse.   Here are the goblets, beakers, basins, amphoras, flowered candelabra of the classic Florentine workshops, and in greater quantity and variety.

On the second floor are the samples, models and goods of the wholesale department.   Then there are, at work, the engravers of initials and other marks required by buyers.   There is a department specially devoted to the business done with hotels.   There are floors with stained-glass windows, and rooms bathed in a light like a chapel for lecturns, with tablets, crosses and chalices.   One large cross of bronze is studded with passion-flowers in relief.   The figures of the lecturns are angels, eagles, annunciation-lilies.   There are all the ecclesiastical art-works.   In buying them, or any object with the Gorham stamp, one buys works truly precious.

THE GORHAM MANUFACTURING COMPANY.
BROADWAY, NORTHWEST CORNER OF 19TH STREET.

Lord & Taylor, wholesale and retail dry-goods merchants, are one of the oldest, largest, and most substantial of New-York business houses. They have two very large stores : one at Broadway and 20th Street, which serves the wants of the wealthy and middle classes, and one at Grand and Chrystie Streets, which is a favorite shopping-place for the enormous population of the East Side. The house is one of the oldest in the dry-goods trade. It was established about 1830 by Samuel Lord, a native of Saddleworth, England, and George W. Taylor, of New York. The original establishment was down-town, in Catharine Street ; and for many years previous to 1871 the principal store was at the corner of Broadway and Grand Street. In the course of time Mr. Taylor retired, and James S. Taylor was admitted to partnership with Mr. Lord.

LORD & TAYLOR, ORIGINAL STORE, CATHARINE STREET.

They were succeeded by John T. Lord, a son of the original senior partner, and John S. Lyle, and these in turn by G. W. T. Lord, Samuel Lord, Jr., and Edward P. Hatch. The firm-name has always been the same, not having been changed in upwards of sixty years, a record not frequent in this country. During that long period the development of the busi- ness has been marvellous, until the small es- tablishment of the early thirties has expanded, by natural growth, into one of the great mer- cantile enterprises of the metropolis. · The principal store is at Broadway and 20th Street. It is of iron, five stories in height, and measures 100 feet on Broadway and 175 feet on 20th Street. It is equipped with Otis elevators, Worthington pumps, and other modern conveniences. A feature of the construc- tion, and a good one from an archi- tectural point of view is a fine large entrance- arch in the centre of the Broadway façade, which extends through two stories. The lower

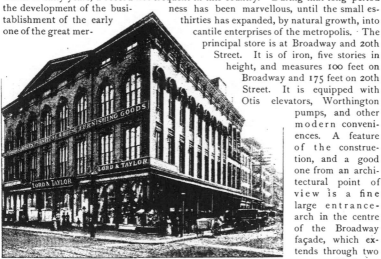

LORD & TAYLOR, GRAND AND CHRYSTIE STREETS.

story is particularly light and bright, the windows on either front being large, and the ceiling high. Silk and dress goods occupy a large portion of the space on this floor, and the departments of hosiery, linens, small wares and men's furnishing goods are also located there. In the second story, which is reached by an elevator, as well as by broad stairways, there are furs, costumes, underwear and cloaks, as well as an extensive millinery department, which the house makes a prominent feature. The third story is devoted to carpets, rugs, upholsteries and Oriental goods. The whole-sale department occupies the fourth and a portion of the fifth stories. The space occupied by this department gives no indication of the volume of business, as it is given up to samples rather than to stock. The rest of the fifth story is given to the manu-facturing department, in which the famous Lord & Taylor costumes are made. The house removed to the present store, which was built for it, in 1871. The up-town establishment is purely a dry-goods store. The Grand-Street house, which is the larger of the two, is not only a dry-goods store, but also, in a sense, a bazaar. The firm-name of Lord & Taylor has been held in high esteem from the outset, and the annual sales of the two stores reach figures away up into the millions of dollars.

Visitors to New York City always find it of great interest to go through the Lord & Taylor establishments. They are always wel-come there, whether patrons or not; they see the newest productions of the world in these lines of goods, and they are waited upon by an attentive and agreeable corps of employees. This house is one which adds greatly to the credit of the mer-cantile firms of New York City.

LORD & TAYLOR, BROADWAY, SOUTHWEST CORNER OF 20TH STREET.

Gilman Collamore & Co., on Fifth Avenue, at the northwest corner of 30th Street, have a veritable art exhibition in their usual display of fancy glass-ware and fine china.   The Collamore name is indelibly identified with the past traditions of this trade, and in houses of wealth and taste it seldom happens that there are not wares obtained through Collamore's.   The firm occupies a handsome sandstone and brick building, which has a frontage of 40 feet on Fifth Avenue, and a depth of 125 feet.   Their grand display-rooms are so laid out and arranged as to promote the artistic effect of the exceedingly choice stock of goods.   A specialty is made of secur- ing the richest and handsomest novelties in glass and china that Europe produces. Its buyers are instructed to look for novelties, rather than to attend to the purchase of staple goods.   The house imports heavily of Sévres, Royal Dresden and Royal Berlin wares, and of the products of the best English and German factories.   A large part of its imported goods cannot be found in any other house in America.   The firm looks for its support to people of wealth, of good taste and refinement, and therefore handles nothing but expensive goods.   Its methods are progressive and brilliant, and at the same time conservative.   It will search all Europe for a novelty of real artistic value, and then will allow that article to make its own appeal to the

purchaser by vir- tue of its place in the general dis- play of stock. The house has been in existence for thirty years, and has always maintained itself at the head and front of its line of trade by virtue of the artistic ex- cellence of its goods.   It has been in its pres- ent location for about two years. Mr.   Collamore, the founder, died some years ago. The firm at pres- ent consists of John J. Gibbons and Timothy J. Martin.   The for- mer pays special attention to pur- chasing, and makes trips to Europe frequently

GILMAN COLLAMORE & CO., FIFTH AVENUE, NORTHWEST CORNER 80TH STREET.

to that end.   Mr. Martin devotes himself to the display and sale of goods.   There is no choicer or more precious stock in this line in America, none more delicately exhibited.

W. & J. Sloane, at the southeast corner of Broadway and 19th Street, whole-sale and retail dealers in carpets, Oriental rugs, lace curtains and upholstery materials, have fifty years of celebrity. In 1843 their house was on Broadway, oppo-site the City Hall ; and, following the march of business up-town, it is at present, as it was then, the centre of the retail furnishing district. The building, of stone, brick and iron, in six stories above and one under the sidewalk, a solid, graceful edifice, is scarcely vast enough for the display of the large stock dealt in by W. & J. Sloane. They con-trol the product of a great number of domestic and for-eign carpet-mills, and moreover im-port the best work of other mills of Germany, Switzer-land, Scotland, England and France. Their goods are in nearly all the carpet and upholstery stores of the country, and have at retail sale a proportionate pat-ronage. Having special advantages, W. & J. Sloane are enabled to offer the

W. & J. SLOANE, BROADWAY, SOUTHEAST CORNER 19TH STREET.

largest assortment of goods, from the cheapest to the most expensive fabric, that exists anywhere. In addition to the large stock of domestic goods, their representa-tives are sent several times every year to the principal markets of Europe and Asia, and they procure all that may by any class reasonably be desired in English and French, Axminster and Aubusson carpets, antique and modern Oriental rugs, China and Japan mattings, and other fabrics. There, also, are found carpets made in special designs to conform to the prevailing styles of interior decoration, and full stocks of conventional patterns. There are upholstery materials for furniture and wall-cover-ing, and window hangings, in the most delicate and beautiful fabrics. There can be found all the luxury which art can give, and a vast assortment of graceful interior deco-rations that may be obtained with limited expenditure. As their retail trade extends throughout the length and breadth of this country, many avail themselves of the privilege of sending for samples, to make selections from. The house of W. & J. Sloane stands indisputably at the head of the carpet and rug industry of this country.

James McCreery & Co., one of the most highly esteemed dry-goods establishments in America, occupy a very large structure on Broadway, at the northwest
corner of 11th Street. The locality is of considerable interest, as Grace Church
and Grace Parish House are almost opposite, just a little below, at the bend in
Broadway. The building is five stories high, built of iron, and is one of the notable
business structures of the city. It measures 75 feet on Broadway, and 225 feet on
11th Street, with a large extension in the rear, reaching toward 12th Street.

The business of this firm is one of the oldest in the dry-goods trade. It was
founded half a century ago, in Canal Street, by Ubsdell & Pearson. Then the firm

JAMES McCREERY & CO., BROADWAY, NORTHWEST CORNER OF 11TH STREET.

became Ubsdell, Pearson & Lake; then Lake & McCreery; and about twenty-five
years ago, James McCreery & Co. The building occupied by the present firm
was erected by its predecessor, and was sold to the Methodist Book Concern just
as James McCreery & Co. moved into it. For twenty years the dry-goods firm was
the tenant of the Book Concern, and occupied a greater part of the building. In
1889 it bought back the property, and now occupies all the five stories, as well as
the basement. The establishment is a dry-goods store, pure and simple, as distin-

guished from the modern bazaar, in which all sorts of things are sold ; and is one of the very few large dry-goods houses in the city which have held closely to their own line of trade. It is preëminently the place at which ladies find materials for dresses, whether they desire simple house-gowns or full wedding *trousseaux.* While the house carries full lines of all staple goods, it pays special attention to the choicest fabrics of rare designs. It has a resident buyer in Europe, whose sole business is to purchase novelties in styles and fabrics, especially in silks and woolens. While it carries goods of all reliable grades, at the lowest practicable prices, the great volume of its trade is in handsome, elegant goods, both staples and novelties. The lower story of the building is peculiarly adapted to the proper display of such materials. There is bright sunlight in the windows of the Broadway and 11th-Street fronts, and

SILK DEPARTMENT OF JAMES McCREERY & CO., BROADWAY AND 11TH STREET.

direct light on the northerly side of the extension toward 12th Street. Besides, the ceiling is nearly 20 feet high, and this of itself gives a bright and airy appearance to the store.

The retail silk department is one of the prominent features of this establishment, and its arrangements are specially good for the most advantageous display of the stock. The other departments have, however, so increased of late years as to make the store a place of very many attractions, either to the cultivated citizen of New York, or to the visitor within the gates of the metropolis.

The trade of James McCreery & Co. is wholesale as well as retail. In the wholesale branch it is confined solely to novelties in styles and fabrics, and extends to every city in the United States. No house in America carries a finer or more extensive line of dress materials of every grade and price that can be considered thoroughly reliable. A peculiarity of the management of the house is that its employees are assured of practically permanent positions, dependent only on good behavior. There are clerks and salesmen now in the house who have been in the service of the firm for twenty years or more, some having begun service with Ubsdell & Pearson, the founders of the house, a full generation ago.

The management of the house is still directly in the hands of the firm, composed of James McCreery, J. C. McCreery, and Thomas Rosevear, all of whom pay close attention to the multitude of details relating to their separate departments.

Pottier, Stymus & Company occupy an extensive, well-built and well-equipped manufactory at 375 and 377 Lexington Avenue, at the northeast corner of 41st Street. The firm is well known, and stands clearly at the head in its line of business. They have a world-wide reputation for the superior grades of furniture and wood-work which they manufacture, as well as for their artistic conceptions in interior decorations and papier-maché work. The articles that they manufacture are from special designs of their own, or from the designs of architects. Their factory and warerooms are the most complete of their kind in the United States. They are built of brick and iron, and are entirely fire-proof. They are five stories high, well lighted, and equipped with unsurpassed facilities for their high grade of work. Many of the richest and finest private residences in America have been furnished by this house. Among these are the homes of Henry M. Flagler, William Rockefeller, J. A. Bostwick, John D. Archbold and Fred T. Steinway, of New-York City; George Westinghouse, Jr., and Robert Pitcairn, of Pittsburg; William Williams, Myron P. Bush and William G. Fargo, of Buffalo; and Mark Hopkins, Leland Stanford, James Flood, Charles Crocker and Henry J. Crocker, of San Francisco. The company has also enjoyed a large business among the first-class hotels, like the palatial Savoy, the superb Plaza, and the world-famous Fifth-Avenue. In Astor's magnificent new Hotel Waldorf they furnished the celebrated State Apartments, which were occupied by the Duke of Veragua in 1893; also the Renaissance, Colonial, Empire and other suites, which are regarded as the most sumptuously furnished and decorated hotel rooms on either continent. Much of the finest work in the gorgeous Ponce de Leon Hotel, at St. Augustine, Florida, came from this wonderful repository and manufactory. Among famous works executed by this house in Washington, were the Cabinet Room of the White House; the Treasury Department, under the administration of Salmon P. Chase; and the Navy Department, under the administration of Gideon Welles, whose residence was also exquisitely furnished by the same house. The choice art-products of Pottier, Stymus & Co., in furniture and decorations, are manufactured under their own vigilant direction, from the best and most durable materials, and by the most skilful artists and artisans. The results are masterpieces, both in substance and form, in most graceful designs, and with rich sculpturesque adornments. All that refined art can do toward the improvement and beautifying of the home is shown in these warerooms. There are no stock patterns, duplicated by myriads in hall and cottage all over the land, but individual creations, unhackneyed, special, unique, and worthy to endure for centuries as noble heirlooms. The foremost point in interior decoration is to have a firm like Pottier, Stymus & Co. attend to all parts of the work, so that the whole may be harmonious.

This business was founded in the year 1856, by Auguste Pottier and William P. Stymus, and for more than a third of a century it advanced slowly and surely, along with the development of true art-ideas among the American people. In the year 1888 the Pottier & Stymus Manufacturing Co. sold out its stock, plant and models to a new coöperative association made up of the prominent men of the old company. It was entitled Pottier, Stymus & Co., and its officers were Adrien Pottier (nephew of Auguste), President; William P. Stymus, Jr., Vice-President; Frank R. Pentz, Treasurer; and William P. Stymus (one of the founders of the original house), Secretary. Adrien Pottier died in 1891. William P. Stymus, Jr., is President; Frank R. Pentz, Vice-President and Treasurer; and William P. Stymus, Secretary.

As the American people become wealthier and more cultivated, there arises a need of such an old, experienced and successful house as Pottier, Stymus & Co.

POTTIER, STYMUS & COMPANY.
LEXINGTON AVENUE, NORTHEAST CORNER 41ST STREET.

Best & Co.'s Liliputian Bazaar is one of the unique business establishments of New York. It occupies the large building at 60 to 62 West 23d Street, and extending through the block, and numbered 49 to 51 West 22d Street. The name of the establishment is significant, as the business is that of fitting children with clothes, shoes, hats, outer garments, and even with the means of amusing themselves. Best & Co. begin with the infants, and their customers do not outgrow the facilities of the establishment until they become men and women. Not only is the Liliputian Bazaar the only establishment of its kind in New York, but it is the largest and most comprehensive one in the world. Its success and in fact its existence illustrate the change in the method of providing children with clothing that has been going on for the past ten years.

As much attention is paid to-day to the artistic appearance of a child's outfit as there is to that of a society belle, and to Best & Co. in considerable measure is due the credit of developing this feeling. The firm manufactures a large proportion of its own goods and supervises the production of its own designs. The lower floor of its double store is devoted to the boys' outfitting department. The second is set apart for the girls' department. The third story is given up to a force of clerks, salesmen and packers, who attend to the mail orders, an important branch of the business, as Best & Co. make shopping for children an easy matter for people who live at a distance. The upper stories are devoted to designing and manufacturing. The growth of the Liliputian Bazaar has been rapid.

BEST & CO., LILIPUTIAN BAZAAR, 60 AND 62 WEST 23D STREET.

Best & Co. began the business of supplying clothing for infants in a small way, twelve years ago. Their store was on Sixth Avenue, between 19th and 20th Streets. In 1882 they removed to 60 West 23d Street, and were among the first of the business men who invaded what was then a residence section of the city. Since then, the fourth building necessary to form a solid square, extending from street to street, has been annexed, to obtain room absolutely needed by the establishment.

Lewis & Conger, at 130 and 132 West 42d Street, between Broadway and Sixth Avenue, are said to be the oldest firm of house-furnishers in the United States. The business was established away back in 1835, by John M. and Cornelius A. Berrian, whose store was at 601 Broadway, near Houston Street. J. & C. Berrian continued the trade here until 1861, when it was taken by Henry H. Casey, to whom the present firm succeeded in 1868. Two years later, following the course of trade, they moved to the Armory Building, at the junction of Broadway, Sixth Avenue and 35th Street, and here they remained until 1891, when the *New-York Herald* took possession of the site. At that time Lewis & Conger bought the two houses at 130 and 132 West 42d Street, which were extensively remodelled, to suit

the needs of their business. As thus practically rebuilt, the new home of the company is a handsome four-story and basement structure, one of the best-arranged for its purposes in the country. The immense show-windows are of heavy plate-glass, the framework being of steel and decorated in white and gold. The main floor covers an area of nearly 5,000 square feet, with finishings of oak and black walnut, a row of substantial columns down the middle, and lines of handsome chandeliers on either side. The floors above, and

LEWIS & CONGER, 130 AND 132 WEST 42D STREET.

the spacious basement and vault, are used for storing the goods. The stock is attractively exhibited on walnut stands, cabinets, counters and shelves on the main floor, and includes numberless articles and varieties used in house-furnishing,—china of all grades; glass, from the ordinary pressed ware to the most exquisite American or French cut goods; tin-ware enough for an empire; cutlery in a thousand forms; and a vast number of other articles used in the comfortable homes of the American people. In many respects it is the foremost house-furnishing goods establishment; the stock being the largest and of the greatest variety. Its patrons include not merely families of New-York City, but are scattered throughout the villages and towns for many miles around, the firm of Lewis & Conger being a familiar name in thousands of households.

THE BOWERY, LOOKING NORTHWARD FROM GRAND STREET.

GRAND STREET, LOOKING EASTWARD FROM THE BOWERY.

F. A. O. Schwarz, in Union Square, is well-known as the most notable dealer in toys in New-York City, where during nearly a quarter of a century he has been diligently building up a great business. He entered this interesting department of trade in the year 1856, with his elder brother Henry, in the city of Baltimore. In 1870, he left the Monumental City and came to New York, where he opened a store at 765 Broadway, nearly opposite A. T. Stewart's retail store. The demands

of business were so active and increasing that ten years later he was compelled to seek more spacious quarters, in his present commodious building. This is at 42 East 14th Street, opposite Union Square, between Broadway and University Place, and extending in the rear to 39, 41 and 43 East 13th Street, and on the side to 77 University Place. The entrance is almost opposite the Lincoln statue. Henry F. Schwarz, the son of the founder of the New-York house, after devoting several years to studying and mastering the business, became a partner in 1891. The stores and the entire buildings of the establishment are filled in autumn with holiday goods in almost infinite variety, and show a much larger stock of toys, from the cheapest to the special high grades, than any other establishment. The motto of the company is: "To offer the best goods, at most reasonable prices, with polite attention."

There are four brothers by the name of Schwarz, having the largest toy stores in New York, Boston, Philadelphia and Baltimore, and by combining their orders they give larger orders than any other toy house in existence, and obtain lower prices, buying also only for strict cash. Many articles in the toy line are made in the United States, under their special direction; but the larger number are made in Europe, where manufacturers are continually at work preparing articles specially designed by Mr. Schwarz. During the last half-century this trade has developed wonderfully in taste for finer and more expensive goods.

F. A. O. SCHWARZ, 42 EAST 14TH STREET,
UNION SQUARE.

Union Square at the vicinity of the Schwarz establishment is conspicuously prominent and interesting. Just here the Broadway cable-cars make their curve around the Lincoln Statue, and with the various crosstown cars passing in front, the University-Place cars passing the side, this becomes a much-frequented spot.

TOMB OF GEN. U. S. GRANT, RIVERSIDE PARK, N. Y.

CENTRAL PARK ENTRANCE, AT SEVENTH AVENUE AND 59TH STREET.

J. Milhau's Son, dispensing chemist, druggist and importer, owns and occupies a store at 183 Broadway, that is one of the landmarks of New-York City.

A brief historical sketch of the founder of this establishment, now in its eightieth year, shows that the late John Milhau, after the death of his father, who had been duly naturalized, established the business in 1813, in Baltimore, the

J. MILHAU'S SON, 183 BROADWAY.

place of his birth, where his parents, of ancient and noble descent, had taken refuge from the insurrection in Saint Domingo during the great French Revolution of 1793. He had received a liberal education, spoke several languages, and inherited his father's ardor for America. Rather than serve a foreign government in any way, he declined the appointment of Consul-General at Baltimore, tendered by the French government without his solicitation, and even before he was of age; the French monarchy having been restored in the person of Louis the Eighteenth. After devoting twelve years to business in Baltimore, and three years to his scientific studies in Paris, he established himself in the present location in New York in 1830. He was moved thereto, in fact, by witnessing the expulsion of Charles the Tenth, although General Lafayette, to whom he was connected and very warmly attached, urgently pressed him to remain in France. He soon became widely prominent as a wholesale and retail dispensing chemist and importer. His productions stood in deserved favor with the medical profession. Some of his notable and disinterested public services, during his forty years of business life in this city, were the incorporation of the New-York College of Pharmacy, in 1831; the pioneering of the beneficent law of 1848, "to prevent the importation into the United States of fraudulent, adulterated, inferior or deteriorated drugs." (This law he carried through Congress, with the zealous coöperation of the colleges of pharmacy, druggists, chemists and medical men, in spite of threats against himself, and the most desperate and determined opposition; initiating, in 1851, the formation of the American Pharmaceutical Association, to guard the proper enforcement of that law; heading the suit, in 1854, that defeated for 32 years Jacob Sharp's grab at Broadway for his railroad; as a director of one of the largest institutions, offering a large loan at legal interest to the Government in the sore crisis of 1861, when some capitalists asked 36 per cent.; contracting for foreign quinine in the interest of the Government, so as to protect it from being cornered in this indispensable supply for the war then commencing ; his active part in the establishment of dispensaries, hospitals, asylums, the American Institute and other corporations ; and his inauguration of the Bogardus system of solid iron fronts on Broadway, erecting the one to his store in the short space of three days. The parts were so accurately fitted beforehand as to require only the insertion of the heavy screw-bolts, as fast as they were lifted into position. The house is now conducted under the firm-name of J. Milhau's Son, by Edward L. Milhau, his only surviving son and former partner, who has successfully maintained the high character impressed on the concern by its founder. The compounding of prescriptions con- tinncs to be one of its notable specialties, the facilities for which are kept fully abreast of the times, requiring several skilled and experienced graduates in phar- macy. The number of prescriptions it has dispensed, exclusive of renewals, amounts to several hundred thousand. In the number were prescriptions held by travellers and others, from nearly every prominent practitioner that has lived during this cen- tury. This house has an important mail-order and export and import business.

Edward L. Milhau, the present proprietor, has over forty years' experience of a high order, having entered this concern in 1850. He graduated from the New- York College of Pharmacy in 1856 ; has held important positions therein, and in the Alumni Association ; is an incorporator for renewal of the original 50-year charter of the College, and for charter of the Alumni ; is life-member of both the above, of the American Pharmaceutical Association, and of the Veteran Association of the Seventh Regiment ; late member of John A. Dix Post, G. A. R., and of the Board of Pharmacy, New-York City ; and Knight of the Order of Bolivar, a decoration conferred by the Republic of Venezuela.

BROADWAY, SIXTH AVENUE AND 32D STREET, SHOWING UNION DIME SAVINGS INSTITUTION.

Randel, Baremore & Billings, diamond importers and cutters, and manufacturers of diamond jewelry, have their offices and factories at 58 Nassau Street and 29 Maiden Lane, New-York City. More than half a century ago, in 1840, Henry Randel and James Baremore began the manufacture of jewelry in this city. After a few years they decided to make a specialty of diamonds. This was a pioneer enterprise, as there were no diamond specialists in this country at that time. They were so successful, that in 1851 they established their present offices and factory, and began the regular importing of cut diamonds. In the same year Chester Billings entered the office as clerk, and in 1860 was made a partner in the business. Mr. Baremore did not live to see the full development of the enterprise which he had been so instrumental in establishing. He died in 1867.

The business and fame of this firm as manufacturers of diamond jewelry steadily increased. In the beginning of the "Eighties" they determined to do their own diamond-cutting. They at once adopted the method which Henry Morse of Boston had introduced in 1870. Before that time European diamond-cutters had sacrificed effect to weight in their work. As a result the stone was finished in any form by which the most substance could be saved. Mr. Morse made effect the paramount object in cutting. His method is now universally adopted in America and Europe.

The firm's manufactory has facilities for fifty employees. Here may be seen those most interesting processes which, beginning with the diamond in the rough,

result in a beautiful transparent stone, scintillating like a star in its gold setting. The cutting is sometimes done in the old-fashioned way by hand, but oftener by machine, which gives more accurate results. The one aim in this cutting is to draw from the finished stone its most brilliant effects. This is generally best accomplished by making the girdle round and the proportions above and below the girdle perfectly symmetrical. The usual proportions are one-third above and two-thirds below. The broad table at the top and the tiny culet at the bottom lie in carefully paralleled planes. The firm, by securing only the most skilled labor for its factory, produces

RANDEL, BAREMORE & BILLINGS: MAIDEN LANE AND NASSAU STREET.

results in the cutting and setting of diamonds that are truly wonderful. Besides diamonds, it imports from its London and Amsterdam offices rubies, sapphires, opals, emeralds and pearls. The designs for the setting of these precious stones are most tastefully executed, and give to Randel, Baremore & Billings a leading rank as manufacturers of jewelry.

STUYVESANT PLACE, 8TH STREET AND ST. MARK'S PLACE. EAST FROM THIRD AVENUE.

UNION SQUARE, LOOKING TOWARDS THE NORTHWEST.

Robert Caterson, the eminent designer and builder of mausoleums, monuments and general monumental work, has perpetuated his own name in the hundreds of specimens of artistic handicraft which he has erected, not only in Woodlawn Cemetery, but also in the cemeteries of various cities in sixteen of the commonwealths of the Union, even as far west as California. His offices, studios, workshops and steam-polishing works are at Woodlawn, just opposite the north entrance of the cemetery. He has been engaged in this industry 37 years, 24 of which have been at Woodlawn, wherein are upwards of 500 of his monuments and mausoleums. His clients include many of the great names of the United States. He designed and built at Woodlawn the Collis P. Huntington mausoleum, which, with its approaches, cost about $300,000 — the most expensive structure of its character on the continent. A few other noted mausoleums erected by him at Woodlawn are those for J. M. Randell, Noe, Edward O. Gould, F. H. Cossitt, Jacob Hays, Jr., Peter F. Meyer, Henry Clews, Frederick B. Taylor, Peter C. Baker, James M. McLean, A. De Bary, Jacob Schmitt, Mandeville-Rice, Whitely, S. P. McClave, Preston-Hays, Watrous,

ROBERT CATERSON, OPPOSITE NORTH ENTRANCE TO WOODLAWN CEMETERY, WOODLAWN.

Herman Leroy Jones, Maurice B. Flynn, D. P. Ingraham, Swan-Callender, Pearson, George A. Osgood, Mix, A. Van Deusen, W. A. Dooley, Cockcroft, Wood, Alfred M. Hoyt, Stephen R. Lesher, and others. At other points might be mentioned these mausoleums: the James Wallace, at Calvary Cemetery, Long Island; the Peck mausoleum, at Meriden, Conn.; the Leland Stanford, Palo Alto, Cal.; the Duclos, Hartford, Conn.; Seth B. Howes, Brewsters, New York; the Hamilton, Philadelphia, Pa.; the Bradley, Meriden, Conn.; and C. Meyer, New Brunswick, N. J. At Harwinton, Conn., is the Elizabeth V. Huntington Memorial Chapel. All of these are exceptionally notable mausoleums, distinctively artistic in their conception, and constructed with a solidity which will defy the ravages of centuries. The monumental work executed by Mr. Caterson varies from the simplest to the grandest; from the most modest to the most costly. His experience and facilities enable him to create satisfactory designs, to furnish absolutely durable materials, and to construct in a thoroughly reliable manner. And as there are eminent architects and builders of temporary palatial homes for the living, so, too, has Mr. Caterson become justly famous as an architect and builder of permanent and artistic homes for the dead.

METROPOLITAN POLICE ANNUAL PARADE REVIEWED BY INFANTA EULALIA IN MADISON SQUARE.

FOOT OF WHITEHALL STREET AND GOVERNOR'S ISLAND, FROM ARMY BUILDING.

The Scott Stamp & Coin Company, Limited, is a unique concern. Its main quarters, at 18 East 23d Street, just opposite Madison Avenue, and its branch rooms, at 183 Broadway, in Milhau's Building, are veritable curiosity shops. Here are to be seen the postage, revenue and other stamps issued by all nations and at all times since stamps were introduced. Here are the headquarters of the stamp-collectors of the world, for the Scott Stamp & Coin Company is indisputably the foremost concern in either continent devoted to the stamp business. Here

SCOTT STAMP & COIN CO., LIMITED, 18 EAST
23D STREET.

comes correspondence from many thousands of amateur collectors making their ordinary collections, and here, too, the advanced collectors are wont to seek the rare and the curious in this peculiar branch of treasure accumulations. Here, too, is published the *American Journal of Philately*, the chief organ of the stamp-collecting fraternity, and also the *Catalogue for Advanced Collectors*, the most elaborate and detailed record yet made of each and every stamp or variety of stamp ever issued. Both publications are edited by Henry Collin and Henry L. Calman, who are respectively the president and secretary of the company. All accessories of stamp collectors are to be obtained here, including stamp albums of various sizes, grades and qualities, the chief one of which is the "International Stamp Album," in its eleventh edition, a large quarto volume, with spaces for about 15,-000 varieties of stamps. Quite naturally this is the foremost concern, for it is also the oldest in this country. The present company succeeded to the business established in 1863 by John W. Scott, who was the first person in this country to devote himself solely to the stamp business, the first to issue a stamp album (1868), the first to issue a stamp-collectors' periodical (1868), and the first to make an elaborate record of the various issues of stamps in the various countries. He sold out to this company in 1885, and then retired from business. Besides the stamp business, with its journals, catalogues, flags, coats-of-arms, portraits, and numerous other incidentals, the Scott Stamp & Coin Company is devoted largely to coins, and leads all other coin concerns in this country. The headquarters on 23d Street are the rendezvous of thousands of stamp and coin collectors, amateur, advanced and professional, from all parts of the world, who, while visiting or sojourning in New-York City, have occasion to seek coins and stamps, or information relating thereto.

BROADWAY AND 29TH STREET, SHOWING IMPERIAL MUSIC HALL AND DALY'S THEATRE.

LEXINGTON AVENUE AND 63D STREET, SHOWING RODOPH SHOLOM SYNAGOGUE.

14TH STREET, FROM UNIVERSITY PLACE TO FIFTH AVENUE.

14TH STREET AND BROADWAY, LOOKING TOWARDS GRACE CHURCH.

Notable Wholesale Establishments.

Some Gigantic Firms and Corporations, Whose Yearly Transactions Involve Millions of Dollars and Extend
to all corners of the Earth.

NEW YORK is the great distributing point for the United States, and to an important extent for the American continent. The fruits of its own immense manufactures, and the mills of New England, the mines of Pennsylvania, the plantations of the South, the grain-fields of the West, are assembled here, as in a great goods clearing-house, for exchange and distribution. New York also has the Western headquarters and offices of hundreds of the great manufactories of Europe, through which the finished products of the Old World are introduced to the favorable consideration and use of the New World. English and Scottish, French and German commercial corporations are represented here by some of their most able men, bent on securing for their products a share of the great Yankee custom. Every transatlantic steamship brings in consignments to these consuls of commerce, whose travelling salesmen seek out every American trade-centre. The quantity of the articles American and foreign, offered here for sale, in large lots, is stupendous; and its variety is bewildering. The wholesale houses of New York set the fashions for the continent, and impose their taste, usually correct and commendable, upon the people of the coasts and mountains, the prairies and plantations. Such illimitable opportunities for commercial conquest, resulting in comfort for the people at large, and competence for their mentors, have developed at New York many generals of commerce, skilled in seizing the strategic points in other localities, in holding them with picked men, and in sending there the supplies most adequate to their needs.

The jobbing trade of the Empire City is colossal in its proportions, and amounts to hundreds of millions of dollars yearly, covering the territory from the Atlantic to the Pacific, and from the Caribbean Sea to Hudson Bay. The wise and careful calculations made by the metropolitan wholesalers include many considerations, the state of the markets, present and future, the conditions of provincial credits, the greater or less permanence of fashions, the durability of materials, the probabilities of all the crops, the possibilities of plagues and pestilences and calamities, the contingencies of threatened and actual wars, the results of possible political or industrial disturbances.

Some exceptionally notable wholesale and jobbing houses of this city are briefly sketched in the following pages. Without the record of these houses the story of New York's greatness would be far from complete. They stand out eminent among tens of thousands of mercantile houses. They have added their full share to the glory of the city.

E. S. Jaffray & Co., of 350 Broadway, and the chronicles of commerce in New York are inseparable.   Their brownstone building at the northeast corner of Broadway and Leonard Street is a landmark.   Their standing as leaders among the dry-goods jobbers is known and appreciated even by those who are not business men. Their history is the history of the gradual advance into commercial supremacy of New York.   The firm is formed of Howard S. Jaffray (son of E. S. Jaffray), J. R. P. Woodriff and Sylvester A. Haver.   Its original founder was Robert Jaffray, who came to New York in 1809, as the representative of the London house of J. R. Jaffray & Co., and soon made its influence predominant.   In 1833 his nephew, E. S. Jaffray, son of J. R. Jaffray, came to work with him.   He was seventeen years of age, and he had the commercial genius of his relatives.   At the death of his uncle he changed the name of the firm to J. R. Jaffray & Sons, but his own name was famous long before it took formally its natural place at the head of the re-organized firm of E. S. Jaffray & Co.   The re-organization occurred after the War for the

E. S. JAFFRAY & CO., BROADWAY AND LEONARD STREET.

Union, in the course of which he had surprised many persons by sacrificing to his patriotic principles the great business interests which he had in the South.   This, however, was E. S. Jaffray's way. When he died, in April, 1892, every phase in his long and admirable business record was as exemplary as his private character. His judgment had been a law; his arbitration definitely settled disputed questions; he was influential independently of his financial position; and he contributed much more than his proportionate share to the commercial triumphs of New York.   He declined the office of mayor, which he would have honored.   He rendered services for which there are no rewards.

The offices and warerooms of the business of Jaffray were at first located in Pearl Street; later they were in Park Place.   For more than a quarter of a century they have been at 350 Broadway.   New York has not a more interesting commercial monument than this wholesale dry-goods house, with its unblemished experience of 83 years.

Dunham, Buckley & Co., importers and jobbers of dry-goods, at 340 to 344 Broadway, rank among the leading houses in the trade. Their establishment stands upon ground of historic interest, as it was the site of the old Broadway Tabernacle, which was the scene years ago of many anniversary gatherings and anti-slavery meetings. The present building was erected in 1858, by George Bliss. The firm of Dunham, Buckley & Co. has been in existence since 1875. The building displays a front of marble on Broadway. It is six stories in height, 70 feet wide, and 225 feet deep, with an extension in the rear, reaching from Worth Street to Catharine Lane. It is fortunately placed, for its long north side rests upon a private street, one-half of which is controlled by the firm. This insures direct sunlight on three sides, an important advantage; and also permits the reception of goods on one side and the delivery on the other. The firm occupies the entire building, and carries an enormous duplicate stock in separate storehouses. The basement is given up to domestic cotton goods, flannels and blankets. On the street floor are displayed British, Continental and domestic dress goods, silks and satins. The second story is assigned to ribbons, trimmings and the notion department; the latter a very important one, not exceeded in magnitude or scope in the country. Then above, on various floors, are the departments of laces, white goods, shawls and wraps,

DUNHAM, BUCKLEY & CO., 340 TO 344 BROADWAY.

and of cloaks manufactured by themselves, in their White-Street store. This is a rapidly growing and important feature. There are also departments of hosiery, underwear and gloves; of woolens, virtually an adjunct to that of dress goods; and of carpets and rugs. The establishment is brilliantly lighted with electricity, supplied by their own plant. The counting-room alone is longer than most banking-houses, and transactions more extensive than those of many banks are carried on within it. Dunham, Buckley & Co., surrounded with bright men as heads of departments, conduct smoothly a business of enormous proportions, which is more than continental in its scope.

Mills & Gibb, importers of laces and kindred goods, occupy an imposing building at the northeast corner of Broadway and Grand Street.   The structure is of iron, seven stories in height, and measures 100 feet on Broadway, and 200 on Grand Street.   The firm has been in existence since April, 1865.   The partners are Philo L. Mills, John Gibb and William T. Evans.   The scope of its dealings includes laces, embroideries, linens, hosiery, and such goods as are known in the dry-goods trade as notions.   The firm accepts no consignments, and transacts no business whatever on commission.   It purchases its goods outright, and to that end maintains offices in Nottingham, Paris, Calais, St. Gall and Plauen.   Thus it is able to secure the choicest products of all the lace and embroidery manufacturing centres of Europe.   Mr. Mills resides altogether in Nottingham, and gives his attention to

MILLS & GIBB, BROADWAY AND GRAND STREET.

purchasing.   Mr. Gibb is at the head of the house in America, and devotes himself to the distribution of goods.   These members of the firm have reversed the usual order of proceeding, in dividing between themselves the responsibilities of business, for Mr. Mills is an American, and Mr. Gibb is a Scotchman.   For the distribution of its goods the firm has branch-houses in Boston, Philadelphia, Baltimore, Chicago, St. Louis, St. Paul and San Francisco.   It employs about 300 people, of whom 50 are travelling salesmen, who sell by samples.   The house of Mills & Gibb is the largest one of its class in America.   Its sales amount in value to several millions of dollars a year.   It has no retail trade.   Mr. Gibb is also principal partner in the dry-goods firm of Frederick Loeser & Company, of Brooklyn.   He and his son, Howard Gibb, have managed the business of that house since 1887.

Sweetser, Pembrook & Co., importers and jobbers of dry goods, occupy a handsome marble building at 374, 376, and 378 Broadway, at the corner of White Street, which has a frontage of 75 feet on Broadway, and is 140 feet deep. The building has some interest from an architectural point of view, for it was erected more than thirty years ago, when the architecture of business blocks was of a plain and unornamental character. Sweetser, Pembrook & Co.'s building is of a much more ambitious style of architecture than most of the others in the vicinity, of equal age. It was originally intended for the occupancy of a dry-goods jobbing house, but the radical changes in business at the outbreak of the war modified the plans of both the owner and prospective tenant, and the building was turned to other uses. It is the property of the estate of William B. Astor. The firm of Sweetser, Pembrook & Co. has been in existence since 1868.

SWEETSER, PEMBROOK & CO., BROADWAY AND WHITE STREET.

It succeeded that of Sweetser & Co., which was organized in 1863. It carries full lines of silks, dress goods, woolens and hosiery; also, an extensive variety of fancy goods which are usually carried in the dry-goods trade. Their stock is sufficiently large to fill the entire building, as well as a separate warehouse near the principal store. The firm has buyers in Europe, who are constantly on the lookout for goods of fine quality. Its travelling salesmen have made the house known to the dry-goods trade all over the United States. For many years the house was located at 365 Broadway. It moved into its present quarters in January, 1885, and thus the building was put into the service for which it was originally intended. The present members of the firm are George D. Sweetser, J. Howard Sweetser, William A. Pembrook, Joseph H. Bumstead, George L. Putnam, Howard P. Sweetser, and Theodore K. Pembrook.

The house of Sweetser, Pembrook & Co. ranks among the most prominent of the dry-goods firms of America.

Tefft, Weller & Co., importers and jobbers of dry goods, of 326, 328 and 330 Broadway, is one of the oldest and most widely esteemed houses in the wholesale dry-goods trade. Its members have been prominently identified with public interests for the past forty years. This business was founded January 1, 1849, by Erastus T. Tefft ; and the firm-name has been successively, E. T. Tefft & Co.; Teffts, Griswold & Kellogg; Tefft, Griswold & Co.; and Tefft, Weller & Co. Through all these changes the house has been steadily advancing, enlarging its trade in all directions, and increasing its capital, facilities and force, as well as its experience. Its founder was a rare man. He was a man of quick perceptions and sound judgment. He was eminently just in all his ways. He was of a conservative disposition, yet was bold, courageous and daring when the occasion demanded these qualities. He was uniformly courteous, kind and gentle, and commanded the confidence and respect of all who knew him. Mr. Tefft died November 10, 1888, at the venerable age of 78 years.

The present firm is composed of his two sons, William E. Tefft and Frank Griswold Tefft, George C. Clarke, John N. Beach and Morton D. Bogue. The firm-name of Tefft, Weller & Co. is retained as a trade-mark, there having been no Weller interest in the house since the death of Joseph H. Weller in 1886, two years previous to the death of E. T. Tefft. The firm occupies the entire seven floors of the spacious iron and granite front building at 326, 328 and 330 Broadway, and three floors of No. 324, together with two floors of Nos. 320 and 322, making in the aggregate 166,250 square feet of floor space. These vast areas are occupied by very full lines of the goods in which the house deals, admirably arranged and ordered. The location of Tefft, Weller & Co.'s buildings, on the east side of Broadway, between Pearl and Worth Streets, is in the midst of the great wholesale dry-goods trade. A view of the Broadway front of the establishment is seen on the opposite page. The business of this house has shown a steady and healthy growth all its years, until it has reached very large proportions, and justly ranks among the first of the great wholesale dry-goods houses in the whole country.

No firm has a better and more reliable constituency than this. The business of the house is thoroughly systematized, each partner giving to it his personal attention, in some special direction. The employees in all the departments number about four hundred and fifty.

A large and well-assorted stock is kept at all seasons, comprising foreign and domestic dress goods, silks, velvets, hosiery, notions, white goods, linens, laces, shawls, cloaks, woolens, flannels, blankets, prints, ginghams, domestics, and an unusually large variety of carpets and mattings, floor oil cloths and upholstery goods. Vast and varied as is the stock, nevertheless its excellent condition is always noticeable, and its arrangement is admirable.

Acting not as commission merchants, but as direct traders, dealing with the chief manufacturers both at home and abroad, Tefft, Weller & Co. have peculiar advantages for the safe and favorable conduct of their business, and for its indefinite expansion, whenever occasion arises therefor. The choicest products of the European looms and workshops are found in their vast stocks, as well as the output of hundreds of American factories, favored by the new birth of industrial activity in the United States.

Tefft, Weller & Co. enjoy facilities for securing every possible advantage in the purchase of goods, both in home and foreign markets, and are always in a position to take excellent care of their customers — a fact which, judging from their constantly growing business, the trade appreciate.

TEFFT, WELLER & COMPANY.
320, 322, 324, 326, 328 AND 330 BROADWAY, EAST SIDE, BETWEEN PEARL AND WORTH STREETS.

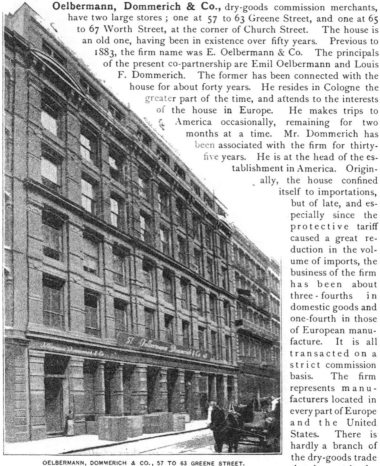

Oelbermann, Dommerich & Co., dry-goods commission merchants, have two large stores ; one at 57 to 63 Greene Street, and one at 65 to 67 Worth Street, at the corner of Church Street. The house is an old one, having been in existence over fifty years. Previous to 1883, the firm name was E. Oelbermann & Co. The principals of the present co-partnership are Emil Oelbermann and Louis F. Dommerich. The former has been connected with the house for about forty years. He resides in Cologne the greater part of the time, and attends to the interests of the house in Europe. He makes trips to America occasionally, remaining for two months at a time. Mr. Dommerich has been associated with the firm for thirty-five years. He is at the head of the establishment in America. Originally, the house confined itself to importations, but of late, and especially since the protective tariff caused a great reduction in the volume of imports, the business of the firm has been about three-fourths in domestic goods and one-fourth in those of European manufacture. It is all transacted on a strict commission basis. The firm represents manufacturers located in every part of Europe and the United States. There is hardly a branch of the dry-goods trade that has not its department in the stores of Oelbermann, Dommerich & Co. The sales amount to about $15,000,000 a year. The Greene-Street store is a seven-story building, and occupies a plot of ground one hundred feet square. It stands on the site of the old Greene-Street Methodist Church. It was built in 1876. The firm owns the estate at 64 to 68 Wooster Street, measuring 65 by 100 feet, adjoining the Greene-Street store in the rear, and intends to build an annex store upon it. Of the Worth-Street building, which is nearly as large as the other, the firm occupies four floors. All the goods at Worth Street are domestic, and both foreign and domestic are handled at ·Greene Street, at which point the general offices of the firm are located.

OELBERMANN, DOMMERICH & CO., 57 TO 63 GREENE STREET.

Frederick Vietor & Achelis, importers and commission merchants in dry goods, occupy a handsome five-story building at 66 to 76 Leonard Street, at the corner of Church Street, in the heart of the dry-goods district. The structure is of brownstone and iron, and is rather more attractive in appearance than its neighbors. It measures $137\frac{1}{2}$ feet on Leonard Street, and 180 feet on Church Street. The firm is the successor of Charles Graebe & Vietor, and has been in existence and under its present title since 1839. Frederick Vietor and Thomas Achelis, the two original partners, died in 1870 and 1872 respectively. The present partners are their sons. They are George F. Vietor, Thomas Achelis, Carl Vietor, and John Achelis. The volume of business transacted by the firm is enormous, reaching a total of from $14,000,000 to $15,000,000 a year. Its dealings in domestic goods

FREDERICK VIETOR & ACHELIS, CHURCH AND LEONARD STREETS.

have increased very largely in the past few years, since the modification of the tariff laws caused a reduction in the volume of imports. The location of the store is peculiarly favorable. It is bounded by streets, and a greater portion of it, therefore, lies under direct sunlight. This is an advantage highly prized by dry-goods men, as many buyers, especially of dress goods, desire to know the appearance of fabrics in a strong light. The business conducted by Frederick Vietor & Achelis is very comprehensive. One department is devoted to domestic woolens, and another to those of foreign manufacture. Another includes woolen dress goods, both imported and American. Then there are departments of silks, domestic and imported ; of silk dress goods ; of millinery silks ; of plushes and velvets ; of shirts, drawers and hosiery ; of cloakings in the piece (of which the firm handle a large variety) ; of cloths and blankets ; and of silks made especially for umbrellas. One important department is that of Philadelphia goods, ginghams and the like. The several floors of the store, if placed side by side on the ground, would cover a tract measuring nearly three acres.

Smith, Hogg & Gardner, dry-goods commission merchants, of 115 and 117 Worth Street, New York, and 66 Chauney Street, Boston, are the successors, in line, of A. and A. (Amos and Abbott) Lawrence & Co., of Boston, who were largely instru-mental during the first half of this century in developing the manufacturing interests of Lowell, Mass. Early in the "fifties" the Lawrences established a branch-house at 43 Broadway, New York, and there represented as selling agents many of the leading textile manufacturing corporations of New England, viz.: The Massachu-setts, Boott, Lawrence, Atlantic, Laconia, Jackson (Indian Head), Tremont and York, who were manufacturers of cotton goods, and also the Lowell Carpet Com-pany. Some years later this firm removed to 79 and 81 Worth Street. In 1865 the Lawrences retired from business, and George C. Richardson & Co., of Boston and New York, became their successors, retaining the majority of the accounts of their predecessors. In 1868 Geo. C. Richardson & Co. moved into the spacious buildings erected by them at 115 and 117 Worth Street, now the property of the Mercantile Real-Estate Company. On January 1, 1884, this firm was succeeded by Geo. C. Richardson, Smith & Co., the latter house being succeeded on July 1, 1885, by Smith, Hogg & Gardner.

Charles S. Smith, now the President of the New-York Chamber of Commerce, and a director in many of the most prominent financial institutions of New York, became connected with this business in 1865, and retained an interest therein for more than twenty years. He was the senior partner of Smith, Hogg & Gardner until 1887, when he retired from active business. The firm is at present composed of John Hogg and Harrison Gardner, of Boston ; Ralph L. Cutter, of Brooklyn ; Walter M. Smith, of Stamford, Conn.; and Stewart W. Smith, of New York. Messrs. Gardner and Cutter entered the employ of the Lawrences, as boys, in 1857, and consequently have been connected with the business for thirty-five years.

The firm of Smith, Hogg & Gardner sell very largely of domestic cotton goods to the export trade, notably to China, Africa and South America, where the products of the Massachusetts and Boott Mills have an extended market and reputation. The volume of business transacted by this house annually reaches the vast sum of many millions of dollars, and it is generally conceded by the trade that no house stands higher or outranks it in amount of business. Its list of mills is a notably strong one, and the products include an extended variety of fabrics. Its salesmen reach every important center of the United States, and in due time the products of the mills represented by this house get into every nook and corner, large and small, of the entire Union of States. This firm occupies four floors of the Mercantile Real-Estate Company's building. The building is a handsome structure, six stories in height, covering some 75 feet on Worth Street and Catharine Lane, and 90 feet on Elm Street, thus giving it the advantage of light on three sides. It is built of marble and iron. Four floors of the building are laid out in offices, some of which are occupied by the New-York representatives of leading Western and other business houses, among whom may be enumerated the John V. Farwell Co., Carson, Pirie, Scott & Co., and Schlesinger & Mayer, of Chicago ; the Hargadine-McKittrick Dry-Goods Co., and the H. T. Simon, Gregory & Co., of St. Louis ; Thomas L. Leedom & Co., of Philadelphia ; Bamberger, Bloom & Co., of Louisville ; Burke, Fitz Simons, Hone & Co., of Rochester ; and Sweet, Orr & Co. and Chadwick Bros., of the Newburgh Bleachery, both of Newburgh, N. Y. This gathering of such a group of nationally eminent business houses tends to give a national importance to the Mercan-tile Real-Estate Company's building, and at the same time brings in close proximity a coterie of a number of the great customers of the house of Smith, Hogg & Gardner.

SMITH, HOGG & GARDNER.

MERCANTILE REAL-ESTATE CO.'S BUILDING, 115 AND 117 WORTH STREET, CORNER OF ELM STREET.

Passavant & Co. is the title of a firm now located at 320 and 322 Church Street, which has been engaged in importing dry-goods for very nearly forty years, and which is well-known throughout Europe and America. The house was founded in July, 1853, by Passavant Brothers, of Frankfort-on-the-Main, in Germany, and it was then a branch of the European establishment. It was at the outset located in Broad Street. The firm has never changed its title, and by virtue thereof, it is now the oldest importing house in the dry-goods trade in the city. Its founders still retain an interest in the establishment. Passavant & Co. conduct a strictly commission business. Their dealings are mainly in silks, ribbons, dress goods and gloves. Of late they have undertaken the distribution of the products of a number of American mills and factories, in order to compensate for the decrease in the volume of imports, and they have been as successful in the management of domestic accounts as of foreign. The present senior partner of the firm, George W. Sutton, is well known in every large trade-centre. He entered the service of the house,

PASSAVANT & CO., CHURCH AND LISPENARD STREETS.

as a salesman, at the beginning, and has been a partner since 1859. Passavant & Co. have occupied their present quarters for twenty-five years. They consist of the large building on Church Street and the adjoining one on Lispenard Street, both of which are five stories in height. The general offices occupy the street floor. The delivery department is located in the basement, and all the space in the stories above the street is required for the salesrooms of the various lines of goods which constitute the trade of the house.

Passavant & Co. is at present composed of the following partners : Gebrüder Passavant, George W. Sutton, Heinrich Meyer, Oscar Passavant, and Arthur W. Watson. The steadfast existence of this old house, maintained for two generations in a career of unquestioned integrity and fidelity, gives to the house of Passavant & Co. a gratifying preëminence which it has fairly earned and well sustains.

Fleitmann & Co. occupy the splendid business building from 484 to 490 Broome Street, with the offices and salesrooms of their representative importing house. Here at all times may be found an immense stock of dry goods, more especially silks of various grades, all kinds of linings and tailors' trimmings, and umbrella silks, besides very choice and beautiful satins and velvets. Although the business is mainly connected with the products of the great and celebrated European mills, the firm has closely observed the rising tendencies of American manufactures in the same line, and has latterly made a feature of goods of domestic make. The business is done on commission, and has attained enormous proportions, the sales reaching from ten to twelve millions of dollars a year, and covering a vast area of the American continent.

The firm was established in 1851 by Herman Fleitmann, who retired from its active direction in 1869, and has since resided in Germany, attending to much of the foreign business of the house. He left the New-York affairs in the hands of his junior partners, Frederick Winkhaus and Ewald Fleitmann (his younger brother). Mr. Winkhaus retired in 1886, and has since died. The present partners are Herman and Ewald Fleitmann, and the two sons of the former, Frederick T. and William M. Fleitmann. The house

FLEITMANN & CO., BROOME AND WOOSTER STREETS.

has gradually moved to its present location from far down-town, its successive homes being in Barclay Street, Reade Street, 14 Greene Street, 23 and 25 Greene Street, southwest corner of Broome and Greene Streets, southeast corner of Broome and Greene Streets, 489 to 493 Greene Street, and thence to its present handsome structure at the northwest corner of Broome and Wooster Streets. Amid all these migrations the strength, credit and resources of Fleitmann & Co. have shown a continual increase until now this house holds a place of the highest honor and influence, occupying one of the most imposing buildings, carrying one of the largest stocks, and enjoying one of the most extensive trades in this important industry.

Woodward, Baldwin & Co. is well-known as a leading dry-goods commission house, and as such has a large business throughout every section of the Union. Besides their large business in this country, they do an extensive export trade, and thus carry American-made fabrics into many countries. Their business is entirely with manufacturers, and is done on an exclusively commission basis. They are the

WOODWARD, BALDWIN & CO., 43 AND 45 WORTH STREET.

agents of various mills producing many lines of cotton fabrics. This concern is one of the oldest in its line, having been formed over half a century ago in the city of Baltimore, where they still carry on business under the same style of Woodward, Baldwin & Co., as in New York. The senior partner, William H. Baldwin, Jr., resides at Baltimore, where he takes the active management of the business in that section. The other partners are Elijah P. Smith, Rignal T. Woodward and William H. Baldwin, who reside in New-York City, and are actively identified with many of the city's prominent social, financial and commercial institutions.

The firm's New-York offices and salesrooms are in the very midst of the dry-goods and allied trades. They occupy spacious quarters in the double five-story and basement, iron and stone-front building, Nos. 43 and 45, on the north side of Worth Street, between Church Street and West Broadway. On this street, a few years ago, stood the New-York Hospital, which, when built, was on the outskirts of the city. A glance through this street, with its two sides lined with substantial structures, occupied by world-famous firms, almost makes one believe that its development has been the work of several generations.

Tebbetts, Harrison & Robins is one of the well and favorably known dry-goods commission houses, although its large business as the agents of various cotton and woolen mills is conducted in the most modest and quietest fashion. For almost twelve years, ever since the firm began business, they have occupied the quarters at 75 and 77 Worth Street. The senior partner is William C. Tebbetts, a New-Englander, who resides in Boston, and has been identified with the dry-goods industry about forty years. At various periods he was an active partner in the houses of Jewett, Tebbetts & Co., and Tebbetts, Baldwin & Davis. It is said that the great Boston fire of 1872 began in the building occupied by his firm ; and also that the great Boston fire, on Thanksgiving Day, in 1891, ended at a party fire-wall which Mr. Tebbetts had had erected in his building. The present firm of Tebbetts, Harrison & Robins was organized in 1882 by the present members, who have remained associates ever since. They comprise William C. Tebbetts, Charles F. Harrison, and Edward B. Robins. Mr. Harrison is the representative of the famous Interlaken Mills, at Arkwright, R. I., which

TEBBETTS, HARRISON & ROBINS, 75 AND 77 WORTH STREET.

produce the various grades of cloth required by book-binders for the covers of books. The vast majority of cloth-covered books bound in this country are covered with Interlaken cloth, of which this firm are the general selling agents. Mr. Harrison is an old-time dry-goods merchant of New York and Philadelphia. In the latter city for three years he represented the house of Minot, Hooper & Co. Afterwards he was connected with the firm of Rhoades, Grosvenor & Co., with whom he remained for ten years, until the formation of his present firm. Mr. Robins, who is a well-known graduate of Harvard University, began his dry-goods career with the famous house of J. C. Howe & Co., with whom he remained twelve years, and whom he left to become a partner in the house of Tebbetts, Harrison & Robins.

Cheney Brothers have their New-York offices and salesrooms at **477, 479 and 481** Broome Street.   They are manufacturers of silk fabrics and silk goods of many descriptions.   Among the chief products of this house are plain silks, of various kinds, dress silks, millinery silks, plushes, velvets, satins, pongees, yarns, printed silks, ribbons and sashes, flags, crapes, and many other articles of kindred character.   They also make a large line of tapestries and decorative upholstery fabrics.

Stocks of these goods are kept at the firm's establishments in New York, Boston and Chicago.   They are sold by the principal wholesalers, jobbers and retailers of dry goods and kindred articles throughout the country.

The great works in which most of the Cheney Brothers' silks are manufactured are located in the village of South Manchester, Connecticut. Most of the houses of the operatives are owned by the manufacturers, who keep them in good order; and each home has its roomy patch of land about it, for the use of the family.

The Cheney Brothers' silk mills employ 2,500 persons, and the value of their yearly output is over $4,000,000, in delicate and beautiful fabrics, of famed durability. The mills are a series of plain, solid and spacious brick buildings, filled with intricate and ingenious machinery. The village is not crowded around the mills, the result being to scatter the population.

The firm's ribbon mills are in the City of Hartford, Connecticut.

Cheney Brothers was founded in 1838, and in 1854 became an incorporated company, but it is practically a private concern; the ownership being in the Cheney family, as it has remained for nearly half a century.

CHENEY BROTHERS, 477, 479 AND 481 BROOME STREET.

E. H. Van Ingen & Co., importers of woolens, occupy one of the handsomest buildings devoted to business purposes in New York. It is the Mohawk Building, called from the famous old Indian tribe, at Fifth Avenue and 21st Street. It was erected by the firm principally for its own use. It was opened May 1, 1892; and is an architectural feature of lower Fifth Avenue. It measures 92 feet on Fifth Avenue and 142½ feet on 21st Street. It is an absolutely fire-proof structure, nine stories high, built of sandstone, St.-Louis brick, and iron. The architecture is simple, showing the lines of construction, with a touch of the Renaissance style. The feature of the Fifth-Avenue front is its projecting entrance-porch in Ionic style. The two upper stories are embraced in a colonnade, which makes them appear as one very high story. The lower floors, from the first to the sixth, are laid out in broad salesrooms, subdivided only by rows of columns. E. H. Van Ingen & Co. occupy the lower floors, the general offices being at the rear end of the entrance story, and the private offices on the floor above. There is a recess on the 21st-Street side which serves as a driveway, and permits loading and unloading goods without encum-

E. H. VAN INGEN & CO., THE MOHAWK BUILDING, FIFTH AVENUE AND 21ST STREET.

bering the sidewalk. The four upper stories are laid out in offices for professional people. They, as well as the warerooms above the ground, are reached by two passenger elevators from the main entrance. The walls of the corridors are wainscoted with handsome tiling, and the floors are laid in mosaic. The building is heated by steam and lighted by electricity. The firm of E. H. Van Ingen & Co. is perhaps the largest one in the woolen trade in the world. For more than twenty years it occupied the building at Broadway and Broome Street. It was the first house in the trade to break away from the wholesale dry-goods centre and build a home up-town.

Siegel Brothers at 65 and 67 Wooster Street and 163 and 165 South Fifth Avenue, are the largest manufacturers of ladies' underwear in the United States. They manufacture ladies', misses' and children's underwear, infants' wear, pillow shams and lawn waists, and, in fact, everything of a kindred nature — of the best grades of muslins, cambric, imported nainsook and silk, with the finest qualities of lace and Hamburg embroideries, of their own importation, for trimming. They occupy two large factories, one in New-York City and the other in Brooklyn, besides having smaller plants distributed throughout the States of New York and New Jersey. They employ more than 1,000 hands.   The superior quality of the

SIEGEL BROTHERS, 65 AND 67 WOOSTER STREET.

Siegel goods was recognized by the judges at the Paris Exposition of 1889, who gave them the very highest awards. Their exhibit at the Columbian Exposition at Chicago is one of the most attractive in this line. The business was established in 1866, by Benjamin and Gerson Siegel, who were associated together for more than twenty-seven years. Its first home was a narrow loft on Reade Street, where, under the stimulus of its directors, the industry rapidly grew, and was transferred to more favorable quarters at 385 Broadway. A subsequent move led to 365 and 367 Canal Street, from which place it finally migrated to its present home on Wooster Street, which is a spacious building of five stories and basement, with lofts measuring 55 by 200 feet. In 1892 Benjamin Siegel, one of the founders, died, and therefore a reorganization of the firm was necessary. On July 1, 1893, the company incorporated with the following officers: Gerson Siegel, President; Joseph Siegel (son of Benjamin Siegel), Vice-President; and Frederick Green, Secretary. Their unusual facilities for importing their materials at low rates, and the sagacious distribution and immense capacity of their factories, together with their many years' experience in the trade, give Siegel Brothers a conspicuous lead in their department of business.

The Siegel Brothers' establishment is not far from Broadway, three short blocks, and only a few doors from Broome Street.

Hornthal, Weissman & Co., whose imposing building is on Broadway, at the northeast corner of Bond Street, stand as the highest type of wholesale clothing manufacturers. The business was started in 1840, and is to-day the oldest existing house in this line in America— an industry which ranks foremost of all the varied manufactures of the Metropolis. The original style of the firm was Hornthal & Whitehead, the founders being Marx Hornthal and Mayer Whitehead. Later it was Hornthal, Whitehead & Co., then Hornthal, Whitehead, Weissman & Co., and in 1892 the present style was adopted, the partners now comprising Lewis M. Hornthal (son of the founder), Leopold Weissman, William E. Lauer, Simon R. Riem and Joseph Benjamin. All of the present members have been actively engaged in the clothing business for a lifetime. Their line of manufacture includes the full range of clothing for men and youths,— overcoats, suitings, trousers, vests, ulsters, dress-suits, liveries, etc., adapted for all seasons, all climates and all localities, and

HORNTHAL, WEISSMAN & CO., BROADWAY AND BOND STREET.

for all grades and conditions of buyers, from the cheapest to the highest. The garments are cut by steam and hand power in their Broadway establishment, and are made by the best hands of New York, Brooklyn and adjacent towns, employ. ment being given to over 2,000 people. More than 20 travelling salesmen cover the whole country from Maine to Alaska.

The site of the building was once in the fashionable centre of this city. Here stood the mansion of Sampson, the East-India merchant, whose daughter became the Duchesse de Dino.

The business was at first at William and Cedar Streets, then on Murray Street, then on Walker Street, and then at 444 to 448 Broadway, in a great building which was destroyed in the notable conflagration of February 8, 1876. After this fire the firm moved to 466 and 468 Broadway, near Grand Street, and then to its present location at Broadway and Bond Street.

W. G. Hitchcock & Co., importing and commission merchants, is a house of the first rank in the dry-goods trade, and in their own specialties unquestionably lead all others in this country, if not in the world. They are the sole agents and control absolutely the product for the United States of the following notable manufacturers : B. Priestley & Co., black dress goods and veilings; S. Courtauld & Co., English crapes; Goodall Worsted Co., American serges, etc.; Lyons Silk & Tapestry Co., broad silks, silk veils and veilings, and American upholstery goods ; Landru Silk Mills, American broad silks; Capitol silks; H. Perinot, Paris kid and Suede gloves; and B. H. & E. E. Elwood, American broad silks. These make a complete line of foreign and domestic dress goods, with all the staple goods and novelties current at each season. They include the general lines sold at large to the trade and the specially confined designs and qualities made to order to suit the demands of their customers in all quarters of the Union. The premises occupied comprise the splendid iron front building six stories high, 50 by 100 feet, on the southwest corner of Broome and Mercer Streets, and the adjoining building on Mercer Street, 25 by 137 feet. The business was established in 1818, nearly three-quarters of a century ago, by Pierre Becar. Among former partners of this house were Aaron Arnold, Richard Arnold and James M. Constable, of Arnold, Constable & Co.

Welcome G. Hitchcock, the present head, and to whom is due its pre-eminent success of to-day, entered its employ in 1854, when it was Noel J. Becar & Co.; after twelve years' service he became a partner, the style then being Becar, Napier & Co., with Alfred Becar and Alex. D. Napier as senior partners; later the style became Hitchcock & Potter, and in 1884 it was changed to its present form, the partners then, as now, comprising W. G. Hitchcock, George Jarvis Geer, A. Howard Hopping, and Charles H. Lane. Mr. Hitchcock came as a poor lad from his native place, Montrose, Penn., and has achieved his success by industry, economy, ability, fidelity to each and every obligation, knowledge of his business and pro-

W. G. HITCHCOCK & CO., BROOME AND MERCER STREETS.

per consideration for his customers. His first situation was with Joseph F. Sanxay, in a men's furnishing goods store, at $2 a week — quite a contrast with his present income. He is identified with various banks and institutions, devoting a part of his incessantly occupied time to matters pertaining to the general welfare.

Langdon, Batcheller & Co., manufacturers of the celebrated "glove-fitting" corsets and kindred goods, occupy the building at 345 and 347 Broadway, one of the prominent structures on this great thoroughfare of commerce. They are the successors in line of W. S. & C. H. Thomson, who organized the business in 1856. This house, like many others, has grown from a very small beginning to be one of the most prominent manufacturing concerns in the United States. Charles H. Langdon was admitted as a partner in 1858, and continued his connection with the firm until January 1, 1893. George C. Batcheller entered the firm in 1865, and is the only member of the present firm who was connected with the original house. In 1862 the style of the firm-name was changed to Thomson, Langdon & Co.; and

in 1889 it was again changed to that of Langdon, Batcheller & Co., the present style. George C. Batcheller, the senior member of the firm, and the controlling spirit of it, has given the best years of his life to the development of the corset industry in this country. In 1876 he conceived the idea of building a large factory in Bridgeport, Ct., for the introduction of hand-made corsets. The success of this venture was assured from the very start, and from it has grown an industry giving em-

LANGDON, BATCHELLER & CO., BROADWAY AND LEONARD STREET.

ployment to thousands of people who produce annually millions of corsets; the output of this house alone being six thousand pairs of corsets a day. The Bridgeport works cover more than an acre; and there is also a factory in up-town New York. The growth of the "glove-fitting" corsets has kept pace with the corset industry, and their reputation is world-wide. This firm has a branch house in Chicago, from which they supply the West and Southwest. The firm is composed of George C. Batcheller, Frank I. Perry, George C. Miller, John A. Kernan and William H. Batcheller. The junior partners have grown up with the business, and are particularly fitted for the work which they have charge of, which enables the firm to handle its immense business with the greatest ease and dispatch. In the corset trade, the foremost position is conceded to Langdon, Batcheller & Co.

The William Clark Company, with its sales department at 295 Church Street, was organized early in 1891, its purpose being to manufacture six-cord sewing thread. William Clark, who owns the controlling interest, and in whose honor it was named, is one of the oldest living thread manufacturers, having spent nearly a half century in the practical management of thread-making, and for over a quarter of a century General Manager of the Clark Thread Company, of Newark, N. J.

WILLIAM CLARK COMPANY, 295 CHURCH STREET.

Mr. Clark was born in Scotland, in 1819, and has a strong personality, effectively felt in every industry he is connected with. Although methodical and strict, he is always fair, which accounts for the fact that he has always had the utmost respect of employees under his charge. The active management of the new company is in the hands of his two sons, William Clark, Jr., and Robert K. Clark, both of whom have had a valuable experience. The thread manufactured by this company is distinguished from others by the letters N-E-W, and notwithstanding the fact that it has been on the market but a short time, it has been favorably received, owing to its meritorious qualities, which have been appreciated in a manner which strengthens the belief that the public is always ready to endorse a good article. The mills at Westerly, R. I., are built after the "slow-burning construction" plan, and are equipped with the best-built and latest machinery, some of which was constructed after plans devised by the management. The company has also constructed many cottages, for homes for the employees, not like ordinary mill tenements, but neat, well-built houses, each upon a plot of ground 60 by 150 feet, where all the comforts of a refined home-life can be enjoyed. The company has also set apart one of these cottages, which is used as a chapel and night-school, both of which are managed solely by the employees, and with extraordinary success. The sales department, at 295 Church Street, is under the management of H. G. Armitage, whose efficiency is shown in the success attending his efforts to popularize the goods of the company. The company has adopted many novel advertising schemes, and has carefully avoided the old ruts in this branch, which has given it the reputation in the trade of being a live and enterprising company. The officers are William Clark, President and Treasurer; Robert K. Clark, Secretary; and William Clark, Jr., General Manager.

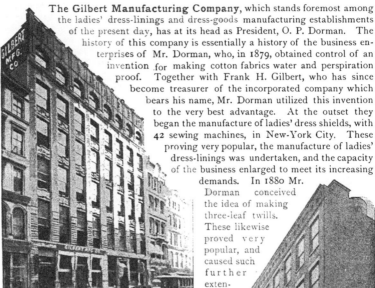

The Gilbert Manufacturing Company, which stands foremost among the ladies' dress-linings and dress-goods manufacturing establishments of the present day, has at its head as President, O. P. Dorman. The history of this company is essentially a history of the business enterprises of Mr. Dorman, who, in 1879, obtained control of an invention for making cotton fabrics water and perspiration proof. Together with Frank H. Gilbert, who has since become treasurer of the incorporated company which bears his name, Mr. Dorman utilized this invention to the very best advantage. At the outset they began the manufacture of ladies' dress shields, with 42 sewing machines, in New-York City. These proving very popular, the manufacture of ladies' dress-linings was undertaken, and the capacity of the business enlarged to meet its increasing demands. In 1880 Mr. Dorman conceived the idea of making three-leaf twills. These likewise proved very popular, and caused such further exten-

GILBERT MANUFACTURING CO.,
514 AND 518 BROADWAY.

sion of the business that in 1881 the firm was incorporated, under its present name. In the same year W. T. McIntire became connected with the company, and three years later was elected to its vice-presidency. For the next three or four years the capacity of the company was taxed to its utmost in meeting the demands for its plain three-leaf twill. Feeling that a slight departure would still further increase the business, a fancy three-leaf twill was introduced. In the early history of the company Mr. Dorman had secured by a contract for five years control of an invention whereby a cotton fabric could be dyed a black, which should be positively and absolutely fast. This discovery was used at the outset exclusively for dress-linings. Later, it was utilized in making black Henrietta cloths,

GILBERT MANUFACTURING CO.,
WAREHOUSE ON CROSBY STREET.

which proved even more successful than the dress-linings. Not satisfied with these results alone, a long series of experiments was undertaken, which at last resulted in the successful manufacture of fast black dress goods with white figures. Further experimenting led to the making of fast black goods with dual and chintz colorings. Looms running in the interest of the company are now scattered through every State in New England, excepting Vermont. The company's main office and salesrooms are at 514 and 516 Broadway, and their warehouses are at 60, 62, 64 and 66 Crosby Street. Branches are established at various points in this and foreign countries.

Belding Brothers & Co. are the foremost representatives of the sewing-silk business in America. From the small beginnings in silk-worm culture at North-

BELDING BROTHERS & CO., 455 AND 457 BROADWAY.

ampton, Massachusetts, have grown the great silk companies of modern times. This business is now one of the most important manufacturing interests of the country. The Belding Brothers, by unremitting push and by placing on the market only the best product of silk-manufacture, have established an enormous business, with a world-wide reputation. Their plant consists of mills at Northampton, Massachusetts; Montreal, Canada; San Francisco, California; Rockville, Connecticut; and Belding, Michigan. These five mills employ over 3,000 hands. Their chief products are machine twist, sewing, knitting and embroidery silks, silk hosiery and lining silks. The total product of the mills during the year 1892 was valued at $5,500,-000. Over 2,250 pounds of raw silk from Asia and Europe, costing $14,000, are daily converted through a great variety of processes into thread. In all branches of the manufacture a single strand of silk must be produced, which is usually doubled for yarns and trebled for machine-twist. This single strand, into which every day at these mills a ton of silk is converted, is long enough to go around the entire globe twelve times. One of the great improvements in the manufacture of silk is the operation of a patented machine which cleans the completed thread, not only taking off all burrs and pluff, but also giving it a gloss which is peculiarly characteristic of the goods of the Belding Brothers.

The principal mills are at Northampton, near the Connecticut-River Railroad and the New-Haven & Northampton Railroad. 175 looms and 20,000 spindles are employed there in weaving silk fabrics, such as sleeve-linings and silk coat-linings for tailors' use. There are also in operation 25 hosiery machines, producing 300 dozen of silk hose each week. This industry is interesting, because of the humble way in which it began. The foundation of it was laid in 1860 by Hiram H. and Alvah N. Belding, who started from Otisco, Michigan, which since has been named Belding, to sell silk from house to house. This method proved so successful that three years later they, together with their brother, Milo M. Belding, started a house in Chicago. In 1863 the three brothers formed a partnership with E. K. Rose, and built a mill at Rockville, Connecticut. Three years later the firm was dissolved. In 1869 the mill at Northampton was built; and subsequently the others. The company's main offices are at 455 and 457 Broadway, New York. The officers are : M. M. Belding, President and Treasurer ; D. W. Belding, Vice-President ; and A. N. Belding, Secretary. The directors are : M. M. Belding and J. R. Emery of New York ; D. W. Belding of Cincinnati ; A. N. Belding, of Rockville ; W. S. Belding, of Chicago ; W. A. Stanton, and E. C. Young of Chicago.

J. R. LEESON & CO., 317 CHURCH STREET.

J. R. Leeson & Co., at Church and Lispenard Streets, is the principal branch of the largest linen-thread importing house of the United States. Besides being the American representatives of the great Scottish house of Finlayson, Bousfield & Co., whose gigantic works are at Johnstone, in Scotland, they are the selling agents of the Grafton Flax Mills, of Grafton, Mass. In addition to their remarkable record as to age, the Scottish house being the oldest established linen-thread manufacturers in Scotland ; as to magnitude, the Johnstone Mills alone giving employment to 3,000 persons ; as to stability, the standing of the concerns being rated at many millions of dollars ; and as to preëminence, being the largest makers of linen and flax threads in the world, and receiving the only Prize Medal awarded for quality in linen threads at the first International Exhibition, London, 1851 : the houses of Finlayson, Bousfield & Co. and J. R. Leeson & Co. have made indelible records in the annals of the growth of their industry by the almost innumerable list of inventions for the better manufacture and the more extended use of the products of linen and flax thread mills. Their introduction of "Real Scotch Linen Floss," and the now universally known "Bargarren Art Threads," for embroidering, crocheting and other ornamental work, created almost a revolution in their way, for they were found to be just as beautiful as silk, and yet far more durable and far less costly. The attachments for book-binders' machines, by which time is saved, with better results and less cost, and without the annoyance of broken needles caused by knotty threads, have become generally used by the book-binders throughout the country. Their peculiarly fine qualities and exceeding strength have made the "Real Scotch" linen threads the especial favorites with the boot and shoe and harness makers and other trades. In 1892 the house introduced a new method of winding threads on tubes, which is destined to revolutionize the entire system of putting up threads for manufacturing and home use, for by this new system the many trials of the old-fashioned balls, bobbins or tubes are avoided, and there is no bulging, no breaking or straining of the thread, no ravelling into knots or loops, no slipping over sides to interfere with machinery, etc. The products of the mills in Scotland and at Grafton include every variety of linen and flax threads now in use for any purposes. They are put up in all conceivable styles of thickness and color for which there is any demand. The headquarters of the firm are at 226 Devonshire Street, Boston; and in addition to the principal branch in New-York City, J. R. Leeson & Co. have agencies at 405 Arch Street, Philadelphia; 323 Main Street, Cincinnati; 240 Franklin Street, Chicago; and in St. Louis, San Francisco, and other important trade-centres.

Francis H. Leggett & Co. is one of the most prominent wholesale grocery-houses of the world; there is none more widely or more favorably known. This house dates back to 1870, at which time Francis H. Leggett associated with himself his brother, Theodore Leggett, and the new house assumed the firm-name as it stands to-day. Leasing the building at 74 Murray Street, a modest beginning was made as a foundation to their present extensive business. Then staple goods, sugars, syrups, molasses, etc., formed the bulk of the stock of all grocery houses, the addition of specialties not coming into vogue until some years later. The new firm was quick to discover any possible opening for adding new and desirable features, and for enlarging the scope of its operations, and it has done much to give the grocery trade its present diversified character. They were, also, among the first in their line to add a complete line of canned goods, imported groceries, and foreign fruits to their lists. The inauguration of each new feature served to increase the popularity and to extend the patronage of the house. In 1873 larger quarters were required, and they removed to 97, 99 and 101 Reade Street. They soon occupied the entire building, and also one adjoining, on Chambers Street. Increasing trade demanded still more space, and in 1881 the firm erected their present building.

By a fire which occurred May 10, 1891, the top floor was destroyed, and the entire stock was seriously damaged by water and smoke. For the ensuing three months the firm occupied temporary quarters in Franklin, Hudson and West Streets, and in the meantime repaired and remodelled their own building. The building is imposing in its dimensions and attractive in its appearance. It is of pressed brick and granite, and comprises ten stories and basement.

The power-plant consists of two horizontal tubular boilers, of 60 horse-power each, and one horizontal automatic cut-off engine, of 90 horse-power. This engine furnishes power for milling and electric-light purposes. The power for milling is transmitted from the engine to the several floors, until it reaches the tenth floor,

FRANCIS H. LEGGETT & CO.'S WHOLESALE GROCERY WAREHOUSE.
FRANKLIN STREET, FROM WEST BROADWAY TO VARICK STREET.

where the Spice Department is located.   The large stock carried by the firm is moved by six powerful steam elevators, of the Otis type.   For electric light purposes there is also used an 80 horse-power high-speed engine, manufactured by the Ball Company of Erie.   The demands upon the boilers have been so great that the firm is contemplating the erection of additional boilers.   The electric-light plant consists of two dynamos.   One is of 700-light capacity, the other of 400-light capacity.

The receiving and shipping departments occupy the first floor, while the private offices, general salesrooms, and counting-room occupy the second floor.   All the stories above are stocked with food-products of all sorts, from every quarter of the globe, and the building contains as large a collection of such as is ever brought under one roof.   The upper floors are used principally for manufacturing purposes, such as grinding spices, milling and packing prepared flour and cereal specialties of every description, flavoring extracts, fruit-syrups, and many other specialties, and the pack- ing of olives, all of which form an important branch of the business.

This firm makes a specialty of high-class groceries of every description, and is a large handler of coffees and teas.   They have a factory at Riverside, N. J., where they pack their own brands of canned goods, jams, and other high-grade specialties, which have a national reputation for excellence.   The firm has also an office at 44 Rue de Traversiere, Bordeaux, France.   They do not sell wines, bitters, or liquors of any description, but deal exclusively in food-products, and their brands are so well-known and popular that their trade extends to all parts of the world.   The steady and prosperous growth of the volume of trade of this house finds its explana- tion in a strict adherence to principles of integrity ; maintaining a high standard of quality for their brands, and dealing fairly and justly with each patron.   The busi- ness is divided into twenty-five departments, each of which is in charge of a com- petent manager.   The present members of the firm are Francis H. Leggett, Albert H. Jones, Lewis Wallace, and John C. Juhring, Theodore Leggett having died in 1883, while absent from the city in the summer of that year.

John Osborn, Son & Co., general merchants, have offices at 45 Beaver Street. The house is a very old one.   John Osborn came to New York from Oporto, where he had a commercial house, and established himself in January, 1836.   Some years later he took his brother Robert into partnership, under the style of John & Robert Osborn ; the place of business being at 111 Wall Street.   In 1854 John Osborn erected the building which they now occupy, then in the centre of the dry-goods trade.   A year or so later that trade began moving farther up-town.   About 1856 the firm removed to 45 Beaver Street, and a year later the firm was dissolved by the death of Robert.   John Osborn continued under his own name.   In April, 1869, he associated with himself his son, Francis Pares Osborn, and Timothy Stevens, under the co-partnership name of John Osborn, Son & Co.   The firm had business rela- tions with foreign countries (particularly with Great Britain, France, Spain and Portugal), and continued until May 16, 1869, when it was dissolved by the death of John Osborn.   Immediately a co-partnership was formed by Francis Pares Osborn, Timothy Stevens and Mary C. Osborn, to continue the business under the same style.   There was no change in the *personnel* until May 1, 1875, when the co-part- nership was dissolved.   Then a limited partnership was formed by Francis Pares Osborn as general, and Mary C. Osborn as special partner, to continue the business under the name of John Osborn, Son & Co.   In 1876 a branch house was opened in Montreal, the head office remaining in New York.   On January 1, 1884, a new limited partnership was formed between Francis Pares Osborn, Charles Spencer Osborn, William Osborn, Robert A. Osborn and Mary C. Osborn, to continue four years under the same name. This partnership was renewed in January, 1888. On December 28, 1891, Mary C. Osborn, the special partner and mother of the general partners, died at her home on Clinton Avenue, Brooklyn, where she had lived for forty-two years, and which was the birthplace of William and Robert A. Osborn. On March 13, 1892, the senior partner, Francis Pares Osborn, died; the firm, however, being a limited partnership, continued. In May, 1892, the firm established a Western Department, with offices at 522 and 523 Monadnock Block, Chicago.

On December 31, 1892, a new firm was formed, under a general partnership, composed of the remaining partners, Charles Spencer Osborn, William Osborn and Robert A. Osborn, under the same style of heretofore. On May 1, 1893, owing to increasing business in the Western Department, and to offer better facilities to all friends who may visit the World's Columbian Exposition, the Western Department removed their offices to the Auditorium Hotel Building, on Michigan Avenue, where they have large and spacious offices on the ground floor, giving them better accommodations to do their increasing business, which is making Chicago the distributing point of the West. Among the agencies which this firm has had control of in its wine and spirit department is that of the old and well-known brand of Piper-Heidsieck Champagne. For years they have imported only one grade of champagne, namely, Piper-Heidsieck, "Sec," but this year, considering that American connoisseurs are demanding also a Brut wine, they have been induced to import a real Brut, known under the name of Piper-Heidsieck, Brut Extra, which is pronounced the highest grade of real Brut that is known on this market. During the many years which this firm has been in existence it has had business relations with all parts of Europe, the South American Republics, and the West Indies, importing and exporting the

JOHN OSBORN, SON & CO., 45 BEAVER STREET.

products of these countries, as well as doing a banking business; and the reputation and high standing of the house are well known throughout the world.

Bulkley, Dunton & Co., whose large paper warehouse and offices are at 75 and 77 Duane Street, is one of the oldest, strongest and most highly esteemed houses in the paper trade. The business was started about 1835 by Jeremiah L. Cross, who in 1838 was joined by Edwin Bulkley and Hiram N. Gookin, under the firm-name of Cross, Bulkley & Gookin. Since then various changes in the firm have taken place, as follows: In 1846 to Bulkley & Gookin, in 1848 to Bulkley & Brother, in 1855 to

Bulkley, Brother & Co., and in 1865 to Bulkley, Dunton & Co., the present style having been continued for nearly thirty consecutive years. Through all these changes and until his death in 1881, Edwin Bulkley remained an active partner, and

from 1846 he was the head of the firm. His record for mercantile sagacity and strictly honorable business methods is of the highest order. His associates, men of kindred character, comprised, besides Messrs. Cross and Gookin, his brother Lewis D. Bulkley, William C. Dunton, Cornelius Perry, his sons Andrew and Moses Bulkley, and the present members of the firm, which is composed of David G. Garabrant, Jonathan Bulkley, and James S. Packard. Mr. Dunton held a prominent place, and, as active manager of the business for many years, is largely to be credited with its success. Moses Bulkley died, a young man, in 1892, but left a reputation for excellent business judgment and the strictest integrity. He was prominent in the directorates of various financial and manufacturing corporations. This house from the beginning has held an influential posi-

BULKLEY, DUNTON & CO., 75 AND 77 DUANE STREET.

tion in the paper trade. The specialties of the house are book and news papers. Besides their own two mills at Middlefield, Mass., they own large interests as stockholders in the Montague Paper Company and Keith Paper Company, at Turner's Falls, Mass., and the Winnipiseogee Paper Company, of Franklin, N. H., three of the most successful paper-manufacturing corporations of New England, and of which they were largely the originators. The products of these mills have an established reputation throughout the country, as unexcelled in their various lines. In the finanelal crises of the United States of the past half century this house has sustained its record of solidity; in 1857 and the following years it carried through several other large firms which otherwise would probably have failed. In 1859, and again in 1864, the house suffered a heavy loss by fire, on both occasions their whole establishment being completely burned out. Heavy losses that arose out of these fires and legally fell upon others were generously assumed, carrying out the liberal policy always maintained. For twenty-seven years they were located at 74 John Street, and in 1891 they moved to their present premises at 75 and 77 Duane Street.

Louis DeJonge & Co., at 71 and 73 Duane Street, a few buildings east of Broadway, is the oldest and the foremost house in America in the manufacture and importation of fancy and silver and gold papers, leathers, cloth and paste-board, pictures and ornaments used by bookbinders, printers, lithographers and box-makers. This now immense business was formed in the year 1846, under the style of J. & L. DeJonge, which was changed in 1868 to Louis DeJonge & Co. In 1891 Louis DeJonge retired from the firm, which is now composed of his son-in-law, Charles F. Zentgraf (admitted in 1873), and his son, Louis DeJonge, Jr. (admitted in 1883). Their spacious factories at Tompkinsville, Staten Island,

began operations in 1858, and now employ nearly 400 workmen. In 1892 the plant was enlarged by a new wing, and its capacity for mak-ing surface-coated paper was materi-ally increased. The product in-cludes fine litho-graphic coated papers for color . work ; plated and glazed surface-coated papers in all colors, for printers, litho-graphers and paper-box mak-ers; plain and embossed leather papers, in endless varieties, for book-binders; marbled and fancy lining and cover papers, Winterbottom's English book-cloth, fine moroc-co and Russia and other foreign and imported leath-ers, likewise buf-fings and roans,

LOUIS DEJONGE & CO., 71 AND 73 DUANE STREET.

skivers, batwings, and fleshers. The glues and wax, brushes and twines, gold leaf and albumen, and other requisites of the book-binders' art are kept in stock. Their sales amount to more than $2,000,000 yearly, and reach all parts of America.

Hermann Boker & Co., wholesale dealers in cutlery, hardware, guns and metals, conduct a business started in 1837 by Hermann Boker, a lineal descendant of an old family of merchants, the Bokers, of Remscheid, in Prussia. The first quarters were in John Street, whence they were removed to 50 Cliff Street, where the firm remained over twenty years, and then, in 1872, built and moved into their own large iron-front business building, 101 and 103 Duane Street, extending through to 10 and 12 Thomas Street, just west of Broadway. The style of the firm was Her-

mann Boker from 1837 until 1857, ever since which time it has been Hermann Boker & Co. By the retirement and death of the older partners, the firm now consists of Ferdinand A. Boker, Carl F. Boker and Albert H. Funke. Both the former are sons of the late Hermann Boker, founder of the business, and the latter is the son of Hermann Funke, and brother of Hermann Funke, Jr., two former partners, who died in 1890. Ferdinand A. Boker has been connected with the firm over thirty years, and resides now in Europe, looking after the European interests. Carl F. Boker and Albert H. Funke entered the firm in 1891, the former adding his business in steel and metals, which he then conducted in John Street under his own name.

The business is one of the largest in its line in the United States. It consists of German and English hardware and cutlery, particularly of the celebrated "Tree Brand," made in Solingen. The firm represents some of the oldest and best-known German and English manufacturers in these lines

HERMANN BOKER & CO., 101 AND 103 DUANE STREET.

and in steel and metals, including the widely celebrated Sheffield firm of Jonas & Colver, Limited. They do a vast export business in copper, and are the European agents of the great Calumet & Hecla Mining Company. They have always done an extensive business in Belgian and English sporting guns, and have a representative in Liége, looking after various interests in Europe. As a matter of fact, it would be the exception not to find at the Boker establishment every desirable article usually sought for in wholesale hardware, cutlery and sporting-gun houses, the completeness of the stock being one of the essential elements of the success of the business.

Everything considered, there is no more highly esteemed business firm in New York than the old house of Hermann Boker & Co.

Wallace, Elliott & Co., of 118 to 124 Duane Street, between Broadway and Church Street, are preëminent as manufacturers, jobbers and wholesalers of boots, shoes, rubbers and slippers. Their five factories, at Poughkeepsie, N. Y., Farmington, N. H., Rochester, N. H., Stoughton, Mass., and Haverhill, Mass., contain the most modern and ingenious machinery in use, and turn out over fifteen thousand pairs of shoes a day. They also manufacture the celebrated "Crest" $2 and $3 shoe for men and women, which is advertised in every nook and corner.

The firm of Wallace & Hollinshed, established more than forty years ago, was succeeded in 1871 by Wallace & Elliott, composed of Edwin Wallace and Henry Elliott. These gentlemen still continue in the business, and have admitted as partners John E. Jacobs (in 1879) and Clinton Elliott, son of Henry Elliott (in 1889). The institution, thus founded and advanced, has developed into one of the most important and interesting of its class in the world, and is still progressing with remarkable business sagacity and financial ability. One cardinal principle has been, never to allow competition to force them to reduce the high quality of their goods, and even in the stormiest periods of under-selling and business chicanery, Wallace, Elliott & Co. have kept their standard high and blameless. The knowledge of this fact has become common property in the trade, and therefore their goods are always in demand. The requirements of their business keep more than fifty sales-

WALLACE, ELLIOTT & CO., DUANE AND CHURCH STREETS.

men busy, and there is not a State in the Union that is not regularly visited by their active salesmen on the road, besides the forces in their branch-offices in Chicago and Philadelphia. Their New-York store is probably the largest in the world, of its class, since it occupies twenty-two floors, all of which contain goods of their own manufacture. Their sample-rooms contain more than one thousand varieties of boots, shoes and slippers, as usually contained in their stock. A fact like this shows how great must be the talent, how careful the training, which prepares the skilful merchant to handle successfully such intricate combinations.

Dan Talmage's Sons & Co., at 115 Wall Street, have passed the half-century mark, and stand at the head and front of the rice traffic in this country. The house was established in 1841 by Daniel Talmage, and is to-day continued by his sons and grandsons, all men in the prime of life, and enjoying a position in the mercantile community fully equal to the worthy founder. Their business is by no means confined to New York, for their largest operations are in the South and Southwest.

DAN TALMAGE'S SONS & CO., 115 WALL STREET.

The house at this point may be termed the financial heart; for out of and to it flow all of its monetary arrangements. Their representatives (all Talmages) at the various points possess marked ability, shrewdness and business sagacity. The Southern houses are located at Charleston and New Orleans, the milling centres of the rice growth in the United States. So intimate are their relations to the growth that they might be termed producers one remove, for they are the right hand of many of the "sons of the soil." The rice crop of the United States is now large enough to supply the home demand, and as the acreage is annually increasing, the time is not far distant when exports of American rice will become an important commercial feature, and form no mean proportion of the amount consumed in Europe. The firm has been very active in stimulating the culture; distributing practical information concerning the industry; and strongly urging upon Southern planters the wisdom of diversifying products, curtailing in a measure any given prominent product,—cotton, sugar or tobacco, as the case might be, in any section,—and the advisability of devoting, among other substitutes, some space to rice. In the distribution of the product the field widens to and throughout the entire country, their shipments entering every prominent city; and in addition they do a large export trade. Their rice-mills in this city and at the South are of large capacity and thoroughly equipped with the latest and best machinery, securing excellent out-turn expeditiously and economically. Supplies of rough rice are derived from shipments by planters who realize the advantage of having their grain milled and sold in the cleaned state. The net results by such course are increased by ten to fifteen per cent., as the producer is brought several steps nearer the consumer and therefore saves many intermediary charges.

Henry A. Rogers, at 19 John Street, is one of the leading American dealers in railroad and machinists' supplies and tools, and enjoys a very large trade with many of the best railroad companies and manufacturing establishments. Commencing with the food, clothing and shelter used by railroad construction parties ; continuing with the rails and tools, such as shovels, picks, graders and rock drills, for

the construction of a railway's road-bed ; and concluding with bridges, cars, locomotives and machinery, lathes, planers, etc., used in every machine-shop, this busy house equips a railroad from its first breaking ground to maintaining it in its fullest operation. Almost equally important with the railroad supplies is his trade in tools and machinery and machinists' supplies, like belting, waste, oil, oil cups, files, hammers, wrenches, etc. He has a large Government business in furnishing machinery and tools for navy yards and military posts. Vast supplies have gone to Australia, Cuba, Mexico and South America. Almost everything used in building the Cartagena Railway, in the United States of Colombia, went from H. A. Rogers's establishment. This house is the sole American agent for the Moncrieff " Perth " glass tubes, which have an immense sale in the United States, leading all makes. These gauge glasses, which show high and low water in boilers, are imported direct from Perth, Scotland. They resist high pressure and great variations of heat, and are so hard outside that a diamond will scarcely scratch them, yet so soft inside that a piece of sharpened steel will cut them. Their high quality, attested by universal adoption as "the best," by engineers all over the world, has won the highest awards and medals.

A quarter of a century has passed since Mr. Rogers left the prominent house of Walton & Co. In 1870 he established himself at 57 John Street ; and in 1871 he formed a partnership with W. C. Duyckinck, under the title of H. A. Rogers & Co. They purchased the entire business of John Ashcroft, and occupied 50 and 52 John Street. Since 1875

H. A. ROGERS, 19 JOHN STREET.

he has conducted the business alone, with marked success. His two brothers are actively connected with him. His branch office at Chicago is managed by John S. Brewer. Mr. Rogers is identified with several banking and other institutions ; was Treasurer of the New-York Athletic Club ; and is a member of many of New-York's famous clubs. He has been for many years a school trustee in the Twenty-second Ward, and largely interested in educational affairs ; is a member of the Chamber of Commerce ; and under three administrations has been U.-S. Commissioner of Jurors.

Canda & Kane, the most extensive dealers in masons' building material in the United States, was formed in 1879 by John M. Canda and John P. Kane, both of whom had been long identified with the business, Mr. Canda as a partner in Morton & Canda, founded in 1850. The firm commenced with two yards in New York, four trucks, and one clerk, and now have four yards in New York and two in Brooklyn, with 70 trucks and 18 clerks, giving means to supply material quickest and in any quantity in both cities. In late years this firm furnished the masons' material of most of the prominent buildings, like the Cotton, Produce and Mercantile Exchanges; the Manhattan Life, Metropolitan Life and Mutual Reserve Insurance Companies; the Potter, Scott & Bowne, United Charities, Havemeyer, Lincoln, *Mail and Express,* New-Jersey Central and Edison Buildings; the Shoe and Leather, Bleecker-Street, Bowery Savings, Market and Fulton, and Manhattan Savings Banks; the New Netherlands, Waldorf, Savoy, Nevada and Sherman-Square Hotels; the Sacred Heart Convent, Seton Hospital, St. Agnes' Church, the Catholic and Colonial Clubs, Clinton Hall, the Manhattan Storage Warehouse, the Delaware, Lackawanna & Western Building, the American and Broadway Theatres, Gansevoort Market, Carnegie Music Hall, Washington Arch, New-York Biscuit Company, the mansions of Cornelius Vanderbilt and C. P. Huntington, and the armories of the 8th, 12th and 71st Regiments. The Potter Building took 11,000,000 bricks and 11,000 barrels of cement, or enough for 110 four-story houses. Music Hall took 7,000,000; the Cotton Exchange, 5,000,000. These amounts are prodigious. They have just completed a handsome office building at the foot of West 52d Street, for their own use, and for the brick manufacturers and representatives of the trade, thereby making it the market and centre of the brick industry. The yearly sales of Canda & Kane have averaged 200,000,000 brick, 75,000 barrels of Portland cement, 300,000 barrels of Rosendale cement, and 300,000 barrels of lime. The quantity of brick sold by them will average one quarter of the whole amount manufactured in this locality. Mr. Kane, the business head of the firm, has given his

CANDA & KANE, WEST 52D STREET, NEAR NORTH RIVER.

SEVENTH AVENUE AND 125TH STREET, SHOWING HARLEM Y. M. C. A.

undivided attention to the establishment of this business, and to his efforts are due the sound credit **and** business reputation the firm enjoys. He resides in a handsome house in West 72d Street, and has a delightful summer residence at Huntington, L. I. Mr. Canda is a popular resident of Brooklyn, and has a summer residence in the Catskills. Canda & Kane do a business of over $3,000,000 a year, are splendidly organized, and are continually increasing their facilities.

RIVERSIDE PARK.

George Borgfeldt & Co. is conspicuously prominent among the great importing commission firms of New-York City. Its specialties are notions, fancy goods, stationery articles, druggists' sundries, dolls, toys, albums, fancy furniture, clocks, bronzes, art goods, bric-a-brac, china, glassware, furnishing goods, etc., etc. Although comparatively a young house (founded in 1881 by George Borgfeldt, Marcel Kahle and Joseph Kahle), and the outgrowth of modest beginnings, it now stands unrivalled in the domain of its operations. It had its commencement at 83 Leonard Street, and later, requiring additional quarters, it removed to 112 and 114 Franklin Street, between West Broadway and Church Street. Still larger premises were occupied at 425 and 427 Broome Street, corner of Crosby Street.

January 1, 1893, the business moved into its present quarters at 18, 20, 22 and 24 Washington Place, at the southwest corner of Greene Street, one of the most elegant and commodious business edifices of New-York City. The present building is eight stories above the sidewalk and two beneath it. On the ground, the dimensions are 100 feet by 100 feet. It was built expressly for its present occupants, and is most advantageously arranged for its uses. It is of fire-proof construction, and affords splendid light and commodious and elegant quarters for the display of its great and varied collections.

Its neighborhood has recently become a well-built-up business section. Tenements and small buildings of a few years ago are giving way to whole blocks of splendid business edifices, the most aristocratic of which is the great and handsome building of George Borgfeldt & Co. In its immediate neighborhood is Washington Square, with its world-famous Washington Arch, and close by are many noted public institutions, such as Cooper Institute, the Astor Library, the Mercantile Library, the University of the City of New York, etc., etc. The location is only a short distance, merely two short blocks, away from Broadway, the main thoroughfare of the Metropolis.

In the departments for which this house is eminently and deservedly noted, samples of the very latest European, Oriental and domestic novelties are to be found; and specimens of the workmanship, skill and style of almost every civilized country on the globe are to be seen. The marvellous and almost infinite variety of the articles is manifest when it is said that it displays over 500,000 distinct and different samples.

Its china, bric-a-brac and art-goods departments are revelations, by virtue of the fact that in them are displayed the ceramics of the most celebrated potteries of the world. That the efforts of their searchers after surprises and the unexpected have been and are appreciated by the merchants of the United States is duly attested to and emphasized by the almost phenomenal growth and development of their business. Its customers extend to every part of the United States and Canada, and the infinite variety of the lines of goods handled brings to it customers in many different branches of trade. The firm has offices and resident representatives in Paris, Berlin, Sonneberg, Solingen, Bodenbach, Fuerth, Stoke-on-Trent, and Limoges.

In 1885, G. F. Pfeiffer (formerly of Strasburger, Pfeiffer & Co.), and Ferdinand Hecht (of Berlin), and a year later Louis P. Twyeffort (formerly with Dunham, Buckley & Co.), were admitted as general partners. In 1889, George Semler, manager of the china department, was admitted to partnership. In 1893, the firm was resolved into a joint-stock corporation, with a paid-in capital of $750,000. Mr. Borgfeldt was chosen President; Marcel Kahle, First Vice-President; George Semler, second Vice-President; George F. Pfeiffer, Secretary; and Joseph Kahle, Treasurer.

GEORGE BORGFELDT & CO.
WASHINGTON PLACE, SOUTHWEST CORNER OF GREENE STREET.

HARLEM RIVER, LOOKING EAST FROM WASHINGTON BRIDGE.

EAST RIVER BRIDGE, FROM NEAR THE BROOKLYN LANDING.

W. H. Schieffelin & Co., wholesale druggists and manufacturers of pharmaceutical preparations, at the corner of William and Beekman Streets, was originated before the beginning of the present century (1794), by Jacob Schieffelin, whose warehouse was at that time at 193 Pearl Street. The location was subsequently changed to Maiden Lane, where the business was conducted until 1841, when the vast increase of its operations demanding more room, the firm, under the style of H. H. Schieffelin & Co., removed to 104 and 106 John Street. In the year of 1849 the style of the firm was changed to Schieffelin Bros. & Co. In 1854, their business having increased so much as to require still more ample accommodations, the establishment was removed to the present spacious warehouse at 170 and 172 William Street, corner of Beekman. In 1865 the firm of Schieffelin Bros. & Co. was re-formed as W. H. Schieffelin & Co. Successive generations of the family have been engaged in the business throughout the past century, and at present the third, fourth and fifth generations are represented in the concern. This is a record of which any mercantile firm may be proud, as it is very unusual to find a house whose business has been carried on and transmitted to several successive generations, and this, together with the high standard of business integrity always maintained, has contributed much to the reputation of the establishment.

The warehouse at 170 and 172 William Street, expressly constructed for themselves, is a brick structure, six stories in height, with basement and sub-cellar, and numerous fire - proof vaults extending under the sidewalk. This firm also has a separate building located at 697 and 699 Water Street, and 400 and 402 Front Street, covering even more ground than their warehouse, a laboratory which is one of the largest and best appointed in the country, where, by the use of the most approved apparatus and machinery (some of which is of their own recent

W. H. SCHIEFFELIN & CO., WILLIAM AND BEEKMAN STREETS.

invention), the greater part of their manufacturing is carried on. A careful investigation of this warehouse and laboratory will satisfy any one that the high reputation enjoyed by its proprietors is a just one, and their prosperity no more than commensurate with their merits. The present members of the firm are William H. Schieffelin, William N. Clark, William S. Mersereau, William L. Brower, William J. Schieffelin and Henry S. Clark, as general partners; and Samuel B. Schieffelin, of New York, and Sidney A. Schieffelin, of Geneva, N. Y., as special partners.

Tarrant & Co., importers and jobbers of drugs and chemicals and manufacturers of pharmaceuticals and perfumery, occupy the building 278-280-282 Greenwich Street and 100 Warren Street.   The name has been displayed on this spot for
nearly 60 years, for James Tarrant opened a drug store at 278 Greenwich Street in
1834.   His establishment was then distinctively the up-town drug store of the business portion of New-York City, and beyond it lay a residence section of almost suburban character.   The New-York Hospital, naturally a rendezvous for the leading
physicians of the time, was then in the vicinity of Broadway and Duane Street, and
Tarrant's drug store, being not far distant, became a supply depot and "house of
call" for the doctors attached to that institution.   In 1844 James Tarrant began the

manufacture of Tarrant's
Seltzer Aperient and various
other specialties for the use
of physicians.   The enterprise proved successful, and
in the course of time this
manufacture became a leading feature of the business.
James Tarrant died in 1852,
and was succeeded by the
firm of John A. Tarrant &
Co., the senior member of
which was a brother of the
founder of the establishment.
In 1861 the firm was incorporated under the style of
Tarrant & Co.   The manu-
facture of pharmaceutical
specialties and perfumery
was continued, and importing and jobbing drugs, chemicals and druggists' sundries
added.   The quaint old
building on which James
Tarrant hung his sign in
1834 was in existence up to
November, 1892, when it
was torn down, to be re-

TARRANT & CO., GREENWICH AND WARREN STREETS.

placed by the handsome and commodious structure shown in the accompanying
illustration.   The new building is built of brick, with terra-cotta trimmings, is
seven stories high, and in addition has large and commodious cellar and vault room.
All modern conveniences, including steam and electric elevators, are prominent features of the new warehouse, which is in every respect admirably adapted to the
requirements of their trade.   Tarrant & Co. are the American representatives of
many European manufacturers of pharmaceutical specialties and druggists' sundries, and their "Seltzer Aperient," first manufactured in 1844, is to-day a household remedy in almost all American homes.   Representatives of the establishment visit every part of the United States, and Central and South America, and
the products of their laboratory are to be found in a great many of the large cities
of Europe.

·Notable Manufacturers·

**An Outline History of Some Preëminent Industries Carried
on or Represented in New York.**

ARTISTS think of New York as the seat of the greatest collections of pictures
and sculpture in America ; authors, as the foremost of publishing centres ;
musicians, as the critical tribunal of the Western World ; theologians, as the seat of
the great Episcopal and Presbyterian schools of the prophets ; financiers, as the
home of the great bank corporations.   Every one has his own point of view in looking
at the Empire City, as port, or fortress, or mart, or mother-city in many ways.

But perhaps few people recognize that a prime distinction of New York is its preëminent position as a manufacturing city, crowded with ingenious artificers, and
pouring its multifarious products all over the Great Republic.   While one section of
the city includes its financial powers, and another is dominated by the clubs and the
theatres, and another by the vast shipping interests, several spacious and thickly
crowded sections are given up to manufactories, and populated with the swarming
families of its mechanics and artisans.

Away back in 1880 this city alone had within her boundaries over 11,000 factories, in which were employed the vast army of 227,342 persons.   These workers
received as wages $97,030,121 a year.   The capital of the manufacturing companies
reached $181,206,356.   Every year their works consumed $288,000,000 worth of
material, which yielded, after the labors of the New-York artisans had enriched
them, articles valued at $473,000,000.   One-sixth of this was in the single article
of clothing, upon whose fabrication nearly 60,000 persons were continually employed.
The preparation of meat for use employs a great army of men, and yields in this one
city a product of about $30,000,000 yearly.   Ten thousand people get their living
by printing and publishing, their yearly product exceeding $20,000,000 in value.
There are armies of brewers, myriads of iron-workers, cohorts of cigar-makers, and
great numbers of makers of pianos and furniture, of boots and shoes, of hats and
caps, of sugar and molasses, of millinery and jewelry.

At the present time New-York City has 12,000 factories, with 500,000 operatives,
and a yearly product valued at above $600,000,000, including an enormous variety
of different articles.   The largest single item of manufacture still is clothing, in a
myriad of different forms.   Next comes the making of books and papers, choice
products of this great publishing centre.   Cigars and tobacco are next in the
importance of their product ; followed by pianos and other kinds of musical
instruments.   Besides the wonderful concentration of manufacturing capital in the
city proper, New York has established large plants in her suburbs, especially in the
New-Jersey and Long-Island sides, with their main headquarters in the metropolis.

A few of the great concerns are noticed in this chapter.

58

The American Bank Note Company conducts one of the most famous industries of the country, and one which has won the respect and admiration of the world for America's artists and skilled mechanics. Its renown has been the result of a rare combination of the highest artistic and mechanical skill through a long experience, and its standing to-day is unequalled. The business was founded in 1795 ; incorporated under the laws of the State of New York in 1858 ; and enlarged and re-organized in 1879. The early and widespread use of paper money rendered it imperative to produce engraved work which could not be counterfeited. The best artists competed in making designs, skilful chemists devised inks to be brilliant and ineradicable, or deleble and sensitive, and inventors applied the principles of mechanics to intricate geometrical engraving. The consolidation of these interests as the American Bank Note Company united the resources and reputation, the safe-guards and facilities, of a century's experience, with abundant capital to test new inventions and acquire new processes. The company has prepared securities to the value of millions and millions of dollars, and bank-notes innumerable, also postage-stamps, bonds, stocks, diplomas, drafts, etc., not only for the Government and financial institutions of the United States, but also for Canada and the West Indies, Costa Rica, Nicaragua, Salvador, Colombia, Ecuador, Peru, Bolivia, the Argentine Republic, Uruguay, Brazil, Russia, Greece, Italy, Spain, England, Sweden, Switzerland, and Japan. Besides its steel-plate engraving, the American Bank Note Company has executed for railroads and various corporations many of the most notable specimens of letter-press printing, in black and in colors. Special styles and grades of paper, suitable for securities, are manufactured exclusively for the use of the company. There is a department of lithographing, and also a department of type-printing, entirely distinct from that of engraving, in which those two important branches of the company's business are conducted. Special attention is paid to making railway-tickets, and the establishment is equipped to produce every variety of numbered or unnumbered tickets, in the improved styles. In its ticket-department are many of the most ingenious machines known in the printing industry. The company built and owns, at 78 to 86 Trinity Place, close by Trinity Church, its commodious and attractive fire-proof establishment, extending through to the next street, covering ten city lots. The buildings are of brick and iron, and are seven to nine stories in height. They overlook Trinity Churchyard, which gives to the windows a view of a busy section of Broadway. This position also assures to the company an unobstructed light for all time, and makes the location especially valuable. The general offices of the company, which occupy the entire second floor of the Trinity-Place front of the building, are exceptionally exquisite and most conveniently arranged. Entrance thereto is had through a large foyer at the northern end, from which leads a massive stairway. The building is thoroughly fire-proof, and has numerous fire-proof vaults. Its equipment of machinery is elaborate, complete and costly. The whole establishment is the most elegant and extensive of its class in the world. The present officers and trustees of the American Bank Note Company are James Macdonough, President ; Augustus D. Shepard and Touro Robertson, Vice-Presidents ; Theodore H. Freeland, Secretary and Treasurer ; John E. Currier, Assistant-Secretary ; J. K. Myers, Assistant Treasurer ; P. C. Lounsbury, W. J. Arkell, T. H. Porter, E. C. Converse, Jos. S. Stout, James B. Ford, Elliott F. Shepard. The officers have been connected with the business represented thirty and forty years, and have had the principal direction of its affairs during all this period. Besides its New-York establishment, the American Bank Note Company has branches in Boston and Philadelphia.

AMERICAN BANK NOTE COMPANY.
TRINITY PLACE, BETWEEN THAMES AND RECTOR STREETS.

The Standard Oil Company of New York, of which William Rockefeller is President, owns the granite building at 26 Broadway, facing Bowling Green. The building is 157 feet high, 209 feet from Broadway through to New Street, contains four acres of floor space, and cost one and one-half millions of dollars. Its architecture is severe but imposing, the interior rich without ornament, and all the rooms large and perfectly lighted and ventilated.

This building is the headquarters of the American petroleum industry, being occupied not only by the company to which it belongs, but by different companies engaged in different branches of the same industry. Here may be found the offices of several producing companies which are engaged in sinking wells and pumping crude petroleum from the bowels of the earth in various parts of the States of New York, Pennsylvania, West Virginia, Ohio and Indiana. Here also are the offices of different pipe-line companies, which receive the crude product from the wells, and convey it in underground pipes to the great refineries in various interior cities and at the sea-board. The company which builds, owns and operates the peculiar boiler-shaped cars which are used to convey refined oil to all parts of the United States has its home in this building ; and likewise the companies which carry oil in bulk across the ocean and deposit it in great tanks at various sea-ports, to be distributed by tank-cars on British and Continental railways. The transatlantic steamships carry each from 800,000 to 1,000,000 gallons, which is loaded or discharged in from 7 to 15 hours. They make seven or eight round trips a year. Side by side with these are found the offices of companies engaged in manufacturing the scores of useful products derived from petroleum, as well as the materials used in such manufacture, and the barrels, tin cans and cases, in which a portion of these products is marketed.

These companies are all separate and independent, but their interests are identified by reason of identity of stockholders.

The business carried on through these agencies is the largest and most successful in this age of large industries, and it is due to the energy and far-sightedness of a comparatively few men. The united investments to-day aggregate over \$100,000,000. Every device which ingenuity could invent, experience suggest, and capital obtain, has been utilized for enlarging the quantity and improving the quality of the products manufactured, and for cheapening the cost of their manufacture and transportation, with the result that the public are supplied, not only with light, but with many new, necessary and useful articles derived from petroleum at a cost which is almost nominal. In its cooperage department the company uses yearly 100,000,000 feet of oak timber, from twenty States ; and at Oswego, N. Y., it has the largest lumber-mill in the world, cutting yearly over 100,000,000 feet of white pine into material for cases for oil sent out in cans.

This industry stands distinct and separate from many large industries, in some respects copied after it, in the fact that it has refrained from stock-jobbing, and, instead of restricting production and increasing prices, it has pursued exactly the opposite policy, and striven by cheapening its products to increase the demand and widen the market for them. A less cost and a larger market is the theory upon which this business has always been conducted, and its great success proves this to be a much wiser business policy than the theory of restricted production and increased prices, which has ruined so many promising industries.

The Standard Oil Companies have extensive refineries in Brooklyn, N. Y. ; Bergen Point, N. J. ; Philadelphia, Penn. ; Baltimore, Md. ; Chicago, Ill. ; Lima, O. ; Buffalo, N. Y., mainly seaboard or lake points, to facilitate transportation ; and they have depots in many cities, and their ramifications extend throughout the world.

THE STANDARD OIL COMPANY.
STANDARD OIL CO.'S BUILDING, 26 BROADWAY, OPPOSITE BOWLING GREEN.

The American Sugar Refining Company is the greatest manufacturing industry in the vicinity of New-York City. No other single local industry begins to compare in magnitude or importance with that of sugar refining. The immense establishments of the American Sugar Refining Company are scattered along the water-front of Brooklyn from the Wallabout to Newtown Creek. The consolidation of the sugar-refining business which took place in 1887 has resulted in a material increase in the capacity of this company's refineries, as also in great improvement in the economy of manufacture. While some of the smaller factories, which were at the time of the consolidation poorly equipped and unable to refine sugar profitably on the close margin on which the business is now done, have been abandoned, radical improvements have been made in others, and in Greenpoint an entirely new and very extensive plant has been erected on the site of the former refinery of the Havemeyer Sugar Refining Company, which was destroyed by fire in June, 1888. This establishment, with a frontage on Newtown Creek and Commercial Street of nearly 1,000 feet, and a depth from the river to the street of about 500 feet, is superior in many respects to any establishment of its kind in the world. Its capacity is from 7,000 to 8,000 barrels of sugar per day.

Of the older refineries, the subject of our illustration, formerly known as the Havemeyer and Brooklyn Houses, now united and worked as one refinery, is the largest. This one establishment, when running full, is capable of producing 14,000 barrels of sugar per day. Add to this the refineries formerly known as the Decastro & Donner houses, at the foot of South Ninth Street and North Third Street, and the sugar refineries of Brooklyn, owned by the American Sugar Refining Company, aggregate a capacity of from 22,000 to 25,000 barrels of sugar a day, which is more than one-half the entire consumption of the United States. This product comprises every grade of sugar known to commerce, from the dominoes and cubes of cut loaf, through the various grades of so-called hard sugars, down to the cheaper grades of yellow, or straw-colored, sugars, which are so popular in many sections of the country.

The collateral industries supported by these refineries alone are vast and varied. Immense cooperage establishments are kept busy supplying the 9,000,000 or more of sugar barrels which they require each year. Hundreds of trucks are necessary to transport daily their product to the various railroad freight stations. The supply of animal charcoal for filtering purposes is drawn from all over the country, and amounts to over 20,000,000 pounds per annum. The consumption of coal is over 400,000 tons for the same period. To handle the immense output of these houses, all the great trunk line railways of the country have been obliged to establish receiving stations and terminal depots in Brooklyn. An army of nearly 4,000 men is required to operate the refineries and their tributaries. The raw sugar used in the process of refining, coming from every quarter of the globe, amounts to nearly 2,000,000,000 pounds per annum, and the ships of all nations can be seen discharging their cargoes day and night at the immense docks and warehouses of the refineries. The capital involved in carrying on this immense industry is $75,000,000. Approximately the above are the working figures for only the Brooklyn refineries owned and operated by the American Sugar Refining Company, which to-day, without doubt, conducts the greatest and most important manufacturing industry in the United States, and supplies to the American consumer of sugar an article which is superior in quality to that of any other country in the world, at prices so low as to leave only a fraction of a cent a pound margin for the cost of refining. The officers of the corporation are : President, H. O. Havemeyer ; Vice-President, Theo. A. Havemeyer ; Secretary and Treasurer, John E. Searles.

AMERICAN SUGAR-REFINING COMPANY.

THE HAVEMEYER AND BROOKLYN HOUSES. REFINERIES IN BROOKLYN. OFFICES, WALL AND SOUTH STREETS, NEW YORK.

The Ansonia Clock Company is, without question, the most extensive manufacturer of clocks in the world. The quality of its output ranges from the most inexpensive nickel clocks for the kitchen mantel, to the most expensive and artistic timekeepers, encased in onyx or gilded bronze. In quantity it is large enough to supply a very large share of the demand of the civilized world. The company was formed in 1876, by the consolidation of several concerns, some of which had been making clocks for forty years. Its original works were at Ansonia, Conn., a little town from which it took its name, and which had already been christened in honor of one of New York's merchant-princes, Anson D. Phelps. Soon after its organization, the company established a plant in Brooklyn, and the works have grown, until they now occupy a whole city block, bounded by Prospect Park, Seventh Avenue, 12th and 13th Streets, four acres in extent. Besides the big main building, a six-story structure laid out in form like a hollow square, there are a dozen buildings in the group. All are substantially constructed of brick, and several are five or six stories in height.

All through the great plant are evidences of the mechanical development of this age, many pieces of unique mechanism performing the most minute details of workmanship, for which not many years ago it was necessary to train the eye, the hand and the intellect of innate mechanics, in order to secure for the finest and most costly clocks the same absolute accuracy now demanded of even the commonest of the clocks which bear the name and trade-mark of the Ansonia Clock Company. These devices not only have made it possible to produce time-pieces of unvarying accuracy, but they have made it also possible to produce them at prices which place them within the means of the whole people.

The company owns a large tract of land in an adjoining block, and contemplates the erection of still another large building. When the company located in Brooklyn, some twelve or more years ago, the territory in the vicinity of its plant was open, unimproved country ; now there is no unoccupied land within many blocks. All is built up and improved. The company has distributed thousands of dollars in salaries and wages every week. The employees have settled themselves in homes in the immediate vicinity of the works. A new field for household trade has been created, and thus the Ansonia Clock Company has not only established a new industry of great proportions, but has also contributed indirectly to the building up of a new section of the city, and to the creating of new real property of great value.

Besides the tremendous output of clocks, the company also produces a great variety of objects of art, in bronzes and other materials. It gives employment to nearly 1,300 people. It has an export trade of enormous proportions, sending its clocks and other products to every part of the known world. As a circulating depot, it maintains a large establishment in London, which is located in its own building, at 23 Fore Street, E. C. For the convenience of its trade in the western part of this country, it has an extensive office and salesroom at 133 Wabash Avenue, Chicago. There is a large staff of clerks and salesmen at each of its branches. There is a salesroom at 11 Cortlandt Street, New-York City, for the display and sale of clocks and bronzes. The headquarters offices are at 11 to 21 Cliff Street, New York, occupying two floors of a large area. From this point all the operations are directed, and the London and Chicago branches are responsible to it. The display of goods in the main salesroom of this establishment, with its fine candelabra, bronze statuettes, onyx clocks and *bric-à-brac*, is an exhibition of art-work, that of its class is unparalleled. There is, in all the range of manufactories in New York, no finer or stronger illustration of the results of energy, intelligent management, and well-directed enterprise, than is found in the establishment of the Ansonia Clock Company.

ANSONIA CLOCK COMPANY.
FACTORIES IN BROOKLYN. OFFICES 11 TO 21 CLIFF STREET, NEW YORK.

Henry R. Worthington, manufacturing pumping machinery, is preëminent among the leading mechanical manufacturing corporations of the world. The first direct-acting steam-pump was patented in September 17, 1841, by its originator and builder, Henry Rossiter Worthington, and in 1845 was established at Brooklyn the nucleus of works which now have an international reputation. The Worthington Direct-Acting Duplex Steam-Pump was the result of attempts to improve the first type of pump, and is to-day universally known and used. The Worthington pumping-engine, in its simplest form, was first applied for water-works service for the city of Savannah, in the year 1854. To this class of machinery has been added the High-Duty attachment, invented by Charles C. Worthington, son of the founder, and by this last and important invention the engines are able to do the same work with one-half the fuel consumption.

In the years 1890 and 1891 145 Worthington engines of the higher types were constructed ; their aggregate daily capacity being 594,000,000 gallons ; and up to January 1, 1893, the total contract-capacity of these engines alone was 2,923,000,000 gallons daily, which is twice the average flow of the Hudson River at Albany. Worthington engines are used for the entire high-service water-supply of New-York City, and perform over 90 per cent. of the pumping done in the prominent business-buildings, such as the Equitable, Mutual-Life, Produce Exchange, Mills Building, City Hall, etc., and on the great ocean steamships, like the *New York, Paris*, and others.

They are used, too, by the Standard Oil Company on their pipe-lines, for forcing petroleum from the oil regions to the Atlantic sea-board and lake-ports. These engines vary in size from 200 to 1,000 horse-power each, some of them being required to deliver from 15,000 to 25,000 barrels of oil a day, against pressure of from 1,000 to 1,500 pounds a square inch. The reputation of this firm soon spread abroad, and resulted in the adoption of the Worthington design for pumping-engines, by the celebrated house of James Simpson & Co., Limited, London, after a test in this

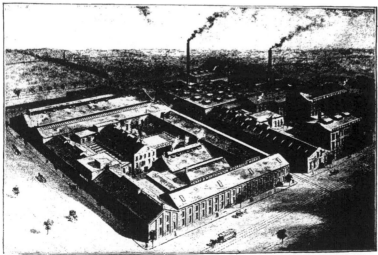

HENRY R. WORTHINGTON HYDRAULIC WORKS, BROOKLYN.   OFFICES : 86 AND 88 LIBERTY STREET, NEW-YORK.

country by representatives of the latter firm ; and Worthington engines are now accepted by the Old World as the most advanced type of pumping machine. The largest sizes are now in successful operation in the principal cities in England, and in Rotterdam, Berlin, St. Petersburg, Calcutta, and Hong Kong, and in Mexico and Australia. The metropolis of London has by far the greatest number of pumping engines of any city in the world, and of the entire water supply of the Metropolitan District sixty per cent. can be furnished by the Worthington engines at present installed in the various stations. During the Soudan war, Worthington engines were purchased by the English Government to supply the army of Sir Garnet Wolseley.

Henry R. Worthington also manufactures pumps for special services, such as mining, wrecking, fire, sewage, etc. The Worthington water-meter is the oldest in use, and is the only type of a positive measure of fluids. It is in use in nearly every city of the United States and in foreign countries. The grand prize for pumping machinery was awarded by the Paris Exposition in 1889 to this company. Their engines were adopted by the authorities of the Centennial in 1876 and the Paris Exposition in 1889 to furnish the entire water-supply. They have been awarded the contract for four large engines by the Commissioners of the World's Columbian Exposition of 1893. These engines will have a capacity of 40,000,000 gallons daily. They also have the contract for special pumps for fire and other purposes, and for supplying condensing water to the amount of 24,000,000 gallons daily. The Worthington Pumping Engine Co., a subsidiary organization, carries on the foreign business, the offices being located in London, Paris, Berlin and other cities. The immense plant, known as the Hydraulic Works, now covers an area of several blocks in Brooklyn, and a larger tract at Elizabethport, N. J.; and upwards of 1,700 men are employed. The company's main offices are at 86 and 88 Liberty Street, New York. The branch-offices are at Boston, Philadelphia, Chicago, St. Louis and Denver.

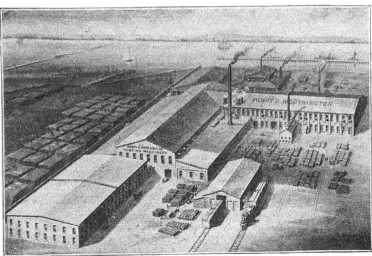

HENRY R. WORTHINGTON HYDRAULIC WORKS, ELIZABETHPORT, N. J.
OFFICES : 86 AND 88 LIBERTY STREET, NEW YORK.

Otis Brothers & Co., whose executive and general offices are at 38 Park Row, are the foremost builders of passenger and freight elevators in the world. They have erected the largest elevators in existence, which convey people from the ferry-landing at Weehawken, N. J., to the Eldorado Garden, at the top of the Palisades. They also constructed the elevators which have made the highest ascent ; and the operating of which required the most intricate machinery ; those with which the Eiffel Tower at Paris was equipped. They have been engaged in elevator-building since 1855, soon after the moving platform began to displace, indoors, the tackle and fall in the handling of heavy merchandise. Their works at Yonkers then consisted of a single two-story building. Early inventions of elevator machinery and appliances, made by E. G. Otis, of Yonkers, and Cyrus W. Baldwin, of Brooklyn, formed the basis upon which their industry was built. Passenger-elevators moved by steam came into use in 1866. Hydraulic apparatus was introduced ten years later, and in 1880 came into general favor. Otis Brothers & Co. were in the field, fully equipped, and they have made probably three-quarters of all the passenger-elevators in use in New-York City.

The firm was incorporated in 1867. The little factory of thirty-seven years ago has grown into a large group of brick buildings, covering several acres, of a capacity for turning out four of their grand elevators a day, with accessory machinery and fittings. Employment is given at Yonkers to about 500 men, and there is a constructing force of about 200, constantly engaged in setting up elevators in New York and other cities. Recently Otis Brothers & Co. have perfected an electric elevator, and have introduced it into several hundred buildings in this country and in Europe. The car, winding machinery, safety-appliances, and controlling devices, are the same as have been in use for many years. The company has adopted, and made part of its system, a motor invented by Rudolph Eickemeyer, of Yonkers. Its valuable features are that it starts and stops with the car, thus economizing power, and is under perfect control of the operator.

The Otis passenger elevators are noted not only for their practical construction, their elegance of finish, their simplicity of operation, their safety under any possible circumstances, but also for their remarkable speed, which is secured with freedom from accident. As any one passes up and down in the public buildings, hotels, clubs, dwellings, business structures, he seems invariably to ride in Otis elevators. An Otis elevator is always beautifully finished, and, above all, safe.

A distinctly valuable feature of the Otis elevator is its safety appliances. Tests made of the safety-appliances of the Otis elevators in the Eiffel Tower resulted in bringing the car to a stop after a fall of eight inches. Similar tests of the Weehawken elevators resulted in a stop after a drop of $3\frac{3}{4}$ inches. The Weehawken elevators, three in number, are each intended to carry 135 people. The cars are 21 feet long and 12 feet wide. The permissible carrying capacity is 20,000 pounds, but either car can lift a much greater weight. They make the ascent of 153 feet at the rate of 200 feet a minute. The machinery is of the hydraulic speed-multiplying type. Otis Brothers & Co. have just completed the construction of the Otis Elevating Railway, 7,000 feet long, in the Catskill Mountains, by means of which visitors ascend to the Catskill Mountain House in ten minutes, and save a journey of four hours by stage.

Otis passenger-elevators are in use in thousands of public buildings, business houses, and residences in New-York City. They are also in use in every city in America, every large city in Europe, and in South America and Australia. The officers of the company are Norton P. Otis, President ; Abraham G. Mills, Vice-President and Secretary ; and William D. Baldwin, Treasurer and General Manager.

OTIS BROTHERS & CO.'S ELEVATOR WORKS.
MANUFACTORY AT YONKERS. NEW-YORK OFFICES AT 38 PARK ROW.

The General Electric Company of New York is a corporation with a special charter, granted early in 1892. Its main work at present is electric lighting, electric railways, and electric transmission of power. In lighting it owns and controls the patents of almost every known method of electric illumination in all its different departments, alternating and direct current, for both arc and incandescent lamps. The two last-named departments have shown most phenomenal growth, and their rapid extension is an accurate gauge of the wide adoption of the electric light in both public and private life. The arc lamps already manufactured and in use number hundreds of thousands, while the incandescent lamps reach millions. The problem of the subdivision of electric illumination, by means of lamps of reduced size and smaller candle-power, has been successfully solved, and the many additional advantages derivable from the use of the electric light in this way rendered still more striking. As a pioneer and careful developer toward perfection in the electric lighting field, the General Electric Company stands to-day preëminent. In street-railway locomotion it has developed, and has in practical operation, the most perfect system, known as the overhead system, while it is now developing high-power locomotives for heavy traction work. So rapid, indeed, have been the strides made in this direction that the substitution of the electric locomotive for the steam locomotive has been brought, by the latest developments of this company, within the range of immediate probabilities. In mining work it manufactures appliances for drilling, hoisting, conveying, pulverizing, extracting, etc., by electricity. In power work it has created appliances for every conceivable kind of portable or stationary motors, from the smallest to the greatest. It has enabled the industrial world to take advantage of the immense energy in the undeveloped water-power of the country. By means of its perfected apparatus the water-falls and water-courses of the country have been laid under contribution, and rendered subservient to the uses of man. Mines heretofore unworkable, on account of the cost of fuel, are now proving sources of great profit, the power to work them having been transmitted to them by means of the electrical devices which this company has invented and constructed. Mills and factories all over the land testify to the almost universal uses to which electricity has been put, all rendered possible and practicable by the inventive talent which the General Electric Company has at its command. It has very extensive electrical works at Schenectady, N. Y., and at Lynn, Mass., and the largest works in the world for the manufacture of incandescent lamps at Harrison, N. J. In its various departments it gives employment to over 10,000 people, many of whom command the highest pay for their skill and knowledge of both the theory and practice of electricity. It is not the exclusive province, however, of the General Electric Company to deal with the public consumer of electricity directly. It is also, as its name implies, the general or "parent" organization under which several thousand distinct local companies, chartered in every State and territory, and also in many foreign countries, are licensed to use its patents, appliances, and products.

The large capital employed by this company, together with its unrivalled corps of inventors, scientists, and experts, permits it to examine and test thoroughly any and all ideas that are likely to develop the science of electricity, and to apply it commercially. The capital of the General Electric Company is $50,000,000.

Its executive offices are located in a large, handsome building, eight stories high, at 44 Broad Street, in New York, and also at 620 Atlantic Avenue, Boston. C. A. Coffin is President; Eugene Griffin, First Vice-President; J. H. Herrick, Third Vice-President; E. I. Garfield, Secretary; A. S. Beves, Treasurer; Joseph P. Ord, Comptroller; and S. Dana Greene, Assistant General Manager.

GENERAL ELECTRIC COMPANY.

EDISON BUILDING, 42 AND 44 BROAD STREET, BETWEEN EXCHANGE PLACE AND BEAVER STREET.

The New-York Belting & Packing Company, Limited, manufacturers of machine belting, hose, rubber springs, and kindred goods, have their offices and warerooms at 15 Park Row.   The main factory is on the Potatook River, near Newtown, Conn.   The business was founded at Boston, Mass., in 1846, two years after the issue to Charles Goodyear of patents for his process of vulcanizing india rubber. At the outset the concern had the personal assistance of Mr. Goodyear.   As the successor of the Boston factory it is the oldest mechanical rubber-goods establishment. It is also the largest concern manufacturing mechanical india-rubber goods in the United States.   It was incorporated about 1856.   The manufacturing establishment at Newtown, Conn., occupies many acres of ground.   The company owns a magnificent water-power on the Potatook River, consisting of two separate falls, each of considerable height.   A portion of the power is utilized by means of a water-wheel fifty feet in diameter.   This is supplemented, whenever the occasion requires, by steam-power, as the works are equipped with an extensive steam-plant.   The factory buildings comprise several mills, fitted for the manufacture of different articles.   With the attached cottages, built for the use of the superintendent and other employees, the establishment constitutes a manufacturing village of considerable size.

Crude india rubber has been known to commerce for several hundred years. Primarily, it is a pale yellow sap, and is taken from trees of several varieties.   It is changed into a gum by the process of evaporation.   Central and South America are the main sources of supply, although rubber is found in considerable quantities in parts of Asia, Africa, and the island of Madagascar.   Most of the crude rubber received in the United States comes from Para, at the mouth of the Amazon River.   Until about fifty years ago there was little use for rubber in manufactures, other than for making overshoes and waterproof fabrics.   The art of vulcanizing the crude material by compounding it with sulphur made it useful in a variety of ways, and upon this art was founded the industry of the New-York Belting & Packing Company, Limited. The process originally discovered by Charles Goodyear was the basis of its operation, but during the years which succeeded many new inventions were made which extended the uses of rubber, and opened up new fields of manufacture.   A large number of these inventions were secured by the company, and thus the breadth and scope of its business have increased.   Among the products of its factories are machine belting, rubber hose for all uses, railroad car-springs, and springs for miscellaneous uses, rubber machine packing, emery wheels, rubber mats, and a variety of small articles.   Its business has grown to enormous proportions, and this growth is not only the natural progress to be expected of a successful concern, but is due in part to the great expansion of the usefulness of rubber, which has gone on year by year.   The house exports large quantities of its goods to Europe and South America.   The principal officers of the company, and the principal stock-holders as well, are John H. Cheever, the treasurer, and J. D. Cheever, the deputy-treasurer. To the former is due much of the credit of creating a new industry, and conducting it successfully until it has reached a position of the first magnitude.

The salesrooms of the New-York Belting & Packing Company are in Park Row, Nos. 13 and 15, immediately opposite the lower end of the United-States Post Office, and not far from the City Hall, Astor House, and St.-Paul's Chapel.   At these salesrooms can be seen the extensive line and great variety of goods which are produced by this company — belting not merely of short lengths and narrow widths, but huge and broad belts for the heaviest conceivable work ; not merely garden hose, but the strongest and most durable needed by fire departments of the metropolis ; and the general products cover the full range of sizes and varieties demanded for all uses.

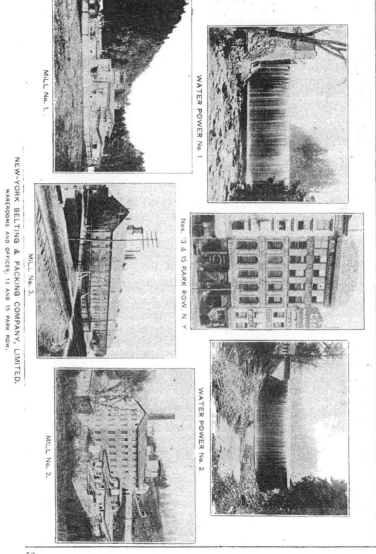

WATER POWER No. 1.

MILL No. 1.

Nos. 13 & 15 PARK ROW, N. Y.

MILL No. 3.

WATER POWER No. 2.

MILL No. 2.

NEW-YORK BELTING & PACKING COMPANY, LIMITED.
WAREROOMS AND OFFICES, 13 AND 15 PARK ROW.

The **Mechanical Rubber Company,** located at 13 Park Row, are manufacturers of the highest grades of soft and hard rubber goods of all descriptions, for
mechanical and domestic purposes, such as hose of all kinds, belting, packing, valves,
gaskets, tubing, matting, wringer rolls, bicycle tires, etc. This company has the
largest and best equipped mills in the country, located both East and West, and
offers unsurpassed facilities, not only for making but for delivering goods more quickly

THE MECHANICAL RUBBER COMPANY, 13 AND 15 PARK ROW.

and at less cost than other manufacturers. The quality of its products will
enlist the interest of buyers who demand the best, and for such are willing
to pay reasonable prices, and the conduct of its affairs is on lines to hold
patronage once acquired. Their hose,
belting and packing are made in two
grades. In their best grade, called
"Amazon," the price has been subor-
dinated to quality, the aim being to entirely eliminate the element of chance,
and to produce goods that are
thoroughly reliable and uniform, and
that will be equal to the sharpest
emergency that may arise in use. This
class of goods is the cheapest because
of the extraordinary service they will
withstand. Their next grade, "Brazilian," is equal if not superior in
quality to the best of other makers,
and is found uniform in quality, reliable in service, reasonable in price
and perfectly satisfactory in every respect to the dealer and consumer.
L. K. McClymonds, recently President of the Cleveland Rubber Co.
and the Chicago Rubber Works, is
Vice-President and General Manager.

**The Fabric Fire Hose Com-
pany,** whose principal offices and
salesrooms are at 13 and 15 Park
Row, in the building also occupied
by the New-York Belting and Packing Co. and the Mechanical Rubber
Co., are the inventors and manufac-
turers of balanced woven-fabric rubber-lined hose for fire and mill purposes. This
company owns the patents for balanced woven hose. It invented the waxing of the
yarn, which protects the hose from mildew and rot, and sheds instead of absorbing
water. The hose of this company is in use in almost every city in this country and
Canada. In the past ten years it has sold over 5,000,000 feet. It put in over 80,000
feet at the World's Fair, obtaining the contract in competition with the world. It
is the largest manufacturer of fire hose in the world. It also manufactures rubber
hose for all uses, such as lawn hose, steam hose, engine hose, etc.

The International Okonite Company, Limited.—Commensurate with the magical extension of applied electricity in the last score of years has been the ever-increasing demand for a more efficient form of insulation for conducting wire, an insulation which should resist the corrosive action of all nature's elements, and insure absolute secrecy in the working of each wire of the hundreds bound in one cable. No company has more nearly succeeded in fulfilling these exacting conditions than The Okonite Company, Limited, of New York and London.

In 1884 J. J. C. and Michael Smith and Herman Gelpcke organized the New-York Insulated Wire and Vulcanite Company, for the manufacture of insulated wire. They established an experimental plant at College Point, L. I. They there began the manufacture of a special form of insulation, which from small beginnings was destined to become of the utmost importance to the continued growth of electrical science. In 1885 the company removed its plant to Passaic, N. J., its name being

INTERNATIONAL OKONITE CO.'S WIRE AND CABLE MILLS.

changed to the "Okonite Company." The active management then passed into the hands of Willard L. Candee and George T. Manson. Under their skilful executive ability the business increased beyond all expectation. The plant became inadequate to the demand made upon it. In 1889 the present plant was erected at Passaic, and the company re-organized under the name of The Okonite Company, Limited, the managers of which are Willard L. Candee and H. Durant Cheever. With them is associated George T. Manson as General Superintendent.

This plant covers about a block, facing on the Dundee Canal, which is used as a water-power. Its main building is 394 feet in length by 63 in width. There is a wing at either end, one of 130 x 57 feet, the other 170 x 53 feet, and other buildings.

The factory can produce every form of the highest grade of insulated wire, from the smallest used in telephone service to the largest used in submarine cables. This company's wire with its efficient insulation has become known to the electrical world as a standard of excellence. It is used by all leading telegraph, telephone, electric-light, railroad and mining companies. The "Okonite" trade-mark, a unique emblem of the company's business, is familiar to all the electrical world.

The company's main offices are in New York, at 13 Park Row. There are agencies in all the principal cities of the United States. Main offices are at London, and a plant, more extensive than at Passaic, at Manchester, England.

The Eaton, Cole & Burnham Company, manufacturers of wrought-iron pipe and brass and iron fittings, valves, cocks, and other appliances for steam, water, oil and gas, began early in the business of the manufacture of these goods, and have grown up with that industry. The company was formed in 1874, by joining the New-York firm of Eaton & Cole with Mr. Burnham, of the Belknap & Burn-ham Manufactur-ing Company in Bridgeport, Conn. The article of their manufacture which is most widely and popu-larly known is, perhaps, the Gem, or Lowell, hose-nozzle. These nozzles are known all over the coun-try by users of small or garden hose, and contain a device by which the stream of water can be changed by a movement of the wrist from a solid stream into the most delicate spray. The com-pany controls the patents on this simple yet valu-able device, and the output exceeds 75,000 annually.

EATON, COLE & BURNHAM CO., FULTON AND GOLD STREETS.

The company also manufactures a full line of pipe threading and cutting machinery, which is becoming extensively known, both in this country and abroad, wherever much piping is carried on. The pipe-lines, through which crude petroleum is pumped for hundreds of miles, from the interior oil regions to the seacoast and to the lakes, have one of this company's large pipe-threading machines at each of their pumping stations. The export business of the Eaton, Cole & Burnham Com-pany covers a large part of the world, more especially South America, England, Germany, Austria, Russia, India and Australia.

In Bridgeport the company has a factory in which over seven hundred employees find work ; and at that place the plant consumes daily from 30 to 35 tons of pig iron and from 8 to 10 tons of copper, together with other metals. The main offices of the Eaton, Cole & Burnham Company are located at 82 and 84 Fulton Street, New York ; and its principal warehouses and depositories of goods are in New-York City, and in Pittsburgh, Penn.

The National Tube Works Company, the New-York offices of which are in the Havemeyer Building, at the corner of Cortlandt and Church Streets, conducts one of the gigantic industries of the country. It was originally a Boston institution, and the office of its Treasurer remains there. The New-York office is that of its General Manager. Its principal works are at McKeesport, Pa. The establishment there covers sixty-five acres, forty being occupied by buildings.

The product includes every variety of wrought-iron pipe, boiler-tubes, pipes or tubes used for artesian, salt, oil or gas wells, rods and columns used in mining grate-bars, hand-rails, telegraph poles, gas and air-brake cylinders, drill-rods, Converse patent lock-joint, wrought iron kalameined and asphalted pipe for water and gas works mains and trunk lines, and locomotive and stationary injectors.

NATIONAL TUBE WORKS CO., NEW-YORK OFFICES, CORTLANDT AND CHURCH STREETS.

An important branch of manufacture is that of sap pan iron, kalameined and galvanized sheet iron, cold rolled iron and steel sheets, and corrugated and curved sheets, for roofs and ceilings. Another specialty is the celebrated "Monongahela" brand of Bessemer, mill and foundry pig-iron.

The company finds a market ·for its goods not only in the United States but also in Central and South America, Mexico, Europe, Australia, and Africa. The works have a capacity of 250,000 tons of tubes and pipe yearly. The company was one of the first to use natural gas as fuel in the manufacture of iron. The gas is brought from its own wells, through twenty miles of pipe, to the works.

The industry was established in Boston in 1869, as the National Tube Works Company; and in 1872 the manufacturing establishment was moved to McKeesport, Pennsylvania, the head-office of the company remaining in Boston. In 1891 the company was re-organized under the laws of New Jersey, with a capital of $11,500,000; and, with its own industry, has consolidated those of the Republic Iron Works of Pittsburgh, the Monongahela Furnace Company, and the Boston Iron & Steel Company (located at McKeesport), allied but not competing concerns. Branch offices are maintained at Pittsburgh, St. Louis and Chicago. The present officers and directors of the company are E. W. Converse, President; D. W. Hitchcock, Vice-President; William S. Eaton, Treasurer; P. W. French, Secretary; E. C. Converse, General Manager; Horace Crosby, W. J. Curtis, J. H. Flagler, and F. E. Sweetser.

The Iron Clad Manufacturing Company, whose offices and salesrooms are at 22 and 24 Cliff Street, was established in 1869 and incorporated in 1876. Its founders were Robert Seaman, at that time a capitalist of wide experience, and well-known as the head of one of the foremost wholesale grocery houses in this city (the firm of Robert Seaman & Co.), and Henry W. Shepard, whose extraordinary business tact and energy, with plans well-made and successfully executed, have placed this company, with its immense lines of specialties, which in quality are synonymous with its trade name "Iron Clad," in the front rank of the manufacturing enterprises of the country. Its extensive factories, covering an area of 139,000 square feet of ground, are located in Brooklyn, N. Y. They are admirably equipped with expensive machinery, and employ over 800 operatives. The manufacturing processes are of much interest, and by exact and very ingenious devices transform the plain sheet metals into myriads of forms of usefulness and value. This company enjoys the reputation of converting into manufactured goods of various forms a greater number of square feet of sheet iron and steel than any competing concern in the country. Among its leading specialties are : steel railroad milk cans, the number annually produced running into the hundreds of thousands ; and galvanized range-boilers, which are also a product of considerable magnitude, their superiority over all others being universally conceded by the best authorities. Other specialties are : coal scuttles, galvanized and japanned, more than half a million of which are manufactured yearly ; wrought steel fire shovels, stove pokers, galvanized ash and garbage cans, water pots, refrigerator pans, ice-cream freezers, well buckets, poultry fountains, wash bowls, dippers and dish pans, tea kettles, water carriers, sap buckets and wash tubs, the latter made very extensively for the Pacific coast and the Southwestern section of the country. The company's great variety of specialties manufactured for engineers and mill supplies, such as cotton or roving cans, oil waste cans, oilers, storing oil cans, fire buckets, sprinklers and elevator buckets, is worthy of mention. Their line of "Yankee" tin-ware for the kitchen, stamped or spun from the black sheets into the desired shape, after which it is dipped or heavily coated with pure tin, would delight any housekeeper. This company also manufactures annually thousands of steel soda-water fountains, with a continuous lining made of pure sheet block tin rolled expressly for the purpose. These fountains the reader may not only have seen in transit to all parts of the country, but doubtless it has been his or her pleasure many a time to quaff from their refreshing contents. Last, but not the least worthy of consideration, is the latest addition that they have made to their lines, of a complete outfit for the kitchen of their enameled iron-ware, the superior finish and durability of which is fast making inroads upon the trade of other wares of similar character. The company's trade-mark (an iron-clad monitor, floating upon the open sea,) is a familiar figure to be found upon practically every piece of goods of their manufacture. Wherever this trade-mark is found upon an article on the shelves or in the store of the dealer, it is not only the surest guarantee of "value received," but also, wherever found, is the best reference that can be furnished that the dealer is disposed to supply his customers with the best goods of their kind manufactured. The exhibit of the Iron Clad Manufacturing Company, in the Manufactures Building of the World's Columbian Exposition, has attracted extensive attention by reason of its practical character and skilful arrangement. The President and Treasurer of the company is Robert Seaman. The Vice-President is Henry B. Haigh. The Secretary is David D. Otis. The General Superintendent is Frank E. Young. Each of these officers has been connected for from ten to twenty years with the Iron Clad Manufacturing Company.

IRON CLAD MANUFACTURING COMPANY.
FACTORIES IN BROOKLYN. OFFICES, 22 AND 24 CLIFF STREET, NEW YORK.

Cooper, Hewitt & Co. was founded in 1847, to continue the business then carried on by Peter Cooper, the philanthropist. Mr. Cooper began his business career about 1815, so that the various establishments now controlled by Cooper, Hewitt & Co. have existed or have been created within the past seventy-five years. His original business, the manufacture of glue, is still carried on by a corporation controlled by his family, under the name of Peter Cooper's Glue Factory. "Cooper's

COOPER, HEWITT & CO., 17 BURLING SLIP.

glue" and "Cooper's gelatine" are household words all over the world. Mr. Cooper very early engaged in the iron business, and after establishing works at Baltimore and New York, finally concentrated them at Trenton, New Jersey, where in 1845 he erected one of the largest mills in the country. Here railroad iron was made as early as 1846. Later the works were changed so as to manufacture iron beams and girders, which were first rolled here, and have continued to be one of the chief products of the New-Jersey Iron & Steel Co., of which the firm are the sole stockholders. Besides the rolling-mill, there is a bridge-shop, capable of producing the heaviest work, and here some of the largest bridges and much elevated railway work have been built. They are now constructing the Bellefontaine bridge, over the Missouri River, and the new structure of the New-York Central Railway, over the Harlem Flats. The firm owns the large works of the Trenton Iron Co., which manufacture wire, wire rope, cables, wire tramways, etc. They have blast furnaces at Durham and Pequest, with a capacity of 75,000 tons of pig iron annually. They own iron mines in New Jersey and Pennsylvania, and coal mines in Pennsylvania and Virginia, so that they can produce the fin-ished article from their own raw material. They have also interests in iron works in the Lake-Superior region, in Tennessee and in Alabama. They are engaged in silver-smelting in the West, and employ a very large capital and many thousands of workmen. In the iron business, the ownership is limited to the members of the firm. The business is done exclusively for cash, and nothing is spared to keep the products up to the highest standard. Peter Cooper was the founder of the Cooper Union in New York, of which city his son, Edward Cooper, and his son-in-law, Abram S. Hewitt, have been mayors. Mr. Hewitt has long been known as a representative in Congress, where he served for twelve years.

In every way,—financially, commercially, socially, and historically—there is no more distinguished business house in America than Cooper, Hewitt & Co.

The Ansonia Brass & Copper Company, whose gigantic works are at Ansonia, Conn., is in fact a New-York industry of the first magnitude, and is one of the concerns that indicate the ability, enterprise and foresight of the old and time-honored house of Phelps, Dodge & Co. Even the city of Ansonia itself is named after Anson G. Phelps of this firm. The main offices and sales-rooms are in New-York City, in Cliff Street, which is nearly all occupied by houses in some branch of the metal industry, and which bears almost the same relation to the metal world that Wall Street does to the financial world. The Ansonia Brass & Copper Co.'s business was established in 1847, and has been steadfastly successful and prosperous. Now it occupies five enormous factories, covering about sixteen acres, and continually employs from 1,200 to 1,500 hands, with a pay-roll of $900,000 per year. The company stands pre-eminent in its production of sheet copper, copper bottoms, copper wire for electrical purposes, and ingot copper. It controls over one hundred patents for lamps, chandeliers and various forms of metal working. It also owns the Cowles patents for insulating wire, and is the sole manufacturer of Tobin bronze, a metal noted for its high tensile and torsional elastic limit, toughness, and non-corrosibility in sea water. At a cherry-red heat it can be forged and stamped as readily as steel. It has a specific gravity of 8.3, and can be welded by the Thomson electric welding process. It is used largely for piston rods, hull plates,

ANSONIA BRASS & COPPER CO., 19 AND 21 CLIFF STREET.

yacht shafting, pump linings, condenser heads, bolts, nuts, valve stems, center boards, rudders, coal chutes and screens, valve faces, powder-mill crush plates and ship fastenings. For the above purposes it is furnished in the form of sheets, plates, and round, square and hexagon bars. Besides this, the company owns various specialties. Among its varied products is an infinite variety of rods, spun brass kettles, brazed and seamless tubes, wires; also brass bedsteads, lamps and chandeliers of the latest designs. The business of the company extends into every nook and corner of the Union; and Ansonia brass or copper, in its simple or manufactured form, is a standard of the whole metal-working industry. The President is Wm. E. Dodge; the Vice-President and Treasurer, Alfred A. Cowles; and the Secretary, W. H. Mathews.

The **Rand D**rill **Company,** the office of which is at 23 Park Place, has played an important part in revolutionizing the methods of mining and tunneling, and in placing America ahead of the world in the production of rock-boring apparatus. The first drill made in which the drilling tool was the extension of the rod of a piston, acted upon by steam or compressed air, was indirectly an outcome of the enterprise begun by private capital and completed by the State of Massachusetts, in cutting a tunnel through the Hoosac Mountain. The use of the Rand Drill has stimulated mining enterprises greatly, not only by virtue of the marked reduction it has made in the cost of cutting out ores, but also because of the even greater advantage of speed in driving tunnels and headings and otherwise opening up new properties, by virtue of which preliminary work — work which formerly required years to accomplish — is now completed in a few months. Vast deposits of iron and copper in the Lake-Superior regions and elsewhere, and of silver in the Far West and in Mexico, are now opened up so expeditiously and so cheaply that the cost of the ores has been

FLOOD ROCK EXPLOSION AT HELL GATE IN OCTOBER, 1885. RAND DRILL COMPANY'S DRILLS AND EXPLOSIVES.

permanently reduced. In Australia and South Africa gold-mining is now carried on by means of the Rand Drill. In fact, to such an extent have the mining enterprises of the Dark Continent been carried on of late, that the production of gold in South Africa for one month recently was estimated to be two-thirds of the output of the United States during a similar period. A great public work in which the Rand Drills were used almost exclusively was the undermining of Flood Rock, an important portion of the work of improving the channel at Hell Gate. Flood Rock was successfully blown up on October 10, 1885, and in the final operation another product of this company, "Rackarock," an explosive of even greater power under water than dynamite, but perfectly safe to handle, was used extensively. The Rand Drill Company supply a large portion of the demand for rock-boring apparatus and safe explosives in this country, and are almost without competition in Australia in the sale of drills. German engineers who are well advanced in the science of tunneling acknowledge the superior efficiency of the Rand Drill. Of the explosives used in Australian mining this company supplies about one-third.

Russell & Erwin Manufacturing Company, which occupies its own five-story marble-front building, at 43 to 47 Chambers Street, is one of the largest concerns producing builders' hardware in the United States. Its business was

founded in 1839 by Russell & Erwin, in New Britain, Conn. Soon a f t e r w a r d, they established an office at 92 John Street, New York, and some time later they removed to 22 and 24 Cliff Street. In 1851, the Russell & Erwin Manufacturing Company was organized. Cornelius B. Erwin was its first president, and Henry E. Russell its first treasurer. When Mr. Erwin died, in March, 1885, Mr. Russell became President, and Mahlon J. Woodruff was elected Treasurer. Mr. Russell died in January, 1893, and

RUSSELL & ERWIN MANUFACTURING CO., 43, 45 AND 47 CHAMBERS STREET.

was succeeded by Mr. Woodruff. The company purchased its present fine sales-room and office building in Chambers Street in 1868.

The corporation is organized under a special charter, obtained from the Legislature of Connecticut. Its principal manufactories are in New Britain, Conn. They consist of many extensive buildings of brick and stone, which cover about nine acres of ground. In 1885 the company purchased the property of the Dayton Screw Company, at Dayton, Ohio, at a cost of about $500,000. It operates the establishment as a branch manufactory, and markets the products through the New-York house. The goods manufactured by the concern are those classed as builders' hardware and house trimmings, and include bronze, brass, wrought-steel and cast-iron door locks, knobs and bolts, and all varieties of wood and machine screws and bolts. The company maintains a warehouse in Philadelphia, and another in London. Its export-trade is very large, although by far the greater portion of its products is sold in the United States. Its capital is $1,000,000, all of which, with its large surplus, is invested in its business. It employs about 1,600 men. The officers and directors are Mahlon J. Woodruff, President ; Henry E. Russell, Vice-President and Treasurer ; George J. Laighton, Assistant Treasurer ; Theodore E. Smith, Secretary ; Isaac D. Russell, Assistant Secretary ; J. Andrew Pickett, Thomas S. Bishop and Wm. G. Smythe.

Charles A. Schieren & Co., of Ferry and Cliff Streets, are preëminent as manufacturers of leather belting and lace leather.   Their factory is considered a model establishment in its line, because of its improved machinery and economic appliances.   The firm owns a number of patents, granted on inventions by Mr. Schieren, and under them manufactures such specialties as electric and perforated

belting for use on dynamos and swift-running electric-light machinery ; leather-link belting, for use in mines and on machinery exposed to water ; and planer belting, suitable for wood-working machinery.   The leather for planer belting is tanned with a view to flexibility and durability.   In order to supply its factory with materials, the firm operates three oak-leather tanneries, in Pennsylvania and Mary-

CHARLES A. SCHIEREN & CO., FERRY AND CLIFF STREETS.

land, and one lace-leather tannery in Brooklyn.   Charles A. Schieren, the founder of the firm, was born in Rhenish Prussia, in 1842, and with his parents emigrated to this country in 1856.   He had received a public-school education in Germany.   In his youth he assisted his father in conducting a cigar and tobacco business in Brooklyn. In 1864, as clerk, he entered the service of Philip F. Pasquay, leather-belting manufacturer, of New York.   By virtue of energy and close application he soon mastered the details of the business, and he became the manager of the establishment, on the death of his employer, in 1866.   Two years later, with limited means, he set up his own establishment.   In a comparatively short time he was at the head of a prosperous manufactory, which to-day ranks as one of the largest in the leather-belting line in the country.   In 1887 Mr. Schieren admitted as partner F. A. M. Burrell, who had been in his service as clerk for ten years.   The firm has branch-houses in Chicago, Boston and Philadelphia, and the products of its factory are shipped to all parts of the civilized world.   Mr. Schieren was one of the founders of the Hide and Leather National Bank, and is now its Vice-President.   He is also identified with many public institutions in Brooklyn, where he resides.

The leather belting made by this house comprises every length and width, and also of heavy and light weights, as their users may require.   Whatever is not carried in general stock can readily be produced by the house of Charles A. Schieren & Co.

Alfred **Dolge**, manufacturer of piano-felt and felt shoes, whose office and sale-rooms are at 122 East 13th Street, has established a new industry in this country, and has also created a manufacturing village. He is of German birth, not yet forty-five years of age, and has been in America since he was sixteen. He had learned the trade of a piano-maker in Saxony, and worked at it for a time in New Haven. Then he began to import materials of a superior quality for piano manufacturers,

ALFRED DOLGE'S DOLGEVILLE FACTORIES.

and at length, perceiving that all the felt used for piano hammers was made in Europe, he set about manufacturing it in America. Mr. Dolge succeeded so well that in 1873, when he was only twenty-five years old, his piano-felt won the first prize at the Vienna Exhibition. Then he went into the wilderness in the southern portion of the Adirondack region, purchased a magnificent water-power, and many thousands of acres of spruce timberland, erected sawmills and shops for turning spruce timber into sounding-boards for pianos, and eventually removed his felt-manufacturing establishment to the new settlement, which, originally known as Brockett's Bridge, was after a time rechristened Dolgeville. The reduction of tariff, which took effect in 1883, made competition with foreign makers of piano-felt almost impossible. Then Mr. Dolge turned his attention to the manufacture of felt shoes, and this industry has now grown to enormous proportions. There are, in the group of factories at Dolgeville, the main felt-mill, a felt-shoe factory, a sounding-board manufactory, a wood-working and planing mill, a grist mill, and several other extensive buildings. Mr. Dolge employs regularly about 600 people. In the winter, during the lumbering season, the number is considerably larger. More than half a million pounds of wool are turned into felt every year. Three million feet of spruce lumber are made into sounding-boards in the same period. The capacity of the felt shoe factory is fifteen hundred pairs of felt shoes every day. And, in addition, Mr. Dolge imports and deals in a great variety of materials, fittings and appliances required in the making of pianos. His catalogue, in fact a large profusely illustrated volume, is an interesting exhibit of the innumerable articles used in the manufacture of a piano. At the New-York establishment is kept the complete line of Alfred Dolge's productions.

Steinway & Sons, at 107-109-111 East 14th Street, in their own building — the white marble portico of which has four Corinthian columns, classic as the lyre which the double "S" of the firm-name forms — have their offices, warerooms and Steinway Hall. The hall attracts the artists that artists applaud. The offices are known to every lover of New York, for the name of William Steinway is the name of a peer among the merchants whom Brander Matthews calls princes. The warerooms are a quick stopping place, a halt for the Steinway pianos. Their cases and actions are made at Steinway, Astoria, L. I. There are a dock and bulkhead 384 feet in length, on the East River, enclosing a basin, 100 feet wide by 300 feet long, filled with logs; there are lumber yards, metal foundries, a saw mill, drying rooms, wherein are constantly 500,000 square feet of air-dried lumber.

A sketch of Steinway Hall, so famous in the annals of music in this country, appears in this volume, in the chapter on Amusement Places.

In the Steinway public-school, English, German and music are taught. In the Steinway public bath are 50 dressing-rooms. The Steinway public park, the Steinway dwellings, the Steinway residence, workmen, artisans of the Steinway pianos, make of Steinway an Arcadia. The finishing manufactory of the Steinway piano is in New-York City, and occupies the whole square from Park to Lexington Avenues and from 52d to 53d Streets. There 500 workmen plane, saw, join, drill, turn, string, fit, varnish and tune the piano works and cases received from the 600 workmen of Steinway, Astoria. A branch piano factory is in Hamburg, Germany. Warerooms in the Neue Rosenstrasse at Hamburg supply the Continent ; warerooms in Lower Seymour Street, London, supply Great Britain and Ireland. At the London International Exhibition in 1862, the Steinway pianos obtained a First Prize Medal ; at the Paris International Exhibition in 1867, a Grand Gold Medal ; at the Vienna International Exhibition in 1873, this flattering comment of the jury : "It is much to be deplored that the celebrated path-breaking firm of Steinway & Sons, to whom the entire pianoforte manufacture is so much indebted, did not exhibit." At the Philadelphia International Exhibition of 1876, the Steinway pianos obtained the highest awards for the best pianofortes and the best pianoforte material. The disposition of the strings in the form of a fan, patented in 1859 ; the duplex scale, patented in 1872 ; the cupola metal frame, patented in 1872 and 1875 ; the special construction of the sound board, patented in 1866, 1869 and 1872 ; the metallic tubular frame action, patented in 1868 and 1875 ; the tone-sustaining pedal, patented in 1874 ; the personal attention given by Steinway & Sons to every detail of their manufacture, account for the excellence of the Steinway pianos. The century has produced four musicians of genius greater than all others : Berlioz, Wagner, Liszt and Rubinstein. They have written enthusiastic praise of the Steinway pianos. The Royal Academy of Fine Arts, of Prussia ; the Royal Academy of Fine Arts, of Sweden ; the Empress of Russia; the Sultan of Turkey ; the Emperor of China ; the Queen of England ; every artistic association, every personage whose judgment is above dispute has given by academic honors, by acquisition for personal use, by words of praise, sanction to the pride with which New-Yorkers regard as the supreme and visible expression of the art of music, the pianos marked with a lyre formed of the initials of Steinway & Sons. During 1890 the Steinways were appointed piano-manufacturers to the Queen of England, and the Prince and Princess of Wales — and further, in 1892, they received from His Majesty Emperor William the appointment as manufacturers to the Royal Court of Prussia.

The Steinway name appears among the directors, officers, and patrons of an endless list of social, financial, commercial, political and other institutions.

STEINWAY & SONS.

The New-York Biscuit Company is a corporation, the business of which is conducted on an enormous scale.   It was organized in 1890, under the laws of Illinois, with a capital stock of $10,000,000.   It now owns most of the profitable plants for the making of biscuits in the East.   Its products are sold in every portion of the United States, and it has also an enormous export trade.   Its brands are held in the highest esteem all over the world.   The company's principal plant, completed and set in full operation in 1892, is at Tenth Avenue and 15th and 16th Streets, New York.   The enormous building, one of the largest of any kind in New-York City, occupies the whole easterly end of the city block, bounded by the streets named, and is 525 feet long, 206 feet wide, and six stories high.   It is arranged in the form of a hollow square, enclosing a court-yard 56 feet wide.   This court-yard is intended for convenience in receiving and shipping goods, and is large enough to accommodate 80 trucks.   The building contains 40 ovens, of a capacity sufficient to convert 1,000 barrels of flour into biscuits of various sorts, every day.   The ovens, as well as all of the machinery of the establishment, are of the newest designs, with the latest and best improvements.   Some portions of the mechanical outfit are of special design, and are not in use in other biscuit manufactories.   There are in the mixing-room 40 mixers, of capacity varying from five to eight barrels of flour in a single operation, and they are so arranged that the process of fermentation may be hastened or retarded, as may be desired.   In full operation, the plant gives employment to from 1,000 to 1,200 people.   The offices of the company occupy the entire western end of the sixth story of the building, and are larger than those of any banking-house in New York.   The new plant, which is the largest and most thoroughly equipped in the world, represents in its operations those formerly owned and operated by Holmes & Coutts, the Vanderveer & Holmes Biscuit Company, John D. Gilmor & Co., and Anger Bros., of New York, and Hetfield & Ducker, of Brooklyn.   The company also operates in New York the plants formerly controlled by E. J. Larrabee & Co. and Brinckerhoff & Co.

While the manufacturing and trade interests of the New-York Biscuit Company naturally centre in this city, it also owns and operates large plants in various other cities.   The one next in size to the New-York establishment is located in Cambridgeport, Mass., and was formerly controlled by the F. A. Kennedy Co.   It contains 16 ovens.   It supplies the goods sold in the New-England States, and is the only very large establishment of the sort in that territory.   The third largest plant owned by the company is located in Chicago.   It contains ten ovens, and its product is distributed through the Northwest, South, and Southwest.   Another large plant is that formerly operated by Sears & Co., in Grand Rapids, Mich.; and still another, that formerly owned by the Wilson Biscuit Company of Philadelphia.   Besides these large establishments, the New-York Biscuit Company also operates the Bent & Co. plant of Milton, Mass., the product of which is the famous hand-made water-cracker; a plant at Newburyport, Mass., which produces Pearson's creams and fine pilot breads; and also establishments in Newark, N. J., and Hartford and New Haven, Conn.

The New-York Biscuit Company, by these numerous and gigantic plants, is not only by far the greatest producer in the world of biscuits, or crackers, but it is also enabled to produce them at the lowest possible figure of cost.   Its enormous purchases of flour and materials give it a purchasing advantage impossible under any other circumstances.   Its varieties cover the whole range of plain and fancy biscuits, popularly called in this country crackers.   It supplies its widespread trade by means of teams, railroads and vessels; its products reach all civilized parts of the world.

NEW-YORK BISCUIT COMPANY.
TENTH AVENUE, FROM 15TH STREET TO 16TH STREET.

The Berwind-White Coal Mining Company was incorporated in 1886 as the successor of Berwind, White & Co., a coal-producing firm which had been organized in 1874 from the still older firms of Berwind & Bradley and White & Lingle. The capital stock of the present corporation is $2,000,000, and its executive officers are : Edward J. Berwind, President ; John E. Berwind, Vice-President ; H. A. Berwind, Secretary, and F. McOwen, Treasurer. The company own and operate extensive coal-mines in the Clearfield and Jefferson County regions, and are mining what is known as the Eureka Bituminous Steam Coal. They operate 29 collieries — 22 of which are at and around Houtzdale ; 2 at Karthaus, and 5 at Horatio, all of which have an aggregate capacity of upward of 15,000 tons a day. The tonnage of the company for 1891 aggregated over 3,500,000 tons. The works of the company are among the best equipped in the bituminous coal regions, being supplied with every modern improvement and labor-saving machinery, and calculated to expedite and economize the cost of the production of coal, as well as to insure its reaching the market in strictly first-class condition.

The company also own and operate 300 coke-ovens, where they are turning out a very superior grade of coke, which finds a ready market among manufacturers and steel-workers.

The Berwind-White Company own 3,000 coal cars and a fleet of 60 coal barges, used exclusively for the delivery of coal to ocean steamships in New York harbor. The coal is of the highest grade of steam coal, and is supplied under yearly contract to nearly all transatlantic and coasting lines running from New York, Philadelphia and Boston, among these steamship lines being the Inman, the North German Lloyd, the Cunard, the Hamburg, and the French lines, whose gigantic and palatial ocean greyhounds have a world-wide reputation. This coal is also supplied to nearly all the railways in the Eastern and Middle States, for locomotive use. It is likewise largely used for rolling-mills, iron-works, forges, glass-works and lime-kilns, in the burning of brick and fire-brick, and for kindred purposes. The mines are located on the Pennsylvania Railroad, or lines accessible thereto, over which they ship to tide-water for shipments coastwise and foreign, and to New York, the New-England States and Canada.

The company's shipping piers are located at Greenwich Point, Philadelphia ; Harsimus, Jersey City, New-York Harbor ; and Canton Piers, Baltimore. The general offices of the company are in the Bullitt Building, Philadelphia ; at 55 Broadway, New York ; at 19 Congress Street, Boston ; and in the Rialto Building, Baltimore. The Berwind-White is the largest bituminous coal mining company in America, employing 5,000 men, and an extensive staff of mining engineers, accountants, etc.

The company's shipping point in New-York harbor is at Harsimus Cove, Jersey City, just north of the Pennsylvania Railroad's freight pier. It consists of an extensive pier which reaches from Henderson Street to the North River, and is supplied with two main tracks, with such sidings as are required for the proper handling of coal cars, and so arranged as to load six barges at the same time. There are extensive coal-sheds capable of storing many thousand tons of coal, and also a weighing-house and suitable offices. The pier reaches to deep water, and can give accommodation to ships of the deepest draught, so that coal may be loaded directly to the ships from the company's sheds or trains. The pier is also the home station of the company's own fleet of specially constructed tugs and barges, which are chiefly engaged in the transhipment of their coal to various points in and around the harbor.

The business transacted by the Berwind-White Company is by far the most extensive in bituminous steam coals, either in Europe or the United States.

THE BERWIND-WHITE COAL-MINING COMPANY.
COAL PIERS AND BARGES AT JERSEY CITY. OFFICES, 55 BROADWAY, NEW YORK.

Chesebrough Manufacturing Company, Consolidated, are the sole manufacturers of Vaseline and Petroleum Jelly. This product from petroleum was discovered by Robert A. Chesebrough of New York in 1869. It was first presented to
the public in 1871, and at once attracted the attention of chemists, physicians, pharmacists and others,
who became speed-
ily interested in it
on account of its
many uses and me-
dicinal virtues. The
name given to it by
its inventor is de-
rived from the
Saxon word *wasser*
(water) and the
Greek *oleon* (oil),
signifying his belief
that from the de-
composition of
water in the earth
and the uniting
of the hydrogen
evolved by this de-
composition with
the carbons of cer-
tain rocks, aided by
natural heat and
pressure, is devel-
oped the substance
known as petro-

CHESEBROUGH MANUFACTURING CO., 24 STATE STREET.

leum. Vaseline appears as a solid jelly of an opal color, free from taste and odor.
It liquefies at 95° Fahr., boils at about 600° Fahr., and will not crystallize or
oxydize. It is the best base for cerates, ointments, pomades, and for many toilet
articles yet presented to the world. In medicine and surgery it has taken a high
rank and has a promising future, not only as an emollient and an antiseptic, but as
possessing remedial and curative effects of a high order. In the treatment of consumption the results obtained are remarkable, although not well understood, but
the discoverer insists that in this direction it is destined to become the remedy of
the future.

The history of Vaseline is remarkable ; for within twenty years, from being regarded as a scientific curiosity it has spread all over the world, has modified several
industries, and its use in the arts and manufactures is constantly extending. As
pharmacists and physicians have been its chief beneficiaries, one would think they
would be its strongest supporters ; but there exists a curious code of ethics amongst
them which seems to require the abandonment of all personal rights of the discoverer
as a condition of support. If not delivered over to them (as demanded), the penalty
is to devise and support imitators and imitations, under names invented by themselves. This practice reminds one of mediæval times and the methods of the robber
barons. It is to be hoped that the day will come when discoverers in medicine and
pharmacy will be recognized and upheld as they are in all other arts and sciences.

F. W. Devoe & C. T. Raynolds Company, the best-known manufacturers of paints, varnishes and artists' materials, have a genealogy as interesting as that of an old family. It was nearly a century and a half ago, in 1755, that William Post started a small business as painter and glazier at 43 Water Street. He extended his business, his sons succeeded him, and various changes took place in the member-ship of the firm until in 1855, just 100 years after the beginning of the business, it became Raynolds, Devoe & Pratt, still, however, occupying its old office on Water Street. Later Mr. Raynolds and Mr. Pratt dropped out, and in 1864 the name became simply F. W. Devoe & Co. In that year the present offices at the corner of Fulton and William Streets were established. In 1892 the old firm was re-united, under the title of F. W. Devoe & C. T. Raynolds Co. In these offices to-day is to be seen an interesting relic of the original house, a life-size painting of William Post. The factory for the manufacture of paints, artists' materials and brushes was built in 1852, on Horatio Street. It has been many times enlarged, until now it extends through to Jane Street and has a floor-space of four acres. For 35 years it has been under the superintendence of James F. Drummond, a member of the firm. The articles there manufactured have obtained an enviable reputation throughout the country for their purity and high quality. The firm has another large factory in Newark, N. J., for the manufacture of varnishes. These are the largest varnish works in the country, and are under the personal supervision of J. Seaver Page, also a member of the firm. That the varnishes made at this factory are held in high repute is well attested to by the fact that they are considered as standards of excellence, and are used by the Pennsylvania, the New-York Central, and other railroads of the country where their wearing qualities are put to the severest tests. The firm, in order to supply the great West, has also established stores and factories in Chicago. In 1882 advantage was taken of the firm's preëminent position to introduce the manufacture of the very highest grade of engineers', architects' and mathematical instruments. Little is now left undone by this firm to give decorators, painters and artists the best of materials for their work.

F. W. DEVOE & C. T. RAYNOLDS COMPANY, FULTON AND WILLIAM STREETS.

Post & McCord are civil engineers and contractors for the iron work in bridges, fire-proof buildings and roofs. The firm consists of Andrew J. Post, C. E., M. A. S. C. E., and William H. McCord. Their offices are in the United Charities Building, at Fourth Avenue and 22d Street, and the works are at North 8th Street and Driggs Avenue, Brooklyn. This firm has constructed many important structures, among which are the roof of the New-Jersey Central train-shed at Communipaw, N. J.; that of the new train-shed at the Grand Central Depot; the roof of the amphitheatre of the Madison-Square Garden, and the frame-work carrying the tower of the same build- ing; and the new iron bridge carrying the tracks of the New-York and New-Haven Railroad over those of the New-York and Harlem Railroad, near Woodlawn Ceme- tery station. It has also furnished and erected the iron work of many of the large fire-proof buildings in New York, among them the Central-Park Apartments, at 58th

POST & McCORD; ARCHITECTURAL AND STRUCTURAL IRON WORKS.

and 59th Streets and Seventh Avenue; the Dakota, at 72d Street and Eighth Ave- nue; the Chelsea, on 23d Street; the new Presbyterian Hospital; Temple Court, at Nassau and Beekman Streets; the Corbin Building, at Broadway and John Street; the Gallatin Bank Building, on Wall Street; the Mechanics' Bank Building, on Wall Street; the Wilks Building, on Wall Street; the 8th-Regiment Armory, New York, and the State Capitol at Trenton, N. J. During the summer of 1892 Post & McCord supplied the iron work for the new Charities Building, at 22d Street and Fourth Avenue; the power station for the Broadway and Seventh-Avenue Cable Railway, at Broadway and Houston Street; and the Metropolitan Realty Company's Building. Mr. Post has had large experience in designing and building railroad bridges, and is well known among civil engineers. Mr. McCord has been connected with some of the largest architectural iron works, and is thoroughly acquainted with the details of that line of construction. The new method of constructing the frames of fire- proof buildings of wrought iron and steel was adopted by this firm in its infancy, and has been elaborated by them to a great extent.

The entire iron work used in the construction of buildings and bridges comes within the province of Post & McCord.

James R. Floyd & Sons are manufacturers and contractors for the iron work used in gas works, the original firm of Herring & Floyd having been the first in this country to make a specialty of that business, their principal work at the time being the making of the Herring safe castings. Mr. Floyd was the patentee of the burglar-proof iron used in the Herring safe, known as Franklinite iron, and the partnership with Silas C. Herring continued until his death in 1881, a period of over twenty-six years. Mr. Floyd then carried on the business alone, until in 1888 he associated with himself two of his sons, the firm now consisting of James R. Floyd, Frederick W. Floyd, C. E., and Henry E. Floyd. The first works were on Greenwich Street, near Hammond Street (now West 11th Street), in the section of the city that was then better known as Greenwich Village, and subsequently as the "old Ninth Ward;" and as it was the custom to give a distinctive name to a new works, and

JAMES R. FLOYD & SONS, OREGON IRON WORKS, 531 TO 543 WEST 20TH STREET.

the question of admitting Oregon into the Union was then warmly debated, it was called the Oregon Iron Works, which name is still retained. In 1886 the present foundry and machine-shops were erected, as shown in our illustration; and the original weather-vane, in the shape of a herring, surmounts the flagstaff over a model foundry. The works are at 531 to 543 West 20th Street, near Eleventh Avenue; and extend through to 21st Street. Here are made the most approved apparatus used in the manufacturing of illuminating gas, retort mouthpieces, scrubbers, condensers, washers, purifiers, valves, station meters, and street connections, as well as a general foundry and machine business. Most of the specialties are covered by patents, and almost all gas-works in the large cities of the United States use some of them. The senior partner is connected with a number of financial and philanthropic institutions.

The Berlin & Jones Envelope Company is one of the great industrial institutions of New-York City. This business was founded in 1849 by J. Berlin, who retired some years ago. It is the oldest in this country in its line, and has remained in possession of the family ever since. It was incorporated in 1868, at which time Mr. Jones (since retired) had an interest, hence its present title. It has occupied its present location — 134 and 136 William Street, near Fulton Street — for 37 years, having

BERLIN & JONES ENVELOPE CO., 134 AND 136 WILLIAM STREET.

moved there in 1856, and is well-known in this section of the city. It is one of the largest envelope manufacturers in the world, having facilities for producing 2,000,000 envelopes each day, employs many people and the finest machinery, which folds, gums and counts envelopes at the rate of 110 a minute. The machinery is their own invention, patented, and has been supplied by them to most of the manufacturers of the present day. They manufacture not only staple envelopes for commercial use, and to supply the necessities of large railroad and other corporations, but their complete printing and binding establishment connected with the envelope works enables them to furnish the general stationery, such as blanks, way-bills, etc., for which they have large contracts. The finest kinds of paper are here also worked up into many forms for wedding and society uses, which, together with the staple goods, find markets in all the States and Territories, as well as in foreign countries, their export business being extensive. The Berlin & Jones Envelope Co., in nearly half a century of successful development, has led the manufacturing stationers in their progressive production of choicer and better goods, and when new processes were needed, some one in this corporation invented the proper mechanism therefor, until now the factory is packed with the finest and most serviceable machinery, acting with almost human intelligence, and with vastly more than human certainty and quickness. The officers of the company are Henry C. Berlin, President; Walter G. Berlin, Treasurer; and H. W. Berlin, Secretary.

The growth of this industry has been very great during the last few years, and the amount of capital invested is much larger than is generally supposed.

The **National Wall Paper Company**, which was organized in 1892, with a capital of $30,000,000, and with its general executive offices in New-York City, is one of the greatest industrial corporations in the United States. It represents the highest success and the fullest development in all that pertains to the interior decorations of homes and public and private buildings. It has united all that age, experience, invention and capital have achieved in this industry. The history of the united concerns would tell the story of the rise, the traditions, and the present state of the wall-paper and interior-decoration industry of this country. Its various branches have offered the largest prizes and paid the greatest prices for designs. They have been awarded great medals for grand exhibits in this country and abroad. The present organization was effected to decrease the cost of the products of the various establishments, by the savings secured through co-operation; to reform abuses which had risen from fierce competition; and to advance and develop the whole industry. When

NATIONAL WALL PAPER CO., BROOME AND ELM STREETS.

one recalls the fact that now almost every room in the land is in some way more or less decorated, it becomes apparent that any effort to extend the possibilities of a higher decoration, at a lower cost, is worthy the support of the entire public. This great organization of the National Wall Paper Company, with its enormous capital, its many extensive and wonderfully equipped factories, and its wide-spread ramifications, has the ability as well as the intention of thus serving the people, and at the same time of yielding to its interested stockholders a fair return for their investments. This company is not founded to carry on any one special line of decoration, but its productions embrace the entire range, from the cheapest possible wall-paper, resulting from unlimited facilities and tremendous output, up to the highest achievements in artistic wall decorations. An idea of its possibilities can be gleaned from the fact that it now owns the business formerly conducted by twenty-five great concerns, including those that have always been acknowledged by the trade and the public to be the absolute leaders in this industry. They include the following establishments: The Robert Graves Co., 483 Fifth Avenue; the F. E. James Co., 483 Tenth Avenue; H. Bartholomae & Co., 124 West 33d Street; Leissner, Midlen & Hughes Co., 432 East 71st Street; the Manhattan Wall Paper Co., 617 West 39th Street; Warren, Fuller & Co., 129 East 42d Street; Robert S. Hobbs & Co., 540 West 58th Street; Henry Gledhill & Co., 541 West 34th Street; Fr. Beck & Co., 206 West 29th Street, and Fifth Avenue and 30th Street; Nevius & Haviland, 42d Street and Tenth

FR. BECK & CO., BRANCH OF THE NATIONAL WALL PAPER CO., FIFTH AVENUE AND 30TH STREET.

THE ROBERT GRAVES CO., BRANCH OF THE NATIONAL WALL PAPER CO., 483 AND 485 FIFTH AVENUE.

Avenue; and Thos. Strahan & Co., Fifth Avenue and 21st Street; all in New-York City: William H. Mairs & Co., 68 Sackett Street; the Robert Graves Co., Third Avenue and 35th Street; J. J. Lindsay & Co., 247 Chestnut Street; and W. N. Peak, 408 Hicks Street; all in Brooklyn: Howell Brothers, Limited, 21st Street and Washington Avenue; Janeway & Co., 621 Market Street; Carey Bros., 2228 North 10th Street; Carey Bros. & Grevemeyer, 817 Market Street; Cresswell & Washburn, 18th Street and Washington Avenue; the Keystone Wall Paper Co., 8th Street and Snyder Avenue; and Janeway & Carpender, 23 North 10th Street; all in Philadelphia: Janeway &

Co., 106 Wabash Avenue;
S. A. Maxwell & Co., 134
and 136 Wabash Avenue;
Nevius & Haviland, 136
Wabash Avenue; Jane-
way & Carpender, 145
Wabash Avenue; the Lartz
Wall Paper Co., 45 Ran-
dolph Street; all in Chi-
cago: Janeway & Co. and
Janeway & Carpender, both
of New Brunswick, N. J.;
the Wilson & Fenimore
Co., Bristol, Pa.; Thos.
Strahan & Co., Chelsea,
Mass.; John S. Roberts,
815 Penn Avenue, Pitts-
burgh, Pa.; and the "Efficient" Shade Roller Fac-
tory of Nevius & Haviland,
at Vergennes, Vt. These
concerns retain their old
styles, but are designated
as branches of the National
Wall Paper Company.

In New-York City the
company maintains several
long-established retail
stores, including those of
Fr. Beck & Co., on Fifth
Avenue and 30th Street,
who introduced "Lincrusta
Walton," one of the finest

WARREN, FULLER & CO., BRANCH OF THE NATIONAL WALL PAPER CO., 42b
STREET, BETWEEN LEXINGTON AVENUE AND GRAND CENTRAL STATION.

wall decorations ever invented; the Robert Graves Co., 483 Fifth Avenue, one
of the largest producers of high-grade wall papers in the country; and Warren,
Fuller & Co., 139 East 42d Street, near the Grand Central Depot, one of the foremost
concerns in this great economic league. Warren, Fuller & Co.'s business was
founded in 1856, and its senior member, James S. Warren, still continues at its head,
as the general manager. This firm has for many years been prominently identified
with this industry, and has done much toward its higher development. They are
widely known throughout the trade, and their products include all grades of wall
paper, from the very cheapest up to the richest and highest class. Their great factories cover a large part of the block between East 42d Street and 43d Street, and
Lexington Avenue and the Grand Central Depot. At Paris, in 1889, Warren,
Fuller & Co. received a medal for the excellence of their exhibit.

One specialty in universal use throughout the land is the "Efficient" shade
roller, myriads of which are manufactured by the Nevius & Haviland Branch.

At various retail stores of the National Wall Paper Co. can be found everything
to decorate the walls and ceilings of any building. The officers are Henry Burn,
President; S. A. Maxwell, Vice-President; Wm. H. Mairs, Treasurer; and J. J. Lindsay, Secretary. The executive offices are at Broome and Elm Streets.

R. Hoe & Co., at 504 Grand Street, the printing-press manufacturers, stand indisputably at the head of their industry in the world. Their presses are in use in all civilized countries, and undoubtedly have been a gigantic force in the civilization of the people of these times. The marvelous development of the press — especially the newspaper press, which is one of the most notable wonders of our age — would not have been possible but for the rare inventive talent, scientific skill, and remarkable power of conceiving and adapting means to ends which have produced the modern Hoe printing-press. The reputation of this firm is as world-wide as its products are world-spread, and its career has been not less spirited than successful.

It was founded in 1804, by Robert Hoe, a cadet of an honorable Lancashire (England) family, who came to New York in 1803, and began manufacturing the usual wooden and also iron hand printing-presses. The firm is now composed of Robert Hoe (a grandson of the founder and son of the late Robert Hoe), Stephen D. Tucker, Theodore H. Mead (also a grandson of the founder), and Charles W. Carpenter. The establishment is located on a commanding site fronting on Grand Street, and occupies the greater part of two blocks, facing respectively on Grand, Broome, Columbia and Sheriff Streets. The floor space is 296,000 square feet, or, 6¾ acres. This immense area is filled with tools, machinery and appliances of the most approved construction and efficiency. The London establishment occupies an entire block on Mansfield Street, and is equally perfect and complete in its equipment. The employees number 2,000. This establishment is well worth a visit from those interested in engineering and mechanical industries, as well as from printers in every department of the art.

Robert Hoe introduced in America, about 1829, the flat-bed cylinder press, then in use in England for newspaper work, and capable, perhaps, at its best, of producing 1,000 impressions an hour. From that small beginning to the magnificent press of to-day, capable of turning out 75,000 eight-page complete and folded newspapers an hour, is as conspicuous and astonishing a result of the cumulative energy and enterprise of the century as any achieved by steam, or electricity, or other "fairy tale of science." This result has been attained by patient and unwearied devotion to a congenial task ; by trained scientific, mechanical and expert ability ; by large expenditures, commensurate with the large ends in view ; by an intelligent, almost a prophetic, perception of the ever-advancing wants of the age ; and by a noble spirit of emulation, and a pride in the reputation and honor of the firm. To a continuous family identity with the undertaking much of its remarkable success and celebrity is due. That New-York journalism and journalistic enterprise leads the world is a fitting corollary to the fact that this New-York firm has placed at its service such delicate, sensitive, and all but sentient machinery, that seems to live and throb with the embodied spirit of the age.

A volume would scarce suffice to trace the interesting and progressive development of the many varieties of the Hoe printing-press. The mechanical experts of the U. S. Patent Office state that "The Sextuple Newspaper Perfecting Press, for originality of invention, perfection of design, accuracy of workmanship, and results accomplished, forms one of the most remarkable productions of the nineteenth century." It is composed of over 16,000 pieces ; weighs 130,000 pounds ; and is 26 feet, 3 inches long, 18 feet wide, and 12 feet high. It prints on both sides of three continuous rolls of paper, and delivers the perfect newspaper, bound, folded, pasted, cut open at the head, and counted. It prints a six-page paper at the rate of 96,000 an hour ; an eight-page at the rate of 75,000 ; a ten or twelve-

R. HOE & CO. PRINTING-PRESS AND SAW WORKS.
GRAND, BROOME, COLUMBIA AND SHERIFF STREETS, NEAR EAST RIVER.

page at the rate of 48,000; a sixteen-page at the rate of 36,000; and up to a twenty-four-page paper at the rate of 24,000 an hour. A late achievement is the construction of rapid color-printing machines for daily papers. The initial press of this kind now prints, at one operation, the daily colored supplements of the *New-York Recorder*, at the speed of 30,000 copies an hour. The firm, as early as 1828, manufactured circular saws, and no less than 25,000 of their patented Chisel-tooth Saws are now in successful operation. Besides newspaper presses and saws, this firm manufactures more cylinder and job, lithographic and book presses than any other firm in the country. They also make all kinds of printers' supplies.

Wyckoff, Seamans & Benedict, sole manufacturers of the Remington Standard Typewriter, with a capital of $3,000,000, have indeed become one of the gigantic and preëminent manufacturing establishments of America. Their executive offices and main selling headquarters occupy the plain and unpretentious, though substantial marble structure on Broadway, near the corner of Worth Street,

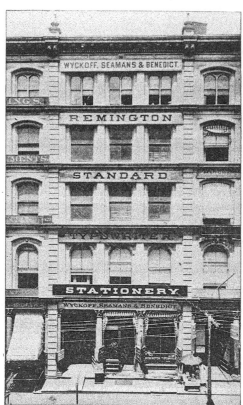

WYCKOFF, SEAMANS & BENEDICT, 327 BROADWAY.

and as the centre of such an industry may well invite the thoughtful attention of all visitors to the city. Here is a business absolutely American, which has its connections with the very ends of the earth. There is nothing in the history of commercial enterprises more strikingly suggestive than the growth of this business. It is estimated that there are in the neighborhood of ten thousand Remington Typewriters in use in New-York City and the immediate vicinity. From very small beginnings, about the year 1873, the growth of the Remington Typewriter business has been simply unprecedented. If, as it has been said, the invention of the typewriter has done more to promote the spread of human intelligence than any one invention since the advent of the printing-press, how great an influence upon the world of thought and action has emanated from this establishment.

Few have any adequate conception of the magnitude of the business done annually at 327 Broadway. From this point general control and supervision is exercised over more than a score of branch-offices located in the leading cities of the United States and Europe. To this office come the reports of an army of representatives stationed in all quarters of the globe, and from thence issue orders to the great factory at Ilion, New York, where the machines are manufactured. The organization and equipment of this business is thorough and admirable throughout.

. To the uninitiated, the number of typewriters made by the Remington factory seems to be simply incredible. Over one hundred complete typewriters each day are turned out by the factory, which employs some seven hundred men. These machines are readily sold, and the demand increases so rapidly that the manufacturing department is often kept running overtime so as to fill the orders promptly. The company's plant is now arranged with a view to increasing the production to one thousand machines a week, in the near future, as it is believed that the day is not far distant when the rapid growth of the trade will require at least this number.

WYCKOFF, SEAMANS & BENEDICT : INTERIOR OF REMINGTON STANDARD TYPEWRITER HEADQUARTERS.

A brick and stone building, which in itself, will be larger than any other typewriter factory in the world is now in course of construction.

The surprising success of the Remington is in no small degree to be attributed to the policy of Wyckoff, Seamans & Benedict. From the first they perceived that in order to keep pace with the demands of users, the machine which was at first a crude and unsatisfactory device, must be constantly improved. A settled policy of steady progress in this direction was, therefore, adopted, and has been faithfully carried out ever since. The result of this, together with the firm's enterprise and skill in making known the merits of the machine, has contributed to procure for the Remington Standard Typewriter its universal recognition as the standard writing machine of the world.

F. A. Ferris & Company, whose name is a household word in the homes of this nation, are conducting a gigantic business that was begun three-quarters of a century ago.   In 1818, a stout German lad of nineteen years landed from a sailing vessel, and walked up Broadway without a penny in his pocket.   Industry, integrity and economy soon enabled this newcomer, John J. Cape, to start a little provision shop, and so well did he prosper that when he was fifty years of age he retired from active business with a comfortable fortune.   He took pride, however, in having his name remain in the succeeding firm of F. A. Ferris & Company until the day of his death.   Through all the exacting war times and wonderful commercial changes since that day, the firm has steadily kept on its way, extending its business to every part of the world that imports fine provisions from the United States, at all times laying as the foundation of further success the crowding of their product towards absolute perfection.   One of their maxims which has a popular ring has

PONTIFEX REFRIGERATING APPARATUS USED BY F. A. FERRIS & CO.

become known to all Americans —"A little higher in price, but ——!" Their establishment, 262, 264, 266, 268, 270 and 272 Mott Street, a plain but substantial brick stone-trimmed businessbuilding without, shows within a most interesting combination of all that science and experience have taught concerning the fine curing and smoking of hams and bacon.   The intricate processes of changing the fresh meats by what is known as "curing" into the smoked hams and bacon which can stand shipment to any ordinary climate now depend fundamentally upon the production of cold by artificial means.   One of the most charming machinery rooms of the country is found in their fire-proof building, where they have in duplicate the Pontifex Refrigerating Plant.   The March, 1893, number of Scribner's Magazine, in an article entitled "Some Notable Food Products," gives a lucid description of the wonderful work accomplished by this mechanical system.   The Ferris Building, standing on the back bone of the lower part of New-York island, has three stories of cellars (excavations having been made thirty feet below the curb through a bed of fine cut sand and gravel), thus adding immensely to the storage capacity of the firm.   It can justly be said that in the preparation of meat-foods this is one of the model establishments of the country.   On the opposite page is a view of the Mott-Street front of the packing establishment of F. A. Ferris & Company.

F. A. FERRIS & COMPANY PACKING ESTABLISHMENT.
MOTT STREET, EAST SIDE, BETWEEN HOUSTON AND PRINCE STREETS.

John Dwight & Co. enjoy the distinction of establishing the pioneer bi-carbo-nate of soda factory in the United States.   Before 1846 pearlash was almost exclusively used throughout the country for domestic purposes.   What bi-carbonate of soda was then used was imported from England.   In that year John Dwight started his soda factory at the foot of West 25th Street, New York.   He there began the manufacture of soda-saleratus and bi-carbonate of soda.   In introducing new articles, subversive of old ideas, he threw down the gage of war to the pearlash-saleratus monopolists at home and bi-carbonate of soda produced by English manufacturers.

JOHN DWIGHT & CO., 11 OLD SLIP.

By placing only the very best articles on the market, he in time educated the house-keepers out of the use of the old-fashioned pearlash-saleratus, and gave them an article much cheaper in price, and of double the carbonic-acid gas strength.   He was aided in this innovation by the fact that at that time, owing to an extensive destruction of the forests from which the raw material for the pearlash was obtained, the prices of the old article were materially advanced.   His bi-carbonate of soda was successfully pushed in the home markets, in opposition to the English importations.   And since that time these latter have never regained a foothold in this country.   The attempts to do so have been various.   They have been sold to the packers of saleratus in America, and placed on the market as pearlash-saleratus.   But this substitute could never usurp the place which Mr. Dwight's pure article has gained.   As a result, the English manufacturers, in order to sell their goods at all in this country, have been obliged to reduce the price of their soda from nine cents a pound, which existed in 1847, at the time of the inception of Mr. Dwight's business, to three cents a pound.   When it was seen that John Dwight could successfully compete with the long-established pearlash-saleratus and the English bi-carbonate of soda, factories for the manufacture of soda-saleratus sprang rapidly into existence.   But from that time to this, in the midst of an ever-increasing competition, Mr. Dwight has maintained his reputation of being the pioneer in the business and standing at its head.   In 1847 he formed a partnership with John R. Maurice, which was continued until 1881.   It was dissolved then on account of Mr. Maurice's increasing years, and Mr. Dwight again carried on the industry alone.

JOHN DWIGHT & CO.

By this time his business had assumed extended proportions, and had become known as the most successful bi-carbonate of soda manufacturing firm in the United States, and the famous " Cow Brand " trade mark is familiar in all households.

In 1885 Mr. Dwight took his son, John E. Dwight, into partnership, and in 1886 William I. Walker was admitted to the firm. These three now constitute the firm of John Dwight & Co., with offices at 11 Old Slip, where Mr. Dwight had established himself in 1856. In 1868 the old factory on 25th Street was given up, and the present one, much larger, established between 112th and 113th Streets. At this factory, besides the bi-carbonate of soda, is manufactured sal soda or washing soda. This article by its extensive consumption makes an additional branch to the business, which by itself is of great importance. The enormous business that this firm does may be realized when it is stated that of the large quantities of bi-carbonate of soda required annually in the United States for domestic uses it supplied one-third in the year 1891.

The New-York Photogravure Co., at 137 West 23d Street, makes perfect pictures for artistic, scientific and commercial purposes, by special, inimitable photogravure, photogelatine and half-tone block processes. They publish *Sun and Shade*, a monthly magazine with one page of descriptive text and plates, wherein the delicacy of the photogelatine and the strength and richness of the photogravure processes are amazingly displayed. The President of the company is Ernest

NEW-YORK PHOTOGRAVURE CO., 137 WEST 23D STREET.

Edwards, inventor of the photogelatine process called heliotype, and manager of the Heliotype Printing Co. from 1872 to 1886. The Art-Director is A. V. S. Anthony, formerly Art-Director for Ticknor & Fields and Fields, Osgood & Co.

The work of the New-York Photogravure Co. is in some of the most valuable art-books of the present time, in Muybridge's *Animal Locomotion* ; in the *Home and Haunts of Shakespeare,* published by Charles Scribner's Sons ; in the *Ada Rehan,* published by Augustin Daly ; in *She Stoops to Conquer,* illustrated by Abbey, published by Harper & Bros. ; in exquisite publications of D. Appleton & Co., Dodd, Mead & Co., Jos. Knight Co., and others. It appears in catalogues, in *menus,* in memorial papers and play bills, and is everywhere acclaimed. It cannot be rivalled in fidelity of execution, finish of workmanship, delicacy of lines, softness of half-tones, by engravers whose tools are not light and chemistry. The ancient xylography has other merits, but not these merits of an art which directs light as the potter's art directs fire.

The New-York Photogravure Co. has a gallery fitted to produce negatives of all sizes up to 24x30, by the best orthochromatic methods. From this department to the packing room there is not a phase of any work, however trivial apparently, not carefully attended with the most zealous supervision. It seems easy, it is extremely difficult ; but it is intensely fascinating. Mr. Edwards has yielded the energy, the incessant labor of a life-time, to that fascination. It is due to him that if the reproduction of paintings made in the United States may be matched abroad, the reproduction of landscapes from original negatives remains an unequalled and unapproachable American art. The New-York Photogravure Co. gives of it extraordinary models.

Sun and Shade reproduces not only the most notable paintings and portraits, but the best work of amateur and professional photographers. If it gave nothing but the latter work it would be deserving of the most liberal patronage that it receives ; but it is an admirable record of the greatest paintings at the Metropolitan Museum of Art, of living American players, of portraits of celebrated Americans, of great American painters with reproductions of their work, and it is a monumental production of the New-York Photogravure Co.

The Automatic Fire-Alarm and Extinguisher Company (Limited) of New York renders an invaluable service to the public by means of its efficient devices for the protection of property from loss by fire. Its apparatus consists of the Watkins Automatic Fire-Alarm, which has been extensively used for many years, and has a record far above all other devices for the early detection of fires. This system has the approval of the fire departments and fire underwriters, and the insurance companies make a decided reduction in the rates where it is introduced. Nearly a thousand important buildings in New-York City alone are protected by the Watkins Automatic Fire-Alarm, besides a large number in Boston and other cities. This system comprises a series of thermostats, or heat detectors, placed at frequent intervals on the ceiling of each room, and made sensitive to heat at any required degree. In case of a fire near any of these thermostats an alarm is automatically sounded at the main office of the company, at 413 Broadway, where the operators, who are on duty day and night, immediately transmit the alarm to the headquarters of the Fire Department and the Insurance Patrol ; the alarm designating the street number and the floor of the building where the fire is located. This immediate automatic notice constitutes the value of the system. The arrival of the firemen is often the first notice the occupants have of fire in their building, and the work done during the first five minutes of a fire is worth more than that of the next five hours.

William B. Watkins was the inventor, and the system in practical operation has been carefully studied and improved by expert electricians for twenty years. It has

some imitators, but no rival. Among the individuals and firms protected by this system in New-York City are such names as William Astor, Arnold, Constable & Co., H. B. Claflin Co., E. S. Jaffray & Co., Mills & Gibb, R. H. Macy & Co., McKesson & Robbins, Rogers, Peet & Co., Tiffany & Co., and Thurber-Whyland Co.

This company is also the New-York representative of the General Fire-Extinguisher Company, which protects property against fire by means of automatic sprinklers (especially the famous Grinnell Sprinkler), and has recently acquired the Neracher, Kane, Harkness and Hill sprinklers. The executive offices are at 413 Broadway, occupying the greater part of the building at the corner of Lispenard Street. The President is Elijah S. Cowles ; the Treasurer, Richard S. Barnes ; and the Secretary, Edward O. Richards.

AUTOMATIC FIRE-ALARM AND EXTINGUISHER CO., 413 BROADWAY, CORNER OF LISPENARD STREET.

WASHINGTON SQUARE AND WASHINGTON ARCH.

The Gamewell Fire-Alarm Telegraph Company, at 1½ Barclay Street, is an institution whose invaluable works are well-known in all American cities and large towns. The first successful employment of electricity for giving fire-alarms was made by Dr. W. F. Channing of Boston and Moses G. Farmer of Salem, whose plan was accepted in 1851 by the city of Boston, where the first official fire-alarm by electricity was sounded in 1852. Three years later, Gamewell

GAMEWELL FIRE-ALARM TELEGRAPH CO.,
1 1-2 BARCLAY STREET.

& Co. secured all the Channing and Farmer patents for the South and West, and soon afterward for the whole country. The Gamewell Fire-Alarm Telegraph Co. was incorporated in 1877, and secured the patents and business of Gamewell & Co. The system is so meritorious, and it has been managed with such business ability, that now more than 500 American cities and towns are equipped with Gamewell fire-alarm telegraphs, and nearly 100 have the Gamewell Police telephone and signal systems. The company has well-managed agencies at Chicago, San Francisco, Boston, Baltimore, Louisville, Utica, and Richmond, Indiana ; and its factory is at Newton, Massachusetts.

The Gamewell apparatus, as manufactured in its own specially equipped factory, is absolutely reliable, and stands as the best, simplest, and most perfectly constructed mechanism yet devised for its purposes. The fire-alarm conveys that prompt and definite notice of the existence and location of a fire without which the best fire-department is unavailable. It saves yearly millions of dollars worth of property, and thousands of lives. The Police Telegraph ensures discipline and attention to duty on the part of patrolmen ; affords means of summoning police assistance and patrol-wagons ; and ensures prompt humane care for victims of accidents, and quick transportation for the drunkard or criminal.

It is a well-recognized tradition of the Gamewell Fire-Alarm Telegraph Company that it has been quick to acquire and to utilize all possible improvements in apparatus which in any way can be utilized for the immediate indication of fires, or for the rapid and convenient method of communication between points of troubles or calamities and the head or central stations of the Police, and thus it is that the Gamewell apparatus is to-day representative for all that has been attained in this line.

The officers are Joseph W. Stover, President ; W. H. Woolverton and D. H. Bates, Vice-Presidents ; H. F. Bender, Treasurer ; Charles W. Cornell, Secretary ; and John N. Gamewell, General Manager.

The Pope Manufacturing Company, whose New-York branch is at 12 Warren Street, is by far the largest concern of the kind in the world. Col. Albert A. Pope, the founder of the bicycle industries in America, organized this company and furnished its capital, in 1877, and he has ever since been its president and active

manager. At first the opposition to the wheel was outspoken and intolerant, but this prejudice was overcome by the free distribution of the best foreign cycling literature, and by interesting home talent. It was in pursuance of this policy that *The American Bicycler* was written, and that Col. Pope founded *The Wheelman,* which is flourishing as the *Outing* of to-day. The Columbia bicycles were made from the outset by the Weed Sewing Machine Co., of Hartford, Conn., a corporation which the Pope Mfg. Co., finally absorbed in 1890, paying the stock-holders 50 per cent. premium for their holdings. Additions have been made to the factory, until it has five acres of flooring, and employs a thousand people. Besides this, the company own an extensive seamless steel tube and forging plant, and have recently purchased and materially enlarged the plant of the Hartford Rubber Works Co.

POPE MANUFACTURING CO., 12 AND 14 WARREN STREET.   Most of the best records for fast riding have been made with Columbias. It was on an Expert Columbia that Stevens made his famous tour around the world. The Standard Columbia, Expert Columbia, and Columbia Light Roadster were the three best-known high wheels, while the Columbia Safety, Light Roadster Safety, and Models 30, 31, and 32 for 1893 mark three important steps of progress in the more modern style of bicycles.

January 1, 1892, the Pope Mfg. Co. took possession of its fine new office-building at 221 Columbus Avenue, Boston. Its architecture is of the early Renaissance school. The front is of Indiana limestone and Perth-Amboy brick, with terra-cotta ornamentations. The store on the first floor, and the general offices, occupying the entire second story, are furnished in quartered oak. The fifth story is devoted to a riding school, equipped with double padded rails, and a fine maple floor. The company has a paid-in capital of $2,000,000, and a very large surplus. It has a number of branch offices in various large cities, and its agents are scattered everywhere.

The New-York branch was opened in 1882, and represents to-day a very important factor of the business. Connected with the Warren-Street store there is a riding-hall. Here may be found at all times a complete line of the Columbia bicycles, together with their hundreds of parts and attachments.

The New-York Boat Oar Company has occupied its present site, at 69 West Street, for many years. It is the representative concern in this line in all America, and its products have vexed the waters of all seas. It is rarely that a business so limited in its variety of articles can be found, for almost the only wares produced here are ash and spruce oars, spoon oars, sweeps, sculls, canoe paddles, mast-hoops, capstan bars, rowlocks and handspikes. These are produced in a variety of sizes and shapes. In this very narrow but important field, the New-York Boat Oar Company has won an undisputed leadership, and its trade not only reaches both coasts of the Americas, but also extends to Europe, Africa ·and Australia. This peculiar industry was founded in the year 1843, by Ezekiel Page, whose excellent oars won such a high reputation that the company still retains his name as a trade-mark, their oars being styled the " Ezekiel Page Brand Oars." He was succeeded by E. W. Page & Sons ; and they by the E. W. Page Co. ; and that by the present corporation, of which Samuel W. Richards was the first president. He was succeeded in 1888 by Frank D. Wilsey, who is now

NEW-YORK BOAT OAR COMPANY, 69 WEST STREET.

the President and Treasurer, F. Clutterbuck being the Secretary. The factories at Bloomville and Jerry City, Ohio, were given up years ago, and the company's chief works now are at Savannah, Georgia, in favorable proximity to their supply of stock. This interesting industry has been brought to a remarkable perfection by the line of ingenious men who have conducted it for the last half century, since the day when Ezekiel Page founded the business. The trade-mark of the New-York Boat Oar Company is a synonym of excellence based on long experience and thorough comprehension of materials and methods ; and the largest shipping interests provide their boats with equipments from the West-Street emporium. It has taken a great number of prizes at important exhibitions, and has always carried off the highest awards whenever it entered for competition. One of its notable honors was an award at the International Maritime Exposition at Havre, in 1887, when its products surpassed those of all the great maritime nations of Europe.

The **A. D. Farmer & Son Type Founding Company** has an establishment at 63 and 65 Beekman Street, and 62 and 64 Gold Street, that is the result of more than three-quarters of a century's growth and development. It is the successor in direct line of the famous old type-foundry of Elihu White, established in 1804, and known to all printers of the past generation.

Aaron D. Farmer, who established the present house, came from Connecticut to New York in 1830, when a boy of twelve years, and entered Mr. White's establishment, at Lombard and Thames Streets, as an apprentice, and here he developed remarkable ability, not only as a manufacturer but also in the business management, and in course of time he became the manager of the establishment. Elihu White was succeeded by Charles T. White & Co., and this firm was followed in 1857 by Farmer, Little & Co., of which house Aaron D. Farmer was at the head. In 1892 two of the partners, Andrew Little and John Bentley, were retired, and Aaron D. Farmer and his son, William W. Farmer, re-organized the house as a private corporation, under the style of A. D. Farmer & Son Type Founding Company. During all these years the products of the house have held first position in the trade, and have been well-known in printing-houses throughout the country. The company manufactures all classes of plain and ornamental type, borders, ornaments, rules and dashes, and, in fact, every article which is required in fitting out a complete composing-room. It builds its own casting-machines, steel-

A. D. FARMER & SON TYPE FOUNDING CO., BEEKMAN AND GOLD STREETS.

punches, matrices, and other apparatus. Its designs for ornamental type are made in its own establishment. It also deals in printing-presses and other machinery required in large printing establishments. It has its own line of patented devices for the making of type; and it owns or controls various patented specialties that are especially valuable in printing establishments. The factory and office-building is a large brick structure, and has a frontage of 65 feet on Beekman Street, and 85 feet on Gold Street, and for the most part is six stories in height. As an evidence of the favor in which the Farmer type is held, it may be stated that many of the great New-York daily newspapers, and also great papers of other cities, are printed with equipments furnished by the predecessors or the present house of A. D. Farmer & Son Type Founding Company.

It is safe to say that every important printing-office — newspaper, periodical, book or job — has the whole or part of its outfit from this establishment. The company has an extensive branch-house at 109 Quincy Street, Chicago, where is kept a full supply of the productions of the New-York house.

F. A. Ringler Company, at 21 and 23 Barclay Street and 26 and 28 Park Place, is called the largest printing-plate establishment in the world. Its president and founder, F. A. Ringler, born at Friedwald, Hesse Cassel, in 1852, came to America in 1866, and learned the electrotyping business at Chicago. He moved to New York in 1871, and bought an interest in Hurst & Crum, which became Crum & Ringler, and in 1880 F. A. Ringler & Co. In 1891 the business was incorporated as F. A. Ringler Co., with F. A. Ringler as President; Max R. Brinkman, Vice-President and Treasurer; George J. Kraemer, Secretary; and Justin Ringler, Manager. The company's building has over 25,000 square feet of floor space, where 175 skilled employees are engaged. Adjoining the office is the art department, where designs for all kinds of illustrations are made. Above is the electrotyping foundry, for which a whole floor, 50 x 175 feet, is used, and every conceivable invention for the perfect production of duplicate plates. The eye takes in the twelve large batteries, four dynamos, six moulding presses, black-leading machines, melting furnaces, and other appliances. On the floor above are the finishing departments for electrotypes, stereotypes and photo-engraved plates. Here are six of the latest and most improved routing machines, circular jig saws, wood and metal planers, trimmers and other kinds of machinery. Above is the photo-engraving department, in which the half-tone, zinc and copper etchings, and the general processes of engraving are conducted. Eight of the largest cameras, each operated by a separate artist, are required to keep up with the orders.

Mr. Ringler has a vivid inventive talent, and he introduced the galvano-plastic process, for various methods of decorating; perfected the process of zinc etching, by which the daily newspapers are now illustrated; and has the only plant where copper and steel engravings are reproduced and steel-faced. He has made the electrotype plates for myriads of books, including many splendid illustrated volumes; and for his excellent work has won over a dozen medals. The F. A. Ringler Co. are the only electrotypers of this country who have an exhibit at the Chicago World's Fair.

F. A. RINGLER CO., CHURCH STREET, FROM BARCLAY STREET TO PARK PLACE.

Baker, Smith & Co. is the most widely known house in the business of warming and ventilating buildings. Before 1854 but little had been done to heat buildings excepting by means of stoves and hot-air furnaces. A few appara- tuses using hot water under a very high pressure had been introduced in England, and a very limited number of open circulation hot-water and high-pressure steam apparatuses in the United States. In 1854, Stephen J. Gold, of New Haven, invented the first low-pressure steam apparatus. It simply warmed the air by direct radiation, without giving any ventilation. William C. Baker was interested in the introduction of Mr. Gold's invention, until 1859, when he entered into a

business partner- ship with John Jewell Smith, of New York, form- ing the firm of Baker & Smith, to engage in the manufacture and erection of an "Improved Low- Pressure Self- regulating Steam Warming and Ven- tilating Appa- ratus." That was the origin of the present firm of Baker, Smith & Co. James L. Wise was admitted to part- nership in 1866; Charles H. Smith, in 1881; and Elias D. Smith in 1888. Mr. Baker retired in 1876 and Mr. Wise in 1887. The firm had a branch

BAKER, SMITH & CO., SOUTH FIFTH AVENUE AND HOUSTON STREET.

house in Chicago until 1886, when, in order to better accommodate the growing demands of that location, the "Baker & Smith Company of Chicago," was incorpor- ated, with John Jewell Smith as President and P. S. Hudson as Vice-President and General Manager. The firm of Baker, Smith & Co. is now composed of John Jewell Smith, Charles H. Smith and Elias D. Smith. They occupy the large building on the corner of South Fifth Avenue and Houston Street, New York, with a branch estab- lishment at 1015 Arch Street, Philadelphia. Very many of the improvements in heating-apparatus now in general use had their origin in the works of Baker, Smith & Co., notable among them being the system of warming railroad cars by heated pipes under the seats, known as the "Baker Heater." Thousands of buildings are fitted with Baker, Smith & Co.'s appliances, which are always of first-class workman- ship, since the financial standing of the firm gives it a choice of the best facilities and skill. Their work may be found in all the large cities of the United States.

The Bradley & Currier Company, Limited, at the corner of Hudson and Spring Streets, is the leading house in their line of business of the country. The business was established in 1867 by Edwin A. Bradley and George C. Currier, under the firm-name of Bradley & Currier, at 44 Dey Street. Very shortly, however, they were obliged to annex the four adjoining stores, which they continued to occupy until 1872, when they were again compelled to seek more room, and took the building at 54 and 56 Dey Street, which they occupied until 1886, when they removed to the large building now occupied by them. It is 75 by 175 feet, eight stories high, and is occupied entirely for ware-rooms, salesrooms and offices, being completely furnished in every respect with all the latest appliances, such as steam elevators, electric lights, etc., to enable them to handle and display their goods to advantage, and to conveniently transact the large volume of business which they control.

In 1885 the present company was organized, with Edwin A. Bradley as President; George C. Currier, Vice-President; and John J. Hughes, Secretary and Treasurer.

The business has largely increased, and requires a force of from forty to fifty salesmen and clerks. In addition to the ware-rooms and the extensive factory, for the manufacture of fine cabinet work, wood mantels, etc., which is a specialty, they have controlling interests in other large factories in various parts of the country, giving steady employment

THE BRADLEY & CURRIER COMPANY, HUDSON AND SPRING STREETS.

to nearly 500 men. Their ware-rooms are the finest, no expense having been spared to render them attractive, and to display the various goods which they manufacture, consisting of the latest designs of mantels, in wood and slate, with their fixtures, tiles, grates, brass and iron fenders, andirons, etc., etc., cabinet trim, screens, doors, windows, blinds, of every grade and style, art glass in great variety,—in fact, all that it is necessary to use in the completion of houses of high or low cost, except the rough lumber, masons' materials and hardware, and it is an important place for people to visit who contemplate using any such goods.

Joseph Loth & Co., manufacturers of "Fair and Square" ribbons, whose store is at 65 Greene Street, were the first business men to invade the historic locality at the northern end of Manhattan Island, known as Washington Heights; a locality that was the site of fortifications and military camps during the War of the Revolu. tion, and which has been a residence section of the city for many years.   Messrs. Loth and Company's factory occupies the block on Amsterdam Avenue between 150th and

JOSEPH LOTH & CO., "FAIR AND SQUARE" RIBBON MANUFACTORY.

151st Streets.   It is a handsome structure of Philadelphia brick and granite, three stories in height, and is in appearance more like a public building than a factory. Good taste and a degree of public spirit were shown by the firm in so designing the outward aspect of their establishment as to avoid the prosiness of business and keep in harmony with the surroundings.   Messrs. Loth & Co. have been engaged in manu- facturing "Fair and Square" ribbons since 1875.   Their present factory was erected in 1886, and they now employ some 600 operatives.   They make fine goods only. They have never put any cheap grades upon the market, but such is the range and scope of their enterprise that the product of their establishment is of 15 different widths, 200 shades of color and from 80 to 90 styles.   The trade-mark, "Fair and Square," is known in every corner of the United States.   The uniform excellence of the goods has spread its fame far and wide, and this has been effectively supple- mented by a free and liberal use of printer's ink.   This firm is the only manufac- turer of ribbons which advertises extensively, and their announcements are striking and effective, as well as dignified, as every one whose range of reading is wide already knows.   It is by means of its unique and liberal advertising that the firm keeps in touch with the public.   It does not sell to the consumer.   It comes in direct con- tact only with the trade, through the efforts of numerous salesmen, but such is the reputation of Joseph Loth & Co. and their "Fair and Square" ribbons that the business has shown a steady and substantial growth from the beginning.

Amasa Lyon & Company of New York may not be the largest or oldest manufacturers of umbrellas, parasols and walking sticks in this country, but there is no house in this industry that stands so prominent for the general high grade of its productions. A "Lyon" umbrella is indicative of taste, durability and reliability as to shape and color. The familiar trade-mark of the upright majestic lion's head, with the assuring legend of "Sans Varier," and the bold autograph of Amasa Lyon, has become known everywhere. No trademark in its line is regarded as so valuable in this trade, and no lines of umbrellas and parasols are so widely known as those of Amasa Lyon & Co. The best evidence of

AMASA LYON & COMPANY, 684 BROADWAY, CORNER OF GREAT JONES STREET.

their acknowledged supremacy is the fact that they are the specially favored wares of the leading establishments throughout the Union wherever fine goods of this character are sold. The business was established in 1877 by Amasa Lyon, who still remains at the head of the establishment, being the president of the corporation known as Amasa Lyon & Co., which was organized in 1889. The main sales-rooms, exhibition rooms and finishing shops are in New York, at the conspicuous corner of Broadway and Great Jones Street, where they have been for about twelve years. The stick factory is at the corner of Hudson and 13th Streets, and here are made all the sticks used by this concern; the woods being imported from all quarters of the globe. The silver and gold shops are in the Broadway building, and here are made all the handles and ornaments, for the style and finish of which the Lyon goods are famous. Any one who has the opportunity of going through these factories becomes amazed at the infinite variety of articles used in the making and ornamenting of umbrellas, parasols and canes: woods, metals, precious stones, ivories, horns, etc., and silks, laces and various fabrics, requiring for their proper use exquisite taste and great skill. These are the only manufacturers who, in their own shops, produce every part of the umbrella, excepting the fabrics and frames, and even these are made on special orders, with furnished designs and under exclusive arrangements. One of the names always seen in first-class establishments is Amasa Lyon. The Amasa Lyon productions rank equal to the highest grades of those made in foreign countries. On account of their high standing and reputation the Lyon umbrellas, parasols and canes were the only make sold on the grounds of the Columbian Exposition.

John Anderson & Company, at 114 Liberty Street, is one of the oldest firms now in business in New York, having been founded very early in the present century. It is also one of the most widely known, and its famous brand of "Solace" tobacco is celebrated all over the world.   John Anderson was the first manufacturer to introduce the idea of wrapping fine-cut tobacco in tin foil, and the result was so

successful, in respect to convenience and cleanliness and the preservation of the tobacco that nothing has yet been found to equal it. "Solace" always has been and is to-day the most widely distributed and best-known brand of tobacco of the fine-cut kind.   Among other largely used articles made here are John Anderson & Co.'s Long-Cut Smoking and Shorts, "Extra," "Honey Dew," and other popular tobaccos, known in all the corner groceries and country stores between the Bay of Fundy and the Gulf of California.   The business is still practically in the hands of the Anderson family and their relatives.   In 1890 the company was incorporated. The President is William H. Catlin, a resident of Rye.   The Secretary

JOHN ANDERSON & COMPANY, 114 AND 116 LIBERTY STREET.

and Treasurer is Alfred Wagstaff, formerly President of the Brooklyn Bridge, and director and trustee in various institutions.   John C. Anderson, son of the original founder of the business, is interested in the company.   The business has made great advances of late years, and especially since the civil war, and is one of the most solid and permanent in the city.   Its office and factory buildings on Liberty Street have long been a familiar down-town landmark.   The statue over the entrance has attracted thousands of people going to and from the ferries.   The company furnishes first-class articles for the use and comfort of a large number of men, and its good reputation of nearly a century is of inestimable value as a trade-mark.   The digger in the ditches, the millionaire half buried in gold-coupons, the sailor on the swinging royal-yard, the lawyer entrancing a jury, the soldier on sentry, the farmer plodding down his brown furrow, the senator discussing the annexation of the world, all stay and inspire themselves with John Anderson & Co.'s tobaccos.

E. R. Durkee & Co., Manufacturers of Spices, Extracts, Sauces, Condiments and Food-Preparations, are more universally known throughout the United States

than any other house in their line. Their goods are the acknowledged standards of excellence, and their trade-mark of the "Gauntlet," coupled with the signature of the firm, always constitute a guarantee of purity. The business was founded in 1850, by E. R. Durkee, and the industry (which is a unique one) has gone on increasing year after year, until now it is one of the most important, in its bearing on the daily life of the people in all parts of the country.

The firm's office and salesrooms are at 135, 137 and 139 Water Street ; and their laboratory, factories and warehouses occupy several large buildings on Water, Pine and Depeyster Streets. Their mills in Brooklyn are very extensive, and well

· E. R. DURKEE & CO., 135 WATER STREET, CORNER OF PINE.

equipped with the newest and most approved machinery. Several hundred trained hands find employment in them, and the whole business is carried on under the personal supervision of the members of the firm. Many of the processes of preparation are their own inventions, and wholly controlled by the firm. Their success is due to the superior excellence, uniformity, and reliability of the various articles put up under their name, and their products are shipped to every quarter of the globe.

The members of the firm are Eugene W. Durkee and David M. Moore, who, with large experience, ample resources, and superior facilities, aim to put up the finest articles in their line that can possibly be produced, and thereby maintain the high

reputation their products have enjoyed for over forty years. In every nook or corner of this whole country one is sure to meet, on the tables of the hotels and restaurants, and also in the private homes, some of the products of the house of E. R. Durkee & Co. And the expressions of approval and commendation at all Food Exhibitions indicate that their goods are not only widely known but are highly appreciated by all who enjoy good living and study domestic comfort.

E. R. DURKEE & CO., BROOKLYN MILLS.

62

Fleischmann & Co., the manufacturers of the celebrated Compressed Yeast, occupy their own offices and headquarters at the corner of Perry and Washington Streets. The introduction of this article into the United States dates back to about 25 years ago, at which time the brothers, Charles and Maximilian Fleischmann, under the firm-name of Fleischmann & Co., started at Cincinnati, Ohio, the first establishment in this country for its production. Since the death, in 1890, of Maximilian Fleischmann, the business has been carried on by the surviving partner, under the same firm-name. Compressed yeast had not, prior to the time of its introduction by Fleischmann & Co., been known on this side of the Atlantic, and its merits had therefore to be demonstrated to the American people. Progress in that direction was necessarily slow, and sales were consequently comparatively small at first, and confined within a limited area. From this small beginning the business of Fleischmann & Co. has steadily grown and spread, until now their compressed yeast is to be found in every city, town and village, while to many a far-away hamlet the dainty little tin-foiled, yellow-labelled packages of this yeast find their way. The consumption of this commodity — which long since attained the dignity of a staple article —is now simply enormous. Nor is it at all surprising that such should be the fact when it is remembered that it is to the use of Fleischmann & Co.'s Compressed Yeast that the marked superiority of the bread found upon our tables and in the bakers' shops to-day, as compared with that made with old-fashioned leavens, is due. Bread made with Fleischmann & Co.'s Compressed Yeast is not only whiter, sweeter

FLEISCHMANN & CO., PERRY AND WASHINGTON STREETS.

and more palatable than that made with other leavening agents, but it is easier of digestion and consequently more healthful ; while for making French and Vienna rolls, buckwheat and other cakes, it is incomparably superior. The practical recognition of this fact by the American public is proved by the wide-spread use to-day of Fleischmann & Co.'s Compressed Yeast. In millions of families and in all of the largest bakeries, hotels and institutions the Fleischmann yeast is used to the exclusion of all others. The manufactories at Cincinnati cover more than 25 acres : the plant in Brooklyn is about as large. More than 6,000 people and over 1,000 horses and wagons are employed.

NEWSPAPER ROW.   ST. PAUL'S CHURCH.   POST OFFICE.

PARK ROW, LOOKING SOUTH FROM MAIL STREET.

UNION SQUARE.   WASHINGTON MONUMENT.

FOURTH AVENUE, LOOKING NORTH FROM UNION SQUARE.

A. R. Whitney & Co., iron and steel merchants, have an enviable record of thirty years' standing. As well as merchants, the firm are manufacturers of and contractors for all kinds of iron and steel work. The construction work erected by them includes the iron and steel work of the Grand Central Depot — one of the greatest railroad stations in the world; the Third-Avenue Elevated Railroad, between 9th and 67th Streets, and also between 98th and 129th Streets; the Second-Avenue Elevated Railroad, between Chatham Square and 67th Street, and including the stations; the Ninth-Avenue Elevated Railroad, including the stations, between 12th and 59th Streets; the great roofs of the armories of the Seventh and Twelfth Regiments; and the structural work of the palatial Hotel Savoy. The firm are the owners of the Portage Iron Company's rolling-mills at Duncansville, Pennsylvania; and also of the Brooklyn Wire Nail Company's plant in Brooklyn.

THIRD-AVENUE ELEVATED RAILROAD, LOOKING NORTH FROM 9TH-STREET STATION,
BUILT BY A. R. WHITNEY & CO.

The latter company is one of the pioneers in the wire nail industry, and the third oldest wire nail factory in this country; and has secured through the quality of its product a large export trade in the West Indies, and South and Central America, in competition with the French and German manufacturers. In addition to the manufacture of wire nails, they also have executed orders for their machines, for use in England and Belgium. This company is also the owner of patents for valuable wire nail machinery, the royalties on which are of considerable magnitude. They are also the exclusive agents for the Carnegie Steel Company's structural material for the district of New York, Brooklyn and Jersey City, and are thus abundantly well qualified to furnish every conceivable variety of structural iron and steel work. The offices occupy the main front of the second floor of the Columbia Building, at 29 Broadway. Besides A. R. Whitney, the members of the firm are J. P. Meday and D. A. Nesbitt. The vast amount of work already executed by this firm in the past three decades thoroughly indicates that A. R. Whitney & Co. are competent to execute any specifications in iron and steel work.

CONEY ISLAND, NEW YORK'S HOLIDAY RESORT.

The J. M. Horton Ice Cream Co. is a name familiar to all New-Yorkers, Brooklynites and neighboring residents; for its delicious creams have been enjoyed by all.   To the epicureans of the table they are indispensable.   Their cool and soft flavors lie upon the palate with a delicacy that only experience can appreciate. Upon transatlantic liners; upon the luxurious dining-cars that speed from city to city ; at balls, at parties, at festivals, at all private or public gatherings in or about our great metropolis, where delicacies vie with one another, Horton's cream is welcomed as an old friend.   Always at its best it stands without an equal.   And Mr.

Horton's name has been so closely associated with the purest i c e cream for many years that the two have become synony- mous.   Indeed, a little girl on being asked how to spell ice cream, said "H-o-r-t-o-n." It was 22 years ago, in 1870, that James M. Horton began the manufacture of ice cream in New York City.   I t took the fastidious public but a short time to realize that there w a s being placed before them creams of the purest quality.   In 1873

J. M. HORTON ICE CREAM CO., PARK ROW BRANCH.

the present company was formed, with James M. Horton, President ; Joseph Cozzino, Secretary ; John J. Frech, Treasurer; and Hugh Stewart and Chauncey E. Horton, Directors.

Of ice creams, the company manufactures both French and American ; the former, made of milk and cream with eggs added, being more expensive and somewhat smoother to the taste than the latter, which is made without eggs.   Besides ice creams, its water-ices, charlotte russe and jellies are well known.   Nearly every steamer that leaves New York carries from 100 to 400 bricks, each brick weighing about 1¾ pounds.   For the Cleveland and Harrison Inaugural balls at Washington there was furnished one-half carload of these creams, a portion of which was made up into appropriate figures, such as Liberty, Washington and Columbia.   At the New-York *World's* festival 15,000 children were fed with 3,000 pounds of Horton's ice cream.   A large share of the public institutions of the city are daily supplied with it.   Indeed, this company furnishes three fifths of all the ice cream used in the city.   The main offices, Fourth Avenue and 23d Street, are in the building owned by The J. M. Horton Co.   There are numerous branch depots scattered throughout New York and Brooklyn.

INDEX.

☞ *Black-faced or heavy-faced figures indicate the pages of illustrations.*

Abbey, H. E., 588, 603, **582, 593**.
Abbey's Theatre, **601**, 594.
Abbott, Austin, 276.
Abbott Collection, 66, 320, 330.
Abbott, Frank, 279.
Aberdeen, Hotel, 148.
Academies, 299.
Academy of Design, **309**, 308, 314, 66, 67.
Academy of Fine Arts, 34.
Academy of Medicine, **490**, 278, 322, 333.
Academy of Music, 603, 68, 583, 587, 633.
Academy of Sciences, 321, 332.
Accounts, Auditors of, 248.
Accounts, Com. of, 257.
Accumulation Policy, 668.
Achelis, Thomas. 879.
Acton, Thomas C., 698, 743.
Actors' Amateur Athletic Association, 565.
Actors' Fund, 446, 592.
Actors' Fund Fair, 44, 586.
Adams, Dr. Wm., 368.
Adams Mem. Church, **369**, 368.
Adee, David, 652.
Adelaide, 75.
Adirondacks, 130.
Adler, Felix, 290, 287, 402.
Advertiser, **623**, 626, 609.
African Methodists, 59.
Africans, 24, 50, 396.
Aged and Infirm Hebrews, **453**, 451.
Aged Couples' Home, 443.
Aged Women's Homes, **441, 442, 445**, 443.
Aguilar Aid Soc., 452.
Aguilar Free Library, 334, 418, 63.
Ahavath Chesed Synagogue, **403, 404**.
Air Line, 120, 132.
Alarm-boxes, 530.
Albany, 7, 34, 103.
Albemarle Hotel, **857**, 148, 228, 230.
Alcazar, 598.
Alcoholic Pavilion, 460.
Alden, H. M., 636.
Aldermen, Board of, 246, 245, 50.
Aldine Club. **554**, 68, 333, 146.
Aldrich Court, **826**, 143.
Alexander, James W., 549.
All Angels' Church, **364**, 361.
Allan-State Line, 83.
Alleghany Mts., 113.
Allen, Timothy F., 279.

All Souls' Church, **385, 359**, 358.
Almshouse, **497**, 256, 459, 496, 500.
Almshouse Chapel, **497**.
Almshouse Hospital, B.I., **499**.
Alpha Delta Phi, 555.
Alvord, A. A., 780.
Amawalk Reservoir, 199.
Amazon River, 102.
Amberg's Theatre, 68, 602.
Ambrosian Ritual, 330.
Ambulance Service, 459, 460, 464.
America, Bank of, **711, 692, 705**, 708, 710.
America Cup, 567.
Americana, 327, 334.
Am. Acad. Dramatic Arts, 299, 606.
Am. Actors' Amateur Athletic Assoc., 565.
American Artists' Soc., 309.
Am. Art School, 288.
Am. Art Union, 320.
Am. Bankers' Assoc., 703.
Am. Bank Note Co., **915**, 914.
Am. Bible Soc., **411, 632**, 409, 410, 412, 59.
American Bishops, 341.
A. B. C. Foreign Missions, 410.
Am. Book Co., 146.
Am. Casualty Insurance & Guarantee Co., **684**, 745.
Am. Chemical Soc., 324.
Am. District Telephone Co., 210.
Am. Experience, 666.
Am. Fine-Arts Soc., **310**.
Am. Fire-Ins. Co., **653**, 652.
Am. Geographical Soc., **321**.
Am. Home Missionary Soc., 412.
Am. Institute, **320**, 321.
Am. Institute Library, 63, 333.
Am. Inst. of Phrenology, **324**.
Am. Jockey Club, 68.
Am. Kennel Club, 68.
American Line Steamships, **77, 79**, 71, 76, 79.
Am. Missionary Assoc., 410.
American Museum of Natural History, **307**, 306, 321, 302, 322.
Am. News Co., 579, 721.
Am. Press Assoc., 314.
Am. Shipmasters' Assoc., 799.
Am. Society of Civil Engineers, 321, 333.

Am. Sugar-Refining Co., **919**, 918, 696.
Am. Sunday-School Union, 409.
Am. Surety Co., 683.
Am. Telephone & Tel. Co., 214.
Am. Theatre, **595**, 594, 579, 583.
Am. Tract Society, 412.
Am. Veterinary College, 281.
Am. Veterinary Hospital, 492.
Am. Water-Color Soc., 309, 67.
Am. Yacht Club, 567.
Amsterdam, 90.
Amsterdam Merchants, 8.
Amusement Hall, B. I., **497**.
AMUSEMENT PLACES.—Play-Houses, Opera-Houses. Theatres, Public Halls, Museums, Outdoor Sports, etc., 575-608.
Amusements, 67, 575.
Anarchists, 42.
Anchorages, 190.
Anchor Line, 82, 91.
Anderson (John) & Co., **976**, 721.
Andrews, Loring, 728.
Andros, Sir Edmund, 23, 24.
Anglo-American Cables, 206, 210.
Animal Industry, 266.
Annexed District, 47, 192.
Ann Street, 23.
Ansonia Brass & Copper Co., **937**.
Ansonia Clock Co., **921**, 920.
Anthropology, Acad. of, 323.
Anti-Abolition Riots, 39.
Antiquities, 304, 330.
Apartment-Houses, 242, 148.
Apgar, A. S., 685, 715, 522, 644.
Apollo Hall, 596.
Appeals, Court of, 260, 261.
Appleton, W. H., 548.
Appraisers' Department, 786, 787.
Apprentices' Library, **330, 417**, 329, 63.
Appropriations, 51, 249.
Aquarium, 141, 578.
Aqueduct, **198**, 54, 197.
Aqueduct Avenue, **189**.
Aqueduct Commissioners, 257.
Arabs, 50.
Arbitration, Court of, 262, 796.
Arcadian Club, 543.
Archæological Institute, 323.
Archbishop's Residence, **392, 394**.
Arch, Central Park, **165**.

Architects, 819.
Architects, Am. Inst. of, 834.
ARCHITECTURAL FEATURES. — Development in Architecture — Notable Office-Buildings and Business Blocks, 817–842.
Architectural League, 310.
Architecture, 66, 273.
Arch, Washington, **173, 966,** 172, 167, 505.
Arc Lamps, 926, 202.
Area, 47.
Arion Society, **319,** 574, 68.
Arizona, 82.
Arkell, W. J., 914, 749.
Arks, 109.
Arlington Hall, **832,** 608.
Armitage, Thomas, 382.
Armories, 531.
Armory Commission, 257, 631.
Army Building, **541, 142, 718, 867.**
Arnold, Aaron, 844.
Arnold, Constable & Co., **845,** 843, 740, 838, 844, 890, 966.
Arnold, Hicks, 844, 740.
Arrests, 51, 526.
Arsenal Building, 528.
Art Amateur, 636.
Art and Architecture, 63.
Art-Collections, Private, 312.
Art Education, 287.
Art-Galleries, **314,** 303, 330, 152.
Art Guild, 311.
Arthur-Kill Bridge, 128, 135.
Arthur, President, 188.
Artillery, 531.
Art-Interchange, 636.
Artist-Artisans, 311, 288.
Artist Materials, 949.
Artists, 314.
Artists' Fund Soc., 311.
Artists' Society, 309.
Art Museum, **304, 305,** 303, 302, 312, 63, 66, 136, 67, 44, 161, 273.
Art Organizations, 311.
Art-Printing, 4.
Art Schools, 288, 289, 309, 310, 311, 306.
Art-Stores, 67, 312.
Art-Students' League, 310, 288.
Art Taste, 66.
Asbury M. E. Church, **374,** 375, 340, 167.
Ascension Church, 356, 152.
Aschenbroedel Verein, **573,** 572.
Asia, 29.
Assay Office, **700,** 699, 55, 155, 698, 721.
Assembly Districts, 44, 51.
Assessed Valuations, 256, 249.
Assessment Value, 51, 256, 249.
Assessors, 216.
Assistant Treasurer, 698, 700, 749, 765.
Associated Artists, **311,** 310.
Associated Banks, 700, 695, 696, 703, 710, 758, 764.
Association Boat-House, 417.
Assoc. for Improving Condition of Poor, 420.

Association Hall, **412, 415.**
Assoc. of the Bar, **557,** 63.
Assyrian Sculptures, 330.
Astor Family, 63, 67, 514, 544.
Astor House, 233, 39, 66, 68, 137, 144, 928.
Astoria, 70.
Astoria Bridge, 195.
Astor, J. J., **441,** 326, 325, 332, 159, 692, 216, 588, 514, 716, 732, 748, 716.
Astor Library, **326,** 325, 63, 146, 159, 838.
Astor Place, **178,** 159, 137, 176, 236, 328.
Astor-Place Opera-House, 328, 579.
Astor-Place Riot, 40, 532.
Astor Vault, 514.
Astor, Wm., 966.
Astor, Wm. B., 325, 326, 342, 544, 875.
Astor, W. W., 218, 326, 606, 716, 756, 758, 771.
Asylums, 59, 62.
Asylums for Insane, **462, 463,** 497, 461.
Asylums for Lying-in, 437.
Atalanta Boat Club, 568.
Athletic Clubs, **564, 565,** 296, 298.
Atlantic Cable, **208,** 210, 258, 304, 820.
Atlantic Docks, 42.
Atlantic Gardens, 17, 215.
Atlantic Mutual Ins. Co., **707, 658, 645,** 758.
Atlantic Transport Line, 83.
Atlas Steamships, **100.**
Atwood, K. C., 685.
Auchmuty, Col. R. T., 291.
Auditors of Accounts, 248.
Audubon, 321, 372, 514.
Audubon Yacht Club, 568.
Aural Institute, 484.
Ausable Chasm, 130.
Austen, Edward, 684.
Australasian Line, **92, 93.**
Authors' Club, 547, 68.
Autographs, 327.
Automatic Fire-Alarm & Extinguisher Co., **966,** 965.
Avery Architectural Library, 332, 834.
Avery, H. O., 314.
Avery, Samuel P., 304, 312, 334.
Avery, S. P., Jr., 314, 315.
Azore Islands, 89.

Babb, Geo. W., Jr., 660.
Babcock, S. D., 558, 743, 764, 769.
Babies' Hospital, **483,** 482.
Babies' Shelter, 456.
Babylonian Cylinders, 304.
Bachelor Apartments, 242.
Baker, Geo. F., 703, 738, 645, 769.
Baker, Geo. H., 332.
Baker Heater, 972.
Baker, Smith & Co., **972.**
Baker, Wm. H., 206.
Baldwin, C. C., 742.
Baldwin, Cyrus W., 924.
Baldwin, Wm., 630.
Baldwin, Wm. D., 924.

Ball Ground, 160.
Ball, Thomas, 180.
Baltimore & Ohio, 126, 110, 135.
Bancroft, George, 321.
Bank Clearings, 700.
Bankers, 750.
Bankers' Safe-Deposit Co., 782.
Bank for Savings, **773,** 464, 715.
Banking Houses, 750.
Bank Note Co., Am., **915,** 914.
Bank of America, **711, 692, 705,** 708, 710, 644.
Bank of Commerce, Nat., **722, 721.**
Bank of New Amsterdam, **743,** 587, 698.
Bank of New York, **704, 25,** 703, 706, 758.
Bank of the Metropolis, **740.**
Bank of the United States, 691, 693, 699, 706, 708.
Banks, 700, 58.
Bank Statement, 703.
Bannard, Otto T., 770.
Banvard's Museum, 594.
Banta, C. V., 706.
Baptist Church, 17, 59, 378.
Baptist Church, First, **379,** 378.
Baptist Mission Soc., 409.
Baptist Home, 444.
Baptist Tabernacle, **331,** 381.
Bar Association, **557.**
Bar Association Library, 63.
Barbey, H. I., 716.
Barclay, Thos., 510.
Bard, Wm., 755.
Barge Office, **71, 719,** 141, 183, 787.
Baring, Magoun & Co., 752.
Barnard College, 273, 274, 63.
Barnard School, 301.
Barnard, F. A. P., 270.
Barnes, Catharine W. 818.
Barnes, H. W., 659.
Barnes, J. S., 743.
Barnes, R. S., 966.
Barney, C. T., 762.
Barnum, P. T., 578, 579, 580.
Barnum's Museum, 579, 583, 614.
Barrett House, 148.
Bartholdi Statue of Liberty, **177,** 174, 42, 66, 176.
Bartholdi Crèche, 426.
Base-Ball Club, 564.
Bastions, 18.
Batcheller, Geo. C., 891.
Bates, D. H., 967.
Bathing Places, 51.
Battalion of Engineers, 72.
Batteries, 531.
Battery, **153,** 10, 16, 24, 28, 29, 33, 54, 139, 140, 70, 71, 141, 135, 183, 539.
Battery Park, **183, 719, 577,** 141, 820.
Battery Place, **71, 141.**
Baumann, G., 226.
Baxter Street, **205,** 158, 422.
Bay and Harbor, **73.**
Bayles, Robert, 728.
Bayne, Samuel G., **818,** 742.
Bay Ridge, 135.
Bazaars, 240.

Beadleston, W. H., 762, 776.
Bears, 792.
Beaver-St. House, 238.
Beck (Fr.) & Co., **954.**
Bedloe's Island, **73, 177,** 72, 66, 174, 177, 541.
Beecher, Schenck & Co., 684.
Beekman, Jas. W., 553, 546.
Beekman Swamp, 19, 25.
Beemer, J. G., 690.
Beer-Gardens, 605.
Beethoven Maennerchor, **317.**
Beethoven Bust, **168,** 178.
Belding Bros. & Co., **894.**
Belgian Society, 448.
Bellevue Hospital, **458, 459,** 460, 455, 62, 63, 277, 489, 490, 498, 500, 501.
Bellevue-Hosp. Medical College, 460, 278.
Bell, Isaac, 771.
Bellomont, Earl of, 25, 328.
Bellows, H. W., 385.
Belmont, August, 312, 620, 732, 746, 752, 766.
Belting, 928, 940.
Belting & Packing Co. (N.Y.), **929,** 928, 930.
Belt Line Surface Roads, 135.
Belvidere, **169,** 161.
Benedict Chambers, 167.
Bennet, W. M., 710.
Bennett Building, **835,** 58.
Bennett, J. G., 208, 210, 519, 622, 614.
Berachah House, 284.
Berean Church, 379.
Beresford, Hotel, 236, 243.
Berg, Louis. 3.
Bergh, Henry, 502.
Berkeley, Hotel, 152.
Berkeley Ladies' Athletic Club, 296, 570.
Berkeley Lyceum, **606,** 68, 300, 323.
Berkeley Oval, 300.
Berkeley School, **300.**
Berlin & Jones Envelope Co., **952,** 714.
Berlin, H. C., 714, 952, 776.
Bermuda, 98.
Bernhardt, Sarah, 600, 582.
Berry, O. F., 714.
Berwind-White Coal Mining Co., **947,** 946.
Best & Co., **856.**
Beth-El, Temple, **402,** 403.
Bethesda Church, **389.**
Bethesda Fountain, **161,** 179.
Beth Israel Bikur Cholim, **405.**
Beth-Israel Hospital, 477.
Bethlehem, Pa., 122.
Bible and Fruit Mission, 453.
Bible House, **411, 632,** 412, 406, 409, 410, 454, 329.
Bibles, Rare, 330.
Bible Society, Am., **411, 632,** 410, 412, 59.
Bible Soc. Library, 63.
Bi-carbonate of Soda, 962.
Bickmore, A. S., 322.
Bicycle Clubs, 68.
Bicycles, 968.
Bijou Theatre, **148,** 598.

Biographical Society, 323, 333.
Births, 251.
Biscuit Co. (N.-Y.), **945,** 944.
Bishop, David Wolfe, 45.
Bissell, G. W., 183.
Bituminous Steam Coal, 946.
Bixby (S. M.) & Co., **980.**
Black-Ball Line, 38, 74.
Black Crook, 604.
Black Friday, 42, 696.
Black Star Ships, 74.
Blackwell, Dr. Emily, 501, 479, 279.
Blackwell Homestead, **497.**
Blackwell's Island, **496, 497, 498, 499,** 456, 14, 47, 62, 438, 455, 459, 460, 461, 261, 493.
Blackwell's - Island Asylum, **462,** 461.
Blackwell's-Island Bridge, 195.
Blagden, Sam. P., 659.
Blake Bros. & Co., 730.
Blanchard, Jas. A., 563.
Blauvelt, C. A., 642.
Bleecker - Street, 40, 439, 167, 236, 240.
Bleecker-Street Savings-Bank, **773.**
Blind, Destitute, **440.**
Blind Institution, **299,** 298.
Blind, Library for, 333.
Bliss, C. N., 764.
Bliss, Geo., 500, 775, 758.
Bliss, John C., 372.
Bliss, Wm. M., 736.
Blizzard of 1888, **41,** 44, 210.
Block, Adriaen, 7, 45.
Block Houses, 17, 162.
Block Statue, 8.
Bloomingdale, 47, 272.
Bloomingdale Asylum, **465,** 466, 463, 464.
Bloomingdale Heights, 166.
Bloomingdale Road, 30, 40, 136.
Bloomingdale Ref. Church, **341.**
B'Nai B'rith, 331.
B'Nai Jeshurun, 400.
Boarding-Houses, 243.
Board of Aldermen, 249, 246, 247.
Board of Brokers, 788.
Board of Education, 257, 269, 292, 51, 62.
Board of Electrical Control, 206.
Board of Estimate, 257, 245, 249.
Board of Excise, 253, 241.
Board of Underwriters, 265.
Board of Health, 457, 794, 251, 244.
Board of Police, 251.
Board of Taxes and Assessments, 256.
Board of Trade and Transportation, 802.
Boat-Houses, **169, 162.**
Boat Oar Co. (N.-Y.), **969.**
Bogardus, Dominie E., 14.
Bogardus Iron Fronts, 863.
Bogardus, Rev. E., 336.
Bogart, John, 321.
Bogue, M. D., 876.

Bohemians, 622, 543.
Boiler-Tubes, 933.
Boker (Herman) & Co., **902.**
Bolivar Statue, **164,** 179.
Bombardments, 29, 30.
Bonded Warehouses, 786, 814.
Bond List, 789.
Bonner, Robert, 626.
Bon Secours Sisters, **441,** 836.
Bookbinders' Materials, 901.
Book-keepers, 294.
Books, 58, 325.
Book-Stores, 152.
Booth, Edwin, 170, 510, 554, 235, 236, 580, 582.
Booth Line, 102.
Booth, R. R., 373.
Booth's Theatre, 600, 582.
Boots and Shoes, 903.
Bordeaux Line, 84.
Boreel Building, 45, 215, 651.
Borgfeldt (Geo.) & Co., **909,** 908.
Boston, 54, 74, 80, 93, 109, 133, 134, 140.
Boston, **99.**
Boston Road, 16, 262.
Botanical Garden, 171.
Boucicault, Dion, 600, 519, 581, 582.
Bouck, W. C., 697.
Bouguereau's Painting, 226.
Boulevard, 140, 148.
Boultan, Bliss & Dallett, 101.
Bouwerie, 351.
Bow Bridge, **167.**
Bowery, **841, 859,** 439, 16, 20, 158, 375, 377, 237, 604, 216.
Bowery Boys, 158.
Bowery Branch, 415.
Bowery Fire-Ins. Co., **642.**
Bowery Mission, 424.
Bowery Savings Bank, **776,** 762, 720.
Bowery Theatre, 216, 604, 578, 583.
Bowling Green, **795, 143, 676, 31,** 13, 17, 18, 28, 30, 32, 45, 67, 76, 79, 85, 86, 93, 142, 148, 167, 215, 382, 820.
Bowne, R., 677.
Box-drains, 204.
Boys' Clubs, 569.
Boys' Lodging-House, **428.**
Boys' Outfitting, 856.
Boys' Protectory, 435.
Brace, C. L., 429.
Bradford, Gov., 20.
Bradford, Wm., 27, 45, 508, 609.
Bradford's Map, **9.**
Bradley & Currier Co., **973.**
Bradley, E. A., 348.
Bradstreet Co., **816,** 814, 4, 767, 630.
Bradstreet's, 816, 630.
Branch Home, 436.
Branch Work-House, 500.
Brass, 937.
Brass and Iron Fittings, 930, 932.
Brazilian Ports, 102.
Bread and Cheese Club, 543.
Brearley School, **606,** 302.
Breese, Sydney, 508.

Breslin, J. H., 762.
Brevoort House, 230, 68, 152.
Brewer's Exchange, **798.**
Brewer, Wm. A., Jr., 677.
Brewster, W. C., 738, 748, 782.
Brice, Lloyd, 636.
Brick. Presb. Church, **366,** 152, 628.
Bridewell, 32, 500, 493.
Bridge of Sighs, 494.
Bridges, 185.
Bridges, Contemplated, 194.
Bridge Street, 17 19.
Brigade Headquarters, 537.
Briggs, C. A., 284.
Brighton-Beach R. R., 135.
Brinckerhoff, G. G., 720, 721, 642.
Bristol-City Line, 83.
Bristol, Hotel, 152, 226.
British Frigates, 30, 552.
British Occupation, 30, 216.
Broad Street, **154, 155,** 18, 23, 25, 26, 30, 33, 156, 822.
Broad-Street Canal, 23.
Broad Street in 1796, **24.**
Broadway, **28, 31, 33, 637,** 17, 18, 23, 30, 137, 914, 142, 236.
Broadway and Astor Place, **659.**
Broadway and Fifth Ave., **144.**
Broadway and 40th St., **595.**
Broadway and Seventh-Ave. R. R., 694.
Broadway and Sixth Ave., **144.**
Broadway and 39th St., 601.
Broadway and 28th St., **601.**
Broadway and 29th St., **869.**
Broadway at City-Hall Park, **145.**
Broadway Athenæum, 581.
Broadway at 32d Street, **863.**
Broadway Central Hotel, **235, 157,** 146, 216.
Broadway, from Bond Street, **157.**
Broadway, from Park Pl., **145.**
Broadway in 1828, **31.**
Broadway Line, 137.
Broadway's Beginning, **676.**
Broadway Surface R. R., 42.
Broadway Tabernacle, **385,** 384, 836, 873.
Broadway Theatre, 148, 598, 594, 582.
Brodhead, Jacob, 336, 340.
Brodie, Stephen, 190.
Brokers, 790.
Brokers' Language, 792.
Bronx Park, 67, 139, 171.
Bronx River, 199.
Bronzes, 920, 304, 846.
Brooklyn, 18, 54, 55, 70, 185, 190.
Brooklyn & Brighton - Beach R. R., 135.
Brooklyn, Bath & West-End R. R., 135.
Brooklyn Bridge, **910, 61, 186, 718, 187,** 107, 185, 93, 257.
Brooklyn Ferry, 17, 27.
Brooklyn Heights, **16,** 185.
Brooklyn Lines, 30.
Brooklyn Mills (E. R. Durkee & Co.), **977.**

Brooks, Arthur, 361.
Brooks, Erastus, 614.
Broome - Street Tabernacle, **389,** 387.
Brougham's Theatre, 597, 580.
Brouner, J. H., 381.
Brown Bros. & Co., 708, 752.
Browne, H. K., 66, 174, 176
Browne, Walter, 721.
Brown, J. Crosby, 758, 773.
Brown, J. T., 762.
Brown, J. W., 354.
Brown, M. B., 745.
Brown, P. A. H., 344.
Brown, T. McKee, 360.
Brown, Vernon H., 726, 774.
Brown, W. H., 729.
Bruce (George) Memorial Library, 332.
Bruce, Catherine Wolfe, 332.
Brunswick, Ga., 98.
Brunswick, Hotel, 230, 68, 152.
Bryan Gallery, 321.
Bryant, W. C., 170, 184, 386, 543, 548, 610.
Bryant Building, 802.
Bryant Park, **172,** 174, 176, 170, 153, 226, 580.
Bryant's Minstrels, 605.
Buccaneers, 25.
Buck, Dudley, 289.
Bucket-shops, 790.
Buckingham Hotel, 68, 152, 226.
Buckley, J. M., 630.
Buell, James, 703.
Buffalo, 110, 113, 114, 116, 125.
Builders' Hardware, 939.
Building Dep't, 257, 584, 818.
Building-Material Exchange, 804.
Buildings, Number of, 51.
Building Stones, 308.
Building-Trades' Club, 558, 836.
Bulkley, Dunton & Co., **900,** 899.
Bulkley, C. E., 749, 748.
Bulkley, Moses, 900.
Bullion, 699, 55.
Bulls, 792.
Bull's Head, 216, 720.
Bumstead, J. H., 875.
Bunner, H. C., 626.
Burbank, W. H., 3.
Bureau of Charities, 256.
Bureau of Combustibles, 530.
Bureau of Corrections, 256.
Bureau of Elections, 525
Bureau of Medical and Surgical Relief, 278.
Burford, Geo. H., 672.
Burn, Henry, 955.
Burgher Guard, 17, 531, 523.
Burgomasters, 523.
Burial Places. 505.
Burlingame. E. L., 636.
Burnet. Gov., 26, 27.
Burnett, G. H., 659.
Burnham, G. W., 179, 180, 230.
Burns's Coffee-House, 215.
Burns's Statue, **168,** 178.
Burr, Aaron, 34, 507, 531, 610, 704, 706.
Burrell, Dr. D. J., 338.
Burtnett, Daniel, 644.

Burton's New London Theatre, 235, 579.
Burton, W. E., 512.
Busby, L. J., 730.
Busk & Jevons, 102.
Bussing Homestead, **818.**
Butchers' & Drovers' Bank, Nat., **720.**
Butler, B. F., 276.
Butler, Charles, 275.
Butler, W. Allen, 557.
Butler, W. S., 329.
Butter and Cheese Exchange, 803.
Byrnes, Thomas, 526.
Byrns, John, 745.

Cabinet Work, 973.
Cable Cars, **139,** 54, 137, 139.
Cable Conduits, 214.
Cables, Submarine, 208.
Cafés, 237.
Café Savarin. 240.
Caissons, 188.
Caledonian Club, **559.**
Caledonian Fire-Ins. Co., 647.
Callisen's School, 301.
Calman, Emil, 658.
Calman, H. L., 868.
Calumet Club, **547,** 546, 153.
Calvary Baptist Church, **381.**
Calvary Cemetery, 522.
Calvary Church, **355,** 380.
Calvary Meth. Church, **376.**
Cambridge, Hotel, **228,** 152.
Camden & Amboy R. R., 118.
Cammack, A., 748.
Campanius, 5.
Campbell, E. T., 659.
Campbellites, 388.
Camp, W. A. 703.
Canadian Pacific Railway, 206.
Canal-boat Fleet, **107.**
Canal Boats, 38, 74, 155.
Canals, 110, 130.
Canal Street, **654, 156,** 10, 36, 38, 204, 344, 144, 809, 852.
Canarsie, 15.
Cancer Hospital, **485,** 155.
Canda, C. J., 698.
Canda & Kane, **906,** 745.
Candee, W. L., 931.
Cannon, H. W., 703.
Canvas Town, 31.
Capture of N. Y., 30.
Caracas, 101.
Carleton, Sir Guy, 31.
Carmansville, 47.
Carnegie, Andrew, 320, 332, 590.
Carnegie Laboratory, 279.
Carnegie Music Hall, **591,** 44, 66.
Carpets, 844, 851.
Carrère & Hastings, 616.
Carrigan, Andrew, 779.
Carrousel, 160.
Cartagena, 98.
Carter, James C., 564.
Carter, O. S., 724.
Cary, Wm. H., 728.
Case, J S., 738.
Casino, **601,** 66, 68, 148, 161, 591.
Casino, Central Park, **163.**

Castle Clinton, 577.
Castle Garden, **577, 539, 719,** 54, 55, 449, 141, 580, 820.
Castle Williams, **542,** 72, 540.
Casualty Ins. Co., **684.**
Caterson, Robert, 866, **518.**
Catharine Market, 808.
Cathedral of St. John the Divine, **363,** 362, 66, 46, 472, 430, 148, 272.
Cathedral of St. Patrick, **136.**
Cathedral Service, 342.
Catholic Apostolic Church, **390, 388.**
Catholic Church, 335.
Catholic Church, B. I., **499.**
Catholic Club, **574,** 556.
Catholic Colleges, 63.
Catholic Protectory, 434, 302.
Catholics, 335.
Catholic Schools, 286.
Catholic World, 636, 397.
Catlin, W. H., **976.**
Cattle, 18, 266.
Cavalry Troop, 538.
Cave, Central Park, **169.**
Cemeteries, 505.
Census, 47.
Central American Steamships, 101.
Central Bridge, 192.
Central Building, **124.**
Central Islip, 461.
Central Nat. Bank, **736.**
Central Park, **105, 160, 861,** 67, 66, 136, 137, 139, 200, 203, 206, 214, 180, 182, 218, 220, 222, 227, 531, 528.
Central-Park Apartments, 243, 950.
Central-Park Reservoir, 197, 198, 199.
Central-Park Sanitorium, 486.
Central Park West, 321, 155.
Central Presb. Church, **370,** 368.
Central R. R. of N. J., **124,** 128.
Central Stores, 814.
Central Trust Co., **763, 815,** 762, 682.
Central Turn Verein, **566.**
Centre Market, **809,** 834.
Centre Street, **56.**
Century Club, **548,** 69, 798.
Century Magazine, 636, 59, 159.
Chamberlain, 245, 248.
Chamberlain, D. H., 386.
Chamber of Commerce, 67, 803, 786, 787, 262, 264, 258, 697, 215, 708, 639.
Chambers Street, **30,** 196, 291.
Chambers, T. W., 337.
Champagne, 899.
Chandler, A. B., 206, 210.
Chandler, C. F., 273.
Channel, 69.
Chantry, 348.
Chapel, Bloomingdale, **465.**
Chapin, E. H., 386.
Chapin, G. S., 781.
Chapin Home, 445.
Chapin's (Dr.) School, 301.
Chapman, J. H., 646.
Chapman, W. R., 318.

Charitable Institutions, 51, 419.
Charitable Societies, 453.
Charities and Corrections, 51, 459, 461, 59, 62, 260, 500.
Charities Building, 950.
CHARITY AND BENEVOLENCE.— Institutions and Associations for the Poor and Unfortunate — Homes and Asylums, and Temporary Relief, 419-456.
Charity Hospital, B. I., **499,** 496, 62, 461.
Charity Organization Soc., 436, 454, 427.
Charleston, 93.
Charter of Liberties, 24.
Charters, 245.
Chase Nat. Bank, 703.
Chase, Wm. H., 720.
Chatham Square, 158, 712, 651.
Chatham-Street Theatre, 582.
Cheap Hotels, 237.
Cheap Restaurants, 241.
Cheap Transportation Assoc., 802.
Cheever, G. B., 371.
Cheever, H. D., 931.
Cheever, J. D., 928.
Cheever, J. H., 928.
Chelsea, 40, 47, 66, 242, 506.
Chelsea Square, 282.
Chemical Nat. Bank, **714,** 703, 746, 732, 778.
Chemical Soc., 323.
Chemistry School, 276.
Chemists, 322, 323.
Cheney Brothers, **886.**
Cherry Street, 19.
Chesapeake, 507.
Chesebrough Mfg. Co., **948.**
Chesebrough, R. A., 948, 794.
Chew, Beverly, 334, 553, 764.
Chiar, Arthur, 4.
Chicago, **99.**
Chickering Hall, 68, 287, 153, 608.
Chief of Fire Dept., 256.
Children Cruelty to, **425.**
Children Homeless, 425.
Children's Aid Soc., **427, 428, 429,** 302, 59, 419.
Children's Charitable Union, 434.
Children's Fold, 433.
Children's Hospital, **481,** 62.
Children's Library, 333.
China, 850, 858.
Chinatown, **158.**
Chinese, 50, 447, 449, 158, 474.
Chinese Bars, 241.
Chinese Guild, St. Bartholomew's, 449.
Chinese Restaurants, 240.
Chinese Rooms, 579.
Chinese Temple, **406.**
Chittenden, S. B., 186.
Choate, J. H., 557, 386, 545, 515.
Chocolate School, 302.
Cholera, 46.
Christ Church, 342, 350.
Christiaensen, 7.
Christian Advocate, **631,** 630.
Christian Aid to Employment Soc., 454.

Christian Brothers, 286.
Christian Commission, 42.
Christian Herald, **632.**
Christian Israelites, 59.
Christian League, 504.
Christian Observances, 14.
Christians, 388.
Christmas Letter Mission, 453.
Christopher Columbus Hospital, 477.
Christopher Street, **84.**
Christus Consolator, 352.
Christy's Minstrels, 579, 597.
Chronic Invalids, 452.
Chronicler, **5.**
Church Chorals, 318.
Church Club, 556.
Churches, 59, 335.
Church Extension Society, 408.
Church for Seamen, **389,** 407.
Church Hospital, 488.
Churchman, **627,** 159.
Church Missionary Society for Seamen, 407.
Church Missions House, **407,** 406, 356.
Church of Disciples, 388.
Church of England, 335, 341.
Church of Heavenly Rest, **351,** 352.
Church of New Jerusalem, 388.
Cienfuegos, 98.
Cilley, J. K., 738.
Cillis, Hubert, 674.
Cisco, J. J., 698.
Citizens' Bridges, 194.
Citizens' Ins. Co. **644.**
Citizens' Savings-Bank, 781.
City and County, 245.
City Bank, **25,** 756.
City Bank, Nat., **713,** 710.
City Cemetery, 461.
City Club, 564.
City Court, 261.
City Debt, 225, 51.
City Dispensary, 487.
City Farm, 461.
City Finances, 249.
City Hall, **5, 33, 52,** 28, **259,** 32, 37, 26, 63, 66, 67, 137, 208, 320, 329, 344, 54, 494, 260, 261, 262, 170, 257, 156, 365, 637.
City-Hall Branch Elevated R. R., **57.**
City-Hall Park, **145, 259, 263, 28, 33, 49, 53, 619, 621,** 54, 190, 18, 28, 32, 505, 493, 262, 144, 170, 257, 156, 265, 487, 500, 216, 237, 824, 830.
City-Hall Park in 1809, **28.**
City-Hall Place, **248.**
City Hotel, 216.
City Improvement Soc., 564.
City Judge, 261, 253.
City Legislature, 246.
City Library, 328.
City Mission and Tract Soc., 387, 412, 500.
City Missionary Soc., 407.
City of Rome, 82.
City Prison, 256.
City Record, 622, 245, 246, 248.
City Reform Club, 563.
City Regiment, 532.

City Revenue, 248.
Civic Pride, 323.
Civil Courts, 261.
Civil Engineering School, 276.
Civil Engineers, Soc. of, 321, 333.
Civil Service Board, 23, 257.
Civil War, 695, 704.
Claflin, John, 736.
Claremont, 47.
Claremont Park, 67, 172.
Clarendon Hall, 608.
Clarendon Hotel, 230.
Clark, Chas. F., 4, 151, 816, 766, 767.
Clark, Col. Emmons, 533, 532.
Clark, H. F., 519.
Clark, J. B., 758.
Clark (William) Co., 892, 767.
Clarke, G. C., 876.
Claussen, Henry, Jr., 798.
Clearing House, 701, 710, 729, 741, 58, 792.
Clearing-House Certificates, 702.
Clement, W. P., 742.
Clergy Club, 556.
Clerk of Arrears, 248.
Clermont, 34.
Cleveland, Grover, 188, 46.
Clews, Henry, 515, 866.
Climatic Cure Fund, 452.
Clinical Soc., 491.
Clinics, 279.
Clinton, Admiral, 26.
Clinton, DeWitt, 320, 270, 129, 258, 519, 773.
Clinton, Gen., 30, 31.
Clinton, Gov., 32, 38, 39, 540.
Clinton Hall, 328, 159, 579, 830, 778.
Clinton-Hall Assoc., 328.
Clinton Market, 808, 809.
Clipper, 626.
Clocks, 921, 920.
Clothing, 58, 889, 913.
Clover Pastures, 25.
Clubs, 68, 152, 543.
Clyde's Steamship Co., 94, 93.
Clyde, Thos., 94.
Clyde West-India and Central-American Line, 102.
Coaching Club, 572, 230.
Coal and Iron Exchange, 131, 130.
Coal Barges, 946.
Coal-Mines, 946.
Coastwise Traffic, 55.
Cobb, H. E., 339.
Cockerill, J. A., 610.
Cod-liver Oil, 828.
Coe, E. B., 338.
Coe, Geo. S., 206, 210.
Coenties Slip, 107, 153, 126, 128, 14, 18, 30, 46, 215.
Coffee, 898.
Coffee Exchange, 804.
Coffee-Houses, 216, 543, 639.
Coffin, C. A., 926.
Coggeshall, E. W., 686.
Cogswell, Dr. J. C., 325.
Cohen, Max, 331.
Coins, 322, 868.
Coke, 946.

Colden, Cadwallader, 28, 787.
Coleman House, 148.
Coles Collection, 304.
Collamore (Gilman) & Co., 850.
Collector of Assessments, 248.
Collector of the Port, 786.
Collect Pond, 36, 493.
Colleges, 269, 26, 62.
College of New York, 269, 268, 62, 290.
College of Physicians and Surgeons, 295, 487, 34.
College Place, 27, 270, 272.
College Settlement, 456, 421.
Collegiate Dutch Church, 336, 337, 338, 782.
Collegiate Church, 48th Street, 336, 338, 152.
Collegiate Church, 7th Street, 337.
Collegiate Church, 29th Street, 337, 782, 338, 152.
Collegiate Church, West-End Avenue, 338.
Collegiate School, 338, 301, 336.
Collingwood, Francis, 321.
Collin, Henry, 868.
Collins Line, 76.
Collis, C. P., 512.
Collyer, Robert, 386.
Colon, 101.
Colonial Club, 550, 549, 68.
Colonnade Row, 627, 628.
Colored Glass Windows, 316.
Colored Home, 450.
Colored Mission, 451.
Colored Orphan Asylum, 450, 42, 372.
Colored People, 24, 50, 396.
Columbia Bicycles, 968.
Columbia Building, 680, 677, 828, 58, 142.
Columbia College, 272, 273, 270, 34, 62, 63, 293, 321, 322, 323, 306, 508, 466, 148, 472, 834.
Columbia-College Law School, 273.
Columbia-College Library, 63, 332.
Columbia Garden, 604.
Columbia Grammar School, 291, 301.
Columbia Heights, 186.
Columbia Restaurant, 240.
Columbia Yacht Club, 567.
Columbus Hospital, 477.
Columbus-Pinzon Monument, 184.
Columbus Statue, 182, 808.
Columbus Theatre, 605.
Combustibles, 530.
Comedy Theatre, 600.
Commerce, 165, 58, 180.
Commerce, Nat. Bank of, 722, 721.
Commerce Statue, 165.
Commercial Advertiser, 609, 610.
Commercial Association, 794.
Commercial Bulletin, 612.
Commercial Cable, 206, 208, 210.
Commercial Preëminence, 783.
Commercial Colleges, 294.

Commissioner of Juries, 51.
Commissioners of Charities and Correction, 434, 459.
Commonalty, 245.
Common Council, 28, 459, 258.
Common Pleas Court, 51, 260, 261.
Commons, 28, 30, 32, 494, 160, 500.
Commonwealth Club, 563.
Communipaw, 123.
Compagnie Generale Transatlantique, 83.
Compañia Trasatlantica, 98.
Compressed Yeast, 978.
Comptroller, 50, 249, 246, 248.
Comstock, Anthony, 503.
Concert Saloons, 67.
Condiments, 977.
Coney Island, 983, 50, 135, 69.
Coney-Island Jockey Club, 68.
Cong'l Church Building Soc., 410.
Congregationalism, 59, 384.
Congregation Singing, 399.
Congressional Districts, 51.
Connecticut. 133.
Connecticut Militia, 29.
Connor, W. E., 152, 567, 515.
Conservatory of Music, 290.
Conservatory Water, 162.
Consistory, 336, 337.
Consistory Building, 339.
Consolers of the Sick, 14.
Consolidated Gas Co., 201.
Consolidated Stock and Petroleum Exchange, 793, 637, 792, 58, 143.
Consolidation Act, 245.
Constable, F. A., 844.
Constable, J. M., 704, 778, 838, 844, 890.
Constables, 524.
Consumptives, 477.
Contemplated Bridges, 194.
Contents, 2.
Continental Hotel, 148.
Continental Ins. Co., 648.
Continental Trust Co., 770.
Contractors, 950.
Convalescents' Homes, 440, 492, 481.
Convent, Sacred Heart, 286.
Converse, E. C., 914, 931, 688.
Converse, E. W., 931, 933.
Conveyances, 17.
Cooke, G. F., 344, 576, 510.
Cooking Schools, 302.
Cooper, Edw., 934, 260, 936, 588, 758.
Cooper, Hewitt & Co., 936.
Cooper Institute, 331, 236.
Cooper, J. F., 543.
Cooper, Myles, 270.
Cooper, Peter, 40, 291, 331, 936.
Cooper-Union, 291, 290, 63, 289, 311, 934, 273, 146.
Cooper-Union Art-School, 311.
Cooper-Union Night Schools, 311.
Cooper-Union Library, 331.
Cooper-Union Schools, 63, 311.
Cooper-Union Woman's Art School, 311.

Cop, 524.
Copper, 935.
Corbin, Austin, 515.
Corbin Bridge, 195.
Cornbury, Lord, 25, 365, 540.
Cornell, J. B., 377.
Corner-Stone, 756.
Corn - Exchange Bank, 731, 730, 794; 703, 729.
Corning, Erastus, 758.
Coroners, 264.
Corporation Attorney, 253.
Corporate Schools, 62, 267.
Corporation Borrowings, 754.
Corporation Counsel, 253, 246.
Corrections, 493.
Corsets, 891.
Cortlandt Street, 117, 129, 211.
Cortlandt-Street Ferry, 129, 119.
Cosmopolitan Growth, 16.
Cosmopolitan Hotel, 237.
Cosmopolitan Magazine, 636.
Cosmopolitan Theatre, 598.
Cosmos Club, 553.
Coster, C. H., 659.
Costumes, 849.
Cotton Exchange, 799, 800, 730, 45, 159, 703.
Cotton Exchange, Main Floor, 800.
Coudert. F. R., 557, 545, 677.
Couldock, C. W., 582.
County Clerk, 264.
County Court-House, 263, 53, 262, 261. 262, 54, 42.
County Medical Soc., 490.
County Officers, 264.
Courrier des Etats-Unis, 612.
Court-House, 53, 54. 42, 66.
Courtney & McCay, 662.
Court of Arbitration, 262.
Court of Chancery, 25
Court, Common Pleas, 49, 261.
Court, General Sessions, 53.
Courts, 260.
Covenant, Church, 369.
Cowles, Elijah S., 966.
Cowles Patents, 935.
Cox, S. S., 178, 176, 159.
Cozens-Smith, E., 662.
Crackers, 944.
Cradle of Methodism, 374.
Crane, J. M., 729.
Crania, 324.
Credit Guarantees, 688.
Credits, 816.
Cremation, 522.
Crematory, 522.
Cremorne Mission, 424.
Crime, Prevention of, 503.
Criminal Law Courts, 255.
Criminals, 494.
Crippled-Boys' School, 429.
Critic, 626.
Crocker, Chas., 587.
Croisic, Marquis de, 230.
Crolius, Wm. H., 652.
Cromwell, Frederic, 556, 769.
Cromwell Steamship Co., 96.
Crosby, Howard, 368, 275, 503, 518.
Cross-Town Lines, 137.
Crotona Park, 67, 171.

Croton Aqueduct, 191, 198, 192, 39.
Croton Dam, 198.
Croton Lake, 134, 197, 199, 200.
Croton Reservoir, 197, 199, 161.
Croton Water-Shed, 54, 197.
Croton Water-System, 512, 706.
Cruelty to Animals, 503, 502.
Cruelty to Children, 425.
Cruger, John, 787, 258.
Cruger, S. V. R., 326, 756.
Crystal Palace, 581, 39, 170, 580, 583.
Cuba Steamships, 98.
Cunard Line, 71, 75, 80.
Curaçoa, 101.
Curbstone Brokers, 792.
Curiosities of Printing, 327, 334.
Curtiss, F., 743.
Cushman, Charlotte, 578.
Custom House, 786, 694, 790, 785, 822, 55, 66, 155, 697, 699.
Cutler's School, 301.
Cutter, R. L., 880.
Cutting. R. F., 152.
Cylinder Press, 956.
Cypress Hill Cemetery, 522.
Cyprus Collection, 304.

Daboll, N. D., 749.
Daily Papers, 623, 625.
Dairy, 160.
Dairy Kitchen, 240.
Dakota Flats, 950, 243.
Dalhousie, The, 105.
Daly, Augustin, 554, 581, 594, 596, 597.
Daly, C. P., 775.
Daly's Theatre, 593, 68, 148.
Damrosch, Leopold, 318, 319, 518, 588.
Damrosch, Walter, 290, 318, 591.
Dana, C. A., 312, 612, 622.
Dancing Schools, 297.
Darling, A. B., 587, 599, 605, 738.
Dauntless Rowing Club, 568.
Dauvray, Helen, 596.
Davenport, E. L., 604.
Davenport, Fanny, 596.
David's Island, 541, 542.
Davis, Howland, 730.
Davis, Jefferson, 94.
Day-Book, 614.
Day, James B., 377.
Day Nursery, 348.
Dayton, C. W., 266.
Deaconess Home, 284.
Deaf and Dumb Inst., 298, 372, 272.
Deaf Mutes, 299, 298.
Death Rate, 457.
Deaths, 51, 251.
Debating Societies, 323.
Deborah Nursery, 452.
Debt, 225, 249, 51.
Debtors' Prison, 494.
Decker, M. S., 770.
Declaration of Independence, 30.
Decorations, 317.
Decorative Art Soc., 311, 288.
Dedication, 4.
Deems, C. F., 387.
Deen, W. M., 688.

DEFENSE AND PROTECTION.— The Police and Fire Departments; Detectives and Fire Patrol; The National Guard; U.-S. Army and Navy Stations and Forts, 523-542.
Defensive Wall, 17.
De Heere Straat, 17.
DeJonge (Louis) & Co., 901.
Delancey's House, 45.
Delaware & Hudson Canal Co., 131, 130, 715.
Delaware, Lackawanna & Western R. R., 125, 127, 126, 54, 740, 712, 752.
Delaware Valley, 129, 130.
Delmonico's, Fifth Ave., 238.
Delmonico's, Beaver Street, 239.
De Long's Grave, 517.
Delta Kappa Epsilon, 153, 555.
Delta Phi Club, 555.
Delta Upsilon, 555.
De Milt Bequest, 330.
De Milt Dispensary, 492, 488.
Democratic Club, 5 2.
Denny, T., 716, 743.
Dent, Dr. E. C., 462.
Dentistry, College of, 279.
Dep't of Arts, 250, 247.
Dep't of the East, 539.
Dep't of Public Parks, 249, 193.
Dep't of Public Works, 250, 193.
Departments and Officers, 243.
Depew, C. M., 545, 418, 152, 522.
De Peyster, 514.
Depot in Jersey City, 117.
Depuy, W. H., 630.
Dermatological Soc., 491.
Desbrosses-St. Ferry, 132.
Design, Academy of, 309, 308, 66, 67, 261. 314.
Destitute Blind, Home, 440.
Destitute Children, 433, 436, 435, 432.
Detective Bureau, 527.
Detectives, 528.
Deutsch-Amerikan. Schuetzen Gesellschaft, 569.
Deutscher Liederkranz, 319.
Deutscherverein, 551, 838.
De Veau. J. M., 742.
De Vinne Press, 159.
De Vlackte, 18, 32.
Devoe, F. W., 949.
Devoe (F. W.) & C. T. Raynolds, 949.
Diamond Cutters, 864.
Diana, 584, 64.
Di Cesnola Collection, 303, 66.
Dickel, C. W., 296.
Dickel's Riding Academy, 296, 297, 568.
Dickey, Chas. D., Jr., 708.
Diet-Kitchen Assoc., 482.
Dilks, G. W., 526, 528.
Dillon, Gregory, 779.
Dillon, Sidney, 515.
Dime-Museum, 68.
Dimock, H. F., 762.
Diocesan House, 408, 627, 407, 159.
Discharged Convicts' Refuge, 504.

Disciples' Church, 388.
Dispensaries, 488, 489, 62.
Dispensary for Women, **480.**
Distributive Trade, 784.
District Attorney, 51.
District Courts, 261.
Divine Paternity, Church, **387,** 386, 152.
Dixey, H. E., 598.
Dix, John A., 514.
Dix, Morgan, 45, 342, 561.
Dixon, Wm. P., 686.
Dock Dept., 250.
Docks, 71.
Dockstader's Minstrels, 600.
Dodge, C. H., 710.
Dodge Statue, **179,** 176.
Dodge, W. E., 518, 522, 176, 516, 756.
Dodsworth's, 295.
Dolge's (Alfred) Factories, **941.**
Dolgeville, 941.
Domestic and Foreign Missionary Soc., 410.
Domestic Architecture, 832.
Domestic Industry, 321.
Domestic Missions, Reformed Church, 409.
Dominican Convent, 434.
Dominican Church, **290.**
Dommerich, L. F., 878.
Donald, E. W., 356.
Donald, Jas. M., 728.
Dongan, Gov., 24, 391.
Doremus, Cornelius, 674.
Dorman, O. P., 893.
Downey, John, 776.
Down-Town Assoc., **558.**
Down-Town Relief Bureau, 422.
Dows, David, 729, 730, 659.
Doyers Street, 158.
Draft Riots, 42, 450, 526, 532.
Drama, 575.
Dramatic Arts Academy, 296.
Dramatic Mirror, 626.
Dramatic News, 626.
Draper, J. W., 275.
Drawbridges, 193.
Drawings, 306.
Drayton, Dr. H. S., 324.
Dreadnaught, 38, 75.
Dress Goods, 844, 849, 853, 893.
Drexel Building, **155.**
Drexel Collection, 304.
Drexel, Morgan & Co., 659, 750, 722, 822.
Drexel-Morgan Building, **155.**
Drexel Musical Library, 337.
Drinking Saloons, 241.
Drisler, Prof. H., 326.
Drugs and Chemicals, 949 862, 911.
Drummond, J. F., 949.
Drunkenness, 260.
Dry-Dock Company, 715.
Dry Docks, 55, 71.
Dry-Dock Savings Inst., **777.**
Dry Goods, 33, 844, 848, 852, 872, 873, 874, 875, 876, 878, 879, 880, 882, 883, 884, 890.
Dry-Goods District, 712.

Dry Goods Economist, **633.**
Dry-Goods Exchange, **633,** 806.
Dry-Goods Store Restaurants, 240.
Duane-Street Church, 367.
Du Bois, Henri Pene, 3.
Ducking-Stool, 26.
Duel, 467, 34.
Duelling Ground at Weehawken, 34.
Duer, John, 686.
Duffield, Howard, 365.
Dugro, Judge P. Henry, 220.
Duke of Veragua, 46, 854.
Duke of York. 8, 20, 23, 260.
Duke's Plan, The, 8.
Duncan, W. B., Jr., 826.
Dunham, Buckley & Co., **873.**
Dunton, W. C., 900.
Durbrow, J. W., 658.
Durkee, E. W., 977.
Durkee (E. R.) & Co., **977.**
Durland's, 297, 569.
Durr Collection, 66, 321.
Dutch Church, **336.**
Dutch Cottage, **7.**
Dutch East India Co., 7.
Dutch Greenland Co., 7.
Dutch Homes, 20.
Dutch Inns, 215.
Dutch Map, **6.**
Dutch Merchants, 7.
Dutch Reform Church, 25.
Dutch *Regime,* 22, 553.
Dutch Seaport, 17.
Dutch Soldiers, 14, 23.
Dutch Vauxhall, 216.
Dutch West India Co., 20, 523, 528.
Duyckinck, Evert A., 327.
Dwelling-Houses, 51.
Dwight (John) & Co., **962, 963.**
Dwight School, 302.
Dwight's (John) House, **150.**

Eagle Cage, **163.**
Eagles and Goat, **179.**
Eagles, Central Park, **165.**
Eames, F. L., 790.
Earle, F. P., 218, 226, 748.
Earle, Guild, 454.
Earle's Hotel, 236.
Earle (Wm. H.) & Sons, 230.
Earl of Bellomont, 25, 328.
Earl of Limerick, 24.
Earl of Stirling, 508.
Eastchester, 50.
East 86th Street Y. M. A. C., 416.
Eastern Dispensary, 488.
Eastern Lines, 103.
Easton, C. H., 386.
Easton Wm., 813.
East River, **16, 107, 126, 180, 718,** 50, 51, 55, 69, 70, 71, 133, 155, 185, 195.
East-River Bridge, **187, 186, 139, 718, 75,** 42, 54, 185, 194, 266, 144, 910.
East-River Park, 170.
East Side, 350, 171, 358, 429, 237, 240, 242, 243.
East-Side Bank, **746, 745.**

East-Side Boys' Lodging-House, **428.**
East-Side Ladies' Aid Society, 454.
Eaton, Cole & Burnham Co., **932.**
Eaton, Dorman B., 386.
Eaton, Wm. S., 933.
Ebraucus, King, 221.
Ecclesiastical Annals, 335.
Eclectic Dispensary, **489.**
Eclectic Medical College, 280.
Eden Musee, 605, 838.
Edgehill Chapel, 373.
Edge, N. J. H., 743.
Edison Building. **927, 154,** 156.
Edison Electric Illuminating Co., **202, 203.**
Edison, Thomas A., 203.
Edson, Franklin, 234, 704.
Educational Institutions, 62, 63, 267-300.
Education, Board of, 257, 269, 292, 51, 62.
Edwards, Ernest, 4, 965.
Edwards-Ficken, H., 599.
Egyptian Obelisk, **819, 160,** 181, 66.
Eidlitz, Leopold, 402.
Eidlitz (Marc) & Son, **836.**
Eiffel Tower, 924.
Eighth Avenue, 155.
Eighth Avenue and 42d St., **595.**
Eighth-Avenue R. R , 137.
Eighth-Avenue Theatre, 605.
Eighth Regiment, **534,** 950, 53.
Eighth-Street Theatre, 159, 605.
Eighth-Ward Mission, 432.
Eldorado Gardens, 923.
Elections, 525.
Electrical Instruments, 926, 212.
Electrical Subways, 206.
Electric Club, 323, 557.
Electric Elevator, 924.
Electric Illumination, 926.
Electricity, 931.
Electric-light Machinery, 940.
Electric Lights, 51, 201, 926.
Electric Railways, 138, 926.
Electric Telegraph, 40.
Electric Wires, 204.
Electrotyping, 971.
Elevated Railroads, **56, 126, 128, 138, 134, 135, 195,** 54.
Elevator and Station, **138.**
Elevators, **138, 83,** 924, 797, 817, 74.
Elgin, 272.
Elliott, C., 903.
Ellis Island, **81,** 266, 55, 71.
Ellsler, Fanny, 577.
Ellsworth, James W., 206.
Elmendorf, Joachim, 339.
Elm-Street Station, **203.**
Ely, George W., 790.
Emanu-El, Temple, **401,** 402.
Embury, Phillip, 373, 377.
Emergency Hospital, 460, 464.
Emery Wheels, 928.
Emigrant Houses, **449.**
Emigrant Industrial Savings-Bank, **779.**
Emmett Monument, **509,** 344.

Empire-State Express, **113**, 140.
Empire Theatre, **595**, 594, 148.
Employment, Aid to, 454.
Employment of Women, 436.
Enameled Iron-Ware, 934.
Engineers' Club, 558.
English Insurance Corporations, 662.
Engine House No. 7, **530**.
Engine No. 15, **530**.
Englishmen, 234.
Engraving, 914, 971.
Eno, Amos R., 738.
Envelopes, 952.
Epileptic Asylum, 460.
Epiphany Bapt. Church, **380**.
Episcopal Church, B. I., **499**.
Episcopal Churches, 341, 407.
Episcopal City Missionary Society, 437.
Episcopal Diocesan House, **627**.
Episcopalians, 29, 627.
Episcopal Seminary, **283**, 281.
Equestrianism. 296.
Equestrian Washington, **180**, 66, 174.
Equitable Building, **671**, **832**, 58, 66, 240, 672.
Equitable Gas Co., 201.
Equitable Life Assurance Soc., **671**, 672, 838.
Erhardt, Joel B., 690.
Ericsson, John, **183**, 304, 511.
Ericsson Line, 94.
Erie Canal, 38, 109, 110, 69, 454, 258, 787, 692.
Erie Railroad, 129, 37, 54.
Erwin, Cornelius B., 939.
Español, Hotel, 236.
Esplanade, 161.
Essex Market, **809**.
Essex - Market Court - House, **257**, **493**.
Estimate and Apportionment, 249.
Estimate, Board of, 249.
Etching Club, 67, 309.
Ethical Culture. **295**, 290, 434, 287.
Ethnological Soc., 322.
Evacuation Day, 31, 46.
Evangelical Aid Soc., 449.
Evangelical Lutheran Church, 384.
Evans, D. L., 742.
Evans, Oliver, 37.
Evans, Wm. T., 874.
Evarts, Wm. M., 545, 557.
Evening Express, 614.
Evening Mail, 614.
Evening Post, **611**, 610, 609, 427, 144.
Evening Schools, 62, 267, 268.
Evening Sun, 622.
Evening Telegram, 622.
Evening World, 622.
Everett House, 230.
Evergreen Cemetery, 522.
Ewer, Dr. F. C., 350.
Exchange for Women's Work, 312.
Exchange Place, 336.
Exchange Street, 25.

Ex-convicts, 501, 504.
Execution of Goff, **14**.
Executive Dep't, 247.
Exempt Firemen's Fund, 446.
Expenditures, 51.
Exports and Imports, 74, 75, 785.
Express, 614.
Eye and Ear Infirmary, **483**, 838, 62.

Fabre Line, 91.
Fabric Fire Hose Co., **930**.
Factories, 913, 58.
Faculty of Medicine, 277.
Fairchild, C. S., 564.
Fairchild. S. W., 279.
Fairmount, 47.
Faith Home, 439.
Falconer Statue, **164**, 180.
Fallen Women, 438, 439.
Fall River, 71.
Fall-River Line, 102.
Falls of Niagara 606.
Fancher, E. L., 410.
Fancuil, Benjamin, 508.
Farmer (A. D.) & Son, **970**.
Farmer's Bridge, 193.
Farmers' Club, 321.
Farmers' Loan & Trust Co., **771**, 712, 752.
Farmers' Market, **807**.
Farragut's Grave, **517**, 516.
Farragut Statue, **182**, 66, 166, 176.
Farrelly, Patrick, 721.
Far Rockaway, 348.
Fashionable Weddings, 350.
Fastest Long-Distance Train, **113**.
Fayerweather, D. B., 516.
Fay, S. W., 726.
Fechter, Chas., 602.
Federal Government, 55.
Federal Hall, **21**, **24**, 33, 258, 174, 156, 697.
Federal Interests, 55.
Fellowcraft Club, 543.
Fellows, E. B., 652.
Felt, 941.
Felt Shoes, 941.
Female Almshouse, **501**.
Female Assistance Soc., 436.
Female Asylum, 437.
Female Guardian Soc , **432**.
Female Insane Pavilion, **497**.
Females, Assoc. for the Relief of Respectable, Aged, Indigent. **441**.
Fencers' Club, 570.
Fencing Classes, 298.
Ferris (F. A) & Co., **961**, **960**.
Ferry-Boats, **132**, 54.
Ferry-Road, 16.
Fidelio Club, **552**, 551.
Fidelity & Casualty Co., 683.
FIDUCIARY INSTITUTIONS.—Trust and Investment Companies, Savings-Banks. Safe-Deposit Companies, etc., 753-782.
Field. B. H., 332.
Field, C. W., 44, 304, 170, 234, 614, 820.

Fielding, M. B., 730.
Fifth Ave., 172, 167, 148, 218, 222, 228, 747
Fifth-Ave. Art Galleries, **314**.
Fifth-Ave. Baptist Church, **382**.
Fifth Ave., Bird's-eye View, **313**.
Fifth-Ave. Collegiate Church, **336**, 338.
Fifth Ave., from 58th St., **747**.
Fifth Ave., from 51st St., **313**, **147**.
Fifth Ave., from 59th St., **160**.
Fifth Ave., from 42d Street, **334**.
Fifth Ave., from 29th St., **782**.
Fifth-Ave. Hotel, **857**, **36**, 40, 68, 148, 152, 599, 605, 580, 218, 782, 738.
Fifth-Ave. Presb. Church, **367**, **147**, 366, 152.
Fifth-Ave. Safe - Deposit Co., 738, 782.
Fifth Ave., from the Cathedral, **413**.
Fifth-Avenue Stage, **136**.
Fifth Avenue, Sunday Morning, **413**.
Fifth-Avenue Theatre, **601**, 596, 597, 44, 68, 148, 581, 583.
Fifty-Eighth Street, **573**.
FINAL RESTING-PLACES.—Cemeteries, Burial-Places, Crematories, Churchyards and Vaults, Tombs, etc., 505-522.
Finance Department, 248.
Finances of the City, 249.
FINANCIAL AND COMMERCIAL ASSOCIATIONS.—The Custom House, Chamber of Commerce, the Stock, Produce, Cotton and other Exchanges, Board of Trade, Mercantile and other Agencies, Warehouses and Markets, 783-816.
Financial Control, 140.
FINANCIAL INSTITUTIONS.—United-States Treasury and Assay Office, Clearing House, National and State Banks, Bankers, Brokers, etc., 783-816.
Financial Organization, 697.
Financial Power, 753.
Fine-Arts Soc., **310**.
Fine Forces, College of, 280.
Finlayson, Bonsfield & Co., 895
Fire-Alarm Telegraphs, 530, 51, 965, 967.
FIRE AND MARINE INSURANCE. —Offices and Companies for Assuming Losses by Fires and Transit, and Fire and Marine Underwriters' Associations, 639-662.
Fireboat *New-Yorker*, **539**.
Fire-buckets, 19.
Fire-company, 19.
Fire Dep't, **529**, 19, 26, 51, 256, 446, 965.
Fire Engines. 26.
Fire Extinguishers, 966.
Fire Hydrants, 200.

Fire Insurance, 639.
Fire-Insurance Companies, 639.
Fire-Island, 46.
Fire Losses 639.
Fire Marshal, 256, 640, 652, 530.
Firemen, 446.
Firemen at Work in 1800, **641.**
Firemen's Monument, 519.
Fire Patrol, 639, 640.
Fire-proof Warehouses, 811.
Fire Protection, 530.
Fires, 51.
Fire Underwriters, 531, 640, 641, 648.
First American Cardinal, 284.
First American Congress, 31.
First-Avenue Line, 137.
First Bapt. Church, **379,** 378.
First Battery, 531, 538.
First Bound Book, 27.
First Boy, 10.
First Brigade, 531.
First British Governor, 22.
First Church, 45.
First Church School, 336.
First Clergyman, 14.
First Collegiate Church of Harlem, 339.
First Compound Engine, 94.
First Cong. Minister, 384.
First Dutch Church, 336.
First Engine-House, 529.
First Ferry, 106.
First Fire Co., 19, 529.
First Great Trunk Line, 37.
First Habitations, 45.
First Insurance Company, 639.
First Judicial District, 260, 261.
First Lawyer, 19.
First Library of Congress, 329.
First Locomotive, 110, 130.
First Mail, 23.
First Market-House, 18.
First Merchants' Exchange, 23.
First Methodist Church, **373.**
First National Bank, 703, 645, 738.
First Newspaper, 45, 508.
First N.-Y. Girl, 10.
First Ocean Steamship, 75.
First Opera, 576.
First Paved Street, 19.
First Presb. Church, **365,** 366, 152, 25.
First President, 697.
First Printer, 508.
First Public School, 267.
First Reformed Presb. Church, 373.
First Schoolmaster, 14, 267.
First Sidewalk, 33.
First Soldiers, 14.
First South Church, 340.
First Steam Ferry, 34.
First Steam Frigate, 34.
First Steam Vessel, 34.
First Steel Steamship, 94.
First Stock Marine Insurance Co., 639.
First Street-Car, 38.
First Street-Railway, 136.
First Tavern 215.
First Unitarians, 385.
First Visitor, 5.

First-Ward Library, 333.
First White Male Child, 10.
Fish Commission, 206.
Fish, Hamilton, 326, 170, 545, 234.
Fish, Nicholas, 706, 720.
Fish, Preserved, 710, 712.
Fish, Stuyvesant, 756.
Fiske, Haley, 678.
Fisk, Jas., Jr., 535.
Fitch, John, 36, 493.
Fitzgerald, Brig.-Gen. L., 531.
Five Points, 158.
Five-Points House of Industry, **422.**
Five-Points House of Industry Infirmary, **487,** 488.
Five-Points in 1859, **38.**
Five-Points Mission, **423, 424,** 302, 333.
Flagler, H. M., 152, 516, 854.
Flagler, J. H., 931, 933.
Flats, 242.
Fleischmann & Co., **978.**
Fleischmann's Vienna Bakery, 240.
Fleitmann & Co., **883.**
Flemish Architecture, 338.
Fletcher, Gov. Benjamin, 25.
Flint, Chas. R., 724, 762.
Flint, G. C., 749.
Flood-Rock Explosion, **938.**
Florence Crittenton Mission, **439.**
Florida, 93, 98.
Florio Line, 91.
Flower, R. P., 354, 152.
Flower Surgical Hospital, 478.
Floyd (James R.) & Sons, **951,** 780.
Flushing, 50.
Flying Cloud, 38.
Folger, Chas. J., 698.
Font Hill, 286.
Food and Shelter Depot, 414.
Foot Post to Albany, 109.
Fordham, 47, 137, 139, 440, 447, 284.
Fordham Heights, 292, 485.
Fordham Hospital, 62.
Ford, Simeon, 231.
Foreign Bankers, 750.
Foreign Commerce, 74, 785.
Foreigners' Churches, 341.
Foreign Exchange, 696.
Foreign Fruit Exchange, 806.
Foreign Insurance Cos., 662.
Foreign Mail, 55.
Foreign Missions, 408, 408, 409.
Foreign Relief Societies, 447.
Forest and Stream, 626.
Forget, Augustin, 84.
Fornes, C. V., 780.
Forrest, Edwin, 40, 286, 159, 582, 578, 577.
Fort Amsterdam, 10, 13, 14, 45, 336, 342.
Fort Chapel, 25.
Fort Columbus, 72, 539, 540.
Fort George, **17,** 24, 30, 193, 172.
Fort Hamilton, 55, 72, 539, 540.
Fort Lafayette, 72, 540.

Fort Nassau, 7.
Fort Schuyler, 72, 55, 539, 541.
Fort Tompkins, 72, 540.
Fortunes, 58.
Fort Wadsworth, **99,** 540, 55, 45², 72, 539.
Fort Washington, 31.
Fort Wood, **73,** 541, 72, 175, 539.
Forty-Second St., from Fourth Ave., **648.**
Forty-Second St. in 1868, **39,** 152.
Forum, 58.
Fosdick, C. B., 738, 743.
Foulke, Wm., 410.
Foundling Asylum, **426.**
Fourteenth Street, **146.**
Fourteenth St. and Broadway, **870.**
Fourteenth St., from University Place, **870.**
Fourteenth-St. Theatre, 602.
Fourth Avenue, **840, 981.**
Fourth-Avenue Line, 37, 137.
Fourth-Avenue Presb. Church, **412,** 368.
Fourth-Avenue Tunnel, 228.
Fourth Nat. Bank, 703.
Fowler & Wells Co., **324, 323.**
Fowler, Lorenzo N., 324.
Fowler, Orson S., 324.
Fraleigh, C. P., 672.
Français, Hotel, 236.
Francis, E. W., 979.
Francis, W. A., 659.
Franconi's Hippodrome, 580.
Frankfort Street, **61.**
Frank Leslie's Illustrated, 626.
Frank Leslie's Illustrirte Zeitung, 626.
Frank Leslie's Monument, **517,** 518.
Franklin Bank, **749,** 698.
Franklin Square, **630,** 19, 156.
Franklin Statue, **176,** 175, 156.
Franklin Theatre, 582.
Fraunce's Tavern, **23,** 31, 46, 215.
Free Banking Act, 693.
Freebooters, 25.
Free Circulating Library, **332,** 331, 63.
Free City, 40.
Free Dispensary, 460.
Freeland, Wm., 301.
Free Library, 329, 446.
Free Public Schools, 257
Free Reading-Rooms, 429.
Free School Society, 34.
Free-Trade Club, 562.
Freight Depot, West St., **119.**
French Benevolent Soc., 448, 474.
French Branch, Y. M. C. A., 416.
French Church, **18.**
French, E. S., 677.
French Evang. Church, 448.
French, F. O., 766.
French Hospital, 474.
French, H. Q., **516.**
French Huguenots, 22.
French Line, 83, 71.

Frenchman, 50, 176.
French, P. W., 933.
French's Hotel, 216, 620.
French, T. Henry, 603, 587, 594, 598.
Fresh-Air Fund, 59.
Fresh-Air Gardens, 70.
Fresh-Pond Crematory, 522
Fresh Water Pond, 34.
Freundschaft Verein. **551.**
Friendless Home for, **432,** 369.
Friends' Meeting-House. **391,** 171, 389.
Friends of Homeless, 437.
Friends' Seminary, **391,** 287, 171.
Friesland, **88.**
Fruit and Flower Mission, 453.
Fruit Exchange, 806.
Fruit Steamers, 74
Fulton Bank, 728.
Fulton Club, 547, 728.
Fulton Ferry, **106.**
Fulton Fish Market, **804.**
Fulton Market, **804,** 808, 576.
Fulton, Robert, 34, 75, 184, 508, 512.
Fulton Street, 612.
Fulton-St. Prayer-Meeting, 339.
Funded Debt, 51.
Funke, A. H, 902.
Furnessia, 82.
Furniture, 854.
Furniture Storage, 810.
Fur Trade, 7, 39, 260.
Fürst Bismarck, **87,** 86.

Gabled Ends, 19.
Gaelic Society, 333.
Gaffney, J. S., 672.
Gage, Gen., 28, 215.
Galilee Rescue Mission, 356.
Gallatin, Albert, 322, 508, 701, 716.
Gallatin Nat. Bank, **705, 717,** 716, 703, 838, 950, 764.
Gallaudet, Dr. T., 358.
Gallows, 17, 32.
Galveston, 97.
Gamewell Fire-Alarm Telegraph Co., **967.**
Gansevoort Market, 809.
Garden Street, 25, 336, 339.
Garden Theatre, 587. 148.
Gardiner's Island, 37.
Gardner, Harrison, 880.
Garfield Safe Deposit Co., 782.
Garibaldi Statue, **170,** 167, 174.
Garrison Chapel, 347.
Garth, H. E., 708.
Gas, 51, 201.
Gaston, Geo. H., 678.
Gas-Works Apparatus, 951.
Gate House, **198.**
Gazette, 27, 45, 609, 820.
Gazeteer, 27.
Gem Minerals, 308.
Genealogical Society, 323, 333.
GENERAL CULTURE.— Educational Institutions — Universities (colleges, Academies, Seminaries; and Public, Private and Parochial Schools, 267–302.

General Electric Co., **927,** 926.
General Fund, 253, 254.
General Sessions, **261,** 262.
General Soc. of Mechanics and Tradesmen, 446, 329, 708.
General Theol. Sem., **283, 281,** 63, 333.
Genoa, 91.
Geographical Society, **321,** 333.
George Bruce Library, 332.
George III., 28, 30.
Georgia-Florida Route, 97.
Gerlach, Hotel, 230.
German American Ins. Co., **654.**
German Catholic Immigrants, 448.
German Clubs, **550.**
German Dispensary, **488,** 838.
German District, 332.
German Evangelical Church, 383.
German Hospital, **476.**
German Hotels, 237.
Germania Life Ins. Co., **673.**
Germania Theatre, 600, 605.
German Legal Aid Soc., 454.
German Lyrism, 319.
German Mission-House Assoc., 447.
German Odd Fellows, **572.**
German Opera, 588.
German Poliklinik, 489.
German Population, 383, 181.
Germans, 50 158, 550, 606, 538.
German Y M. C. A., **415,** 416.
Gerry, E. T., 425, 588.
Gibb, John, 874.
Gibbons, John J., 850.
Gibson, R. W., 338, 362, 406.
Gilbert, Alex., 728.
Gilbert, F H., 893.
Gilbert Manufacturing Co., **893.**
Gilbert, W. B., 344.
Gilder, R. W., 636.
Gilman, Collamore & Co., **850.**
Gilman, E. W., 410.
Gilmore, P. S., 587.
Gilroy, T. F., 360.
Gilsey Building, **601.**
Gilsey House, 2.6, 148.
Girls' Protectory, 435.
Gladstone, Hotel, 148.
Glass, 3 6, 858, 850.
Glen Summit, 122.
Glue, 916.
Godey's Magazine, 636.
Godkin, E. L., 610.
God's Acres, 505.
Goelet Family, 152, 714, 743, 838, 756, 760.
Gold and Silver, 699.
Gold & Stock Telegraph, 790.
Gold Bars. 699.
Gold Board, 790.
Golden Eagle Inn, 216.
Golden Hill, 28.
Gold Room, 695.
Good, Brent, 596, 749.
Goodrich, T. F., 647.
Good Samaritan Disp., 488.
Good Shepherd, Chapel, 282, 500.

Goodyear, Charles, 928.
Gorham Mfg. Co., **847,** 846, 183, 226.
Gotham Art-Students, 288.
Gotham Club, 547.
Gotham Wheelmen, 569.
Gould, Jay, 67, 515, 695, 603.
Gould's Mausoleum, 516.
Gouverneur Hospital, **460,** 461.
Government, 245.
Government House, 45, 320.
Government Loans, 695, 738.
Governor's Island, **867,** 72, 14, 47, 55, 347, 539, 540.
Governor's Room, 67, 258.
Grace Chapel, 348.
Grace Church, **232, 349,** 66, 67, 144, 146, 236, 233, 391, 407, 852.
Grace House, 348.
Grace Memorial House, **350,** 348.
Grace, W. R., 260, 814.
Graduate Law School, 277.
Graduate Sem., 276.
Grain, 74, 797.
Grain-Laden Steamships, 74.
Gramercy Park, 40, 170, 234, 389.
Grammar Schools, **268,** 62, 267.
Grand Army, 561, 44.
Grand Central Hotel, 236.
Grand Central Station, **111, 231, 115, 123,** 112, 133, 193, 196, 195, 950, 955, 132, 360, 417, 230, 515.
Grand Hotel, 148.
Grand Opera House, 603, 608.
Grand Street, **859,** 14.
Grand Union Hotel, **231.**
Grange, **355.**
Granniss, Jas. E., 688, 690, 714.
Grant, Hugh J., 260.
Grant Mausoleum, **861,** 66, 148.
Grant, U. S., 258, 376.
Gravesend, 30.
Graves (Robert) Co., **954.**
Gravity Road, 130.
Gray, W. S., 744.
Great Barn Island, **78.**
Greater New York, 50.
Great Fire of 1776, 33.
Great Western, 76.
Greek Benevolent Soc., 447.
Greek Church, 406.
Greeley, Horace, 44, 324, 156, 175, 519, 612, 616.
Greeley Statue, **178,** 44, 66, 184.
Green, Andrew H., 50.
Greene, Thomas B., 651.
Green Goods, 503.
Green, J. C., 329, 773.
Green, Robert S., 672.
Greenwich Ins. Co., **643.**
Greenwich Savings-Bank, **775,** 154.
Greenwich Street, 26.
Greenwich-Street Theatre, 583.
Greenwich Village, 15, 29, 40, 47, 66, 951, 381, 431, 355, 498, 216, 242, 979.
Green-Wood Cemetery, 519.
Greer, D. H., 358.
Grenoble, Hotel, **227, 243.**

Griffin, Eugene, 926.
Griffon, Hotel, 236.
Grinnell, Minturn & Co., 38.
Grinnell Sprinkler, 966.
Grinnell, W. M., 742.
Grolier Club, 553, 334.
Guayra, La, 101.
Guernsey Building, 690, 681.
Guild of St. Elizabeth, 455.
Guion Line, 82, 71,
Gustavus Adolphus Church, 384.
Gutenberg, 178.

Hahnemann, Hospital, 475.
Haigh, H. B., 934.
Haight, C. C., 350, 272, 688.
Haldeman, I. M., 378.
Hale, Nathan, 184.
Half-Moon, 7.
Half-Orphans 432.
Hall, A. C., 738.
Hall, A. Oakey, 258, 260, 582.
Hall, Chas. B. 703.
Halleck, Fitz Greene, 39, 326, 543.
Halleck Statue, 168, 178,
Hallgarten (Julius) Fund, 452, 332.
Hall, James, 721.
Hall, John, 418, 367, 275, 519.
Hall of Records, 619, 31, 32, 54, 262, 170, 494, 252.
Halls, 608.
Hall's, Dr., Church, 367, 366.
Halls, Wm., Jr., 728.
Halsey, Jacob L., 670, 672.
Halve-Maen, 7.
Hamburg-American Packet Co, 87, 86, 88, 91, 83.
Hamilton, A., 164, 28, 34, 326, 180, 270, 355, 507, 703, 700, 610, 743.
Hamilton Bank, 744, 743.
Hamilton Statue, 164, 180.
Hammerstein, Oscar, 605, 594.
Hammond, D. S., 748.
Hammond, F. A., 222.
Hanan, J. H., 716.
Hanover Fire-Ins. Co., 649, 648, 647.
Hanover Nat. Bank, 726.
Hanover Square, 17, 159, 799.
Harbor, 73, 75, 69, 70.
Harbor Defenses, 541, 72.
Harbor in 1893, 75.
Harbor Police, 525.
Hardenbergh, H. J., 312, 400, 218.
Harding & Gooch, 224.
Harding, Geo. Edw., 208.
Hardman Hall, 68, 608.
Hardware, 902, 939.
Hargous, 514.
Harlem, 152, 19, 29, 47, 139, 339, 361, 364, 371, 166, 161, 243, 743.
Harlem Art Assoc., 288.
Harlem Bridges, 193, 194.
Harlem Club, 548, 549.
Harlem Dem. Club, 562.
Harlem Dispensary, 489.
Harlem Heights, 30, 372, 466.
Harlem Hospital, 62, 460.
Harlem Law Library, 332.

Harlem Library, 334.
Harlem Med. Assoc., 491.
Harlem Mere, 161.
Harlem Mission, 377.
Harlem Municipal Building, 254.
Harlem Opera-House, 605.
Harlem Railroad, 115, 196, 132, 134.
Harlem Republican Club, 563.
Harlem River, 189, 191, 194, 257, 822, 70, 54, 67, 112, 134, 138, 69, 192, 193, 196, 198, 204, 910.
Harlem Y. M. C. A., 907, 414.
Harmonie Club, 550, 838.
Harper & Brothers, 828, 626, 630, 965.
Harper, E. B., 682.
Harper, Jas., 40, 260, 524, 780.
Harper's Bazaar, 626.
Harper's Magazine, 58, 636.
Harper's Weekly, 626.
Harper's Young People, 626.
Harrigan & Hart's Theatre, 581.
Harrigan, Edw., 598, 600.
Harrigan's Theatre, 598, 148.
Harriman, Oliver, 710, 769, 770.
Harrison, C. F., 885.
Harrison, President, 44, 76.
Harry Howard Square, 156.
Harsha, W. J., 339.
Harteau, Henry, 683.
Hart, Josh, 600.
Hart's Island, 62, 455, 461, 500, 522.
Hart's-Island Asylum, 462.
Hart's-Island Hospital, 460, 462.
Harvard Club, 556, 760.
Harvard School, 301.
Harvey, Chas. C., 138.
Hatch, Edw. P., 848.
Hatié, J. C., 658.
Havana, 98.
Havemeyer Building, 827, 826, 58, 931, 933.
Havemeyer, Henry O., 918, 152, 519.
Havemeyer, John C., 770.
Havemeyer, Theo. A., 918, 826.
Havemeyer, Wm. F., 258, 260.
Havemeyers & Elder. 723.
Haven, Geo. G., 312, 588, 710, 743, 769, 776.
Haver, Sylvester A., 872.
Havre Packets, 38.
Hawks, Dr. F. L., 352.
Haxtun, Wm., 677.
Haynes, Tilly, 236.
Hays, D. C., 645, 760, 781, 790.
Heald, Daniel, 651.
Health Dep't, 251, 256.
Health Officer, 457, 264, 251.
Healy Building, 61.
Heavenly Rest, Church, 351, 352, 152, 67.
Hebrew Actors. 604, 605.
Hebrew Americans, 447.
Hebrew Benevolent Orphan Asylum, 451.
Hebrew Charities, 451, 418.
Hebrew Children, 451, 452.
Hebrew-Christian Church, 390.

Hebrew Congregations, 400.
Hebrew Free Schools, 301.
Hebrew Immigrants, 452.
Hebrew Institute, 418.
Hebrew Lying-in Soc., 483.
Hebrew Operas, 604.
Hebrew Orphan Asylum, 451.
Hebrew Relief Society, 451.
Hebrew Restaurants, 240.
Hebrews, 50, 469.
Hebrew Sheltering Guardian Soc., 451.
Hebrew Sheltering Home, 452.
Hebrew Technical School, 297.
Hecker, Isaac, 397.
Hegeman, John R., 678, 729, 767.
Hegger's Photographs, 315.
Heimath, Isabella, 445, 838.
Heins & LaFarge, 362.
Hell Gate, 78, 938, 70, 26, 37, 42, 265.
Hell-Gate Pilots, 265.
Hempstead, 50.
Herald, 624, 614, 39, 144, 208, 576, 858.
Herald Buildings, 624.
Herdsman, 18.
Herold, 622.
Herring, Silas C., 951.
Herrmann's Theatre, 601, 600, 148.
Herzog Teleseme, 224.
Hewitt, A. S., 936, 188, 260, 170, 234, 721.
Hickok. Geo. S., 732.
High Altar, 395, 392.
High Bridge, 191, 822, 192, 197, 198, 200, 910.
High-Bridge Park, 192, 170.
HIGHER CULTURE — Art Museums and Galleries, Scientific, Literary, Musical and Kindred Institutions and Organizations, 303-324.
Highlands, 104, 105, 113, 128.
High-Service Station, 199.
High-Service Water, 922.
Hillhouse, Thos., 698, 764, 765, 773.
Hill, J. M., 600, 602.
Hine, C. C., 634, 673.
Hippodrome, 580.
Hirsch (Baron) Fund, 292, 301.
HISTORICAL.—New York of the Past, from the Earliest Times to the Present, 5-46.
Historical Portraits, 321.
Historic Ground. 50.
Historical Society, 331, 330, 329, 34, 45, 63, 66, 358, 381, 778.
Hitchcock, D. W., 933.
Hitchcock, Hiram, 587.
Hitchcock, W. G., 890, 738.
Hitchcock (W. G.) & Co., 890.
Hlas Lindu, 622.
Hobart Hall, 282.
Hoboken, 27, 34, 84, 85, 88, 90.
Hoboken Ferry Pier, 84.
Hoe (R.) & Co., 957, 956, 765.
Hoe, Robert, 334, 765, 956.
Hoffman House, 857, 226, 68, 148.

Hoffman Island, 458, 73, 264.
Hoffman, John T., 186.
Hoffman, Josiah O., 706.
Hofheimer, Henry, 720.
Hogg, John, 880.
Holland, 7.
Holland, Dr. J. G., 636.
Holland House, **225, 782,** 224, 66, 68, 152.
Holland's Map, **12.**
Holland Society, 553, 44, 45, 46.
Holley Bust, **171,** 174.
Holloway, J. F., 559.
Holt, R. S., 773.
Holy Comforter, House, 440.
Holy Communion, Church, 357, 456, 472.
Holy Cross, Church, **398,** 4-0.
Holy Cross School, **293, 398,** 286.
Holy Family, House, **436.**
Holy Rosary, School, 286.
Holy Spirit, Church, 258.
Holy Trinity, **151, 360' 362,** 361.
Homans, Sheppard, 678, 680
Home for Destitute Blind, **440.**
Home for Aged Hebrews, **453,** 451.
Home for Incurables, 440.
Home for Old Men, 443.
Home Insurance Co., **650,** 651.
Home Journal, 628.
Homeless Children, 433.
Home Life, 241.
Home Life Ins. Building, **675, 674,** 674, 676, 144.
Home Life Ins. Co., **674, 675.**
Home Missions, 408. 409, 412.
Home of Industry, **504.**
Homer Ramsdell Transportation Co., **104.**
Homes for the Aged, **441, 442, 443, 444, 445.**
Homœopathic Dispensary, 489.
Homœopathic Hospital, **475,** 481.
Homœopathic Medical Coll., 279, 63.
Hone Club, 543.
Hone, Philip, 258, 512, 532, 710, 773.
Hop-Dealers' Exchange, 806.
Hope Chapel, 380, 368.
Hopper, Isaac T., Home, 438.
Hornthal, Weissman & Co., **889.**
Horse-and-Cart Lane, 378.
Horse-Boats, 106.
Horse-Railroads, 37, 136.
Horse-Sales, 812.
Horticultural Soc., 323.
Horton (J. M.) Ice Cream Co., **984.**
Hosack, Dr. D., 272, 482.
Hose, 928, 930.
Hosmer, Chas. R., 206, 210.
Hospital for Incurables, 440, 496, 62.
Hospital Graduates' Club, 491.
Hospital Newspaper Soc., 454.
Hospitals, 458, 62, 59.
Hospitals for Children, 428.
Hospital Ship, 458.

Hospital Sunday Assoc., 492.
Hotel Brunswick, 230.
Hotel, Cambridge, **228.**
Hotel de Logerot, 230.
Hotel District, 216.
Hotel Grenoble, **227,** 154.
Hotel Imperial, 226, 148, 66, 68.
Hotel Monico, 236.
Hotel New Netherland, **219,** 218.
Hotel Normandie, **601,** 226.
Hotel Rates in 1650, 215.
Hotels, 216, 68, 148.
Hotel Savoy, **221,** 220, 854, 982.
Hotel Waldorf, **217,** 218, 854.
Houghton, Dr. G. H., 357.
House and School of Industry, **437.**
House Furnishers, 858.
House of Industry, **422,** 302.
House of Mercy, 438.
House of Nazareth, 436.
House of Refuge, 501, 40, 62, 302, 500, 778.
House of Relief, 464.
House of Rest, 407.
Houston Street, 36, 352.
House of the Good Shepherd, 438.
House of the Holy Comforter, 440.
Howard, Gen. O. O., 539.
Howard, Harry, 519.
Howard Mission, 433.
Howe, G. C., 647.
Howland, Dr. R. S., 352.
Howland, Gardiner G., 210.
Hoyt, A. M., 715, 773.
Hoyt & Thomas, 597.
Hoyt, Chas. H., 597.
Hoyt, G. L., 751.
Hoyt's Madison-Square Theatre, **597.**
Hubbard, L. P., 454.
Hubbard, S. T., 742.
Hubbell, C. O., 742.
Hubert Street, **32.**
Hudson, Henry, **5,** 7.
Hudson River, **103,** 50, 54, 55, 69, 70, 75, 109, 112, 128, 129.
Hudson-River Bridge, 194.
Hudson-River Day Line, **103,** 71.
Hudson-River Railroad, 115, 37.
Hudson-River Tunnel, 195.
Hudson-St. Freight Depot, 814.
Hughes, Archbishop, **184,** 42, 183, 284, 391.
Huguenot Graveyard, 522.
Huguenots, 22, 25, 509.
Huguenot Society, 332.
Humboldt Statue, **168,** 180.
Hume, W. H., **681,** 451, 682, 549.
Humphreys, Solon, 659.
Hungarian Assoc., 447.
Hungarians, 241.
Hunt & Eaton, 630.
Hunt, A. S., 410.
Hunter, Gov , 25.
Hunter's Island, 171.
Hunter's Point, 135.
Huntington, C. P., 67, 312, 152, 222, 764.

Huntington, Daniel, 548.
Huntington Mansion, 66.
Huntington Mausoleum, **518,** 866.
Huntington, W. R., 350, 418.
Hunt, R. H., 747.
Hunt, Richard M., 130, 312, 327, 175, 257, 272, 834.
Hunt, Sanford, 716.
Hurlbert, H. C., 756.
Hurlbut, H. A., 737.
Hutchins, Rev. John, 337.
Hutton, Prof. F. R., 322.
Hyde, E. F., 764.
Hydrants, 51.
Hydraulic Works, **922,** 923.

Ice Bridge, 44. .
Ice Cream, 984.
Ide, Geo. E , 676.
Idiot Asylum, 62, 500.
Iglehart, F. C., 377.
Immaculate Virgin, House, **435,** 159.
Immigrant Bureau, 81, 266, 141.
Immigrants, 578.
Immigration, 55, 448.
Immigration, Commissioners, 247.
Imperial Hotel, 226, 68, 66, 148.
Imperial Insurance Co , **661.**
Importers' and Traders' Club, 558.
Importers' and Traders' Bank, 703, 724.
Imports, 785, 74.
Inauguration of Washington, **21,** 31, 44, 344.
Incandescent Lamps, 926, 202, 203.
Incarnation, Church, **361,** 836.
Incurables, 460.
Incurables, Home for, 440, 500.
Incurables Ward B. I., **499.**
Indian Antiquities, 330.
Indian Councils, 18.
Indian Hunter, **165,** 66, 179.
Indians, 20.
Indian Slaves, 23.
Indian War, 15.
India-rubber, 928.
Indigent Females' Home, **441,** 442, 443.
Industrial Art-Education, 288.
Industrial Life-Insurance, 677.
Industrial Schools, **437.**
Industrial Training, 290.
Industrial Trusts, 696.
Infant Asylum, **425.**
Infanta Eulalia, 397.
Infants' Hospitals, 460, 500, 62.
Infirmaries, 62.
Infirmary for Women and Children, **479,** 279.
Infirmary, N.-Y., **479.**
Ingleside, 433.
Inman Line, 76.
Insane Asylum, B. I., **462,** 461.
Insane Asylum for Males, 460, 462, 62.
Insane Asylums, 461, 462.
Insane Asylum, Ward's Id., **463,** 462.
Insane Pavilion, 459, 466.

Inspection of Buildings, 251.
Inspection of Combustibles, 256.
Institute of Artist-Artisans, 311.
Institution for Savings of Merchants' Clerks. **778.**
Institute of Mercy, 437, 435.
Insular Navigation Co., 89.
Insulated Wire, 931.
Insulation, 931.
Insurance, 641.
Insurance Club, 557
Insurance Dep't, 640, 641.
Insurance Legislation, 640.
Insurance Monitor, **634.**
Insurance Patrol, 5;0, 965.
Insurance Reports, 640
Insuring of Vessels, 646.
Intemperate Men, Home for, 487.
Interlaken Cloth. 885.
International Banking-Houses, 750.
Internat. Medical Missionary Institute, 284.
International Navigation Co., **77, 76,** 79.
International Okonite Co., **931.**
Invalids' Homes, 440.
Inventions, 321.
Inwood, 47, 438.
Irish Emigrant Society, 448.
Irishmen, ςo, 536.
Irish Regiment, 536.
Iron, 931, 934, 951, 936.
Iron Clad Mfg. Co., **935,** 934. 715.
Iron Pier, Coney Id., **983.**
Iron Skeletons, 818.
Iron Work, **950, 951,** 306, 982.
Iroquois Club, 562.
Irving Hall, 6ɔ3.
Irvingites, 389.
Irving Place, 234.
Irving-Place Theatre, 6ɔ2.
Irving Savings Institution, 782.
Irving, W., **172,** 176, 39, 325, 326, 160, 170, 134, 817.
Irvin, Richard, Jr., 21ɔ.
Isaac T. Hopper Home, 438.
Isabella Heimath, **445,** 838.
Iselin, Adrian, 588, 71ɔ, 773.
Iselin, Adrian, Jr., 716, 764, 769, 838.
Iselin. C. O., 756.
Isham, Wm. B., 740.
Island Mission, 453.
Islip, 62.
Istituto, Italiano, **456, 455.**
Italian Benevolent Soc., 447.
Italian Club, **489.**
Italian Home, **456,** 4ςς.
Italian Immigrants, 4ςς, 474.
Italian Institute, **456,** 455.
Italiɑn Quarter, **159.**
Italian Restaurants, 241.
Italians, 5ɔ, 3ɔ2, 174, 18c.

Jackson, H. M., 659.
Jackson, J. J., 684.
Jacksonville, 93.
Jaffray (E. S.) & Co., **872.**
Jaffray, H. S., 872.

Jaffray, Robert, 872.
Jamaica, 5ɔ, 100.
James, C. F., 749.
James Fountain, **179,** 182.
James, Thomas L., 266.
Jans, Roelof, 14.
Japanese Club, 240.
Japanese Restaurant, 240.
Japanese Swords, 304.
Jarvie, Jas. N., 71ɔ.
Jay, John. 27ɔ.
Jeanette Park, **82, 153, 107.**
Jefferson, Joseph, 581.
Jefferson Market, 8 9.
Jefferson-Market Court, **839,** 253, 494, 493, 154, 828.
Jenkins, E. F., 425.
Jerome Avenue, 192.
Jerome Park, 192, 198, 199, 200.
Jersey, 3', 542.
Jersey Central Building, 58.
Jersey City, 27, 119, 118 121, 129.
Jesuit Institutions, 285.
Jesuits, 284, 285, 391, 397.
Jesup, Chas. M., 764.
Jesup, M. K., 366, 423, 764.
Jewelers' Association, 528.
Jewish Cemetery, 505, 522.
Jewish Church 5ɔ, 1 2, 400.
Jewish Immigrants' Protective Soc., 447.
Jewish Infants, 451.
Jewish Literature, 331, 610.
Jewish Philanthropies, 451, 447.
Jewish Poor, 452.
Jewish Reform, 403.
Jewish Theol. Seminary, 284.
Jobbing Trade, 871-912.
Jogues, Father, 391.
Johnson, Geo. P., 749.
Johnson, Isaac G., 644.
Johnson, Samuel, 27ɔ.
Johnston, John S., 4, 43.
Johnston, J. T., 315, 304, 275.
John Street, 28.
John-Street M. E. Church, **374,** 35ɔ, 377, ɔ86.
John-Street Theatre, 576.
Jones, A. H., 898.
Jones, George, 618.
Jones, J. D., 645, 646.
Jordan, Conrad N., 698.
Journal, 622, 609, 27.
Journalism, 6ɔ9, 27.
JOURNALISM AND PUBLISHING.—
Newspapers and Periodicals, Book, Music and other Publishing, 609-638.
Journal of Commerce, 612, 609, 610.
Judaism, 452.
Judge, **635,** 1ςɔ, 626, 749.
Judiciary, 26ɔ, 51.
Judiciary Salaries, 51.
Judson Memorial Church, **378,** 173, 379, 456, 167.
Juhring, J. C., 898.
Juilliard, A. D., 71ɔ, 764, 769.
Jumel Mansion, **22.**
Jurors, ɔ62.
Juvenile Asylum, **501,** 302, 372.

Kahle, J. 908.
Kahle, M., 908.

Kaiser Wilhelm, **85.**
Kane, J. P., 745, 906.
Kean, Charles, 51ɔ.
Kean, Edmund, 51ɔ, 576.
Kean Riot, 5;6.
Kearny, Gen. Phil., 509.
Keene, Laura, 58!.
Keener, Wm. A., 273.
Keep, Mrs. E. A., 484.
Kelly, Eugene, 704, 732, 780,830.
Kelly, Hugh, 721.
Kelsey, C. H., 73ɔ.
Kendrick, A. C., 381.
Kennedy Collection, 327.
Kennedy, H. V. R., 771.
Kennedy (F. A.) Co., 944.
Kennedy, J. S., 722, 764.
Kennedy, R. L., 773.
Kenny, W. J. K., 622.
Kensico Cemetery, **521,** 52ɔ.
Kensico Lake, **521.**
Kent's Commentaries, 273, 543.
Kernan, J. A., 891.
Kernɔchan, J. P., 756.
Kerr, Walter, 756.
Keys, J. G., 742.
Kidd, Capt. Robert, 25.
Kieft, Wm., 14, 215, 523.
Kimball, F. H., 670.
Kimber, A. C., 347.
Kindergarten Assoc., 302.
Kindergartens,302, 269, 298,434.
King, C. W., 304.
King, David H., Jr., 688, 618, 762, 832.
King, Edward, 326, 556, 645, 76ɔ, 781.
King George, 787.
King, Richard, 722.
King's Arms Tavern, 17, 215.
Kingsbridge, 192.
Kingsbridge Road, 193, 148.
King's College, 27ɔ, 27, 34.
King's Daughters, **455.**
King's Farm, 14, 25.
King's (John) House, **151.**
Kingsland, A C., 26ɔ, 780.
Kingsley, W. C., 185, 186, 188.
King's Model Houses, 832.
Kinsley, H. M., 226.
Kipp's Bay, 3ɔ.
Kirk's, 241.
Kitchin's Map, **15.**
Kit-Kat Club, 3ɔ9, 314.
Kittredge. A. E., 34ɔ.
Klopsch, Louis, 632.
Knapp, Shepherd, 372.
Knevals, Caleb B., 519.
Knickerbocker Canoe Club, 568.
Knickerbocker Casualty Co., 681.
Knickerbocker Club, **546,** 68, 153.
Knickerbocker, Diedrich, **5.**
Knickerbocker Fire-Ins. Co., 639.
Knickerbocker Hotel, 220.
Knickerbocker Trust Co., **760.**
Knights Templar, 571.
Knox, John Jay, 44, 724.
Koburger Bible, 33ɔ.
Koster & Bial's, 6ɔ5, 148.
Krigier's Tavern, 17, 215.

Lace Leather, 940.
Laces, 874.
Lackawanna Building, 58.
Lackawanna System, 125.
Ladenburg, Adolph, 587.
Ladies' Christian Union, 436.
Ladies' Deborah Nursery, 452.
Ladies' Fuel Society, 454.
Ladies' Health Protective Association, 492.
Ladies' Mission, 455.
Ladies' N.-Y. Club, 571.
Ladies' Union Relief Association, 454.
LaFarge, John, 352, 354, 356, 366, 398 399, 545.
LaFarge House, 235.
Lafayette, 14', 175, 258, 532.
Lafayette Place, **326, 328,** 159, 325, 358, 347, 146, 236, 628.
Lafayette Statue, **180,** 176, 166.
Lafayette Theatre, 583.
Laffan, W. M., 613.
Lahn, **85.**
Lake, Central Park, **162.**
Lake, Kensico, **521.**
Lake, Woodlawn, **517.**
Lamb, Martha J , 636.
Lambs, 792.
Lamb's Artillery, 532.
Lambs' Club, 552.
Lamar, G. B , 724.
LaMontagne Garden, 216.
Lamp Posts, 201.
Lancey, J. De, 509.
Landon, C. G., 764.
Lane, Barent H., 814.
Lane, I. R., 648.
Langdon, Batcheller & Co., **891.**
Langdon, Edwin, 736.
Langdon W G., 748.
Langdon, Woodbury, 722, 736.
Langham, Hotel, 132.
Langill, C. C., 4, 41.
Langtry, Mrs., 582, 593.
Lanier, Charles, 306, 587, 764.
Lanterns, 26.
Larocque, Joseph, 748.
Laryngological Assoc., 491.
La Salle Institute, 286.
Las Novedades, 622.
Laura Franklin Hospital, **482,** 481.
Laura Keene's Varieties, 580, 581.
Law Dep't, 276.
Law Institute, 332, 260.
Law Libraries, 332.
Lawrence (A. & A.) & Co., 880.
Lawrence, Capt., 507.
Lawrence, F R., 549.
Law Schools, 270, 273, 276, 63.
Lawyers, 19.
Lawyers' Club, 557, 332.
Lawyers' Surety Co., 690.
Lawyers' Title Insurance Co. of New York, **687,** 686.
Lazarus Collection, 304.
Lazarus Guild, 413.
L. A. W., 669.
Leake and Watts Orphan Home, 430, 362.
Leather Belting, 940.

Leather Heads, 524.
Leather Trade, 778.
Lebanon Hospital, **474,** 473, 62.
Le Brun, N., 678.
Le Brun (Napoleon) & Sons, 257, 157, 674.
L'Eco d'Italia, 618.
Ledger, 626.
Lee, Gen., 29.
Leeson (J. R) & Co., **895.**
Leggett (F. H.) & Co., **897,** 896, 776.
Legislative Dept., 246.
Lehigh River, 122.
Lehigh Valley, 125.
Lehigh-Valley Railroad, **121.**
Leisler, Jacob, 24, 25.
Lenox-Avenue Unit. Church, 386.
Lenox Collection, 330.
Lenox Hill, 354, 282.
Lenox Institute, 331.
Lenox, James, 326, 370, 468.
Lenox Library, **327,** 326, 63, 66, 67, 153.
Lenox Lyceum, 606, 68, 320.
Lenox Medical Soc., 491.
Lenox Nineveh Marbles, 66.
Lenox, Robert, 482, 751.
Leo House, **449,** 448.
Leonard, Robert, 776.
Leslie, Frank, 626.
Leupp, W. H., 771.
Leverich, C. P., 704.
Lewis & Conger, **858.**
Lewis, R V , 743.
Lexington Ave. and 63d St., **869.**
Lexington-Ave. Opera-House, 606.
Liautard, Dr. A., 281.
Libbey, A. F , 738.
Libbey, Wm., 758.
Liberty Enlightening the World, **177,** 42, 72, 174.
Liberty Pole, 28.
Libraries, 6 , 325.
Libraries for Ships, 414.
Library, Columbia College, 332.
Library of Congress, 329.
Licenses, 253.
Liederkranz, **318,** 319, 68, 290.
Life, 626.
LIFE-INSURANCE.— Companies for Protection of Widows, Orphans and others, and for Providing Incomes in Advanced Age, etc., and Life-Insurance Associations, 663-682.
LIFE IN THE METROPOLIS.— Hotels, Inns, Cafés, Restaurants, Apartment-Houses, Flats, Homes, Tenements, etc., 215-244.
Life-Underwriters, 662.
Light House, B. I., **497.**
Lighting Streets, 201.
Liliputian Bazaar, **856.**
Lily Pond, 162.
Lincoln Club, 562.
Lincoln Statue. **181,** 176, 166.
Lincrusta Walton 055.

Lind, Jenny, 141, 578, 580, 235, 236.
Linen Thread, 895.
Lioness. **165.**
Lion Insurance Co., 662.
Lispenard Meadows, 34.
Listy, 622.
LITERARY CULTURE. — Libraries, Public, Club, Society and Private, 325-334.
Lithographing, 914.
Little Church Around the Corner, **357.**
Little Mothers' Aid, 427.
Little Sisters of the Poor, **443, 444.**
Little Wanderers. 433.
Little Water Street, **38.**
Liverpool, London & Globe Ins. Co., 662.
Livingston, Chancellor, 34, 36.
Livingston, Edw., 32, 258.
Livingston Ref. Church, 340.
Livingston, R. S., 512.
Livingston, 28.
Lloyds Plate Glass Ins. Co., **690.**
Local Traffic, 54.
Local Transit 135.
Locomotive, First, 110, 130.
Lodging-Houses, 243.
Lodging-Houses Boys', 429.
Loeser (Frederick) & Co., 874.
Loew Bridge, **44.**
Loew, E. V., 742, 762.
Logerot, Hotel de, 230, 152.
London Theatre, 605.
London Steamships, 83.
Long Branch, 55, 124.
Long-Distance Telephone, 210.
Long Island, 62, 55, 50, 69, 72, 185, 195.
Long-Island City, 50, 54, 134, 195.
Long-Island Railroad, 54, 134, 135, 195.
Long-Island Sound, 34, 50, 55, 60, 73, 102, 170.
Loomis Laboratory, **276,** 277, 838.
Loomis, Mathematician, 276.
Lord & Taylor, Broadway, **849.**
Lord & Taylor, Grand Street, **848, 838.**
Lord & Taylor, Old Store, **848.**
Lord, Daniel, 326.
Lord, G. W. T., 848.
Lord, Samuel, 848.
Lorillard, C. L., 515.
Lorillard, Pierre, 383.
Lorraine Library, 334.
Loss, G. W., 742.
Loth (Joseph) & Co., **974.**
Lotos Club, **549,** 68.
Lounsbury, P. C., 522, 685, 715, 767.
Lovelace, Col. F., 23, 109.
Lovers' Walk, **163.**
Lower Bay, 69, 72, 264.
Lower Broadway, **143.**
Lower Market Landing, **19.**
Lower Quarantine, 73.
Low, Nicholas, 703.
Low, Seth, 270.

Loyal Legion, 561.
Ludlow-Street Jail, **494, 257,** 256.
Lumber-Trade Assoc., 806.
Lummis, Wm., 767.
Lunacy Law Reform, 504.
Lunatic Asylums, 461.
Lutheran Cemetery, 522.
Lutheran Pilgrim House, **449.**
Lutherans, 17, 449, 382, 383, 389, 522.
Lutheran Society, 36, 383.
Luther's Bible, 330.
Lyceum Opera-House, 606.
Lyceum Theatre, 596.
Lying-in Hospital, 482, 778.
Lyman, Frank, 758.
Lyne's Map, **11.**
Lyon (Amasa) & Co., **975.**

MacArthur, R. S., 380.
Macdonald, Gordon, 770.
Macdonough, Jas., 914.
Mackay, Donald, 708.
Mackay, John W., 206, 208, 210.
Macready Riot, 579.
Macy, W. H., 758, 774.
Madison Avenue, 154, 243.
Madison-Ave. Baptist Church, **382,** 381.
Madison-Ave. Church, **375.**
Madison Ave.,from 42d St.,**151.**
Madison Ave., from 69th St., **151.**
Madison-Ave. Line, 137.
Madison-Ave. Presb. Ch., 369.
Madison-Ave. Ref. Ch., **341.**
Madison Cottage, 580.
Madison Square, **737,** 181, **182, 183, 144,** 166, 40, 153, 176, 152, 501, 505, 218, 230, 738.
Madison-Square Garden, **585, 583,** 584, 44. 66, 68, 446, 950, 148, 579.
Madison-Square Theatre, 597, 68, 148, 592.
Madison-Square Tower, 66.
Madison-Square Tower, Views from, **734, 735.**
Madison-Square Presbyterian Church, **368.**
Maennerchors, **317,** 319.
Magdalen Asylum, 438.
Magoun, G. C., 760, 774.
Mahommedanism, 406.
Maiden Lane, 18, 23, 24, 185, 505, 548.
Maidens' Path, 18.
Mail and Express, **615, 207,** 614, 46, 144.
Maimonides Library. 331, 745.
Maine Steamship Co:, 93.
Maitland, Phelps & Co., **751,** 662.
Maitland, T., 662.
Majestic, 79.
Mall, Central Park, **163,** 161, 178.
Mallory, Dr. G. S., 627.
Mallory Line, **97,** 92.
Mallory, Marshall H., 627.
Manhattan, 5, 7.
Manhattan Athletic Club, **564, 151,** 68.

Manhattan Bank, **705.**
Manhattan Bicycle Club, 568.
Manhattan Club, **545,** 68, 314, 153, 150.
Manhattan College, **284,** 286.
Manhattan Co., 645, 706, 758.
Manhattan Dispensary, **476.**
Manhattan Eye and Ear Hospital, **484.**
Manhattan Hospital, **476.**
Manhattan Island, 47, 50, 54, 192, 104, 69.
Manhattan Life-Ins. Co., **669, 637,** 668, 645, 143.
Manhattan Medical Soc., 491.
Manhattan Opera-House, 594.
Manhattan Railway, 138.
Manhattan Safe-Deposit and Storage Co., 666, 782.
Manhattan Savings - Institution, **780.**
Manhattan Square, 170, 306.
Manhattan Storage & Warehouse Co., **810, 811,** 838.
Manhattan Trust Co., **765.**
Manhattanville, 47. 137. 286.
Manhattan Water Works, **30,** 39, 196.
Manners, T. R., 745.
Manson, Geo. T., 931.
Manual Training Schools, 268.
MANUFACTURERS.—An Outline History of some Preëminent Industries Carried on or Represented in New York, 913-984.
Maps, **6, 8, 9, 11, 12, 13, 15.**
Marble Arch, **165,** 161.
Marble Cemetery, **506,** 510.
Marble Church. **337,** 338.
Maretzek, Max, 603, 578, 579.
Margaret Louisa Home, **417.**
Margaret Strachan Home, 439.
Marine Court, 261.
Marine Hospital, 483.
Marine Insurance, 639, 640.
Mariners' Church, 414.
Mariners' Family Asylum, 447.
Marine Underwriters, 799.
Maritime Association, 801.
Maritime Exchange, 802, 58.
Market and Fulton Bank, **727,** 728, 838.
Markets, 808.
Markets, Sup't of, 248.
Marlborough, Hotel, 236, 148.
Marquand, H. G., 304, 306, 314, 312, 332.
Marquand Pavilion. 459.
Martin, Hotel. 236.
Martyrs' Monument, **507,** 508.
Mason, E. S., 704.
Masonic Hall, 154, 608.
Masonic Library, 333.
Masonic Temple, **570,** 571.
Massage, College of, 280.
Materia Medica Soc., 491.
Maternity Home, 280, 482.
Mathematical Soc., 323.
Matsell, Geo. W., 524, 526.
Matthews, Geo. E., 4.
Matthews, Jas. M., 340.
Matthews-Northrup Co., 4.
Mausoleums, 866.

Maverick's Map, **13.**
Mayors, 258, 245, 247, 249.
Mayor, Aldermen and Commonalty, 245.
Mazzini Statue, **168,** 180.
McAlpin, D. H., 652, 672, 724.
McAnerney, John, 721.
McAuley, Jerry, 424.
McCall, John A., 736, 780.
McCay, John R., 662.
McCloskey, John, 284.
McClure, S. S., 636.
McClymonds, L. K., 930.
McComb's-Dam Bridge, 192.
McCord, Wm. H., 950.
McCreery (James) & Co., **852, 853,** 294, 146, 233.
McCurdy, R. A., 666, 769.
McGowan's Pass, 162.
McIntyre, T. A., 730.
McKim, Mead & White, 154, 272, 379, 545, 614.
McLean, Alex., 410.
McLean, J. M., 644.
McLoughlin, J., 749.
McVickar, Wm., 350.
Mechanical Engineers, **322.**
Mechanical Rubber Co., **930.**
Mechanics' and Traders' Exchange, 794.
Mechanics' and Tradesmen's Soc., 446, 329, 708.
Mechanics' Nat. Bank, **709,** 708, 950.
Meday, J. P., 981.
Medical College for Women. **481,** 280, 480.
Medical Inspectors, 457.
Medical Libraries, 333.
Medical Schools, 63, 272, 277.
Medical Societies, 491.
Medicine, Acad. of, 278.
Medico-Chirurgical Soc., 490.
Medico-Historical Soc., 491.
Medico-Legal Soc., 491.
Memorial Arch, **173, 966,** 172, 167, 505.
Menagerie. **166,** 161.
Menlo-Park Ceramic, **838.**
Mercantile Agency, 816.
Mercantile Credit Guarantee Co., **688.**
Mercantile Exchange, 803.
Mercantile Library, **328, 723,** 63, 150, 146. 579.
Mercantile Nat. Bank, **744, 207.**
Merchants' Bank, **692, 705.**
Merchants' Central Club, 558.
Merchants' Clerks' Savings Bank, **778.**
Merchants' Club, **558.**
Merchants' Coffee-House. 216.
Merchants' Exchange, 785, 790. 697, 522.
Merchants' Exchange Nat. Bank, **715,** 674.
Merchants' Nat. Bank, 706.
Meridian Club, 570.
Messiah Church, **386.**
Meteorological Observations, 672.
Methodist Book-Concern. **631,** 630, 150, 333, 408, 716, 852.

Methodist Church Home, **444.**
Methodist-Episcopal Church, 59, 374, 433.
Methodist Mission House, **631,**
Metropole, Hotel, 148, 236.
Metropolis, Bank of the, **740.**
Metropolitan Casino, 508.
Metropolitan Club, 68. 153, 545.
Metropolitan College of Music, 289.
Metropolitan Hotel, 233, 604.
Metropolitan Life - Ins. Co., **679,** 154, 677, 729, 838, 840.
Metropolitan Line, 93.
Metropolitan Museum, **304, 305,** 303, 44, 63, 66, 67, 136, 312, 407, 836.
Met. Museum Schools, 288.
Metropolitan Opera-House, **589, 743,** 587, 603, 66, 46, 67, 68, 148, 583, 838.
Metropolitan Plate-Glass Ins. Co., 683.
Metropolitan Railway, 138.
Metropolitan Telephone & Telegraph Co., **211, 212, 213, 214,** 210.
Metropolitan Trust Co., **764, 707,** 698.
Meyer, Heinrich, 882.
Meyer, Oscar R., 658.
Meyer, P. F., 866.
Michaelius. Rev. J., 336.
Microscopical Soc., 323.
Middle Dutch Church, **18, 337,** 25, 31, 45, 156, 329, 337, 505.
Midgley, Wm. E., 684.
Midnight Mission, 439.
Milhau's (J.) Son, **862,** 863.
Military Defences, 72.
Military Department of the East, 55, 72.
Military Museum, 72.
Military Service Inst., 72, 540.
Militia, 531, 40, 54.
Miller, C. R., 618.
Miller, G. C., 891.
Millionaires, 58.
Millionaires' Club, 545.
Mills & Gibb, **874.**
Mills, Andrew, 672, 777.
Mills Building, **823, 155,** 822, 154, 156, 58.
Mills, D. O., 312, 152, 280, 492, 704, 764, 771, 822.
Mills (D. O.) Training School, **281,** 280, 490, 587.
Mills, P. L., 874.
Mills, W. M., 748.
Milmine, Geo., 742.
Mines, School of, 273.
Mining, 938.
Mining Engineers, 322.
Minturn, R. B., 545, 721, 779.
Minuit, Peter, **5,** 336, 10, 12, 13, 20, 241, 523.
MISCELLANEOUS INSURANCE. — Companies for Providing against Accidents, Explosions, Broken Plate - Glass, Dishonest Employees. Loss of Salaries, and for Furnishing Bonds, 683–690.

Missionary College, 284.
Missionary Societies, 406, 59.
Mission of Our Lady of the Rosary, **449.**
Mitchell, Pringle, 317.
Mohawk & Hudson - River Railroad, 110, 114.
Mohawk Building, **887,** 150.
Monico, Hotel, 236.
Montague, Geo., 721, 738, 776, 782.
Montefiore Home, **452,** 440.
Montgomery, Col. John, 26.
Montgomery, Richard, **510,** 509, 344.
Monthly Publications, 634–636, 58.
Monumental Work, 866.
Moore, David M., 977.
Moore (E. C.) Collection, 304.
Moore Statue, **168,** 180.
Moravians, 59, 381, 390.
Morgan, A. J., 979.
Morgan, Dr. D. P., 352.
Morgan, E. D., 567, 764.
Morgan (Enoch) Sons Co., **979.**
Morgan, G. F., 979.
Morgan, J. Pierpont, 291, 308, 351, 312, 545, 587. 588, 751, 722, 838.
Morgan Line, **120,** 96, 71.
Morgen Journal, 622.
Morgue, 461, 470.
Morning Advertiser, 626.
Morning Journal, 622.
Morningside Heights. 293.
Morningside Park, **363, 473,** 364, 148, 166, 67.
Morrisania, **114,** 47, 172, 493.
Morris Building, 45, 730.
Morrison, D. M., 766, 767, 776.
Morse Building, **831,** 830, 561, 628.
Morse, S. F. B., **164,** 40, 308, 326, 287, 275, 276, 180, 508.
Morse Statue, **164.**
Mortimer Building, **842.**
Morton, Bliss & Co., 752, 766.
Morton House, 148, 233.
Morton, L. P., 312, 348, 677, 742, 290.
Moss, Theodore, 593, 600.
Most Holy Redeemer, 66.
Mothers' Home, 482.
Mott Haven, **112, 132,** 47.
Mott Memorial Library, **333.**
Mott Street, **158,** 439.
Mott, Valentine, 333, 184. 277.
Mounted-Police Station, **527.**
Mount Hope Cemetery, 519.
Mount-Morris Bank, **742.**
Mount-Morris Park, **175, 150.**
Mount-Sinai Hospital, **470, 471, 290,** 469, 62.
Mount-Sinai Nurses' Home, **529.**
Mount St. Vincent, **288,** 286, 47.
Muhlenberg, W. A., 357, 472.
Mulberry-Bend, **159,** 171.
Municipal Administration, 50.
Municipal Art Society, 312.
Municipal Ordinances, 246.
Murray, H. A., 769.
Murray Hill, 28, 30, 38.

Murray-Hill Hotel, **840,** 230, 68.
Murray Street, **52.**
Murray, Wm., 526, 528.
Museum of Art. **304, 305,** 303, 302, 63, 68, 66, 67, 136, 181, 312.
Museum of Natural History, **307,** 306, 321, 333, 322, 236, 302.
Music, 317.
Music, Acad. of, 68.
Music Hall, **591,** 590, 406, 44, 68.
Mutual Fire Ins. Co., **657.**
Mutual Life Building, 58, 66, 45, 788.
Mutual Life-Ins. Co., **665, 769,** 664, 647, 337, 144, 156, 505, 522, 752.
Mutual Reserve Life Assoc., **681,** 680, 824, 144.
Mygatt, L. C., 301.

Name New York, 22, 23.
Narrows, 33, 37, 50, 55, 69, 72, 73, 93, 540, 576.
Nash, W. A., 703, 730.
Nassau Boat Club, 568.
Nassau Street, **619,** 26, 156.
Nation, The, **611,** 628.
Nat. Acad. of Design, **309,** 308, 314, 66, 67, 287.
National Banking Act, 695.
National Banking Assoc., 703.
Nat. Bank of Commerce, **722.**
National Bank of the Republic, **725,** 724, 703.
National City Bank, **713,** 710.
National Guard, **568,** 39, 46, 54, 171, 262, 538, 531, 532.
National Hospitals, 474.
National Line, 83.
Nat. Park Bank, **733,** 732, 144, 830, 838.
Nat. Shoe and Leather Bank, **728,** 838.
National Tube Works, **933.**
National Wall-Paper Co., **955, 953, 954,** 953.
Natural History Museum, **307,** 306, 321, 302, 322, 333, 170, 266, 155, 273, 236.
Nautical School, 62, 292.
Naval Battalion, **539,** 538, 531.
Naval Militia, 538.
Naval Officer, 786.
Navarro Flats, 243.
Navy-Yard, 55, 71, 542.
Nazro, H. H., 740.
Needlework Guild, 454.
Negroes, 24, 42, 158, 505, 808.
Negro Riot of 1741, 335, 391.
Neighborhood Guild, 421.
Nelson, Stuart G., 742.
Nesbitt, D. A., 982.
Netherlands-Am. Co., **90,** 84.
Nevius & Haviland, 955.
New Amsterdam, 44, 245, 523.
New Amsterdam, Bank, 698.
New-Amsterdam Eye and Ear Hospital, 485.
Newark, **99.**
Newburgh, 104, 105, 113.
New City Hall, 257, 262, 581.

New Club, 547.
New - England Soc., 454, 449, 180, 563.
New Hampshire, 539, 538.
New-Jersey Central R. R., 124, 54.
New-Jersey Southern, 54.
New Jerusalem Church, 388,
New Netherland, Hotel, 219, 105, 218, 68, 152.
New - Orleans Steamers, 70, 96.
New Park System, 171.
News, 623, 620.
Newsboys' Lodging, 60.
Newspaper Row, 623, 581.
Newspapers, 58, 331.
New Year's, 32.
New York, 77, 76, 70.
N.-Y. & Cuba S. S. Co., 98.
N.-Y. & Harlem R. R., 111, 54, 115, 136.
N.-Y. & New-England R. R., 133, 134.
N.-Y. & N.-J. Bridge Co., 194.
N.-Y. & Northern Railway, 54, 134, 192, 193.
N.-Y. & Texas Steamers, 97.
N.-Y. Athletic Club, 565, 68.
New York, Bank of, 692, 701.
N.-Y. Belting & Packing Co., 929, 928, 930.
N.-Y. Biscuit Co., 945, 944, 746.
N.-Y. Boat Oar Co., 969.
N.-Y. Bowery Fire-Ins. Co., 642.
N.-Y. Central & Hudson River R. R., 110, 111, 112, 113, 197, 814, 83, 114, 115, 116, 131, 192, 193, 194, 54, 37, 417, 587, 522.
N.-Y. City Consolidation Act, 245.
N.-Y. City Dispensary. 487.
N.-Y. City Mission. 59
New-York Club, 546, 68, 314, 153, 545.
N.-Y. College of Music, 290.
N.-Y. College of Pharmacy, 280, 279.
N.-Y. College of Veterinary Surgeons, 281.
N.-Y. Conservatory, 290.
N.-Y. Eye and Ear Infirmary. 62.
N.-Y. Fruit Exchange, 806.
N.-Y. Guarantee, Indem. & Security Co., 769.
New-York Harbor, 331, 69.
N.-Y. Historical Soc., 331, 330, 34, 66, 63, 67, 320, 45.
N.-Y. Hospital, 464, 463, 333, 62, 280, 466, 482, 483, 491, 884.
New York in 1728. 11.
New York in 1746, 18, 19.
New York in 1775, 17.
New York in 1778, 15.
New York in 1779, 13.
New York in 1805, 26.
New York in 1851, 35.
N.-Y., Lake-Erie & Western R. R., 129.
N.-Y. Life-Insurance & Trust Co., 757, 755, 663.
N.-Y. Life-Ins. Co., 667, 666, 663, 144.

N.-Y. Maennerchor 317, 319.
N.-Y. Marble Cemetery, 511.
N.-Y., New-Haven & Hartford, R. R., 111, 54, 132, 133, 193.
N.-Y. Observer, 629, 628.
NEW YORK OF THE PRESENT.— A Comprehensive Outline of the Whole City—Area, Population, Wealth, etc., 47-68.
New-York, Ontario & Western R. R., 128.
N.-Y. Photogravure Co., 964, 4.
N.-Y. Plate-Glass Ins. Co., 690.
N.-Y. Press Club, 555, 554.
N.-Y. Produce Exchange. 795, 796, 794.
N.-Y. Security & Trust Co., 755.
N.-Y. Society Library, 329, 63.
New York, The Name, 22.
N.-Y. Times, 619, 42, 625.
N.-Y. Trade School, 274, 291.
N.-Y. Turn-Verein, 567, 566.
N.-Y. Underwriters' Agency, 656, 648, 657.
New-York University, 320, 323, 332, 340.
N.-Y. Yacht Club, 567, 106.
Niagara Fire-Ins. Co., 647.
Niblo's Theatre, 146, 582, 233.
Niblo, Wm., 543, 604.
Night Schools, 311.
Niles, Nathaniel. 830.
Nilsson, Christine, 588.
Nineteenth-Ward Bank, 745, 744.
Ninth-Avenue Line, 137.
Ninth National Bank, 739, 738, 144.
Ninth Regiment. 531, 535.
Nivin, W. B., 745.
Noble, W.. 227.
Normal College, 270, 271, 260, 268, 62.
Normandie, Hotel, 226, 148.
North America. Bank, 692.
North American Review, 636.
North Battery, 32, 40.
North British & Mercantile Ins. Co. 658, 7, 2.
North Brother Island, 62.
Northern Assurance Co . 660.
Northern Dispensary 488.
North German Lloyd Line, 85, 84, 91, 83.
North-River Bridge, 194, 195.
North-River Ferry-Boat, 119.
Northrop, H. D., 748.
Northwestern Dispensary, 489.
Norwegian Relief Soc., 447, 474.
Norwich Line, 102, 133.
Numbering of Houses, 33, 51.
Numismatic Society, 322, 333.
Nursery and Child's Hospital, 480.
Nurses' Homes 471, 497, 499.
Nurses' Training-Schools, 460.

Obelisk, 160 181, 819.
Observer, 629, 628, 824, 372.
Ocean Greyhounds, 55, 75, 155.
Ocean Steamship Co., 95.
Odd-Fellows' Library, 333.

Oelbermann, Dommerich & Co., 878.
Oelbermann. E., 656.
Oelrichs & Co., 86, 708.
Office-Buildings, 819, 58.
Ogden, D. B., 686.
Ogilvie, J. H., 760.
Ohio Society, 560.
Okonite Co.. 931.
Old Brewery. 424, 423.
Old Custom House in 1825, 29.
Old Dominion Steamships 94.
Old Fort, Central Park, 169.
Old Guard, 560.
Old London Streets, 581.
Old Merchants' Exch., 784.
Olympic Theatre, 582, 645.
Omnibuses, 136.
110th-Street Trestle. 135.
123d Street, 150.
Opera, 67.
Ophthalmic Institute, 484, 480.
Ophthalmic Hospital, 473, 62, 280. 483
Ophthalmological Society, 491.
Orangemen, 42.
Orange Riots, 532.
Oratorio Society, 68, 318, 320.
Oregon Iron Works, 951.
Oriental Hotel, 595, 148.
Orphan Asylums, 430.
Orphan Asylum Society, 431.
Orphans' Home. 431.
Orr, Alex. E., 708. 723, 742, 758, 769.
Ortgies & Co , 315.
Orthopedic Dispensary, 486.
Osborn (John), Son & Co., 899.
Otis Bros. & Co., 925, 924, 824.
Otis Elevators, 227, 672, 826, 830, 848.
Otis, Norton P., 924.
Ottendorfer Library, 488.
Ottendorfer, Oswald, 445, 312, 312, 6 3.
Our Lady of the Rosary, 449.
Outing, 636.
OVERHEAD AND UNDERFOOT.— Bridges, Tunnels, Sewers, Water, Aqueducts, Reservoirs, Lighting, Telegraph, Telephone, etc. 185-214.
Oyer & Terminer, 260, 262, 254.
Oyster Market, 802, 809.

Packard's Business College, 294.
Pacific Mail Line, 101.
Packard, Edwin, 769.
Packard's Business College, 294.
Packard, S. S., 295.
Packet Lines, 74.
Page, J. Seaver, 949.
Paintings, 320, 314, 306, 327, 326.
Palmer A. M., 446, 602, 554, 592, 537.
Palmer's Theatre, 592, 593, 68, 148.
Paper, 899, 901.
Paris, 77, 76.
Parish, Henry, 755, 756.
Parish School, 295.

Park Avenue, 150, **197**, 193, 42.
Park-Avenue Hotel, **229.**
Park-Ave. M. E. Church, **377.**
Park Bank, Nat., **733,** 732, 144.
Park Commissioners, 249.
Parker, Jas. H., 545.
Parkhurst, C. H., 368, 504.
Park Row, from Mail St., 681.
Park Place, from Broadway, **247.**
Park Police, 528.
Park Presb. Church, **371,** 370.
Park Row, **366, 251, 619, 623,** 190, 156, 262, 144, 266, 577, 600.
Parks 67, 159, 249.
Parks, Dep't of Pub , 249, 51, 191, 578.
Park Theatre, 576, 33, 148, 562, 583, 600.
Parkways, 172.
Passavant & Co., **882.**
Pastels, Painters in. 311.
Pastor's (Tony) Theatre, 604, 605, 5b3.
Pathological Cabinet, 463.
Patrol, **526,** 525, 74.
Patrol Wagon, 525.
Patroons, .6. 17.
Patti, Adelina, 578, 579, 580, 586, 236.
Paulist Fathers, 397, 636.
Paxton, J. R., 367.
Peabody (Henry W.) & Co., **92, 93.**
Pearl Street, 10, 17, 18, 23.
Pearson, H. G., 266.
Pease, Geo. L., 729.
Peck Slip, **80,** 17.
Pelham-Bay Park, 67, 171.
Pembrook, T. K., 875
Pembrook, W. A., 875.
Penitentiary, **496, 499,** 459.
Pennsylvania Railroad, **117, 118, 119,** 54, 116, 133. 70.
Penny Provident Fund, 454.
Pension Office, 542, 781.
People's Church, 370.
Perkins. E. H., Jr , 703, 672.
Perkins Geo. W., 723.
Perkins, Wm. H., 710.
Perry, F. I., 891.
Personal Property, 51.
Peters, Dr. T. M., 433. 362.
Peters, Madison C., 341.
Petroleum, 916, 930, 932, 792.
Petroleum Jelly, 048.
Pfeiffer, G. F., 908.
Pharmacy, College of, **280,** 270, 863, 862.
Phelps, Dodge & Co., 712.
Phelps, W. W., 758.
Phenix Insurance Co., 662.
Philadelphia, 26, 47, 74, 79, 94, 32, 34 40, 109, 116, 118, 122, 128, 131, 712.
Philharmonic Soc . 317, 68.
Phillips Presb. Church, 370
Photograph Depot, 315.
Photogravure (N.-Y.) Co., **964.**
Phrenological Journal, 324.
Phrenology Institute of, **324.**
Physical Culture, 296.

Physicians and Surgeons, 274, 487, 467, 479.
Pianos, 942.
Picture-Sales, 315.
Piers. 70, 69, 51.
Pilgrim Statue, **165,** 180.
Pilots. 264.
Pim, Forwood & Co., 101.
Pintard, John, 320. 639, 773.
Pipe Lines, 185, 930. 932.
Pitcher, J. R., 688, 714.
Plate-Glass Insurance 690, 683.
Platt, Edw. C., 206, 210.
Players, **554,** 553. 68 313, 170.
Playgrounds for Children, 455.
Play-houses, 148, 582.
Plaza Bank, **747.**
Plaza Hotel **223,** 222, **105,** 152.
Plymouth. 14, 20.
Pneumatic Tubes, 210.
Police, .57, 5', 73.
Police Boat *Patrol,* **526.**
Police Courts, **56,** 493, 501, 261, 254, 525.
Police Dept., 245, 523, 524, 527, 525, 240, 504.
Police Headquarters. **525,** 526.
Police Justices 51. 253.
Police Parade, **867.**
Police Pension Fund. 541, 527.
Polish Benevolent Soc., 447.
Polish Jews. 400.
Political Clubs, 561.
Political Divisions, 51.
Political-Science School, 273.
Polytechnic Assoc., 321.
Pope Manufacturing Co., **968.**
Popular Science Monthly, 636.
Population, 47.
Portraits, 258, 310. 557, 788.
Port Society Library, 333, 414.
Portuguese, 400.
Port-Wardens. 264, 265.
Postal Telegraph Cable Co., **209,** 206, 208. 144. 676.
Post & McCord, **950.**
Post, G. B., 618. 626
Post-Graduate Medical School, **278,** 490, 477, 279.
Postmasters, 266.
Post-Office, **37, 251, 265, 619,** 260, 55, 137, 332, 45, 144, 156, 170. 838, 981.
Post-Office Stations, 266
Post, William 949.
Potter, Bishop, 341, 364, 381, 556.
Potter Building, **825,** 824, **251.** 810, 58, 144, 622, 626.
Potter, O. B., 758, 773, 824.
Potter's Field, 40, 505, 167, 256.
Potter, W. A., 348, 362.
Pottier, Stymus & Co., **855.**
Powers, Jas. G., 715.
Powers, Jesse W., 715.
Pratt, Dallas B., 425, 710, 751.
Prayer-Meetings, 339.
Precincts. 575.
Preferred Mutual Accident Association, **685.**
Presbyterian Home. **442.**
Presbyterian Hospital, **151,** 469, 468, 62, 836, 950.
Presbyterian House, **409,** 408.
Presbyterians, 59, 282, 365.

Press, 622, 824.
Press Bureau, 501.
Press Club, **555,** 554, 522.
Prevention of Crime Soc., 503.
Prevention of Cruelty. **503.**
Primary Schools, **619,** 62.
Printing, 27, 327, 913, 971.
Printing-House Square, **178, 176,** 156, 835, 618
Printing-House Sq. in 1868,**614.**
Printing-Presses, 956.
Prisons, 212.
Private Detectives, 528.
Private Schools, 299, 63.
Private Watchmen, 528.
Proctor's 23d-Street Theatre, **599,** 601.
Produce Exchange, **795, 64, 128, 141, 143, 676, 155,** 794, 66, 203, 333, 58, 802, 142, 730, 541, 821.
Produce-Exchange Bank, 729.
Progreso Italo-Americano, 182, 622
Progress Club, **551,** 153.
Property Clerk 526.
Protection Against Fire, 528.
Protectories, 434. 302.
Protestant Episcopalians, 59, 438, 439, 440, 443, 445, 341.
PROTECTION AND DEFENSE.— Police Department, Military and Militia, Army and Pension Offices, Fire Department, Fire Patrol, Detectives, etc.. 523-542.
Providence Line, 102.
Provident-Savings Life-Assurance Soc. **680,** 678.
Provincial Congress, 29, 787
Public Administration, 253.
Public Charities and Correction, **421,** 419, 434, 450, 459, 460, 453, 461. 494, 498, 496, 256.
Public Parks Dep't, 51, 204, 193.
Public Schools. 267.
Public Works Dep't, 246, 249.
Publishing, 27 58, 913.
Puck Building, **638,** 636.
Pulitzer Building, 58, 216, 620.
Pulitzer, Joseph, 620
Pullen, Eugene H., 703, 724.
Pumping Machinery, 922.
Pure Science, 274.
Puritans, Church of, **371.**
Pyne, Percy R., 710, 771.

Quadrangle, Columbia, **273.**
Quakers. 335, 389.
Quarantine, 72, 46, 457, 251.
Quarantine Com., 252.
Quill Club, 552.
Quinlan, Jr., Wm. J., 714.
Quinlan, James, 775, 776.
Quintard, G. W., 720, 672.

Rachel, 236, 580.
Racquet and Tennis Club, **566,** 296, 298.
Railroad Y. M. C. A., **415,** 417.
Railways, 37, 97, 110, 695.
Rainsford, W. S., 351.
Ramble, 161, 181.
Ramsdell Line. **104.**

Randall's Island, 47, 62, 455, 460. 426, 500, 501.
Rand, A. C., 559, 740.
Rand Drill Co., **938**, 559.
Randel, Baremore & Billings, **864.**
Rapid Transit, 140, 744.
Rate of Taxation, 249.
Raymond, R. W., 322.
Raynolds, C. T., 049.
Reading Railroad System, **121.**
Reading-Rooms, 325, 429.
Real Estate, 804, 805.
Real Estate Valuation, 51.
Receiving Department, **499.**
Receiving Tomb, **521.**
Reception Hospital, 62, 457.
Reconciliation, Chapel, 361.
Recorder, 253, 51, 261.
Recorder, 626.
Record of Am. Shipping, 799.
Red Cross Steamships, 92.
Red " D " Line, 101.
Red Star Line, **89**, 88, 79, 38.
Reference Library, 326.
REFORMATORIES AND CORREC-
TIONS.--The Police Courts, Prisons, House of Refuge, Penitentiaries, House of Correction. etc., 493-504.
Reform Club, **563**, 152, 564.
Reformed Church Building, 409.
Ref. Dutch Church, 59, 323, 335, 337, 339.
Reformed Episcopal Church, **391**, 390.
Reformed Presb. Church, 365, 371, 59.
Refuge for Convicts. **504.**
Regina Sodalium, **184.**
Register of Records, **252.**
Register's Hall, 252.
Register's Office, 252.
Reid, Whitelaw, 154, 618.
Relief of Respectable Indigent Females, **441.**
Religious Papers, 610 627-633.
Religious Work, 59, 418.
Remensnyder, J. B., 383.
Remington Typewriter, 958.
Renwick, James, 350, 373, 391.
Republican Club, **563**, 153.
Republic, Nat. Bank of, **725.**
Reservoir, Fifth Avenue, **200.**
Reservoir, Old, **30.**
Reservoir Park, 170.
Reservoirs, 54, 199, 161, 153, 170.
Restaurants. 237.
RETAIL ESTABLISHMENTS.-- Interesting and Prominent Retail Concerns, nearly all being Leading Houses, 843-870.
Revolution, Sons of, 184.
Revenue, City, 249.
Rhine Steamboats, 90.
Rhoades, J. H., 758, 775.
Rice Traffic. 904.
Richards, E. O., 966.
Richardson (G. C.) & Co.. 880.
Riding Club, **568**, 569, 572.
Riding School, **291, 297.**
Riker, John L., 704, 644, 686, 738, 743, 748, 776.

Ringler (F. A.) Co., **971.**
Riverdale Presb. Church, 373.
Riverdale Station, **112**, 286.
Riverside Drive, **818**, 431.
Riverside Hospital, 62, 457.
Riverside Park, **861**, **907**, 67, 174, 148, 162.
Riverside Rest Assoc., 438.
Rivington's Gazetteer, 27, 29.
Robbins, G. A., 756.
Roberts, Ellis H., 698, 749.[1]
Roberts, M. O , 518, 602, 844.
Robertson, R. H., 355, 417, 419.
Robins, E. B., 885.
Robinson, G. B., 742.
Robinson, T. W., 742.
Rockaway Beach, 50, 134, 481.
Rockefeller, Wm., 152, 726, 758, 840, 854, 916.
Rodoph Sholom Synagogue, **869, 404.**
Roebling, 185, 186, 188.
Roelandsen, Adam, 14, 267, 336.
Rogers, Henry A., **905**, 721.
Rogers, Theodore, 740.
Rogue's Gallery. 527.
Rollins, Daniel G., 454
Rolston, Roswell G., 712, 771.
Roman Cath. Cathedral, **393**, **392, 394**, 391.
Roman-Catholic Orphan Asylum, **394.**
Roman Catholics, 59, 391.
Rome, Watertown & Ogdensburg R. R., 116.
Roosevelt Hospital, **467**, 466.
Roosevelt, J. A., 643, 644, 714, 743, 756, 773.
Root, C. F.. 806. 634.
Rose Hill, 284, 381.
Rosevear, Thomas, 853.
Rossiter Stores 814.
Rossiter, Wm. W., 730.
Roumania Opera-House, 605.
Royal Blue Line, 123, 128, 140.
Royal Dutch Line, 102.
Royal Exchange, 26.
Rubenstein Soc., 318.
RULE OF THE CITY.--The City, County, State and National Government -- Officers and Buildings, Courts. 245-266.
Ruptured and Crippled, **486.**
Russell & Erwin Mfg. Co., **939.**
Russian Immigrants, 453.
Russian Restaurants, 240.
Rutgers College, 298, 352.
Rutgers Fire-Ins. Co., **651.**
Rutgers Presb. Church, **372.**
Rylance, Dr. J. H., 352.

Sabbath Committee, 412.
Sacred Heart Academy, **287, 286.**
Safe-Deposit Vaults, 811, 753.
Sagamore Club, **562.**
Sage, Russell, 44, 155.
Sailors' Snug Harbor, 446.
St. Agnes' Chapel, **348**, 342, 347.
St. Agnes' Hall, 438.
St. Ambrose Chapel, 407.
St. Andrew's Church, **400, 356.**
St. Andrew's Coffee-Stands, 241.
St. Andrew's Hospital, 482.

St. Andrew's M. E. Church, **375,** 376.
St. Andrew's Society, 447.
St. Ann's Church, 350, 358.
St.-Ann's Home, 435.
St.-Anthony Club, **552.**
St. Anthony's Monastery, **834.**
St Augustine's Chapel, **347,** 346, 519, 342.
St.-Barnabas' House, 437, 407.
St.-Barnabas Library, 334.
St. Bartholomew's Chinese Guild, 449.
St. Bartholomew's Church, **358, 151**, 449.
St. Bartholomew's Hospital, 486.
St. Bartholomew's House, **359.**
St. Benedict's Church, **396.**
St. Bernard's Church, **401**, 400.
St. Catharine's Convent, **289.**
St. Cecilia's Church, **399**, 400.
St. Christopher's Home. 433.
St. Chrysostom's Chapel, **346.**
St. Chrysostom's Disp., 489.
St. Cloud Hotel, 148.
St. Cornelius' Chapel. 347.
St. David's Society, 448.
St.-Denis Hotel, **232**, 148.
St. Elizabeth's Hospital, 476.
St.-Francis Hospital, 836, 475.
St. Francis Xavier, **285**, 397.
St.-Francis Xavier Coll.. **285.**
St. Gaudens, Augustus, 66, 176, 352, 312, 354, 356, 385.
St. George, 123, 135, 170.
St. George's Church, **351**, 350, 66, 341, 342.
St. George's Club, 559.
St. George's Memorial House, **352,** 351.
St. Ignatius' Church, 350.
St. James' Church, **354.**
St.-James Hotel, 226, 148, 857.
St. James' Luth. Church, **383.**
St. James' M. E. Church, **378,** 377.
St. James' Theatre, 596, 598.
St. John's Burying Ground, 512.
St. John's Chapel, **344, 654.**
St. John's College, **184**, 183, 284.
St. John's Guild, 427.
St. John's River, 93.
St. John the Divine, **363**, 362.
St. John, Wm. P., 723, 724, 744, 738.
St. Joseph's Asylum, 430.
St. Joseph's Day Nursery, 426.
St. Joseph's Deaf Mutes Institute. 298.
St. Joseph's Home, 302, 435.
St. Joseph's Home for the Aged, **442**, 443.
St. Joseph's Hospital, **477.**
St. Joseph's Refuge, 439.
St. Joseph's Union, **435.**
St. Lazarus' Guild, 440, 485.
St.-Louis College, 286.
St. Luke's Chapel, **353**, 342.
St. Luke's **355**, 442, 519.
St. Luke's Churchyard, 512.
St. Luke's Home, 412.
St. Luke's Hospital, **472. 473**, 471, 62, 153, 357.

St. Mark's Church, **351**, 22, 342.
St. Mark's Churchyard, 511.
St. Mark's Hospital, 477.
St. Mark's Library, 334.
St. Mark's Place, **865**.
St. Mary's, **99**, 292.
St. Mary's Free Hospital, **481**.
St. Mary's Lodging-House, 437.
St. Mary's Park, 67, 477, 172.
St. Mary's School, 287.
St. Mary the Virgin **353**, 360.
St. Matthew's Academy, 287.
St. Matthew's Church, 382.
St. Michael's, **353**, 433, 438, 362.
St. Nicholas, 636.
St. Nicholas' Church, 14, 336, 341.
St.-Nicholas Club, **547**, 546, 153.
St.-Nicholas Soc., 572.
St. Patrick's Cathedral, **392**, **393, 394**, 391, 395, 66, 67, 152, 522
St. Patrick's Church, **396**, 394, 506, 559.
St. Paul's Chapel, **345**, 49, 144, 431.
St. Paul's Churchyard, **509**.
St. Paul the Apostle, **397**.
St. Peter's Church, **394**.
St. Stephen's, 396.
St. Thomas' Chapel, 354.
St. Thomas' Church, **353**, **147**, 152, 67.
St. Timothy, **353**, 359.
St. Vincent de Paul, 421.
St. Vincent de Paul's Soc., 422.
St. Vincent de Paul's Asylum, **434**.
St. Vincent Ferrers, **290**, 286.
St. Vincent's Hospital, 62, 474, 836.
Salmagundi Club, 311, 552.
Salvation Army, 414.
Samaritan Home for Aged, 444.
Samson, G. W., 298.
Sands, B. A., 814.
Sandy Hook, 54, 55, 69, 72, 73, 93.
Sandy-Hook Bay, 69.
Sandy-Hook Pilots, 265.
Sandy-Hook Route, 123.
San Francisco, 120.
San-Francisco Minstrels, 600.
Santiago de Cuba, 98.
Sanitary Aid Society, 492.
Sanitary Code, 457.
Sanitary Commission, 42, 545, 385.
Sanitary Condition, 457.
SANITARY ORGANIZATIONS.—
Board of Health and Health Statistics, Hospitals, Dispensaries, Morgue, Curative Institutions, Insane and other Asylums, 457–492.
Sanitary Superintendent, 251.
San Remo, Hotel, 155, 236, 243.
Sapolio, 979.
Saunders, Frederick, 326.
Saunders, Henry M., 381.
Savannah Steamships, **95**, 71.
Savings, Bank for, **773**, 772.
Savings Banks, 720, 730, 772, 782, 58.

Savings of Merchants' Clerks, **778**.
Savoy, Hotel, **221**, 220, **105**, 66, 68, 937, 152.
Scandinavians, 376.
Scheffer's (Ary) *Christus Consolator*, 352.
Schell, Edw., 721, 670, 645, 780.
Schell, Robert, 740.
Schenck, V. R., 684.
Schieffelin (W. H.) & Co., **911**.
Schieren (C. A.) & Co., **940**.
Schiff, J. H., 332.
Schiller Bust, **164**, 181.
Schwab, G. H., 708.
Scientific Organizations, 320.
School Buildings, 62, 267.
Schoolcraft, H. R., 322.
School of Mines, 270.
School-Ship **99**.
Schwab, Gustav H., 758.
Schwartz, F. A. O., **860**.
Schwartz, H. F., 860.
Science, Night School of, 290, 311
Sciences, Academy of, 321.
Scotch Presb. Church, 365.
Scots, 178, 559.
Scott & Bowne Building, **829**, 828.
Scott, Col. Thos. A., 118.
Scottish Rite Hall, 571, 608.
Scott, J. W., 868.
Scott's Emulsion, 828.
Scott Stamp & Coin Co., 868.
Scott Statue, **168**, 178.
Scribner, G. H., 743.
Scribner's (Chas.) Sons, 965, 732.
Scribner's Magazine, 636, 59.
Sculpture, 172.
Seaboard Nat. Bank, **741**.
Seal of the City, 260.
Seaman, Robert, 715, 932, 934.
Seaman's Bank for Savings, **774**, 838, 715.
Seamen's Children, 447.
Seamen's Christian Assoc., 447.
Seamen's Friend Soc., 333, 414.
Seamen's Libraries, 333.
Seamew, 10.
Searle, H. A., 738.
Searles, John E., 814.
Searls, W. D., 771.
Sears, Isaac, 29.
Seaside Hospital, 428.
Seawanhaka Yacht Club, **567**.
Secession War, 534.
Second Avenue, 158.
Second-Avenue Bridge, **196**.
Second-Avenue Elevated Railroad, 137, 937.
Second Battery, 538, 537, 531.
Second Collegiate Church, **339**.
Second National Bank, **737**, 721.
Seep, Joseph, 742.
Seidl, Anton, 318.
Seligman, Jesse, 743.
Seminaries, 299.
Semler, George, 908.
Senatorial Districts, 51.
Seton Hospital, 477.
Seventh Avenue, **861**, 154.
Seventh Ave. and 125th St., **907**.

Seventh-Avenue Line, 137.
Seventh Nat. Bank, **857**, **721**.
Seventh Reg., **533**, 531, 532, 982, 40.
Seventh-Reg. Statue, **165**, 180.
Seventh-Reg. Veteran Club, 561, 153, 747.
Seventh-Street Church, 374.
Seventy-First Reg., **537**, 531.
79th Regiment Armory, 599.
Seward (W. H.) Club, 563.
Seward (W. H.) Statue, **181**, 176, 166.
Sewell, Robert, 684.
Sewers, 204, 51, 185.
Shade-Rollers, 955.
Shaarai Tephila, **403**.
Shakespeare Society, 553.
Shakespeare Statue, **168**, 173.
Shakespeariana, 63, 553.
Sheldon, Henry, 708.
Sheldon, R. K., 745.
Sheltering Arms, **433**.
Shepard, A. D., 914.
Shepard, E. F., 616, 914, 46, 418, 147.
Sherer, Wm., 703.
Sheriff, 264, 51, 494, 256.
Sherman, A. W., 716.
Sherman Bank, **748**.
Sherman, George, 738, 762.
Sherman Statue, 184.
Sherman, W. W., 722.
Sherry's Hall, 608.
Shillaber, William, 820.
Shipbuilders' Home, 292.
Shipbuilding, 274, 778.
Ship Canal, 194, 70.
Shipman, J. S., 350.
Shipping, 55.
Shoe & Leather Bank, **728**.
Shooting Clubs, 569.
Shopping, 843.
Shot Tower, **64**.
SHRINES OF WORSHIP.—Cathedrals, Churches, Synagogues and other Places of Worship and Work, 335–418.
Sichron Ephraim Synagogue, **404**, 405.
Sick Children's Mission, 429.
Siegel Bros., **888**.
Sigma Phi Club, 555.
Signal Corps, 537, 531.
Silberhorn, Henry, 642, 652, 720.
Silks, 853, 886.
Silleck, D. C., 782.
Sill, T. H., 346.
Silvey, J. A., 656.
Simmons, J. E., 703.
Sinking Fund, 249, 51.
Sisters of Charity, 260, 286, **426**.
Sisters of Mercy, 435, 437.
Sisters of Notre Dame, 430.
Sisters of St. Dominic, 434.
Sisters of Good Shepherd, 435.
Sisters of the Poor of St. Francis, 475, 477.
Sixth Avenue, 154.
Sixth-Avenue Railroad, 137.
Sixty-Ninth Regiment, 536, 531.
Skating in the Park, **746**.
Skin and Cancer Hosp., 440, 485.
Skinner, Thomas, 210.

Slaves, 24.
Slip Battery, 18.
Sloane Brothers, 516.
Sloane Maternity Hospital, 62, 274, 478, 417.
Sloane, Wm. D., 478, 274, 147, 740.
Sloane, W. & J., **851**, 846, 740.
Sloan, Samuel, 712 740, 771.
Sloughter, Gov., 25, 351, 512.
Slum Posts, 414.
Smith, C. S., 708, 758, 788, 880.
Smith, C. V., 688.
Smith, E. P., 706. 884.
Smith, Hogg & Gardner, **881.**
Smith, Jer. T., **838**, 678.
Smith, J. J., 972.
Smith, J. W., 645.
Smith, Sir Donald A., 210.
Smith, S. W., 880.
Smith, Wm. A., 770.
Smith, W. Merle. 370.
Snug Harbor, 446.
SOCIABILITY AND FRIENDSHIP.
—Clubs and Social Associa-
·tions, Secret and Friendship
Organizations. 543-574.
Société Français, 448.
Society of War of 1812, 561.
Society Library, **329**, 666.
Society for Ethical Culture, 434, 290.
Soda, 962.
Soldiers 531. 42.
Somerville, Robert, 315.
Sons of Liberty, 28, 29, 216.
Sons of the Revolution, 184.
Sorosis, 323. 570, 152.
Soulard, A. L, 683.
Sounding Boards, 941.
South-American Coast, 93.
South-American Shipping, 155.
Southampton, 76, 86.
South Battery, 540.
Southern Pacific Company, **120, 96.**
Southern Society, 560.
South Ferry, **134,** 137, 139.
South Manchester, 886.
South Ref. Church, **340,** 339.
South River, 70.
South Street, **82, 153,** 155.
Spaarndam, **90.**
Spanish Mail Line, 98.
Spanish Residents, 50, 449, 184.
Spanish Benevolent Soc., 447.
Spanish Cooking. 240.
Spanish Synagogue, 310.
Sparrow Cops, 828.
Spaulding, H. F., 708.
Special Libraries, 333.
Special Sessions, 262, 253, 254, 494.
Spining. G. L., 370, 618.
Spire Cross, 346, 379.
Spirit of the Times, 626.
Spiritualists, 406.
Sprague, C. E., 781.
Spree, **85.**
Spring, Gardiner, 366, 275.
Spuyten Duyvil, 47, 114, 193, 194, 19', 140, 148 477. 373.
Spuyten-Duyvil Creek, 25, 70.
Staats Zeitung, **56, 57,** 144, 613.

Stadt Huys, 17, 18, 23, 46, 215.
Stadt Huys Battery, 18.
Stage Coaches, 26, 109, 136.
Stamp Act, 27, 45, 576.
Stamp Collectors, 868.
Stamped Paper, 28.
Standard Oil Co., **917,** 916, 74, 142, 922, 696, 519, 516, 742, 726.
Standard Theatre, 148, 583, 600.
Star Theatre. 68, 146, 580, 600.
State Arsenal, **538,** 154.
State Banks, 58.
State Camp-Ground, 531.
State Church, 341.
State Courts. 260.
State Emigrant Hospital, 62.
State Line. 83.
Staten Island, 23, 27, 50, 55, 128, 135, 195, 68, 73, 72, 106.
Staten-Island R. R., 126, 135.
State of California, 83.
State Prison, 40.
State Street, **143,** 19, 449.
State Taxes, 51.
State Trust Company, **768,** 767.
State Vote, 51.
Station-Houses, 525.
Station, Kensico, **520.**
Statue of Liberty, **177,** 174, 50, 66, 533, 541, 820.
Statues, **164, 165, 168, 169,** 172.
Steamboats, 54, 74.
Steamboat Squad, 525.
Steam Company, 214.
Steam Engines, 37.
Steam Navigation, 34, 54, 75.
Steam Railways, 54.
Steamship Lines, 69, 785.
Steamship Row, **143, 676,** 76.
Steel-Plate Engraving, 914.
Steel Turrets, 72.
Steel Work 937. 817.
Steers, Henry, 768.
Steinway & Sons, **943,** 942, 740.
Steinway, F. T., 854.
Steinway Hall, **607,** 838.
Steinway, Wm., 319, 740, 942.
Stenography, School of, 294.
Stephenson, John, **136,** 38.
Stetson, John, 596, 582.
Stevens, F. W., 756, 714.
Stevens, J. A., 721.
Stevens, John, 34, 75.
Stevens, John O., 206.
Stevens, W. E., 683.
Steward, D. J., 306.
Stewart, A. T, 146, 312, 512, 545, 229, 581, 604, 715, 706.
Stewart Building, **767,** 505, 144. 233.
Stewart, J. A., 698, 708, 743.
Stewart Mansion, 66.
Stewart's Store, 241.
Still Hunt, **164,** 181, 66.
Stillman, Jas. 814, 710, 712, 771.
Stillman, T. E., 820.
Stimson, John Ward, 289, 311.
Stirling, Earl of, 30, 508.
Stock Exchange, **789, 791, 154, 155,** 788, 793, 754, 58, 156, 691, 692, 695, 760, 822, 767, 770.
Stoddard, Dr. C. A., 372, 628.
Stoddart, Alexander, 655, 656.
Stokes, A. P., 758.

Stokes, H. B., 645, 672, 670, 781.
Stokes, Spencer C.. 519.
Stone, Mason A., 644, 643.
Stone Street, 16, 19.
Stonington Line, 102.
Storage Buildings, 810, 814.
Storrs, R S., 43, 188.
Story, J. B., 745.
Stourbridge Lion, 110.
Stout, A. V., 728.
Stout, Chas. H., 724.
Stout, Jos. S., 914, 729.
Stover, J. W., 967.
Strangers, Church of, **388, 387,** 367.
Straus, Isidor, 728.
Street-Cars, 38, 54, 70.
Street Cleaning, 26, 51, 250.
Street Department, 457.
Street Improvements, 256.
Street-Lighting, 51.
Streets, Sewers, Water, 51.
Strong, C. E., 686, 756.
Strong, Wm. L., 560, 736, 948.
Stryker, Peter, 340.
Stuart, R L., 306.
Sturges, Frederick, 790.
Sturges, Jonathan, 545, 721.
Sturges, Wm C., 774.
Sturgis Pavilion, **459.**
Sturgis, Russell, 310.
Stuyvesant Ins. Co., 178.
Stuyvesant, Peter. 17, 18, 19, 20, 45, 441, 339, 351, 352, 794, 511, 158, 382, 267, 215, 245, 389, 390.
Stuyvesant Square, **351, 865,** 350, 383, 170, 279.
Stymus, W. P., 854.
Sub-Treasury, **698,** 697. 43, 55, 66, 155, 156, 174, 822, 765.
Subways, 206, 212.
Sud, El, **96.**
Sugar Refinery Co., Am., **919,** 918.
Summer-Gardens, 241.
Sun, **613, 614, 616,** 25, 39, 612, 817.
Sun and Shade, 964, 965.
Sunset Route, 120.
Superintendent of Police, 524.
Superior Court. 51, 260, 261.
Suppression of Vice Soc., 503.
Supreme Court, 51, 796, 800, 802, 260, 261.
Surrogates, 51, 261.
Surveyor's Department, 787.
Sutton, G. W., 882.
Svenska Kyrka. **384.**
Swedes, 266, 384.
Swedish Church, **384.**
Swedish Luth. Church, **384,** 389.
Swedish M. E. Church, **376.**
Sweetser, Pembrook & Co., **875.**
Swinburne Island, 458, 73, 264.
Swiss Benevolent Soc., **448.**
Swiss Club, 559.
Swiss Home, 474.
Switch-Room, **212, 210.**
Symphony Soc., 68, 318.
Syms Operating Theatre, **467.**
Synagogues, 402.

Table d'Hote Dinners, 240.
Tablets, Historical, 45.
Talmage's (Dan) Sons, **904.**
Tammany Hall, **562,** 612.
Tammany Society, 561, 32, 46.
Tank-Steamships, 74.
Tapestry, 288, 886.
Tappen, F. D., 703, 716, 764, 773.
Tariff Duties, 786.
Tarrant & Co., **912.**
Tattersalls, **812, 813,** 154.
Taxes and Assessments, 257.
Taxes Dept., 249, 256.
Tax Rate, 51, 249.
Taylor, A. J., 715.
Taylor. H. A. C., 712, 756, 771.
Teachers College, 293, 273, 472.
Tebbetts, Harrison & Robins, **885.**
Tefft, Weller & Co., **877,** 876, 738.
Telegram, Evening, 622.
Telephone & Telegraph Co., **210, 211.**
Teleseme, 224.
Temple Beth-El, **402,** 403.
Temple Court, **833,** 58, 328, 576, 732, 950.
Temple Emanu-El, **401,** 402, 66.
Temple Shearith Israel, **404,** 405.
Tenderloin Club, 574.
Tenements, 452, 455, 257, 244.
Terminal Warehouse Co., **815,** 814, 730.
Terrace, Central Park, **161.**
Terrace Garden, 606.
Texas Route, 97.
Thalia Theatre, 68, 579, 216, 604.
Theatre Fires, 582.
Theatres, 375, 67, 68.
Theatres, Construction of, 583.
Theological Libraries, 333.
Theology, 277, 281, 282.
Theosophical Workers, 456, 422.
Thingvalla Line, 91.
Third-Avenue Elevated Railroad, **937, 982.**
Third-Avenue R. R., **137.**
Thirteen Club, 571.
Thirty-Second Precinct Station, **527.**
Thomas, Chas. W., 597.
Thomas (Theodore) Orchestra, 607.
Thompson, Chas. L., 370.
Thompson G. K., 670.
Thompson's, Corporal, **36,** 40, 580.
Thornell, H. L., 758.
Thorne, Samuel, 764.
THOROUGHFARES AND ADORNMENTS. — Streets, Avenues, Boulevards, Alleys, Ways, Parks, Squares, Drives, Monuments, Statues, Fountains, etc., 141–184.
Throgg's Neck, 55, 541.
Tiemann, D. P., 260, 721.
Tiffany, C. L., **149,** 66, 545, 154, 740.
Tiffany Glass & Decorating Co., **316,** 337, 340, 348, 383, 740.

Tiffany House, **149,383,** 154.
Tiffany, Louis C., 316, 154.
Tilden, S. J., 63, 44, 170, 234.
Tillinghast, Wm. H., 724, 765.
Times, 619, 618, **250, 614,** **48, 49,** 748, 58, 66, 42, 144.
Tombs, **495, 255,** 36, 54, 66, 501, 493, 494, 262, 253, 254.
Tompkins Market,**801,** 809,537.
Tow-Boats, 106.
Toys, 860.
Trade Associations, 58.
Trade Schools, 291, 63, 446, 274.
Tradesmen's Nat. Bank, **712.**
Train-House, **123.**
Training-Schools for Nurses, 62, 461, 463, 470, 489.
Transatlantic Navigation, 36, 76.
Transfiguration Church, **357.**
TRANSPORTATION AND TRANSIT. — Railroads, Steam, Elevated, Cable, Horse and Electric.—Stages, 109–140.
Transportation, Board of, 802.
Treasure-Vault, 732.
Trenholm, W. L., 681, 708.
Tribune, 616, 614, 48, 39, 66, 42, 154, 427, 175, 144.
Tribune Fresh-Air Fund, 427.
Trimble, Merritt, 464, 677, 773, 778.
Trinity Chapel, **346,** 342, 344.
Trinity Church, **343, 677, 693, 757, 27,** 66, 67, 335, 346, 350, 342, 14, 25, 26, 3, 36, 914, 14, 156, 270, 506, 834, 513.
Trinity Church Association, 421, 489.
Trinity-Church Cemetery, **515,** 514.
Trinity Church in 1789, **21.**
Trinity Church Schools, 286.
Trinity Churchyard, 511.
Trinity Churchyard, **507, 514,** 506, 183, 215.
Trinity Luth. Church, 384.
Trinity Place, 914.
Tripler Hall, 235, 583, 580.
Troop A, **568,** 538, 531, 534, 297, 298.
Trust Companies, 753, 755, 58, 140, 657.
Turnverein, **567,** 296, 298, 566.
Tweed, W. M., 42, 54, 188, 220, 259, 529, 618.
Twelfth Reg., **535, 531,** 982.
Twenty - Second Reg., **536,** 531.
Twenty-Second Reg. Armory, **536.**
Two-Mile-Stone Meeting House, 352, 374, 375.
Tyng, Stephen H., 351, 360.
Typewriters, 958, 959.

Underground Cables, 212.
Underwriters' Agency, N.-Y., 656.
Union Club, **544,** 543, 68, 152.
Union Dime Savings, Inst., **781,** 154.
Union League Club, **544,** 66, 68, 303, 314, 153.

Union Square, **179, 180, 181, 865,** 981, 39, 49, 4, 5, 182, 175, 176, 166, 146, 371, 233, 234, 740, 860.
Union-Square Fountain, **179,** 182.
Union-Square Hotel, 233.
Union-Square Theatre, 583, 602, 592.
Union Theol. Seminary, **282,** 63, 333, 368, 277, 273.
Union Trust Co., **761,** 758, 143, 645.
Unitarians, 59, 385.
United Bank Building, **725,** 724.
United Charities, **420,** 409, 412, 950, 302, 419.
United Hebrew Charities, 451, 483.
United Relief Works, 434, 590.
United Service Club, **560.**
U.-S. Army Building, **541, 142, 718, 867.**
U.-S. Nat. Bank, **707,** 714, 749.
U.-S. Barge Office, **71, 719,** 141, 183, 787.
U.-S. Bonded Warehouses, 786, 814.
U.-S. Courts, 260, 55.
U.-S. District Court, 260.
U.-S. Guarantee Co., 690.
U.-S. Life Ins. Co., 672.
U.-S. Military Headquarters, 539.
United-States Mutual Accident Assoc., 668.
U.-S. Nat. Bank, **707.**
U.-S. Navy Yard, 542, 71.
U.-S. Trust Co., **759,** 758, **707,** 698.
Universalism, 59, 386.
University Club **549,** 68.
University Med. College, **277.**
University of New York, **275,** 39, 40, 63, 323, 332, 340, 358, 269, 167, 146, 387, 388.
University Settlement, 456, 421.
Upjohn, Richard, 342, 344, 352, 272, 357, 834.

Valuation, 225, 49.
Value of Exports, 785.
Van Cortlandt Park, 67, 134.
Vanderbilt, C., 34, 59, 312, 417, 418, 353, 178, 695, 222, 588, 387, 515.
Vanderbilt Clinic, **491,** 487, 62.
Vanderbilt Family, 62, 67, 367.
Vanderbilt, G. W, 310, 332.
Vanderbilt Houses, **147,** 152.
Vanderbilt's (Mrs. W. H.) House, **135,** 312, 147.
Vanderbilt, W. H., 181, 358, 277, 478, 487.
Vanderbilt, W. K., **147,** 312.
Van Horne, W. C., 206, 210.
VanIngen (E. H.) & Co, **887,** 776.
Van Nest, A. T., 644, 730, 771, 776.
Van Twiller, Wouter, 14, 301.
Vaseline, 948.
Vauxhall, 28, 39, 216, 583.
Vendome, Hotel, 148, 236.

Veragua, Duke of, 46.
Vermilye & Co., 708, 715.
Vermilye, W. G., 708.
Verplanck, G. C., 548, 704, 777.
Veterinary Colleges, 280, 281, 492.
Vice, Suppression of, 503.
Victoria, Hotel, 152, 148, 230.
Vietor (F.) & Achelis, 879.
Vital Statistics, 664, 666.
Votes, 47, 51.

Wagstaff, Alfred, 721, 976.
Waldorf, 217, 68, 218, 152.
Walker Street, 156.
Wallace, Elliot & Co., 903.
Wall Paper Co., 955, 953.
Wallack, Lester, 68, 146, 600, 592.
Wallack's Theatre, 580, 600.
Walling, G. W., 526, 528.
Wall Paper Co., 955, 953.
Wall Street, 705, 707, 765, 786, 694, 692, 693, 709, 343, 21, 27, 527, 25, 55, 140, 31, 33, 10, 155, 174, 258.
Wall-Street, from Assay Office, 693.
Wall-Street, Custom House to Broad Street, 694.
Wall Street, from Custom House, 694.
Wall Street in 1789, 21.
Wall Street in 1800, 25.
Wall Street in 1860, 692.
Walter, Henry, 228.
Walton, E. A. 644, 645, 672, 780.
Ward Steamships, 98.
Ward, Geo. G., 206, 210.
Ward, J. Q. A., 66, 174, 175, 176, 178, 179, 180, 184, 312.
Wards, 23.
Ward's Island, 47, 62, 455, 256.
Ward's Island Asylum, 463.
Ward's Mexican Line, 98.
Warehouses, 786, 810, 811.
Ware, Wm. R., 257, 273, 674.
Warner, L. C., 744.
Warner, L. P., 742.
Warner, O. L., 312, 166.
Warren, Fuller & Co., 955.
Washington Arch, 173, 966, 172, 167, 66, 505.
Washington Bridge, 822, 189, 190, 54, 192.
Washington Bridge, View from, 910.
Washington Building, 821, 141, 820, 142, 97, 58, 120, 208.
Washington Building Views, 108, 689.
Washington Centennial, 43.
Washington, George, 43, 180, 30, 31, 32, 109, 113, 344, 576, 142, 171, 172, 174, 258, 697, 215, 533.
Washington Heights, 22, 47, 137, 192, 193, 54, 67, 355, 161, 166, 148, 172, 372, 569, 514.
Washington-Heights Presb. Church, 372.
Washington-Heights Y. M. C. A., 416.

Washington Life-Ins. Co., 677, 676.
Washington Market, 797, 808.
Washington Square, 374, 378, 173, 171, 275, 167, 39, 40, 196, 323, 340, 172, 375, 379, 153, 170, 148, 146, 505, 236, 242, 244, 966, 908.
Washington Statues, 176, 166.
Washington Trust Co., 767, 766.
Watchmen, 25, 524, 528.
Waterbury, J. I., 766.
Water-Color Society, 309, 311.
Water Front, 69, 70, 155.
Water Mains, 51, 200.
Water Supply, 54, 196.
Water Tower, 822.
WATERWAYS.—The Harbor and Rivers, Piers and Shipping, Fortifications and Quarantine, Exports and Imports, Oceanic and Coastwise Lines, etc., 69-108.
Watkins Fire Alarm, 965.
Watson, James, 449.
Watts' Statue, 514, 183.
Weather Bureau, 832, 672.
Webb's Academy, 292, 447.
Webster, Daniel, 168, 129, 180, 543.
Webster Statue, 168, 179.
Weehawken, 34, 115, 128, 507.
Weingart Institute, 301.
Wendell, Evert J., 501, 556.
Wendell, Jacob, 659, 708.
West-End Avenue Church, 338.
West-End Presb. Church, 370.
Western Electric Co., 837, 838.
Westernland, 89, 88.
Western Union Tel. Co., 207, 210, 58, 206, 790.
West Farms, 47, 137, 139.
West India Co., 10, 12, 17, 19, 20, 15, 215.
Westminster Hotel, 234.
Westminster Presb. Church, 370, 369.
West Presb. Church. 367.
West-72d Street Y. M. C. A., 417.
West Side, 155. 237, 242, 832.
West-Side German Disp., 489.
West Street, 122, 155.
West Washington Market, 807, 809.
Wetmore Home, 439, 502.
Wheelmen's Clubs, 568.
White, Charles E., 659.
Whitehall, 142, 135, 18, 19, 29.
Whitehall Battery, 18, 30.
Whitehall, Foot of, 867.
White Squadron, 99.
White, Stanford, 66, 154, 172, 356.
White Star Line, 79, 71.
White Train, 133, 140.
Whitney (A. R) & Co., 982, 937.
Whitney, W. C., 152, 588, 519, 748, 769.
Winter Garden, 235, 580, 583.

WHOLESALE ESTABLISHMENTS.
—Some Gigantic Firms and Corporations whose Yearly Transactions Involve Millions of Dollars and Extend over the Earth, 871-912.
Wilks Building, 155, 950.
Willett's Point, 55, 72, 541.
Williamsburgh City Fire-Ins. Co., 655, 143, 652.
Williams, G. G., 672, 703, 714, 760.
William Street, 57, 65, 379.
Wilsey, F. D., 969.
Windmills, 10, 14, 19.
Windsor Hotel, 152, 218, 512.
Windsor Theatre, 583, 604.
Winser, J. H., 306.
Winston, F. S., 306, 666, 522.
Wolfe, Miss C. L., 306, 348, 350, 407.
Woman's Art School, 311, 289, 291.
Woman's Hospital, 478, 479.
Women's Medical College, 279, 480.
Women's Press Club, 570.
Wood, Edw., 762, 776.
Wood, Fernando, 40, 258, 260, 160, 514.
Woodlawn Cemetery, 517, 515.
Woodward, Baldwin & Co., 884, 726.
Woodward, Jas. T., 587, 726, 760.
Work-House, 498, 496, 256.
Workingmen's School, 295, 434.
World, 614, 621, 251, 620, 39, 66, 144, 175, 984.
World Building, Views from, 48, 49, 52, 53, 56, 57, 60, 61, 64, 65.
Worthington, Henry R., 922, 923.
Worthington Pumps, 922, 923, 672, 445, 200, 794, 274, 586, 654, 830, 848.
Worth Monument, 183, 857, 166, 176.
Wright, Ebenezer K., 732, 768.
Wrought-iron pipe, 930, 931, 932, 933.
Wyckoff, Seamans & Benedict, 958, 959.

Xavier Club, 556.

Yachting, 566, 106.
Yale Alumni, 555.
Y. M. C. A., 417, 412, 414, 59, 63, 368.
Y. M. C. A. Hall, 608.
Y. M. C. A. Library, 63, 330.
Young Men's Hebrew Assoc., 418
Young Men's Institute, 414, 416, 59.
Young Women's Christian Association, 416, 333, 543.
Young Women's Hebrew Association, 452, 418.

Zion and St. Timothy Church, 353, 359.